ELEVENTH EDITION

The Developing Person
Through the Life Span

Kathleen Stassen Berger
Bronx Community College of the
City University of New York

worth publishers
Macmillan Learning
New York

Senior Vice President, Content Strategy: Charles Linsmeier
Program Director, Social Sciences: Shani Fisher
Executive Program Manager: Christine Cardone
Developmental Editor: Andrea Musick Page
Assistant Editor: Dorothy Tomasini
Executive Marketing Manager: Katherine Nurre
Marketing Assistant: Steven Huang
Executive Media Editor: Laura Burden
Director, Content Management Enhancement: Tracey Kuehn
Senior Managing Editor: Lisa Kinne
Senior Content Project Manager: Peter Jacoby
Project Manager: Jana Lewis, Lumina Datamatics, Inc.
Media Project Manager: Brian Nobile
Senior Workflow Supervisor: Susan Wein
Senior Photo Editor: Sheena Goldstein
Photo Researcher: Donna Ranieri, Lumina Datamatics, Inc.
Director of Design, Content Management: Diana Blume
Design Services Manager: Natasha A. S. Wolfe
Cover Designer: John Callahan
Interior Design: Studio Montage and Lumina Datamatics, Inc.
Art Manager: Matthew McAdams
Illustrations: Lumina Datamatics, Charles Yuen, Matthew McAdams
Composition: Lumina Datamatics, Inc.
Printing and Binding: LSC Communications
Cover Photograph: Stephen Simpson/DigitalVision/Getty Images

Library of Congress Control Number: 2019940136
ISBN-13: 978-1-319-19175-7
ISBN-10: 1-319-19175-4

Printed in the United States of America

1 2 3 4 5 6 24 23 22 21 20 19

Worth Publishers
One New York Plaza
Suite 4600
New York, NY 10004-1562
www.macmillanlearning.com

ABOUT THE AUTHOR

Kathleen Stassen Berger received her undergraduate education at Stanford University and Radcliffe College, and then she earned an M.A.T. from Harvard University and an M.S. and a Ph.D. from Yeshiva University. Her broad experience as an educator includes directing a preschool, serving as chair of philosophy at the United Nations International School, and teaching child and adolescent development to graduate students at Fordham University and undergraduates at Montclair State University and Quinnipiac University. She also taught social psychology to inmates at Sing Sing Prison who were earning their paralegal degrees.

Currently, Berger is a professor at Bronx Community College of the City University of New York, as she has been for most of her professional career. She began as an adjunct in English, and for the past decades she has been a full professor in the Social Sciences Department, which includes sociology, economics, anthropology, political science, human services, and psychology. She has taught introduction to psychology, social psychology, abnormal psychology, human motivation, and all four developmental courses—child, adolescent, adulthood, and life span. Her students—who come from many ethnic, economic, and educational backgrounds, with varied ages, interests, and ambitions—consistently honor her with the highest teaching evaluations.

Berger is also the author of *Invitation to the Life Span* and *The Developing Person Through Childhood and Adolescence*. Her developmental texts are currently being used at more than 700 colleges and universities worldwide and are available in Spanish, French, Italian, and Portuguese, as well as English. She is among the top 100 female authors assigned in colleges in the United States and the United Kingdom, an honor she shares with Jane Austen, Toni Morrison, and 97 other well-respected women.

Berger's research interests include adolescent identity, immigration, bullying, and grandparents, and she has published articles on development in the *Wiley Encyclopedia of Psychology* and in publications of the American Association for Higher Education and the National Education Association. She continues teaching and learning from her students, as well as from her four daughters and three grandsons. She has recently published a trade book, *Grandmothering: Building Strong Ties with Every Generation*.

BRIEF CONTENTS

Cultura/JFCreatives/Cultura Exclusive/Getty Image

PART I: The Beginnings 1

1 The Science of Human Development 3

2 Theories 33

3 The New Genetics 61

4 Prenatal Development and Birth 89

Paul Thomas / EyeEm/Getty Images

PART II: The First Two Years 115

5 The First Two Years: Biosocial Development 117

6 The First Two Years: Cognitive Development 143

7 The First Two Years: Psychosocial Development 167

baona/iStock/Getty Images

PART III: Early Childhood 195

8 Early Childhood: Biosocial Development 197

9 Early Childhood: Cognitive Development 221

10 Early Childhood: Psychosocial Development 247

EdZbarzhyvetsky/Deposit Photos

PART IV: Middle Childhood 273

11 Middle Childhood: Biosocial Development 275

12 Middle Childhood: Cognitive Development 299

13 Middle Childhood: The Social World 323

Pixel- Shot/Shutterstock.com

PART V: Adolescence 351

14 Adolescence: Biosocial Development 353

15 Adolescence: Cognitive Development 377

16 Adolescence: Psychosocial Development 403

RapidEye/iStock/E+/Getty Images

PART VI: Emerging Adulthood 429

17 Emerging Adulthood: Biosocial Development 431
18 Emerging Adulthood: Cognitive Development 453
19 Emerging Adulthood: Psychosocial Development 479

iko/Shutterstock

PART VII: Adulthood 505

20 Adulthood: Biosocial Development 507
21 Adulthood: Cognitive Development 531
22 Adulthood: Psychosocial Development 555

Image Source/Divine Images/Media Bakery

PART VIII: Late Adulthood 583

23 Late Adulthood: Biosocial Development 585
24 Late Adulthood: Cognitive Development 611
25 Late Adulthood: Psychosocial Development 635

EPILOGUE: Death and Dying 661

APPENDIX: More About Research Methods A-1

Glossary G-1
References R-1
Name Index NI-1
Subject Index SI-1

CONTENTS

Preface xv

Cultura/JFCreatives/Cultura Exclusive/Getty Images

PART I

The Beginnings

Leren Lu/DigitalVision/Getty Images

1 The Science of Human Development 3

Understanding How and Why 4

The Scientific Method 4

The Nature–Nurture Controversy 5

A VIEW FROM SCIENCE: Priming 6

The Life-Span Perspective 7

Development Is Multidirectional 7

Development Is Multicontextual 8

Development Is Multicultural 10

Chapter App 1: Culture Compass

Development Is Multidisciplinary 13

Development Is Plastic 14

INSIDE THE BRAIN: Thinking About Marijuana 15

A CASE TO STUDY: David 16

Using the Scientific Method 18

Observation 18

The Experiment 20

The Survey 21

Meta-Analysis 22

Studying Development over the Life Span 22

Cautions and Challenges from Science 25

Correlation and Causation 25

Quantity and Quality 26

Ethics 26

VISUALIZING DEVELOPMENT: Diverse Complexities 31

AlexSava/E+/Getty Images

2 Theories 33

Grand Theories 34

What Theories Are 34

Psychodynamic Theory: Freud and Erikson 34

Behaviorism: Conditioning and Learning 36

Cognitive Theory: Piaget and Information Processing 40

INSIDE THE BRAIN: Measuring Mental Activity 41

A VIEW FROM SCIENCE: Walk a Mile 44

Newer Theories 46

Sociocultural Theory: Vygotsky and Beyond 46

Evolutionary Theory 49

Chapter App 2: My Token Board

What Theories Contribute 53

OPPOSING PERSPECTIVES: Toilet Training—How and When? 54

VISUALIZING DEVELOPMENT: Historical Highlights of Developmental Science 58

Philip Nealey/Photodisc/Getty Images

3 The New Genetics 61

The Genetic Code 61

46 to 21,000 to 3 Billion 61

Same and Different 62

Matching Genes and Chromosomes 64

A CASE TO STUDY: Women Engineers 66

OPPOSING PERSPECTIVES: Too Many Boys? 68

New Cells, New People 69

Cells and Identity 69

Twins and More 71

From Genotype to Phenotype 72

Many Factors 73

Gene–Gene Interactions 73

Nature and Nurture 75

Practical Applications 78

Chromosomal and Genetic Problems 78

Not Exactly 46 78

Gene Disorders 80

Genetic Counseling and Testing 81

A VIEW FROM SCIENCE: The Genes of Psychological Disorders 82

Chapter App 3: Gene Screen

VISUALIZING DEVELOPMENT: One Baby or More? 87

kupicoo/E+/Getty Images

4 Prenatal Development and Birth 89

Prenatal Development 90

Germinal: The First 14 Days 90

Embryo: From the Third Week Through the Eighth Week 90

Fetus: From the Ninth Week Until Birth 91

Chapter App 4: What to Expect Pregnancy and Baby Tracker

INSIDE THE BRAIN: Essential Connections 93

Birth 94

The Newborn's First Minutes 95

Medical Assistance at Birth 95

Problems and Solutions 96

OPPOSING PERSPECTIVES: Interventions in the Birth Process 97

Risk Analysis 98

Harmful Substances 98

A CASE TO STUDY: Behavioral Teratogens 99

Prenatal Diagnosis 102

Low Birthweight: Causes and Consequences 103

A VIEW FROM SCIENCE: What Is Safe? 103

The New Family 107

The Newborn 107

New Mothers 108

New Fathers 109

Family Bonding 109

CAREER ALERT: The Genetic Counselor 112

VISUALIZING DEVELOPMENT: The Apgar 113

PART II The First Two Years

Paul Thomas / EyeEm/Getty Images

Tetra Images - Jessica Peterson/Brand X Pictures/Getty Images

5 The First Two Years: Biosocial Development 117

Body Changes 118

Body Size 118

Chapter App 5: Sprout Baby

Sleep 119

OPPOSING PERSPECTIVES: Where Should Babies Sleep? 120

Brain Development 121

INSIDE THE BRAIN: Brains from Back to Front 122

Necessary and Possible Experiences 124

Harming the Body and Brain 125

Perceiving and Moving 126

The Senses 126

A VIEW FROM SCIENCE: Addiction in Newborns 129

Motor Skills 130

Cultural Variations 131

Surviving and Thriving 132

Immunization 133

A CASE TO STUDY: Scientist at Work 133

Nutrition 136

Malnutrition 137

VISUALIZING DEVELOPMENT: Immunization 141

Ed Fox/Getty Images

6 The First Two Years: Cognitive Development 143

The Eager Mind 144

Listening to Learn 144

Looking to Learn 145

Core Knowledge 146

A VIEW FROM SCIENCE: Face Recognition 147

Chapter App 6: The Wonder Weeks

Theories of the Infant Mind 148

Infant Memory 149

Piaget's Sensorimotor Intelligence 151

Stages One and Two: Primary Circular Reactions 152

Stages Three and Four: Secondary Circular Reactions 153

OPPOSING PERSPECTIVES: Object Permanence 154

Stages Five and Six: Tertiary Circular Reactions 154

Language: What Develops in the First Two Years? 155

The Universal Sequence 155

The Naming Explosion 157

A CASE TO STUDY: Early Speech 157

Theories of Language Learning 159

VISUALIZING DEVELOPMENT: Early Communication and Language 165

David A Land/Blend Images/Media bakery

7 The First Two Years: Psychosocial Development 167

Emotional Development 167

Early Emotions 168

Toddlers' Emotions 169

Temperament 170

INSIDE THE BRAIN: The Growth of Emotions 172

The Development of Social Bonds 173

Synchrony 173

Chapter App 7: Red Rover
Attachment 175
A VIEW FROM SCIENCE: Measuring Attachment 177
A CASE TO STUDY: Can We Bear This Commitment? 179
Social Referencing 180
Fathers as Social Partners 181
Theories of Infant Psychosocial Development 182
Psychodynamic Theory 182
Behaviorism 182
Cognitive Theory 183
Evolutionary Theory 184
Sociocultural Theory 185
Who Should Care for Babies? 185
Complications of Interpretation 185
Exclusive Mother-Care 186
OPPOSING PERSPECTIVES: Why Doesn't Everyone Agree? 186
Problems with Nonmaternal Care 188
Cohort Differences 189
CAREER ALERT: The Pediatrician and the Pediatric Nurse 192
VISUALIZING DEVELOPMENT: Developing Attachment 193

PART III

Early Childhood

baona/iStock/Getty Images

LightField Studios/Shutterstock.Com

8 Early Childhood: Biosocial Development 197
Body Changes 198
Growth Patterns 198
Nutrition 198
Brain Growth 201
Myelination 201
INSIDE THE BRAIN: Connected Hemispheres 202
Maturation of the Prefrontal Cortex 202
Inhibition and Flexibility 203
Advancing Motor Skills 204
Chapter App 8: Wuf Shanti Yoga Fun Machine
Harm to Children 206
Avoidable Injury 207
A CASE TO STUDY: "My Baby Swallowed Poison" 208
Prevention 209
A VIEW FROM SCIENCE: Lead in the Environment 210
Child Maltreatment 212
Preventing Harm 215
VISUALIZING DEVELOPMENT: Developing Motor Skills 219

Westend61/Getty Images

9 Early Childhood: Cognitive Development 221
Thinking During Early Childhood 221
Executive Function 222
Piaget: Preoperational Thought 223
A CASE TO STUDY: Stones in the Belly 226
Vygotsky: Social Learning 226
Children's Theories 229
INSIDE THE BRAIN: The Role of Experience 231
Language Learning 232
The Sensitive Time for Language Learning 232
The Vocabulary Explosion 232
Acquiring Grammar 234
Chapter App 9: FaceTalker
Learning Two Languages 235
Early-Childhood Schooling 236
Homes and Schools 236
Child-Centered Programs 237
Teacher-Directed Programs 238
OPPOSING PERSPECTIVES: Comparing Child-Centered and Teacher-Directed Preschools 239
Intervention Programs 240
Long-Term Gains from Intensive Programs 240
VISUALIZING DEVELOPMENT: Early-Childhood Schooling 245

Henryk T. Kaiser/Age Fotostock/Media Bakery

10 Early Childhood: Psychosocial Development 247
Emotional Development 247
Initiative Versus Guilt 248
A VIEW FROM SCIENCE: Waiting for the Marshmallow 249
Chapter App 10: Daniel Tiger's Grr-ific Feelings
Motivation 250
Play 251
Playmates 251
Social Play 252
Challenges for Caregivers 254
Styles of Caregiving 254
Discipline 256
OPPOSING PERSPECTIVES: Spare the Rod? 258

Becoming Boys and Girls: Sex and Gender 260
A CASE TO STUDY: The Berger Daughters 262
Teaching Right and Wrong 265
CAREER ALERT: The Preschool Teacher 270
VISUALIZING DEVELOPMENT: More Play Time, Less Screen Time 271

PART IV

Middle Childhood

EdZbarzhyvetsky/Deposit Photos

Image Source/DigitalVision/Getty Images

11 Middle Childhood: Biosocial Development 275

A Healthy Time 276
Statistics on Health 276
Health Habits 276
Physical Activity 276
Motor Skills and School 278
Health Problems in Middle Childhood 280

Brain Development 282
Brains and Motion 282
Measuring the Mind 283
A VIEW FROM SCIENCE: The Flynn Effect 285

Children with Special Brains and Bodies 287
Many Causes, Many Symptoms 287
OPPOSING PERSPECTIVES: Drug Treatment for ADHD and Other Disorders 288
Specific Learning Disorders 290
Chapter App 11: Model Me Going Places 2
Special Education 292
A CASE TO STUDY: The Gifted and Talented 293
VISUALIZING DEVELOPMENT: Childhood Obesity Around the World 297

Marc Romanelli/Blend Images/Getty Images

12 Middle Childhood: Cognitive Development 299

Thinking 300
Piaget on Middle Childhood 300
Vygotsky and Culture 301
Information Processing 302
OPPOSING PERSPECTIVES: Two or Twenty Pills a Day 303
INSIDE THE BRAIN: Coordination and Capacity 304

Language 306
Vocabulary 307
Speaking Two Languages 307
Poverty and Language 308

Teaching and Learning 309
The Curriculum 310
Chapter App 12: Khan Academy
International Testing 312
A CASE TO STUDY: Happiness or High Grades? 315
Schooling in the United States 316
VISUALIZING DEVELOPMENT: Education in Middle Childhood 321

altrendo images/Stoked/Media Bakery

13 Middle Childhood: The Social World 323

The Nature of the Child 323
Industry and Inferiority 323
Parental Reactions 324
Self-Concept 325
Resilience and Stress 326

Families During Middle Childhood 329
Shared and Nonshared Environments 329
Function and Structure 329
A VIEW FROM SCIENCE: "I Always Dressed One in Blue Stuff . . ." 330
Various Family Structures 331
Connecting Family Structure and Function 332
A CASE TO STUDY: How Hard Is It to Be a Kid? 336
Family Trouble 336

The Peer Group 338
The Culture of Children 338
Friendships 339
Popular and Unpopular Children 340
Bullying 340
Chapter App 13: Daisy Chain
Children's Morality 343
OPPOSING PERSPECTIVES: Parents Versus Peers 344
CAREER ALERT: The Speech Therapist 348
VISUALIZING DEVELOPMENT: Family Structures Around the World 349

Pixel-Shot/Shutterstock.com

PART V
Adolescence

Stephen Simpson/Divine Images/Media Bakery

14 Adolescence: Biosocial Development 353

Puberty Begins 353
Sequence 353
Unseen Beginnings 354
Chapter App 14: Sleep Cycle
Brain Growth 356
When Will Puberty Begin? 357
INSIDE THE BRAIN: Lopsided Growth 358
Too Early, Too Late 360
A VIEW FROM SCIENCE: Stress and Puberty 361

Growth and Nutrition 363
Growing Bigger and Stronger 363
Diet Deficiencies 364
Eating Disorders 366

Sexual Maturation 367
Sexual Characteristics 367
Sexual Activity 367
Sexual Problems in Adolescence 369
VISUALIZING DEVELOPMENT: Satisfied with Your Body? 375

AE Pictures Inc./DigitalVision/Getty Images

15 Adolescence: Cognitive Development 377

Logic and Self 378
Egocentrism 378
Formal Operational Thought 380

Two Modes of Thinking 382
Intuitive and Analytic Processing 383
A CASE TO STUDY: Biting the Policeman 384
Better Thinking 385
Chapter App 15: HappiMe for Young People
INSIDE THE BRAIN: Stop and Think? No! 385

Technology and Cognition 386
Digital Natives 387
Technology in Schools 387
Sexual Abuse? 388
Computer Addiction 389
Cyber Danger 390

Secondary Education 391
Definitions and Facts 392
Middle School 392
High School 394
OPPOSING PERSPECTIVES: High-Stakes Testing 396
Variability 398
VISUALIZING DEVELOPMENT: How Many Adolescents Are in School? 401

Marc Romanelli/Tetra images/Getty Images

16 Adolescence: Psychosocial Development 403

Identity 403
Not Yet Achieved 404
Arenas of Identity Formation 404

Close Relationships 407
Family 407
A VIEW FROM SCIENCE: Teens and Genes 407
Peer Power 410
A CASE TO STUDY: The Naiveté of Your Author 411
Learning About Sex 414

Sadness and Anger 416
Depression 416
Chapter App 16: My3 - Support Network
Delinquency and Defiance 417
INSIDE THE BRAIN: Impulses, Rewards, and Reflection 420

Drug Use and Abuse 421
Age Trends 421
Harm from Drugs 422
OPPOSING PERSPECTIVES: E-Cigarettes: Path to Addiction or Health? 423
Preventing Drug Abuse: What Works? 424
CAREER ALERT: The Teacher 426
VISUALIZING DEVELOPMENT: Adolescent Bullying 427

PART VI
Emerging Adulthood

RapidEye/iStock/E+/Getty Images

Tempura/E+/Getty Images

17 Emerging Adulthood: Biosocial Development 431

Biological Universals 432

A New Stage 432

Body Systems 432

A VIEW FROM SCIENCE: Universal or WEIRD? 433

Health and Sickness 433

Chapter App 17: First Aid: American Red Cross

Capacity for Recovery 434

Examples of Load and Balancing 435

Appearance 439

Sexual Activity 440

Births 440

Universal Sex Drives 440

OPPOSING PERSPECTIVES: Premarital Sex 441

Taking Risks 444

Who Are the Risk Takers? 444

Benefits of Risk Taking 445

A CASE TO STUDY: A Hero for Millions 446

VISUALIZING DEVELOPMENT: Highlights in the Journey to Adulthood 451

AJ_Watt/E+/Getty Images

18 Emerging Adulthood: Cognitive Development 453

A New Level of Thinking 454

Postformal Thought 454

INSIDE THE BRAIN: A New Stage? 455

Dialectical Thought 457

Ethics and Religion 461

Doing the Right Thing 461

Faith and Practice 463

Cognitive Growth and Higher Education 466

Health and Wealth 466

A VIEW FROM SCIENCE: Women and College 468

College and Cognition 469

A CASE TO STUDY: Generation to Generation 471

Improving the College Experience 472

Technology in College 473

Chapter App 18: SimpleMind Pro+ Mind Mapping

Why Learn? 475

VISUALIZING DEVELOPMENT: Why Study? 477

pixelfit/E+/Getty Images

19 Emerging Adulthood: Psychosocial Development 479

Identity Achievement 479

Moratoria 480

Ethnic Identity 480

Chapter App 19: Countable

Vocational Identity 483

Identity and Intimacy 485

Emerging Adults and Their Parents 486

Friendship 488

Romantic Partners 491

The Dimensions of Love 491

A CASE TO STUDY: My Students, My Daughters, and Me 495

Cohabitation 496

OPPOSING PERSPECTIVES: Making Divorce More Likely? 497

Concluding Hopes 500

CAREER ALERT: The Career Counselor 502

VISUALIZING DEVELOPMENT: Marital Status in the United States 503

PART VII
Adulthood

iko/Shutterstock

PhotoAlto/Frederic Cirou/PhotoAlto Agency RF Collections/Getty Images

20 Adulthood: Biosocial Development 507

Growing Older 508

Senescence 508

INSIDE THE BRAIN: Neurons Forming in Adulthood 510

Outward Appearance 511

The Senses 512

The Sexual-Reproductive System 513

Sexual Responsiveness 513

The Sexual-Reproductive System in Middle Age 516

Habits: Good and Bad 518

Exercise 519

Chapter App 20: Couch to 5K

Drugs 520
Nutrition 523
Correlating Income and Health 524
VISUALIZING DEVELOPMENT: Adult Overweight Around the World 529

Plan Shoot/Multi-bits/ImaZinS/Getty Images

21 Adulthood: Cognitive Development 531

Intelligence Changes During Adulthood? 532
Inborn IQ 532
Age and IQ 533
OPPOSING PERSPECTIVES: Who Is Smarter, the College Student or the Retiree? 534
Putting It All Together 536

Components of Intelligence: Many and Varied 537
Two Clusters of Intelligence 537
Three Forms of Intelligence 538

Selective Gains and Losses 541
Optimization with Compensation 541
Chapter App 21: Freedom
Expert Cognition 543
A VIEW FROM SCIENCE: Who Wins in Soccer? 545
Expertise, Age, and Experience 548
A CASE TO STUDY: Parenting Expertise 550
VISUALIZING DEVELOPMENT: Media Use Among U.S. Adults 553

Cecilie_Arcurs/E+/Getty Images

22 Adulthood: Psychosocial Development 555

Personality Development in Adulthood 556
Erikson's Theory 556
Maslow's Theory of Personality 557
The Big Five 558
Common Themes 559

Intimacy: Connecting with Others 560
Romantic Partners 560
A CASE TO STUDY: The Benefits of Marriage 562
Friends and Acquaintances 564
Family Bonds 564

Generativity: The Work of Adulthood 566
Parenthood 566
Chapter App 22: Cozi Family Organizer
Caregiving 571
A VIEW FROM SCIENCE: The Skipped-Generation Family 571
Employment 572
OPPOSING PERSPECTIVES: Accommodating Diversity 575
Finding the Balance 577
CAREER ALERT: The Physical Therapist 580
VISUALIZING DEVELOPMENT: Family Connections 581

PART VIII Late Adulthood

Image Source/Divine Images/Media Bakery

23 Late Adulthood: Biosocial Development 585

Prejudice and Predictions 586
The Special Harm 586
A VIEW FROM SCIENCE: I'm Not Like Those Other Old People 587
Demography and Ageism 590

Adjusting to Changes 594
Microsystem Compensation: Sex 594
A CASE TO STUDY: Sex Among Older Adults 595
Macrosystem Compensation: Driving 596
Exosystem Compensation: The Senses 597
Chapter App 23: Magnifying Glass with Light
Primary and Secondary Aging 599

Theories of Aging 602
Wear and Tear 602
It's All Genetic 604
Aging of the Cells 605
VISUALIZING DEVELOPMENT: Elders Behind the Wheel 609

Uwe Umstätter/Westend 61/Media Bakery

24 Late Adulthood: Cognitive Development 611

The Brain During Adulthood 612
Ongoing Development 612
OPPOSING PERSPECTIVES: Slower Thinking 614

Step-by-Step Processing 615
Input 615
Memory 616
Control Processes 617
Output 618

Neurocognitive Disorders 619

Mild Cognitive Impairment 619
The Ageism of Words 620
Prevalence of NCDs 620
The Many Neurocognitive Disorders 621
Preventing Impairment 624
Reversible Neurocognitive Disorder? 624
Chapter App 24: Medisafe
A CASE TO STUDY: The More You Know . . . 627

New Cognitive Development 628
Erikson and Maslow 628
Aesthetic Sense and Creativity 628
Wisdom 630
VISUALIZNG DEVELOPMENT: Global Prevalence of Major NCD 633

Ronnie Kaufman/Corbis/Getty Images

25 Late Adulthood: Psychosocial Development 635

Theories of Late Adulthood 636
Self Theories 636
Stratification Theories 638
A CASE TO STUDY: Saving Old Newspapers 639

Activities in Late Adulthood 641
Working 641
Home Sweet Home 643
Religious Involvement 644
Political Activity 645
Friends and Relatives 645

The Frail Elderly 649
Activities of Daily Life 649
Preventing Frailty 649
Cognitive Failure 651
Caring for the Frail Elderly 651
Chapter App 25: Caring Bridge
Long-Term Care 653
A CASE TO STUDY: A Trusted Sister 654
CAREER ALERT: The Developmental Scientist 658
VISUALIZING DEVELOPMENT: Living Independently After Age 65 659

EPILOGUE: Death and Dying 661

APPENDIX: More About Research Methods A-1

Glossary G-1
References R-1
Name Index NI-1
Subject Index SI-1

PREFACE

If human development were simple, universal, and unchanging, there would be no need for a new edition of this textbook. Nor would anyone need to learn anything about human growth. But humans are complex, varied, and never the same.

This is evident to me as I apply what I know. Since the tenth edition of this textbook, I have learned more about birth (my close friend had her first child), about schools (two of my grandsons entered new schools), about adult employment (two of my daughters changed jobs), and, sadly, about death (my brother died). I have improved my exercise and eating habits, and I continue to teach, learning about current trends from my students.

Although this book is personal to me and to everyone else (we all are developing persons) it also highlights new evidence on many controversies, about conception, breast-feeding, early education, college costs and benefits, ethnic identity, immigration, family dynamics, addictive drugs, and more. All these topics benefit from a better understanding of human development, and all of them—as you will read—raise new issues that are not yet settled.

That is why I wrote this eleventh edition, which presents both enduring and current findings from the science of human development. Some of those findings have been recognized for decades, even centuries, and some are new, as thousands of scientists continue to study how humans grow and change. I hope their conclusions will add insight as we live our personal and public lives, moving us all forward from the moment of conception until the last breath. Accordingly, the need for evidence, alternatives, and ethics is often highlighted in this eleventh edition, even more so than in previous editions.

sarahwolfephotography/Moment/Getty Images

NEW TOPICS AND RESEARCH

Every year, scientists discover and explain new concepts and research. The best of these are integrated into the text, including hundreds of new references on many topics such as epigenetics, prenatal nutrition, the microbiome, early-childhood education, autism spectrum disorder, vaping, high-stakes testing, opioid addiction, cohabitation, gender nonconformity, the grandmother hypothesis, living wills, continuing bonds, and diversity of all kinds—ethnic, economic, and cultural.

Cognizant that the science of human development is interdisciplinary, I include recent research in biology, sociology, neuroscience, education, anthropology, political science, and more—as well as my home discipline, psychology. A list highlighting this material is available at macmillanlearning.com.

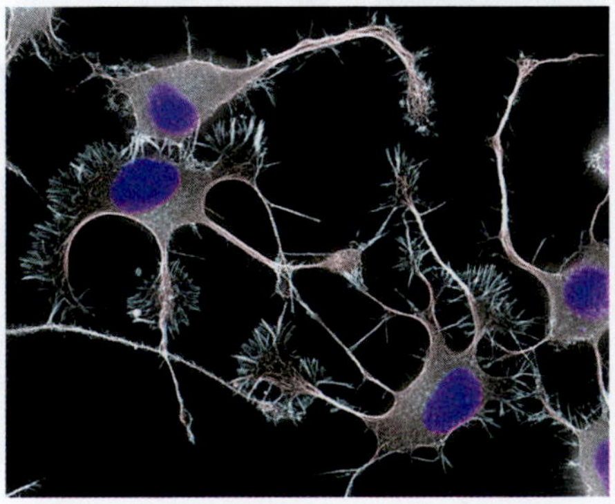

DR TORSTEN WITTMANN/SCIENCE PHOTO LIBRARY/Getty Images

NEW and Updated Coverage of Neuroscience

Of course, neuroscience continues in the text as well. In addition to the Inside the Brain features, cutting-edge research on the brain appears in virtually every chapter, often with charts, figures, and photos. A list highlighting this material is available at macmillanlearning.com.

NEW! Career Alerts

At the end of each Part, students will read about career options for various applied settings related to life-span development. These Career Alerts are informed by the Bureau of Labor Statistics' Occupational Outlook Handbook, which describes duties, education and training, pay, and outlook for hundreds of occupations.

NEW! Chapter Apps

Chapter Apps that students can download to their smartphones have been added, offering a real-life application of the science of life-span development. Call-outs to the Chapter Apps (one per chapter) appear in the margins, along with brief descriptions and links to their iTunes and/or Google Play downloads.

Klaus Vedfelt/Getty Images

Renewed Emphasis on Critical Thinking in the Pedagogical Program

Critical thinking is essential for all of us lifelong. Virtually every page of this book presents not only facts but also questions with divergent interpretations, sometimes with references to my own need to reconsider my assumptions. Marginal Think Critically questions encourage students to examine the implications of what they read.

Every chapter is organized around learning objectives. Much of what I hope students will always remember from this course is a matter of attitude, approach, and perspective—all hard to quantify. The What Will You Know? questions at the beginning of each chapter indicate important ideas or provocative concepts—one for each major section of the chapter. In addition, after every major section, What Have You Learned? questions help students review what they have just read. Some of these questions are straightforward, requiring only close attention to the chapter. Others are more complex, seeking comparisons, implications, or evaluations. Cognitive psychology and research on pedagogy show that vocabulary, specific knowledge, and critical thinking are all part of learning. These features are designed to foster all three; I hope students and professors will add their own questions and answers, following this scaffolding.

fatihhoca/iStock/Getty Images

Updated Features: Opposing Perspectives, A View from Science, A Case to Study, and Inside the Brain

In this edition of *The Developing Person Through the Life Span*, I've included four unique features. Opposing Perspectives focuses on controversial topics—from prenatal sex selection to e-cigarettes. I have tried to present information and opinions on both sides of each topic so that students will weigh evidence, assess arguments, and recognize their biases while reaching their own conclusions. A View from Science, which explains research, and A Case to Study, which illustrates development via specific individuals, have been extensively updated. Since new discoveries in neuroscience abound, Inside the Brain features explore topics such as the intricacies of prenatal and infant brain development, brain specialization and speech development, and brain maturation and emotional development.

NEW and Updated Visualizing Development Infographics

Data are often best understood visually and graphically. Every chapter of this edition includes a full-page illustration of a key topic that combines statistics, maps, charts, and photographs. These infographics focus on key issues such as immunization trends, college and later income, and global prevalence of neurocognitive disorders. My editors and I worked closely with noted designer and 2018 Guggenheim Fellow Charles Yuen to develop these Visualizing Development infographics.

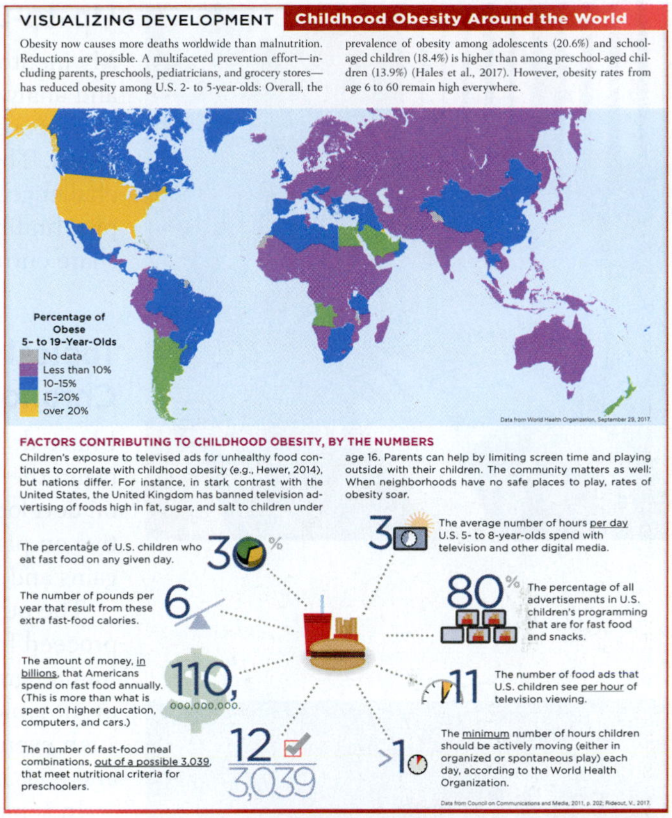

Macmillan Learning

Updated Online Data Connections Activities

Evidence is crucial for scientists, and I hope students will understand this experientially via the interactive activities that require interpretation of the latest data on important topics, from child care to risk-taking to demographic shift. These activities engage students in active learning, promoting a deeper understanding of the science of development. Instructors can assign the Data Connections in the online LaunchPad that accompanies this book.

ONGOING FEATURES

Many characteristics of this book have been acclaimed since the first edition.

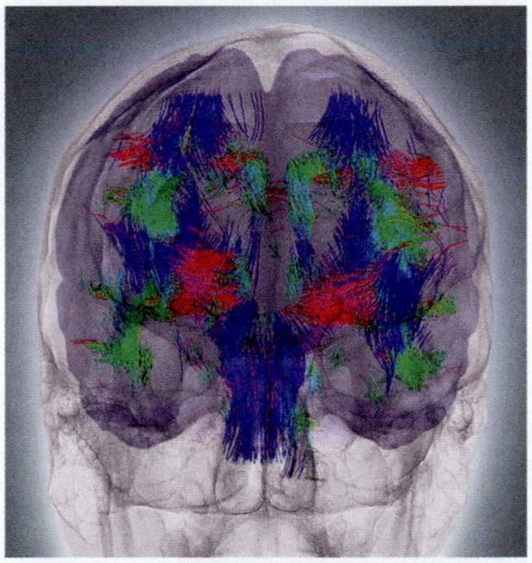

Zephyr/SPL/Science Source

Writing That Communicates the Excitement and Challenge of the Field

An overview of the science of human development should be lively, just as real people are. To that end, each sentence conveys tone as well as content. Chapter-opening vignettes describe real (not hypothetical) situations to illustrate the immediacy of development. Examples and explanations abound, helping students make the connections between theory, research, and their own experiences.

Coverage of Diversity

Cross-cultural, international, intersectional, multiethnic, sexual orientation, socioeconomic status, age, gender identity—all of these words and ideas are vital to appreciating how people develop. Research uncovers surprising similarities and notable differences: We have much in common, yet each human is unique. From the emphasis on contexts in Chapter 1 to the coverage of historical and religious differences in death in the Epilogue, each chapter highlights variations.

New research on family structures, immigrants, bilingualism, and ethnic differences are among the many topics that illustrate human diversity. Respect for human diversity is evident throughout. Examples and research findings from many parts of the world are included, not as add-ons but as integral parts of each age. A list highlighting multicultural material is available at macmillanlearning.com.

Photosindia.com/Exotica/AGE Fotostock

Up-to-Date Coverage

My mentors welcomed curiosity, creativity, and skepticism; as a result, I read and analyze thousands of articles and books on everything from how biology predisposes infants to autism spectrum disorder to the determination of brain death. The recent explosion of research in neuroscience and genetics has challenged me once again, first to understand and then to explain many complex findings and speculative leaps. My students ask nuanced questions and share current experiences, always adding perspective.

Topical Organization Within a Chronological Framework

I have devoted much thought to the organization of this text. Four chapters begin the book with discussions of definitions, theories, genetics, and prenatal development. These chapters provide a foundation for a life-span perspective on plasticity, nature and nurture, multicultural awareness, risk analysis, gains and losses, family bonding, and many other basic concepts.

The other seven parts correspond to the major stages of development and proceed from biology to cognition to emotions to social interaction because human growth usually follows that path. Each stage begins when a new life event typically occurs: Puberty begins adolescence, for instance. The ages of such events vary among people, but 0–2, 2–6, 6–11, 11–18, 18–25, 25–65, and 65+ are the approximate and traditional ages of the various parts.

Milatas/iStock/Getty Images

In some texts, emerging adulthood (Chapters 17, 18, and 19) is subsumed in a stage called early adulthood (ages 20 to 40), which is followed by middle adulthood (ages 40 to 65). I decided against that for two reasons. First, there is no event that starts middle age, especially since the evidence for a "midlife crisis" has crumbled. Second, as these chapters explain, current young adults merit their own part because they are distinct from both adolescents and adults.

I know, as you do, that life is not chunked—each passing day makes us older, each aspect of development affects every other aspect, and each social context affects us in a multitude of ways. However, we learn in sequence, with each thought building on the previous one. Thus, a topical organization within a chronological framework scaffolds comprehension of the interplay between age and domain.

Dinendra Haria / SOPA Images/Sipa USA (Sipa via AP Images)

Photographs, Tables, and Graphs That Are Integral to the Text

Students learn a great deal from this book's illustrations because Worth Publishers encourages their authors to choose the photographs, tables, and graphs and to write captions that extend the content. Observation Quizzes accompany some of them, directing readers to look more closely at what they see. The online Data Connections further this process by presenting numerous charts and tables that contain detailed data for further study.

Integration with LaunchPad

Call-outs to accompanying online materials are in the margins throughout the book. These point to special videos (e.g., a video featuring Susan Beal, M.D., one of the Australian researchers who discovered a link between infant sleep position and sudden infant death syndrome).

Child Development and Nursing Career Correlation Guides

Many students taking this course seek to become licensed nurses or educators. This book and its accompanying testing materials are fully correlated to the NAEYC (National Association for the Education of Young Children) career preparation goals and the NCLEX (nursing) licensure exams. These two supplements are available in this book's accompanying online LaunchPad.

Kyodo/AP Images

TEACHING AND LEARNING AIDS

Supplements can make or break a class, as I and every other experienced instructor knows. Instructors use many electronic tools that did not exist a few decades ago. The publisher's representatives are trained every year to guide students and professors in using the most effective media for their classes. I have adopted texts from many publishers; the Worth representatives are a cut above the rest. Ask them for help with media, with testing, and with content.

LaunchPad with Developing Lives, LearningCurve Quizzing, and Data Connections Activities

Built to solve key challenges in the course, LaunchPad provides everything students need to prepare for class and exams, and it gives instructors everything they need to set up a course, shape the content, craft lectures, assign homework, and monitor the learning of each student and the class as a whole.

LaunchPad (preview at www.launchpadworks) includes:

- An **interactive e-book,** which integrates the text and all student media, including Data Connections activities, videos, and much more.

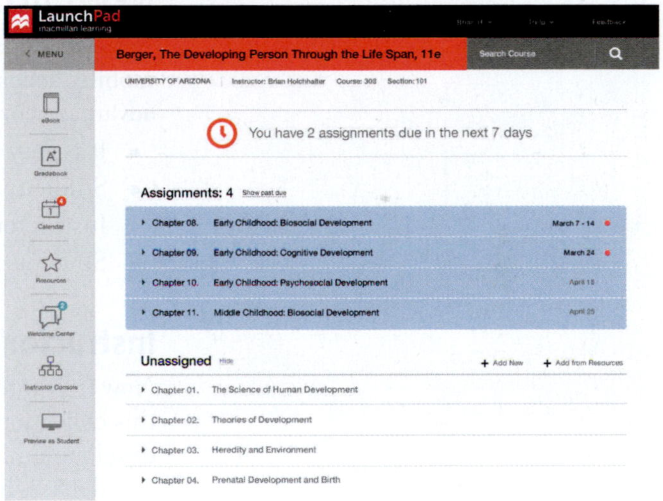

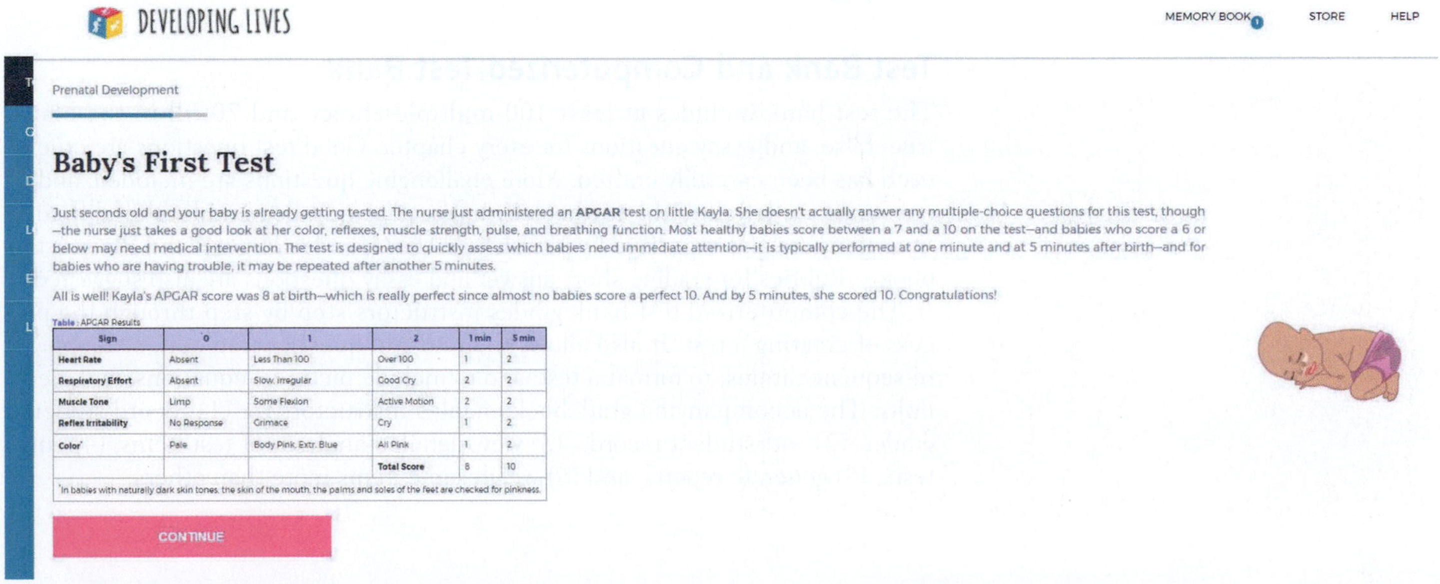

DEVELOPING LIVES
MEMORY BOOK
STORE
HELP
Prenatal Development
Baby's First Test
Just seconds old and your baby is already getting tested. The nurse just administered an APGAR test on little Kayla. She doesn't actually answer any multiple-choice questions for this test, though —the nurse just takes a good look at her color, reflexes, muscle strength, pulse, and breathing function. Most healthy babies score between a 7 and a 10 on the test—and babies who score a 6 or below may need medical intervention. The test is designed to quickly assess which babies need immediate attention—it is typically performed at one minute and at 5 minutes after birth—and for babies who are having trouble, it may be repeated after another 5 minutes.
All is well! Kayla's APGAR score was 8 at birth—which is really perfect since almost no babies score a perfect 10. And by 5 minutes, she scored 10. Congratulations!
Table: APGAR Results
Sign | 0 | 1 | 2 | 1 min | 5 min
Heart Rate | Absent | Less Than 100 | Over 100 | 1 | 2
Respiratory Effort | Absent | Slow, irregular | Good Cry | 2 | 2
Muscle Tone | Limp | Some Flexion | Active Motion | 2 | 2
Reflex Irritability | No Response | Grimace | Cry | 1 | 2
Color* | Pale | Body Pink, Extr. Blue | All Pink | 1 | 2
Total Score | 8 | 10
*In babies with naturally dark skin tones, the skin of the mouth, the palms and soles of the feet are checked for pinkness.
CONTINUE

- **Developing Lives,** the robust interactive experience in which students "raise" their own virtual child. This simulation integrates more than 200 videos and animations, with quizzes and questions to assign and assess.
- **Data Connections**, interactive activities that allow students to interpret data.
- **LearningCurve adaptive quizzing,** based on current research on learning and memory. It combines individualized question selection, immediate and valuable feedback, and a gamelike interface to engage students. Each LearningCurve quiz is fully integrated with other resources in LaunchPad through the Personalized Study Plan, so students can review using Worth's extensive library of videos and activities. Question analysis reports allow instructors to track the progress of individuals and the entire class.
- Worth's **Video Collection for Human Development** is an extensive archive of video clips that covers the full range of the course, from classic experiments (like Ainsworth's Strange Situation and Piaget's conservation task) to illustrations of many topics. Instructors can assign these videos to students through LaunchPad or choose from 50 activities that combine videos with short-answer and multiple-choice questions. (For presentations, our videos are also available on flash drive.)

NEW! Achieve Read & Practice

Achieve Read & Practice combines LearningCurve adaptive quizzing and our mobile, accessible e-book in one easy-to-use and affordable product. Among the advantages of Achieve Read & Practice are the following:

- It is easy to get started.
- Students are better prepared: They can read and study in advance.
- Instructors can use analytics to help their students.
- Students learn more.

Instructor's Resources

Now fully integrated with LaunchPad, and available with Achieve Read & Practice, this collection has been hailed as the richest collection of instructor's resources in developmental psychology. Included are learning objectives, topics for discussion and debate, handouts for student projects, course-planning suggestions, ideas for term projects, and a guide to videos and other online materials.

Test Bank and Computerized Test Bank

The test bank includes at least 100 multiple-choice and 70 fill-in-the-blank, true–false, and essay questions for every chapter. Good test questions are crucial; each has been carefully crafted. More challenging questions are included, and all questions are keyed to the textbook by topic, page number, and level of difficulty. Questions are also organized by NCLEX, NAEYC, and APA goals and Bloom's taxonomy. Rubrics for grading short-answer and essay questions are also suggested.

The computerized test bank guides instructors step by step through the process of creating a test. It also allows them to add questions; to edit, scramble, or re-sequence items; to format a test; and to include pictures, equations, and media links. The accompanying gradebook enables instructors to: (1) record students' grades, (2) sort student records, (3) view detailed analyses of test items, (4) curve tests, (5) generate reports, and (6) weigh some items more than others.

THANKS

Hundreds of academic reviewers and hundreds of thousands of students have read this book in every edition. Many have provided suggestions, criticisms, references, and encouragement. Because of them, every edition is better than the previous one. I especially thank those who have formally reviewed this edition:

Dr. Stephanie Babb, *University of Houston-Downtown*
Renee Babcock-Wolf, *Central Michigan University*
Aileen M. Behan-Collins, M.S., *Chemeketa Community College*
Gina Brelsford, *Penn State Harrisburg*
Melissa L. Cannon, *Western Oregon University*
Catherine Deering, Ph.D., ABPP, *Clayton State University*
Bailey Drechsler, *Cuesta College*
Donnell Griffin, *Davidson County Community College*
Diane Gillooly, DNP, RN-BC, APN, *Rutgers School of Nursing*
Dr. Catherine Hollis, *Harold Washington College, City College of Chicago*
Katie M. Lawson, *Ball State University*
Ariana Lopez, *John Jay College of Criminal Justice, CUNY*
Robert Pasnak, *George Mason University*
Laura Pirazzi, *San Jose State University*
Katelyn E. Poelker, *Hope College*
Pamela Schuetze, *SUNY Buffalo State College*
Brooke R. Spangler Cropenbaker, *Miami University*
Ruth Tincoff, *The College of Idaho*
Virginia Tompkins, *Ohio State University at Lima*

The editorial, production, and marketing people at Worth Publishers are dedicated to high standards. They devote time, effort, and talent to every aspect of publishing, a model for the industry. I am particularly grateful to my executive program manager, Chris Cardone; my developmental editor, Andrea Musick Page; and Macmillan's senior vice president, Charles Linsmeier. I also thank other members of my Macmillan team: Diana Blume, Laura Burden, Matthew Christensen, Shani Fisher, Sheena Goldstein, Noel Hohnstine, Peter Jacoby, Lisa Kinne, Tracey Kuehn, Jana Lewis, Jennifer MacMillan, Matthew McAdams, Michael McCarty, Hilary Newman, Brian Nobile, Katherine Nurre, Donna Ranieri, Steven Huang, Dorothy Tomasini, Susan Wein, and Charles Yuen.

New York, September 2019

APPLICATION TO DEVELOPING LIVES PARENTING SIMULATION

INTRODUCTION AND PRENATAL DEVELOPMENT

In the Introduction module of Developing Lives, you will begin to customize the developmental journey of your child with information about your personality, cognitive abilities, and demographic characteristics. Next, as you progress through the Prenatal simulation module, how you decide the following will impact the biosocial, cognitive, and psychosocial development of your baby.

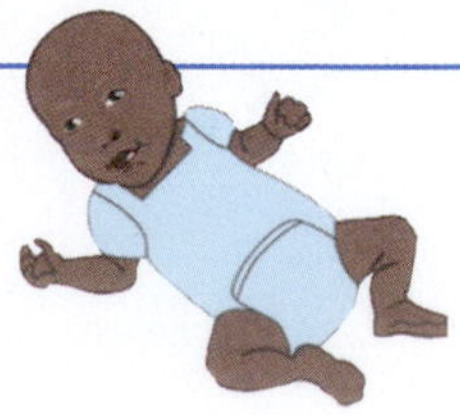

Biosocial

- Will you modify your behaviors and diet during pregnancy?
- Will you find out the gender of your baby prior to delivery?
- What kind of delivery will you and your partner plan for (in the hospital with medication, at home with a doula, etc.)?

Cognitive

- Are you going to talk to your baby while he or she is in the womb?
- How much does your baby understand during prenatal development?

Psychosocial

- How will your relationship with your partner change as a result of the pregnancy?
- Will you begin bonding with your baby prior to birth?

CHAPTERS 1 • 2 • 3 • 4

PART I

The Beginnings

The science of human development includes many beginnings. Each of the first four chapters of this text forms one corner of a solid foundation for our study.

Chapter 1 introduces definitions and dimensions, explaining research strategies and methods that help us understand how people develop. The need for science, the power of culture, and insights from the life-span perspective are explained.

Without theories, our study would be only a jumble of haphazard observations. **Chapter 2** provides organizing guideposts: clusters of theories, each leading to hypotheses and controversies, are described.

Heredity is explained in **Chapter 3.** Genes never act alone, yet no development—anywhere in the body or brain of anyone at any time—is unaffected by epigenetics.

Chapter 4 details the growth of each developing person from a single-celled zygote to a breathing, grasping newborn. Many circumstances—from the mother's diet to the father's care, from the place of birth to the customs of the culture—affect every moment of embryonic and fetal growth.

As you see, the science and the wonder of human life begin long before the first breath. Understanding the beginnings prepares us to understand all the rest.

Left: Monkey Business Images/Stockbyte/Getty Images
Right: Cultura/JFCreatives/Cultura Exclusive/Getty Images

CHAPTER 1

The Science of Human Development

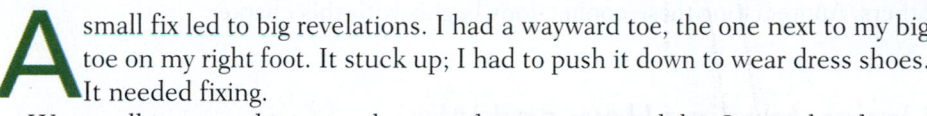

What Will You Know?*

1. Why is science crucial for understanding how people develop?
2. Are people the same, always and everywhere, or is each person unique, changing from day to day and place to place?
3. How are the methods of science used to study development?
4. What must scientists do to make their conclusions valid and ethical?

- **Understanding How and Why**
  - The Scientific Method
  - A VIEW FROM SCIENCE: Priming
  - The Nature–Nurture Controversy
- **The Life-Span Perspective**
  - Development Is Multidirectional
  - Development Is Multicontextual
  - Development Is Multicultural
  - Development Is Multidisciplinary
  - Development Is Plastic
  - INSIDE THE BRAIN: Thinking About Marijuana
  - A CASE TO STUDY: David
- **Using the Scientific Method**
  - Observation
  - The Experiment
  - The Survey
  - Meta-Analysis
  - Studying Development over the Life Span
- **Cautions and Challenges from Science**
  - Correlation and Causation
  - Quantity and Quality
  - Ethics
- **VISUALIZING DEVELOPMENT: Diverse Complexities**

A small fix led to big revelations. I had a wayward toe, the one next to my big toe on my right foot. It stuck up; I had to push it down to wear dress shoes. It needed fixing.

We are all immersed in our culture, and mine suggested that I consult a doctor. I did. The podiatrist also followed cultural norms: She sent me for X-rays and then recommended surgery and a month with very little walking to recuperate. I told her I didn't have a month, that I walk for hours every day. She smiled: "That's what everyone says."

I tried to retrain the toe, taping it down. I failed. Reluctantly I scheduled surgery, postponing it for six months until the school year was over.

Three life-span issues appeared.

The first was that the doctor wrote a prescription for 20 pills.

"These are addictive," I told her.

She laughed and said that I would need them, and that I could not become addicted.

Some doctors discount the harm that often results from opioid use. But as a developmentalist, I read the data: Every day almost 200 Americans die of an opioid overdose. Addiction can happen to anyone. I took two pills the day after the surgery. I was afraid to take more.

What to do with the rest of the pills? Life-span development considers the environment and anticipates future possibilities. Given that, I could not flush them down the toilet; that would contaminate the water supply. I could not store them high in the medicine cabinet in case I needed them someday; that might harm my curious, climbing grandsons. The solution — informed by science — was to crush, dissolve, and incinerate them.

The second problem was a clash between my daughters and me. One daughter insisted on coming with me to surgery. She obtained a wheelchair and ordered a car and driver to get me home. All four daughters arranged their schedules so that at least one of them would be with me day and night for a month. Not necessary, I said; they insisted.

*What Will You Know? questions are a preview *before* each chapter, one for each major heading. They are big ideas that you will still know a decade from now, unlike "What Have You Learned?" questions that are more specific, *after* each major heading.

Left: Leren Lu/DigitalVision/Getty Images
Top: Cultura/JFCreatives/Cultura Exclusive/Getty Images

Two weeks after surgery I went to an evening meeting. When I arrived home at 10 P.M., my daughter Elissa was frantic, on the phone with another worried daughter, Sarah.

"You didn't tell us you had a meeting," Elissa accused me.

I replied with anger of my own.

"I never tell you when I have a meeting. I am old enough to go out at night by myself."

I had forgotten a long-standing insight from life-span development: Everyone has a personal perspective. I wanted to be independent; they wanted to be caregivers; we all behaved as people our age usually do. I should have told Elissa about the meeting.

The final lesson occurred a month later, when the surgeon sent me to physical therapy. Ridiculous, I thought. I expected the therapist to shake her head and say that P.T. was for legs, arms, and backs, not toes.

She did not. Instead she massaged my toe and taught me six exercises to do every day.

"Your toe is connected to your entire body," she explained.

All three lessons illustrate human development. As you will see in this chapter, our science is multidirectional, multicontextual, multicultural, multidisciplinary, and plastic. Each small event, just like every toe and every relative, connects to the others. Appreciating these connections begins with this chapter.

Understanding How and Why

science of human development The science that seeks to understand how and why people of all ages and circumstances change or remain the same over time.

The **science of human development** *seeks to understand how and why people—all kinds of people, everywhere, of every age—change over time.* The goal is for the almost 8 billion people on Earth to fulfill their potential. Growth is *multidirectional, multicontextual, multicultural, multidisciplinary,* and *plastic,* five terms that will be explained soon.

First, however, we need to emphasize that developmental study is a *science.* It depends on theories, data, analysis, critical thinking, and sound methodology, like every other science. All scientists ask questions and seek answers in order to ascertain "how and why."

scientific method A way to answer questions beginning with hypotheses that are then tested with empirical research before drawing conclusions.

Science is especially useful when we study people: Our lives depend on it. What should pregnant women eat? How much should babies cry? When should children be punished, and how, and for what? Under what circumstances and at what age should adults marry, divorce, retire, die? People disagree about all this and more, sometimes vehemently.

The Scientific Method

Facts are often misinterpreted. Applications may spring from assumptions, not from data. To avoid unexamined opinions and to rein in personal biases, researchers follow the five steps of the **scientific method** (see **Figure 1.1**):

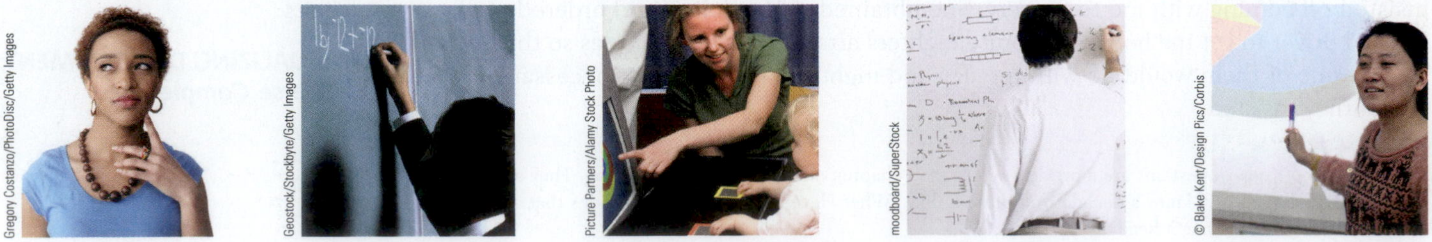

1. Curiosity **2.** Hypothesis **3.** Test **4.** Analyze data and draw conclusions **5.** Report the results

FIGURE 1.1

Process, Not Proof Built into the scientific method—in questions, hypotheses, tests, and replication—is a passion for possibilities, especially unexpected ones.

1. *Begin with curiosity.* On the basis of theory, prior research, or a personal observation, pose a question.
2. *Develop a hypothesis.* Shape the question into a **hypothesis,** a specific prediction that can be tested.
3. *Test the hypothesis.* Design and conduct research to gather **empirical evidence** (data).
4. *Analyze the evidence.* Conclude whether the hypothesis is supported or not, and analyze any interesting nuances, such as age and gender differences. Interpret strong or weak results.
5. *Report the results.* Share data, conclusions, and alternative explanations.

hypothesis A specific prediction that can be tested. Hypotheses that turn out to be false are as meaningful as those that are confirmed.

empirical evidence Evidence that is based on data, i.e., that is demonstrated, not assumed.

As you see, developmental scientists begin with curiosity and then seek facts, drawing conclusions after careful research. The scientific method is especially enlightening when the results are unexpected—that is, when the hypothesis is not supported. Then scientists change their cherished opinions, publishing the empirical evidence so that others can also rethink assumptions. This is often the best part of science: Questions lead to new research and then a better understanding of human behavior (Nash, 2018).

A Replication Crisis? Replication—repeating the procedures and methods of a study with different participants—is often a sixth step of the scientific method. Scientists study the reports of other scientists (Step 5) and build on what has gone before (back to Step 1). Sometimes they try to duplicate a study exactly; often they follow up with related research (Stroebe & Strack, 2014). Conclusions are revised, refined, rejected, or confirmed after replication.

replication Repeating a study, usually using different participants but similar or identical procedures and measures.

Obviously, the scientific method is not foolproof. Scientists may draw conclusions too hastily, misinterpret data, or ignore alternative perspectives (Bouter, 2015).

Ideally, before any conclusion is accepted, results are replicated, not only by performing the same study again (Step 3) but also by designing other studies that can verify and extend the same hypothesis (Larzelere et al., 2015).

An effort to replicate 100 published studies in psychology found that about one-third did not replicate and another one-third were less conclusive than the original (Bohannon, 2015), causing what has been termed a *replication crisis.* That conclusion itself needed replication: A new analysis (Step 4) found a failure rate of one in seven, not one in three (Gilbert et al., 2016).

When problems arose with those 100 studies, usually something was amiss in the research design (Step 3), and researchers and editors were too eager to publish surprising results (Step 5). They did not wait for reanalysis and replication. Thus, "there is still more work to do to verify whether we know what we think we know" (Open Science Collaboration, 2015, p. 943).

The replication crisis has led to better research. Hypotheses are often stated in advance; details of the data are available to other scientists; studies are likely to include more participants to prevent a few outliers from skewing the results.

Of course, the fact that we study humans, who develop in diverse contexts and cultures, means that no study will exactly duplicate another (De Boeck & Jeon, 2018). Perfect replication is impossible; that is why new research is inspired by what has gone before. (See A View from Science on page 6.)

The Nature–Nurture Controversy

An easy example of the need for science concerns a great puzzle of life, the *nature–nurture debate.* **Nature** refers to the influence of the genes that people inherit. **Nurture** refers to environmental influences, beginning with the health, diet, and stress of

nature The genetic influences on a person.

nurture The non-genetic influences on each developing person, which is everything from the mother's nutrition while pregnant to the national culture.

Chopin's First Concert Frederick Chopin, at age 8, played his first public concert in 1818, before photographs. But this photo shows Piotr Pawlak, a contemporary prodigy playing Chopin's music in the same Polish Palace where that famous composer played as a boy. How much of talent is genetic and how much is cultural? This is a nature–nurture question that applies to both boys, 200 years apart.

the future person's mother at conception and continuing lifelong, including experiences in the family, school, community, and nation.

The nature–nurture debate has many manifestations, among them *heredity–environment, maturation–learning,* and *sex–gender.* Under whatever name, the basic question is, "How much of any characteristic, behavior, or emotion is the result of genes, and how much is the result of experience?"

Born That Way? Some people believe that most traits are inborn, that children are innately good ("an innocent child") or bad ("beat the devil out of them"). Others stress nurture, crediting or blaming parents, or neighborhoods, or drugs, or even additives in the food, when someone is good or bad, a hero or a villain.

Neither belief is accurate. As one group of scholars explains, human characteristics are neither born nor made (Hambrick et al., 2018). Genes and the environment *both* affect every characteristic: Nature always affects nurture, and then nurture affects nature. Any attempt to decide exactly how much of a trait is genetic and how much is environmental is bound to fail, because genetic and environmental influences continuously interact, sometimes increasing the influence of the other and sometimes decreasing it.

A further complication is that the impact of any good or bad experience might be magnified or inconsequential because of particular genes or past events. For example, a beating, or a beer, or a blessing might be a turning point in someone's life, or it might not matter at all.

Every adult can remember a remark or an incident from childhood that is seared in memory because it caused pain, or shame, or joy. That very remark

A VIEW FROM SCIENCE*

Priming

An impressive attempt at replication has focused on *priming,* in which study participants are induced (primed) to think in a certain way and then assessed to find out whether those thoughts affect their later thinking or behavior. For example, they may contemplate (often via reading a passage or writing a short essay) one set of thoughts, such as about death, or old age, or race. They might be given some task (answering questions, walking, confronting a bully) that might be influenced by the prime.

Thousands of studies at the end of the twentieth century found that priming affects later performance. In one of these studies, psychology students were primed to think of themselves either as a professor or as a "soccer hooligan." (This study was in the Netherlands, where soccer hooligans were infamous for cursing, fighting, and drinking too much beer.)

Then they took a test in which they answered some trivia questions. The effects were dramatic: Those who imagined themselves as professors scored 13 percent higher than those who thought of themselves as hooligans (Dijksterhuis & van Knippenberg, 1998).

That prompted a massive replication effort: 40 laboratories in 19 nations repeated the procedures with a total of 6,554 college students (O'Donnell et al., 2018). Replication failed! The data from the labs varied (some positive, some negative), but none approached the original results.

Two reasons for replication failure were suggested.

1. Cultural changes: Students worldwide may now consider the intelligence of professors less, or soccer hooligans more, than those Dutch students did two decades ago.
2. Knowledge: Current psychology students may know about priming, suspect that this study was a replication attempt, and resist it (Dijksterhuis, 2018).

You can probably think of a third possibility: The original result might have been a fluke, which would have made replication impossible even then. With a careful scientific approach, this is unlikely, but always possible, especially with relatively few select local participants. Perhaps those Dutch students were unlike students anywhere else. That is why replication is needed.

*Many chapters of this text feature A View from Science, which explains surprising insights from scientific research.

might have been forgotten by the person who said it, or it might have been said to another child with no effect. Each aspect of nature and nurture depends on other aspects of nature and nurture in ways that themselves vary because of the nature and nurture of each individual.

Differential Susceptibility

The effect of an offhand remark illustrates **differential susceptibility** (Ellis et al., 2011a). People vary in how sensitive they are to any particular words, or drugs, or experiences, either because of the particular genes they have inherited or because of events years earlier.

differential susceptibility The idea that people vary in how sensitive they are to particular experiences, either because of their genes or because of past events. The same experience might harm some people and help others. (Also called *differential sensitivity.*)

Asthma is an obvious example of differential susceptibility: Some people begin wheezing when they are near a cat, but others never do. Because of their parents' reactions in their early years, some older children are terrified at the first signs of an attack; others are nonchalant.

A more dramatic example involves dogs as well as cats (Krzych-Fałta et al., 2018). If a person lives in a rural area, fur-bearing pets reduce the rate of asthma; but in urban areas, such animals increase the incidence. That is differential susceptibility.

Developmentalists use a floral metaphor to express this idea. Some people are like *dandelions*—hardy, growing, and thriving in good soil or bad, with or without ample sun and rain. Other people are like *orchids*—quite wonderful, but only when ideal growing conditions are met (Ellis & Boyce, 2008; Laurent, 2014). The child who takes asthma or any other illness in stride is a dandelion; the one who experiences terror may be an orchid.

THINK CRITICALLY: Why not assign a percent to nature and a percent to nurture so that they add up to 100 percent?*

*Think Critically questions occur several times in each chapter. They are intended to provoke thought, not simple responses, and hence have no obvious answers.

WHAT HAVE YOU LEARNED?*

1. What are the five steps of the scientific method?
2. What is the difference between asking a question (Step 1) and developing a hypothesis (Step 2)?
3. Why is replication important for scientific progress?
4. What basic question is at the heart of the nature–nurture controversy?
5. When in development does nurture begin to influence nature?
6. How might differential susceptibility apply to responses to a low exam grade?

The Life-Span Perspective

The **life-span perspective** (Fingerman et al., 2011; Lerner et al., 2010; Baltes et al., 2006) considers all aspects of the entire life. That leads to the realization that human development is multidirectional, multicontextual, multicultural, multidisciplinary, and plastic.

life-span perspective An approach to the study of human development that takes into account all phases of life, not just childhood or adulthood.

Development Is Multidirectional

The study of life-span development highlights *how and why people change over time*: Approximate ages for each period in this book appear in **Table 1.1**. Other stages could be listed: middle adulthood, or old-old age, and much more.

But a crucial realization regarding any life stage is that *gains and losses* are continual. Even in old age, gains are apparent. A simplistic understanding of the

*What Have You Learned? questions test your specific knowledge of what you have just read. Some of the questions can be answered by a close reading of the text; others require application of the ideas you have learned.

TABLE 1.1

Age Ranges for Different Developmental Stages

Infancy	0 to 2 years
Early childhood	2 to 6 years
Middle childhood	6 to 11 years
Adolescence	11 to 18 years
Emerging adulthood	18 to 25 years
Adulthood	25 to 65 years
Late adulthood	65 years and older

As you will learn, developmentalists are reluctant to specify chronological ages for any period of development, because time is only one of many variables that affect each person. However, age is a crucial variable, and development can be segmented into periods of study. Approximate ages for each period are given here.

direction of development from birth to death—up, steady, and down—is imprecise and sometimes flat-out wrong.

That is the first maxim of the life-span perspective: Multiple changes, in every direction, characterize life. Traits appear and disappear, with increases, decreases, and zigzags (see **Figure 1.2**). Do not let anyone tell you that so-and-so will never change: People change in expected and unexpected ways.

Sometimes *discontinuity* is evident. Change can occur rapidly and dramatically: Caterpillars become butterflies; loners fall in love. Sometimes *continuity* is found. Growth can be gradual: Redwoods add rings over hundreds of years; golfers incrementally lower their score.

Critical and Sensitive Periods The timing of losses and gains, impairments or improvements, is affected by age and maturation. Some changes are sudden and profound because of a **critical period,** which is either when something *must* occur to ensure normal development or the only time when an abnormality might occur.

critical period A crucial time when certain events (either biological or social) must occur in order for development to proceed normally.

For instance, the human embryo grows arms and legs, hands and feet, fingers and toes, each over a critical period between 28 and 54 days after conception. After that, it is too late: Unlike some insects, humans never grow replacement limbs.

We know this because of a tragedy. Between 1957 and 1961, thousands of newly pregnant women in 30 nations took *thalidomide,* an antinausea drug. This change in nurture (via the mother's bloodstream) disrupted nature (the embryo's genetic program).

If an expectant woman ingested thalidomide during the critical period for limb formation, her newborn's arms or legs were malformed or absent (Moore et al., 2015). Whether all four limbs or just arms, hands, or fingers were missing depended on exactly when the drug was taken. If thalidomide was ingested only after day 54, no harm occurred.

Life has few critical periods. Often, however, a particular development occurs more easily—but not exclusively—at a certain time. That is called a **sensitive period.**

sensitive period A time when a certain development is most likely to occur. For example, early childhood is considered a sensitive period for language learning.

An example is learning language (Werker & Hensch, 2015). If children do not communicate in their first language between ages 1 and 3, they might do so later (these years are not critical), but their grammar is impaired (these years are sensitive). Childhood is a particularly sensitive period for learning to pronounce a second or third language with a native accent.

One review of the brain structures for second language learning strongly recommends hearing both languages during the first year of life. Adults who learn a new language after adolescence almost never master a native accent "even after years of practice, and despite high proficiency in all other aspects of language function" (Berken et al., 2017, p. 222). The critical period for hearing and repeating nuances of accent is over.

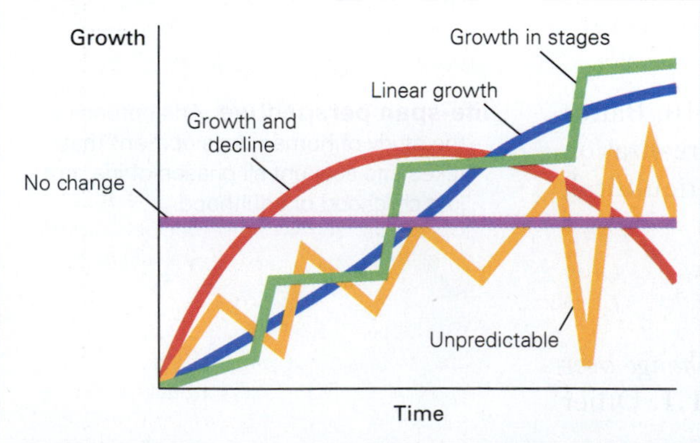

FIGURE 1.2
Patterns of Developmental Growth Many patterns of developmental growth have been discovered by careful research. Although linear (or nonlinear) progress seems most common, scientists now find that almost no aspect of human change follows the linear pattern exactly.

Development Is Multicontextual

The second insight from the life-span perspective is that "human development is fundamentally contextual" (Pluess, 2015, p. 138). Among the many contexts are three obvious clusters: physical surroundings (including climate, noise, trees), family structures

(marital status, family size, ages), and community characteristics (urban, suburban, or rural; diverse or not).

The Social Context Humans are intensely social creatures, so a fourth category, the social context, is crucial. The social context includes all other people who influence each individual.

For example, a 20-year-old college student might be persuaded to stop by a party instead of heading to the library. The host furnishes the setting, with drinks, food, and music. The people—friends, acquaintances, strangers—provide the immediate social context, which affects whether the student will stay till 3 A.M. or leave soon after arriving. On the following morning, the context of the party will affect the student's attention in class—another social context.

In the same way, we each experience several contexts each day, some by choice and some involuntarily, and they affect our later thoughts and actions. A hard day at work might make a parent impatient with the children—or a family conflict might spill over to work. Sexual liaisons change neurotransmitters and hormones, and that affects other social contexts.

In these examples, the effect is almost immediate, but much of development is affected by contexts over the long term. Childhood social play may affect adult work habits, for instance. A child's family and neighborhood contexts predispose adult psychological disorders—always with differential susceptibility (Keers & Pluess, 2017).

Ecological Systems A leading developmentalist, Urie Bronfenbrenner (1917–2005), emphasized the power of contexts. Just as a naturalist studying an organism examines the ecology (the relationship between the organism and its environment) of a tiger, or tree, or trout, Bronfenbrenner told developmentalists to take an **ecological-systems approach** (Bronfenbrenner & Morris, 2006).

This approach recognizes three nested levels (see **Figure 1.3**).

- Most obvious is the **microsystem** (each person's immediate social contexts, such as family and peer group).
- Also important is the **exosystem** (local institutions such as school and church).
- Beyond that is the **macrosystem** (the larger social setting, including cultural values, economic policies, and political processes).

Two more systems affect these three.

- One is the **chronosystem** (literally, "time system"), which is the historical context.
- The other is the **mesosystem,** consisting of the connections among the other systems.

In the student-at-party example, the student's immediate social circle is the microsystem, the college culture (is it a "party school"?) is the exosystem, and the national emphasis on higher education is part of the macrosystem. The party itself is a mesosystem, in that it connects the microsystem and the exosystem. Every gathering reflects the chronosystem. Party food and drink vary by year, and the fact that students attend parties reflects the century. (Many 20-year-olds a century ago were married parents.)

Bronfenbrenner's perspective remains useful. For example, children who have been sexually abused are likely to be abused again, in childhood and adulthood. Why? Is there something amiss in the person or is the fault in the culture?

Psychologists have used Bronfenbrenner's systems approach to answer that question, finding causes in all systems simultaneously (Pittenger et al., 2016). For example, an abused adult is likely to have been abused by a family member as a child (macrosystem), to belong to a church that is silent about sexuality

ecological-systems approach A perspective on human development that considers all of the influences from the various contexts of development. (Later renamed *bioecological theory.*)

microsystem In Bronfenbrenner's ecological approach, the immediate social contexts that directly affect each person, such as family, peer group, work team.

exosystem In Bronfenbrenner's ecological approach, the community institutions that affect the immediate contexts, such as churches and temples, schools and colleges, hospitals and courts.

macrosystem In Bronfenbrenner's ecological approach, the overarching national or cultural policies and customs that affect the more immediate systems, such as the effect of the national economy on local hospitals (an exosystem) or on families (a microsystem)

chronosystem In Bronfenbrenner's ecological approach, the impact of historical conditions (wars, inventions, policies) on the development of people who live in that era.

mesosystem In Bronfenbrenner's ecological approach, a connection between one system and another, such as parent–teacher conferences (connecting home and school) or workplace schedules (connecting family and job).

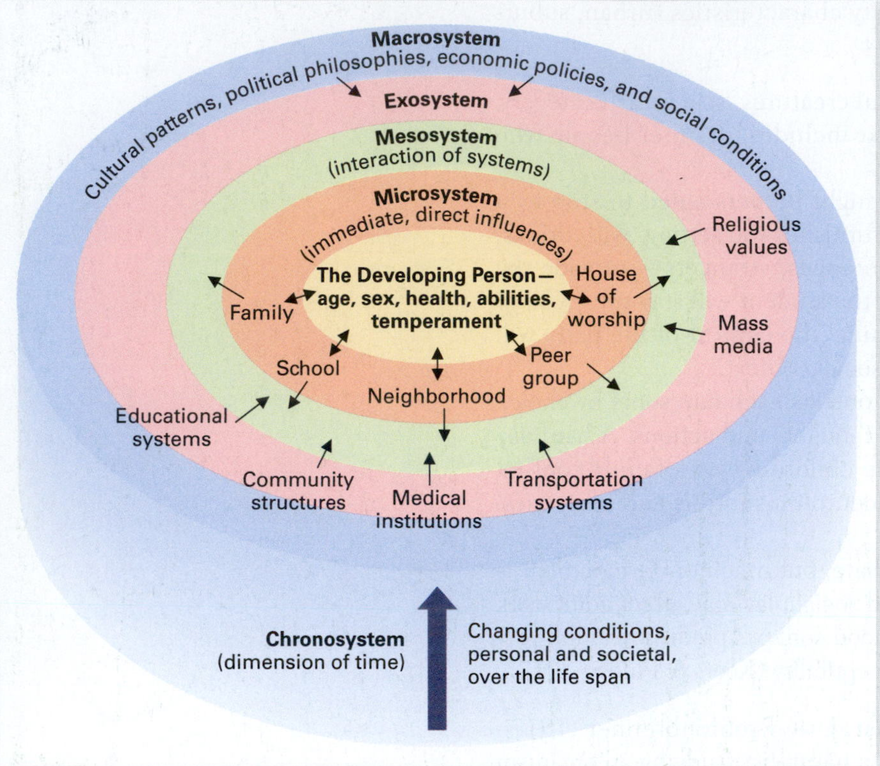

FIGURE 1.3

The Ecological Model According to developmental researcher Urie Bronfenbrenner, each person is significantly affected by interactions among a number of overlapping systems, which provide the context of development. *Microsystems*—family, peer group, classroom, neighborhood, house of worship—intimately and immediately shape human development. Surrounding and supporting the microsystems are the *exosystems*, which include all the external networks (such as community structures and local educational, medical, employment, and communications systems) that affect the microsystems. Influencing both of these systems is the *macrosystem*, which includes cultural patterns, political philosophies, economic policies, and social conditions. *Mesosystems* refer to interactions among systems, as when parents and teachers coordinate to educate a child. Bronfenbrenner eventually added a fifth system, the *chronosystem*, to emphasize the importance of historical time.

(exosystem), and to live within a culture that does not prosecute abuse (macrosystem).

The Historical Context All persons born within a few years of one another are called a **cohort,** a group defined by its members' shared age. Cohorts travel through life together, experiencing at each age particular values, events, and technologies. Imagine growing up before contraception, or color television, or social media—as is true for people over age 70. Their entire lives would be different from those of the current generation.

Consider a person's name. If you know someone named Emma, she is probably young: Emma is the most common name for girls born between 2014 and 2018 but was not in the top 100 until 1996, nor in the top 1,000 in 1990. If you know someone named Mary, she is probably old: Mary was the first or second most popular name from 1900 to 1965; now only 1 baby in 800 is named Mary.

These rankings are from the United States (U.S. Social Security Administration, 2019) (see **Table 1.2**). Variation is evident by nation, by culture, and by region—within the United States and elsewhere. For example, Wyatt is the third most common boy's name in Alaska, but it isn't in the top 100 in California.

The Socioeconomic Context Some scholars believe that the economic context is even more important than the historical one. Each person's **socioeconomic status,** abbreviated **SES** (SES is an abbreviation that is basic to understanding human development, so it is used often in this text), affects every stage of development.

SES is not solely about income. It also reflects education, occupation, and neighborhood. The combination affects development much more than money alone.

Imagine two U.S. families comprised of an infant, an unemployed mother, and a father who earns less than $17,000 a year. That family income is markedly below the 2018 federal poverty line for a family of three ($20,780).

However, that income does not determine SES. If one family lives in a crime-ridden neighborhood, headed by parents who never completed high school and dependent on the father's minimum wage job that provides $16,965 in annual income ($7.25 per hour × 45 hours a week × 52 weeks), their SES would be low. If the other father is a postdoctoral student living on campus with his college graduate wife and teaching part time, the family would be middle class.

cohort People born within the same historical period who therefore move through life together, experiencing the same events, technologies, and cultural shifts at the same ages. For example, the effect of the Internet varies depending on what cohort a person belongs to.

socioeconomic status (SES) A person's position in society as determined by income, occupation, education, and place of residence. (Sometimes called *social class*.)

Development Is Multicultural

In order to learn about "all kinds of people, everywhere, at every age," it is necessary to study people of many cultures. For social scientists, **culture** is "the system

culture A system of shared beliefs, norms, behaviors, and expectations that persist over time and guide behavior and assumptions.

of shared beliefs, conventions, norms, behaviors, expectations and symbolic representations that persist over time and prescribe social rules of conduct" (Bornstein et al., 2011, p. 30).

Social Constructions Thus, culture is far more than food or clothes; it is a set of ideas, beliefs, and patterns. Culture is a powerful **social construction,** that is, a concept created, or *constructed,* by a society. Social constructions affect how people think and act—what they value, ignore, and punish.

Each group of people creates a culture, which means there are ethnic cultures, national cultures, family cultures, college cultures, economic cultures, and so on. Thus, everyone is multicultural and everyone sometimes experiences a clash between their cultures. One of my students wrote:

> My mom was outside on the porch talking to my aunt. I decided to go outside; I guess I was being nosey. While they were talking I jumped into their conversation which was very rude. When I realized what I did it was too late. My mother slapped me in my face so hard that it took a couple of seconds to feel my face again.
>
> [C., *personal communication*]

Notice that my student reflects her family culture; she labels her own behavior "nosey" and "very rude." She later wrote that she expects children to be seen but not heard and that her own son makes her "very angry" when he interrupts.

However, her "rude" behavior may have been encouraged by the culture of her school, as she attended a New York public school, far from her mother's native land. In the United States, many teachers want children to speak up, so children's talk is welcomed. Do you think my student was nosey or, on the contrary, that her mother should not have slapped her? Or do you think she was rude *and* that the mother should have responded less harshly? Your answer reflects your culture.

Deficit or Just Difference? As with my student's mother, everyone is inclined to believe that their culture is better than others. This tendency has benefits: Generally, people who appreciate their own culture are happier, prouder, and more willing to help strangers. However, that belief becomes destructive if it reduces respect for people from other groups. Too quickly and without conscious thought, differences are assumed to be problems (Akhtar & Jaswal, 2013).

Developmentalists recognize the **difference-equals-deficit error,** which is the belief that people unlike us (different) are inferior (deficit). Sadly, when humans realize that their ways of thinking and acting are not universal, they may believe that people who think or act differently are to be pitied, feared, and encouraged to change.

The difference-equals-deficit error is one reason that a careful multicultural approach is necessary. Never assume that another culture is wrong and inferior—or the opposite, right and superior. Assumptions can be harmful.

For example, one immigrant child, on her first day in a U.S. school, was teased about the food she brought for lunch. The next day, she dumped the contents of her lunchbox in the garbage soon after she arrived at school, choosing hunger over being different.

This example illustrates the problem with judging another culture: A child's lunch of another culture might, or might not, be more nutritious than conventional peanut butter and jelly sandwiches.

TABLE 1.2

First Names

Girls	
2018:	Emma, Olivia, Ava, Isabella, Sophia
1998:	Emily, Hannah, Sarah, Samantha, Ashley
1978:	Jennifer, Melissa, Jessica, Amy, Heather
1958:	Mary, Susan, Linda, Karen, Patricia
1938:	Mary, Barbara, Patricia, Betty, Shirley
Boys	
2018:	Liam, Noah, William, James, Oliver
1998:	Michael, Jacob, Matthew, Joshua, Christopher
1978:	Michael, Jason, Christopher, David, James
1958:	Michael, David, James, Robert, John
1938:	Robert, James, John, William, Richard

Information from U.S. Social Security Administration.

social construction An idea that is built on shared perceptions, not on objective reality. Many age-related terms (such as *childhood, adolescence, yuppie,* and *senior citizen*) are social constructions, connected to biological traits but strongly influenced by social assumptions.

difference-equals-deficit error The mistaken belief that unusual behavior or conditions are necessarily inferior.

CHAPTER APP 1

Culture Compass

RELATED TOPIC:
The role of culture and context in human development

IOS:
https://tinyurl.com/y3uo6y3e

ANDROID:
https://tinyurl.com/y2bfjx7r

This app prepares users for personal and professional encounters with people from other backgrounds and cultures, offering insight and guidance about national and cultural differences in values, behavior, rituals, and symbols.

MYRTO PAPADOPOULOS FOR THE WASHINGTON POST VIA GETTY IMAGES

Difference, But Not Deficit This Syrian refugee living in a refugee camp in Greece is quite different from the aid workers who assist there, as evident in her head covering (hijab) and the cross on her tent. But the infant, with a pacifier in her mouth and a mother who tries to protect her, illustrates why developmentalists focus on similarities rather than on differences.

In this example, the children did not consider culture or nutrition; the mothers thought the lunch they packed was best; the student wanted to be accepted. The difference was misjudged as a deficit, and then it harmed that student (hungry children learn less). Later consequences might be lifelong shame about her heritage.

THINK CRITICALLY: How does the difference-equals-deficit error apply to attitudes of native-born citizens about immigrants, and vice versa?

Ethnic and Racial Groups Cultural clashes fuel wars and violence when differences are seen as deficits. To prevent that, we need to understand the terms *ethnicity* and *race*. Members of an **ethnic group** almost always share ancestral heritage and often have the same national origin, religion, and language.

ethnic group People whose ancestors were born in the same part of the world, often sharing language, culture, and religion.

race Categorizing people based on inherited traits. Anthropologists and biologists no longer think race is a valid biological concept, although it is a powerful social construction.

Ethnicity is a social construction, a product of the social context, not biology. Ethnic groups often share a culture, but not necessarily.

There are "multiple intersecting and interacting dimensions" to ethnic identity (Sanchez & Vargas, 2016, p. 161). People may share ethnicity but differ culturally (e.g., people of Irish descent in Ireland, Australia, and North America), and people of one culture may come from several ethnic groups (consider British culture). [**Life-Span Link:** The major discussion of ethnic identity is in **Chapter 19**.]

Historically, most North Americans were taught that race was an inborn biological characteristic that differentiated members of one group from another, each distinct. According to this belief, a person could not be multiracial. Races were categorized by skin color: white, black, red, and yellow (Coon, 1962).

It was not obvious that color words are a gross exaggeration of relatively minor physical differences. No one is really white (like this page) or black (like these letters) or red or yellow (both terms offensive).

Biologists now recognize **race** as a social construction. One team writes:

> We believe the use of biological concepts of race in human genetic research—so disputed and so mired in confusion—is problematic at best and harmful at worst. It is time for biologists to find a better way.
>
> [*Yudell et al., 2016, p. 564*]

The fact that race is a social construction does not make it meaningless, given history. Adolescents who are proud of their racial ancestry are likely to achieve academically, resist drugs, and feel better about themselves (Zimmerman et al., 2013).

The relationship between racial pride and racial prejudice is complex. Ethnic pride, but not personal experiences with discrimination, predicts more positive attitudes about oneself and about other groups. In the United States, this was found in a study of 15- to 25-year-old African American and Hispanic American youth, but it was not apparent among European American youth—who usually did not consider themselves as belonging to a racial group (Sullivan & Ghara, 2015).

That involves an interesting historical twist. A hundred years ago, Americans of Irish, Italian, and Greek ethnicity were *not* considered part of the "White race" (Gordon, 2017). This confirms, of course, that race is a social construction.

intersectionality The idea that the various identities need to be combined. This is especially important in determining if discrimination occurs.

Intersectionality **Intersectionality** begins with the idea that we each are pushed and pulled—sometimes strongly, sometimes weakly, sometimes by ourselves, sometimes by authorities—by our gender, religion, generation, nation, age, and ethnic group. Our many identities interact with and influence each other (see

Figure 1.4). Intersectionality then recognizes that those identities can be used to discriminate by dividing people—White women versus Black women, Asian men versus Latino men, and so on—instead of uniting us.

Intersectionality focuses attention on power differences between groups, bringing special attention to the needs of people who are simultaneously in several marginalized groups. They are most harmed when their intersectional identities are ignored.

When Kimberlé Crenshaw (1989) first introduced the term "intersectionality," she recognized that the courts allowed discrimination against African American women because the laws did not acknowledge that racism and sexism combined to harm them.

Intersectionality highlights discrimination in many institutions. For example, do judges give African American people harsher prison sentences than European American people for the same crimes? The data say yes, and that is unfair. But the unfairness may be more extensive than that.

A careful study of all sentences meted out to convicted criminals in Pennsylvania found age and gender disparities more notable than ethnic ones. For the same crime, young adults are sentenced more harshly than older ones, and men more harshly than women (Steffensmeier et al., 2017). Thus young African American men may be particularly misjudged.

More generally, like interlocking gears, systems of social categorization and group power intersect to influence everyone, every day. How would your life be different if you were of another gender identity, ethnicity, family background, sexual orientation, health status, ability, and so on?

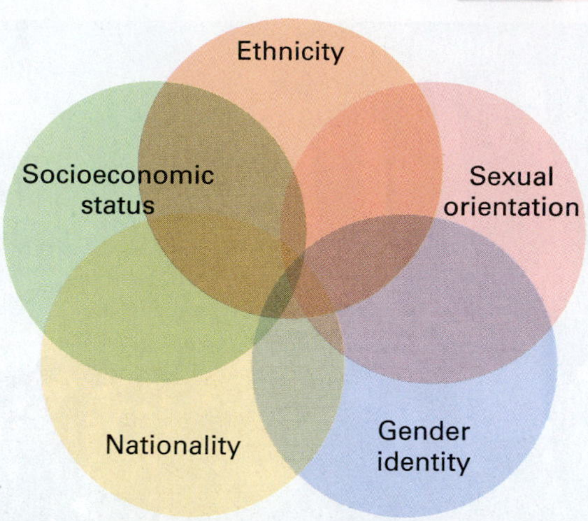

FIGURE 1.4

Identities Interacting We all are in the middle, with many identities. Our total selves are affected by them all, with variation by culture and context as to which are more salient.

Development Is Multidisciplinary

In order to examine each aspect of human growth, development is often considered in three domains—*biosocial*, *cognitive*, and *psychosocial*. Each domain is the focus of several academic disciplines:

- Biosocial includes biology, neuroscience, and medicine.
- Cognitive includes psychology, linguistics, and education.
- Psychosocial includes economics, sociology, and history.

Typically, each scholar follows a particular thread within one discipline and one domain, using clues and conclusions from other scientists who have concentrated on that same thread.

Accordingly, human development requires insights and information from many scientists, past and present, in many disciplines. Our understanding of every topic benefits from multidisciplinary research; scientists hesitate to apply general conclusions about human life until they are substantiated by several disciplines, each specializing.

Genetics The need for multidisciplinary research is obvious when considering genetic analysis. When the human genome was first mapped in 2003, some people assumed that humans became whatever their genes destined them to be—heroes, killers, or ordinary people. However, multidisciplinary research quickly showed otherwise.

Yes, genes affect every aspect of behavior. But even monozygotic twins, with identical genes, differ biologically, cognitively, and socially. [**Life-Span Link:** Twins are discussed in **Chapter 3**.] Among the many reasons are their position in the womb and non-DNA influences in utero, both of which affect birthweight and birth order, and then dozens of other epigenetic influences throughout life

MIKE COPPOLA/GETTY IMAGES Entertainment/Getty Images

Fitting In The best comedians are simultaneously outsider and insider, giving them a perspective that helps people laugh at the absurdities in their lives. Trevor Noah—son of a Xhosa South African mother and a German Swiss father—grew up within, yet outside, his native culture. For instance, he was seen as "Coloured" in his homeland but as "White" on a video, which once let him escape arrest!

Lloyd Wolf

Criminology and Medicine Punishment of criminals and the health of newborns are central concerns of the disciplines of criminology and medicine, not psychology or political science. However, here you see 100 psychologists about to inform the U.S. Congress about the hazards of using restraints (e.g., handcuffs) on women giving birth, which is the practice in many prisons. As in this example, many human problems require a multidisciplinary approach.

(Carey, 2012). Thus, to understand any person, one must consider findings from many disciplines: genetics, nutrition, psychology, sociology, education, and more.

Every academic discipline risks becoming a *silo*—that is, a storage tank for research in that discipline, isolated from other disciplines. Breaking out of silos can illuminate topics that mystified scientists who were stuck in their own discipline.

A dramatic example comes from autism spectrum disorder (ASD). Autism was not recognized as distinct from schizophrenia until about 1940, and then it remained in the silo of psychiatry for decades.

For most of the twentieth century, psychiatrists traced psychological disorders to early mother–child relationships. Accordingly, since many children with ASD do not look at people or let their mothers hug them, some blamed cold, unaffectionate "refrigerator mothers," reflecting a perspective of many psychiatrists (Bettelheim, 1972).

Thousands of mothers suffered from that judgment (Jack, 2014). Then a reversal came from biology, specifically genetics: A discipline once thought to be irrelevant to mental disorders was now considered pivotal for autism spectrum disorder, schizophrenia, mood disorders, and so on (Kandel, 2018).

Geneticists collected data proving that autism is genetic. However, although the genetic evidence released mothers from guilt, it convinced people that nothing could be done to help such children. Then another silo weighed in: Educators found that children "on the spectrum" can be taught language and social skills.

Soon neuroscientists found signs of autism in the brain; nutritionists suggested dietary changes; medical doctors prescribed drugs; public health workers were appalled when parents blamed vaccinations; demographers traced the increase in cases (now estimated among U.S. 8-year-old boys at about 1 in 23) (Baio et al., 2018); and so on.

We still do not know all the causes and treatments of ASD [**Life-Span Link:** Autism spectrum disorder is discussed in **Chapter 11**.] But we do know that insights from many disciplines are needed. If anyone suggests *the* cause or *the* cure for autism spectrum disorder, a life-span perspective declares that silo approach mistaken.

Overall, multidisciplinary research broadens and deepens our knowledge of human development. People are complex, and to properly grasp all of the systems—from the workings of the microbiome in the gut to the effects of climate change throughout the entire world—requires a multidisciplinary approach. Adding to this complexity: People change. That leads to the final theme of the life-span perspective, plasticity.

Development Is Plastic

plasticity The concept that suggests that abilities, personality, neurons, and so on are moldable, not immutable.

dynamic-systems approach A view of human development as an ongoing, ever-changing interaction between the physical, cognitive, and psychosocial influences. This approach recognizes that development is never static.

The term **plasticity** denotes two complementary aspects of development: Human traits can be molded (as plastic can be), yet people maintain a certain durability of identity (as plastic does). The concept of plasticity in development provides both hope and realism—hope because change is possible, and realism because development builds on what has come before.

Dynamic Systems Plasticity is basic to our contemporary understanding of human development. This is evident in the **dynamic-systems approach.** The idea is that human development is an ongoing, ever-changing interaction between the

body and mind and between each person and every aspect of the environment. This includes all of the systems of the ecological-systems approach.

Note the word *dynamic*: Physical contexts, emotional influences, the passage of time, each person, and every aspect of the ecosystem are always active, always in flux, always in motion.

Thus, a dynamic-systems approach to understanding the role of fathers takes into account the gender and age of the child, the role of the mother, and the cultural norms of fatherhood. The result is a complex mix of complementary effects—and this dynamic mix affects each child in diverse ways (Cabrera, 2015).

Plasticity is also apparent in social norms. Inside the Brain highlights plasticity in culture as well as in the brain.

INSIDE THE BRAIN*

Thinking About Marijuana

Brains are affected by drugs, for better or worse. This is evident both in structure (parts of the brain change size because of drug exposure) and activity (connections between neurons are strengthened or weakened).

Consider marijuana. The intensity of fear in the amygdala and pleasure from the basal ganglia precede drug use, and the size and activity of both are powerfully affected by childhood. Then those parts of the brain continue to be molded, evident in how various generations of adults think about marijuana as well as whether they use the drug.

The plasticity of attitudes is dramatic. In the United States in the 1930s, marijuana was declared illegal. The 1936 movie *Reefer Madness* was shown until about 1960, with vivid images connecting marijuana with a warped brain, suicide, and insanity. Before 1960, most Americans feared and shunned marijuana.

The 1960s cohort of adolescents rebelled; listened to the music of the Beatles, Bob Dylan, James Brown, and Bob Marley (all of whom sang about smoking marijuana); and rejected adult fears, values, and rules about drugs, sex, and everything else. This is charted in the annual *Monitoring the Future* report (Miech et al., 2018). By 1978, only 12 percent of high school students thought experimental use of marijuana was harmful, and more than half had tried the drug.

That worried older adults, whose emotional reactions to marijuana had been formed decades earlier. President Nixon declared drug abuse (especially marijuana, but not cigarettes or alcohol) "Public Enemy Number One," and Nancy Reagan (First Lady from 1981 to 1989) exhorted, "Just say no" to drugs.

Marijuana was declared a "gateway drug," likely to lead to heroin use and addiction (Kandel, 2002). People were arrested and jailed for possession of even a few grams. By 1991, 80 percent of high school seniors thought there was "great risk" in regular use of marijuana, and only 21 percent of high school seniors had ever smoked it. Many of them were part of a subculture (the "druggies," not the "jocks") that defiantly used marijuana.

Obviously, attitudes continue to shift, in part because those in the antimarijuana generation are now quite old. Few teenagers think regular use of marijuana is "a great risk." By 2018, marijuana had become legal in Canada, Uruguay, Argentina, and Ecuador, and in 30 U.S. states (often only for medical use) (see Figure 1.5). According to a Gallup poll, two-thirds of Americans believe smoking marijuana should be legal for adults. About half of all high school seniors have smoked marijuana.

Since we know that the brain is plastic, affected by many drugs, scientists ask: "How does marijuana change the brain?" Some find that marijuana relieves pain by decreasing pain neurons, with less addiction or neurological risk than opioids and improved thinking (Gruber et al., 2018). By contrast, some find a correlation between marijuana use and "structural abnormalities in the brains of young people" (DuPont & Lieberman, 2014, p. 557).

Evidently, not only are attitudes about marijuana plastic but so are its effects on the brain, influenced by the age of the user, the user's genes, and perhaps the specifics of the marijuana (where it is grown, additives, etc.) (Dow-Edwards & Silva, 2017; Mandelbaum & de la Monte, 2017). Marijuana may impair brain structures that support memory and motivation—but not for everyone. Plasticity!

In all of these ebbs and flows of public attitudes, scientists have reached no consensus about the long-term effects of marijuana because the federal government made it illegal for scientists to undertake objective research. Currently, many researchers are concerned that the political push to accept marijuana did not consider the neurological effects.

We know that the effects of the drug on the brain vary and that simply thinking about marijuana triggers neurotransmitters, causing phobias, ecstasy, and many emotions in between those extremes. We know that adults who smoked marijuana decades ago are a select group, so we cannot be sure that their current situation is caused by their past drug use. Are current attitudes (mostly positive) more rational than those (mostly negative) of our great-grandparents? More science is needed.

*The brain is crucial for all of development, so many findings from the study of the brain appear as regular text. Sometimes, however, more details from neuroscience add to our understanding. Inside the Brain features present these details.

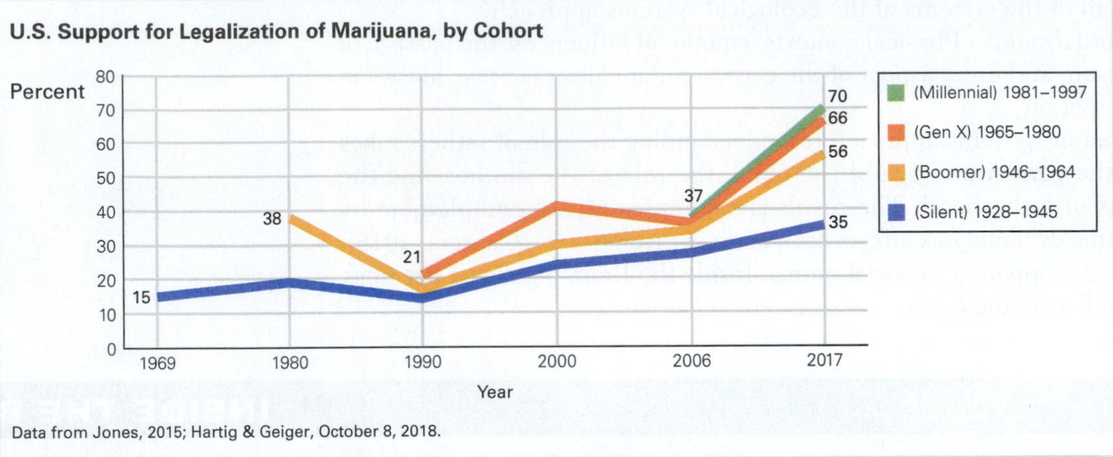

FIGURE 1.5

Double Trends Both cohort and generational trends are evident. Note that people of every age are becoming more accepting of marijuana, but the effect is most obvious for adults who never heard about "reefer madness."

Observation Quiz Why is the line for the 1981–1997 cohort much shorter than the line for the older cohorts? (see answer, page 30)* ↑

*Observation Quizzes are designed to help students practice a crucial skill, specifically to notice small details that indicate something about human development. Answers appear on the next page or two.

This underlies all of the other four aspects of the life-span perspective: multidirectional, multicontextual, multicultural, and multidisciplinary. With any topic, stage, or problem, the dynamic-systems approach urges consideration of all interrelated aspects, every social and cultural factor, over days and years.

Individuals, families, and societies are moldable. In the United States 20 years ago, no one predicted that teen births, cigarette smoking, and midlife cardiovascular death would be down by half, or that rates of same-sex marriage and single parenthood would double. Each of those changes has altered development for children and adults.

Plasticity is apparent when developmentalists consider the life of any human being. Everyone's brain and body would have been different if they had been born in another culture, grown up in another era, eaten other food, witnessed particular events, with different parents, friends, teachers, and so on. My nephew David is one example as As Case to Study explains.

A CASE TO STUDY*

David

My sister-in-law, Dot, contracted rubella (also called German measles) early in her third pregnancy. The disease was not diagnosed until David was born, blind and dying. Immediate heart surgery saved his life, but surgery to remove a cataract destroyed one eye.

The doctor was horrified that operating disturbed the virus and killed the eye, so he did not remove the other cataract until David was 5. One dead eye and one thick cataract meant that young David's visual system was severely impaired. It soon became apparent that other parts of his body—thumbs, ankles, teeth, toes, spine, and brain—were also damaged.

Blindness and brain damage affect social learning. For instance, 3-year-old David connected with other children by pulling their hair and laughing. Fortunately, the virus occurred after the critical prenatal period for hearing. Because of plasticity, David's diminished sight led to excellent audition. He cried often but was quieted when his parents sang to him.

*Many chapters include the feature A Case to Study. Each person is unique; it is not valid to generalize from one case. However, sometimes one case makes a general concept clear.

David attended three special preschools—for the blind, for children with cerebral palsy, for children who were intellectually disabled. At age 6, when surgery removed the remaining cataract, David entered regular public school, learning academic but not social skills—partly because he was excluded from physical education and recess.

By age 10, David had blossomed intellectually. He read (large print) at the eleventh-grade level. To spare him from the social demands of adolescence, he attended a boarding school for blind children, where he gained some social skills and learned to swim. Before age 20, he spoke a second and a third language. In emerging adulthood, he enrolled in college.

The interplay of developmental systems was evident. David's family and community contexts (Appalachia, where people are more accepting of disabilities) helped him to become a productive and happy adult. He told me, "I try to stay in a positive mood."

David's listening skills continue to be impressive. He once told me:

> I am generally quite happy, but secretly a little happier lately, especially since November, because I have been consistently getting a pretty good vibrato when I am singing, not only by myself but also in congregational hymns in church. [*I asked, what is vibrato? David answered.*] When a note bounces up and down within a quartertone either way of concert pitch, optimally between 5.5 and 8.2 times per second.

David works as a translator of German texts, which he enjoys because, as he says, "I like providing a service to scholars, giving them access to something they would otherwise not have."

Plasticity does not undo a person's genes, childhood, or permanent damage. The prenatal brain destruction remains, and David, age 50, still lives with his mother. When his father died in 2014, David was better than the rest of us in accepting the death (he said, "Dad is in a better place").

Glen Stassen

My Brother's Children Michael, Bill, and David *(left to right)* are adults now, with quite different personalities, abilities, numbers of offspring (4, 2, and none), and contexts (in Massachusetts, Pennsylvania, and California). Yet despite genes, prenatal life, and contexts, I see the shared influence of Glen and Dot, my brother and sister-in-law—evident here in their similar, friendly smiles.

He comforted his mother. She applied to enter a senior citizen residence, but they would not allow David; he is too young. Instead of getting angry, Dot found another apartment for both of them near one of her other children. She laughingly said that David gives her a reason for living, because in another 12 years they will be able to stay in senior housing together.

As his aunt, I have seen him repeatedly overcome handicaps. Plasticity is dramatically evident; my intellectually disabled nephew became a very intelligent adult. Thus, this case illustrates all five aspects of the life-span perspective (see Table 1.3).

TABLE 1.3

Five Characteristics of Development

Characteristic	Application in David's Story
Multidirectional. Change occurs in every direction, not always in a straight line. Gains and losses, predictable growth, and unexpected transformations are evident.	David's development seemed static (or even regressive, as when early surgery destroyed one eye), but then it accelerated each time he entered a new school or college.
Multidisciplinary. Numerous academic fields—especially psychology, biology, education, and sociology, but also neuroscience, economics, religion, anthropology, history, medicine, genetics, and many more—contribute insights.	Two disciplines were particularly critical: medicine (David would have died without advances in surgery on newborns) and education (special educators guided him and his parents many times).
Multicontextual. Human lives are embedded in many contexts, including historical conditions, economic constraints, and family patterns.	The high SES of David's family made it possible for him to receive daily medical and educational care. His two older brothers protected him.
Multicultural. Many cultures—not just between nations but also within them—affect how people develop.	Appalachia, where David lived, is more accepting of people with disabilities.
Plasticity. Every individual, and every trait within each individual, can be altered at any point in the life span. Change is ongoing, although it is neither random nor easy.	David's measured IQ changed from about 40 (severely intellectually disabled) to about 130 (far above average), and his physical disabilities became less crippling as he matured.

WHAT HAVE YOU LEARNED?

1. What aspects of development show continuity?
2. What is the difference between a critical period and a sensitive period?
3. Why is it useful to know when sensitive periods occur?
4. What did Bronfenbrenner emphasize in his ecological-systems approach?
5. What are some of the social contexts of life?
6. How does cohort differ from age group?
7. How might male–female differences be examples of the difference-equals-deficit error?
8. What is the difference between race and ethnicity?
9. What factors comprise a person's SES?
10. What is the problem with each discipline having its own silo?
11. How is human development plastic?

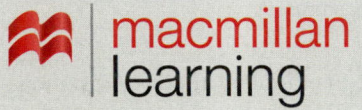

VIDEO ACTIVITY: What's Wrong with This Study? explores some of the major pitfalls of the process of designing a research study.

Using the Scientific Method

To verify or refute a hypothesis (Step 2 in the scientific method), researchers seek the best of hundreds of research designs, choosing exactly who and what to study, how and when (Step 3), in order to gather results that will lead to valid conclusions (Step 4) that are worth publishing (Step 5). Often they use statistics to discover relationships between various aspects of the data. (See **Table 1.4**.)

Accordingly, every student of development needs to understand the basic research designs used to reach conclusions. We now describe three research strategies and then three ways in which developmentalists study change over time.

Observation

scientific observation A method of testing a hypothesis by systematically watching and recording participants' behavior, in a natural setting, in a laboratory, or in archival data.

Scientific observation requires researchers to record behavior systematically and objectively. Observations can occur in three ways: a naturalistic setting such as a home; in a laboratory, where scientists observe human reactions; or by analyzing data collected for other reasons.

In the latter, smartphones, Twitter messages, voting totals, spending records, and census numbers have all been mined for insights about development. Such observation is not direct and therefore needs interpretation, but it can be intriguing.

All three kinds of observation evoke hypotheses, providing questions that need to be studied further. This is evident is a study of the 2016 Thanksgiving holiday, which occurred 16 days after the bitterly partisan U.S. presidential election. Many families still gathered together for the traditional meal, but when the politics of the host community differed from the politics of the travelers, the latter did not stay as long as they had the year before (Chen & Rohla, 2018).

Shortened visits were particularly likely when travelers from Republican communities, who had been subject to extensive pro-Trump advertising, visited

relatives in Democratic-leaning areas. They left about an hour earlier in 2016 than they had in 2015. Earlier leaving was also evident among Democrats who were visiting Republicans.

How did the researchers discern this? They used smartphone data, which showed where people lived (tracking revealed where they slept at night, and where they traveled) as well as detailed voting data for the precinct where they were located between 1 and 5 P.M. on Thanksgiving. Thus, if a smartphone owner came from, say, Minneapolis, which voted heavily for Clinton, to celebrate Thanksgiving in North Dakota, where many Trump voters live, they did not stay as long after dinner as they had stayed the year before, or as long as other people from Minneapolis who traveled to Chicago, where many Clinton voters live.

TABLE 1.4

Statistical Measures Often Used to Analyze Search Results

Measure	Use
Effect size	There are many kinds, but the most useful in reporting studies of development is called *Cohen's d*, which can indicate the power of an intervention. An effect size of 0.2 is called small, 0.5 moderate, and 0.8 large.
Significance	Indicates whether the results might have occurred by chance. If chance would produce the results only 5 times in 100, that is significant at the 0.05 level; once in 100 times is 0.01; once in 1,000 is 0.001.
Cost-benefit analysis	Calculates how much a particular independent variable costs versus how much it saves. This is useful for analyzing public spending, such as finding that preschool education programs or preventative health measures save money.
Odds ratio	Indicates how a particular variable compares to a standard, set at 1. For example, one study found that although less than 1 percent of all child homicides occurred at school, the odds were similar for public and private schools. The odds of it in high schools, however, were 18.47 times that of elementary or middle schools (set at 1.0) (MMWR, January 18, 2008).
Factor analysis	Hundreds of variables could affect any given behavior. In addition, many variables (such as family income and parental education) overlap. To take this into account, analysis reveals variables that can be clustered together to form a factor, which is a composite of many variables. For example, SES might become one factor, child personality another.

The fact that partisan polarization interfered with "close family settings" (Chen & Rohla, 2018) is troubling for developmentalists, because relatives usually provide affection and support for every family member. Further, contact with people who differ is the best way to expand understanding and reduce prejudice (Hodson et al., 2018). Thus, conversations among people who disagree are likely to help Republicans and Democrats understand each other.

Therefore, shorter Thanksgiving visits may impair both intellectual growth and family support. Indeed, lack of family communication is a major cause of adolescent rebellion, of divorce, even of suicide, so these data are ominous. Other data reveal that drug abuse and midlife suicide have increased since 2016—might that be connected to less family harmony?

But wait. These data were observational. We are not even sure that people who traveled a distance for Thanksgiving were visiting family, or that hosts who lived in pro-Trump or pro-Clinton areas reflected the opinions of their neighbors. Data on other family interactions lead to the assumption that more time together would have fostered a better family support system, but we do not *know* that.

Indeed, we cannot be sure why visits were shorter. Did talking about politics make people angry enough to storm out? Or did people follow the maxim, "Never discuss politics or religion at the dinner table," so they didn't have much else to say?

Maybe shorter visits preserved family harmony rather than signified problems? Might people have avoided talking politics in order to protect family closeness? Now you see why observation is intriguing, but it requires other research to confirm hypotheses. Experiments are needed.

experiment A research method in which the researcher seeks to discover what causes what. One variable (called the *independent variable*) is added. Then the scientist observes and records the effect on the other variable (called the *dependent variable*).

independent variable In an experiment, the variable that is introduced to see what effect it has on the dependent variable. (Also called *experimental variable.*)

dependent variable In an experiment, the variable that may change as a result of whatever new condition or situation the experimenter adds. In other words, the dependent variable *depends* on the independent variable.

Especially for Nurses*

In the field of medicine, why are experiments conducted to test new drugs and treatments? (see response, page 30)

*Since many students reading this book are preparing to be teachers, health care professionals, police officers, or parents, every chapter contains Especially For questions, which encourage you to apply important developmental concepts just as experts in the field do.

The Experiment

The **experiment** establishes what causes what. In the social sciences, experimenters typically impose a particular treatment on a group of participants or expose them to a specific condition and then note whether their behavior changes.

Standard Terminology In technical terms, the experimenters manipulate an **independent variable,** which is the extra treatment or special condition (also called the *experimental variable*; a *variable* is anything that can vary). They note whether this independent variable affects whatever they are studying, called the **dependent variable** (which *depends* on the independent variable).

Thus, the independent variable is the new, special treatment; any change in the dependent variable is the result. The purpose of an experiment is to find out what causes what, that is, whether an independent variable affects the dependent variable.

A typical experiment (as diagrammed in **Figure 1.6**) has two groups of participants. One group, the *experimental group,* experiences the particular treatment or condition (the independent variable); the other group, the *comparison group* (also called the *control group*), does not.

Experimental Design To follow up on the observation study above, researchers could design an experiment. To create two equal groups, they could assess the political perspectives of hundreds of people before Thanksgiving. For instance, they might ask, "What proportion of Republicans earn more than $250,000 a year?" or "What proportion of Democrats are atheists or agnostics?"

Generally, Democrats overestimate the proportion of Republicans who are rich (estimates are 44 percent; actual is 2.2 percent), and Republicans overestimate how many Democrats are atheist or agnostic (estimate is 36 percent; actual is 9 percent) (Ahler & Sood, 2018). The answers to such questions would ensure that researchers include the same proportion of partisan individuals in both the experimental and the control groups.

The experimenters would also need to find out how important family is. They might ask, "If you needed advice and support, how likely would you be to ask your . . . [various relatives]?" They might ask about affection, respect, or appreciation between the generations.

Thus, they would form two groups, equal in political and family attitudes. As the independent variable, one group could be assigned to talk with their families about politics at Thanksgiving and the other told not to do so. The researchers could again record length of stay. The hypothesis is that time spent together is affected by discussion of politics.

FIGURE 1.6

How to Conduct an Experiment The basic sequence diagrammed here applies to all experiments. Many additional features, especially the statistical measures listed in Table 1.4 and various ways of reducing experimenter bias, affect whether publication occurs. (Scientific journals reject reports of experiments that were not rigorous in method and analysis.)

The Experiment

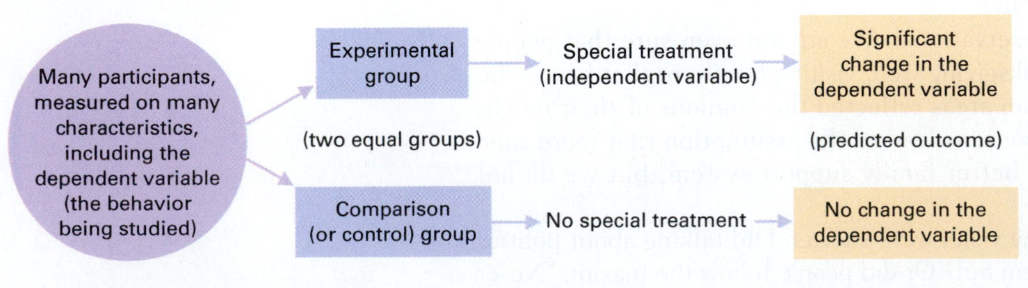

Procedure:

1. Divide participants into two groups that are matched on important characteristics, especially the behavior that is the dependent variable on which this study is focused.
2. Give special treatment, or intervention (the independent variable), to one group (the experimental group).
3. Compare the groups on the dependent variable. If they now differ, the cause of the difference was probably the independent variable.
4. Publish the results.

After the holiday, the people would be queried again to ascertain whether they followed the experimental instructions and whether their attitudes about Republicans, Democrats, or family members changed. Did conversations improve understanding? Or did political conversations provoke yelling and rapid departures? A well-designed experiment would find out.

Such an experiment would involve significant effort. Ideally hundreds of families planning to visit relatives in other parts of the nation for Thanksgiving would need to be recruited. Creating equal experimental and control groups would require careful assessments, balancing not only political and family connections but ethnic and generational relationships as well.

The best way to find out whether the experimental instructions were followed would be to provide wearable recording microphones for all participants. After the event, scientists who did not know the hypothesis or what instructions the families had been given could analyze the recordings, noting emotional words. Audiograms could assess shouting, interrupting, awkward silences.

As you can see, this experiment would be costly and difficult. Moreover, three aspects are artificial: being told to talk or not talk about politics, wearing a microphone, and knowing that an experiment is under way. Thus, the results may differ from normal life. But without an experiment, we cannot be sure whether and how a divisive political climate affects family gatherings. Observation provides clues; experiments suggest proof.

Rick Friedman/Corbis/Getty Images

What Can You Learn? Scientists first establish what is, and then they try to change it. In one recent experiment, Deb Kelemen (shown here) established that few children under age 12 understand a central concept of evolution (natural selection). Then she showed an experimental group a picture book illustrating the idea. Success! The independent variable (the book) affected the dependent variable (the children's ideas), which confirmed Kelemen's hypothesis: Children can understand natural selection if instruction is tailored to their ability.

The Survey

A third research method is the **survey,** in which information is collected from a large number of people by interview, questionnaire, or some other means. This is a quick, direct way to obtain data. Surveys keep us from assuming that everyone is like the people we know.

survey A research method in which information is collected from a large number of people by interviews, written questionnaires, or some other means.

For example, perhaps you know a 16-year-old who is pregnant, or a 40-year-old who hates his job, or a 70-year-old who watches television all day. You might think that most 16- or 40- or 70-year-olds are like them. But surveys of thousands of teenagers, or adults, or older people from many regions, cultures, and incomes find that teenage pregnancy is now uncommon, that most adults like their jobs, and that the elderly watch less television than the young.

As you see, surveys may uncover information that is contrary to popular assumptions. Unfortunately, however, the data may not be totally accurate. Wording matters.

For example, a survey described the epidemic of opioid deaths and explained life-saving sites, where medical rescues are available for people to take drugs purchased elsewhere. Such sites are common in Europe but rare in the United States, because local authorities believe that the public is adamantly opposed. Public health doctors administered a survey to find out if the authorities were right.

THINK CRITICALLY: What other titles would increase or decrease approval?

U.S. adults read a description and were asked whether such sites should be legal. Although the descriptions were identical in every survey, 45 percent approved "Overdose Prevention" sites but only 29 percent approved "Safe Consumption" sites (Davis et al., 2018). This illustrates a problem with every survey: Exactly how questions are asked influences the result.

Survey respondents may lie to researchers, or to themselves. For instance, every two years since 1991, high school students in the United States have been surveyed confidentially in the Youth Risk Behavior Surveillance. Always, a wide and diverse sample is sought: 14,956 students from all kinds of schools from all 50 states contributed to the most recent survey (MMWR, June 15, 2018).

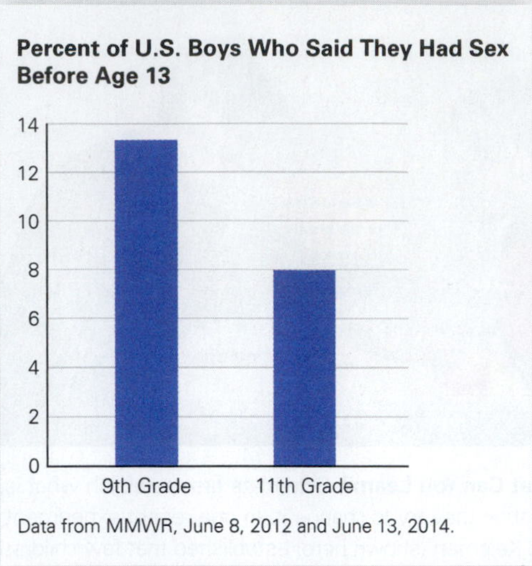

FIGURE 1.7
I Forgot? If these were the only data available, you might conclude that ninth-graders have suddenly become more sexually active than eleventh-graders. But we have 20 years of data—those who are ninth-graders now will answer differently by eleventh grade.

meta-analysis Combining the results of many studies, each of which may have small, and limited samples, to reach a general conclusion.

Students are asked whether they had sexual intercourse *before* age 13. Every year, more ninth-grade boys than eleventh-grade boys say they had sex before age 13, yet those eleventh-graders were ninth-graders two years before (see **Figure 1.7** for a dramatic example of this discrepancy). Why? Are teenage boys likely to lie, with the ninth-graders bragging or the eleventh-graders denying? Or have eleventh-graders forgotten?

Meta-Analysis

As you see, every research design, method, and statistic has strengths as well as weaknesses. To assess conclusions, developmentalists analyze the data, participants, and methods of other scientists. Questioning and replicating are part of the process. No single study is conclusive.

One way to overcome potential bias is through the **meta-analysis,** which is an analysis that combines many studies and summarizes the results. This makes sense, in that some studies might have too few participants, or some unknown bias in the design, or some oddity in the results. But when dozens of studies are gathered, a meta-analysis might reveal significant trends.

In the best meta-analyses, the researchers begin by stating exactly how they chose studies that are the grist for their analysis. Care is taken to find all relevant studies, published and unpublished, on a particular topic. Only those that are scientifically rigorous are included.

Accordingly, in meta-analysis, no single study determines the conclusions: It is the weight of all of the studies that matters. A meta-analysis "has become widely accepted as a standardized, less biased way to weigh the evidence" (de Vrieze, 2018, p. 1186).

However, even meta-analyses do not always reach clear conclusions. For instance, does media violence encourage actual violence? President Trump blamed the shooting deaths at a high school in Parkland, Florida, on video games. Is he right? Does shooting in video games provoke real deaths? One meta-analysis says yes (Anderson et al., 2010), another no (Ferguson & Kilburn, 2010), and a third says yes but not very much (Hilgard et al., 2017).

The main reason for these differences is that, in order to avoid publication bias (journals tend to publish only dramatic results, called the *file-drawer problem*), the authors included unpublished studies, but they disagreed about which unpublished studies to use. For scientists, that is a healthy disagreement: All of the foregoing descriptions of methods and analysis confirm that alternate explanations are part of science.

Aaron Bacall/Cartoon Collections/Cartoonstock

"It's a one-year timer. It gives an added sense of urgency to my research grant."

Not Long Enough For understanding the human life span, scientists wish for grants that are renewed for decades.

cross-sectional research Research that compares people who differ in age but are similar in other important characteristics.

Studying Development over the Life Span

In addition to conducting observations, experiments, and surveys, developmentalists must measure how people *change or remain the same over time,* as the definition stresses. Remember that systems are dynamic, ever-changing. To capture that dynamism, developmental researchers use one of three basic research designs: cross-sectional, longitudinal, and cross-sequential.

Cross-Sectional Versus Longitudinal Research The quickest and least expensive way to study development over time is with **cross-sectional research,** in which groups of people of one age are compared with people of another age. You saw that with attitudes about marijuana: Younger people are more likely to approve of legalization than older people.

Cross-sectional design seems simple. However, the people being compared may differ in several ways, not just age. For example, attitudes about many political and

Six Times of Life These photos show Sarah-Maria, born in 1980 in Switzerland, at six periods of her life: infancy (age 1), early childhood (age 3), middle childhood (age 8), adolescence (age 15), emerging adulthood (age 19), and adulthood (age 36).

social issues originate in childhood and are solidified in early adulthood. Since the oldest adults were taught that marijuana was a dangerous gateway drug, their opinions are still influenced by their beliefs at age 16. Attitudes of the oldest generation about same-sex marriage, war, religion, and so on are influenced by what their cohort believed decades ago.

To help discover whether age itself rather than cohort causes a developmental change, scientists undertake **longitudinal research.** They collect data repeatedly on the same individuals over time. Longitudinal research can span a few years, but for insight about the life span, the same individuals may be studied for decades. Long-term research requires patience and dedication from many scientists, but it can pay off.

For example, a longitudinal study of 790 infants born in Baltimore to low-income parents found that only 4 percent of them had graduated from college by age 28 (Alexander et al., 2014). Why don't more low-SES people complete college? Many people blame high school guidance counselors, or college admission practices, or university faculty for this result.

However, this longitudinal study traced when children were pushed away from college or toward it. It began very early in life. Early education and friendly neighbors turned out to be more significant than high school or college!

Thus, longitudinal data are cherished by developmentalists; they show at what point in the life span to focus on better health practices, education, family interactions. For instance, we now know that the best way to reduce lung cancer deaths is not better diagnosis but instead prevention of adolescent smoking. People who do not smoke before age 21 are unlikely to develop lung cancer decades later, because people rarely start smoking after those sensitive teenage years.

Of course, the historical context may compromise useful conclusions from longitudinal research. Technology, culture, and politics alter life experiences. Data collected on people born decades ago may not be relevant for today.

For example, many recent substances might be harmful or beneficial, among them *phthalates* and *bisphenol A* (BPA) (chemicals used in manufacturing plastic containers), *hydrofracking* (a process used to get gas for fuel from rocks), *e-waste* (from old computers and cell phones), and *chlorpyrifos* (an insecticide). Some nations and states ban or regulate each of these; others do not. Verified, longitudinal data are not yet possible.

A current conundrum is climate change. Some predict global civil wars, agriculture failure, disaster-related deaths—and that life on our planet may be snuffed out within a century because of the current warming of the atmosphere. Others call that alarmist, suggesting that mitigation can protect humanity (C. Murphy et al., 2018). We will not know until it is too late.

Cross-Sequential Research Scientists have discovered a third strategy, combining cross-sectional and longitudinal research. This combination is called **cross-sequential research** (also referred to as *cohort-sequential* or *time-sequential research*). With this design, researchers study several groups of people of different ages (a cross-sectional approach), follow them over the years (a longitudinal

Observation Quiz Longitudinal research best illustrates continuity and discontinuity. For Sarah-Maria, what changed over 30 years and what didn't? (see answer, page 30) ↑

longitudinal research Research in which the same individuals are followed over time, as their development is repeatedly assessed.

cross-sequential research Research that begins by comparing people of different ages (a cross-sectional approach) and then follows those people over the years (a longitudinal approach). (Also called *cohort-sequential research* or *time-sequential research.*)

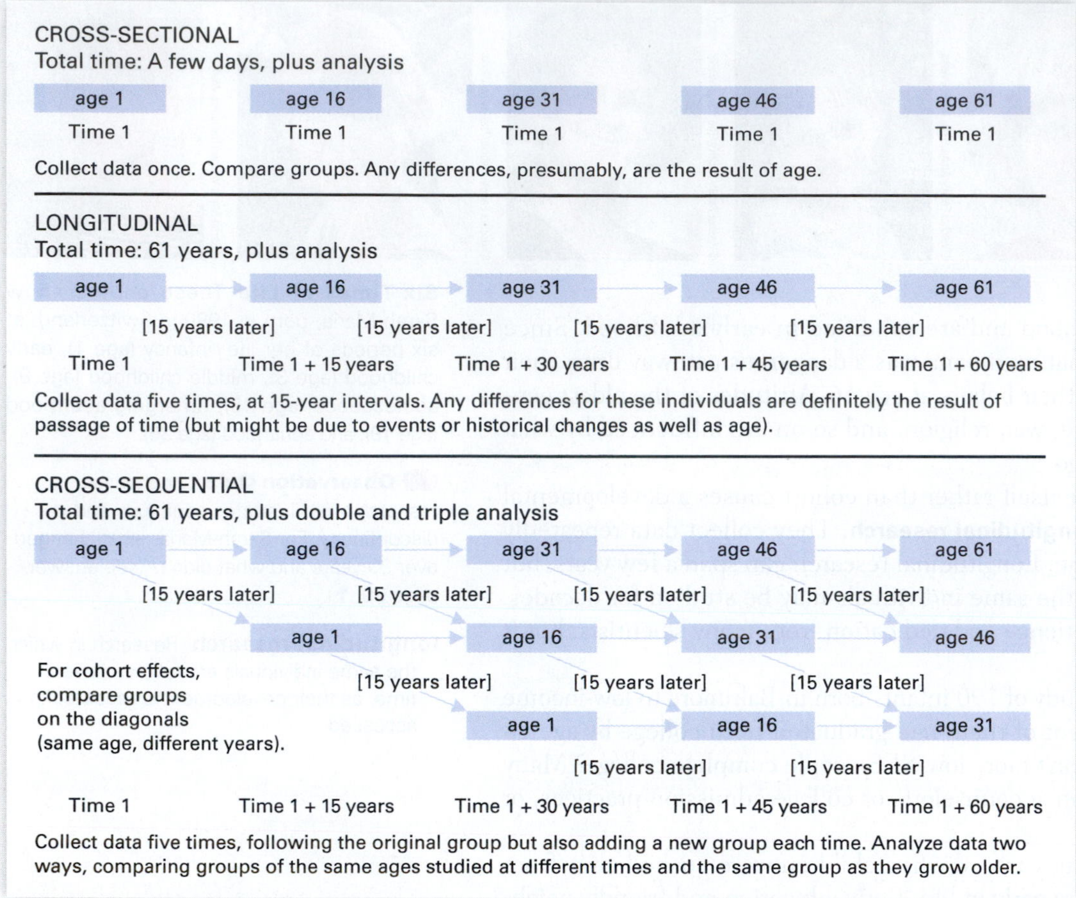

FIGURE 1.8

Which Approach Is Best? Cross-sequential research is the most time-consuming and complex, but it yields the best information. One reason that hundreds of scientists conduct research on the same topics, replicating one another's work, is to gain some advantages of cohort-sequential research without waiting for decades.

Especially for Future Researchers
What is the best method for collecting data? (see response, page 30)

approach), and then combine the results.

A cross-sequential design lets researchers compare findings for, say, 16-year-olds with findings for the same individuals at age 1, as well as with data for people who were 16 long ago, who are now ages 31, 46, and 61 (see **Figure 1.8**). Cross-sequential research is complicated, in recruitment and analysis, but it lets scientists disentangle age from history.

The first well-known cross-sequential study (the *Seattle Longitudinal Study*) found that some intellectual abilities (vocabulary) increase even after age 60, whereas others (speed) start to decline at age 30 (Schaie, 2005/2013), confirming that development is multidirectional. This study also discovered that declines in adult math ability are more closely related to education than to age, something neither cross-sectional nor longitudinal research could reveal.

Cross-sequential research is useful for young adults as well. For example, drug addiction (called *substance use disorder,* or *SUD*) is most common in the early 20s and decreases by the late 20s. But one cross-sequential study found that the origins of SUD are much earlier, in adolescent behaviors and in genetic predispositions (McGue et al., 2014).

Other research finds that heroin deaths are more common after age 30, but the best time to intervene seems to be in emerging adulthood (Carlson et al., 2016). [**Life-Span Link:** The major discussions of SUD are in Chapters 16 and 17.]

WHAT HAVE YOU LEARNED?

1. Why do careful observations not prove "what causes what"?
2. Why do experimenters use a control (or comparison) group as well as an experimental group?
3. What are the strengths and weaknesses of the survey method?
4. Why would a scientist conduct a cross-sectional study?
5. What are the advantages and disadvantages of longitudinal research?
6. Why do developmentalists prefer cross-sequential research, even though it takes longer and is more expensive?

Cautions and Challenges from Science

The scientific method illuminates and illustrates human development as nothing else does. Facts, consequences, and possibilities have emerged that would not be known without science—and people of all ages are healthier, happier, and more capable because of it.

For example, thanks to science, infectious diseases in children, illiteracy in adults, depression in late adulthood, and sexism and racism at every age are much less prevalent today than a century ago. Young adults, aware of Black Lives Matter and the Me Too movement, might doubt that progress is evident, but they need to ask someone over age 70 what life was like for women, African Americans, and other marginalized groups decades ago. Early death—from violence, war, or disease—is also less likely, with scientific discoveries and education as likely reasons (Pinker, 2018).

Developmentalists have also discovered unexpected sources of harm. Video games, cigarettes, television, shift work, lead, asbestos, and even artificial respiration are all less benign than people first thought.

The benefits of science are many, in improving lives and discovering hazards. However, science also entails complications that can lead us all astray. We now discuss three of them: misinterpreting correlation, depending on numbers, and ignoring ethics.

Correlation and Causation

Probably the most common mistake in interpreting research is confusing correlation with causation. A **correlation** exists between two variables if one variable is more (or less) likely to occur when the other does. A correlation is *positive* if both variables tend to increase together or decrease together, *negative* if one variable tends to increase while the other decreases, and *zero* if no connection is evident. (Try the quiz in **Table 1.5**.)

correlation A number between +1.0 and –1.0 that indicates the relationship between two variables, expressed in terms of the likelihood that one variable will (or will not) change when the other variable does (or does not). A correlation indicates that two variables are somehow related, NOT that one variable causes the other to occur.

Expressed in numerical terms, correlations vary from +1.0 (the most positive) to –1.0 (the most negative). Correlations are almost never that extreme; a correlation of +0.3 or –0.3 is noteworthy; a correlation of +0.8 or –0.8 is astonishing.

Many correlations are unexpected. For instance: First-born children are more likely to develop asthma than are later-born children; teenage girls have higher rates of mental health problems than do teenage boys; and counties in the United States with more dentists have fewer obese residents. That last study controlled for the number of medical doctors and the poverty of the community. The authors suggest that dentists provide information about nutrition that improves health (Holzer et al., 2014).

That dentist explanation may be wrong. Every scientist knows the mantra: *Correlation is not causation.* Just because two variables are correlated does not mean that one causes the other—even if it seems logical that it does. It proves only that the variables are connected somehow. Either one could cause the other or a third variable may cause the correlation.

TABLE 1.5

Quiz on Correlation

Two Variables	Positive, Negative, or Zero Correlation?	Why? (Third Variable)
1. Ice cream sales and murder rate	________	________
2. Reading ability and number of baby teeth	________	________
3. Adult's sex assigned at birth and average number of offspring	________	________

For each of these three pairs of variables, indicate whether the correlation between them is positive, negative, or nonexistent. Then try to think of a third variable that might determine the direction of the correlation. The correct answers appear on the next page.

Thaves/Universal Uclick

A Pesky Third Variable Correlation is often misleading. In this case, a third variable (the supply of fossil fuels) may be relevant.

> **Answers:**
> 1. Positive; third variable: heat
> 2. Negative; third variable: age
> 3. Zero. Each child must begin with a sperm from a male and an ovum from a female. No third variable.

Unless people remember that correlation is not causation, they may draw mistaken and even dangerous conclusions.

Quantity and Quality

A second caution concerns whether scientists should rely on data produced by **quantitative research** (from the word *quantity*). Quantitative research data can be ranked or numbered, allowing easy translation across cultures. One example of quantitative research is using children's achievement scores to assess education within a school or a nation.

Since quantities can be easily summarized, compared, charted, and replicated, many scientists prefer quantitative research. Statistics require numbers. Quantitative data are easier to replicate and less open to bias.

However, when data are presented in categories and numbers, some nuances and individual distinctions are lost. Many developmental researchers thus turn to **qualitative research** (from the word *quality*)—asking open-ended questions, reporting answers in narrative (not numerical) form.

quantitative research Research that provides data that can be expressed with numbers, such as ranks or scales.

qualitative research Research that considers qualities instead of quantities, and hence includes narratives and other aspects of development that express individuality.

Qualitative researchers are "interested in understanding how people interpret their experiences, how they construct their worlds . . ." (Merriam, 2009, p. 5). Qualitative research reflects cultural and contextual diversity, but it is also more vulnerable to bias and harder to replicate. Both types of research are needed (Morgan, 2018).

For that reason, some studies now use both methods, which provides richer, but also more verifiable, details. For example, one study compared the very old (over age 90) and their children (age 51–75) (Scelzo et al., 2018). Research compared scores on various measures of psychological and physical health and reported the numbers. Generally, the very old were in poorer physical shape but better psychological health than the merely old.

This study also reported qualitative data. For example, one man over age 90 said:

> I lost my beloved wife only a month ago and I am very sad for this. We were married for 70 years. I was close to her during all her illness and I have felt very empty after her loss. But thanks to my sons I am now recovering and feeling much better. I have 4 children, 10 grandchildren, and 9 great-grandchildren. I have fought all my life and I am always ready for changes. I think changes bring life and give chances to grow. I have had a heart condition for which I have undergone surgery but I am now okay. I have also had two very serious car accidents and I have risked losing my life. But I am still here!! I am always thinking for the best. There is always a solution in life. This is what my father had taught me: to always face difficulties and hope for the best. I am always active. I do not know what stress is. Life is what it is and must be faced. . . . I feel younger now than when I was young!
>
> [Scelzo et al., 2018, p. 33]

Ideally, qualitative research illustrates quantitative research, as was true in this study. This man is in poor physical health (heart condition) but good psychological health (much hope, no stress). As you see, any one study, with any one method, benefits from other studies and methods.

Ethics

The most important challenge for all scientists is to follow ethical standards. Each professional society involved in research of human development has a *code of*

ethics (a set of moral principles). Most colleges and hospitals have an *Institutional Review Board* (IRB), a group that permits only research that follows certain guidelines set by the federal government.

Although IRBs often slow down scientific study, some research conducted before they were established was clearly unethical, especially when the participants were children, members of minority groups, prisoners, or animals. Even with IRBs, serious ethical dilemmas remain, particularly when research occurs in developing nations (Leiter & Herman, 2015).

Ebola Many ethical dilemmas arose in the 2014–2015 West African Ebola epidemic (Rothstein, 2015; Gillon, 2015). Among them:

- Is it fair to use vaccines whose safety is unproven when such proof would take months?
- What kind of informed consent is needed to avoid both false hope and false fears?
- Is it justified to keep relatives away from people who have Ebola, even though social isolation might harm patients and their families?
- Is justice served by a health care system that is inadequate in some countries and high-tech in others?

Especially for Future Researchers and Science Writers Do any ethical guidelines apply when an author writes about the experiences of family members, friends, or research participants? (see response, page 30)

Medicine tends to focus on individuals, ignoring the customs and systems that make some people more vulnerable. One observer noted:

> When people from the United States and Europe working in West Africa have developed Ebola, time and again the first thing they wanted to take was not an experimental drug. It was an airplane that would cart them home.
>
> [Cohen, 2014, p. 911]

A systemic understanding of the Ebola crisis has led to an effort to establish secure, biocontainment laboratories in many nations, in order to quickly recognize deadly diseases (Le Duc & Yuan, 2018).

Public health doctors note that the political and economic cooperation necessary for world health tends to respond only when a crisis is immediate: A life-span perspective is needed. Developmental scientists need to bring their expertise to international research, with a longitudinal, multicultural, multidirectional perspective—and understanding of plasticity.

But before coasting on that optimism, remember that everyone has strong opinions that they expect research to confirm. Scientists might try (sometimes without noticing it) to achieve the results they want while maintaining national and cultural values. As one team explains:

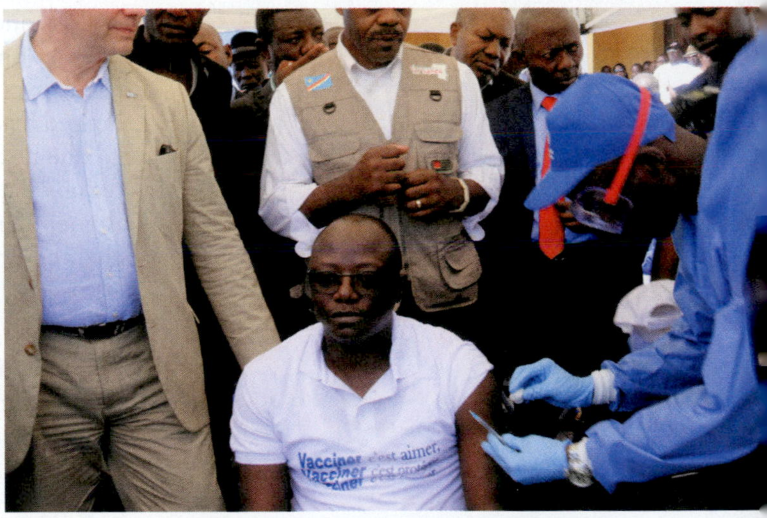

AP Images/John Bompengo/Associated Press

Risky Shot? Most vaccines undergo years of testing before they are used on people, but vaccines protecting against Ebola were not ready until the 2014 West African epidemic finally waned after 11,000 deaths. Thus, the effectiveness of Ebola vaccines is unknown. However, when deadly Ebola surfaced again in the Democratic Republic of Congo in 2018, public health doctors did not wait for longitudinal data. Here Dr. Mwamba, a representative of Congo's Expanded Program on Immunization, receives the vaccine. He hopes that it will protect him and thousands of other Congolese. We will know by 2021 if the vaccine halted an new epidemic.

> Our job as scientists is to discover truths about the world. We generate hypotheses, collect data, and examine whether or not the data are consistent with those hypotheses . . . . [but we] often lose sight of this goal, yielding to pressure to do whatever is justifiable to compile a set of studies we can publish. This is not driven by a willingness to deceive but by the self-serving interpretation of ambiguity . . .
>
> [Simmons et al., 2011, pp. 1359, 1365]

Obviously, collaboration, replication, and transparency are essential ethical safeguards. Hundreds of questions regarding human development need answers, and researchers have yet to find them. That is the most important ethical mandate of all. For instance:

- Do we know enough about prenatal drugs to protect every fetus?
- Do we know enough about world poverty to enable everyone to be healthy?

- Do we know enough about transgender children, or single parenthood, or divorce, or same-sex marriages to ensure optimal development?
- Do we know enough about dying to enable everyone to die with dignity?

The answers to these questions are *NO, NO, NO,* and *NO*.

Scientists and funders tend to avoid questions that might produce unwanted answers. People have strong opinions about drugs, income, families, and death (the four questions above) that may conflict with scientific findings and conclusions. Religion, politics, and customs shape scientific research, sometimes stopping investigation before it begins.

In one final example, consider gun legislation. In 1996, the U.S. Congress, in allocating funds for the Centers for Disease Control, passed a law stating that "None of the funds made available for injury prevention and control at the Centers for Disease Control and Prevention may be used to advocate or promote gun control." This has stopped some research on the most common means of suicide in the United States, or the most used weapons in homicides, because it might—or might not—be used to advocate gun control.

As two highly respected scientists explain:

> There is only very sparse scientific evidence [regarding] . . . which policies will be effective. . . . Even the seemingly popular view that violent crime would be reduced by laws prohibiting the purchase or possession of guns by individuals with mental illness was deemed to have only moderate supporting evidence.
>
> *[Leshner & Dzau, 2018, p. 1195]*

It may be unfair to blame Congress or focus on guns. Indeed, there are unanswered questions about almost every aspect of human development. Even worse are the "unknown unknowns," the topics that we think we understand but do not or the hypotheses that have not yet occurred to anyone because human thinking is limited by culture and context.

The next cohort of developmental scientists will build on what is known, mindful of what needs to be explored, raising questions that no one has asked before. Remember that the goal is to help everyone fulfill their potential. The next 24 chapters are a beginning.

macmillan learning

VIDEO ACTIVITY: Eugenics and the "Feebleminded": A Shameful History illustrates what can happen when scientists fail to follow a code of ethics.

THINK CRITICALLY: Can you think of an additional question that researchers should answer?

WHAT HAVE YOU LEARNED?

1. Why does correlation not prove causation?
2. What are the advantages and disadvantages of quantitative research?
3. What are the advantages and disadvantages of qualitative research?
4. What is the role of the IRB?
5. Why might a political leader avoid funding developmental research?
6. What questions about human development remain to be answered?

SUMMARY

Understanding How and Why

1. The study of human development is a science that seeks to understand how people change or remain the same over time. As a science, it begins with questions and hypotheses and then gathers empirical data.

2. Replication confirms, modifies, or refutes conclusions, which are not considered solid until they are confirmed by several studies. A replication crisis has strengthened the science of human development.

3. The universality of human development and the uniqueness of each individual's development are evident in both nature (the genes) and nurture (the environment); no person is quite like another. Nature and nurture always interact, and each human characteristic is affected by that interaction.

4. Differential susceptibility is evident when we study nature and nurture. Each person's genes and experiences affect his or her vulnerability to developmental change, for better or worse. Asthma is an example.

The Life-Span Perspective

5. The assumption that growth is linear has been replaced by the realization that both continuity and discontinuity are part of every life. Developmental gains and losses are apparent lifelong.

6. Time is a crucial variable. Everyone changes with age. Critical periods are times when something *must* occur for normal development; sensitive periods are times when a particular kind of development occurs most easily.

7. Development occurs within many contexts and cultures, as Urie Bronfenbrenner's ecological-systems approach emphasizes. Each person is situated within larger systems of family, school, community, and culture.

8. Each cohort is influenced by the innovations and events of their historical period, and each person is affected by their socioeconomic status (SES), with affects of both cohort and SES varying depending on the age and circumstances of the person.

9. *Culture, ethnicity,* and *race* are social constructions, concepts created by society. Culture includes beliefs and patterns; ethnicity refers to ancestral heritage. Race is also a social construction, sometimes mistakenly thought to be biological.

10. Humans have many ways to think or act, influenced by age, gender, and culture. Developmentalists try to avoid the difference-equals-deficit error. A multidisciplinary, dynamic-systems approach is needed because each person develops in many ways—biosocially, cognitively, and psychosocially—simultaneously.

11. Throughout life, human development is plastic. Brains and behaviors are molded by experiences. Cultures also adjust to social needs.

Using the Scientific Method

12. Commonly used research methods are observation, experiments, and surveys. Each can provide insight, yet each is limited. Replication, or using other methods to examine the same topic, is needed. Meta-analyses summarize conclusions of many studies.

13. Developmentalists study change over time, often with cross-sectional and longitudinal research. Cross-sequential research, which combines the other two methods, attempts to avoid the pitfalls of cross-sectional and longitudinal studies.

Cautions and Challenges from Science

14. A correlation is a statistic that indicates that two variables are connected, both increasing in tandem or in opposite directions. Correlation does not prove cause. Even when it seems logical that one variable causes the other to occur, the cause may be in the opposite direction, or a correlation between two variables may occur because of a third variable.

15. Quantitative research provides numerical data. This makes it best for comparing contexts and cultures via verified statistics. By contrast, more nuanced data come from qualitative research, which reports on individual lives. Both are useful.

16. Ethical behavior is crucial in all of the sciences. Results must be fairly gathered, reported, and interpreted. Participants must be informed and protected.

17. The most important ethical question is whether scientists are designing, conducting, analyzing, publishing, and applying the research that is most critically needed. This does not always occur: The next cohort of developmental scholars will add to our scientific knowledge.

KEY TERMS

science of human development (p. 4)
scientific method (p. 4)
hypothesis (p. 5)
empirical evidence (p. 5)
replication (p. 5)
nature (p. 5)
nurture (p. 5)
differential susceptibility (p. 7)
life-span perspective (p. 7)
critical period (p. 8)
sensitive period (p. 8)
ecological-systems approach (p. 9)
microsystem (p. 9)
exosystem (p. 9)
macrosystem (p. 9)
chronosystem (p. 9)
mesosystem (p. 9)
cohort (p. 10)
socioeconomic status (SES) (p. 10)
culture (p. 10)
social construction (p. 11)
difference-equals-deficit error (p. 11)

ethnic group (p. 12)
race (p. 12)
intersectionality (p. 12)
plasticity (p. 14)
dynamic-systems approach (p. 14)
scientific observation (p. 18)
experiment (p. 20)
independent variable (p. 20)
dependent variable (p. 20)
survey (p. 21)
meta-analysis (p. 22)
cross-sectional research (p. 22)
longitudinal research (p. 23)
cross-sequential research (p. 23)
correlation (p. 25)
quantitative research (p. 26)
qualitative research (p. 26)

APPLICATIONS

1. It is said that culture is pervasive but that people are unaware of it. List 30 things you did *today* that you might have done differently in another culture. Begin with how and where you woke up.

2. How would your life be different if your parents were much higher or lower in SES than they are? Consider all three domains.

3. A longitudinal case study can be insightful but is also limited in generality. Interview one of your older relatives, and explain what aspects of his or her childhood are unique, what might be relevant for everyone of their cohort, and what might be relevant today.

Especially For ANSWERS

Response for Nurses (from p. 20) Experiments are the only way to determine cause-and-effect relationships. If we want to be sure that a new drug or treatment is safe and effective, an experiment must be conducted to establish that the drug or treatment improves health.

Response for Future Researchers (from p. 24) There is no best method for collecting data. The method used depends on many factors, such as the age of participants (infants can't complete questionnaires), the question being researched, and the time frame.

Response for Future Researchers and Science Writers (from p. 27) Yes. Anyone you write about must give consent and be fully informed about your intentions. They can be identified by name only if they give permission. For example, family members gave permission before anecdotes about them were included in this text. My nephew David read the first draft of his story (see pages 16–17) and is proud to have his experiences used to teach others.

Observation Quiz ANSWERS

Answer to Observation Quiz (from p. 16) Surveys rarely ask children their opinions, and the youngest cohort on this graph did not reach adulthood until about 2005.

Answer to Observation Quiz (from p. 23) Of course, much changed and much did not change, but evident in the photos is continuity in Sarah-Maria's happy smile and discontinuity in her hairstyle (which shows dramatic age and cohort changes).

VISUALIZING DEVELOPMENT Diverse Complexities

It is often repeated that "the United States is becoming more diverse," a phrase that usually refers only to ethnic diversity and not to economic and religious diversity (which are also increasing and merit attention). From a developmental perspective, two other diversities are also important—age and region, as shown below. What are the implications for schools, colleges, employment, health care, and nursing homes in the notable differences in the ages of people of various groups? And are attitudes about immigration, or segregation, or multiracial identity affected by the ethnicity of one's neighbors?

THE CHANGING ETHNIC MAKEUP OF THE UNITED STATES

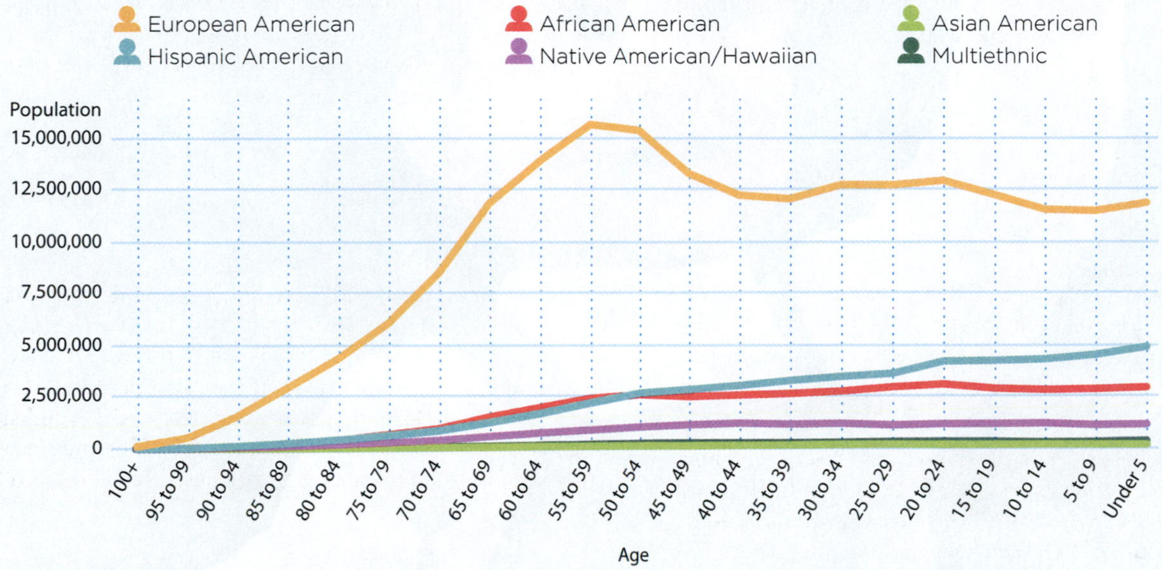

Regional Differences in Ethnicity Across the United States

In the United States, there are regional as well as age differences in ethnicity. This map shows which counties have an ethnic population greater than the national average. Counties where more than one ethnicity or race is greater than the national average are shown as multiethnic. Areas for which data are unavailable are left unshaded.

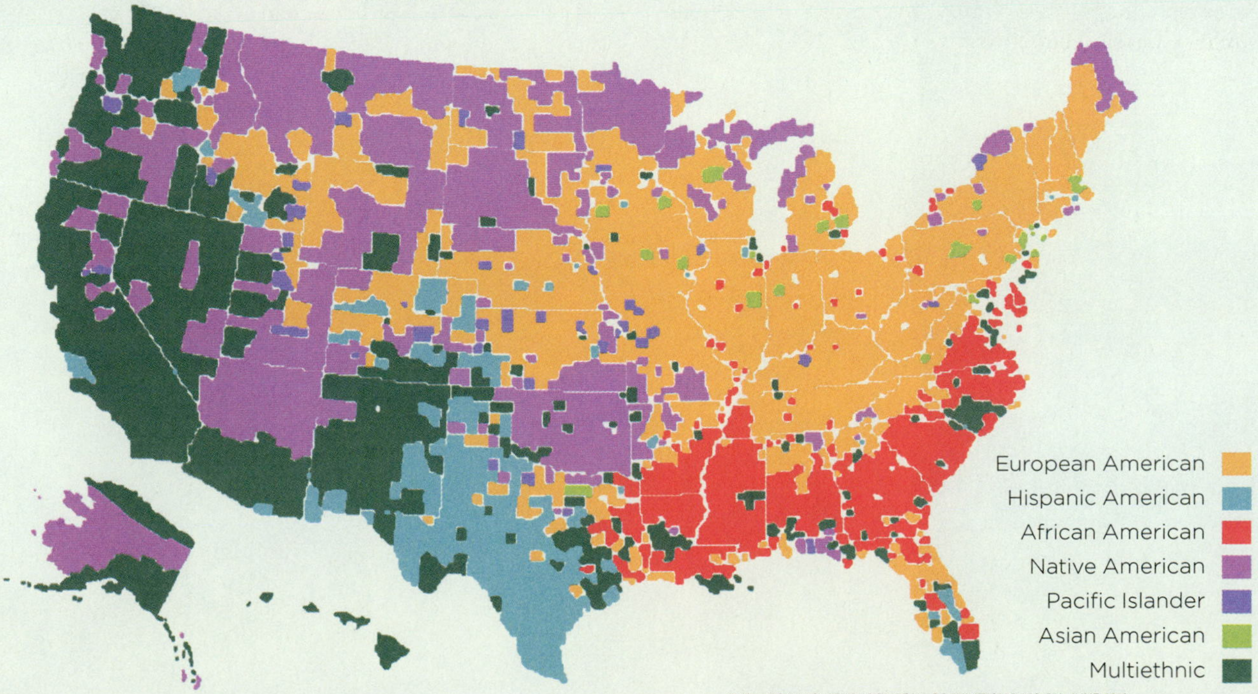

DATA FROM U.S. CENSUS BUREAU, POPULATION DIVISION, JUNE 2010.

CHAPTER 2

Theories

What Will You Know?

1. Do childhood experiences affect adults?
2. Would you be a different person if you grew up in another place or century?
3. Why do we need so many theories?

- **Grand Theories**
  - What Theories Are
  - Psychodynamic Theory: Freud and Erikson
  - Behaviorism: Conditioning and Learning
  - Cognitive Theory: Piaget and Information Processing
  - A VIEW FROM SCIENCE: Walk a Mile
  - INSIDE THE BRAIN: Measuring Mental Activity
- **Newer Theories**
  - Sociocultural Theory: Vygotsky and Beyond
  - Evolutionary Theory
- **What Theories Contribute**
  - OPPOSING PERSPECTIVES: Toilet Training—How and When?
- **VISUALIZING DEVELOPMENT: Highlights of the Science of Human Development**

Linda (not her real name) has been my friend since 2002, when she was single and childless. She swore me to secrecy about her exciting romance with a man we both idealized. She thought our other friends would gossip and criticize them both. A year later she was furious at him for lying to her. No one, including the man himself, knew that I knew.

Happily, Linda soon became involved with another man, Mike, who was honestly devoted to her. I liked him, but Linda wanted a husband and a baby and she worried that Mike was afraid of commitment: He had no steady job, and he feared marriage because his parents' marriage was unhappy. Mike and Linda were together for a year. Then Linda said, "Marry me or leave."

In all this, Linda was following her own theories. My role was to be a friend—someone who listened. I kept my opinions and theories quiet, although I thought her ultimatum to Mike was harsh. It turned out well: He found a steady job; I was part of their large church wedding.

Two years later, Linda became pregnant and my role changed from friend to expert. She asked me about nutrition, c-sections, mothers-in-law, breast-feeding, postpartum depression, hired caregivers, and more. I happily answered; she made good decisions. Her marriage and daughter thrived; I was proud of both of us.

But when her daughter, Mya, was 1 year old, Linda asked about sleep training. Should Mya go to sleep in her arms? Should Linda let Mya cry herself to sleep?

When Mya had a cold, both parents responded immediately to their congested, unhappy daughter. When the cold was gone, Mya's demanding cries continued every few hours all night long. Linda was exhausted but feared that if she did not respond, Mya would be traumatized and Mike would awaken, tend to the baby, and resent his wife.

Linda was asking me to choose between two opposing grand theories. This chapter describes those two, and three others. At the end of this chapter, you will read how Linda managed to get everyone in the family to sleep in peace.

Left: AlexSava/E+/Getty Images
Top: Cultura/JFCreatives/Getty Images

Aaron Bacall/Cartoon Collections/Cartoon Stock

"I'm going to refer to an educational theory which was first published in February and is still applicable today."

The Test of Time Grand theories have endured for decades and still guide contemporary scientists.

developmental theory A group of ideas, assumptions, and generalizations that interpret and illuminate the thousands of observations that have been made about human growth.

Grand Theories

In the first half of the twentieth century, two opposing theories—psychodynamic and behaviorism—dominated psychology, each with extensive applications to human development from birth to death. In about 1960, a third theory—cognitive—arose, and it, too, was applied to the entire life span.

These three are called "grand theories" because they are comprehensive, enduring, and far-reaching. But before describing them, we must explain why we need theories.

What Theories Are

A **developmental theory** is a comprehensive statement of general principles that provides a framework for understanding how and why people change as they grow older. Theories organize scattered facts and confusing observations into patterns, weaving the details into a meaningful whole. A developmental theory is more than a hunch or a hypothesis; it has emerged from data, survived analysis, led to experiments, and raised new questions.

To be more specific:

- Theories produce *hypotheses*.
- Theories generate *discoveries*.
- Theories offer *practical guidance*.

Sometimes people say dismissively, "that's just a theory," as if theories were disconnected from facts. However, facts—accepted as true—are crucial for every good theory. When scientists imagine a world without facts, "a world of ignorance where many possibilities seem equally likely. . . . [with] unreliable conclusions. . . . [and] shoddy evidence," they confirm that science must collect empirical facts (Step 3 of the scientific method) (Berg, 2018, p. 379).

Step 3 is the pivot, but notice that it is in the middle of the five steps. Scientists begin with a question and then a hypothesis (Steps 1 and 2), which often arises from a theory, and then collect facts to be analyzed, interpreted, and shared with other scientists (Steps 4 and 5), which again relates to a theory.

As Kurt Lewin (1945) once quipped, "Nothing is as practical as a good theory." Like many other scientists, he knew that theories help analysis and move us toward understanding.

For example, imagine trying to build a house without a design. You might have all the raw materials—the bricks, the wood, the nails. But without tools and a plan you could not proceed. Science provides the tools; theories provide the plan.

Of course, every theory is limited by when and where it arose. Each of the three grand theories began with a man in Europe more than a century ago (Freud, Pavlov, Piaget). These theories have inspired thousands of scientists to revise, refute, and then restructure them, and each has led to newer, better theories (Erikson, Skinner, information processing). That ongoing process is evidence that these grand theories are still useful, which is why we begin with them.

AKG/Science Source

Freud at Work In addition to being the world's first psychoanalyst, Sigmund Freud was a prolific writer. His many papers and case histories, primarily descriptions of his patients' symptoms and sexual urges, helped make the psychoanalytic perspective a dominant force for much of the twentieth century.

Psychodynamic Theory: Freud and Erikson

Inner drives, deep motives, and unconscious needs rooted in childhood—especially the first six years—are the focus of the first grand theory. These unconscious forces are thought to influence every aspect of thinking and behavior, from the smallest details of daily life to the crucial choices of a lifetime.

Freud's Ideas Sigmund Freud (1856–1939) was an Austrian physician who treated patients with mental illness. He listened to their remembered dreams and to their uncensored streams of thought. From that, he constructed an elaborate, multifaceted theory.

According to Freud, development in the first six years of life occurs in three stages. His theory is sometimes called a theory of *psychosexual* development, because each stage is characterized by sexual interest and pleasure arising from a particular part of the body.

In infancy, the erotic body part is the mouth (the *oral stage*); in early childhood, it is the anus (the *anal stage*); in the preschool years, it is the penis (the *phallic stage*), a source of pride and fear among boys and a reason for sorrow and envy among girls. After a quiet, nonsexual period (*latency*), the *genital stage* arrives at puberty, lasting throughout adulthood. (**Table 2.1** describes the stages in Freud's theory.)

One of Freud's most influential ideas was that each stage includes its own struggles. Conflict occurs, for instance, when parents wean their babies (oral stage), toilet-train their toddlers (anal stage), deflect the sexual curiosity and fantasies of their 5-year-olds (phallic stage), and limit the sexual interests of adolescents

TABLE 2.1

Comparison of Freud's Psychosexual and Erikson's Psychosocial Stages

Approximate Age	Freud (psychosexual)	Erikson (psychosocial)
Birth to 1 year	*Oral Stage* The lips, tongue, and gums are the focus of pleasurable sensations in the baby's body; sucking and feeding are the most stimulating activities.	*Trust vs. Mistrust* Babies either trust that others will satisfy their basic needs, including nourishment, warmth, cleanliness, and physical contact, **OR** develop mistrust about the care of others.
1–3 years	*Anal Stage* The anus is the focus of pleasurable sensations in the baby's body, and toilet training is the most important activity.	*Autonomy vs. Shame and Doubt* Children either become self-sufficient in many activities, including toileting, feeding, walking, exploring, and talking, **OR** doubt their own abilities.
3–6 years	*Phallic Stage* The phallus, or penis, is the most important body part, and pleasure is derived from genital stimulation. Boys are proud of their penises; girls wonder why they don't have them.	*Initiative vs. Guilt* Children either try to undertake many adultlike activities **OR** internalize the limits and prohibitions set by parents. They feel either adventurous **OR** guilty.
6–11 years	*Latency* Not really a stage, latency is an interlude. Sexual needs are quiet; psychic energy flows into sports, school work, and friendship.	*Industry vs. Inferiority* Children busily practice and then master new skills **OR** feel inferior, unable to do anything well.
Adolescence	*Genital Stage* The genitals are the focus of pleasurable sensations, and the young person seeks sexual stimulation and satisfaction in heterosexual relationships.	*Identity vs. Role Confusion* Adolescents ask themselves "Who am I?" They establish sexual, political, religious, and vocational identities **OR** are confused about their roles.
Adulthood	Freud believed that the genital stage lasts throughout adulthood. He also said that the goal of a healthy life is "to love and to work."	*Intimacy vs. Isolation* Young adults seek companionship and love **OR** become isolated from others, fearing rejection. *Generativity vs. Stagnation* Middle-aged adults contribute to future generations through work, creative activities, and parenthood **OR** they stagnate. *Integrity vs. Despair* Older adults try to make sense of their lives, either seeing life as a meaningful whole **OR** despairing at goals never reached.

Ted Streshinsky/The LIFE Images Collection/Getty Images

A Legendary Couple In his first 30 years, Erikson never fit into a particular local community, since he frequently changed nations, schools, and professions. Then he met Joan. In their first five decades of marriage, they raised a family and wrote several books. If Erikson had published his theory at age 73 (when this photograph was taken) instead of in his 40s, would he still have described life as a series of crises?

(genital stage). Freud thought that the experiences surrounding these conflicts determine adult personality.

Freud did not believe that new stages occurred after puberty; rather, he believed that adult personalities and habits were influenced by unconscious memories of childhood experiences. Unconscious conflicts rooted in early life are evident in adulthood—for instance, in smoking cigarettes (oral) or cleaning house (anal) or falling in love with a much older partner (phallic).

Erikson's Ideas Many of Freud's followers became famous theorists themselves—Carl Jung, Alfred Adler, and Karen Horney among them. They agreed with Freud that early-childhood emotions affect everyone, often unconsciously, but they also expanded and modified Freud's ideas.

For scholars in human development, one neo-Freudian, Erik Erikson (1902–1994), is particularly insightful. He proposed a comprehensive developmental theory of the entire life span. [**Life-Span Link:** Each of Erikson's stages is described in detail in the relevant psychosocial chapter—Chapters 7, 10, 13, 16, 19, 22, and 25.]

Erikson emphasized the social contexts of development; his theory is called *psychosocial*. He understood that the people—family, friends, and the larger community—who nurture each person are crucial for that person's development. Those people follow the norms of their culture in raising their children. Erikson was intrigued by Native American child rearing, for instance.

Erikson described eight developmental stages, each characterized by a particular challenge, or *developmental crisis* (summarized in Table 2.1). Typically, development at each stage leads to neither extreme but to something in between.

Especially for Teachers Your kindergartners are talkative and always moving. They almost never sit quietly and listen to you. What would Erik Erikson recommend? (see response, page 57)

For example, in the fifth stage (*intimacy versus isolation*), young adults seek closeness with another person—a socially recognized commitment such as marriage that involves emotional, practical, and sexual intimacy. The opposite would be people who always keep to themselves, trusting no one, never sharing, unable to commit to another person.

In actuality, of course, it is rare for a romance to be totally open and intimate for years. The other extreme is also rare: Very few people keep to themselves all the time. What Erikson recognized is that the prime emotional need for young adults is to connect with other people—a drive that is far stronger than it was earlier or will be in later stages. Intimacy is not always totally achieved.

In two crucial aspects, Erikson's theory diverges from Freud's:

1. Erikson's stages emphasized family and culture, not sexual urges.
2. Erikson recognized that development continues lifelong, with three stages after adolescence.

Behaviorism: Conditioning and Learning

The comprehensive theory that dominated psychology in the United States for most of the twentieth century was **behaviorism**. This theory began in Russia, with Pavlov (1849–1936), who first described conditioning.

behaviorism A grand theory of human development that studies observable behavior. Behaviorism is also called *learning theory* because it describes the laws and processes by which behavior is learned.

Classical Conditioning In the first years of the twentieth century, Ivan Pavlov performed hundreds of experiments to examine the link between something that affected a living creature (such as a sight, a sound, a touch) and the reaction of that creature. Technically, he was interested in how a *stimulus* effects a *response*.

This began with Pavlov's medical research on salivation. He noticed that the dogs in his research drooled (response) not only at the smell of food (stimulus) but also, eventually, at the sound of the footsteps of the people bringing food. This

observation led him to perform a famous experiment: He conditioned dogs to salivate (response) when hearing a particular noise (stimulus).

Pavlov began by sounding a tone just before presenting food. After a number of repetitions of the tone-then-food sequence, dogs began salivating at the sound even when there was no food. This simple experiment demonstrated **classical conditioning** (also called *respondent conditioning*).

In classical conditioning, a person or animal learns to associate a neutral stimulus with a meaningful one, gradually responding to the neutral stimulus in the same way as to the meaningful one.

In Pavlov's original experiment, the dog associated the tone (the neutral stimulus) with food (the meaningful stimulus) and eventually responded to the tone as if it were the food itself. The conditioned response to the tone (no longer neutral but now a conditioned stimulus) was evidence that learning had occurred.

Behaviorists see dozens of examples of classical conditioning in humans. Infants learn to smile at their parents because they associate them with food and play; toddlers become afraid of busy streets if the noise of traffic repeatedly frightens them; students enjoy—or fear—school, depending on what happened in kindergarten.

One application of this theory regards *substance use disorder (SUD)*. Of course, some reasons for addiction are biological—the body depends on the specific ingredients of the drug. But addiction is also a product of learning. The neutral objects that accompany drug use—the shape of the glass, the picture on the package, the line of the powder—become meaningful, triggering craving.

Behaviorists notice many reactions linked to stimuli that once were neutral. Think of how some people react to a bumblebee, or a baby's cry, or a final exam, or a police car in the rearview mirror. Such reactions are learned. An announcement about a future exam makes some students get chills—as no young child would. Many students, taking an exam, find that the stress makes them forget what they know—again, a conditioned response from past learning.

Hulton-Deutsch/Hulton-Deutsch Collection/Corbis/ Getty Images

A Contemporary of Freud Ivan Pavlov was a physiologist who received the Nobel Prize in 1904 for his research on digestive processes. It was this line of study that led to his discovery of classical conditioning, when his research on dog saliva led to insight about learning.

Observation Quiz How is Pavlov similar to Freud in appearance, and how do both look different from the other theorists pictured? (see answer, page 57) ↑

classical conditioning The learning process in which a meaningful stimulus (such as the smell of food to a hungry animal) is connected with a neutral stimulus (such as the sound of a tone) that had no special meaning before conditioning. (Also called *respondent conditioning*.)

Behaviorism in the United States Pavlov's ideas seemed to bypass most Western European developmentalists but were welcomed in the United States, since many North American scientists disputed Freud's emphasis on the unconscious.

The first of three famous Americans who championed behaviorism was John B. Watson (1878–1958). He argued that if psychology was to be a true science, psychologists should examine only what they could see and measure, not invisible impulses. In his words:

> Why don't we make what we can *observe* the real field of psychology? Let us limit ourselves to things that can be observed, and formulate laws concerning only those things. . . . We can observe *behavior—what the organism does or says*.
>
> [Watson, 1924/1998, p. 6]

According to Watson, everything is learned. He wrote:

> Give me a dozen healthy infants, well-formed, and my own specified world to bring them up in and I'll guarantee to take any one at random and train him to become any type of specialist I might select—doctor, lawyer, artist, merchant-chief, and yes, even beggar-man and thief, regardless of his talents, penchants, tendencies, abilities, vocations, and race of his ancestors.
>
> [Watson, 1924/1998, p. 82]

Other North American psychologists agreed. They developed behaviorism to study observable behavior, objectively and scientifically. For living creatures at every age, they believe that behavior follows natural laws.

Archives of the History of American Psychology/The University of Akron]

An Early Behaviorist John Watson was an early proponent of learning theory. His ideas are still influential and controversial today.

They seek to uncover those laws, experimenting with mice, dogs, and birds, because they believe that all learning follows the same laws. For behaviorists, everything that people do and feel is learned, step by step, via conditioning.

For example, newborns need to *learn* to suck on a nipple; infants *learn* to smile at a caregiver; preschoolers *learn* to hold hands when crossing the street. Such learning is conditioned and generalized to other situations and stimuli.

Once they are conditioned to suck on nipples for nourishment, children suck lollipops, and adults suck on cigars. Similarly, I still grab my adult children's hands when we cross the street. They say, "Mom, I know how to avoid cars now." I have been conditioned to help them cross. They have been conditioned to feel joy when they see me but to resist my impulse to restrict their independence.

Behaviorists believe that development occurs not in stages but bit by bit. A person learns to talk, read, socialize, and even love—one tiny step at a time.

operant conditioning The learning process by which a particular action is followed by something desired (which makes the person or animal more likely to repeat the action) or by something unwanted (which makes the action less likely to be repeated). (Also called *instrumental conditioning*.)

reinforcement When a behavior is followed by something desired, such as food for a hungry animal or a welcoming smile for a lonely person.

Operant Conditioning The most influential North American proponent of behaviorism was B. F. Skinner (1904–1990). Skinner agreed with Watson that psychology should focus on observable behavior. He did not dispute Pavlov's classical conditioning, but, as a good scientist, he built on Pavlov's conclusions.

Skinner's most famous contribution was to recognize another type of conditioning—**operant conditioning** (also called *instrumental conditioning*)—in which animals (including people) act and then something follows that action.

In other words, Skinner went beyond learning by association, in which one stimulus is paired with another stimulus (in Pavlov's experiment, the tone with the food). He focused instead on what happens *after* the response. If the consequence that follows is enjoyable, the creature (any living thing—a bird, a mouse, a child) tends to repeat the behavior; if the consequence is unpleasant, the creature does not do that action again.

This learning process is called **reinforcement** (Skinner, 1953). According to behaviorism, almost all of our daily behavior, from saying "Good morning" to earning a paycheck, is the result of past reinforcement.

Pleasant consequences are *reinforcers*. Behaviorists do not like to call them rewards because what some people consider a reward may actually be a *punishment*, an unpleasant consequence. For instance, a teacher might reward good behavior by giving the class extra recess time, but some children hate recess. Then recess is not a reinforcer.

The opposite is true as well: Something thought to be a punishment may actually be a reinforcement. For example, parents "punish" their children by withholding dessert. But a particular child might dislike the dessert, so being deprived of it is no punishment. The crucial question is "what works as a reinforcement or punishment for that individual?"

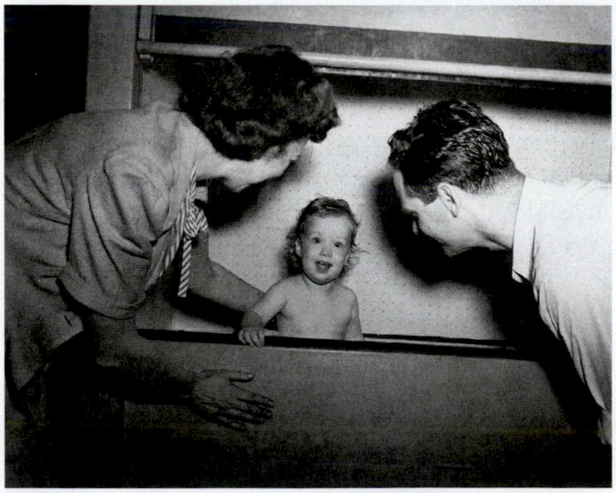

AP Images

Rats, Pigeons, and People B. F. Skinner is best known for his experiments with rats and pigeons, but he also applied his knowledge to human behavior. For his daughter, he designed a glass-enclosed crib in which temperature, humidity, and perceptual stimulation could be controlled to make her time in the crib enjoyable and educational. He encouraged her first attempts to talk by smiling and responding with words, affection, or other positive reinforcement.

The answer varies by age. For instance, adolescents find risk and excitement particularly reinforcing and consider punishments much less painful than adults do. That was one conclusion of a study of violent teenagers: For them, the thrill of breaking the law was reinforcing, outweighing the possible pain of getting caught (Shulman et al., 2017).

Consider a common practice in some schools, punishing children by suspending them. Most children who are suspended once are suspended again, and those children who are repeatedly suspended are more likely to be boys, to be African American, and/or to have special educational needs.

Those statistics raise a troubling question: Is suspension a punishment or reinforcement for those children? Might suspension be reinforcing for the teachers, who temporarily are rid of a misbehaving child (Tajalli & Garba, 2014; Shah, 2011)?

Children who are suspended from school are more likely to be imprisoned years later, the infamous school-to-prison pipeline (Barnes & Motz, 2018). That is a correlation; it does not prove that suspension *causes* later prison. [**Life-Span Link:** See the discussion of correlation and causation in Chapter 1.] But behaviorists suggest that it might (Mallett, 2016).

Remember, behaviorists focus on the *effect* that a consequence has on future behavior, not whether it is intended to be a reward or a punishment. Children who misbehave again and again have been reinforced, not punished, for their actions, perhaps by their parents or teachers, perhaps by their friends, perhaps by themselves.

Social Learning At first, behaviorists thought all behavior arose from a chain of learned responses, the direct result of (1) the association between one stimulus and another (classical conditioning) or (2) past reinforcement (operant conditioning). Thousands of experiments inspired by learning theory have demonstrated that both classical conditioning and operant conditioning occur in everyday life. We are all conditioned to react as we do.

However, people at every age are social and active, not just reactive. Instead of responding merely to their own conditioning, "people act on the environment. They create it, preserve it, transform it, and even destroy it . . . [in] a socially embedded interplay" (Bandura, 2006, p. 167).

That social interplay is the foundation of **social learning theory** (see **Table 2.2**), which holds that humans sometimes learn without personal reinforcement. This learning often occurs through **modeling**, when people copy what they see others do (also called *observational learning*) (Bandura, 1986, 1997).

Modeling is not simple imitation: People copy only some actions, of some individuals, in some contexts. They may do the opposite of what they observed. All that is social learning.

Generally, modeling is most likely when the observer is uncertain or inexperienced (modeling is especially powerful in childhood) and when the model is admirable, powerful, nurturing, or similar to the observer. Social learning occurs not

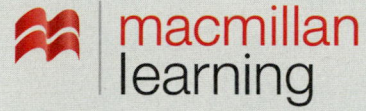

VIDEO ACTIVITY: Modeling: Learning by Observation features the original footage of Albert Bandura's famous experiment.

social learning theory An extension of behaviorism that emphasizes the influence that other people have over a person's behavior. Even without specific reinforcement, every individual learns many things through observation and imitation of other people. (Also called *observational learning*.)

modeling The central process of social learning, by which a person observes the actions of others and then copies them.

THINK CRITICALLY: Is your speech, hairstyle, or choice of shoes similar to those of your peers, or someone famous? Why?

TABLE 2.2

Three Types of Learning

Behaviorism is also called *learning theory* because it emphasizes the learning process, as shown here.

Type of Learning	Learning Process	Result
Classical Conditioning	Learning occurs through association.	Neutral stimulus becomes conditioned stimulus leading to a conditioned response.
Operant Conditioning	Learning occurs through reinforcement and punishment.	Weak or rare responses become strong and frequent—or, with punishment, unwanted responses become extinct.
Social Learning	Learning occurs through modeling what others do.	Observed behaviors become copied behaviors.

Would You Talk to This Man? Children loved talking to Jean Piaget, and he learned by listening carefully—especially to their incorrect explanations, which no one had paid much attention to before. All his life, Piaget was absorbed with studying the way children think. He called himself a "genetic epistemologist"—one who studies how children gain knowledge about the world as they grow.

cognitive theory A grand theory of human development that focuses on changes in how people think over time. According to this theory, our thoughts shape our attitudes, beliefs, and behaviors.

cognitive equilibrium In cognitive theory, a state of mental balance in which people are not confused because they can use their existing thought processes to understand current experiences and ideas.

assimilation The reinterpretation of new experiences to fit into old ideas.

accommodation The restructuring of old ideas to include new experiences.

only for behavior (why do teenagers style their hair as they do?) but also for morals, which people may think they decided for themselves but instead have been powerfully affected by other people (Bandura, 2016).

Cognitive Theory: Piaget and Information Processing

According to **cognitive theory**, thoughts and expectations profoundly affect attitudes, values, emotions, and actions. This is obvious now, but it was not always so. Social scientists describe a "cognitive revolution," around 1980, when *how* and *what* people think became important to understanding how and what people do.

This added to psychodynamic theory (which emphasized hidden impulses) and behaviorism (which emphasized observed actions). Thoughts come between those impulses and actions, and they are crucial.

Piaget's Stages of Development Jean Piaget (1896–1980) transformed our understanding of cognition, leading some people to consider him "the greatest developmental psychologist of all time" (Haidt, 2013, p. 6). His academic training was in biology, with a focus on shellfish—a background that taught him to look closely at small details.

Before Piaget, most scientists believed that babies could not yet think. But Piaget used scientific observation with his own three infants. He took meticulous notes, finding the infants to be curious and thoughtful, developing new concepts month by month.

Later he studied hundreds of schoolchildren. From this work emerged the central thesis of cognitive theory: *How* children think changes with time and experience, and those thought processes affect behavior. According to cognitive theory, to understand humans of any age, one must understand what they are thinking.

Piaget maintained that cognitive development occurs in four age-related periods, or stages: *sensorimotor, preoperational, concrete operational,* and *formal operational* (see **Table 2.3**). Each period fosters certain cognitive processes: Infants think via their senses; preschoolers have language but not logic; school-age children have simple logic; adolescents and adults can use formal, abstract logic (Inhelder & Piaget, 1958/2013b; Piaget, 1952/2011). [**Life-Span Link:** These stages are described in detail in Chapters 6, 9, 12, and 15.]

Piaget found that, at every age, intellectual advancement occurs because humans seek **cognitive equilibrium**—a state of mental balance. The easiest way

TABLE 2.3

Piaget's Periods of Cognitive Development

	Name of Period	Characteristics of the Period	Major Gains During the Period
Birth to 2 years	Sensorimotor	Infants use senses and motor abilities to understand the world. Learning is active, without reflection.	Infants learn that objects still exist when out of sight (*object permanence*) and begin to think through mental actions. (The sensorimotor period is discussed in Chapter 6.)
2–6 years	Preoperational	Children think symbolically, with language, yet children are *egocentric,* perceiving from their own perspective.	The imagination flourishes, and language becomes a significant means of self-expression and social influence. (The preoperational period is discussed in Chapter 9.)
6–11 years	Concrete operational	Children understand and apply logic. Thinking is limited by direct experience.	By applying logic, children grasp concepts of conservation, number, classification, and many other scientific ideas. (The concrete-operational period is discussed in Chapter 12.)
12 years through adulthood	Formal operational	Adolescents and adults use abstract and hypothetical concepts. They can use analysis, not only emotion.	Ethics, politics, and social and moral issues become fascinating as adolescents and adults use abstract, theoretical reasoning. (The formal-operational period is discussed in Chapter 15.)

to achieve this balance is to interpret new experiences through the lens of preexisting ideas.

For example, infants grab new objects in the same way that they grasp familiar objects. Similarly, children's concept of God as a loving—or punishing—parent depends on their experience with their own parents. That is true universally, which is why people of many faiths call themselves "a child of God" and pray to their heavenly *Father*, or respect *Mother* Earth.

At every age, people interpret other people's behavior by assuming that everyone thinks as they themselves do. Once people get an idea, they usually stick to it—even when logic or facts say otherwise. Have you noticed how hard it is to convince anyone that they are wrong?

However, a flood of unexpected experiences or questions may be jarring, disturbing one's simple thoughts. Then the person experiences *cognitive disequilibrium,* an imbalance that creates confusion.

As **Figure 2.1** illustrates, disequilibrium advances cognition if it leads to adaptive thinking. Piaget describes two types of adaptation:

- **Assimilation**: New experiences are reinterpreted to fit, or *assimilate,* into old ideas.
- **Accommodation**: Old ideas are restructured to include, or *accommodate,* new experiences.

Accommodation is more difficult than assimilation, but it advances thought. New concepts are developed when old ones fail. In Piagetian terms, people *construct* ideas based on their experiences; the idea of constructed knowledge implies that people build their cognition. One purpose of college is to challenge students, helping them build a new worldview.

Ideally, when two people disagree, adaptation is mutual. Think of a lovers' quarrel. If both parties listen to the other, they both accommodate. Then the quarrel strengthens their relationship, and they reach a new, better equilibrium.

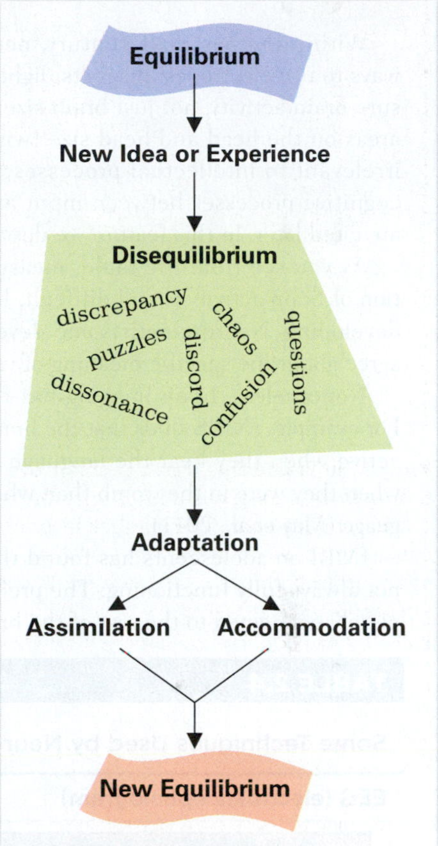

FIGURE 2.1

Challenge Me Most of us, most of the time, prefer the comfort of our conventional conclusions. According to Piaget, however, when new ideas disturb our thinking, we have an opportunity to expand our cognition with a broader and deeper understanding.

Information Processing Piaget is credited with discovering that mental constructs affect behavior, an idea that is now accepted by most social scientists. However, many think Piaget's theories were limited. Neuroscience and cross-cultural studies have extended our understanding of cognition.

This is most evident in **information-processing theory**, a newer expression of cognitive theory inspired by the input, programming, memory, and output of the computer. When conceptualized in that way, thinking is affected by the synapses and neurons of the brain. (See Inside the Brain.)

information-processing theory A perspective that compares human thinking processes, by analogy, to computer analysis of data, including sensory input, connections, stored memories, and output.

INSIDE THE BRAIN

Measuring Mental Activity

A hundred years ago, people thought that emotions came from the heart. That's why we still send hearts on Valentine's Day and why we speak of "broken hearts" or people who are "soft-hearted" or have "hardened their hearts."

But now we know that everything begins inside the brain. It is foolish to dismiss a sensation with "It's all in your head." Of course it is in your head; everything is.

Until quite recently, the only way scientists estimated brains was to measure heads. Of course, measuring produced some obvious discoveries—babies with shrunken brains (microcephaly) suffered severe intellectual disability, and brains grew bigger as children matured.

Measuring also led to some obvious errors. In the nineteenth and early twentieth centuries, many scientists believed the theory that bumps on the surface of the head reflected intelligence and character, a theory known as *phrenology*. Psychiatrists would run their hands over a person's skull to measure 27 traits, including spirituality, loyalty, and aggression.

Another discredited example was suggesting that women could never be professors because their brains were too small (Swaab & Hofman, 1984).

Within the past half-century, neuroscientists developed ways to use electrodes, magnets, light, and computers to measure brain activity, not just brain size (see **Table 2.4**). Raised areas on the head and head size (within limits) were proven irrelevant to intellectual processes. Researchers now study cognitive processes between input and output. Some results are cited later. In this feature we describe methods.

As you see from the table, measurement and interpretation of brain activity is still difficult, but newer techniques are developing. Neuroscientists and developmentalists often disagree about the specific meaning of various results.

Nonetheless, brain imaging has revealed many surprises. For example, fNIRS finds that the brains of newborns are more active when they hear the language that their mother spoke when they were in the womb than when they hear another language (May et al., 2011).

fMRI on adolescents has found that a fully grown brain is not always fully functioning: The prefrontal cortex is not completely connected to the rest of the brain until about age 25.

Individual differences in brain development are intriguing. Some adolescents are much more cognitively mature than others, as measured by their brains (Foulkes & Blakemore, 2018), and brain scans of new mothers reveal that babies change their mothers' brains (P. Kim et al., 2016).

All of the tools indicated in Table 2.4 have discovered brain plasticity and variations not imagined in earlier decades. However, sensitive machines and advanced computer analysis are required for accurate readings.

Changes in light absorption, or magnetism, or oxygenated blood flow in the brain are miniscule from one moment to the next. Interpretation is complex.

Variations within and between people make it difficult to know what someone is thinking via brain scans. Once again, this confirms the need for theory: Without an idea of what to look for, or what it might mean, the millions of data points from all brain images might lead to the same trap as earlier measurements of the skull—human bias.

TABLE 2.4

Some Techniques Used by Neuroscientists to Understand Brain Function

EEG (electroencephalogram)

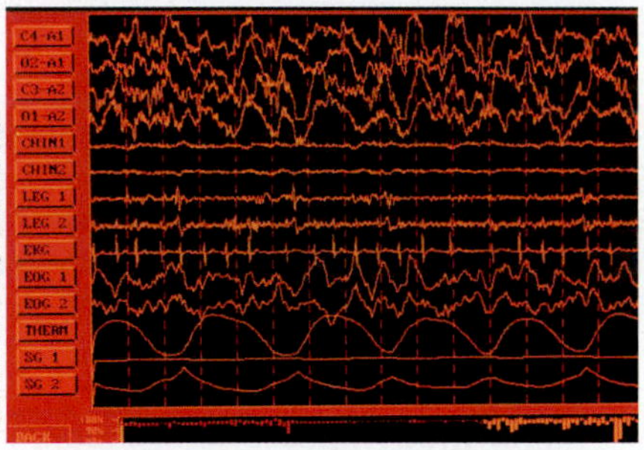

Robert J. Herko/The Image Bank/Getty Images

The EEG measures electrical activity in the cortex. This can differentiate active brains (beta brain waves—very rapid, 12 to 30 per second) from sleeping brains (delta waves—1 to 3 per second) and brain states that are half-awake, or dreaming. Complete lack of brain waves, called flat-line, indicates brain death.

ERP (event-related potential)

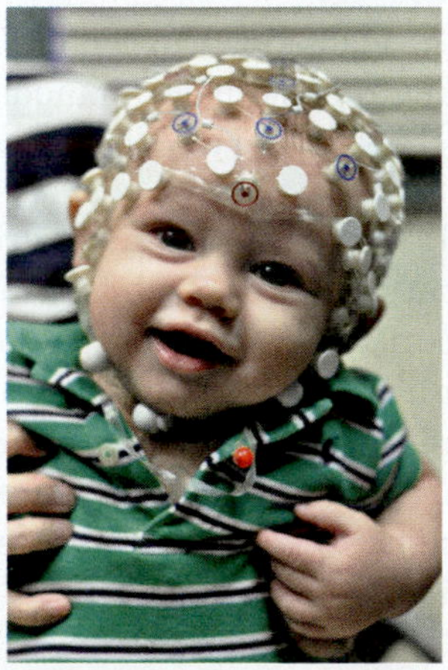

Langlois Social Development Lab

The amplitude and frequency of brain electrical activity changes when a particular stimulus (called an event) occurs. First, the ERP establishes the usual patterns, and then researchers present a stimulus (such as a sound, an image, a word) that causes a blip in electrical activity. ERP indicates how quickly and extensively people react—although this method requires many repetitions to distinguish the response from the usual brain activity.

MRI (magnetic resonance imaging)

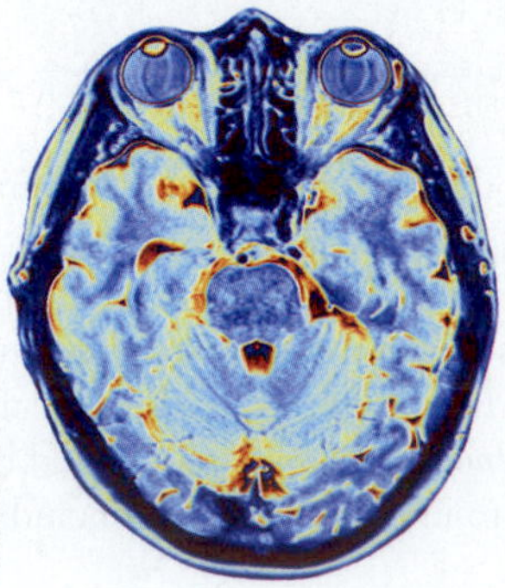

Pasieka/Science Source

The water molecules in various parts of the brain each have a magnetic current, and measuring that current allows measurement of myelin, neurons, and fluid in the brain.

fMRI (functional magnetic resonance imaging)

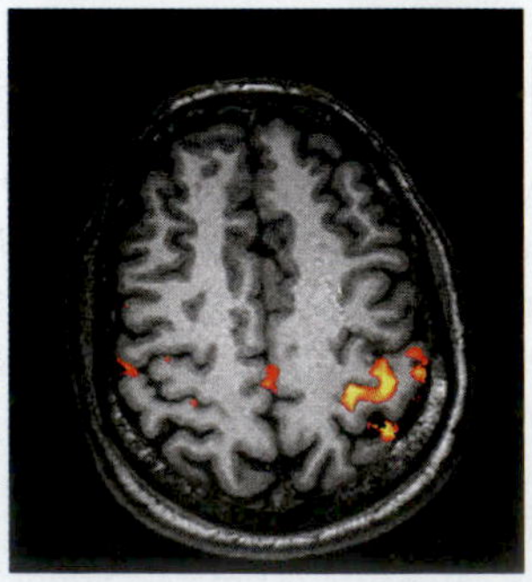

Kul Bhatia/Science Source

In advanced MRI, function is measured as more oxygen is added to the blood flow when specific neurons are activated. The presumption is that increased blood flow means that the person is using that part of the brain. fMRI has revealed that several parts of the brain are active at once—seeing something activates parts of the visual cortex, but it also may activate other parts of the brain far from the visual areas.

PET (positron emission tomography)

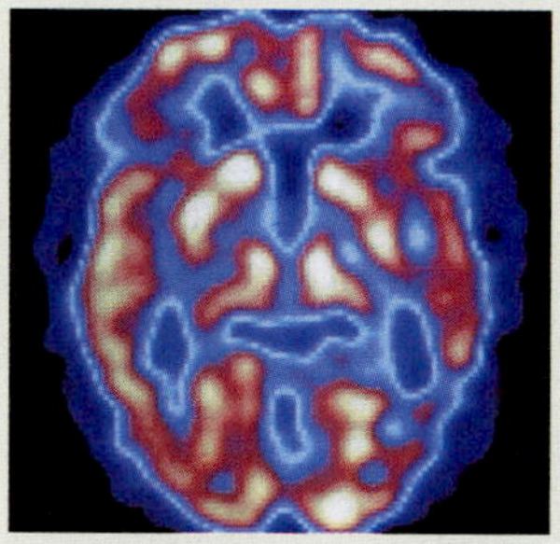

Tim Beddow/Science Source

When a specific part of the brain is active, the blood flows more rapidly in that part. If radioactive dye is injected into the bloodstream and a person lies very still within a scanner while seeing pictures or other stimuli, changes in blood flow indicate thought. PET can reveal the volume of neurotransmitters; the rise or fall of brain oxygen, glucose, amino acids; and more. PET is almost impossible to use with children (who cannot stay still) and is very expensive with adults.

fNIRS (functional near-infrared spectroscopy)

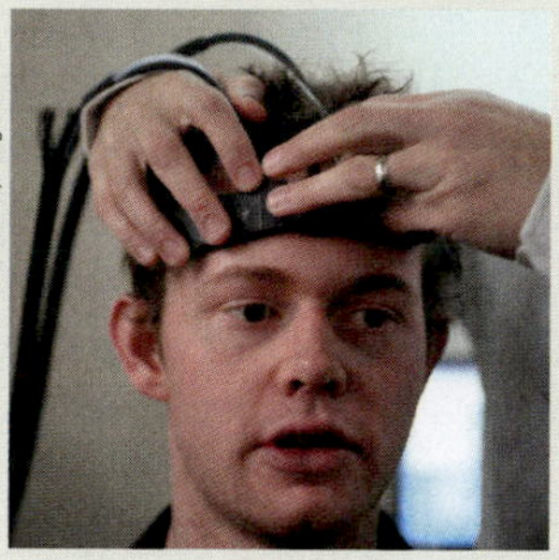

Pat Greenhouse/The Boston Globe/Getty Images

This method also measures changes in blood flow. But, it depends on light rather than magnetic charge and can be done with children, who merely wear a special cap connected to sensors and do not need to lie still in a noisy machine (as they do for PET or fMRI). By measuring how each area of the brain absorbs light, neuroscientists infer activity of the brain (Ferrari & Quaresima, 2012).

DTI (diffusion tensor imaging)

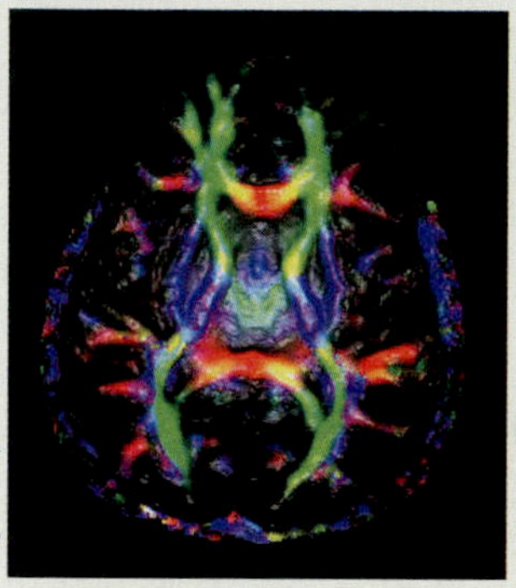

Living Art Enterprises/Science Source

DTI is another technique that builds on the MRI. It measures the flow (diffusion) of water molecules within the brain, which shows connections between one area and another. This is particularly interesting to developmentalists because life experiences affect which brain areas connect with which other ones. Thus, DTI is increasingly being used by clinicians who want to individualize treatment and monitor progress (Van Hecke et al., 2016).

For both practical and ethical reasons, it is difficult to use these techniques on large, representative samples. One of the challenges of neuroscience is to develop methods that are harmless, quick, acceptable to parents and babies, and comprehensive. A more immediate challenge is to depict the data in ways that are easy to interpret and understand.

Information processing is "a framework characterizing a large number of research programs" (Miller, 2011, p. 266). Instead of interpreting *responses* by infants and children, as Piaget did, this cognitive theory focuses on the *processes* of thought—that is, when, why, and how neurons fire before a response.

Brain activity is traced back to what activated those neurons. Information-processing theorists examine stimuli and responses from the senses, body movements, hormones, and organs, all of which affect thinking (Glenberg et al., 2013). These scientists believe that details of cognitive processes shed light on what people think and know. We can understand the product of the mind when we better understand how ideas originated.

For example, we sometimes feel happy, or sad, or whatever. Our feelings affect how we think about everything we experience. But until we consider the origins of those feelings—the gut and brain connections that led to those emotions—we cannot fully understand why people feel and think as they do (Damasio, 2018).

Hundreds of scientists focus on *biomarkers* (signs in the body), such as activity of the parasympathetic and sympathetic nervous systems, or hormones in the bloodstream, or heart rate, that reveal how thoughts affect actions (Buss et al., 2018).

Brain Cells in Action Neurons reach out to other neurons, shown here in an expansion microscopy photo that was impossible even a decade ago. No wonder Piaget's description of the four stages of cognition needs revision from the information-processing perspective.

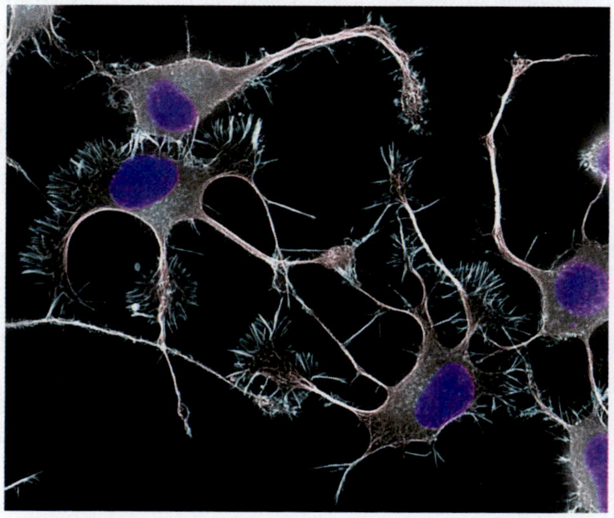

DR TORSTEN WITTMANN/SCIENCE PHOTO LIBRARY/Getty Images

With the aid of neuroscience and sensitive technology (see Inside the Brain), information-processing research has overturned some of Piaget's findings, as you will later read. However, the basic tenet of cognitive theory is equally true for Piaget, neuroscience, and information processing: *Ideas matter*.

Thus, how children interpret a hypothetical social situation, such as whether they anticipate welcome or rejection, affects the quality of their actual friendships; how teenagers think about heaven and hell influences their sexual activity; how adults view the proper role of women affects whether or not they have sex, marry, become parents, divorce. For everyone, ideas frame situations and affect actions (see A View from Science).

A VIEW FROM SCIENCE

Walk a Mile

The folk saying "walk a mile in my shoes," memorialized in a song that asks if "I could be you and you could be me for just an hour," reflects the importance of *social perspective-taking*. When humans understand the circumstances of each other's lives, that might lead to more caring behavior because according to cognitive theory, thoughts guide actions.

As you have read, the information-processing perspective encourages scientists to connect thinking, behavior, and brain structures, not in stages but bit by bit. An international team of seven scientists did just that, with 293 participants, aged 7 to 26 (Tamnes et al., 2018).

In that study, the main test of perspective-taking was a modification of the dictator task (Keysar et al., 2000). In that task, the participants view objects in a display case that has 16 cubicles, 5 of which have backs so that the contents are not seen by someone on the other side while the other 11 are open front and back. A man on the other side (the dictator) supposedly tells the participant to move one of the objects. (See **Figure 2.2**.)

The objective of this perspective-taking challenge is for the participant to realize that the dictator cannot see the objects in some of the boxes. For example, three of the cubicles hold balls—large, medium, and small—but the dictator can see only the first two.

Thus, when the dictator commands "Move the small ball," the participant must decide whether to move the medium ball or the smallest ball. The correct answer would be the medium ball, because, from the dictator's restricted view, that ball is smallest.

Perspective-taking increases gradually with development. In this study, children (up to age 11) were wrong about one-third of the time; adolescents (ages 12 to 18) were wrong about one-seventh of the time; and emerging adults were wrong about one-twentieth of the time, (Tamnes et al., 2018).

This replicates many other studies: Maturation brings gradual increases in perspective-taking, with adults still not able to always understand another person's views. Contrary to Piaget, there is no discontinuity, that is, no stage at which perspective-taking suddenly appears.

The researchers in this study then gave many of the participants a survey called the Strength and Difficulties questionnaire, which asks children and adults 25 questions about behavior—their own or someone else's. This questionnaire has been carefully vetted and often used (Goodman et al., 1998).

In the social perspective-taking study, the participants were asked six questions from that questionnaire, including whether they never, sometimes, or always were "helpful if someone is hurt, upset, or feeling ill."

Accuracy on perspective-taking in the dictator task correlated with prosocial behavior on the Strength and Difficulties questionnaire. Even when the effects of age were taken into account, those participants who were better at figuring out what the dictator could see were also better at caring for other people (Tamnes et al., 2018).

Finally—and this is the feature that makes this study innovative—the scientists used neurological measures, specifically how thick the distance was between gray and white matter in various regions of the cortex. Previous work had shown that the cortex thins with maturation: When a particular region is thinner, that suggests more advanced thinking in that area.

Each of the three components above had been studied in isolation many times before. The information-processing perspective led these scientists to put all three together.

Cognition, behavior, and brain were correlated: Those with the thinner cortexes—especially in regions of the brain known for social cognition (the medial prefrontal, lateral prefrontal, and anterior cingulate)—were most likely to help other people and to understand the views of others.

This study is far from definitive, as the scientists themselves reported, using the words "might," "may," "modest," and the need for "further study." The behavior was self-reported and

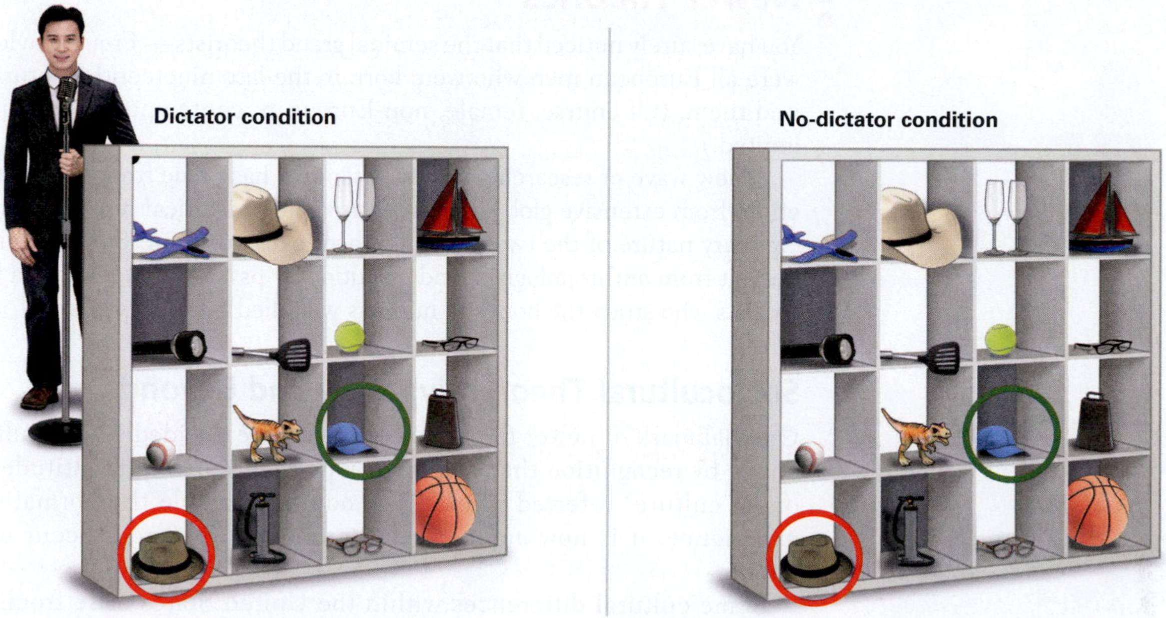

FIGURE 2.2

Do You See What I See? If a man behind a set of shelves, some open and some closed, told you to move the small hat or the big ball, what would you do? Probably you would move the mid-sized objects because you would realize that he could not see what you see. Young children, however, might move the wrong objects. (This illustration is more complex than the one in the experiment, to help you understand the complications of perspective-taking.)

cross-sectional (remember the limitations described in Chapter 1), and correlations among the three kinds of measures was relatively low (although significant).

Nonetheless, this raises the possibility that advancing perspective-taking (perhaps by having people read biographies, or engage in conversations with people unlike them) might increase prosocial behaviors and might be seen longitudinally in brain imaging. Longitudinal research might verify with brain imagery that empathy benefits from experience.

In this way, cognitive theory can promote social understanding via social interactions in schools, camps, workplaces. As you see, the information-processing perspective can suggest new ways to help humans advance their cognition and thus their actions.

This is *not* what Piaget advocated. He dubbed "How to accelerate cognition?" the American question, because Americans asked him that much more often than Europeans.

However, many developmentalists think that the American question is not an obsession but a goal. They hope to understand how people process information, and that might advance the goal of our study—to help all 8 billion people on Earth fulfill their potential.

WHAT HAVE YOU LEARNED?

1. What is the basic emphasis of psychodynamic theory?
2. What similarities and differences are found between Freud's and Erikson's theories of adulthood?
3. How does the central focus of behaviorism differ from psychodynamic theory?
4. When is social learning most powerful?
5. What did Piaget discover that earlier psychologists did not realize?
6. How does information processing contribute to the cognitive revolution?
7. What does neuroscience make possible that was impossible for Freud, Skinner, or Piaget?

Newer Theories

You have surely noticed that the seminal grand theorists — Freud, Pavlov, Piaget — were all European men who were born in the late nineteenth century. That limited them. (Of course, female, non-European, contemporary theorists also are limited.)

A new wave of research and understanding has come from scientists who benefited from extensive global, cross-cultural, and historical research. The multidisciplinary nature of the two emerging theories is apparent: Sociocultural theorists benefit from anthropologists, and evolutionary psychologists use data from archeologists who study the bones of humans who died 100,000 years ago.

Sociocultural Theory: Vygotsky and Beyond

One hallmark of newer theories is that they are decidedly multicultural, influenced by recognition that cultures shape experiences and attitudes. Whereas once "culture" referred primarily to oddities outside the normative Western experience, it is now apparent that cultural differences occur within each nation.

Some cultural differences within the United States arise from ethnic and national origins — people with grandparents in Pakistan versus those with grandparents from Poland, for instance. Some arise from education, when college graduates are contrasted with high school dropouts. And some are related to region, age, and gender: The sociocultural perspective of an 80-year-old woman in Montana differs from that of a 15-year-old boy in Mississippi, even if they share SES, citizenship, and ethnicity. Sociocultural theory values all of those differences, not in insolation but in intersectionality. [**Life-Span Link:** The concept of intersectionality is introduced in Chapter 1.]

sociocultural theory A newer theory which holds that development results from the dynamic interaction of each person with the surrounding social and cultural forces.

apprenticeship in thinking Vygotsky's term for how cognition is stimulated and developed in people by more skilled members of society.

The central thesis of **sociocultural theory** is that human development results from the dynamic interaction between developing persons and their surrounding society. Culture is not something external that impinges on developing persons but is internalized, integral to everyday attitudes and actions. This idea is so central to our current understanding of human development that it was already stressed in Chapter 1. Now we explain sociocultural theory in more detail.

Dr. James Wertsch

Affection for Children Vygotsky lived in Russia from 1896 to 1934, when war, starvation, and revolution led to the deaths of millions. Throughout this turmoil, Vygotsky focused on learning. His love of children is suggested by this portrait: He and his daughter have their arms around each other.

Teaching and Guidance The pioneer of the sociocultural perspective was Lev Vygotsky (1896–1934), a psychologist from the former Soviet Union. Like the other theorists, he was born at the end of the nineteenth century, but unlike them, he traveled extensively as he was developing his ideas. Russia was a huge, multicultural nation: Vygotsky studied Asian and European groups of many faiths, languages, and social contexts.

Vygotsky saw that people were taught whatever beliefs and habits were relevant within their culture, from rural Siberia to urban Moscow. He was particularly struck by the many variations, a contrast to the universal stages and laws favored by the grand theories. For example, Vygotsky chronicled how farmers think about tools, how nonreading people grasp abstract ideas, and how deaf children learn to communicate.

In Vygotsky's view, everyone, schooled or not, develops with the guidance of more skilled members of their society. Those skilled people become mentors in an **apprenticeship in thinking** (Vygotsky, 2012).

The word *apprentice* once had a quite specific meaning, sometimes spelled out in a legal contract that detailed what an apprentice would learn from a master. For example, in earlier centuries, a young person wanting to repair shoes might become a cobbler's apprentice, learning the trade while assisting the teacher.

Vygotsky believed that children become apprentices to people who know more. Mentors teach them how to think within that culture, explaining ideas, asking questions, and reinforcing values.

To describe this process, Vygotsky developed the concept of **guided participation**, the method used by parents, teachers, and entire societies to teach novices the skills and habits expected within their culture. Tutors engage learners (*apprentices*) in joint activities, offering "mutual involvement in several widespread cultural practices with great importance for learning: narratives, routines, and play" (Rogoff, 2003, p. 285).

guided participation The process by which people learn from others who guide their experiences and explorations.

Active apprenticeship and sensitive guidance are central to sociocultural theory because everyone depends on others to learn. All cultural beliefs are social constructions, not natural laws, according to sociocultural theorists.

Customs are needed to protect and unify a community, yet some cultural assumptions need to change. Because they are social constructions, communities can reconstruct them. For example, Vygotsky stressed that children with disabilities should be educated (Vygotsky, 1994b). This belief has been enshrined in U.S. law since about 1970, a sociocultural shift.

The Zone of Proximal Development According to sociocultural theory, all learning is social, whether people are learning a manual skill, a social custom, or a language. As part of the apprenticeship of thinking, a *mentor* (parent, peer, or professional) finds the learner's **zone of proximal development**, an imaginary area surrounding the learner that contains the skills, knowledge, and concepts that are close (proximal) to being grasped but not yet reached.

zone of proximal development In sociocultural theory, a metaphorical area, or "zone," surrounding a learner that includes all of the skills, knowledge, and concepts that the person is close ("proximal") to acquiring but cannot yet master without help.

Through sensitive assessment of each learner, mentors engage mentees within their zone. Together, in a "process of joint construction," new knowledge is attained (Valsiner, 2006). The mentor must avoid two opposite dangers: boredom and failure. Some frustration is permitted, but the learner must be actively engaged, never passive or overwhelmed (see **Figure 2.3**).

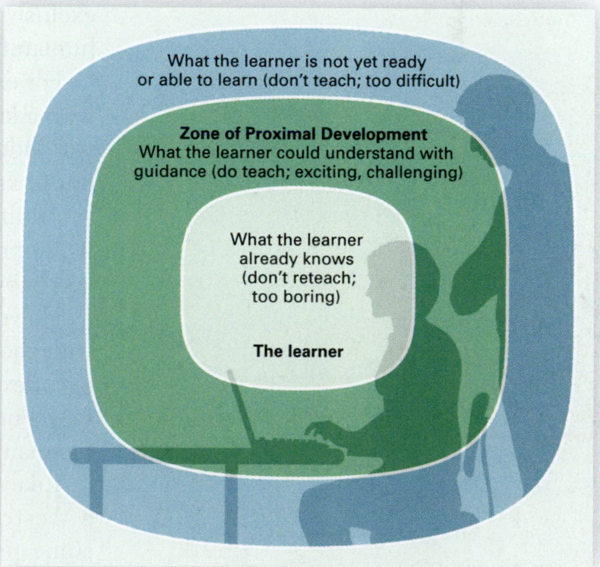

FIGURE 2.3

The Magic Middle Somewhere between the boring and the impossible is the zone of proximal development, where interaction between teacher and learner results in knowledge never before grasped or skills not already mastered. The intellectual excitement of that zone is the origin of the joy that both instruction and study can bring.

A mentor must sense whether support or freedom is needed and how peers can help (they may be the best mentors). Skilled teachers know when a person's zone of proximal development expands and shifts.

Excursions into and through the zone of proximal development are everywhere. One recent innovation from the medical profession is for adults with illnesses of many sorts. The strategy builds on adults' need to thrive within their particular context. For that reason, adults are given the tools they need to monitor their health, such as wearable technology that measures insulin, or blood pressure, or heart rate, or whatever. They are then sent text messages encouraging and advising them about diet, exercise, and prescriptions.

Text messages are geared to each person's particular zone, helping that person take the next best step toward health. For example, if people want to stop smoking cigarettes, it is effective to have them receive text messages geared to their level and stage of quitting (Head et al., 2013).

The success of sensitive mentoring is evident. For example, for those 84 million U.S. adults who are considered prediabetic, text messages alone were shown to be as effective as formal education in diabetes prevention (Fischer et al., 2018).

Mentoring within the zone of proximal development requires sensitive teachers (who know exactly what the next step is for the individual) and motivated learners (who are willing the leave their familiar comfort zone to learn something new).

Examples from other people and equipment provided by the culture also teach children, according to sociocultural theory. Children in the United States want to learn to ride a bike because they have seen other children biking. Unlike a few decades ago, training wheels and small bikes without pedals are available to advance learning, and laws require helmets even for the youngest children. Those cultural artifacts guide safe learning.

In another culture, everything might be different. Perhaps no children ride bicycles. Recognizing such cultural differences is crucial for understanding development, according to this theory.

Universals and Specifics By emphasizing the impact of all the specific aspects of each culture, sociocultural theory aims to apply to everyone, everywhere. Perhaps paradoxically, becoming attuned to the specifics of each time and place furthers what sociocultural theorists believe is universal for humans—everyone learns and thrives within a particular community.

Thus, mentors, attuned to ever-shifting abilities and motivation, continually urge a new competence—the next level, not the moon. For their part, learners ask questions, show interest, and demonstrate progress, all of which informs and inspires the mentors. When education goes well, both mentor and learner are fully engaged and productive within the zone. Particular skills and processes vary enormously, but the overall process is the same.

Within each culture, learners have personal traits, experiences, and aspirations, all part of the differential susceptibility described in Chapter 1. Consequently, education must be attuned to the individual. Some people need more assurance; some seek independence. However, the idea that each person has a particular learning style (e.g., by listening or watching) is more myth than fact; all humans learn using all of their modalities (Kirschner, 2017).

Consequently, mentors need to be sensitive to the needs, abilities, and motives of the learner; but they must not pigeonhole anyone's learning mode. The sociocultural perspective likewise notes that it is shortsighted to consider any culture exclusively one type or another; everyone, and every culture, expresses common humanity, albeit in various ways.

For example, every Western adult has learned to sit at the dinner table and eat with a knife and fork. The learning process begins with babies being fed and ends with adults eating with utensils, sometimes using salad forks, soup spoons, and butter knives all appropriately.

Adults teach others how to eat, including the manners of a particular culture, while providing appropriate tools and guidance—beginning with the sippy cup and baby spoon.

However, given that a third of the world's people eat with knives and forks, a third with chopsticks, and a third with their hands, it would be foolish to measure a 3-year-old's dexterity by noting how that child used utensils, unless culture were considered first. Further, many table manners are quite specific to each culture. When I lived in Germany, I ate with my fork in my left hand, changing my American habit.

Likewise, insights from sociocultural theory have revealed the limitations of a Western analysis of children's drawings (Rübeling et al., 2011). Specifically, some psychologists thought that children who drew their families as small people with neutral facial expressions and arms downward were less securely attached to their families than those who drew smiling, arms-up families (Fury et al., 1997).

But comparing drawings from children in Berlin with those from children in Cameroon found that the latter usually drew small figures with neutral expressions and often with arms down (see **Figure 2.4**). Nonetheless, those children in Cameroon were well adjusted and flourished within their families (Gernhardt et al., 2016).

Prof. i.R. Dr. Heidi Keller & Dr. rer. nat. Ariane Gerhardt

FIGURE 2.4

Standing Firm When children draw their families, many child therapists look for signs of trouble—such as small, frowning people with hands down floating in space. But cross-cultural research shows that such depictions reflect local norms. The Cameroonian 6-year-olds were as well adjusted in their local community as the three German children.

Evolutionary Theory

You are familiar with Charles Darwin and his ideas, first published 150 years ago, regarding the evolution of plants, insects, and birds over billions of years (Darwin, 1859). But you may not realize that serious research on human development inspired by this theory is quite recent (Simpson & Kenrick, 2013). As a leader in this theory recently wrote:

> Evolutionary psychology . . . is a revolutionary new science, a true synthesis of modern principles of psychology and evolutionary biology.
>
> [Buss, 2015, p. xv]

This perspective is increasingly important for understanding life-span development. A noted scholar wrote that **evolutionary theory** "is becoming the

evolutionary theory When used in human development, the idea that many current human emotions and impulses are a legacy from thousands of years ago.

Sanjay Kanojia/AFP/Getty Images

A Sacred River? This is the Ganges river at Allahabad in 2013, which the Indian government is working to clean—a monumental task. No nation is working to rid the Pacific Ocean of a much bigger garbage site. What would evolutionary theory recommend?

Observation Quiz Beyond the pollution of the Ganges by humans' garbage, what characteristics of the river, visible here, contribute to the pollution? (see answer, page 57) ↑

foundation of modern psychology and of developmental psychology" (Bjorklund, 2018, p. 2291).

This theory has led to new hypotheses and provocative ideas relevant to human development. One leading psycholinguist wrote, "there are major spheres of human experience—beauty, motherhood, kinship, morality, cooperation, sexuality, violence—in which evolutionary psychology provides the only coherent theory" (Pinker, 2003, p. 135).

The basic idea of evolutionary theory in development is that in order to understand the emotions, impulses, and habits of humans over the life span, we need to understand how those same emotions, impulses, and habits developed in *Homo sapiens* over the past 200,000 years.

Why We Fear Snakes More Than Cars Evolutionary developmental theory has intriguing explanations for many issues, including a pregnant woman's nausea, 1-year-olds' attachment to their parents, the obesity epidemic, and psychopathology. All of these may have evolved to help people survive millennia ago.

For example, many people are terrified of snakes; they scream and sweat upon seeing one. That is a phobia, which can be a serious psychology disorder.

Yet snakes currently cause less than one death in a million, while cars cause more than a thousand times that (OECD, 2014). Why is virtually no one terrified of automobiles? The explanation is that human fears have evolved since ancient times, when snakes were common killers. Thus,

> ancient dangers such as snakes, spiders, heights, and strangers appear on lists of common phobias far more often than do evolutionarily modern dangers such as cars and guns, even though cars and guns are more dangerous to survival in the modern environment.
>
> *[Confer et al., 2010, p. 111]*

Since our fears have not caught up to automobiles, we use our minds to pass laws regarding infant seats, child-safety restraints, seat belts, red lights, and speed limits. Humanity is succeeding in such measures: The U.S. motor-vehicle death rate has been cut in half over the past 20 years.

Other modern killers—climate change, opioid addiction, extreme obesity, particulate pollution—also require social management because long-standing instincts are contrary to current dangers. Instincts that have allowed *Homo sapiens* to survive over 200,000 years—such as the instinct to stop pain and to drink water from a stream—are now killers. For example:

> For millennia, the Ganges River, holy to Hindus, has provided livelihoods, food, and water for Nepal, India, and Bangladesh. . . .[is] now one of the world's worst polluted rivers.
>
> *[Shah et al., 2018]*

Evolutionary theory contends that recognizing the ancient origins of destructive urges—such as the deadly desire to eat calorie-dense, sugary desserts—is the first step in controlling them (King, 2013).

Applied to the Ganges, industries and agriculture seeking profit, added to the once-beneficial practice of funerals that sent corpses down the river, now destroy life. Protecting the river requires understanding why people and nations continue to pollute it and finding better ways to express those same instincts (Shah et al., 2018).

Why We Protect Babies According to evolutionary theory, every species has two long-standing, biologically-based drives: survival and reproduction. Understanding these two drives provides insight into protective parenthood, the death of newborns, infant dependency, child immaturity, the onset of puberty, the formation of families, and much more (Konner, 2010).

Here is an example. Adults consider babies to be cute—despite the reality that babies have little hair, no chins, stubby legs, and round stomachs—none of which is considered attractive in adults. The reason, evolutionary theory contends, is that adults are instinctually attuned to protect and cherish infants more than adults. That was essential when survival of the species was in doubt.

Especially for Teachers and Counselors of Teenagers Teen pregnancy is destructive of adolescent education, family life, and sometimes even health. According to evolutionary theory, what can be done about this? (see response, page 57)

But humans do not always protect every baby. Indeed, another evolutionary instinct is that all creatures seek to perpetuate their own descendants more than those of unrelated people. That might lead to the killing of infants who are not one's own.

Some primates do exactly that: Chimpanzee males who take over a troop kill babies of the deposed male. This occurred among ancient humans as well. The Bible chronicles many examples, including two in the story of Moses and one in the birth of Jesus. Modern humans, of course, have created laws against such practices—necessary because evolutional instincts are murderous (Hrdy, 2009).

Laws do not always remedy destructive instincts. Even today, humans are much less concerned about deaths of unknown babies than of their own kin. From a distance, it is paradoxical that parents willingly sacrifice sleep, money, and even life itself for their offspring, while adults seem indifferent to wars and epidemics that kill thousands of children in distant lands. This makes sense when we consider ancient instincts to protect one's own progeny and those of one's own tribe.

THINK CRITICALLY: What would happen if lust were the only reason one person would mate with another?

An application of evolutionary theory is found in research on grandmothers. When female scientists studied grandmothers, they analyzed historic data from Africa, Japan, India, and elsewhere. That itself is evidence of the diversity of current research. This scholarship led to the *grandmother hypothesis,* that menopause and female longevity were evolutionary adaptations arising from the need to protect future generations (Hawkes & Coxworth, 2013).

Genetic Links This inborn urge to protect is explained by a basic concept from evolutionary theory: **selective adaptation**. The idea is that both nature and nurture promote survival and reproduction. According to one version of selective adaptation, genes for traits that aid survival and reproduction have been selected over time. (see **Figure 2.5**).

selective adaptation The process by which living creatures (including people) adjust to their environment. Genes that enhance survival and reproductive ability are selected, over the generations, to become more prevalent.

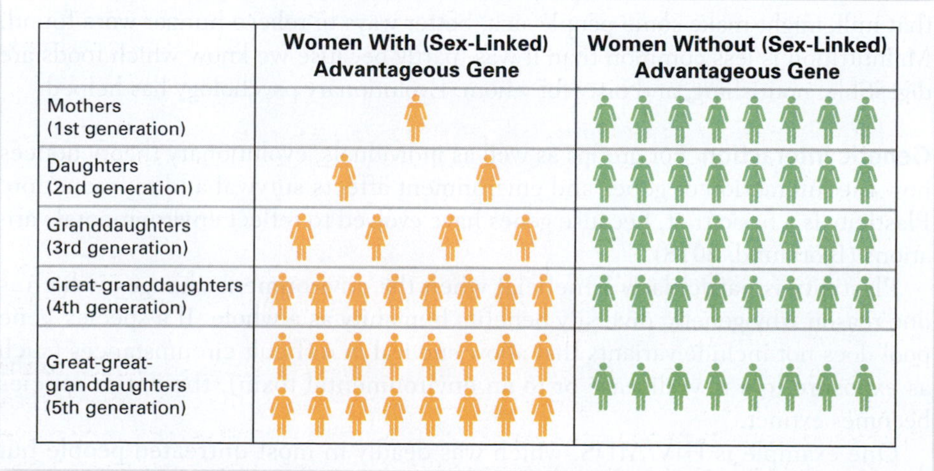
Women With (Sex-Linked) Advantageous Gene
Women Without (Sex-Linked) Advantageous Gene
Mothers (1st generation)
Daughters (2nd generation)
Granddaughters (3rd generation)
Great-granddaughters (4th generation)
Great-great-granddaughters (5th generation)

FIGURE 2.5
Selective Adaptation Illustrated Suppose only one of nine mothers happened to have a gene that improved survival. The average woman had only one surviving daughter, but this gene mutation might mean more births and more surviving children such that each woman who had the gene bore two girls who survived to womanhood instead of one. As you see, in 100 years, the "odd" gene becomes more common, making it a new normal.

"Why don't you just stay and work on being a better fish?"

Mick Stevens/Conde Nast/Cartoonbank

What Next? Evolution is ongoing, from the first land creature to the current brain adaptations in humans.

Some of the best qualities of people—cooperation, spirituality, and self-sacrifice—may have originated thousands of years ago when such qualities protected life in our species (Rand & Nowak, 2016). Overall, many traits of human development—infant curiosity, adolescent risk taking, grandmother babysitting—can be harmful to the individuals but beneficial to the community (Bjorklund, 2018).

This is evident in selective adaptation. If one person happens to have a trait that makes survival more likely, allowing them to live long enough to mate and reproduce, the gene (or combination of genes) responsible for that trait is passed on to the next generation. That individual would then have more children than their siblings without that gene—and that trait would become common.

For example, originally almost all human babies lost the ability to digest lactose at about age 2, when they were weaned from breast milk. Older children and adults were *lactose-intolerant*, unable to digest milk (Suchy et al., 2010).

In a few regions thousands of years ago, cattle were domesticated. In those places, "killing the fatted calf" provided a rare feast for the entire community.

In those cattle-raising regions, occasionally a young woman would chance to have an aberrant but beneficial gene for the enzyme that maintained digestion of cow's milk. If she drank milk intended for a calf, she would gain weight. That would allow her to experience early puberty, sustain many pregnancies, and have ample breast milk for her offspring.

For all of those reasons, her genes would spread to many children. Thus, the next generation would include more people who inherited that aberrant gene, becoming lactose-tolerant unlike most people. With each generation, their numbers would increase. Eventually, that gene would become the new norm, as it is for most Americans today.

Interestingly, there are several genetic versions of lactose tolerance: Apparently distinct aberrant genes appeared in several cattle-raising regions, among them eastern Africa and northern Europe. Selective adaptation increased the prevalence of that odd gene (Ranciaro et al., 2014). No genetic protection evolved in another region that domesticated livestock (Mongolia); they developed another way—yogurt and cheese—to allow digestion of milk (Curry, 2018).

Selective adaptation takes thousands of years, but it is especially useful when we seek to promote healthy development worldwide. Once humanitarians understood that milk might make some people sick, better ways to relieve hunger were found. Malnutrition is less common than it was, partly because we know which foods are digestible, nourishing, and tasty for whom. Evolutionary psychology has helped.

CHAPTER APP 2

My Token Board

IOS: https://tinyurl.com/yy6hmbuq

RELEVENT TOPIC: Behaviorism and positive reinforcement for children

My Token Board is a visual reward system for children of all ages and abilities that helps motivate them to learn and complete tasks. The app's use of reinforcers is based on the principles of operant conditioning and effective with children who are on the autism spectrum.

Genetic interaction For groups as well as individuals, evolutionary theory notices how the interaction of genes and environment affects survival and reproduction. Plasticity is a basic trait, because genes have evolved to reflect environmental variations (Bjorklund, 2018).

Plasticity is particularly beneficial when the environment changes, which is one reason why genetic diversity benefits humanity as a whole. If a species' gene pool does not include variants that allow survival in difficult circumstances (such as exposure to a new disease or to an environmental toxin), the entire species becomes extinct.

One example is HIV/AIDS, which was deadly in most untreated people but not in a few who were genetically protected. The same was true for Ebola. Some

people have inborn protection, and genetic influences on lifestyle, that make contracting Ebola less likely (Kilgore et al., 2015). No wonder biologists worry when a particular species becomes inbred. Inbreeding eliminates variations, risking extinction. Diversity is protective.

People do not always act as evolutionary theory predicts: Parents sometimes abandon newborns; adults sometimes handle snakes. Nonetheless, evolutionary theorists believe that understanding ancient impulses enables control. Cars are safer and teenage driving is limited, because we know that risk-taking adolescents find speed irrationally attractive rather than instinctually frightening.

WHAT HAVE YOU LEARNED?

1. Why is the sociocultural perspective particularly relevant within the United States?
2. How do mentors and mentees interact within the zone of proximal development?
3. Why would behaviors and emotions that benefited ancient humans be apparent today?
4. How are human tastes affected by what people ate 100,000 years ago?
5. What human behaviors were protective centuries ago but are harmful now?

What Theories Contribute

Considering the entire life span, many more theories have aided our understanding of human development. Among those that have inspired developmentalists for decades are *humanism* (Maslow, 1943), *selective adaptation with compensation* (Baltes & Baltes, 1986), and *socioemotional selectivity* (Carstensen et al., 1999)—all discussed in the second half of this book.

This chapter reviews only the most comprehensive life-span theories. Each has contributed to our understanding of human development (see **Table 2.5**):

- *Psychodynamic theories* make us aware of the impact of early-childhood experiences, remembered or not, on subsequent development.
- *Behaviorism* shows the effect that immediate responses, associations, and examples have on learning, moment by moment and over time.

TABLE 2.5

Five Perspectives on Human Development

Theory	Area of Focus	Fundamental Depiction of What People Do	Relative Emphasis on Nature or Nurture?
Psychodynamic theory	Psychosexual (Freud) or psychosocial (Erikson) stages	Battle unconscious impulses and overcome major crises.	More nature (biological, sexual impulses, and parent–child bonds)
Behaviorism	Conditioning through stimulus and response	Respond to stimuli, reinforcement, and models.	More nurture (direct environment produces various behaviors)
Cognitive theory	Thinking, remembering, analyzing	Seek to understand experiences while forming concepts.	More nature (mental activity and motivation are key)
Sociocultural theory	Social control, expressed through people, language, customs	Learn the tools, skills, and values of society through apprenticeships.	More nurture (interaction of mentor and learner, within cultures)
Evolutionary	Needs and impulses that originated thousands of years ago	Develop impulses, interests, and patterns to survive and reproduce.	More nature (needs and impulses apply to all humans)

- *Cognitive theories* bring an understanding of intellectual processes, that thoughts and beliefs affect every aspect of our development.
- *Sociocultural theories* remind us that development is embedded in a rich and multifaceted cultural context, evident in every social interaction.
- *Evolutionary theories* suggest that human impulses need to be recognized before they can be guided.

Remember that each theory is designed to be practical. This is evident with a very practical issue for many parents: how to toilet-train their children (see Opposing Perspectives).

OPPOSING PERSPECTIVES

Toilet Training—How and When?

Parents hear opposite advice about almost everything regarding infant care, including feeding, responding to cries, bathing, and exercise. Often a particular parental response springs from one of the theories explained in this chapter—no wonder advice is sometimes contradictory.

One practical example is toilet training. In the nineteenth century, many parents believed that bodily functions should be controlled as soon as possible in order to distinguish humans from lower animals.

Pushed by that theory (and opposed to the theory of evolution), many parents began toilet training in the first months of life (Accardo, 2006). Then, Freud pegged the first year as the oral stage, not anal (when toilet training was supposed to occur), and Erikson stressed that infants need to develop trust.

Accordingly, *psychoanalytic theory* recommended postponing training to avoid serious personality problems later on. This was soon part of many manuals on child rearing.

For example, a leading pediatrician, T. Berry Brazelton, wrote a popular book for parents. He advised delaying toilet training until the child was cognitively, emotionally, and biologically ready—around age 2 for daytime training and age 3 for nighttime dryness.

> As a society, we are far too concerned about pushing children to be toilet trained early. I don't even like the phrase "toilet training." It really should be toilet learning.
>
> *[Brazelton & Sparrow, 2006, p. 193]*

When *behaviorism* took hold in the United States, that led to the belief that toilet training could occur whenever the parent wished, not at a particular age.

What did parents want? Early training before disposable diapers (about 1970). But now, stores carry diapers designed for 4-year-olds, so parents postpone training. Behaviorism supported that.

In one application of behaviorism, children drank quantities of their favorite juice, sat on the potty with a parent nearby to keep them entertained, and then, when the inevitable occurred, the parent praised and rewarded them—a powerful reinforcement for the child and soon for the adult as well. Children were conditioned (in one day, according to some behaviorists) to head for the potty whenever the need arose (Azrin & Foxx, 1974).

Cognitive theory would consider such a concerted effort unnecessary, suggesting that parents wait until the child can understand why they should urinate and defecate in the toilet. Thinking leads to behavior—which explains why older adults are mortified by urinary incontinence.

This raises the importance of the *sociocultural view*. In some African communities, children toilet-train themselves by following slightly older children to the surrounding trees and bushes. This is easier, of course, if toddlers wear no diapers—a practice that makes sense in some climates and ecosystems. Sociocultural practices differ because of the context.

Finally, *evolutionary theory* notes that control of urination and defecation is part of every human culture, because it promotes survival by reducing the spread of pathogens. That is why dogs and cats readily learn where to eliminate waste (and instinctively scratch to bury their feces) and why humans worldwide learn bathroom hygiene. The contemporary emphasis on handwashing is the latest manifestation of ancient impulses.

Note how each of these theories would be critical of one U.S. mother who began training her baby just 33 days after birth. She noticed when her son was about to defecate, held him above the toilet, and had trained him by 6 months (Sun & Rugolotto, 2004).

- Psychodynamic theorists would wonder what made her such an anal person, valuing cleanliness and order without considering the child's needs.
- Behaviorists would say that the mother was trained, not the son. She taught herself to be sensitive to his body; she was reinforced when she read his clues correctly.
- Cognitive theory would question the mother's thinking. For instance, did she have an irrational fear of normal body functions?
- Sociocultural theory would be aghast that the U.S. drive for personal control took such a bizarre turn.
- Evolutionary theory would expect that such early training would be a rare event unless it was adaptive to the species—and would note that every mother reading about this woman would probably consider her more whacky than wise.

What is best? Some parents are reluctant to train, and the result, according to one book, is that many children are still in diapers at age 5 (Barone, 2015). Dueling theories and diverse parental practices have led the authors of an article for pediatricians to conclude that "despite families and physicians having addressed this issue for generations, there still is no consensus regarding the best method or even a standard definition of toilet training" (Howell et al., 2010, p. 262).

That may return us to the multicontextual, multicultural perspectives of Chapter 1 that explain the vast differences from one community to another. A study of parents' opinions in Belgium found that single mothers who were of low SES waited until age 3 or so to train their children, which was too long according to those researchers (van Nunen et al., 2015). Of course, both "too soon" and "too late" are matters of opinion.

There is no easy answer, but many parents firmly believe in one approach or another. We all have theories, sometimes strongly held, whether we know it or not.

No comprehensive view of development can ignore any of these theories, yet each has encountered severe criticism: *psychodynamic theory* for being too subjective; *behaviorism* for being too mechanistic; *cognitive theory* for undervaluing emotions; *sociocultural theory* for neglecting individual choice; *evolutionary theory* for ignoring current morals, laws, and norms.

Most developmentalists prefer an **eclectic perspective**, choosing what they consider to be the best aspects of each theory. Rather than adopt any one of these theories exclusively, they make selective use of all of them.

eclectic perspective The approach taken by most developmentalists, in which they apply aspects of each of the various theories of development rather than adhering exclusively to one theory.

Obviously, all theories reflect the personal background of the theorist, as do all criticisms of theories. Being eclectic, not tied to any one theory, is beneficial because everyone, scientist as well as layperson, is biased. But even being eclectic may be criticized: Choosing the best from each theory may be too picky or the opposite, too tolerant.

For developmentalists, all of these theories merit study and respect. It is easy to dismiss any one of them, but using several perspectives opens our eyes and minds to aspects of development that we might otherwise ignore.

As you will see in many later chapters, theories provide a fresh look at behavior. Imagine a mother, father, teacher, coach, and grandparent discussing the problems of a particular child. Each might suggest a possible explanation that makes the others say, "I never thought of that." If they listen to each other with an open mind, together they might understand the child better and figure out how best to help the child.

Using five theories is like having five perceptive observers. Each of the five may sometimes be off target, but each offers another perspective. Thus, each avoids assumptions that are too narrow and restrictive. A hand functions best with five fingers, although each finger is different, and some fingers are more useful than others.

Back to Linda and her crying baby. The real test of theories is how practical and useful they are, and Linda eventually combined them all. She understood the psychodynamic view that mother–infant bonding is important and also the behaviorist perspective that she was reinforcing frequent nighttime waking.

As a result, she combined three strategies: cuddling Mya often during the day, giving her a hearty meal at night (evolutionary, so Mya was not hungry at midnight), and then letting her cry at night (not reinforcing nighttime waking).

Cognitive theory led her to talk to Mike to explain her strategy, so he would not think her neglectful. Sociocultural theory led her to talk with other mothers, including me.

Evolutionary theory helped Linda understand why she herself felt an urge to tend to her daughter all night long. For that she needed to recognize that her innate response was no longer adaptive: Neither parent had jobs that allowed napping, unlike mothers of old who slept whenever their baby napped.

After several difficult nights, Linda's family slept through the night. The baby adjusted, and the parents were less stressed. Mya is now 3 years old, and Linda, Mike, and Mya are thriving.

WHAT HAVE YOU LEARNED?

1. What are the criticisms of each of the five theories?
2. Why are most developmentalists eclectic in regard to theories?
3. Why is it useful to know more than one theory to explain human behavior?

SUMMARY

Grand Theories

1. A theory provides general principles to guide research and to explain observations. Each of the three grand theories—psychodynamic, behaviorist, and cognitive—interprets human development from a distinct perspective, providing a framework for understanding human emotions, experiences, and actions.

2. Psychodynamic theory emphasizes that adult actions and thoughts originate from unconscious impulses and childhood conflicts. Freud theorized that sexual urges arise during three stages of childhood—oral, anal, and phallic—and continue, after latency, in the genital stage.

3. Erikson described eight successive stages of development, each involving a crisis to be resolved. The early stages are crucial, with lifelong effects, but the emphasis is on social, not just sexual, needs. Erikson stressed that societies, cultures, and families shape development.

4. Behaviorists, or learning theorists, believe that scientists should study observable and measurable behavior. Behaviorism emphasizes conditioning—a lifelong learning process in which an association between one stimulus and another (classical conditioning) or the consequences of reinforcement and punishment (operant conditioning) guide behavior.

5. Social learning theory recognizes that people learn by observing others, even if they themselves have not been reinforced or punished. Children are particularly susceptible to social learning, but all humans are affected by what they notice in other people.

6. Cognitive theorists believe that thoughts and beliefs powerfully affect attitudes, actions, and perceptions, which in turn affect behavior. Piaget proposed four age-related periods of cognition, each propelled by an active search for cognitive equilibrium.

7. Information processing focuses on each aspect of cognition—input, processing, and output. This perspective has benefited from technology—first from understanding computer functioning and more recently by the many ways neuroscientists monitor the brain and body.

Newer Theories

8. Sociocultural theory emphasizes the guidance, support, and structure provided by each social group through culture and mentoring. Vygotsky described how learning occurs through social interactions; mentors guide learners through their zone of proximal development.

9. Sociocultural learning is also encouraged by the examples and tools that each society provides. These are social constructions, which guide everyone but which also can change.

10. Evolutionary theory contends that contemporary humans have genes and customs that have fostered survival and reproduction for tens of thousands of years. Through selective adaptation, certain fears, impulses, and reactions that were useful millennia ago continue. Sometimes they are now more destructive than beneficial.

What Theories Contribute

11. Many other theories focus specifically on adult development and are discussed later. All theories, however, can provide hypotheses for researchers and insights for us all.

12. Psychodynamic, behavioral, cognitive, sociocultural, and evolutionary theories have aided our understanding of human development. Each is also criticized for being too narrow to describe the full complexity of human life.

13. Since no single theory captures the diversity of contemporary human experience, most developmentalists are eclectic, drawing on many theories.

KEY TERMS

developmental theory (p. 34)
behaviorism (p. 36)
classical conditioning (p. 37)
operant conditioning (p. 38)
reinforcement (p. 38)
social learning theory (p. 39)
modeling (p. 39)
cognitive theory (p. 40)
cognitive equilibrium (p. 40)
assimilation (p. 41)
accommodation (p. 41)
information-processing theory (p. 41)
sociocultural theory (p. 46)
apprenticeship in thinking (p. 46)
guided participation (p. 47)
zone of proximal development (p. 47)
evolutionary theory (p. 49)
selective adaptation (p. 51)
eclectic perspective (p. 55)

APPLICATIONS

1. Developmentalists sometimes talk about "folk theories," which are theories developed by ordinary people who may not know that they are theorizing. Choose three sayings that are commonly used in your culture, such as (from the dominant U.S. culture) "A penny saved is a penny earned" or "As the twig is bent, so grows the tree." Explain the underlying assumptions, or theory, that each saying reflects.

2. Cognitive theory suggests the power of thoughts, and sociocultural theory emphasizes the power of context. Find someone who disagrees with you about some basic issue (e.g., abortion, immigration, socialism) and listen carefully to the ideas and reasons. Then analyze how cognition and experience shaped the other person's ideas *and* your own.

3. Ask three people to tell you their theories about male–female differences in mating and sexual behaviors. Which of the theories described in this chapter is closest to each explanation, and which theory is not mentioned?

Especially For ANSWERS

Response for Teachers (from p. 36) Erikson would note that the behavior of 5-year-olds is affected by their developmental stage and by their culture. Therefore, you might design your curriculum to accommodate active, noisy children.

Response for Teachers and Counselors of Teenagers (from p. 51) Evolutionary theory stresses the basic human drive for reproduction, which gives teenagers a powerful sex drive. Thus, merely informing teenagers of the difficulty of caring for a newborn (some high school sex-education programs simply give teenagers a chicken egg to nurture) is not likely to work. A better method would be to structure teenagers' lives so that pregnancy is impossible—for instance, with careful supervision or readily available contraception.

Observation Quiz ANSWERS

Answer to Observation Quiz (from p. 37) Both are balding, with white beards. Note also that none of the other theorists in this chapter have beards—a cohort difference, not an ideological one.

Answer to Observation Quiz (from p. 50) The river is slow-moving (see the boat) and shallow (see the man standing). A fast-moving, deep river is able to flush out contaminants more quickly.

VISUALIZING DEVELOPMENT Historical Highlights of Developmental Science

As evident throughout this textbook, much more research and appreciation of the brain, social context, and the non-Western world has expanded our understanding of human development in the 21st century. This timeline lists a few highlights of the past.

200,000–50,000 BCE With their large brains, long period of child development, and extensive social and family support, early humans were able to sustain life and raise children more effectively than other primates.

©2016 Macmillan

c. 400 BCE In ancient Greece, ideas about children from philosophers like Plato (c. 428-348 BCE) and Aristotle (384-322 BCE) influenced further thoughts about children. Plato believed children were born with knowledge. Aristotle believed children learn from experience.

©2016 Macmillan

©2016 Macmillan

1650–1800 European philosophers like John Locke (1632–1704) and Jean Jacques Rousseau (1712–1778) debate whether children are born as "blank slates" and how much control parents should take in raising them.

1797 First European vaccination: Edward Jenner (1749–1823) publicizes smallpox inoculation, building on vaccination against smallpox in Asia, the Middle East, and Africa.

1750–1850 Beginning of Western laws regulating child labor and protecting the rights of children.

1879 First experimental psychology laboratory established in Leipzig, Germany.

1885 Sigmund Freud (1856–1939) publishes *Studies on Hysteria*, one of the first works establishing the importance of the subconscious and marking the beginning of psychodynamic theory.

©2016 Macmillan

1895 Ivan Pavlov (1849–1936) begins research on dogs' salivation response.

Agency Animal Picture/Stockbyte/Getty Images

1905 Max Weber (1864–1920), the founder of sociology, writes *The Protestant Work Ethic*, about human values and adult work.

1905 Alfred Binet's (1857–1911) intelligence test published.

1907 Maria Montessori (1870–1952) opens her first school in Rome.

Harvey Watts Photography/Moment/Getty Images

1913 John B. Watson (1878–1958) publishes *Psychology As the Behaviorist Views It*.

50,000 BCE | 400 BCE | 0 | 500 | 1000 | 1500 | 1650 | 1700 | 1750

140 BCE In China, imperial examinations are one of the first times cognitive testing is used on young people.

500–1500 During the Middle Ages in Europe, many adults believed that children were miniature adults.

Scala/Art Resource, NY

1100–1200 First universities founded in Europe. Young people pay to be educated together.

Ralf Hettler/Grafissimo/Getty Images

1837 First kindergarten opens in Germany, part of a movement to teach young children before they entered the primary school system.

1859 Charles Darwin (1809–1882) publishes *On the Origin of Species*, sparking debates about what is genetic and what is environmental.

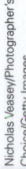

Nicholas Veasey/Photographer's Choice/Getty Images

1900 Compulsory schooling for children is established for most children in the United States and Europe.

Ralf Hettler/Grafissimo/Getty Images

1903 The term "gerontology," the branch of developmental science devoted to studying aging, first coined.

Fuse/Corbis/Getty Images

1920 Lev Vygotsky (1896–1934) develops sociocultural theory in the former Soviet Union.

1923 Jean Piaget (1896–1980) publishes *The Language and Thought of the Child*.

©2016 Macmillan

1933 Society for Research on Child Development, the preeminent organization for research on child development, founded.

1939 Mamie (1917–1983) and Kenneth Clark (1914–2005) receive their research grants to study race in early childhood.

JGI/Jamie Grill/Blend Images/Getty Images

1943 Abraham Maslow (1908–1970) publishes *A Theory of Motivation*, establishing the hierarchy of needs.

1950 Erik Erikson (1902–1994) expands on Freud's theory to include social aspects of personality development with the publication of *Childhood and Society*.

©2016 Macmillan

1951 John Bowlby (1907–1990) publishes *Maternal Care and Mental Health*, one of his first works on the importance of parent–child attachment.

Monkey Business Images/Shutterstock.com

1953 Publication of the first papers describing DNA, our genetic blueprint.

AlonzoDesign/DigitalVision Vectors/Getty Images

1957 Harry Harlow (1905–1981) publishes *Love in Infant Monkeys*, describing his research on attachment in rhesus monkeys.

Martin Rogers/The Image Bank/Getty Images

1961 The morning sickness drug thalidomide is banned after children are born with serious birth defects, calling attention to the problem of teratogens during pregnancy.

1961 Alfred Bandura (b. 1925) conducts the Bobo Doll experiments, leading to the development of social learning theory.

1979 Urie Bronfenbrenner (1917–2005) publishes his work on ecological systems theory

1986 John Gottman (b. 1942) founded the "Love Lab" at the University of Washington to study what makes relationships work.

1987 Carolyn Rovee-Collier (1942–2014) shows that even young infants can remember in her classic mobile experiments.

1990–Present New brain imaging technology allows pinpointing of brain areas involved in everything from executive function to Alzheimer's disease.

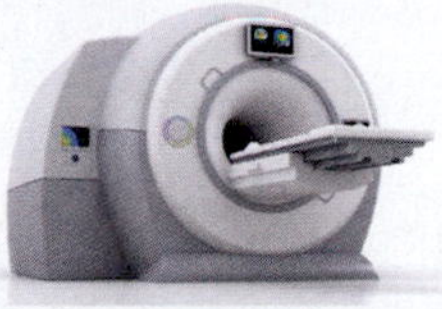
adventtr/E+/Baris Simsek/Getty Images

1994 Steven Pinker (b. 1954) publishes *The Language Instinct*, focusing attention on the interaction between neuroscience and behavior, helping developmentalists understand the need for physiological understanding as part of human growth. These themes continue in *How the Mind Works* (1997).

1996 Giacomo Rizzolatti publishes his discovery of mirror neurons.

2000 Jeffrey Arnett conceptualizes emerging adulthood.

2003 Mapping of the human genome is completed.

2013 DSM-5, which emphasizes the role of context in understanding mental health problems, is published.

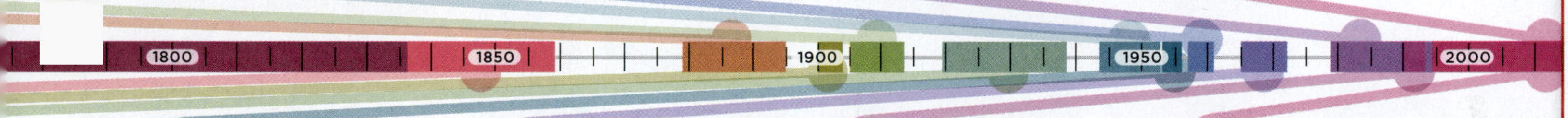

anyaivanova/iStock/Getty Images

1953 B.F. Skinner (1904–1990) conducts experiments on rats and establishes operant conditioning.

1955 Emmy Werner (b. 1929) begins her Kauai study, which focuses on the power of resilence.

Donna Day/Exactostock-1598/Superstock

1956 K. Warner Schaie's (b. 1928) Seattle Longitudinal Study of Adult Intelligence begins.

1965 Head Start, an early childhood education program, launched in the United States.

1965 Mary Ainsworth (1913–1999) starts using the "Strange Situation" to measure attachment.

©2016 Macmillan

1966 Diana Baumrind (b. 1928) publishes her first work on parenting styles.

1972 Beginning of the Dunedin, New Zealand, study—one of the first longitudinal studies to include genetic markers.

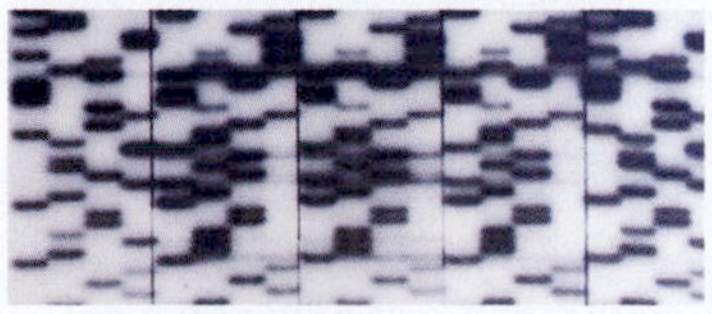
Tetra Images/Getty Images

1990 Barbara Rogoff (b. 1950) publishes *Apprenticeship in Thinking*, making developmentalists more aware of the significance of culture and context. Rogoff provided new insights and appreciation of child-rearing in Latin America.

1993 Howard Gardner (b. 1943) publishes *Multiple Intelligences*, a major new understanding of the diversity of human intellectual abilities. Gardner has since revised and expanded his ideas in many ways.

TongRo Images Inc/Getty Images

2013 U.S. President Barack Obama announces his administration's Brain Research through Advancing Innovative Neurotechnologies (BRAIN) Initiative, which helps researchers seek new ways to treat, cure, and prevent brain disorders.

JEWEL SAMAD/Getty Images

2014–2020 Onward. Many more discoveries are chronicled in this book, as researchers continue to test and explore.

CHAPTER 3

The New Genetics

What Will You Know?

1. Genetically, how is each zygote unique?
2. How do twins differ from other siblings?
3. Who is likely to carry genes that they do not know they have?
4. When should people see a genetic counselor?

- **The Genetic Code**
  - 46 to 21,000 to 3 Billion
  - Same and Different
  - A CASE TO STUDY: Women Engineers
  - Matching Genes and Chromosomes
  - OPPOSING PERSPECTIVES: Too Many Boys?
- **New Cells, New People**
  - Cells and Identity
  - Twins and More
- **From Genotype to Phenotype**
  - Many Factors
  - Gene–Gene Interactions
  - Nature and Nurture
  - Practical Applications
- **Chromosomal and Genetic Problems**
  - Not Exactly 46
  - Gene Disorders
  - Genetic Counseling and Testing
  - A VIEW FROM SCIENCE: The Genes of Psychological Disorders
- **VISUALIZING DEVELOPMENT: One Baby or More?**

For 30 years I have spent Thanksgiving with my four daughters. Now adults, they fly or drive many miles to gather together; they have their own jobs and homes. One tradition is that each of us says what we are thankful for in the past year, and that typically includes each other. The family connections are strong.

It is apparent that we are closely related. Strangers say we look alike, people on the phone mistake us for one another, we laugh in the same way at the same jokes. Our similarities go far deeper. We all express strong opinions (disagreeing on specifics but sharing values); we all make our living by teaching and writing (in different places and professions); and we all have similar habits (we pick up litter; yesterday we had a robust discussion about the best strategy to encourage our neighbors to do so).

Our differences are obvious, at least to us. When we are together, each prepares her own coffee—caf or decaf, brewed or instant, black or not, canned or bottled milk, sugar or honey or neither. One daughter was upset this year that I didn't have two-percent milk in a carton. Without telling her, I asked our neighbor, who gave me some, and then another daughter was troubled that I bothered that neighbor. That illustrates a general truth: We each are distinct—in cooking, eating, cleaning, sleeping, socializing, . . . and so on.

In all of this, my family reflects the themes of this chapter. Genes and family background shape human lives, yet each person is unique. The rest of this chapter continues those themes—nature and nuture interwoven, from conception onward.

The Genetic Code

First, we begin with biology. All living things are composed of cells. The work of cells is done by proteins, aided by other cells. Cells manufacture proteins according to a code of instructions stored by molecules of **deoxyribonucleic acid (DNA)** at the heart of the cell. These coding DNA molecules are on a **chromosome.**

46 to 21,000 to 3 Billion

Humans have 23 pairs of chromosomes (46 in all, half from each parent), which direct the manufacture of proteins needed for life and growth. The instructions on the 46 chromosomes are organized into genes, with every **gene** usually situated at a precise location on a particular chromosome.

Left: Philip Nealey/Photodisc/Getty Images
Top: Cultura/JFCreatives/Cultura Exclusive/Getty Images

deoxyribonucleic acid (DNA) The chemical composition of the molecules that contain the genes, which are the chemical instructions for cells to manufacture various proteins.

chromosome One of the 46 molecules of DNA (in 23 pairs) that virtually every cell of the human body contains and that, together, contain all the genes. Other species have more or fewer chromosomes.

gene A small section of a chromosome; the basic unit for the transmission of heredity. A gene consists of a string of chemicals that provide instructions for the cell to manufacture certain proteins.

gamete A reproductive cell. These sperm (for males) and ova (for females) each contain 23 chromosomes, so the zygote will contain 46 chromosomes, in 23 pairs.

zygote The single cell formed from the union of two gametes, a sperm and an ovum.

genome The full set of genes that are the instructions to make an individual member of a certain species.

When one **gamete** (a reproductive cell, sperm from a man or ovum from a woman) combines with another, those two gametes create a new cell called a **zygote.** Each gamete is formed from a particular combination of chromosomes and genes. Each man or woman produces many possible versions of their 46 chromosomes on each gamete—8 million possible combinations of 23 chromosomes (2^{23}, or 8,388,608).

Zygotes have a total of about 21,000 coding genes, each directing the formation of specific proteins made from a string of 20 amino acids. The instructions on those 21,000 genes are on about 3 billion *base pairs,* which are pairs of four chemicals (adenine paired with thymine, and guanine paired with cytosine).

The entire packet of instructions to make a living organism is called the **genome.** There is a genome for every species and variety of plant and animal—even for every bacterium and virus. Most human genes are also present in other creatures, yet genes define each species.

Having more genes or chromosomes does not necessarily make a more advanced creature. For instance, chimpanzees have 48 chromosomes, and rice—the world's most important food crop—has about 38,000 genes.

A few human genes are ours alone. For example, we are the only species with extensive language, a genetic innovation that may have originated in our Neanderthal ancestors (Frayer, 2017). Other animals communicate as well, but not as elaborately as humans do.

Members of the same species are similar genetically—more than 99 percent of any human's base pairs are identical to those of any other person because, although they differ in tiny details, all human chromosomes contain the same basic genes. The definition of a species is that its members can interbreed successfully. Since humans are one species, couples with wide ethnic differences mate and produce new humans, each with all the genes that define a person.

Same and Different

Decoding the genome of *Homo sapiens* was a major breakthrough in genetic research in 2001. Since then, the genomes of hundreds of other species have been decoded and thousands of variations in the human genome have been discovered.

allele A variation that makes a gene different in some way from other genes for the same characteristics. Many genes never vary; others have several possible alleles.

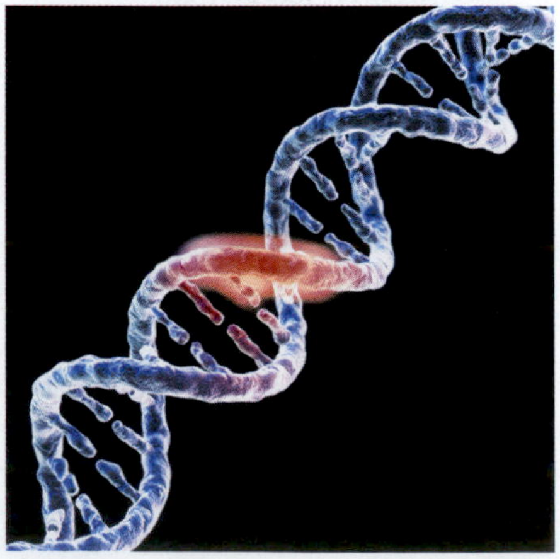

Hybrid Medical Animation/Science Source

Twelve of 3 Billion Pairs This is a computer illustration of a small segment of one gene. Even a small difference in one gene can cause major changes in a person's phenotype.

It is human nature to notice differences. For that reason, before we follow our usual bent to focus on individuality, keep in mind the most important truth: All people are basically the same, genetically. Not only do all humans have similar bodies (two eyes, hands, and feet; the same organs, blood, and bones), but also we all use words, we all love and hate, we all hope and fear, for ourselves and for descendants, friends, and strangers.

Yet none of us is exactly like anyone else, and those differences start with genes. Any variation in a gene, such as a difference in the precise sequence of the base pairs—sometimes with a seemingly minor transposition, deletion, or repetition—is called an **allele.**

Most alleles cause small differences (such as the shape of an eyebrow), but some are crucial. Another way to state this is that some genes are *polymorphic* (literally, "many forms"). Many have *single-nucleotide polymorphisms* (abbreviated SNPs, pronounced "snips"), which is a variation in only one part of the code, causing an allele of that gene.

Beyond the Genes *RNA* (*ribonucleic acid,* another molecule) and additional DNA surround each gene. In a process called *methylation,* this material enhances, transcribes, connects, empowers, silences, and alters genetic instructions. Methylation continues throughout life, from conception until death.

This noncoding material used to be called *junk*—*but* no longer. Obviously, genes are crucial, but even more crucial is whether and how genes are expressed. RNA regulates and transcribes genetic instructions, turning some genes and alleles on or off.

In other words, a person can have the genetic tendency for a particular trait, disease, or behavior, but that tendency might never appear because it was never turned on. Think of a light switch: A lamp might have a new bulb and be plugged into power, but the room stays dark unless the switch is flipped.

Scientists continually discover new functions—for good or ill—of the noncoding genetic material (Larsen, 2018). Applications are many—treating and controlling diseases, genetically modifying crops to resist pathogens, developing vaccines to protect people and animals.

Scientists are thrilled, the public is wary, and nations differ in their laws regarding genetic material. No one understands all the implications of genetic research, which may benefit or harm humankind.

As one article explains, we have "fast science and sluggish policy . . . enveloped by UN procedures that promote inclusiveness but are typically slow, lumbering, and inflexible, making it difficult to adapt to fast-moving events in the outside world" (Wynberg & Laird, 2018, p. 1). This is only one of the several ethical dilemmas presented by innovative research.

Roz Chast/The New Yorker Collection/The Cartoon Bank

Not All Genetic Every child becomes their own person—not what their parents fantasize.

Epigenetics The science of the interaction between nature and nurture is explored in **epigenetics,** the study of how the environment alters genetic expression, beginning at conception and continuing lifelong. The Greek root *epi-*, meaning "around, above, below," focuses attention on the vital noncoding elements.

epigenetics The study of how environmental factors affect genes and genetic expression—enhancing, halting, shaping, or altering the expression of genes.

Events and circumstances surrounding (around, above, below) the genes determine whether genes are expressed or silenced (Ayyanathan, 2014). This is contrary to the traditional notion of genetics still held by many people who think that genes determine whether or not a person can learn a particular skill or develop a talent. They do not.

We now know that, although brain formation begins with genes inherited at conception, nutrients and toxins affect prenatal and postnatal brain development. Epigenetic interactions continue lifelong, part of the plasticity highlighted in Chapter 1.

The long reach of epigenetics is easy to understand when the force is biological, such as a poison, but social experiences, such as chronic loneliness, also can change brain structures (Cacioppo et al., 2014). The influence of factors other than genes continues throughout the body. For instance, diet and exercise affect everything genetic—muscles, shape, skin, and so on.

Sometimes protective factors, either in nature or nurture, outweigh liabilities. As one review explains, "there are, indeed, individuals whose genetics indicate exceptionally high risk of disease, yet they never show any signs of the disorder" (Friend & Schadt, 2014, p. 970). Why? Epigenetics.

The Microbiome One aspect of both nature and nurture that profoundly affects each person is the **microbiome,** which refers to all of the microbes (bacteria, viruses, fungi, archaea, yeasts) that live within every part of the body. The microbiome includes "germs," the target of disinfectants and antibiotics. Nonetheless, most microbes are helpful, enhancing life, not harming it.

microbiome All the microbes (bacteria, viruses, and so on) with all their genes in a community; here, the millions of microbes of the human body.

Microbes have their own DNA, reproducing every day. There are thousands of varieties, and together they have an estimated 3 million genes—influencing immunity, weight, diseases, moods, and much more (Dugas et al., 2016; Koch, 2015). Particularly crucial is how the microbiome affects nutrition, since bacteria in the gut break down food for nourishment.

Experiments find that obese or thin mice change body size when the microbiota from another mouse with the opposite problem is added (Dugas et al., 2016). Thus, when a child weighs too little or too much, the microbiome may be more to blame than the parents.

One innovation of modern medicine is to implant feces (which are rich in microbes) from one person into another to cure illnesses. This works particularly well for certain infections (especially *C difficile*) and gastrointestinal diseases (Vaughn et al., 2019).

Siblings Not Alike Siblings differ in their microbiomes and much more. With a rare exception (monozygotic twins, discussed soon), siblings have only half of their genes in common, because each gamete has only one of the two chromosomes that a man or a woman has at each of the 23 locations. Thus, you could have an astronomical number of siblings, from your same parents, none just like you.

Especially for Medical Doctors Can you look at a person and then write a prescription that will personalize medicine to their particular genetic susceptibility? (see response, page 86)

genotype An organism's entire genetic inheritance, or genetic potential.

Remember that each parent contributes 23 chromosomes, or half the genetic material, for each child. When the man's chromosomes pair with the woman's (chromosome 1 from his gamete with chromosome 1 from hers, chromosome 2 with chromosome 2, and so on), each gene connects with its counterpart from the other parent, and the interaction between the two determines the inherited traits of the future person.

Since some alleles from the father differ from the alleles from the mother, their combination produces a zygote unlike either parent. Thus, each new person is a product of two parents but is unlike either one.

Usually, genetic diversity helps the species, because creativity, prosperity, and survival are enhanced when one person is unlike another. There is an optimal balance between diversity and similarity for each species: Human societies are close to that optimal level (Ashraf & Galor, 2013).

Matching Genes and Chromosomes

The genes on the chromosomes constitute an organism's genetic inheritance, or **genotype,** which endures throughout life. Growth requires duplication of the code of the original cell again and again, with expansion of the noncoding material as well.

Autosomes In 22 of the 23 pairs of chromosomes, both members of the pair (one from each parent) are closely matched. As already explained, some of the genes have alternate alleles, but each chromosome finds its comparable chromosome, making a pair. Those 44 chromosomes are called *autosomes*, which means that they are independent (*auto-* means "self") of the sex chromosomes (the 23rd pair).

Each autosome, from number 1 to number 22, contains hundreds of genes in the same positions

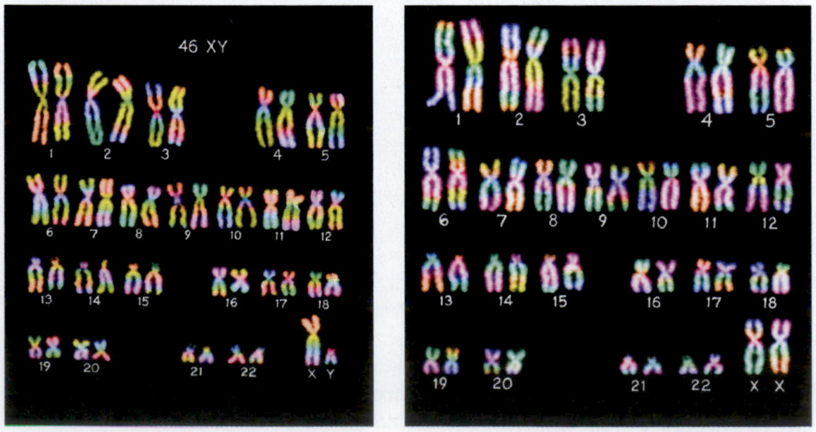

Uncertain Sex Every now and then, a baby is born with "ambiguous genitals," meaning that the child's sex is not abundantly clear. When this happens, analysis of the chromosomes reveals whether the 23rd pair is XY or XX. The karyotypes shown here indicate a typical baby boy *(left)* and girl *(right)*.

Biophoto Associates/Science Source

and sequence. If the code of a gene from one parent is exactly like the code on the same gene from the other parent, the gene pair is **homozygous** (literally, "same-zygote"). Most of our gene pairs are homozygous.

Indeed, every person in the world has most of the same genes, so it does not matter who your parents are—you still would be homozygous for the number of legs, for instance.

homozygous Referring to two genes of one pair that are exactly the same in every letter of their code. Most gene pairs are homozygous.

However, the match is not always letter-perfect. The mother might have a different allele of a particular gene than the father has. If a gene's code differs from that of its counterpart, the two genes still pair up, but the zygote (and, later, the person) is **heterozygous.** This can occur with any of the gene pairs on any of the autosomes, but a few genes are particularly likely to be heterozygous.

heterozygous Referring to two genes of one pair that differ in some way. Typically one allele has only a few base pairs that differ from the other member of the pair.

Given that only half of a man's genes are on each sperm and only half of a woman's genes are on each ovum, the combination creates siblings who will be, genetically, similar and different from each other.

Thus, which particular homozygous or heterozygous genes my brother and I inherited on our autosomes from our parents is a matter of chance, and it has no connection to the fact that I am the younger sister, not the older brother.

Sex Chromosomes However, for the **23rd pair** of chromosomes, a marked difference is apparent between my brother and me. My 23rd pair matched, but his did not. In that, he is like all males: When gametes combine to form the zygote, half of the time a dramatic mismatch occurs, because some sperm carry an X and some a Y.

23rd pair The chromosome pair that, in humans, determines sex. The other 22 pairs are autosomes, inherited equally by males and females.

XY A 23rd chromosome pair that consists of an X-shaped chromosome from the mother and a Y-shaped chromosome from the father. XY zygotes become males.

XX A 23rd chromosome pair that consists of two X-shaped chromosomes, one each from the mother and the father. XX zygotes become females.

This is how it happens. In males, the 23rd pair has one X-shaped chromosome and one Y-shaped chromosome. It is called **XY.** In females, the 23rd pair is composed of two X-shaped chromosomes. Accordingly, it is called **XX.**

Because a female's 23rd pair is XX, when her chromosomes split to make ova, each ovum contains an X from her mother or an X from her father—but always an X. And because a male's 23rd pair is XY, half of a man's sperm carry an X chromosome from his mother and half a Y from his father.

The X chromosome is bigger, with about 100 more genes, but the Y has a crucial gene, called *SRY,* that directs the embryo to make male hormones and organs. Thus, sex depends on which sperm penetrates the ovum—a Y sperm with the SRY gene 1, creating a boy (XY), or an X sperm, creating a girl (XX) (see **Figure 3.1** on page 67).

The fact that X deactivation occurs in girls but not in boys is only one example of the significance of the embryo's sex. Sometimes the same allele affects male and female embryos differently. For instance, women develop multiple sclerosis more often than men, and they usually inherit it from their mothers, not their fathers, probably for genetic as well as epigenetic reasons (Huynh & Casaccia, 2013).

It may matter whether a gene came from the mother or the father, a phenomenon called *parental imprinting.* The best-known example occurs with a small deletion or duplication on chromosome 15 (Kalsner & Chamberlain, 2015).

If a harmful allele on chromosome 15 came from the father, the child will develop Prader-Willi syndrome and be obese, slow-moving, and stubborn. If that same allele came from the mother's chromosome 15, the child will have Angelman syndrome and be thin, hyperactive, and happy—sometimes too happy, laughing when no one else does.

Other diseases and conditions are affected by imprinting, again sometimes in opposite ways (Couzin-Frankel, 2017).

Maria Platt-Evans/Science Source

She Laughs Too Much No, not the smiling sister, but the 10-year-old on the right, who has Angelman syndrome. She inherited it from her mother's chromosome 15. Her two siblings inherited the mother's other chromosome 15 and do not have the condition. If she had inherited the identical deletion on her father's chromosome 15, she would have developed Prader-Willi syndrome, which would cause her to be overweight as well as always hungry and often angry. With Angelman syndrome, however, laughing, even at someone's pain, is a symptom.

A CASE TO STUDY

Women Engineers

Typically, A Case to Study uses quotes from one individual, but here the "case" is engineering, particularly women in that profession.

It was once thought that genes made females inferior in math, specifically that prenatal neurological connections made their brains less adept at spatial understanding. That explained why women scored lower than men on tests of math.

For that reason, if a girl wanted to be an engineer, she was advised to choose another career because she would not be as capable as the men. Moreover, she was told that continuing in her ambition would be to deny her feminine and maternal nature—and no man would marry her. (I myself was the only girl in my high school trigonometry class, which I might not have chosen if I had realized how odd that was.)

The only way a woman could be an engineer was as a dutiful wife. For example, Emily Roebling was called the "secret engineer" of the Brooklyn Bridge (completed in 1883), because the man designated as chief engineer was her husband, and he became so ill that he could not leave his bed (Dougherty, 2019; Wagner, 2017). No college would allow her to study engineering; she educated herself so that she could do his job.

I identify with another woman, Sheri Sheppard, who became a professor of engineering. In the 1970s, her father, an engineering professor, suggested that she take an engineering class. She did, partly to please him. At first she thought that she did not belong. She remembers:

> My second year in college [at the University of Michigan], I hit my first engineering class. And at the time I was, in most of my engineering classes, the only woman. And the professor got in front of us and was lecturing and he was using words that I had no idea what he was speaking. And I'm thinking that every guy in the room knows exactly what he's talking about, I mean they were born knowing that. [still feeling that I did not belong] I went to the next class and one of the other students . . . raised his hand right at the beginning of the class and he said to the professor, "I don't have the foggiest notion of what you're talking about." And it was just like, "they don't know it either!" And after that it became really fun because education is all about asking questions.
>
> *[Retelas, 2017]*

Beginning in the 1960s, millions of women insisted that nurture, not nature, kept women from advanced math, and thus from professions that required it. Sheppard was one of the first women to study engineering; now she is a professor of engineering at Stanford, mentoring many female students. Adults no longer discourage girls from studying geometry and calculus. Currently, high school math achievement of the two sexes is quite similar, with boys slightly ahead in most nations but girls slightly ahead in others (Russia, Singapore, Algeria, Iran).

More college women now major in engineering, physics, and chemistry (Brown & Lent, 2016). This does not erase genetic tendencies: Some people excel at math and others struggle with it, but it does suggest that those genes are not exclusive to people of one sex or another, or, for that matter, one family or ethnic background or another.

Genetic sex differences no longer dissuade people from any profession. Of course, gender-based prejudices still affect career choice. Part of the engineering curriculum in college is to work as an engineering intern. Male students describe internships as rewarding, but some women are discouraged by them. One said:

> The environment was creepy, with older weirdo man engineers hitting on me all the time and a sexist infrastructure was in place that kept female interns shuffling papers while less experienced male counterparts had legitimate engineering assignments.
>
> *[Aurora, quoted in Seron et al., 2016, p. 201]*

Many women hired as engineers quit, with a third of them citing hostility from male co-workers as the reason (Silbey, 2016). Others leave because of another genetic force—the urge to become a mother, coupled with the assumption that motherhood and engineering are incompatible.

Fortunately, a recent study of female engineers in large British companies found that social support and role models are changing. Some of the women were explicitly encouraged and protected by their male colleagues, especially after the women pointed out the gender-related problems they encountered (Fernando et al., 2018).

Since we know that development—in the brain as well as in daily life—is plastic, having a role model enhances cognition. For example, one young woman engineer said:

> My boss' boss is a woman. She has a daughter. The team leader for one of the other big assets in the North Sea is a woman and she works four days a week. She's very well respected as an engineer. . . . so there is hope for me—in the beginning I didn't think there was any hope especially if I wanted to have children. But now it makes sense to develop a career here.
>
> *[Rosie, quoted in Fernando et al., 2018, p. 489]*

Currently, not only are more women employed as engineers, but their brains also reflect their profession: They can envision spatial relations with the best of them—and far better than their mothers and grandmothers. That is an epigenetic result.

More Than Sex Organs Although biology and culture (nature and nurture) constantly interact, the word *sex* generally refers to one's assigned sex at birth, and the word *gender* refers to social and cultural constructs. This distinction is useful in understanding the relationship between genes and male–female differences.

The Y chromosome directs the embryo to grow a penis, and much more. Typically, the SRY gene causes hormone production that affects the brain, skeleton, body fat, and muscles, beginning in the first weeks of prenatal development and continuing to the last breath in old age. As you have surely noticed, sex differences vary among individual men and women, influenced by the genes, hormones, and culture.

One review suggests "gender identity is a multifactorial complex trait with a heritable polygenic component" (Polderman et al., 2018, p. 95). That review sought to explain transgender and other gender-nonbinary individuals, but for everyone many traits are affected by the sex chromosomes.

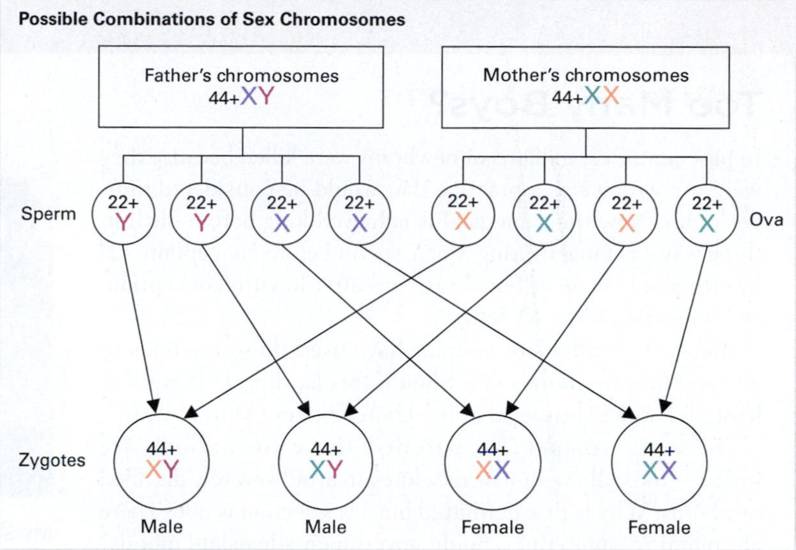

FIGURE 3.1

Determining a Zygote's Sex Any given couple can produce four possible combinations of sex chromosomes; two lead to female children and two to male children. In terms of the future person's natal sex, it does not matter which of the mother's Xs the zygote inherited. All that matters is whether the father's Y sperm or X sperm fertilized the ovum. However, for X-linked conditions it matters a great deal because typically one, but not both, of the mother's Xs carries the trait.

For example, at conception, about 120 male zygotes are conceived for every 100 females, probably because the sperm with fewer genes have a slight advantage in the race to the ovum. From that moment on, male life is more fragile, as more male embryos die.

At birth, the male/female ratio is 105:100 in developed nations and 103:100 in the poorest ones. That ratio not only reveals that male embryos die at higher rates but also that, when pregnant women are sick and malnourished, surviving embryos are more often female.

Males continue to have a higher death rate at every age. In the United States, after age 85, there are two surviving women for each man.

Remember, however, that sex is influential but not determinative. Gender differences begin at birth, when newborns are named and wrapped in blue or pink. Gender also influences late life survival: Old women are more likely to see a doctor and control blood pressure, obesity, and other late-life hazards.

Although XX or XY is determined at conception, for most of history people could not learn the sex of the fetus until birth, when someone looked at the genitals and shouted "It's a ------!" Because they didn't know better, millions of pregnant women ate special foods, slept on one side, or repeated certain prayers, all to control their baby's sex—which was already determined.

Now prospective parents can learn whether a fetus is male or female. One consequence is that biological sex might be fatal because of gender differences in the culture (see Opposing Perspectives).

WHAT HAVE YOU LEARNED?

1. How many chromosomes and genes do people have?
2. What is an allele?
3. What effect does the microbiome have?
4. Does it matter whether a gene pair is homozygotic or heterozygotic?
5. What determines a baby's sex?

OPPOSING PERSPECTIVES

Too Many Boys?

In past centuries, millions of newborns were killed because they were the wrong sex, a practice that would be considered murder today. Now the same goal is achieved long before birth in three ways: (1) inactivating X or Y sperm before conception, (2) inserting only male or female zygotes after in vitro conception, or (3) aborting XX or XY fetuses.

Recently, millions of couples have used these methods to choose their newborn's sex. Should this be illegal? It is, in at least 36 nations. It is legal in the United States (Murray, 2014).

To some prospective parents, those 36 nations are unfair—most allow similar measures to avoid severely disabled newborns. Why is that permitted but sex selection is not? There are moral reasons. But, should governments legislate morals? People disagree (Wilkinson, 2015).

One nation that forbids prenatal sex selection is China. This was not always so. In about 1979, China began a "one-child" policy, urging and sometimes forcing couples to have only one child. That achieved the intended goal: fewer children to feed . . . or starve. Severe poverty was almost eliminated.

But advances in prenatal testing combined with the Chinese tradition that sons, not daughters, care for aging parents led many couples to want their only child to be male. Among the unanticipated results of the one-child policy:

- Since 1980, an estimated 9 million abortions of female fetuses
- Adoption of thousands of newborn Chinese girls by Western families
- By 2010, far more unmarried young men than women

In 1993, the Chinese government forbade prenatal testing for sex selection. In 2013, China rescinded the one-child policy. Yet from 2005 to 2015, the ratio of preschool boys to girls was about 116:100, an imbalance that continues (United Nations, Department of Economic and Social Affairs, Population Division, 2018). Despite government policies, Chinese couples still prefer to have only one child, a boy, and abort female embryos.

The argument in favor of sex selection is freedom from government interference. Some fertility doctors and many individuals believe that each couple should be able to decide how many children to have and what sex they should be (Murray, 2014).

Why would anyone object to personal choice? The reason is social harm. This is evident in China. Thirty years after the one-child policy began, many more young Chinese men than women die. In part because of the high male mortality, the 2010 Chinese census found that women lived eight years longer than men.

The developmental explanation is that unmarried men take risks to attract women. They become depressed if they remain alone. Thus, the skewed sex ratio among adults in China increases early deaths, from accidents, suicide, drug overdoses, and poor health practices (Srinivasan & Li, 2018).

AP Images/MANISH SWARUP

My Strength, My Daughter That's the slogan these girls in New Delhi are shouting at a demonstration against abortion of female fetuses in India. The current sex ratio of children in India suggests that this campaign has not convinced every couple.

This is a warning to other nations. A society with an excess of males might also have an excess of problems, since males are more likely to be drug addicts, commit crimes, kill each other, die of heart attacks, and start wars. This is true in every nation.

For instance, the U.S. Department of Justice reports that, since 1980, 85 percent of the prison population are men, and, primarily because of heart disease, suicide, and accidents, men are about twice as likely as women to die before age 50 (Centers for Disease Control and Prevention, 2018). Increasing the number of men might mean increasing all these problems.

But wait: Chromosomes and genes do not *determine* behavior. Every gender difference is influenced by culture. Even traits that originate with biology, such as the propensity to heart attacks, are affected more by environment (in this case, diet and cigarettes) than by XX or XY chromosomes.

Already, improved diagnosis and declines in smoking (changes in nurture) have reduced heart attacks in men. In 1950, four times as many middle-aged men as women died of heart disease; by 2015, the rate was lower for both sexes, but especially for men (2:1, not 4:1). Lifelong, rates of cardiovascular deaths in the United States are currently close to sex-neutral (Centers for Disease Control and Prevention, 2018).

Indeed, every sex difference is strongly influenced by culture and policy. Historically, some cultures have adjusted to an excess of women by accepting divorce and remarriage, or polygamy, thus providing husbands and children for most women. Societies could change customs to adapt to an excess of males as well. Should they?

THINK CRITICALLY: Might laws against prenatal sex selection be unnecessary if culture shifted?

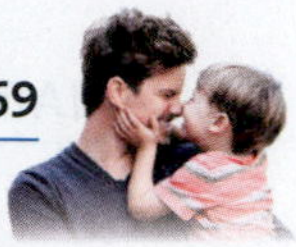

New Cells, New People

Within hours after conception, the zygote begins *duplication* and *division*. First, the 23 pairs of chromosomes (carrying all of the genes) duplicate to form two complete sets of the genome. These two sets move toward opposite sides of the zygote, and the single cell splits neatly down the middle into two cells, each containing the original genetic code.

These first two cells duplicate and divide, becoming four, which duplicate and divide, becoming eight, and so on. The name of the developing mass changes as cells multiply—the zygote (one cell) becomes a *morula,* then a *blastocyst,* then an *embryo,* then a *fetus*—*and* then, at birth, a *baby*. [**Life-Span Link:** Prenatal growth from then on is detailed in Chapter 4.]

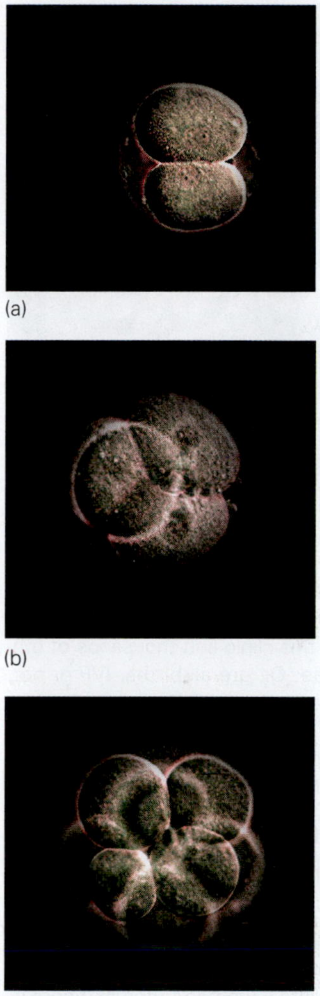

(a)

(b)

(c)

Anatomical Travelogue/Science Source

First Stages of the Germinal Period The original zygote as it divides into *(a)* two cells, *(b)* four cells, and *(c)* eight cells. Occasionally at this early stage, the cells separate completely, forming the beginning of monozygotic twins, quadruplets, or octuplets.

Cells and Identity

Nine months after conception, a newborn has about 26 billion cells, all influenced by nutrients, drugs, hormones, viruses, microbes, and so on from the pregnant woman. Almost every human cell carries a complete copy of the genetic instructions of the original cell. Half of those instructions came from each parent, but every zygote also has a few mutations—about 40 base pair variations that were not inherited.

Adults have about 37 trillion cells, each with the same 46 chromosomes and the same thousands of genes of the original zygote. This explains why DNA testing of any body cell, even from a drop of saliva or a snip of hair, can identify "the real father," "the guilty criminal," "the long-lost brother."

DNA lingers long after death. Several living African Americans claimed Thomas Jefferson as an ancestor: DNA proved some right and some wrong (Foster et al., 1998).

Indeed, because the Y chromosome is passed down to every male descendant, and because the Y changes very little from one generation to the next, men today have the Y of their male ancestors who died thousands of years ago.

Female ancestors also live on. Each zygote has *mitochondria,* biological material that provides energy for the cell. The mitochondria come from the mother, and her mother, and her mother, and thus each person carries evidence of maternal lineage.

As with all genetic material, mitochondria sometimes predispose a person to disease, especially problems with the heart (Bonora et al., 2019). Although males are more vulnerable to heart attacks than females are, the problem may originate with their mothers!

Stem Cells The cells that result from the early duplication and division are called **stem cells;** they can produce any other cell and thus become a complete person. After about the eight-cell stage, although duplication and division continue, a third process called *differentiation* begins.

stem cells Cells from which any other specialized type of cell can form.

In differentiation, cells specialize, taking different forms and reproducing at various rates depending on where they are located. For instance, some cells become part of an eye, others part of a finger, still others part of the brain. They are no longer stem cells.

Scientists have discovered several ways in the laboratory to reprogram cells, making them like stem cells again (Papapetrou, 2016). This can control many genetic illnesses and conditions, but it is not yet known how to use reprogrammed cells without risking serious harm to patients.

Another new method, called CRISPR, has been developed to edit genes, with the potential to control the mosquitos that spread malaria, Zika virus, and other

Stuart Atkins/Shutterstock.com

From Miracle to Routine Here is Louise Brown, whose birth was an international front-page headline when she became the first IVF baby born decades ago. Here she is holding twins who were also born via IVF, now a routine event at this clinic and thousands of others worldwide. Or, are all births, IVF or not, now and always a miracle? Perhaps you agree with an Indian mystic who once said that "every newborn is a sign that God has not yet given up on the world."

in vitro fertilization (IVF) Fertilization that takes place outside a woman's body (as in a glass laboratory dish). The procedure involves mixing sperm with ova that have been surgically removed from the woman's ovary. If a zygote is produced, it is inserted into a woman's uterus, where it may implant and develop into a baby.

diseases. Although human genes could theoretically be edited with CRISPR, the prospect of "designer babies" raises serious ethical questions.

Therefore, at least at the moment, CRISPR is forbidden for human organisms (Lander, 2016; Green, 2015). An attempt (unverified) to use CRISPR in a human embryo caused a storm of protest (Cohen, 2018).

In Vitro Fertilization The ethical implications of CRISPR raise the issue of **in vitro fertilization (IVF),** which was pronounced "sacrilegious" and "against God" when first attempted in 1960. That did not stop the scientists, who finally succeeded with a live baby, Louise Brown, in 1978.

Over the past half-century, procedures have improved and IVF has become "a relatively routine way to have children" (C. Thompson, 2014, p. 361). The European Society of Human Reproduction and Embryology estimated in 2018 that 8 million IVF babies have been born, some from every nation.

The two daughters of former president Barack Obama were both conceived via IVF. So was the younger sister of Louise Brown. Both Brown daughters have had babies of their own, conceived naturally, but they have said they would use IVF if need be.

A study of more than 2 million ninth-graders in Sweden reported that specifics of conception made little difference in school achievement (Norrman et al., 2018). Psychologically, IVF children have also fared well. For all children, genes and family life are far more influential than details of conception.

IVF differs markedly from typical conceptions, almost half of which are unintended (Finer & Zolna, 2016). When a couple opts for IVF, the woman takes hormones to increase the number of ripe ova, and then several are surgically removed while the man ejaculates into a sterile container. Then a technician combines ova and sperm in a laboratory dish (*in vitro* means "in glass"), often by inserting one viable sperm into each ovum.

Zygotes that fail to duplicate properly are rejected, but several days after conception, one or more blastocysts are inserted into the uterus. Implantation succeeds about half the time, with the age of the couple an important predictor. Since young eggs are more viable, young women who do not yet want children may freeze their ova for IVF years later.

Some nations forbid IVF unless a couple provides proof of heterosexual marriage, of infertility, and even of financial and emotional health. Several European nations limit the numbers of blastocysts inserted into the uterus at one time, partly because national health care pays for both IVF and infant care.

The United States has no legal restrictions, although income matters. The cost varies from clinic to clinic within the United States, perhaps $20,000 for drugs, monitoring, and the procedure itself.

Medical societies provide some oversight. For example, the California Medical Board revoked the license of the physician who inserted 12 blastocysts in Nadya Suleman. She gave birth to eight surviving babies in 2009, a medical miracle but a developmental disaster.

Another IVF miracle is that adults can have children who are not biologically theirs because others have donated the sperm, the ova, and/or the womb. The word *donate* is misleading, since most donors—often college students—are paid. Some couples travel to other nations (especially India) with less restrictive laws and more women willing to be surrogate mothers (Reddy et al., 2018). Is that international exploitation?

As you see, many aspects of fertility and infertility raise moral questions, within nations and between them. Should anyone other than the prospective parents decide whether or not a child is born?

Twins and More

Thus far we have described conception as if one sperm and one ovum resulted in one baby. That is typical, but there is an important exception. Sometimes one sperm and one ovum results in two babies, or even four. To understand this, you need to understand the difference between monozygotic and dizygotic twins.

Monozygotic Twins Remember that each stem cell contains the entire genetic code. If parents who carry destructive genes use IVF, at about the eight-cell stage, before implantation, one cell can be removed and analyzed. If that cell carries a known destructive gene, or if the chromosomes are not exactly 46, then that blastocyst is not inserted into the uterus.

If genetic testing finds no problems, the remaining cell mass is inserted, where it might implant and grow normally. Removing one stem cell does not harm development, because every one of the remaining stem cells has all of the instructions needed to create a person.

Twins *could* be created by separating the cells of the blastocyst before implantation, which could create two or more identical babies if the separated cells were implanted and then grew. This is illegal with human zygotes in IVF. However, about once in every 250 pregnancies, nature within the woman's body does what doctors are forbidden to do—it splits those early cells. If each separated cell duplicates, divides, differentiates, implants, grows, and survives, multiple births occur.

One separation results in **monozygotic (MZ) twins,** so called because they came from one (*mono-*) zygote (also called *identical twins*). Separations at the four- or eight-cell stage create monozygotic quadruplets or octuplets. Because monozygotic multiples originate from one zygote, they have identical genetic instructions for appearance, psychological traits, disease vulnerability, and everything else genetic.

Remember, however, that epigenetic influences begin as soon as conception occurs: Monozygotic twins look and act very much alike, but their environment is not identical. Epigenesis begins within hours of conception, and thus the developing blastocysts may differ.

For example, the particular spot in the uterus where each twin implants may allow one fetus to be better nourished than the other, which affects that person lifelong. One twin is born first, and from that moment on each twin will have a slightly different experience.

Monozygotic twins are fortunate in several ways. They can donate a kidney or other organ to their twin with no organ rejection. They can also befuddle their parents and teachers, who may need visible ways (such as different earrings or haircuts) to tell them apart.

Usually, the twins themselves establish their own identities. For instance, both might inherit athletic ability, but one decides to join the basketball team while the other plays soccer.

As one monozygotic twin writes:

> Twins put into high relief *the* central challenge for all of us: self-definition. How do we each plant our stake in the ground, decide how sensitive, callous, ambitious, conciliatory, or cautious we want to be every day? . . . Twins come with a built-in constant comparison, but defining oneself against one's twin is just an amped-up version of every person's life-long challenge: to individuate—to create a distinctive persona in the world.
>
> *[Pogrebin, 2010, p. 9]*

sarahwolfephotography/Moment/Getty Images

Not Exactly Alike These two 4-year-old boys in South Carolina are identical twins, which means they originated from one zygote. But one was born first and heavier, and, as you see here, one appears to be more affectionate to his brother.

monozygotic (MZ) twins Twins who originate from one zygote that splits apart very early in development. (Also called *identical twins*.) Other monozygotic multiple births (such as triplets and quadruplets) can occur as well.

macmillan learning

VIDEO ACTIVITY: Identical Twins: Growing Up Apart gives a real-life example of how genes play a significant role in people's physical, social, and cognitive development.

That woman and her twin sister married and had a son and then a daughter within months of each other. Coincidence? Genetic? Sister pressure?

To improve the chance of implantation, the technician may puncture (called *hatching*) a minuscule hole in the blastocyst. This slightly increases the rate of monozygotic twins (Knopman et al., 2014).

dizygotic (DZ) twins Twins who are formed when two separate ova are fertilized by two separate sperm at roughly the same time. (Also called *fraternal* twins.)

Dizygotic Twins Before any fertility treatments, about once in 60 natural conceptions, **dizygotic (DZ) twins** are conceived. They begin life when two ova are fertilized by two sperm at about the same time. Usually, women release only one ovum per month, so most human newborns are singletons. However, sometimes multiple ovulation occurs and dizygotic twins are possible.

Dizygotic twins are sometimes called *fraternal twins,* although because *fraternal* means "brotherly" (as in *fraternity*), fraternal is inaccurate. Of course, MZ twins are always the same sex (their 23rd chromosomes are either XX or XY), but for DZ twins just as for any two siblings in the same family, some are brothers, some are sisters, and some are brother and sister.

People say that twinning "skips a generation," but really it skips fathers, not mothers. Since dizygotic twinning requires multiple ovulation, the likelihood of a woman ovulating two ova and thus conceiving twins depends on her genes from her parents. The father's genes are irrelevant.

However, half of a man's genes are from his mother. If a male DZ twin inherited his mother's gene for multiple ovulation, there is a 50 percent chance that his genes include the multiple ovulating one. Then his daughters may have twins because their paternal grandmother did.

When dizygotic twinning occurs naturally, the incidence varies by ethnicity. For example, about 1 in 11 Yorubas in Nigeria is a twin, as are about 1 in 45 European Americans, 1 in 75 Japanese and Koreans, and 1 in 150 Chinese. Age matters, too: Older women more often double-ovulate and thus have more twins.

Like all children from the same parents, dizygotic twins have about half of their genes in common. They can differ markedly in appearance, or they can look so much alike that only genetic tests determine whether they are MZ or DZ. In the rare incidence that a woman releases two ova at once *and* has sex with two men over a short period, twins can have different fathers. Then they share only one-fourth of their genes.

WHAT HAVE YOU LEARNED?

1. How does DNA establish identity?
2. What makes a cell a "stem cell"?
3. Why is CRISPR illegal for humans?
4. What is similar and different in an IVF pregnancy and a traditional pregnancy?
5. What is the difference between monozygotic and dizygotic twins?
6. For whom is twinning more likely?

From Genotype to Phenotype

phenotype The characteristics of a person, including appearance, personality, intelligence, and all other traits.

As already explained, when a sperm and an ovum create a zygote, the *genotype* (all the genes of the developing person) is established. This initiates several complex processes that form the **phenotype**—the person's actual appearance, behavior, and brain and body functions.

Nothing is totally genetic, not even physical traits such as height or hair color; but nothing is wholly untouched by genes, either. Genes affect behavior as well as bodies: People who work overtime, get divorced, or spank their children do so partly for genetic reasons (Knopik et al., 2017). (Of course, culture and context are crucial as well.)

Many Factors

The phenotype depends on the combination of the genotype and the environment, from the moment of conception until the moment of death. The environment changes genes directly, in epigenesis. It also affects the phenotype via culture and context. As you remember, human development is remarkably plastic.

Almost every trait is *polygenic* (affected by many genes) and *multifactorial* (influenced by many factors). A zygote might have the alleles for becoming, say, a musical genius, but that potential may never be expressed.

Remember that nearly all important human characteristics are epigenetic. This is easiest to see with conditions that are known to be inherited, such as cancer, schizophrenia, and autism spectrum disorder (Kundu, 2013; Knopik et al., 2017). It is also apparent with cognitive abilities and personality traits.

Diabetes is a notable example. People who inherit genes that put them at risk do not always become diabetic. Lifestyle factors—weight and exercise—awaken that genetic risk. Yet some people are overweight and inactive but never develop diabetes because it is not in their genotype.

The same may be true for other developmental changes over the life span. Substance abuse—cocaine, cigarettes, alcohol, and so on—may produce epigenetic changes. Once addicted, people who have not used the drug for years are still vulnerable and can never use that drug again as an unaffected person could (Bannon et al., 2014). Their brain has changed; they are "clean" but still have a substance use disorder.

Gene–Gene Interactions

Many discoveries have followed the completion of the **Human Genome Project** in 2001. One surprise was shared genes: All humans have virtually the same genes, and 98 percent of human genes are shared with other mammals.

Human Genome Project An international effort to map the complete human genetic code. This effort was essentially completed in 2001, though analysis is ongoing.

Then why are people markedly unlike other species? Why is each person so different from any other person? Such questions led to increased interest in the complex interactions between one human gene and its counterpart from the other parent.

Additive Heredity

Interactions among genes and alleles are often called *additive* because their effects *add up* to influence the phenotype. The phenotype then reflects the contributions of every additive gene. Height, hair curliness, and skin color, for instance, are usually the result of additive genes. Indeed, height is probably influenced by 180 genes, each contributing a very small amount (Enserink, 2011).

Most Americans have ancestors of varied height, hair curliness, skin color, and so on. Their children's phenotypes do not mirror the parents' phenotypes (although the phenotype always reflects the genotype) because of the interactions of their unique set of genes.

I see this in my family: Our daughter Rachel is of average height, shorter than her father and me but taller than either of our mothers. She apparently inherited some of her grandmothers' height genes via our gametes. And none of my children

Genetic Mix Dizygotic twins Olivia and Harrison have half their genes in common, as do all siblings from the same parents. If the parents are close relatives who themselves share most alleles, the nonshared half is likely to include many similar genes. That is not the case here, as mother (Nicola) is from Wales and father (Gleb) is from the nation of Georgia, which includes many people of Asian ancestry. Their phenotypes, and the family photos on the wall, show many additive genetic influences.

Especially for Future Parents Suppose you wanted your daughters to be short and your sons to be tall. Could you achieve that? (see response, page 86)

has exactly my skin color—apparent when we borrow clothes from each other and notice that a particular shade is attractive on one but ugly on another.

How any additive trait turns out depends partly on all the genes a child happens to inherit (half from each parent, which means one-fourth from each grandparent, one-eighth from each great-grandparent, and so on). Some of those genes amplify or dampen the effects of other genes, aided by all the other DNA and RNA (not junk!) in the zygote.

Genetic variations are apparent in every family, particularly among African Americans in the United States. Historically, the continent of Africa was, genetically, the most diverse (Choudhury et al., 2018). Added to that, current North Americans who identify as Black are not only the product of African diversity but also carry genes from many parts of Europe and from many tribes of indigenous Americans.

dominant Reflected in the phenotype. Dominant genes have more influence on traits than recessive genes.

recessive Hidden, not dominant. Recessive genes are carried in the genotype and are not evident in the phenotype, except in special circumstances.

carrier A person whose genotype includes a gene that is not expressed in the phenotype. The carried gene occurs in half of the carrier's gametes and thus is passed on to half of the carrier's children. If such a gene is inherited from both parents, the characteristic appears in the phenotype.

Dominant–Recessive Heredity Not all genes are additive. In one nonadditive form, some alleles are **dominant** and others are **recessive.** The *dominant gene* is more influential for whatever trait that pair of genes affects. It overpowers a *recessive gene,* which may be hidden on the genotype, not apparent in the phenotype.

A person is called a **carrier** of the recessive gene when it is on their genotype but not their phenotype. In other words, they carry that gene in their DNA, and they will transmit it to half of their sperm or ova. Only when a person inherits a recessive gene from both parents, and therefore no dominant gene is inherited for that trait, does the recessive characteristic appear on the phenotype.

Most recessive genes are harmless. One example is eye color. Brown eyes are dominant. Everyone with brown eyes has at least one dominant brown-eye gene. They could, of course, have two brown-eye genes—one from each parent. But it is not obvious by looking at them, since one brown-eye gene is enough.

Blue eyes are determined by a recessive allele. If both parents have blue eyes—that is, every eye-color gene on every gamete has a blue-eye gene—their children will all have blue eyes. If a child has one blue-eyed parent (who always has two recessive blue-eye genes) and one brown-eyed parent, that child will *usually* have brown eyes.

Observation Quiz Who has the genetic condition? (see answer, page 86) ↓

Courtesy Kate Nurre

Sisters, But Not Twins, In Iowa From their phenotype, it is obvious that these two girls share many of the same genes, as their blond hair and facial features are strikingly similar. And you can see that they are not twins; Lucy is 7 years old and Ellie is only 4. It may not be obvious that they have the same parents, but they do—and they are both very bright and happy because of it. This photo also shows that their genotypes differ in one crucial way: One of them has a dominant gene for a genetic condition.

Usually, not always. Brown-eyed parents all have one brown-eye gene (otherwise they would not have brown eyes), but they might carry a blue-eye gene. In that case, in a blue-eyed/brown-eyed couple, every child has at least one blue-eye gene (from the blue-eyed parent), and half of the children will have a blue-eye recessive gene (from the carrier parent).

They will have blue eyes because they have no dominant brown-eye gene. The other half will have a brown-eye dominant gene. Their eyes will be brown, but they will be carriers of the blue-eye gene, just like their brown-eyed parent.

Sometimes both parents are carriers. If two brown-eyed parents both have the blue-eye recessive gene, the chances are one in four that their child will have blue eyes (see **Figure 3.2**).

This example is simplified because it presumes that only one pair of genes determines eye color. However, as with almost every trait, eye color is polygenic, so other genes have some influence. Eyes are various shades of blue and brown, green or gray, because of many genes.

Again, most recessive genes are carried on the genotype but hidden on the phenotype. A recessive trait appears on the phenotype *only* when a person inherits the same recessive gene from both parents. No need for parents to blame each other's ancestors if their child has a recessive disease, nor for fathers to suspect infidelity if a child is unexpectedly blue-eyed.

Mother to Son A special case of the dominant–recessive pattern occurs with genes that are **X-linked** (located on the X chromosome). If an X-linked gene is recessive—as are the genes for red–green color blindness (by far the most common type of color blindness), several allergies, a few diseases, and some learning disorders—the fact that it is on the X chromosome is critical (see **Table 3.1**). Boys might have the phenotype; girls might be carriers.

To understand this, remember that the Y chromosome is much smaller than the X, containing far fewer genes. Consequently, the X has many genes that are unmatched on the Y. If one of those X genes is recessive, there is no chance for a dominant gene on the Y to keep it hidden.

Thus, if a boy (XY) inherits a recessive gene on his X from his mother, he will have no corresponding dominant gene on his Y from his father to counteract it, so his phenotype will be affected. Girls, however, need to inherit a double recessive to be unable to see red and green.

This explains why males inherit X-linked disorders from mothers, not fathers. A study of color-blind children from six ethnic groups in northern India found a sex ratio of nine boys to one girl. The fact that people tend to marry within their ethnic group revealed that color blindness was affected by genes: The incidence of color blindness was 7 percent in one group but only 3 percent in another (Fareed et al., 2015).

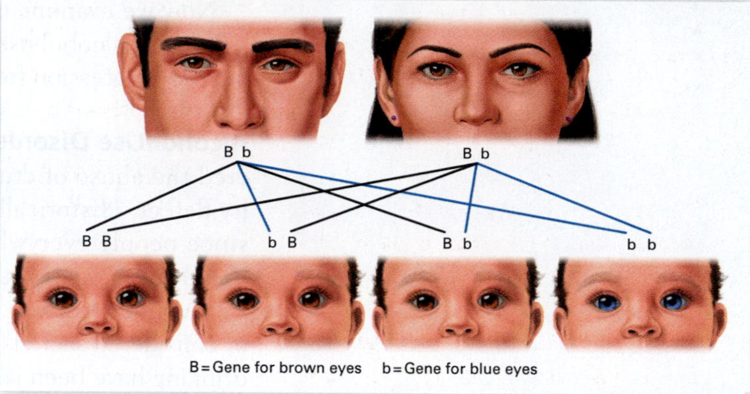

FIGURE 3.2

Changeling? No. If two brown-eyed parents both carry the blue-eye gene, they have one chance in four of having a blue-eyed child. Other recessive genes include the genes for red hair, Rh negative blood, and many genetic diseases.

Observation Quiz Why do these four offspring look identical except for eye color? (see answer, page 86) ↑

X-linked A gene carried on the X chromosome. If a male inherits an X-linked recessive trait from his mother, he expresses that trait because the Y from his father has no counteracting gene. Females are more likely to be carriers of X-linked traits but are less likely to express them.

Nature and Nurture

One goal of this chapter is for readers to grasp the complex interaction between genotype and phenotype. This is not easy. For decades, millions of scientists have struggled to understand this complexity. Each year brings advances in statistics and molecular analysis with new data to uncover various patterns, all resulting in hypotheses to be explored.

TABLE 3.1

The 23rd Pair and X-Linked Color Blindness

23rd Pair	Phenotype	Genotype	Next Generation
1. XX	Typical woman	Not a carrier	No color blindness
2. XY	Typical man	Typical X from mother	No color blindness
3. ⓍX	Typical woman	Carrier from father	Half her children will inherit her Ⓧ. The girls with her Ⓧ will be carriers; the boys with her Ⓧ will have color blindness.
4. XⓍ	Typical woman	Carrier from mother	Half her children will inherit her Ⓧ. The girls with her Ⓧ will be carriers; the boys with her Ⓧ will have color blindness.
5. ⓍY	Color-blind man	Inherited from mother	All his daughters will have his Ⓧ. None of his sons will have his Ⓧ. All his children will have typical vision, unless their mother also had an Ⓧ for color blindness.
6. ⓍⓍ	Color-blind woman (rare)	Inherited from both parents	Every child will have one Ⓧ from her. Therefore, every son will have color blindness. Daughters will be only carriers, unless they also inherit an Ⓧ from the father, as their mother did.

Ⓧ = X that carries recessive gene for color blindness

Now we examine two traits, addiction and visual acuity, in two specific manifestations, alcohol use disorder and nearsightedness. As you will see, understanding the progression from genotype to phenotype has many practical implications.

Alcohol Use Disorder At various times throughout history, people have considered the abuse of drugs to be a moral weakness, a social scourge, or a personality defect. Historically and internationally, the main focus has been on alcohol, since people everywhere discovered fermentation thousands of years ago—to the joy of many and the addiction of some.

Alcohol has been declared illegal (as in the United States from 1919 to 1933) or considered sacred (as in many religious rituals). Those who cannot control their drinking have been jailed, jeered, or burned at the stake.

Especially for Drug Counselors Is the wish for excitement likely to lead to addiction? (see response, page 86)

We now know that inherited biochemistry affects alcohol metabolism. Punishing those with the genes does not stop addiction. There is no single "alcoholism gene," but alleles that make alcohol use disorder more likely have been identified on every chromosome except the Y (Epps & Holt, 2011).

To be more specific, alleles create an addictive pull that can be overpowering, extremely weak, or somewhere in between. Each person's biochemistry reacts to alcohol in a particular way, causing sleep, nausea, aggression, joy, relaxation, forgetfulness, or tears.

If metabolism allows people to "hold their liquor," they might drink too much; others (including many East Asians) sweat and become red-faced after just a few sips. That embarrassing response may lead to abstinence. This inherited "flushing" tendency not only mitigates alcohol use disorder but also improves metabolism (Kuwahara et al., 2014).

Although scientists first sought the genes that affected the *biology* of addiction, they soon learned that genetic personality traits (including a quick temper, sensation seeking, and high anxiety) are as crucial as biology (Macgregor et al., 2009).

Age matters too. Teenagers feel the pressure to drink if their best friends are drinking, while adults find it easier to say "no thank you" if they choose. Social contexts also are influential. Fraternity parties encourage drinking; church socials in a "dry" county make it difficult to swallow anything stronger than lemonade.

Finally, both sex and gender are relevant. For biological reasons (body size, fat composition, metabolism), women become drunk on less alcohol than men. Heavy-drinking females double their risk of mortality compared to heavy-drinking males (Wang et al., 2014). That may be why many cultures encourage men to drink but not women (Chartier et al., 2014). Or, sexism and chauvinism may be the reason.

Hero Images Inc./Alamy Stock Photo

Welcome Home For many women in the United States, white wine is part of the celebration and joy of a house party, as shown here. Most people can drink alcohol harmlessly; there is no sign that these women are problem drinkers. However, danger lurks. Women get drunk on less alcohol than men, and females with alcohol use disorder tend to drink more privately and secretly, often at home, feeling more shame than bravado. All that makes their addiction more difficult to recognize.

As you see by all this, explaining a particular habit—drinking alcohol—quickly becomes very complex. Alcohol use disorder is genetic, but it also is much more. Again, phenotype is affected by both genotype and environment.

Nearsightedness Age, genes, and culture affect vision as well. Consider *myopia* (nearsightedness), the most common visual problem.

The effects of age are evident universally, for humans everywhere. Newborns focus only on things within 1 to 3 feet of their eyes; vision improves steadily until about age 10. The eyeball changes shape at puberty (increasing myopia) and again in middle age (decreasing myopia). Vision of all kinds becomes less acute in late adulthood, and serious problems increase.

Added to those developmental patterns that affect all people, nearsightedness is strongly influenced by genes that vary from one person to another. Heritability is about 75 percent—which is quite high (Williams & Hammond, 2016). If one monozygotic twin is nearsighted, the other twin is virtually always nearsighted, too.

However, **heritability** indicates only how much of the variation in a particular trait, *within a particular population, in a particular context and era,* can be traced to genes. For example, the heritability of height is very high (about 95 percent) when children receive good medical care and nutrition, but it is low (about 20 percent) when children are severely malnourished. Children who are chronically underfed are quite short, no matter what their genes. Similarly, although nearsightedness is highly heritable, nurture may be crucial.

Indeed, it is. In some African and Asian communities, heritability of nearsightedness is close to zero because of diet. Due to severe "vitamin A deficiency, more than 250,000 children become blind every year, and half of them die within a year of losing their sight" (Ehrenberg, 2016, p. 25). Obviously, for them, the genetic tendency to be nearsighted is irrelevant.

To prevent blindness, scientists have developed strains of local staples such as "golden rice" that are high in vitamin A, although use is limited by fears of genetically modified food (Ehrenberg, 2016). Some nations (Zambia and Cameroon) avoid genetic food modification by adding vitamin A directly to cooking oil and sugar. This must be carefully done—excessive, nonfood vitamin A causes health problems, but the risks are far less serious than blindness (Tanumihardjo et al., 2016).

What about children who consume adequate vitamin A in their food? Is their vision entirely inherited? No. Changes in the environment led one ophthalmologist to predict "an epidemic of pathological myopia . . . in the next few decades in Asia" (Saw, quoted in Seppa, 2013a, p. 23).

That prediction is based on three decades of research. Nearsightedness increased from 26 percent to 43 percent in one decade (1980 to 1990) in the army-mandated medical exams of all 17-year-old males in Singapore (Tay et al., 1992). Similar increases were evident in China. Asia is not the only continent with increasing nearsightedness. One summary claims that myopia is "out of control" in the United States (Holden, 2010).

An article in the leading British medical journal (*The Lancet*) suggests that although genes are usually to blame for severe myopia, "any genetic differences may be small" for common nearsightedness (I. Morgan et al., 2012, p. 1739). Nurture must somehow be involved. But how?

One possible culprit is homework. As Chapter 12 describes, contemporary East Asian children are amazingly proficient in math and science. Fifty years ago, most Asian children were working outside; now almost all are diligent students. As their developing eyes focus on their books, those with a genetic vulnerability to myopia may lose acuity for objects far away—which is exactly what nearsightedness means.

A related culprit is too much time indoors. Data from the United States on children playing sports have led some ophthalmologists to suggest that the underlying cause is inadequate exposure to daylight (I. Morgan et al., 2012). If North American children spent more time outside, would fewer need glasses?

Between the early 1970s and the early 2000s, nearsightedness in the U.S. population increased from 25 percent to 42 percent (Vitale et al., 2009). Urbanization, screen time, and fear of strangers have kept many U.S. children indoors most of the time, unlike children of earlier generations. The result may be reduced visual flexibility.

One ophthalmologist comments that "we're kind of a dim indoors people nowadays" (Mutti, quoted in Holden, 2010, p. 17). Decades ago, genetically vulnerable children did not necessarily become nearsighted; now they do. Nurture affecting nature, again.

©Imaginechina/Corbis

Applauding Success These eager young men are freshmen at the opening convocation of Shanghai Jiao Tong University. They have studied hard in high school, scoring high on the national college entrance exam. Now their education is heavily subsidized by the government. Although China has more college students than the United States, the proportions are far lower, since the population of China is more than four times that of the United States.

Observation Quiz Name three visible attributes of these young men that differ from a typical group of freshmen in North America. (see answer, page 86) ↑

heritability A statistic that indicates what percentage of the variation in a particular trait within a particular population, in a particular context and era, can be traced to genes.

Practical Applications

Since genes affect every disorder, no one should be blamed or punished for inherited problems. We all have them: They are not our fault, nor the fault of our parents.

However, knowing that genes never act alone opens the door to prevention. For instance, if alcohol use disorder is in the genes, parents can keep alcohol out of the home and explain the dangers of addiction (neither exaggerating nor ignoring), hoping their children become cognitively and socially mature before drinking. If nearsightedness runs in the family, parents can play outdoors with their children every day.

Of course, avoiding alcohol and playing outdoors are recommended for all children, as are dozens of other behaviors, such as flossing twice a day, saying "please," sleeping 10 hours each night, eating five servings of vegetables, and promptly writing thank-you notes. It is unrealistic to expect parents to make their children do all of these; awareness of genetic risks can guide priorities.

WHAT HAVE YOU LEARNED?

1. Why do humans vary so much in skin color and height?
2. What is the difference between additive and dominant–recessive inheritance?
3. How can a blue-eyed child have brown-eyed parents?
4. Why are sons more likely to inherit recessive conditions from their mothers instead of their fathers?
5. What genes increase the risk of alcohol use disorder?
6. What suggests that nearsightedness is affected by nurture?
7. What does *heritability* mean?

VIDEO: Genetic Disorders offers an overview of various genetic disorders.

Chromosomal and Genetic Problems

We now focus on conditions caused by an extra chromosome or a single destructive gene. Each person carries about 40 alleles that *could* cause serious diseases—including some very common ones such as strokes, heart disease, and cancer—but most of those require at least two SNPs, plus aspects of the environment (drugs, diet, smoking).

If all notable anomalies and disorders are included, 92 percent of people do *not* develop a serious genetic condition by early adulthood—but that means 8 percent have a serious condition in their phenotype as well as their genotype (Chong et al., 2015).

Not Exactly 46

As you know, most humans have 46 chromosomes, created by two gametes, each with 23 chromosomes. However, sperm and ova do not always split exactly in half to make gametes.

About half of all zygotes have more than or fewer than 46 chromosomes (Milunsky & Milunsky, 2016). Almost all of them fail to duplicate, divide, differentiate, and implant, or they are spontaneously aborted before anyone knows that conception occurred.

If implantation does occur, many embryos with chromosomal miscounts are aborted, either spontaneously (miscarried) or deliberately. Ninety-nine percent of fetuses that survive until birth have the usual 46 chromosomes. If a newborn has 45, 47, or, rarely, 48 or 49 chromosomes, their first days of life are often their last (Benn, 2016).

Survival is more common if only some cells have 47 chromosomes and the others 46 (a condition called *mosaicism*), or if only a piece of a chromosome is missing or added. Analysis suggests that mosaicism of some sort "may represent the rule rather than the exception" (Lupski, 2013, p. 358). Usually mosaicism has no marked effect, although cancer is more likely with extra or missing genetic material.

Claudia Daut/REUTERS

Universal Happiness All young children delight in painting brightly colored pictures on a big canvas, but this scene is unusual for two reasons: Daniel has trisomy-21, and this photograph was taken at the only school in Chile where normal and special-needs children share classrooms.

Trisomies If an entire chromosome is missing or added, that leads to a recognizable *syndrome*, a cluster of distinct characteristics that tend to occur together. Usually the cause is three chromosomes at a particular location instead of the typical two (a condition called a *trisomy*).

One in 10,000 newborns has three chromosomes at the 13th site (*Patau syndrome*), and 1 in 5,000 has three at the 18th (*Edwards syndrome*). Most newborns with these trisomies die soon after birth (Acharya et al., 2017).

A much more common trisomy is at the 21st site, which occurs about once in 700 births (S. E. Parker et al., 2010). Then survival is likely. In 1868, Dr. Langdon Down and his wife opened a home for children with three chromosomes at the 21st site (then called "Mongolian Idiots"), demonstrating that such children could be quite capable. A century later, Dr. Down was honored by the World Health Organization when trisomy-21 was called **Down syndrome.**

Down syndrome A condition in which a person has 47 chromosomes instead of the usual 46, with 3 rather than 2 chromosomes at the 21st site. People with Down syndrome typically have distinctive characteristics, including unusual facial features, heart abnormalities, and language difficulties. (Also called *trisomy-21.*)

Some 300 distinct characteristics can result from trisomy-21. No individual with Down syndrome is identical to another, but this trisomy usually produces telltale characteristics—a thick tongue, round face, and slanted eyes, as well as distinctive hands, feet, and fingerprints. The brain is somewhat smaller; the hippocampus (important for memory) is especially affected.

The impact of that third chromosome varies over the life span. By the time they reach middle age, many people with Down syndrome develop Alzheimer's disease (AD), because chromosome 21 has a gene that increases amyloid plaque—a symptom and maybe a cause of AD. A blood test may indicate that triple gene early enough to forestall the disease in Down syndrome individuals and perhaps in everyone else (Hamlett et al., 2018).

That extra chromosome always affects the brain and other organs lifelong, but specific outcomes depend on other genes and the family, education, and medical help. Some medication may reduce disability: "people with Down syndrome are achieving success in school and employment and are very satisfied with their lives" (Skotko, in Underwood, February 28, 2014).

Especially for Teachers Suppose you know that one of your students has a sibling who has Down syndrome. What special actions should you take? (see response, page 86)

Problems of the 23rd Pair Every human has at least 44 autosomes and one X chromosome; an embryo cannot develop without those 45. However, miscounts at the 23rd pair are more common and less deadly than miscounts in the autosomes. About 1 in every 300 infants is born with only one sex chromosome (no Y) or with three or more (not just two) (Benn, 2016). Most of them reach adulthood.

Each particular combination of sex chromosomes results in a specific syndrome (see **Table 3.2**), but all affect cognition, fertility, and sexual maturation (Hong & Reiss, 2014). Sometimes the problem is evident at birth. For example, Turner syndrome, when a girl has only one X, causes a wide neck and a low hairline. On the other hand, some children with an extra sex chromosome (XXY, for instance) are not diagnosed until adolescence or adulthood.

TABLE 3.2

Common Abnormalities Involving the Sex Chromosomes

Chromosomal Pattern	Physical Appearance	Psychological Characteristics	Incidence *
XXY (Klinefelter syndrome)	Males. Usual male characteristics at puberty do not develop—penis does not grow, voice does not deepen. Usually sterile. Breasts may develop.	Can have some learning disabilities, especially in language skills.	1 in 700 males
XYY (Jacob's syndrome)	Males. Typically tall.	Risk of intellectual impairment, especially in language skills.	1 in 1,000 males
XXX (Triple X syndrome)	Females. Normal appearance.	Impaired in most intellectual skills.	1 in 1,000 females
XO (only one sex chromosome) (Turner syndrome)	Females. Short, often "webbed" neck. Secondary sex characteristics (breasts, menstruation) do not develop.	Some learning disabilities, especially related to math and spatial understanding; difficulty recognizing facial expressions of emotion.	1 in 6,000 females

*Incidence is approximate at birth.
Information from Hamerton & Evans, 2005; Aksglaede et al., 2013; Powell, 2013; Benn, 2016.

Gene Disorders

More common than chromosomal problems are gene disorders. Everyone carries a dozen or more alleles that *could* produce diseases or disabilities in the next generation. Most such genes have no serious consequences because they are rare and recessive.

The phenotype is affected only when the inherited gene is dominant or when both parents carry the same allele. Even with such parents, only one unlucky child in two (for dominant disorders) or four (for recessive disorders) inherits the genetic problem.

Dominant Disorders Many of the 7,000 *known* single-gene disorders are dominant (Milunsky & Milunsky, 2016). Most of them are relatively mild, because a severe disorder would result in death. The gene is not passed on to another generation.

However, a few dominant disorders do not appear until adulthood. One is *Huntington's disease,* a fatal central nervous system condition caused by a copy number variation—more than 35 repetitions of a particular set of three base pairs.

Although the Huntington's gene sometimes affects children or adolescents (Milunsky & Milunsky, 2016), symptoms usually do not arise until midlife. By then an adult could have had several children, half of whom are affected.

The folk singer Woody Guthrie, who wrote "This Land Is Your Land," died of Huntington's, as did two of his daughters. Fortunately, his son Arlo inherited his talent but not his disorder.

Who Has the Fatal Dominant Disease? The mother, but not the children. Unless a cure is found, Amanda Kalinsky will grow weak and experience significant cognitive decline, dying before age 60. She and her husband, Bradley, wanted children without Amanda's dominant gene for a rare disorder, Gerstmann-Straussler-Scheinker disease. Accordingly, they used IVF and pre-implantation testing. Only zygotes without the dominant gene were implanted. This photo shows the happy result.

Nathan Morgan/The New York Times/Redux

Recessive Disorders Recessive diseases are more numerous than dominant ones because they are passed down by carriers. Most are on the autosomes, which means that either parent could have that gene on their genotype (Milunsky & Milunsky, 2016).

Only when two carriers have a child who inherits the recessive gene from both of them (true for one child in four from such a couple) is it apparent that something is amiss. There are thousands of recessive diseases; advance carrier detection is currently possible for several hundred.

A few recessive conditions are X-linked, including hemophilia, Duchenne muscular dystrophy, and **fragile X syndrome,** which is caused by more than 200 repetitions on one stretch of one gene (Plomin et al., 2013). (Some repetitions are normal, but not this many.)

fragile X syndrome A genetic disorder in which part of the X chromosome seems to be attached to the rest of it by a very thin string of molecules. The cause is a single gene that has more than 200 repetitions of one triplet.

Common Recessive Disorders About 1 in 12 North American adults carries an allele on their autosomes for cystic fibrosis, thalassemia, or sickle-cell disease, all devastating for those who inherit two recessive genes. These conditions are common because carriers have benefited from the gene.

Consider the most studied example: sickle-cell disease. Carriers of the sickle-cell gene die less often from malaria, which is prevalent and lethal in parts of Africa. Indeed, four distinct alleles cause sickle-cell disease, each originating in a malaria-prone region.

Selective adaptation allowed the gene to become widespread because it protected more people (the carriers) than it killed (those who inherited the recessive gene from both parents). Odds were that if a couple were both carriers and had four children, one would die of sickle-cell disease, one would not be a carrier and thus might die of malaria, and two would be carriers, protected against a common, fatal disease. Consequently, carriers were more likely than noncarriers to become parents. Over the millennia, the recessive trait became widespread.

This connection between genes and local diseases is not unusual. Almost every disease and risk of death is more frequent in one place than in another (Weiss & Koepsell, 2014). Whenever a particular genetic condition is common, there are benefits for carriers.

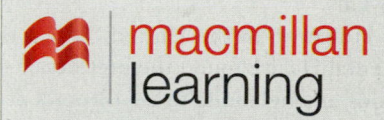

macmillan learning

Visit **Data Connections activity: Common Genetic Diseases and Conditions** to learn more about several different types of gene disorders.

About 11 percent of Americans with African ancestors have the recessive gene for sickle-cell disease—they are protected against malaria. Cystic fibrosis is more common among people with ancestors from northern Europe, because carriers may have been protected from cholera.

Benefits are apparent for additive genes as well. Dark skin is protective against skin cancer, a benefit if a person is often exposed to direct sun. Light skin allows more vitamin D to be absorbed from the sun—a benefit if a baby lives where sunlight is scarce. Being relatively short is beneficial in cold climates, or when food is scarce.

Genetic Counseling and Testing

Until recently, after the birth of a child with a severe disorder, couples blamed witches or fate, not genes or chromosomes. That has changed, with many young adults concerned about their genes long before parenthood. Virtually everyone has a close family member with a serious condition that is partly genetic.

Knowing the entire genome of a person takes extensive analysis, but the cost has plummeted in recent years from more than a million dollars to less than a thousand. If someone has their entire genome analyzed, the results may suggest the best treatment for a disease, or a way to avoid the condition completely.

Experts do not recommend full genome screening because most SNPs are "variants of unknown significance" (Couzin-Frankel, 2016, p. 442). In other words, the screening often finds something unusual, but no one knows what such oddities signify.

Some people pay for commercial genetic testing, which often provides misleading information. From the perspective of genetic counselors, even worse is that the emotional needs of the person are not addressed.

Many Options A genetic counselor may explain that serious problems are unusual no matter the age of the parents. Counselors also know about organizations of parents with children of all kinds of special needs, about adoption

Randy Pench/Sacramento Bee/TNS/Getty Images

Double Trouble or Genetic Joy? Six-year-old Ethan Dean inherited two recessive genes for cystic fibrosis. That may prevent him from fulfilling his wish—to become a garbage man. But another genetic trait is evident: Humans want to care for children, especially those with deadly conditions. The Sacramento Department of Sanitation, and the Make-a-Wish Foundation, gave Ethan a day collecting trash, to his apparent delight.

(both nationally and internationally), about treatment that is experimental but that might soon be proven (which may suggest that parents who are carriers might postpone conception), and so on. Counselors are trained to help clients understand and explore many possibilities.

This requires up-to-date information. New genetic disorders—and treatments—are revealed almost weekly. An inherited disorder than once meant lifelong neurological impairment (e.g., phenylketonuria, or PKU) might now mean a normal life. Accuracy, effect, and interpretation of testing varies: Sometimes a particular gene increases the risk of a problem by only a tiny amount, perhaps 0.1 percent. Counselors need to help clients understand both risks and uncertainty.

A VIEW FROM SCIENCE

The Genes of Psychological Disorders

Misinformation and mistaken fears are particularly common if someone has a close relative with a psychological disorder. This is true for many people. Exactly what qualifies as mental illness, and the line between mild, moderate, and several, is not obvious.

However, in the United States, the National Institute of Mental Health found the prevalence of mental illness (usually mild) among adults to be 18 percent. A study of severe emotional disorders among 13- to 17-year-olds within the previous year reported a prevalence rate of 8 percent (Kessler et al., 2012).

Among the common disorders with genetic origin are depression, bipolar disorder, schizophrenia, and autism spectrum disorder. No doubt genes increase the risk in all of these (Knopik et al., 2017). Yet, as with addiction and vision, the environment is crucial—not only the microsystem, but also the macrosystem and exosystem.

This was confirmed by a study of the entire population of Denmark, where good medical records and decades of free public health care make research accurate (Gottesman et al., 2010). If *both* Danish parents developed schizophrenia, 27 percent of their children developed it; if one parent had it, 7 percent of their children developed it. Evidence for genes?

These same statistics can be presented in another way: Even if both parents had schizophrenia, almost three-fourths (73 percent) of their children did not. (Some of them developed other psychological disorders, again providing evidence for epigenetics and additive genes.)

The genetic link is particularly obvious in studies of monozygotic twins. If one identical twin develops schizophrenia, often—but not always—the other twin also develops a psychological disorder of some sort (Gottesman et al., 2010).

Recent research on MZ twins found specific risk factors (Pepper et al., 2018). One is age: If one MZ twin is diagnosed with schizophrenia before age 23, almost half the time (54 percent) the other twin later will be diagnosed with the disorder. However, if the first diagnosis does not occur until after age 30, the incidence is less than a third (30 percent).

Another risk factor is the family context. If one parent has schizophrenia, and one MZ twin develops it as well, chances are 63 percent that the genetic twin will also develop the disease. However, if neither parent had schizophrenia but one MZ does, odds are reduced by a third..

Similar results come from studies of mood disorders. No doubt there is a genetic risk, but also no doubt that childhood experiences matter (Sullivan et al., 2000; Ottesen et al., 2018). Again, this alerts caretakers to the importance of nurture. If mental illness is in the family, it is especially important that a child's life be stable, not chaotic, and that the child experiences reliable emotional support, not hostility.

Since we know that prevalent diseases, such as sickle cell, became common partly because carriers benefited, could genes for psychological disorders ever be beneficial?

Perhaps. Anxiety, for instance, makes people anticipate problems. Is it beneficial for some people to anticipate disaster, if that makes the community better prepared for hurricanes, earthquakes, ethnic warfare, disease epidemics, and so on?

The Greek mythological character Cassandra envisioned wars and other devastation in the future. No one believed her; they thought she was insane. She became depressed, was shunned and eventually murdered. According to the myth, she was later considered a prophet, not a madwoman.

Even schizophrenia may have a benefit. Bruce Springsteen's father was an angry, emotionally abusive man and probably had schizophrenia (Springsteen, 2017).

Did that somehow help his son become a creative, musical genius? Indeed, many great artists and writers apparently suffered from serious mental illness, from Van Gogh to Virginia Woolf, from Anthony Bourdain to Andrew Solomon—you can think of many more. Is there any connection here?

That is speculation. Many would disagree. However, two conclusions seem solid:

1. Genes are powerful influences on psychological disorders, and
2. No disorder is entirely genetic.

Between those two is the obvious question: How much, for whom, and what are the triggers, the interactions, the treatments, the outcomes?

Progress is evident regarding the identification of environmental influences on schizophrenia, including fetal malnutrition, birth in the summer, adolescent use of psychoactive drugs, emigration in young adulthood, and family emotionality during adulthood.

Some adults learn to live with mental illness — the rate of recent illness declines from adolescence on, according to the National Institute of Mental Health (see **Figure 3.3**). Is that because experiences gradually allow mastery of harmful DNA? Plasticity again?

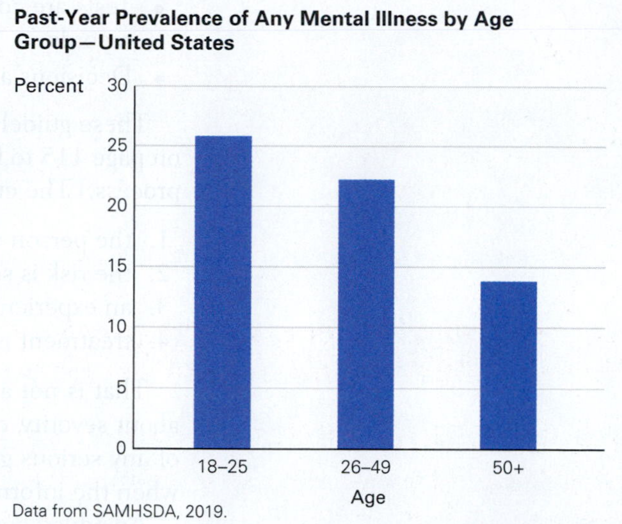

FIGURE 3.3

Getting Better How much of this improvement is because of therapy and medication, and how much is the self-understanding that helps adults know that feelings are not always facts?

Who Needs Counseling? Rational and informed understanding is elusive, not only among prospective parents but also among professionals not trained in counseling. Consider the experience of one of my students. A month before she became pregnant, Jeannette's employer required her to have a rubella vaccination. Hearing that Jeannette had had the shot, her obstetrician gave her the following prognosis:

> My baby would be born with many defects, his ears would not be normal, he would be intellectually disabled. . . . I went home and cried for hours and hours. . . . I finally went to see a genetic counselor. Everything was fine, thank the Lord, thank you, my beautiful baby is okay.
>
> *[Jeannette, personal communication]*

Jeannette may have misunderstood what she was told, but that is exactly why the doctor should have spoken more carefully. Genetic counselors are trained to make information clear. If sensitive counseling is available, then preconception, prenatal, or even prenuptial (before marriage) testing is especially useful for:

- individuals who have a parent, sibling, or child with a serious genetic condition
- couples who have had several spontaneous abortions or stillbirths
- couples who are infertile
- women over age 35 and men over age 40
- couples from the same ethnic group, particularly if they are relatives

The latter is especially crucial among populations who often intermarry. This is true for Greeks in Cyprus, where about one-third of the population carries the recessive gene for thalassemia (either A or B). In the 1970s, about one out of every 158 Cypriot babies was born with serious thalassemia, which led to repeated hospitalization and premature death.

Then Cyprus encouraged everyone to be tested, before conception or at least prenatally. Some couples decided not to marry. Now virtually no newborns in Cyprus have thalassemia (Hvistendahl, 2013).

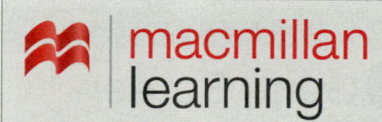

macmillan learning

VIDEO: Genetic Testing examines the pros and cons of knowing what diseases may eventually harm us or our offspring.

MICHELLE DEL GUERCIO/Science Source

Reassurance and Gratitude Karen is pregnant and just learned that a relative has the gene for a serious condition. Here, a genetic counselor is explaining all the possibilities. Several months after this photo was taken, she gave birth to a healthy baby!

The Ethics of Counseling Genetic counselors follow two ethical rules:

- Tests are confidential, beyond the reach of insurance companies and public records.
- Decisions are made by the clients, not by the counselors.

These guidelines are not easy to follow (A. Parker, 2012). (See the Career Alert on page 115 to learn more about how genetic counselors help clients navigate this process.) The current consensus is that information should be shared if:

1. the person wants to hear it;
2. the risk is severe and verified;
3. an experienced counselor explains the data; and
4. treatment is available.

That is not as straightforward as it appears. Scientists and physicians disagree about severity, certainty, and treatment. Some experts advocate informing patients of any serious genetic disorder, even when the person does not want to know and when the information might be harmful (Couzin-Frankel, 2013a).

An added complication is that individuals differ in their willingness to hear bad news. What if one person wants to know but other family members—perhaps a parent or a monozygotic twin who has the same condition—do not? We all are carriers. Do we all want to know?

Always the professional explains probabilities; always the clients decide. Often people need time to understand their risks. A wise genetic counselor notes the many relevant factors in nature and nurture, writes a letter explaining the genetic facts and future possibilities, and follows up months and years later to find out what needs more explanation.

Treatment options are described. For instance, if parents decide to conceive an embryo with high risk of a disorder, prenatal testing is described along with newborn diagnosis, early intervention, parental support groups, and medical specialists. Sometimes experimental treatments are promising, and parents learn that postponing conception is the best option.

Overall, the deeper ethical question is whether the twenty-first-century emphasis on genes distracts us from public health hazards (poverty, pollution, pesticides, and so on) that harm health more than genes do (Plows, 2011). Developmentalists recognize genes, but they also know that context and culture have a major effect; plasticity characterizes development.

As you have read many times in this chapter, genes are part of the human story, influencing every page, but they do not determine the plot or the final paragraph. The remaining chapters describe the rest of the story.

CHAPTER APP 3

Gene Screen

IOS:
https://tinyurl.com/yxvxbzun

RELEVANT TOPIC:
Genetic disorders, counseling, and testing

The Gene Screen app provides information about the inheritance and prevalence of recessive genetic diseases in different cultures and ethnicities.

THINK CRITICALLY: Instead of genetic counseling, should we advocate health counseling?

WHAT HAVE YOU LEARNED?

1. What chromosomal miscounts might result in a surviving child?
2. What is the cause and consequence of Down syndrome?
3. How common are recessive conditions?
4. Why is sickle-cell disease very common in some parts of Africa?
5. What is the role of the genetic counselor?
6. What ethical mandates are required of genetic counselors?

SUMMARY

The Genetic Code

1. Genes are the foundation for all development, first instructing the developing creature to form the body and brain, and then affecting thought, behavior, and health lifelong. Human conception occurs when two gametes (a sperm with 23 chromosomes and an ovum with 23 chromosomes) combine to form a single cell called a zygote.

2. A zygote usually has 46 chromosomes (half from each parent), which carry a total of about 21,000 genes. Genes and chromosomes from each parent match up to make the zygote, but the match is not always letter-perfect because of genetic variations called alleles, or polymorphisms.

3. Genetic variations occur in many ways, from the chromosomes of the parent to the epigenetic material surrounding the zygote and the microbiome of every body part. Spontaneous mutations, copy number variations, and much more make each person unique.

4. The most notable mismatch is in the 23rd pair of chromosomes, which is XX in females and XY in males. The sex of the embryo depends on the sperm, since only men have a Y chromosome and thus can make Y gametes.

New Cells, New People

5. The first duplications of the one-celled zygote create stem cells, each of which could become a person if it developed.

6. Monozygotic twins occur if those first stem cells split completely. Dizygotic twins occur if two ova are fertilized by two sperm at about the same time. Genetically, they have half of their genes in common, as do all full siblings.

7. In vitro fertilization (IVF) has led to millions of much-wanted babies and also to an increase in multiple births, who often are preterm and of low birthweight. Ethical concerns regarding standard IVF have quieted, but new dilemmas appear. CRISPR is the most recent example.

From Genotype to Phenotype

8. Genes interact in many ways, sometimes additively with each gene contributing to development and sometimes in a dominant–recessive pattern. If a recessive trait is X-linked, it is passed from mother to son.

9. Genetic makeup can make a person susceptible to many conditions. Examples include substance use disorder (especially alcohol use disorder) and poor vision (especially nearsightedness). Culture and family affect both of these conditions dramatically.

10. Every adult is a carrier of harmful genes. Their expression depends on the genes of the other parent, as well as on many influences from the environment. Genetic understanding can help caregivers protect people from potentially harmful genes.

Chromosomal and Genetic Problems

11. Often a gamete has fewer or more than 23 chromosomes, which may create a zygote with 45, 47, or 48 chromosomes. Usually such zygotes do not duplicate, implant, or grow.

12. Infants may survive if they have three chromosomes at the 21st site (Down syndrome). These individuals may have fulfilling lives, although they are vulnerable to heart and lung problems, and, in midlife, to Alzheimer's disease.

13. Another possible problem is a missing or extra sex chromosome. Such people have intellectual disabilities or other problems, but they may also lead a fulfilling life.

14. Everyone is a carrier for genetic abnormalities. Usually these conditions are recessive, not apparent unless the mother and the father both carry the gene. Serious dominant disorders usually do not appear until midlife.

15. Serious recessive diseases can become common if carriers have a health advantage. This is true for sickle-cell disease, which protected carriers against malaria.

16. Genetic testing and counseling can help many couples. Testing provides information about possibilities, which are difficult for people to understand when their emotions are overwhelming. The final decision about what to do with the information rests with the client, not the counselor.

KEY TERMS

deoxyribonucleic acid (DNA) (p. 61)
chromosome (p. 61)
gene (p. 61)
gamete (p. 62)
zygote (p. 62)
genome (p. 62)
allele (p. 62)
epigenetics (p. 63)
microbiome (p. 63)
genotype (p. 64)
homozygous (p. 65)
heterozygous (p. 65)
23rd pair (p. 65)
XY (p. 65)
XX (p. 65)
stem cells (p. 69)
in vitro fertilization (IVF) (p. 70)
monozygotic (MZ) twins (p. 71)
dizygotic (DZ) twins (p. 72)
phenotype (p. 72)
Human Genome Project (p. 73)
dominant (p. 74)
recessive (p. 74)
carrier (p. 74)
X-linked (p. 75)
heritability (p. 77)
syndrome (p. 79)
Down syndrome (p. 79)
fragile X syndrome (p. 81)

APPLICATIONS

1. Pick one of your traits and explain the influences that both nature *and* nurture have on it. For example, if you have a short temper, explain its origins in your genetics, your culture, and your childhood experiences.

2. Many adults have a preference for having a son or a daughter. Interview adults of several ages and backgrounds about their preferences. If they give the socially preferable answer ("It does not matter"), ask how they think the two sexes differ. Listen and take notes—don't debate. Analyze the implications of the responses you get.

3. Draw a genetic chart of your biological relatives, going back as many generations as you can and listing all serious illnesses and causes of death. Include ancestors who died in infancy. Do you see any genetic susceptibility? If so, how can you overcome it?

4. List a dozen people you know who need glasses (or other corrective lenses) and a dozen who do not. Are there any patterns? Is this correlation or causation?

Especially For ANSWERS

Response for Medical Doctors (from p. 64): No. Personalized medicine is the hope of many physicians, but appearance (the phenotype) does not indicate alleles, recessive genes, copy number variations, and other genetic factors that affect drug reactions. Many medical researchers seek to personalize chemotherapy for cancer, but although this is urgently needed, success is still experimental, even when the genotype is known.

Response for Future Parents (from p. 74): Possibly, but you wouldn't want to. You would have to choose one mate for your sons and another for your daughters, and you would have to use sex-selection methods. Even so, it might not work, given all the genes on your genotype. More important, the effort would be unethical, unnatural, and possibly illegal.

Response for Drug Counselors (from p. 76): Maybe. Some people who love risk become addicts; others develop a healthy lifestyle that includes adventure, new people, and exotic places. Any trait can lead in various directions. You need to be aware of the connections so that you can steer your clients toward healthy adventures.

Response for Teachers (from p. 79): As the text says, "information combats prejudice." Your first step would be to make sure you know about Down syndrome by reading material about it. You would learn, among other things, that it is not usually inherited (your student need not worry about his or her progeny) and that some children with Down syndrome need extra medical and educational attention. This might mean you need to pay special attention to your student, whose parents might focus on the sibling.

Observation Quiz ANSWERS

Answer to Observation Quiz (from p. 74): Ellie has a gene for achondroplasia, the most common form of dwarfism, which affects her limb growth, making her a little person. Because of her parents and her sister, she is likely to have a long and accomplished life: Her problems are less likely to come from her genotype than from how other people perceive her phenotype.

Answer to Observation Quiz (from p. 75): This figure was drawn to illustrate the recessive inheritance of blue eyes, and thus eyes are the only difference shown. If this were a real family, each child would have a distinct appearance.

Answer to Observation Quiz (from p. 77): Not nearsightedness! Rates of corrective lenses (estimated at 85 percent) might be as high among university students in the United States, but Americans would typically have contacts. Two other visible differences: uniforms and gender. Except for in the military, no U.S. university issues uniforms, and the majority of North American students are women. A fourth difference may be inferred from their attentiveness: The graduation rate of incoming college students in China is about 90 percent, compared to about 50 percent in the United States.

VISUALIZING DEVELOPMENT One Baby or More?

Humans usually have one baby at a time, but sometimes twins are born. Most often they are from two ova fertilized by two sperm (*lower left*), resulting in dizygotic twins. Sometimes, however, one zygote splits in two (*lower right*), resulting in monozygotic twins; if each of these zygotes splits again, the result is monozygotic quadruplets.

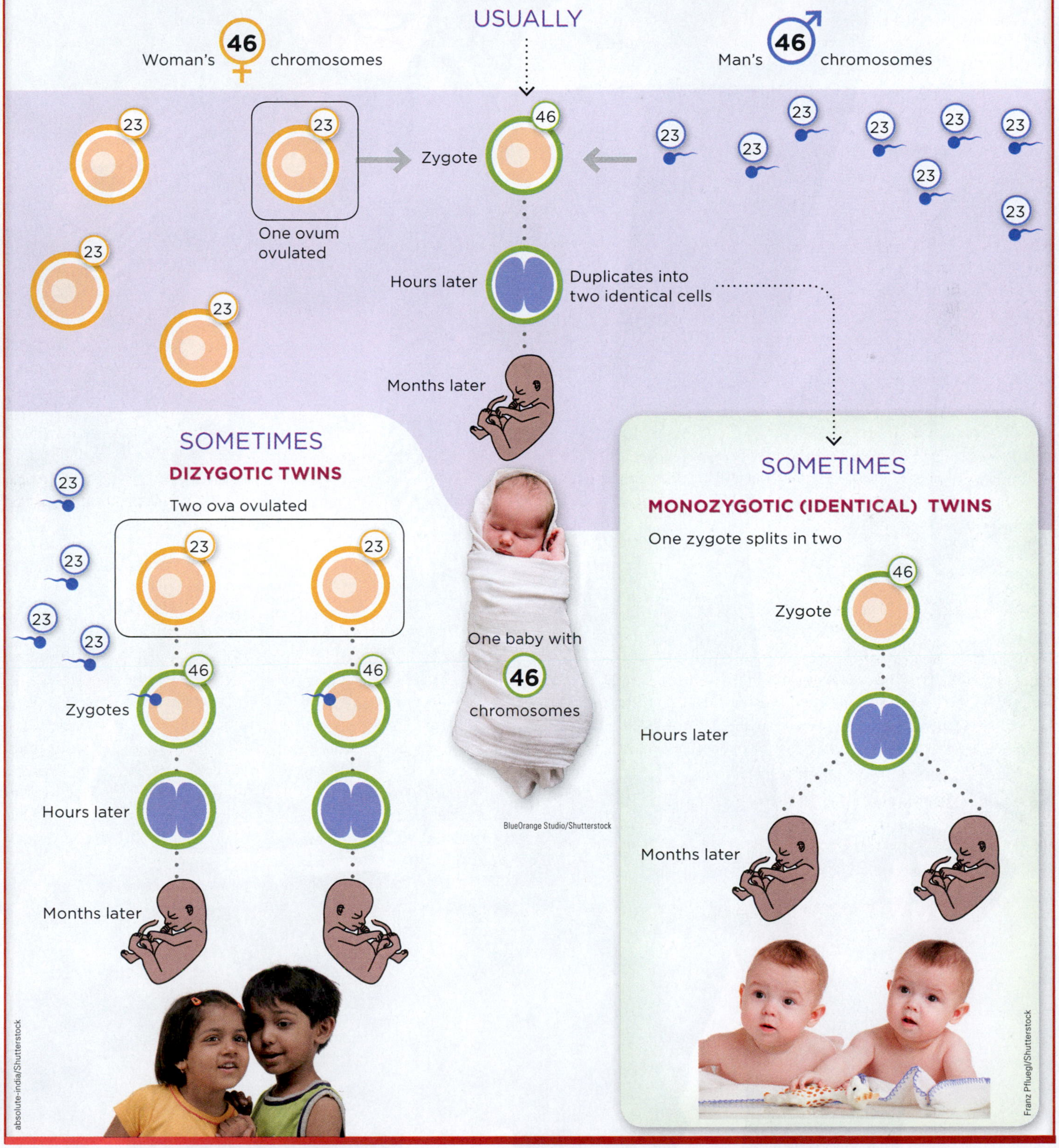

CHAPTER 4

Prenatal Development and Birth

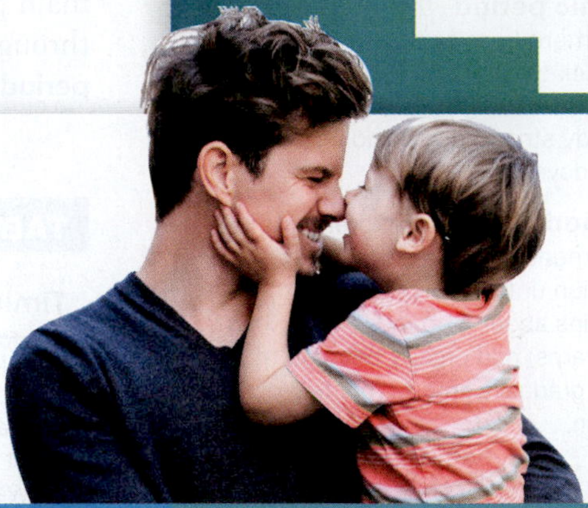

What Will You Know?

1. Why do most zygotes never become babies?
2. Are home births ever best?
3. What can a pregnant woman do to ensure a healthy newborn?
4. Why do new mothers and fathers sometimes become depressed?

- **Prenatal Development**
  - Germinal: The First 14 Days
  - Embryo: From the Third Week Through the Eighth Week
  - Fetus: From the Ninth Week Until Birth
  - INSIDE THE BRAIN: Essential Connections
- **Birth**
  - The Newborn's First Minutes
  - Medical Assistance at Birth
  - OPPOSING PERSPECTIVES: Interventions in the Birth Process
- **Problems and Solutions**
  - Risk Analysis
  - Harmful Substances
  - A CASE TO STUDY: Behavioral Teratogens
  - Prenatal Diagnosis
  - A VIEW FROM SCIENCE: What Is Safe?
  - Low Birthweight: Causes and Consequences
- **The New Family**
  - The Newborn
  - New Mothers
  - New Fathers
  - Family Bonding
- **CAREER ALERT: The Genetic Counselor**
- **VISUALIZING DEVELOPMENT: The Apgar**

My daughter Elissa had a second child. At 6 A.M. she and her husband were in the labor room of the birthing center; I was with Asa, age 5, in the family waiting room. Several times Asa walked down the hall to see his parents. Usually the midwife let us in. Sometimes we had to wait until a contraction was over, before both parents smiled at Asa again.

When the baby was born, a nurse came to say, "There's a new person who wants to meet you."

"Let me put this last Lego piece in," Asa said. I was eager to see my daughter and new grandson, but people at every age have their own priorities. Soon Asa was ready to bring his new creation to his parents. They introduced him to Isaac, sucking on his mother's breast. Six hours later, the entire family was home again.

The scientific study of human development is not only about how individuals change over time; it is about historical change—Bronfenbrenner's chronosystem. This struck me forcefully when I remembered Elissa's birth.

Back then, midwives and children were banned, fathers sat in waiting rooms, and new mothers were not allowed to touch their babies for 24 hours. As soon as she was born, Elissa was wiped, weighed, wrapped, and wheeled away. The nurse told me that I had no milk, that I needed rest, and that my baby was tired, too.

I now know that Elissa and I would both have benefited if she had sucked some colostrum from my breasts before she disappeared into the hospital nursery.

This chapter describes what we know about prenatal growth and birth, and some of the vast differences from one era, one culture, and even one family to another. Possible harm is noted: causes and consequences of diseases, malnutrition, drugs, pollution, stress, and of forbidding the mother to nurse at birth, as occurred at Elissa's birth a few decades ago and is still taboo in some West African cultures today (Bee et al., 2018).

In most places, thankfully, fathers and other family members now are active birth partners, midwives facilitate more births than doctors, and newborns are breast-fed within an hour of birth. In many ways, everyone—medical professionals, governments, and family members—affect each developing person, from conception on.

germinal period The first two weeks of prenatal development after conception, characterized by rapid cell division and the beginning of cell differentiation.

embryonic period The stage of prenatal development from approximately the third week through the eighth week after conception, during which the basic forms of all body structures, including internal organs, develop.

fetal period The stage of prenatal development from the ninth week after conception until birth, during which the fetus gains about 7 pounds (more than 3,000 grams) and organs become more mature, gradually able to function on their own.

embryo The name for a developing human organism from about the third week through the eighth week after conception.

Prenatal Development

The most dramatic and extensive transformation of the life span occurs before birth. To make it easier to study, prenatal development is often divided into three main periods. The first two weeks are called the **germinal period**; the third week through the eighth week is the **embryonic period**; from then until birth is the **fetal period**. (Alternative terms are presented in **Table 4.1**.)

TABLE 4.1

Timing and Terminology

Popular and professional books use various phrases to segment the stages of pregnancy.
• *Beginning of pregnancy:* Pregnancy begins at conception, which is also the starting point of *gestational age*. However, the organism does not become an *embryo* until about two weeks later, and pregnancy does not affect the woman (and is not confirmed by blood or urine testing) until implantation. Some obstetricians and publications count from the woman's last menstrual period (LMP), usually about 14 days *before* conception.
• *Length of pregnancy:* Full-term pregnancies last 266 days, or 38 weeks, or 9 months. If the LMP is used as the starting time, pregnancy lasts 40 weeks, sometimes expressed as 10 lunar months. (A lunar month is 28 days long.)
• *Trimesters:* Instead of *germinal period, embryonic period,* and *fetal period,* as used in this text, some writers divide pregnancy into three-month periods called *trimesters.* Months 1, 2, and 3 are called the *first trimester;* months 4, 5, and 6, the *second trimester;* and months 7, 8, and 9, the *third trimester.*
• *Due date:* Although a specific due date based on the LMP is calculated, only 5 percent of babies are born on that exact day. Babies born between two weeks before and one week after that date are considered *full term.* [This is recent; until 2012, three weeks before and two weeks after were considered full term.]

Germinal: The First 14 Days

You learned in Chapter 3 that the one-celled zygote duplicates, divides, and multiplies. Soon after the 16-cell stage, a fourth crucial process, *differentiation* begins. About a week after conception, the developing mass of cells forms two distinct parts—a shell that will become the *placenta* and a nucleus that will become the *embryo*.

The first task of the cell mass is implantation, embedding into the nurturing lining of the uterus. This is far from automatic; most zygotes never implant (Niakan et al., 2012) (see **Table 4.2**).

Embryo: From the Third Week Through the Eighth Week

The start of the third week after conception initiates the *embryonic period,* during which the mass of cells takes shape—not yet recognizably human but worthy of a new name, **embryo**. (The word *embryo* is often used loosely, but each early stage has a particular name; here, embryo refers to day 14 to day 56.)

Day by Day At about day 14, a thin line called the *primitive streak* appears down the middle of the cell mass; it forms the neural tube 22 days after conception. The neural tube develops into the central nervous system, that is, the brain and spinal column (Sadler, 2015). Soon the head appears, as eyes, ears, nose, and mouth start to form and a minuscule blood vessel that will become the heart begins to pulsate.

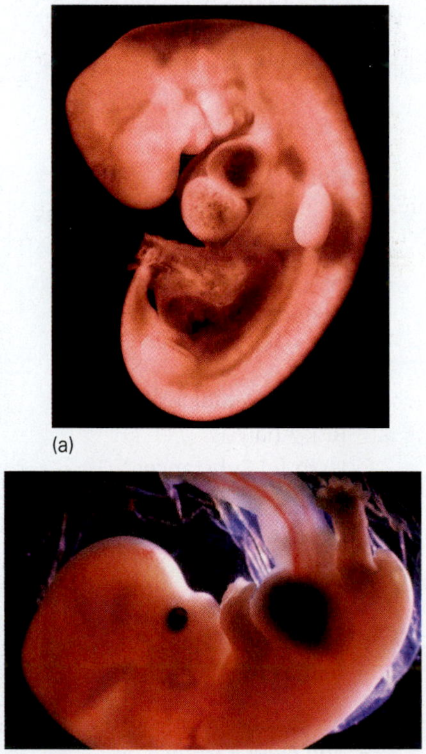

Omikron/Science Source

(a)

Petit Format/Science Source

(b)

The Embryonic Period *(a)* At 4 weeks past conception, the embryo is only about 1/8 inch (3 millimeters) long, but already the head has taken shape. *(b)* By 7 weeks, the organism is somewhat less than an inch (2 centimeters) long. Eyes, nose, the digestive system, and even the first stage of toe formation can be seen.

By the fifth week, buds that will become arms and legs emerge. Upper arms and then forearms, palms, and webbed fingers grow. Legs, knees, feet, and webbed toes, in that order, appear a few days later, each with the beginning of a skeleton. Then, 52 and 54 days after conception, respectively, the fingers and toes separate (Sadler, 2015).

At the end of the eighth week after conception (56 days), the embryo weighs just one-thirtieth of an ounce (1 gram) and is about 1 inch (2½ centimeters) long. It moves frequently, about 150 times per hour, imperceptible to the woman. Random arm and leg movements are more frequent early in pregnancy than later on (Rakic et al., 2016).

By eight weeks postconception, the developing embryo has all of the organs and body parts of a human being, including elbows and knees. Development is **cephalocaudal** (literally, "head-to-tail") and **proximodistal** (literally, "near-to-far"), with the head forming first and the extremities last. This directional pattern continues until puberty, when it reverses. (Feet first, brain last!)

The early embryo has both male (via *Wolffian ducts*) and female (via *Müllerian ducts*) potential, in a tiny intersex gonad. At the end of the embryonic period, hormonal and genetic influences typically cause one or the other to shrink, and then ovaries or testes, and a vagina or penis, grow from that omnipotent gonad (Zhao et al., 2017).

TABLE 4.2

Surviving Prenatal Development

The Germinal Period An estimated 60 percent of all zygotes do not grow or implant properly and thus do not survive the germinal period.
The Embryonic Period About 20 percent of all embryos are aborted spontaneously. This is usually called an early *miscarriage,* a misleading term. The usual cause is a chromosomal abnormality.
The Fetal Period About 5 percent of all fetuses are aborted spontaneously before viability at 22 weeks or are *stillborn,* defined as born dead after 22 weeks. This is much more common in poor nations.
Birth Because of all these factors, only about 31 percent of all zygotes become newborns.

Information from Bentley & Mascie-Taylor, 2000; Laurino et al., 2005; Cunningham et al., 2014.

cephalocaudal Growth and development that occurs from the head down.

proximodistal Growth and development that occurs from the center or core in an outward direction.

Fetus: From the Ninth Week Until Birth

The organism is called a **fetus** from the beginning of the ninth week after conception until birth. The fetal period encompasses dramatic change, from a tiny creature smaller than the final joint of your thumb to a newborn about 20 inches (51 centimeters) long.

fetus The name for a developing human organism from the start of the ninth week after conception until birth.

Early growth is rapid. By three months, the fetus weighs about 3 ounces (87 grams) and is about 3 inches (7.5 centimeters) long. Those numbers—3 months, 3 ounces, 3 inches—are approximate. (Metric measures—100 days, 100 grams, 100 millimeters—are similarly imprecise.)

The Middle Three Months The 4-month-old fetus is very active, with "large body movements—whole body flexion and extension, stretching and writhing, and vigorous leg kicks that somersault the fetus through the amniotic fluid" (Adolph & Franchak, 2017). The heartbeat becomes stronger and faster when the fetus is awake and moving. Digestion and elimination develop. Fingernails, toenails, and buds for teeth form, and hair grows (including eyelashes).

All of those developments inspire awe, but the crucial mid-pregnancy development is that the central nervous system becomes active, regulating heart rate, breathing, and sucking. Brain maturation allows the fetus to reach the **age of viability**, when a fetus born far too early might survive.

age of viability The age (about 22 weeks after conception) at which a fetus might survive outside the mother's uterus if specialized medical care is available.

Every day of prenatal life within the uterus increases viability. If birth occurs before 22 weeks, death is certain because advanced technology cannot maintain life without some brain response. (Reports of survivors born before 22 weeks are unreliable, because the date of conception is unknown.)

After the age of viability, life is still fragile. Currently, if birth occurs in an advanced neonatal unit, some very preterm babies survive, and some of those

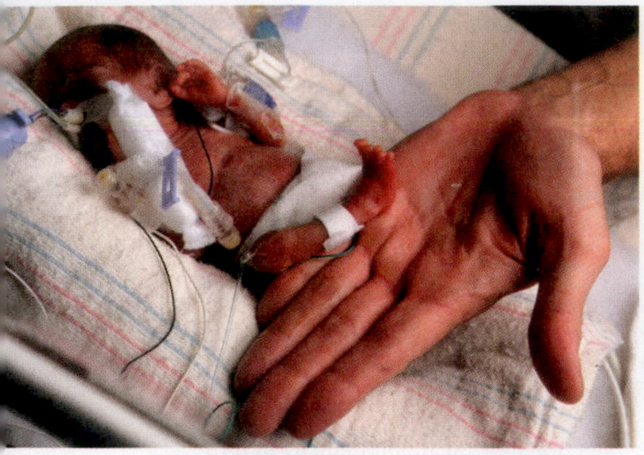

Loyola Univ. Medical Center/Getty Images News/Getty Images

One of the Tiniest Rumaisa Rahman was born after 26 weeks and 6 days, weighing only 8.6 ounces (244 grams). Nevertheless, she has a good chance of living a full, normal life. Rumaisa gained 5 pounds (2,270 grams) in the hospital and then, six months after her birth, went home. Her twin sister, Hiba, who weighed 1.3 pounds (590 grams) at birth, had gone home two months earlier. At their one-year birthday, the twins seemed normal, with Rumaisa weighing 15 pounds (6,800 grams) and Hiba 17 pounds (7,711 grams) (Nanji, 2005).

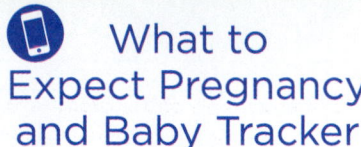

reach age 2 without major impairments. Rates vary by nation, by sex (girls do better), and by medical advances.

Among the best survival rates are those in Japan and France. In Japan, about half of 22-week-old newborns born alive survive the first week of life, and about half of those survivors escape major cognitive disabilities (Kono et al., 2018).

In France, when labor is induced prematurely because continued pregnancy might be fatal, only 11 percent of 22-week fetuses without cerebral palsy survive to age 2 (most died at birth or soon thereafter), but 66 percent do so if they were born 25 weeks past conception (Lorthe et al., 2018).

The Final Three Months Each day of the final three months benefits the fetal brain and body. Many aspects of prenatal life are awe-inspiring; the fact that an ordinary woman provides a far better home for a fetus than the most advanced medical technology is one of them.

The neurological, respiratory, and cardiovascular systems all develop. The lungs expand and contract, and breathing muscles strengthen as the fetus swallows and spits out amniotic fluid. The valves of the heart go through a final maturation, as do the arteries and veins throughout the body; the testicles of the male fetus descend; brain pathways form.

The various lobes and areas of the brain are also established, and pathways between one area and another are forged. For instance, sound and sight become coordinated: Newborns quickly connect voices heard during pregnancy with faces. That may be why they recognize their mother after seeing her only once or twice.

That phenomenal accomplishment occurs within a day or two after birth. Indeed, the fetal brain is attuned to voices much more than to other noises: Neurological plasticity is designed to recognize the voices of familiar people by the sixth month after conception (Webb et al., 2015). When a baby is born very prematurely, impairments are often evident in movement, intelligence, and/or vision but less often in audition (Kono et al., 2018).

By full term, human brain growth is so extensive that the cortex has become wrinkled, with *gyri* and *sulci*, as the hills and valleys of the cortex are called (see **Figure 4.1**). Although some huge mammals (whales, for instance) have bigger brains than humans, no other creature needs as many folds because, relative to body size, the human brain is much larger.

Beyond brain growth, with an estimated 86 billion neurons at birth, another process occurs in the final three months of pregnancy—cell death. Programmed cell death, called *apoptosis,* occurs in two prenatal waves. The first wave is easy to understand: Abnormal and immature neurons, such as those with missing or extra chromosomes, are lost.

Later in development, however, seemingly normal neurons die: Almost half of all newly formed brain cells are gone before birth (Underwood, 2013).

The final months of pregnancy are crucial to protect the brain. During this time, the membranes and bones covering the brain thicken. This helps prevent "brain bleeds," a hazard of preterm birth if paper-thin blood vessels in the cortex collapse.

Newborns have two areas on the top of their heads (*fontanels*) where the bones of the skull have not yet fused. Fontanels enable the fetal head to become narrower during birth. They gradually close during infancy. Fontanels are larger in preterm babies, making these babies more vulnerable to brain damage.

The average American fetus gains about 4½ pounds (2.1 kilograms) in the third trimester, increasing to about 7½ pounds (about 3.4 kilograms) at birth, with boys a few ounces heavier than girls. The World Health Organization reports that some well-nourished mothers give birth to healthy newborns weighing 6 pounds,

CHAPTER APP 4

What to Expect Pregnancy and Baby Tracker

IOS:
https://tinyurl.com/y6esrn5a

ANDROID:
https://tinyurl.com/nufnyqg

RELEVANT TOPIC:
Prenatal health and development, birth, and the new family

This pregnancy tracker app, based on the tried and true *What to Expect When You're Expecting,* guides users through pregnancy day-by-day and week-by-week, based on their baby's due date. Users receive personalized updates, tips, and articles on their baby's development, and are joined with a virtual community of parents-to-be with similar due dates. New parents can then access expert advice and support for baby's first year and beyond.

INSIDE THE BRAIN

Essential Connections

In earlier decades, a newborn's chance of survival was pegged to how much the baby weighed. Today we know that weight is a crude predictor—some 1-pound babies live and some 3-pound babies die. The crucial factor is brain maturation. Whether the brain developed for nine months in utero, or several weeks or a few months less than that, makes a marked difference in a child's ability to think, talk, and move.

As you now know, the central nervous system is the first body system to begin development. The embryonic stage starts with the primitive streak, which becomes the neural tube even before the facial features are formed and before the first pulsating blood vessel appears. In the two years after birth, the most rapid organ development of the infant is, again, in the brain (Gilmore et al., 2018).

Already by the third week after conception some cells specialize to become *neural progenitor cells,* which duplicate and multiply many times until some of them create neurons (brain cells). Neurons do not duplicate, but some endure lifelong. Those early neurons migrate to a particular part of the brain (brain stem, cerebellum, hypothalamus, visual cortex, and so on) and specialize. For example, some neurons are dedicated to seeing faces, others to seeing red and green, others to blue and yellow, and so on.

By mid-pregnancy, the brain has developed billions of neurons (*neurogenesis*). Earlier, the cortex (the outer part of the brain) had been smooth, but now folds and wrinkles (the gyri and sulci) allow the human brain to be larger and more complex than the brains of other animals (Stiles & Jernigan, 2010).

[**Life-Span Link:** The cortex and other brain structures are described in Chapter 5.]

Following the proximodistal (near-to-far) sequence, the six layers of the cortex are produced, with the bottom (sixth) layer first and then each new layer above the previous one so that the top, outer layer is the last to form. Similarly, the brain stem above the back of the neck, then the midbrain, and finally the forebrain develop and connect.

Synchronized connections between parts of the brain indicate that they are working together—as in an adult who sees and smells something delicious, experiences hunger, and reaches for the food, all in a flash. These four responses arise together from different brain regions, a synchrony that begins prenatally.

One study found that a relative lack of synchronized coordination after 20 weeks predicted preterm delivery, indicating that something was amiss in the prenatal environment (Thomason et al., 2017).

Detailed study of one crucial brain region, the *hippocampus* (the major site for memory formation), reveals an explosion of new cells during the fourth prenatal month, followed by a gradual slowdown as other parts of the fetal body increase (Ge et al., 2015).

This mid-gestation burst of neurogenesis and then slowdown is characteristic of the entire brain, with each specific area following its own timetable, prenatally and postnatally (Gilmore et al., 2018). This is an example of the biosocial development detailed in every later biosocial chapter: Each age has a particular pattern of growth.

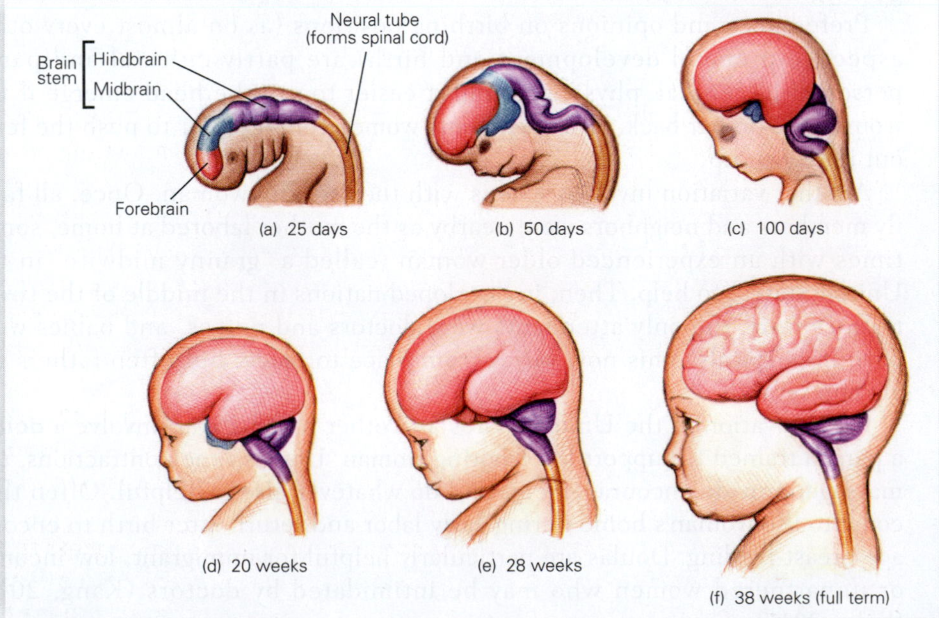

FIGURE 4.1
Prenatal Growth of the Brain Just 25 days after conception *(a)*, the central nervous system is already evident. The brain looks distinctly human by day 100 *(c)*. By the 28th week of gestation *(e)*, at the very time brain activity begins, the various sections of the brain are recognizable. When the fetus is full term *(f)*, all parts of the brain, including the cortex (the outer layers), are formed, folding over one another and becoming more convoluted, or wrinkled, as the number of brain cells increases.

while others have babies weighing 10 pounds, with variation by nation (northern European newborns tend to be heavier) (Kiserud et al., 2018).

Reflexes (listed at the end of this chapter) are a better indication of health than weight. Unless something is amiss, most newborns are ready by the end of prenatal life to thrive at home on Mother's milk—no expert help, oxygenated air, or special feeding required. For thousands of years, that is how humans survived: We would not be alive if any of our ancestors had been born before the last three months of pregnancy.

WHAT HAVE YOU LEARNED?

1. What are the three stages of prenatal development?
2. Why are the first days of life the most hazardous?
3. What parts of the embryo form first?
4. When do sex organs appear?
5. What is the prognosis of a baby born before 25 weeks of gestation?
6. What occurs in the final three months of pregnancy?

Birth

About 38 weeks (266 days) after conception, the fetal brain signals massive increases in the hormone *oxytocin* to start labor. Birth occurs after 12 hours of active labor for first births and 7 hours for subsequent ones. These are averages: Birth is still *full term* two weeks before or after the due date, and labor may take twice or half as long. Some women believe they are in active labor for days, and others say 10 minutes.

Women's birthing positions vary—sitting, squatting, lying down. Some women labor in a tub of warm water, which helps the woman relax (the fetus continues to get oxygen via the umbilical cord).

Preferences and opinions on birthing positions (as on almost every other aspect of prenatal development and birth) are partly cultural and partly personal. In general, physicians find it easier to see the head emerge if the woman lies on her back. However, many women find it easier to push the fetus out if they sit up.

Another variation involves who is with the birthing woman. Once, all family members and neighbors were nearby as the mother labored at home, sometimes with an experienced older woman (called a "granny midwife" in the United States) to help. Then, in developed nations in the middle of the twentieth century, the only attendants were doctors and nurses, and babies were born in hospitals. This now varies from place to place, but often fathers are also present.

An innovation in the United States and other nations is to involve a **doula**, a person trained to support the laboring woman. Doulas time contractions, use massage, provide encouragement, and do whatever else is helpful. Often they come to the woman's home during early labor and return after birth to encourage breast-feeding. Doulas are particularly helpful for immigrant, low-income, or unpartnered women who may be intimidated by doctors (Kang, 2014; Saxbe, 2017).

doula A woman who helps with the birth process. Traditionally in Latin America, a doula was the only professional who attended childbirth. Now doulas are likely to arrive at the woman's home during early labor and later work alongside a hospital's staff.

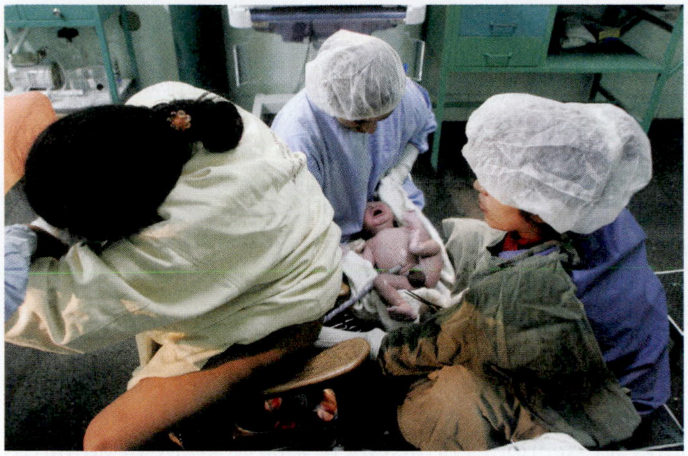

Enrique Castro-Mendivil/REUTERS

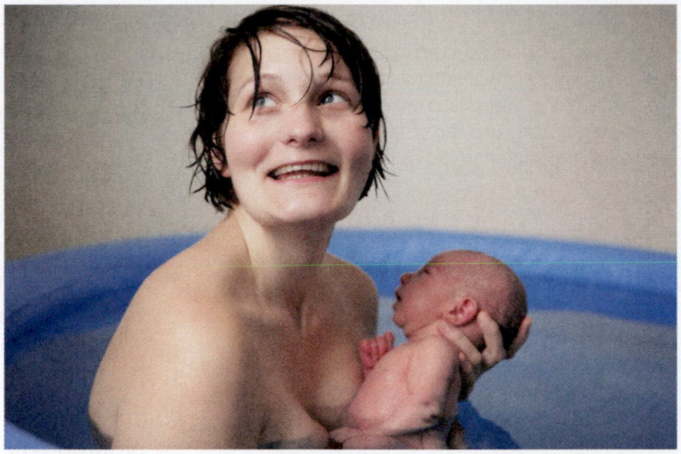

Frank Herholdt/The Image Bank/Getty Images

Choice, Culture, or Cohort? Why do it that way? Both of these women (in Peru, on the *left*, and in England, on the *right*) chose methods of labor that are unusual in the United States, where birth stools and birthing pools are uncommon. However, in all three nations, most births occur in hospitals—a rare choice a century ago.

The Newborn's First Minutes

Newborns usually breathe and cry on their own. The first breaths of air bring oxygen to the lungs and blood, and the infant's color changes from bluish to pinkish. (Pinkish refers to blood color, visible beneath the skin, and applies to newborns of all skin tones.) Eyes open wide; tiny fingers grab; even tinier toes stretch and retract. The full-term baby is instantly, zestfully, ready for life.

Newborn health is often measured by the **Apgar scale**, first developed by Dr. Virginia Apgar. When she earned her M.D. in 1933, Apgar wanted to work in a hospital but was told that only men did surgery. She became an anesthesiologist, present at many births but never the doctor in charge.

Apgar scale A quick assessment of a newborn's health, from 0 to 10. Below 5 is an emergency—a neonatal pediatrician is summoned immediately. Most babies are at 7, 8, or 9—almost never a perfect 10.

Apgar saw that "delivery room doctors focused on mothers and paid little attention to babies. Those who were small and struggling were often left to die" (Beck, 2009, p. D1). To save those young lives, Apgar developed a simple rating scale of five vital signs—color, heart rate, cry, muscle tone, and breathing. Nurses could use the scale and sound the alarm immediately if a newborn was in crisis.

Since 1950, birth attendants worldwide have used the Apgar (often using the name as an acronym: Appearance, Pulse, Grimace, Activity, and Respiration) at one minute and again at five minutes after birth, assigning each vital sign a score.

A study comparing Apgar rates in 23 nations found that birth attendants were affected by culture: In some nations 97 percent of newborns scored 9 or 10, whereas in other nations only 73 percent had such scores. High scores did not necessary indicate excellent obstetric practice, but an Apgar below 7 always indicated risk (Siddiqui et al., 2017). Thus, worldwide to this day, a low Apgar signals "baby emergency" (see Visualizing Development, p. 113).

Medical Assistance at Birth

The specifics of birth depend on the fetus, the mother, the birth attendant, the birthplace, and the culture. In the United States 98 percent of births occur in hospitals, with sterile procedures, electronic monitoring, and drugs to dull pain or speed contractions.

Fifty years ago in developed nations, hospitals banned midwives, but now many hospitals allow certified midwives to deliver babies. Midwife births have lower rates of various complications and interventions than physician births, in part because midwives emphasize breathing, massage, and social support (Bodner-Adler et al., 2017; Renfrew et al., 2014; Raipuria et al., 2018).

cesarean section (c-section) A surgical birth in which incisions through the mother's abdomen and uterus allow the fetus to be removed quickly instead of being delivered through the vagina. (Also called simply *section*.)

Especially for Conservatives and Liberals Do people's attitudes about medical intervention at birth reflect their attitudes about medicine at other points in their life span, in such areas as assisted reproductive technology (ART), immunization, and life support? (see response, page 112)

Surgery Nonetheless, most U.S. births are attended by physicians. They are the only ones allowed to perform certain medical measures, including **cesarean sections**, when the fetus is removed though incision in the mother's abdomen instead of being pushed by contractions through the vagina.

C-sections were once rare, a last-ditch effort to save a new life when the mother was dying and vaginal birth was impossible. Now, with much better anesthesia and fetal monitoring, more than one birth in five worldwide (21 percent in 2015, compared to 12 percent in 2000) is a c-section (Boerma et al., 2018). This surgery is safe for mother and baby, who feel no pain.

Cesareans are medically indicated for about 10 percent of births. Among the circumstances that suggest a c-section are multiple births (twins or more), breech births (fetus is not positioned head down), prior c-section, long active labor (more than 24 hours), a narrow pelvis, a large fetus, and advanced maternal age.

None of these *requires* a c-section. For instance, a large study of all births (78,880) in the state of Washington focused on the relationship between age and various complications. Sixty percent of new mothers aged 50 or older delivered via c-section; 40 percent delivered vaginally (Richards et al., 2016).

Public health experts are troubled by increases in c-sections in the past decade and by international disparities. Too few (4 percent) cesareans are performed in central Africa, including about 1 percent in South Sudan, where childbirth is still a leading cause of death. Too many occur in the Caribbean and Latin America (44 percent), with the highest of all in the Dominican Republic (58 percent) (Boerma et al., 2018).

Nations with very low cesarean rates also have high levels of childbirth deaths, but nations with high cesarean rates are not necessarily healthier. In the United States, the cesarean rate rose between 1996 and 2008 (from 21 percent to 34 percent) and since has declined slightly—about 31 percent in 2018.

Cesareans have immediate advantages for hospitals (easier to schedule, quicker, and more expensive than vaginal deliveries) and for women (advance planning, quick birth).

Disadvantages appear later. After a c-section, mothers less often breast-feed and more often develop medical complications. Their babies have higher rates of asthma and obesity (Chu et al., 2017; Mueller et al., 2017). One reason: Babies delivered surgically have less beneficial microbiomes than those delivered vaginally (Wallis, 2014).

WHAT HAVE YOU LEARNED?

1. What is the typical birth process?
2. Who was Virginia Apgar and what did she do?
3. What are the immediate and long-term results of a cesarean birth?
4. Why do cesarean rates vary internationally?
5. What are the advantages and disadvantages of a hospital birth?

Problems and Solutions

The early days of life place the future person on the path toward health and success—or not. Problems can begin before conception, if the sperm, the ovum, or the uterus was affected by the parents' health. Indeed, the grandmothers' health when the mother and father were born may affect the grandchild (Arshad et al., 2017).

OPPOSING PERSPECTIVES

Interventions in the Birth Process

Opposing views are evident in opinions about the birth process. Is it a natural process that should be left alone or a medical event that requires doctors, technology, and hospitals? This is evident in discussions about cesareans. Public health professionals consider the worldwide rates too high, but many doctors and women choose them.

Other controversial measures include drugs to start or speed labor, or to reduce pain. Some drugs are similar to what is prescribed for headaches or minor pain, but another drug, an *epidural,* is injected in the spine to alleviate all sensation in the lower body.

An epidural can cause complications in the mother (later headaches), reduce Apgar in the baby, increase the rate of cesarean sections, decrease newborn sucking, and lead to other complications—at least according to a large study in Pennsylvania (Kjerulff, 2014). But many medical professionals and laboring women consider an epidural a wonderful innovation.

Another medical intervention is adding oxytocin (usually in Pitocin) intravenously, as occurs in about 25 percent of U.S. births and an estimated 10 percent worldwide. Oxytocin is produced naturally to start labor, promote breast-feeding, and encourage infant care. Thus, oxytocin starts or strengthens labor.

Induction and augmentation of labor correlate with complications, including higher rates of cesareans (Mikolajczyk et al., 2016; Grivell et al., 2012). But correlation is not causation. Concerns about harm to the fetus are considered "premature" when induction is medically indicated (Lønfeldt et al., 2018).

Questions abound for every medical measure. For instance, intervention rates vary more by doctor than by medical conditions. Are some doctors too quick to intervene or too slow to help women in pain? Birth rates are higher during weekdays than on nights and weekends because of more c-sections and oxytocin (Fischetti & Armstrong, 2017). Does that indicate better care or too much intervention?

One reaction to high rates of intervention is to have a baby at home, where interventions are minimal and family members are around. However, in the United States less than 1 percent of babies are born at home. Planned home births are controversial, with some suggesting that they are less safe than hospital births and others saying that they may be better for women and their families (Wendland, 2018).

Home births are more common in other nations. It is British policy that a woman can choose where to give birth "based on her wishes and cultural preferences and any medical and obstetric needs she and her baby may have" (quoted in Hinton et al., 2018). About 90 percent choose hospitals; 8 percent choose a birthing center; 2 percent choose home.

In the Netherlands, home births are chosen by about a third of the low-risk women, because special ambulances called *flying storks* speed mother and newborn from home to hospital if needed. According to one source, in nations where low-risk mothers can choose home births and good medical care is available, mothers have fewer complications and infants are at least as likely to survive in the first days and weeks after birth (de Jonge et al., 2015).

No one doubts that babies *can* be born at home, with little intervention—that is how our ancestors were born. Before the twentieth century, many newborns died: Death was as common as life during childbirth in some nations. But some say that birth was better when it was more natural; others are grateful for all that modern medicine has brought.

Eliot Elisofon/The LIFE Picture Collection/Getty Images

They Called It "Catching" the Baby Midwife Mahala Couch shows her strong hands that "caught" thousands of newborns in the back woods of Southern Appalachia. Midwife births became illegal in about 1920, but many women preferred home birth with Mahala over hospital birth with a doctor. Currently, midwives are trained, certified, and legal in most states and nations.

WANG ZHAO/AFP/Getty Images

Pick Up Your Baby! Probably she can't. In this maternity ward in Beijing, China, most patients are recovering from cesarean sections, making it difficult to cradle, breast-feed, or carry a newborn until the incision heals.

Fortunately, healthy newborns are the norm, not the exception. However, if something is amiss, it is often part of a sequence that may become overwhelming (Rossignol et al., 2014).

Risk Analysis

Life requires risks: We routinely decide which chances to take and how to minimize harm. For example, we know the danger as well as the benefits of crossing the street, so we hold the hands of young children, teaching them how to safely cross.

That is a small illustration of risk analysis. Risks need to be taken, but they also need to be controlled. Pregnancy and birth entail many risks, but the outcome—a new baby—seems well worth it. The challenge is to avoid problems and to mitigate damage. Development is a long process; no single event causes a problem, but sometimes a cascade of events does.

You just read a small example of such a cascade: Induced labor increases the need for an epidural, which increases the likelihood of a cesarean, which reduces the likelihood of breast-feeding. None of this is necessarily harmful if the fetus is full term and healthy. But if other problems occur during prenatal life, then the circumstances of birth may result in a newborn who begins life with handicaps.

cerebral palsy A disorder that results from damage to the brain's motor centers. People with cerebral palsy have difficulty with muscle control, so their speech and/or body movements are impaired.

A dramatic example is **cerebral palsy** (a disease marked by difficulties with movement), which was once thought to be caused solely by birth procedures (excessive medication, slow breech birth, or misused forceps). However, it now seems that cerebral palsy begins with genetic sensitivity, prenatal insults, and maternal infection (Mann et al., 2009) and is exacerbated by insufficient oxygen to the fetal brain at birth.

anoxia A lack of oxygen that, if prolonged, can cause brain damage or death.

This lack of oxygen is called **anoxia**. Anoxia often occurs for a second or two during birth, indicated by a slower fetal heart rate, with no harm done. Because their birth takes longer, twins and breech births are more likely to experience anoxia.

To prevent prolonged anoxia, the fetal heart rate is monitored during labor, and often a cesarean is used to prevent problems. If the Apgar indicates slow breathing or bluish color, immediate oxygen is given.

How long anoxia can continue without harming the brain depends on genes, birthweight, gestational age, drugs in the bloodstream (either taken by the mother before birth or given by the doctor during birth), and many other factors. Thus, anoxia is part of a cascade that may cause cerebral palsy. Almost every other birth complication is also the result of many factors.

Harmful Substances

teratogen An agent or condition, including viruses, drugs, and chemicals, that can impair prenatal development and result in birth defects or even death.

Monthly, even weekly, scientists discover another **teratogen**, which is anything—drugs, viruses, pollutants, malnutrition, stress, and more—that increases the risk of prenatal abnormalities and birth complications.

But don't be like one of my students, who said that now that she knew all the things that can go wrong, she never wanted a baby. As I told her, problems can be avoided, and damage can be remedied. Pregnancy is not a dangerous period to be feared; it is a natural process to be protected.

Visible and Invisible Damage People once thought that the placenta protected the fetus against all harm. Then, about six decades ago, rubella and thalidomide (both explained in Chapter 1) proved otherwise.

A CASE TO STUDY

Behavioral Teratogens

About 20 percent of all children have difficulties in thinking and behavior that *could* be connected to teratogens. One of my students wrote:

> I was nine years old when my mother announced she was pregnant. I was the one who was most excited. . . . My mother was a heavy smoker, Colt 45 beer drinker and a strong caffeine coffee drinker.
>
> One day my mother was sitting at the dining room table smoking cigarettes one after the other. I asked "Isn't smoking bad for the baby?" She made a face and said "Yes, so what?"
>
> I said "So why are you doing it?"
>
> She said, "I don't know.". . .
>
> During this time I was in the fifth grade and we saw a film about birth defects. My biggest fear was that my mother was going to give birth to a fetal alcohol syndrome (FAS) infant. . . . My baby brother was born right on schedule. The doctors claimed a healthy newborn. . . . Once I heard healthy, I thought everything was going to be fine. I was wrong, then again I was just a child. . . .
>
> My baby brother never showed any interest in toys . . . he just cannot get the right words out of his mouth . . . he has no common sense . . .
>
> Why hurt those who cannot defend themselves?
>
> [*J., personal communication*]

As you remember from Chapter 1, one case is not proof. J. blames her mother, but probably genetic risks, inadequate prenatal care, and troubling postnatal experiences are part of her brother's sorry cascade. Her mother was of low SES (itself a correlate of harm), and her cigarette addiction suggests that she was poorly nourished. Boys and later-born children are more vulnerable, which may help explain why J. was a good student, unlike her brother.

However, as with this case, a newborn may appear to have escaped a teratogen, but the brain is nonetheless damaged. The best proven example is the thousands of newborns—born to women who drank alcohol only on weekends—who appear normal but will nonetheless experience fetal alcohol spectrum disorder (Hoyme et al., 2016).

The long reach of a seemingly harmless teratogen is evident in the Zika virus (ZIKV), not recognized until 2015, when an epidemic led to dozens of Brazilian newborns with abnormally small brains (*microcephaly*). Zika is caused by the bite of an infected mosquito and is more common in poor regions (as are all teratogens). Poor Brazilians are likely to live in homes without screens situated near mosquito breeding grounds.

Zika has probably harmed fetuses for centuries, but once it was recognized, Zika appeared in dozens of other nations, including the United States. We now know that fetuses infected with ZIKV often appear typical but may be impaired, particularly in their senses and emotions (they are very irritable) (Van den Pol, 2017; Rosen, 2016).

In the past several years, many scientists have worked to detect ZIKV. Apparently, many people were infected and now are immune. The epidemic has subsided for the moment because of that immunity.

Research continues. Some scientists are working to develop a vaccine, and others to use CRISPR to stop the mosquitos who carry the virus. Some researchers deliberately infected pregnant monkeys. Follow-up on monkeys who appeared normal at birth evidenced "a spectrum of subtle fetal brain injuries" that correlate with schizophrenia, major depression, and Alzheimer's (Waldorf et al., 2018, p. 370). That result was corroborated by other scientists (Christian et al., 2018).

It is clear that many factors, prenatal and postnatal, affect the brain. Prenatal toxins are one factor: The rest of development can mitigate or exacerbate the effects. I hope J. learned how to help her brother. Her question "Why hurt those who cannot defend themselves?" still echoes in my mind.

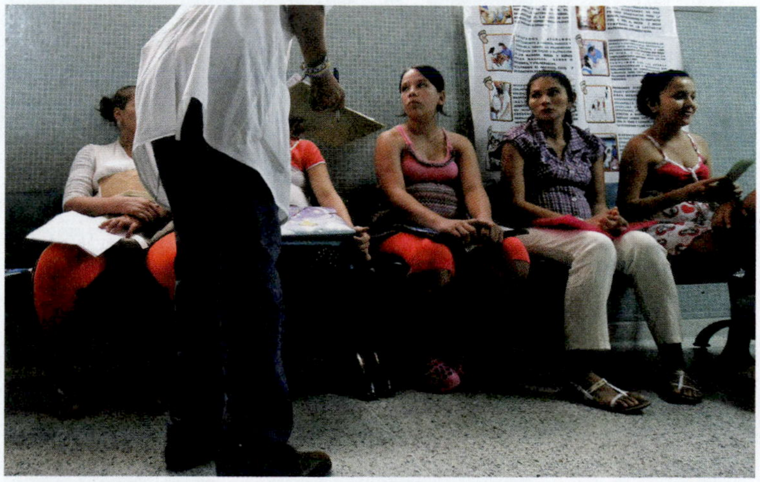

Schneyder Mendoza/European Pressphoto Agency/CÃºcuta/Norte de Santander/Colombia/Newscom

No One Knows Dozens of newborns in northern Brazil led doctors to discover that mosquitos carrying the Zika virus could cause microcephaly (small heads). More is now known: Zika brain damage is sometimes invisible, and newborns in North, Central, and South America are affected. However, certain diagnosis and long-term damage are still unknown. No wonder these pregnant women in a clinic in Colombia are worried, especially Sandra Ovallos (in the middle), who recently had a fever and rash.

behavioral teratogens Agents and conditions that can harm the prenatal brain, impairing the future child's intellectual and emotional functioning.

More recently, people knew that teratogens caused birth defects—such as blindness from rubella or the missing limbs from thalidomide—but they didn't know that teratogens could affect behavior. Now it is known that **behavioral teratogens**, might cause no visible harm but instead make a child hyperactive, antisocial, or intellectually disabled.

The Critical Time Timing is crucial. Some teratogens cause damage only during a *critical period,* which may occur before a woman knows she is pregnant (see **Figure 4.2**). [**Life-Span Link:** Critical and sensitive periods are described in Chapter 1.] Consequently, women need to avoid drugs, supplement a balanced diet with folic acid and iron, update their immunizations, and gain or lose weight if needed *before* pregnancy occurs.

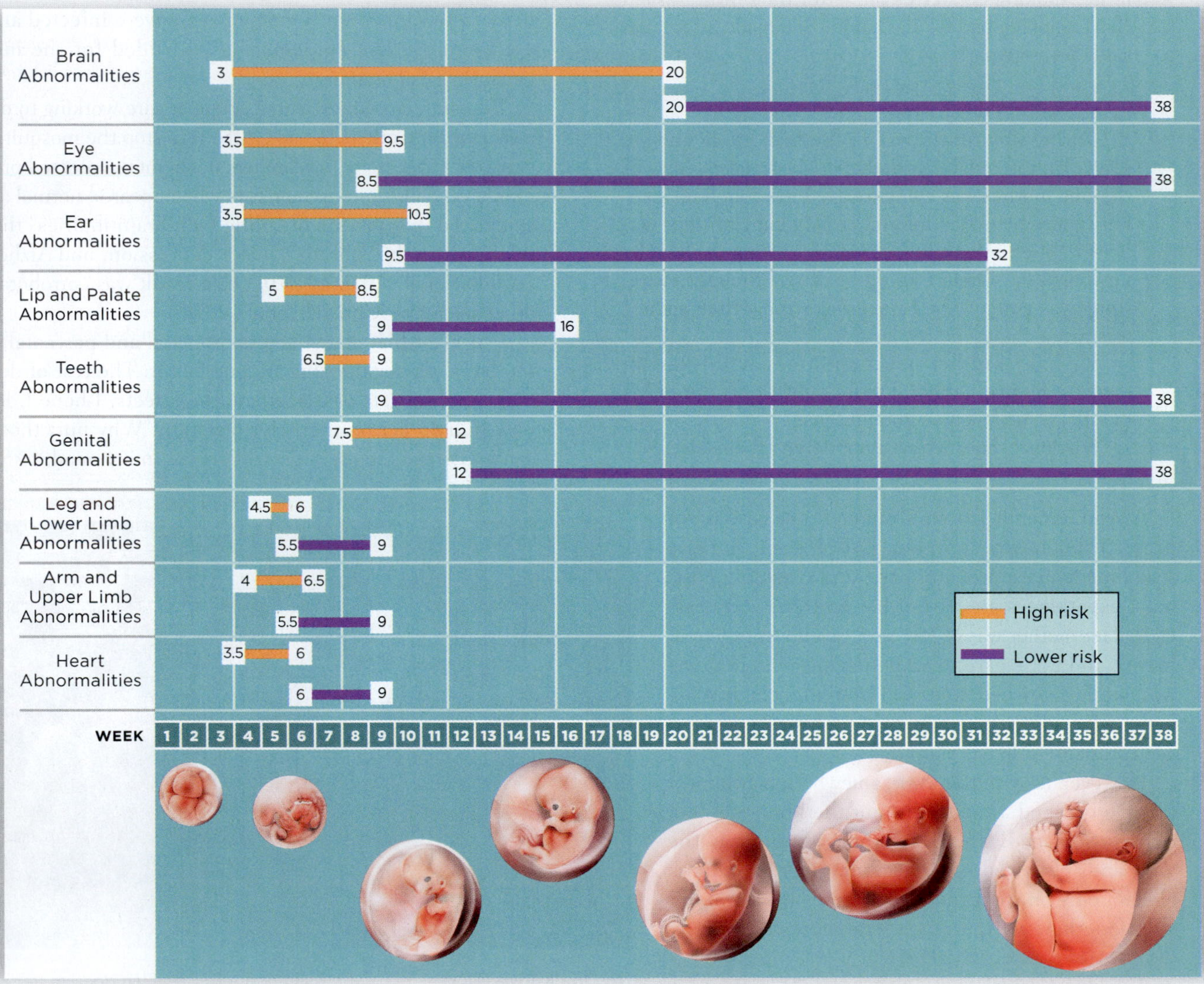

FIGURE 4.2

One More Reason to Plan a Pregnancy The embryonic period, before a woman knows she is pregnant, is the most sensitive time for causing structural birth defects. However, at no time during pregnancy is the fetus completely safe from harm. Individual differences in susceptibility to teratogens may be caused by a fetus's genetic makeup or peculiarities of the mother, including the effectiveness of her placenta or her overall health. The dose and timing of the exposure are also important.

Observation Quiz What part of the embryo and fetus has the longest period of vulnerability? What has the shortest? (see answer, page 112)

The first days and weeks after conception (the germinal and embryonic periods) are critical for body formation, but behavioral teratogens affect the fetus at any time. Cigarettes, for instance, are harmful when the mother smokes before or during pregnancy, but quitting by mid-pregnancy has a major impact on newborn birthweight (Kvalvik et al., 2017). Similarly, a longitudinal study of 7-year-olds found that, although alcohol affects the form of the face early in pregnancy, binge drinking is an especially potent behavioral teratogen in the second half of pregnancy (Niclasen et al., 2014).

macmillan learning

Data Connections Activity: Teratogens examines both the effects of various teratogens and the preventive measures that mitigate their risk to a developing fetus.

Timing may be important in another way. When pregnancy occurs soon after a previous pregnancy, risk increases. For example, one study found that second-born children are twice as likely to have autism spectrum disorder if they are born within a year of the first-born child (Cheslack-Postava et al., 2011).

How Much Is Too Much? A second factor that affects the harm from teratogens is the dose and/or frequency of exposure. Some teratogens have a **threshold effect**; they are virtually harmless until exposure reaches a certain level, at which point they "cross the threshold" and become damaging.

threshold effect In prenatal development, when a teratogen is relatively harmless in small doses but becomes harmful once exposure reaches a certain level (the threshold).

Is there a safe dose or timing for psychoactive drugs? Research has focused on alcohol, a drug ingested by many young women. Early in pregnancy, a woman's heavy drinking can cause **fetal alcohol syndrome (FAS)**, which distorts the facial features of a child (especially the eyes, ears, and upper lip). Later in pregnancy, behavior can be affected; *fetal alcohol effects (FAE)* occur, not FAS (Hoyme et al., 2016).

fetal alcohol syndrome (FAS) A cluster of birth defects, including abnormal facial characteristics, slow physical growth, and reduced intellectual ability, that may occur in the fetus of a woman who drinks alcohol while pregnant.

Currently, pregnant women are advised to avoid all alcohol, but many women in France (between 12 and 63 percent, depending on specifics of the research) do not heed that message (Dumas et al., 2014). Most of their babies seem fine. Should all women who *might* become pregnant refuse a legal substance that most men use routinely? Wise? Probably. Necessary? Maybe not.

Especially for Judges and Juries
How much protection, if any, should the legal system provide for fetuses? Should women with alcohol use disorder who are pregnant be jailed to prevent them from drinking? What about people who enable them to drink, such as their partners, their parents, bar owners, and bartenders? (see response, page 111)

Innate Vulnerability Genes are a third factor that influences the effects of teratogens. When a woman carrying dizygotic twins drinks alcohol, for example, the twins' blood alcohol levels are equal, yet one twin may be more severely affected because of different alleles for the enzyme that metabolizes alcohol. Similar differential susceptibility occurs for many teratogens (McCarthy & Eberhart, 2014).

Although the links from genes to teratogens to damage are sometimes difficult to verify, two examples of genetic susceptibility are proven. First, male fetuses are more often spontaneously aborted, stillborn, or harmed by teratogens than are female fetuses. Precise impact is difficult to specify, because the male–female hazard rate differs from one teratogen to another (Lewis & Kestler, 2012).

false positive The result of a laboratory test that reports something as true when in fact it is not true. This can occur for pregnancy tests, when a woman might not be pregnant even though the test says she is, or during pregnancy, when a problem is reported that actually does not exist.

Second, one maternal allele reduces folic acid, and that deficit can produce *neural-tube defects*—either *spina bifida,* in which the tail of the spine is not enclosed properly (enclosure normally occurs at about week 7), or *anencephaly,* when part of the brain is missing. Neural-tube defects are more common in certain ethnic groups (e.g., Irish, English, and Egyptian). Nonetheless, most women with the gene have healthy babies.

In one study (Smithells et al., 2011), about half of a group of 550 mothers of a child with a neural-tube disorder (and hence genetically at risk) took folic acid supplements. The other half ate normally. The rate of newborns with neural-tube defects was 1 in 250 among the supplemented mothers and 13 in 300 in the non-supplemented ones. That was proof that folic acid helps.

But, note that almost 96 percent of the women who were at genetic risk and did *not* take supplements had healthy babies. Also, one supplemented

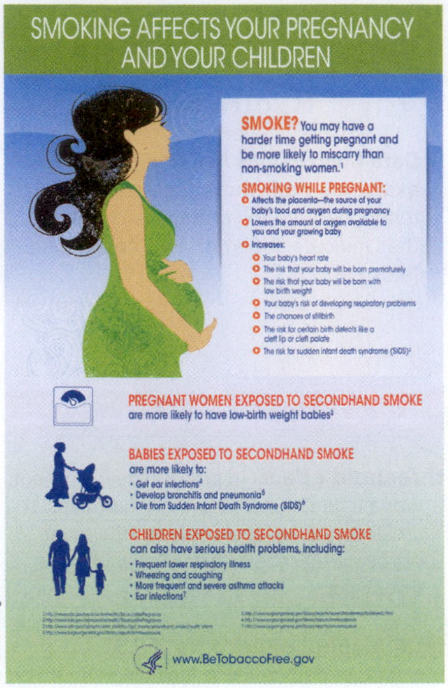

BeTobaccoFree.gov

Smoke-Free Babies Posters such as this one have had an impact. Smoking among adults is only half of what it was 30 years ago. One-third of women smokers quit when they know they are pregnant, while the other two-thirds cut their smoking in half. Unfortunately, the heaviest smokers are least likely to quit—they need more than posters to motivate them to break the habit.

woman bore a second child with a neural-tube defect. Why? Was the dose too low, or did she skip taking the pills, or was some other genetic risk the problem? Questions regarding teratogens abound.

Prenatal Diagnosis

Early prenatal care has many benefits: Women learn what to eat, what to do, and what to avoid. Some serious conditions, syphilis and HIV among them, can be diagnosed and treated in the first prenatal months before they harm the fetus.

Tests of blood, urine, fetal heart rate, and ultrasound reassure parents, facilitating the crucial parent–child bond. It is now possible to know the sex of the fetus within the first few months. This allows parents to name the fetus, considering him or her a person, long before birth.

In general, early care protects fetal growth, connects women to their future child, makes birth easier, and renders parents better able to cope. When complications (such as twins, gestational diabetes, and infections) arise, early recognition increases the chance of a healthy birth.

Unfortunately, however, about 20 percent of early pregnancy tests *raise* anxiety instead of reducing it. For instance, the level of alpha-fetoprotein (AFP) may be too high or too low, or ultrasound may indicate multiple fetuses, abnormal growth, Down syndrome, or a mother's narrow pelvis. Many such warnings are **false positives**; that is, they falsely suggest a problem that does not exist. On the other hand, advice about fetal growth can alert women to avoid underweight newborns, a serious problem.

Advice from Experts Even doctors need to be more careful. One concern is pain medication. Opioids (narcotics) may damage the fetus. Yet, a recent study found that 23 percent of pregnant women on Medicaid were given a prescription for a narcotic (Desai et al., 2014).

Worse still is that some obstetricians do not ask about harmful life patterns. One example is diet. Optimal weight gain depends on preconception weight: Underweight women need to gain more and obese women need to gain less. But few obstetricians tailor nutritional advice to the specific patient (Phelan et al., 2011).

In another example, one Maryland study found that almost one-third of pregnant women were *not* asked about alcohol consumption (Cheng et al., 2011). Those least likely to be queried were college-educated women over age 35, yet older, educated women are more likely to drink alcohol. The rate for pregnant woman overall is 10 percent, but the rate for college-educated women is 13 percent, and for older pregnant women 19 percent (Tan et al., 2015).

Many women assume that herbal medicines or over-the-counter drugs are safe. Not so. As pediatrics professor Allen Mitchell explains, "Many over-the-counter drugs were grandfathered in with no studies of their possible effects during pregnancy" (quoted in Brody, 2013, p. D5). ("Grandfathered" means that if they were legal in days past, they remain legal—no testing needed.)

To learn which medications are safe, women consult the Internet. However, a study of 25 Web sites that, together, listed 235 medications as safe found that TERSIS (a group of expert teratologists who analyze drug safety) had declared only 60 (25 percent) safe. The rest were not *proven* harmful, but TERSIS found insufficient evidence to confirm safety (Peters et al., 2013). Internet sites sometimes use unreliable data: Some drugs on the safe list of one site were on the danger list of another (Peters et al., 2013).

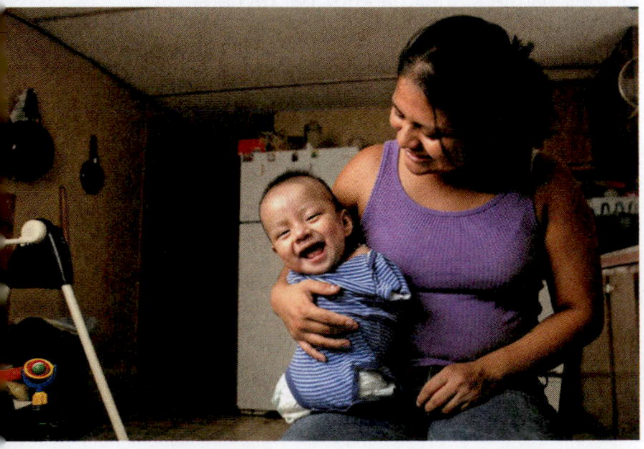
Taylor Jones/ZUMA Press/Florida City/FL/USA/Newscom

No More Pesticides Carlos Candelario, shown here at age 9 months, was born without limbs, a birth defect that occurred when his mother (Francisca, show here) and father (Abraham) worked in the Florida fields. Since his birth in 2004, laws prohibit spraying pesticides while people pick fruit and vegetables, but developmentalists worry about the effect of the residue on developing brains.

Low Birthweight: Causes and Consequences

The World Health Organization defines **low birthweight (LBW)** as under 2,500 grams (5 ½ pounds). LBW babies are further grouped into **very low birthweight (VLBW)**, under 1,500 grams (3 pounds, 5 ounces), and **extremely low birthweight (ELBW)**, under 1,000 grams (2 pounds, 3 ounces).

low birthweight (LBW) A body weight at birth of less than 2,500 grams (5½ pounds).

very low birthweight (VLBW) A body weight at birth of less than 1,500 grams (3 pounds, 5 ounces).

extremely low birthweight (ELBW) A body weight at birth of less than 1,000 grams (2 pounds, 3 ounces).

With modern hospital care, even very small newborns born after the age of viability usually survive, but they are more vulnerable to harm. Ranking worse than most developed nations—and tied with Uruguay, Tanzania, Romania, and Spain—is the United States, whose low birthweight rate is 46th in the world (World Bank, 2014).

It would be better for everyone—mother, father, baby, and society—if all newborns were in the womb for at least 36 weeks and weighed more than 2,500 grams (5½ pounds). (Usually, this text gives pounds before grams. But hospitals worldwide report birthweight using the metric system, so grams precede pounds and ounces here.)

Too Soon or Too Small Babies born **preterm** (two or more weeks early; no longer called *premature*) are often LBW, because fetal weight normally doubles in the last trimester of pregnancy, with 900 grams (about 2 pounds) of that gain occurring in the final three weeks. As already mentioned, every week past week 22 adds weight and maturation.

preterm A birth that occurs two or more weeks before the full 38 weeks of the typical pregnancy—that is, at 36 or fewer weeks after conception.

A VIEW FROM SCIENCE

What Is Safe?

As explained in Chapter 1, the scientific method is designed to be cautious. It takes years—for replication, for alternate designs, and for exploration of conflicting hypotheses—to reach sound conclusions. On almost any issue, scientists disagree until the weight of evidence is unmistakable.

For example, it took decades before all researchers agreed on such (now obvious) teratogens as lead and cigarettes, and decades more for laws to reflect that agreement, eliminating lead from gasoline, and cigarette ads from television.

No biologist doubts that pesticides harm frogs, fish, and bees, but the pesticide industry insists that careful use (e.g., spraying plants, not workers) benefits people, in the form of fresh, low-cost food. That certain benefit may outweigh any possible risk.

Developmentalists, however, fear that pregnant women who breathe or ingest these toxins will bear brain-damaged babies (Heyer & Meredith, 2017). One scientist said, "Pesticides were designed to be neurotoxic. Why should we be surprised if they cause neurotoxicity?" (Lanphear, quoted in Mascarelli, 2013, p. 741).

Since 2000, the United States removed one pesticide, *chlorpyrifos*, from household use (it had been used to kill roaches and ants). It was banned from U.S. agriculture in the last month of the Obama administration but reinstated in the first year of the Trump administration—to the distress of many scientists and doctors (Lipton, 2017; Rauh, 2018).

Is that a developmental issue, an economic issue, or a political issue? Chlorpyrifos is widely used in other nations, in homes as well as farms, and is very profitable.

Analysis of umbilical cord blood finds that fetuses exposed to chlorpyrifos become children with lower IQs and more behavior problems than other children (Horton et al., 2012). However, the companies that sell chlorpyrifos argue that confounding factors need to be considered (Mascarelli, 2013).

What might those confounding factors be? For one thing, pregnant women who use roach spray are more likely to live in stressful, inner-city neighborhoods, a context that reduces learning whether pesticides are used or not. Likewise, parents who pick sprayed crops are often migrants who move from place to place and fear deportation. Moving, and fear, disrupts children's schooling.

Could factors such as these be a third variable that explains the correlation between pregnant women exposed to pesticides and their children's education? Further, even if chlorpyrifos is a teratogen, does that outweigh the economic benefits for farmers, chemical companies, and parents who need to buy fruits and vegetables? Risk analysis is needed.

To make all of this more difficult, stress and anxiety affect the fetus, yet pregnancy itself increases fear (Rubertsson et al., 2014). Prospective parents want clear, immediate answers. Scientists take years to find them; laws take even longer.

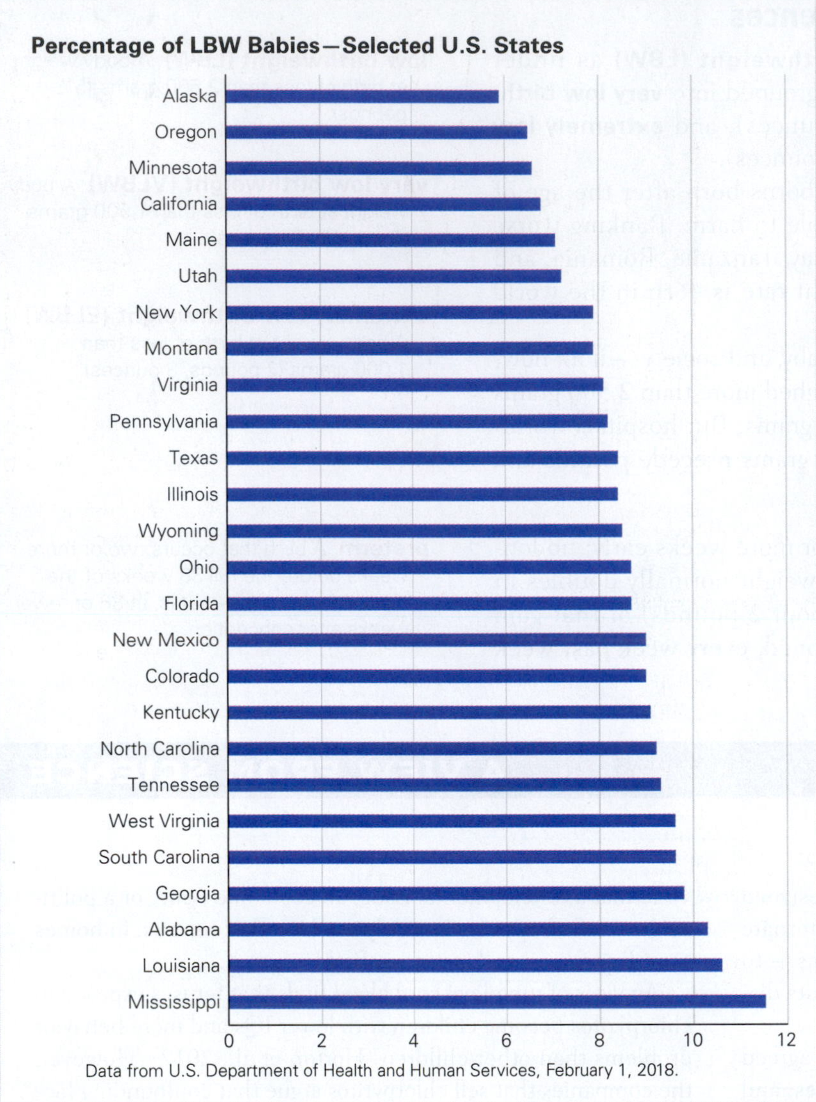

FIGURE 4.3
Where Were You Born? Rates of low birthweight vary by nation, from about 4 to 20 percent, and, as you see here, *within* nations. Why? Poverty is a correlate—is it also a cause?

small for gestational age (SGA) A term for a baby whose birthweight is significantly lower than expected, given the time since conception. For example, a 5-pound (2,265-gram) newborn is considered SGA if born on time but not SGA if born two months early. (Also called *small-for-dates*.)

immigrant paradox The surprising, paradoxical fact that low-SES immigrant women tend to have fewer birth complications than native-born peers with higher incomes.

Other LBW babies have gained weight slowly throughout pregnancy and are *small-for-dates*, or **small for gestational age (SGA)**. A full-term baby weighing only 2,600 grams and a 30-week-old fetus weighing only 1,000 grams are both SGA, even though the first is not technically low birthweight. Low birthweight varies dramatically from nation to nation, and, within the United States, from county to county as both a cause and a predictor of lifelong poverty (Robertson & O'Brien, 2018) (see **Figure 4.3**).

In most nations, malnutrition is the most common reason for slow fetal growth. Women who begin pregnancy underweight, who eat poorly during pregnancy, or who gain less than 3 pounds (1.3 kilograms) per month in the last six months often have underweight infants. This problem is particularly common in Africa and South Asia, but it can occur in developed nations as well.

The second common reason, particularly in developed nations, is drug use. Almost every psychoactive drug—including legal ones such as cigarettes and alcohol—reduces nutrition and birthweight.

A third reason is multiple births. Twins gain weight more slowly in pregnancy and are born, on average, three weeks early. As you remember from Chapter 3, multiple births are more common in IVF, with some hopeful parents choosing to implant several blastocysts—against medical advice.

Unfortunately, many risk factors tend to occur together. For example, undernourished mothers often live in urban neighborhoods where pollution is high—another risk factor (Erickson et al., 2016). Women in rural areas have yet another cascade of risks—distance from prenatal care, unwanted pregnancies, and exposure to pesticides (Committee on Health Care for Underserved Women, 2014).

What About the Father? The causes of low birthweight rightly focus on the pregnant woman. However, "Fathers' attitudes regarding the pregnancy, fathers' behaviors during the prenatal period, and the relationship between fathers and mothers . . . influence risk for adverse birth outcomes" (Misra et al., 2010, p. 99).

Indeed, everyone who affects a pregnant woman also affects a fetus. Her mother, her boss, her mother-in-law, her doctor, and especially her partner can add to her stress, or reduce it. Thus, it is not surprising that unintended pregnancies increase the incidence of low birthweight and birth defects, a link strongest in women of low income (Finer & Zolna, 2016). Obviously, intentions are in the mind, not in the body, and are affected by the father and the community, all influencing a woman's behavior.

Evidence for this is in the **immigrant paradox**. As already mentioned, low SES correlates with low birthweight, especially in the United States (Martinson & Reichman, 2016). Many immigrants have difficulty getting education and well-paid jobs; their socioeconomic status is low.

Nonetheless, babies born to immigrants generally are heavier and healthier than newborns of native-born women of the same SES and ethnicity (Marks et al., 2014). This is true not only when women from Latin America are compared to Hispanics whose families have lived in the United States for generations but also for women born in the Caribbean, Africa, eastern Europe, and Asia compared to U.S.-born women with similar genes.

Why? One hypothesis is that fathers and the entire communities are supportive of pregnant women, keeping them drug-free and well-fed, appreciated and healthy, buffering the stress of poverty (Luecken et al., 2013). By contrast, with more time in the United States, the community protection decreases (Fox et al., 2018).

DARREN HAUCK/The New York Times/Redux

Does She Belong in Jail? Alicia Beltran, age 28, shown here pregnant with her first child, confided at her initial prenatal visit that she had been addicted to a painkiller but was now clean (later confirmed by a lab test). She refused a prescription to keep her away from illegal drugs, prompting the police to take her to court in handcuffs and shackles when she was 14 weeks pregnant. A state-appointed lawyer for the fetus successfully argued that she should be detained. After more than two months, a nonprofit lawyer got her released. More than a year later, a judge conceded that her constitutional rights had been violated but dismissed the case because the state had dropped the charges.

Consequences of Low Birthweight Low birthweight is a problem, not only at birth but for years. At birth, life itself is uncertain and Apgar scores are lower. Then every developmental milestone — smiling, holding a bottle, walking, talking — is, on average, delayed, with cognitive difficulties and visual and hearing impairments more common. As toddlers, LBW children cry often, pay attention less, and disobey more (Aarnoudse-Moens et al., 2009; Stolt et al., 2014).

Problems continue, especially if birthweight was very low. Children who were extremely SGA or preterm tend to have neurological problems in middle childhood, including smaller brain volume, lower IQ, and behavioral difficulties (Clark et al., 2013; Hutchinson et al., 2013; Howe et al., 2016). Even in adulthood, risks persist, with higher rates of diabetes, obesity, heart disease, and depression (Lyall et al., 2016).

However, remember plasticity. By age 4, some ELBW infants exhibit typical brain development, especially if they had no medical complications and their mother was well educated.

In adulthood, for the fortunate ones, early arrival may no longer be relevant. This was evident for adults whose birthweight was less than 1,000 grams. They tended to have higher rates of shyness — except when adult experiences, particularly a happy marriage, reduced the impact of ELBW (Xu et al., 2018).

International Comparisons As you remember from Chapter 1, scientists collect empirical data and then draw conclusions based on facts. Regarding low birthweight, the facts are clear; the conclusions are not. No less than six hypotheses might explain a puzzling fact: Low birthweight is less common in most nations than it was, but it is increasing in some nations — the United States among them. We begin with what is known.

In some northern European nations, only 4 percent of newborns weigh under 2,500 grams; in several South Asian and African nations, including India, Pakistan, Mali, and Yemen, more than 20 percent do. Two conclusions are proven: First, there is worldwide improvement. Less malnutrition resulted in fewer underweight, fragile newborns in 2017 than a decade ago. One happy result: In the first month of life, the rate of death per thousand newborns was 19 in 2017, compared to 36 in 1990 (UNICEF, 2018).

Second, national goals matter. In China, Cuba, and Chile low birthweight has plummeted since 2000 because prenatal care has become a national priority. That is one conclusion of a study provocatively titled *Low birth weight outcomes: Why better in Cuba than Alabama?* (Neggers & Crowe, 2013).

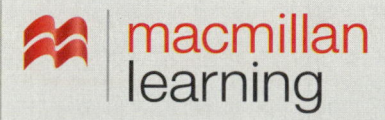

macmillan learning

VIDEO: Low Birthweight in India discusses the causes of LBW among babies in India.

THINK CRITICALLY: Food scarcity, drug use, and unmarried parenthood have all been suggested as reasons for the LBW rate in the United States. Which is it—or are there other factors?

In other nations, the LBW rate is rising. Many of those nations are in sub-Saharan Africa, and the rise is troubling but not puzzling: Global warming, HIV/AIDS, food shortages, wars, and other problems affect pregnancy.

However, in other nations, an increasing rate of LBW is puzzling. The LBW rate in the United States fell throughout most of the twentieth century, reaching a low of 7.0 percent in 1990. But then it rose, dipping slightly around 2010 but increasing every year since 2012 and reaching 8.17 percent in 2016 (Martin et al., 2018). That is higher than almost every other developed nation.

Added to the puzzle is that several changes in maternal ethnicity, age, and health since 1990 should have *decreased* LBW. For instance, although the rate of LBW among African Americans is higher than the national average (14 percent compared with 8 percent), and although teenagers have smaller babies than do women in their 20s, the birth rate among both groups was much lower in 2016 than in 1990. Thus, the average should have fallen, not risen.

Similarly, unintended pregnancies are less common (Finer & Zolna, 2016), and two conditions that produce heavier babies (maternal obesity and diabetes) have increased since 1990. Paradoxically, more underweight babies are born in the United States currently than decades ago.

Is prenatal care the crucial variable? In some nations, but not in the United States. The rates of women giving birth without prenatal care have decreased.

Another hypothesis is that IVF increased multiple births, which are often LBW. However, LBW rates are rising for naturally conceived singletons.

Perhaps the problem is nutrition. The U.S. Department of Agriculture (Coleman-Jensen et al., 2015) reported an increase in the rate of *food insecurity* (measured by skipped meals, use of food stamps, and outright hunger) between the first seven years of the twenty-first century and the next seven, from about 11 percent to about 15 percent (see **Figure 4.4**).

The group most likely to be food insecure are young mothers. Some undereat so that their children can eat—unaware that they are harming a future child. Their undernourishment adds stress to their children, who become stressed in return, affecting everyone—including weight gain of a future baby (King, 2018).

Perhaps lack of health care? Untreated infections and chronic illness correlate with LBW, and many of the poorest young women have no health insurance.

A fifth possible culprit is drug use. In the United States, the birth rate is highest among 20- to 24-year-olds, and so is drug use—in that age group, 11 percent smoke during pregnancy (Drake et al., 2018).

Observation Quiz Is the gap between single mothers and single fathers increasing or decreasing? (see answer, page 112)

FIGURE 4.4
And Recovery? As you can see, all family types were affected by the Great Recession that began in 2007—especially single fathers, who were most likely to lose their jobs and not know how to get food stamps. But why are children of single mothers hungry more often than children of single fathers and three times as often as children of married parents? The data show correlation; researchers do not agree about causes.

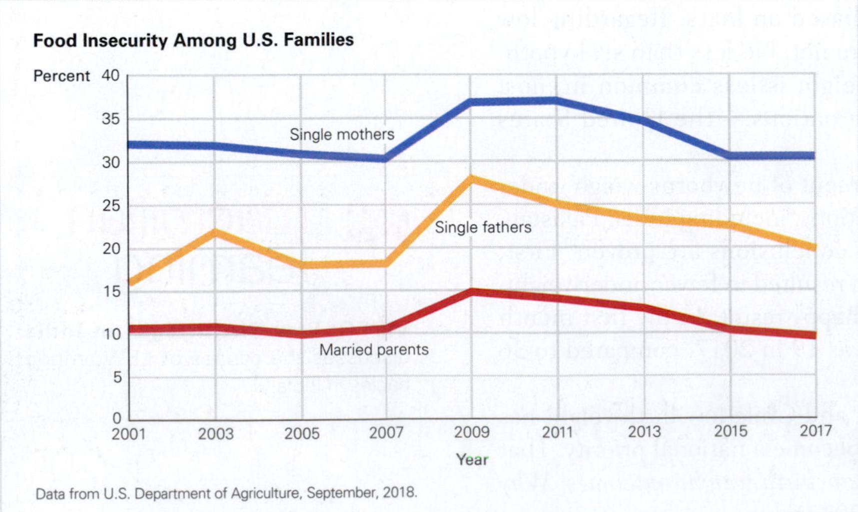

Looking beyond the United States, some trends are ominous. In recent years, low birthweight has decreased markedly in Asia, but smoking and drinking among young women are now increasing in those nations.

In Japan, low birthweight was slightly more than 6 percent in 2000 but almost 10 percent in 2015. Smoking and drinking are among the possible culprits, but so are low weight gain during pregnancy, increasing mercury in food, and more births after age 35 (Tamura et al., 2018).

In every hypothesis, we must distinguish correlation from causation. Low birthweight varies from nation to nation and year to year, so something in nurture is crucial. Since LBW correlates with problems throughout life, we need to know more about causes so that we can prevent the

consequences. For developing nations, the first steps are obvious—less hunger and better prenatal care. But for developed nations, more science is needed: Many hypotheses need to be explored.

WHAT HAVE YOU LEARNED?

1. How do we know that the placenta does not screen out all harmful substances?
2. What factors increase the harm from a teratogen?
3. Why is it difficult to be certain that a behavioral teratogen affected a child?
4. What is the difference between low, very low, and extremely low birthweight?
5. What are the causes and consequences of low birthweight?
6. What is puzzling about national and ethnic differences in low birthweight?

The New Family

Humans are social creatures, seeking interaction with their families and their societies. We have already seen how crucial social support is during pregnancy. Social interaction may become even more important when a child is born.

The Newborn

Before birth, humans already affect their families. Fetal movements and hormones that trigger maternal nurturance (food aversions, increased sleep, and more). At birth, a newborn's appearance (big hairless head, tiny feet, and so on) stirs the human heart, evident in adults' brain activity and heart rate. Fathers are often enraptured by their scraggly newborns and protective of the exhausted mothers, who may appreciate their partners more than before, for hormonal as well as practical reasons.

Newborns are responsive social creatures in the first hours of life (Zeifman, 2013). They listen, stare, cry, stop crying, and cuddle. In the first day or two, a professional might administer the **Brazelton Neonatal Behavioral Assessment Scale (NBAS)**, which records 46 behaviors, including 20 reflexes. Parents watching this assessment are amazed at the newborn's responses—and this fosters early parent–child connection (Hawthorne, 2009).

Technically, a **reflex** is an involuntary response to a particular stimulus. The strength of a reflex varies from one newborn to the next depending on genes, drugs in the bloodstream, and overall health. Newborns have three sets of reflexes that aid survival.

- *Reflexes that maintain oxygen supply*. The *breathing reflex* begins even before the umbilical cord, with its supply of oxygen, is cut. Additional reflexes that maintain oxygen are reflexive *hiccups* and *sneezes,* as well as *thrashing* (moving the arms and legs about) to escape something that covers the face.
- *Reflexes that maintain constant body temperature*. When infants are cold, they *cry, shiver,* and *tuck their legs* close to their bodies. When they are hot, they try to *push away* blankets and then stay still.
- *Reflexes that manage feeding*. The *sucking reflex* causes newborns to suck anything that touches their lips—fingers, toes, blankets, and rattles, as well as natural and artificial nipples of various textures and shapes. In the *rooting reflex,* babies turn their mouths toward anything that brushes against their cheeks—a reflexive search for a nipple—and start to suck. *Swallowing* also aids feeding, as does *crying* when the stomach is empty and *spitting up* when too much is swallowed quickly.

Brazelton Neonatal Behavioral Assessment Scale (NBAS) A test that is often administered to newborns which measures responsiveness and records 46 behaviors, including 20 reflexes.

reflex An unlearned, involuntary action or movement in response to a stimulus. A reflex occurs without conscious thought.

macmillan learning

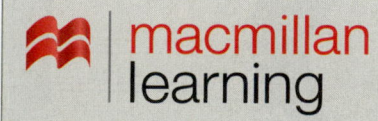

VIDEO: Newborn Reflexes shows several infants displaying the reflexes discussed in this section.

Other reflexes beyond these 13 promoted survival in ancient times but now only signify brain and body maturation. Among them are the:

- *Babinski reflex*. When a newborn's feet are stroked, the toes fan upward.
- *Stepping reflex*. When newborns are held upright, feet touching a flat surface, they move their legs as if to walk.
- *Swimming reflex*. When held horizontally on their stomachs, newborns stretch out their arms and legs.
- *Palmar grasping reflex*. When something touches newborns' palms, they grip it tightly.
- *Moro reflex*. When someone bangs on the table they are lying on, newborns fling their arms outward and then bring them together on their chests, crying with wide-open eyes.

These 18 reflexes (in italics) and more are evident in most newborns. The senses are also responsive. New babies listen more to voices than to traffic, for instance. Thus, in many ways newborns connect with the people of their family, who themselves are genetically predisposed to respond (Zeifman, 2013). If the baby tested on the Brazelton NBAS were your own, you would be proud and amazed.

New Mothers

postpartum depression A new mother's feelings of inadequacy and sadness in the days and weeks after giving birth.

When birth hormones decrease, between 8 and 15 percent of women experience **postpartum depression**, a sense of inadequacy and sadness (called *baby blues* in the mild version and *postpartum psychosis* in the most severe form). That 8 to 15 percent may be an underestimate: Some sources say that for low-SES and adolescent mothers the rate is 25 percent (Kozhimannil & Kim, 2014).

With postpartum depression, baby care (feeding, diapering, bathing) feels very burdensome. The newborn's cry may not compel the mother to carry and nurse her infant. Instead, the mother may have thoughts of neglect or abuse, thoughts so terrifying that she is afraid of herself. She may be overprotective, insisting that no one else care for the baby. This signifies a fearful mother, not a healthy one.

The first sign that something is amiss may be euphoria after birth. A new mother may be unable to sleep, stop talking, or eat normally. She may be overwhelmed with exaggerated or irrational worries.

After that initial high, severe depression may set in, with long-term impact on the child. Postpartum depression may not be evident right away; anxiety and depression symptoms are strongest two or three months after birth (Kozhimannil & Kim, 2014).

Postpartum depression is not due to hormonal changes alone. From a developmental perspective, some causes (such as financial stress) predate pregnancy. Others (such as marital problems) occur during pregnancy; still others correlate with birth itself (especially if the mother is alone and imagined a different birth than what actually occurred).

In addition, the baby may be disappointing. One single mother who experienced postpartum depression thought:

> My only problem in life was that I didn't have a baby. On the day I had a baby, I discovered that no, I had other problems. I hadn't any money, I was in debt, the family was fighting about the debt, it was partly my fault . . . and I started to see I wasn't such a good mother as I had thought I would be. I used to think what could be difficult? It's enough for you to love the baby and everything will be fine. This didn't happen because the baby didn't respond. I'm affectionate, I'd come and take her, hug her and the baby didn't like this. She didn't like to be hugged, she didn't like affection.
>
> *[O'Dougherty, 2013, p. 190]*

Marty Bucella/CartoonStock

"Of course I know what he wants when he cries. He wants you."

Successful breast-feeding mitigates maternal depression, but although most new mothers try to nurse their newborn, many quit—which increases depression. A supportive family member, friend, midwife, or lactation consultant allows the mother to recover—as most women with postpartum depression do by six months after the birth.

New Fathers

Not every depressed mother impedes her baby's development. If she manages to respond sensitively to her baby's needs, within a well-functioning, supportive family (with good emotional management, communication, and clear roles and routines), the baby develops well (Parade et al., 2018). Fathers may be crucial in keeping the family supportive and caring for the baby.

Fathers may experience pregnancy and birth biologically, not just psychologically. Many fathers gain weight and experience indigestion during pregnancy and feel pain during labor (Leavitt, 2009).

Paternal experiences of pregnancy and birth are called **couvade**, expected in some cultures, a normal variation in many, and considered pathological in others (M. Sloan, 2009). A study in India found that couvade was common (Ganapathy, 2014). In the United States, many fathers are intensely involved during prenatal development, birth, and infancy (Brennan et al., 2007; Raeburn, 2014).

Fathers are usually the first responders when the mother experiences postpartum depression; they may get the support that the mother and baby need. But fathers are vulnerable to depression, too, with the same stresses that mothers feel (Gutierrez-Galve et al., 2015). Indeed, sometimes the father experiences more emotional problems than the mother (Bradley & Slade, 2011). Friends and relatives need to help both parents in the first weeks after birth.

A study of fathers found that many men not only felt stressed but also felt ashamed and avoided talking about it.

One father acknowledged that he did not sleep well during pregnancy; several fathers worried intensely about the birth, their partner, and the baby; and yet many men felt they had no right to complain. One said, "I'm always conscious that my wife has it a lot worse." Another said at the birth, "I felt a bit more like a spare part, but then again they were very good with [partner]. I just felt in the way."

Several men found relief at work, where they could put the stress of fatherhood behind them or talk about their feelings with other men. A man who is part of a group of engineers said,

> "we probably spend half the day talking about babies and kids and that sort of thing. . . . I know that there's guys there that have had similar experiences and they know what it's like. They know how I'm feeling if I say Oh, we've had a rough night. . . . Some people have had worse experiences so you think, oh, what we're going through is normal."
>
> *(quoted in Darwin et al., 2017).*

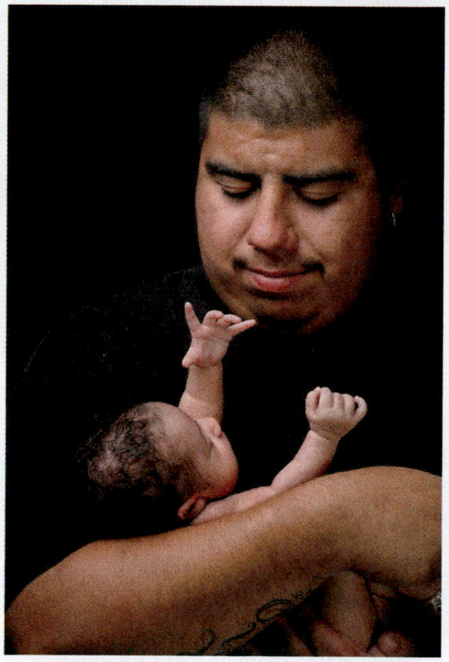

Nathan Allred/Alamy Stock Photo

Mutual Joy For thousands of years, hormones and instincts have propelled fathers and babies to reach out to each other, developing lifelong connections.

Especially for Nurses in Obstetrics Can the father be of any practical help in the birth process? (see response, page 111)

couvade Symptoms of pregnancy and birth experienced by fathers.

Family Bonding

To what extent are the first hours after birth crucial for the **parent–infant bond**, the strong, loving connection that forms as parents hold, examine, and feed their newborn? It has been claimed that this bond develops when a mother touches her newborn, just as sheep and goats must immediately smell and nuzzle their newborns if they are to nurture them (Klaus & Kennell, 1976).

parent–infant bond The strong, loving connection that forms as parents hold, examine, and feed their newborn.

However, the hypothesis that early skin-to-skin contact is *essential* for human nurturance is false (Eyer, 1992; Lamb, 1982). Substantial research on monkeys begins with *cross-fostering,* when newborns are removed from their biological

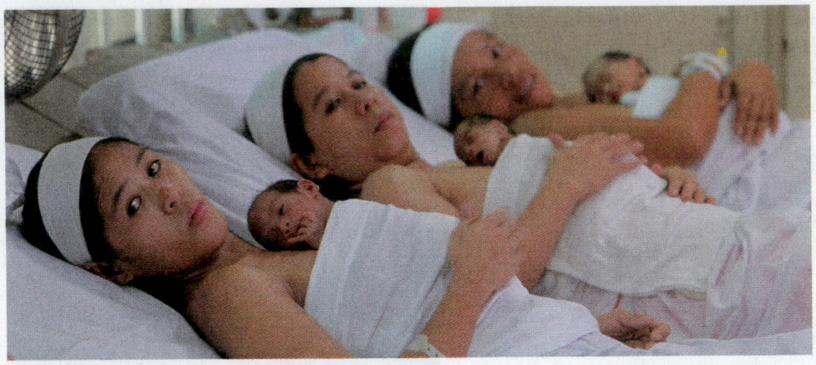

ROLEX DELA PENA/European Pressphoto Agency/MANILA/Philippines/Newscom

Better Care Kangaroo care benefits mothers, babies, and hospitals, saving space and medical costs in this ward in Manila. Kangaroo care is one reason Filipino infant mortality in 2010 was only one-fifth of what it was in 1950.

kangaroo care A form of newborn care in which mothers (and sometimes fathers) rest their babies on their naked chests, like kangaroo mothers that carry their immature newborns in a pouch on their abdomen.

mothers in the first days of life and raised by another monkey, female or male. A strong and beneficial relationship between the infant and the foster parent may develop (Suomi, 2002).

For people, bonding can begin before birth, or it may not arise until days after birth. Overall, the active involvement of both parents in pregnancy, birth, and care of the newborn benefits all three. Factors that encourage parents to nurture their newborns have lifelong benefits, proven with mice, monkeys, and humans (Champagne & Curley, 2010). Beneficial, but not essential.

The benefits of early contact are evident with **kangaroo care**, in which the newborn lies between the mother's breasts, skin-to-skin, listening to her heartbeat and feeling her body heat. A review of 124 studies confirms that kangaroo-care newborns sleep more deeply, gain weight more quickly, and spend more time alert than do infants with standard care, as well as being healthier overall (Boundy et al., 2016). Father involvement, including father–infant kangaroo care, also fosters newborn's health (Feeley et al., 2013).

As we will see in later chapters, the relationship between parent and child develops over decades, not merely hours. Birth is one step of a lifelong journey for every family member.

WHAT HAVE YOU LEARNED?

1. How can a newborn be socially interactive?
2. What causes postpartum depression?
3. How are fathers affected by birth?
4. Why is kangaroo care beneficial?
5. When does the parent–infant bond form?

SUMMARY

Prenatal Development

1. In the first two weeks of prenatal growth (the germinal period), the single-celled zygote multiplies into more than 100 cells that will eventually form both the placenta and the embryo. About half the time, the growing organism fails to implant in the uterus, ending pregnancy.

2. The embryonic period (the third week through the eighth week after conception) begins with the primitive streak, the beginning of the central nervous system. The future heart begins to pulsate, and eyes, ears, nose, mouth, and brain form. By the eighth week, the first traces of all of the basic organs and features are present.

3. Early in the fetal period (ninth week until birth), male and female organs form, and hormones start to shape the brain. At 22 weeks, the brain can regulate basic body functions, and viability is possible but unlikely. Babies born that early are at high risk of death or disability.

4. In the final three months, the average fetus gains approximately 4½ pounds (2,040 grams), weighing 7½ pounds (3,400 grams) at birth. Maturation of brain, lungs, and heart ensures survival of more than 99 percent of all full-term babies.

Birth

5. Ideally, hormones (oxytocin) start labor and birth approximately 38 weeks after conception. The Apgar scale provides a quick evaluation of the newborn's health.

6. Medical assistance speeds contractions, dulls pain, and saves lives. However, many interventions, including about half of cesarean sections, have been criticized as impersonal and unnecessary.

Problems and Solutions

7. Every birth complication, such as an unusually long and stressful labor that includes anoxia, has a combination of causes. Long-term handicaps are not inevitable.

8. Some teratogens cause physical impairment. Others, called behavioral teratogens, harm the brain and therefore impair cognitive abilities and affect personality.

9. Whether a teratogen harms an embryo or fetus depends on timing, dose, and genes. Family members affect the pregnant woman's health.

10. Low birthweight (under 5½ pounds, or 2,500 grams) may arise from early or multiple births, placental problems, maternal illness, malnutrition, smoking, drinking, illicit drug use, and age.

11. Underweight babies experience more medical difficulties and psychological problems for many years. Babies that are small for gestational age (SGA) are especially vulnerable.

The New Family

12. Newborns are primed for social interaction. The Brazelton Neonatal Behavioral Assessment Scale measures 46 newborn behaviors, 20 of which are reflexes.

13. Fathers can be supportive during pregnancy as well as helpful in birth. Paternal support correlates with shorter labor and fewer complications. Some fathers become very involved with the pregnancy and birth, experiencing couvade.

14. Many women feel unhappy, incompetent, or unwell after giving birth. Postpartum depression gradually disappears with appropriate help; fathers can be crucial in baby care, or they can experience depression themselves.

15. Kangaroo care benefits all babies, but especially those who are vulnerable. The parent–infant bond depends on many factors in addition to birth practices.

KEY TERMS

germinal period (p. 90)
embryonic period (p. 90)
fetal period (p. 90)
embryo (p. 90)
cephalocaudal (p. 91)
proximodistal (p. 91)
fetus (p. 91)
age of viability (p. 91)
doula (p. 94)
Apgar scale (p. 95)
cesarean section (p. 96)
cerebral palsy (p. 98)
anoxia (p. 98)
teratogen (p. 98)
behavioral teratogens (p. 100)
threshold effect (p. 101)
fetal alcohol syndrome (FAS) (p. 101)
false positive (p. 101)
low birthweight (LBW) (p. 103)
very low birthweight (VLBW) (p. 103)
extremely low birthweight (ELBW) (p. 103)
preterm (p. 103)
small for gestational age (SGA) (p. 104)
immigrant paradox (p. 104)
Brazelton Neonatal Behavioral Assessment Scale (NBAS) (p. 107)
reflex (p. 107)
postpartum depression (p. 108)
couvade (p. 109)
parent–infant bond (p. 109)
kangaroo care (p. 110)

APPLICATIONS

1. Go to a nearby greeting-card store and analyze the cards about pregnancy and birth. Do you see any cultural attitudes (e.g., variations depending on the sex of the newborn or of the parent)? If possible, compare those cards with cards from a store that caters to another economic or ethnic group.

2. Interview three mothers of varied backgrounds about their birth experiences. Make your interviews open-ended—let the mothers choose what to tell you, as long as they give at least a 10-minute description. Then compare and contrast the three accounts, noting especially any influences of culture, personality, circumstances, and cohort.

3. People sometimes wonder how any pregnant woman could jeopardize the health of her fetus. Consider your own health-related behavior in the past month—exercise, sleep, nutrition, drug use, medical and dental care, disease avoidance, and so on. Would you change your behavior if you were pregnant? Would it make a difference if you, your family, and your partner did not want a baby?

Especially For ANSWERS

Response for Conservatives and Liberals (from p. 96): Yes, some people are much more likely to want nature to take its course. However, personal experience often trumps political attitudes about birth and death; several of those who advocate hospital births are also in favor of spending one's final days at home.

Response for Judges and Juries (from p. 101): Some laws punish women who jeopardize the health of their fetuses, but a developmental view would consider the micro-, exo-, and macrosystems.

Response for Nurses in Obstetrics (from p. 109): Usually not, unless they are experienced, well taught, or have expert guidance. But their presence provides emotional support for the woman, which makes the birth process easier and healthier for mother and baby.

Observation Quiz ANSWERS

Answer to Observation Quiz (from p. 100): Brain. Legs.

Answer to Observation Quiz (from p. 106): Decreasing. The reason may be related to greater gender equity. Note, however, that the recession impacted fathers dramatically, as many wage-earners lost their jobs and did not immediately know how to get public or private help in feeding their families.

CAREER ALERT The Genetic Counselor

An understanding of life-span development is useful for every career. No matter what career a student considers, it is useful to consult career counselors and to check the Occupational Outlook Handbook from the U.S. Department of Labor, which lists prospects, salary, and qualifications. I reference some of that here.

Beyond those basics, however, the Career Alert features raise questions and issues from a developmental perspective, issues that might not be found in a standard description of the career. You will see this in this discussion of genetic counseling.

There is far greater demand for genetic counselors than there are people trained in this area, so job prospects are good. Salary is good, too: The median in 2017 was $77,500. Training requires a master's degree, and then passing an exam to be certified (not required in every state). That all seems simple, but the reality is much more challenging.

The first challenge is to understand and communicate difficult biological and statistical material, so that clients understand the implications of whatever genes they have. This is difficult: Not only are new discoveries made every day, but every disorder is polygenic and multifactorial, and mosaicism, methylation, and the microbiome are all relevant.

One reason this is a rapidly growing career is that many people are curious about their ancestry and pay for commercial tests (such as 23 and Me) to identify where their ancestors lived. In the process, they may discover confusing implications for their health, making genetic counseling essential (Smart et al., 2017).

Further, since is it now apparent that almost every disease is partly genetic, many people are concerned about their own health, the health of their family members, or the health of their prospective children, and they want answers. This is complex even when the issue is the genes of an adult, but it is doubly difficult when discussing a prospective child, who will inherit only half of the genes from each parent.

Facts, medical treatments, and quality of life for an affected child are difficult to explain, but even harder to understand are the prospective parents' emotions, assumptions, and values. People differ greatly in risk-taking, in culture, in religious beliefs, and in personal experiences. They also misunderstand results; counselors must draw charts, rephrase results, and repeat basic facts so that the message is understood.

Then couples may disagree with each other or decide something contrary to their counselor's clear conclusions. Thus, counselors must not only know facts and be able to explain odds and consequences, but they must also work with complex social dynamics, respecting everyone—no matter what they decide.

Theoretical decisions often conflict with reality. If a woman knows that her embryo has trisomy-21, should she terminate the pregnancy? About two-thirds of prospective parents say no, but about two-thirds of pregnant women at high risk (for example, over age 35) say yes, as do almost all (87 to 96 percent) women who know they are carrying an embryo with Down syndrome (Choi et al., 2012).

Similarly, variation was evident when 152 pregnant women in Wisconsin learned that their embryo had trisomy-13 or trisomy-18. Slightly more than half of the women decided to abort; most of the rest decided to give birth but provide only comfort care for the newborn. Three chose full intervention to preserve life (their three babies lived for a few days but died within the first weeks) (Winn et al., 2018).

Many factors—including children, religion, opinions of others—make a difference (Choi et al., 2012). Unfortunately, no matter what the decision, outsiders sometimes tell parents they made the wrong choice—something genetic counselors never do.

Before deciding on this profession, ask yourself what you would do in the following situations, each of which has occurred:

- Parents of a child with a disease caused by a recessive gene from both parents ask whether another baby will suffer the same condition. Tests reveal that the husband does not carry that gene. Should the counselor tell the parents that their next child won't have this disease because the husband is not the father of the first child?
- A woman learns that she is at high risk for breast cancer because she carries the BRAC1 gene. She wants to have her breasts removed, but she refuses to inform her four sisters, half of whom probably carry BRAC1.
- A couple both are little people, with genes for short stature. They want to know whether they might have a child of typical height. They plan to abort such a fetus.
- A person is tested for a genetic disease that runs in the family. The results are good (not a carrier) and bad (the person carries another serious condition). Should the counselor reveal a risk that the client did not ask about?

This fourth issue is new: Even a few years ago, the cost of testing precluded learning about unrequested results. But now genome-wide association study (GWAS) is routine, capturing the entire genome, so counselors learn about thousands of unsuspected conditions.

Even with careful counseling, people with identical genetic conditions often make opposite choices. For instance, 108 women who had one child with fragile X syndrome were told that another pregnancy would have a 50/50 chance of fragile X. Most decided to avoid pregnancy, but some (20 percent) deliberately conceived another child (Raspberry & Skinner, 2011).

In another study, pregnant women learned that their fetus had an extra sex chromosome. Half the women aborted; half did not (Suzumori et al., 2015). That highlights why this career is not for everyone. Professionals explain facts and probabilities; people decide. Can you live with that?

VISUALIZING DEVELOPMENT The Apgar

Just moments after birth, babies are administered their very first test. The APGAR score is an assessment tool used by doctors and nurses to determine whether a newborn requires any medical intervention. It tests five specific criteria of health, and the medical professional assigns a score of 0, 1, or 2 for each category. A perfect score of 10 is rare—most babies will show some minor deficits at the 1-minute mark, and many will still lose points at the 5-minute mark.

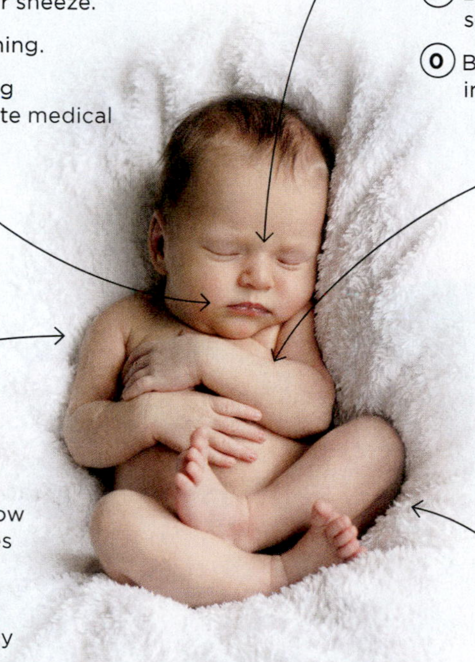

GRIMACE RESPONSE/REFLEXES

(2) A healthy baby will indicate his displeasure when his airways are suctioned—he or she will grimace, pull away, cough, or sneeze.

(1) Baby will grimace during suctioning.

(0) Baby shows no response to being suctioned and requires immediate medical attention.

RESPIRATION

(2) A good strong cry indicates a normal breathing rate.

(1) Baby has a weak cry or whimper, or slow/irregular breathing.

(0) Baby is not breathing and requires immediate medical intervention.

PULSE

(2) A pulse of 100 or more beats per minute is healthy for a newborn.

(1) Baby's pulse is less than 100 beats per minute.

(0) A baby with no heartbeat requires immediate medical attention.

APPEARANCE/COLOR

(2) Body and extremities should show good color, with pink undertones indicating good circulation.

(1) Baby has some blueness in the palms and soles of the feet. Many babies exhibit some blueness at both the 1- and 5-minute marks; most warm up soon after.

(0) A baby whose entire body is blue, grey, or very pale requires immediate medical intervention.

ACTIVITY AND MUSCLE TONE

(2) Baby exhibits active motion of arms, legs, and body.

(1) Baby shows some movement of arms and legs.

(0) A baby who is limp and motionless requires immediate medical attention.

REFLEXES IN INFANTS

Never underestimate the power of a reflex. For developmentalists, newborn reflexes are mechanisms for survival, indicators of brain maturation, and vestiges of evolutionary history. For parents, they are mostly delightful and sometimes amazing.

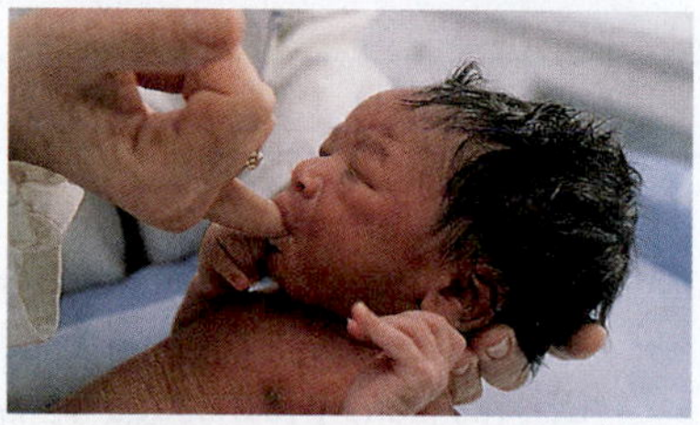

THE SUCKING REFLEX A newborn, just a few minutes old, demonstrates that he is ready to nurse by sucking on a doctor's finger.

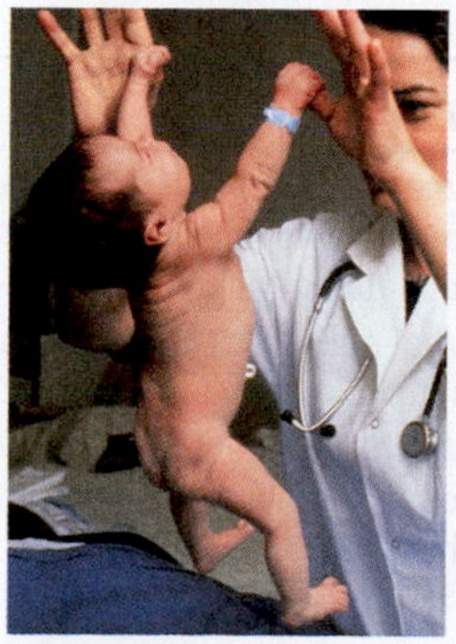

THE GRASPING REFLEX When the doctor places a finger on the palm of a healthy infant, he or she will grasp so tightly that the baby's legs can dangle in space.

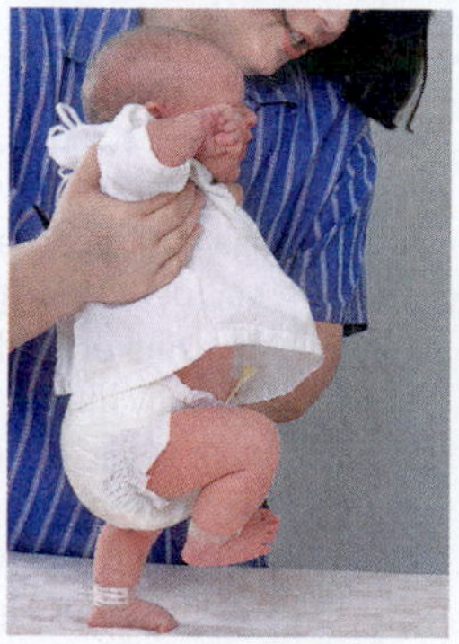

THE STEP REFLEX A 1-day-old girl steps eagerly forward on legs too tiny to support her body.

Sekundator/Shutterstock.com; Astier/BSIP/Science Source; Petit Format/Science Source; Jennie Woodcock; Reflections Photolibrary/Corbis Documentary/Getty Images

APPLICATION TO DEVELOPING LIVES PARENTING SIMULATION

BABIES AND TODDLERS

As you progress through the Babies and Toddlers simulation module, how you decide the following will impact the biosocial, cognitive, and psychosocial development of your child.

Biosocial

- Will you vaccinate your baby?
- Will you breast-feed your baby? If so, for how long?
- What kind of foods will you feed your baby during the first year?
- How will you encourage motor skill development?
- How do your baby's height and weight compare to national norms?

Cognitive

- What activities will you expose your baby to (music class, reading, educational videos)?
- What activities will you do to promote language development?
- Which of Piaget's stages of cognitive development is your child in?

Psychosocial

- How will you soothe your baby when he or she is crying?
- Can you identify your baby's temperament style?
- Can you identify your baby's attachment style?
- What kind of discipline will you use with your child?

PART II

The First Two Years

Adults don't change much in a year or two. They might have longer, grayer, or thinner hair; they might gain or lose weight; they might learn something new. But if you saw friends you hadn't seen for two years, you'd recognize them immediately.

Imagine caring for a newborn every day for a month. You would learn everything about that baby — how to diaper and bathe, when to play and rock, when, where, and how to put the baby to sleep. Then imagine you moved to a distant city for two years. When you returned and were asked to pick up the child at a day-care center, you would have to ask the teacher which child to take! And that toddler would hesitate to come with you.

In those two years, the child's weight would have quadrupled, height increased by a foot, and hair grew. The child would now understand words and photographs (ideally your photo had been shown often) and express new emotions — with new fears, including of you, now a stranger.

Two years are less than 3 percent of the average human life. However, in those 24 months, people reach half of their adult height; learn to run, climb, and talk in sentences; and express every emotion — not just joy and fear but also love, jealousy, and shame. Invisible growth of the brain is even more awesome. The next three chapters describe this transformation.

Left: twomeows/Moment/Getty Images
Right: Paul Thomas / EyeEm/Getty Images

CHAPTER

5

The First Two Years: Biosocial Development

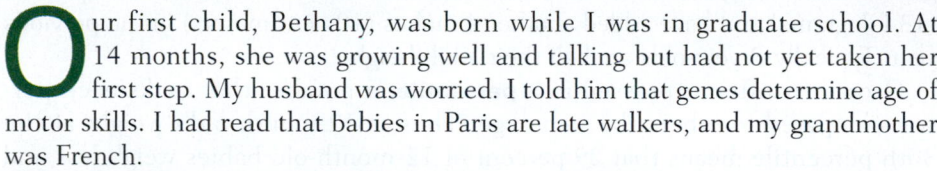

What Will You Know?

1. What part of an infant grows most in the first two years?
2. Are babies essentially blind and deaf at birth?
3. What happens if a baby does not get his or her vaccinations?

Our first child, Bethany, was born while I was in graduate school. At 14 months, she was growing well and talking but had not yet taken her first step. My husband was worried. I told him that genes determine age of motor skills. I had read that babies in Paris are late walkers, and my grandmother was French.

To my relief, Bethany soon took a few steps, and she was running by 18 months. By kindergarten, she was the fastest runner in her class; years later she ran a marathon. My genetic explanation was bolstered when our next two children, Rachel and Elissa, were also slow to walk. My students with Guatemalan and Ghanaian ancestors bragged about their infants who walked at 10 months; those from China had later walkers. Proof of genes?

Fourteen years after Bethany, Sarah was born. I could finally afford a full-time caregiver, Mrs. Todd. She thought Sarah was the most advanced baby she had ever known, except for her own daughter, Gillian.

"She'll be walking by a year," Mrs. Todd told me. "Gillian walked at 10 months."

"We'll see," I graciously replied.

I underestimated Mrs. Todd. She bounced my delighted baby on her lap, day after day, and spent hours giving her "walking practice." Sarah took her first step at 12 months—late for a Todd, early for a Berger, and a humbling lesson for me.

As a scientist, I know that a single case proves nothing. The two-month age gap between Bethany and Sarah might indeed be partly genetic, especially since Sarah shares only half her genes with Bethany and since my daughters are only one-eighth French (a fraction I had ignored when I needed reassurance about my late-walking first-born).

Nonetheless, every developmental scientist is now well aware that caregivers influence every aspect of growth. You will soon read about caregiving that enables babies to grow, move, see, and learn. Genes provide the scaffold, but every day shapes and guides each infant to become a distinct—and special—human being.

- **Body Changes**
  - Body Size
  - Sleep
  - OPPOSING PERSPECTIVES: Where Should Babies Sleep?
  - Brain Development
  - INSIDE THE BRAIN: Brains from Back to Front
  - Necessary and Possible Experiences
  - Harming the Body and Brain
- **Perceiving and Moving**
  - The Senses
  - A VIEW FROM SCIENCE: Addiction in Newborns
  - Motor Skills
  - Cultural Variations
- **Surviving and Thriving**
  - A CASE TO STUDY: Scientist at Work
  - Immunization
  - Nutrition
  - Malnutrition
- **VISUALIZING DEVELOPMENT: Immunization**

Left: Tetra Images - Jessica Peterson/Brand X Pictures/Getty Images
Top: Paul Thomas / EyeEm/Getty Images

macmillan learning

VIDEO: Physical Development in Infancy and Toddlerhood offers a quick review of the physical changes that occur during a child's first two years.

percentile A point on a ranking scale of 0 to 100. The 50th percentile is the midpoint; half of the people in the population being studied rank higher and half rank lower.

CHAPTER APP 5

Sprout Baby

RELATED TOPIC:
Physical development and well-being during infancy

IOS:
http://tinyurl.com/y33575ce

This app enables parents of infants to log growth spurts, periods of illness and medications, as well as sleeping routines, diaper changes, and feeding times. Informed by CDC and WHO data, the app also helps parents compare their baby's progress against that of the general population. Sprout Baby offers users extras like a photo and memory recording tool and advice and tip sheets on what kinds of development transpires during infancy and toddlerhood.

Body Changes

In infancy, growth is so rapid and the consequences of neglect so severe that gains are closely monitored. Medical checkups, including measurement of height, weight, and head circumference, indicate whether an infant is progressing as expected—or not.

Body Size

Newborns lose several ounces in the first three days and then gain an ounce a day for months. Their weight at birth has doubled by 4 months and tripled by a year, so a 7-pound newborn might be 21 pounds at 12 months (9,525 grams, up from 3,175 grams at birth).

That is an average, but variation is substantial, depending not only on genes and nutrition but also on birthweight. Small babies may double their weight in two months and quadruple by age 1.

Height also increases rapidly: A typical newborn grows 10 inches (25 centimeters) by age 1, measuring about 30 inches (76 centimeters). Physical growth then slows, but not by much. Most 24-month-olds weigh about 28 pounds (13 kilograms) and have added another 4 inches (10 centimeters) in the previous year. Typically, 2-year-olds are half their adult height.

Growth is often expressed in a **percentile,** a number that ranks each person compared to others the same age. Thus, a 12-month-old's weight at the 30th percentile means that 29 percent of 12-month-old babies weigh less and 70 percent weigh more.

Any percentile between 10 and 90 may be fine: The crucial factor is whether the percentile is close to the previous one for that individual (see **Figure 5.1**). Healthy big babies continue to be big for their age; healthy small babies continue to be small.

When an infant's weight percentile moves markedly up or down, or when the weight and height percentiles are far apart, that signifies trouble. A notable drop, say, from the 50th to the 20th percentile, suggests poor nutrition. A sudden increase—perhaps with weight increasing from the 30th to the 60th, especially if height stays at the 30th percentile—signifies overfeeding.

Parents were once blamed. Especially when the percentile dropped, it was thought that parents made feeding stressful, leading to *failure to thrive.* Now pediatricians consider it "outmoded" to blame parents, because failure to thrive may be caused by allergies, the microbiome, or diseases (Jaffe, 2011, p. 100). Similarly,

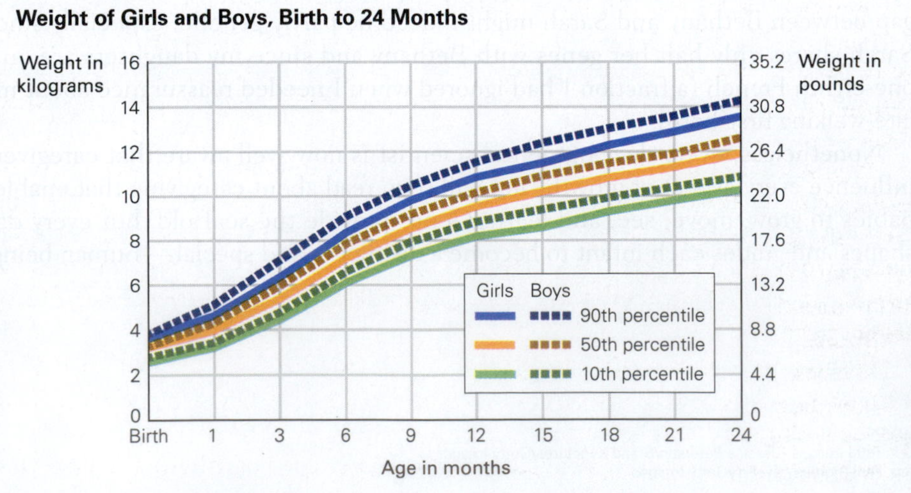

FIGURE 5.1
Averages and Individuals Norms and percentiles are useful—most 1-month-old girls who weigh 10 pounds should be at least 25 pounds by age 2. Obviously, individuals do not always follow the norms, which is not necessarily a problem.

babies are overweight because of the social context: Blaming parents alone is not fair, nor is blaming genes alone.

Sleep

Throughout life, health and growth correlate with regular and ample sleep (El-Sheikh & Kelly, 2017). As with many health habits, sleep patterns begin in the first year.

Newborns sleep about 15 to 17 hours a day. Every week brings a few more waking minutes. For the first two months, the norm for total time asleep is 14¼ hours; for the next three months, 13¼ hours; for the next 12 months, 12¾ hours. Preterm and breast-fed infants wake up often, sometimes needing another meal soon after the previous one (called *cluster feeding*).

Remember that norms are averages; about 5 percent of babies sleep 19 hours a day and another 5 percent sleep 9 hours or less, according to parent reports (Sadeh et al., 2009). National averages vary as well. Two-year-olds in New Zealand sleep two hours more each day than those in Japan (13 1/3 hours compared to 11 2/3) (Sadeh et al., 2010).

"Sleeping through the night" is sought by every exhausted parent, but when this occurs depends not only on the baby but on the parent's definition of "night." If night is from midnight to 5 A.M., many babies occasionally sleep "all night" at 3 months. But if night is from 8 P.M. to 6 A.M., almost no infant sleeps through the night (C. Russell et al., 2013).

Over the first few months, the time spent in each stage of sleep changes. Preterm newborns seem to be frequently dozing, never in deep sleep, but that may be caused partially by the constant bright lights and frequent feedings in the traditional NICU (neonatal intensive care unit). When they come home, they usually adjust to a day–night schedule (Bueno & Menna-Barreto, 2016).

About half of the sleep of full-term newborns is **REM (rapid eye movement) sleep,** with flickering eyelids and rapid brain waves. That indicates dreaming, now thought to consolidate memories. REM sleep declines over the early weeks, as does "transitional sleep," the half-awake stage. At 3 or 4 months, quiet sleep (also called *slow-wave sleep*) increases markedly.

Sleep varies not only because of biology (maturation and genes) but also because of culture and caregivers. Infants who are fed formula and cereal sleep longer and more soundly—easier for parents but not better for the baby.

Where the baby sleeps varies markedly by culture. **Bed-sharing** (in the parents' bed) or **co-sleeping** (in the parents' room) is the norm in some places but rare in others (Esposito et al., 2015).

Feeding patterns are also influential. Bed-sharing is more common in breast-fed babies. A study in Sweden found that most breast-fed preterm infants (who need feeding every two or three hours) sleep with their mothers—especially if the mother had trouble getting back to sleep if she got up to feed her infant (Blomqvist et al., 2017).

The brain patterns of newborns do not allow long stretches of deep sleep. Some infants develop longer sleep patterns within a few months, but some do not—and that affects the entire family (Piteo et al., 2013). This could be a cause or a consequence. Mothers' sleep patterns correlate with those of partners and children, so everyone's sleep is disturbed if the baby keeps waking up the mother (El-Sheikh & Kelly, 2017).

Parents "are rarely well-prepared for the degree of sleep disruption a newborn infant engenders." As a result, many become "desperate" and institute patterns that they may later regret (C. Russell et al., 2013, p. 68). But what patterns are best? Experts, strangers, and relatives give conflicting advice (see Opposing Perspectives).

Adey Bryant/Cartoonstock

Danger Here Not with the infant (although those pillows should be removed), but for the family. It is hard to maintain a happy marriage if the parents are exhausted.

REM (rapid eye movement) sleep A stage of sleep characterized by flickering eyes behind closed lids, dreaming, and rapid brain waves.

bed-sharing When two or more people sleep in the same bed.

co-sleeping A custom in which parents and their children (usually infants) sleep together in the same room.

Especially for New Parents You are aware of cultural differences in sleeping practices, which raises a very practical issue: Should your newborn sleep in bed with you? (see response, page 140)

OPPOSING PERSPECTIVES

Where Should Babies Sleep?

In Asia, Africa, and Latin America, infants usually sleep beside their mothers. By contrast, most U.S. infants sleep in cribs in their own rooms.

Each culture criticizes other patterns. In developing nations, separating mother and child at night may be considered abusive; in Western nations, some psychiatrists feared that children would be traumatized if they woke when their parents had sex. Many North American pediatricians note that sudden infant death (SIDS) is more common among bed-sharing babies.

A 19-nation study found that Asian and African mothers worry about separation, whereas mothers with European roots worry more about privacy. In the extremes of that study, 82 percent of Vietnamese babies slept with their mothers, as did only 6 percent in New Zealand (Mindell et al., 2010) (see **Figure 5.2**). Sleeping alone may encourage independence for both child and adult—a quality valued in some cultures, discouraged in others.

Sleeping patterns are changing in the United States. Since 2000, co-sleeping has been recommended by North Americans who advocate *attachment parenting* (Sears & Sears, 2001).

Many companies sell "co-sleepers" that allow babies to sleep beside their mothers without the SIDS risk posed by a soft mattress or blankets. Bed-sharing itself (not just co-sleeping) is becoming more popular in the United States: The rate doubled from 1993 to 2010 (6.5 percent to 13.5 percent) (Colson et al., 2013).

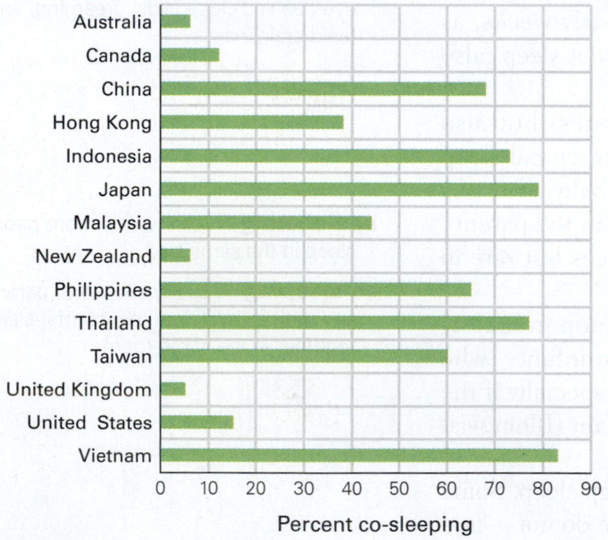

Data from Mindell et al., 2010.

FIGURE 5.2

Awake at Night Why the disparity between Asian and non-Asian rates of co-sleeping? It may be that Western parents use a variety of gadgets and objects—monitors, night-lights, pacifiers, cuddle cloths, sound machines—to accomplish some of what Asian parents do by having their infant next to them.

Many experts seek to safeguard infants who sleep with their parents (Ball & Volpe, 2013). Their advice includes *never* sleeping beside a baby if the parent has been drinking alcohol or taking psychoactive drugs, and *never* using a soft comforter, pillow, or mattress near a sleeping infant. Beyond that, much depends on the family. One issue is how co-sleeping affects the mother's sleep.

If co-sleeping continues for months and years, that might disrupt the relationship between the parents, which affects the entire family. One study found that when infants and mothers sleep in the same room, the mothers do not sleep as well. They wake up more often during the night, not only to feed the baby but also when the baby is simply stirring for a few moments (Volkovich et al., 2015).

The typical pattern in the United States in the twenty-first century is for infants to sleep in the parents' bedroom at first but have their own room by 6 months. One study found that when babies continued to sleep with their mothers, the mothers were more often depressed and unhappy with the father's lack of involvement in child care (Teti et al., 2015).

According to these authors, in cultures where co-sleeping is the norm, the practice does not affect the parental relationship. However, even in Japan bed-sharing and marital strain often occur together. One Japanese mother wrote:

> I take care of my baby at night, since my husband would never wake up until morning whatever happens. Babies, who cannot turn over yet, are at risk of suffocation and SIDS because they would not be able to remove a blanket by themselves if it covers over their face. In my case, I sleep with my older child and baby. By the way, my husband sleeps in a separate room because of his bad snoring.
>
> [*Shimizu et al., 2014*]

Contrary to this woman's rationalization, *sudden infant death syndrome* (or *SIDS*, discussed later) is twice as likely when babies sleep beside their parents. Researchers pinpoint the reason: Many parents occasionally sleep beside their baby after drinking or taking drugs. Then bed-sharing can be fatal (P. Fleming et al., 2015).

As one review explained, "There are clear reasons . . . [for bed-sharing] . . . warmth, comfort, bonding, and cultural tradition, but there are also clear reasons against doing so, such as increased risk of sudden infant death syndrome" (Esposito et al., 2015).

As with many aspects of child care, deciding sleep location is complicated, cultural, and complex. Over time, sleep patterns of each family member affect the sleep of the others.

A good night's rest benefits everyone, so parents need to establish *sleep hygiene* (calming routines and regular schedules) (Bathory & Tomopoulos, 2017; El-Sheikh & Kelly, 2017). Exactly what that means is . . . opposing perspectives.

Brain Development

From two weeks after conception to two years after birth, the brain grows more rapidly than any other organ. If teething or a stuffed-up nose temporarily slows eating, body weight is affected but not brain weight, a phenomenon called **head-sparing.** That term expresses well what nature does—protecting the cells of the brain.

Those brain cells are called *neurons,* which are specialized cells that transmit messages, activating movement, senses, memories, and more. Neurons are found in every part of the body, but they are particularly numerous and significant in the brain. The adult human brain has about 86 billion neurons.

head-sparing A biological mechanism that protects the brain when malnutrition disrupts body growth. The brain is the last part of the body to be damaged by malnutrition.

Dendrites, Axons, and Synapses Messages from one neuron to another are transmitted via fibers that reach toward other neurons. Those fibers are either **dendrites,** which bring messages to the cell body, or **axons,** extending out to reach dendrites of other cells. Most neurons have one axon and several dendrites. Axons and dendrites do not touch; the tiny gap between them is a **synapse.**

At birth, the brain contains far more neurons than a person needs. By contrast, the newborn's brain has far fewer dendrites, axons, and synapses than the person will eventually have, and much less **myelin**—the whitish substance that coats the axons to speed transmission. Because of the new dendrites, axons, and myelin, the brain is twice as large at age 1 as its size at birth, and three times as large by age 2.

To be specific, an estimated fivefold increase in dendrites in the cortex occurs in the 24 months after birth, with about 100 trillion synapses present at age 2. According to one expert, "40,000 new synapses are formed every second in the infant's brain" (Schore & McIntosh, 2011, p. 502).

The rapid brain growth in infancy is one reason that head circumference is a measure of infant growth. Although thousands of dendrites and axons develop, the particular ones that grow depend on experience, an example of the plasticity described in Chapter 1. Plasticity is crucial, allowing evolution of our species and of every developing person: Human brains need to be flexible to adjust to whatever the context of their life might be.

dendrite A fiber that extends from a neuron and receives electrochemical impulses transmitted from other neurons via their axons.

axon A fiber that extends from a neuron and transmits electrochemical impulses from that neuron to the dendrites of other neurons.

synapse The intersection between the axon of one neuron and the dendrites of other neurons.

myelin The coating on axons that speeds transmission of signals from one neuron to another.

Hormones The brain produces many hormones, which are chemicals that pulse through the body affecting appetite, emotions, sleep, and many other aspects of development. During infancy, two hormones in a mother's bloodstream are known to be crucial: *cortisol* and *oxytocin* (Ludmer et al., 2018). These affect the quality of her caregiving, and that, in turn, affects hormones in the infant.

Research on **cortisol** is most definitive. Too much cortisol can disrupt thinking and brain development lifelong. If a mother is highly stressed, with high levels of cortisol during pregnancy and the first few months of an infant's life, her baby is likely to have high levels of cortisol during the first year (Jonas et al., 2018). Children who are mistreated in infancy are impaired in learning later on, partly because of a flood of cortisol affecting their developing brains.

The connection between cortisol in the mother and in the baby is most evident with breast-feeding mothers. The mother's cortisol is in her breast milk. Usually breast-feeding reduces stress in both mother and child, because touch and gaze reduce cortisol. But highly stressed breast-feeding mothers can increase cortisol. Generally, formula-fed infants experience higher cortisol from their own stress (Lester et al., 2018).

The crucial hormone for social bonding is **oxytocin.** Parents who are particularly nurturant with their babies have higher levels of oxytocin (Gordon et al., 2010; Vittner et al., 2018), and their babies respond in kind. It is proven that oxytocin increases the flow of breast milk and that breast-feeding increases oxytocin, so it is also likely that infants' oxytocin increases when they are breast-fed—although research in this area is just beginning.

cortisol The primary stress hormone; fluctuations in the body's cortisol level affect human emotions.

oxytocin The primary bonding hormone, evident lifelong but particularly high at birth and in lactation.

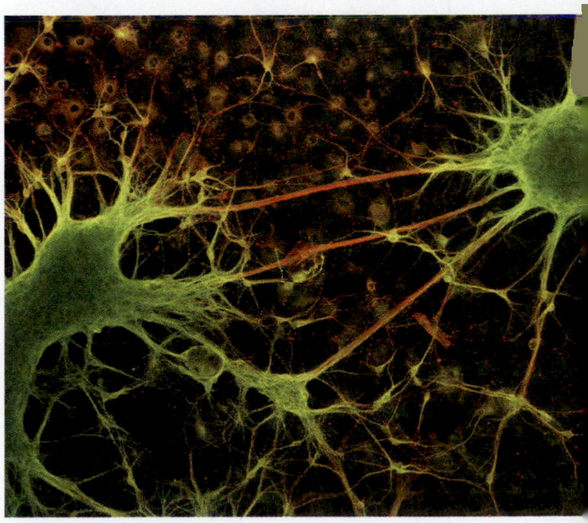

Francois Paquet-Durand/SPL/Science Source

Connecting The color staining on this photo makes it obvious that the two cell bodies of neurons (stained chartreuse) grow axons and dendrites to each other's neurons. This tangle is repeated thousands of times in every human brain. Throughout life, those fragile dendrites will grow or disappear as the person continues thinking.

INSIDE THE BRAIN

Brains from Back to Front

To further understand brain development over the life span, it helps to understand more about the parts of the brain. Every small area of the brain has a name and location (see **Figure 5.3**), and each connects to other areas. Scientists are often amazed at the specifics. For example, one particular area controls the thumb (Bauer et al., 2014).

Scientists are also amazed at the interconnections: A single thought or impulse activates several parts, with details that vary by age and culture. Like the rest of human development (Chapter 1), brains are multidirectional and multicultural.

The parts we now describe are not isolated parts. Mammal brains have several regions that develop in sequence: hindbrain (be*hind*, at the lower back of the head), cerebellum, midbrain, and forebrain (also called the *cerebrum,* the site of the cortex). Each specializes, but each also connects to all the other parts.

The *hindbrain* begins with the first structure to arise from that bulb at the top of the neural tube, at about five weeks after conception. The basics of life preservation—automatic breathing, sleeping, beating of the heart—are in the hindbrain.

Envisioning the brain from back to front, the next part is the *cerebellum,* a structure that refines basic movement. The cerebellum allows smoother coordination: People dance and draw, not just walk and scribble.

The role of the cerebellum is obvious when it is impaired: Alcohol is toxic to this part of the brain. This can be temporary, as when a drunk person cannot talk clearly or walk a straight line, or permanent, as in fetal alcohol syndrome, when a pregnant woman's drinking damages the cerebellum of her fetus.

Next to the cerebellum is the midbrain, which processes inputs from the hindbrain. The term *midbrain* suggests a large middle structure. That is accurate in some creatures, and in the human embryo. For the human fetus, baby, child, and adult, however, the midbrain is soon overwhelmed by the forebrain.

The forebrain becomes by far the biggest part, with 90 percent of the volume of the human brain. The forebrain includes the *cerebral cortex,* which covers the cerebrum with six layers of cells. This cortex is large, "comprising 80 percent of the human brain overall" (Kolb & Whishaw, 2013, p. 55).

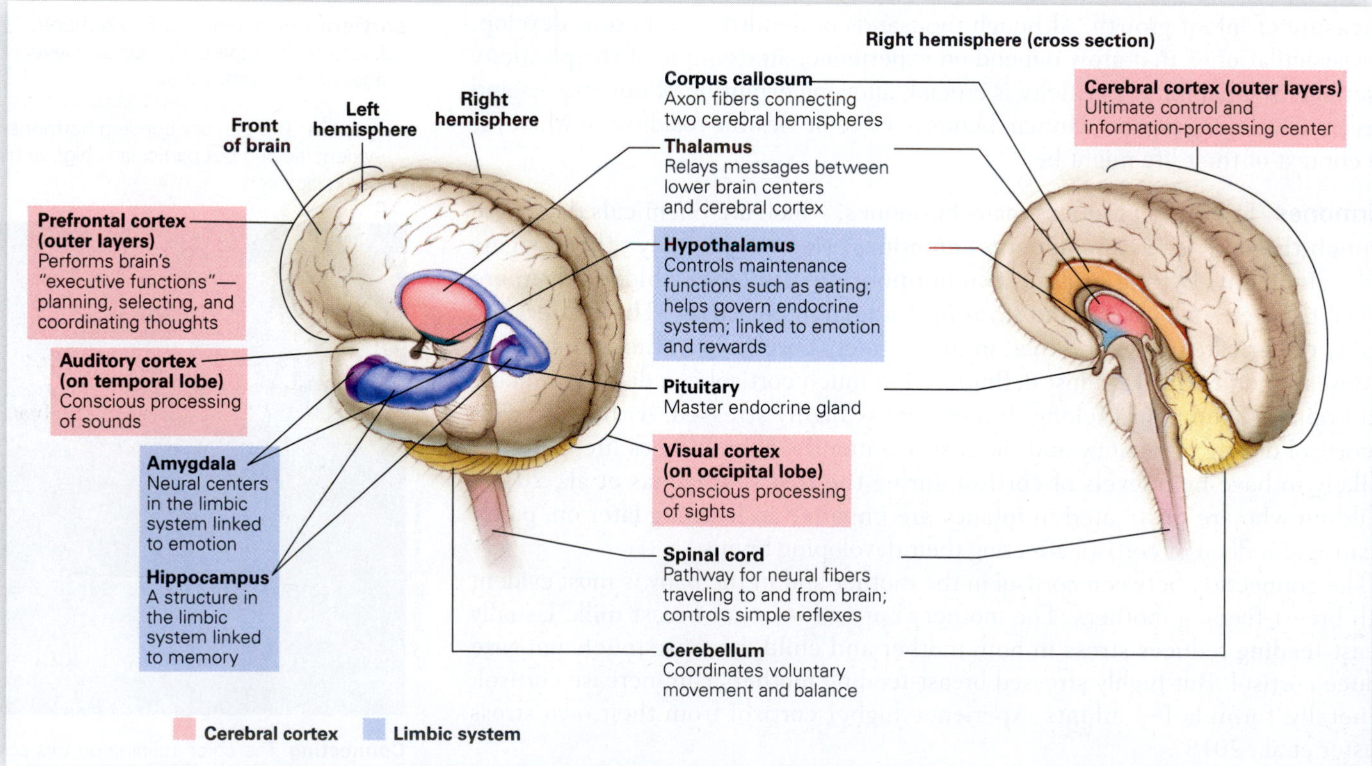

FIGURE 5.3

Connections A few of the hundreds of named parts of the brain are shown here. Although each area has particular functions, the entire brain is interconnected. The processing of emotions, for example, occurs primarily in the limbic system, where many brain areas are involved, including the amygdala, hippocampus, and hypothalamus.

Different parts of the cerebral cortex have different names. The *visual cortex* contains about 20 distinct parts that allow recognition of colors, shapes, motion, and so on; the *auditory cortex* interprets words, music, and other sounds; the *motor cortex* has areas for each body part, from the right pinky finger to the left foot and so on.

An area at the very front of the brain (right behind the forehead) is the *prefrontal cortex,* which specializes in anticipation, planning, reflection, and reasoning. This area is crucial for human development, but it is the last to reach maturity. It is virtually absent in infants (babies cannot decide whether, when, and how to cry, as adults do) and is not fully developed until about age 25 (which is why teenagers sometimes seem irrational). Within each of these parts (hindbrain, cerebellum, midbrain, cerebrum) are dozens of specific areas.

This book does not mention most of them, and some are explained in later chapters. However, three areas in one region merit mention now. That region is the *limbic system,* a cluster of brain areas deep in the brain where the cerebellum meets the midbrain, which is heavily involved in emotions.

The limbic system contains many parts. Three (amygdala, hippocampus, hypothalamus) are crucial for understanding human development, because their activity in infancy affects fear, depression, and anxiety lifelong (Ng et al., 2017; Qiu et al., 2015; Braun, 2011).

The *amygdala* is a tiny structure, about the same shape and size as an almond. It registers strong emotions. Frightening a baby is likely to increase amygdala size and activity, causing terrifying nightmares or sudden terrors later on.

Another structure in the emotional network is the *hippocampus,* located next to the amygdala. The size and structure of the hippocampus are markedly affected by cortisol in infancy (Dahmen et al., 2018). The hippocampus is a central processor of memory, especially memory for locations, and it affects the amygdala by summoning memory. Some places feel comforting (perhaps a mother's chest), and others evoke fear (perhaps a doctor's office).

Emotions that first emerged in infancy continue even when the experiences that originated those emotions are long gone. For instance, the touch of another person makes some adults cringe but is welcomed by those who enjoy being caressed and massaged. The cause may be an amygdala activated by the unconscious memories from the hippocampus.

Sometimes considered part of the limbic system is the *hypothalamus,* which responds to signals from the amygdala and to memories from the hippocampus by producing hormones, especially cortisol. Stress affects the hypothalamus, and vice versa.

The first months of life are crucial for every aspect of brain development, including how all these structures and parts connect to the other parts. Adult personality—how quickly a person becomes angry, for instance, or how readily amused they are—may be the result of brain connections and regions molded by early experiences.

The transmission of oxytocin occurs lifelong. People respond to the hormonal levels of oxytocin in their caregivers, a finding that extends from grandparent to parent to infant (Fujiwara et al., 2019). This is partly genetic, as well as a product of experience.

Exuberance and Pruning Early dendrite growth is called **transient exuberance:** *exuberant* because it is so rapid and *transient* because some of it is temporary.

transient exuberance The great but temporary increase in the number of dendrites that develop in an infant's brain during the first two years of life.

Thinking and learning require connections among many parts of the brain, and eliminating some unused neural connections makes the brain more efficient (Gao et al., 2017). Just as a gardener might prune a rose bush by cutting away some growth to enable more, or more beautiful, roses to bloom, inactive brain connections atrophy and die while new dendrites form.

As one expert explains it, there is an "exuberant overproduction of cells and connections followed by a several-year sculpting of pathways by massive elimination" (Insel, 2014, p. 1727). Notice the word *sculpting,* as if a gifted artist created an intricate sculpture from raw marble or wood. Human infants are gifted artists, developing their brains to adjust to whatever family, culture, or society they are born into.

For example, to understand any sentence in this text, you need to know the letters, the words, the surrounding sentences, the ideas they convey, and how they relate to your other thoughts and knowledge. Those connections are essential for your understanding, which is unlike that of other people whose brains developed in homes unlike yours.

Thus, your brain automatically interprets these Roman letters, and, for most of you, is befuddled when viewing Arabic, Cyrillic, or Chinese. You may not notice the differences between one Chinese word and another, but you immediately see that a "b" is not a "d," despite obvious similarities.

Further evidence of the benefit of cell death comes from a sad symptom of fragile X syndrome (described in Chapter 3), "a persistent failure of normal synapse pruning" (Irwin et al., 2002, p. 194). Without pruning, the dendrites of children with fragile X syndrome are too dense and long, making thinking difficult.

Similar problems occur for children with autism spectrum disorder: Their brains are unusually large and full, making communication between neurons less efficient and some sounds and sights overwhelming (Lewis et al., 2013).

Thus, pruning is essential. Normally, as brains mature, the process of extending and eliminating dendrites is exquisitely attuned to experience, as the appropriate links in the brain are established, protected, and strengthened (Gao et al., 2017). As with the rose bush, pruning needs to be done carefully, allowing further growth.

Necessary and Possible Experiences

A scientist named William Greenough identified two experience-related aspects of brain development (Greenough et al., 1987). Adults who understand these two avoid the difference-equals-deficit error explained in Chapter 1, while still providing the experiences every baby needs.

experience-expectant growth Brain functions that require certain basic common experiences (which an infant can be expected to have) in order to develop normally.

experience-dependent growth Brain functions that depend on particular, variable experiences and therefore may or may not develop in a particular infant.

- **Experience-expectant growth.** Certain functions require basic experiences in order to develop, just as a tree requires water. Those experiences are part of almost every infant's life, and thus, almost all human brains grow as their genes direct. Brains *expect* such experiences; development suffers without them.
- **Experience-dependent growth.** Human brains are quite plastic. Some brain connections are affected by specific experiences. These experiences are not essential: They happen in some families and cultures but not in others.

Aaron McCoy/Photolibrary/Getty Images

Face Lit Up, Brain Too Thanks to scientists at the University of Washington, this young boy enjoys the EEG of his brain activity. Such research has found that babies respond to language long before they speak. Experiences of all sorts connect neurons and grow dendrites.

Thus, basic expected experiences *must* happen for normal brain maturation to occur, and they almost always do. For example, in deserts and in the Arctic, on isolated farms and in crowded cities, babies have things to see, objects to manipulate, and people to love them.

Infants everywhere welcome such experiences: They look around, grab for objects, smile at people. As a result, their brains develop. Without expected experiences, brains wither.

In contrast, dependent experiences *might* happen; because of them, one brain differs from another. Babies' experiences vary in the languages they hear, the faces they see, the emotions their caregivers express, and, as you just read, where they sleep.

Depending on those particulars, infant brains are structured and connected one way or another; some neurons and dendrites grow and thrive while others die (Stiles & Jernigan, 2010). If you know someone who cannot sleep peacefully alone, you can wonder about their early life (when the hindbrain connected with the limbic system). Overall, all people are both similar (experience-expectant) and unique (experience-dependent).

One example comes from face recognition: All infants need to see faces (experience-expectant), and they all are attracted to face-like structures—a round form with eyes above a mouth. (Toy manufacturers know this very well.) But which particular facial feature they notice depends on whom they see (experience-dependent).

Harming the Body and Brain

Most infants develop well. Feeding and health care vary, but every family tries to ensure that their children survive in good health and thrive within their culture.

For brain development, it does not matter whether a person learns French or Farsi, or expresses emotions dramatically or subtly (e.g., throwing themselves to the floor or merely pursing their lips, a cultural difference). However, infant brains do not grow normally if they lack basic expected experiences.

Necessary Stimulation Some adults imagine that babies need quiet, perhaps in a room painted one neutral color. That is a mistake.

Babies need stimulation—sights and sounds, emotional expression, and social interaction that encourages movement (arm waving, then crawling, grabbing, and walking). Severe lack of stimulation stunts the brain: "Enrichment and deprivation studies provide powerful evidence of . . . widespread effects of experience on the complexity and function of the developing system" of the brain (Stiles & Jernigan, 2010, p. 345).

Proof came first from rodents! Some "deprived" rats (raised alone in small, barren cages) were compared with "enriched" rats (raised in large cages with toys and other rats). At autopsy, the brains of the enriched rats were larger, with more dendrites (Diamond, 1988; Greenough & Volkmar, 1973).

Subsequent research with other mammals confirms that isolation and sensory deprivation stunt development. That is now sadly evident in longitudinal studies of orphans from Romania, described in Chapter 7.

Especially for Parents of Grown Children Suppose you realize that you seldom talked to your children until they talked to you and that you often put them in cribs and playpens. Did you limit their brain growth and their sensory capacity? (see response, page 140)

Stress and the Brain Some infants experience the opposite problem, too much of the wrong kind of stimulation. Overstimulated infants—as when televisions are blaring and lights are blinking throughout the first year—may have trouble concentrating years later. That is the main symptom of ADHD (attention deficit/hyperactivity disorder) (Christakis et al., 2018).

Likewise, if the brain produces an overabundance of cortisol early in life (as when an infant is frequently terrified), that derails the connections from parts of the brain, causing atypical responses to stress lifelong. Years later, that child or adult may be hypervigilant (always on the alert) or emotionally flat (never happy or sad).

Note that infants respond to emotions, not directly to physical pain. Occasional pain—from routine inoculations, brief hunger, an unwanted bath or diaper change—are part of normal infant life. However, intense and frequent fear can lead to a harmful flood of cortisol (Propper & Holochwost, 2013).

Understanding this distinction is crucial for caregivers. All babies cry. As already noted, infants cannot *decide* to stop crying on command. In this case, adults with overactive limbic systems might yell at their babies (frightening the baby), or worse, shake them.

Because infants have immature brains, the whiplash from shaking ruptures blood vessels and breaks neural connections, causing **shaken baby syndrome,** an example of *abusive head trauma* (Christian & Block, 2009). Death is possible; intellectual impairment is likely.

shaken baby syndrome A life-threatening injury that occurs when an infant is forcefully shaken back and forth, a motion that ruptures blood vessels in the brain and breaks neural connections.

Not every infant who has neurological symptoms of head trauma is the victim of abuse: Legal experts worry about false accusations (Byard, 2014). Nonetheless, infants are vulnerable, so the response to a screaming, frustrating baby should be to comfort or walk away, never to shake, yell, or hit.

WHAT HAVE YOU LEARNED?

1. What facts indicate that infants grow rapidly in the first year?
2. Why are pediatricians not troubled when an infant is at the 20th percentile in height and weight, month after month?
3. How do sleep patterns change from birth to 18 months?
4. What are the arguments for and against bed-sharing?
5. How can pruning increase brain potential?
6. What is the difference between experience-expectant and experience-dependent growth?
7. What should caregivers remember about brain development when an infant cries?

sensation The response of a sensory organ (eyes, ears, skin, tongue, nose) when it detects a stimulus.

perception When the brain is conscious of a sensation or idea. Perception sometimes combines several senses and ideas: You might suddenly perceive that your mother is angry because of her face and voice and your past experience of her anger.

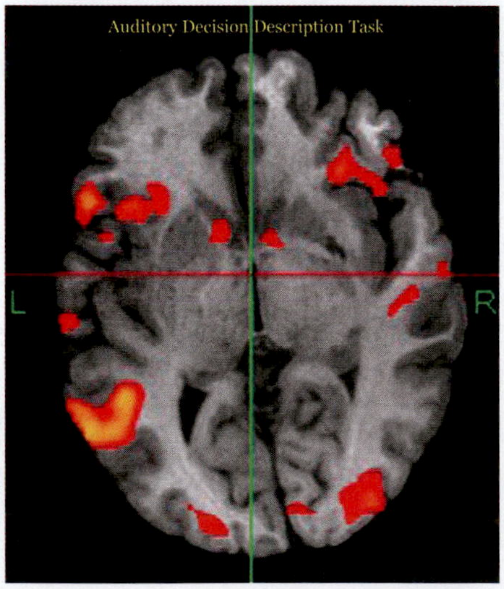

NEIL M. BORDEN/Science Source

Listen, Imagine, Think, and Tap A person has just heard "banana" and "round, red fruit," and is told to tap if the two do not match. An MRI reveals that 14 areas of the brain are activated. As you see, this simple matching task requires hearing (the large region on the temporal lobe), imagined seeing (the visual cortex in the occipital lobe at the bottom), motor action (the parietal lobe), and analysis (the prefrontal cortex at the top). Imagine how much more brain activation is required for the challenges of daily life.

Perceiving and Moving

Young human infants combine motor ineptness and sensory acuteness (Konner, 2010). Most mammals have the opposite combination. Kittens, for instance, are born deaf, with eyes sealed shut, but they can walk immediately. By contrast human senses are crucial from birth on, but skilled movement takes months and years.

Thus, newborns listen and look from day 1, and then they gradually master deliberate movement by practicing whatever they can do. The interaction between the senses and movement is continuous in the early months, with every sensation propelling the infant to attempt new motor skills. Here are the specifics.

The Senses

Sensation occurs when a sensory system detects a stimulus, as when the inner ear reverberates with sound, or the eye's retina and pupil intercept light. Thus, sensations begin when an outer organ (eye, ear, nose, tongue, or skin) meets anything that can be seen, heard, smelled, tasted, or touched.

Perception occurs when a sensation reaches the brain and the person is aware of it. For example, right this moment, if you stop to listen, you can hear sounds—perhaps voices in the hall, the hum of an air conditioner, a car on the street, your own stomach gurgling—that you did not notice before. You could sense them, but you did not perceive them.

All of the senses function at birth. Newborns have open eyes, sensitive ears, and responsive noses, tongues, and skin. Very young babies use all those senses to attend to everything, developing perceptions. For instance, in the first months of life, they smile at everyone, listen attentively to every voice, and suck almost anything. By two months, they are more selective.

Genes developed over a million years affect all of the senses. Humans cannot hear what mice hear, or see what bats see, or smell what puppies smell; humans do not need those sensory abilities. However, survival requires that human babies respond to people, and newborns innately do so with every sense they have (Konner, 2010; Zeifman, 2013).

Hearing Even before birth, fetal hearing responds to the social world: Loud sounds trigger reflexes, and voices make the fetus stop to listen—or at least slows down its movement and speeds up the heart rate—in the last trimester. Newborns recognize their mother's voice (Voegtline et al., 2013; Lee & Kisilevsky, 2014). They also respond to the father's voice if he often spoke to the fetus.

Newborn hearing is tested in every U.S. hospital, and, if necessary, remediation begins in the early weeks. Deaf babies are given hearing aids; parents of infants are taught to use signs. Some infants undergo surgery to get *cochlear implants,* which bypass damage to the structures of the ear via a microphone attached to the skull that converts sound waves into electrical impulses and transmits them to the auditory cortex. If this surgery occurs by age 1, the child's ability to understand and produce spoken language is not delayed (Tobey et al., 2013).

Since early hearing is so crucial, developmentalists worry about two problems with universal newborn hearing tests. Very few babies are profoundly deaf; most are able to hear some noises. But a positive result means a deficit: More testing is needed. However, parents and pediatricians must follow up. They understand deafness, but they may not realize the damage from impaired hearing (Nikolopoulos, 2015).

Second, sometimes infants are born with normal hearing, but ear infections harm later ability. That slows down language learning (Friedmann & Rusou, 2015). Ear infections are common, and painful, during infancy—one reason that good medical care is crucial.

Especially for Nurses and Pediatricians The parents of a 6-month-old have just been told that their child is deaf. They don't believe it because, as they tell you, the baby babbles as much as their other children did. What do you tell them? (see response, page 140)

Seeing Vision is probably the least mature sense at birth, but it develops rapidly. Many newborns seem "apparently blind" (Brodsky, 2016). The reason is limited experience; the fetus had nothing much to see. Newborns focus only on things quite close to their eyes, such as the face of their breast-feeding mother, and even that may be blurry.

Almost immediately, experience combines with maturation of the visual cortex to improve vision. By 2 months, infants not only stare at faces but also, with perception and the beginning of cognition, smile. (Smiling can occur earlier but not because of perception.)

binocular vision The ability to focus the two eyes in a coordinated manner in order to see one image.

Binocular vision (coordinating both eyes to see one image) cannot develop in the womb (nothing is far enough away), so many newborns use their two eyes independently, momentarily appearing wall-eyed or cross-eyed. Usually, experience allows both eyes to focus on a single thing between 2 and 4 months (Seemiller et al., 2018). However, if cataracts or other problems affect vision, remediation is needed in the first weeks so that the brain can correctly process what the eyes sense (Lambert & Lyons, 2016).

As perception builds, visual scanning improves. Thus, 3-month-olds look closely at the eyes and mouth, smiling more at happy faces than at angry or expressionless ones. They pay attention to patterns, colors, and motion—the mobile above the crib, for instance.

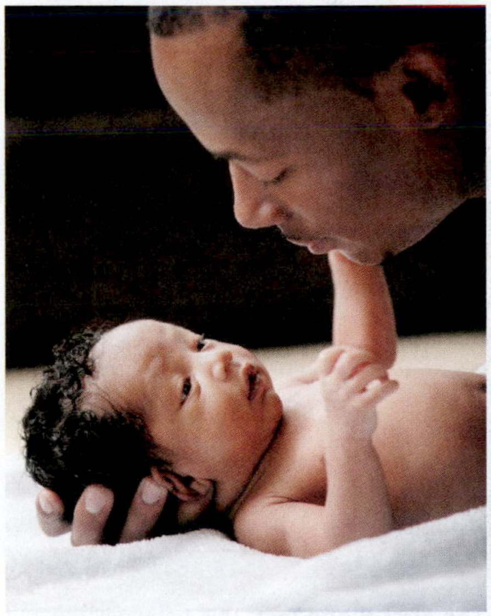

Blend Images - Mike Kemp/Brand X Pictures/Getty Images

Who's This? Newborns don't know much, but they look intensely at faces. Repeated sensations become perceptions, so in about six weeks this baby will smile at Dad, Mom, a stranger, the dog, and every other face. If this father in Utah responds like typical fathers everywhere, cognition will be apparent by 6 months: The baby will chortle with joy at seeing him but become wary of unfamiliar faces.

Because of this rapid development, babies should be allowed to see many sights. A crying baby might be distracted by being taken outside to watch passing cars. Infant vision is attracted to movement and to the eyes (more than the hair, for instance). By age 1, infants have learned to interpret facial expressions, to follow the eyes of someone else to see what they are looking at, and to use their own eyes to communicate (Grossman, 2017).

Tasting and Smelling As with vision and hearing, smell and taste also function at birth. Infants prefer the taste of their pregnant mothers' diet, spices and all, which they swallowed as amniotic fluid (part of preparing the lungs to function).

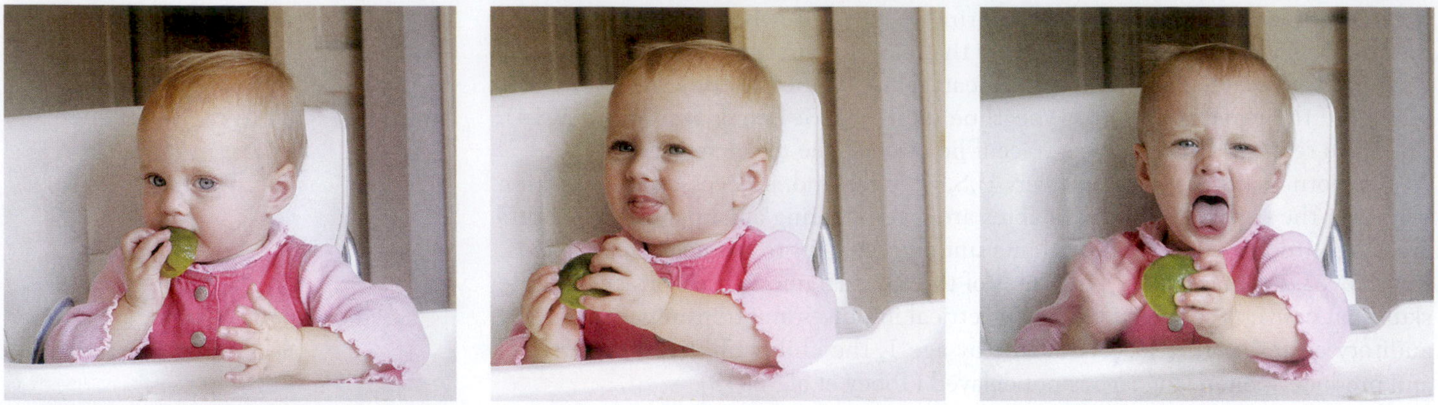

Cindy Charles/PhotoEdit

Learning About a Lime As with every other normal infant, Jacqueline's curiosity leads to taste and then to a slow reaction, from puzzlement to tongue-out disgust. Jacqueline's responses demonstrate that the sense of taste is acute in infancy and that quick brain perceptions are still to come.

Each culture's smells and tastes not only prepare infants to adjust to their families but also aid survival. For example, bitter foods provide some defense against malaria, hot spices help preserve food and may prevent food poisoning, some spices slow cancer, and so on (Kuete, 2017; Aggarwal & Yost, 2011; Prasad et al., 2012).

Notice plasticity again: Early experiences affect sensations, which become perceptions and then preferences. Taste sensations endure when a person leaves home. Immigrants buy expensive ingredients in specialty stores because a particular food was cheap and plentiful when they were children. Thousands of miles away, those foods are imported luxuries.

Early adaptation also occurs for the sense of smell. When breast-feeding mothers used a chamomile balm to ease cracked nipples, their babies preferred that smell two years later, in contrast to babies whose mothers used an odorless ointment (Delaunay-El Allam et al., 2010).

Because babies recognize each person's scent, they prefer to sleep next to their favorite caregivers, and they nuzzle into their caregivers' cheeks and chests—especially when the adults are shirtless. Parents help infants who are frightened of the bath (some love bathing; some hate it) by joining the baby in the tub: The smell of the adult's body mixes with the smell of soap and with the familiar touch, sight, and voice of the caregiver. The entire experience provides sensory comfort.

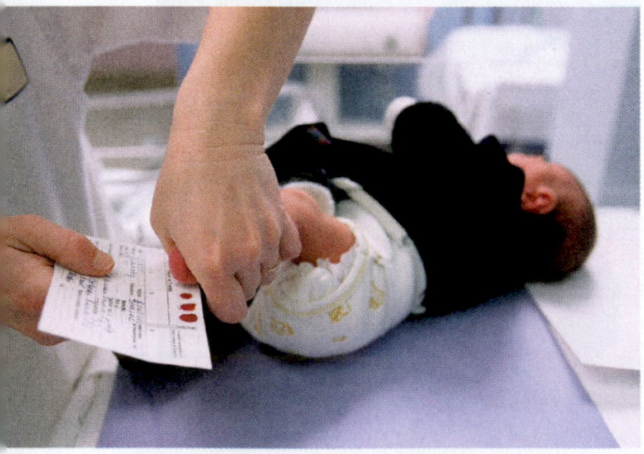

BSIP/Universal Images Group/Getty Images

The First Blood Test This baby will cry, but most experts believe the heel prick shown here is well worth it. The drops of blood will reveal the presence of any of several genetic diseases, including sickle-cell anemia, cystic fibrosis, and phenylketonuria. Early diagnosis allows early treatment, and the cries subside quickly with a drop of sugar water or a suck of breast milk.

Touch and Pain The senses of touch and pain are closely connected in infants. Touch may cause pain, and yet often it relieves pain. Wrapping, rubbing, massaging, and cradling are soothing. Even when their eyes are closed, some infants stop crying and visibly relax when held securely. In the first year of life, the heart rate slows and muscles relax when babies are stroked gently and rhythmically on their arms (Fairhurst et al., 2014).

Everywhere, parents cuddle their infants, rocking, carrying, and so on. Some touch (gentle of course) seems experience-expectant, essential for normal growth. Beyond that, how much a baby is touched is experience-dependent, varying by culture. In some regions of the world, daily massage begins soon after birth (Trivedi, 2015).

As with other senses, cultural traditions regarding touch are not always ideal. In rural India, mothers immediately bathe and massage their newborns. This may chill a fragile infant. Instead, public health workers now teach mothers to wipe their newborns gently and breast-feed immediately—preserving body heat and reducing death (Acharya et al., 2015).

By contrast, some mothers in Western nations do not caress their infants enough: They need to know that, in the first months of life, maternal touch pleases babies and increases joy in motherhood.

In theory, birth itself might be painful for the fetus, who is squeezed through the birth canal. One famous twentieth-century psychiatrist wrote about the trauma of being born (Rank, 1929). However, that idea is no longer popular.

Pain receptors are undeveloped early in life: Some experiences that adults find very painful (circumcision, setting a broken bone) seem much less so to newborns. Indeed, some twentieth-century doctors thought that newborns felt no pain (Rodkey & Riddell, 2013).

Experts now believe that infants feel some pain—as indicated by changes in cortisol, heartbeat, and brain waves—but that immature infant brains protect them against the intensity of pain that adults and older children feel (Moultrie et al., 2016). Especially in infancy, the other senses reduce pain: A drop of sugar water before a heel stick decreases crying and listening to their mother's voice, or even to calming music, reduces distress (Filippa et al., 2017).

It was once assumed that babies in a NICU were impervious to the intravenous lines, blood draws, alarms, lights, pokes, and so on. Now many NICUs have eliminated bright lights and noisy monitors, reduced distress through careful swaddling and positioning, and taught parents how to touch their fragile newborns (Wallace & Jones, 2017). That improves later social and cognitive development (Montirosso et al., 2017).

Because all of the senses mature rapidly over the first year, infants increasingly seem to feel pain over the first months of life. Some cry inconsolably for more than three hours, more than three days a week. Digestive pain (colic) caused by the gut microbiome is the usual explanation (Pärtty & Kalliomäki, 2017).

Pediatricians know that colic usually disappears by 3 months, so they are not troubled by it, but many parents are overwhelmed. Therefore, developmentalists take crying seriously; it may impair the relationship between infant and caregiver. That relationship—in which all of the senses are attuned to human caregiving—is the crucial aspect of early sensation and perception.

THINK CRITICALLY: What political controversy makes objective research on newborn pain difficult?

A VIEW FROM SCIENCE

Addiction in Newborns

In 2018, almost 200 people *per day* died of opioids in the United States, and thousands more are addicted. Some of them are pregnant women; four times as many newborns are born addicted now than a few years ago (Haight et al., 2018). If an addicted pregnant woman is weaned to methadone, that helps her quit heroin, fentanyl, and so on, which is better for her fetus. However, the newborn may still experience withdrawal, with convulsions and inconsolable crying.

Usually addicted newborns are treated in the NICU, where they are given morphine for withdrawal symptoms. Gradually, less morphine is needed, and the babies are sent home, morphine-free, 22 days (on average) after birth.

Doctors in one hospital decided to put addicted newborns, not in the NICU but in quiet, dimly lit, private rooms (Grossman et al., 2017). A caregiver (mother, father, partner, grandparent, or volunteer) was always with the infant, providing sensory care—cradling, singing, rocking. Ideally the mother breast-fed on demand.

The message to the family, conveyed in the last weeks of pregnancy, is that the most important medical treatment is human comfort. Nurses in this hospital were taught to appreciate the mother instead of condemning her addiction. Morphine was administered to the infant only if nothing else worked to mitigate the pain.

By focusing on sensory calming, much less morphine was needed. In this study, infants were able to leave the hospital, on average, after 6 days—compared to 22 days under the previous NICU and morphine treatment (Grossman et al., 2017).

Advancing and Advanced At 8 months, she is already an adept crawler, alternating hands and knees, intent on progress. She will probably be walking before a year.

motor skill The learned abilities to move some part of the body, in actions ranging from a large leap to a flicker of the eyelid. (The word *motor* here refers to movement of muscles.)

gross motor skills Physical abilities involving large body movements, such as walking and jumping. (The word *gross* here means "big.")

Motor Skills

The most dramatic **motor skill** (any movement ability) is independent walking, which explains why I worried when my 14-month-old daughter had not yet taken a step (as described in the introduction to this chapter). All basic motor skills, from the newborn's head-lifting to the toddler's stair-climbing, develop in infancy.

Responsive movement begins with reflexes, as explained in Chapter 4. Reflexes become skills if they are practiced and encouraged. As you saw in the chapter's beginning, Mrs. Todd set the foundation for my fourth child's walking when Sarah was only a few months old. Similarly, some very young babies can swim—if adults build on the swimming reflex by floating with them in calm, warm water.

Gross Motor Skills Deliberate actions that coordinate many parts of the body, producing large movements, are called **gross motor skills.** These skills emerge directly from reflexes and proceed in a *cephalocaudal* (head-down) and *proximodistal* (center-out) direction. Infants first control their heads, lifting them up to look around. Then they control their upper bodies, their arms, and finally their legs and feet. (See At About This Time, which shows age norms for gross motor skills.)

Each motor skill requires maturation and practice. For example, sitting requires muscles to steady the torso, no simple feat. By 3 months, most infants can sit propped up in a lap.

By 6 months, babies can usually sit unsupported, but "novice sitting and standing infants lose balance just from turning their heads or lifting their arms" (Adolph & Franchak, 2017). Babies never propped up (as in some institutions for orphaned children) sit much later, as do blind babies who cannot use vision to adjust their balance.

All humans move forward (inching, bear-walking, scooting, creeping, or crawling) before they walk, but many resist being placed on their stomachs. Another variation is that heavier babies master gross motor skills later than leaner ones because practice and balance are harder when the body is heavy.

As soon as they are able, babies stand and then take some independent steps, falling frequently at first, about 32 times per hour. They persevere because walking

Observation Quiz Which of these skills has the greatest variation in age of acquisition? Why? (see answer, page 140) →

AT ABOUT THIS TIME

Age Norms (in Months) for Gross Motor Skills

	When 50% of All Babies Master the Skill	When 90% of All Babies Master the Skill
Sit unsupported	6	7.5
Stands holding on	7.4	9.4
Crawls (creeps)	8	10
Stands not holding	10.8	13.4
Walking well	12.0	14.4
Walk backward	15	17
Run	18	20
Jump up	26	29

Note: As the text explains, age norms are affected by culture and cohort. The first five norms are based on babies from countries on five continents [Brazil, Ghana, Norway, United States, Oman, and India] (World Health Organization, 2006). The next three are from a U.S.-only source [Coovadia & Wittenberg, 2004; based on Denver II (Frankenburg et al., 1992)]. Mastering skills a few weeks earlier or later does not indicate health or intelligence. Being very late, however, is a cause for concern.

is much quicker than crawling, and it has other advantages — better sight lines and free hands (Adolph & Tamis-LeMonda, 2014).

Once toddlers can walk by themselves, they practice obsessively, barefoot or not, at home or in stores, on sidewalks or streets, on lawns or in mud. Some caregivers encourage practice, holding infants upright in the bath or after diapering. Indeed, "practice, not merely maturation, underlies improvements . . . in 1 hour of free play, the average toddler takes about 2400 steps, travels the length of about 8 U.S. football fields, and falls 17 times" (Adolph & Franchak, 2017).

That illustrates the drive that underlies every motor skill: Children are powerfully motivated to do whatever they can as soon as they can.

skynesher/E+/Getty Images

No Stopping Him Something compels infants to roll over, sit, stand, and walk as soon as their bodies allow it. This boy will fall often, despite his balancing arms, but he will get up and try again. Soon he will run and climb. What will his cautious mother (behind him) do then?

fine motor skills Physical abilities involving small body movements, especially of the hands and fingers, such as drawing and picking up a coin. (The word *fine* here means "small.")

Fine Motor Skills Small body movements are called **fine motor skills.** The most valued fine motor skills are finger movements, enabling humans to write, draw, type, tie, and so on. Movements of the tongue, jaw, lips, and toes are fine movements, too.

- Newborns have a strong reflexive grasp but lack control.
- During their first two months, babies excitedly stare and wave their arms at objects dangling within reach.
- By 3 months, they can usually touch such objects, but because of limited eye–hand coordination, they cannot yet grab and hold on unless an object is placed in their hands.
- By 4 months, infants sometimes grab, but their timing is off: They close their hands too early or too late.
- By 6 months, with a concentrated, deliberate stare, most babies can reach, grab, and hold on to almost any graspable object. Some can even transfer an object from one hand to the other.

Finger skills improve toward the end of the first year and throughout the second, as babies master the *pincer movement* (using thumb and forefinger to pick up tiny objects) and self-feeding (first with hands, then fingers, then utensils) (Ho, 2010). (See At About This Time.)

As with gross motor skills, fine motor skills are shaped by practice, which is relentless from the third month of prenatal development throughout childhood. Practice is especially obvious in the first year, when "infants flap their arms, rotate their hands, and wiggle their fingers, and exhibit bouts of rhythmical waving, rubbing, and banging while holding objects" (Adolph & Franchak, 2017).

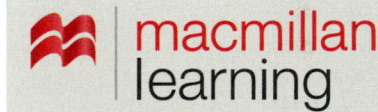

macmillan learning

VIDEO: Fine Motor Skills in Infancy and Toddlerhood shows the sequence in which babies and toddlers acquire fine motor skills.

Cultural Variations

Mastery of every motor skill depends, not only on maturation and practice, but also on culture and opportunity. For example, when given "sticky mittens" (with Velcro) that allow grabbing, infants master hand skills sooner than usual. Their perception advances as well (Reid et al., 2019).

Indeed, all senses and motor skills expand cognitive awareness, with practice advancing both skill and cognition (Libertus & Hauf, 2017). The importance of context is illustrated by follow-up studies on the "sticky mittens" experiments.

Some researchers have given 2-month-olds practice in reaching for toys without sticky mittens. The infants advanced as much as those

AT ABOUT THIS TIME

Age Norms (in Months) for Fine Motor Skills

	When 50% of All Babies Master the Skill	When 90% of All Babies Master the Skill
Grasps rattle when placed in hand	3	4
Reaches to hold an object	4.5	6
Thumb and finger grasp	8	10
Stacks two blocks	15	21
Imitates vertical line (drawing)	30	39

Data from World Health Organization, 2006.

Success At 6 months, this baby is finally able to grab her toes. From a developmental perspective, this achievement is as significant as walking, as it requires coordination of feet and fingers. Note her expression of determination and concentration.

with special mittens (Williams et al., 2015). It seems that practice of every motor skill advances development, not only of the skill but overall (Leonard & Hill, 2014).

In another example, when U.S. infants are grouped by ethnicity, African American babies generally are ahead of Hispanic American babies when it comes to walking. In turn, Hispanic American babies are ahead of those of European descent.

The reason may be cultural traditions that began with ancestors and continue when their descendants live in the United States. It is known that, internationally, the earliest walkers are in sub-Saharan Africa, where many well-nourished and healthy babies walk at 10 months.

How might culture affect this? In many African communities, babies are massaged and stretched from birth onward and are encouraged to walk as soon as possible (Adolph & Franchak, 2017). Some cultures encourage running over long distances: The fastest, strongest people are admired, likely to have many children. Selective adaptation, plus childhood practice, may explain why African runners are often the fastest in the world.

The latest walkers may be in Mongolia (15 months), where infants cannot practice because they are bundled up against the cold (Adolph & Robinson, 2013). The other reason some cultures discourage walking is that danger (poisonous snakes, open fires) is nearby, so toddlers are safer if they cannot wander.

Remember that difference is not deficit. Cultures differ, and hence babies differ. However, slow development *relative to local norms* may indicate a problem that needs attention; lags are much easier to remedy during infancy than later on.

Also remember dynamic systems: If one sense or motor skill is impaired, the other parts are affected as well. This is true throughout childhood: Fine motor skills are aided by the ability to sit; language development depends on hearing; reading depends on vision—so careful monitoring of basic sensory and motor skills in infancy is part of good infant care.

WHAT HAVE YOU LEARNED?

1. What particular sounds capture infant attention?
2. How does an infant's vision change over the first year?
3. Why is hearing more acute than vision in the early weeks?
4. Why do some babies prefer certain tastes and smells that others dislike?
5. What is known and unknown about infant pain?
6. What is universal and what is cultural in the development of motor skills?
7. What is the relationship between motor skills and the senses?
8. Why do caregivers vary in which motor skills they encourage?

Surviving and Thriving

None of this discussion of infant body size, senses, and motor skills would matter if babies did not thrive and grow. In North America, most people now take that for granted. However, more than a billion infants worldwide died in the past half-century.

sudden infant death syndrome (SIDS) A situation in which a seemingly healthy infant, usually between 2 and 6 months old, suddenly stops breathing and dies unexpectedly while asleep.

Regarding infant survival, life on this planet is improving. In 1950, one young child in seven died, but only about one child in thirty died in 2017 (United Nations, 2017). Some nations have improved dramatically. Chile's rate of infant mortality, for instance, was almost four times higher than the rate in the United States in 1970; now their rates are virtually identical.

As more children survive, parents focus more attention and resources on each child, and that reduces the birth rate. The average woman had five (4.96) births in 1950; she now has two or three (2.52) (United Nations, 2017).

Maternal education is a major reason for lower birth rates and better infant health. Educated women are more likely to plan their families, and they are aware of research on the benefits of breast-feeding, immunization, and other practices that protect health.

A dramatic example of the difference education can make is evident for **sudden infant death syndrome (SIDS),** called *crib death* in North America and *cot death* in England. Before about 1980, in all cities and villages, thousands of tiny infants smiled, waved their arms at rattles that small fingers could not yet grasp, went to sleep, and never woke up. That is much less common today, thanks to the work of one scientist who looked closely at cultural differences (see A Case to Study).

Louise Gubb/Corbis Historical/Getty Images

Well Protected Disease and early death are common in Ethiopia, where this photo was taken, but neither is likely for 2-year-old Salem. He is protected not only by the nutrition and antibodies in his mother's milk but also by the large blue net that surrounds them. Treated bed nets, like this one provided by the Carter Center and the Ethiopian Health Ministry, are often large enough for families to eat, read, as well as sleep in together, without fear of malaria-infected mosquitoes.

Immunization

Diseases that killed many infants (including measles, chicken pox, polio, mumps, rotavirus, and whooping cough) are now rare because of **immunization,** which primes the body's immune system to resist a particular disease. Immunization (often via *vaccination*) is said to have had "a greater impact on human mortality reduction and population growth than any other public health intervention besides clean water" (Baker, 2000, p. 199).

In the first half of the twentieth century, almost every child had measles and chicken pox; many had other childhood diseases. Usually they recovered, and then they were immune. That prevented the disease in adulthood when it was much more serious. Indeed, some parents took their toddlers to play with children who were sick with an infectious disease, hoping their child would catch it and become immune.

immunization A process that stimulates the body's immune system by causing production of antibodies to defend against attack by a particular contagious disease. Creation of antibodies may be accomplished either naturally (by having the disease), by injection, by drops that are swallowed, or by a nasal spray.

A CASE TO STUDY

Scientist at Work

Susan Beal studied medicine, married, and beginning at age 30, bore five children. At age 40, she began to study SIDS.

She was often phoned at dawn and told that another baby had died. Her husband became the sole caregiver while Beal drove to interview the families (eventually 500 of them) who just lost their baby. Parents were grateful. Some blamed themselves and each other; Beal reassured them that no one knew why SIDS occurred.

Thousands of scientists were testing hypotheses (the cat? the quilt? natural honey? homicide? spoiled milk?) to no avail. They found correlations (winter, formula feeding, baby aged 2–6 months) but no explanations. Beal learned additional factors that mattered (parental cigarette-smoking) and others that did not (birth order).

During those years, many Australians were anti-immigrant, but Beal put prejudice aside. That allowed her to notice that among the Australian infants with Chinese immigrant parents or grandparents, almost none died of SIDS. She observed that, contrary to usual Australian practice or the recommendation of pediatricians in every developed nation, Chinese parents put their babies to sleep on their backs, not their stomachs.

Beal convinced a large group of non-Chinese parents to put their babies to sleep on their backs. Almost no back-sleeping babies died.

Beal published her findings in the *Medical Journal of Australia* (Beal, 1988). Two scientists in the Netherlands read the article and then recommended back-sleeping (Engelberts & de Jonge, 1990). Many new mothers followed that advice. SIDS was reduced in the Netherlands by 40 percent in a year — a stunning replication.

Worldwide, putting babies "Back to Sleep" has now cut the SIDS rate dramatically (Mitchell & Krous, 2015). According to the Centers for Disease Control and Prevention (the official body that tracks health throughout the United States), the SIDS death rate is less than a third of what it was (38 per 100,000 live births in 2016 compared to 130 in 1990) (see **Figure 5.4**). In the United States alone, at least 100,000 children and young adults are alive who would be dead if they had been born before 1990.

Although SIDS is much less common than it was, some U.S. parents still put newborns to sleep on their stomachs, partly because of past tradition. Education matters as well. SIDS rates are much higher among low-SES families than high-SES ones, and rates are five times higher among African American babies than among Asian American ones. (Babies of European descent are midway between those two.)

macmillan learning

Interview with Susan Beal
https://tinyurl.com/y2a5n7wq

Sleeping position is not the only risk. Other risks are low birthweight, exposure to cigarette smoke, soft pillows, bed-sharing, and abnormalities in the brain stem, heart, or microbiome (Neary & Breckenridge, 2013; Hauck & Tanabe, 2017).

Most SIDS victims experience several risks, a cascade of biological and social circumstances. But thanks to cross-cultural research and one perceptive woman, the major risk — stomach-sleeping — need not occur.

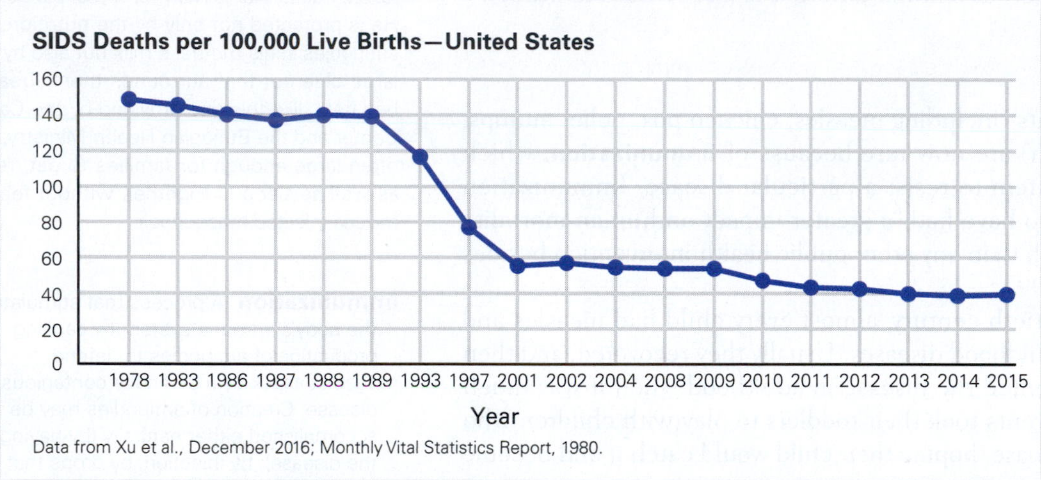

FIGURE 5.4

Alive Today As more parents learn that a baby should be on his or her "back to sleep," the SIDS rate continues to decrease. Other factors are also responsible for the decline—for example, fewer parents smoke cigarettes in the baby's room.

Scott Eels/Redux

True Dedication This young Buddhist monk lives in a remote region of Nepal, where until recently measles was a common, fatal disease. Fortunately, a UNICEF porter carried the vaccine over mountain trails for two days so that this boy—and his whole community—could be immunized.

Success and Survival Beginning with smallpox in the nineteenth century, doctors discovered that giving a small dose of a virus to healthy people stimulates antibodies and provides protection. By 1980, smallpox, the most lethal disease for children in the past, disappeared; vaccination against smallpox is no longer needed.

Other diseases that every child once contracted are now rare. Only 784 cases of polio were reported anywhere in the world in 2003, and, since 2000, 21 million children who would have died of complications of measles are alive—all because of increases in global vaccination rates (Dabbagh et al., 2018).

Unfortunately, two problems are apparent: war and ignorance. Civil war in Nigeria, combined with false rumors, halted immunization of young children. Polio reappeared, sickening almost 2,000 West Africans in 2005. Over the next several years, public health workers and community leaders rallied. Nigeria's polio rate fell again, to six cases in 2014.

However, in 2014, more than 300 children in Pakistan and Afghanistan were diagnosed with polio. A rush to immunize led to fewer cases in 2015, but until no cases are reported worldwide for several years (as with smallpox), no nation can afford to relax for polio or any other disease (Martinez et al., 2017).

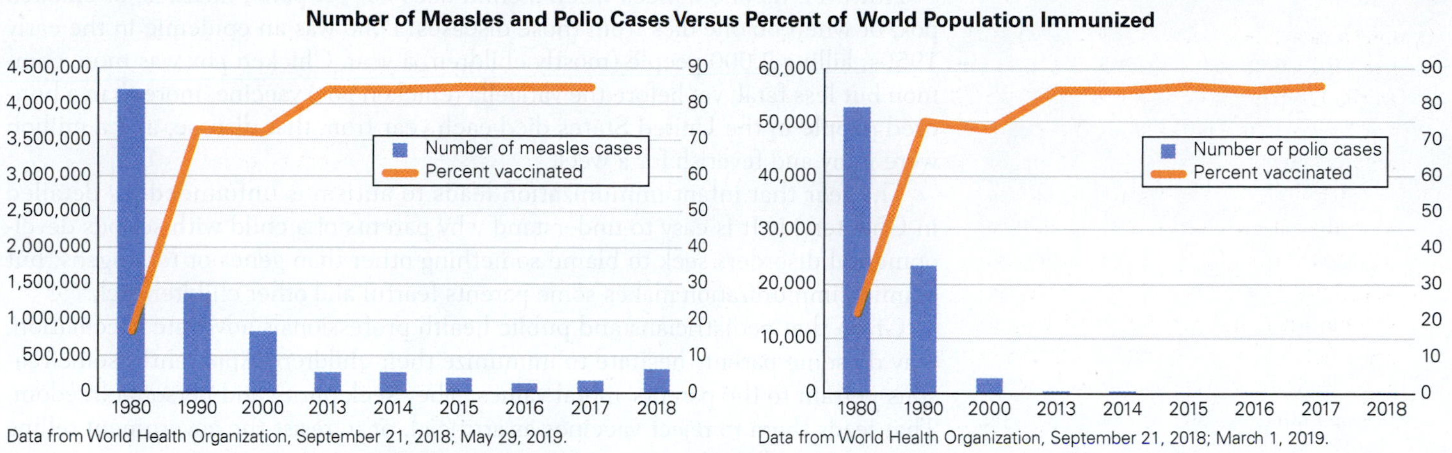

FIGURE 5.5

Ask Grandma Neither polio nor measles is completely eradicated, because some parents do not realize the danger. They may never have seen the serious complications of these diseases.

Another troubling example is measles. Once almost every child contracted that virus, but rates fell dramatically with infant immunization (the MMR—measles, mumps, and rubella), But recently, measles has increased in many nations of Europe and the Middle East because vaccination rates have fallen (Dabbagh et al., 2018) (see **Figure 5.5**).

This problem is evident in the United States as well. In the spring of 2017, an outbreak of measles in Minnesota put 20 people (mostly infants) in the hospital and led to emergency immunization of thousands (Hall et al., 2017). In 2018, a measles outbreak appeared in New York City, with 92 cases—mostly among Orthodox Jewish children who, for religious and cultural reasons, have low rates of immunization. A thousand more were affected in 2019.

Worldwide, the data show that 8 percent more infants were immunized in the past decade, but variations are evident by region, and about 14 percent of all infants still do not get the basic protection (VanderEnde et al., 2018).

Immunization protects not only from temporary sickness but also from complications, including deafness, blindness, sterility, and meningitis. Sometimes such damage is not apparent until decades later. Having a virus (e.g., mumps, measles, or chicken pox) in childhood doubles the risk of schizophrenia in adulthood (Khandaker et al., 2012). If a young boy contracts mumps, the result can be infertility in adulthood.

Immunization also protects those who cannot be safely vaccinated, such as infants under 3 months and people with impaired immune systems (HIV-positive, aged, or undergoing chemotherapy). Fortunately, each vaccinated child stops transmission of the disease, a phenomenon called *herd immunity.* Usually, if 90 percent of the people in a community (a herd) are immunized, no one dies of that disease.

Everywhere, some children are not vaccinated for valid medical reasons, but Minnesota is one of the 20 states that allow a child to be unvaccinated because a parent has a "personal belief." When rates of immunized children fall below herd immunity, outbreaks harm infants.

Many parents are concerned about the potential side effects of vaccines, in part because of the media attention when an individual is sickened by vaccination. Humans tend to overestimate the frequency of a memorable case, and thus they avoid immunization.

Especially for Nurses and Pediatricians A mother refuses to have her baby immunized because she wants to prevent side effects. She wants your signature for a religious exemption, which in some jurisdictions allows the mother to refuse vaccination. What should you do? (see response, page 140)

However, no one notices when a child does *not* get polio, measles, or chicken pox, or when no one dies from those diseases. Polio was an epidemic in the early 1950s, killing 2,000 people (mostly children) a year. Chicken pox was more common but less fatal, yet before the varicella (chicken pox) vaccine, more than a hundred people in the United States died each year from that disease, and a million were itchy and feverish for a week.

The fear that infant immunization leads to autism is unfounded, as detailed in Chapter 11. It is easy to understand why parents of a child with serious developmental disorders seek to blame something other than genes or teratogens, but blaming immunization makes some parents fearful and other children sick.

Given that pediatricians and public health professionals advocate vaccination, why do some parents hesitate to immunize their children? Apparently, some reasons pertain to the parents' moral values: They seek purity and personal freedom. That leads them to reject vaccines as artificial, or to resist the government telling them what to do.

Instead of fighting against parental values, public health workers might frame the message to respect such values. For instance, "Boost your child's natural defenses. Keep your child free of infection." "Take personal control over your child's health" (Amin et al., 2017).

Nutrition

As already explained, infant mortality worldwide has plummeted for several reasons: fewer sudden infant deaths, advances in prenatal and newborn care, clean water, and, as you just read, immunization. One more measure is making a huge difference: better nutrition.

Breast Milk The best defense against malnutrition is the one humans have relied on for a million years or more: breast milk. The World Health Organization now recommends *exclusive* (no formula, juice, cereal, or water) breast-feeding for the first six months of life.

That recommendation is based on extensive research from all nations of the world. The specific fats and sugars in breast milk make it more digestible and better for the brain than any substitute (Drover et al., 2009; Wambach & Riordan, 2014).

Ideally, nutrition starts with *colostrum,* a thick, high-calorie fluid secreted by the mother's breasts at birth. This benefit is not understood in some cultures, where mothers are forbidden to breast-feed until their milk "comes in" two or three days after birth. (Sometimes other women nurse the newborn; sometimes herbal tea is given.) This is one time when culture is harmful: Colostrum saves infant lives, especially if the infant is preterm (Moles et al., 2015; Andreas et al., 2015).

Breast-feeding mothers should be well nourished and hydrated; then their bodies will make the perfect food for their babies. Formula is preferable only in unusual cases, such as when the mother is HIV-positive or uses toxic or addictive drugs.

Even with HIV, however, exclusive breast-feeding may be best. In some

Same Situation, Far Apart: Breast-Feeding Breast-feeding is universal. None of us would exist if our fore-mothers had not successfully breast-fed their babies for millennia. Currently, breast-feeding is practiced worldwide, but it is no longer the only way to feed infants, and each culture has particular practices.

SelectStock/Vetta/Getty Images

hadynyah/Vetta/E+/Getty Images

TABLE 5.1

The Benefits of Breast-Feeding

For the Baby	For the Mother
Balance of nutrition (fat, protein, etc.) adjusts to age of baby	Easier bonding with baby
Breast milk has micronutrients not found in formula	Reduced risk of breast cancer and osteoporosis
Less infant illness, including allergies, ear infections, stomach upsets	Natural contraception (with exclusive breast-feeding, for several months)
Better childhood vision	Pleasure of breast stimulation
Less adult illness, including diabetes, cancer, heart disease	Satisfaction of meeting infant's basic need
Protection against many childhood diseases, since breast milk contains antibodies from the mother	No formula to prepare; no sterilization
Stronger jaws, fewer cavities, advanced breathing reflexes (less SIDS)	Easier travel with the baby
Higher IQ, less likely to drop out of school, more likely to attend college	**For the Family**
Later puberty, fewer teenage pregnancies	Increased survival of other children (because of spacing of births)
Less likely to become obese or hypertensive by age 12	Increased family income (because formula and medical care are expensive)
	Less stress on father, especially at night

Information from Victora et al., 2016; Horta et al., 2018; Wambach & Riordan, 2014.

nations, infants' risk of catching HIV from their infected mothers is lower than the risk of dying from infections, diarrhea, or malnutrition as a result of bottle-feeding (A. Williams et al., 2016).

In China, a study of more than a thousand babies in eight cities compared three groups of babies: those exclusively breast-fed (by their own mothers or wet nurses), those fed no breast milk, and those fed a combination of foods, formula, and breast milk. Based on all of the data, the researchers suggest that the WHO recommendation for exclusive breast-feeding for the first six months "should be reinforced in China" (Ma et al., 2014, p. 290).

The more research is done, the better breast milk seems (see **Table 5.1**). For instance, the composition of breast milk adjusts to the age of the baby, with milk for premature babies distinct from that for older infants. Quantity increases to meet the demand: Twins and even triplets can be exclusively breast-fed for months.

Each generation of scientists, and consequently each generation of mothers, knows more about breast milk. Indeed, the benefits of breast milk are recognized by doctors in every nation.

Fifty years ago in the United States, breast-feeding mothers were considered old-fashioned or ignorant. Now formula-feeding mothers are unfairly criticized. Some authors write about a prejudice called *lactivism*, the idea that every mother who loves her baby *must* breast-feed (Jung, 2015). Not so.

Malnutrition

Protein-calorie malnutrition occurs when a person does not consume enough food to sustain normal growth. This form of malnutrition affects roughly one-third of children in developing nations (World Health Organization, 2014).

protein-calorie malnutrition
A condition in which a person does not consume sufficient food of any kind. This deprivation can result in several illnesses, severe weight loss, and even death.

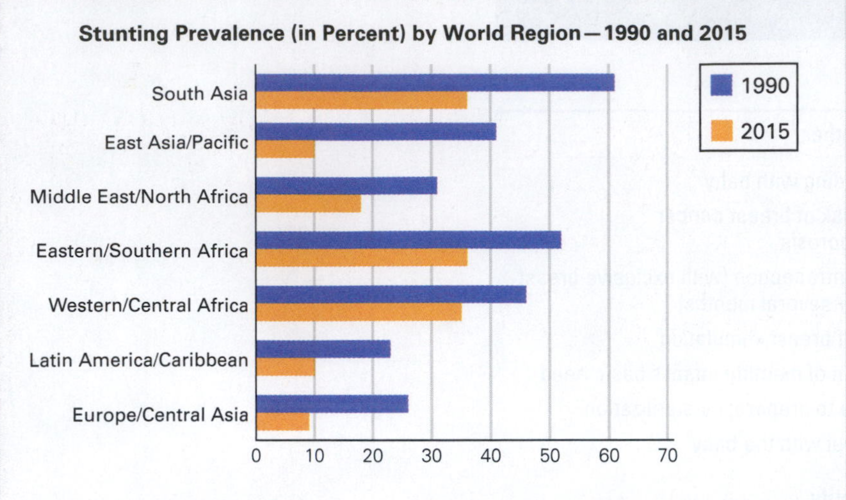

Data from UNICEF, January 13, 2017.

FIGURE 5.6

Evidence Matters Genes were thought to explain height differences among Asians and Scandinavians, until data on hunger and malnutrition proved otherwise. The result: starvation down and height up almost everywhere—especially in Asia. Despite increased world population, far fewer young children are stunted (255 million in 1970; 156 million in 2015). Evidence now finds additional problems: Civil war, climate change, and limited access to contraception have increased stunting in East and Central Africa, from 20 to 28 million in the past 50 years.

Observation Quiz Which regions have the most and least improvement since 1990? (see answer, page 140) ↑

stunting The failure of children to grow to a normal height for their age due to severe and chronic malnutrition.

wasting The tendency for children to be severely underweight for their age as a result of malnutrition.

Some diseases result directly from malnutrition. One is *marasmus,* which occurs during the first year, when body tissues waste away. Another is *kwashiorkor*, which occurs after age 1. In kwashiorkor, growth slows down, hair becomes thin, skin becomes splotchy, and the face, legs, and abdomen swell with fluid (edema).

Worldwide, about half of all childhood deaths occur because malnutrition makes a childhood disease lethal. This is true not just for the leading causes of childhood deaths (diarrhea and pneumonia), but also for milder diseases such as measles (Walker et al., 2013; Roberts, 2017).

If a malnourished child survives, growth may be affected. Some experience **stunting** (being short for their age), because chronic malnutrition kept them from growing. Severe stunting is 3 standard deviations from typical height. Among well-fed children, less than 1 percent are naturally that short, but in many nations, 35 percent are stunted.

Even worse is **wasting,** when children are severely underweight for their age and height (3 or more standard deviations below average). Many nations, especially in East Asia, Latin America, and central Europe, have seen improvement in child nutrition in the past decades, with an accompanying decrease in wasting and stunting (see **Figure 5.6**).

India is one such nation (Dasgupta et al., 2016). However, much more is necessary: Improvement means that in 2014, instead of most children in India being severely malnourished, only 17 percent of children were severely stunted, and 5 percent were severely wasted (UNICEF, 2015). Of course, that is still too many.

In other nations, primarily in Africa, wasting is increasing. In northern Nigeria, many people have fled from Boko Haram, a jihadist military organization. The children suffer from malnutrition, measles, and malaria, and this combination makes child deaths several times higher than emergency levels (Roberts, 2017).

Most adults who were severely malnourished as infants have lower IQs throughout life, even if they eat enough later on (Waber et al., 2014). Some of this is directly related to brain growth.

Some long-term effects of malnutrition in infancy are indirect. For instance, severely malnourished infants have less energy and reduced curiosity. As you have seen, young children naturally want to do whatever they can: A child with no energy is a child who is not learning. When they become adults, children who were malnourished tend to be cognitively impaired (Waber et al., 2018).

Prevention, more than treatment, is needed. Ideally, prenatal nutrition, then breast-feeding, and then supplemental iron and vitamin A, stop malnutrition before it starts.

Once malnutrition is apparent, highly nutritious formula (usually fortified peanut butter) often restores weight, and antibiotics can help. Unfortunately, some children hospitalized for marasmus or kwashiorkor die even with good medical care because their digestive systems are already failing (M. Smith et al., 2013; Gough et al., 2014).

macmillan learning

VIDEO: Nutritional Needs of Infants and Children: Breast-Feeding Promotion shows UNICEF's efforts to educate women on the benefits of breast-feeding.

That sad outcome is less common than it was. Indeed, this entire chapter can be seen as good news: Infants are more likely to live and learn in the twenty-first century than at any previous time.

Back to the opening anecdote: Babies have always been genetically primed to develop (see, hear, walk, talk, and so on), but we now have a better understanding of the impact of good caregiving. That is a reason to be thankful. My daughter Sarah makes me proud. Should I be grateful to Mrs. Todd for that?

WHAT HAVE YOU LEARNED?

1. What is the best protection against SIDS?
2. What are four reasons that immunization benefits a community?
3. What are the advantages of breast-feeding?
4. When should a woman not breast-feed?
5. Which is worse and why: stunting or wasting?

SUMMARY

Body Changes

1. In the first year, infants triple their birth weight, grow almost a foot, and increase in head circumference. These all indicate development and are measured by percentiles, which compare each baby to others the same age.

2. Sleep is crucial for good health lifelong. Infants gradually sleep less every day, but frequent waking is common. Whether a child sleeps beside their parents, or in the same room, or in their own room is a decision profoundly affected by culture.

3. Brains develop rapidly, increasing in size from about 25 percent to 75 percent of the adult brain's weight in the first two years. Brain growth of synapses, axons, and dendrites is dramatic in the early months. Two hormones, cortisol and oxytocin, can affect later development.

4. Some stimulation is experience-expectant, needed for normal brain development, and other events are experience-dependent, shaping the brain. Exuberant growth and extensive pruning aid cognition.

5. Experience is vital for brain development. An infant who is socially isolated, over-stressed, or deprived of stimulation may be impaired lifelong. Too much stimulation also damages the brain.

Perceiving and Moving

6. At birth, the senses already respond to stimuli. Prenatal experience makes hearing the most mature sense. Vision is the least mature, but it improves quickly, with binocular vision.

7. The senses of smell, taste, and touch are present at birth and help infants respond to their social world. Pain may be felt, with researchers seeking to understand how infant pain differs from pain later on.

8. Infants gradually improve their motor skills as they begin to grow, and brain maturation continues. Gross motor skills are soon evident, from rolling over to sitting up (at about 6 months), from standing to walking (at about 1 year), and from climbing to running (before age 2).

9. Fine motor skills also improve, as infants learn to grab, aim, and manipulate almost anything within reach. With all motor skills, infants are motivated to use their bodies as much as possible.

Surviving and Thriving

10. The first days and months of life were often fatal a century ago. Now cultural awareness has reduced SIDS by ensuring that babies sleep on their back, and immunization has eliminated smallpox and reduced the rate of many childhood diseases.

11. Public health workers are concerned that immunization rates are below herd immunity in some regions of the world and in some U.S. states. Epidemics of polio, measles, and other preventable diseases still occur.

12. Most babies are breast-fed at birth, with life-giving colostrum before the mother's milk "comes in." Many infants are breast-fed at 6 months, sometimes exclusively (as doctors recommend), providing protection against diseases and malnutrition.

13. Severe malnutrition can cause death, both directly and indirectly if a child catches measles, an intestinal virus, or some other illness. Both stunting and wasting are less common than they were a decade ago, but both still harm children in developing nations.

KEY TERMS

percentile (p. 118)
REM (rapid eye movement) sleep (p. 119)
bed-sharing (p. 119)
co-sleeping (p. 119)
head-sparing (p. 121)
dendrite (p. 121)
axon (p. 121)
synapse (p. 121)
myelin (p. 121)
cortisol (p. 121)
oxytocin (p. 121)
transient exuberance (p. 123)
experience-expectant growth (p. 124)
experience-dependent growth (p. 124)
shaken baby syndrome (p. 125)
sensation (p. 126)
perception (p. 126)
binocular vision (p. 127)
motor skill (p. 130)
gross motor skills (p. 130)
fine motor skills (p. 131)
sudden infant death syndrome (SIDS) (p. 133)
immunization (p. 133)
protein-calorie malnutrition (p. 137)
stunting (p. 138)
wasting (p. 138)

APPLICATIONS

1. Immunization regulations and practices vary, partly for social and political reasons. Ask at least two faculty or administrative staff members what immunizations the students at your college must have and why. If you hear "It's a law," ask why.

2. Observe three infants (whom you do not know) in public places such as a store, playground, or bus. Look closely at body size and motor skills, especially how much control each baby has over his or her legs and hands. From that, estimate the baby's age in months, and then ask the caregiver how old the infant is.

3. *This project can be done alone, but it is more informative if several students pool responses.* Ask 3 to 10 adults whether they were bottle-fed or breast-fed and, if breast-fed, for how long. If someone does not know, or expresses embarrassment, that itself is worth noting. Do you see any correlation between adult body size and infant feeding?

Especially For ANSWERS

Response for New Parents (from p. 119): From the psychological and cultural perspectives, babies can sleep anywhere as long as the parents can hear them if they cry. The main consideration is safety: Infants should not sleep on a mattress that is too soft, nor beside an adult who is drunk or on drugs. Otherwise, families should decide for themselves.

Response for Parents of Grown Children (from p. 125): Probably not. Brain development is programmed to occur for all infants, requiring only the stimulation that virtually all families provide—warmth, reassuring touch, overheard conversation, facial expressions, movement. Extras such as baby talk, music, exercise, mobiles, and massage may be beneficial but are not essential.

Response for Nurses and Pediatricians (from p. 127): Urge the parents to begin learning sign language and investigating the possibility of cochlear implants. Babbling has a biological basis and begins at a specified time in deaf as well as hearing babies. If their infant can hear, sign language does no harm. If the child is deaf, however, lack of communication may be destructive.

Response for Nurses and Pediatricians (from p. 135): It is difficult to convince people that their method of child rearing is wrong, although you should try. In this case, listen respectfully and then describe specific instances of serious illness or death from a childhood disease. Suggest that the mother ask her grandparents whether they knew anyone who had polio, tuberculosis, or tetanus (they probably did). If you cannot convince this mother, do not despair: Vaccination of 95 percent of toddlers helps protect the other 5 percent. If the mother has genuine religious reasons, talk to her clergy adviser.

Observation Quiz ANSWERS

Answer to Observation Quiz (from p. 130): Jumping up, with a three-month age range for acquisition. The reason is that the older an infant is, the more impact both nature and nurture have.

Answer to Observation Quiz (p. 138): Most is East Asia, primarily because China has prioritized public health. Least is Western and Central Africa, primarily because of civil wars. In some nations, high birth rates have dramatically increased the *numbers* of stunted children, even though *rates* in the region are lower.

VISUALIZING DEVELOPMENT Immunization

Before the measles vaccine was introduced in 1963, 30 million people globally contracted measles each year. About 2 million of them died, usually because they were both malnourished and sick. (World Health Organization, April 28, 2017). Thankfully, worldwide vaccination efforts now mean that no child need die of measles.

Measles is highly infectious, so 95 percent of the population needs to be immunized in order for "herd immunity" to protect the entire community. The United States achieved that: A decade ago, the measles incidence was close to zero. Experts thought measles would soon be eliminated in all developed countries, so public health workers focused on the very poorest nations.

ESTIMATED MEASLES VACCINE COVERAGE – SELECTED NATIONS

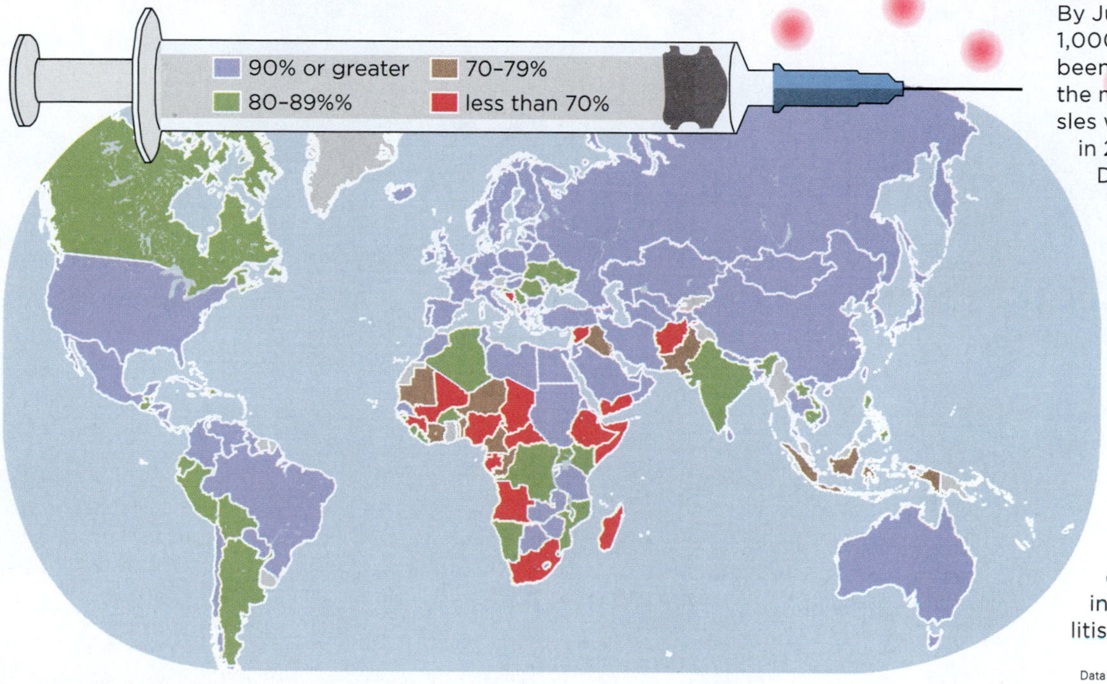

By June 2019, more than 1,000 measles cases had been reported in 28 states, the most since 1992 (measles was declared eliminated in 2000) (Centers for Disease Control and Prevention, June 17, 2019). To understand what went wrong, note that many states allow personal or religious exemptions to immunization requirements. Thus, as the U.S. map shows, several states are not at that safe 94 percent—leaving many vulnerable, not only to discomfort but also to complications, including pneumonia, encephalitis, and even death.

Data from World Health Organization, May 29, 2019.

MMR COVERAGE AND EXEMPTION RATES – UNITED STATES

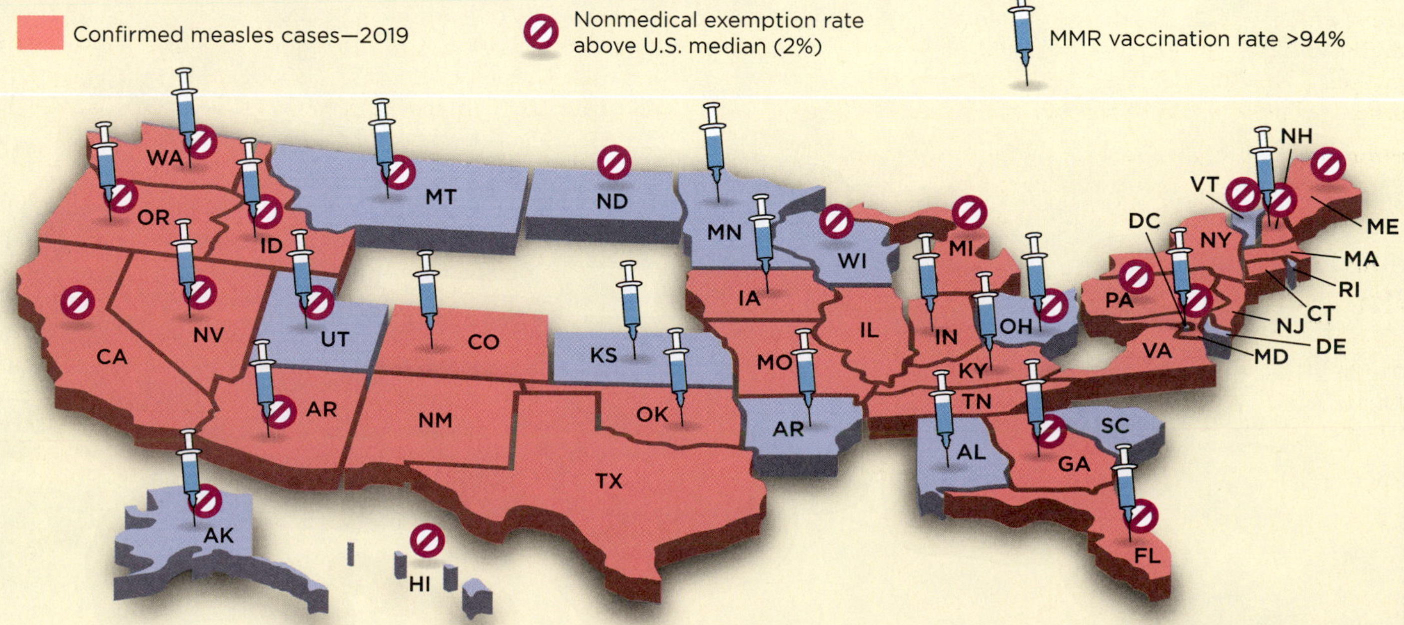

Data from Mellerson et al., 2018.

CHAPTER 6

The First Two Years: Cognitive Development

What Will You Know?

1. What will infants remember before they can talk?
2. Why did Piaget compare 1-year-olds to scientists?
3. When and how do infants learn to talk?

- **The Eager Mind**
  - Listening to Learn
  - Looking to Learn
  - Core Knowledge
  - A VIEW FROM SCIENCE: Face Recognition
  - Theories of the Infant Mind
  - Infant Memory
- **Piaget's Sensorimotor Intelligence**
  - Stages One and Two: Primary Circular Reactions
  - Stages Three and Four: Secondary Circular Reactions
  - OPPOSING PERSPECTIVES: Object Permanence
  - Stages Five and Six: Tertiary Circular Reactions
- **Language: What Develops in the First Two Years?**
  - The Universal Sequence
  - A CASE TO STUDY: Early Speech
  - The Naming Explosion
  - Theories of Language Learning
- **VISUALIZING DEVELOPMENT: Early Communication and Language Development**

A neuroscientist learned about a Korean fortune-telling ritual for 1-year-olds:

> The unsuspecting baby is placed in front of an assortment of objects and is encouraged to pick one. . . . If the baby picks up a banana, she will never go hungry; choosing a book means she is destined for academia; a silver coin foretells wealth, or a paintbrush, creativity.
>
> I was intrigued. That very same evening, I placed Livia in front of a collection of items: a stethoscope (would she become a doctor?), a stuffed dog (a vet?), a plant (a Greenpeace activist?), a piece of pastry (a chef?), and a colorful model of the brain (a neuroscientist?). Livia inspected the options closely, took her time, and then went straight for the iPhone I had happened to leave at the corner of the table.
>
> I shouldn't have been surprised. The little girl was obsessed with this piece of machinery. She would skillfully roll herself from one side of the room to the other to grab hold of it. . . . When she finally grabbed hold of the phone she would quickly insert it into her mouth and attempt to chew. . . .
>
> She had other bright, musical toys that she did not desire as much. The iPhone was the item she wanted because from the day she was born she had observed her parents constantly interacting with it with great interest. Although she was only a few months old, and could not even say a word she was able to infer that these metal rectangles must be extremely valuable. Little Livia's fondness for iPhones tells us something important about how our brains work.
>
> [*Sharot, 2017*, pp. 152–153]

This incident introduces the chapter on cognitive development during infancy for three reasons.

First, this topic is intriguing: We all wonder what thoughts, aspirations, and abilities the newest humans will have. We also hope they will choose our own professions, interests, and values.

Did you notice that the stethoscope meant doctor (not some other medical profession), that a plant signified Greenpeace (not farmer), and that a model of the brain was among the options (for the daughter of a neuroscientist)?

The second reason is to highlight that infants are curious and social. Of course all those Korean babies reach for something, as Olivia did—every baby would. And of course they are influenced by what they have observed in their parents.

Left: Ed Fox/Getty Images
Top: Paul Thomas / EyeEm/Getty Images

The third is that caregiver behavior is pivotal. Without realizing it, every family and each culture molds the infant mind. This social influence on infants is obvious when babies begin to speak their native language, not any of the 600 other languages that infants elsewhere speak. Caregivers also affect curiosity, persistence, and logic, as you will soon learn.

This chapter describes the process of infant cognition, as well as its accomplishments. From the brief moment when newborns open their eyes to the seemingly constant grabbing, experimenting, and talking of 2-year-olds, infants are active learners.

The Eager Mind

Chapter 5 chronicled the intense human drive to use every sensory and motor ability. Newborns look and listen; toddlers run and climb. Brain growth makes these sensory and motor developments possible; babies obsessively use each of their abilities as soon as they can.

In this chapter you will see that the same phenomenon occurs with cognitive development. One team suggested that infants are "scientist[s] in the crib" (Gopnik et al., 1999), a suggestion that was "frequently met with incredulity" (Halberda, 2018, p. 1215).

Recently, however, incredulity met evidence. "The field of developmental neuroscience has burgeoned over the last 20 years with advances in technology and methods that are well-suited for measuring the human brain in vivo in infants...." (Guyer et al., 2018, p. 687).

As scientists discover more about the infant brain, they are increasingly impressed by its inborn motivation to learn. One team wrote, "from early on in development, infants display perceptual biases and attentional patterns that strongly suggest a motive to acquire information" (Lucca & Wilbourn, 2018, p. 942).

"IS THIS THE WAY YOU PLAN TO SPEND YOUR PEAK LEARNING YEARS?"
S. Harris
SIDNEY HARRIS/CARTOONSTOCK

Still Wrong Parents used to ignore infant cognition. Now some make the opposite mistake, assuming that infants learn via active study, as adults might.

Listening to Learn

Remember that newborns' hearing is acute. Infants can hear all noises—traffic on the street, clanking of dishes in the kitchen, the hum or crackle of the radiator—but they ignore most of what they hear.

Sensation does not usually become perception, and perception does not necessarily become cognition. Instead, babies listen closely to sounds that can teach them, particularly the human voice.

Distinguishing Speech Sounds Newborns do not understand words, of course, but they have an inborn affinity for language, probably because, for humans, most learning occurs via words.

Vast differences are audible in adult speech: Russian does not sound like a tonal language such as Chinese; English does not pronounce the "r" as French does; the cadence of German is quite different from that of Spanish. Babies need to learn from whatever language their caregivers speak, which means that every linguistic nuance must be perceived.

That is what happens. Even in the early weeks, babies distinguish the difference between the sound of *pa* and *ba*, for example, and they hear the nuances of many other speech sounds—some insignificant in one language but crucial in another. They are called *universalists* because they hear the differences in any language (Kuhl, 2004).

By one year after birth, however, their ability to distinguish sounds in never-heard languages deteriorates, a loss that continues throughout childhood. Babies at first attend to all linguistic sounds; by adulthood people literally cannot hear some sound differences that are crucial in languages they have never learned. That is evidence for cognitive maturation.

Babies from English-speaking families were shown pictures of 17 common objects while hearing the names of the objects (Bergelson & Swingley, 2018). Sometimes the name was deliberately mispronounced, as in the examples shown in **Table 6.1**.

Six-month-olds were tested for knowledge of these words. Performance overall was poor, but some babies already knew a few of the 17. Importantly, their understanding was equally good in three conditions: (1) their mother saying the words correctly; (2) their mother mispronouncing the words; and (3) a stranger saying the words correctly.

By 1 year of age, however, not only did they know more but also their brains had already learned correct U.S. English pronunciation. They were significantly better at understanding correct speech from strangers than mispronunciation by their own mothers.

This study shows, first, that very young babies are primed to learn language, and second, that 1-year-olds already know the accepted way to pronounce words. (English-speaking babies in Jamaica, or England, or India learn other nuances.)

Learning Two Languages Bilingual proficiency begins in the first year of life—every young human brain can learn several languages. Ideally, parents often speak in two languages, and then their children become doubly fluent as well. The brains of bilingual 1-year-olds respond to both (Ramírez et al., 2017). Infant brains are primed to learn whatever speech they hear.

However, most bilingual adults use one language with friends and family and the other one in more formal settings. Very young infants figure out which language is most important and respond preferentially to that one.

This was one conclusion from a study of 94 newborns (age 0 to 5 days) in Vancouver, Canada (Byers-Heinlein et al., 2010). For half of them, their mother spoke English and Tagalog (a language native to the Philippines); for one-third, their mothers spoke only English; and for one-sixth, their mothers spoke English and Chinese.

The infants in all three groups sucked on a pacifier connected to a recording of 10 minutes of English and 10 minutes of Tagalog. The two languages were matched for pitch, duration, and number of syllables.

As evident in the rate and intensity of their sucking (which activated the recording), babies with English-only mothers preferred English and those with bilingual mothers preferred Tagalog (Byers-Heinlein et al., 2010). Because of what they heard in the womb, they connected Tagalog with more animated, emotional talk—and that is what they wanted to learn first.

Looking to Learn

Developmentalists have long known that very young infants spend most of their time looking around while awake. Thus, one good way to quiet fussy 3-month-olds is to carry them to see different sights—traffic on the street, dogs coming to be petted, toys that move.

Gaze-Following Until recently, however, developmentalists were unaware of how important vision is for cognition. Very young babies choose to look at whatever is likely to advance their understanding. They wisely focus on their caregivers'

TABLE 6.1

Mispronunciation Examples in the Bergelson & Swingley Study

Apple	*opel*
Banana	*banoona*
Milk	*mulk*
Hair	*har*
Mouth	*mith*
Nose	*nazz*

macmillan learning

VIDEO: Event-Related Potential (ERP) Research shows a procedure in which the electrical activity of an infant's brain is recorded to see whether the brain responds differently to familiar versus unfamiliar words.

Especially for Educators An infant day-care center has a new child whose parents speak a language other than the one the teachers speak. Should the teachers learn basic words in the new language, or should they expect the baby to learn the teachers' language? (see response, page 164)

No Fear Like all infants, this 11-month-old girl is eager to explore through sight and touch. Praise to all three—this mother for encouraging learning, this baby for reaching out, and this dog for licking the hand. Most dogs recognize babies, tolerating actions they would not accept from adults of any species.

attention, via *gaze-following*, instinctively knowing that what caregivers look at might tell them something important.

For example, following adults' lead, they look at the face of someone entering the room, ignoring the ceiling, the floor, or the person's feet. Have they learned that adults look at faces because expressions are informative, or is gaze-following natural for infants?

Both. It was thought that gaze-following occurred only as a response to adults, who alert the babies to opportunities to learn. Adults say, "Javier, look, here comes Daddy," or "Sophia, here is your teddy bear." Such guides to gaze-following are part of adults' natural tendency to teach babies through *natural pedagogy* (Gergely & Csibra, 2013).

Natural pedagogy is evident when caregivers direct the baby's gaze, calling their name, pointing at an object, and so on. Adults try to advance infant cognition; very young babies respond by looking at whatever the adult shows.

But we now know that infants will follow an adult's gaze even without caregiver cues (Gredebäck et al., 2018). If a tilt of the head and the movement of the pupils indicates that something interests the caregiver, the baby follows the gaze. Thus, gaze-following arises from both nature and nurture.

Early Logic Nature and nurture may also give babies some understanding of the laws of physics. In one study, a toy dinosaur was removed from a display where it had been next to a flower. A screen then covered the display. A moment later, the screen was lifted to reveal the dinosaur instead of the flower (Cesana-Arlotti et al., 2018).

Cameras and computers measured how long the babies looked at that unexpected event. Infants stared longer when the flower was surreptitiously replaced with the dinosaur than when the flower was still there. This indicated that they knew how things should be and were surprised when their basic understanding was wrong.

Many other events (such as a ball that is suspended in the air rather than falling, or a toy that becomes two toys) that are contrary to the basic laws of how things work elicit the same surprise. From such research, many developmentalists believe that infants have some innate logic. Scientific reasoning may not be a "hard-won accomplishment mastered later in life" but rather an "inherent attribute of the mind" (Halberda, 2018, p. 1214).

Core Knowledge

To explain infants' impressive cognition, some scientists suggest that newborns have a basic understanding of how the world works, which they call *core knowledge* (Stahl & Feigenson, 2017). Core knowledge includes the understanding that gravity makes objects fall, moving objects are stopped by a solid wall, and adult gaze signals important information.

Core expectations not only prime learning but also alert the infant when something unexpected happens. Surprises arouse babies' curiosity, and they learn more. No one thinks that babies are born with the knowledge and logic they will display in a few months or years. But core knowledge makes rapid learning possible as the brain grows (remember, it triples in size by age 2) and experiences accumulate.

Consider how this works when infants see pictures (LoBue, 2013). Infants are *not* instinctively afraid of snakes. However, when they look at pictures of flowers and snakes, they focus more on the snakes. Their brains seem to know that snakes may be important; then, during early childhood, they are taught whether or not to be afraid.

Recognizing Faces Another example comes from attention to faces. Unless you have *prosopagnosia* (face blindness), the *fusiform face area* of your brain is astonishingly adept. This is innate. Newborns are quicker to recognize a face that they have seen just once than are older children and adults (Zeifman, 2013).

Because of experience-expectant brain development, every face is fascinating: Babies stare at pictures of monkey faces and photos of human ones, at drawings and toys with faces, as well as at live faces. At 6 weeks, they smile at almost anyone whose face is about 2 feet away.

Soon, with experience-dependent learning, babies smile more readily at familiar people, differentiate men from women, and distinguish among faces from their own ethnic group (called the *own-race effect*). This fact could be worrisome: Does it suggest that humans are naturally sexist and racist? No, as A View from Science explains. Brains are primed to pay attention to familiar faces, and most babies see faces of a particular kind.

A VIEW FROM SCIENCE

Face Recognition

The *own-race effect* is the finding that infants are much better at recognizing individuals from their own ethnic group than at distinguishing individuals from other groups. Experience, not racism, is the reason: Most babies see only people like them.

When the viewing experience of the baby is multiracial, the own-race effect is not evident. Indeed, children of one ethnicity who are adopted and raised exclusively among people of another ethnicity recognize differences among people of their adopted group more readily than differences among people of their biological group (Sangrigoli et al., 2005).

The importance of experience is confirmed by three studies. In the first study, parents repeatedly "read" a book to their 6-month-old infants (Scott & Monesson, 2010). The book depicted six monkey faces. One-third of the infants' parents read the name of each monkey while showing the pictures; another one-third said only "monkey" as they turned each page; the final one-third simply turned the pages with no verbal labeling.

At 9 months, infants in all three groups viewed pictures of six *unfamiliar* monkeys. The infants who had heard names of monkeys were better at distinguishing one new monkey from another than were the infants who saw the same picture book but did not hear each monkey's name (Scott & Monesson, 2010).

Evidently, by hearing the names, the babies learned what features distinguish one monkey from another. This applies to humans' understanding of racial and national groups as well. Interacting with several named people of any group helps people understand that members of that group are individuals, not stereotypes (Thorup et al., 2018).

The second study occurred in Malaysia, where many people of two ethnic groups (Malay and Chinese) live and where the custom is for women, but not men, to interact with babies. A group of Chinese infants recognized individuality among Chinese women by 3 months and among Malaysian women by 8 months. However, they did not perceive individuality among Europeans or among men—apparently because they had limited experience with them (Tham et al., 2019).

As with almost every type of infant development, experience combines with inborn brain proclivities. This is evident for face recognition in other primates, not just for humans.

In a third study, researchers prevented macaque monkeys from seeing faces (including those of other monkeys and of humans) for the first three months of life. Then they showed pictures, some with faces and some not. Those deprived 3-month-olds looked more attentively at photos of faces than photos of other objects. Every face—of chimpanzees, otters, humans, as well as monkeys—was almost equally interesting.

By 6 months, they had some experiences with other macaques and consequently paid more attention to photos of faces of their own species than of other primates (Simpson et al., 2017). That is just what human babies do: They look intently at every face-like image at first but zero in on the faces that are most important to them.

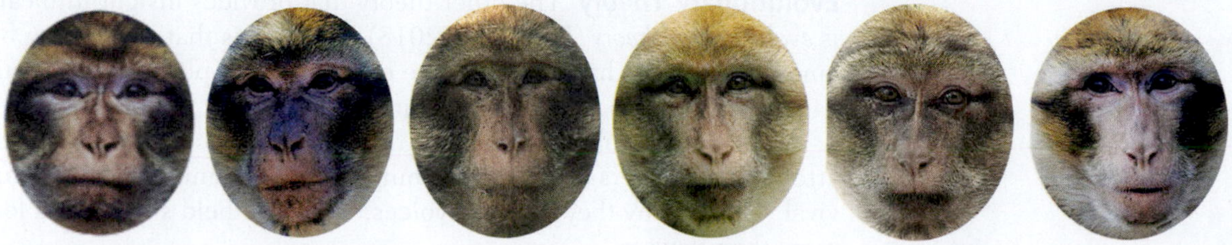

Dario Boris Anice Iona Flora Louis

Iona Is Not Flora If you heard that Dario was not Louis or Boris, would you stare at unfamiliar monkey faces more closely in the future? For 6-month-olds, the answer is yes.

CHAPTER APP 6

The Wonder Weeks

IOS:
https://tinyurl.com/yxkmmf2w

ANDROID:
https://tinyurl.com/y2rkeelf

RELEVANT TOPIC:
Cognitive development during infancy

This award-winning app contains video explanations, over 500 facts about infant cognition, week-by-week updates, and a notes feature, ensuring that parents learn at their own pace.

How to Learn One final area of cognition merits mention—babies learn how to learn. As you remember from Chapter 4, infants are born with reflexes. Some of those reflexes fade and others build, depending on experience.

Curiosity is an inborn reflex; newborns look at and listen to everything. Then, some infants are allowed to explore and experiment (fingering their toys, reaching for people, and so on); others are not ("Don't touch!"). It matters whether caregivers encourage curiosity, respond to noises, and shape reflexes (as Mrs. Todd did in Chapter 5). For example, if a baby utters a sound, some caregivers stop and respond, other ignore the sound, and some others tell the baby to be quiet.

By the second year of life, some toddlers are eager to explore and investigate while others are much more hesitant. One quality, sometimes called *grit* (persistent effort) fosters learning throughout life.

In one experiment, 15-month-olds observed adults trying to get a toy from a container (Leonard et al., 2017). The adult said, "How can I get this toy out of here?" and then worked to do so. Half the infants saw the toy come out quickly, and the other half watched the adult working hard for half a minute to release the toy.

Then the babies were handed another toy. The experimenter pushed a button to demonstrate that the toy played music. The babies did not know that the toy was rigged not to play again. Every baby tried to make the toy play music. That is what babies do naturally; they manipulate objects to see what will happen.

Some babies were much more persistent than others. A few quickly threw the toy to the floor in frustration. Others kept trying for two minutes. The babies' reactions depended on what they had just observed. The average baby pushed the button 22.5 times if the adult had persisted for half a minute before getting the toy, but if they had seen the adult succeed quickly, they pushed, on average, only 12 times (Leonard et al., 2017).

The authors conclude that adults should sometimes let children see them struggle to complete a task. The idea that hard work pays off is a learning strategy that helps throughout a person's education—and it may begin in infancy.

Theories of the Infant Mind

Two theories are relevant to this new understanding of the infant mind: information-processing theory and evolutionary theory.

Information Processing As you remember from Chapter 2, *information-processing theory* originated from computers, which gather millions of bits of information and then compute a result. The central idea of this theory is that the human mind is like a computer, accumulating experiences and then establishing knowledge.

Thus, this theory leads to the hypothesis that the infant mind is programmed for cognition: The myriad sights and sounds produce understanding.

Evolutionary Theory The other theory that provides insight into early cognition is *evolutionary theory* (Bjorklund, 2018). The idea is that the human brain, unique among mammals, has evolved to be extraordinarily plastic so that human babies can learn everything they need within their culture.

According to evolutionary theory, this occurs in two steps. First, infants innately attend to caregivers as well as to things that, millennia ago, were crucial for survival. That is why they listen to voices, like to be held snugly, and look at snakes more than flowers.

Second, the diversity of human culture required that the infant brain be amazingly plastic, allowing rapid cognitive growth as inborn predispositions adapt to whatever life may bring. Over the millennia, those people with the most flexible brains were most likely to survive and procreate, so that the genes for plasticity continued.

The Sucking Reflex For hundreds of thousands of years, evolution has required the sucking/swallowing/breathing reflexes to function well in newborns, even though every other motor ability takes months to develop. You also remember that breast milk is good for the brain; babies who are breast-fed tend to have higher IQs than those who are formula-fed. These two facts are particularly relevant for babies born very early.

The sucking reflex does not begin until about 33 weeks after conception, which meant that, in prior centuries, preterm babies died. Now respirators, incubators, and so on allow viable preterm babies to live. They are tube-fed, ideally with breast milk that their mothers have expressed with a breast pump. At about 34 weeks, in the hospital, they begin to suck, either via a special bottle and nipple designed for their tiny mouths or directly from the nipples of their mothers.

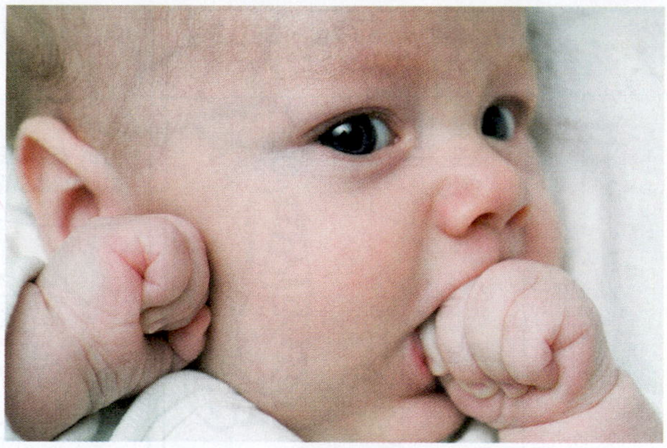

Vladimir Godnik/Getty Images

Time for Adaptation Sucking is a reflex at first, but adaptation begins as soon as an infant differentiates a pacifier from her mother's breast or realizes that her hand has grown too big to fit into her mouth. This infant's expression of concentration suggests that she is about to make that adaptation and suck just her thumb from now on.

NICU professionals prefer the bottle approach, since the mothers do not need to be physically present and nurses can more easily measure nutrition. Doctors thought that babies could easily switch to direct breast-feeding at home. However, that idea ignored what cognitive psychologists now know about infant learning: Sucking for nourishment is core knowledge, evident in newborns.

Tiny babies who are bottle-fed learn that this is how sucking brings milk. By contrast, those who are directly breast-fed in the hospital (for very preterm infants this means many times a day, often supplemented with tube-feeding) learn that breasts give milk. Babies who are breast-fed in the hospital are released earlier and are more often breast-fed at home (Suberi et al., 2018), which benefits their cognition.

This is an example of the infant's eager mind, because these tiny babies quickly learned to adapt an inborn ability (sucking) with experience (as both information processing and evolutionary theory suggest).

Infant Memory

Are infant skills and cognition impressive, or are they markedly immature? Both. To further understand this, we need to look at one more ability—memory, which "is crucial for the acquisition of the tremendous amount of knowledge and skills infant[s] and children acquire in the first years of life" (Vöhringer et al., 2018, p. 370).

People remember what they need to remember. Babies quickly remember who their caregivers are, and they learn how their own behaviors can affect their experiences.

Forget About Infant Amnesia! Piaget, Freud, and other early developmentalists described *infant amnesia,* the idea that people forget everything that happened to them before age 3. Wrong. Infant brains are adapted to learn, which means that they can remember.

An insight regarding infant amnesia begins with the distinction between *implicit* and *explicit* memory. Implicit memory is not verbal; it is memory for movement, emotions, or thoughts that are not put into words. Implicit memory is evident by 3 months, begins to stabilize by 9 months, and varies from one infant to another as well as within each infant during the early months.

The reason it appears so early is partly because it comes from old parts of the brain—including the cerebellum and the amygdala (Vöhringer et al., 2018). Those brain parts develop in the first months of life.

Explicit memory takes longer to emerge, as it depends on language. It arises mainly from the cortex. Explicit memory improves dramatically throughout childhood (Hayne et al., 2015). Verbal memory, especially vocabulary, continues to increase throughout adulthood. When experts tested memory by asking questions, they were testing explicit memory, which seemed absent for the early years. Infant amnesia? That is an adult conclusion.

macmillan learning

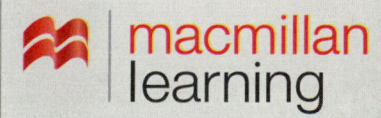

VIDEO: Contingency Learning in Young Infants shows Carolyn Rovee-Collier's procedure for studying instrumental learning during infancy.

Selective Amnesia As we grow older, we forget about spitting up, nursing, crying, and almost everything else from our early years. However, strong emotions (love, fear, mistrust) leave lifelong traces.

Thus, when people say "I don't remember," they mean "I cannot recall," because it is not in explicit memory. Unconsciously and implicitly, a memory might be present. A person might have an irrational fear of doctors or hospitals, for instance, because of early terrifying and painful experiences—experiences they do not consciously recall.

Remind Me! The most dramatic proof of very early memory comes from a series of innovative experiments in which 3-month-olds learned to move a mobile by kicking their legs (Rovee-Collier, 1987, 1990). The infants lay on their backs connected to a mobile by means of a ribbon tied to one foot.

Virtually all babies realized that kicking made the mobile move. They then kicked more vigorously and frequently, sometimes laughing at their accomplishment. So far, this is no surprise—observing self-activated movement is highly reinforcing to infants.

When infants as young as 3 months had the mobile-and-ribbon apparatus reinstalled and reconnected *one week later,* most started to kick immediately, proof that they remembered their previous experience. But when other 3-month-old infants were retested *two weeks later,* they kicked randomly. Had they forgotten? It seemed so.

But then, *two weeks after* the initial training, the lead researcher, Carolyn Rovee-Collier, allowed some infants to watch the mobile move when they were not connected to it. The next day, when a ribbon again tied their leg to the mobile, they kicked almost immediately.

Apparently, watching the mobile the previous day reminded them about what they had previously experienced. Other research similarly finds that reminders are powerful. If Daddy routinely plays with a 3-month-old, goes on a long trip, and the mother shows Daddy's picture and says his name on the day before his return, the baby might grin broadly when he reappears.

At 12 months, memory improves. Brains have added tens of thousands of dendrites and synapses.

Every day of their young lives, infants process information and store memories. Indeed, if you saw a photo of a grandmother who cared for you every day when you were an infant and who died when you were 2, your brain would still react, even though you thought you forgot her. Information-processing research finds evidence of early memories, with visual memories particularly strong (Leung et al., 2016; Gao et al., 2017).

Observation Quiz Do you see anything here that is less than ideal? (see answer, page 164) ↓

He Remembers! Infants are fascinated by moving objects within a few feet of their eyes—that's why parents buy mobiles for cribs and why Rovee-Collier tied a string to a mobile and a baby's leg to test memory. Babies not in her experiment, like this one, sometimes flail their limbs to make their cribs shake and thus make their mobiles move. Piaget's stage of "making interesting sights last" is evident to every careful observer.

WHAT HAVE YOU LEARNED?

1. What is the developmental pattern of hearing the sound of speech?
2. Why do babies look at whatever they look at?
3. What suggests that infants have an understanding of how objects move?
4. What does face recognition tell us about infant cognition?
5. What suggests that infants develop strategies for learning by watching adults?
6. Why is information-processing theory relevant for infant cognition?
7. Why is evolutionary theory relevant for infant cognition?

Piaget's Sensorimotor Intelligence

Now we turn to Jean Piaget, the groundbreaking theorist who studied infant cognition a century ago. Of course, Piaget lacked the technological advances that undergird our current understanding of infant cognition, but many contemporary developmentalists consider Piaget's six stages of infant cognition a foundation on which to build.

In 1918, when Piaget earned his doctorate in biology, most scientists thought infants only ate, cried, and slept. His Ph.D. research was on shellfish, specifically how they adapt to their environment. That required meticulous observation to understand details such as how a clam interacted with sandy water, or how a snail moved along a particular surface.

When he became a father, Piaget used his scientific observation skills with his own three infants. Contrary to conventional wisdom, he detailed active learning from birth on, recording his children's cognitive development day by day.

Early reflexes, senses, and body movements are the raw materials for infant cognition, Piaget surmised. That is why he called cognition in the first two years **sensorimotor intelligence**. He subdivided this period into six stages (see **Table 6.2**). [**Life-Span Link:** Piaget's theory of cognitive development is introduced in Chapter 2.]

TABLE 6.2

The Six Stages of Sensorimotor Intelligence

For an overview of the stages of sensorimotor thought, it helps to group the six stages into pairs.

Primary Circular Reactions	
The first two stages involve the infant's responses to his or her own body.	
Stage One (birth to 1 month)	*Reflexes:* sucking, grasping, staring, listening *Example:* sucking anything that touches the lips or cheek
Stage Two (1–4 months)	*The first acquired adaptations:* accommodation and coordination of reflexes *Examples:* sucking a pacifier differently from a nipple; attempting to hold a bottle to suck it
Secondary Circular Reactions	
The next two stages involve the infant's responses to objects and people.	
Stage Three (4–8 months)	*Making interesting sights last:* responding to people and objects *Example:* clapping hands when mother says "patty-cake"
Stage Four (8–12 months)	*New adaptation and anticipation:* becoming more deliberate and purposeful in responding to people and objects *Example:* putting mother's hands together in order to make her start playing patty-cake
Tertiary Circular Reactions	
The last two stages are the most creative, first with action and then with ideas.	
Stage Five (12–18 months)	*New means through active experimentation:* experimentation and creativity in the actions of the "little scientist" *Example:* putting a teddy bear in the toilet and flushing it
Stage Six (18–24 months)	*New means through mental combinations:* thinking before doing; new ways of achieving a goal without resorting to trial and error *Example:* before flushing the teddy bear again, hesitating because of the memory of the toilet overflowing and mother's anger

sensorimotor intelligence Piaget's term for the way infants think—by using their senses and motor skills—during the first period of cognitive development.

primary circular reactions The first of three types of feedback loops in sensorimotor intelligence, this one involving the infant's own body. The infant senses motion, sucking, noise, and other stimuli and tries to understand them.

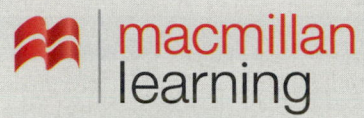

macmillan learning

VIDEO: Sensorimotor Intelligence in Infancy and Toddlerhood shows how senses and motor skills fuel infant cognition.

Stages One and Two: Primary Circular Reactions

Piaget described the interplay of sensation, perception, action, and cognition as *circular reactions,* emphasizing that, as in a circle, there is no beginning and no end. Each experience leads to the next, which loops back (see **Figure 6.1**).

In **primary circular reactions,** the circle is within the infant's body. Stage one, called the *stage of reflexes,* lasts only a month. Reflexes become deliberate; sensation leads to perception, perception leads to cognition, and then cognition leads back to sensation.

Stage two, called *first acquired adaptations* (also called *stage of first habits*), begins as the mind of the infant allows adjustment to whatever responses they elicit. Adaptation is cognitive; it includes repeating old patterns (assimilation) and developing new ones (accommodation). [**Life-Span Link:** Assimilation and accommodation are explained in Chapter 2.]

Here is one example. As you remember, full-term newborns reflexively suck anything that touches their lips (stage one). They must learn to suck, swallow, and suck again without spitting up too much—a major circular reaction that takes a few days to learn.

Then, infants *adapt* their sucking reflex to bottles or breasts, pacifiers or fingers, each requiring specific types of tongue pushing. You already read about this in preterm babies who, at 33 weeks, first are able to suck (Suberi et al., 2018). Soon adaptation signifies that infants have begun to interpret sensations; as they *accommodate,* they are thinking—ready for stage two.

During stage two, which Piaget pegged from about 1 to 4 months of age, additional adaptation of the sucking reflex begins. Infant cognition leads babies to suck in some ways for hunger, in other ways for comfort—and not to suck fuzzy blankets or hard plastic. Once adaptation occurs, it sticks.

Adaptation is specific. For instance, 4-month-old breast-fed babies may reject milk from the nipple of a bottle if they have never experienced it. Early cognition can endure, as evolutionary theory contends. That explains why children like to suck lollipops and why some adults still like to suck other things.

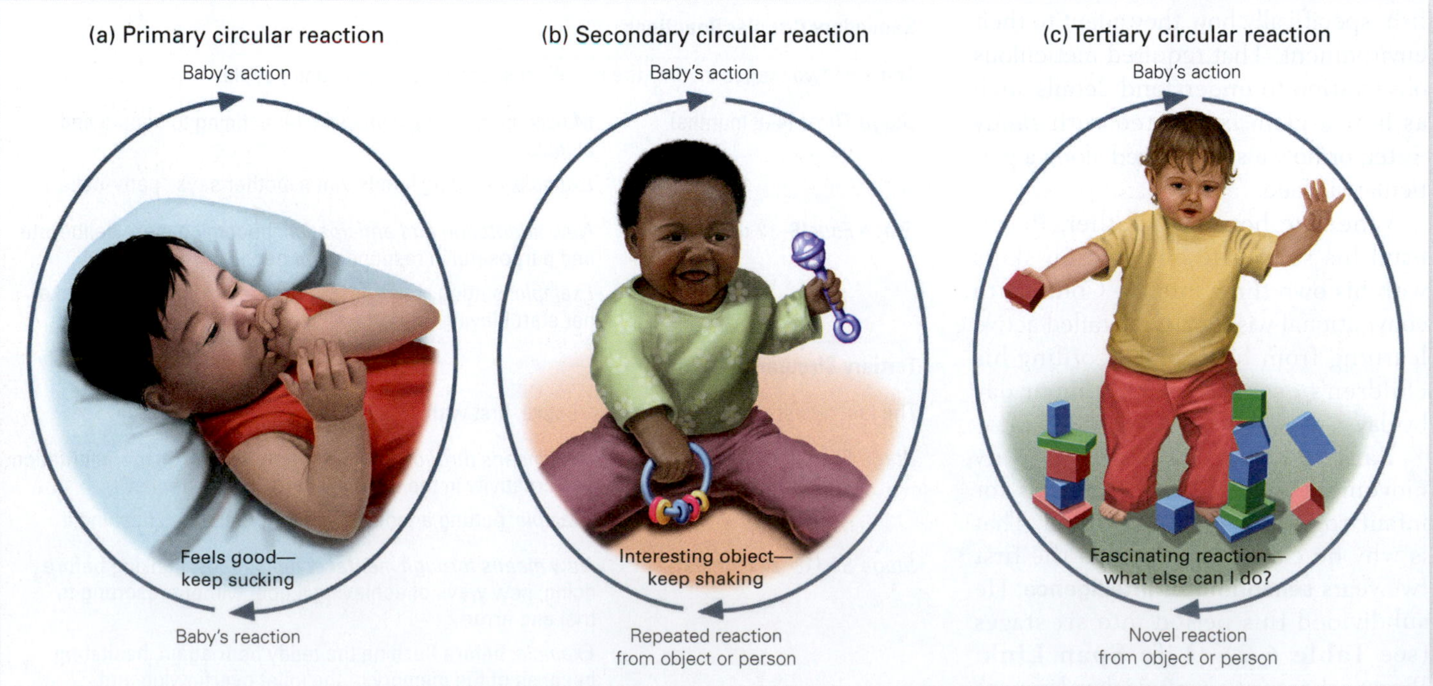

FIGURE 6.1
Never Ending Circular reactions keep going because each action produces pleasure that encourages more action.

Now, suppose 4-month-olds have discovered how to suck their thumbs and have practiced thumb-sucking to their joy and satisfaction. Then, when this stage is over, suppose at 6 months the parents decide that a pacifier is better—perhaps healthier for teeth. Too late! Babies reject a new object. Adaptation has already occurred.

In the same way at every age, Piaget found that older children and adults tend to stick to their early learning. This is apparent if you ever try to convince someone that something they have done all their life is wrong. Habits of thought and deed are hard to change, from infancy on.

Stages Three and Four: Secondary Circular Reactions

In stages three and four, development advances from primary to **secondary circular reactions**. These reactions extend beyond the infant's body; this circular reaction is between the baby and something else.

During stage three (4 to 8 months), infants attempt to produce exciting experiences, a stage called *making interesting sights last.* Realizing that rattles make noise, for example, they wave their arms and laugh whenever someone puts a rattle in their hand. The sight of something delightful—a favorite squeaky toy, a smiling parent—can trigger active efforts for interaction.

Next comes stage four (8 months to 1 year), called *new adaptation and anticipation* (also called the *means to the end*). Babies may ask for help (fussing, pointing, gesturing) to accomplish what they want. Thinking is more innovative because adaptation is more complex. For instance, instead of always smiling at Grandpa, an infant might first assess his mood. Stage-three babies continue an experience; stage-four babies initiate and anticipate.

Pursuing a Goal An impressive attribute of stage four is that babies work hard to achieve their goals. A 10-month-old girl might crawl over to her mother, bringing a bar of soap to signal she loves baths, and then start to remove her clothes—finally squealing with delight when the bath water is turned on. Similarly, if a 10-month-old boy sees Dad putting on a coat to leave, he might get his own jacket.

In both cases, infants have learned from repeated experience—Daddy may have often brought his son along when he went out. With a combination of experience and brain maturation, babies become attuned to the goals of others, an ability that is more evident at 10 months than 8 months (Brandone et al., 2014).

According to Piaget, a major accomplishment of stage four is **object permanence**—the concept that objects or people continue to exist when they are not visible. At about 8 months—not before—infants look for toys that have fallen from the crib, rolled under a couch, or disappeared under a blanket.

As another scholar explains:

> Many parents in our typical American middle-class households have tried out Piaget's experiment in situ: Take an adorable, drooling 7-month-old baby, show her a toy she loves to play with, then cover it with a piece of cloth right in front of her eyes. What do you observe next? The baby does not know what to do to get the toy! She looks around, oblivious to the object's continuing existence under the cloth cover, and turns her attention to something else interesting in her environment. A few months later, the same baby will readily reach out and yank away the cloth cover to retrieve the highly desirable toy. This experiment has been done thousands of times and the phenomenon remains one of the most compelling in all of developmental psychology.
>
> [*Xu, 2013, p. 167*]

This is one of Piaget's most well-known, as well as most controversial, insights (see Opposing Perspectives).

Especially for Parents When should parents decide whether to feed their baby only by breast, only by bottle, or using some combination of the two? When should they decide whether or not to let their baby use a pacifier? (see response, page 164)

secondary circular reactions The second of three types of feedback loops in sensorimotor intelligence, this one involving people and objects. Infants respond to other people, to toys, and to any other object that they can touch or move.

object permanence The realization that objects (including people) still exist when they can no longer be seen, touched, or heard.

Bambu Productions/The Image Bank/Getty Images

Family Fun Peek-a-boo makes all three happy, each for cognitive reasons. The 9-month-old is discovering object permanence, his sister (at the concrete operational stage) enjoys making Brother laugh, and their mother understands more abstract ideas—such as family bonding.

OPPOSING PERSPECTIVES

Object Permanence

Piaget found that:

- Infants younger than 8 months do not search for an attractive object momentarily covered by a cloth.
- At about 8 months, infants remove the cloth immediately after the object is covered but not if they have to wait a few seconds.
- At 18 months, infants search after a wait. However, if they have seen the object put first in one place (A) and then moved to another (B), they search in A but not B.
- By 2 years, children fully understand object permanence, progressing through several stages of ever-advanced cognition (Piaget, 1954/2013a).

This research provides many practical suggestions. If young infants fuss because they see something they cannot have (keys, a cell phone, candy), caregivers are advised to put that coveted object out of sight. Fussing stops if object permanence has not yet appeared.

By contrast, for toddlers, hiding is not enough. It must be securely locked up, lest the child later retrieve it, climbing onto the kitchen counter or under the bathroom sink to do so.

Piaget believed that failure to search before 8 months meant that infants had no concept of object permanence—that "out of sight" literally means "out of mind." That is where the controversy begins.

Does a baby need to be able to remove a cover from a hidden toy to demonstrate object permanence? No, according to information-processing research. The best-known example is a series of studies by Renee Baillargeon which proved that 3-month-old infants grasp object permanence, long before when Piaget said it emerged (8 months). How was this discovered?

Baillargeon devised clever experiments that entailed showing infants an object, then covering it with a screen, and then removing the screen. If the object vanished behind the screen, the babies' brain waves, heart rate, or focused eyes showed surprise. This meant that they expected the object to still be present—that is, they believed an object's existence was permanent (Baillargeon & DeVos, 1991; Spelke, 1993).

Later research on object permanence has continued to question Piaget's conclusions. Many other creatures (cats, monkeys, dogs, birds) develop object permanence faster than human infants. The animal ability seems to be innate, not learned—wolves can develop it as well as dogs, but neither is adept at A-not-B displacement (Fiset & Plourde, 2013).

How quickly infants master the A-not-B displacement depends partly on brain maturation, which varies. Current research finds that early experiences, plus inherited brain dispositions, make the age of object permanence (especially A-not-B displacements) much more variable than Piaget described (MacNeill et al., 2018).

There are opposing perspectives on exactly how infant cognition and surprise should be measured (Dunn & Bremner, 2017). But, everyone agrees that babies are thinking long before they can move their hands to uncover a hidden object.

Stages Five and Six: Tertiary Circular Reactions

In their second year, infants start experimenting in thought and deed—or, rather, in the opposite sequence, deed and thought. They act first (stage five) and think later (stage six).

tertiary circular reactions The third of three types of feedback loops in sensorimotor intelligence, this one involving active exploration and experimentation. Infants explore a range of new activities, varying their responses as a way of learning about the world.

"little scientist" The stage-five toddler (age 12 to 18 months) who experiments without anticipating the results, using trial and error in active and creative exploration.

Tertiary circular reactions begin when 1-year-olds take independent actions to discover the properties of other people, animals, and things. Infants no longer respond only to their own bodies (primary reactions) or to other people or objects (secondary reactions). Their cognition is more like a spiral than a closed circle, increasingly creative with each discovery.

Piaget's stage five (12 to 18 months), called *new means through active experimentation,* builds on the accomplishments of stage four. Now, goal-directed and purposeful activities become more expansive.

Toddlers delight in squeezing all the toothpaste out of the tube, in drawing on the wall or uncovering an anthill—activities they have never observed. Piaget referred to the stage-five toddler as a **"little scientist"** who "experiments in order

BruesWu/MomentOpen/Getty Images

Imitation Is Lifelong As this photo illustrates, at every age, people copy what others do—often to their mutual joy. The new ability at stage six is "deferred imitation"—this boy may have seen another child lie on a tire a few days earlier.

to see." Scientists who study 12- to 19-month-olds report that "flexible and productive hypothesis testing does begin in infancy, with a vengeance" (Cesana-Arlotti et al., 2018, p. 1263).

The toddlers' preferred research method is trial and error. Their devotion to discovery is familiar to every adult scientist—and to every parent. Protection is needed. A curious toddler might swallow bleach, flush a doll down the toilet, or throw a cat out the window, all to see what happens next.

Finally, in the sixth stage (18 to 24 months), toddlers use *mental combinations,* intellectual experimentation via imagination that can supersede the active experimentation of stage five. Because they combine ideas, stage-six toddlers can pretend as well as think about the consequences of what they do, hesitating a moment before yanking the cat's tail or dropping a raw egg on the floor.

Stage-six toddlers remember what they have seen and repeat it later themselves, an ability Piaget called *deferred imitation.* (Newer research finds that some accomplishments that Piaget pegged for stage six—including pretending and deferred imitation—begin much earlier.)

However, although he was wrong on the timing of his stages, Piaget was right to describe babies as avid and active learners who "learn so fast and so well" (Xu & Kushnir, 2013, p. 28). His main mistake was underestimating how rapidly their learning occurs.

Especially for Parents One parent wants to put all breakable or dangerous objects away because the toddler is able to move around independently. The other parent says that the baby should learn not to touch certain things. Who is right? (see response, page 164)

WHAT HAVE YOU LEARNED?

1. Why did Piaget call cognition in the first two years "sensorimotor intelligence"?
2. How does stage one of sensorimotor intelligence lead to stage two?
3. In sensorimotor intelligence, what is the difference between stages three and four?
4. What is the significance of the concept of object permanence for infant cognition?
5. What does the active experimentation of the stage-five toddler suggest for parents?
6. Why did Piaget underestimate infant cognition?

Language: What Develops in the First Two Years?

Human linguistic ability by age 2 far surpasses that of full-grown adults from every other species. Very young infants listen intensely, responding as best they can. One scholar explains, "infants are acquiring much of their native language before they utter their first word" (Aslin, 2012, p. 191). How do they do it?

The Universal Sequence

The sequence of language development is the same worldwide (see At About This Time). Some children learn several languages, some only one; some learn rapidly, others slowly. But all follow the same path.

AT ABOUT THIS TIME

The Development of Spoken Language in the First Two Years

Age*	Means of Communication
Newborn	Reflexive communication—cries, movements, facial expressions.
2 months	A range of meaningful noises—cooing, fussing, crying, laughing.
3–6 months	New sounds, including squeals, growls, croons, trills, vowel sounds.
6–10 months	Babbling, including both consonant and vowel sounds repeated in syllables.
10–12 months	Comprehension of simple words; speechlike intonations; specific vocalizations that have meaning to those who know the infant well. Deaf babies express their first signs; hearing babies also use specific gestures (e.g., pointing) to communicate.
12 months	First spoken words that are recognizably part of the native language.
13–18 months	Slow growth of vocabulary, up to about 50 words.
18 months	Naming explosion—three or more words learned per day. Much variation: Some toddlers do not yet speak.
21 months	First two-word sentence.
24 months	Multiword sentences. Half of the toddler's utterances are two or more words long.

*The ages in this table reflect norms. Many healthy, intelligent children attain each linguistic accomplishment earlier or later than indicated here.

Listening and Responding In every spoken language, adults use higher pitch, simpler words, repetition, varied speed, and exaggerated emotional tone when talking to infants. Babies respond with attention and emotion. By 7 months, they begin to recognize words that are distinctive: *Bottle, doggie,* and *mama,* for instance, might be differentiated, not *baby, Bobbie,* and *Barbie.*

Infants also like alliteration, rhymes, repetition, melody, rhythm, and varied pitch. Think of your favorite lullaby (itself an alliterative word); obviously, babies prefer sounds over content and singing over talking (Tsang et al., 2017). Early listening abilities and preferences are the result of brain function.

Babbling and Gesturing Between 6 and 9 months, babies repeat certain syllables (*ma-ma-ma, da-da-da, ba-ba-ba*), a vocalization called **babbling** because of the way it sounds. Babbling is experience-expectant; all babies babble.

babbling An infant's repetition of certain syllables, such as *ba-ba-ba*, that begins when babies are between 6 and 9 months old.

Caregivers usually encourage those noises, and it is wise that they do so. Babbling predicts later vocabulary, even more than the other major influence — the education of the mother (McGillion et al., 2017).

Expectations in babies regarding speech appear early. Before uttering their first word, infants notice patterns of speech, such as which sounds are commonly spoken together. A baby who often hears that something is "pretty" expects the sound of *prit* to be followed by *tee* (MacWhinney, 2015) and is startled if someone says "prit-if."

Infants also learn the relationship between mouth movements and sound. In one study, 8-month-olds watched a film of someone speaking, with the audio a fraction of a second ahead of the video. Even when the actor spoke an unknown language, babies noticed the mistiming (Pons & Lewkowicz, 2014).

Ariel Skelley/Getty Images

Who Is Babbling? Probably both the 6-month-old and the 27-year-old. During every day of infancy, mothers and babies communicate with noises, movements, and expressions.

Some caregivers, recognizing the power of gestures, teach "baby signs" to their 6- to 12-month-olds, who communicate with hand signs months before they move their tongues, lips, and jaws to make words. There is no evidence that baby signing accelerates talking (as had been claimed), but it may make parents more responsive (Kirk et al., 2013).

For deaf babies, sign language is crucial in the first year: It not only predicts later ability to communicate with signs but also advances crucial cognitive development (M. Hall et al., 2017).

Even without adult signing, gestures become a powerful means of communication (Goldin-Meadow, 2015). One early gesture is pointing and responding to pointing from someone else. The latter requires something quite sophisticated — understanding another person's perspective.

Infants younger than a year old who are adept at pointing tend to be those who will soon begin talking. That is one reason adults need to respond to pointing as if it is intended to communicate—which it is (Bohn & Köymen, 2018).

First Words Finally, at about a year, the average baby utters a few words, understood by caregivers if not by strangers. Spoken vocabulary increases gradually (perhaps one new word a week). Meanings are learned rapidly; babies understand about 10 times more than they can say.

Initially, the first words are merely labels for familiar things (*mama* and *dada* are common), but each early word soon becomes a **holophrase,** a single word that expresses an entire thought, accompanied by gestures, facial expressions, and nuances of tone, loudness, and cadence (Saxton, 2010). (See A Case to Study.) Imagine meaningful communication in "Dada," "Dada?" and "Dada!" Each is a holophrase.

Show Me Where Pointing is one of the earliest forms of communication, emerging at about 10 months. As you see here, pointing is useful lifelong for humans.

The Naming Explosion

Spoken vocabulary builds rapidly once the first 50 words are mastered, with 21-month-olds typically saying twice as many words as 18-month-olds (Adamson & Bakeman, 2006). This language spurt is called the **naming explosion** because many early words are nouns, that is, names of persons, places, or things.

Before the explosion, names are already favored. Infants learn the names of each significant caregiver (often *dada, mama, nana, papa, baba, tata*), sibling, and pet. (See Visualizing Development, p. 166.) Other frequently uttered words refer to favorite foods (*nana* can mean "banana" as well as "grandma") and to elimination (*pee-pee, wee-wee, poo-poo, ka-ka, doo-doo*).

holophrase A single word that is used to express a complete, meaningful thought.

naming explosion A sudden increase in an infant's vocabulary, especially in the number of nouns, that begins at about 18 months of age.

A CASE TO STUDY

Early Speech

As you read, sensitive caregiving is crucial for early cognition, as babies innately look at and listen to their caregivers in order to learn. For their part, caregivers need to be sensitive and responsive. Often parents understand what an infant is trying to communicate long before other people do.

Consider the early words of Kyle, who at 13 months was advanced in language development. He knew standard words such as *mama,* but he also knew *da, ba, tam, opma,* and *daes,* which his parents knew to be, respectively, "downstairs," "bottle," "tummy," "oatmeal," and "starfish." He also had a special sound that he used to call squirrels (Lewis et al., 1999).

When acquaintances came to visit the parents, they were often mystified by Kyle's attempts to speak. Who would know that *daes* meant "starfish," or how a person might call squirrels? Only Kyle and his very astute parents.

Even a caring grandmother might not understand a baby. Of course, the thought in the baby's mind may not be what the adult understands. I know this personally. I was caring for my 16-month-old grandson when he said, "Mama, mama." He looked directly at me, and he didn't seem wistful.

"Mommy's not here," I told him. That didn't interest him; he repeated "mama, mama," more as a command than a complaint. I offered him milk in his sippy cup. He said, "No, no."

When his father appeared, Isaac repeated "mama." Then his dad lifted him, and Isaac cuddled in his arms. I asked what "mama" means. The reply: "Pick me up."

I now understand Isaac's logic: When he saw his mother, he said "mama" and she picked him up. His parents understood and responded to his words and gestures.

Now Isaac is a proficient talker, explaining about bird families (pigeons are the parents, because they are bigger), about who should get a seat on the subway (it is Isaac, because, as he says very plaintively to other riders, "I need to sit down"—and to my embarrassment, he usually gets a seat), and about what his brother has done wrong (explained in detail to his parents, who listen attentively but almost never punish).

I also listen to his chatter, repeating some of his phrases, knowing that early responses affect later talking.

Josep Rovirosa/Westend61 RF/medicalimages.com

What Does He See? All children stare out of windows, but only some are told the names of the various cloud formations and the landscape below. Does this matter for language learning?

Notice that all of these words have two identical syllables, a consonant followed by a vowel. Many words follow that pattern—not just *baba* but also *bobo, bebe, bubu, bibi*. Other early words are only slightly more complicated—*ma-me, ama*.

The meaning of these words varies by language, but every baby says such words, and every culture assigns meaning to them. Words that are hard for babies to say are simplified: Rabbits are "bunnies," stomachs are "tummies," and a man may not wait to be called "Father," choosing "Daddy" or "Papa" instead.

Cultural Differences Early communication transcends culture. In one study, 102 adults listened to 40 recorded infant sounds and were asked which of five possibilities (pointing, giving, protesting, action request, food request) was the reason for each cry, grunt, or whatever. Half of the sounds, and about half of the adults, were from Scotland and the other half from Uganda.

Adults in both cultures scored significantly better than chance (although no one got everything right). It did not matter much whether the sounds came from Scottish or Ugandan infants, or whether the adults were parents or not (Kersken et al., 2017).

However, cultures and families vary in how much child-directed speech children hear. Some parents read to their infants, teach them signs, and respond to every burp or fart as if it were an attempt to talk. Other parents are much less verbal. They use gestures and touch; they say "hush" and "no" instead of expanding vocabulary.

Traditionally, in small agricultural communities, the goal was for everyone to be "strong and silent." If adults talked too much, they might be called blabbermouths or gossips; a good worker did not waste time in conversation.

In some rural areas of the world, that notion remains. One such place is in Senegal, where mothers traditionally feared talking to their babies lest that might encourage evil spirits to take over the child (Zeitlin, 2011).

However, communication is crucial in the twenty-first-century global economy. Government, teachers, and most parents recognize this: A child's first words are celebrated as much or more than a child's first steps.

In one study in Senegal, professionals from the local community (fluent in Woloff, the language spoken by the people) taught mothers in some villages about infant development. A year later those babies were compared to babies in similar villages where the educational intervention had not been provided.

The newly educated mothers talked more to their babies, who, in turn, talked more than the control group (A. Weber et al., 2017). Those who designed this study were careful not to dispute traditional notions directly; instead they taught how early language development advanced infant cognition. The mothers did the rest.

grammar All of the methods—word order, verb forms, and so on—that languages use to communicate meaning, apart from the words themselves.

Putting Words Together **Grammar** includes all of the methods that languages use to communicate meaning. There are many ways to add letters to words and to put words together—that is grammar.

Word order, prefixes, suffixes, intonation, verb forms, pronouns and negations, prepositions and articles—all of these are aspects of grammar. Grammar can be discerned in holophrases because one word can be spoken differently depending on meaning. Grammar becomes essential when babies combine words (Bremner & Wachs, 2010). That typically happens between 18 and 24 months.

For example, "Baby cry" and "More juice" follow grammatical word order. Children do not usually ask "Juice more," and even toddlers know that "Cry baby" is not the same as "Baby cry." By age 2, children combine three words. English grammar uses subject–verb–object order. Toddlers say, "Mommy read book" rather than any of the five other possible sequences of those three words.

Children's proficiency in grammar correlates with sentence length, which is why **mean length of utterance (MLU)** is used to measure a child's language progress (e.g., Miyata et al., 2013). The child who says, "Baby is crying" is more advanced than the child who says, "Baby crying" or simply, "Baby!"

mean length of utterance (MLU) The average number of words in a typical sentence (called utterance because children may not talk in complete sentences). MLU is often used to measure language development.

Theories of Language Learning

Worldwide, people who are not yet 2 years old express hopes, fears, and memories — sometimes in more than one language. By adolescence, people communicate with nuanced words and gestures, some writing poems and lyrics that move thousands of their co-linguists. How is language learned so easily and so well?

Answers come from at least three schools of thought. The first theory says that infants are directly taught, the second that social impulses propel infants to communicate, and the third that infants understand language because of genetic brain structures that arose more than 100,000 years ago.

Theory One: Infants Need to Be Taught One idea arises from behaviorism. The essential idea is that learning is acquired, step by step, through association and reinforcement.

B. F. Skinner (1957) noticed that spontaneous babbling is usually reinforced. Typically, when a baby says "ma-ma-ma-ma," a grinning mother appears, repeating the sound and showering the baby with attention, praise, and perhaps food.

Behaviorists note that some 3-year-olds converse in elaborate sentences; others just barely put one simple word with another. Such variations correlate with the amount of language each child has heard.

Indeed, to some extent infants are "statistical learners" of language, deciding the meanings and boundaries of words based on how often those sounds are heard (Saffran & Kirkham, 2018). Parents of the most verbal children teach language throughout infancy — singing, explaining, listening, responding, and reading to their babies, giving their children a rich trove of verbal data, long before the infant utters a first spoken word (see **Figure 6.2**).

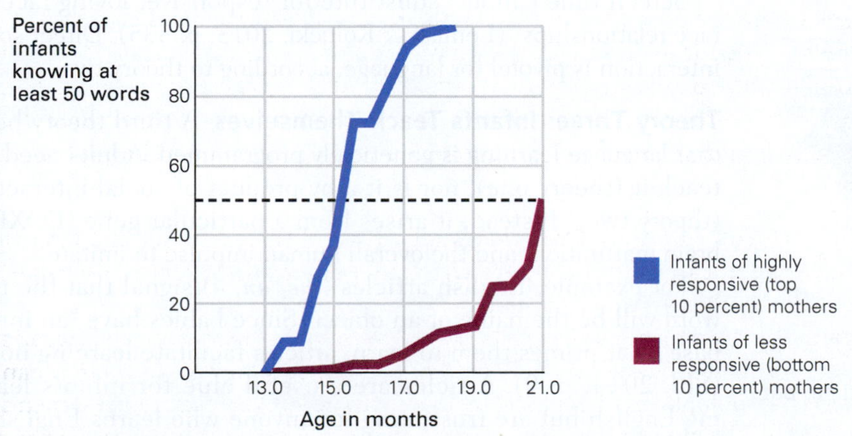

Data from Tamis-LeMonda et al., 2001, p. 761.

FIGURE 6.2

Maternal Responsiveness and Infants' Language Acquisition Learning the first 50 words is a milestone in early language acquisition, as it predicts the arrival of the naming explosion and the multiword sentence a few weeks later. Researchers found that half of the infants of highly responsive mothers (top 10 percent) reached this milestone at 15 months. The infants of less responsive mothers (bottom 10 percent) lagged significantly behind, with half of them at the 50-word level at 21 months.

Theory Two: Social Impulses Foster Infant Language The second theory arises from the sociocultural reason for language: communication. According to this perspective, infants communicate because humans are social beings, dependent on one another for survival and joy.

All human infants (and no chimpanzees) seek to master words and grammar in order to join the social world (Tomasello & Herrmann, 2010). According to this perspective, the social function of speech, not the words, undergirds early language.

This theory challenges child-directed videos, CDs, and downloads named to appeal to parents (*Baby Einstein, Brainy Baby,* and *Mozart for Mommies and Daddies—Jumpstart Your Newborn's I.Q.*). Since early language development is impressive, even explosive, some parents who allow infants to watch such programs believe that the rapid language learning is aided by video. Commercial apps, such as *Shapes Game HD* and *VocabuLarry,* have joined the market.

However, developmental research finds that screen time during infancy may be harmful, because it avoids the social interaction that is essential for learning to communicate. One recent study found that toddlers could learn a word from either a book or a video but that only book-learning, not video-learning, enabled children to use the new word in another context (Strouse & Ganea, 2017).

Another study focused particularly on teaching "baby signs," 18 hand gestures that refer to particular objects (Dayanim & Namy, 2015). The babies in this study were 15 months old, an age at which all babies use gestures and are poised to learn object names. The 18 signs referred to common early words, such as *baby, ball, banana, bird, cat,* and *dog*.

In this study, the toddlers were divided into four groups: video only, video with parent watching and reinforcing, book instruction with parent reading and reinforcing, and no instruction. Not surprisingly, the no-instruction group learned words (as every normal toddler does) but not signs, and the other three groups learned some signs. The two groups with parent instruction learned most, with the book-reading group remembering signs better than either video group. Why?

The crucial factor is parent interaction. When parents watch a video with their infants, they talk less than when they read a book or play with toys (Anderson & Hanson, 2016). Since adult input is essential for language learning, cognitive development is reduced by video time. Infants are most likely to understand and apply what they have learned when they learn directly from another person (Barr, 2013).

Screen time cannot "substitute for responsive, loving face-to-face relationships" (Lemish & Kolucki, 2013, p. 335). Direct social interaction is pivotal for language, according to theory two.

Emily Flake the New Yorker Collection/The Cartoon Bank

"Keep in mind, this all counts as screen time."

Caught in the Middle Parents try to limit screen time, but children are beguiled and bombarded from many sides.

Theory Three: Infants Teach Themselves A third theory holds that language learning is genetically programmed. Adults need not teach it (theory one), nor is it a by-product of social interaction (theory two). Instead, it arises from a particular gene (FOXP2), brain maturation, and the overall human impulse to imitate.

For example, English articles (*the, an, a*) signal that the next word will be the name of an object. Since babies have "an innate base" that primes them to learn, articles facilitate learning nouns (Shi, 2014, p. 9). Articles are a useful clue for infants learning English but are frustrating for anyone who learns English as an adult. Adults may be intelligent and motivated, but they are past the best language-learning time.

Our ancestors were genetically programmed to imitate for survival, but until a few millennia ago, no one needed to learn any language other than their own. Thus, human genes allow experience-dependent language learning, pruning unneeded language connections. If those nuances are needed by another language that we want to learn in adulthood, our brains cannot resurrect them.

The prime spokesman for this perspective was Noam Chomsky (1968, 1980). Although behaviorists focus on variations among children in vocabulary size, Chomsky focused on similarities in language acquisition—the evolutionary universals, not the differences.

Noting that all young children master basic grammar according to a schedule, Chomsky hypothesized that children are born with a brain structure he called a **language acquisition device (LAD),** which allows children, as their brains develop, to derive the rules of grammar quickly and effectively.

language acquisition device (LAD) Chomsky's term for a hypothesized mental structure that enables humans to learn language, including the basic aspects of grammar, vocabulary, and intonation.

For example, everywhere, a raised tone indicates a question, and infants prefer questions to declarative statements (Soderstrom et al., 2011). This suggests that infants are wired to talk. Caregivers universally ask them questions long before they can answer back.

According to theory three, language is experience-expectant, as the developing brain quickly and efficiently connects neurons to support whichever language the infant hears. Because of this experience-expectancy, the various languages of the world are all logical, coherent, and systematic. Then some experience-dependent learning occurs as each brain adjusts to a particular language.

The LAD works for deaf infants as well. All 6-month-olds, hearing or not, prefer to look at sign language over nonlinguistic pantomime. For hearing infants, this preference disappears by 10 months, but deaf infants begin signing at that time, which is their particular expression of the universal LAD.

All True? A master linguist explains that "the human mind is a hybrid system," perhaps using different parts of the brain for each kind of learning (Pinker, 1999, p. 279).

The idea that every theory is partially correct may seem idealistic. However, many scientists who are working on extending and interpreting research on language acquisition have arrived at this conclusion. They contend that language learning is neither the direct product of repeated input (behaviorism) nor the result of a specific human neurological capacity (LAD). Rather, "different elements of the language apparatus may have evolved in different ways," and thus, a "piecemeal and empirical" approach is needed (Marcus & Rabagliati, 2009, p. 281).

Neuroscience is the most recent method to investigate the development of language. It was once thought that language was located in two specific regions of the brain (Wernicke's area and Broca's area). But now neuroscientists are convinced that language arises from other regions as well. Some genes and regions are crucial, but hundreds of genes and many brain regions contribute to linguistic fluency.

Neuroscientists describing language development write about "connections," "networks," "circuits," and "hubs" to

Observation Quiz If this is a typical scene, what family values are evident? (see answer, page 164) ↓

Steven J. Kazlowski / Alamy

Family Values Every family encourages the values and abilities that their children need to be successful adults. For this family in Ecuador, that means strong legs and lungs to climb the Andes, respecting their parents, and keeping quiet unless spoken to. A "man of few words" is admired. By contrast, many North American parents babble in response to infant babble, celebrate the first spoken word, and stop their conversation to listen to an interrupting child. If a student never talks in class, or another student blurts out irrelevant questions, perhaps the professor should consider cultural influences.

capture the idea that language is interrelated and complex (Pulvermüller, 2018; Dehaene-Lambertz, 2017). Even when the focus is simply on talking, one neuroscientist notes that "speech is encoded at multiple levels in different parallel pathways" (Dehaene-Lambertz, 2017, p. 52).

That neuroscientist begins her detailed description of the infant brain and language with the same amazement that traditional linguists have expressed for decades:

> For thousands of years and across numerous cultures, human infants are able to perfectly master oral or signed language in only a few years. No other machine, be it silicon or carbon based, is able to reach the same level of expertise.
>
> *[Dehaene-Lambertz, 2017, p. 48]*

In the early months, language is closely linked with cognition. As one review of the many pathways between learning to talk and understanding the world concludes:

> A constellation of factors that are unique to human development—infants' prolonged period of dependency, exquisite sensitivity to experience, and powerful learning strategies—collectively spark a cascade of developmental change whose ultimate result is the acquisition of language and its unparalleled interface with cognition.
>
> *[Perszyk & Waxman, 2018, p. 246]*

The words "constellation" and "cascade" signify that many brain structures and social inputs result in both language and learning.

From this we are led to an overall conclusion. Infants are amazing and active learners—through understanding of people, objects, memory, and communication. Before Piaget, many experts assumed that babies did not yet learn or think. How wrong they were!

WHAT HAVE YOU LEARNED?

1. What aspects of language develop in the first year?
2. When does vocabulary develop slowly and when does it develop quickly?
3. What is typical of the first words that infants speak?
4. What indicates that toddlers use some grammar?
5. According to behaviorism, how do adults teach infants to talk?
6. According to sociocultural theory, why do infants try to communicate?
7. Do people really have a language acquisition device?
8. Why do developmentalists accept several theories of language development?

SUMMARY

The Eager Mind

1. Infants learn so quickly that developmentalists now suggest that some basic understanding is programmed into the brain—no experience necessary.

2. All of the possible sounds of human languages are heard by infants. This ability decreases as babies become more attuned to whatever languages they hear.

3. Infants observe events and people to learn what merits their attention. Face recognition seems to be an inborn ability that is refined by experience.

4. Information-processing theory, which looks at each step of the thinking process, helps researchers understand that every moment of experience aids cognition, enhanced by the innate programming of the infant mind.

5. Evolutionary theory is also relevant, as it emphasizes the basic cognitive capacities that humans have needed to survive. The emphasis is not only on inborn cognitive structures but also on plasticity, which allows each infant to adapt to the environment.

6. Infant memory is fragile but not completely absent. Reminder sessions help trigger memories, and young brains learn motor sequences and respond to repeated emotions (their own and those of other people) long before explicit memory.

Piaget's Sensorimotor Intelligence

7. Piaget realized that very young infants are active learners who seek to understand their complex observations and experiences. The six stages of sensorimotor intelligence involve early adaptation to experience.

8. Sensorimotor intelligence begins with reflexes and ends with mental combinations. The six stages occur in pairs, with each pair characterized by a circular reaction.

9. Infants first react to their own bodies (primary), then respond to other people and things (secondary), and finally, in the stage of tertiary circular reactions, infants become more goal-oriented, creative, and experimental as "little scientists."

10. Infants gradually develop an understanding of objects. According to Piaget's classic experiments, infants understand object permanence and begin to search for hidden objects at about 8 months. Newer research finds that Piaget underestimated infant cognition.

Language: What Develops in the First Two Years?

11. Attempts to communicate are apparent in the first weeks and months, beginning with noises, facial expressions, and avid listening. Infants babble at about 6 months, understand words and gestures by 10 months, and speak their first words at about 1 year.

12. Vocabulary builds slowly until the infant knows approximately 50 words. Then the naming explosion begins. Grammar is evident in the first holophrases. Combining words in proper sequence is further evidence that babies learn grammar as well as vocabulary.

13. Toward the end of the second year, toddlers express wishes and emotions in short sentences. Variation is evident, in part because of caregiver attention. Some babies are already bilingual.

14. Theories differ in explaining how infants learn language—whether infants must be taught, or that social impulses foster language learning, or that brains are genetically attuned to language as soon as the requisite maturation occurs.

15. Each theory of language learning is confirmed by research. Developmental scientists find that many parts of the brain, and many strategies for learning, result in early language accomplishments.

KEY TERMS

sensorimotor intelligence (p. 151)
primary circular reactions (p. 152)
secondary circular reactions (p. 153)
object permanence (p. 153)
tertiary circular reactions (p. 154)
"little scientist" (p. 154)
babbling (p. 156)
holophrase (p. 157)
naming explosion (p. 157)
grammar (p. 158)
mean length of utterance (MLU) (p. 159)
language acquisition device (LAD) (p. 161)

APPLICATIONS

1. Elicit vocalizations from an infant—babbling if the baby is under age 1, using words if the baby is older. Write down all of the baby's communication for 10 minutes. Then ask the primary caregiver to elicit vocalizations for 10 minutes, and write these down. What differences are apparent between the baby's two attempts at communication? Compare your findings with the norms described in the chapter.

2. Many educators recommend that parents read to babies every day, even before 1 year of age. What theory of language development does this reflect and why? Ask several parents whether they did so, and why or why not.

3. Test a toddler's ability to pretend and to imitate, as Piaget would expect. Use a doll or a toy car and pretend with it, such as feeding the doll or making the car travel. Then see whether the child will do it. This experiment can be more elaborate if the child succeeds.

Especially For ANSWERS

Response for Educators (from p. 145): Probably both. Infants love to communicate, and they seek every possible way to do so. Therefore, the teachers should try to understand the baby and the baby's parents, but they should also start teaching the baby the majority language of the school.

Response for Parents (from p. 153): Both decisions should be made within the first month, during the stage of reflexes. If parents wait until the infant is 4 months or older, they may discover that they are too late. It is difficult to introduce a bottle to a 4-month-old who has never sucked on an artificial nipple or a pacifier to a baby who has already adapted the sucking reflex to a thumb.

Response for Parents (from p. 155): It is easier and safer to baby-proof the house because toddlers, being "little scientists," want to explore. However, it is important for both parents to encourage and guide the baby. If having untouchable items prevents a major conflict between the adults, that might be the best choice.

Observation Quiz ANSWERS

Answer to Observation Quiz (from p. 150): The mobile is a good addition—colorful and too high for the baby to reach. (Let's hope it is securely fastened and those strings are strong and tight!) But there are two things that are not what a cognitive developmentalist would recommend. First, the crib and the wall are both plain white, limiting what the baby can focus on, and second, the crib bumper is a SIDS risk.

Answer to Observation Quiz (from p. 161): Not social interaction, not talking. Instead, all quietly stare at sky and terrain; awe of nature may be a family value. Hierarchy and gender seem significant: The father is distant and above all, the mother is busy, the children are below the parents. Do only males wear hats?

VISUALIZING DEVELOPMENT Early Communication and Language

Communication Milestones: The First Two Years

These are norms. Many intelligent and healthy babies vary in the age at which they reach these milestones.

Months	Communication Milestone
0	Reflexive communication—cries, movements, facial expressions
1	Recognizes some sounds Makes several different cries and sounds Turns toward familiar sounds
3	A range of meaningful noises—cooing, fussing, crying, laughing Social smile well established Laughter begins Imitates movements Enjoys interaction with others
6	New sounds, including squeals, growls, croons, trills, vowel sounds Meaningful gestures including showing excitement (waving arms and legs) Deaf babies express their first signs Expresses negative feelings (with face and arms) Capable of distinguishing emotion by tone of voice Responds to noises by making sounds Uses noise to express joy and unhappiness Babbles, including both consonant and vowel sounds repeated in syllables
10	Makes simple gestures, like raising arms for "pick me up" Recognizes pointing Makes a sound (not in recognizable language) to indicate a particular thing Responds to simple requests
12	More gestures, such as shaking head for "no" Babbles with inflection, intonation Names familiar people (like "mama," "dada," "nana") Uses exclamations, such as "uh-oh!" Tries to imitate words Points and responds to pointing First spoken words
18	Combines two words (like "Daddy bye-bye") Slow growth of vocabulary, up to about 50 words Language use focuses on 10–30 holophrases Uses nouns and verbs Uses movement, including running and throwing, to indicate emotion Naming explosion may begin, three or more words learned per day Much variation: Some toddlers do not yet speak
24	Combines three or four words together; half the toddler's utterances are two or more words long Uses adjectives and adverbs ("blue," "big," "gentle") Sings simple songs

Information from American Academy of Pediatrics

Universal First Words

Across cultures, babies' first words are remarkably similar. The words for mother and father are recognizable in almost any language. Most children will learn to name their immediate family and caregivers between the ages of 12 and 18 months.

Language	Mother	Father
English	mama, mommy	dada. daddy
Spanish	mama	papa
French	maman, mama	papa
Italian	mamma	bebbo, papa
Latvian	mama	te-te
Syrian Arabic	mama	babe
Bantu	be-mama	taata
Swahili	mama	baba
Sanskrit	nana	tata
Hebrew	ema	abba
Korean	oma	apa

ampyang/iStock/Getty Images

Mastering Language

Children's use of language becomes more complex as they acquire more words and begin to master grammar and usage. A child's spoken words or sounds (utterances) are broken down into the smallest units of language to determine their length and complexity:

MEAN LENGTH OF UTTERANCE (MLU), ILLUSTRATED

"Baby!" = 1

"Baby + Sleep" = 2

"Baby + Sleep + ing" = 3

"Shh! + Baby + Sleep + ing" = 4

"Shh! + Baby + is + Sleep + ing" = 5

"Shh! + The + Baby + is + Sleep + ing" = 6

CHAPTER 7

The First Two Years: Psychosocial Development

What Will You Know?

1. Does a difficult newborn become a difficult child?
2. What do infants do if they are securely attached to their caregivers?
3. Is it ideal for infants to be cared for exclusively by their mothers?

- **Emotional Development**
  - Early Emotions
  - Toddlers' Emotions
  - Temperament
  - INSIDE THE BRAIN: The Growth of Emotions
- **The Development of Social Bonds**
  - Synchrony
  - Attachment
  - A VIEW FROM SCIENCE: Measuring Attachment
  - A CASE TO STUDY: Can We Bear This Commitment?
  - Social Referencing
  - Fathers as Social Partners
- **Theories of Infant Psychosocial Development**
  - Psychodynamic Theory
  - Behaviorism
  - Cognitive Theory
  - Evolutionary Theory
- **Who Should Care for Babies?**
  - Complications of Interpretation
  - Exclusive Mother-Care
  - OPPOSING PERSPECTIVES: Why Doesn't Everyone Agree?
  - Problems with Nonmaternal Care
  - Cohort Differences
- **CAREER ALERT: The Pediatrician and the Pediatric Nurse**
- **VISUALIZING DEVELOPMENT: Developing Attachment**

My daughter Bethany came to visit her newest nephew, 7-month-old Isaac. She had visited him many times before, expressing joy and excitement with her voice, face, and hands. At 3 months, he always responded in kind, with big smiles and waving arms. Not surprising: Mutual delight is typical for babies and aunts. But at 7 months, Bethany approached and Isaac turned away, nuzzling into his mother. Later Bethany tried again, and this time he kept looking and smiling.

"You like me now," she said.

"He always liked you; he was just tired," said Elissa, his mother.

"I know," Bethany told her. "I didn't take it personally."

I appreciated both daughters. Elissa sought to reassure Bethany, and Bethany knew that Isaac's reaction was not really to her. But the person I appreciated most was Isaac, responsive to people as well-loved babies should be, but newly wary and seeking maternal comfort. Emotions change month by month in the first two years; ideally caregivers adjust.

We open this chapter by tracing infants' emotions as their brains mature and their experiences accumulate. Next we explore caregiver–infant interaction, particularly *synchrony, attachment,* and *social referencing,* and some theories that explain those developments.

Finally, we explore a controversy: Who should care for infants? Only mothers, or should other relatives, nannies, and day-care teachers provide major care? Families and cultures answer this question in opposite ways. Fortunately, as this chapter explains, despite diversity of temperament and caregiving, most infants develop well, as long as their basic emotional needs are met. Isaac, Elissa, and Bethany continue to thrive.

Emotional Development

Psychosocial development during infancy can be seen as two interwoven strands—nature/nurture, or universal/particular, or experience-expectant/experience-dependent. To portray these strands with words in a book, we must pull them apart; so this chapter is a zigzag, turning from universal to particular again and again.

Left: David A Land/Blend Images/Media bakery
Right: Paul Thomas/EyeEm/Getty Images

AT ABOUT THIS TIME

Developing Emotions

Birth	Distress; contentment
6 weeks	Social smile
3 months	Laughter; curiosity
4 months	Full, responsive smiles
4–8 months	Anger
9–14 months	Fear of social events (strangers, separation from caregiver)
12 months	Fear of unexpected sights and sounds
18 months	Self-awareness; pride; shame; embarrassment

As always, culture and experience influence the norms of development. This is especially true for emotional development after the first 8 months.

social smile A smile evoked by a human face, normally first evident in infants about 6 weeks after birth.

Early Emotions

We begin with universal: In their first two years, all infants progress from reactive pain and pleasure to complex patterns of socioemotional awareness, a movement from basic instincts to learned responses (see At About This Time).

At first, comfort predominates: Newborns are happy and relaxed when fed and drifting off to sleep. Discomfort is also part of daily life: Newborns cry when they are hurt or hungry, tired or frightened (as by a loud noise or a sudden loss of support).

By the second week, some infants have bouts of uncontrollable crying, called *colic,* probably the result of immature digestion. Others have *reflux,* probably the result of immature swallowing. About 20 percent of babies cry "excessively," defined as more than three hours a day, more than three days a week, for more than three weeks (J. Kim, 2011).

Fortunately, early emotions are universal and do not predict later life. A longitudinal study of 291 infants found that, by age 2, infants with colic were no more likely to have behavioral problems than those without (Bell et al., 2018).

Smiling and Laughing Soon, crying decreases and additional emotions become recognizable. Happiness is expressed by a fleeting **social smile,** evoked by a human face at about 6 weeks (Wörmann et al., 2012).

Preterm babies smile later because the social smile is affected by age since conception, not age since birth (White-Traut et al., 2018). In other words, the social smile is another universal—all babies do it when they are old enough.

Laughter builds over the first months, often in tandem with curiosity: A typical 6-month-old chortles upon discovering new things, particularly social experiences that balance familiarity and surprise, such as Daddy making a funny face. That is what Piaget would call "making interesting experiences last." Very young infants prefer seeing happy faces over sad ones, even if the happy faces are not looking at them (Kim & Johnson, 2013).

Soon happiness becomes more discriminating. In one study, infants first enjoyed a video of dancing to music as it normally occurs, on the beat. Then some watched a video in which the soundtrack was mismatched with dancing. Eight- to 12-month-old babies, compared to younger ones, were quite curious—but less delighted—about offbeat dancing. The researchers came to the conclusion that "babies know bad dancing when they see it" (Hannon et al., 2017).

REUTERS/Suzanne Plunkett

Developmentally Correct Both Santa's smile and Olivia's grimace are appropriate reactions for people of their age. Adults playing Santa must smile no matter what, and if Olivia smiled, that would be troubling to anyone who knows about 7-month-olds. Yet every Christmas, thousands of parents wait in line to put their infants on the laps of oddly dressed, bearded strangers.

Anger and Sadness Crying in pain and smiling in pleasure are soon joined by emotions that are more responsive to external experience. Anger is notable at 6 months, usually triggered by frustration.

For example, to study infant emotions, researchers "crouched behind the child and gently restrained his or her arms for 2 min[utes] or until 20 s[econds] of hard crying ensued" (Mills-Koonce et al., 2011, p. 390). "Hard crying" was not rare: Infants hate to be strapped in, caged in, closed in, or just held in place when they want to explore.

In infancy, anger is a healthy response to frustration, unlike sadness, which also may appear in the first months (Thiam et al., 2017). Sadness indicates withdrawal instead of a bid for help, and it is accompanied by a greater increase in the body's production of cortisol. For that reason, developmentalists are troubled if a very young baby is sad.

Fear Fear begins with events, such as fear of falling or of loud noises, but soon it involves human interaction. Two kinds of social fear are typical:

- **Separation anxiety**—clinging and crying when a familiar caregiver is about to leave. Some separation anxiety is normal at age 1, intensifies by age 2, and then usually subsides.
- **Stranger wariness**—fear of unfamiliar people, especially when they move too close, too quickly. Wariness indicates memory: When Isaac hesitated at seeing Bethany, that meant his memory was maturing.

separation anxiety An infant's distress when a familiar caregiver leaves; most obvious between 9 and 14 months.

stranger wariness An infant's expression of concern—a quiet stare while clinging to a familiar person, or a look of fear—when a stranger appears.

Many 1-year-olds are wary of anything unexpected, from a flush of the toilet to the pop of a jack-in-the-box, from closing elevator doors to the tail-wagging approach of a dog. With repeated experience and reassurance, older infants might enjoy flushing the toilet (again and again) or calling the dog (crying if the dog does *not* come). Note the transition from instinct to learning to thought (Panksepp & Watt, 2011).

Especially for Nurses and Pediatricians Parents come to you concerned that their 1-year-old hides her face and holds onto them tightly whenever a stranger appears. What do you tell them? (see response, page 191)

If separation anxiety and stranger fear remain intense after age 3, impairing a child's ability to leave home, to go to school, or to play with other children, that is an emotional disorder. According to *DSM-5*, separation anxiety becomes a disorder when it lingers into childhood or adolescence (American Psychiatric Association, 2013); some clinicians diagnose it in adults, as well (Bögels et al., 2013). Likewise, stranger wariness may continue, becoming social phobia or general anxiety later on (Rudaz et al., 2017).

Toddlers' Emotions

Emotions take on new strength during toddlerhood, as both memory and mobility advance. For example, throughout the second year and beyond, anger and fear become less frequent but more focused, targeted toward infuriating or terrifying experiences. Similarly, laughing and crying are louder and more discriminating.

Temper Tantrums The new strength of emotions is apparent in temper tantrums. Toddlers are famous for fury. When something angers them, they might yell, scream, cry, hit, and throw themselves on the floor. Logic is beyond them: If adults tease or get angry, that makes it worse. Parental insistence on obedience exacerbates the tantrum (Cierpka & Cierpka, 2016).

One child said, "I don't want my feet. Take my feet off. I don't want my feet." Her mother tried logic, which didn't work, and then offered to get scissors and cut off the offending feet. A new wail erupted, with a loud shriek "Nooooo!" (Katrina, quoted in Vedantam, 2011).

With temper tantrums, soon sadness comes to the fore. Then comfort—not punishment—is helpful (Green et al., 2011). Outbursts of anger are typical at age 1 and 2, but if they persist and become destructive, that signifies trouble, in parent or child (Cierpka & Cierpka, 2016).

As with these examples, a toddler's innate reactions may evolve into moral values and psychic responses, with specifics depending on parents and experiences. For example, many children take off their clothes in public, unaware that nakedness is taboo. Children are born curious and uninhibited: Shame and self-consciousness are learned.

Joseph Farris/CartoonStock

Empathy Wins Crying babies whose caregivers empathize often become confident, accomplished, and caring children. Sleep deprivation makes anyone unhappy, but this man's response is much better for both of them than anger or neglect.

Self and Others Temper can be seen as an expression of selfhood, as can other common toddler emotions: pride, shame, jealousy, embarrassment, disgust, and guilt. These emotions may begin with inborn sensitivities, but they involve social awareness.

THINK CRITICALLY: Which does your culture consider more annoying, people who brag or people who put themselves down?

Such awareness typically emerges from family interaction, especially the relationship between caregiver and baby. For instance, in a study of infant jealousy, mothers ignored their own baby and attended to another infant. That made the babies move closer to their mothers, bidding for attention. Their brain activity also registered social emotions (Mize et al., 2014).

Positive emotions also show social awareness and learning. Most toddlers try to help a stranger who has dropped something or who is searching for a hidden object. Their response seems to be natural empathy, quite apart from any selfish motives (Warneken, 2015).

Over time, children learn when and whom to help by watching adults. Some adults donate to beggars, others look away, and still others complain to the police. Attitudes about ethnicity (or immigration, or clothing) begin with the infant's preference for the familiar and interest in novelty, and then upbringing adds appreciation or rejection.

self-awareness A person's realization that he or she is a distinct individual whose body, mind, and actions are separate from those of other people.

temperament Inborn differences between one person and another in emotions, activity, and self-regulation. It is measured by the person's typical responses to the environment.

Recognizing the Self In addition to social awareness, another foundation for emotional growth is **self-awareness,** the realization that one's body, mind, and activities are distinct from those of other people (Kopp, 2011). Closely following the new mobility that results from walking is an emerging sense of individuality.

In a classic experiment (Lewis & Brooks, 1978), 9- to 24-month-olds looked into a mirror after a dot of rouge had been surreptitiously put on their noses. If they reacted by touching the red dot on their noses, that meant they knew the mirror showed their own faces. None of the babies younger than 12 months did that, although they sometimes smiled and touched the dot on the "other" baby in the mirror.

My Finger, My Body, and Me Mirror self-recognition is particularly important in her case, as this 2-year-old has a twin sister. Parents may enjoy dressing twins alike and giving them rhyming names, but each baby needs to know she is an individual, not just a twin.

Between 15 and 24 months, babies become self-aware, touching their own red noses with curiosity and puzzlement. Self-recognition in the mirror/rouge test (and in photographs) usually emerges with two other advances: pretending and using first-person pronouns (*I, me, mine, myself, my*) (Lewis, 2010).

This illustrates the interplay of infant abilities—walking, talking, social awareness, and emotional self-understanding all combine to make the 18-month-old quite unlike the 8-month-old. Timing and expression are affected by the social context (Ross et al., 2017).

Some cultures value independence and others do not, and values differ among individuals as well. If you asked a toddler to put away some toys and were told "No," would you be angry or amused? Your answer reflects your culture; babies learn to reflect that as well.

macmillan learning

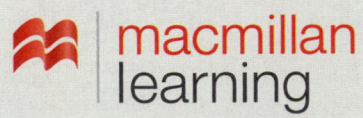

VIDEO ACTIVITY: Self-Awareness and the Rouge Test shows the famous assessment of how and when self-awareness appears in infancy.

Temperament

The early emotions are universal, but the intensity of those emotions reflects temperament. That varies from one baby to the next.

Temperament is defined as the "biologically based core of individual differences in style of approach and response to the environment that is stable across time and situations" (van den Akker et al., 2010, p. 485). "Biologically based" means temperament begins with genes.

Are babies really born with different temperaments? Yes! One team recorded the tone, duration, and intensity of infant cries after the first inoculation, before much experience outside the womb. Cries at this very early stage correlated with later temperament: Those who screamed loudest and longest became quickest to protest later on (Jong et al., 2010).

Dimensions of Temperament In laboratory studies of temperament, 4-month-old infants might see spinning mobiles or hear unusual sounds, and older babies might confront a clown who approaches quickly. During such experiences, some children laugh, some cry, and others are quiet.

A summary of research (Lengua et al., 2019) reports a general agreement among scientists that three distinct aspects of temperament are apparent in infants:

- Effortful control (regulating attention and emotion, self-soothing)
- Negative mood (fearful, angry, unhappy)
- Exuberance (active, social, not shy)

Temperament is *not* the same as personality, although temperament may lead to personality differences. Together, they make us "who we are" (Rothbart, 2011). Generally, personality traits (e.g., honesty and humility) are learned, whereas temperamental traits (e.g., shyness and aggression) are genetic.

Of course, nature and nurture always interact. For both temperament and personality, family influences are powerful: While parents affect their children in temperament and personality, children also affect their parents (Lengua et al., 2019).

In general, infants with difficult temperaments are more likely than other babies to develop emotional problems, especially if their mothers had a difficult pregnancy and were depressed or anxious caregivers (Garthus-Niegel et al., 2017). In that case, the difficult baby affects the stressed parent, and vice versa.

Denis Doyle/Getty Images Entertainment/Getty Images

Feliz Navidad Not only is every language and culture distinct, but each individual also has his or her own temperament. Here children watch the Cortylandia Christmas show in Madrid, Spain, where the Christmas holiday begins on December 24 and lasts through January 6, which is Three Kings Day. As you see from the fathers and children, each person has his or her own reaction to the same event.

Observation Quiz What indicates that each father has his own child on his shoulders? ↑ (see answer, page 192)

Temperament Over the Years One longitudinal study analyzed temperament at least eight times, in infancy, early childhood, middle childhood, adolescence, and adulthood. The scientists designed laboratory experiments to evoke emotions appropriate for the age of the participants, collected detailed reports from mothers and later from participants themselves, and gathered observational data and physiological evidence, including brain scans (Fox et al., 2001, 2005, 2013; Williams et al., 2010; Jarcho et al., 2013; Shechner et al., 2018).

In early childhood, change was most likely for the inhibited, fearful infants and least likely for the exuberant ones (see **Figure 7.1**). Why was that? Do some parents coax frightened infants to be brave, letting exuberant babies stay happy?

When the fearful children grew up, about half were still fearful. The half who overcame their anxiety had more activation in another part of the brain (the anterior cingulate cortex), which signals safety (Shechner et al., 2018).

Perhaps if fearful infants were quickly reassured by their caregivers, a neurological link formed between fear and comfort. Then, when anxiety rose later in life, the brain automatically counteracted it.

The researchers found unexpected gender differences. As teenagers, formerly inhibited boys had relatively high rates of drug abuse, but the opposite was found for inhibited girls (Williams et al., 2010). A likely explanation is cultural: Shy boys use drugs to mask their social anxiety, but shy girls may be more accepted as they are. Other research also finds that shyness is more stable in girls than boys (Poole et al., 2017).

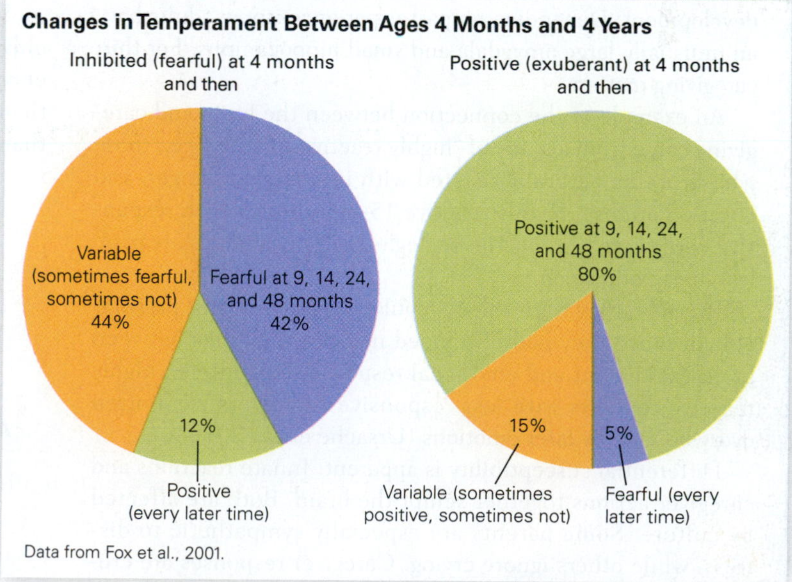

FIGURE 7.1

Do Babies' Temperaments Change? Sometimes it is possible—especially if they were fearful babies. Adults who are reassuring help children overcome fearfulness. If fearful children do not change, it is not known whether that's because their parents are not sufficiently reassuring (nurture) or because the babies themselves are temperamentally more fearful (nature).

Especially for Nurses Parents come to you with their fussy 3-month-old. They have read that temperament is "fixed" before birth, and they are worried that their child will always be difficult. What do you tell them? (see response, page 191)

Brain Variations You read earlier that temperament is "biologically based." This means that brain maturation is crucial for emotional development, particularly for emotions that respond to other people.

Experience connects the amygdala and the prefrontal cortex (van Goozen, 2015), teaching infants to align their own feelings with those of their caregivers (Missana et al., 2014). Joy, fear, and excitement become shared, mutual experiences—as anyone who successfully makes a baby laugh knows.

Essentially, connections between innate emotional impulses from the amygdala and experience-based learning shows "dramatic age-dependent improvement," with genes, prenatal influences, and early caregiving all affecting brain growth (Gao et al., 2017, p. 180). Infant experience leads to adult reactions: If you know someone who cries, laughs, or angers quickly, ask about their first two years of life.

All social emotions, particularly sadness and fear, affect the hormones and hence the brain (see Inside the Brain). Caregiving matters. Sad and angry infants whose mothers are depressed become fearful toddlers and depressed children (Dix & Yan, 2014).

Abuse and unpredictable responses from caregivers are likely among the "early adverse influences [that] have lasting effects on developing neurobiological systems in the brain" (van Goozen, 2015, p. 208). Even worse is a lack of any social responses: That leads to significant brain shrinkage (Marshall, 2014; Sheridan et al., 2018). In-depth studies of the brain and emotions confirm this.

INSIDE THE BRAIN

The Growth of Emotions

As you read in Chapter 5, the regions of the brain that comprise the limbic system are particularly crucial in emotional development. Depending on past experience, some adults have an unusually large amygdala and small hippocampus. For this, caregiving matters.

An example of the connection between the brain and caregiving came from a study of "highly reactive" infants (i.e., those whose brains naturally reacted with intense fear, anger, and other emotions). Highly reactive 15-month-olds with responsive caregivers (not hostile or neglectful) became less fearful, less angry, and so on.

By age 4, they were able to regulate their emotions, presumably because they had developed neurological links between brain excitement and emotional response. By contrast, highly reactive toddlers with less responsive caregivers were often overwhelmed by later emotions (Ursache et al., 2013).

Differential susceptibility is apparent: Innate reactions and caregiver actions together sculpt the brain. Both are affected by culture: Some parents are especially sympathetic to distress, while others ignore crying. Caregiver responses are crucial in infancy, even though the emotional manifestations are more apparent later on (Cole & Hollenstein, 2018).

Genes and prenatal influences on the brain are evident. Some fetuses are exposed to toxic drugs; some inherit genes that make them vulnerable to autism spectrum disorder; some preterm newborns spend their early days in the hospital. For all such infants, postnatal experiences are crucial for emotional development in the brain (Gao et al., 2017; White-Traut et al., 2018) (see **Figure 7.2**).

The social smile, for instance, is fleeting when 2-month-olds see almost any face. As the brain develops and experience builds, infants smile more quickly at a familiar caregiver than a stranger, and more at responsive, smiling caregivers than at less interactive caregivers. When neurons repeatedly

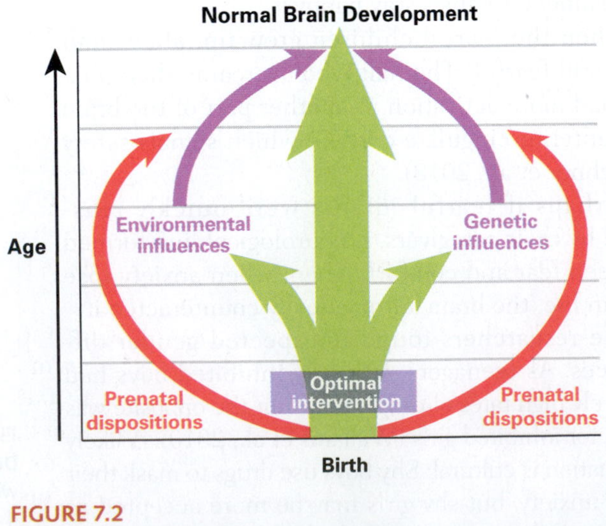

FIGURE 7.2
Seven Arrows Pointing Up This figure is intended to show the ongoing development of the brain. Prenatal, genetic, and experiential influences continue lifelong.

fire together, the dendrites become closely connected, with one quickly triggering another. Even at 2 months, experience matters.

In classic research, the brains of infant mice released more serotonin when their mothers licked them. That not only increased the mouselings' pleasure but also started epigenetic responses, reducing cortisol from brain and body, including the adrenal glands. The effects were lifelong; those baby mice became smarter and more social adults, with larger brains.

That research with mice has been replicated and extended. Neuroscientists are awed by the early "remarkable capacity for plastic changes that influence behavioural outcomes throughout the lifetime" (Kolb et al., 2017, p. 1218).

Too much fear and stress harms the hippocampus and hypothalamus, which then grow more slowly. If infants are maltreated, they develop abnormal responses to stress, anger, and other emotions, apparent in many brain areas (hypothalamus, amygdala, hippocampus, prefrontal cortex) (Bernard et al., 2014; Cicchetti, 2013a).

The immune system is also impaired (Hostinar et al., 2018). Consequently, abused children may become sickly, slow-thinking adults with erratic emotions, because of what has happened inside their brains decades earlier.

WHAT HAVE YOU LEARNED?

1. What experiences trigger happiness, anger, and fear?
2. How do emotions differ between the first and second year of life?
3. What is the significance of how toddlers react to seeing themselves in a mirror?
4. What is the difference between temperament and personality?
5. How do temperamental traits affect later behavior?

The Development of Social Bonds

Now we return to what is universally true. Humans are, by nature, social creatures. The specifics of social interaction during infancy depend on the age of the baby, with *synchrony, attachment,* and *social referencing* each evident in sequence during the first two years of life.

Synchrony

Early parent–infant interactions are described as **synchrony,** a mutual exchange with split-second timing. Metaphors for synchrony are often musical—a waltz, a jazz duet—to emphasize that each partner must be attuned to the other, with moment-by-moment responses. Synchrony increases over the first year.

To be specific, long before they can reach out and grab, infants respond excitedly to caregiver attention by waving their arms. Adults with animated expressions move close so that a waving arm can touch a face or, even better, a hand can grab hair. This is the eagerness to "make interesting events last" that was described in Chapter 6.

Synchronizing adults open their eyes wide, raise their eyebrows, smack their lips, and emit nonsense sounds. Hair-grabbing might make adults bob their heads back and forth, in a playful attempt to shake off the grab, to the infants' joy. Over time, an adult and an infant might develop a routine of hair-grabbing in synchrony.

Another adult–infant pair might develop another routine, perhaps with hand-clapping, or lip-smacking, or head-turning. Synchrony may become a mutual dance, with both knowing the steps. Often mothers and infants engage in "social games," which are routines passed down from adult to infant in that culture. Social games soon become synchronized, with the infant anticipating and reacting to each move (Markova, 2018).

synchrony A coordinated, rapid, and smooth exchange of responses between a caregiver and an infant.

CHAPTER APP 7

Red Rover

IOS:
https://tinyurl.com/nasyoxg

RELEVANT TOPIC:
Psychosocial development and the caregiver–infant bond

This free location-based app and private social network helps parents connect with friends and members of their community to find kid-friendly activities, restaurants, museums, and even clean bathrooms. Fun features include location sharing, Facebook and Twitter sharing, photo sharing, and one-touch emergency management.

BSIP/UIG via Getty Images

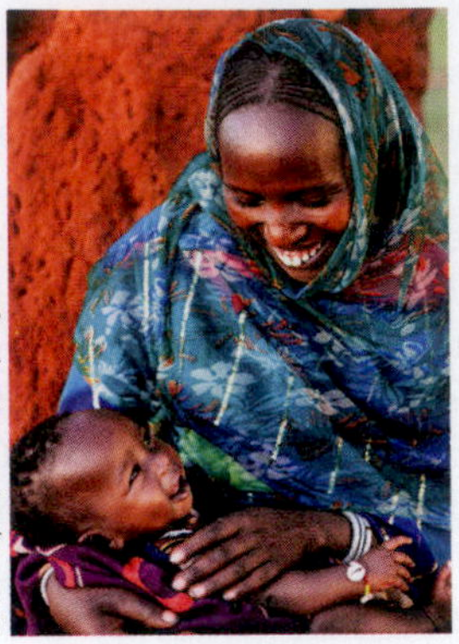

Bartosz Hadyniak/Photodisc/Getty Images

Nancy Honey/Cultura/Getty Images

Open Wide Synchrony is evident worldwide. Everywhere, babies watch their parents carefully, hoping for exactly what these three parents—each from quite different cultures—express, and responding with such delight that adults relish these moments.

Both Partners Active Direct observation reveals synchrony; anyone can see it when watching a caregiver play with an infant who is far too young to talk. Adults rarely smile much at newborns until that first social smile, weeks after birth. Smiling is like a switch that lights up the adult and the baby. Soon both partners synchronize smiles, eyes, noises, and movements.

Detailed research, typically with two cameras, one focused on the infant and one on the caregiver, examines the timing of every millisecond of arched eyebrows, widening eyes, pursed lips, and so on. That confirms the tight relationship between adult and infant (Messinger et al., 2010).

Physiological measures, such as heart rate and brain waves, also measure synchrony. This reveals how maternal depression leads to infant depression—the baby picks up on the mother's responses (Atzil et al., 2014).

In every interaction, infants read others' emotions and develop social skills, taking turns and watching expressions. Synchrony usually begins with adults imitating infants (not vice versa), responding to barely perceptible facial expressions and body motions (Beebe et al., 2016). This helps infants connect their internal state with expressions and behavior.

still-face technique An experimental practice in which an adult keeps his or her face unmoving and expressionless in face-to-face interaction with an infant.

Neglected Synchrony Experiments involving the **still-face technique** suggest that synchrony is experience-expectant (needed for normal brain growth) (Tronick, 1989; Tronick & Weinberg, 1997; Hari, 2017). [**Life-Span Link:** Experience-expectant and experience-dependent brain functions are described in Chapter 5.]

In still-face studies, at first an infant is propped in front of an adult who responds normally. Then, on cue, the adult stops all expression, staring quietly with a "still face" for a minute or two.

Sometimes by 2 months, and clearly by 6 months, infants are upset when their parents are unresponsive. Babies frown, fuss, drool, look away, kick, cry, or suck their fingers. By 5 months, they also vocalize, as if to say, "React to me!"

Synchrony is experience-expectant, not simply experience-dependent. Responsiveness aids psychosocial and biological development, evident in heart rate, weight gain, and brain maturation.

THINK CRITICALLY: What will happen if no one plays with an infant?

One study looked in detail at 4-month-old infants during and immediately after a still-face episode (Montirosso et al., 2015). The researchers found three clusters: "socially engaged" (33 percent), "disengaged" (60 percent), and "negatively engaged" (7 percent).

When the mothers were still-faced, the socially engaged babies remained active, looking around at other things, apparently expecting that the caregivers would soon resume connection. When the still face was over, they quickly reengaged.

By contrast, the disengaged group became passive, looking sad. When the still face was over, they did not quickly return to normal. Finally, the negatively engaged babies were upset and angry, crying during and after the still face.

The mothers of each type differed in how they played with their infants before and after the still face. The socially engaged mothers matched the infants' actions (bobbing heads, opening mouth, and so on), but the negatively engaged mothers almost never matched and sometimes expressed anger—not sympathy—when the baby cried (Montirosso et al., 2015).

Attachment

Responsive and mutual relationships are important throughout childhood and beyond. However, once infants can walk, the moment-by-moment, face-to-face synchrony is less common. Instead, **attachment**—the connection between one person and another, measured by how they respond to each other—comes to the fore. Two signs indicate attachment: *contact-maintaining* and *proximity-seeking*.

attachment According to Ainsworth, "an affectional tie" that an infant forms with a caregiver—a tie that binds them together in space and endures over time.

Research on mother–infant attachment began with John Bowlby (1983) in England and Mary Ainsworth (1967) in Uganda. Over the past four decades, attachment has been studied on every continent and in virtually every nation, in both atypical populations (e.g., infants with Down syndrome or autism spectrum disorder) and typical ones, with fathers and others, not just mothers.

Attachment is lifelong, beginning before birth and influencing relationships during early and late childhood, adolescence, and adulthood (e.g., Simpson & Rholes, 2015; Grossmann et al., 2014; Tan et al., 2016; Hunter & Maunder, 2016). Developmentalists are convinced that attachment is basic to the survival of *Homo sapiens,* with the manifestation dependent on culture and the age of the person.

Thus, attachment is a universal; expression is particular. For instance, Ugandan mothers never kiss their infants, but they often massage them, contrary to Westerners. American adults may phone their mothers every day—even when the mothers are a thousand miles away. Or attached family members may all sit in the same room of a large house, each reading quietly, speaking only a few words every so often. All of these signify attachment.

Attachment is mutual. During infancy, caregivers often keep a watchful eye on their baby, initiating contact with expressions, gestures, and sounds. Before going to sleep at midnight they might tiptoe to the crib to gaze at their sleeping infant, or, in daytime, absentmindedly smooth their toddler's hair.

For their part, 1-year-olds look to their caregivers. Their attachment is physical: They grab a hand, a leg, a sleeve.

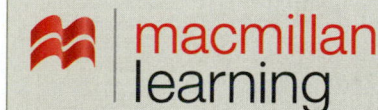

macmillan learning

VIDEO ACTIVITY: Mother Love and the Work of Harry Harlow features classic footage of Harlow's research, showing the setup and results of his famous experiment.

Secure and Insecure Attachment

Attachment is classified into four types: A, B, C, and D (see Visualizing Development, page 193). Infants with **secure attachment** (type B) feel comfortable and confident. The caregiver is a *base for exploration,* providing assurance and enabling discovery.

secure attachment A relationship in which an infant obtains both comfort and confidence from the presence of his or her caregiver.

A securely attached toddler might, for example, scramble down from the caregiver's lap to play with an intriguing toy but periodically look back and vocalize (contact-maintaining) or bring the toy to the caregiver for inspection (proximity-seeking).

The caregiver's presence gives the child courage to explore; departure causes distress; return elicits positive contact (such as smiling or hugging) and then more playing. This balanced reaction—the child concerned but not overwhelmed by comings and goings—indicates security.

By contrast, insecure attachment (types A and C) is characterized by fear, anxiety, anger, or indifference. Some insecurely attached children play independently without seeking contact; this is **insecure-avoidant attachment** (type A). The

insecure-avoidant attachment A pattern of attachment in which an infant avoids connection with the caregiver, as when the infant seems not to care about the caregiver's presence, departure, or return.

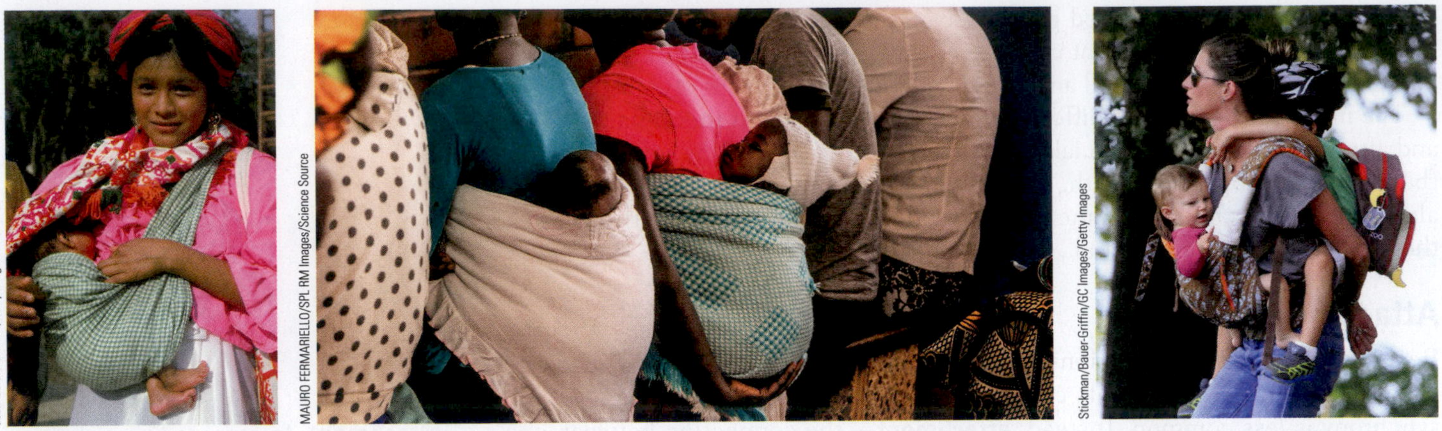

Jean-Gerard Sidaner/Getty Images

MAURO FERMARIELLO/SPL RM Images/Science Source

Stickman/Bauer-Griffin/GC Images/Getty Images

Same or Different? A theme of this chapter is that babies and mothers are the same worldwide, yet dramatically different in each culture. Do you see more similarities or differences between the Huastec mother in Mexico (left), the mothers waiting in a clinic in Uganda (middle), and supermodel Gisele Bündchen in Boston, Massachusetts (right)? (Her husband is Tom Brady, star quarterback of the New England Patriots.)

insecure-resistant/ambivalent attachment A pattern of attachment in which an infant's anxiety and uncertainty are evident, as when the infant becomes very upset at separation from the caregiver and both resists and seeks contact on reunion.

disorganized attachment A type of attachment that is marked by an infant's inconsistent reactions to the caregiver's departure and return.

opposite reaction is **insecure-resistant/ambivalent attachment** (type C). Children with type C cling to their caregivers and are angry at being left.

Infants may be securely or insecurely attached to mothers, fathers, or other caregivers—sometimes just to one person, sometimes to several. Is secure attachment innate? Are difficult children always insecurely attached? No. Every baby seeks attachment: Temperament may affect the expression, but not the need (Groh et al., 2017).

Ainsworth's original schema differentiated only types A, B, and C. Later researchers discovered a fourth category (type D), **disorganized attachment.** Type D infants may suddenly switch from hitting to kissing their mothers, from staring blankly to crying hysterically, from pinching themselves to freezing in place.

Among the general population, almost two-thirds of infants are secure (type B). About one-third are insecure, either indifferent (type A) or unduly anxious (type C), and about 5 to 10 percent are disorganized (type D).

Type D infants are especially worrisome to developmentalists. They have no consistent strategy for social interaction, even avoidance or resistance. They are at high risk for later psychopathology, including severe aggression and major depression (Cicchetti, 2016; Groh et al., 2012).

Recently, some people have advocated *attachment parenting,* which prioritizes the mother–infant relationship during the first three years of life far more than Ainsworth or Bowlby did (Sears & Sears, 2001; Komisar, 2017). Attachment parenting mandates that mothers should always be near their infants (co-sleeping, "wearing" the baby in a wrap or sling, breast-feeding on demand). Some experts suggest that attachment parenting is too distant from the research concept and evidence (Ennis, 2015).

Orphanages in Romania No scholar doubts that attachments should develop in the first year of life and that the lack of close caregiver–infant relationships risks dire consequences. Unfortunately, thousands of children born in Romania are proof.

When Romanian dictator Nicolae Ceaușescu forbade birth control and abortions in the 1980s, illegal abortions became the leading cause of death for Romanian women aged 15 to 45 (Verona, 2003), and 170,000 children were abandoned and sent to crowded, impersonal, state-run orphanages (Marshall, 2014). The children were severely deprived of social contact, experiencing virtually no synchrony, play, or conversation.

A VIEW FROM SCIENCE

Measuring Attachment

Scientists take great care to develop valid measurements. They seek to develop an "operational definition," an observable behavior that indicates the construct, so that other scientists know what is measured and can replicate the study.

For instance, if you wanted to study love between romantic partners, what would your empirical measurement be? Ask on a questionnaire? Record a video of their interaction and count how often they made eye contact, or expressed agreement, or moved closer together? Note whether they cohabited, married, divorced, had sex, shared finances? None of these is exactly what people call "love," but all might be useful.

Mary Ainsworth (1973) developed a now-classic laboratory procedure called the *Strange Situation* to measure attachment. In a well-equipped playroom, an infant is observed for eight episodes, each lasting no more than three minutes. First, the child and mother are together. Next, according to a set sequence, the mother and then a stranger come and go. Infants' responses to their mothers indicate which type of attachment they have formed.

Researchers focus on the following:

- *Exploration of the toys.* A secure toddler plays happily.
- *Reaction to the caregiver's departure.* A secure toddler notices when the caregiver leaves and shows some sign of missing him or her.
- *Reaction to the caregiver's return.* A secure toddler welcomes the caregiver's reappearance, seeks contact, and then plays again.

Scientists who measure attachment in 1-year-olds are carefully trained, via watching videos, calibrating ratings, and studying manuals. Researchers are certified only when they reach a high standard of accuracy. They learn that some common behaviors signify insecurity. For instance, clinging to the caregiver may be type C; being too friendly to the stranger suggests type A.

In attachment research, some other measures—again empirical—are used. This is particularly needed when studying adult attachments. A sign of a past insecure childhood is not only rejection of mother ("I never want to see her again") but also sanctification of her ("she was a saint"). It is especially troubling if an adult is confused and incoherent, with few details about their awful or perfect childhood.

The measurement of attachment via the Strange Situation has made longitudinal studies possible, with interesting results that could not have been established unless the measurement was understood and procedures were carefully followed. Attachment affects brain development and the immune system (Pietromonaco & Powers, 2015).

Insecure attachment does not always lead to later problems (Keller, 2014); links from one generation to another are weaker than originally thought (Fearon & Roisman, 2017). Anxious attachment peaks in adolescence and declines over adulthood, according to several longitudinal studies (Fraley, 2019).

Nonetheless, thanks to procedures developed by Mary Ainsworth half a century ago, we now know that securely attached infants *are* more likely to become secure toddlers, socially competent preschoolers, high-achieving schoolchildren, partners in loving couples, capable parents, and healthy adults (Fraley, 2019; Raby et al., 2017).

THINK CRITICALLY: Is the Strange Situation a valid way to measure attachment in every culture, or is it biased toward the Western idea of the ideal mother–child relationship?

Excited, Troubled, Comforted This sequence is repeated daily for 1-year-olds, which is why the same sequence is replicated to measure attachment. As you see, toys are no substitute for mother's comfort if the infant or toddler is secure, as this one seems to be. Some, however, cry inconsolably or throw toys angrily when left alone.

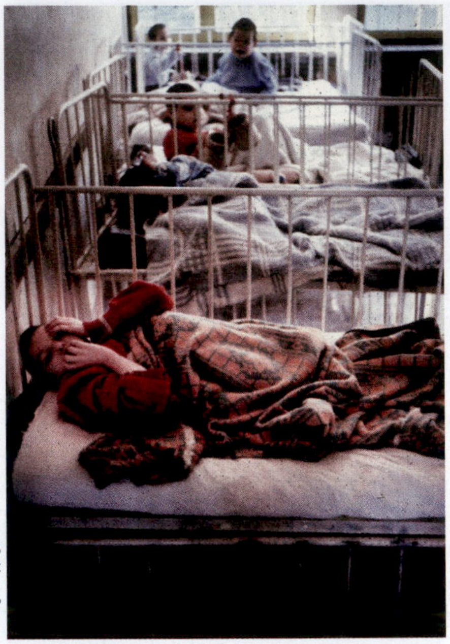

All images copyrighted Thomas B. Szalay

Hands on Head These children in Romania, here older than age 2, probably spent most of their infancy in their cribs, never with the varied stimulation that infant brains need. The sad results are evident here—that boy is fingering his own face, because the feel of his own touch is most likely one of the few sensations he knows. The girl sitting up in the back is a teenager. This photo was taken in 1982; Romania no longer destroys children so dramatically.

In the two years after Ceauseşcu was ousted and killed in 1989, thousands of those children were adopted by North American, western European, and Australian families. Infants under 6 months of age fared best; their adoptive parents established synchrony and attachment, play and caregiving. Many adopted at slightly older ages also fared well.

For those adopted after age 1, early signs were encouraging: Skinny toddlers gained weight, started walking, and grew quickly, developing the motor skills they had lacked (H. Park et al., 2011). However, if their social deprivation had lasted more than a year, their emotions and intellect suffered.

Many of the late adoptees were overly friendly to strangers, a sign of insecure attachment. By age 11, their average IQ was only 85, which is 15 points lower than the statistical norm. The older they had been at adoption, the worse they fared (C. Nelson et al., 2014). Some became impulsive, angry teenagers. Apparently, the stresses of adolescence and emerging adulthood exacerbated their cognitive and social deficits (Merz & McCall, 2011). (See **Table 7.1**.)

These children are now adults, many with serious emotional or conduct problems (Sonuga-Barke et al., 2017). Some overly friendly 4-year-olds suffer as adolescents from *disinhibited social engagement disorder* (Guyon-Harris et al., 2018). That makes them vulnerable throughout adulthood: They follow people who will harm them.

None of this is inevitable. Other research on children adopted nationally and internationally finds that many develop well. However, every stress—such as parental maltreatment, institutional life, and the adoption process—makes it more difficult for children to become happy, well-functioning adults (Grotevant & McDermott, 2014).

Romania no longer permits international adoption, even though some infants are still institutionalized. Research confirms that early emotional deprivation, not genes or nutrition, is their greatest problem. Infants develop best in their

TABLE 7.1

Predictors of Attachment Type

***Secure* attachment (type B) is more likely if:**

- The parent is usually sensitive and responsive to the infant's needs.
- The infant–parent relationship is high in synchrony.
- The infant's temperament is "easy."
- The parents are not stressed about income, other children, or their marriage.
- The parents have a working model of secure attachment to their own parents.

***Insecure* attachment is more likely if:**

- The parent mistreats the child. (Neglect increases type A; abuse increases types C and D.)
- The mother is mentally ill. (Paranoia increases type D; depression increases type C.)
- The parents are highly stressed about income, other children, or their marriage. (Parental stress increases types A and D.)
- The parents are intrusive and controlling. (Parental domination increases type A.)
- The parents have alcohol use disorder. (Father with alcoholism increases type A; mother with alcoholism increases type D.)
- The child's temperament is "difficult." (Difficult children tend to be type C.)
- The child's temperament is "slow-to-warm-up." (This correlates with type A.)

own families, second best in foster families, and worst in institutions (C. Nelson et al., 2014).

This is true for infants everywhere: Families usually nurture their babies better than strangers who provide good physical care but not emotional attachment. The longer children live in hospitals and orphanages, the more social and intellectual harm occur (Julian, 2013).

Fortunately, most institutions have improved or closed, although many (an estimated 8 million) children worldwide are still in institutions (Marshall, 2014). Recent adoptees are much less impaired than those Romanian orphans (Grotevant & McDermott, 2014), and many adoptive families are as strongly attached as any biological family, as A Case to Study demonstrates.

A CASE TO STUDY

Can We Bear This Commitment?

Parents and children capture my attention, wherever they are. Today I spotted one mother ignoring her stroller-bound toddler on a crowded subway (I wanted to tell her to talk to her child) and another mother breast-feeding a 7-month-old in a public park (I smiled approvingly, because that was illegal three decades ago).

I notice signs of secure or insecure attachment — the contact-maintaining and proximity-seeking moves that parents do, seemingly unaware that they are responding to primordial depths of human love. I particularly observe families I know. I am struck by the powerful bond between parent and child, as strong (or stronger) in adoptive families as in genetic ones.

One adoptive couple is Macky and Nick. They echo my own responses to my biological children. Two examples:

- When their first daughter, Alice, was a tiny baby, I overheard Nick phone another parent, discussing detergents that are gentle but effective for washing baby clothes. That reminded me that I switched detergents for my newborn.
- Years later, at a social event when Macky was engrossed in conversation, Nick interrupted to tell him that they needed to go home because the girls needed their naps. Parents everywhere do that, with one telling the other it's time to leave.

My appreciation of their attachment was cemented by a third incident. In Macky's words:

> I'll never forget the Fourth of July at the spacious home of my mother-in-law's best friend. It was a perfect celebration on a perfect day. Kids frolicked in the pool. Parents socialized nearby, on the sun-drenched lawn or inside the cool house. Many guests had published books on parenting; we imagined they admired our happy, thriving family.
>
> My husband and I have two daughters, Alice who was then 7 and Penelope who was 4. They learned to swim early and are always the first to jump in the pool and the last to leave. Great children, and doesn't that mean great parents?
>
> After hours of swimming, the four of us scrambled up to dry land. I went inside to the library to talk with my father, while most people enjoyed hot dogs, relish, mustard, and juicy watermelon.
>
> Suddenly we heard a heart-chilling wail. Panicked, I raced to the pool's edge to see the motionless body of a small child who had gone unnoticed underwater for too long. His blue-face was still. Someone was giving CPR. His mother kept wailing, panicked, pleading, destroyed. I had a shameful thought — thank God that is not my child.
>
> He lived. He regained his breath and was whisked away by ambulance. The party came to a quick close. We four, skin tingling from the summer sun, hearts beating from the near-death of a child who was my kids' playmate an hour before, drove away.
>
> Turning to Nick, I asked, "Can we bear this commitment we have made? Can we raise our children in the face of all hazards — some we try to prevent, others beyond our control?"
>
> That was five years ago. Our children are flourishing. Our confidence is strong and so are our emotions. But it takes only a moment to recognize just how entwined our well-being is with our children and how fragile life is. We are deeply grateful.

Victor J. Blue/The New York Times/Redux

A Grateful Family This family photo shows (from *left* to *right*) Nick, Penelope, Macky, and Alice with their dog Cooper. When they adopted Alice as a newborn, the parents said, "This is a miracle we feared would never happen."

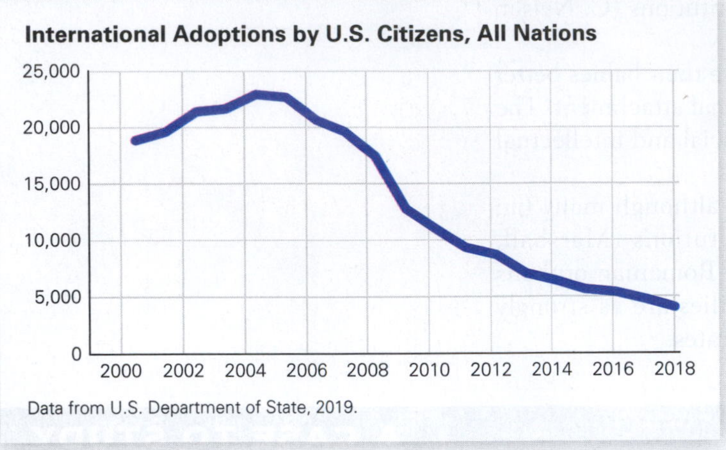

FIGURE 7.3
Declining Need? No. More couples seek to adopt internationally, and millions of children in dozens of nations have no families. This chart does not reflect changing needs of families; it reflects increasing nationalism within and beyond the United States. Sadly, babies have become weapons in national politics.

Politics and Children Without Parents Many nations now restrict international adoptions, in part because some children were literally snatched from their biological parents to be sent abroad. According to government records, the number of international adoptees in the United States was 4,058 in 2018, down from 22,884 in 2004 (Budiman & Lopez, 2017) (see **Figure 7.3**).

The decrease may be influenced more by international politics than by infant needs. For example, Russia was one of the top three "sending" nations for international adoptions (China and Ethiopia were the other two), but when the United States imposed sanctions on Russian officials accused of human rights violations, Russia retaliated by banning adoptions.

Ideally, every baby would be wanted, every parent would be supported, and no infant would be institutionalized. But if that ideal is not reached, scientists advocate family care over institutional care, because attachment to a dedicated caregiver is crucial for well-being (McCall, 2013).

Developmentalists of every political stripe are horrified that thousands of children of immigrants are separated from their parents at the border between Mexico and the United States (Roth et al., 2019). Attachment research confirms that children need dedicated caregivers and that disruption of this relationship causes lifelong harm. Again politics, rather than what we know about attachment, interferes with good care.

Social Referencing

social referencing Seeking information about how to react to an unfamiliar or ambiguous object or event by observing someone else's expressions and reactions. That other person becomes a social reference.

The third social connection that developmentalists look for during infancy, after synchrony and attachment, is **social referencing.** Much as a student might consult a dictionary or other reference work, social referencing means seeking emotional responses or information from other people. A reassuring glance, a string of cautionary words, a facial expression of alarm, pleasure, or dismay—those are social references.

As you read in Chapter 6, gaze-following begins in the first months of life, as part of cognition. After age 1, when infants can walk and are "little scientists," their need to consult others becomes urgent and more accurate—for emotional input, not merely cognition.

Toddlers search for clues in gazes, faces, and body position, paying close attention to emotions and intentions. They focus on their familiar caregivers, but they also use relatives, other children, and even strangers to help them assess objects and events.

From early infancy to late adolescence, children are remarkably selective, noticing that some strangers are reliable references and others are not (Fusaro & Harris, 2013). Emotions and desires spring from social referencing (Wellman, 2014).

Social referencing has many practical applications. Consider mealtime. Caregivers the world over pretend to taste and say "yum-yum," encouraging toddlers to eat beets, liver, or spinach. Toddlers read expressions, insisting on the foods that the adults *really* like.

If a mother enjoys eating a particular food and then presents some to her toddler, the child will eat it. Otherwise not (Shutts et al., 2013). Some tastes (spicy, bitter, sour) are rejected by very young infants, but if they see their caregivers eat such food, they learn to like it (Forestell & Mennella, 2017).

Through this process, some children develop a taste for raw fish or curried goat or smelly cheese—foods that children in other cultures refuse. Similarly, toddlers use social cues to understand the difference between real and pretend eating, as well as to learn which objects, emotions, and activities are forbidden.

Rotini Pasta? Look again. Every family teaches their children to relish delicacies that other people avoid. Examples are bacon (not in Arab nations), hamburgers (not in India), and, as shown here, a witchetty grub. This Australian aboriginal boy is about to swallow an insect larva.

Bill Bachman/Alamy Stock Photo

Fathers as Social Partners

Synchrony, attachment, and social referencing are evident with fathers as well as with mothers. Indeed, fathers tend to elicit more smiles and laughter from their infants than mothers do. They play more exciting games, swinging and chasing, while mothers do more caregiving and comforting (Fletcher et al., 2013).

This gender division—women as caregivers and men as playmates—is apparent in every nation. But children develop well when the roles are reversed, or when both parents are male or both parents are female. Each couple coordinates; children thrive (Shwalb et al., 2013).

One researcher reported that "fathers and mothers showed patterns of striking similarity: they touched, looked, vocalized, rocked, and kissed their newborns equally" (Parke, 2013, p. 121). He found only one gender difference: Women did more smiling.

Gender differences in child rearing vary more by nation, by income, by cohort, and by ideology than by natal sex or by ethnic background. Variation is dramatic, from fathers who had nothing to do with infants to fathers who are intensely involved. The latter is common in the United States in the twenty-first century, unlike in former times (Abraham & Feldman, 2018).

Contemporary fathers worldwide are more active caregivers than their own fathers were (Sriram, 2019). The effects are evident not only in infants but in fathers themselves. As one man in India said, "My child transformed me" (Kaur, 2019).

For all parents, stress decreases their involvement. That brings up another difference between mothers and fathers. When money is scarce and stress is high, some fathers opt out. That choice is less possible for mothers (Roopnarine & Hossain, 2013; Qin & Chang, 2013).

The reactions of caregivers to infants is also affected by the parents' temperament, genes, and early-childhood experiences (Senese et al., 2019). This is another reason why all babies need responsive caregiving: The effects will endure decades later when they have children of their own.

WHAT HAVE YOU LEARNED?

1. Why does synchrony affect early emotional development?
2. How are proximity-seeking and contact-maintaining attachment expressed by infants and caregivers?
3. How does infant behavior differ in each of the four types of attachment?
4. How might each of the four types of attachment be expressed in adulthood?
5. What has been learned from the research on Romanian orphans?
6. How is social referencing important in toddlerhood?
7. How do mothers and fathers differ in infant care?

Theories of Infant Psychosocial Development

That infants are emotional, social creatures is one of those universal truths, recognized by everyone who studies babies. However, each of the theories discussed in Chapter 2 has a distinct perspective on this universal reality, as you will now see.

Especially for Nursing Mothers You have heard that if you wean your child too early, he or she will overeat or develop alcohol use disorder. Is it true? (see response, page 191)

Psychodynamic Theory

Psychodynamic theory connects biosocial and psychosocial development. Sigmund Freud and Erik Erikson each described two distinct stages of early development, one in the first year and one beginning in the second year.

Freud: Oral and Anal Stages According to Freud (1935/1989, 2001), the first year of life is the *oral stage,* so named because the mouth is the young infant's primary source of gratification. In the second year, with the *anal stage,* pleasure comes from the anus—particularly from the sensual satisfaction of bowel movements and, eventually, the psychological pleasure of controlling them.

Freud believed that the oral and anal stages are fraught with potential conflicts. If a mother frustrates her infant's urge to suck—weaning too early or too late, for example, or preventing the baby from sucking a thumb or a pacifier—that may later lead to an *oral fixation.* Adults with an oral fixation are stuck (fixated) at the oral stage, and therefore they eat, drink, chew, bite, or talk excessively, still seeking the mouth-related pleasures of infancy.

Similarly, if toilet training is overly strict or if it begins before maturation allows sufficient control, that causes a clash between the toddler's refusal—or inability—to comply and the wishes of the adult, who denies the infant normal anal pleasures. That may lead to an *anal personality*—an adult who seeks self-control, with a strong need for regularity and cleanliness in all aspects of life.

JOSE MIGUEL GOMEZ/REUTERS/Newscom

All Together Now Toddlers in an employees' day-care program at a flower farm in Colombia learn to use the potty on a schedule. Will this experience lead to later personality problems? Probably not.

trust versus mistrust Erikson's first crisis of psychosocial development. Infants learn basic trust if the world is a secure place where their basic needs (for food, comfort, attention, and so on) are met.

autonomy versus shame and doubt Erikson's second crisis of psychosocial development. Toddlers either succeed or fail in gaining a sense of self-rule over their actions and their bodies.

Erikson: Trust and Autonomy According to Erikson, the first crisis of life is **trust versus mistrust,** when infants learn whether or not the world can be trusted to satisfy basic needs. Babies feel secure when food and comfort are provided with "consistency, continuity, and sameness of experience" (Erikson, 1993a, p. 247). If social interaction inspires trust, the child (and later the adult) confidently explores the social world.

The second crisis is **autonomy versus shame and doubt,** beginning at about 18 months, when self-awareness emerges. Toddlers want autonomy (self-rule) over their own actions and bodies. Without it, they feel ashamed and doubtful. Like Freud, Erikson believed that problems in early infancy could last a lifetime, creating adults who are suspicious and pessimistic (mistrusting) or easily shamed (lacking autonomy).

Behaviorism

From the perspective of behaviorism, emotions and personality are molded as adults reinforce or punish children. Behaviorists believe that parents who respond joyously to every glimmer of a grin will have children with a sunny disposition. The opposite is also true:

> Failure to bring up a happy child, a well-adjusted child—assuming bodily health—falls squarely upon the parents' shoulders. [By the time the child is 3] parents have already determined . . . [whether the child] is to grow into a happy person, wholesome and good-natured, whether he is to be a whining, complaining neurotic, an anger-driven, vindictive, over-bearing slave driver, or one whose every move in life is definitely controlled by fear.
>
> *[Watson, 1928/1972, pp. 7, 45]*

Empathy, for instance, is an emotion that appears in direct proportion to the parents' responses (Grady & Hastings, 2018; Heyes, 2018). Shy boys in particular become more outgoing if their fathers talk with them about emotions (Grady & Hastings, 2018).

Social Learning Behaviorists also recognize that infant behavior reflects *social learning,* from observing other people. You already saw an example, social referencing. Social learning occurs throughout life (Shneidman & Woodward, 2016). Toddlers express emotions in various ways—from giggling to cursing—just as they see their parents or older siblings do.

For example, a boy might develop a hot temper if his father's outbursts seem to win his mother's respect; a girl might be coy, or passive-aggressive, if that is what she has seen at home. These examples are deliberately sexist: Gender roles, in particular, are learned.

"Which one generates the most synapses?"

Barbara Smaller/The New Yorker Collection/The Cartoon Bank

Brainy Baby Fortunately, infant brains are designed to respond to stimulation of many kinds. As long as the baby has moving objects to see (an animated caregiver is better than any mobile), the synapses proliferate.

Keeping Baby Close Parents often unwittingly encourage certain traits in their children. Should infants explore, or should they learn that danger lurks if they wander off? Should toddlers have many toys, or will that make them greedy? When babies cry, should the mother pick them up, feed them, give them a pacifier, ignore them? Should an infant be breast-fed until age 2, switch to a bottle, or sip from a cup?

These questions highlight the distinction between **proximal parenting** (being physically close to a baby, often holding and touching) and **distal parenting** (keeping some distance—providing toys, encouraging self-feeding, talking face-to-face instead of communicating by touch). Caregivers tend to behave in proximal or distal ways very early, when infants are only 2 months old (Kärtner et al., 2010). Each pattern reinforces some behavior.

proximal parenting Caregiving practices that involve being physically close to the baby, with frequent holding and touching.

distal parenting Caregiving practices that involve remaining distant from the baby, providing toys, food, and face-to-face communication with minimal holding and touching.

For instance, toddlers who, as infants, were often held, patted, and soothed (proximal) become toddlers who are more obedient to their parents but less likely to recognize themselves in a mirror. This has been found in Greece, Cameroon, Italy, Israel, Zambia, Scotland, and Turkey. Distal child rearing correlates with cultures that value individual independence; proximal care correlates with cultures that value collective action and family interdependence (Scharf, 2014; Keller et al., 2010; Ross et al., 2017; Carra et al., 2013; Borke et al., 2007; Kärtner et al., 2011).

Cognitive Theory

Cognitive theory holds that thoughts determine a person's perspective. Early experiences are important because beliefs, perceptions, and memories make them so, not because they are buried in the unconscious (psychoanalytic theory) or burned into the brain's patterns (behaviorism).

From this perspective, cognitive processes, including language and information, affect attachment, as children and caregivers develop a mutual understanding. Together they build (co-construct) a **working model,** which is a set of assumptions that becomes a frame of reference for later life (Posada & Waters, 2018).

working model In cognitive theory, a set of assumptions that the individual uses to organize perceptions and experiences. For example, a person might assume that other people are trustworthy and be surprised by an incident in which this working model of human behavior is erroneous.

It is a "model" because early relationships form a prototype, or blueprint. It is "working" because it is a work in progress, not fixed or final. It is cognitive because the child's understanding and interpretation are crucial.

Ideally, infants develop "a working model of the self as lovable and competent" because the parents are "emotionally available, loving, and supportive of their mastery efforts" (Harter, 2012, p. 12). Reality does not always conform to this ideal.

A 1-year-old girl might develop a model, based on her parents' erratic actions, that people are unpredictable. She will continue to apply that model to everyone: Her childhood friendships will be insecure, her adult relationships guarded.

Especially for Pediatricians A mother complains that her toddler refuses to stay in the car seat, spits out disliked foods, and almost never does what she says. How should you respond? (see response, page 191)

The crucial idea, according to cognitive theory, is that early experiences themselves are not necessarily pivotal, but the interpretation of those experiences is (Olson & Dweck, 2009). Children may misinterpret, or parents may offer inaccurate explanations, and this may form ideas that affect later thinking and behavior.

In this way, working models formed in childhood echo lifelong. A hopeful message from cognitive theory is that people can rethink and reorganize their thoughts, developing new models. Our mistrustful girl might marry someone who is faithful and loving, so she may gradually develop a new working model.

Evolutionary Theory

Remember that evolutionary theory stresses two needs: survival and reproduction. Human brains are extraordinarily adept at those tasks. However, not until decades of maturation is the human brain fully functioning. A child must be nourished, protected, and taught much longer than offspring of any other species. Infant and parent emotions ensure this lengthy protection (Hrdy, 2009).

Emotions for Survival Infant emotions are part of this evolutionary mandate. All of the reactions described in the first part of this chapter—from the hunger cry to the temper tantrum—can be seen from this perspective (Konner, 2010).

For example, newborns are extraordinarily dependent, unable to walk or talk or even sit up and feed themselves for months after birth. They must attract adult devotion—and they do. That first smile, the sound of infant laughter, and their role in synchrony are all powerfully attractive to adults—especially to parents.

Adults call their hairless, chinless, round-faced, big-stomached, small-limbed offspring "cute," "handsome," "beautiful," "adorable"—yet all of these characteristics are often considered ugly in adults. Parents willingly devote hours to carrying, feeding, changing, and cleaning their infants, who never express gratitude. The love of a parent for a child is part of evolution: Humans need that love to survive.

Adaptation is evident. Adults have the ability to be caregivers, and grandparents have done it before. However, according to evolutionary psychology, behavior arises from an evolutionary need: Busy adults become devoted caregivers and dependent infants become emotional magnets because species survival requires it.

If humans were motivated solely by money or power, no one would have children. Yet evolution has created adults who find parenting worth every sacrifice, and when they provide the care that evolution has ordained, children develop well (Narvaez et al., 2013). We can all be grateful for that.

Fabrice Trombert Photography Inc./The Image Bank/Getty Images

Chau Doan/LightRocket/Getty Images

Same Situation, Far Apart: Safekeeping Historically, grandmothers were sometimes crucial for child survival. Now, even though medical care has reduced child mortality, grandmothers still do their part to keep children safe, as shown by these two—in the eastern United States *(left)* and Vietnam *(right)*.

Evolutionary theory holds that the emotions of attachment — love, jealousy, and even clinginess and anger — keep toddlers near caregivers who remain vigilant. Infants fuss at still faces, fear separation, and laugh when adults play with them — all to sustain caregiving. Emotions are our genetic legacy; we would die without them.

Allocare Evolutionary social scientists note that if mothers were the exclusive caregivers of each child until children were adults, a given woman could rear only one or two offspring — not enough for the species to survive. Instead, before the introduction of reliable birth control, the average interval between births for humans was two to four years.

Humans birth children at relatively short intervals because of **allocare** — the care of children by *alloparents,* caregivers who are not the mother. Allocare is essential for *Homo sapiens'* survival.

allocare Literally, "other-care"; the care of children by people other than the biological parents.

Compared with many other species (mother chimpanzees space births by four or five years and never let another chimp hold their babies), human mothers let other people help with child care. This is because evolution has programmed the human brain so that other people, especially fathers and grandparents, want to help (Abraham & Feldman, 2018).

Allocare is universal for our species — but each community has distinct values and preferences regarding who should care for children and when (Konner, 2018). This is explored in the next section.

Sociocultural Theory

The fifth theory described in Chapter 2 is sociocultural, which emphasizes the role of culture. Rather than describe it here, we turn now to infant day care. As you will see, widely different views are evident. The entire topic shows the power of sociocultural influences.

WHAT HAVE YOU LEARNED?

1. According to Freud, what might happen if a baby's oral needs are not met?
2. How might Erikson's crisis of "trust versus mistrust" affect later life?
3. How do behaviorists explain the development of emotions and personality?
4. What does the term *working model* mean within cognitive theory?
5. What is the difference between proximal and distal parenting?
6. How does evolution explain the parent–child bond?
7. Why is allocare necessary for survival of the human species?

Who Should Care for Babies?

As you see, cultures and theories differ in every aspect of infant care. We have already described cultural differences in breast-feeding, co-sleeping, and language development. Now one final example: All babies need care, but there are many ways to provide it.

Complications of Interpretation

Summarizing the research on infant care is difficult, because people assume that the practices of their own family or culture are best and that other patterns are

Ted Richardson/Raleigh News & Observer/MCT/Getty Images

Compare This with That In stark contrast with the Romanian orphanage shown on page 182, this infant day-care center provides excellent care.

Observation Quiz What three things do you see that suggest good care? (see answer, page 192)

harmful. This is an example of the difference-equals-deficit error first described in Chapter 1.

Everyone is inclined to give greater weight to the studies that confirm their own perspective. As a scientist, I try to avoid personal biases, but—full disclosure—I was the director of a small day-care center when my eldest children were young. Does that distort my perspective?

Another complication is that conclusions vary from one study to another, depending on what aspects are considered, how caregivers act, and which infants are studied. A strength of the scientific method is that various measures and populations lead to divergent conclusions; cumulative research studies rather than any one study or personal experience make good science.

At least there is some consensus on four principles:

1. Mutual attachment to one or several familiar caregivers is pivotal.
2. Quality of care, whether at home or in a day-care program, matters.
3. Babies benefit from warm and responsive caregivers.
4. Frequent changes and instability in care are problematic.

Regarding the last item on this list, it is now apparent that every disruption undercuts infants' efforts to understand their world. If a neighbor, a grandmother, a day-care center, and then another grandmother each provide care on a different day of the week, or if the infant lives with the biological mother, then a foster mother, then with the biological father, then back with the biological mother, that is harmful. By age 3, children with unstable care histories are more aggressive than those with stable care (Pilarz & Hill, 2014).

Exclusive Mother-Care

Beyond the need for attachment and stability, experts and cultures differ on who should provide care, which makes this topic worthy of students' careful consideration. Some people think exclusive mother-care is best; others believe that other relatives (father, grandmothers, older siblings, aunts, grandfathers) should be involved; some contend that professional infant day care is beneficial. These divergent views are expressed in national policies as well as individual attitudes, as described in Opposing Perspectives.

OPPOSING PERSPECTIVES

Why Doesn't Everyone Agree?

Opinions are shaped by personal experience (adults who, as infants, were in nonparental care are more likely to approve of it), by gender (males are more likely to think that mothers should provide exclusive care), and by education (higher education increases support for nonparental care) (Galasso et al., 2017; Rose et al., 2016; Shpancer & Schweitzer, 2016).

Beyond that, for cultural, ideological, and economic reasons, nations differ. Some nations consider infant care a public right, just as emergency services, schooling, and medical care are available to everyone. By contrast, infant care paid by the government is rare in South Asia, Africa, and Latin America, where many lawmakers believe it is harmful.

Thus, center-based infant care is common in France, Israel, China, Chile, Norway, and Sweden, where it is heavily subsidized by the government. Quality varies. In France, subsidized care can begin at 12 weeks, although there is a long waiting list and as many as seven infants are cared for by one caregiver, a ratio that would indicate poor quality to Americans.

Norwegians believe that babies under age 1 are best cared for by their mothers. Consequently, new mothers are paid full salary to stay home with their babies for 47 weeks, and high-quality, center day care is heavily subsidized by the government from age 1 on. Many (62 percent) Norwegian 1-year-olds are in center care, as are more (84 percent) 2-year-olds and most (93 percent) 3-year-olds.

Longitudinal research of early center care in Norway finds no detrimental results. What U.S. researchers consider behavioral problems are not seen as such in Norway: Instead, Norwegian researchers suggest that early experiences with other children make shy children become bolder (Solheim et al., 2013).

Likewise, a study in the Netherlands found that, if anything, children who attended high-quality day care were less likely to have emotional problems than similar children with less day-care experience (Broekhuizen et al., 2018). In that nation, day care may begin before age 1, but most children attend center care part time, two or three days a week.

In other nations, notably the United States, government funding rarely pays for center care for children younger than 4 years old. Reflecting the U.S. preference for mother-care, the federal government supports more than a thousand home-visiting programs to help low-income mothers provide educational experiences. Some programs add guidance for increasing secure attachment (Berlin et al., 2018).

Most nations are in between, and most parents are conflicted as well. Germany recently began offering paid infant care, not because the government decided it was best but rather as a strategy to increase the birth rate.

Similar policies are found in Australia, where the government attempted to increase the birth rate by paying parents $5,000 for each newborn, providing paid parental leave, and offering low-cost child-care centers. Yet many Australians still believe that babies should have exclusive maternal care (Harrison et al., 2014).

For example, one Australian mother of a 12-month-old boy used center care but said:

> I spend a lot of time talking with them about his day and what he's been doing and how he's feeling and they just seem to have time to do that, to make the effort to communicate. Yeah they've really bonded with him and he's got close to them. But I still don't like leaving him there.
>
> *[Paula, quoted in Boyd et al., 2013, p. 172]*

Obviously, all of these differences are affected by culture, economics, and politics more than by universal needs of babies. What is your opinion?

If you are, for instance, a well-educated North American woman whose mother was employed when you were young, you may think favorably of infant day care. Or if you are a man with roots in Latin America, you may look askance at any family who would entrust their infant to center care. Everyone needs to ask: Are opinions based on evidence?

Underlying every opinion are theories about what is best, as well as other concerns. In the United States, each employer sets policies, with some offering paid maternal leave and others providing on-site child care—which may be a way to encourage employees with young children to stay on the job. Paternal leave is almost never paid, publicly or privately, with one exception: The U.S. military allows 10 days of paid leave for fathers.

In poor nations, mothers have no choice: They must be primary caregivers, although variations are nonetheless found in allocare. In wealthy nations, variations abound (see **Figure 7.4**). All human infants are born with the same needs, but nations and families differ dramatically in who cares for them at 6 months, at a year, and beyond.

Worldwide, an increasing number of women are employed. If a nation considers maternal care best, that nation often provides paid leave for working mothers (see **Figure 7.5**), and sometimes for fathers, too. Laws often require that the mother's job be available when she returns to work.

In many other nations, the government subsidizes group infant care, because it is thought that young children benefit from caregivers who know how to facilitate cognitive stimulation and social interaction beyond what most homes provide.

In the United States, only 20 percent of infants are cared for *exclusively* by their mothers (i.e., no other relatives or babysitters) throughout their first year. This is in contrast to Canada, which has far more generous maternal leave and lower rates of maternal employment. In the first year of life, most Canadians are cared for only by their mothers (Babchishin et al., 2013). Why is that?

The United States is one of the few developed nations that provides neither paid parental leave nor subsidized infant care, even though more than half of the mothers of infants under 1 year of age are in the labor force (58 percent in 2015, according to the U.S. Bureau of Labor Statistics). Since the cost of child care is

AP Images/Jeff Chiu

Double Winner For the father in this photo, baby and victory in the same year! He is one of many parents who are advocating for six weeks of paid family leave. The San Francisco Board of Supervisors voted yes, making this the first jurisdiction in the United States to mandate fully paid leave. The law went into effect in 2017—too late for both the mother and father shown here. Perhaps their next babies?

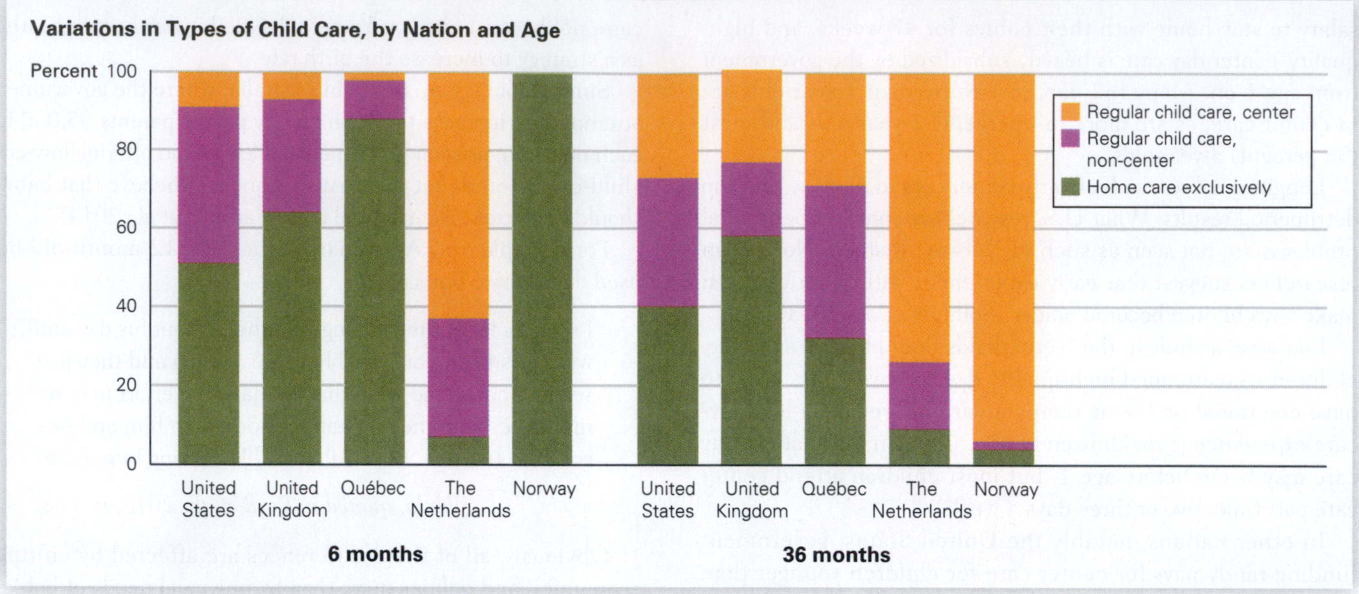

FIGURE 7.4
Who Cares for the Baby? Infants are the same everywhere, but cultures and governments differ dramatically. Does a 6-month-old need Mother more than a 3-year-old? Norway and Quebec say yes; the United States, United Kingdom, and the Netherlands say no.

borne by the families, many family members (especially fathers and grandmothers) help mothers care for babies.

Problems with Nonmaternal Care

Is there anything wrong with allocare? It depends: Some relatives provide good care, some not. Some day-care centers are excellent; many are not. Decisions about caregivers should not rest on financial considerations, but they often do. Two worries are often expressed: (1) Without exclusive maternal care, infants will be insecurely attached; and (2) with extensive day care, children will develop behavioral problems.

The first worry has been disproven. Secure mother–infant attachment (as measured by the Strange Situation) is evident for infants with regular father-care, with professional day care, with care from other caregivers. In retrospect, this makes sense: Even when fathers or daycare centers provide major care, mothers still spend many hours each week (especially nights and weekends) interacting with their babies.

The data are not as reassuring for emotional development. Some research suggests that boys, particularly, who were in organized programs of care are likely to be more aggressive and less obedient than other children (Coley et al., 2013).

A review of many studies (Dearing & Zachrisson, 2017) found conflicting results: In half of the studies of children with many hours of group care (more than 20 a week), the rate of externalizing problems increased. However, that was not found in the other half, which included one study that found *better* emotional adjustment in children with extensive day-care experience.

The best longitudinal research in the United States comes from a study by the Early Child Care Network of the National Institute of Child Health and Human Development (NICHD), which has followed the development of more than 1,300 children born in 1991. Early day care correlated with many cognitive advances, especially in language. Children who were enrolled in high-quality preschools had higher achievement throughout childhood and adolescence.

The social consequences were less clear, however. As one summary explained:

> higher quality of child care was linked to higher academic-cognitive skills in primary school and again at age 15. Higher hours of child care were associated with teacher reports of behavior problems in early primary school and youth reports of greater impulsivity and risk taking at age 15.
>
> [Burchinal et al., 2014, p. 542]

Overall, infants with neglectful mothers benefit from day care; infants with good homes suffer in day care of poor quality. As one review explained, "This evidence now indicates that early nonparental care environments sometimes pose risks to young children and sometimes confer benefits" (Phillips et al., 2011, p. 44).

When are the benefits seen? Adolescents who had extensive nonmaternal care in infancy but who had sensitive parenting in middle childhood tended to demonstrate higher achievement without the detrimental effects (high impulsivity) found in other teenagers (Burchinal et al., 2014). Attachment matters at every age.

Cohort Differences

Scientists criticize some of these longitudinal results, primarily because current infant care is of higher quality and more common than it was in the twentieth century. High-quality infant care advances cognition and socialization with no evidence of emotional harm, especially when it is followed by good preschool care (W. Li et al., 2013; Huston et al., 2015).

For example, in the United States, the National Association for the Education of Young Children updated its standards for care of babies from birth to 15 months, based on current research (NAEYC, 2014). Group size is small (no more than eight infants), and the ratio of adults to babies is 1:4 or fewer (see **Table 7.2**).

Thus, each infant is given personal attention. Emotional and intellectual growth are central to the curriculum. For instance, teachers are told to "engage infants in frequent face-to-face social interactions"—including talking, singing, smiling, and touching (NAEYC, 2014, p. 4). Teachers also must respect cultural differences among families. Maternal involvement is encouraged, including breastfeeding (bottles of pumped milk are stored for each baby).

All of the research on infant day care confirms that sociocultural differences matter. What seems best for one infant in one culture may not be best for another infant elsewhere. Good infant care—whether by mother, father, grandmother, or day-care center—depends on specifics, not generalities.

As is true of many topics in child development, questions remain. But one fact is without question: Each infant needs personal responsiveness. Someone should serve as a partner in the

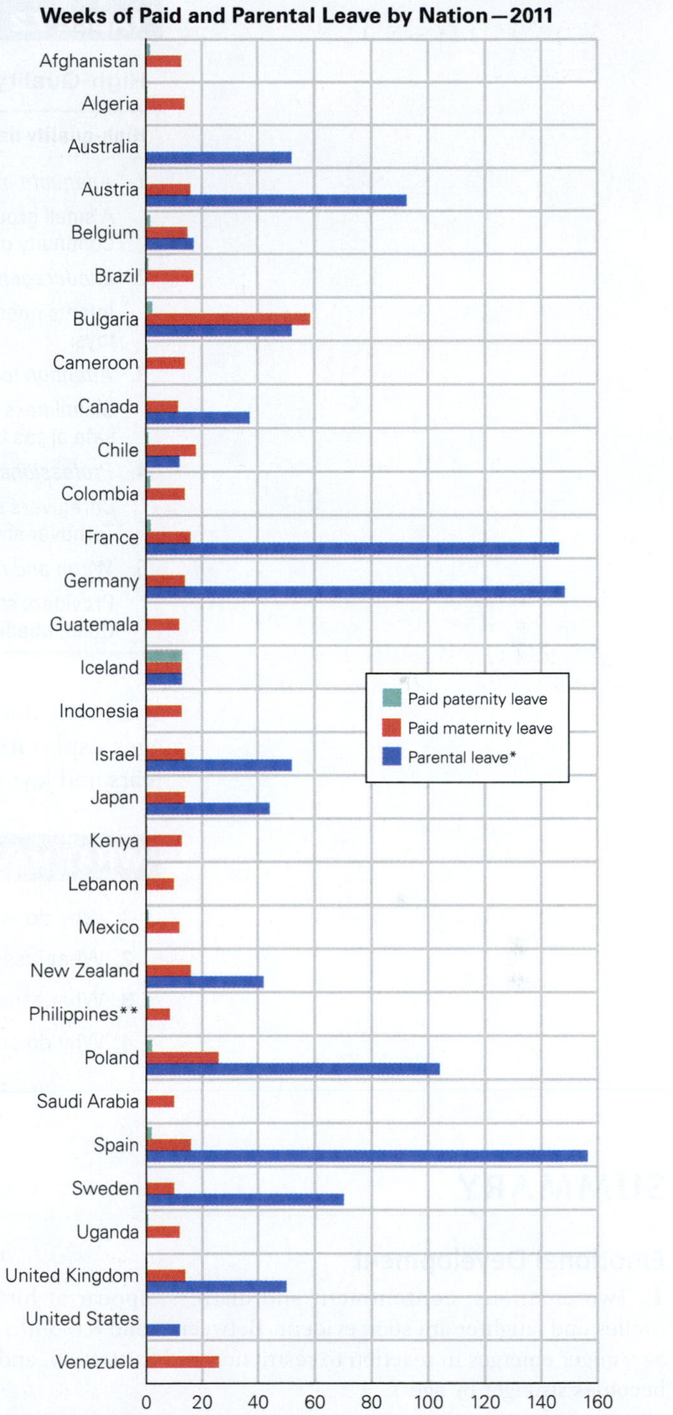

Data from Addati et al., 2014, pp. 150–163.

Notes: *In some cases, leave can be shared between parents or other family members. Many nations have increased leave since these data were gathered. **In the Philippines, parents must be married in order to receive paid leave.

FIGURE 7.5

A Changing World Maternity leave did not exist a century ago because the only jobs that mothers had were unregulated. Now, virtually every nation has a maternity leave policy, revised every decade or so. As of 2019, only Belgium, Denmark, France, Latvia, Luxembourg, and Sweden have laws ensuring gender equality. That may be the next innovation in many nations.

TABLE 7.2

High-Quality Day Care

High-quality day care during infancy has five essential characteristics:
1. *Adequate attention to each infant* A small group of infants (no more than eight) needs two reliable, familiar, loving caregivers. Continuity of care is crucial.
2. *Encouragement of language and sensorimotor development* Infants need language—songs, conversations, and positive talk—and easily manipulated toys.
3. *Attention to health and safety* Cleanliness routines (e.g., handwashing), accident prevention (e.g., no small objects), and safe areas to explore are essential.
4. *Professional caregivers* Caregivers should have experience and degrees/certificates in early-childhood education. Turnover should be low, morale high, and enthusiasm evident.
5. *Warm and responsive caregivers* Providers should engage the children in active play and guide them in problem solving. Quiet, obedient children may indicate unresponsive care.

synchrony duet, a base for secure attachment, and a social reference who encourages exploration. Then, infant emotions and experiences — cries and laughter, fears and joys — will ensure that development goes well.

WHAT HAVE YOU LEARNED?

1. Why do cultures differ on the benefits of infant nonmaternal care?
2. What lessons can be learned from the experiences of infant care in Norway?
3. What aspects of infant care are agreed on by everyone?
4. Why do some nations pay mothers to stay home with their babies and some do not?

SUMMARY

Emotional Development

1. Two emotions, contentment and distress, appear at birth. Smiles and laughter are soon evident. Between 4 and 8 months of age, anger emerges in reaction to restriction and frustration, and it becomes stronger by age 1.

2. Reflexive fear is apparent in very young infants. Fear of something specific, including fear of strangers and of separation, typically arises in the second half of the first year, is strong by age 1, and continues until age 2.

3. In the second year, social awareness and self-awareness produce more selective and intense fear, anger, and joy. Emotions arise from the interaction of the self and others; specifically, these include pride, shame, and affection as well as explosive temper. Self-recognition (measured by the mirror/rouge test) emerges at about 18 months.

4. Temperament is inborn, but the expression of temperament is influenced by the context, with evident plasticity.

The Development of Social Bonds

5. Often by 2 months, and clearly by 6 months, infants become more responsive and social. Synchrony is evident. Caregivers and infants engage in reciprocal interactions, with split-second timing.

6. Attachment is the relationship between two people who try to be close to each other (proximity-seeking and contact-maintaining). It is measured in infancy by a baby's reaction to the caregiver's presence, departure, and return in the Strange Situation.

7. Secure attachment provides encouragement for infant exploration, and its influence is lifelong. Adults are attached as well, evident not only as parents but also as romantic partners.

8. As they become more mobile and engage with their environment, infants use social referencing (looking to other people's facial expressions and body language) to detect what is safe, frightening, or fun.

9. Infants frequently use fathers as partners in synchrony, as attachment figures, and as social references, developing emotions and exploring their world. Contemporary fathers often play with their infants.

Theories of Infant Psychosocial Development

10. According to all major theories, caregivers are especially influential in the first two years. Freud stressed the mother's impact on oral and anal pleasure; Erikson emphasized trust and autonomy. Both believed that the impact of these is lifelong.

11. Behaviorists focus on learning. They note that parents teach their babies many things, including when to be fearful or joyful, and how much physical and social distance (proximal or distal parenting) is best.

12. Cognitive theory holds that infants develop working models based on their experiences. Interpretation is crucial, and that can change with maturation.

13. Evolutionary theorists recognize that both infants and caregivers have impulses and emotions that have developed over millennia to foster the survival of each new member of the human species. Attachment is one example.

Who Should Care for Babies?

14. Research confirms that every infant needs responsive caregiving, secure attachment, and cognitive stimulation. These three can occur at home or in a good day-care center. Quality matters, as does consistency of care.

15. Some people believe that infant day care benefits babies and that governments should subsidize high-quality infant care, just as governments pay professional firefighters to put out any fire. Other cultures believe the opposite—that infant care is best done by mothers, who are solely responsible for providing it.

KEY TERMS

social smile (p. 168)
separation anxiety (p. 169)
stranger wariness (p. 169)
self-awareness (p. 170)
temperament (p. 170)
synchrony (p. 173)
still-face technique (p. 174)
attachment (p. 175)
secure attachment (p. 175)
insecure-avoidant attachment (p. 175)
insecure-resistant/ambivalent attachment (p. 176)
disorganized attachment (p. 176)
social referencing (p. 180)
trust versus mistrust (p. 182)
autonomy versus shame and doubt (p. 182)
proximal parenting (p. 183)
distal parenting (p. 183)
working model (p. 183)
allocare (p. 185)

APPLICATIONS

1. One cultural factor that influences infant development is how infants are carried from place to place. Ask four mothers whose infants were born in each of the past four decades how they transported them—front or back carriers, facing out or in, strollers or carriages, in car seats or on mother's laps, and so on. Why did they choose the mode(s) they chose? What are their opinions and yours on how such cultural practices might affect infants' development?

2. Record video of synchrony for three minutes. Ideally, ask the parent of an infant under 8 months of age to play with the infant. If no infant is available, observe a pair of lovers as they converse. Note the sequence and timing of every facial expression, sound, and gesture of both partners.

3. Contact several day-care centers to try to assess the quality of care they provide. Ask about factors such as adult/child ratio, group size, and training for caregivers of children of various ages. Is there a minimum age for the children? Why or why not? Analyze the answers, using Table 7.2 as a guide.

Especially For ANSWERS

Response for Nurses and Pediatricians (from p. 169): Stranger wariness is normal up to about 14 months. This baby's behavior actually might indicate secure attachment.

Response for Nurses (from p. 172): It's too soon to tell. Temperament is not truly "fixed" but variable, especially in the first few months. Many "difficult" infants become happy, successful adolescents and adults, if their parents are responsive.

Response for Nursing Mothers (from p. 182): Freud thought so, but there is no experimental evidence that weaning, even when ill-timed, has such dire long-term effects.

Response for Pediatricians (from p. 184): Consider the origins of the misbehavior—probably a combination of the child's inborn temperament and the mother's distal parenting. Acceptance and consistent responses (e.g., avoiding disliked foods but always using the car seat) is more warranted than anger. Perhaps this mother is expressing hostility toward the child—a sign that intervention may be needed. Find out.

Observation Quiz ANSWERS

Answer to Observation Quiz (from p. 171) Watch the facial expressions.

Answer to Observation Quiz (from p. 186) Remontia Green is holding the feeding baby in just the right position as she rocks back and forth—no propped-up bottle here. The two observing babies are at an angle and distance that makes them part of the social interaction, and they are strapped in. Finally, look at the cribs—no paint, close slats, and positioned so the babies can see each other.

CAREER ALERT The Pediatrician and the Pediatric Nurse

Many people studying human development hope to enter the medical field as doctors, nurses, physical therapists, or in dozens of related careers. Often their ultimate goal is to become a pediatrician, a medical doctor who helps children grow strong and healthy.

From an educational perspective, that is a lofty goal indeed. To become a pediatrician, one must first become a medical doctor (M.D.) after earning a bachelor's degree. This entails entering medical school, first with two years of advanced classes and then working as an intern for two more years in many aspects of medicine.

At that point, a fledgling doctor might decide to be a pediatrician, which requires a residency in pediatrics for at least three more years. Finally, the doctor can be licensed in pediatrics. The pediatrician can then work in a hospital or other institution that treats children or begin a private practice.

If someone wants to work directly for the health of children, yet remaining a student for more than ten years after college graduation seems impossible, then the person should consider one of many other medical professions that help children, among them nurses, physician assistants, physical therapists, and pediatric psychologists. Nursing itself consists of many levels, from aide, to practical nurse (L.P.N), to registered nurse (R.N.), to nurse practitioner (who can do many of the same things as an M.D.).

For all these, the job outlook is good: The Occupational Outlook Handbook reports that the United States will need 15 percent more pediatricians in the next decade. Nurses fare even better: The projection for registered nurses is 16 percent; for nurse-midwives, 22 percent; and for nurse practitioners, 36 percent. Nurse practitioners must complete two more years of education after earning a bachelor's degree and becoming a registered nurse (RN), but the reward is higher salary, more responsibility, and job security.

How can child health be an expanding field, since the birth rate is falling? There are two reasons: First, the field of medicine is increasingly focused on prevention, and child health is the foundation for adult health. That means that well-child care is increasingly important. Second, as parents have fewer children, they have become more intensely concerned about each child.

The joy of all these professions is working with children and watching them grow into happy and successful adults. However, the children who need the most care are the ones in poor health. Often medicine can cure an illness, or at least pave a path toward a satisfying adulthood. This is now true for many common problems, such as sickle cell anemia or Down's syndrome, that once led to suffering and death. However, some children still suffer and a few die, which is devastating not only to the parents but also to medical professionals.

The other problem is that helping children requires helping caregivers. Often parents are grateful for medical advice, but sometimes they are not. Specializing in child health requires a person to also specialize in providing information and respect to whomever is responsible for the direct care of the child. That may be difficult.

For example, currently, many parents hesitate to vaccinate their children. Medical professionals know the evidence and have treated children with measles, mumps, and other childhood diseases that could have been prevented. That makes them understandably impatient with parents who choose not to protect their children. Yet parents have picketed and sued doctors who advocate vaccination. Thus, becoming a medical professional in child health requires courage as well as knowledge.

Worst of all, some parents mistreat their children, and the doctor or nurse is the first one to notice it. They are "mandated reporters"; they must report their concerns. However, as this text makes clear, reporting is only the first step toward helping a mistreated child. Medical professionals may be the best ones to support caregivers and children, making sure that the child recovers from any harm.

Thus, caring for children is a noble and joyous task, but it requires courage and strong human relations skills. As your study of human development makes clear, children do not grow in isolation: A skill medical professional is a crucial team member, allowing every child to thrive.

VISUALIZING DEVELOPMENT **Developing Attachment**

Attachment begins at birth and continues lifelong. Much depends not only on the ways in which parents and babies bond, but also on the quality and consistency of caregiving, the safety and security of the home environment, and individual and family experience. While the patterns set in infancy may echo in later life, they are not determinative.

How Many Children are Securely Attached?

The specific percentages of children who are secure and insecure vary by culture, parent responsiveness, context, and specific temperament and needs of both the child and the caregiver. Generally, about a third of all 1-year-olds seem insecure.

50–70%	10–20%	10–20%	5–10%
Secure Attachment (Type B)	Avoidant Attachment (Type A)	Ambivalent Attachment (Type C)	Disorganized Attachment (Type D)

Attachment in the Strange Situation May Influence Relationships Through the Life Span

Attachment patterns formed in infancy affect adults lifelong, but later experiences of love and rejection may change early patterns. Researchers measure attachment by examining children's behaviors in the Strange Situation where they are separated from their parent and play in a room with an unfamiliar caregiver. These early patterns can influence later adult relationships. As life goes on, people become more or less secure, avoidant, or disorganized.

Securely Attached [Type B] In the Strange Situation, children are able to separate from caregiver but prefer caregiver to strangers.	Later in life, they tend to have supportive relationships and positive self-concept.
Insecure-Avoidant [Type A] In the Strange Situation, children avoid caregiver.	Later in life, they tend to be aloof in personal relationships, loners who are lonely.
Insecure-Resistant/Ambivalent [Type C] In the Strange Situation, children appear upset and worried when separated from caregiver; they may hit or cling.	Later in life, their relationships may be angry, stormy, unpredictable. They have few long-term friendships.
Disorganized [Type D] In the Strange Situation, children appear angry, confused, erratic, or fearful.	Later in life, they can demonstrate odd behavior—including sudden emotions. They are at risk for serious psychological disorders.

The Continuum of Attachment

Avoidance and anxiety occur along a continuum. Neither genes nor cultural variations were understood when the Strange Situation was first developed (in 1965). Some contemporary researchers believe the link between childhood attachment and adult personality is less straightforward than this table suggests.

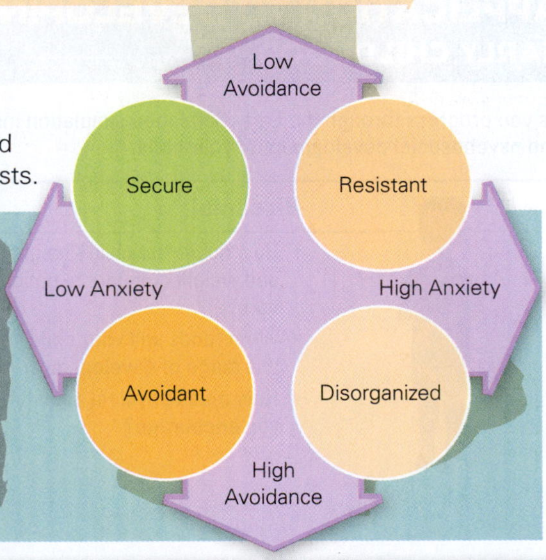

APPLICATION TO DEVELOPING LIVES PARENTING SIMULATION

EARLY CHILDHOOD

As you progress through the Early Childhood simulation module, how you decide the following will impact the biosocial, cognitive, and psychosocial development of your child.

Biosocial

- How does your child's height and weight compare to national norms?
- What foods will your child eat at this stage of development?
- How much physical activity will you encourage?

Cognitive

- Which of Piaget's stages of cognitive development is your child in?
- In what kind of school will you enroll your child?
- Will your child be able to demonstrate impulse control?
- How will your child compare to national averages in reading, math, and language?

Psychosocial

- In what kind of social environment will you place your child?
- How will your child react if you and your partner split up?
- How will you discipline your child at this age?
- How does your stress level impact your child's emotional health?

PART III

Early Childhood

From ages 2 to 6, children spend most of their waking hours discovering, creating, laughing, and imagining — all the while acquiring the skills they need. They chase each other and attempt new challenges (developing their bodies); they play with sounds, words, and ideas (developing their minds); they invent games and dramatize fantasies (learning social skills and morals).

These were once called the *preschool years* because school started in first grade. But first grade is no longer first; most children begin school long before age 6. Instead, these years are called *early childhood,* because those who were once called *preschoolers* are now *young children.* By whatever name, the years from 2 to 6 are a time for extraordinary growth, impressive learning, and spontaneous play, joyful not only for young children but also for anyone who knows them.

Left: Karina Mireya Sanchez Andino/EyeEm/Getty Images
Right: baona/iStock/Getty Images

CHAPTER 8

Early Childhood: Biosocial Development

What Will You Know?

1. Do young children eat too much, too little, or the right amount?
2. If children never climb trees or splash in water, do they suffer?
3. Why is injury control needed more than accident prevention?
4. Which is worse, neglect or abuse?

- **Body Changes**
  - Growth Patterns
  - Nutrition
- **Brain Growth**
  - Myelination
  - INSIDE THE BRAIN: Connected Hemispheres
  - Maturation of the Prefrontal Cortex
  - Inhibition and Flexibility
  - Advancing Motor Skills
- **Harm to Children**
  - Avoidable Injury
  - A CASE TO STUDY: My Baby Swallowed Poison
  - Prevention
  - A VIEW FROM SCIENCE: Lead in the Environment
  - Child Maltreatment
  - Preventing Harm
- **VISUALIZING DEVELOPMENT: Developing Motor Skills**

I often took 5-year-old Asa and his female friend, Ada, by subway from kindergarten in Manhattan to their homes in Brooklyn. Their bodies were quite similar (no visible gender differences yet), but they were quite distinct from the hundreds of other subway riders. Of course they were shorter and thinner, with rounder heads and smaller hands. Like all 5-year-olds in this subway designed for adults, their feet did not touch the floor, and the two of them could easily sit together in one seat. But none of those body characteristics was the most noticeable difference from the other passengers. Movement was.

I tried to keep their swinging feet from kicking other riders; I told them again and again to hold on to the pole; I asked them to sit beside me instead of careening up and down the subway car, looking out the window, oblivious to the strangers they bumped into or squeezed by. Enforcing proper subway behavior with 5-year-olds is difficult; I often failed.

That is how nature makes young children: full of energy and action, unaware of the social disapproval they might cause. Might the strangers on that train judge Asa and Ada as rude and undisciplined, and blame me? Or maybe my worries were my problem, not a problem for Asa, Ada, or onlookers.

My task was to get us all off at the right stop and to keep the children from falling when the train jerked. For that, I succeeded. Adults must guide young children, keeping them safe while enjoying their exuberance. Most of the tired subway riders did that; they smiled, admired, and sent me sympathetic glances.

This chapter describes growth during early childhood—in body, brain, and motor skills—and what adults do to protect it. As you will read, accidents are the leading cause of childhood deaths: Adults need to keep children safe and happy.

With Asa and Ada, I held their hands when we crossed the street; remembered to bring their coats, lunchboxes, and backpacks from school to train to home; made sure they didn't leave my sight. Success. They are both older now, usually quietly reading when on the train, still safe and happy.

Left: LightField Studios/Shutterstock.Com
Top: baona/iStock/Getty Images

Marc Romanelli/Tetra images/Getty Images

Short and Chubby Limbs No Longer Siblings in New Mexico, ages 7 and almost 1, illustrate the transformation of body shape and skills during early childhood. Head size is almost the same, but the older child's arms are twice as long, evidence of proximodistal growth.

Observation Quiz Can this toddler pedal the tricycle? (see answer, page 218) ↑

Body Changes

In early childhood, as in infancy, the body and brain grow according to powerful epigenetic forces—biologically driven and socially guided, experience-expectant and experience-dependent. [**Life-Span Link:** Experience-expectant and experience-dependent brain development are explained in Chapter 5.]

Growth Patterns

Compare an unsteady 24-month-old with a cartwheeling 6-year-old. Physical differences are obvious. Height and weight increase in those four years (by about a foot and 16 pounds, or almost 30 centimeters and 8 kilograms).

Dramatic changes occur in shape: Children slim down, the lower body lengthens, fat is replaced by muscle. The average *body mass index* (or *BMI,* a ratio of weight to height) is lower at ages 5 and 6 than at any other time of life. [**Life-Span Link:** Body mass index is defined in Chapter 11.]

Gone are the infant's protruding belly, round face, short limbs, and large head. The center of gravity moves from the breast to the belly, enabling cartwheels, somersaults, and many other accomplishments. The joys of dancing, gymnastics, and pumping legs on a swing become possible; changing proportions enable new achievements.

During each year of early childhood, well-nourished children grow about 3 inches (about 7½ centimeters) and gain almost 4½ pounds (2 kilograms). By age 6, the average child in a developed nation:

- is at least 3½ feet tall (more than 110 centimeters).
- weighs between 40 and 50 pounds (between 18 and 23 kilograms).
- looks lean, not chubby.
- has adultlike body proportions (legs constitute about half the total height).

Nutrition

Although they rarely starve, young children sometimes are malnourished, even in nations with abundant food. Small appetites are often satiated by unhealthy snacks, crowding out needed vitamins.

Obesity Among Young Children Older adults often encourage children to overeat, protecting them against famine that was common a century ago. Unfortunately, that encouragement is now destructive. As family income decreases, obesity increases—a sign of poor nutrition, likely to reduce immunity and later increase disease (Rook et al., 2014).

There are many explanations for the connection between obesity and low SES. Families with little money or education are more likely to have family habits—less exercise, more television, fewer vegetables, more sweetened drinks, frequent fast food—that correlate with overweight (Cespedes et al., 2013). In addition, low-income children may have grandmothers who cling to feeding patterns that, in other times and places, protected against starvation.

Problems endure lifelong. Children who grow up in food-insecure households learn to eat whenever food is available, becoming less attuned to hunger and satiety signals in their bodies. Consequently, as adults, they overeat when they are not hungry, risking obesity, diabetes, and strokes (S. Hill et al., 2016).

Appetite naturally decreases between ages 2 and 6, as growth slows down. Parents need to know this, neither enticing children to eat nor feeding them candy or cake that will fill them up. However, parents often underestimate their children's weight. A review of 69 studies found that half of the parents of overweight children believe their children are thinner than they actually are (Lundahl et al., 2014).

Early childhood is the best time for prevention, because overweight increases with age. In 2016, 14 percent of 2- to 5-year-olds, 18 percent of 6- to 11-year-olds, and 21 percent of 12- to 19-year-olds in the United States were obese (Fryar et al., 2018).

Surprisingly, parental recognition that a child is overweight may lead to an *increase* in that child's weight, according to research on 2,823 Australian 4- and 5-year-olds followed until mid-adolescence (Robinson & Sutin, 2017). Similar results were found in Ireland and the United States.

The reason may be, according to the authors of that Australian study, that parents add stress without changing family eating patterns. If parents criticize the child, the child may react by cycling between dieting and overeating. Childhood obesity is linked to childhood depression (Sutaria et al., 2019) as well as lack of exercise and excessive screen time.

Sadly, people in many other nations are adopting Western diets, buying cars and other labor-saving devices, and moving to cities where long walks outside are unusual. As a result, "childhood obesity is one of the most serious public health challenges of the 21st century. The problem is global and is steadily affecting many low- and middle-income countries, particularly in urban settings" (Sahoo et al., 2015, pp. 187–188).

There has been some good news, however. In the United States, school lunches include more fruit and less fat, and the rate of obesity in 2- to 5-year-olds has not shown a steady increase. Pediatric awareness, corporate policies, and parental action are all credited with this improvement, as is former First Lady Michelle Obama, who made child nutrition and exercise her major goal. The real credit may go to her pediatrician, who told her in 2007 that her children were gaining weight more quickly than was ideal (Obama, 2018).

Many day-care centers have successfully prevented increases in obesity rates among 2- to 5-year-olds by promoting exercise and improving snacks—carrot sticks and apple slices, not cookies and chocolate milk (Sisson et al., 2016). Similar trends are apparent in Germany, with rates of childhood obesity steady among older children and dropping slightly among young children (Schienkiewitz et al., 2018).

Sadly, after leveling off for a few years, preschool obesity in the United States has risen again to 13.9 percent (Fryar et al., 2018). That bad news has a hopeful twist: Since weight gain in early childhood is fluid, parents and communities can make a difference if they so choose.

Nutritional Deficiencies Although many young children consume more than enough calories, they do not always obtain adequate iron, zinc, and calcium. For example, North American children now drink less milk than formerly, which means they ingest less calcium and have weaker bones later on.

Eating a wide variety of fresh foods may be essential for optimal health. Compared with the average child, young children who eat more dark-green and orange vegetables and less fried food benefit in many ways. They gain bone mass but not fat, according to a study that controlled for other factors that might correlate with body fat, such as gender (girls have more), ethnicity (people of some ethnic groups are genetically thinner), and income (poor children have worse diets) (Wosje et al., 2010).

Sugar is a major problem. Many cultural customs entice children to eat sweets—in birthday cake, holiday candy, desserts, sweetened juice, soda, and

DAVE CARPENTER
"IT SAYS RIGHT HERE IN THE INGREDIENTS, 'THIS PRODUCT CONTAINS NO YUCKY STUFF'."
Dave Carpenter/Cartoonstock

Who Is Fooling Whom? He doesn't believe her, but maybe she shouldn't believe what the label says, either. For example, "low fat" might also mean high sugar.

so on. In early childhood, the American Heart Association recommends no more than six teaspoons of natural or added sugars, such as high-fructose corn syrup. The average child consumes three times that. Too much sugar causes poor circulation—with heart attacks likely 50 years later (Vos et al., 2017).

Advertisements may mislead. For example, vitamin C is usually found in abundance in the normal diet of young children and is a cheap vitamin to add to food, so sweetened juice with 100 percent of the daily requirement of vitamin C is no bargain.

Oral Health The most immediate harm from sugar is cavities and decaying teeth before age 6. Thus, children should see a dentist and brush their teeth regularly during early childhood—practices that were unnecessary before widespread sugar consumption (Gibbons, 2012).

"Baby" teeth are replaced naturally from ages 6 to 10. The schedule is genetic, with girls a few months ahead of boys. However, tooth brushing and dentist visits should become habitual in early childhood because poor oral health harms those permanent teeth (forming below the first teeth) and can cause jaw malformation, chewing difficulties, and speech problems.

Teeth are affected by diet and illness, so a young child's teeth can alert a professional to other health problems. The process works in reverse as well: Infected teeth can affect the rest of the child's body. In adulthood, tooth infections can cause preterm births (Puertas et al., 2018).

Allergies and Food An estimated 6 to 8 percent of children are allergic to a specific food, almost always a common, healthy one: Milk, eggs, peanuts, tree nuts (such as almonds and walnuts), soy, wheat, fish, and shellfish are the usual culprits. Diagnostic standards for allergies vary (which explains the range of estimates), and treatment varies even more.

Some experts advocate total avoidance of the offending food—there are peanut-free schools, where no one is allowed to bring a peanut-butter sandwich for lunch. However, carefully giving children who are allergic to peanuts a tiny bit of peanut powder (under medical supervision) is usually a safe and effective way to decrease preschool children's allergic reaction (Couzin-Frankel, 2018).

Indeed, exposure to peanuts can begin before birth: A study of pregnant women who ingested peanuts found that their children were less likely to be allergic (Frazier et al., 2014). Fortunately, many childhood food allergies are outgrown, but ongoing allergies make a balanced diet even harder to maintain.

Other allergies may increase as children grow older, depending on various preventive measures—for example, avoiding air pollution or having a pet (Nowak & Schaub, 2018). Diet might matter. Children who eat fewer fast foods (which have relatively high levels of saturated fatty acids, trans fatty acids, sodium, carbohydrates, and sugar) are less likely to have asthma, nasal congestion, watery eyes, and itchy skin allergies.

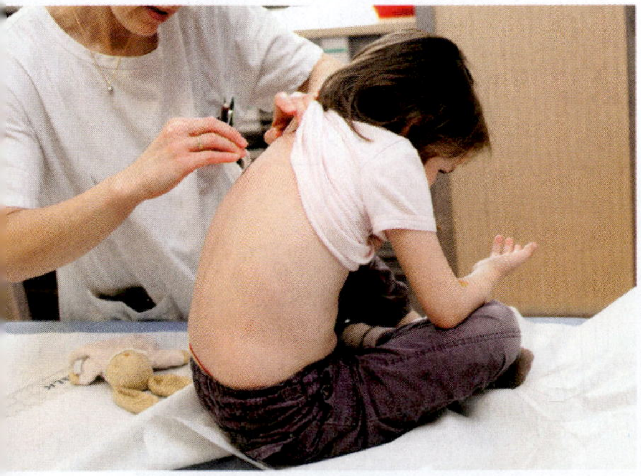

©Burger/Phanie/The Image Works

Not Allergic Anymore? Many food allergies are outgrown, so young children are more likely to have them than older ones. This skin prick will insert a tiny amount of a suspected allergen. If a red welt develops in the next half hour, the girl is still allergic. Hopefully, no reaction will occur; but if her breathing is affected, an EpiPen is within reach.

WHAT HAVE YOU LEARNED?

1. About how much does a well-nourished child grow in height and weight from age 2 to age 6?
2. Why do some adults overfeed children?
3. How do childhood allergies affect nutrition?
4. Why are today's children more at risk of obesity than children 50 years ago?

Brain Growth

By age 2, most neurons have connected to other neurons and substantial pruning has occurred. The 2-year-old's brain already weighs 75 percent of what it will weigh in adulthood; the 6-year-old's brain is 90 percent of adult weight.

Since most of the brain is already present and functioning by age 2, what remains to develop? The most important parts! Most important for people, that is.

Myelination

After infancy, most of the increase in brain weight occurs because of **myelination**. *Myelin* (sometimes called the *white matter* of the brain; the *gray matter* is the neurons themselves) is a fatty coating on the axons that protects and speeds signals between neurons.

myelination The process by which axons become coated with myelin, a fatty substance that speeds the transmission of nerve impulses from neuron to neuron.

Myelin helps every part of the brain, especially the connections between neurons that are far from each other. It is far more than mere insulation around the axons: "Myelin organizes the very structure of network connectivity . . . and regulates the timing of information flow through individual circuits" (Fields, 2014, p. 266).

Lateralization Myelination is especially evident in the major link between the left and the right halves of the brain, the **corpus callosum** (see Inside the Brain).

corpus callosum A long, thick band of nerve fibers that connects the left and right hemispheres of the brain and allows communication between them.

Left-handed people tend to have thicker, better myelinated corpus callosa than right-handed people do, perhaps because they often need to switch between the two sides of their bodies, depending on the task. Naturally they use their dominant left hand (e.g., brushing their teeth), but socially they use their right hand because that is what is expected (e.g., shaking hands).

Acceptance of left-handedness is more widespread now than a century ago. More adults in Great Britain and the United States claim to be left-handed today (about 10 percent) than in 1900 (about 3 percent) (McManus et al., 2010). Developmentalists now advise against forcing a left-handed child to become right-handed, since the brain is the origin of handedness.

lateralization Literally, sidedness, referring to the specialization in certain functions by each side of the brain, with one side dominant for each activity. The left side of the brain controls the right side of the body, and vice versa.

Indeed, the brain is the source of all types of **lateralization** (literally, *sidedness*). The entire human body is lateralized, apparent not only in right- or left-handedness but also in the feet, the eyes, the ears, and the brain itself.

Genes, prenatal hormones, and early experiences all affect which side does what, and then the corpus callosum puts it all together. Left lateralization is an advantage in some professions, especially those involving creativity and split-second, emotional responses.

A disproportionate number of artists, musicians, and sports stars were/are left-handed, including Pele, Babe Ruth, Monica Seles, Bill Gates, Oprah Winfrey, Jimi Hendrix, Lady Gaga, and Justin Bieber. Five of the past seven presidents of the United States were/are lefties: Gerald Ford, Ronald Reagan, George H.W. Bush, Bill Clinton, and Barack Obama. Each was able to coordinate with many nations and opinions in Congress: Political flexibility allowing respect for diverse populations may correlate with a strong corpus callosum. (See Inside the Brain.)

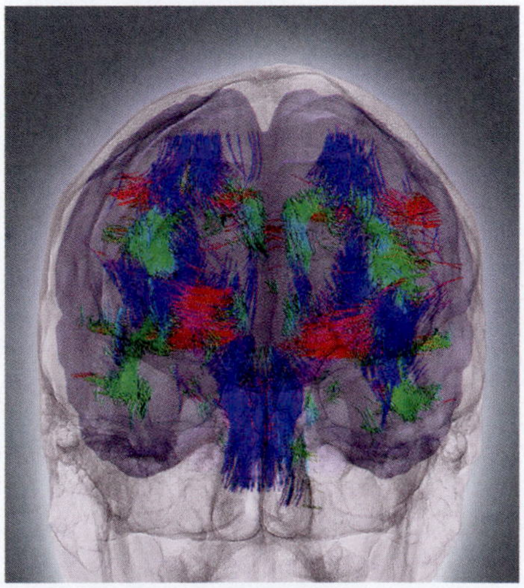

Zephyr/SPL/Science Source

Mental Coordination? This brain scan of a 38-year-old depicts areas of myelination (the various colors) within the brain. As you see, the two hemispheres are quite similar, but not identical. For most important skills and concepts, both halves of the brain are activated.

Humans and Other Animals Although the brains and bodies of other primates are better than those of humans in some ways (other primates climb trees earlier and faster, for instance), and although many animals have abilities that humans lack (smell in dogs, hearing in bats), humans have intellectual capacities far beyond any other animal. Much of this is the ability to use many parts of the brain at once, an ability aided by extensive white matter.

With other creatures, evolution is sometimes called "survival of the fittest." But humans have developed "a mode of living built on social cohesion,

INSIDE THE BRAIN

Connected Hemispheres

The brain is divided into two halves called hemispheres. Those two are connected by the corpus callosum, a long, thick band of nerve fibers that myelinates and grows particularly rapidly in early childhood (Ansado et al., 2015). For that reason, compared to toddlers, young children become much better at coordinating the two sides of their brains and, hence, both sides of their bodies. They can hop, skip, and gallop at age 5, unlike at age 2.

Both sides of the brain are usually involved in every skill, not only gross motor skills such as hopping, skipping, and galloping but also fine motor skills such as eating with utensils or buttoning one's coat. Intellectual skills also use many parts of the brain, as do social responses to other people.

That is why the corpus callosum is crucial. As myelination progresses, signals between the two hemispheres become quicker and clearer, enabling children to become better thinkers, to be less clumsy, and eventually to read, write, and add—all skills that require the whole brain.

The development of the corpus callosum is easy to see when comparing infants and older children. For example, no 2-year-old can hop on one foot, but most 6-year-olds can—an example of brain balancing. Many songs, dances, and games that young children love involve moving their bodies in some coordinated way—challenging, but fun because of that. Logic (left brain) without emotion (right brain) is a severe impairment, as is the opposite (Damasio, 2012).

Emotions also need to be balanced. In adulthood, depression is more common in people with impaired balance between the two sides of the brain (Bruder et al., 2017).

Serious disorders are caused when the corpus callosum fails to develop. That almost always results in intellectual disability (Cavalari & Donovick, 2014). Abnormal growth of the corpus callosum is one symptom of autism spectrum disorder, as well as of dozens of other disorders (Travers et al., 2015; J. Wolff et al., 2015; Al-Hashim et al., 2016). This is partly genetic, but it also is prenatal, as evidenced by smaller corpus callosa when the mother drank heavily during pregnancy (Biffen et al., 2018).

Astonishing studies of humans whose corpus callosa were severed to relieve severe epilepsy, as well as research on humans and other vertebrates with intact corpus callosa, reveal how the brain's hemispheres specialize. Typically, the left half controls the body's right side as well as areas dedicated to logical reasoning, detailed analysis, and the basics of language.

The brain's right half controls the body's left side and areas dedicated to emotional and creative impulses, including appreciation of music, art, and poetry. Thus, the left half notices details and the right half grasps the big picture.

This left–right distinction has been exaggerated, especially when broadly applied to people. No one is exclusively left-brained or right-brained, except individuals with severe brain injury in childhood, who may use half of their brain to do all of the necessary thinking. Nonetheless, we should all be grateful that many parts of our brains coordinate with other parts. We have our corpus callosa to thank for that.

cooperation and efficient planning. It was a question of survival of the smartest" (Corballis, 2011, p. 194). Myelination from ages 3 to 6 is crucial for that, because it enables the parts of the brain to communicate with each other (Forbes & Gallo, 2017).

Maturation of the Prefrontal Cortex

The entire frontal lobe continues to develop for many years after early childhood; dendrite density and myelination are still increasing in emerging adulthood. Nonetheless, neurological control advances significantly between ages 2 and 6, evident in several ways:

- Sleep becomes more regular.
- Emotions become more nuanced and responsive.
- Temper tantrums subside.
- Uncontrollable laughter and tears are less common.

One example of the maturing brain is evident in the game Simon Says. Players are supposed to follow the leader *only* when orders are preceded

Especially for Early-Childhood Teachers You know you should be patient, but frustration rises when your young charges dawdle on the walk to the playground a block away. What should you do? (see response, page 218)

by the words "Simon says." Thus, if leaders touch their noses and say, "Simon says touch your nose," players are supposed to touch their noses; but when leaders touch their noses and say, "Touch your nose," no one is supposed to follow the example. Young children lose at this game because they impulsively do what they see and hear.

Another example is the sudden fear that young children experience. Because the amygdala is not well connected to more reflective and rational parts of the brain, many young children become suddenly terrified—even of something that exists only in imagination. With maturation and reassurance, the fearful child becomes the confident adult.

"I would share, but I'm not there developmentally."

Barbara Smaller/The New Yorker Collection/Cartoonbank.com

Good Excuse It is true that emotional control of selfish instincts is difficult for young children because the prefrontal cortex is not yet mature enough to regulate some emotions. However, family practices can advance social understanding.

Inhibition and Flexibility

Neurons have only two kinds of impulses: on–off or, in neuroscience terms, *activate–inhibit*. Each is signaled by biochemical messages from dendrites to axons to neurons. (The consequences are evident in *executive function* and *emotional regulation*, both crucial aspects of cognition that are discussed in the next two chapters.)

Impulsiveness A balance of activation and inhibition (on/off) is necessary for thoughtful adults, who neither leap too quickly nor hesitate too long, neither lash out angrily nor freeze in fear. Neurological equilibrium is best lifelong: One sign of cognitive loss is when a person becomes too cautious or too impulsive.

Some preschool teachers tell the children to sit on their hands during "circle time", assigning each child to a designated spot on the carpet, because children have difficulty not touching their neighbor. Poor **impulse control** signifies a personality disorder in adulthood but not in early childhood. Few 3-year-olds are capable of sustained attention to tasks that adults organize.

impulse control The ability to postpone or deny the immediate response to an idea or behavior.

Perseveration The opposite reaction is also apparent. Some young children **perseverate**, which is to stick to (persevere) one thought or action. A child might play with one toy or hold one fantasy for hours. This is characteristic of children on the autism spectrum but can also be quite typical for a 3-year-old.

perseverate To stay stuck, or persevere, in one thought or action for a long time. The ability to be flexible, switching from one task to another, is beyond most young children.

Young children may repeat a phrase or question again and again, or they may not be able to stop giggling once they start. That is perseveration. Crying may become uncontrollable because the child is stuck in whatever triggered the outburst.

A study of children from ages 3 to 6 found that the ability to attend to what adults requested gradually increased. That correlated with academic learning and behavioral control (fewer outbursts or tears) (Metcalfe et al., 2013). Development continues as brain maturation (innate) and emotional regulation (learned) allow most children to pay attention and switch activities as needed, with neurological maturation related to cultural demands (Posner & Rothbart, 2017).

In childhood as well as adulthood, perseveration leads to procrastination ("Not now, I am busy"). Impulsivity and procrastination may seem to be opposites, but they are closely correlated, because the same brain regions (particularly the left dorsolateral prefrontal cortex) are involved in both (Liu & Feng, 2017).

Stress and the Brain The relationship between stress and brain activity depends partly on the age of the person and partly on the degree of stress. Both too much and too little impair learning.

fatihhoca/iStock/Getty Images

Open Your Arms! But four children keep their arms closed because Simon didn't say to do so. You can almost see their prefrontal cortices (above the eyes) hard at work.

macmillan learning

VIDEO ACTIVITY: The Childhood Stress-Cortisol Connection examines how high cortisol levels can negatively impact a child's overall health.

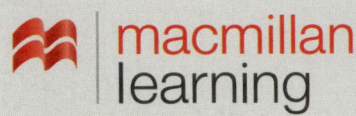

In an experiment, brain scans and hormone measurements were taken of 4- to 6-year-olds immediately after a fire alarm (Teoh & Lamb, 2013). As measured by their cortisol levels, some children were upset and some were not. Two weeks later, they were questioned about the event. Those with higher cortisol reactions to the alarm remembered more details than did those with lower cortisol. That is found in other research as well—some stress, but not too much, aids cognition (Keller et al., 2012).

However, especially with children, if an adult creates stress by asking questions sternly and demanding immediate yes-or-no answers, memories are less accurate. There are good evolutionary reasons for that: People need to remember experiences that arouse their emotions so that they can avoid, or adjust to, similar experiences in the future. On the other hand, the brain protects itself from too much stress by shutting down.

Generally, a balance between arousal and reassurance is needed, again requiring coordination among many parts of the brain. For instance, if children are witnesses to a crime (a stressful experience) or experience abuse, memory is more accurate when an interviewer is warm and attentive, listening carefully but not suggesting answers (Johnson et al., 2016).

Direct maltreatment is worse, causing not only shrinkage of various regions of the brain but also decreases in white matter—and thus reduced connections between parts of the brain (Puetz et al., 2017; Rock et al., 2018). A person who was abused as a child might get stuck—perhaps on fear, or on fantasy, or even on a happy or neutral thought, unable to coordinate the mixed emotions of most experiences.

Sadly, this topic leads again to the Romanian children mentioned in Chapter 7. When some adopted Romanian children saw pictures of happy, sad, frightened, or angry faces, their limbic systems were less reactive than were those of Romanian children who were never institutionalized. Their brains were also less lateralized, suggesting less efficient thinking (C. Nelson et al., 2014). Thus, institutional life, without stress reduction provided by loving caretakers, impaired their brains.

Advancing Motor Skills

Maturation and myelination allow children to move with greater speed, agility, and grace as they age (see Visualizing Development, page 219). Brain growth, motivation, and guided practice undergird all motor skills.

Gross Motor Skills Gross motor skills improve dramatically during early childhood. When playing, many 2-year-olds fall down and bump clumsily into each other. By contrast, some 5-year-olds perform coordinated dance steps, tumbling tricks, or sports moves.

There remains much for them to learn, especially in the ability to adjust to other people and new circumstances. Thus, a 5-year-old can sometimes kick a ball with precision, but it is much harder for that child to be a good team player on a soccer team. (Learning about people and controlling emotions are discussed in the next two chapters.)

Many North American 5-year-olds can ride a tricycle, climb a ladder, and pump a swing, as well as throw, catch, and kick a ball. A few can do these things by age 3, and some 5-year-olds can already skate, ski, dive, and ride a bike—activities that demand balanced coordination and both brain hemispheres. Elsewhere, some 5-year-olds swim in oceans or climb cliffs.

Adults need to make sure that children have a safe space to play, with time, appropriate equipment, and playmates. Children learn best from peers who demonstrate whatever the child is ready to try, from catching a ball to climbing a tree. Of course, culture and locale influence particulars: Some small children learn to skateboard, others to sail.

TIMOTHY A. CLARY/AFP/Getty Images

STR/AFP/Getty Images

Practice with the Big Kids Ava is unable to stand as Carlyann can *(left)*, but she is thrilled to be wearing her tutu in New York City's Central Park with 230 other dancers in a highly organized attempt to break a record for the most ballerinas on pointe at the same moment. Motor skills are developing in exactly the same way on the other side of the world *(right)* as children in Beijing perform in ballet class.

Crowded, busy, or violent streets not only impede development of gross motor skills but also add to the natural fears of the immature amygdala, compounded by the learned fears of adults. Gone are the days when parents told their children to go out and play, only to return when hunger, rain, or nightfall brought them home. Now many parents fear strangers and traffic, keeping their 3-to 5-year-olds inside (R. Taylor et al., 2009).

Learning from Nature That worries many childhood educators who believe that children need space and freedom in order to develop well (Moore & Sabo-Risley, 2017). Balancing on branches and jumping over fences, squeezing mud and throwing pebbles, chasing birds and catching bugs—each forbidden now by some adults—educated millions of children in former cohorts.

Play is considered crucial for every aspect of child development, cognitive and social as well as physical. It is discussed in Chapter 10. Here we acknowledge that children develop their motor skills—running, climbing, leaping, jumping—when they play outside with other children.

Accordingly, some researchers have studied which environments are most likely to encourage active play. A study found that children were most likely to play actively outside on dead-end streets, cul-du-sacs, or side streets where there was some visible litter (Kaczynski et al., 2018). The "counterintuitive" discovery that streets with litter correlated with play was explained by the researchers as an indication of more playmates and fewer authorities.

Fine Motor Skills Fine motor skills also improve dramatically in early childhood. This is particularly apparent in eating. Most 1-year-olds grab their food in their hands, and they prefer finger foods of all kinds—sandwiches, chips, carrots, cookies. Indeed, many very young children eat spaghetti, or ice cream, or mashed potatoes with their hands—despite the obvious difficulties.

Gradually, however, children learn to use spoons, and then forks, and eventually, knives. This is culture-specific, of course. Chopsticks are mastered by 4-year-olds in Asia, even though many 40-year-olds in North America cannot manipulate them.

Other fine motor skills are gradually mastered. Two-year-olds try to mash a puzzle piece into a space, not only because their spatial visualization needs maturation

CHAPTER APP 8

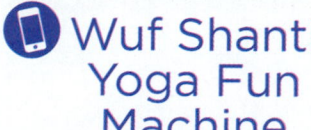

Wuf Shanti Yoga Fun Machine

iOS:
https://tinyurl.com/y5hzbsmc

RELATED TOPIC:
Motor skills and general well-being in early childhood

Based on a book and South Florida PBS series and featuring the motto "Think well to be well," this app for young children includes brief videos of yoga poses, songs, meditations, and positive thoughts. There are also games and coloring pages on the app, all of which encourage health, wellness, happiness, and positivity in children.

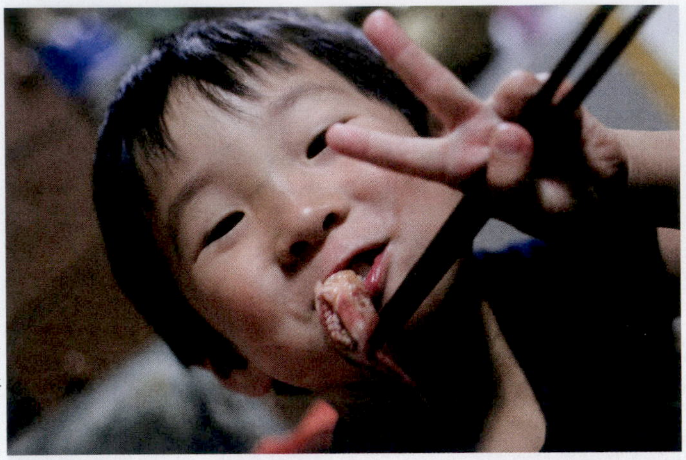

Wilfried Maisy / REA / Redux

Nils Hendrik Mueller/Cultura/Getty Images

Same Situation, Far Apart: Finger Skills Children learn whatever motor skills their culture teaches. Some master chopsticks, with fingers to spare; others cut sausage with a knife and fork. Unlike children in Japan *(above left)* and Germany *(above right)*, some never master either, because about one-third of adults worldwide eat directly with their hands.

but also because their fingers are not yet adept at rotation. That is why many puzzles for young children have wooden pieces with knobs for easier manipulation. Sewing, knitting, drawing, buttoning, and much more develops gradually. Ideally, equipment for children takes immaturity into account—as seen in children's shoes, now never tied, always velcroed or slip-on.

Gender differences are evident. In part, that is because maturation is quicker in girls than boys—already apparent in when baby teeth fall out. But part of it may be practice: Girls are more often given sewing cards, or Barbie dolls that have clothes that require fine motor skills. [**Life-Span Link:** This tension between nature and nurture for gender issues is discussed in Chapter 10.]

WHAT HAVE YOU LEARNED?

1. Why is myelination important for thinking and motor skills?
2. How does brain maturation affect impulsivity and perseveration?
3. How do stress hormones affect brain development?
4. What factors help children develop their gross motor skills?
5. What are the advantages and disadvantages of organized sports programs?
6. What factors help children develop their fine motor skills?

Harm to Children

The goal of the study of human development is to help everyone develop their full potential lifelong. All cultures cherish the young. Communities provide education, health care, and playgrounds; parents, grandparents, and strangers of every income, ethnicity, and nation seek to protect children while fostering their growth.

Nevertheless, far more children are harmed by acts of commission or omission (action or neglect), by deliberate or accidental violence, than from any specific disease. In the United States, almost four times as many 1- to 4-year-olds die of accidents than of cancer, which is the leading cause of disease death during these years (National Center for Health Statistics, 2018).

Avoidable Injury

Worldwide, injuries cause millions of premature deaths. Not until age 40 does any specific disease overtake accidents as a cause of mortality.

In some nations, malnutrition, malaria, and other infectious diseases *combined* cause more infant and child deaths than injuries do, but those nations also have high rates of child injury. For example, southern Asia and sub-Saharan Africa have the highest rates of child motor-vehicle deaths, even though the number of cars is relatively low (World Health Organization, 2015). Most children who die in such accidents are pedestrians, or are riding—without a helmet—on motorcycles.

Age-Related Dangers In accidents overall, 2- to 6-year-olds are more often seriously hurt than 6- to 10-year-olds. Why are young children so vulnerable?

Immaturity of the prefrontal cortex makes young children impulsive; they plunge into danger. Unlike infants, their motor skills allow them to run, leap, scramble, and grab in a flash, before a caregiver can stop them. Their curiosity is boundless; their impulses are uninhibited.

Meanwhile, adults tend to overestimate what their children understand (Morrongiello, 2018). Parents teach not to run with scissors, for example, and are proud that their children can repeat that rule and obey when the parents are nearby. But those same parents think that their children know the reason for that rule—but most do not. A child who suddenly feels angry may deliberately break a rule—unaware of the danger.

Especially for Urban Planners Describe a neighborhood park that would benefit 2- to 5-year-olds. (see response, page 218)

Parents think they can predict what hazards will be attractive to their children, yet "young children routinely do unpredictable things that lead to injuries" (Morrongiello, 2018, p. 218). A child who has never seemed interested in, for instance, the kitchen knife rack might one day want to carve, cut, or stab, never having learned that knives can be dangerous. I did exactly that when I was learning to write: One of my parents' cherished coffee tables had "KAT" carved in it.

Almost all young children do something that they know is forbidden and hide it from their parents. This could be quite harmless, such has hiding broccoli in their napkin or sweeping up shards of the glass that should have stayed on the shelf. But it could also be dangerous: Children run away and get lost, start a fire and try to extinguish it, or swallow pills but never tell their parents that they feel sick.

Age-related trends are apparent in particulars. Falls are more often fatal for the youngest (under 24 months) and oldest (over 80 years) people; 1- to 4-year-olds have high rates of poisoning and drowning; motor-vehicle deaths peak from age 15 to 25.

Generally, as income falls, accident rates rise, but not for every cause. In the United States, young children drown in swimming pools six times more often than

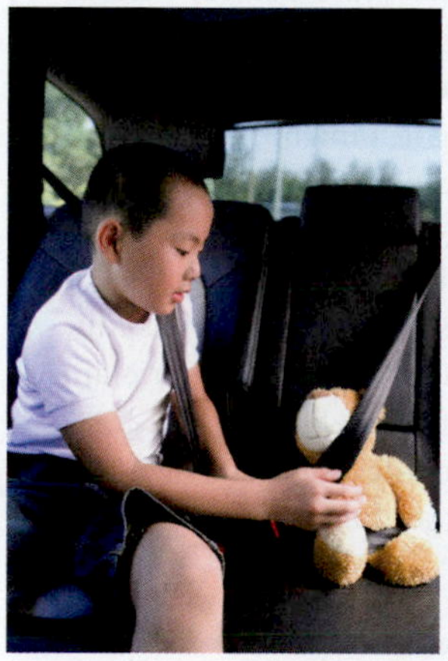

Blue Jean Images / Alamy

© DAVID R. FRAZIER/DANITADELIMONT.COM

Same Situation, Far Apart: Keeping Everyone Safe Preventing child accidents requires action by both adults and children. In the United States *(left)*, adults passed laws and taught children to use seat belts—including this boy who buckles his stuffed companion. In France *(right)*, teachers stop cars while children hold hands to cross the street—each child keeping his or her partner moving ahead.

older children and adults (Gilchrist & Parker, May 16, 2014). Usually the deadly pool is in their own backyard, a luxury few low-income families enjoy.

injury control/harm reduction Practices that are aimed at anticipating, controlling, and preventing dangerous activities; these practices reflect the beliefs that accidents are not random and that injuries can be made less harmful if proper controls are in place.

Injury Control Instead of using the term *accident prevention,* public health experts prefer **injury control** (or **harm reduction**). Consider the implications. *Accident* implies that an injury is random, unpredictable; if anyone is at fault, it's a careless parent or an accident-prone child. Instead, *injury control* suggests that the impact of an injury can be limited, and *harm reduction* implies that harm can be minimized.

If young children are allowed to play to develop their skills, minor mishaps (scratches and bruises) are bound to occur. As already explained, children benefit from play. A child with no scrapes may be overprotected.

However, playing children need protection. Serious injury is unlikely if a child falls on a safety surface instead of on concrete, if a car seat protects the body in a crash, if a bicycle helmet cracks instead of a skull, or if swallowed pills come from a tiny bottle. Reducing harm requires effort from professionals and parents, as I know too well from my own experience (see A Case to Study).

Less than half as many 1- to 5-year-olds in the United States were fatally injured in 2015 as in 1980, thanks to laws that limit poisons, prevent fires, and regulate cars. Control has not yet caught up with newer hazards, however.

For instance, many new homes in California, Florida, Texas, and Arizona have swimming pools: In those states, drowning is a leading cause of child death. Children under age 5 are now less often poisoned from medicines and more often poisoned by cosmetics or personal care products (deodorant, hair colorant, etc.) (Mowry et al., 2015, p. 968).

A CASE TO STUDY

"My Baby Swallowed Poison"

Many people think that the way to prevent injury to young children is to educate parents. However, public health research finds that laws that apply to everyone are more effective than education, especially if parents are overwhelmed by the daily demands of child care and money management. Injury rates rise when parents have more than one small child, and not enough money.

For example, thousands of lives have been saved by infant car seats. However, many parents do not voluntarily install car seats. Research has found that parents are more likely to use car seats if they are given them to take their newborn home from the hospital, and if an expert installs the seat and shows the parents how to use it—not simply tells them or makes them watch a video (Tessier, 2010).

Laws mandating car seats and hospital programs have had an effect. In 2013 in the entire United States, only 60 infant passengers died in car accidents, one-eighth the number in 2003.

The research concludes that motivation and education help, but laws mandating primary prevention are more effective. I know this firsthand. Our daughter Bethany, at age 2, climbed onto the kitchen counter to find, open, and swallow most of a bottle of baby aspirin. Where was I? In the next room, nursing our second child and watching television. I did not notice what Bethany was doing until I checked on her during a commercial.

Bethany is alive and well today, protected by all three levels of prevention. Primary prevention included laws limiting the number of baby aspirin per container; secondary prevention included my pediatrician's written directions from when Bethany was a week old to buy syrup of ipecac; tertiary prevention was my phone call to Poison Control.

I told the helpful stranger who answered the phone, "My baby swallowed poison." He calmly asked me a few questions and then advised me to give Bethany ipecac to make her throw up. I did, and she did.

That ipecac had been purchased two years before, when I was a brand-new mother and ready to follow every bit of my pediatrician's advice. If the doctor had waited until Bethany was able to climb before recommending it, I might not have followed his advice, because by then I had more confidence in my ability to prevent harm.

I still blame myself, but I am grateful for all three levels of prevention that protected my child. In some ways, my own education helped avert a tragedy. I had chosen a wise pediatrician; I knew the number for Poison Control (FYI: 1-800-222-1222).

As I remember all the mistakes I made in parenting (only a few mentioned in this book), I am grateful for every level of prevention.

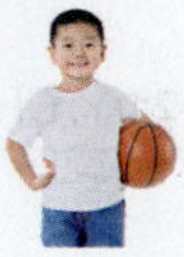

Prevention

Prevention begins long before any particular child, parent, or legislator does something foolish. Unfortunately, few people notice injuries and deaths that did not happen. Scientists analyze data, however, and advocate prevention. That has reduced accidental deaths dramatically.

Levels of Prevention Three levels of prevention apply to every health and safety issue.

- **Primary prevention** considers the overall conditions that affect the likelihood of harm. Laws and customs reduce injury for people of every age.
- **Secondary prevention** is more targeted, averting harm in high-risk situations or for vulnerable individuals.
- **Tertiary prevention** begins after an injury has occurred, limiting damage.

primary prevention Actions that change overall background conditions to prevent some unwanted event or circumstance, such as injury, disease, or abuse.

secondary prevention Actions that avert harm in a high-risk situation, such as holding a child's hand when crossing the street.

tertiary prevention Actions, such as immediate and effective medical treatment, that are taken after an adverse event (such as illness or injury) and that reduce harm.

Tertiary prevention is the most visible, but primary prevention is the most effective. Much of the research has focused on sports injuries among older children and adults (Emery, 2018), but the same principles apply at every age.

An example comes from data on motor-vehicle deaths. As compared with 50 years ago, far more cars are on the road; but the rate of children killed by cars is only one-fourth of what it was (Insurance Institute for Highway Safety, 2018) (see **Figure 8.1**). How does each level of prevention contribute?

Primary prevention includes sidewalks, pedestrian overpasses, streetlights, and traffic circles. Cars have been redesigned (e.g., better headlights, windows, and brakes), and drivers' competence has improved (e.g., stronger penalties for drunk driving). Reduction of traffic via improved mass transit provides additional primary prevention.

Secondary prevention reduces danger in high-risk situations. Crossing guards and flashing lights on stopped school buses are secondary prevention, as are salt on icy roads, warning signs before blind curves, speed bumps, and walk/don't walk signals at busy intersections. Laws require safety seats for child passengers.

Finally, *tertiary prevention* reduces damage after an accident. Examples include speedy ambulances, efficient emergency room procedures, effective follow-up care, and laws against hit-and-run drivers, all of which have been improved from

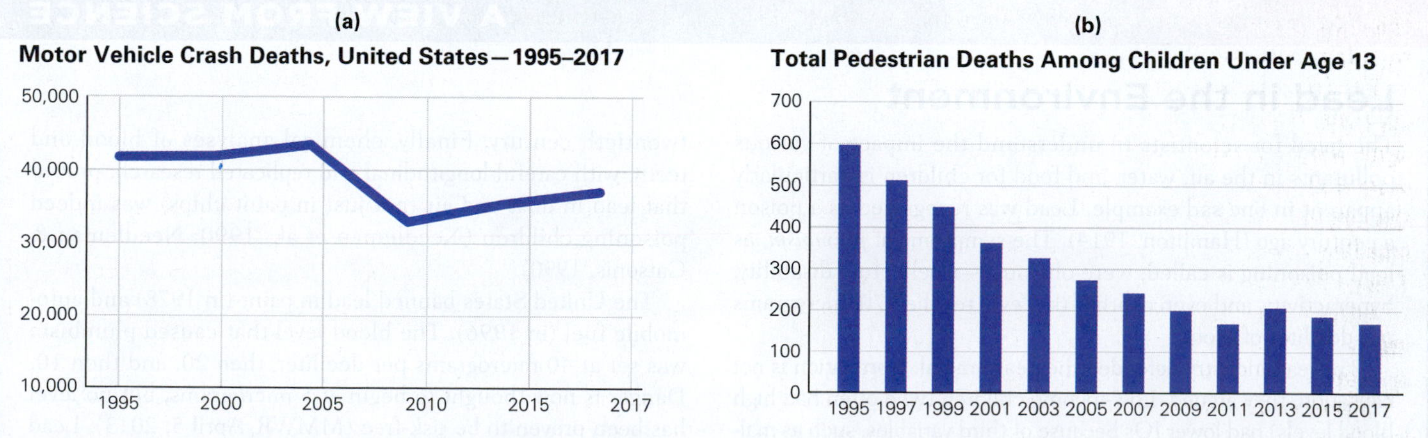

Data from Insurance Institute for Highway Safety, December, 2018.

FIGURE 8.1

No Matter What Statistic Motor-vehicle fatalities of pedestrians, passengers, and drivers, from cars, trucks, and motorcycles, for people of all ages, were all lower in 2017 than in 1995, a dramatic difference since the population had increased by a third and the number of cars increased as well. Proof could be shown in a dozen charts, but here is one of the most telling: deaths of child pedestrians. All three levels of prevention—in roads, cars, drivers, police, caregivers, and the children themselves—contributed to this shift.

Solent News/Splash News/Newscom

Forget Baby Henry? Infants left in parked cars on hot days can die from the heat. Henry's father invented a disc to be placed under the baby that buzzes his cell phone if he is more than 20 feet away from the disc. He hopes all absentminded parents will buy one.

decades ago. Medical personnel speak of the *golden hour,* the hour following an accident, when a victim should be treated. Of course, there is nothing magical about 60 minutes in contrast to 61 minutes, but the faster an injury victim reaches a trauma center, the better the chance of recovery (Dinh et al., 2013).

The child death rate is lower for other reasons, as well. Air pollution has been reduced, so fewer children die of asthma. Poison control is more readily available, so fewer children die of swallowing toxins. And many pesticides are banned from home use, so fewer children swallow them.

A most dramatic advance in harm prevention has been in accidental firearm death. In 1970 that rate was 10 per million children ages 1 to 14; in 2015, the rate was half that (National Center for Health Statistics, 2018), even though more guns have been sold.

Evidence matters. It has led to community awareness and prevention. Children are no less curious than they were, and guns are no less common. Indeed, "the civilian gun stock has roughly doubled since 1968, from one gun per every two persons to one gun per person" according to a 2012 report to the U.S. Congress (Krouse, 2012). Other sources also find more guns in homes. However, more parents hide and lock their guns, so only half as many children die of gun deaths.

Many pediatricians now advise safe firearm storage when they counsel about locking up poisons. Sadly, the school shooting in Sandy Hook, Connecticut, was followed by increases in both gun purchases and accidental gun deaths of children (Levine & McKnight, 2017). Newly purchased guns are more likely to cause deaths of family members, because new buyers are less careful.

For all of these problems, the focus has been on physical injury, not on intellectual harm. That is the next challenge for developmentalists, as it is apparent that pollutants in air and water, and chemicals in household products and food, may harm the brain, particularly in infancy and childhood. It continues lifelong (Babadjouni et al., 2017).

It is difficult for any one person to prevent this harm, and government regulations are notoriously slow. Lead is a sobering example of this, as explained in A View from Science.

A VIEW FROM SCIENCE

Lead in the Environment

The need for scientists to understand the impact of various pollutants in the air, water, and food for children is particularly apparent in one sad example. Lead was recognized as a poison a century ago (Hamilton, 1914). The symptoms of *plumbism,* as lead poisoning is called, were obvious—intellectual disability, hyperactivity, and even death if the level reached 70 micrograms per deciliter of blood.

The lead industry defended the heavy metal. Correlation is not causation, they argued. Low-income children (who often had high blood levels) had lower IQs because of third variables, such as malnutrition, inadequate schools, and parents who let their children eat flaking chips of lead paint (which tastes sweet). This made sense to some developmental psychologists (Scarr, 1985) and, I confess, to me in the first edition of my textbook (Berger, 1980).

Lead remained a major ingredient in paint (it speeds drying) and in gasoline (it raises octane) for most of the twentieth century. Finally, chemical analyses of blood and teeth, with careful longitudinal and replicated research, proved that lead in dust and air (not just in paint chips) was indeed poisoning children (Needleman et al., 1990; Needleman & Gatsonis, 1990).

The United States banned lead in paint (in 1978) and automobile fuel (in 1996). The blood level that caused plumbism was set at 40 micrograms per deciliter, then 20, and then 10. Danger is now thought to begin at 5 micrograms, but no level has been proven to be risk-free (MMWR, April 5, 2013). Lead is especially destructive of fetal, infant, and young child brains (Hanna-Attisha et al., 2016).

Regulation has made a difference: The percentage of U.S. 1- to 5-year-olds with more than 5 micrograms of lead per deciliter of blood was 8.6 percent in 1999–2001, 4.1 percent in 2003–2006, 2.6 percent in 2007–2010, and less than 1 percent

in 2010–2014 (Raymond & Brown, January 20, 2017) (see **Figure 8.2**).

Prevention matters. Many parents now know to wipe window ledges clean, avoid child exposure to construction dust, test drinking water, discard lead-based medicines and crockery (available in some other nations), and prevent children from eating chips of lead-based paint. A new measure is to make sure that children drink milk, since dairy products eliminate lead from the body (Kordas et al., 2018).

However, private actions alone are not sufficient to protect health. Developmentalists note many examples when blaming parents (for obesity, injury, abuse, low achievement, high blood pressure, neglect, and so on) distracts from blaming industries, laws, or the wider community.

A stark example occurred in Flint, Michigan, where in April 2014 cost-saving officials (appointed by the state to take over the city when the tax base shrunk as the auto industry left) changed the municipal drinking water from Lake Huron to the Flint River. That river contained chemicals from industrial waste that increased lead leaching from old pipes, contaminating tap water for drinking and mixing infant formula.

The percent of young children in Flint with blood lead levels above 5 micrograms per deciliter doubled in two years, from 2.4 to 4.9 percent, and more than tripled in one neighborhood from 4.6 to 15.7 percent (Hanna-Attisha et al., 2016).

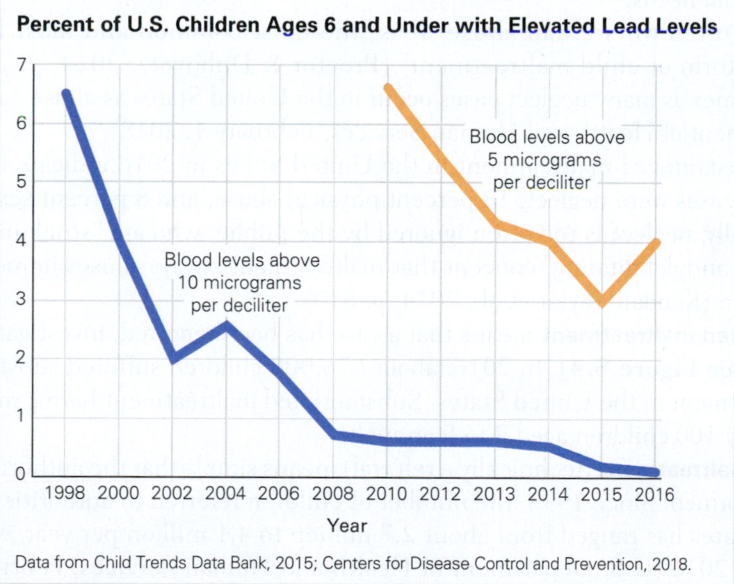

FIGURE 8.2

Dramatic Improvement in a Decade When legislators finally accepted the research establishing the damage from lead in paint, gasoline, and water, they passed laws that helped to make it exceedingly rare for any child to die or suffer intellectual disability because of plumbism. A decade ago, 10 micrograms per deciliter of blood was thought to be completely safe; now less than 1 child in 200 tests at that level, and even 5 micrograms per deciliter alerts pediatricians and parents to find the source. These national data make the tragedy in Flint, Michigan, especially shocking.

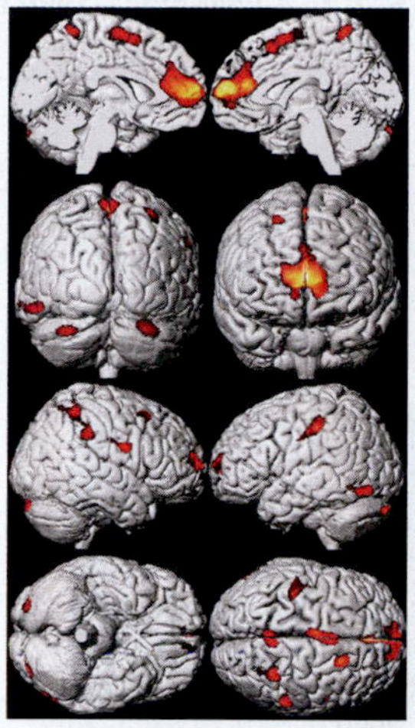

Cecil, Kim M.; Brubaker, Christopher J.; Adler, Caleb M.; Dietrich, Kim N.; Altaye, Mekibib; Egelhoff, John C., . . . Lanphear, Bruce P. (2008). Decreased Brain Volume in Adults with Childhood Lead Exposure. *PLoS Med 5*(5): e112. doi:10.1371/journal.pmed.0050112.

Toxic Shrinkage This composite of 157 brains of adults who, as children, had high lead levels in their blood shows reduced volume. The red and yellow hot spots are all areas that are smaller than areas in a normal brain. No wonder lead-exposed children have multiple intellectual and behavioral problems.

The consequences may harm these children lifelong, not only in their education but also in their activity level (hyperactivity is more common in lead-poisoned children). Some of those children will be in prison later in life because of the lead in their brains.

What? The children will be in prison, not the bureaucrats? Yes. Teenagers whose brains were damaged by lead are more likely to commit violent crimes than other teenagers.

At least that is what epidemiology suggests. In the United States, about 15 years after the sharp decline in blood lead levels in young children, the rates of violent crimes committed by teenagers and young adults fell sharply (Nevin, 2007).

Research in Canada, Germany, Italy, Australia, New Zealand, France, and Finland finds the same trends. Those nations that were earlier to legislate against lead had earlier crime reductions, about 20 years after the new laws. Research in many nations finds that blood lead levels predict attention deficits, school suspensions, and aggression (Amato et al., 2013; Goodlad et al., 2013; Nkomo et al., 2018).

Not surprisingly, some people think that connecting crime reduction to legislation to reduce lead is unfair, since other factors—fewer unwanted births, improved law enforcement, better education—have also reduced crime. But scientists in Sweden, where meticulous longitudinal research is possible, recently concluded that reduced lead levels in children directly reduced all crimes by 7 to 14 percent (Grönqvist et al., 2014).

There is now no doubt that lead, even at low levels in a young child, harms the brain. That makes the Flint tragedy more troubling. Developmentalists have known about the dangers of lead for decades. Why didn't the Michigan administrator know better?

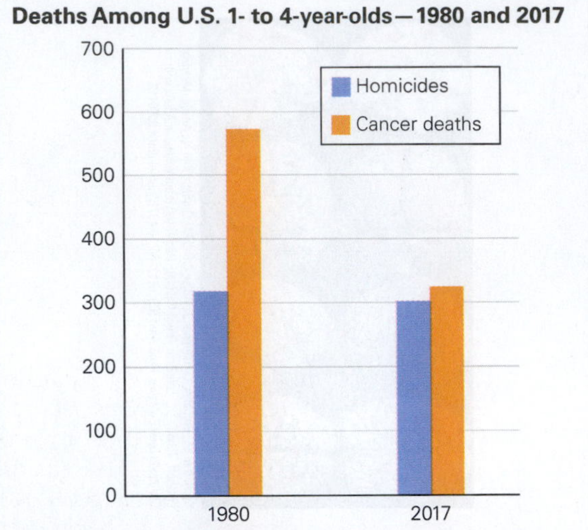

Data from National Center for Health Statistics, 2012 and 2019.

FIGURE 8.3
Scientists at Work Medical researchers have reduced child cancer deaths in half, primarily because new drugs are discovered to destroy cancer cells. Why haven't scientists learned how to stop homicides?

child maltreatment Intentional harm to or avoidable endangerment of anyone under 18 years of age.

child abuse Deliberate action that is harmful to a child's physical, emotional, or sexual well-being.

child neglect Failure to meet a child's basic physical, educational, or emotional needs.

substantiated maltreatment Harm or endangerment that has been reported, investigated, and verified.

reported maltreatment Harm or endangerment about which someone has notified the authorities.

Child Maltreatment

Accidental deaths are common worldwide, but the data reveal a related problem. Many children are harmed not accidentally but deliberately. Indeed, in recent years, almost as many 1- to 4-year-old U.S. children have been murdered as have died of cancer. This was not always true (see **Figure 8.3**).

In the Past 50 Years Childhood disease deaths have decreased markedly with immunization and better nutrition, but this is not true for maltreatment deaths. We need to better understand maltreatment in order to prevent it.

Until about 1960, people thought child abuse was rare and consisted of a sudden attack by a disturbed stranger, usually a man. Today we know better, thanks to a pioneering study based on careful observation in one Boston hospital (Kempe & Kempe, 1978).

Maltreatment is neither rare nor sudden, and more than 90 percent of the time the perpetrators are one or both of the child's parents—more often the mother than the father (U.S. Department of Health and Human Services, February 1, 2018). That makes it worse: Ongoing maltreatment at home, with no protector, is much more damaging than a single outside incident.

Definitions and Statistics **Child maltreatment** now refers to all intentional harm to, or avoidable endangerment of, anyone under 18 years of age. Thus, child maltreatment includes both **child abuse,** which is deliberate action that is harmful to a child's physical, emotional, or sexual well-being, and **child neglect,** which is failure to meet essential needs.

Neglect is often worse than abuse. It is "the most common and most frequently fatal form of child maltreatment" (Proctor & Dubowitz, 2014, p. 27). About three times as many neglect cases occur in the United States as abuse cases (U.S. Department of Health and Human Services, February 1, 2018).

Data on *substantiated* maltreatment in the United States in 2016 indicate that 75 percent of cases were neglect, 18 percent physical abuse, and 8 percent sexual abuse. Ironically, neglect is too often ignored by the public, who are "stuck in an overwhelming and debilitating" concept that maltreatment always causes immediate bodily harm (Kendall-Taylor et al., 2014, p. 810).

Substantiated maltreatment means that a case has been reported, investigated, and verified (see **Figure 8.4**). In 2016, about 676,000 children suffered substantiated maltreatment in the United States. Substantiated maltreatment harms more than 1 in every 100 children aged 2 to 5 annually.

Reported maltreatment (technically a referral) means simply that the authorities have been informed. Since 1993, the number of children referred to authorities in the United States has ranged from about 2.7 million to 4.1 million per year, with 4.1 million in 2016 (U.S. Department of Health and Human Services, February 1, 2018).

The 6-to-1 ratio of reported versus substantiated cases occurs because:

1. Each child is counted only once, so six verified reports about a single child result in one substantiated case.
2. Substantiation requires proof. Most investigations do not find unmistakable harm or a witness.
3. Many professionals are *mandated reporters,* required to report any signs of *possible* maltreatment. In 2014, two-thirds of all reports came from

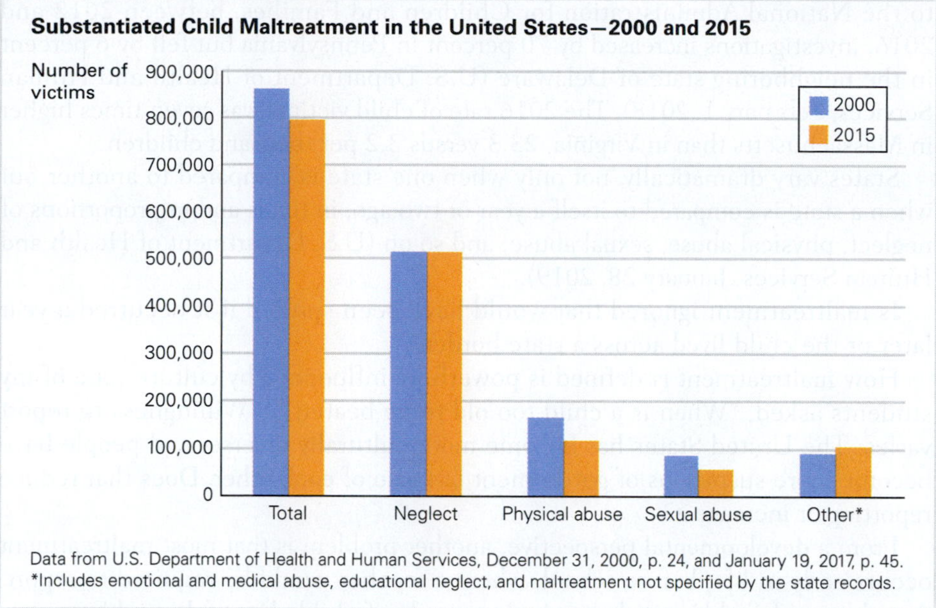

FIGURE 8.4

Getting Better? As you can see, the number of victims of child maltreatment in the United States has declined in the past decades, an especially good result because the total number of children has increased. One possible explanation is that the legal, social work, and community responses have improved, so fewer children are mistreated. Other less sanguine explanations are possible, however.

professionals. An investigation usually finds no harm (Pietrantonio et al., 2013).

4. Some reports are "screened out" as belonging to another jurisdiction, such as the military or a Native American tribe, who have their own systems, or the report is not about a child who is the victim of maltreatment. About one-third of all reports are screened out.
5. A report may be false or deliberately misleading (though few are) (Sedlak & Ellis, 2014).

Frequency of Maltreatment How often does maltreatment occur? We cannot be sure. Not all instances are noticed, not all that are noticed are reported, and not all reports are substantiated. Part of the problem is in drawing the line between harsh discipline and abuse, and between momentary lapses and ongoing neglect. If the standard were perfect parenting all day and all night from birth to age 18, as judged by neighbors, professionals, as well as parents, then every child has been mistreated. Only severe cases are tallied.

If we rely on official U.S. statistics, positive trends are apparent. Substantiated child maltreatment increased from about 1960 to 1990 but decreased thereafter. Other sources also report declines, particularly in sexual abuse.

Perhaps national awareness has led to better reporting and then more effective prevention. However, trends between 2010 and 2017 suggest that rates are increasing again (see **Figure 8.5**) (U.S. Department of Health & Human Services, January 28, 2019). There are many possible explanations. The growing gap between rich and poor families is the most plausible, but no matter what the reason, it is obvious that more work is needed.

Unfortunately, official reports raise doubt about the prevalence of child maltreatment. For example, in data reported

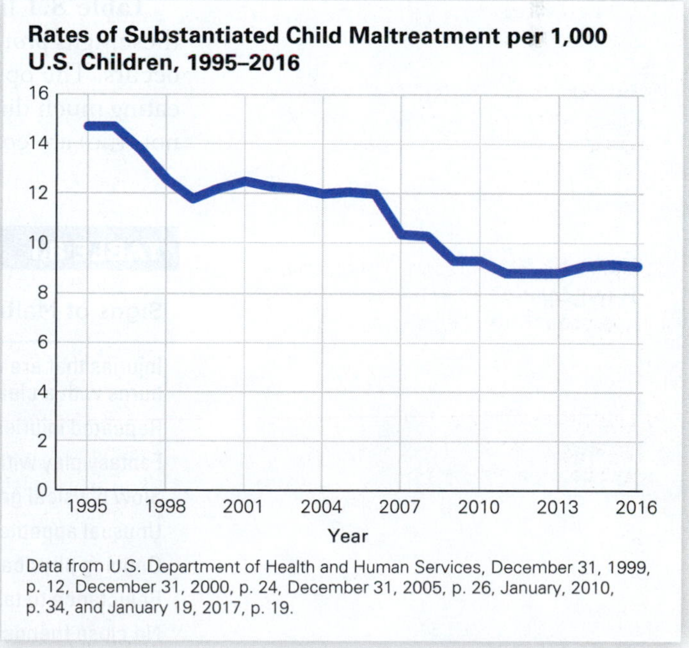

FIGURE 8.5

Still Far Too Many The number of substantiated cases of maltreatment of children under age 18 in the United States is too high, but there is some good news: The rate has declined significantly from its peak (15.3) in 1993.

to the National Administration for Children and Families, between 2012 and 2016, investigations increased by 70 percent in Pennsylvania but fell by 6 percent in the neighboring state of Delaware (U.S. Department of Health and Human Services, February 1, 2018). The 2016 rate of child victims was seven times higher in Massachusetts than in Virginia, 23.3 versus 3.2 per thousand children.

States vary dramatically, not only when one state is compared to another but when a state is compared to itself a year or two ago, in totals and in proportions of neglect, physical abuse, sexual abuse, and so on (U.S. Department of Health and Human Services, January 28, 2019).

Is maltreatment ignored that would have been spotted if it occurred a year later or the child lived across a state border?

How maltreatment is defined is powerfully influenced by culture (one of my students asked, "When is a child too old to be beaten?"). Willingness to report varies. The United States has become more culturally diverse, and people have become more suspicious of government but also of each other. Does that reduce reporting or increase it?

From a developmental perspective, another problem is that most maltreatment occurs early in life, before school, where a teacher would be required to report. An additional problem is that a single episode of child abuse followed by parental protection and love—never blaming the child—allows children to recover. By contrast, if one family member is abusive and another family member neglects to intervene, that is likely to cause lifelong harm.

Especially for Nurses While weighing a 4-year-old, you notice several bruises on the child's legs. When you ask about them, the child says nothing and the parent says that the child bumps into things. What should you do? (see response, page 218)

Warning Signs Instead of relying on official statistics and mandated reporters, every reader of this book can recognize developmental problems and prevent maltreatment. Often the first sign is delayed development, such as slow growth, immature communication, lack of curiosity, or unusual social interactions. These are all evident in infancy and early childhood.

Table 8.1 lists signs of child maltreatment, both neglect and abuse. None of these signs *proves* maltreatment, but investigation is needed whenever any of them occurs. The opposite is also true: Some things that many young children do (not eating much dinner, crying when they must stop playing, imagining things that are not true) are common, not usually signs of abuse.

TABLE 8.1

Signs of Maltreatment in Children Aged 0 to 10
Injuries that are unlikely to be accidents, such as bruises on both sides of the face or body; burns with a clear line between burned and unburned skin
Repeated injuries, especially broken bones not properly tended (visible on X-ray)
Fantasy play with dominant themes of violence or sex
Slow physical growth
Unusual appetite or lack of appetite
Ongoing physical complaints, such as stomachaches, headaches, genital pain, sleepiness
Reluctance to talk, to play, or to move, especially if development is slow
No close friendships; hostility toward others; bullying of smaller children
Hypervigilance, with quick, impulsive reactions, such as cringing, startling, or hitting
Frequent absence from school
Frequent change of address
Frequent change in caregivers
Child seems fearful, not joyful, on seeing caregiver

Maltreated young children may seem fearful, easily startled by noise, defensive and quick to attack, and confused between fantasy and reality. These are symptoms of **post-traumatic stress disorder (PTSD),** first identified in combat veterans, then in adults who had experienced some emotional injury or shock (after a serious accident, natural disaster, or violent crime).

For children abused during early childhood, PTSD may appear, either immediately or later on (Dunn et al., 2017).

post-traumatic stress disorder (PTSD) An anxiety disorder that develops as a delayed reaction to exposure to actual or threatened death, serious injury, or sexual violence. Its symptoms may include flashbacks to the event, hyperactivity and hypervigilance, displaced anger, sleeplessness, nightmares, sudden terror or anxiety, and confusion between fantasy and reality.

Consequences of Maltreatment It has been said that abused children become abusive parents, but this is not necessarily true (Widom et al., 2015a). Many people avoid the mistakes of their parents, especially if their friends, partners, or the reformed parents show them a better way.

Nonetheless, the consequences of maltreatment may last for decades. Immediate impairment is obvious, as when a child is bruised, broken, afraid to talk, or failing in school. Later on, however, deficits in social skills and self-esteem are more crippling than physical or intellectual damage.

Maltreated children tend to hate themselves and distrust everyone else. Even if the child was mistreated in the early years and then not after age 5, emotional problems (externalizing for the boys and internalizing for the girls) linger (Godinet et al., 2014). Adult drug abuse, social isolation, and poor health may result from maltreatment decades earlier (Sperry & Widom, 2013; Mersky et al., 2013).

Hate is corrosive. A warm and enduring friendship can repair some damage, but maltreatment makes such friendships less likely. Many studies find that mistreated children typically regard other people as hostile; hence, they become less friendly, more aggressive, and more isolated than other children.

The earlier that abuse starts and the longer it continues, the worse the children's relationships are, with physically and sexually abused children likely to be irrationally angry and neglected children often withdrawn (Petrenko et al., 2012). That makes healthy romances and friendships difficult lifelong.

Preventing Harm

For accidents, child abuse, and child neglect, the ultimate goal is *primary prevention,* a social network of customs and supports that help parents, neighbors, and professionals protect every child. Neighborhood stability, parental education, income support, and fewer unwanted children all reduce injury.

Such primary prevention measures are more effective over the years to reduce maltreatment and injuries. However, governments and private foundations are more likely to fund secondary prevention, with projects that focus on high-risk families (Nelson & Caplan, 2014). The media's focus on shocking examples of parental abuse or social worker neglect ignores the families, communities, and professionals who stop harm before it begins.

Secondary prevention includes spotting warning signs and intervening to keep a risky situation from getting worse. For example, insecure attachment, especially of the disorganized type, is a sign of a disrupted parent–child relationship. Thus, insecure attachment should be repaired before it becomes harmful, leading to abuse, neglect, or lack of supervision. [**Life-Span Link:** Attachment types are explained in detail in Chapter 7.]

Tertiary prevention limits harm after injury has occurred. Reporting is the first step; investigating and substantiating is

Where Is Mama? These would-be immigrant children are in U.S. custody in Homestead, Florida, without their parents. Here they are having their daily outside play time. We know that the presence of a parent is both physically and emotionally protective, which is one reason that, in 2019, about one immigrant child per month died in custody, separated from parents. Of course, separation was not the cause of death, but developmentalists believe it is a contributing factor.

AP Photo/Brynn Anderson

She Recovered and Sings Maya Angelou was abused and neglected as a child, but she also was loved and protected by her brother and other family members. The result was extraordinary insight into the human condition, as she learned "why the caged bird sings."

second. The final step, however, is helping the caregiver provide better care. That may include treating addiction, assigning a housekeeper, locating family helpers, securing better living quarters, and helping the child recover, with special medical, psychological, or education assistance. The child must be protected, either in the same family or in another one where better care is available.

In every case, **permanency planning** is needed: This is planning that addresses how to nurture the child until adulthood (Scott et al., 2013). Uncertainty, moving, a string of temporary placements, and frequent changes in schools are all destructive.

When children are taken from their parents and entrusted to another adult, that is **foster care**. The other adult might be a stranger or a relative, in which case it is called **kinship care**. Foster care sometimes is informal—a grandmother provides custodial care because the parents do not—or may result from Child Protective Services provided by the government.

Every year for the past decade in the United States, almost half a million children have been officially in foster care. At least another million are unofficially in kinship care, because relatives realize that the parents are unable or unwilling to provide good care.

Most foster children are from low-income, ethnic-minority families—a statistic that reveals problems in the macrosystem as well as the microsystem. In the United States, most foster children have physical, intellectual, and emotional problems that arose in their original families—evidence of their abuse and neglect (Jones & Morris, 2012). Obviously, foster parents need much more than financial subsidies to provide good care for such children.

Sometimes, a child's best permanency plan is adoption by another family, who will provide care lifelong. However, adoption is difficult, for many reasons:

- Judges and biological parents are reluctant to release children for adoption.
- Most adoptive parents prefer infants, but few infants are available. One problem is that immature and abusive parents do not know how hard child care can be until they have tried, and failed, to provide for their children.
- Some agencies screen out families not headed by heterosexual couples.
- Some professionals insist that adoptive parents be of the same ethnicity and/or religion as the child.

As you have seen in this chapter, caring for the nutrition, brain development, and safety of a 2- to 6-year-old is not easy for any parent—biological, foster, or adoptive. Yet these years are vital, with consequences lasting for decades. This is as true for cognitive and psychosocial development as for biosocial, as you will soon read.

permanency planning An effort by child-welfare authorities to find a long-term living situation that will provide stability and support for a maltreated child. A goal is to avoid repeated changes of caregiver or school, which can be particularly harmful to the child.

foster care A legal, publicly supported system in which a maltreated child is removed from the parents' custody and entrusted to another adult or family, who is reimbursed for expenses incurred in meeting the child's needs.

kinship care A form of foster care in which a relative of a maltreated child, usually a grandparent, becomes the approved caregiver.

WHAT HAVE YOU LEARNED?

1. What can be concluded from the data on rates of childhood injury?
2. How do injury deaths compare in developed and developing nations?
3. What is the difference between primary, secondary, and tertiary prevention?
4. Why have the rates of child accidental death declined?
5. Why is reported abuse six times higher than substantiated abuse?
6. Why is neglect considered worse than abuse?
7. What are the long-term consequences of childhood maltreatment?
8. Why does permanency planning rarely result in adoption?

SUMMARY

Body Changes

1. Well-nourished children gain weight and height during early childhood at a lower rate than infants do. Proportions change, allowing better body control.

2. Worldwide, an increasing number of children are obese, which puts them at risk for many health problems. Further, many children have an unbalanced diet. Sugar, particularly, is harmful, reducing appetite and harming teeth.

Brain Growth

3. The brain continues to grow in early childhood, reaching about 75 percent of its adult weight at age 2 and 90 percent by age 6. Much of the increase is in myelination, which speeds transmission of messages from one part of the brain to another.

4. Maturation of the prefrontal cortex allows more reflective, coordinated thought and memory, but this takes decades. Many young children gradually become less impulsive and less likely to perseverate.

5. Childhood trauma may create a flood of stress hormones (especially cortisol) that damage the brain and interfere with learning.

6. Gross motor skills continue to develop; clumsy 2-year-olds become 6-year-olds who move their bodies well, guided by their peers, practice, motivation, and opportunity—all varying by culture. Playing with other children develops skills that benefit children's physical, intellectual, and social development.

Harm to Children

7. Accidents cause more child deaths than diseases, with young children more likely to suffer a serious injury or premature death than older children. Close supervision and public safeguards can protect young children from their own eager, impulsive curiosity.

8. In the United States, various preventive measures have reduced the rate of serious injury, and medical measures have reduced disease deaths even faster. Four times as many young children die of injuries than of cancer, the leading cause of disease death in childhood.

9. Injury control occurs on many levels, including long before and immediately after each harmful incident. Primary prevention protects everyone, secondary prevention focuses on high-risk conditions and people, and tertiary prevention occurs after an injury. All three are needed.

10. Child maltreatment includes ongoing abuse and neglect, usually by a child's own parents. In 2016, about 4 million cases of child maltreatment were reported in the United States; about a fifth of them were substantiated, with the annual rate of maltreatment about 1 child in 100.

11. Physical abuse is the most obvious form of maltreatment, but neglect is more common and more harmful. Health, learning, and social skills are all impeded by abuse and neglect, not only during childhood but also decades later.

12. Primary prevention is needed to stop child maltreatment before it starts. Secondary prevention should begin when someone first notices a possible problem.

13. Tertiary prevention may include placement of a child in foster care, including kinship care, or in an adoptive family. Permanency planning is required because frequent changes are harmful to children.

KEY TERMS

myelination (p. 201)
corpus callosum (p. 201)
lateralization (p. 201)
impulse control (p. 203)
perseverate (p. 203)
injury control/harm reduction (p. 208)
primary prevention (p. 209)
secondary prevention (p. 209)
tertiary prevention (p. 209)
child maltreatment (p. 212)
child abuse (p. 212)
child neglect (p. 212)
substantiated maltreatment (p. 212)
reported maltreatment (p. 212)
post-traumatic stress disorder (PTSD) (p. 215)
permanency planning (p. 216)
foster care (p. 216)
kinship care (p. 216)

APPLICATIONS

1. Keep a food diary for 24 hours, writing down what you eat, how much, when, how, and why. Did you eat at least five servings of fruits and vegetables, and very little sugar or fat? Did you get too hungry, or eat when you were not hungry? Then analyze when and why your food habits began.

2. Go to a playground or another place where young children play. Note the motor skills that the children demonstrate, including abilities and inabilities, and keep track of age and sex. What differences do you see among the children?

3. Ask several parents to describe each accidental injury of each of their children, particularly how it happened and what the consequences were. What primary, secondary, or tertiary prevention measures were in place, and what measures were missing?

4. Think back to your childhood and the friends you had at that time. Was there any maltreatment? Considering what you have learned in this chapter, why or why not?

Especially For ANSWERS

Response for Early-Childhood Teachers (from p. 202): One solution is to remind yourself that the children's brains are not yet myelinated enough to enable them to quickly walk, talk, or even button their jackets. Maturation has a major effect, as you will observe if you can schedule excursions in September and again in November. Progress, while still slow, will be a few seconds faster.

Response for Urban Planners (from p. 207): The adult idea of a park—a large, grassy, open space—is not best for young children. For them, you would design an enclosed area, small enough and with adequate seating to allow caregivers to socialize while watching their children. The playground surface would have to be protective (since young children are clumsy), with equipment that encourages motor skills. Teenagers and dogs should have their own designated areas, far from the youngest children.

Response for Nurses (from p. 214): Any suspicion of child maltreatment must be reported, and these bruises are suspicious. Someone in authority must find out what is happening so that the parent as well as the child can be helped.

Observation Quiz ANSWERS

Answer to Observation Quiz (from p. 198): No. There are no pedals! Technically this is not a tricycle; it has four wheels. The ability to coordinate both legs follows corpus callosum development in the next few years, as explained on page 201.

VISUALIZING DEVELOPMENT | Developing Motor Skills

Every child can do more with each passing year. These examples detail what one child might be expected to accomplish from ages 2 to 6. But each child is unique, and much depends on culture, practice, and maturity.

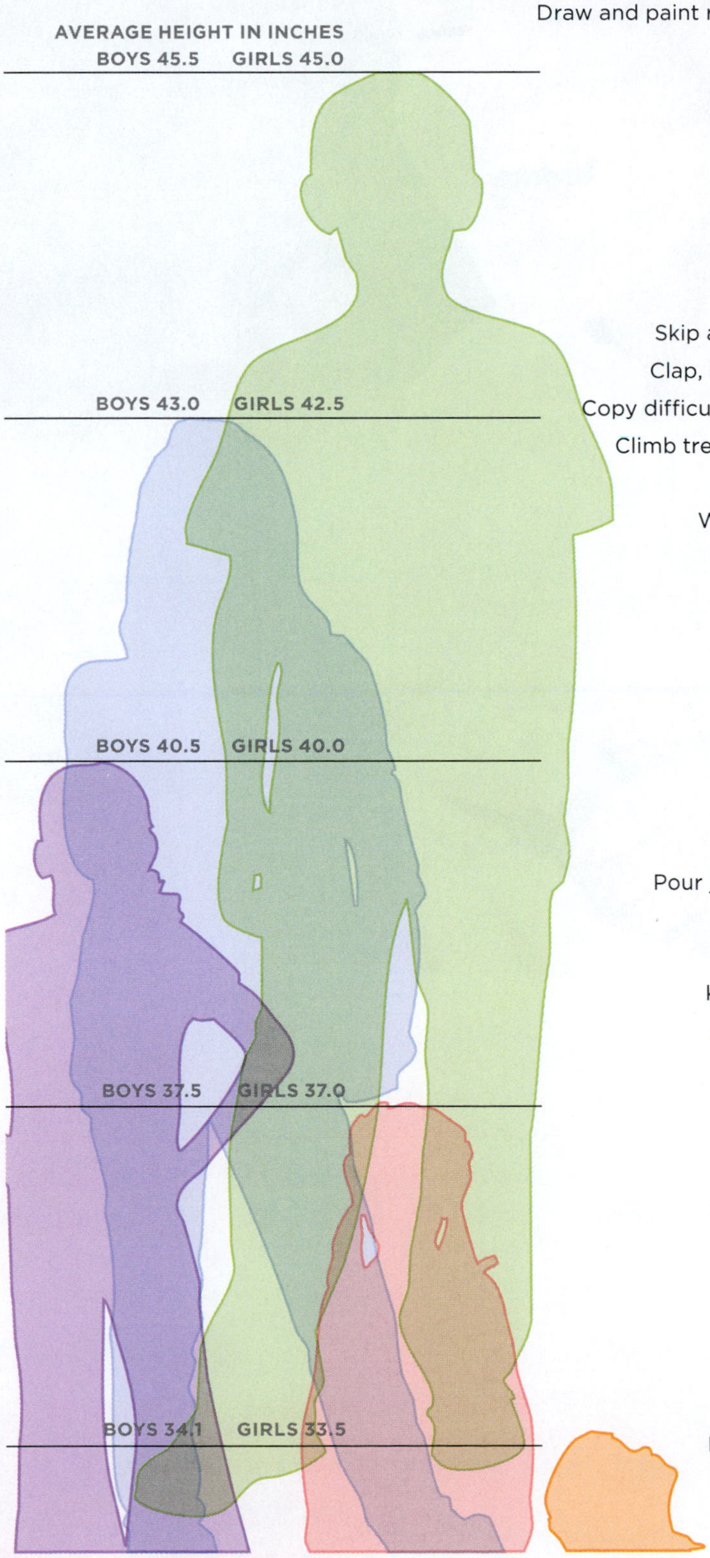

SKILLS

6 years

Draw and paint recognizable images
Write simple words
Read a page of print
Tie shoes
Catch a small ball

Jose Luis Pelaez Inc/DigitalVision/Getty Images

5 years

Skip and gallop in rhythm
Clap, bang, sing in rhythm
Copy difficult shapes and letters
Climb trees, jump over things
Use a knife to cut
Wash face, comb hair

Ramona Heim/Shutterstock.com

4 years

Catch a beach ball
Use scissors
Hop on either foot
Feed self with fork
Dress self
Copy most letters
Pour juice without spilling
Brush teeth

naluwan/Shutterstock.com

3 years

Kick and throw a ball
Jump with both feet
Pedal a tricycle
Copy simple shapes
Walk down stairs
Climb ladders

Nejron Photo/Shutterstock.com

2 years

Run without falling
Climb out of crib
Walk up stairs
Feed self with spoon
Draw spirals

Artem Efimov/Shutterstock.com

Early Childhood: Cognitive Development

CHAPTER 9

What Will You Know?

1. Are young children selfish or just self-centered?
2. Do children get confused if they hear two languages?
3. Is it a mistake to let children play all day at preschool?

- **Thinking During Early Childhood**
  - Executive Function
  - Piaget: Preoperational Thought
  - A CASE TO STUDY: Stones in the Belly
  - Vygotsky: Social Learning
  - Children's Theories
  - INSIDE THE BRAIN: The Role of Experience
- **Language Learning**
  - The Sensitive Time for Language Learning
  - The Vocabulary Explosion
  - Acquiring Grammar
  - Learning Two Languages
- **Early-Childhood Schooling**
  - Homes and Schools
  - Child-Centered Programs
  - Teacher-Directed Programs
  - OPPOSING PERSPECTIVES: Comparing Child-Centered and Teacher-Directed Preschools
  - Intervention Programs
  - Long-Term Gains from Intensive Programs
- **VISUALIZING DEVELOPMENT: Early-Childhood Schooling**

Asa, not yet 3 feet tall, held a large rubber ball. He wanted me to play basketball with him.

"We can't play basketball; we don't have a hoop," I told him.

"We can imagine a hoop," he answered, throwing the ball up.

"I got it in," he said happily. "You try."

I did.

"You got it in, too," he announced, and did a little dance.

Soon I was tired, and sat down.

"I want to sit and think my thoughts," I told him.

"Get up," he urged. "You can play basketball and think your thoughts."

Asa is typical. Imagination comes easily to him, and he aspires to the skills of older, taller people in his culture. He thinks by doing, and his vocabulary is impressive; but he does not yet understand that my feelings differ from his, that I would rather sit than throw a ball at an imaginary basket. He does know, however, that I usually respond to his requests.

This chapter describes these characteristics of young children—imagination, active learning, vocabulary, but also their difficulty in understanding another person's perspective. I hope it also conveys the joy that adults gain when they understand how young children think. When that happens, you might do what I did—get up and play.

Thinking During Early Childhood

You learned in Chapter 8 about the rapid advances in motor skills, brain development, and impulse control from ages 2 through 6, enabling the young child to do somersaults by kindergarten. Part of the reason this is possible is maturation of the body. Its changing proportions enable head-over-heels moves, because the legs are now much longer than the torso. And part of it is social influence. Few children do somersaults unless they have seen another child do one.

The same two forces allow the mental somersaults of early childhood. Soon you will read about the two major developmental theorists, Piaget and Vygotsky, who focused on young children. Piaget describes cognitive maturation, as children

Left: Westend61/Getty Images
Top: baona/iStock/Getty Images

advance from preoperational thought to concrete operational thought. Vygotsky stressed the impact of social forces, as young children learn to talk, think, and explain.

But before describing the contributions of each of these theorists to childhood thinking, we note another aspect of thought that comes to the fore in early childhood.

Executive Function

At every age, a person's ability to think depends on what has been called *executive function,* a cognitive ability that is nascent at age 2 and that continues to improve throughout life (Diamond, 2012). It is evident, and can be measured, in early childhood (Eisenberg & Zhou, 2016; Espy et al., 2016).

Indeed, executive function has been measured at every stage of life. It protects adolescents from destructive emotional outbursts (Poon, 2018), promotes coping skills in adulthood (Nieto et al., 2019), and forestalls death in old age (Reimann et al., 2018).

executive function A combination of memory, inhibition, and cognitive flexibility that allows better thinking, so people can anticipate, strategize, and plan behavior.

Definitions

Executive function combines three essential abilities: (1) memory, (2) inhibition, and (3) flexibility. Each of the three requires some further explanation.

The aspect of memory emphasized in executive function is short-term or working memory, which is memory for what was seen a minute ago or yesterday, not for what happened years ago. Young children who are proficient in this aspect of cognition are able to remember what they had for lunch, where they put their mittens, what they saw at the science museum.

Inhibition is the ability to control responses, to stop and think for a moment before acting or talking. Young children with this ability are able to restrain themselves from hitting or crying when someone else accidentally bumps them, and to raise their hands without blurting out an answer to a teacher's question.

Flexibility (also called *shifting*) is the ability to see things from another perspective rather than staying stuck in one idea. One example from early childhood is when children want to play with a toy that another child has. Executive function enables the child with the toy to share, and it allows the onlookers to switch to another activity or wait for a turn.

The result, as a leading expert explains, is that young children gain "core skills critical for cognitive, social, and psychological development" that allow "playing with ideas, giving a considered response rather than an impulsive one, and being able to change course or perspectives as needed, resist temptations, and stay focused" (Diamond, 2016).

Developmentalists have many creative ways to measure executive function in young children. To measure memory, for instance, 3- to 5-year-olds are shown a series of barnyard animals and asked to remember them in order. For inhibition, they are asked to push a button when they see a fish but not a shark. For flexibility, they are asked to alternate stamping on a picture of a dog and one of a bone (both are presented together, again and again). Scores on all of these improve with age during early childhood (Espy, 2016).

The Joy of Rivalry Look closely at this sister and brother in Johannesburg, South Africa. Just as 1-year-olds run as soon as they are able, siblings everywhere quarrel, fight, and compromise, ideally testing their physical and intellectual skills, which, as seems to be the case here, is fun.

Grant Difford/Greatstock/Alamy

A Sensitive Time

It is thought that early childhood is a particularly important time to develop executive function skills. Compared to older children, 2- to 6-year-olds are more open to learning, have much to learn (remember the impulsive and perseverative responses explained in Chapter 8), and are open to suggestion (Walk et al., 2018).

Many educators and parents focus on young children's intelligence and vocabulary. That is not wrong: Children's minds need to be engaged, and their language

development must be encouraged. However, for success in kindergarten and beyond, executive function seems especially crucial. It correlates more with brain development than with scores on intelligence tests (Friedman & Miyake, 2017).

An important book with 14 chapters from many experts focuses on executive function in preschool children (Griffin et al., 2016). Two points are repeated throughout the research.

1. Executive function skills are foundational. They undergird later cognitive abilities and school achievement, including in reading and math.
2. Executive function skills are not inborn. Instead, they can and should be taught during early childhood.

What practices help young children advance in executive function? Family life and early schooling are crucial. Regarding education programs, instead of explicit, time-limited lessons, executive function skills permeate the entire curriculum. Young children need to verbalize their emotions, plan their actions, sustain activity, and work with another child or two—not the whole group.

One suggested activity, for example, is for two children to develop a pretend scenario together. They need to decide on their roles and actions (advance planning) and then carry out the play, with the flexibility required to react to their playmates' actions. In order to develop executive function, children are guided and encouraged, rarely criticized or punished (Diamond & Lee, 2011).

Families and Executive Function Much of executive function among young children hinges on how their caregivers respond to them. Generally, living in a low-income household impedes development of executive function. However, a detailed study found that it wasn't low income per se but the stress caused by poverty that impeded the child's ability to remember what just happened, to postpone gratification, and to cooperate with siblings (the triad of memory, inhibition, and flexibility) (Rhoades et al., 2011).

Many cognitive psychologists now focus on executive function, particularly on efforts to improve it during early childhood. But this does not reduce the importance of Piaget, Vygotsky, language development, and early education. Indeed, all four of those topics are enhanced, not erased, by our understanding of executive function. We begin with the grandfather of cognitive development, Jean Piaget.

Piaget: Preoperational Thought

Early childhood is the time of **preoperational intelligence,** the second of Piaget's four periods of cognitive development (described in Table 2.3 on page 40). Piaget referred to early-childhood thinking as *pre*operational because children do not yet use logical operations (reasoning processes) (Inhelder & Piaget, 1964/2013a).

preoperational intelligence Piaget's term for cognitive development between the ages of about 2 and 6; it includes language and imagination (which involve symbolic thought), but logical, operational thinking is not yet possible.

Preoperational children are beyond sensorimotor intelligence because they think in symbols, not just via senses and motor skills. In **symbolic thought,** an object or a word can stand for something else, including something out of sight or imagined. Language is the most apparent example of symbolic thought. Words make it possible to think about many things at once.

symbolic thought A major accomplishment of preoperational intelligence that allows a child to think symbolically, including understanding that words can refer to things not seen and that an item, such as a flag, can symbolize something else (in this case, a country).

However, although vocabulary and imagination soar in early childhood, logical connections between ideas are not yet *operational,* which means that Piaget found that young children cannot yet apply their impressive new linguistic ability to comprehend reality.

Consider how the word *dog,* for instance, changes in Piaget's description of cognition. During the sensorimotor level, "dog" means only the family dog sniffing at the child, not yet a symbol (Callaghan, 2013). By age 2, in preoperational thought, the word *dog* becomes a symbol: It can refer to a remembered dog, or a plastic dog, or an imagined dog.

Walt Disney Studios Motion Pictures/Photofest

Red-Hot Anger Emotions are difficult for young children to understand, since they are not visible. The Disney-Pixar movie *Inside Out* used symbolic thought to remedy that.

Observation Quiz What emotions are associated with green, red, and violet? (see answer, page 244) ↑

animism The belief that natural objects and phenomena are alive, moving around, and having sensations and abilities that are human-like.

Symbolic thought allows for the language explosion (detailed later in this chapter), which enables children to talk about thoughts and memories. Nonetheless, because the child is not yet operational, if asked to define the differences between dogs and cats, preschoolers have difficulty contrasting the essential qualities of "dogness" from those of "catness."

Symbolic thought helps explain **animism,** the belief of many young children that natural objects (such as trees or clouds) are alive and that nonhuman animals have the same characteristics as humans, especially the human the child knows best, him- or herself. Many children's stories include animals or objects that talk and listen (Aesop's fables, *Winnie-the-Pooh, Goodnight Gorilla, The Day the Crayons Quit*). Preoperational thought is symbolic and magical, not logical and realistic.

Several scholars contend that many preindustrial peoples believed in animism, praying to the sky and to rivers, for instance, and that human history is best understood by considering Piaget's understanding of cognitive development (e.g., Oesterdiekhoff, 2014). Other scholars think that the child's "enchanted animism"—that is, their imagination and delight in trees, rocks, clouds, and so on—is a much-needed corrective to climate change, pollution, and deforestation (Merewether, 2018).

centration A characteristic of preoperational thought in which a young child focuses (centers) on one idea, excluding all others.

egocentrism Piaget's term for children's tendency to think about the world entirely from their own personal perspective.

focus on appearance A characteristic of preoperational thought in which a young child ignores all attributes that are not apparent.

static reasoning A characteristic of preoperational thought in which a young child thinks that nothing changes. Whatever is now has always been and always will be.

irreversibility A characteristic of preoperational thought in which a young child thinks that nothing can be undone. A thing cannot be restored to the way it was before a change occurred.

Obstacles to Logic Piaget described symbolic thought as characteristic of preoperational thought. He also noted four limitations that make logic difficult: *centration, focus on appearance, static reasoning,* and *irreversibility.*

Centration is the tendency to focus on one aspect of a situation to the exclusion of all others. For example, young children may insist that Daddy is a father, not a brother, because they center on the role that he fills for them. This illustrates a particular type of centration that Piaget called **egocentrism**—literally, "self-centeredness." Egocentric children contemplate the world exclusively from their personal perspective.

Egocentrism is *not* selfishness. One 3-year-old chose to buy a model car as a birthday present for his mother: His "behavior was not selfish or greedy; he carefully wrapped the present and gave it to his mother with an expression that clearly showed that he expected her to love it" (Crain, 2011, p. 133).

A second characteristic of preoperational thought is a **focus on appearance** to the exclusion of other attributes. For instance, a girl given a short haircut might worry that she has turned into a boy. In preoperational thought, a thing is whatever it appears to be—evident in the joy young children have in wearing the hats or shoes of a grown-up, clomping noisily and unsteadily around the house.

Third, preoperational children use **static reasoning.** They believe that the world is stable, unchanging, always in the state in which they currently encounter it. Many children cannot imagine that their own parents were ever children. If they are told that Grandma is their mother's mother, they still do not understand how people change with maturation. One child asked his grandmother to tell his mother not to spank him because "she has to do what her mother says."

The fourth characteristic of preoperational thought is **irreversibility.** Preoperational thinkers fail to recognize that reversing a process might restore whatever existed before. A young girl might cry because her mother put lettuce on her sandwich. She might reject the food even after the lettuce is removed because she believes that what is done cannot be undone.

Conservation and Logic Piaget reported many examples of the ways in which preoperational intelligence disregards logic. A famous series of experiments involved **conservation,** the notion that the amount of something remains the same (is conserved) despite changes in its appearance.

conservation The principle that the amount of a substance remains the same (i.e., is conserved) even when its appearance changes.

Suppose two identical glasses contain the same amount of pink lemonade, and the liquid from one of these glasses is poured into a taller, narrower glass. When young children are asked whether one glass contains more or, alternatively, if both glasses contain the same amount, those younger than 6 answer that the narrower glass (with the higher level) has more. (See **Figure 9.1** for other examples.)

All four characteristics of preoperational thought are evident in this mistake. Young children fail to understand conservation because they focus (*center*) on what they see (*appearance*), noticing only the immediate (*static*) condition. It does not occur to them that they could pour the lemonade back into the wider glass and re-create the level of a moment earlier (*irreversibility*).

Note that this reveals one of the key aspects of cognition that is central to executive function. Unless they are taught, children younger than 6 do not have the memory or flexibility to grasp conservation.

This is an important lesson for teachers of young children. They can, and do, encourage children to develop their understanding of quantity to further their knowledge of math, but teachers also need to recognize the limitations of preschoolers' thinking (McCray et al., 2018). To develop an understanding of conservation, a teacher might ask the child to remember how much lemonade there was before pouring it, for example, and then let the child and a friend pour it again and again.

macmillan learning

VIDEO ACTIVITY: Achieving Conservation focuses on the cognitive changes that enable older children to pass Piaget's conservation-of-liquid task.

Tests of Various Types of Conservation

Type of Conservation	Initial Presentation	Transformation	Question	Preoperational Child's Answer
Volume	Two equal glasses of pink lemonade.	Pour one into a taller, narrower glass.	Which glass contains more?	The taller one.
Number	Two equal lines of candy.	Increase spacing of candy in one line.	Which line has more candy?	The longer one.
Matter	Two equal balls of cookie dough.	Squeeze one ball into a long, thin shape.	Which piece has more dough?	The long one.
Length	Two pencils of equal length.	Move one pencil.	Which pencil is longer?	The one that is farther to the right.

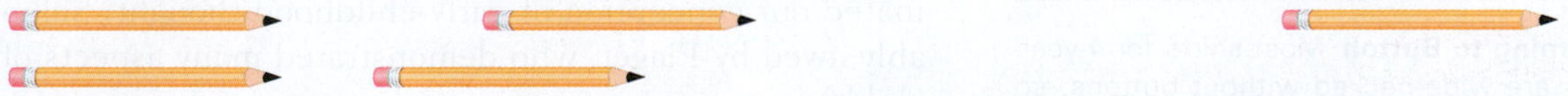

FIGURE 9.1

Conservation, Please According to Piaget, until children grasp the concept of conservation at (he believed) about age 6 or 7, they cannot understand that the transformations shown here do not change the total amount of liquid, candies, cookie dough, and pencils.

A CASE TO STUDY

Stones in the Belly

As we were reading a book about dinosaurs, my 3-year-old grandson, Caleb, told me that some dinosaurs (*sauropods*) have stones in their bellies. It helps them digest their food and then poop and pee.

I was amazed, never having known this before.

"I didn't know that dinosaurs ate stones," I said.

"They don't eat them."

"Then how do they get the stones in their bellies? They must swallow them."

"They don't eat them."

"Then how do they get in their bellies?"

"They are just there."

"How did they get there?"

"They don't eat them," said Caleb. "Stones are dirty. We don't eat them."

I dropped it, as I knew that his mother had warned him not to eat pebbles, and I didn't want to confuse him. However, my question apparently puzzled him. Later he asked my daughter, "Do dinosaurs eat stones?"

"Yes, they eat stones so they can grind their food," she answered.

At that, Caleb was quiet.

In all of this, preoperational cognition is evident. Caleb is bright; he can name several kinds of dinosaurs, as can many young children.

But logic eludes Caleb. He is preoperational, not operational.

It seemed obvious to me that the dinosaurs must have swallowed the stones. However, in his static thinking, Caleb said the stones "are just there." He rejected the thought that dinosaurs ate stones because he has been told that stones are too dirty to eat.

Caleb is egocentric, reasoning from his own experience, and animistic, in that he thinks other creatures think and act as he himself does. He trusts his mother, who told him never to eat stones, or, for that matter, sand from the sandbox, or food that fell on the floor.

My authority as grandmother was clearly less than the authority of his mother, but at least he considered what I said. He was skeptical that a dinosaur would do something he had been told not to do, but the idea lingered rather than being completely rejected. Of course, the implications of my status as his mother's mother are beyond his static thinking.

Like many young children, Caleb is curious, and my question raised his curiosity.

Should I have expected him to tell me that I was right when his mother agreed with me? No. That would have required far more understanding of reversibility and far less egocentrism than most young children can muster.

There are additional ways to encourage cognition in young children. Piaget's original tests of conservation required children to respond verbally to an adult's questions. Contemporary researchers have made tests of logic simple and playful, and then young children sometimes succeed.

Moreover, before age 6, children indicate via eye movements or gestures that they can understand some logic, even though they cannot yet put their understanding into words (Goldin-Meadow & Alibali, 2013). Conservation and many other logical ideas can be grasped bit by bit, with active, guided experience. Glimmers of understanding may be apparent in children as young as age 4 (Sophian, 2013).

As with sensorimotor intelligence in infancy, Piaget underestimated preoperational children. Piaget was right about his basic idea, however: Young children are not very logical (Lane & Harris, 2014). Their cognitive limits make smart 3-year-olds sometimes foolish, as Caleb is.

Hero Images/DigitalVision/Getty Images

Learning to Button Most shirts for 4-year-olds are wide-necked without buttons, so preschoolers can put them on themselves. But the skill of buttoning is best learned from a mentor, who knows how to increase motivation.

Vygotsky: Social Learning

For decades, the magical, illogical, and self-centered aspects of cognition dominated our conception of early-childhood thought. Scientists were understandably awed by Piaget, who demonstrated many aspects of egocentric thought in children.

Vygotsky emphasized another side of early cognition—that each person's thinking is shaped by other people. His focus on the sociocultural context contrasts with Piaget's emphasis on the individual.

Mentors Vygotsky believed that cognitive development is embedded in the social context at every age (Vygotsky, 1987). He stressed that children are curious and observant of everything in their world.

Young children are famous for their exasperating penchant to ask questions. They want to know how machines work, why weather changes, where the sky ends. They seek answers from more knowledgeable mentors, who might be their parents, teachers, older siblings, or just a stranger. The answers they get are affected by the mentors' perceptions and assumptions. In this way, according to Vygotsky, culture shapes thought.

As you remember from Chapter 2, children learn through *guided participation*, as mentors teach them. Parents are their first guides, although young children are guided by many others, especially in an interactive preschool (Broström, 2017).

According to Vygotsky, children learn because their mentors do the following:

- Present challenges.
- Offer assistance (without taking over).
- Add crucial information.
- Encourage motivation.

Scaffolding As you read in Chapter 2, Vygotsky believed that all individuals learn within their *zone of proximal development (ZPD)*, an intellectual arena in which new ideas and skills can be mastered. *Proximal* means "near," so the ZPD includes the ideas and skills that children are close to mastering but cannot yet demonstrate independently. Learning depends, in part, on the wisdom and willingness of mentors to provide **scaffolding,** or temporary sensitive support, to help children within their developmental zone (Mermelshtine, 2017).

Good mentors provide plenty of scaffolding, encouraging children to look both ways before crossing the street (pointing out speeding trucks, cars, and buses while holding the child's hand) or letting them stir the cake batter (perhaps covering the child's hand on the spoon handle, in guided participation). Crucial in every activity is joint engagement, when both learner and mentor are actively involved together in the ZPD (Adamson et al., 2014).

Culture matters. In some families and cultures, book-reading is a time for conversation and questions; in others, it is a time for telling the child to be quiet and listen. Parents scaffold whatever they deem important.

One study of U.S. parents found that many book-reading parents who are Chinese Americans pointed out how misbehavior caused problems for the book's characters, while many Mexican Americans highlighted the emotions of the characters (Luo et al., 2014). From this contrast, a possible conclusion is that Chinese Americans teach their children to become well-behaved adults, while Mexican Americans encourage their children to notice the emotions that accompany behavior.

Overimitation Sometimes scaffolding is inadvertent, as when children copy something that adults would rather the child not do. Young children curse, kick, and worse because someone else showed them how.

More benignly, children imitate meaningless habits and customs, a trait called **overimitation.** Children are eager to learn from mentors, allowing for "rapid, high-fidelity intergenerational transmission of tool-use skills and for the perpetuation and generation of cultural forms" (Nielsen & Tomaselli, 2010, p. 735).

Overimitation was demonstrated in a series of experiments with 3- to 6-year-olds, 64 of them from San communities (pejoratively called "Bushmen") in South Africa and Botswana, and, for comparison, 64 from cities in Australia and 19 from aboriginal communities within Australia. Australian middle-class adults

scaffolding Temporary support that is tailored to a learner's needs and abilities and aimed at helping the learner master the next task in a given learning process.

overimitation When a person imitates an action that is not a relevant part of the behavior to be learned. Overimitation is common among 2- to 6-year-olds when they imitate adult actions that are irrelevant and inefficient.

Observation Quiz Is the girl above right-handed or left-handed? (see answer, page 244) ↓

Tim Hall/The Image Bank/Getty Images

Count by Tens A large, attractive abacus could be a scaffold. However, in this toy store the position of the balls suggests that no mentor is nearby. Children are unlikely to grasp the number system without a motivating guide.

often scaffold for children with words and actions, but San adults rarely do. The researchers expected the urban Australian children but not the San children to follow adult demonstrations (Nielsen et al., 2014). The researchers were wrong.

In part of the study, one by one some children in each group watched an adult open a box, which could easily and efficiently be opened by pulling down a knob by hand. Instead, the adult waved a red stick above the box three times and used that stick to push down the knob to open the box. Then children were given the stick and asked to open the box. No matter what their culture, they followed the adult example, waving the stick three times, not using their hands directly on the knob.

Other San and Australian children did not see the demonstration. When they were given the stick and asked to open the box, they simply pulled the knob. Then they observed an adult do the stick-waving opening—and they copied those inefficient actions, even though they already knew the easy way. Apparently, children everywhere learn from others not only through explicit guidance but also through observation. Across cultures, overimitation is striking and generalizes to other similar situations.

Overimitation is universal: Young children follow what adults do. They are naturally "socially motivated," which allows them to learn as long as the adults structure and guide that learning. Adults worldwide teach children in that way, using eye contact and facial expressions to facilitate learning (Heyes, 2016).

This imitation process is exquisitely designed. Adults enjoy transmitting knowledge, and for their part, children are automatic imitators—especially when copying is not too difficult: They imitate adults who seem to know what they are doing, even if the adults are not deliberately teaching (Tomasello, 2016; Keupp et al., 2016).

That is exactly what Vygotsky expected and explained: Children are attuned to culture.

private speech The internal dialogue that occurs when people talk to themselves (either silently or out loud).

social mediation Human interaction that expands and advances understanding, often through words that one person uses to explain something to another.

Language as a Tool Although all of the elements of a culture guide children, Vygotsky thought language is pivotal.

First, talking to oneself, called **private speech,** is evident when young children talk aloud to review, decide, and explain events to themselves (and, incidentally, to anyone else within earshot) (Al-Namlah et al., 2012). With time, children become more circumspect, sometimes whispering. Audible or not, private speech aids cognition and self-reflection; adults should encourage it (Perels et al., 2009; Benigno et al., 2011). Many adults use private speech as they talk to themselves when alone or write down ideas.

Second, language advances thinking by facilitating social interaction which is vital to learning (Vygotsky, 2012). This **social mediation** function of speech occurs as mentors guide mentees in their zone of proximal development, learning numbers, recalling memories, and following routines.

Michelle Del Guercio/Science Source/Getty Images

Future Engineers in the Bronx Playing with Legos helps children learn about connecting shapes, which makes math and geometry easier to learn in school and makes STEM careers more likely. Once, Legos were only marketed to boys, but no longer—there now are kits designed to appeal to girls.

STEM Learning A practical use of Vygotsky's theory concerns STEM (science, technology, engineering, math) education. Many adults are currently concerned that too few college students choose a STEM career.

Developmentalists find that a person's interest in such vocations begins with learning about numbers and science (counting, shapes, fractions, molecular structure, the laws of motion) in early childhood. Spatial understanding—how one object fits with another—is an accomplishment of early childhood that enhances later math skills (Verdine et al., 2017). During the preschool years, an understanding of math and physics develops month by month. Before first grade, children learn to:

- Count objects, with one number per item (called *one-to-one correspondence*).
- Remember times and ages (bedtime at 8 P.M., a child is 4 years old, and so on).
- Understand sequence (first child wins, last child loses).

- Know which numbers are greater than others (e.g., that 7 is greater than 4).
- Understand how to make things move, from toy cars to soccer balls.
- Appreciate temperature effects, from ice to steam.

By age 3 or 4, children's brains are mature enough to comprehend numbers, store memories, and recognize routines. Whether or not children actually demonstrate such understanding depends on what they hear and how they participate in various activities within their families, schools, and cultures. "Scaffolding and elaboration from parents and teachers provides crucial input to spatial development," which itself leads to math understanding, which underpins STEM expertise (Verdine et al., 2017, p. 25).

Some 2-year-olds hear sentences such as "One, two, three, takeoff," "Here are two cookies," or "Dinner in five minutes" several times a day. They are encouraged to touch an interesting bit of moss, or are alerted to the phases of the moon outside their window, or play with toys that fit shapes, or learn about the relationship between pace and steepness of a hill they are climbing.

Other children never have such experiences—and they have a harder time with math in first grade, with science in the third grade, and with physics in high school. If, as Vygotsky believed, words mediate between brain potential and comprehension, STEM education begins long before formal education.

Educational software becomes "a conduit for collaborative learning" (Cicconi, 2014, p. 58), as Web 2.0 (interactive) programs respond to the particular abilities and needs of each child. Several children can work together, each mentoring the others, talking aloud as the computer prompts them.

For executive function, however, interactive software needs to be carefully chosen. Video games, for instance, usually encourage rapid responses—the opposite of the planning, inhibition, and memory that are the bedrock of executive function.

Educators disapprove if a screen replaces human interaction (that is opposite to what Vygotsky advocates), but they also recognize that computers, carefully used (no more than an hour a day), might be learning tools, just as books might be (Alper, 2013; American Academy of Pediatrics, 2016).

Children's Theories

Every scholar who studies learning during early childhood notices that children are eager to understand everything. Young children do more than gain words and concepts; they develop theories to help them understand and remember—theories that arise from both brain maturation and personal experience (Baron-Cohen et al., 2013).

Theory-Theory In **theory-theory**, the *theory* about how children think is that they construct a *theory*.

theory-theory The idea that children attempt to explain everything they see and hear by constructing theories.

Humans always want theories (even false ones sometimes suffice) to help them understand the world. Especially in childhood, theories are subject to change as new evidence accumulates (Meltzoff & Gopnik, 2013; Bridgers et al., 2016).

Children ask questions, and, if they are not satisfied with the answers, they develop their own theories. For example, one child thought his grandpa died because God was lonely; another thought thunder occurred because God was rearranging the furniture.

Children follow the same processes that scientists do: asking questions, developing hypotheses, gathering data, and drawing conclusions. As a result, "preschoolers have intuitive theories of the physical, biological, psychological, and social world" (Gopnik, 2012, p. 1623).

One common theory-theory is that everyone intends to do things correctly. For that reason, when asked to repeat something ungrammatical that an adult says, children often correct the grammar. They theorize that the adult intended to speak grammatically but failed to do so (Over & Gattis, 2010).

Theory of Mind Mental processes—thoughts, emotions, beliefs, motives, and intentions—are among the most complicated and puzzling phenomena that humans encounter every day. Adults wonder why people fall in love with the particular persons they do, why they vote for the candidates they do, or why they make foolish choices—from signing for a huge mortgage to buying an overripe cucumber. Children are likewise puzzled about a playmate's unexpected anger, a sibling's generosity, or an aunt's too-wet kiss.

Especially for Social Scientists Can you think of any connection between Piaget's theory of preoperational thought and 3-year-olds' errors in this theory-of-mind task? (see response, page 244)

theory of mind A person's theory of what other people might be thinking. In order to have a theory of mind, children must realize that other people are not necessarily thinking the same thoughts that they themselves are. That realization seldom occurs before age 4.

To know what goes on in another's mind, people develop a *folk psychology,* which includes ideas about other people's thinking, called **theory of mind.** Theory of mind is an emergent ability, slow to develop but typically evident in most children by about age 4 (Carlson et al., 2013).

Part of theory of mind is understanding that someone else might have a mistaken belief. For example, a child watches a puppet named Max put a toy dog into a red box. Then Max leaves and the child sees the dog taken out of the red box and put in a blue box.

When Max returns the child is asked, "Where will Max look for the dog?" Without a theory of mind, most 3-year-olds confidently say, "In the blue box"; most 6-year-olds correctly say, "In the red box."

macmillan learning

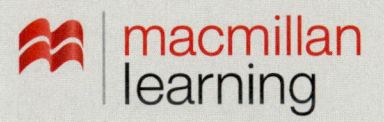

VIDEO: Theory of Mind: False-Belief Tasks demonstrates how children's theory of mind develops with age.

Theory of mind actually develops gradually, progressing from knowing that someone else might have different desires (at about age 3) to knowing that someone might hide their true feelings (about age 6).

The development of theory of mind can be seen when young children try to escape punishment by lying. Their faces often betray them: worried or shifting eyes, pursed lips, and so on. Parents sometimes say, "I know when you are lying," and, to the consternation of most 3-year-olds, parents are usually right.

In one experiment, 247 children, aged 3 to 5, were left alone at a table that had an upside-down cup covering dozens of candies (Evans et al., 2011). The children were told *not* to peek, and the experimenter left the room.

For 142 children (57 percent), curiosity overcame obedience. They peeked, spilling so many candies onto the table that they could not put them back under the cup. The examiner returned, asking how the candies got on the table. Only one-fourth of the participants (more often the younger ones) told the truth (see **Figure 9.2**).

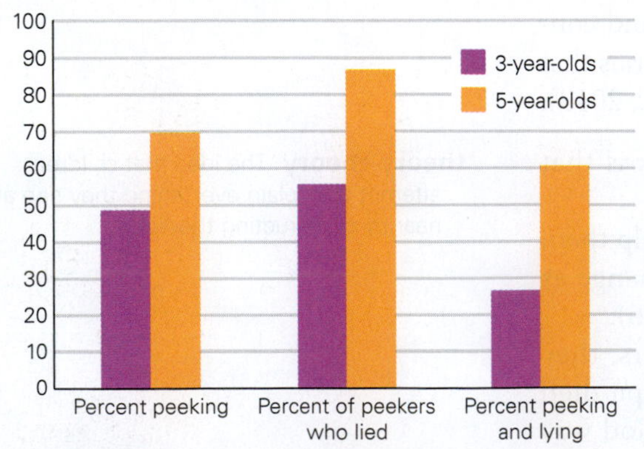

Data from Evans et al., 2011.

FIGURE 9.2
Better with Age? Could an obedient and honest 3-year-old become a disobedient and lying 5-year-old? Apparently yes, as the proportion of peekers and liars in this study more than doubled over those two years. Does maturation make children more able to think for themselves or less trustworthy?

The rest lied, and their skill at lying increased with their age. The 3-year-olds typically told hopeless lies (e.g., "The candies got out by themselves"); the 4-year-olds told unlikely lies (e.g., "Other children came in and knocked over the cup"). Some of the 5-year-olds, however, told plausible lies (e.g., "My elbow knocked over the cup accidentally").

A study of prosocial lies (saying that a disappointing gift was appreciated) found that children who were advanced in theory of mind and in executive function were also better liars, able to stick to the lie that they liked the gift (S. Williams et al., 2016). This study was of 6- to 12-year-olds, not preschoolers, but the underlying abilities are first evident at about age 4.

Evidence for crucial brain maturation comes from other research on the same 3- to 5-year-olds whose lying was studied. The children who were asked to say "day" when they saw a picture of the moon and "night" when they saw a picture of the sun needed to inhibit their automatic reaction. Their success indicated advanced executive function, which correlated with maturation of the prefrontal cortex.

INSIDE THE BRAIN

The Role of Experience

Why do executive control, concrete operational thought, social interaction, and even lying improve with age? There are many factors, of course, but developmentalists increasingly recognize the crucial maturation of the prefrontal cortex. With modern neuroscience, this can be traced quite precisely: A notable advance in all of these abilities occurs between ages 4 and 5, probably because the prefrontal cortex matures markedly at this point (Devine & Hughes, 2014).

Children who are slow in language development are also slow in theory of mind, a finding that makes developmentalists suggest that underlying deficits—genetic or neurological—may be crucial for both. Remember the plasticity of the brain: The early years may be particularly important for neurological control.

In studies of adults as well, many brain regions are involved in theory of mind and much depends on past history and context (Preckel et al., 2018). Developmentalists suggest that when a young child is slow in language learning, in addition to targeted work on vocabulary, articulation, and so on, therapists and teachers need to advance executive function (Nilsson & de López, 2016).

Social interactions with other children promote brain development, advancing both theory of mind and executive function. This is especially evident when those other children are siblings of about the same age (McAlister & Peterson, 2013). As one expert in theory of mind quipped, "Two older siblings are worth about a year of chronological age" (Perner, 2000, p. 383).

Indeed, many studies have found that a child's ability to develop theories correlates with neurological maturation, which also correlates with advances in executive processing—the reflective, anticipatory capacity of the mind (Mar, 2011; Baron-Cohen et al., 2013). Detailed studies find that theory of mind activates several brain regions (Koster-Hale & Saxe, 2013).

This makes sense, as theory of mind is a complex ability that humans develop in social contexts, so it is not likely to reside in just one neurological region. Brain research finds that, although each cognitive ability arises from a distinct part of the brain, experience during childhood advances neurological coordination.

Remember that experience strengthens neuronal connections. This is true not only within each neuron and the dendrites reaching another neuron but also in regions of the brain. Thus, while theory of mind promotes empathy in one brain region, and executive function promotes flexibility and memory in another, the prefrontal cortex is able to coordinate the two (Wade et al., 2018).

That is why a correlation is found between theory of mind and executive function. As a child advances in one, that child also advances in the other. Repeated coordination in the brain allows the child, for instance, to comfort a sad friend in exactly the way that sad friend is best comforted.

Even when compared to other children who were the same age, those who failed the day–night tests typically told impossible lies. Their age-mates who were higher in executive function told more plausible lies (Evans et al., 2011).

Does the crucial role of neurological maturation make culture and context irrelevant? Not at all: Nurture is always important. The reason that formal education traditionally began at about age 6 is that this is when maturation of the prefrontal cortex naturally allows sustained attention. However, experiences before age 6 advance brain development and thus prepare children for school (Blair & Raver, 2015).

Some helpful experiences before age 6 occur naturally: Children develop theory of mind in talking with adults and in playing with other children. Games that require turn-taking encourage memory and inhibitory control, two crucial components of executive control. In daily life, as brothers and sisters argue, agree, compete, and cooperate, and as older siblings fool younger ones, it dawns on 3-year-olds that not everyone thinks as they do, a thought that advances theory of mind.

By age 5, children have learned how to persuade their younger brothers and sisters to give them a toy. Meanwhile, younger siblings figure out how to gain sympathy by complaining that their older brothers and sisters have victimized them. Parents, beware: Asking, "Who started it?" may be irrelevant.

Chris Wildt/Cartoon Stock

"Another milestone: the first step, first word, first excuse..."

The Dog Did It If only all parents were aware of cognitive development.

WHAT HAVE YOU LEARNED?

1. What three abilities comprise executive function?
2. What is not logical about preoperational thought?
3. What is the difference between egocentrism in a child and selfishness in an adult?
4. How does guided participation increase a child's zone of proximal development?
5. Why did Vygotsky think that talking to oneself is an aid to cognition?
6. Why does theory-theory develop?
7. What advances theory of mind?

Language Learning

Learning language is often considered the premier cognitive accomplishment of early childhood. Two-year-olds use short, telegraphic sentences ("Want cookie," "Where Daddy go?"), omitting adjectives, adverbs, and articles. By contrast, 5-year-olds seem to be able to say almost anything (see At About This Time) using every part of speech. Some preschoolers understand and speak two or three languages, an accomplishment that many adults struggle for years to achieve.

AT ABOUT THIS TIME

Language in Early Childhood

Approximate Age	Characteristic or Achievement in First Language
2 years	*Vocabulary:* 100–2,000 words *Sentence length:* 2–6 words *Grammar:* Plurals; pronouns; many nouns, verbs, adjectives *Questions:* Many "What's that?" questions
3 years	*Vocabulary:* 1,000–5,000 words *Sentence length:* 3–8 words *Grammar:* Conjunctions, adverbs, articles *Questions:* Many "Why?" questions
4 years	*Vocabulary:* 3,000–10,000 words *Sentence length:* 5–20 words *Grammar:* Dependent clauses, tags at sentence end (". . . didn't I?" ". . . won't you?") *Questions:* Peak of "Why?" questions; many "How?" and "When?" questions
6 years and up	*Vocabulary:* 5,000–30,000 words *Sentence length:* Some seem unending (". . . and . . . who . . . and . . . that . . . and . . .") *Grammar:* Complex, depending on what the child has heard, with some children correctly using the passive voice ("Man bitten by dog") and subjunctive ("If I were . . .") *Questions:* Some about social differences (male–female, old–young, rich–poor) and many other issues

The Sensitive Time for Language Learning

Brain maturation, myelination, scaffolding, and social interaction make early childhood ideal for learning language. As you remember from Chapter 1, scientists once thought that early childhood was a *critical period* for language learning—the *only* time when a first language could be mastered and the best time to learn a second or third one.

A first language (even a sign language) is a scaffold for learning. Thus, talking, listening, and reading to young children is crucial for education, including learning a second language (Mayberry & Kluender, 2018). Although new language learning in adulthood is possible, it is not easy. Early childhood is a *sensitive period* for language learning—for rapidly mastering vocabulary, grammar, and pronunciation. Young children are language sponges; they soak up every verbal drop they encounter.

Language comes easily partly because preoperational children are not self-critical about their fluency. Egocentrism has advantages; this is one of them.

The Vocabulary Explosion

The average child knows about 500 words at age 2 and more than 10,000 at age 6 (Herschensohn, 2007). That's more than six new words a day. As with many averages in development, the range is vast: The number of root words (e.g., *run* is a root word, not *running* or *runner*) that 5-year-olds know ranges from 2,000 to 6,000 (Biemiller, 2009). In fact, it is very difficult to determine vocabulary size, although almost everyone agrees that building vocabulary is crucial (Milton & Treffers-Daller, 2013).

To understand why vocabulary is difficult to measure, consider the following: Children listened to a story about a raccoon that saw its reflection in the water. The children were asked what *reflection* means. Five of the answers:

1. "It means that your reflection is yourself. It means that there is another person that looks just like you."
2. "Means if you see yourself in stuff and you see your reflection."
3. "Is like when you look in something, like water, you can see yourself."
4. "It mean your face go in the water."
5. "That means if you the same skin as him, you blend in."

[*Hoffman et al., 2014, pp. 471–472*]

In another example, a story included "a chill ran down his spine." Children were asked what *chill* meant. One answer: "When you want to lay down and watch TV—and eat nachos" (Hoffman et al., 2014, p. 473).

Which of the five responses indicated that the child knew what *reflection* means? None? All? Some number in between? The last child was given zero credit for "chill"; is that fair?

Fast-Mapping Children develop interconnected categories for words, a kind of grid or mental map that makes speedy vocabulary acquisition possible. Learning a word after one exposure is called **fast-mapping** (Woodward & Markman, 1998) because, rather than figuring out the exact definition after hearing a word used in several contexts, children hear a word once and quickly stick it into a category in their mental language grid. For 2-year-olds, *mother* can mean any caregiving woman, for instance.

Picture books offer many opportunities to advance vocabulary through scaffolding and fast-mapping. A mentor might encourage the next steps in the child's zone of proximal development, such as that tigers have stripes and leopards spots, or, for an older child, that calico cats are almost always female and that lions with manes are always male.

This process explains children's learning of colors. Generally, 2-year-olds fast-map color names (K. Wagner et al., 2013). For instance, "blue" is used for some greens or grays.

Children apply words they know to broad categories and have not yet learned the boundaries that adults use, or specifics such as chartreuse, turquoise, olive, navy. As one team of scientists explains, adults' color words are the result of slow-mapping (K. Wagner et al., 2013), which is not what young children do.

Words and the Limits of Logic Closely related to fast-mapping is a phenomenon called *logical extension:* After learning a word, children use it to describe other objects in the same category. One child told her father that she had seen some "Dalmatian cows" on a school trip to a farm. Instead of criticizing her error, he remembered the Dalmatian dog she had petted the weekend before. He realized that she saw Holstein cows, not Jersey ones.

Bilingual children who don't know a word in the language they are speaking often insert a word from the other language, code-switching in the middle of

VIDEO ACTIVITY: Language Acquisition in Young Children features video clips of a new sign language created by deaf Nicaraguan children and provides insights into how language evolves.

fast-mapping The speedy and sometimes imprecise way in which children learn new words by tentatively placing them in mental categories according to their perceived meaning.

Jason Lindsey/Alamy Stock Photo

What Is It? These two children at the Mississippi River Museum in Iowa might call this a crocodile, but really it is an alligator. Fast-mapping allows that mistake, and egocentrism might make them angry if someone tells them they chose the wrong name.

a sentence. That mid-sentence switch may be considered wrong, but it is actually evidence of the child's drive to communicate. By age 5, bilingual children realize who understands which language, and they avoid substitutions when speaking to a monolingual person. That illustrates theory of mind.

Some words are particularly difficult for every child, such as, in English, *who/whom, have been/had been, here/there, yesterday/tomorrow*. More than one child has awakened on Christmas morning and asked, "Is it tomorrow yet?" A child told to "stay there" or "come here" may not follow instructions because the terms are confusing. It might be better to say, "Stay there on that bench," or "Come here to hold my hand." Every language has difficult concepts that are expressed in words; children everywhere learn them eventually.

Abstractions are particularly difficult; actions are easier to understand. A hole is to dig; love is hugging; hearts beat.

Acquiring Grammar

Remember from Chapter 6 that *grammar* includes structures, techniques, and rules that communicate meaning. Knowledge of grammar is essential for learning to speak, read, and write. A large vocabulary is useless unless a person knows how to put words together. Each language has its own grammar rules; that's one reason children speak in one-word sentences first.

Children apply rules of grammar as soon as they figure them out, using their own theories about how language works and their experience regarding when and how often various rules apply (Meltzoff & Gopnik, 2013). For example, English-speaking children quickly learn to add an *s* to form the plural: Toddlers follow that rule when they ask for two cookies or more blocks.

Soon they add an *s* to make the plural of words they have never heard before, even nonsense words. If preschoolers are shown a drawing of an abstract shape, told it is called a *wug,* and are then shown two of these shapes, they say there are two *wugs* (Berko, 1958). Children realize that words have a singular and a plural before they demonstrate proper use.

overregularization The application of rules of grammar even when exceptions occur, making the language seem more "regular" than it actually is.

Sometimes children apply the rules of grammar when they should not. This error is called **overregularization.** By age 4, many children overregularize that final *s,* talking about *foots, tooths,* and *mouses.* This signifies knowledge, not lack of it: Many children first say words correctly (*feet, teeth, mice*), repeating what they have heard. Later, they are smart enough to apply the rules of grammar, and over-regularize, assuming that all constructions follow the rules.

Melba/AGE Fotostock

Terraxplorer/iStock/Getty Images

Camels Protected, People Confused Why the contrasting signs? Does everyone read English at the international airport in Chicago (O'Hare) but not on the main road in Tunisia?

More difficult to learn is an aspect of language called **pragmatics**—knowing which words, tones, and grammatical forms to use with whom (Siegal & Surian, 2012). In some languages, it is essential to know which set of words to use when a person is older, or when someone is not a close friend, or when grandparents are on the mother's side or the father's.

English does not make those distinctions, but pragmatics are important for early-childhood learning nonetheless. Children learn variations in vocabulary and tone depending on the context, and once theory of mind is established, on the audience.

Knowledge of pragmatics is evident when a 4-year-old pretends to be a doctor, a teacher, or a parent. Each role requires different speech. On the other hand, children often blurt out questions that embarrass their parents ("Why is that lady so fat?" or "I don't want to kiss Grandpa because his breath smells."): The pragmatics of polite speech require more social understanding than many young children possess.

pragmatics The practical use of language that includes the ability to adjust language communication according to audience and context.

CHAPTER APP 9

FaceTalker

RELATED TOPIC:
Language learning in early childhood

IOS:
https://tinyurl.com/y5xycx6p

Many teachers find FaceTalker to be a fun classroom tool for demonstrating the sounds animals make, introducing literature or poetry, and for many other learning activities. The app can enliven lessons on basic arithmetic, ancient Egypt, music, art, and more. Even better: Online reviews of the app suggest it is easy to get started.

Learning Two Languages

Language-minority people (those who speak a language that is not their nation's dominant one) suffer if they do not also speak the majority language (Rosselli et al., 2016). In the United States, those who lack fluency in English have lower school achievement, diminished self-esteem, and inadequate employment.

Some of the problem is prejudice from those who speak English well, but some is directly connected to language. Fluency in English erases some liabilities; fluency in another language then becomes an asset.

Neuroscience finds that if adults mastered two languages before age 6, both languages are located in the same areas of the brain with no detriment to the cortex structure (Klein et al., 2014). Being bilingual seems to benefit the brain lifelong, further evidence for plasticity (Bialystok, 2017). Indeed, the bilingual brain may provide some resistance to neurocognitive disorder due to Alzheimer's disease in old age (Costa & Sebastián-Gallés, 2014).

By contrast, if a new language is learned in adulthood, pronunciation and grasp of idioms and exceptions to the rules usually lag behind use of proper grammar and vocabulary. Thus, many immigrants speak the majority language with an accent but are proficient in comprehension and reading (difference is not deficit).

From infancy on, hearing is more acute than vocalization. Almost all young children mispronounce whatever language they speak, blithely unaware of their mistakes. They comprehend more than they say, they hear better than they speak, and they learn rapidly as long as people speak to them.

Language Loss and Gains

Language-minority parents have a legitimate fear: Their children might make a *language shift,* becoming fluent in the school language and not in their home language. Language shift occurs whenever theory-theory leads children to conclude that their first language is inferior to another one (Bhatia & Ritchie, 2013).

Some language-minority children in Mexico shift to Spanish; some children of Canada's First Nations shift to French; some children in the United States shift to English. In China, all speak some form of Chinese, but some shift from Mandarin, Cantonese, and so on, troubling their parents.

Remember that young children are preoperational: They center on the immediate status of their language (not on future usefulness or past glory), on appearance more than substance. No wonder many children shift toward the language of the dominant culture.

Since language is integral to culture, if a child is to become fluently bilingual, everyone who speaks with the child should respect both cultures, in song, books,

ATTILA KISBENEDEK/AFP/Getty Images

Bilingual Learners These are Chinese children learning a second language. Could this be in the United States? No, this is a class in the first Chinese-Hungarian school in Budapest. There are three clues: the spacious classroom, the letters on the book, and the large windows and many trees outside.

Especially for Immigrant Parents You want your children to be fluent in the language of your family's new country, even though you do not speak that language well. Should you speak to your children in your native tongue or in the new language? (see response, page 244)

and daily conversation. Children learn from listening and talking, so they need to hear twice as much talk to become fluent in two languages.

The same practices make a child fluently trilingual, as some 5-year-olds are. Young children who are immersed in three languages may speak all three with no accent—except the accent of their mother, father, and friends. [**Life-Span Link:** Bilingual education is also discussed in Chapter 12.]

Sadly, most young children who are bilingual or trilingual are language deficient in both, or all three, languages. Crucial is exposure "to both languages in ways that do not diminish the amount of exposure to each" (Hoff, 2018, p. 84). This means that, during early childhood, language that is to be learned must be used often in daily conversation—twice as often as for a monolingual child.

WHAT HAVE YOU LEARNED?

1. What is the evidence that early childhood is a sensitive time for learning language?
2. How does fast-mapping aid the language explosion?
3. How is overregularization a cognitive advance?
4. What in language learning shows the limitations of logic in early childhood?
5. What are the advantages of teaching a child two languages?
6. How can the language shift be avoided in children?

Early-Childhood Schooling

Today, virtually every nation provides some early-childhood education, sometimes financed by the government, sometimes private, sometimes for a privileged few, and sometimes for every child (Georgeson & Payler, 2013).

In many European nations, more than 95 percent of all 3- to 5-year-olds are enrolled in government-funded schools. Almost every parent and politician realizes that young children are amazingly capable and eager to learn.

Tricky Indeed Young children are omnivorous learners, picking up habits, curses, and attitudes that adults would rather not transmit. Deciding what to teach—by actions more than words—is essential.

"We teach them that the world can be an unpredictable, dangerous, and sometimes frightening place, while being careful not to spoil their lovely innocence. It's tricky."

Homes and Schools

Developmental research does not translate directly into specific practices in early education, so no program can legitimately claim to follow Piaget or Vygotsky exactly (Hatch, 2012). This general finding should reassure parents: Young children learn in a variety of settings. Parents are influential even if a young child is in a day-care center from 8 A.M. to 6 P.M., five days a week. Nonetheless, developmental theories and scientific research inform educators, suggest hypotheses, and shape the curriculum of every program.

Beyond the amazing potential of young children to learn, another robust conclusion from research on children's learning seems not yet universally understood: Quality matters (Gambaro et al., 2014).

Quality cannot be judged by the name of a program or by its sponsorship. Educational institutions for 3- to 5-year-olds are called preschools, nursery schools, day-care centers, pre-primary programs, pre-K classes, and kindergartens. Sponsors can be public (federal, state, or city), private, religious, or corporate. Each child is an individual and cultures differ; an excellent program for one child might be less effective for another.

Indeed, quality is notoriously difficult to judge (Votruba-Drzal & Dearing, 2017). "[B]ecause quality is hard for parents to observe, competition seems to be dominated by price" (Gambaro et al., 2014, p. 22). That is a problem, because to make a profit, programs hire fewer teachers — so low cost may indicate low quality.

However, high cost does not necessarily mean high quality. As you have learned, children are active learners who benefit from social interaction with other children and with adults who guide them. A quiet preschool, with adults who are not actively engaged with talkative children, is low quality.

Professional assessment of quality also seems inadequate (Sabol et al., 2013). However, one aspect — child–teacher interaction — correlates with learning. A bad sign is a teacher who sits and watches; effective teachers talk, laugh, guide, and play with the children. (See Visualizing Development, page 245.)

In order to sort through this variety, we review some distinctions among types of programs. One broad distinction concerns the program goals. Is the goal to encourage each child's creative individuality (*child-centered*) or to prepare the child for formal education (*teacher-directed*), or is it to prepare low-SES children for school (*intervention,* such as *Head Start*)?

Child-Centered Programs

Many programs are called *child-centered,* or *developmental,* because they stress each child's development and growth. Teachers in such programs believe children need to follow their own interests rather than adult directions. For example, they agree that "children should be allowed to select many of their own activities from a variety of learning areas that the teacher has prepared" (Lara-Cinisomo et al., 2011). The physical space and the materials (such as dress-up clothes, art supplies, puzzles, blocks, and other toys) are arranged to allow exploration.

Most child-centered programs encourage artistic expression, including music and drama (Bassok et al., 2016). Some educators argue that young children are gifted in seeing the world more imaginatively than older people do. According to advocates of child-centered programs, this peak of creative vision should be encouraged; children need many opportunities to tell stories, draw pictures, dance, and make music for their own delight.

That does not mean that academics are ignored. Advocates of math learning, for instance, believe that children have a natural interest in numbers and that child-centered schools can guide those interests as children grow (Stipek, 2013).

Child-centered programs are often influenced by Piaget, who emphasized that each child will discover new ideas if given a chance, or by Vygotsky, who thought that children learn from playing, especially with other children.

Montessori Schools One type of child-centered school began in the slums of Rome, Italy, in 1907, when Maria Montessori opened a nursery school (Standing, 1998). She believed that children needed structured, individualized projects to give them a sense of accomplishment. Her students completed puzzles, used sponges and water to clean tables, traced shapes, and so on.

Contemporary **Montessori schools** still emphasize individual pride and achievement, presenting many literacy-related tasks (e.g., outlining letters and looking at books) to young children. Specific materials differ from those that Maria Montessori developed, but the underlying philosophy is the same. Children seek out learning tasks; they do not sit quietly in groups while a teacher instructs them. That makes Montessori programs child-centered (Lillard, 2013).

Tibet, China, India, and . . . Italy? Over the past half-century, as China increased its control of Tibet, thousands of refugees fled to northern India. Tibet traditionally had no preschools, but young children adapt quickly, as in this preschool program in Ladakh, India. This Tibetan boy is working a classic Montessori board.

Malie Rich-Griffith/infocusphotos.com/Alamy Stock Photo

Montessori schools Schools that offer early-childhood education based on the philosophy of Maria Montessori, which emphasizes careful work and tasks that each young child can do.

Reggio Emilia A program of early childhood education that originated in the town of Reggio Emilia, Italy, and that encourages each child's creativity in a carefully designed setting.

ELIZABETH FLORES/Tribune News Service/PLEASANT PRAIRIE/WI/USA/Newscom

Child-Centered Pride How could Rachel Koepke, a 3-year-old from a Wisconsin town called Pleasant Prairie, seem so pleased that her hands (and cuffs) are blue? The answer arises from northern Italy—Rachel attended a Reggio Emilia preschool that encourages creative expression.

Waldorf schools An early-childhood education program that emphasizes creativity, social understanding, and emotional growth. It originated in Germany with Rudolf Steiner, and now is used in thousands of schools throughout the world.

Especially for Teachers In trying to find a preschool program, what should parents look for? (see response, page 244)

Reggio Emilia Another form of early-childhood education is **Reggio Emilia,** named after the town in Italy where it began. In Reggio Emilia, children are encouraged to master skills that are not usually taught in North American schools until age 7 or so, such as writing and using tools. Although many educators worldwide admire the Reggio philosophy and practice, it is expensive to duplicate in other nations—there are few dedicated Reggio Emilia schools in the United States.

Reggio schools do not provide large-group instruction, with lessons in, say, forming letters or cutting paper. Instead, hands-on activities chosen by individual children, such as drawing, cooking, and gardening, are stressed. Measurement of achievement, such as standardized testing to see whether children recognize the 26 letters of the alphabet, is antithetical to the conviction that each child should explore and learn in his or her own way. Each child's learning is documented via scrapbooks, photos, and daily notes—not to measure progress but to help the child and the parent take pride in accomplishments (Caruso, 2013).

Appreciation of the arts is evident. Every Reggio Emilia school originally had a studio, an artist, and space to encourage creativity (Forbes, 2012). Children's art is displayed on white walls and hung from high ceilings, and floor-to-ceiling windows open to a spacious, plant-filled playground. Big mirrors are part of the schools' décor—again, with the idea of fostering individuality and self-expression. However, individuality does not mean that children do not work together. On the contrary, group projects are encouraged.

Often those group projects include exploring the natural world. One analysis of Reggio Emilia in the United States found "a science-rich context that triggered and supported preschoolers' inquiries and effectively engaged preschoolers' hands, heads, and hearts with science" (Inan et al., 2010, p. 1186).

Waldorf Schools A third type of child-centered program is called a **Waldorf school,** first developed by Rudolf Steiner in Stuttgart, Germany, in 1919. The emphasis again is on creativity and individuality—with no homework, no tests, no worksheets. As much as possible, children play outdoors; appreciation of nature is basic to Waldorf education. Children of various ages learn together, because older children serve as mentors for younger ones, and the curriculum follows the interests of the child, not the age of the child.

There is a set schedule—usually circle time in the beginning and certain activities on certain days (always baking on Tuesdays, for instance)—but children are not expected to master specific knowledge at certain ages. All child-centered schools emphasize creativity; in Waldorf schools, imagination is particularly prized (Kirkham & Kidd, 2017).

Teacher-Directed Programs

Teacher-directed preschools stress academics, often taught by one adult to the entire group. The curriculum includes learning the names of letters, numbers, shapes, and colors according to a set timetable; every child naps, snacks, and goes to the bathroom on schedule as well. Children learn to sit quietly and listen to the teacher. Praise and other reinforcements are given for good behavior, and time-outs (brief separation from activities) are imposed to punish misbehavior.

The goal of teacher-directed programs is to make all children "ready to learn" when they enter elementary school. For that reason, basic skills are stressed, including precursors to reading, writing, and arithmetic, perhaps with teachers asking questions that children answer together in unison. Behavior is taught: Children learn to listen quietly, to follow schedules, to hold hands when they go out.

Many teacher-directed programs were inspired by behaviorism, which emphasizes step-by-step learning and repetition, with reinforcement (praise, gold stars, prizes) for accomplishment. Another inspiration comes from information-processing research indicating that children who have not learned basic skills by kindergarten often fall behind in primary school.

OPPOSING PERSPECTIVES

Comparing Child-Centered and Teacher-Directed Preschools

Most developmentalists advocate child-centered programs (Christakis, 2016; Golinkoff & Hirsh-Pasek, 2016). They believe that from ages 3 to 6 young children learn best when they can interact in their own way with materials and ideas (Sim & Xu, 2017). On the other hand, many parents and legislators want proof that early education will improve later school achievement.

The developmental critics of teacher-directed education fear trading "emotional grounding and strong language skills known to support learning for assembly-line schooling that teaches children isolated factoids" (Hirsh-Pasek & Golinkoff, 2016, p. 1158).

As Penelope Leach wrote, "Goals come from the outside. . . . It is important that people see early learning as coming from inside children because that's what makes clear its interconnectedness with play, and therefore the inappropriateness of many 'learning goals'" (Leach, 2011, p. 17). Another developmentalist asks, "why should we settle for unimaginative goals . . . like being able to identify triangles and squares, or recalling the names of colors and seasons" (Christakis, 2016).

However, children who enter kindergarten without knowing names and sounds of letters may become first-graders who cannot read (Ozernov-Palchik et al., 2017). Understanding how written symbols relate to sounds is crucial, and children are unlikely to learn literacy skills in creative play (Gellert & Elbro, 2017).

Early familiarity with numbers and shapes predicts school achievement later on. As you will soon read, Head Start programs have shifted over the past decades to be more teacher-directed, largely because national policy directives from the government have advocated that change—to the distress of many developmentalists (Walter & Lippard, 2017).

Finding the right balance between child-centered and teacher-directed learning is needed so that all young children learn in the manner that is best for them (Fuligni et al., 2012). The current trend is toward teacher-directed learning, according to a survey of kindergarten teachers (Bassok et al., 2016) (see **Figure 9.3**).

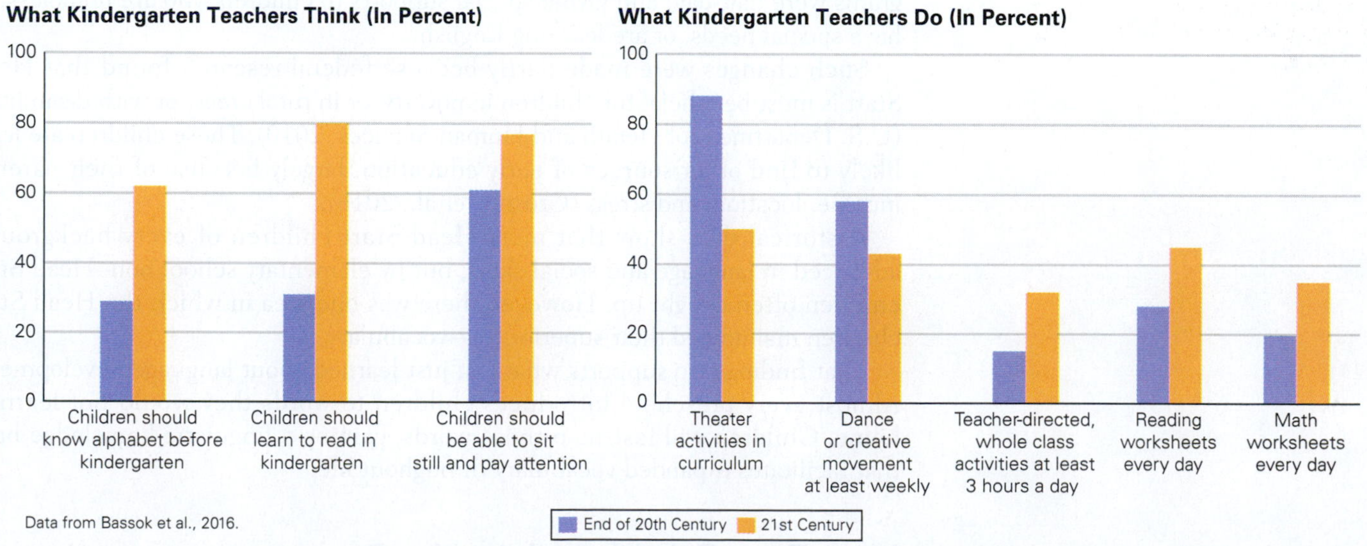

FIGURE 9.3

Less Play, More Work These data come from a large survey of more than 5,000 public school teachers throughout the United States. In 1998 and 2010, kindergarten teachers were asked identical questions but gave different answers. Smaller, more recent surveys suggest that these trends continue, and they now involve teachers in preschools. Some use worksheets for 3-year-olds.

Octavio Jones/Tampa Bay Times/ZUMAPRESS.com

If You're Happy and You Know It Gabby Osborne (pink shirt) has her own way of showing happiness, not the hand-clapping that Lizalia Garcia tries to teach. The curriculum of this Head Start class in Florida includes learning about emotions, contrary to the wishes of some legislators, who want proof of academics.

Head Start A federally funded early-childhood intervention program for low-income children of preschool age.

Intervention Programs

Several programs designed for children from low-SES families were established in the United States decades ago. Some solid research on the results of these programs is now available.

Head Start In the early 1960s, millions of young children in the United States were thought to need a "head start" on their formal education to foster better health and cognition before first grade. Consequently, since 1965, the federal government has funded a massive program for 4-year-olds called **Head Start.**

The goals for Head Start have changed over the decades, from lifting families out of poverty to promoting literacy, from providing dental care and immunizations to teaching Standard English, from focusing on 4-year-olds to including 2- and 3-year-olds. In 2015, more than 8 billion dollars in federal funds were allocated to Head Start, which enrolled almost 1 million children.

Head Start is a massive program, but there are about 8 million 3- and 4-year-olds in the United States, which means that only about 12 percent of U.S. children that age attend Head Start. Many of the other children are in private programs (about 83 percent of 4-year-olds from the wealthiest families are enrolled in private preschools). Many more are in state-sponsored programs, which range in quality from excellent to woefully inadequate (Barnett et al., 2016).

As you read in Opposing Perspectives, although most Head Start programs were child-centered initially, they have become increasingly teacher-directed as waves of legislators have shaped them. Children learn whatever their particular teachers emphasize. Not surprisingly, specific results vary by program and cohort.

In 2016, new requirements were put in place for Head Start, mandating that programs be open at least 6 hours a day and 180 days a year (initially, most programs were half-day) and giving special supports to children who are homeless, or have special needs, or are learning English.

Such changes were made partly because federal research found that Head Start is most beneficial for children in poverty, or in rural areas, or with disabilities (U.S. Department of Health and Human Services, 2010). Those children are least likely to find other sources of early education, largely because of their parents' income, location, and stress (Crosnoe et al., 2016).

Historical data show that most Head Start children of every background advanced in language and social skills, but by elementary school non–Head Start children often caught up. However, there was one area in which the Head Start children maintained their superiority—vocabulary.

That finding also supports what you just learned about language development. Almost every preschool introduces children to words they would not learn at home. Children will fast-map those words, gaining a linguistic knowledge base that facilitates expanded vocabulary throughout life.

Long-Term Gains from Intensive Programs

This discussion of philosophies, practices, and programs may give the impression that the research on early-childhood cognition is contradictory. That is not true. Specifics are debatable, but empirical evidence and longitudinal evaluation find that preschool education advances learning. Ideally, each program has a curriculum that guides practice, all of the adults collaborate, and experienced teachers respond to each child.

The best longitudinal evidence comes from three intensive programs that enrolled children for years — sometimes beginning with home visits in infancy, sometimes continuing in after-school programs through first grade. One program, called *Perry* (or *High/Scope*), was spearheaded in Michigan (Schweinhart & Weikart, 1997); another, called *Abecedarian,* got its start in North Carolina (Campbell et al., 2001); a third, called *Child–Parent Centers,* began in Chicago (Reynolds, 2000). They all focused on children from low-SES families.

Frank Porter Graham Child Development Institute.

Lifetime Achievement The baby in the framed photograph escaped the grip of poverty. The woman holding the photograph proved that early education can transform children. She is Frances Campbell, who spearheaded the Abecedarian Project. The baby's accomplishments may be the more impressive of the two.

All three programs compared experimental groups of children with matched control groups, and all reached the same conclusion: Early education has substantial long-term benefits that become most apparent when children are in the third grade or later.

By age 10, children in these programs scored higher on math and reading tests than did other children from the same backgrounds, schools, and neighborhoods. Fewer were placed in classes for children with special needs, or repeated a year of school, or left high school before graduation.

An advantage of decades of longitudinal research is that teenagers and adults who received early education can be compared with those who did not. For all three programs, early investment paid off.

In adolescence, the children who had undergone intensive preschool education had higher aspirations, possessed a greater sense of achievement, and were less likely to have been abused. As young adults, they were more likely to attend college and less likely to go to jail. As middle-aged adults, they were more often employed, paying taxes, healthy, and not needing government subsidies (Reynolds & Ou, 2011; Schweinhart et al., 2005; Campbell et al., 2014).

All three research projects found that providing direct cognitive training, with specific instruction in various school-readiness skills, was useful. Each child's needs and talents were considered — a circumstance made possible because the child/adult ratio was low. This combined child-centered and teacher-directed programs, with all of the teachers working together on the same goals so that children were not confused. In all three, teachers deliberately involved parents, and each program included strategies to enhance the home–school connection.

These programs were expensive (ranging from $6,500 to $20,000 annually per young child in 2016 dollars). From a developmental perspective, the decreased need for special education and other social services later on made early education a "wise investment" (Duncan & Magnuson, 2013, p. 128). Additional benefits to society over the child's lifetime, including increased employment and tax revenues, as well as reduced crime, are worth much more than the cost of the programs.

Between 2010 and 2017, some states (e.g., Oklahoma, Georgia, Florida, New Jersey, and Illinois) and some cities (e.g., New York, Boston, Cleveland, San Antonio, and Los Angeles) have offered preschool to every 4-year-old. Overall, 29 percent of all 4-year olds were in state-sponsored preschool, twice as many as a decade earlier (Barnett et al., 2015); another 10 percent attended Head Start; and about 3 percent were in publicly funded programs for children with disabilities (U.S. Department of Education, 2015).

The increases in government-sponsored preschool—either child-centered or teacher-directed—for 4-year-olds is good news. But developmentalists note that in the United States, unlike in Europe, almost half of all 4-year-olds and most 3-year-olds are not in any educational program. The children *least* likely to be in such programs are Spanish-speaking, or from families with income slightly above poverty-level, or whose mother is not employed.

Ironically, these are precisely the children for whom early education may be especially helpful, a conclusion found not only in Head Start but in other research as well (Weiland & Yoshikawa, 2013).

In the United States, economic and political pressures are reducing government funds for preschool education. Adjusted for inflation, per-pupil spending by states was $5,129 per child in 2002 and $4,121 in 2014 (Barnett et al., 2015). Head Start funding is also down per pupil, and cuts of more than 10 percent were projected for 2018.

Any cuts to preschool education not only mean less child-centered learning (which is more expensive) but also less high-quality teacher-directed learning. Further, in most states, kindergarten (always locally funded) is optional, and sometimes unavailable: Only 13 of the 50 states are required to offer full-day kindergarten (E. Parker et al., 2016). Scientists who know the research are dismayed when the wishes of the adults (lower taxes) supersede the needs of the children.

Compared to a decade ago, much more is known about early cognition: 2- to 4-year-olds are capable of learning languages, concepts, math, theory of mind, and much more. What a child learns before age 6 is pivotal for later life. That is evident in the next chapter, as well.

WHAT HAVE YOU LEARNED?

1. What do most preschools provide that most homes do not?
2. In child-centered programs, what do the teachers do?
3. What makes the Reggio Emilia program different from most other preschool programs?
4. Why are Montessori schools still functioning 100 years after the first such schools opened?
5. What are the advantages and disadvantages of teacher-directed preschools?
6. What are the goals of Head Start?
7. What are the long-term gains from intervention preschools?

SUMMARY

Thinking During Early Childhood

1. An important part of developing cognition during early childhood is the emergence of executive function, or cognitive control, as children learn to regulate and control their sensory impulses in order to use their minds more effectively.

2. Three components are usually included in executive function: memory, inhibition, and flexibility. Executive function can be improved during early childhood, and that advances later learning more than a high score on an IQ test or extensive vocabulary.

3. Piaget stressed the egocentric and illogical aspects of thought during early childhood. He called this stage of thinking preoperational intelligence because young children do not yet use logical operations to think about their observations and experiences.

4. Young children, according to Piaget, sometimes focus on only one thing (centration) and see things only from their own viewpoint (egocentrism), remaining stuck on appearances and current reality. They may believe that living spirits reside in inanimate

objects and that nonhuman animals have the same characteristics they themselves have, a belief called animism.

5. Vygotsky stressed the social aspects of childhood cognition, noting that children learn by participating in various experiences, guided by more knowledgeable adults or peers. Such guidance assists learning within the zone of proximal development.

6. According to Vygotsky, the best teachers use various hints, guidelines, and other tools to provide a child with a scaffold for new learning. Language is a bridge that provides social mediation between the knowledge that the child already has and the learning that society hopes to impart. Words are tools for learning.

7. Children develop theories, especially to explain the purpose of life and their role in it. One theory about children's thinking is called "theory-theory"—the hypothesis that children develop theories because all humans innately seek explanations for everything they observe.

8. An example of the developing cognition of young children is theory of mind—an understanding of what others may be thinking. Theory of mind begins at around age 4, partly as a result of maturation of the brain. Culture and experiences also influence its development.

Language Learning

9. Language develops rapidly during early childhood, a sensitive period but not a critical one for language learning. Vocabulary increases dramatically, with thousands of words added between ages 2 and 6. In addition, basic grammar is mastered.

10. The child's ability to learn language is evident in fast-mapping (the quick use of new vocabulary words) and in overregularization (applying the rules of grammar even when they are not valid).

11. Many children learn to speak more than one language, gaining cognitive as well as social advantages. Early childhood is the best time to learn two languages. The benefits of bilingualism are lifelong.

Early-Childhood Schooling

12. Organized educational programs during early childhood advance cognitive and social skills, although specifics vary a great deal. The quality of a program cannot be judged by the name or by appearance.

13. Montessori and Reggio Emilia are two child-centered programs that began in Italy and are now offered in many nations. Waldorf, which began in Germany, is another child-centered program.

14. Behaviorist principles led to many specific practices of teacher-directed programs. Children learn to listen to teachers and become ready for kindergarten. Teacher-directed programs are preferred by many parents and legislators, and these programs are increasingly popular—to the consternation of many child developmentalists.

15. Head Start is a U.S. federal government program primarily for low-income children. Longitudinal research finds that early-childhood education reduces the risk of later problems, such as needing special education. High-quality programs increase the likelihood that a child will become a law-abiding, gainfully employed adult.

KEY TERMS

executive function (p. 222)
preoperational intelligence (p. 223)
symbolic thought (p. 223)
animism (p. 224)
centration (p. 224)
egocentrism (p. 224)
focus on appearance (p. 224)
static reasoning (p. 224)
irreversibility (p. 224)
conservation (p. 225)
scaffolding (p. 227)
overimitation (p. 227)
private speech (p. 228)
social mediation (p. 228)
theory-theory (p. 229)
theory of mind (p. 230)
fast-mapping (p. 233)
overregularization (p. 234)
pragmatics (p. 235)
Montessori schools (p. 237)
Reggio Emilia (p. 238)
Waldorf schools (p. 238)
Head Start (p. 240)

APPLICATIONS

The best way to understand thinking in early childhood is to listen to a child, as Applications 1 and 2 require. If some students have no access to children, they should do Application 3 or 4.

1. Replicate one of Piaget's conservation experiments. The easiest one is conservation of liquids (Figure 9.1). Work with a child under age 5 who tells you that two identically shaped glasses contain the same amount of liquid. Then carefully pour one glass of liquid into a narrower, taller glass. Ask the child whether one glass now contains more or the glasses contain the same amount.

2. To demonstrate how rapidly language is learned, show a preschool child several objects and label one with a nonsense word that the child has never heard. (*Toma* is often used; so is *wug*.) Or choose a word that the child does not know, such as *wrench, spatula,* or the name of a coin from another nation. Test the child's fast-mapping.

3. Theory of mind emerges at about age 4, but many adults still have trouble understanding other people's thoughts and motives. Ask several people why someone in the news did whatever he or she did (e.g., a scandal, a crime, a heroic act). Then ask your informants how sure they are of their explanation. Compare and analyze the reasons as well as the degrees of certainty. (One person may be sure of an explanation that someone else thinks is impossible.)

4. Think about an experience in which you learned something that was initially difficult. To what extent do Vygotsky's concepts (guided participation, zone of proximal development) explain the experience? Write a detailed, step-by-step account of your learning process as Vygotsky would have described it.

Especially For ANSWERS

Response for Social Scientists (from p. 230): According to Piaget, preschool children focus on appearance and on static conditions (so they cannot mentally reverse a process). Furthermore, they are egocentric, believing that everyone shares their point of view. No wonder they believe that they had always known the puppy was in the blue box and that Max would know that, too.

Response for Immigrant Parents (from p. 236): Children learn by listening, so it is important to speak with them often. Depending on how comfortable you are with the new language, you might prefer to read to your children, sing to them, and converse with them primarily in your native language and find a good preschool where they will learn the new language. The worst thing you could do is to restrict speech in either tongue.

Response for Teachers (from p. 238): Tell parents to look at the people more than the program. Parents should see the children in action and note whether the teachers show warmth and respect for each child.

Observation Quiz ANSWERS

Answer to Observation Quiz (from p. 224): Green with jealousy, red-hot anger, and shrinking violet for fear.

Answer to Observation Quiz (from p. 227): Right-handed. Her dominant hand is engaged in something more comforting than exploring the abacus.

VISUALIZING DEVELOPMENT Early-Childhood Schooling

Preschool can be an academic and social benefit to children. Around the world, increasing numbers of children are enrolled in early-childhood education.

Programs are described as "teacher-directed" or "child-centered," but in reality, most teachers' styles reflect a combination of both approaches. Some students benefit more from the order and structure of a teacher-directed classroom, while others work better in a more collaborative and creative environment.

TEACHER-DIRECTED APPROACH

Focused on Getting Preschoolers Ready to Learn

Direct instruction
Teacher as formal authority
Students learn by listening
Classroom is orderly and quiet
Teacher fully manages lessons
Rewards individual achievement
Encourages academics
Students learn from teacher

CHILD-CENTERED APPROACH

Focused on Individual Development and Growth

Teacher as facilitator
Teacher as delegator
Students learn actively
Classroom is designed for collaborative work
Students influence content
Rewards collaboration among students
Encourages artistic expression
Students learn from each other

Worth Publishers

DIFFERENT STUDENTS, DIFFERENT TEACHERS

There is clearly no "one right way" to teach children. Each approach has potential benefits and pitfalls. A classroom full of creative, self-motivated students can thrive when a gifted teacher acts as a competent facilitator. But students who are distracted or annoyed by noise, or who are shy or intimidated by other children, can blossom under an engaging and encouraging teacher in a more traditional environment.

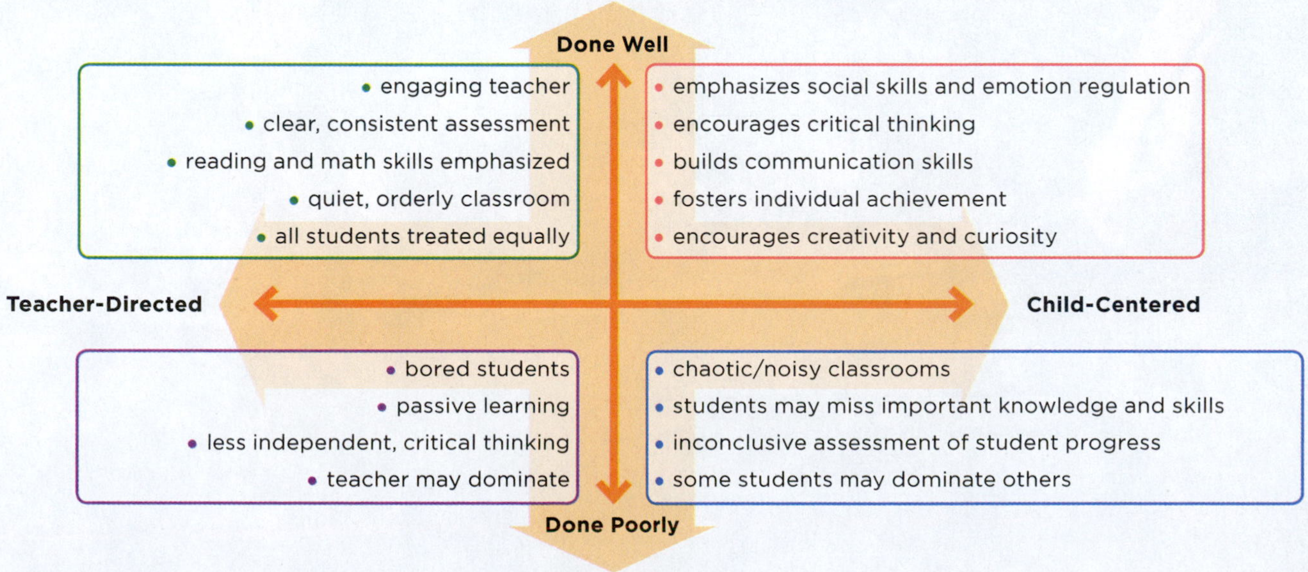

Early Childhood: Psychosocial Development

CHAPTER 10

What Will You Know?

- Why do 2-year-olds have more sudden tempers, tears, and terrors than 6-year-olds?
- What happens if parents let their children do whatever they want?
- How does spanking affect children?

- Emotional Development
  - A VIEW FROM SCIENCE: Waiting for the Marshmallow
  - Initiative Versus Guilt
  - Motivation
- Play
  - Playmates
  - Social Play
- Challenges for Caregivers
  - Styles of Caregiving
  - Discipline
  - OPPOSING PERSPECTIVES: Spare the Rod?
  - Becoming Boys and Girls: Sex and Gender
  - A CASE TO STUDY: The Berger Daughters
  - What Is Best?
  - Teaching Right and Wrong

CAREER ALERT: The Preschool Teacher

VISUALIZING DEVELOPMENT: More Play Time, Less Screen Time

At age 4, Isaac is now a "big kid." When we wait for the bus, he begs his older brother to play "the monster game." Asa usually says, "No, I don't want to play." Then Isaac cries. At that point, Asa stops the wailing by pretending to be a blind monster, clomping around with arms outstretched to catch Isaac, who laughs as he runs ahead, never caught. Should I intervene, telling Isaac not to cry or telling Asa not to reward the tears?

In running, Isaac sometimes bumps into strangers who are also waiting for the bus. Some strangers smile, some seem annoyed, but no one expresses anger. I would not mind if they did; I want Isaac to be more aware of the people around him. One friendly man asked Isaac his name, which he readily gave, as well as his address.

"Don't tell strangers where you live," the man said.

Isaac repeated his address.

Isaac is self-confident, emotional, and playful, all typical of 4-year-olds, as you will see in this chapter. Yet with both his brother and the strangers, it is apparent that Isaac has much to learn. Adults—parents and, in this case, grandmothers—need to figure out when and how to guide, encourage, and discipline.

Emotional Development

Controlling the expression of feelings, called **emotional regulation,** is the preeminent psychosocial task between ages 2 and 6. Emotional regulation is a lifelong endeavor, a crucial aspect of executive function, which develops most rapidly in early childhood (Gross, 2014; Lewis, 2013).

By age 6, most children can be angry, frightened, sad, anxious, or proud without the explosive outbursts of temper, or terror, or tears. Depending on a child's training and temperament, some emotions are easier to control than others, but even temperamentally angry or fearful children learn to regulate their emotions.

Overall, many factors affect the development of emotional regulation. Three have been proven again and again:

1. **Maturation matters.** Emotional regulation improves every year.
2. **Learning matters.** In the zone of proximal development, children learn from mentors, who offer tactics for managing emotions.

Left: Henryk T. Kaiser/Age Fotostock/Media Bakery
Top: baona/iStock/Getty Images

Allen Brown/dbimages/Alamy Stock Photo

Learning Emotional Regulation Like this girl in Hong Kong, all 2-year-olds burst into tears when something upsets them—a toy breaks, a pet refuses to play, or it's time to go home. Mothers who comfort young children and help them calm down are teaching them to regulate their emotions.

emotional regulation The ability to control when and how emotions are expressed.

self-concept A person's understanding of who they are, in relation to self-esteem, appearance, personality, and various traits.

effortful control The ability to regulate one's emotions and actions through effort, not simply through natural inclination.

initiative versus guilt Erikson's third psychosocial crisis, in which young children undertake new skills and activities and feel guilty when they do not succeed at them.

3. **Culture matters.** In the United States, many parents tell their children not to be afraid; in Japan, parents tell children not to brag; in the Netherlands, not to be moody. Children regulate their emotions in accord with their national culture as well as their family one.

In the process of emotional regulation, children develop their **self-concept,** which is their idea of who they are. Remember that 1-year-olds begin to recognize themselves in the mirror, the start of self-awareness. From then on, the self-concept builds rapidly.

By age 6, children can describe some of their characteristics, including what emotions they feel and how they express them. That is probably true for all children everywhere, although parental guidance and encouragement aid in self-awareness (LeCuyer & Swanson, 2016).

Emotional regulation is also called **effortful control** (Eisenberg et al., 2014), a term that emphasizes that controlling outbursts is not easy. Effortful control is more difficult when a person—of any age—is in pain, or tired, or hungry.

Effortful control, executive function, and emotional regulation are related constructs, with much overlap, at least in theory (Scherbaum et al., 2018; Slot et al., 2017). Executive function emphasizes cognition; effortful control emphasizes temperament; both undergird emotional regulation. Many neurological processes underlie these abilities; all advance during early childhood. (See A View from Science.)

Initiative Versus Guilt

Emotional regulation is part of Erikson's third developmental stage, **initiative versus guilt.** *Initiative* includes saying something new, beginning a project, expressing an emotion. Depending on what happens next, children feel proud or guilty. Gradually, they learn to rein in boundless pride and avoid crushing guilt.

Pride is particularly common in early childhood. As one team expressed it:

> Compared to older children and adults, young children are the optimists of the world, believing they have greater physical abilities, better memories, are more skilled at imitating models, are smarter, know more about how things work, and rate themselves as stronger, tougher, and of higher social standing than is actually the case.
>
> *[Bjorklund & Ellis, 2014, p. 244]*

That *protective optimism* helps young children try new things, and thus, initiative advances learning. As Erikson predicted, their optimistic self-concept protects young children from guilt and shame and encourages them to learn.

Young children often brag about what they have accomplished. As long as the boast is not a lie, other young children like them for it. At about age 7 a developmental shift occurs, when children as well as adults appreciate modesty more than boasting (Lockhart et al., 2018). That shows marked emotional regulation, when children finally are able to keep quiet about how wonderful they are.

Pride and Prejudice In many cultures, a young child's self-concept usually includes being proud of all their attributes, including age, size, and maturation. They are very glad that they aren't babies. "Crybaby" is an insult; praise for being a "big kid" is welcomed.

Indeed, many young children believe that whatever they are is good. They may feel superior to children of another nationality or religion. This arises because of maturation: Cognition enables them to understand group categories, not only of ethnicity, gender, and nationality but even categories that are irrelevant.

A VIEW FROM SCIENCE

Waiting for the Marshmallow

You may be familiar with the famous marshmallow test, which now has longitudinal results (Mischel et al., 1972; Mischel, 2014). Young children were told that they could eat one marshmallow immediately or eat two if they waited—sometimes as long as 15 minutes.

Some gobbled up the marshmallow immediately, but those who waited used various tactics—they looked away, closed their eyes, or sang to themselves. Young children who waited became more successful as teenagers, young adults, and even middle-aged adults—doing well in college, for instance, and having happy marriages.

Of course, this is correlation, not causation: Some impatient preschoolers in the original study nonetheless became successful adults. However, in general, many studies have found that emotional regulation is a key component of academic achievement and later success. Three overall conclusions about 2- to 6-year-olds are:

1. National differences are evident between nations. Some cultures may encourage instant gratification; others may expect people to wait patiently. For example, in a replication of the marshmallow test, children from the Nso people of Cameroon waited longer than the California children in Mischel's original experiment (Lamm et al., 2018).
2. Cultural differences are also apparent in personal experience. When children in a replication of the marshmallow test experienced an unreliable examiner (who previously had reneged on a promise), they ate the marshmallow right away (Kidd et al., 2013). Thus, the ability to delay gratification is not innate; it is a result of parents and cultures who do, or do not, teach patience and keep their promises.
3. Finally, age matters. Delaying gratification is an ability that usually increases with age. College students schedule a party after exams are over, adults save money for a vacation, and older adults postpone retirement until the best pension income is available. All these vary from one person to another: Are you one of those who saves until you have two marshmallows?

One amusing example occurred when preschoolers were asked to explain why one person would steal from another, as occurred in a story about two fictional tribes, the Zazzes and the Flurps. As you would expect from theory-theory, the preschoolers readily found reasons. Their first explanation illustrated their belief that group loyalty was more important than any personal characteristic.

> "Why did a Zaz steal a toy from a Flurp?"
> "Because he's a Zaz, but he's a Flurp . . . They're not the same kind . . ."

Then they were asked to explain a more difficult case

> "Why did a Zaz steal a toy from a Zaz?"

In that case, group loyalty could not be the explanation. The children had to consider character, morality, and personality. They gave this answer:

> "Because he's a very mean boy."
> [*Rhodes, 2013, p. 259*]

An interesting developmental pattern is evident for group loyalty. Already by age 3, children generally believe that people should not harm someone from their own group. This applies not only to logical categories that a child might understand (such as girls should not hurt other girls or neighbors should not hurt neighbors) but also to arbitrary categories, such as Zazzes and Flurps, or children wearing red versus children wearing blue.

Brain Maturation The new initiative that Erikson described results from myelination in the limbic system, growth of the prefrontal cortex, and a longer attention span—all indicative of neurological maturation. Emotional regulation and cognitive maturation develop together, each enabling the other to advance (Bell & Calkins, 2011; Lewis, 2013; Bridgett et al., 2015).

Jose Luis Pelaez Inc/Blend Images - KidStock/Brand X Pictures/Getty Images

Both Accomplished Note the joy and pride in this father and daughter in West New York, New Jersey. Who has achieved more?

THINK CRITICALLY: At what age, if ever, do people understand when pride becomes prejudice?

CHAPTER APP 10

Daniel Tiger's Grr-ific Feelings

RELATED TOPIC:
Emotional development in early childhood

IOS:
https://tinyurl.com/jc9jwxc

This early-learning app from PBS Kids helps 2- to 5-year-old children identify and express emotions through games and songs. It incorporates words like *jealous*, *patient*, *frustrated*, and *proud* to encourage children to express their feelings verbally and guides children through a simple calming technique.

Normally, at about age 4 or 5 due to brain maturation, with family and preschool experiences, the capacity for self-control becomes more evident. For example, a child might *not* open a present immediately if asked to wait and might *not* express disappointment at an undesirable gift.

Emotional regulation is evident when someone opens a gift. If the receiver is a young child, you can probably tell whether the child liked the present. If the receiver is an adult, you may not be sure (Galak et al., 2016).

Children strengthen and develop their neuronal connections in response to the emotions of other people. The process is reciprocal and dynamic: Anger begets anger, which leads to more anger; joy begets joy, and so on.

This reciprocity is not just a matter of words and facial expression, it also directly involves the brain. For instance, researchers scanned the brains of mothers and children as they solved a difficult puzzle together. When the mothers became frustrated, the children did too—and vice versa. As the scientists explain, "mothers and children regulate or deregulate each other" (Atzaba-Poria et al., 2017, p. 551).

This shared emotionality benefits adults as well as children. If a happy young boy runs to you, try to laugh, pick him up, and swing him around; if a grinning young girl drums on the table, try to catch the rhythm and pound in return, smiling broadly. Your stress hormones will decrease and your endorphins will increase. Of course, reciprocal joy is not always possible, but since emotions are infectious, catch the good ones and drop the bad ones.

Motivation

intrinsic motivation A drive, or reason to pursue a goal, that comes from inside a person, such as the joy of reading a good book.

extrinsic motivation A drive, or reason to pursue a goal, that arises from the wish to have external rewards, perhaps by earning money or praise.

Motivation is the impulse that propels someone to act. It comes either from a person's own desires or from the social context.

Intrinsic motivation arises from within, when people do something for the joy of doing it: A musician might enjoy making music even if no one else hears it; the sound is intrinsically rewarding. Intrinsic motivation is thought to advance creativity, innovation, and emotional well-being (Weinstein & DeHaan, 2014).

All of Erikson's psychosocial needs—including the young child's initiatives—are intrinsic: A child feels inwardly compelled to act. This is very evident to adults, especially when they are in a hurry as they walk with a child. The adult might say "come quickly, we are late," but their young companion's response to intrinsic motivation is to explore. The child may jump up to walk along a ledge, may stop to throw a snowball, or may pick up a piece of trash to explore.

Extrinsic motivation comes from outside the person, when external praise or some other reinforcement is the goal, such as when a musician plays for applause or money. A 4-year-old might brush his teeth because he is praised, sometimes even rewarded with musical toothbrushes and tasty toothpaste; another 4-year-old might put on her own shoes because she is promised a walk after she does so.

If an extrinsic reward is removed, the behavior may stop unless it has become a habit. Young children might not brush their teeth if parents don't notice and praise them. For most of us, tooth brushing was extrinsically rewarded at first, and that continued long enough for it to become a habit. Then motivation is intrinsic. As adults, tooth brushing has become a comforting, internally motivated routine.

MECKY/The Image Bank/Getty Images

More Fun With Mommy Emotions splash as water does. Thankfully, worries about getting wet did not drown out the joy.

Spontaneous Joy of Children Intrinsic motivation is evident in childhood. Young children play, question, exercise, create, destroy, and explore for the sheer joy of it. That serves them well. For example, a longitudinal study found that 3-year-olds who were strong in intrinsic motivation were, two years later, advanced in early math and literacy (Mokrova et al., 2013). The probable reason: They enjoyed counting things and singing songs—when alone.

In contrast, exaggerated external praise ("Your drawing is amazingly wonderful!") undercuts motivation (Brummelman et al., 2017). If young children believe the praise, they might be afraid to try again, thinking they will not be able to do as well. If they suspect that the praise was inaccurate, they may discount the entire activity.

When playing a game, few young children keep score; intrinsic joy is the goal, more than winning. In fact, young children often claim to have won when objective scoring would say they lost; in this case, the children may really be winners.

Imaginary Friends Intrinsic motivation is also apparent when children invent dialogues for their toys, concentrate on creating a work of art or architecture, or converse with imaginary friends. Invisible companions are rarely encouraged by adults (thus, no extrinsic motivation), but many 2- to 7-year-olds have them.

An international study of 3- to 8-year-olds found that about one child in five said that they had one or more invisible companions, with notable variation by culture: 38 percent of children in the Dominican Republic, but only 5 percent in Nepal, said they had such a friend (Wigger, 2018). Is that because some cultures discourage imagination, so some children did not tell adults about their imaginary friends?

Especially for College Students Is extrinsic or intrinsic motivation more influential in your study efforts? (see response, page 269)

WHAT HAVE YOU LEARNED?

1. How might protective optimism lead to new skills and competencies?
2. What did Erikson think was crucial for young children?
3. Why might impulse control, as with marshmallows, predict adult success?
4. What is an example (not in the text) of intrinsic motivation?
5. What is an example (not in the text) of extrinsic motivation?

Play

Play is timeless and universal—apparent in every part of the world over thousands of years. Many developmentalists believe that play is children's most productive, enjoyable activity (Elkind, 2007; Bateson & Martin, 2013; P. Smith, 2010).

Playmates

Young children play best with *peers,* that is, people of about the same age and social status. Although infants are intrigued by other children, babies play only with toys or adults because peer play requires some social maturation (Bateson & Martin, 2013). Gradually, from age 2 to 6, most children learn how to join a peer group, manage conflict, take turns, find friends, and keep the action going (Şendil & Erden, 2014; Göncü & Gaskins, 2011).

The Historical Context As you remember, one dispute in early education is finding the proper balance between child-centered creative play and teacher-directed learning. This was not an issue a century ago: Most families had many children, few mothers had jobs, and all of the children played outside with neighboring boys and girls of different ages. The older children looked out for the younger ones, and games like tag, hide-and-seek, and stickball allowed everyone to play at their own level.

REUTERS/Akhtar Soomro

Good Over Evil or Evil Over Good? Boys everywhere enjoy "strong man" fantasy play, as the continued popularity of Spider-Man and Superman attests. These boys follow that script. Both are Afghan refugees now in Pakistan.

In 1932, American sociologist Mildred Parten described five stages of play, each more advanced than the previous one:

1. *Solitary:* A child plays alone, unaware of other children playing nearby.
2. *Onlooker:* A child watches other children play.
3. *Parallel:* Children play in similar ways but not together.
4. *Associative:* Children interact, sharing toys, but not taking turns.
5. *Cooperative:* Children play together, creating dramas or taking turns.

Research on contemporary children finds much more age variation than Parten did, perhaps because family size is smaller and parents invest heavily in each child, rarely telling their children to "go out and play and come back when it gets dark." An only child who stayed home, without peers, until kindergarten might stand at the edge of the recess yard, watching (stage 2).

Social Play

Play can be divided into two kinds: solitary *pretend play* and *social play* that occurs with playmates. One meta-analysis of the research on both types of play reports that evidence is weak or mixed regarding pretend play but that social play has much to commend it (Lillard et al., 2013). If social play is prevented, children are less happy and less able to learn.

Children need playmates, because even the most playful parent is outmatched by another child at negotiating the rules of tag, at play-fighting, at pretending to be sick, at killing dragons, and so on. As they interact with peers, children learn emotional regulation, empathy, and cultural understanding. Specifics vary, but "play with peers is one of the most important areas in which children develop positive social skills" (Xu, 2010, p. 496).

rough-and-tumble Play that seems to be rough, as in play wrestling or chasing, but in which there is no intent to harm.

Rough-and-Tumble One form of play is called **rough-and-tumble,** because it looks rough and children seem to tumble over one another. The term was coined by British scientists who studied animals in East Africa (Blurton-Jones, 1976). They noticed that young monkeys often chased, attacked, rolled over in the dirt, and wrestled quite roughly without injuring one another, all while seeming to smile (showing a *play face*).

When the scientists who studied monkeys in Africa returned to London, they saw that puppies, kittens, and even their own children engaged in rough-and-tumble play. Children chase, wrestle, and grab each other, with established rules, facial expressions, and gestures to signify "just pretend."

THINK CRITICALLY: Is "play" an entirely different experience for adults than for children?

Developmentalists now recognize that rough-and-tumble play happens everywhere, with every mammal species, and it has for many thousands of years (Fry, 2014). It is more common among males than females, and it flourishes best in ample space with minimal supervision (Pellegrini, 2013).

Neurological benefits from such play are evident in experiments with rodents. Young rats try to bite the nape of another's neck. If a bite occurs, the two rats switch roles and the bitten tries to bite the other's nape. This is all playful. If rats want to hurt each other, they try to bite organs, not napes. Rat rough-and-tumble play increases rat brain development (Pellis et al., 2018).

Controlled experiments on humans—with some children allowed to play and a matched control group never playing—would be unethical, but correlations suggest that the limbic system connects more strongly with the prefrontal cortex because children engage in rough-and-tumble play. Indeed, longitudinal research on boys who played carefully but roughly with peers and parents finds that they become caring, compassionate men (Fry, 2014; Raeburn, 2014).

Sociodramatic Play

Sociodramatic Play Another major type of play is **sociodramatic play,** in which children act out various roles and plots. Through such acting, children:

- explore and rehearse social roles.
- learn to explain their ideas and persuade playmates.
- practice emotional regulation by pretending to be afraid, angry, brave, and so on.
- develop self-concept in a nonthreatening context.

sociodramatic play Pretend play in which children act out various roles and themes in plots or roles that they create.

Sociodramatic play builds on pretending, which emerges in toddlerhood. But remember that solitary pretending does not advance social skills; dramatic play with peers does. As children combine their imagination with that of their friends, they advance in theory of mind, gaining emotional regulation as they do so (Kavanaugh, 2011; Goldstein & Lerner, 2018).

The prevalence of sociodramatic play varies by culture, with parents and then children following cultural norms. Some cultures find make-believe play frivolous and discourage it; in other cultures, parents teach toddlers to be lions, or robots, or ladies drinking tea. Then children elaborate on those themes (Kavanaugh, 2011). Many young children are avid television watchers, and they act out superhero themes from their favorite shows.

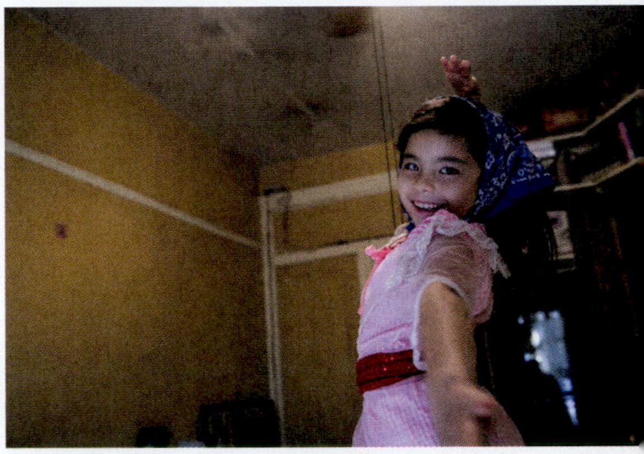

2016 Macmillan

Joy Supreme Pretend play in early childhood is thrilling and powerful. For this dancing 7-year-old from Park Slope, Brooklyn, pretend play overwhelms mundane realities, such as an odd scarf or awkward arm.

Screen Time In North America, most children watch screens more than an hour a day (Carson et al., 2013; Fletcher et al., 2014). That troubles developmentalists for many reasons. One is simply time—the more children are glued to screens, especially when they have their own hand-held device, the less time they have for active play (see **Figure 10.1**). Pediatricians, psychologists, and teachers all report extensive research indicating that screen time reduces conversation, imagination, and outdoor activity (Downing et al., 2017).

Might it be that some children are naturally less active and less talkative, and that makes them less likely to develop language skills and physical health, as well as more likely to use screens? In other words, is the connection between watching television and other problems a correlate, not a cause? That would exonerate the parents who let their children use screens.

Sadly, no. A recent study in Canada of 2,441 children, followed longitudinally from before birth until age 5, found that the average 3-year-old watched more than two hours a day (Madigan et al., 2019). (See Visualizing Development, page 271.)

One result was to "disrupt interactions with caregivers"; another was to reduce cognitive and emotional development. Because this was a careful longitudinal study, these results were not merely correlational (as had been shown many times before) but also causational. These authors suggest screen-free zones or times (e.g., not at dinner, not before bed).

Similar results are found in many nations, with many young children using screens three hours a day, and with far reaching consequences, in obesity, emotional immaturity, intellectual growth. Overall, the American Academy of Pediatrics (2016) recommends no more than an hour a day of any screen time for 2- to 6-year-olds. This organization also urges parents never to let their children watch programs or play games that include

FIGURE 10.1

Learning by Playing Fifty years ago, the average child spent three hours a day in outdoor play. Video games and television have largely replaced that, especially in cities. Children seem safer if parents can keep an eye on them, but what are they learning? The long-term effects on brain and body may be dangerous.

Daily Screen Time for 0- to 8-year-olds in the United States, 2011–2017

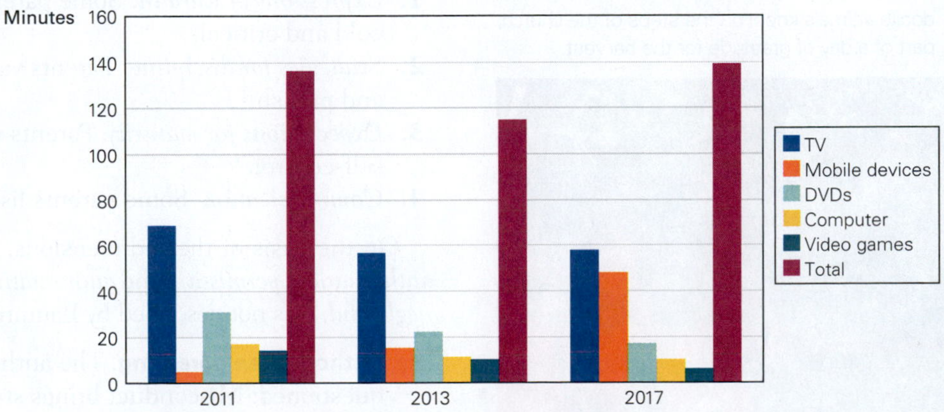

Data from Common Sense Media, 2017.

VIDEO: The Impact of Media on Early Childhood explores how screen time can affect young children's cognition.

violent or sexual media, or racist and sexist stereotypes, and always to watch with the child, interpreting or reinforcing rather than letting the child watch uncritically.

However, most young children watch more than recommended, unsupervised. If you have no children, you might wonder why any parent would allow children to look at screens more than occasionally, or, worse, give a child an iPad for Christmas. If you are a parent, you know why.

WHAT HAVE YOU LEARNED?

1. What are children thought to gain from play?
2. Why does playing with peers increase physical development and emotional regulation?
3. What do children learn from rough-and-tumble play?
4. What do children learn from sociodramatic play?
5. Why do pediatricians want to limit children's screen time?

Challenges for Caregivers

Every developmentalist and every parent realizes that caring for a young child is difficult. Young children are energetic and curious but not wise, and that tests the emotions and skills of every caregiver. Some children, by temperament, are especially challenging. Even more so than compliant children, they need patient parents (Ayoub et al., 2018).

Styles of Caregiving

One challenge for caregivers is choosing how strict or permissive to be. Variations in parenting styles are astonishing: Some are so strict that they seem abusive, and others are so lenient that they seem neglectful. Variations are apparent within nations, within ethnic groups, within neighborhoods, and sometimes within marriages.

authoritarian parenting An approach to child rearing that is characterized by high behavioral standards, strict punishment of misconduct, and little communication from child to parent.

Baumrind's Categories Although thousands of researchers have traced the effects of parenting on child development, the work of one person, 60 years ago, remains influential. Diana Baumrind (1967, 1971) studied 100 preschool children, all from California, almost all middle-class European Americans.

She found that parents differed on four important dimensions:

1. *Expressions of warmth.* Some parents are warm and affectionate; others are cold and critical.
2. *Strategies for discipline.* Parents vary in how they explain, criticize, persuade, and punish.
3. *Expectations for maturity.* Parents vary in expectations for responsibility and self-control.
4. *Communication.* Some parents listen patiently; others demand silence.

Observation Quiz Is the father below authoritarian, authoritative, or permissive? (see answer, page 269) ↓

Protect Me from the Water Buffalo These two are at the Carabao Kneeling Festival. In rural Philippines, hundreds of these large but docile animals kneel on the steps of the church, part of a day of gratitude for the harvest.

REUTERS/Erik de Castro

On the basis of these dimensions, Baumrind identified three parenting styles: *authoritarian, permissive,* and *authoritative* (summarized in **Table 10.1**). A fourth style, *neglectful,* was not described by Baumrind but was suggested by other researchers.

1. **Authoritarian parenting.** The authoritarian parent's word is law, not to be questioned. Misconduct brings strict punishment, usually physical. Authoritarian parents set down clear rules and hold high standards. Discussion about emotions and expressions of affection are rare. One adult raised by

TABLE 10.1

Characteristics of Parenting Styles Identified by Baumrind

				Communication	
Style	**Warmth**	**Discipline**	**Expectations of Maturity**	**Parent to Child**	**Child to Parent**
Authoritarian	Low	Strict, often physical	High	High	Low
Permissive	High	Rare	Low	Low	High
Authoritative	High	Moderate, with much discussion	Moderate	High	High

authoritarian parents said that "How do you feel?" had only two possible answers: "Fine" and "Tired."

2. **Permissive parenting.** Permissive parents (also called *indulgent*) make few demands. Discipline is lax, partly because expectations are low. Permissive parents are nurturing and accepting, listening to whatever their offspring say, which may include "I hate you"—a remark that authoritarian parents would not tolerate.
3. **Authoritative parenting.** Authoritative parents set limits, but they are flexible. They consider themselves guides, not authorities (unlike authoritarian parents) and not friends (unlike permissive parents). The goal of punishment is for the child to understand what was wrong and what should have been done differently.
4. **Neglectful/uninvolved parenting.** Neglectful parents are oblivious to their children's behavior; they seem not to notice. Their children do whatever they want. The child's behavior may be similar to those of the permissive parent, but the parents' attitude is quite different: Neglectful parents do not care, whereas permissive parents care very much.

permissive parenting An approach to child rearing that is characterized by high nurturance and communication but little discipline, guidance, or control.

authoritative parenting An approach to child rearing in which the parents set limits and enforce rules but are flexible and listen to their children.

neglectful/uninvolved parenting An approach to child rearing in which the parents seem indifferent toward their children, not knowing or caring about their children's lives.

Long-term effects of parenting styles have been reported in many nations. Cultural and regional differences are apparent, but authoritative parenting seems best everywhere (Pinquart & Kauser, 2018). The following trends have been found in many studies, although you will soon read that results are not as universal as the early research found.

- *Authoritarian* parents raise children who become conscientious, obedient, and quiet but not especially happy. Such children may feel guilty or depressed, internalizing their frustrations and blaming themselves when things don't go well. As adolescents, they sometimes rebel, striking out on their own before age 20. As adults, they are quick to blame and punish.
- *Permissive* parents raise children who lack self-control. Inadequate emotional regulation makes them immature and impedes friendships, so they are unhappy. They tend to continue to live at home, still dependent on their parents in adulthood.
- *Authoritative* parents raise children who are successful, articulate, happy with themselves, and generous with others. These children are usually liked by teachers and peers, especially in cultures that value individual initiative (e.g., the United States).
- *Neglectful/uninvolved* parents raise children who are immature, sad, lonely, and at risk of injury and abuse, not only in early childhood but also lifelong.

I NEED LOVE
"He's just doing that to get attention."

Harry Bliss/The New Yorker Collection/The Cartoon Bank

Pay Attention Children develop best with lots of love and attention. They shouldn't have to ask for it!

Cultural Differences Given a multicultural and multicontextual perspective, developmentalists realize that many parenting practices are sometimes effective. Indeed, some children are temperamentally happy and wise, and they may become happy and wise adults despite authoritarian or neglectful parents.

But that does not mean that all families function equally well—far from it. Signs of emotional distress, including a child's anxiety, aggression, and inability to play with others, indicate that the family may not be the safe haven of support and guidance that it should be. Neglectful parenting is always harmful, with some children more harmed than others.

A detailed study of Mexican American mothers of 4-year-olds noted 1,477 instances when the mothers tried to change their children's behavior. Most of the time the mothers simply uttered a command and the children complied (Livas-Dlott et al., 2010).

This simple strategy, with the mother asserting authority and the children obeying without question, might be considered authoritarian. Almost never, however, did the mothers use physical punishment or even harsh threats when the children did not immediately do as they were told—which happened 14 percent of the time. For example:

> Hailey [the 4-year-old] decided to look for another doll and started digging through her toys, throwing them behind her as she dug. Maricruz [the mother] told Hailey she should not throw her toys. Hailey continued to throw toys, and Maricruz said her name to remind her to stop. Hailey continued her misbehavior, and her mother repeated "Hailey" once more. When Hailey continued, Maricruz raised her voice but calmly directed, "Hailey, look at me." Hailey continued but then looked at Maricruz as she explained, "You don't throw toys; you could hurt someone." Finally, Hailey complied and stopped.
>
> *[Livas-Dlott et al., 2010, p. 572]*

Note that the mother's first three efforts failed, and then a "look" accompanied by an explanation (albeit inaccurate, no one could be hurt) succeeded. These Mexican American families did not fit any of Baumrind's categories. Respect (*respeto*) did not mean an authoritarian style. Instead, the relationship shows evident caring (*cariño*) (Livas-Dlott et al., 2010).

As in this example, parenting practices may arise from cultural values that sometimes work well (Butler & Titus, 2015). Adults may prematurely judge other adults as too strict or too permissive. However, some parents *are* too strict or too permissive. Harsh or cold parenting is always harmful, increasing child anger and aggression no matter what the culture or the nature of the child (Dyer et al., 2014; Wang & Liu, 2018).

Discipline

Children misbehave. They do not always do what adults want them to do. Sometimes they do not know better, or the adults demand too much of an immature child. However, sometimes children deliberately ignore a request or even do exactly what they have been told not to do.

Misbehavior is part of growing up, but children need guidance to keep them safe and strong. Parents must respond when the child does something forbidden, dangerous, or mean. Most parents find some way to punish their children, especially during early childhood.

Rates of punishment increase dramatically after infancy (when it is rare) and later decrease, when children are more capable of self-discipline. During early childhood, most parents use several methods to discipline their children (Thompson et al., 2017). Every form of discipline has critics as well as defenders (Larzelere et al., 2017).

Physical Punishment In the United States, young children are slapped, spanked, or beaten more often than are infants or older children, and more often than children in Canada or western Europe. Spanking is more frequent:

- in the southern United States than in New England.
- by mothers than by fathers.
- among conservative Christians than among nonreligious families.
- among African Americans than among European Americans.
- among European Americans than among Asian Americans.
- among U.S.-born Hispanics than among immigrant Hispanics.
- in low-SES families than in high-SES families (MacKenzie et al., 2011; S. Lee et al., 2015; Lee & Altschul, 2015).

These are general trends, but be careful of stereotypes. Contrary to these generalizations, some African American mothers living in the South never spank, and some secular, European American, high-SES fathers in New England routinely do. Local norms matter, but individual parents make their own decisions, and neighbors may disagree.

Many people are especially troubled about physical punishment (called **corporal punishment** because it hurts the body). Such punishment usually succeeds momentarily because children become quiet, but longitudinal research finds that corporally punished children are more disobedient later on and are more likely to become child bullies, adolescent delinquents, and then abusive adults (Gershoff et al., 2012).

Variation in norms is evident. In most developed nations, corporal punishment is illegal; in many other nations, it is the norm. A massive international study of low- and moderate-income nations found that 63 percent of 2- to 5-year-olds had been physically punished (slapped, spanked, hit with an object) in the past month (Deater-Deckard & Lansford, 2016).

Many spanked children become fine adults. Nonetheless, a correlation between spanking and aggression is found in all ethnic groups, in many nations (Lansford et al., 2014; Wang & Liu, 2018). Children who are *not* spanked are *more* likely to develop self-control. (See Opposing Perspectives on page 258.)

Although some adults believe that physical punishment will "teach a lesson" to behave, others argue that the lesson learned is that "might makes right." Children who were physically disciplined tend to become more aggressive (Thompson et al., 2017). They also are more likely to use corporal punishment on others—first on their classmates, later on their partners, and then on their children.

Paddling in Schools In more than 100 nations, physical punishment is illegal in any educational setting. However, each state of the United States sets its own law, and teachers may legally paddle children in 22 of them. Overall, in the United States in one recent year, 218,466 children were corporally punished at school. Sixteen percent of those children had intellectual disorders, and a disproportionate number were African American boys (Morones, 2013; Gershoff et al., 2015).

A study in one American state that allows corporal punishment in school (Arkansas) reports that whether or not a child is physically punished depends more on the school culture than on the state or district policy. The rate of discipline in Arkansas in the 2015–2016 school year was 59 per 100 students, with 5 per 100 including physical punishment.

Interpret those statistics carefully. A ratio of 59 punishments per 100 students does not mean that more than half of the students were disciplined. Instead, some students experienced more than 10 punishments (some were paddled several

UrbanZone/Alamy Stock Photo

Smack Will the doll learn never to disobey her mother again?

corporal punishment Disciplinary techniques that hurt the body (*corpus*) of someone, from spanking to serious harm, including death.

Especially for Parents Suppose you agree that spanking is destructive, but you sometimes get so angry at your child's behavior that you hit him or her. Is your reaction appropriate? (see response, page 269)

OPPOSING PERSPECTIVES

Spare the Rod?

Opinions about spanking are influenced by past experience and cultural norms. That makes it hard for opposing perspectives to be understood by people on the other side (Ferguson, 2013). Try to suspend your own assumptions as you read this.

What might be right with spanking? Over the centuries, many parents have done it, so it has stood the test of time and has been a popular choice. Spanking is less common in the twenty-first century than in the twentieth (Taillieu et al., 2014).

However, 85 percent of U.S. adolescents who were children at the end of the twentieth century recall being slapped or spanked by their mothers (Bender et al., 2007). In low- and middle-income nations, more than a third of the mothers believe that physical punishment is essential to raise a child well (Deater-Deckard & Lansford, 2016).

Those who are pro-spanking need to explain the correlations reported by developmentalists (between spanking and later depression, low achievement, aggression, crime, and so on). They suggest that a third variable, not spanking itself, is the reason for that connection. One possible third variable is misbehavior: Perhaps disobedient children cause spanking, not vice versa. Such children may become delinquent, depressed, and so on not *because* they were spanked but *in spite of* being spanked.

Noting problems with correlational research, one team explains, "Quite simply, parents do not need to use corrective actions when there are no problems to correct" (Larzelere & Cox, 2013, p. 284). As these authors explain, although it is true that children who are spanked frequently are also children who misbehave frequently, the punishment may be the result of the child's actions, not the cause.

Further, since parents who spank their children often have less education and money than other parents, low SES may be another crucial variable. Perhaps spanking is a symptom of poverty and poor parenting. If that is true, the way to reduce the low achievement, aggression, and depression that correlates with spanking is to increase education and reduce poverty, not to ban spanking (Ferguson, 2013).

Another criticism is the way in which the scientists define spanking. If they do not distinguish between severe corporal punishment and milder, occasional spanking, then the data will show that spanking is harmful—but that conclusion may reflect the harmful effects of severe punishment (Larzelere et al., 2017).

What might be wrong with spanking? One problem is adults' emotions: Angry spankers may become abusive. Children have been seriously injured and even killed by parents who use corporal punishment.

Another problem is the child's immature cognition. Parents assume that the transgression is obvious, but children may think that the parents' anger, not the child's actions, caused spanking (Harkness et al., 2011). Most parents tell their children why they are being spanked, but when they are hit, children are less likely to listen or understand.

Almost all of the research finds that children who are physically punished suffer overall (Grogan-Kaylo et al., 2018). Compared to children punished in other ways, they are more depressed, antisocial, and lonely. Many hate school and have few close friends. Emotional and social problems in adulthood are more common in people who were spanked as children—true for relatively mild spanking as well as for more severe spanking.

One reason for these correlations is that spanked children more often have angry, depressed, unloving parents. However, even among children of warm and loving parents, spanked children tend to be more anxious, worried about doing something to lose their parents' affection (Lansford et al., 2014).

Of course, there are exceptions—spanked children who become happy and successful adults. For example, one U.S. study found that conservative Protestant parents spanked their children more often than other parents, but if that spanking occurred *only* in early (not middle) childhood, the children did not develop low self-esteem and increased aggression (Ellison et al., 2011).

The authors of the study suggest that, since spanking was the norm in that group, the children believed they were loved. Moreover, religious leaders tell parents never to spank in anger. As a result, their children may "view mild-to-moderate corporal punishment as legitimate, appropriate, and even an indicator of parental involvement, commitment, and concern" (Ellison et al., 2011, p. 957).

Another study of conservative Christians found that many thought their faith condoned spanking. Only when they learned biblical lessons opposing spanking (e.g., that "sparing the rod" refers to the guiding rod that shepherds use, which was never used to punish), and learned research on the long-term harm, did they change their minds (Perrin et al., 2017). Many then conclude that physical punishment is contrary to their belief in love and forgiveness.

As I write these words, I know which perspective is mine. I am one of many developmentalists who believe that alternatives to spanking are better for children and a safeguard against abuse. Indeed, the same study that found spanking common in developing nations also reported that 17 percent of the children experienced severe violence that no developmentalist would condone (Bornstein et al., 2016). That alone is reason to stop.

Nonetheless, a dynamic-systems, multicultural perspective reminds me that everyone is influenced by background and context. I know that I am; so is every scientist, and so are you.

times), while most (especially the younger girls) were never punished. Rates were much higher in middle schools than elementary schools. The most common infractions were "minor, non-violent," when students did not obey their teacher or follow school guidelines.

THINK CRITICALLY: The varying rates of physical punishment in schools could be the result of prejudice, or they could be because some children misbehave more than others. Which is it?

In Arkansas as well as nationwide, school culture is changing. In most communities, paddling decreased over the past decade. However, suspensions (the school equivalent of time-out) increased (McKenzie & Ritter, 2017).

Alternatives to Spanking If spanking is bad but discipline is good, what is a parent to do? Some employ **psychological control,** using children's shame, guilt, and gratitude to control their behavior (Barber, 2002). But this has its own problems (Alegre, 2011).

psychological control A disciplinary technique that involves threatening to withdraw love and support, using a child's feelings of guilt and gratitude to the parents.

Consider Finland, where corporal punishment is forbidden. In one study, psychological control was measured by how much parents agreed with the following statements:

1. "My child should be aware of how much I have done for him/her."
2. "I let my child see how disappointed and shamed I am if he/she misbehaves."
3. "My child should be aware of how much I sacrifice for him/her."
4. "I expect my child to be grateful and appreciate all the advantages he/she has."

The higher the parents scored on these four measures of psychological control, the lower the children's math scores were—and this connection grew stronger over time. Moreover, the children tended to have negative emotions (depression, anger, and so on) (Aunola et al., 2013).

Another disciplinary technique that is often used in North America is the **time-out,** in which a misbehaving child is required to sit quietly, without toys or playmates, for a short time. Time-out is not to be done in anger, or for too long; it is recommended that parents use a calm voice and that the time-out last only one to five minutes (Morawska & Sanders, 2011). Time-out is punishment if the child enjoys "time-in," when the child is engaged with parents or with peers.

time-out A disciplinary technique in which a person is separated from other people and activities for a specified time.

induction A disciplinary technique in which the parent tries to get the child to understand why a certain behavior was wrong. Listening, not lecturing, is crucial.

Time-out is favored by many experts. For example, in the large, longitudinal evaluation of Head Start cited in Chapter 9, an increase in time-outs and a decrease in spankings were considered signs of improved parental discipline (U.S. Department of Health and Human Services, 2010).

However, the same team who criticized the correlation between spanking and misbehavior also criticized the research favoring time-out. They added, "misbehavior is motivated by wanting to escape from the situation . . . time-out reinforces the misbehavior" (Larzelere & Cox, 2013, p. 289).

Often combined with the time-out is another alternative to physical punishment and psychological control—**induction,** in which the parents discuss the infraction with their child, hoping the children themselves will realize why their behavior was wrong. Ideally, a strong and affectionate parent–child relationship allows children to express their emotions and allows parents to listen.

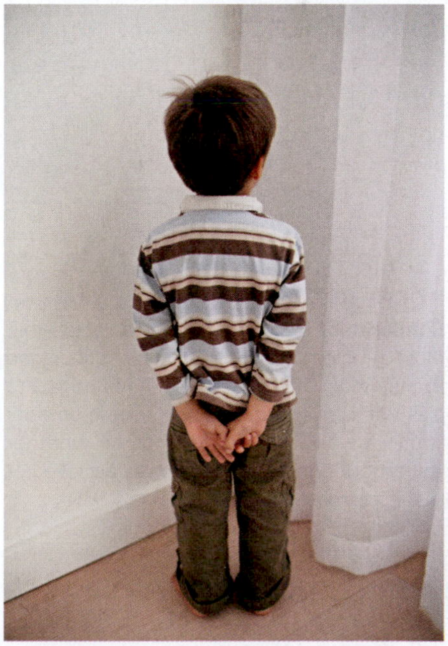

PeopleImages/E+/DigitalVision/Getty Images

Bad Boy or Bad Parent? For some children and in some cultures, sitting alone is an effective form of punishment. Sometimes, however, it produces an angry child without changing the child's behavior.

Induction takes time and patience, and, like other disciplinary measures, it does not always succeed. One problem is that young children confuse causes with consequences and tend to think they behaved properly, given the situation. Simple induction ("Why did he cry?") may be appropriate, but even that is hard before a child develops theory of mind. Nonetheless, induction may pay off over time. Children whose parents used induction when they were 3-year-olds became children with fewer externalizing problems in elementary school (Choe et al., 2013b).

What do parents actually do? A survey of discipline in early childhood found that most parents use more than one method (Thompson et al., 2017). In the United States, time-out is the most common punishment, and about half of the parents sometimes spank. The survey found that other methods—induction, counting, distraction, hand-smacking, removal of a toy or activity—were also used.

Specifics of parenting style and punishment seem less crucial than whether or not children know that they are loved, guided, and appreciated (Grusec et al., 2017). Some parents may seem to be authoritarian, but the crucial variable is how loving and warm they are: If that love is evident, their children may have higher achievement and pride than their peers (Pinquart & Kauser, 2018).

Becoming Boys and Girls: Sex and Gender

Another challenge is to promote a healthy understanding of sex and gender so that children are proud of themselves and accepting of others (Wilcox & Kline, 2013).

Biology determines whether an embryo is male or female (except in rare cases): Those XX or XY chromosomes shape organs and produce hormones, creating **sex differences,** which are physiological. That is distinct from **gender differences,** which are both social and cultural. In theory this distinction seems simple; in practice it is complex. Regarding sex and gender, scientists need to "treat culture and biology not as separate influences but as interacting components of nature and nurture" (Eagly & Wood, 2013, p. 349).

sex differences Biological differences between males and females, in organs, hormones, and body shape.

gender differences Differences in male and female roles, behaviors, clothes, and so on that arise from society, not biology.

Although infants already show some awareness of gender differences (in their use of pronouns, for instance), ages 3 to 5 are when children develop their gender identities. Boys and girls typically choose toys, clothes, and so on that are designated for their sex. Indeed, many children are quite rigid, with girls choosing frilly pink dresses and boys avoiding anything "girly" (Halim et al., 2014).

Many, but not all, adults try to be gender-neutral, believing that they treat their sons and daughters the same; but in practice most follow long-standing gender norms. A 2017 survey found that most adults thought parents should encourage their children to play with toys associated with the other sex, but a sizable minority disagreed (Parker et al., 2017) (see **Figure 10.2**).

The strongest disagreement was expressed by men regarding boys: 43 percent of the men thought boys should not be encouraged to do things usually stereotyped for girls, such as care for dolls, jump rope, or wear bracelets.

Transgender Children Sex and gender issues are complex. Some children identify as *transgender,* identifying as being a gender which is not their assigned sex at birth. This presents their parents with a new awareness of childhood gender variance (Rahilly, 2015). It is one thing to allow young girls to climb trees and

FIGURE 10.2
Similarities? What is more remarkable—that most people think girls should be encouraged to play with trucks and boys encouraged to play with dolls, or that some people do not? Your answer probably depends on whether you thought gender equality was achieved or is still far away.

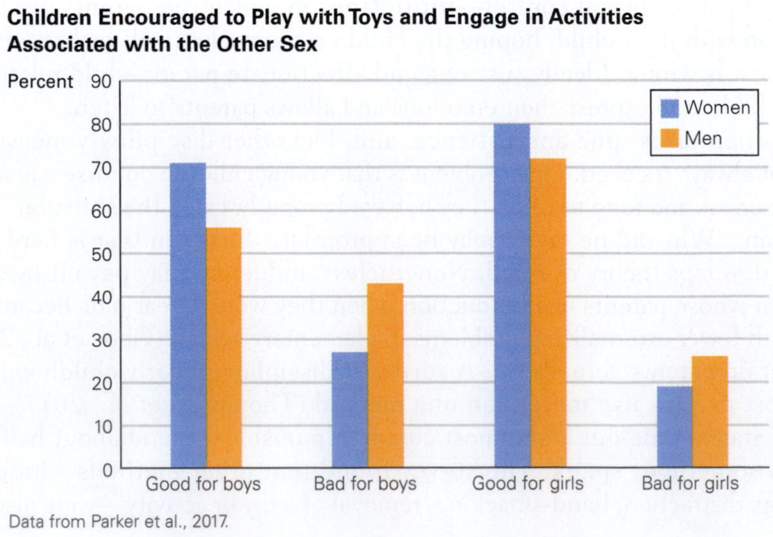

young boys to jump rope, but it may be harder to accept that a child has quite distinct ideas about what gender they are, when that gender is not the one on their birth certificate. One mother said:

> Since he was two, all he can say is that he wants to be a girl, or that he is a girl. He knows that he is not, but there is no way to change his mind. He is 6 now, and he still asks me everyday "Mom, can I be a girl when I grow up?"
>
> [*quoted in Malpas, 2011, p. 453*]

In that case, the parents were counseled in ways to protect the child, although the father, particularly, wanted his son to become a man.

Unlike in that family, some parents during early childhood (when gender nonconforming children are insistent) accept their gender nonconforming child. That is made easier if the parents see their children as individuals and are able to handle any anxiety they experience about having a child who is gender nonconforming (Ehrensaft, 2011).

A study of 36 transgender children, whose parents accepted their transition to the other sex before age 6, compared them with their siblings and with gender-typical children who were the same age. The study found that all of the children had definite ideas of what clothes, toys, and activities they preferred. The transgender children chose whatever conformed to their gender, just as the gender-typical children did (Fast & Olsen, 2018).

Mike Belleme

Not Emma In a North Carolina kindergarten, each child had an "All About Me" day in which the teacher would draw a picture of the child for all of the other children to copy. Emma was born with male sex organs but identifies as a girl. On her day, she proudly wore a light-pink shirt with a heart, pink glittery shoes, and long hair—and she came home bawling because the teacher drew this picture with her "boy name" (barely visible here). Her parents consoled her, had her edit her name and draw longer hair, with some other additions. Should children be allowed to be who they believe they are?

Gender in Early Childhood Already by age 2, children use gender labels (*Mrs., Mr., lady, man*) consistently. By age 4, children believe that certain toys (such as dolls or trucks) and roles (Daddy, Mommy, nurse, teacher, police officer, soldier) are reserved for one sex or the other, even when their experience is otherwise. As one expert explains:

> [F]our-year-olds say that girls will always be girls and will never become boys. . . . they are often more absolute about gender than adults are. They'll tell their very own pants-suited doctor mother that girls wear dresses and women are nurses.
>
> [*Gopnik, 2016, p. 140*]

Although they do not understand the biology of sex differences, many children accept rigid male–female roles. Despite their parents' and teachers' wishes, children say, "No girls [or boys] allowed." Most older children consider ethnic discrimination immoral, but they accept some sex discrimination (Møller & Tenenbaum, 2011). Transgender children, likewise, are insistent that they are not the sex that their parents thought (Rahilly, 2015), rather than suggesting that gender roles themselves are too narrow.

Why are male and female distinctions recognized by 2-year-olds, significant to 5-year-olds, and accepted as proper by 10-year-olds? All of the major theories "devote considerable attention to gender differences" (Bornstein et al., 2016, p. 10) because they all recognize that this is a major concern in middle childhood. Each, however, "attributes distinct causes for gender differences" (Bornstein et al., 2016, p, 11). Consider the theories in Chapter 2.

Psychodynamic Theory Freud (1938/1995) called the period from about ages 3 to 6 the **phallic stage,** named after the *phallus,* the Greek word for penis. At age 3 or 4, according to Freud, boys become aware of their male sexual organ. They masturbate, fear castration, and develop sexual feelings toward their mother.

These feelings make every young boy jealous of his father—so jealous, according to Freud, that he wants to replace his dad. Freud called this the **Oedipus complex,** after Oedipus, son of a king in Greek mythology.

Abandoned as an infant and raised in a distant kingdom, Oedipus returned to his birthplace and, without realizing it, killed his father and married his mother. When he discovered the horror, he blinded himself.

phallic stage Freud's third stage of development, when the penis becomes the focus of concern and pleasure.

Oedipus complex The unconscious desire of young boys to replace their fathers and win their mothers' exclusive love.

Freud believed that this ancient story (immortalized in *Oedipus Rex,* a play written by Sophocles and first presented in Athens in 429 B.C.E.) is still presented every year somewhere in the world because it evokes unconscious wishes in everyone.

Freud hypothesized that every young boy feels guilty about his incestuous and murderous impulses. In self-defense, the boy develops a powerful conscience called the **superego,** which is quick to judge and punish.

superego In psychodynamic theory, the judgmental part of the personality that internalizes the moral standards of the parents.

That marks the beginning of morality, according to psychodynamic theory. This theory contends that a small boy's fascination with superheroes, guns, kung fu, and the like arises from his unconscious impulse to kill his father. Further, an adult man's homosexuality, homophobia, or obsession with guns, pornography, prostitutes, or hell arises from problems at the phallic stage.

Freud thought that girls also want to eliminate their same-sex parent (mother) and become intimate with the opposite-sex parent (father). For Freud, that explained why many 5-year-old girls dress in frills and lace and are happy to be "Daddy's girl."

Many psychologists criticize psychodynamic theory as being unscientific. That was my opinion in graduate school, so I dismissed Freud's ideas and deliberately dressed my baby girls in blue, not pink, so that they would not follow stereotypes. However, scientists seek to reconcile theory and experience. My daughters made me reconsider. (See A Case to Study.)

A CASE TO STUDY

The Berger Daughters

It began when my eldest daughter, Bethany, was about 4 years old:

Bethany: When I grow up, I'm going to marry Daddy.
Me: But Daddy's married to me.
Bethany: That's OK. When I grow up, you'll probably be dead.
Me: *[Determined to stick up for myself]* Daddy's older than me, so when I'm dead, he'll probably be dead, too.
Bethany: That's OK. I'll marry him when he gets born again.

I was dumbfounded, without a good reply. Bethany saw my face fall, and she took pity on me:

Bethany: Don't worry, Mommy. After you get born again, you can be our baby.

The second episode was a conversation I had with Rachel when she was about 5:

Rachel: When I get married, I'm going to marry Daddy.
Me: Daddy's already married to me.
Rachel: *[With the joy of having discovered a wonderful plan]* Then we can have a double wedding!

The third episode was considerably more graphic. It took the form of a "Valentine" left on my husband's pillow on February 14th by my daughter Elissa (see **Figure 10.3**).

FIGURE 10.3
Pillow Talk Elissa placed this artwork on my husband's pillow. My pillow, beside it, had a less colorful, less elaborate note—an afterthought. It read, "Dear Mom, I love you too."

Finally, when Sarah turned 5, she also said she would marry her father. I tried one more time: I told her she couldn't, because he was married to me. Her response revealed the hazard of screen time: "Oh, yes, a man can have two wives. I saw it on television."

As you remember from Chapter 1, a single example (or four daughters from one family) does not prove that Freud was correct. I still think he was wrong on many counts. But, his description of the phallic stage seems less bizarre than I once thought.

Behaviorism Behaviorists believe that virtually all roles, values, and morals are learned. To behaviorists, gender distinctions result from reinforcement, punishment, and social learning, evident in early childhood.

Indeed, the push toward traditional gender-typed behavior in play and chores (washing dishes versus fixing cars) is among the most robust findings of decades of research on this topic (Eagly & Wood, 2013). For example, a 2-year-old boy who asks for a train and a doll for his birthday is more likely to get the train. Gender differences are taught more to boys than girls.

Gender differentiation may be subtle, with adults unaware that they are reinforcing traditional masculine or feminine behavior. For example, parents talking to young children mention numbers and shapes more often with their sons (Chang et al., 2011; Pruden & Levine, 2017).

This may be a precursor to the boys becoming more interested in math and science later on. Even with infants, fathers interact differently with their children, singing and talking more to their daughters but using words of achievement, such as *proud* and *win,* more with their sons (Mascaro et al., 2017).

According to *social learning theory*, people model themselves after people they perceive to be nurturing, powerful, and yet similar to themselves. For young children, those people are usually their parents. Adults are the most gender-typed of their entire lives when they are raising young children, so, according to social learning theory, children also are gender-typed.

Generally, if an employed woman is ever to leave her job to become a housewife, it is when she has a baby. Fathers tend to work longer hours—they are home less often—and mothers work fewer hours when children arrive. Since children learn gender roles from their parents, it is no surprise that they are quite sexist (Hallers-Haalboom et al., 2014). They follow the examples they see, unaware that their very existence is the reason for that behavior.

Reinforcement for distinct male and female actions is widespread. As the president of the Society for Research in Child Development observes, "parents, teachers, and peers . . . continue to encourage, model, and enforce traditional gender messages" (Liben, 2016, p. 24). The 3-year-old boy who brings his Barbie doll to preschool will be punished—not physically, but with words and social exclusion—by his male classmates. As social learning increases from age 2 to 22, so does gender divergence.

Observation Quiz How can you tell that she is going out and he is staying home? (see answer, page 269)

Robert Houser/UpperCut Images/Getty Images

Remarkable Social Learning No, not both children brushing their teeth at the same time while their parents watch, but the husband staying home while the wife gets ready for her job. This family is similar to about a million other families with employed moms and child-care dads.

Cognitive Theory Cognitive theory offers an alternative explanation for the strong gender identity of 5-year-olds (Kohlberg et al., 1983). Remember that cognitive theorists focus on how children understand various ideas. Children develop a **gender schema,** which is their own concept of male–female differences (Bem, 1981; Martin et al., 2011).

gender schema A child's cognitive concept or general belief about male and female differences.

As cognitive theorists point out, young children tend to perceive the world in simple, egocentric terms, explained in Chapter 9. Therefore, they categorize male and female as opposites. Nuances, complexities, exceptions, and gradations about gender (and about everything else) are beyond them.

During the preoperational stage, appearance is stronger than logic. One group of researchers who endorse the cognitive interpretation note that "young children pass through a stage of gender appearance rigidity; girls insist on wearing dresses, often pink and frilly, whereas boys refuse to wear anything with a hint of femininity" (Halim et al., 2014, p. 1091).

Cognitive theory explains some of the amusing mistakes that children make in their theories of gender. In one preschool, the young children themselves decided

Same Situation, Far Apart: Culture Clash? He wears the orange robes of a Buddhist monk, and she wears the hijab of a Muslim girl. Although he is at a weeklong spiritual retreat led by the Dalai Lama and she is in an alley in Pakistan, both carry universal toys—a pop gun and a bride doll, identical to those found almost everywhere.

DIPTENDU DUTTA/AFP/GETTY IMAGES

Ilyas Dean/The Image Works

that one wash-up basin was for boys and the other for girls. That fits the cognitive schema that everything can be divided into male or female.

But another cognitive mandate for 3-year-olds is to do whatever it takes to get what you want. A young girl started to use the boys' basin.

> **Boy:** This is for the boys.
> **Girl:** Stop it. I'm not a girl and a boy, so I'm here.
> **Boy:** What?
> **Girl:** I'm a boy and also a girl.
> **Boy:** You, now, are you today a boy?
> **Girl:** Yes.
> **Boy:** And tomorrow what will you be?
> **Girl:** A girl. Tomorrow I'll be a girl. Today I'll be a boy.
> **Boy:** And after tomorrow?
> **Girl:** I'll be a girl.
>
> *[Ehrlich & Blum-Kulka, 2014, p. 31]*

This incident occurred in Israel, where women have been drafted into the army and have served as national leaders for decades. Probably this girl had been told that some gender restrictions are unfair to females, and she appropriated that message when she wanted to wash up. Neither she nor the boy questioned the overall binary, however.

Sociocultural Theory Gender distinctions are pervasive in every culture (Starr & Zurbriggen, 2016). Even in the most gender-equal nations, women do much more child care, house cleaning, and meal preparation than do men. This is true even when women are the primary wage earners for their families (as are about 40 percent of mothers in the United States) (Bornstein & Putnick, 2016).

Furthermore, cultures socialize young girls and boys differently. For example, two 4-year-old girls might hug each other and hear "how sweet," but a boy who hugs a boy might be pushed away. Already by age 6, rough-and-tumble play is the only accepted way that boys touch each other. It is no surprise that such play is much more common in boys than girls.

Parents encourage gender differences sometimes without realizing it. For instance, a massive study of 41 low- and middle-income nations found that fathers took their young boys outside more often than their girls. They also were more likely to read to, tell stories to, and count with their sons. The mothers tended to be more unisex in their activities (Bornstein & Putnick, 2016).

By age 6, children are astute "gender detectives," seeking out ways that males and females differ in their culture and then trying to follow the lead of others of their sex. Mia is one example:

> On her first day of school, Mia sits at the lunch table eating a peanut butter and jelly sandwich. She notices that a few boys are eating peanut butter and jelly, but not one girl is. When her father picks her up from school, Mia runs up to him and exclaims, "Peanut butter and jelly is for boys! I want a turkey sandwich tomorrow."
>
> *[quoted in C. Miller et al., 2013, p. 307]*

Evolutionary Theory Evolutionary theory holds that sexual passion is a basic human drive because all creatures must reproduce. Since conception requires an ovum and a sperm, males and females follow their evolutionary mandate by seeking to attract the other sex—walking, talking, and laughing in traditional feminine or masculine ways. That awakens sexual impulses in the other sex, assuring that the species will continue.

Evolutionary theory emphasizes the urge to survive as well as the urge to reproduce. Over millennia of human history, genes, chromosomes, and hormones dictate that young boys are more active (rough-and-tumble play) and girls more domestic (playing house). That prepared them for adulthood, when fathers needed to defend against predators and mothers needed to feed the children.

That is not needed today. No tigers and bears prowl outside and children, but evolution still produces impulses needed 100,000 years ago.

Biz Jones / ImageSource /Age Fotostock

Gender-Nonconforming The dad, not the daughter. Like many 6-year-olds, she loves wearing her frilly dress, and like many fathers he allows her to follow traditional roles, here by letting her put a tiara on his head.

Teaching Right and Wrong

Parents want their children to develop a morality that is in accord with the parents' values. Young children are ready to learn morality from their parents, an outgrowth of bonding, attachment, and cognitive maturation. Even infants have a sense of right and wrong, believing it is better to be helpful to someone else and it is wrong to hurt them (Hamlin & Van de Vondervoort, 2018).

The survival of our species depended on protection, cooperation, and even sacrifice for one another. Humans needed group defense against harsh conditions and large predators. Morality evolved because humans need each other to survive (Dunning, 2011). Thus, hormones (oxytocin, vasopressin) push people toward trust, love, and morality (Zak, 2012).

macmillan learning

VIDEO: Interview with Lawrence Walker discusses what parents can do to encourage their children's moral development.

Empathy With the cognitive advances of early childhood, and increased interaction with peers, these innate moral impulses are strengthened. Children develop **empathy,** an understanding of other people's feelings and concerns.

Empathy leads to compassion and **prosocial behavior**—helpfulness and kindness without any obvious personal benefit. Expressing concern, offering to share, and including a shy child in a game are examples of children's prosocial behavior. The opposite is **antisocial behavior,** intentionally hurting other people.

Prosocial behavior seems to result more from emotion than from intellect, more from empathy than from theory (Eggum et al., 2011). The origins of prosocial behavior can be traced to parents who help children understand their own

empathy The ability to understand the emotions and concerns of another person, especially when they differ from one's own.

prosocial behavior Actions that are helpful and kind but that are of no obvious benefit to the person doing them.

antisocial behavior Actions that are deliberately hurtful or destructive to another person.

Liz Banfield/Photolibrary/Getty Images

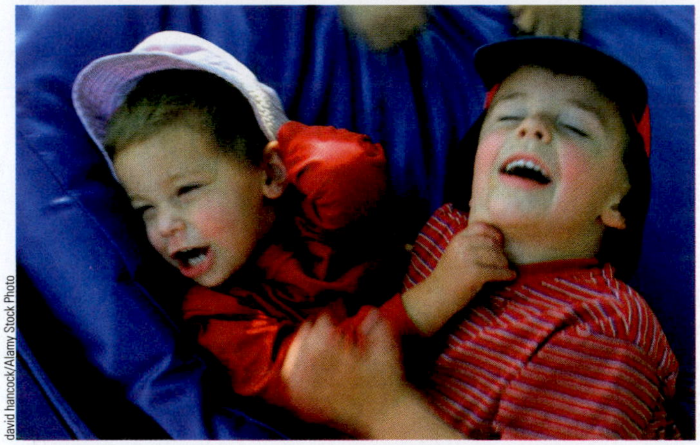

david hancock/Alamy Stock Photo

Pinch, Poke, or Pat Antisocial and prosocial responses are actually a sign of maturation: Babies do not recognize the impact of their actions. These children have much more to learn, but they already are quite social.

emotions, not from parents who tell children what emotions others might have (Brownell et al., 2013).

Prosocial reactions are inborn but not automatic. Some children limit empathy by "avoiding contact with the person in need [which illustrates] . . . the importance of emotion development and regulation in the development of prosocial behavior" (Trommsdorff & Cole, 2011, p. 136). Feeling distress may be a part of nature, but whether and how a child expresses it is nurture.

Antipathy Empathy is evident even in 2-month-olds, who mirror the smiles of other people. However, by early childhood, **antipathy** is also apparent, as children express a strong dislike for some people.

Antipathy leads to antisocial actions, which include verbal insults, social exclusion, and physical assaults. A 2-year-old might look at another child, scowl, and then kick hard without provocation. Generally, parents and teachers teach better behavior, and children become more prosocial and less antisocial with age (Ramani et al., 2010).

An interesting example comes from attitudes about possessions. Two-year-olds find it hard to share, even to let another child use a crayon that they have already used and no longer need. They have a sense of ownership: A teacher's crayon should be shared, but if a child brought it, the other children believe that child is allowed to be selfish (Neary & Friedman, 2014).

The rules of ownership are understood by children as young as 3, who apply them quite strictly. Consider how this develops over time. Some adolescents come to blows over sunglasses or shoes; some adults kill over what belongs to whom. Others are much more willing to lose, share, or give away.

Aggression Early childhood is prime time for both aggressive behavior and victimization: Almost every young child is both an aggressor and a victim at some point (Saracho, 2016). Not surprisingly, given their moral sensibilities, young children judge whether another child's actions are fair or not.

The focus at first is on effects, not motives: A child who accidentally spilled water on another's painting may be the target of that child's anger.

As young children gain in social understanding, particularly theory of mind, they gradually become better at understanding intentions, and that makes them more likely to forgive an accident (Choe et al., 2013a) and to understand harm from omission not just commission.

Researchers recognize four general types of aggression, each of which is evident in early childhood (see **Table 10.2**).

Instrumental aggression is common among 2-year-olds, who often want something and try to get it. This is called *instrumental* because it is a tool, or instrument, for getting something that is desired. The harm in grabbing a toy, and hitting if someone resists, is not understood.

Because instrumental aggression occurs, **reactive aggression** also is common among young children. Almost every child reacts when hurt, whether or not the hurt was deliberate. The reaction may be aggressive—a child might punch in response to an unwelcome remark.

THINK CRITICALLY: How much of your own readiness to share or not is innate, and how much is learned?

antipathy Feelings of dislike or even hatred for another person.

instrumental aggression Hurtful behavior that is intended to get something that another person has.

reactive aggression An impulsive retaliation for another person's intentional or accidental hurtful action.

TABLE 10.2

The Four Forms of Aggression

Type of Aggression	Definition	Comments
Instrumental aggression	Hurtful behavior that is aimed at gaining something (such as a toy, a place in line, or a turn on the swing) that someone else has	Apparent from age 2 to 6; involves objects more than people; quite normal; more egocentric than antisocial.
Reactive aggression	An impulsive retaliation for a hurt (intentional or accidental) that can be verbal or physical	Indicates a lack of emotional regulation, characteristic of 2-year-olds. A 5-year-old can usually stop and think before reacting.
Relational aggression	Nonphysical acts, such as insults or social rejection, aimed at harming the social connections between the victim and others	Involves a personal attack and thus is directly antisocial; can be very hurtful; more common as children become socially aware.
Bullying aggression	Unprovoked, repeated physical or verbal attack, especially on victims who are unlikely to defend themselves	In both bullies and victims, a sign of poor emotional regulation; adults should intervene before the school years. (Bullying is discussed in Chapter 13.)

Relational aggression (usually verbal) destroys self-esteem and disrupts social networks. A child might tell another, "You can't be my friend" or "You are fat," hurting another's feelings. Worse, a child might spread rumors, or tell others not to play with so-and-so.

relational aggression Nonphysical acts, such as insults or social rejection, aimed at harming the social connection between the victim and other people.

bullying aggression Unprovoked, repeated physical or verbal attack, especially on victims who are unlikely to defend themselves.

The fourth and most ominous type is **bullying aggression**, which is done to dominate. Bullying aggression occurs among young children but should be stopped before kindergarten, when it becomes more destructive. Not only does it destroy the self-esteem of victims, it also impairs the later development of the bullies, who learn behavior habits that harm them lifelong.

Three-year-old bullies need to learn the effects of actions, because 10-year-old bullies may be feared and admired and 50-year-old bullies may be hated and lonely. (An in-depth discussion of bullying appears in Chapter 13.)

Most types of aggression, including bullying, become less common from ages 2 to 6, as the brain matures and empathy increases. In addition, children learn to use aggression selectively, which decreases victimization (Ostrov et al., 2014). Parents, peers, and preschool teachers are pivotal mentors in this learning process.

Adults tend to regard relational aggression as normal in young children. However, relational aggression may be more hurtful than physical aggression. Children who learn to understand another's viewpoint are less likely to become bullies. Thus, early childhood is a time when teachers and parents should prevent relational aggression as well as physical aggression (Swit et al., 2018).

It is a mistake to expect children to regulate their emotions and become prosocial on their own. If they are not guided, they may develop destructive patterns. It is also a mistake to punish aggressors too harshly: That may increase their reactive aggression rather than teaching them how to regulate their anger.

In other words, although there is evidence that children spontaneously judge others who harm people, there also is evidence that prosocial and antisocial behavior are affected by early learning (Smetana, 2013). Who teaches them? By middle childhood (next three chapters), lessons need to be learned.

WHAT HAVE YOU LEARNED?

1. What are the four main styles of parenting?
2. What are the consequences of each style of parenting?
3. Why is discipline part of being a parent?
4. What are the arguments for and against corporal punishment?
5. When is time-out effective and when is it not?
6. What are the differences between the psychodynamic and behaviorist theories of gender development?
7. What are the differences between the cognitive and evolutionary theories of sex-role development?
8. How might children develop empathy and antipathy as they play with one another?
9. How much of moral development is innate and how much is learned?
10. What are the similarities and differences of the four kinds of aggression?

SUMMARY

Emotional Development

1. Emotional regulation is crucial during early childhood. It occurs in Erikson's third developmental stage, initiative versus guilt. Children normally feel pride when they demonstrate initiative, but sometimes they feel guilt or even shame at an unsatisfactory outcome.

2. Intrinsic motivation is apparent when a child concentrates on a drawing or a conversation with an imaginary friend. It may endure when extrinsic motivation stops.

Play

3. All young children enjoy playing—preferably with other children of the same sex, who teach them lessons in social interaction that their parents do not.

4. Play with other children gradually changes as children mature. Peer experiences, videos, and television affect children's play as they progress from being onlookers to engaging in cooperation.

5. Active play takes many forms, with rough-and-tumble play fostering social skills and sociodramatic play developing emotional regulation. Boys tend to engage in the former and girls in the latter, although experts disagree on whether this is nature or nurture.

Challenges for Caregivers

6. Three classic styles of parenting are authoritarian, permissive, and authoritative. Generally, children are happier and more successful when their parents express warmth and set guidelines.

7. A fourth style of parenting, neglectful/uninvolved, is always harmful. The particulars of parenting reflect the culture as well as the temperament of the child.

8. Parental punishment can have long-term consequences, with both corporal punishment and psychological control teaching lessons that few parents want their children to learn.

9. Even 2-year-olds correctly use sex-specific labels. Young children become aware of gender differences in clothes, toys, playmates, and future careers, and they typically become quite strict about male–female distinctions. Transgender children show strong gender preferences in early childhood.

10. Every major theory interprets children's awareness of gender differences in a particular way. Freud emphasized attraction to the opposite-sex parent; behaviorists stress reinforcement; cognitive theory focuses on gender schemas; sociocultural theory on social norms; and evolutionary theory on the need for species survival.

11. Young children's sense of self and social awareness become the foundation for morality, influenced by both nature and nurture.

12. Prosocial emotions lead to caring for others; antisocial behavior includes instrumental, reactive, relational, and bullying aggression.

13. Early childhood is an ideal time to teach children how to control their aggression, as well as to learn other aspects of how to navigate the social world in which they find themselves.

KEY TERMS

emotional regulation (p. 248)
self-concept (p. 248)
effortful control (p. 248)
initiative versus guilt (p. 248)
intrinsic motivation (p. 250)
extrinsic motivation (p. 250)
rough-and-tumble (p. 252)
sociodramatic play (p. 253)
authoritarian parenting (p. 254)
permissive parenting (p. 255)
authoritative parenting (p. 255)
neglectful/uninvolved parenting (p. 255)
corporal punishment (p. 257)
psychological control (p. 259)
time-out (p. 259)
induction (p. 259)
sex differences (p. 260)
gender differences (p. 260)
phallic stage (p. 261)
Oedipus complex (p. 261)
superego (p. 262)
gender schema (p. 263)
empathy (p. 265)
prosocial behavior (p. 265)
antisocial behavior (p. 265)
antipathy (p. 266)
instrumental aggression (p. 266)
reactive aggression (p. 266)
relational aggression (p. 267)
bullying aggression (p. 267)

APPLICATIONS

1. Children's television programming is rife with stereotypes about ethnicity, gender, and morality. Watch an hour of children's TV, especially on a Saturday morning, and describe the content of both the programs and the commercials. Draw conclusions about stereotyping, citing specific evidence, not generalities.

2. Gender indicators often go unnoticed. Go to a public place (park, restaurant, busy street) and spend at least 10 minutes recording examples of gender differentiation, such as articles of clothing, mannerisms, interaction patterns, and activities. Quantify what you see, such as baseball hats on eight males and two females. Or (better, but more difficult) describe four male–female conversations, indicating gender differences in length and frequency of talking, interruptions, vocabulary, and so on.

3. Ask three parents about punishment, including their preferred type, at what age, for what misdeeds, and by whom. Ask your three informants how they were punished as children and how that affected them. If your sources all agree, find a parent (or a classmate) who has a different view.

Especially For ANSWERS

Response for College Students (from p. 251): Both are important. Extrinsic motivation includes parental pressure and the need to get a good job after graduation. Intrinsic motivation includes the joy of learning, especially if you can express that learning in ways others recognize. Have you ever taken a course that was not required and was said to be difficult? That was intrinsic motivation.

Response for Parents (from p. 257): No. The worst time to spank a child is when you are angry. You might seriously hurt the child, and the child will associate anger with violence. You would do better to learn to control your anger and develop other strategies for discipline and for prevention of misbehavior.

Observation Quiz ANSWERS

Answer to Observation Quiz (from p. 254): It is impossible to be certain based on one moment, but the best guess is authoritative. He seems patient and protective, providing comfort and guidance, neither forcing (authoritarian) nor letting the child do whatever he wants (permissive).

Answer to Observation Quiz (from p. 263): The best clue is their shoes. Women do not wear high heels when caring for children, and men do not wear slippers to work.

CAREER ALERT The Preschool Teacher

Preschool teachers are increasingly in demand, as more and more families and communities understand how much young children can learn, and more and more mothers enter the job market. Added to that is the growing realization by public leaders that social skills and self-confidence developed in early childhood continue lifelong: A child who has good early education is likely to become an adult who is a competent and compassionate member of the community.

For developmentalists, important new insights come from neurological research, which helps preschool teachers understand what, how, and when young children learn. For example, since the auditory, visual, and motor cortexes are undergoing rapid myelination, children need to coordinate both hemispheres of brain and body by running, climbing, and balancing. But the immature motor cortex is not yet ready for writing, or tying shoelaces, or sitting quietly in one place.

Research on the developing brain finds that early childhood is the best time for learning language, so the curriculum should be language-rich—talking, listening, singing, hearing stories, making rhymes, engaging in verbal play. Young children can learn to recognize and name letters just as they learn to distinguish a baseball from a soccer ball.

Fostering control of gross motor skills may be particularly important for children who are at risk for ADHD (attention-deficit/hyperactivity disorder), the label given to active children who find it especially hard to concentrate, quietly, on one activity. Such children need to exercise their bodies, which helps their brains mature (Halperin & Healey, 2011; Hillman, 2014).

That is another reason for preschool education—children are most likely to develop their brains by playing with other children. Screen time, a common activity for children who are not in preschool, does not foster the brain regulation that children need.

Moreover preschool teachers help children learn how to cooperate with other children, a valuable life lesson that is best learned in childhood. Thus, preschool teachers can be proud that they are nurturing compassionate, prosocial adults.

The joy and satisfaction of working with young children is crucial, because at the moment, salary and working conditions are not yet what they should be. The U.S. Bureau of Labor Statistics reports that, compared to teachers overall, preschool teachers are most in demand and least well paid—the average annual salary is below $30,000 a year. There is marked variation in state-by-state certification requirements and in neighborhood-by-neighborhood salary levels.

This is changing, but students should enter this field for emotional reasons, not financial ones. If you are interested in early-childhood education, you can find more details from a professional group called the National Association for the Education of Young Children (NAEYC).

VISUALIZING DEVELOPMENT More Play Time, Less Screen Time

Play is universal—all young children do it when they are with each other, if they can. According to a 2017 study, U.S. 2- to 10-year-olds average 19 hours per week of screen time, exceeding the 15 hours they spend in indoor screen-free play by themselves or with others. Although children play outside for an additional 11 hours per week, parents report that when indoors, their children's screen time crowds out screen-free play.

WHAT 2- TO 10-YEAR-OLDS DO WITH THEIR FREE TIME

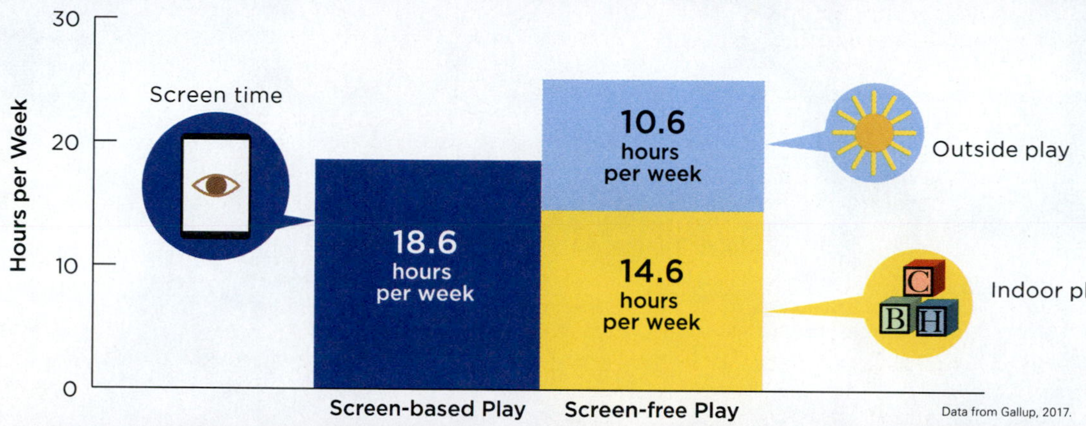

Data from Gallup, 2017.

WAY TOO MUCH SCREEN TIME

Very few children have the recommended less than an hour of screen time per day. Some have much more. This is particularly evident on weekends, when they should be playing outside or interacting with their families. What did children do before 1950, without TV or computers? Talking, reading, cooking, cleaning, board games, ball games, playing music, drawing pictures, writing letters ... the list of things that some children never do could go on and on!

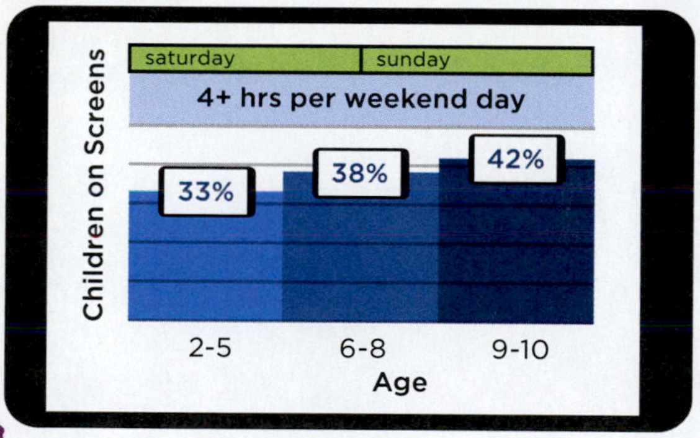

Data from Gallup, 2017.

WHAT CAREGIVERS CAN DO TO ENCOURAGE PLAY

at Ages 1–3

Choose childcare and preschools that emphasize unstructured playtime.

Offer simple, inexpensive objects (blocks, empty containers, puzzles, etc.), not screens or fancy gadgets.

Organize caregiver-supervised playdates with peers.

Encourage make-believe play.

Sing songs and play rhythms that invite participation.

at Ages 4–6

Provide opportunities for singing and dancing.

Encourage a variety of movements in a safe environment—e.g., hopping, swinging, climbing, and somersaulting.

Blend make-believe games and reality—e.g., "playing house" and helping with chores.

Encourage school officials to offer recess and play-centered learning approaches, not just reading, memorization, and worksheets.

Information from American Academy of Pediatrics, 2018.

APPLICATION TO DEVELOPING LIVES PARENTING SIMULATION
MIDDLE CHILDHOOD

As you progress through the Middle Childhood simulation module, how you answer the following questions will impact the biosocial, cognitive, and psychosocial development of your child.

Biosocial	Cognitive	Psychosocial
• How will you adjust your child's diet and activity level in middle childhood? • Will you follow the recommended immunization schedule? • Will you regulate your child's screen time?	• Which of Piaget's stages of cognitive development is your child in? • How will your child score on an intelligence test? • Will you put your child in tutoring if needed? • Will you help with your child's homework?	• Will you eat meals as a family around the table or have a different routine? • What kind of elementary school will you choose for your child? • What stage of moral development is your child in? • Will your child be popular?

CHAPTERS 11 • 12 • 13

PART IV

Middle Childhood

Every year has joys and sorrows, gains and losses. But if you were pushed to choose one best period, you might select middle childhood. The years from age 6 to 11 are usually a time of good health and steady growth. Children master new skills, learn thousands of words, and enter a wider social world. They are safe and happy; the dangers of adolescence (drugs, early sex, violence) are distant.

But not always. For some children, these years are the worst, not the best. They hate school or fear home; they suffer with asthma or disability; they are bullied or lonely.

Nor are these years straightforward for every adult who cares for these children. Instead, controversies abound. Should hyperactive children be medicated? Should reading and math crowd out music, or handwriting, or free play? Does single parenthood, divorce, cohabitation, or poverty harm children? The next three chapters explore the joys and complications of middle childhood.

Left: Hero Images/Getty Images
Right: EdZbarzhyvetsky/Deposit Photos

CHAPTER 11

Middle Childhood: Biosocial Development

What Will You Know?

- Who is at fault if a child is obese?
- How does playing a musical instrument affect brain development?
- Why are so many children on the autism spectrum?

- **A Healthy Time**
  - Statistics on Health
  - Health Habits
  - Physical Activity
  - Motor Skills and School
  - Health Problems in Middle Childhood
- **Brain Development**
  - Brains and Motion
  - Measuring the Mind
  - A VIEW FROM SCIENCE: The Flynn Effect
- **Children with Special Brains and Bodies**
  - Many Causes, Many Symptoms
  - OPPOSING PERSPECTIVES: Drug Treatment for ADHD and Other Disorders
  - Specific Learning Disorders
  - Special Education
  - A CASE TO STUDY: The Gifted and Talented
  - Teaching the Gifted and Talented
- **VISUALIZING DEVELOPMENT: Childhood Obesity Around the World**

After school I sit on a bench, watching two of my grandsons and hundreds of other children play. Many parents, grandparents, and babysitters are there also, sometimes talking to each other, sometimes reading, sometimes interacting with a child who is temporarily hurt or who wants a snack (I always bring fruit; other adults bring cookies, or dried seaweed, or chips).

I admire the parents who are more active: One father pretends to chase the children, including his daughter, to their shrieks of joy. Another father plays soccer, encouraging both the novices ("Nice kick!") and his own skilled son. One mother walks beside her daughter, who is blind but nonetheless climbs up the ladder to go down the slide. But most adults, like me, sit and watch.

What do we see? Much running, chasing, and climbing. Why do children hang on to metal rings, swinging their legs and grabbing for another metal ring? Why do they run across a bridge designed to be unsteady? Why do they grab each other, falling to the ground (it is rubberized), or, depending on the season, collect leaves, or throw snow, or chase pigeons?

The older children organize games—four square, touch football, kickball—but they do not keep score. Teams are fluid: When a parent takes a player away, the remaining children quickly rebalance the teams. Games continue until only two or three children remain or until someone takes the ball home.

Even with my warmest coat, I am cold sitting on the bench. Meanwhile, my older grandson wears only a T-shirt. Shivering, I bring his coat to him; he laughs and runs away. ("No. No. I am not cold.") Weather, even drizzle and snow, does not hinder the play.

The equipment is designed to be safe (there is a fence around the swings), but children sometimes run into things. Injury does not stop them. My younger grandson once came to me crying, "I bumped my head." Remembering the animism of young children, I tried to distract him, saying "Tell me what pole hit you, and I will tell that pole not to hurt you again." He said, "I bumped it on another head" and ran off, happy again.

I am awed by their energy and social interaction, a marked contrast to my bench-sitting. This chapter is about that: the actions of children in middle childhood and the adults who try to manage them, not always well. Examples include

Left: Image Source/DigitalVision/Getty Images
Top: EdZbarzhyvetsky/Deposit Photos

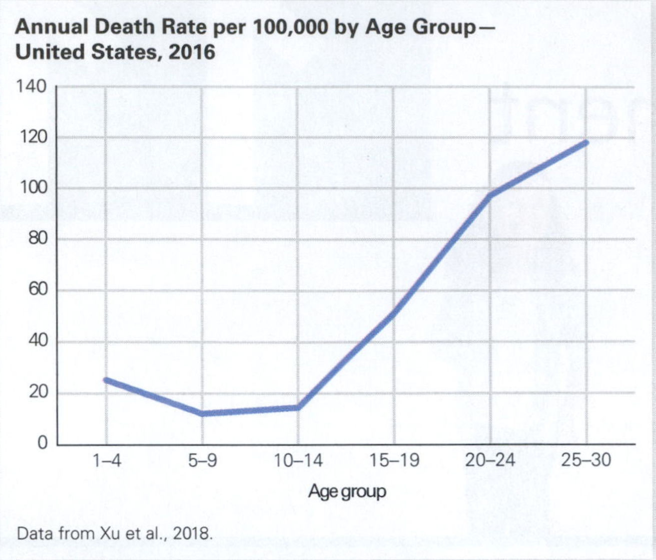

FIGURE 11.1
Rates continue to rise with age, up to 13,392 for those aged 85 and older, so this figure cannot portray the entire life span. Details are remarkable as well. Not only are fatal diseases rare, thanks to immunization, but accidents and homicides also dip during middle childhood—and rise rapidly thereafter.

allergies, asthma, obesity, and special needs. I hope the mother of the "other head" responded better than I did.

A Healthy Time

Unlike the first five years or the next ten, middle childhood is a time of slow and steady growth. Children gain about 2 inches and 5 pounds a year (5 centimeters and 2 kilograms). Nature and nurture combine to make these the healthiest years of life.

Statistics on Health

To be specific, the death rate in middle childhood is by far the lowest of any age (Murphy et al., 2017) (see **Figure 11.1**). Genetic diseases are more threatening in infancy or old age; infectious diseases are kept away via immunization; fatal accidents—although the most common cause of child death—are relatively uncommon until late adolescence.

This low death rate is becoming even lower, thanks to better injury control and modern medicine. In the United States in 1950, the death rate per 100,000 5- to 14-year-olds was 60; in 2017, it was 14 (National Center for Health Statistics, 2018). Minor illnesses—ear infections, inflamed tonsils, and flu—are also reduced.

Oral health has improved, with more brushing and fluoride. A survey found that 75 percent of U.S. children saw a dentist for preventive care in the past year, and for 70 percent of them, the condition of their teeth was very good (Iida & Rozier, 2013).

AP Images/Aijaz Rahi

Global Decay Thousands of children in Bangalore, India, gathered to brush their teeth together, part of an oral health campaign. Music, fast food, candy bars, and technology have been exported from the United States, and many developing nations have their own versions (Bollywood replaces Hollywood). Western diseases have also reached many nations; preventive health care now follows.

Observation Quiz Beyond toothbrushes, what other health tools do most children here have that their parents did not? (see answer, page 296) ↑

Health Habits

Children maintain good health if adults teach them good habits and if regular doctor and dentist visits are part of their lives. Every child needs adequate medical care; without it, health many years later is impaired. If people have good care in adulthood but had poor health and care in childhood, their adult health is still impacted (McEwen & McEwen, 2017; Juster et al., 2016).

Peers and parents are particularly influential in the early years. If children see others routinely caring for their own health, social learning pushes them to do the same. Camps for children with asthma, cancer, diabetes, sickle-cell anemia, and other chronic illnesses are recommended, because peers and knowledgeable adults teach self-care.

Middle childhood is an ideal time for this, as these children are less likely to question parental guidelines. Health habits should be established before teenage rebellion erupts: Many adolescents resist special diets, pills, warning signs, and doctors (Dean et al., 2010; Naughton et al., 2014).

Physical Activity

Beyond the sheer fun of playing, the benefits of physical activity—especially games with rules, which children now can follow—last a lifetime. Exercise advances physical, emotional, and mental health, as well as learning in school. That could entail the free play of running around (as I saw in the playground) or organized sports, as most parents choose.

Team sports teach cooperation, self-control, and emotional regulation — all essential lessons in middle childhood. Harm from sports is also possible.

Organizations have developed guidelines to prevent concussions among 7- and 8-year-olds in football and to halt full-body impact from ice hockey among children under age 12. The fact that regulations are needed to protect children from brain injury is sobering (Toporek, 2012).

The Influence of Parents Generally, parental involvement and encouragement of physical activity has increased over recent years, which benefits the children. In some nations, boys and girls are influenced equally by both parents, but in other nations, they follow the adults of their gender. In Portugal, for instance, a child's participation in physical activity follows that of the parent of the same sex (Rodrigues et al., 2018).

Adult emotions may be affected by children's competitive sports. A study found that fathers' testosterone and cortisol levels rose when they watched their children in a soccer tournament. Effects were stronger for sons than daughters, especially if the men thought the referee was unfair. Before judging these men, you should know that hormones were unaffected by winning or losing, as long as the fathers thought the children played as well as they could (Alvarado et al., 2018).

An important cohort change has occurred. Both parents are much more engaged in their children's sports activities than they were a few decades ago, according to a detailed study in Norway (Stefansen et al., 2018). Many parents consider this a way to connect with their children, as one father said:

> It's about being acknowledged sort of. To be praised and to be able to talk about [the game] later. [. . .]. And to share experiences. For instance when [our son] played [soccer] when he was eight and we could see him score a goal, or [our daughter] for that matter and enjoy that experience then. . .yes. I played football [soccer] all through my childhood and youth, but my parents did not attend one match. Not one.
>
> *[quoted in Stefansen et al., 2018, p. 166]*

This is echoed in many other nations. In the United States, parental involvement in children's sports is part of parental investment in each child, which is both a benefit (children know their parents care) and a liability (children feel pressured to perform) (Putnam, 2015).

The Need for Movement It may be tempting to criticize parents who are too enmeshed in their children's competitive play, but since physical activity is crucial for health and learning, many developmentalists are more troubled when indoor activities crowd out active play. Parents used to tell their children to "go out and play"; now they say, "don't leave the house."

Many parents enroll their children in after-school sports that vary by culture — tennis, karate, cricket, yoga, rugby, baseball, or soccer. However, the children who most need to connect their bodies and their minds — those from low-SES families or who have physical disabilities — are least likely to join Little League and the like, even when enrollment is free. The reasons are many, the consequences sad (Dearing et al., 2009).

Idyllic Two 8-year-olds, each with a 6-year-old sister, all four daydreaming or exploring in a very old tree beside a lake in Denmark — what could be better? Ideally, all of the world's children would be so fortunate, but most are not.

Henrik Sorensen/Cultura Creative (RF)/Alamy Stock Photo

Physical Exercise in Japan The idea that exercise improves the brain is evident in Japan, where children score high on international tests, and where many schools have more than an hour of recess (in several segments) a day in addition to gym classes. The Japanese believe that physical activity promotes learning and character development (Webster & Suzuki, 2014). Thus, many public schools in Japan have swimming pools, indoor gyms, and outdoor yards with structures for climbing, swinging, and so on.

This emphasis on exercise is for everyone lifelong. That may explain why the Japanese live longer, on average, than people in any other nation. Of course, longevity could result from many other factors: Correlation is not causation.

Motor Skills and School

Traditional school necessitates fine motor skills and brain maturation, with increasing expectations for writing and reading as the prefrontal cortex matures and connections between parts of the brain improve.

Gross Motor Skills Children learn various skills and also exercise their bodies in school. Why do some schools have more time than others for sports, recess, and gym? A study of all elementary schools in Illinois found that schools with the least time scheduled for physical activity tend to be those with the most low-SES children, as well as the lowest reading scores (Kern et al., 2018).

In this example, understanding correlation provides a novel way to interpret the relationship between reading scores and recess. Remember that correlation does not indicate the direction of the connection.

From that Illinois study, one might conclude that more reading instruction is needed in schools with low scores. If that is valid, then school leaders are making the right choice when academic instruction crowds out time for physical education. But, the correlation might occur in the opposite direction: Less physical activity might cause less learning (Kern et al., 2018).

Or a third variable—perhaps less support for cluster teachers, such as coaches, counselors, and reading specialists—might underlie both restricted exercise and low reading achievement. Other studies also find that as student income decreases, so does school time for physical exercise (Van Dyke et al., 2018).

Fine Motor Skills Writing requires finger control, reading print requires eye control, and sitting at a desk requires impulse control. Consequently, even the brightest 3-year-old is not ready for traditional elementary school.

Same Situation, Far Apart Given the contrast between the Russian children in front of their rural school *(left)* and the Japanese girls beside their urban school *(right)*, you might see the differences here. But child psychologists notice that children everywhere chase and catch, kick and throw, and as in these photos, jump rope while chanting rhymes.

Vladimir Grigorev/Alamy Stock Photo

Milatas/iStock/Getty Images

Even at age 6, many children are frustrated if their teachers demand that they write neatly, sit still, and cut in a straight line. Some educators suggest waiting until a child is "ready" for school; some suggest that early education should focus on readiness; others suggest that schools should adjust to children, not vice versa.

Some children seem to need to move their bodies (walking around, jiggling their feet, tapping their pencils) in order to concentrate. As you will see later in this chapter, some of these children may be diagnosed with *attention deficit/hyperactivity disorder* (ADHD). There are two opposite dangers here: A typically squirmy, active child may be given medication to quiet down, or an overactive child may be shamed and punished instead of diagnosed and treated.

Fine motor skills—like many other biological characteristics, such as bones, brains, and teeth—mature about six months earlier in girls than in boys. By contrast, boys often are ahead of girls in gross motor skills. These differences may be biological, or they may result from practice: Young girls more often dress up and play with dolls (fine motor skills), while boys more often climb and kick (gross motor skills) (Saraiva et al., 2013).

THINK CRITICALLY: How is a person "ready" for school? Are you "ready" for your current education?

Artistic Expression Children are imaginative and creative, developing all types of motor skills in the process. They love to express themselves, especially if their parents applaud their performances, display their artwork, and otherwise communicate approval.

The fact that their fine motor skills are immature, and thus their drawings lack precision, does not matter. Similarly, there is the deep, emotional significance of children's theater productions. Walking across the stage at the appropriate moment, making the required facial expression, gesturing in the right direction—all of these require skill at execution and inhibition, not the impulsive actions of the younger child.

Making Music Playing a musical instrument is a fine motor skill, in that the fingers need to move precisely. But as for all motor skills, physical movement is connected to brain function. This seems to be particularly apparent with music.

Some parents enroll their young children in music lessons, hoping they will learn to play. As a result, those children become better at listening to sounds—in speech and music alike. Neurological evidence finds that their brains reflect their new auditory abilities, a remarkable testament to the connection between motor skills, family influences, and learning (Strait et al., 2013; Zuk et al., 2014).

Music education can also occur as part of school curriculum, with an impact on the brain. In one study, students were divided into groups: (1) music lessons, (2) visual arts, and (3) education as usual (Jaschke et al., 2018).

Both special curricula were carefully designed for elementary school children. For example, the music curriculum included singing, clapping in rhythm, and learning to play an instrument of the student's choice.

The children in the visual arts curriculum not only became better at drawing but also became better at seeing shapes and objects and remembering what they had seen, an ability called *visual-spatial memory*. This was measured, before and after the special curriculum, by asking children to reproduce from memory a configuration of dots (on a 4-by-4 matrix) that they had seen.

The effects of the music curriculum were more far-reaching. The children became better at various executive control skills, including planning ahead and inhibiting unwanted responses (Jaschke et al., 2018). [**Life-Span Link:** Executive control is explained in Chapter 9.]

Buddhism in Maine? Yes. These schoolchildren are performing a play called *Buddha Walks* on St. Patrick's Day (March 17) in 2017. There are many ways to teach children about other cultures: Drama is one of the best, as in this Lebanon, Maine elementary school.

Especially for Medical Professionals You notice that a child is overweight, but you are hesitant to say anything to the parents, who are also overweight, because you do not want to offend them. What should you do? (see response, page 296)

Health Problems in Middle Childhood

Some chronic health conditions, including Tourette syndrome, stuttering, and allergies, may worsen during the school years, drawing unwanted attention to the affected child. Even minor problems—wearing glasses, repeatedly coughing or blowing one's nose, or having a visible birthmark—can affect children's self-esteem. We will now look at two more obvious examples of physical conditions that affect how children feel about themselves.

childhood overweight In a child, having a BMI above the 85th percentile, according to the U.S. Centers for Disease Control's 1980 standards for children of a given age.

childhood obesity In a child, having a BMI above the 95th percentile, according to the U.S. Centers for Disease Control's 1980 standards for children of a given age.

asthma A chronic disease of the respiratory system in which inflammation narrows the airways from the nose and mouth to the lungs, causing difficulty in breathing. Signs and symptoms include wheezing, shortness of breath, chest tightness, and coughing.

Childhood Obesity

Childhood overweight is usually defined as a BMI above the 85th percentile for children of a particular age. **Childhood obesity** is defined as a BMI above the 95th percentile. Those percentiles are based on weights of children in the United States, as published in growth charts at the end of the twentieth century. Now more children weigh as much as those former 5 percent did (see **Figure 11.2**). To be specific, in 2016, 18 percent of U.S. 6- to 11-year-olds were obese (Hales et al., 2017).

What affects children's weight? Genes were once blamed, but many other circumstances make a difference. Obesity rates rise if newborns are born too early, if infants are not breast-fed and begin eating solid foods before 4 months, if young children have televisions in their bedrooms and drink large quantities of soda, if older children sleep too little but have several hours of screen time each day, if they rarely play outside (Hart et al., 2011; Taveras et al., 2013).

During middle childhood, children themselves have *pester power*—the ability to get adults to do what they want (Powell et al., 2011), which often includes pestering their parents to buy calorie-dense snacks that are advertised on television or that other children eat. Parents need to say no, which is easier if only healthy food is in the house and if children never come grocery shopping.

There is hope both for parents and for pestering children. Rather than targeting parents *or* children, educating parents and their overweight children together improves weight and health, not just during the intervention but also over the long term (Yackobovitch-Gavan et al., 2018).

A dynamic-systems approach that considers individual differences, parenting practices, school lunches, fast-food restaurants, television and Internet ads, and community norms is needed. Prevention must be tailored to the particular child, family, and culture (Harrison et al., 2011; Baranowski & Taveras, 2018). That makes progress slow—treatments in isolation seem to have little impact.

Observation Quiz Are boys more likely to be overweight than girls? (see answer, page 296) ↓

FIGURE 11.2

Ethnic or Economic? Obesity increases as income decreases. Is that obvious from this figure?

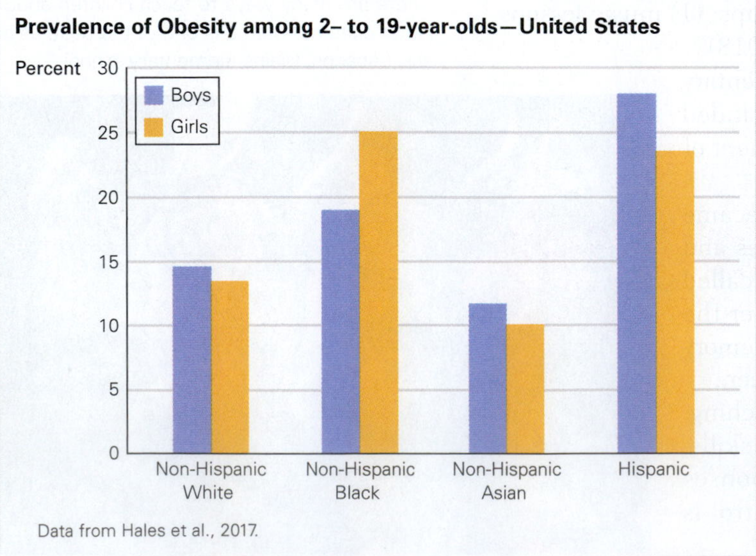

Every nation is worried about childhood obesity (see Visualizing Development, page 297). But, practices and policies are diverse, and solutions in one culture are resisted in another (Bagchi, 2019). For example, Mexico taxes sugar-sweetened beverages to reduce obesity, a tax that has met stiff opposition in the United States (Paarlberg et al., 2018). On the other hand, efforts to increase exercise in school seem to be adopted by more school districts in the United States.

Asthma

Another childhood condition that can affect learning is **asthma,** a chronic inflammatory disorder of the airways that makes breathing difficult. Sufferers have periodic attacks, sometimes requiring a rush to the hospital emergency room, a frightening experience for children who know that asthma might kill them (although it almost never does in childhood).

If asthma continues in adulthood, which it does about half the time, it can be fatal (Banks & Andrews, 2015). But children's most serious problem related to asthma is frequent absence from school. This impedes not only learning but also friendships, which thrive between children who see each other every day.

In the United States, childhood asthma rates more than doubled from 1980 to 2000, increased more gradually from 2000 to 2010, and then decreased somewhat (probably because smog has become less prevalent as clean-air regulations have taken effect) (Zahran et al., 2018).

Currently, about 1 in every 10 U.S. 5- to 11-year-olds has been diagnosed with asthma and still suffers from the condition. For more than half of them, asthma has meant missing school and having an attack in the past year, with rates somewhat higher for boys, African Americans, and children of Puerto Rican descent (Zahran et al., 2018).

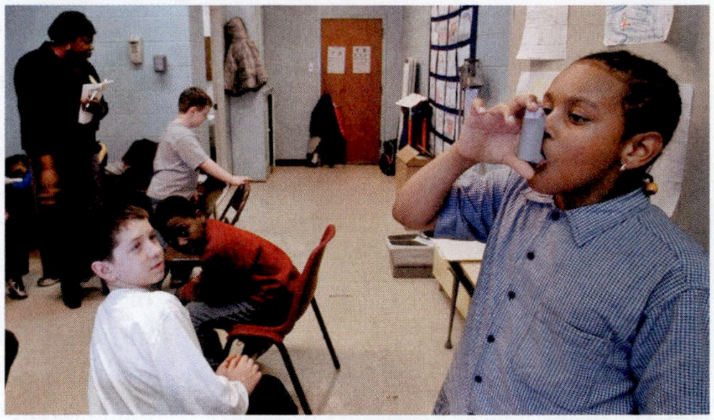

Kathy McLaughlin/The Image Works

Pride and Prejudice In some city schools, asthma is so common that using an inhaler is a sign of pride, as suggested by the facial expressions of these two boys. The "prejudice" is beyond the walls of this school nurse's room, in a society that allows high rates of childhood asthma.

Rates increase as income falls. For children whose families are under the poverty threshold, 12 percent currently have asthma, as do only 7 percent of those whose annual family income is above $100,000 (Zahran et al., 2018).

Researchers have found many causes. Some genetic alleles have been identified, as have many aspects of modern life—carpets, pollution, house pets, airtight windows, parental smoking, cockroaches, dust mites, less outdoor play. None acts in isolation. A combination of genetic sensitivity to allergies and early respiratory infections increases wheezing and shortness of breath (Mackenzie et al., 2014).

Some experts suggest a *hygiene hypothesis:* that "the immune system needs to tangle with microbes when we are young. . . . despite what our mothers told us, cleanliness sometimes leads to sickness" (Leslie, 2012, p. 1428). Children may be overprotected from viruses and bacteria, especially in modern nations. In their concern about hygiene, parents prevent exposure to minor infections, germs, and family pets that would strengthen their child's immunity. As you remember, this is suggested as the reason for the increases in all allergies as well as asthma (Liu, 2015).

This hypothesis is supported by data showing that:

1. first-born children develop asthma more often than later-born ones;
2. asthma and allergies are less common among farm-dwelling children; and
3. children born by cesarean (very sterile) have a greater incidence of asthma.

Remember the microbiome—the many bacteria within our bodies. Some microbes in the lungs affect asthma (Singanayagam et al., 2017). Accordingly, changing the microbiome—via diet, drugs, or exposure to animals—may treat asthma. However, asthma has multiple, varied causes and types; no single treatment will help everyone.

WHAT HAVE YOU LEARNED?

1. How does growth during middle childhood compare with growth earlier or later?
2. Why is middle childhood considered a healthy time?
3. How does physical activity affect a child's education?
4. What are several reasons why some children are less active than they should be?
5. What are the short-term and long-term effects of childhood obesity?
6. Why is asthma more common now than it once was?

Brain Development

As already mentioned many times, the most important part of the maturation process for children is in the brain, which enables the entire body to function. As you remember from Chapter 8, the child's brain develops better connections between its various parts every year. This process continues during middle childhood.

One of the distinguishing traits of humans is that the brain is not fully mature until about age 25, which enables all of the cognitive and psychosocial aspects of development in middle childhood described in the next two chapters. Sadly, children born far too early (under 27 weeks), who escape any obvious brain malfunction, may still have subtle signs of brain abnormalities that impair motor skills (Bolk et al., 2018).

macmillan learning

VIDEO ACTIVITY: Brain Development: Middle Childhood depicts the changes that occur in a child's brain from age 6 to age 11.

Brains and Motion

Body movement improves intellectual functioning and vice versa. How could this be? A review of the research suggests several possible mechanisms, including direct benefits for cerebral blood flow and neurotransmitters as well as indirect results from better moods (Singh et al., 2012). Those better moods themselves loop back to more body movement.

Many studies have found that children's brains benefit from physical exercise (Voelcker-Rehage et al., 2018). This can be quite specific: One study found that for boys (not girls), the size of the hippocampus correlated with sports activities (Gorham et al., 2019).

While sports and aerobic exercise may directly affect brain structures, movement of every part of the body, in fine and gross motor skills, can foster learning. Children learn by doing and then express what they know by moving. This is part of a concept called *embodied cognition,* the idea that thinking is connected to body movement (Pexman, 2017).

Remember that the study of music and arts education also had a control group. Their abilities improved over the two years, as you would expect, but not as much as the children in the more active learning groups. Moreover, IQ scores, which are thought to reflect brain functioning, also rose in the active groups (Jaschke et al., 2018).

In another example, the physical act of handwriting helps children learn to read (James, 2017). This has implications for students at every level: Taking a screen shot, or printing out a PowerPoint slide, is less useful than writing out the assignment.

Paying Attention As you remember, one specific aspect of executive control is the ability to inhibit some impulses to focus on others. Neurological advances allow children to pay special heed to the most important elements of their environment. *Selective attention,* concentrating on some stimuli while ignoring others, improves markedly at about age 7.

Selective attention is partly the result of brain maturation, but it is also greatly affected by experience, particularly active play. School-age children not only notice various stimuli (which is one form of attention) but also select appropriate responses when several possibilities conflict (Wendelken et al., 2011). In kickball, soccer, basketball, and baseball, it is crucial to attend to the ball, not to dozens of other stimuli.

For example, in baseball, young batters learn to ignore the other team's attempts to distract them; fielders start moving into position as soon as the bat connects; and pitchers adjust to the height, handedness, and past performance of the person at bat. Another physical activity that seems to foster *executive function* is karate, which requires inhibition of some reactions in order to execute others (Alesi et al., 2014).

Reaction Time Physical play combined with brain maturation improves **reaction time,** which is how long it takes to respond to a stimulus. Preschoolers are sometimes frustratingly slow in putting on their pants, eating their cereal, throwing a ball. Reaction time is reduced every year of childhood, thanks to increasing myelination. As a result, older children can react more quickly.

Skill at games is an obvious example, from scoring on a video game, to swinging at a pitch, to kicking a soccer ball toward a teammate—timing on all of these improve every year from age 6 to 11, depending partly on practice, partly on body growth, and partly on brain connections.

Typical 7-Year-Old? In many ways, this boy is typical. He likes video games and school, he usually appreciates his parents, and he gets himself dressed every morning. This photo shows him using blocks to construct a design to match a picture, one of the ten kinds of challenges that comprise the WISC, a widely used IQ test. His attention to the task is not unusual for children his age, but his actual performance is more like that of an older child. That makes his IQ score significantly above 100.

Measuring the Mind

In ancient times, if adults were strong and hardworking, they were solid members of the community. A child needed to be well fed, protected from injury, and tended to when sick in order to grow into a capable adult. No one was singled out if they could not think quickly, read well, or sit still. Those who had an obvious impairment, such as being blind or deaf, received special care; no need for diagnosis.

Over the centuries, however, humans have placed more value on brain functioning. Books were printed, making reading important; money was exchanged, so calculating was needed; voters chose leaders instead of kings inheriting kingdoms. All of this required learning. It became evident that some people were much better at reading, at math, at analysis. Schools were built, and some students learned more quickly than others.

The slower ones struggled and quit, but adults wanted to know whether they did so because of lack of effort (they could be beaten or forced to stand in a corner wearing a dunce cap) or because their brains made them inherently incapable of learning. It became important to measure intelligence.

reaction time The time it takes to respond to a stimulus, either physically (with a reflexive movement such as an eyeblink) or cognitively (with a thought).

***g* (general intelligence)** The idea of *g* assumes that intelligence is one basic trait, underlying all cognitive abilities. According to this concept, people have varying levels of this general ability.

Aptitude, Achievement, and IQ The *potential* to master a specific skill or to learn a certain body of knowledge is called *aptitude.* A child might have the intellectual aptitude to be a proficient reader, for instance, even though that child has not learned to read or write. Some children have the potential to become a talented athlete, artist, architect, and so on. Most aptitudes are not developed, since motivation and opportunity (or some would say, money and luck) are needed as well.

Aptitude is distinct from *achievement,* which is what is actually mastered. For children, academic achievement is measured by comparing that child with expected accomplishments at each grade. As you remember, children should be able to walk at 1 year, scribble with a marker at 2 years, and catch a ball at 4 years (depending on the size of the ball). These are achievements of motor skills; the same principle underlies achievement of brain skills.

Yes, But... Measuring anything is biased! The assumption is that whatever is measured is important.

Thus, a child who is at a second-grade reading level might actually be in the second grade, but it is just as likely for that child to be in the first or third grade. If that second-grade reader is 9 years old and therefore should be reading at the fourth-grade level, then something is amiss—perhaps with aptitude. That reasoning led to IQ tests, to find out whether low achievement was caused by low aptitude or something else.

People assumed that, for intelligence, one general aptitude—often referred to as ***g* (general intelligence)**—could be assessed by answers to a series of questions (vocabulary, memory, and so on). The number of correct answers was compared to the average for children of a particular age to compute an IQ, thought to measure brain functioning (Spearman, 1927).

"MY FATHER SAYS, THESE INTELLIGENCE TESTS ARE BIASED TOWARD THE INTELLIGENT."

Scores on IQ tests correlated with school achievement: Children with high IQs were able to perform at above grade level, because their intellectual potential enabled them to learn quickly. On the other hand, a low IQ score indicated that a child did not have the aptitude to be a quick learner. People with psychological disorders such as schizophrenia or obsessive-compulsive disorder tend to have lower average IQ scores, because their brains do not process ideas as quickly or as well as other people's brains (Abramovitch et al., 2018).

The original IQ tests were developed by Alfred Binet in France at the beginning of the twentieth century. He sought a way to distinguish children who were unable to learn as fast as other children. Thanks to Binet, such children were no longer beaten and shamed. The test he developed has been revised many times and is now called the Stanford-Binet Intelligence Scale.

An American, David Wechsler, also developed intelligence tests in the twentieth century. Because he recognized the importance of maturation, Wechsler developed different tests for young children, older children, and adults, specifically the WIPPSI (Wechsler Preschool and Primary Scale of Intelligence), the WISC (Wechsler Intelligence Scale for Children), and the WAIS (Wechsler Adult Intelligence Scale). Each of these tests has five indicators of Verbal Intelligence (including vocabulary, math problems, and logic) and five indicators of Performance Intelligence (puzzles, pictures with something missing, and so on).

Calculating IQ Originally, IQ (intelligence quotient) tests produced a number that was literally a quotient: Mental age (the average age of those who answered a specific number of questions correctly) was divided by the actual age of a person taking the test. The answer from that division (the quotient) was multiplied by 100. An IQ of 100 was exactly average, because when mental age was the same as chronological age, the quotient was 1, and $1 \times 100 = 100$.

Thus, if the average 9-year-old answered, say, exactly 60 questions correctly, then everyone who got 60 questions correct—no matter what their chronological age—would have a mental age of 9. Obviously, for children whose mental age was the same as their chronological age (such as a 9-year-old who got 60 questions right), the IQ would be 100 ($9 \div 9 = 1 \times 100 = 100$), exactly average.

If a 6-year-old answered the questions as well as a typical 9-year-old, the score would be $9 \div 6 \times 100$, or 133. If a 12-year-old answered only 60 questions correctly, the IQ would be 75 ($9 \div 12 \times 100$). The current method of calculating IQ is more complex, but the basic idea is the same: *g* is calculated based on the average mental age of people of a particular chronological age. (See **Figure 11.3**.)

Plasticity and Intelligence You have probably already spotted the underlying problem with the assumptions about mental age. Intelligence is much more

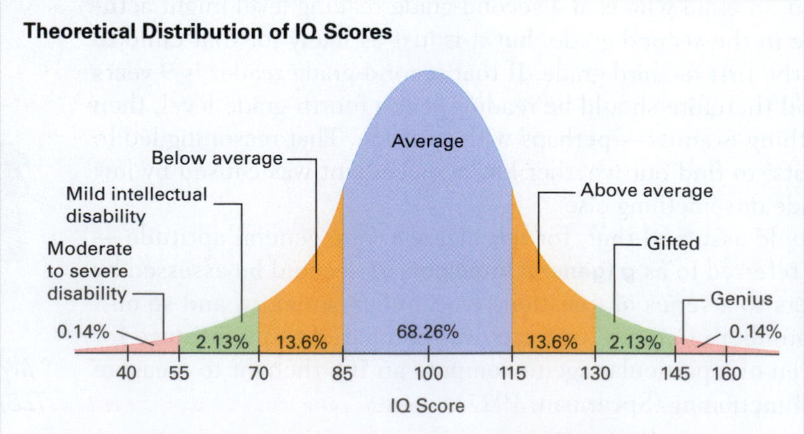

FIGURE 11.3
In Theory, Most People Are Average Almost 70 percent of IQ scores fall within the "average" range. Note, however, that this is a norm-referenced test. In fact, actual IQ scores have risen in many nations; 100 is no longer exactly the midpoint. Furthermore, in practice, scores below 50 are slightly more frequent than indicated by the normal curve (shown here) because severe disability is the result not of normal distribution but of genetic and prenatal factors.

Observation Quiz If a person's IQ is 110, what category are they in? (see answer, page 296) →

plastic than people once thought. This is particularly apparent for brain development in childhood, but it also may be true in adulthood (Glenn et al., 2018; Patton et al., 2019).

Aptitude is not a fixed characteristic, present at birth, that determines how much a person can learn or whether an individual can become an artist or architect. Young children with a low IQ can become above average or even gifted adults, like my nephew David (discussed in Chapter 1).

An added complication is the relationship between intelligence and creativity. A child who scores very high on IQ tests qualifies as gifted, but how that aptitude leads to achievement depends on another trait that differs among people. Some are *divergent thinkers,* who find many solutions and even more questions for every problem, and others are *convergent thinkers,* who quickly find one, and only one, correct answer for every problem.

Many Intelligences Since scores change over time (see A View from Science), IQ tests are much less definitive than they were once thought to be, but aptitude remains a useful concept. Every human has a mix of aptitudes and abilities. Some aptitudes are nurtured, and they may become notable achievements; some aptitudes are never developed.

An ongoing debate is whether *g* exists, and thus whether any single test can measure the complexities of the human brain. People may inherit and develop many abilities, some high and some low (e.g., Q. Zhu et al., 2010).

Flynn effect The rise in average IQ scores that has occurred over the decades in many nations.

A VIEW FROM SCIENCE

The Flynn Effect

The average IQ scores of more than 30 nations has risen substantially every decade for the past century. This phenomenon is called the **Flynn effect** (Pietschnig & Voracek, 2015; Trahan et al., 2014).

When James Flynn first suggested in the 1980s that the IQ scores had risen throughout the twentieth century, critics said he did not understand the data and was misled by biased samples. Some added that if Flynn had realized the strong genetic inheritance of IQ, and if he recognized how genes are passed from one generation to the next, he would know that grandchildren could not be much smarter than their grandparents.

In the past half-century, those critics have been silenced, as hundreds of studies found rising scores in nation after nation. Most of those studies have been in industrialized nations of Europe because the longitudinal, large-scale, valid comparisons are difficult, but the Flynn effect is also evident in poorer nations. For instance, a study in Kenya found that scores on the Raven's matrix (supposed to be culture-free) increased from 12.8 to 17.3 over a 14-year period (Daley et al., 2003).

Scientists no longer question whether the Flynn effect exists; they ask why it does. Better education? Better nutrition? Better medical care? More widespread information from newspapers, television, the Internet?

The Flynn effect is more apparent for women than for men, and in southern Europe more than northern Europe, as nutrition and education improved (D. Weber et al., 2017). Rising average IQs are less apparent for upper-class European men. The suggestion is that even in the early-twentieth century, most of them had good nutrition, education, and opportunity.

Once those benefits are available to everyone, IQ will stabilize. In fact, in the most advanced nations of northern Europe, recent evidence suggests that the Flynn effect may be moving in the other direction, decreasing over time (Pietschnig & Voracek, 2015).

The fact that IQ scores vary by social conditions has changed perceptions. Most psychologists now agree that the brain is like a muscle, affected by mental exercise—which often is encouraged or discouraged by the social setting. This is proven in language and music (brains literally grow with childhood music training), and it is probably true in other domains (Moreno et al., 2015; Zatorre, 2013).

Both speed and memory are crucial for *g*, and they are affected by experience, evident in the Flynn effect. Moreover, every test of intelligence is designed to measure what is considered to be intelligence within that culture.

Think of someone you believe to be very smart, and then ask yourself whether someone in an entirely different context (a rural village, for instance) would also think that person to be smart. When I ask myself that question, I realize how proud I am of my intellectual ability. Some humility is needed.

A Gifted Child Gardner believes every person is naturally better at some of his nine intelligences, and then the social context may or may not appreciate the talent. In the twenty-first century, verbal and mathematical intelligence is usually prized far more than artistic intelligence, but Georgie Pocheptsov was drawing before he learned to speak. The reason is tragic: His father suffered and died of brain cancer when Georgie was a toddler, and his mother bought paints and canvases to help her son cope with his loss. By middle childhood (shown here), Pocheptsov was already a world-famous artist. Now as a young adult his works sell for hundreds of thousands of dollars—often donated to brain tumor research.

multiple intelligences The idea that human intelligence is composed of a varied set of abilities rather than a single, all-encompassing one.

Especially for Teachers What are the advantages and disadvantages of using Gardner's nine intelligences to guide your classroom curriculum? (see response, page 296)

neurodiversity The idea that each person has neurological strengths and weaknesses that should be appreciated, in much the same way diverse cultures and ethnicities are welcomed. Neurodiversity seems particularly relevant for children with disorders on the autism spectrum.

Two leading developmentalists (Robert Sternberg and Howard Gardner) are among those who believe that humans have **multiple intelligences,** not just one. Sternberg originally described three kinds of intelligence: *analytic, creative,* and *practical* (Sternberg, 2008; Gardner, 2011). Children who are unusually creative, or very practical, may not be the best students in school, but they may flourish later on. [**Life-Span Link:** This is explained more in Chapter 21.]

Gardner originally described seven intelligences: *linguistic, logical-mathematical, musical, spatial, bodily-kinesthetic* (movement), *interpersonal* (social understanding), and *intrapersonal* (self-understanding), each associated with a particular brain region (Gardner, 1983). He subsequently added an eighth (*naturalistic*: understanding nature, as in biology, zoology, or farming) and a ninth (*spiritual/existential*: thinking about life and death) (Gardner, 1999, 2006; Gardner & Moran, 2006).

Although everyone has some of all nine intelligences, Gardner believes that each individual excels in particular ones. For example, someone might be gifted spatially but not linguistically (a visual artist who cannot describe her work) or might have interpersonal but not naturalistic intelligence (an astute clinical psychologist whose houseplants die).

Schools, cultures, and families dampen or expand particular intelligences. If two children are born with creative, musical aptitude, the child whose parents are musicians is more likely to develop musical intelligence than the child whose parents are tone-deaf. Gardner (2011) believes that schools often are too narrow, teaching only some aspects of intelligence and thus stunting children's learning.

Scanning the Brain Another way to indicate aptitude is to measure the brain directly. In childhood, brain scans do not correlate with IQ scores (except for children with abnormally small brains), but they do later on (Brouwer et al., 2014). Brain scans can measure activity (reaction time, selective attention, emotional excitement) or the size of various brain areas, but they are not accurate in diagnosing cognitive disorders in childhood (Goddings & Giedd, 2014).

Neuroscientists and psychologists agree, however, on four generalities:

1. *Brain development depends on experiences*. Thus, a brain scan is accurate only at the moment, not for the future.
2. *Dendrites form and myelination changes throughout life*. Middle childhood is crucial, but developments before and after these years are also significant.
3. *Children with disorders often have unusual brain patterns, and training may change those patterns*. Normal variation means that diagnosis and remediation based on brain patterns are far from perfect.
4. *Each brain functions in a particular way, a concept called* ***neurodiversity.*** Diverse neurological patterns are not necessarily better or worse; they are simply different, an example of the *difference is not deficit* idea explained first in Chapter 1 (Kapp et al., 2013).

WHAT HAVE YOU LEARNED?

1. What is the difference between selective attention and quick reaction time?
2. Why were intelligence tests originally developed?
3. What are the arguments for and against *g*?
4. Are aptitude and achievement distinct ideas, or are they part of the same trait?
5. How might the concept of multiple intelligences be useful in school?

Children with Special Brains and Bodies

Developmental psychopathology links typical with atypical development, especially when the atypical development results in special needs (Cicchetti, 2013b; Hayden & Mash, 2014). This topic is relevant lifelong because "[e]ach period of life, from the prenatal period through senescence, ushers in new biological and psychological challenges, strengths, and vulnerabilities" (Cicchetti, 2013b, p. 458).

developmental psychopathology The field that uses insights into typical development to understand and remediate developmental disorders.

Most disorders are **comorbid,** which means that more than one problem is evident in the same person. Comorbidity is now considered "the rule, rather than the exception" (Krueger & Eaton, 2015, p. 27). Turning points, opportunities, and past influences are always apparent. Many people of every age have differences that do not meet a diagnostic threshold but that nonetheless impact their lives, making other problems more likely.

comorbid Refers to the presence of two or more unrelated disease conditions at the same time in the same person.

At the outset, four general principles should be emphasized.

1. *Abnormality is normal,* meaning that everyone has some aspects of behavior that are unusual. The opposite is also true: Everyone with a diagnosed disorder is, in many respects, like everyone else.
2. *Disability changes year by year* (Clark et al., 2017). A severe childhood disorder may become insignificant, but a minor problem may become disabling. Some children with significant disabilities (e.g., blindness) become productive adults. Conversely, some conditions (e.g., conduct disorder) become more disabling.
3. *Plasticity and compensation are widespread.* Many conditions, especially those that originate in the brain, seem to disappear with age and treatment (Livingston & Happé, 2017).
4. *Diagnosis and treatment reflect the social context.* Each individual interacts with the surrounding settings—including family, school, community, and culture—which modify, worsen, cause, or eliminate psychopathology.

DSM-5 (the fifth edition of the *Diagnostic and Statistical Manual of Mental Disorders,* published by the American Psychiatric Association in 2013) is used as a reference here. However, the cutoff between what is and what is not a disorder varies (Clark et al., 2017). Because of the four principles above, it is not always obvious whether a particular child has a disorder or not.

DSM-5 is only one set of criteria—the World Health Organization has another (ICD-11); some experts use a third (RDoC) for research. Psychiatrists are discussing DSM-6, which again will redefine various disorders (Clark et al., 2017).

Many Causes, Many Symptoms

To help children with special needs, it is helpful to know what caused their differences. Perhaps a child has a chemical imbalance that might be corrected with a drug, or perhaps a parent or a school has exacerbated a small vulnerability into a huge disorder, or perhaps an inherited physical weakness requires targeted exercise. Finding the appropriate cause and treatment, however, is more complex than it appears.

One cause can have many final manifestations, a phenomenon called **multifinality** (many final forms). The opposite is also apparent: One symptom can result from several different causes, a phenomenon called **equifinality** (equal in final form). Thus, a direct line from cause to consequence cannot be drawn with certainty.

multifinality A basic principle of developmental psychopathology which holds that one cause can have many (multiple) final manifestations.

equifinality A basic principle of developmental psychopathology which holds that one symptom can have many causes.

For example, in multifinality, an infant who has been flooded with stress hormones may become a child who is hypervigilant or irrationally placid, may be easily angered or quick to cry, or may not be affected. Or in equifinality, a child who does not talk may have autism or hearing impairment, be electively mute or pathologically shy.

Jeff Gritchen/Digital First Media/Orange County Register via Getty Images

Expressing Surprise You would be surprised as Vincent Saporita was when he was named Teacher of the Year in Huntington Beach, California. But you might not express your surprise as he did. His students are hearing impaired, so he has learned to use gestures to express emotions.

To illustrate the complexities in psychopathology, we discuss three disorders: attention-deficit/hyperactivity disorder (ADHD), specific learning disorders, and autism spectrum disorder (ASD). The general principles illustrated by these three apply to everyone. We all have quirks and oddities.

attention-deficit/hyperactivity disorder (ADHD) A condition characterized by a persistent pattern of inattention and/or by hyperactive or impulsive behaviors; ADHD interferes with a person's functioning or development.

Attention-Deficit/Hyperactivity Disorder Someone with **attention-deficit/hyperactivity disorder (ADHD)** is inattentive, active, and impulsive. DSM-5 says that symptoms must start before age 12 (in DSM-IV it was age 7) and must impact daily life. (DSM-IV said *impair,* not merely *impact.*)

Partly because the definition now includes older children, the rate of children diagnosed with ADHD has increased worldwide (Polanczyk et al., 2014). In 1980, about 5 percent of all U.S. 4- to 17-year-olds were diagnosed with ADHD; more recent rates are 8 percent of 4- to 11-year-olds, and 14 percent of 12- to 17-year-olds (G. Xu et al., 2018).

Every young child is sometimes inattentive, impulsive, and active, gradually settling down with maturation. However, those with ADHD "are so active and impulsive that they cannot sit still, are constantly fidgeting, talk when they should be listening, interrupt people all the time, can't stay on task, . . . accidentally injure themselves." All of this makes them "difficult to parent or teach" (Nigg & Barkley, 2014, p. 75).

Because many adults are upset by children's moods and actions, and because any physician can write a prescription to quiet a child, thousands of U.S. children may be too readily diagnosed and medicated. *But,* because many parents do not recognize that their child needs help, and many adults are suspicious of drugs and psychologists (Moldavsky & Sayal, 2013; Rose, 2008), thousands of children may suffer needlessly. This dilemma is explored in Opposing Perspectives.

OPPOSING PERSPECTIVES

Drug Treatment for ADHD and Other Disorders

Many child psychologists believe that the public discounts the devastation and lost learning that occur when a child's serious disorder is not recognized or treated. On the other hand, many parents are suspicious of drugs and psychotherapy, so they avoid recommended treatment (Gordon-Hollingsworth et al., 2015).

In the United States, a non-Hispanic White child is more likely to be diagnosed with ADHD than is a non-Hispanic Black child. As for Hispanic children, their rates of diagnosed ADHD are much lower than non-Hispanic children of any race (G. Xu et al., 2018). What do you make of these ethnic differences? Do they reflect prejudice, poverty, genes, or culture?

The question of proper diagnosis and treatment is controversial among experts as well. A leading book argues that drug companies and doctors are far too quick to push pills, making ADHD "by far, the most misdiagnosed condition in American medicine" (Schwarz, 2016, p. 2). A critical review of that book notes a failure to mention the millions of people who "have experienced life-changing, positive results" from treatment—including medication (Zametkin & Solanto, 2017, p. 9).

In the United States, more than 2 million people younger than 18 take prescription drugs to regulate their emotions and behavior. The rates are about 14 percent for teenagers (Merikangas et al., 2013), about 10 percent for 6- to 11-year-olds, and less than 1 percent for 2- to 5-year-olds (Olfson et al., 2010). Most children in the United States who are diagnosed with ADHD are medicated; in England and Europe, less than half are (Polanczyk et al., 2014).

In China, psychoactive medication is rarely prescribed for children: A child with ADHD symptoms is thought to need correction, not medication (Yang et al., 2013). In Africa, an inattentive, overactive child is more likely to be beaten than sent to a psychiatrist. Wise or cruel?

The most common drug for ADHD is Ritalin (methylphenidate), but at least 20 other psychoactive drugs are prescribed for children to treat depression, anxiety, intellectual disability, autism spectrum disorder, disruptive mood dysregulation disorder, and many other conditions. Some parents welcome the relief that drugs may provide; others refuse to medicate their children because they fear later consequences.

Children with ADHD, with or without medication, are more likely to have psychological and substance abuse problems in adulthood. Those comorbid aspects should be attributed to the underlying cause, not to the medication, which seems to reduce, but not erase, the likelihood of later problems (Uchida et al., 2018).

A meta-analysis finds that medication is likely to help when it is combined with cognitive-behavioral therapy, but also that ADHD is not one simple disorder but a condition that varies from one child, one context, and one nation to another. Thus, no particular drug, and no particular therapy, works for every child (López-Pinar et al., 2018).

Some research finds a correlation between medicating children and the rate of mental illness in adulthood (Moran et al., 2015). On the other hand, one expert argues that if children with ADHD are not diagnosed and treated, that increases another outcome—prison. This may be particularly likely for African American boys who are disruptive. If they are punished, not treated, for ADHD symptoms, they may enter the "school-to-prison pipeline" (Moody, 2016).

All professionals agree that finding the best drug at the right strength is difficult, in part because each child's genes and personality are unique, and in part because children's weight and metabolism change every year. Given that, why are most children who are prescribed psychoactive drugs seen only by a general practitioner who does not follow up on dose and outcome (Patel et al., 2017)? Do pharmaceutical companies mislead parents about the benefits and liabilities of ADHD drugs?

Most professionals believe that contextual interventions (instructing caregivers and schools on child management, changing the diet, increasing outdoor play, eliminating screens) should be tried before drugs. Good advice, but not easy to take if a parent or teacher is trying to manage an overactive, disruptive child every day.

Genes, culture, health care, education, religion, and stereotypes all affect ethnic and economic differences. As two experts explain, "disentangling these will be extremely valuable to improving culturally competent assessment in an increasingly diverse society" (Nigg & Barkley, 2014, p. 98). Given the emotional and practical implications of that tangle, opposing perspectives are not surprising.

In general, three problems are apparent.

- *Misdiagnosis*. If ADHD is diagnosed when another disorder is the problem, treatment might make the problem worse (Miklowitz & Cicchetti, 2010). Many psychoactive drugs alter moods, so a child with *disruptive mood dysregulation disorder* might be harmed by ADHD medication.
- *Drug abuse*. Although drugs may be therapeutic for true ADHD cases, some adolescents want an ADHD diagnosis in order to obtain amphetamines legally (McCabe et al., 2014). Parents or teachers may also overuse medication to quiet children.
- *Typical behavior considered pathological*. If a child's activity, impulsiveness, and curiosity are diagnosed as ADHD, that child's exuberance and self-confidence may suffer.

"Typical considered pathological" is one interpretation of data on 378,000 children in Taiwan, a Chinese nation whose rates of ADHD are increasing (M.-H. Chen et al., 2016). Boys who were born in August, and hence entered kindergarten when they had just turned 5, were diagnosed with ADHD at the rate of 4.5 percent, whereas boys born in September, starting kindergarten when they were almost 6, were diagnosed at the rate of 2.8 percent.

Diagnosis for these Chinese boys typically occurred years after kindergarten, but August birthday boys were at risk throughout their school years. (See **Figure 11.4**.) The data suggest that a year of maturation would have reduced the rate of ADHD by a third.

The example in Taiwan highlights another concern. For ADHD diagnosis, one source reported that "boys

Observation Quiz This chart also shows medication rate. Are those August birthdays more likely to be medicated than the September birthdays? (see answer, page 296)

FIGURE 11.4

One Month Is One Year In the Taiwanese school system, the cutoff for kindergarten is September 1, so some boys enter school a year later because they were born a few days later. Those who are relatively young among their classmates are less able to sit still and listen. They are twice as likely to be given drugs to quiet them down.

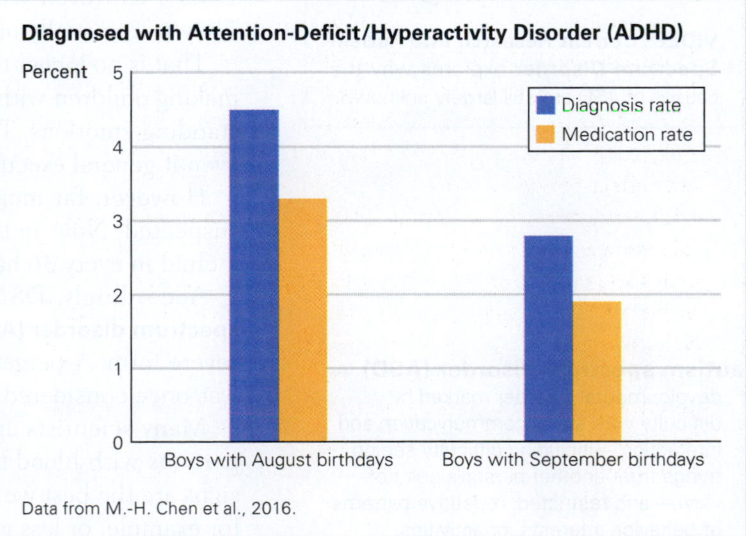

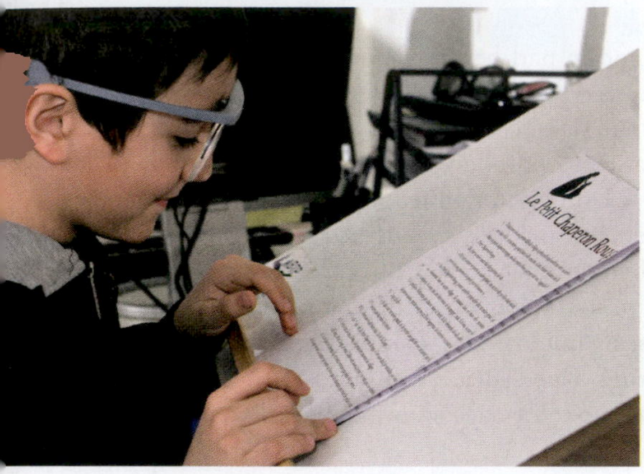

BSIP/UIG/Getty Images

Happy Reading Those large prism glasses keep the letters from jumping around on the page, a boon for this 8-year-old French boy. Unfortunately, each child with dyslexia needs individualized treatment: These glasses help some, but not most, children who find reading difficult.

outnumber girls 3-to-1 in community samples and 9-to-1 in clinical samples" (Hasson & Fine, 2012, p. 190). (Clinical samples are those children whose ADHD receives ongoing profession care.) Could typical boy activity be troubling to mothers and teachers? Could that be the reason for this male/female ratio?

Specific Learning Disorders

The DSM-5 diagnosis of **specific learning disorders** now includes problems in both perception and information processing that cause low achievement in reading, math, or writing (including spelling) (Lewandowski & Lovett, 2014). Differences in these areas undercut academic achievement, destroy self-esteem, and qualify a child for special education (according to U.S. law) or formal diagnosis (according to DSM-5).

The most commonly diagnosed learning disorder is **dyslexia** — unusual difficulty with reading. Historically, some children with dyslexia figured out themselves how to cope — as did Hans Christian Andersen and Winston Churchill.

Early theories hypothesized visual difficulties — for example, reversals of letters (reading *god* instead of *dog*) and mirror writing (*b* instead of *d*) — as causing dyslexia. That hypothesis was tested and found not to be the usual explanation. Instead, dyslexia more often originates with speech and hearing difficulties (Gabrieli, 2009; Swanson, 2013). Language development in the early years correlates with reading development later on.

dyslexia Unusual difficulty with reading; thought to be the result of some neurological underdevelopment.

specific learning disorder A marked deficit in a particular area of learning that is not caused by an apparent physical disability, by an intellectual disability, or by an unusually stressful home environment.

dyscalculia Unusual difficulty with math, probably originating from a distinct part of the brain.

Another common learning disorder is **dyscalculia,** unusual difficulty with math. For example, when asked to estimate the height of a normal room, second-graders with dyscalculia might answer "200 feet," or, when shown both the 5 and 8 of hearts from a deck of playing cards and asked which is higher, schoolchildren might use their fingers to count the hearts on each card (Butterworth et al., 2011).

Although learning disorders can appear in any skill, DSM-5 recognizes only dyslexia, dyscalculia, and one more — *dysgraphia,* difficulty in writing. Few children write neatly at age 5, but practice allows most children to write easily and legibly by age 10.

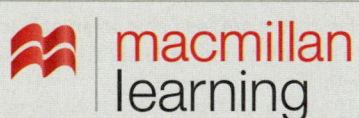

macmillan learning

VIDEO: Current Research into Autism Spectrum Disorder explores why the causes of ASD are still largely unknown.

Autism Spectrum Disorder

Autism was once a rare disorder affecting fewer than 1 in 1,000 children, who exhibited "an extreme aloneness that, whenever possible, disregards, ignores, shuts out anything . . . from the outside" (Kanner, 1943). Children with autism were usually nonverbal and severely impaired. They were usually institutionalized, and they died young.

That is no longer true. The defining symptom is still impaired social interaction, making children with autism less adept at conversion, at social play, and at understanding emotions. Theory of mind (explained in Chapter 9) develops much later, even if general executive function skills remain (Jones et al., 2018).

However, far more children and adults have signs of autism than once was suspected. Now, in the United States, among all 3- to 17-year-olds, an estimated 1 child in every 36 has been diagnosed as having ASD (Xu et al., 2019).

Accordingly, DSM-5 has changed the terminology from autism to **autism spectrum disorder (ASD).** People "on the spectrum" may have a mild, moderate, or severe form. Asperger's syndrome (people who are highly verbal but socially inept) was once considered a separate disorder; now Asperger's is part of that spectrum.

autism spectrum disorder (ASD) A developmental disorder marked by difficulty with social communication and interaction — including difficulty seeing things from another person's point of view — and restricted, repetitive patterns of behavior, interests, or activities.

Many scientists are searching for biological ways to detect autism early in life, perhaps with blood tests or brain scans before age 1. At the moment, behavioral signs are the best we have. ASD signs may appear in early infancy (no social smile, for example, or less gazing at faces and eyes).

Early diagnosis can produce early treatment, which benefits children and their parents. Currently, some children improve by age 3; others deteriorate (Klinger et al., 2014). Some children who were diagnosed with autism in early childhood have compensated so well that they are no longer on the spectrum (Livingston & Happé, 2017).

Remember neurodiversity, the concept that each person's brain functions differently? That is apparent with ASD, as those with this disorder seem to have a mixture of perceptions, abilities, and deficiencies that are unlike most children. Because of the diverse abilities of these children, adults should neither be dazzled by their talents nor saddened by their deficits. Some children with ASD have special talents in art or math. Many score above average in IQ (MMWR, March 28, 2014).

The neurodiversity perspective leads to new criticisms of the many treatments for ASD. When a child is diagnosed with ASD, parental responses vary from irrational hope to deep despair, from blaming doctors and chemical additives to feeling guilty for their genes, for their behavior during pregnancy, or for the circumstances of their child's birth.

A sympathetic observer describes one child who was medicated with

> Abilify, Topamax, Seroquel, Prozac, Ativan, Depakote, trazodone, Risperdal, Anafranil, Lamictal, Benadryl, melatonin, and the homeopathic remedy, Calms Forté. Every time I saw her, the meds were being adjusted again . . . [he also describes] physical interventions—putting children in hyperbaric oxygen chambers, putting them in tanks with dolphins, giving them blue-green algae, or megadosing them on vitamins . . . usually neither helpful nor harmful, though they can have dangers, are certainly disorienting, and cost a lot.
>
> *[Solomon, 2012, pp. 229, 270]*

Six Hypotheses Why is autism so much more common than it once was? Two hypotheses were suggested that now have been proven false. One is that unaffectionate or unavailable mothers (the so-called "refrigerator mothers") caused children to withdraw so far from social interaction as to develop autism. Before that idea was proven wrong, thousands of mothers were blamed.

The other disproven hypothesis was that infant vaccinations caused autism. Thousands of studies in many nations refute this idea (only one discredited, fraudulent study backed it), but some parents still refuse to immunize their children.

The current quest of millions of health professionals is to figure out how to prevent epidemics of measles and mumps that can harm children lifelong. A recent article focused on nurses. They are the medical professionals who are closest to the parents, and thus nurses may be able to convince parents to immunize their children to stop the resurgence of childhood diseases (Kubin, 2019).

Four new groups of hypotheses are suggested.

1. One cluster focuses on the environment, such as new chemicals in food, air, or water.
2. Another cluster considers prenatal influences: More mothers may use drugs, eat foods with traces of pesticides or hormones, contract viruses such as some strains of influenza.
3. A third set of hypotheses is that ASD itself has not increased, but diagnosis has. In 2000 in the United States, education for children with ASD became publicly funded, so parents may be more willing to seek a diagnosis and doctors to provide one.
4. Finally, DSM-5 itself may be the reason. Since the definition is expanded, more children fit the category and more doctors recognize the symptoms, so children who once were overlooked are now categorized as having ASD.

AF archive/Alamy Stock Photo

Not a Cartoon At age 3, Owen Suskind was diagnosed with autism. He stopped talking and spent hour after hour watching Disney movies. His father said his little boy "vanished," as chronicled in the Oscar-nominated documentary *Life Animated*. Now, at age 23 (shown here), Owen still loves cartoons, and he still has many symptoms of autism spectrum disorder. However, he also has learned to speak and has written a movie that reveals his understanding of himself, *The Land of the Lost Sidekicks*.

THINK CRITICALLY: Many adults are socially inept, insensitive to other people's emotions, and poor at communication—might they have been diagnosed as on the spectrum if they had been born more recently?

CHAPTER APP 11

Model Me Going Places 2

RELATED TOPIC:
Autism spectrum disorder and other childhood disorders

IOS:
http://tinyurl.com/y6qj2j27

Model Me Going Places 2 is a social skills aid designed for children with autism spectrum disorder or other differences, but the tutorials are useful for any child who needs help building social skills. Six sets of photos with narration demonstrate appropriate and expected behaviors in public settings, helping children learn about emotion labels and characterics, as well as cause and effect.

Kathryn Scott/The Denver Post/Getty Images

How It Should Be But Rarely Is In this well-equipped classroom in Centennial, Colorado, two teachers are attentively working with three young children, indicating that each child regularly receives individualized instruction. At this school, students with developmental disabilities learn alongside typical kids, so the earlier a child's education begins the better. Sadly, few nations have classrooms like this, and in the United States, few parents can find or afford special help for their children. Indeed, most children with special needs are not diagnosed until middle childhood.

least restrictive environment (LRE) A legal requirement that children with special needs be assigned to the most general educational context in which they can be expected to learn.

response to intervention (RTI) An educational strategy intended to help children who demonstrate below-average achievement in early grades, using special intervention.

individual education plan (IEP) A document that specifies educational goals and plans for a child with special needs.

Special Education

The overlap of the biosocial, cognitive, and psychosocial domains is evident to developmentalists, as is the need for parents, teachers, therapists, and researchers to work together to help each child. However, deciding whether a child should be educated differently than other children is not straightforward, nor is it closely related to individual needs. Parents, schools, and therapists often disagree.

According to the 1975 Education of All Handicapped Children Act, all children can learn, and all must be educated in the **least restrictive environment (LRE)**. This means that children with special needs are usually educated within a regular class (a practice once called *mainstreaming*) rather than restricted to a special class.

Sometimes a class is an *inclusion class,* which means that children with special needs are "included" in the general classroom, with "appropriate aids and services" (ideally from a trained teacher who works with the regular teacher).

A more strategy is called **response to intervention (RTI)** (Al Otaiba et al., 2019; Miciak et al., 2019). First, all children are taught specific skills—for instance, learning the sounds that various letters make. Then the children are tested, and those who did not master the skill receive special "intervention"—practice and individualized teaching, within the regular class.

After the first round of intervention, the children are tested again, and, if need be, intervention occurs again. According to the RTI strategy, only when children do not respond adequately to repeated, focused intervention are they referred for special education.

At that point, the school proposes an **individual education plan (IEP),** ideally designed for the particular child. Unfortunately, educators do not always know effective strategies, partly because research on remediation focuses on the less common problems. For example, in the United States "research funding in 2008–2009 for autistic spectrum disorder was 31 times greater than for dyslexia and 540 times greater than for dyscalculia" (Butterworth & Kovas, 2013, p. 304).

As **Figure 11.5** shows, the proportion of children designated with special needs in the United States rose from 10 percent in 1980 to 13 percent in 2016. The greatest rise was in children with learning disorders (National Center for Education Statistics, 2018).

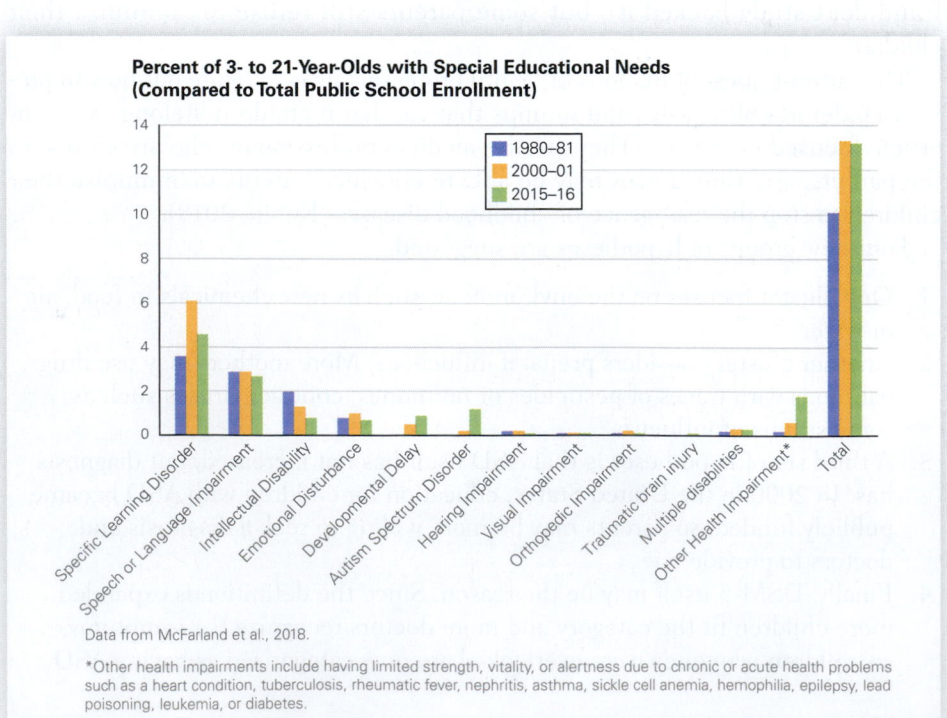

Percent of 3- to 21-Year-Olds with Special Educational Needs (Compared to Total Public School Enrollment)

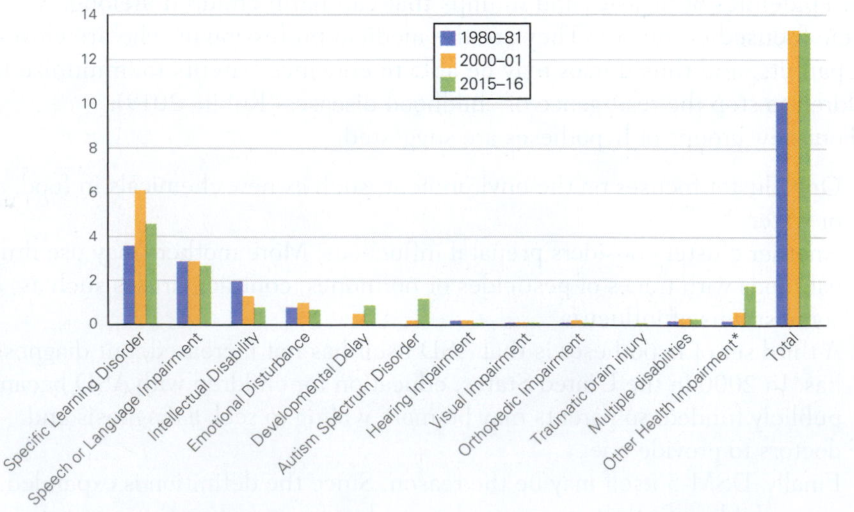

Data from McFarland et al., 2018.

*Other health impairments include having limited strength, vitality, or alertness due to chronic or acute health problems such as a heart condition, tuberculosis, rheumatic fever, nephritis, asthma, sickle cell anemia, hemophilia, epilepsy, lead poisoning, leukemia, or diabetes.

FIGURE 11.5

Changing Labels Note that fewer children have intellectual disability but more have autism. Many experts think that is a change in name, not substance.

The U.S. school system designates more children as having special needs than does any other nation: Whether or not this is a reason for national pride depends on whether one considers special education a benefit to children, to parents, or to teachers.

How many children really need special education? Some U.S. experts fear that neurodiversity, RTI, and inclusion may limit help for children with special needs. If everyone is special, will that prevent help for children who desperately need it (Kauffman et al., 2017)? (See A Case to Study.)

A CASE TO STUDY

The Gifted and Talented

Usually chapters focus on one case to study, but one lesson is apparent from all children with special needs: They vary among themselves a great deal. A diagnosis does not signify that all children with the same label have the same needs, or that they all need the same remediation.

To illustrate this point, we highlight another group of children who are sometimes thought to require special education, those who are unusually gifted and talented. Such children are so diverse that it seems best to describe several such children.

Historically, parents taught such children themselves or hired a special coach or tutor. For example, Mozart composed music at age 3 and Picasso created works of art at age 4. Both boys had fathers who recognized their talent. Mozart's father transcribed his earliest pieces and toured Europe with his gifted son; Picasso's father removed him from school in second grade so that he could create all day.

Although intense early education nourished their talent, neither Mozart nor Picasso had a happy adult life. Mozart had a poor understanding of math and money. He had six children, only two of whom survived infancy, and he died in debt at age 35. Picasso regretted never fully grasping how to read or write. He married at age 17 and had a total of four children by three women.

When school attendance became universal about a century ago, gifted children were allowed to skip early grades and join other children of the same mental age, not their chronological age. Many accelerated children never learned how to get along with others. As one woman remembers:

> Nine-year-old little girls are so cruel to younger girls. I was much smaller than them, of course, and would have done anything to have a friend. Although I could cope with the academic work very easily, emotionally I wasn't up to it. Maybe it was my fault and I was asking to be picked on. I was a weed at the edge of the playground.
>
> *[Rachel, quoted in Freeman, 2010, p. 27]*

Calling herself "a weed" suggests that Rachel never overcame her conviction that she was less cherished than the other children. Her intellectual needs may have been met by skipping two grades, but her emotional and social needs were severely neglected.

My own father skipped three grades, graduating from high school at age 14. Because he attended a one-room school, and because he was the middle child of five, his emotional and social needs were met until he began college, where he almost failed because of his immaturity. He recovered, but some other children do not. A chilling example comes from:

> Sufiah Yusof [who] started her maths degree at Oxford [the leading University in England] in 2000, at the age of 13. She too had been dominated and taught by her father. But she ran away the day after her final exam. She was found by police but refused to go home, demanding of her father in an email: "Has it ever crossed your mind that the reason I left home was because I've finally had enough of 15 years of physical and emotional abuse?" Her father claimed she'd been abducted and brainwashed. She refuses to communicate with him. She is now a very happy, high-class, high-earning prostitute.
>
> *[Freeman, 2010, p. 286]*

The fate of creative children may be worse than that of intellectually gifted children. If not given an education that suits them, they joke in class, resist drudgery, ignore homework, and bedevil their teachers. They may become innovators, inventors, and creative forces in the future, but they also may use drugs or drop out of school.

They may find it hard to earn a degree or get a steady job because they are eager to try new things and feel stifled by normal life. Among the well-known creative geniuses who were less-than-exemplary students were Bill Gates, Richard Branson, Steve Jobs, and hundreds of thousands of others, probably some of whom you know personally.

One such person was Charles Darwin, whose "school reports complained unendingly that he wasn't interested in studying, only shooting, riding, and beetle-collecting" (Freeman, 2010, p. 283). At the behest of his physician father, Darwin entered college to study medicine, but he dropped out.

Without a degree, he began his famous five-year trip around South America at age 22, collecting specimens and developing the theory of evolution—which disputed conventional religious dogma as only a highly creative person could do.

All of these examples suggest that extraordinary children may become extraordinary adults, but they bear some problems because of their abilities. As you see, educators are still not sure what the ideal schooling should be for the gifted and talented.

Steve Granitz/WireImage/Getty Images

And Tomorrow? The education of gifted children is controversial, as is the future of Sunny Pawar, "just a normal boy" from the slums of Mumbai (shown here at age 8) and also a talented star in *Lion,* a 2016 Oscar-nominated film made in Australia. After a worldwide tour to promote the film, he returned to his one-room home and attends school, where he gets none of the perks of being a movie star. What next?

Early Intervention One conclusion from all of the research on special education is that diagnosis and intervention often occur too late, or not at all. The numbers of children in public schools who are designated as needing special education increase as children grow older, which is the opposite of what would occur if early intervention were successful. This is apparent in each of the disorders we have discussed.

Sometimes the current approach is called "wait to fail," when ADHD and learning disorders are not diagnosed until a child has been struggling for years without help for sensory, familial, or cultural problems. As one expert says, "We need early identification, and. . . . early intervention. If you wait until third grade, kids give up" (Shaywitz, quoted in Stern, 2015, p. 1466).

A similar problem occurs with autism spectrum disorder. You read that autism appears in infancy, but children are not usually diagnosed until age 4, on average (MMWR, March 28, 2014). This is long after many parents have noticed something amiss in their child, and it is years after the most effective intervention can begin.

Teaching the Gifted and Talented Children who are unusually gifted are often thought to have special educational needs, although federal laws in the United States do not include them as a special category. Instead, each U.S. state selects and educates gifted and talented children in a particular way. Should children who are unusually intelligent, talented, or creative be home-schooled, skipped, segregated, or enriched? Each of these solutions has been tried and found lacking.

Since both acceleration and intense home schooling have led to later social problems, a third education strategy has become popular, at least in the United States. Children who are bright, talented, and/or creative—all the same age but each with special abilities—are taught as a group in their own separate class. Ideally, such children are neither bored nor lonely; each is challenged and appreciated by classmates and teachers.

Such classes require unusual teachers—bright and creative, and able to individualize instruction. For example, a 7-year-old artist may need freedom, guidance, and inspiration for magnificent art but also may need patient, step-by-step instruction in sounding out simple words.

Similarly, a 7-year-old classmate who already reads at the twelfth-grade level might have immature social skills, so the teacher must find another child to befriend him or her and then must help both of them share, compromise, and take turns. The teacher must also engage the child who is advanced in reading in conversation about books that most children cannot read until college.

The argument against gifted-and-talented classes is that *every* child needs such teachers, no matter what the child's abilities or disabilities. If each school district (and sometimes each school principal) hires and assigns teachers, as occurs in the United States, then the best teachers may have the most able students, and the school districts with the most money (the most expensive homes) may have the highest paid teachers. Should it be the opposite?

High-achieving students are especially likely to have great teachers if the hidden curriculum includes *tracking,* putting children with special needs together, sorting regular classes by past achievement of the students. Most private or charter schools select only certain students and expel difficult ones.

Every Child Special? Mainstreaming, IEPs, and so on were developed when parents and educators saw that segregation of children with special needs led to less learning and impaired adult lives. The same may happen if gifted and talented children are separated from the rest.

Some nations (China, Finland, Scotland, and many others) educate all children together, assuming that all children could become high achievers if they put in the effort and are guided by effective teachers. Since every child is special, should every child have special education?

WHAT HAVE YOU LEARNED?

1. What are the four principles of psychopathology?
2. What is the difference between multifinality and equifinality?
3. What is the difference between ADHD and typical child behavior?
4. What are dyslexia, dyscalculia, and dysgraphia?
5. What are the symptoms of autism spectrum disorder?
6. How might the concept of neurodiversity affect treatment for special children?
7. What is the difference between mainstreaming and inclusion?

SUMMARY

A Healthy Time

1. Middle childhood is the healthiest period of the entire life span. Death and disease rates are low, and typically good health habits protect every part of the body.

2. Physical activity aids health and joy in many ways. Benefits are apparent in bodies (strength and coordination) and brains (quicker reaction time, more selective attention). However, children who most need physical activity may be least likely to have it.

3. Both gross and fine motor skills increase during middle childhood. One particular way to improve fine motor skills is through art and music.

4. Worldwide, rates of obesity and asthma are increasing. Children suffer, particularly if they miss time with friends in school and in play.

5. International research finds that family habits and national policies interact to increase or decrease the rate of obesity and asthma.

Brain Development

6. Body movement affects brain maturation through blood flow and connections between one part of the brain and another.

7. During middle childhood, children gradually become better at paying attention and at reacting quickly. These are valuable skills in the classroom, as well as on sports teams. Athletic participation of all kinds develops the brain as well as the body.

8. Intellectual aptitude is usually measured with IQ tests, with scores that can change over time. Achievement is what a person has actually learned, a product of aptitude, motivation, and opportunity.

9. Critics of IQ testing contend that intelligence is manifested in multiple ways, which makes *g* (general intelligence) too narrow and limited. Gardner describes nine distinct intelligences.

Children with Special Brains and Bodies

10. Developmental psychopathology uses an understanding of typical development to inform the study of unusual development. Most disorders are comorbid.

11. Four general lessons apply to psychopathology at every age: Abnormality is normal; disability changes over time; plasticity and compensation are common; the social context affects manifestation, diagnosis, and treatment. Medication should not be the first response.

12. Children with attention-deficit/hyperactivity disorder (ADHD) have potential problems in three areas: inattention, impulsiveness, and activity. DSM-5 recognizes learning disorders, specifically dyslexia (reading), dyscalculia (math), and dysgraphia (penmanship).

13. Children on the autism spectrum typically have problems with social interaction and language. ASD originates in the brain, with genetic and prenatal influences, but neurodiversity suggests caution in treatment and analysis.

14. Education of children with special needs targets needed treatment. Response to remediation is a first step, before a child is formally adjudicated as a special-needs child.

KEY TERMS

childhood overweight (p. 280)
childhood obesity (p. 280)
asthma (p. 280)
reaction time (p. 283)
g (general intelligence) (p. 283)
Flynn effect (p. 285)
multiple intelligences (p. 286)
neurodiversity (p. 286)
developmental psychopathology (p. 287)
comorbid (p. 287)
multifinality (p. 287)
equifinality (p. 287)
attention-deficit/hyperactivity disorder (ADHD) (p. 288)
specific learning disorder (p. 290)
dyslexia (p. 290)
dyscalculia (p. 290)
autism spectrum disorder (ASD) (p. 290)
least restrictive environment (LRE) (p. 292)
response to intervention (RTI) (p. 292)
individual education plan (IEP) (p. 292)

APPLICATIONS

1. Compare play spaces and school design for children in different neighborhoods—ideally, urban, suburban, and rural areas. Note size, safety, and use. How might this affect children's health and learning?

2. Parents of children with special needs often consult Internet sources. Pick one disorder and find 10 Web sites that describe causes and educational solutions. How valid, how accurate, and how objective is the information? What disagreements do you find? How might parents react to the information provided?

3. Should every teacher be skilled at teaching children with a wide variety of needs, or should some teachers specialize in particular kinds of learning difficulties? Ask professors in your education department. Then ask parents of children with special needs.

4. How inclusive are the elementary schools (public, charter, and private) in your community? Get data on ethnic, economic, and ability grouping. Then analyze whether this is best.

Especially For ANSWERS

Response for Medical Professionals (from p. 280): You need to speak to the parents, not accusingly (because you know that genes and culture have a major influence on body weight) but helpfully. Alert them to the potential social and health problems that their child's weight poses. Most parents are very concerned about their child's well-being and will work with you to improve the child's snacks and exercise levels.

Response for Teachers (from p. 286): The advantages are that all of the children learn more aspects of human knowledge and that many children can develop their talents. Art, music, and sports should be an integral part of education, not just a break from academics. The disadvantage is that they take time and attention away from reading and math, which might lead to less proficiency in those subjects on standardized tests and thus to criticism from parents and supervisors.

Observation Quiz ANSWERS

Answer to Observation Quiz (from p. 276): Water bottles, sun visors, and I.D. badges—although the latter might not be considered a healthy innovation.

Answer to Observation Quiz (from p. 280): Overall, no. But in some groups, yes. Rates of obesity among Asian American boys are almost three times higher than among Asian American girls.

Answer to Observation Quiz (from p. 284): The person is average. Anyone with a score between 85 and 115 has an average IQ.

Answer to Observation Quiz (from p. 289): Yes, not only overall but also in response to the diagnosis. When a September birthday boy is diagnosed with ADHD, he is less likely to be medicated than an August birthday boy—the opposite of what would be expected if only boys with real problems were diagnosed.

VISUALIZING DEVELOPMENT Childhood Obesity Around the World

Obesity now causes more deaths worldwide than malnutrition. Reductions are possible. A multifaceted prevention effort—including parents, preschools, pediatricians, and grocery stores—has reduced obesity among U.S. 2- to 5-year-olds: Overall, the prevalence of obesity among adolescents (20.6%) and school-aged children (18.4%) is higher than among preschool-aged children (13.9%) (Hales et al., 2017). However, obesity rates from age 6 to 60 remain high everywhere.

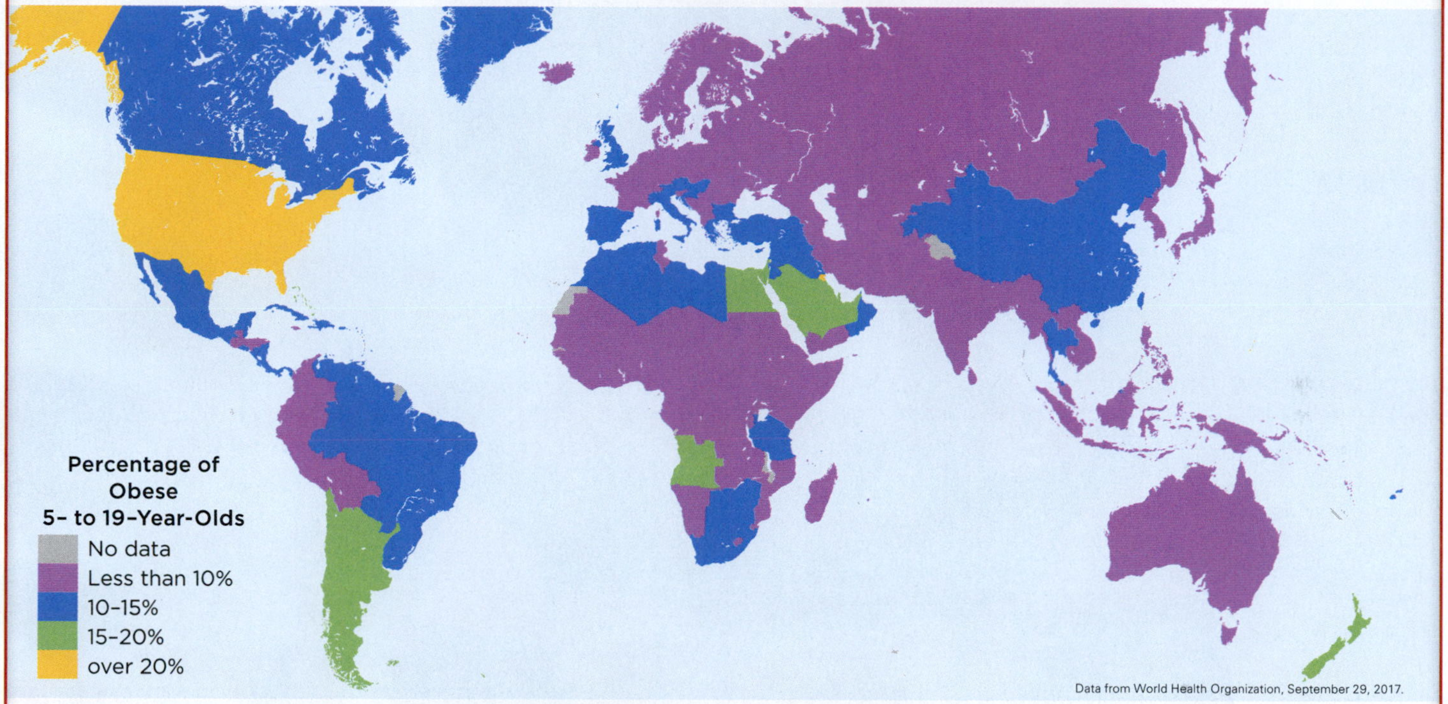

Data from World Health Organization, September 29, 2017.

FACTORS CONTRIBUTING TO CHILDHOOD OBESITY, BY THE NUMBERS

Children's exposure to televised ads for unhealthy food continues to correlate with childhood obesity (e.g., Hewer, 2014), but nations differ. For instance, in stark contrast with the United States, the United Kingdom has banned television advertising of foods high in fat, sugar, and salt to children under age 16. Parents can help by limiting screen time and playing outside with their children. The community matters as well: When neighborhoods have no safe places to play, rates of obesity soar.

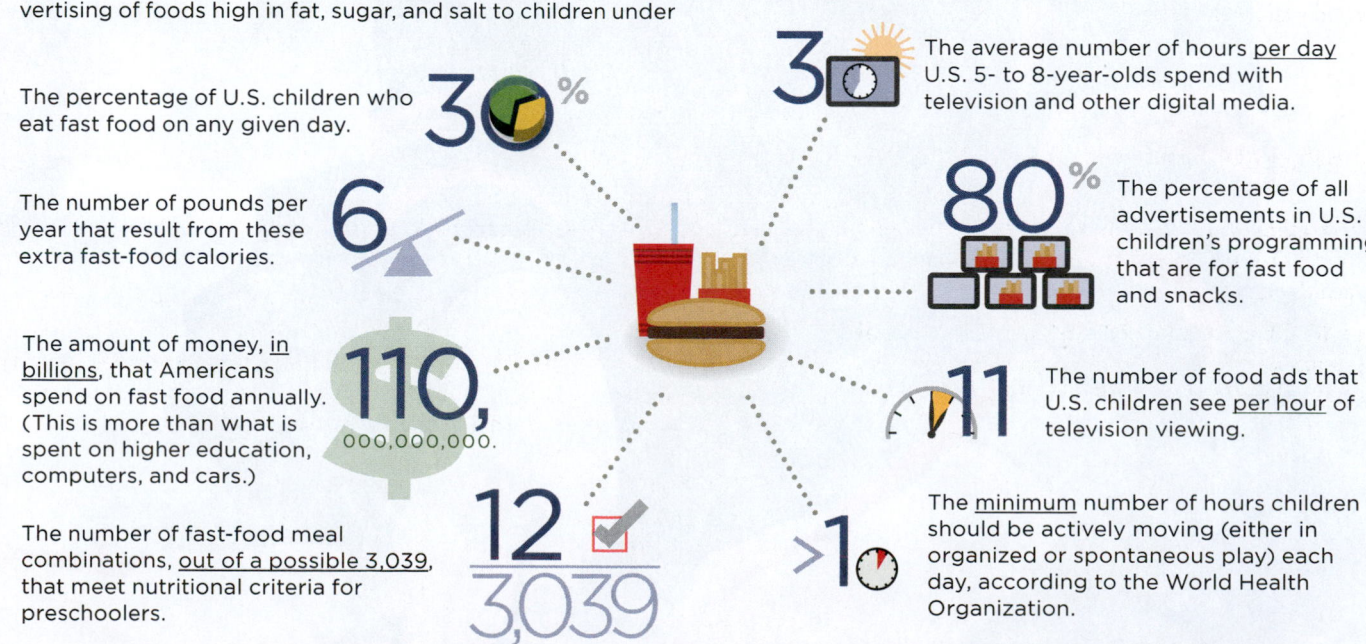

30% The percentage of U.S. children who eat fast food on any given day.

6 The number of pounds per year that result from these extra fast-food calories.

110,000,000,000 The amount of money, in billions, that Americans spend on fast food annually. (This is more than what is spent on higher education, computers, and cars.)

12/3,039 The number of fast-food meal combinations, out of a possible 3,039, that meet nutritional criteria for preschoolers.

3 The average number of hours per day U.S. 5- to 8-year-olds spend with television and other digital media.

80% The percentage of all advertisements in U.S. children's programming that are for fast food and snacks.

11 The number of food ads that U.S. children see per hour of television viewing.

>1 The minimum number of hours children should be actively moving (either in organized or spontaneous play) each day, according to the World Health Organization.

Data from Council on Communications and Media, 2011, p. 202; Rideout, V., 2017.

CHAPTER 12

Middle Childhood: Cognitive Development

What Will You Know?

1. Does cognition improve naturally with age, or is teaching crucial to its development?
2. Why do children use slang, curse words, and bad grammar?
3. What type of school is best during middle childhood?

- **Thinking**
  - Piaget on Middle Childhood
  - Vygotsky and Culture
  - OPPOSING PERSPECTIVES: Two or Twenty Pills a Day
  - Information Processing
  - INSIDE THE BRAIN: Coordination and Capacity
- **Language**
  - Vocabulary
  - Speaking Two Languages
  - Poverty and Language
- **Teaching and Learning**
  - The Curriculum
  - International Testing
  - A CASE TO STUDY: Happiness or High Grades?
  - Schooling in the United States
- **VISUALIZING DEVELOPMENT: Education in Middle Childhood**

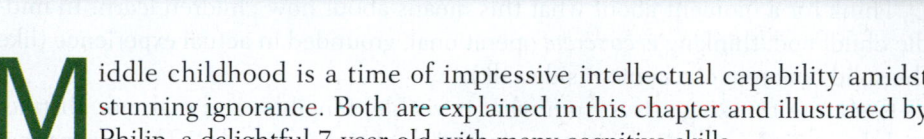

Middle childhood is a time of impressive intellectual capability amidst stunning ignorance. Both are explained in this chapter and illustrated by Philip, a delightful 7-year-old with many cognitive skills.

Philip speaks French to his mother and English to everyone else; he can read fluently and calculate Pokémon trades; he does his schoolwork conscientiously. Everyone likes Philip, in part because he has developed excellent pragmatic language skills: He knows when to use "bathroom words" that make his peers laugh and when to use polite phrases that adults appreciate. Thus, his cognition is impressive, which is true for many children in middle childhood. But not always.

Last year, Phillip's mother, Dora, needed open-heart surgery. She and her husband, Craig, told Philip that his mother would be in the hospital for a few days. They explained what this would mean for him, such as that his father would pick him up from school and several others would help with cooking and cleaning. Craig did the explaining; Dora did not want to show her fear.

Philip mirrored his parents' attitude: factual, not emotional. He had a few questions, mostly about exactly what the surgeon would do. A day later he told his parents that when he told his classmates that his mother was having heart surgery, one of them asked, "Is she going to die?" Philip reported this to show his parents how foolish his friend was; he seemed unaware of the insensitivity. His parents, wisely, exchanged wide-eyed glances but simply nodded.

Later, Craig asked Dora: "What is wrong with him? Does he have no heart?"

As you will read, Piaget described concrete operational thought, evident in 6- to 11-year-olds, and Vygotsky explained the power of the social context. Philip's thinking is typical of his age. During these years, if they are told that their parents are divorcing, children might ask, "Where will I live?" instead of expressing sympathy, surprise, or anger. Aspects of cognition that adults take for granted—empathy, emotional sensitivity, hope and fears for the future—develop gradually.

Dora's operation went well; no repeat surgery is expected. Someday Philip might blame his 7-year-old self for his nonchalance; Craig and Dora can reassure him that he reacted as a child normally does. Later, as adolescents, Philip and his classmates will have more than enough "heart."

Left: Marc Romanelli/Blend Images/Getty Images. Licensed Material is being used for illustrative purposes only; any person depicted in the licensed Material is a model.
Top: EdZbarzhyvetsky/Deposit Photos

Thinking

The human mind from age 6 to 11 is ready to explore and learn from every experience, as children move from the shelter of their family to the wider world of school and community. New intellectual capacities are evident, as described somewhat differently by Piaget, Vygotsky, and information-processing theory.

Piaget on Middle Childhood

concrete operational thought Piaget's term for the ability to reason logically about direct experiences and perceptions.

Piaget called this stage of development **concrete operational thought,** characterized by new logical abilities. *Operational* comes from the Latin verb *operare,* meaning "to work; to produce."

By calling this period operational, Piaget emphasized productive thinking. By using the word *concrete,* Piaget stressed that the logic of children is focused on specific experiences and observations, not on abstractions. Piaget's theory is a classic stage theory: Concrete operational thinking follows preoperational thought and precedes formal operational cognition, when abstractions become possible.

Think for a moment about what this means about how children learn. In middle childhood, thinking is *concrete* operational, grounded in actual experience (like the solid concrete of a cement sidewalk).

Concrete thinking arises from what is visible, tangible, and real, not abstract and theoretical (as at the next stage, formal operational thought). This means that thinking benefits from personal experience. Play, excursions, classroom interactions, games with objects—all of this is grist for concrete thought.

classification The logical principle that things can be organized into groups (or categories or classes) according to some characteristic that they have in common.

seriation The concept that things can be arranged in a logical series, such as the number sequence or the alphabet.

A Hierarchy of Categories One logical operation is **classification,** the organization of things into groups (or *categories* or *classes*) according to some characteristic that they share. For example, *family* includes parents, siblings, and cousins. Other common classes are animals, toys, transportation, and food. Each class includes some elements and excludes others; each is part of a hierarchy.

Food, for instance, is an overarching category, with the next-lower level of the hierarchy being meat, grains, fruits, and so on. Most subclasses can be further divided: Meat includes poultry, beef, and pork, each of which can be divided again.

Adults grasp that items at the bottom of a classification hierarchy belong to every higher level: Bacon is always pork, meat, and food. They also know that each higher category includes many lower ones, but not vice versa (most food, meat, and pork are not bacon). This mental operation of moving up and down the hierarchy is beyond preoperational children.

Gradually, with personal experience (such as eating a variety of foods, meeting many relatives, using several forms of transportation), concrete operational children can classify. They begin to understand, for instance, that planes and motor vehicles are both transportation and that each can be subdivided and further subdivided (buses/trucks/cars, and then sedans/limousines/station wagons, and so on).

Observation Quiz What indicates that his caregivers are protective of his welfare? (see answer, page 320) ↓

Divine Images/Hero Images/Media Bakery

Notebook and Weeds "Write about it," said the teacher to the students on a field trip near San Diego, California. Will this boy describe the air, the plants, the trees—or will his canvas bag distract him? Concrete operational thought is not abstract: He probably won't write about Mother Earth, global warming, or God's kingdom.

Piaget devised many classification experiments. In one, he showed a child a bunch of nine flowers—seven yellow daisies and two white roses. Then the child is asked, "Are there more daisies or more flowers?" Until about age 7, most children answer, "More daisies."

The youngest children offer no justification, but some 6-year-olds explain that "there are more yellow ones than white ones" or "because daisies are daisies, they aren't flowers" (Piaget et al., 2015). By age 8, most children can classify: "More flowers than daisies," they say.

Understanding Sequence Another example of concrete logic is **seriation,** the knowledge that things can be arranged in a logical *series.* Seriation is crucial for using (not merely memorizing) the alphabet or the number sequence. By age 5, most children can count up to 100, but because they do not yet grasp seriation, most cannot correctly estimate where any particular two-digit number would be placed on a line that starts at 0 and ends at 100.

The ability to remember a sequence of events or actions develops gradually in middle childhood. For example, when children are shown four actions in sequence (for instance, dropping a button into a tube, moving two toys together, putting a stick through a hole, tapping a toy animal with a stick) and are asked to do them in order, most 5-year-olds are unable to do so. By age 8, children are better at this task (Loucks & Price, 2019).

This ability to follow a series may seem inconsequential, but in fact there are dozens of practical applications. Gradually during middle childhood, children learn to get ready for school by performing a series of actions: pee, eat breakfast, brush teeth, put on underwear, then pants and shirt, then socks, then shoes, and so on. This is very hard for 6-year-olds, who need to be reminded what to do next. It is easier with age—and with a list that can be checked off.

Toby Maudsley/The Image Bank/Getty Images

Numbers and Sequence Their lockers are numbered, not named, as was true in preschool. Are these children (from Stockholm, Sweden) also aware that their lockers were assigned according to how many inches tall each child is?

Learning Math Math begins with familiarity with numbers. As you remember from Chapter 9, some children hear numbers often, such as 10 minutes to play, you are 4 years old, push the elevator button for the third floor. However, to understand math, children need to grasp the logic behind the numbers, and that develops gradually during concrete operational thought.

Every logical concept helps with math. Concrete operational thinkers begin to understand that 15 is always 15 (conservation); that numbers from 20 to 29 are all in the 20s (classification); that 134 is less than 143 (seriation); and that because $5 \times 3 = 15$, it follows that $15 \div 5$ must equal 3 (reversibility). By age 11, children use mental categories and subcategories flexibly, inductively, and simultaneously, unlike at age 7.

This learning occurs best when hands-on math (using manipulatives such as blocks, coins, or beans) and verbal descriptions of concepts are both part of instruction (Bachman et al., 2015). Children need to work out math problems together: Social interaction is part of concrete thought.

There are cultural and family differences in how quickly children apply concepts to their math understanding: Those differences are related to specifics of preschool and family education. But all children need cognitive maturation before they can, for instance, perform the necessary steps of multidigit multiplication or grasp that four-fifths is greater than seven-tenths.

Vygotsky and Culture

Like Piaget, Vygotsky felt that educators should consider children's thought processes, not just the outcomes of those processes. He also believed that middle childhood was a time for much learning, with the specifics dependent on the family, school, and culture.

Vygotsky appreciated children's curiosity and creativity. For that reason, he believed that an educational system based on rote memorization rendered the child "helpless in the face of any sensible attempt to apply any of this acquired knowledge" (Vygotsky, 1994a, pp. 356–357).

Vygotsky would consider a repressive school particularly destructive of cognitive development, because "development depends heavily on the existing diverse social structures" (Lourenço, 2012, p. 284). Thus, the specifics of school organization and curriculum, as well as of family interactions and values, and of cultural mandates and practices, are crucial for Vygotsky.

Especially for Teachers How might Piaget's and Vygotsky's ideas help in teaching geography to a class of third-graders? (see response, page 320)

The Role of Instruction Unlike Piaget, Vygotsky welcomed direct instruction from teachers and other mentors. They provide the scaffold between potential and knowledge, engaging children in their own zone of proximal development.

Vygotsky would not be surprised that children who begin school at age 4 or 5, not 6 or 7, tend to be ahead in academic achievement compared to those who enter later. This effect is still apparent at age 15, although not in every nation (Sprietsma, 2010).

Vygotsky would expect children with more social interactions within their zone of proximal development (as would happen in any good kindergarten) to benefit intellectually. The impact of an extra year of early schooling will vary, because some nations have encouraged more interactive education than others.

School is one arena for guided participation, but Vygotsky noted many others. Play with peers, dinner with family, tapping on a screen, greeting neighbors—every experience, from birth on, teaches a child, according to Vygotsky. On their own, children gradually become more logical during middle childhood, but Vygotsky emphasized the role of mentoring.

By the end of middle childhood, some children understand that *if* birds can fly, and *if* elephants are birds, *then* elephants can fly (Christoforides et al., 2016). That logic is not spontaneously understood until formal operational thought, but when children are taught, they can master logical arguments (even counterfactual ones) by age 11. Note that this is not what Piaget stressed. Piaget advocated discovery; Vygotsky stressed guidance.

Vygotsky knew that the lessons a child learns vary by culture and school and are not simply the result of maturation. He recognized, however, that children are limited by experience and age, as in comprehending philosophical issues of life and death. They tend to be quite matter-of-fact, absorbing whatever their parents and culture teach rather than seeking the deeper meaning—as was true for Philip (opening anecdote).

Information Processing

Contemporary educators and psychologists find both Piaget and Vygotsky insightful. International research confirms the merits of their theories (Wright, 2018; Mercer & Howe, 2012). One scholar wrote:

> [A]sked who are the two main geniuses in the field of developmental psychology, many, if not all, developmentalists would certainly point to Jean Piaget (1896–1980) and Lev Vygotsky (1896–1934).
>
> *[Lourenço, 2012, p. 281]*

Piaget described universal changes; Vygotsky noted cultural impact. However, neither grand theory describes the year-by-year details of cognition in middle childhood. Each domain of achievement may follow a particular path (Siegler, 2016). Developmentalists recognize the need for a third approach to understanding cognition.

As you read in earlier chapters, the *information-processing perspective* benefits from technology that allows much more detailed data and analysis than were possible for Piaget or Vygotsky. Like computers that process information, people accumulate large amounts of facts. They then (1) seek relevant facts (as a search engine does) for each cognitive task, (2) analyze (as software programs do), and (3) express conclusions (as the totals on a spreadsheet might). By tracing the paths and links of each of these functions, scientists better understand the learning process.

The usefulness of the information-processing approach is evident in data on children's school achievement year by year and even month by month. Absences, vacations, new schools, and even new teachers set back a child's learning because each day builds on the learning of the previous day.

A Boy In Memphis Moziah Bridges (known as Mo Morris) created colorful bowties, which he first traded for rocks in elementary school. He then created his own company (Mo's Bows) at age 9, selling $300,000 worth of ties to major retailers by age 14. He is shown here with his mother, who encouraged his entrepreneurship.

ABC/Photofest

OPPOSING PERSPECTIVES

Two or Twenty Pills a Day

As you have seen, adults often have opposite points of view on many developmental issues, from racial differences to breast-feeding, from immunization to cesarean births. Here, we present a different kind of opposing perspective, one directly related to the logic and experience of the child.

Researchers presented adults and two groups of children, some at the beginning and some at the end of middle childhood, with the following:

> Marty's ear is red and swollen and hurts a lot. Marty goes to the doctor with his badly infected ear. The doctor takes a look at Marty and gives him some medicine to solve the problem. He tells Marty to take two pills each day, one in the morning when he wakes up, and one at night before he goes to bed. He should take those pills for 10 days—so that if Marty takes two pills a day for ten days, that would be 20 pills in all.
>
> *[Lockhart & Keil, 2018, p. 66]*

The participants were asked what would happen if Marty did not take the pills as prescribed but instead:

Took one a day for 20 days.

Took two every morning and none at night for 10 days.

Took two every morning, two at night, for five days.

Took all 20 at once, immediately.

Would Marty get better (rated a 3), stay the same (2), or get worse (rated 1)? The overall results are shown in **Figure 12.1**. As you see, 20 pills at once was quite acceptable to many of the youngest children. Other data showed that only half of them thought this megadose would be harmful, as did 77 percent of the 8- to 11-year-olds and 93 percent of the adults.

This is dramatic evidence that logic by itself is not enough, nor is experience. Virtually all of these children, in their first five years of life, had taken pills prescribed over a period of days, but that experience did not teach them. At the beginning of middle childhood, some understanding began. However, simple logic (more is better) led to a dangerous perspective unless it was tempered by experience. From a developmental perspective, Piaget is inadequate without Vygotsky.

As you also see from these data, children grow wiser in middle childhood, but their concrete, literal thinking is evident. The 8- to 11-year-olds were less willing to deviate from the prescribed dose than the adults were.

Most of the adults thought Marty would still get better if he took two pills every morning or only one every day, but many children disagreed. Balanced cognition, using both logic and experience, is not yet available to every 8- to 11-year-old.

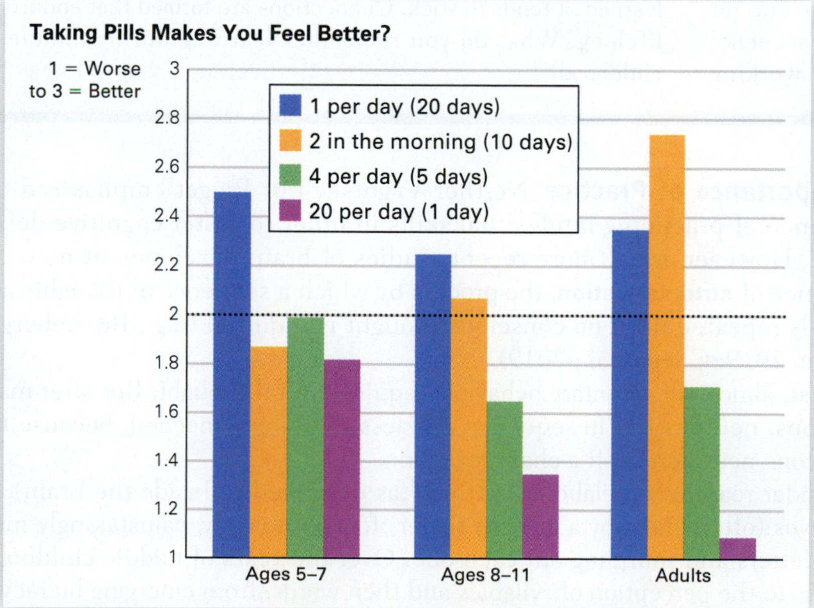

FIGURE 12.1

Not Doctor's Orders A doctor diagnosed an infected ear and prescribed 20 pills, with instructions to take one in the morning and one in the evening for ten days. People of various ages were asked how the person would feel if they didn't follow orders. A rating of 3 means "better"; 1 means "worse." The chart shows the average responses, by age. As you see, almost every adult expected improvement if the person took two each morning, and they knew that taking 20 at once was a terrible idea. About half of the youngest children did not know that—most thought the person would still feel okay, and some thought taking 20 pills at once would be fine! Most also thought that one pill a day would be good enough. Given how children think, no wonder their accident rate is so high.

Brain connections and pathways are forged from repeated experiences, allowing advances in processing. Without careful building and repetition, fragile connections between neurons break. Middle childhood is a crucial time for brain connections between one region and another, with the specifics of cultural emphasis aiding those links.

INSIDE THE BRAIN

Coordination and Capacity

Recall that emotional regulation, theory of mind, and left–right coordination emerge in early childhood. The maturing corpus callosum connects the hemispheres of the brain, enabling balance and two-handed coordination, while myelination adds speed. Maturation of the prefrontal cortex—the executive part of the brain—allows the child to plan, monitor, and evaluate.

In middle childhood, increasing maturation results in connections between the brain's various lobes and regions. Connections are crucial for the complex tasks that children must master, which require "smooth coordination of large numbers of neurons" (P. Stern, 2013, p. 577).

Certain areas of the brain, called *hubs,* are locations where massive numbers of axons meet. Hubs tend to be near the corpus callosum, and damage to them correlates with notable brain dysfunction (Crossley et al., 2014).

Because of hubs, brain connections forming in middle childhood are crucial (Wierenga et al., 2018). Consider learning to read. Reading is not instinctual: Our ancestors never did it, and until recent centuries, only a few scribes and scholars could interpret letters written on papyrus, carved in wood, or chiseled into stone. Consequently, the brain has no areas dedicated to reading in the way it does for talking or gesturing (Sousa, 2014).

Instead, reading uses many parts of the brain—one for sounds, another for recognizing letters, another for sequencing, another for comprehension, and more. By working together, these parts first foster listening, talking, and thinking, and then they put it all together (Lewandowski & Lovett, 2014).

Children with reading difficulties are variable. That makes their reading erratic (Tamm et al., 2014). Fluent reading—possible at age 8 or so—requires:

1. seeing a long sequence of letters;
2. segmenting them as words;
3. differentiating words spelled alike (such as *read* and *read, bark* and *bark*);
4. considering context to grasp unfamiliar words;
5. recognizing oddities and ironies; and
6. understanding meaning related to the previous sentences.

For fluency, reactions must be quick and automatic.

More broadly, it is now evident that the prefrontal cortex coordinates many hubs and subcortical regions of the brain "very rapidly (prior to conscious awareness)" as the brain automatically responds to stimulation (Blair, 2016, p. 3). This rapid, unconscious processing is the result of all of the neurotransmitters and neurological hubs of early and middle childhood.

The brain of a typical 6- to 11-year-old is ready to learn rapidly and well; and because of plasticity, once something is learned, it tends to stick. Connections are formed that endure lifelong. What do you remember learning during middle childhood?

automatization A process in which repetition of a sequence of thoughts and actions makes the sequence routine so that it no longer requires conscious thought.

The Importance of Practice Neither Vygotsky nor Piaget emphasized the importance of practicing intellectual skills in order to foster cognitive development. However, many more recent studies of brain development note the importance of **automatization,** the process by which a sequence of thoughts and actions is repeated until no conscious thought is required (e.g., Rønneberg & Torrance, 2019; Chen et al., 2019).

At first, almost all voluntary behaviors require careful thought. But after many repetitions, neurons fire in sequence and less thinking is needed, because the firing of one neuron sets off a chain reaction.

Consider reading, an elaborate activity (as described in Inside the Brain). At age 6, eyes (often aided by a guiding finger) focus intensely, painstakingly making out letters and sounding out each one. Over the years of middle childhood, this leads to the perception of syllables and then words, from emerging literacy at about age 6 to fluent reading by age 10. Eventually, the process becomes so automatic that people driving along a highway read billboards with a glance when they have no interest in doing so.

Automatization aids all academic skills. One longitudinal study of second-graders—from the beginning of the school year to the end—found that each type of academic proficiency aided each other type. Thus, learning became more automatic as automatization fostered more learning (Lai et al., 2014).

Learning a second language, reciting the multiplication tables, and writing one's name are all slow at first, but automatization makes each effortless as the school years go by. Not just academic knowledge but also habits and routines from childhood echo lifelong—and adults find them hard to break. If you have a bad habit that you can't stop, blame your brain. That's automatization.

For instance, being able to calculate when to utter a witty remark and when to stay quiet is something few 6-year-olds can do. By the end of middle childhood, children can (1) realize that a comment could be made and (2) decide what it could be, (3) think about the other person's possible response and, in the same split second, (4) know when something should NOT be said.

Some responses—saying "thank you" for a compliment, "good morning" to an acquaintance, "please" to a stranger—are learned in early childhood (often slowly, with reminders from adults) and become automatic in middle childhood.

Abaca Press/Sipa USA via AP Images

Following Instructions In middle childhood, children become quite capable of following adults' instructions, as these children in Tallinn, Estonia are. Their teacher told them to put out their right hand, so that Pope Francis could greet each child quickly. The teacher must not have given the most important instruction about greeting a pope: Keep your eyes open.

Siegler on Math Learning One of the leaders of the information-processing perspective is Robert Siegler, who studies day-by-day details of children's cognition in math (Siegler & Braithwaite, 2017). Siegler compares the acquisition of knowledge to waves on an ocean beach when the tide is rising. After ebb and flow, eventually a new level is reached.

Like those waves, math understanding accrues gradually, with new and better strategies for calculation tried, ignored, half-used, abandoned, and finally adopted (Siegler, 2016). The specifics are influenced by the culture, which may or may not emphasize math concepts, and the teachers, who may or may not understand the need for patience and practice. Counting itself is the product of culture: Some languages lack words for large numbers, fractions, and so on (Everett, 2017).

Using computer testing and analysis, Siegler and his colleagues have been able to pinpoint lapses in children's understanding of math concepts with precision, unlike Piaget and Vygotsky. For example, many children at age 10 are quite capable of adding and subtracting whole numbers, but they are woefully inadequate with fractions (Braithwaite et al., 2018). Research uncovers the particular needs that children have.

macmillan learning

VIDEO: Arithmetic Strategies: The Research of Robert Siegler demonstrates how children acquire math understanding.

Knowledge Leads to Knowledge The more people already know, the better they can learn. Having an extensive **knowledge base,** or a broad body of knowledge in a particular subject, makes it easier to remember and understand related new information. As children gain knowledge during the school years, they become better able to judge (1) accuracy, (2) what is worth remembering, and (3) what is not important (Woolley & Ghossainy, 2013).

knowledge base A body of knowledge in a particular area that makes it easier to master new information in that area.

Past experience, current opportunity, and personal motivation all facilitate increases in the knowledge base. Motivation explains why a child may not know what facts parents or teachers prefer.

Some schoolchildren memorize words and rhythms of hit songs, calculate the worth of dozens of game cards, or recite names and statistics of basketball (or soccer, baseball, or cricket) stars. Yet they do not know whether World War I was in the nineteenth or twentieth century, or whether Pakistan is in Asia or Africa.

Concepts are learned best when linked to personal and emotional experiences. For example, children from South Asia, or those with classmates from there, learn the boundaries of Pakistan if teachers appreciate and connect with their students' heritage. On the other hand, children who are new to a nation or a neighborhood may be confused by some concepts that are easy for those who have always lived there.

control processes Mechanisms (including selective attention, metacognition, and emotional regulation) that combine memory, processing speed, and knowledge to regulate the analysis and flow of information within the information-processing system. (Also called *executive processes*.)

Control Processes The neurological mechanisms that put memory, processing speed, and the knowledge base together are **control processes;** they regulate the analysis and flow of information within the brain. Two terms are often used to refer to cognitive control—*metacognition* (sometimes called "thinking about thinking") and *metamemory* (knowing about memory).

Control processes require the brain to organize, prioritize, and direct mental operations. For that reason, control processes are also called executive processes, and the ability to use them is called executive function (already explained in Chapter 9).

Control processes allow a person to step back from the specifics to consider more general goals and cognitive strategies, with the flexibility, memory, and inhibition that characterize executive processing. The finding, again and again, is that how children use their minds provides the foundation for learning. Maturation and experience matter.

All of these abilities develop spontaneously as the prefrontal cortex matures, but they can also be taught (de Oliveira Cardoso et al., 2018). Examples that may be familiar include spelling rules ("*i* before *e* except after *c*") and ways to remember how to turn a lightbulb ("lefty-loosey, righty-tighty").

Preschoolers ignore such rules or use them only on command; 7-year-olds begin to use them; 9-year-olds can create and master more complicated rules. Efforts to teach executive control succeed if the particular neurological maturation of the child is taken into account, which is exactly what information-processing theorists would predict (Karbach & Unger, 2014).

Michael Prince/Getty Images

What Does She See? It depends on her knowledge base and personal experiences. Perhaps this trip to an aquarium in North Carolina is no more than a break from the school routine, with the teachers merely shepherding the children to keep them safe. Or, perhaps she has learned about sharks and dorsal fins, about scales and gills, about warm-blooded mammals and cold-blooded fish, so she is fascinated by the swimming creatures she watches. Or, if her personal emotions shape her perceptions, perhaps she feels sad about the fish in their watery cage or finds joy in their serenity and beauty.

Theory of Mind Closely related to control processes is the ongoing development of theory of mind (Wilson et al., 2018). As you remember, theory of mind begins in early childhood. It continues to develop, including more nuanced beliefs and desires, in middle childhood and beyond (Wellman, 2018).

Theory of mind turns out to be pivotal for cognitive development. For example, it aids 6- to 11-year-olds in understanding the scientific process and mathematics. Both of those aspects of cognitive development are far from merely factual; they are facilitated by social awareness (Piekny & Maehler, 2013; Peng et al., 2017; Libertus et al., 2013).

WHAT HAVE YOU LEARNED?

1. What did Piaget mean when he called cognition in middle childhood *concrete operational thought*?
2. How do Vygotsky and Piaget differ in their explanations of cognitive advances in middle childhood?
3. How does information-processing theory differ from traditional theories of cognitive development?
4. According to Siegler, what is the pattern of learning math concepts?
5. How and why does the knowledge base increase in middle childhood?
6. How might control processes help a student learn?

Language

Language is crucial for cognition in middle childhood. It is the means by which children learn new concepts, and it also indicates how much children have learned. A school-age child who can explain ideas with complex sentences is a child who is thinking well. Every aspect of language—vocabulary, comprehension, communication skill, and code-switching—advances each year from age 6 to 11.

Vocabulary

Vocabulary builds during middle childhood. Because concrete operational children are logical, they can use prefixes, suffixes, compound words, phrases, and metaphors. That enables them to understand the meaning of a word they have never heard before, a decided advantage over younger children.

For example, 2-year-olds know *egg,* but 10-year-olds also know *egg salad, egg-drop soup, egghead, a good egg,* and *"last one in is a rotten egg"*—a metaphor from my childhood that a 2017 Google search found still relevant today. By age 10, a child who has never smelled a rotten egg nor heard that phrase can figure out the meaning.

In middle childhood, some words become pivotal for understanding the curriculum, such as *negotiate, evolve, allegation, deficit, molecule.* Consequently, vocabulary is taught in every elementary school classroom.

JONAS GRATZER/LIGHTROCKET/GETTY IMAGES

Go With the Flow This boat classroom in Bangladesh picks up students on shore and then uses solar energy to power computers linked to the Internet as part of instruction. The educational context will teach skills and metaphors that peers of these students will not understand.

Adjusting Language to the Context A crucial aspect of language that advances markedly in middle childhood is pragmatics, defined in Chapter 9. Pragmatics is evident when a child knows which words to use with teachers (never calling them a rotten egg) and informally with friends (who can be called rotten eggs or worse). For this, the social interaction foundation for cognition is apparent.

As children master pragmatics, they become more adept at making friends. Shy 6-year-olds cope far better with the social pressures of school if they use pragmatics well (Coplan & Weeks, 2009). By contrast, children with autism spectrum disorder are usually very poor at pragmatics (Klinger et al., 2014).

Mastery of pragmatics allows children to change styles of speech, or *linguistic codes,* depending on their audience. Each code includes many aspects of language—not just vocabulary but also tone, pronunciation, grammar, sentence length, idioms, and gestures. Sometimes the switch is between *formal code* (used in academic contexts) and *informal code* (used with friends); sometimes it is between standard (or proper) speech and dialect or vernacular (used on the street).

All children need instruction because the logic of grammar and spelling (whether *who* or *whom* is correct, or how to spell *you*) is almost impossible to deduce. Since they will be judged by ability to speak and write the formal code, children need to learn it.

THINK CRITICALLY: Do children from some backgrounds need to become especially adept at code-switching? Does this challenge advance cognitive development?

Speaking Two Languages

Code changes are obvious when children speak one language at home and another at school. Every nation includes many such children; most of the world's 6,000 languages are not school languages.

In the United States, about one school-age child in five speaks something other than English at home (see **Figure 12.2**). Many other U.S. children speak one or more of the 20 or so English dialects that reflect regional or ethnic word use, pronunciation, and grammar.

A child's comfort using the home language or regional dialect correlates with pride and motivation. At the same time, in the United States, a child's ability to use standard English correlates with school achievement.

Consequently, teachers need to respect the home language while teaching the school language (Terry et al., 2016). However, this is not as simple as it may seem, as

FIGURE 12.2

Home and Country Do you see good news, or do you see trouble? A dramatic increase in the number of bilingual children is a benefit for the nation, but the increase in the number who have trouble with English suggests that more education is needed.

Bilingual 5- to 17-Year-Olds in the United States

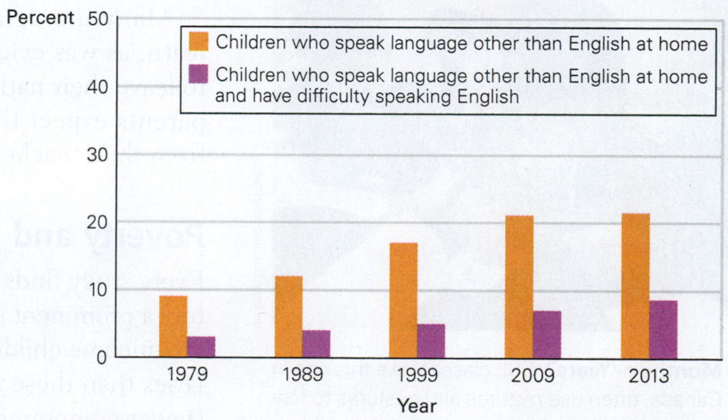

Data from Aud et al., 2010, p. 33; U.S. Census Bureau, 2016a; U.S. Census Bureau, 2016b.

adult ideology many conflict with what is best for the child (MacSwan, 2018). It is known, however, that language is crucial for school achievement from early childhood on. Children can learn several codes—easily before age 5, with some help in middle childhood, and with effort after puberty.

Educators and political leaders in the United States argue about how to teach English to **English Language Learners (ELLs),** students whose first language is not Standard English. About 12 percent of the children in middle childhood are designated as ELLs (McFarland et al., 2018). Note that this is significantly lower than the percent who speak another language at home. Many of them are bilingual before they reach primary school.

How should children learn the school language if they have not already done so in early childhood? One strategy is called **immersion,** in which instruction occurs entirely in the new code. The opposite strategy is to teach children in their first language initially and then to add instruction of the second as a "foreign" tongue (a strategy that is rare in the United States but common elsewhere).

Between these extremes lies **bilingual education,** with instruction in two languages, and **English as a Second Language (ESL),** with all non-English speakers taught English in one multilingual group, preparing them to join English-only classes. Every method for teaching a second language sometimes succeeds and sometimes fails. A major problem is that language-learning abilities change with age: The youngest children learn a new language fastest, so immersion might succeed for them.

For cognitive advances during middle childhood, the information-processing approach suggests that children should learn two languages. When bilingual individuals are asked to reason about something in their second language, they tend to be more rational and less emotional—which usually (but not always) leads to better thought (Costa et al., 2017).

Bilingual children who are fluent in both languages are able to inhibit one language while using another, advancing in cognitive control. This is obvious in language but also is an asset in other aspects of executive function (Bialystok, 2018). The emphasis here is on proficiency: Children who are not fluent in at least one language are also impaired in cognitive skills.

Parents influence the language fluency of their children, but they are not alone. Children benefit from conversations with relatives, strangers, friends, and teachers, which is one reason going to school every day and playing with children who are proficient in other languages are recommended for language development in middle childhood.

One of my African students speaks five languages, all learned before puberty. His mother and father came from different ethnic groups, so he learned two home languages. He was schooled in Senegal (French-speaking) and Sierra Leone (English-speaking). Finally, he learned Arabic to study the Quran.

Many immigrant children have another advantage, powerful motivation to learn, as was evident in my student. They seek to validate their parents' decision to leave their native land (Ceballo et al., 2014; Fuller & García Coll, 2010). Their parents expect them to learn the school language and to study hard. With help from their teachers and friends, they do.

English Language Learners (ELLs) Children in the United States whose proficiency in English is low—usually below a cutoff score on an oral or written test. Many children who speak a non-English language at home are also capable in English; they are *not* ELLs.

immersion A strategy in which instruction in all school subjects occurs in the second (usually the majority) language that a child is learning.

bilingual education A strategy in which school subjects are taught in both the learner's original language and the second (majority) language.

English as a Second Language (ESL) A U.S. approach to teaching English that gathers all of the non-English speakers together and provides intense instruction in English. Students' first languages are never used; the goal is to prepare students for regular classes in English.

Especially for Parents You've had an exhausting day but are setting out to buy groceries. Your 7-year-old son wants to go with you. Should you explain that you are so tired that you want to make a quick solo trip to the supermarket this time? (see response, page 320)

Ian Taylor/First Light/Getty Images

Months or Years? ESL classes, like this one in Canada, often use pictures and gestures to foster word learning. How soon will these children be ready for instruction in English or French?

Poverty and Language

Every study finds that SES affects cognitive development, with poor language mastery a prominent sign and perhaps the major cause of low academic achievement in low-income children. Children from low-SES families usually have smaller vocabularies than those from higher-SES families, and they also are impaired in grammar (fewer compound sentences, dependent clauses, and conditional verbs) (Hart & Risley, 1995; Hoff, 2013). That slows down school learning in every subject.

Brain scans confirm that language proficiency is related to brain activity (Romeo et al., 2018). The development of the hippocampus (crucial for memory) is particularly affected by SES, and that may be critical for language learning (Jednoróg et al., 2012).

How can poverty affect the brain? Possibilities include inadequate prenatal care, no breakfast, lead in the bloodstream, crowded and noisy households, few books at home, teenage parents, authoritarian child rearing, inexperienced teachers, air pollution, neighborhood violence, lack of role models . . . the list could go on and on (Cree et al., 2018; Kolb & Gibb, 2015; Rowe et al., 2016). All of these conditions correlate with low SES, slower language development, and less learning.

One factor seems to be a cause, not just a correlate: language heard early on (Neuman et al., 2018). The mother's education is influential, especially if she continues her quest for learning by reading and asking questions. Children who grow up in homes with many books accumulate, on average, three more years of education than children who live in homes with no books (Evans et al., 2010).

Of course, the books cannot merely sit on shelves. A study of 16,000 11-year-olds in England found that language proficiency was heavily influenced by how much the parents read to the child—which could begin before the first birthday and continue after the children are able to read on their own (Law et al., 2018).

Remember the plasticity of the brain. In some families, neuronal connections are strengthened and dendrites grow to support language. This process continues in middle childhood (Perone et al., 2018).

Low income per se is not as influential as parental talk and listening. Educated parents are more likely to take their children to museums, zoos, and libraries as well as to engage children in conversation about the interesting sights around them. Many sing to their children, not just a few simple songs but dozens of songs with varied vocabulary.

Overall, a child's *perception* of whether or not they are poor is as important as their actual deprivation. That perception is heavily influenced by the actions and attitudes of their parents and of their teachers (McLoyd, 2019).

JW LTD/Photographer's Choice/Getty Images

Priorities This family in London is low-income, evident in the stained walls, peeling paint, and old toilet, but that does not necessarily limit the girl's future. More important is what she learns about values and behavior. If this scene is typical, this mother is teaching her daughter about appearance and obedience. What would happen if the child had to care for her own grooming? Tangles? Short hair? Independence? Linguistic advances?

Observation Quiz What in the daughter's behavior suggests that maternal grooming is a common event in her life? (see answer, page 320)

WHAT HAVE YOU LEARNED?

1. How does language benefit from cognition in middle childhood?
2. What is the relationship between language and cognition?
3. Why would a child's linguistic code be criticized by teachers but admired by peers?
4. How does a person most readily become bilingual?
5. How does family income affect language development?

Teaching and Learning

In middle childhood, anything can be learned. Some children, by age 11, beat their elders at chess, play music that adults pay to hear, publish poems, and solve complex math problems. Others survive on the streets or fight in civil wars, using automatic weapons that are almost too big to carry.

AT ABOUT THIS TIME

Math

Age	Norms and Expectations
4–5 years	• Count to 20. • Understand one-to-one correspondence of objects and numbers. • Understand *more* and *less.* • Recognize and name shapes.
6 years	• Count to 100. • Understand *bigger* and *smaller.* • Add and subtract one-digit numbers.
8 years	• Add and subtract two-digit numbers. • Understand simple multiplication and division. • Understand word problems with two variables.
10 years	• Add, subtract, multiply, and divide multidigit numbers. • Understand simple fractions, percentages, area, and perimeter of shapes. • Understand word problems with three variables.
12 years	• Begin to use abstract concepts, such as formulas and algebra.

Math learning depends heavily on direct instruction and repeated practice, which means that some children advance more quickly than others. This list is only a rough guide meant to illustrate the importance of sequence.

AT ABOUT THIS TIME

Reading

Age	Norms and Expectations
4–5 years	• Understand basic book concepts. For instance, children learning English and many other languages understand that books are written from front to back, with print from left to right, and that letters make words that describe pictures. • Recognize letters—name the letters on sight. • Recognize and spell own name.
6–7 years	• Know the sounds of the consonants and vowels, including those that have two sounds (e.g., *c, g, o*). • Use sounds to figure out words. • Read simple words, such as *cat, sit, ball, jump.*
8 years	• Read simple sentences out loud, 50 words per minute, including words of two syllables. • Understand basic punctuation, consonant–vowel blends. • Comprehend what is read.
9–10 years	• Read and understand paragraphs and chapters, including advanced punctuation (e.g., the colon). • Answer comprehension questions about concepts as well as facts. • Read polysyllabic words (e.g., *vegetarian, population, multiplication*).
11–12 years	• Demonstrate rapid and fluent oral reading (more than 100 words per minute). • Vocabulary includes words that have specialized meaning in various fields. • For example, in civics, *liberties, federal, parliament,* and *environment* all have special meanings. • Comprehend paragraphs about unfamiliar topics. • Sound out new words, figuring out meaning using cognates and context. • Read for pleasure.
13+ years	• Continue to build vocabulary, with greater emphasis on comprehension than on speech. Understand textbooks.

Reading is a complex mix of skills, dependent on brain maturation, education, and culture. The sequence given here is approximate; it should not be taken as a standard to measure any particular child.

Children worldwide learn whatever adults in their culture teach, whenever their brains are ready. (See the accompanying At About This Time tables for some of the sequences of learning to read and do arithmetic.) Traditionally, children were educated at home, but now almost all of the world's 7-year-olds are in school. It is crucial that adults develop the schools and the curriculum to prepare children for adult life.

Indeed, in many developing nations, the number of students in elementary school exceeds the number of school-age children, because many older children as well as adults now seek basic education. In 2014, Ghana, El Salvador, and China were among the nations with significantly more students in primary school than the total number of children in middle childhood (UNESCO, 2014).

The Curriculum

What should children learn? Every nation seeks to teach reading, writing, and arithmetic—the classic "three R's." But beyond literacy and math, nations vary in what they expect.

Brendan Fitterer/ZUMA Press/New Port Richey/Florida/U.S./Newscom

ROMEO GACAD/AFP/Getty Images

Room to Learn? In the elementary school classroom in Florida *(left)*, the teacher is guiding two students who are working to discover concepts in physics—a stark contrast to the Filipino classroom *(right)* in a former storeroom. Sometimes the hidden curriculum determines the overt curriculum, as shown here.

For example, every nation wants children to become good citizens, but nations disagree about what good citizenship entails or how children can learn it (Cohen & Malin, 2010). Accordingly, many children simply follow their parents' example regarding everything from picking up trash to supporting a candidate for president.

Religious education also varies. The U.S. Constitution forbids overt teaching of religion in public schools (although, of course, children can pray, express beliefs, or wear religious symbols), but other nations believe religious education is part of learning. In the United States, many private schools also teach religion.

Another variation is in how much importance is placed on each particular subject. As already mentioned in the previous chapters, the time spent on physical education, on the arts, and on other aspects of the curriculum varies from nation to nation, and, in the United States, from school district to school district.

The Hidden Curriculum Differences between nations, and between schools in the United States, are stark in the **hidden curriculum**—all of the implicit values and assumptions of schools. Schedules, tracking, teacher characteristics, discipline, teaching methods, sports competitions, student government, and extracurricular activities are all part of the hidden curriculum. This teaches children far beyond the formal, published curriculum that lists what is taught in each grade.

hidden curriculum The unofficial, unstated, or implicit patterns within a school that influence what children learn. For instance, teacher background, organization of the play space, and tracking are all part of the hidden curriculum—not formally prescribed, but instructive to the children.

An obvious example is the physical surroundings. Some schools have spacious classrooms, wide hallways, and large, grassy playgrounds; others have cramped, poorly equipped classrooms and cement play yards. In some nations, school is held outdoors, with no chairs, desks, or books; classes are canceled when it rains. What does that tell the students?

Teacher Ethnicity Another aspect of the hidden curriculum is who the teachers are. If their gender, ethnicity, or economic background is unlike that of their students, children may conclude that education is irrelevant for them.

School organization is also significant. If the school has gifted classes, the non-gifted may conclude that they are not capable of learning.

The United States is experiencing major demographic shifts. Since 2010, half of the babies born are from Hispanic, Asian, African, or Native American families, whereas more than two-thirds of adults are of European background. Given the past history of sexual and racial discrimination, many experienced teachers are older women whose ancestors lived in western or northern Europe.

CHAPTER APP 12

Khan Academy

RELATED TOPIC:
Schooling and academic development in middle childhood

IOS:
http://tinyurl.com/y34g8v4f

ANDROID:
http://tinyurl.com/ybrxqdh3

Appropriate for students of all ages, Khan Academy's free learning library app contains thousands of interactive exercises, videos, and articles pertaining to arithmetic and pre-algebra, science, grammar, history, and much more. Students can take practice exercises, quizzes, and tests, receiving instant feedback and step-by-step hints. The app enables offline learning, as well: Content can be bookmarked and downloaded for access without an Internet connection.

Because of changes in the population's age and ethnic distribution, most children never have an elementary school teacher who is a man of minority background. Of course, many older women are excellent teachers, but schools also need more excellent male, non-white, younger teachers—not only for the non-white boys. The hidden curriculum could teach that caring educators come from many backgrounds. Does it?

Teacher Expectations Less visible, yet probably more influential, is the hidden message that comes from attitudes. If a teacher expects a child to be disruptive, or unable to learn, that child is likely to confirm those expectations. Fortunately, teacher expectations are malleable: Learning increases and absences decrease when teachers believe all of their students are educable and they teach accordingly, encouraging every child (Sparks, 2016).

One teacher expectation is whether students should talk or be quiet. In the United States, adults are expected to voice opinions. Accordingly, many teachers welcome student questions, call on children who do not speak, ask children to work in pairs so that each child talks, and grant points for participation.

As a result of their schooling, North American students learn to speak, even when they do not know the answers. Elsewhere, children are expected to be quiet.

This was dramatically apparent to me when I taught at the United Nations International School. Some of my students shouted out answers, some raised their hands, some never spoke except when I called on them. When I called on one quiet student from South Asia, he immediately stood up to answer—to the surprise of his classmates.

This aspect of the hidden curriculum affects learning if the teachers' assumptions differ from the students' assumptions. In one study, middle-class children asked questions and requested help from their teachers more often than low-SES students did (Calarco, 2014).

The researchers suggested that the low-SES students sought to avoid teacher attention, fearing it would lead to criticism. Might that have given teachers the impression that they were disinterested? Thus, the hidden curriculum might prevent students who most need encouragement from getting it. Student attitudes affect teacher attitudes as well as vice versa.

International Testing

Every nation now wants to improve education, because they believe longitudinal data showing that the national economy advances when school achievement rises (Hanushek & Woessmann, 2015). Better-educated children become healthier and more productive adults. That is one reason many developing nations are building more schools and colleges.

Nations also want to make education more effective for all students. To measure that, almost 100 nations have participated in at least one massive international test of children's learning.

Achievement in science and math is tested in the *Trends in Math and Science Study (TIMSS)*. The main test of reading is the *Progress in International Reading Literacy Study (PIRLS)*. A third test is the *Programme for International Student Assessment (PISA)*, which is designed to measure the ability to apply learning to everyday issues. East Asian nations always rank high, and scores for more than a dozen nations (some in Europe, most in Asia) surpassed those for the United States (see **Tables 12.1** and **12.2**).

THINK CRITICALLY: Finland's success has been attributed to many factors, some mentioned here and some regarding the geography and population of the nation. What do you think is the most influential reason?

One surprising example is that Finland's scores increased dramatically after a wholesale reform of its public education system. Reforms occurred in several waves (Sahlberg, 2011, 2015). In 1985 ability grouping was abolished, and in

1994 the curriculum began to encourage collaboration and active learning rather than competitive passive education.

Currently, in Finland, all children learn together—no tracking—and teachers are mandated to help each child. If some children need special help to master the formal curriculum, teachers provide it within the regular class.

Over the past two decades, strict requirements for becoming a teacher have been put in place. Only the top 3 percent of Finland's high school graduates are admitted to teachers' colleges. They study for five years at the university at no charge, earning a master's degree in the theory and practice of education.

Finnish teachers are granted more autonomy within their classrooms than is typical in other nations. Since the 1990s, they have had more time and encouragement to work with colleagues (Sahlberg, 2011, 2015). They are encouraged to respond to each child's temperament as well as the child's skills. This strategy has led to achievement, particularly in math (Viljaranta et al., 2015).

Problems with International Comparisons

Elaborate and extensive measures are in place to make the PIRLS, TIMSS, and PISA valid. Test items are designed to be fair and culture-free, and participating children represent the diversity (economic, ethnic, etc.) of each nation's child population. Thousands of experts work to ensure validity and reliability. Consequently, most social scientists respect the data gathered from these tests.

The tests are far from perfect, however. Creating questions that are equally valid for everyone is impossible. For example, in math, should fourth-graders be expected to understand fractions, graphs, decimals, and simple geometry? Nations introduce these concepts at different ages, and some schools stress math more than others: Should every fourth-grader be expected to divide fractions?

After such general issues are decided, items are written. The following item tested math:

> Three thousand tickets for a basketball game are numbered 1 to 3,000. People with ticket numbers ending with 112 receive a prize. Write down all the prize-winning numbers.

Only 26 percent of fourth-graders worldwide got this one right (112; 1,112; 2,112—with no additional numbers). About half of the children in East Asian nations and 36 percent of the U.S. children were correct. Those national scores are not surprising; children in Singapore, Japan, and China have been close to the top on every international test for 20 years, and the United States has been above average but not by much.

TABLE 12.1

TIMSS Average Scores of Math Achievement for Fourth-Graders, 2011 and 2015

	2011	2015
Singapore	606	618
Hong Kong	602	615
Korea	605	608
Chinese Taipei	591	597
Japan	585	593
N. Ireland	562	570
Russia	542	564
England	542	546
Belgium	549	546
United States	541	539
Canada (Quebec)	533	533
Finland	545	532
Netherlands	540	530
Germany	528	522
Sweden	504	519
Australia	516	517
Canada (Ontario)	518	512
Italy	508	507
New Zealand	486	491
Iran	431	431
Kuwait	342	353

TABLE 12.2

PIRLS Average Scores of Reading Achievement for Fourth-Graders, 2011 and 2016

	2011	2016
Hong Kong	571	569
Russia	568	581
Finland	568	566
Singapore	567	576
N. Ireland	558	565
United States	556	549
Denmark	554	547
Chinese Taipei	553	559
Ireland	552	567
England	552	559
Canada	548	543
Italy	541	548
Germany	541	537
Israel	541	530
New Zealand	531	523
Australia	527	544
Poland	526	565
France	520	511
Spain	513	528
Iran	457	428

Information from Mullis et al., 2012b, 2017.

"Big deal, an A in math. That would be a D in any other country."

Children from North Africa did especially poorly; only 2 percent of Moroccan fourth-graders were correct. Is basketball, or 3,000 tickets for one game, or a random prize as common in North Africa as in the United States?

Another math item gives ingredients—4 eggs, 8 cups of flour, ½ cup of milk—and asks:

> The above ingredients are used to make a recipe for 6 people. Sam wants to make this recipe for only 3 people. Complete the table below to show what Sam needs to make the recipe for 3 people. The number of eggs he needs is shown.

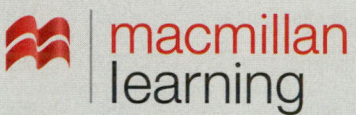

Eggs	2
Flour	?___
Milk	?___

The table (see margin) lists 2 eggs, and the child needs to fill in amounts of flour and milk. Fourth-grade children in Ireland and England scored highest on this item (about half got it right), while those in Korea, China, and Japan scored lower (about 33 percent). The United States scored higher than East Asian nations but lower than England.

This is puzzling, since East Asians usually surpass others in math. Why not here? Are English and Irish children experienced with recipes for baked goods that include eggs, flour, and milk, unlike Japanese children? Or are Asian children distracted by the idea of a boy cooking?

macmillan learning

VIDEO ACTIVITY: Educating the Girls of the World examines the situation of girls' education around the world while stressing the importance of education for all children.

Who Takes the Test? Beyond the problem of writing items that are fair for children throughout the world is the problem of student selection. In theory, all children in school at a particular grade level take the test, but in practice the school dropout rate in some nations means that many of the lowest achieving children are not tested.

China has consistently scored far higher than the United States, but some critics say that comparison is unfair (Singer & Braun, 2018). For one thing, the Chinese children who take the test are in the major cities, not rural areas. For another, some say that the American children who take the test are not motivated, since the scores are not tied to them. The Chinese, by contrast, are highly motivated to do well.

Related to motivation is how much a culture values high scores on achievement tests. A major controversy in the United States is whether children are over-tested, with a narrow focus on high achievement. This is discussed in Chapter 15, but the underlying issue is whether or not personality traits that push toward high scores should be encouraged at home.

Gender Differences in School Performance In addition to marked national, ethnic, and economic differences, gender differences in achievement scores are reported. The PIRLS finds fourth-grade girls ahead of boys in reading in every nation, by an average of 19 points (Mullis et al., 2017).

The 2016 female verbal advantage on the PIRLS in the United States is 8 points, which is a difference of less than 2 percent. Several other nations are close to the U.S. norms, including France, Spain, and Hong Kong. Does this mean that those nations are more gender-equitable than the nation with the widest gender gap—Saudi Arabia, with a 65-point gap (464/399)? Maybe, maybe not.

Future Engineers After-school clubs now encourage boys to learn cooking and girls to play chess, and both sexes are active in every sport. The most recent push is for STEM (Science, Technology, Engineering and Math) education—as in this after-school robotics club.

Steve Debenport/asiseeit/Getty Images

Historically, boys were ahead of girls in math and science. However, TIMSS reported that those gender differences among fourth-graders in math have narrowed, disappeared, or reversed. In many nations, boys are still slightly ahead, with the United States showing a male advantage (7 points—less than 2 percent). However, in other nations, girls are ahead, sometimes significantly, such as 10 points in Indonesia and 20 points in Jordan. Why? Is there an anti-male bias in the schools or culture?

In middle childhood, girls in every nation have higher report card grades, including in math and science. Is that biological (girls are better able to sit still, to

A CASE TO STUDY

Happiness or High Grades?

Thousands of social scientists — psychologists, educators, sociologists, economists — have realized that for cognitive development from middle childhood through late adulthood, characteristics beyond IQ scores, test grades, and family SES are sometimes pivotal.

One leading proponent of this idea is Paul Tough, who wrote: "We have been focusing on the wrong skills and abilities in our children, and we have been using the wrong strategies to help nurture and teach those skills" (Tough, 2012, p. xv). Instead of focusing on test scores, Tough believes we should focus on characteristics, particularly *grit* (persistence and effort).

Many scientists agree that executive control processes with many names (grit, emotional regulation, conscientiousness, resilience, executive function, effortful control) develop over the years of middle childhood. Over the long term, these aspects of character predict achievement in high school, college, and adulthood. Developmentalists disagree about exactly which qualities are crucial for achievement, with grit considered crucial by some but not others (Ivcevic & Brackett, 2014; Duckworth & Kern, 2011). However, no one denies that success depends on personal traits.

The opposing perspective is that parental encouragement is more important for academic achievement and that the focus on grit makes it seem as if the child is to be blamed for failure when parents, schools, and community may make learning very difficult for the child. Grit could make a child spend large amounts of time studying and feeling inadequate, never enjoying life.

Remember that school-age children are ready for intellectual growth (Piaget) and are responsive to mentors (Vygotsky). These universals were evident in one study that occurred in two places, 12,000 miles apart: the northeastern United States and Taiwan.

In that study, more than 200 mothers were asked to recall and then discuss with their 6- to 10-year-olds two learning-related incidents that they knew their child had experienced. In one incident, the child had a "good attitude or behavior in learning"; in the other, "not perfect" (J. Li et al., 2014, p. 1210).

All of the mothers were married and middle-class, and all tried to encourage their children, stressing the value of education and the importance of doing well in school. The researchers noted that the mothers differed in the attitudes they were trying to encourage in their children. The Taiwanese mothers were far more likely to mention what the researchers called "learning virtues," such as practice, persistence, and concentration — all of which are part of grit. The American mothers were more likely to mention "positive affect," such as happiness and pride.

This distinction is evident in the following two excepts:

First, Tim and his American mother discussed a "not perfect" incident.

Mother: I wanted to talk to you about . . . that time when you had that one math paper that . . . mostly everything was wrong and you never bring home papers like that. . . .

Tim: I just had a clumsy day.

Mother: You had a clumsy day. You sure did, but there was, when we finally figured out what it was that you were doing wrong, you were pretty happy about it . . . and then you were happy to practice it, right? . . . Why do you think that was?

Tim: I don't know, because I was frustrated, and then you sat down and went over it with me, and I figured it out right with no distraction and then I got it right.

Mother: So it made you feel good to do well?

Tim: Uh-huh.

Mother: And it's okay to get some wrong sometimes.

Tim: And I, I never got that again, didn't I?

The next excerpt occurred when Ren and his Taiwanese mother discuss a "good attitude or behavior."

Mother: Oh, why does your teacher think that you behave well?

Ren: It's that I concentrate well in class.

Mother: Is your good concentration the concentration to talk to your peer at the next desk?

Ren: I listen to teachers.

Mother: Oh, is it so only for Mr. Chang's class or is it for all classes?

Ren: Almost all classes like that. . . .

Mother: So you want to behave well because you want to get an . . . honor award. Is that so?

Ren: Yes.

Mother: Or is it also that you yourself want to behave better?

Ren: Yes. I also want to behave better myself.

[J. Li et al., 2014, p. 1218]

Both Tim and Ren are likely to be good students in their respective schools. When parents support and encourage their child's learning, the child almost always masters the basic skills required of elementary school students, and almost never does the child become crushed by life experiences. Instead, the child has sufficient strengths to overcome most challenges (Masten, 2014).

The specifics of parental encouragement affect the child's achievement. Some research has found that parents in Asia emphasize that education requires hard work, whereas parents in North America stress the joy of learning. Could it be, as one group of researchers contend, that U.S. children are happier but less accomplished than Asian ones (F. Ng et al., 2014)? If so, and if a child cannot have both, which is more important: high self-esteem or high grades?

manipulate a pencil)? Or cultural (girls have been taught to do as they are told)? Or does the hidden curriculum favor girls (most of their elementary school teachers were women)?

The popularity of various explanations has shifted. Analysts once attributed girls' higher grades in school to their faster physical maturation. Now explanations are more often sociocultural—that parents and teachers expect girls to be good students and that schools are organized to favor female strengths. The same switch in explanations, from biology to culture, appears for male advantages in science. Is that change itself cultural?

Schooling in the United States

Many international tests indicate improvements in U.S. children's academic performance over the past decades. However, the United States has the largest disparities between income and ethnic groups. Some blame the disparity on immigration, but other nations (e.g., Canada) have more ethnic groups and immigrants than the United States, yet the Canadian achievement gap between groups is not as large.

National Assessment of Educational Progress (NAEP) An ongoing and nationally representative measure of U.S. children's achievement in reading, mathematics, and other subjects over time; nicknamed "the Nation's Report Card."

National Standards For decades, the United States government has sponsored the **National Assessment of Educational Progress (NAEP),** which is a group of tests designed to measure achievement in reading, mathematics, and other subjects. The NAEP finds fewer children proficient than do state tests. For example, New York's tests reported 62 percent proficient in math, but the NAEP found only 32 percent; 51 percent were proficient in reading on New York's state tests, but only 35 percent according to NAEP (Martin, 2014).

The NAEP also finds that Hispanic American and African American fourth-graders are about 10 percent lower than their European American peers in reading and 7 percent lower in math (National Assessment of Educational Progress, 2019). "Federal civil rights data show persistent and widespread disparities among disadvantaged students from prekindergarten through high school" with low-SES children, English Language Learners, and minority ethnic groups all suffering (McNeil & Blad, 2014, p. 8).

Especially for School Administrators Children who wear uniforms in school tend to score higher on reading tests. Why? (see response, page 320)

For some statistics—high school graduation, for instance—Asian American children achieve at higher rates than European Americans. However, this contributes to the "model minority" stereotype, which obscures disadvantages for many children of Asian heritage. For instance, Asian children may suffer from parental pressure or peer jealousy (Cherng & Liu, 2017).

The reason for disparities within the United States seems more economic than ethnic, because African Americans in some of the wealthier states (Massachusetts) score higher than European Americans in the poorer states (Mississippi). Indeed, on international tests, students in Massachusetts are close to the highest-scoring nations, those in East Asia (Singer & Braun, 2018).

Many suggest that the disparity in local funding for schools is at the root of the problem: High-SES children of all groups attend well-funded schools. That raises the first of several issues within U.S. education, 10 of which are mentioned now.

Ten Questions

1. Should public schools be well-supported by public funds, or should smaller class sizes, special curricula, and expensive facilities (e.g., a stage, a pool, a garden) be available only in *private schools*, paid via tuition from wealthy parents? All told, about 11 percent of students in the United States attend private schools (see **Figure 12.3**). Other nations have higher or lower rates.

2. Should parents be given *vouchers* to pay for some tuition at a private school? Each state regulates vouchers differently, but a detailed look at vouchers in Wisconsin found that most parents who used vouchers were inclined to send their children to nonpublic schools in any case, partly for religious and safety reasons (Cowen et al., 2013). Thus, vouchers subsidize schools that differ from public schools, which may allow parents to choose a school that does not follow public school policy or curriculum. Is that fair?
3. Should more *charter schools* open or close? Charter schools are funded and licensed by states or local districts. Thus, they are public schools but are exempt from some regulations, especially those negotiated by teacher unions (hours, class size, etc.). Most have some control over admissions and expulsions, which makes them more ethnically segregated, with fewer children with special needs (Stern et al., 2015). Quality varies. Overall, more children (especially African American boys) and teachers leave or are expelled from charter schools than from other public schools, a disturbing statistic. However, some charters report that children who stay learn more and are more likely to go to college than their peers in regular public schools (Prothero, 2016).
4. In 35 of the 50 U.S. states, and in several other nations, parents can choose to *home-school* their children, never sending them to an educational institution, public or private. In the United States, home-schooled children must learn certain subjects (reading, math, and so on), but each family decides schedules and discipline.

   About 2 percent of all U.S. children were home-schooled in 2003 and about 3 percent in 2007. Since then, numbers have leveled off (Snyder & Dillow, 2013; Ray, 2013; Grady, 2017). Home schooling requires intense family labor, typically provided by an educated, dedicated, patient mother in a two-parent family.

   The major disadvantage for home-schooled children is not academic (some have high test scores) but social: no classmates. To compensate, many parents plan activities with other home-schooling families.
5. Should public education be free of *religion* to avoid bias toward one religion or another? In the United States, thousands of parochial schools were founded when Catholics perceived Protestant bias in public schools. In the past 20 years, many Catholic schools have closed, but schools teaching other religions—Judaism, Islam, evangelical Christianity—have opened.
6. Should *the arts* be part of the curriculum? Music, drama, dance, and the visual arts are essential in some places, not in others. Half of all U.S. 18- to 24-year-olds say that they had no arts education in childhood, either in school or anywhere else (Rabkin & Hedberg, 2011). By contrast, schools in Finland consider arts education essential, with a positive impact on learning (Nevanen et al., 2014).
7. Should children learn a *second language* in primary school? In Canada and in most European nations, almost every child studies two languages by age 10. In the United States, less than 5 percent of children under age 11 study a language other than English in school (Robelen, 2011).

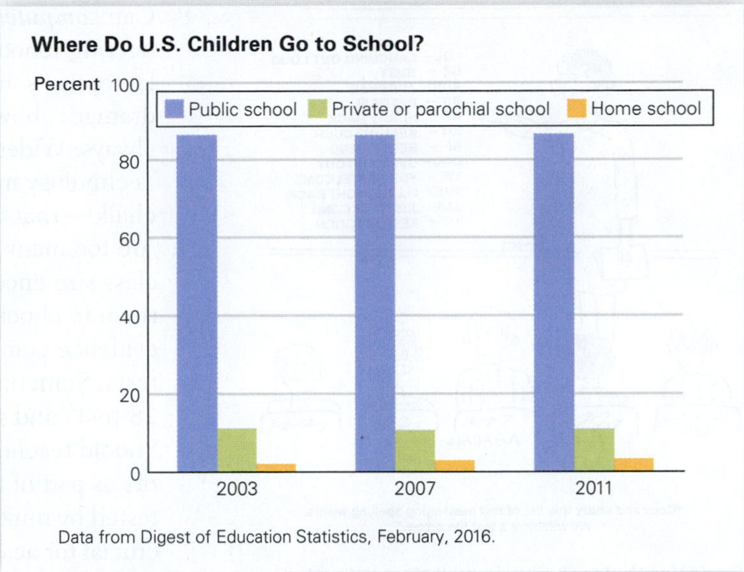

FIGURE 12.3

Where'd You Go to School? Note that although home schooling is still the least-chosen option, the number of home-schooled children is increasing. Not shown is the percentage of children attending the nearest public school, which is decreasing slightly because of charter schools and magnet schools. More detailed data indicate that the average home-schooled child is a 7-year-old European American girl living in a rural area of the South with an employed father and a stay-at-home mother.

Ten Questions
1. Private schools?
2. Vouchers?
3. Charter schools?
4. Home schooling?
5. Religion?
6. The arts?
7. Second language?
8. Computers?
9. Class size?
10. Soft skills?

William Widmer/Redux

Plagiarism, Piracy, and Public School Charter schools often have special support and unusual curricula, as shown here. These four children are learning about copyright law in a special summer school class at the ReNEW Cultural Arts Academy, a charter school in New Orleans.

Aaron Bacall/cartoon stock

"Copy and study this list of text messaging spelling words. We will have a test tomorrow."

Basic Vocabulary? Should educators instruct children in texting? Maybe the adults are the ones who need instruction. One adult e-mailed a sympathy note to a friend whose mother died, and she signed it "LOL." She thought that meant "Lots of Love."

8. Can *computers* advance education? Some enthusiasts hope that connecting schools to the Internet or, even better, giving every child a laptop (as some schools do) will advance learning. The results are not dramatic, however. Sometimes computers improve achievement, but not always. Widespread, sustainable advances are elusive (Lim et al., 2013). Technology may be only a tool—a twenty-first-century equivalent of chalk—that depends on a creative, trained teacher to use well.
9. Are too many students in each class? Parents typically think that smaller class size encourages more individualized education. That belief motivates them to choose private schools or home schooling. However, mixed evidence comes from nations where children score high on international tests. Sometimes they have large student–teacher ratios (Korea's average is 28-to-1) and sometimes small (Finland's is 14-to-1).
10. Should teachers nurture *soft skills* such as empathy, cooperation, and integrity as part of the school curriculum, even though these skills cannot be tested by multiple-choice questions? Many scholars argue that soft skills are crucial for academic success and later for employment (Reardon, 2013).

Who Decides? Overall, research in human development guides teachers who want to know exactly which concepts and skills are crucial foundations for mastery of reading, writing, science, math, and human relations. However, the science of child cognition is not necessarily understood by those who determine what children learn.

An underlying issue for almost any national or international school is the proper role of parents. In most nations, matters regarding public education—curriculum, funding, teacher training, and so on—are set by the central government.

Generally, when governments are responsible for education, almost all children attend the local school, whose resources and standards are similar to those of the other schools in that nation. If there are serious religious or cultural differences in the nation, public schools offer alternatives—religious or secular, in one language or another, and so on. The parents' job is to support the teachers and the child's learning.

In the United States, however, public schools are open to everyone, which means that no specific religious instruction occurs. Local districts provide most of the funds and guidelines, and parents, as voters and volunteers, are active within the school.

Welcome Home Laura Stevens returns to her Maine elementary school after a whirlwind trip in Washington, D.C. She received the Presidential Award for Excellence in Math and Science Teaching, and $10,000. Which do you think makes her happier, the award, the hero's welcome from her students and colleagues, or the joy of teaching?

Gregory Rec/Portland Press Herald/Getty Images

Although most U.S. parents send their children to the nearest public school, almost one-fifth send their children to private schools (11 percent) or charter schools (6 percent), or they educate their children at home (3 percent) (McFarland et al., 2018). Parental choices may vary for each child, depending on the child's characteristics, the parents' current economic status, and the political rhetoric at the time. Every option has strengths and weaknesses, both for the child and for society.

It is difficult for parents to determine the best school for their child, partly because neither the test scores of students in any of these schools, nor the moral values a particular school may espouse, correlate with the cognitive skills that developmentalists seek to foster (Finn et al., 2014).

Thus, parents may choose a school that advertises what they value, but that does not mean that the school provides the best educational experience for their child. It is not uncommon for parents to pull children from one school to enroll them in another, a phenomenon that has increased in recent years. That undercuts lasting friendships.

Statistical analysis raises questions about home schooling, vouchers, and charter schools; but continuity benefits children, so the parents' restlessness may not be wise (Lubienski et al., 2013; Finn et al., 2014). However, the data allow many interpretations.

As one review notes, "the modern day, parent-led home-based education movement . . . stirs up many a curious query, negative critique, and firm praise" (Ray, 2013, p. 261). Indeed, for all public and private schools, partisan political controversies swirl around school choice, which makes it hard to make a definitive conclusion about what school is best for a particular child (Quinn & Cheuk, 2018).

Schoolchildren's ability to be logical and teachable — now that they are no longer preoperational and egocentric — makes this a good time to teach them. They will learn whatever adults deem important. Parents, politicians, and developmental experts all agree that school is vital for development, but disagreements about teachers and curriculum — hidden or overt — abound.

WHAT HAVE YOU LEARNED?

1. How does the hidden curriculum differ from the stated school curriculum?
2. What are the TIMSS, the PIRLS, and the PISA?
3. Which nations score highest on international tests?
4. How do boys and girls differ in school achievement?
5. How do charter schools, private schools, and home schools differ?
6. How is it decided what curriculum children should receive?

SUMMARY

Thinking

1. According to Piaget, middle childhood is the time of concrete operational thought, when egocentrism diminishes and logical thinking begins. Among the most important yet most difficult aspects are the concepts of classification and seriation.

2. By contrast, Vygotsky stressed the social context of learning, including the specific lessons of school and learning from peers, adults, and culture.

3. An information-processing approach examines each step of the thinking process, from input to output, using the computer as a model. Repeated practice is essential, as cognitive functions become automated.

4. One famous researcher who used the information-processing approach is Robert Siegler, who compared learning math to the waves lapping on a beach. Concepts are not learned suddenly.

5. Both the knowledge base and intellectual control processes are crucial aspects of the cognitive advances of middle childhood. Information-processing research has helped describe these developments.

Language

6. Language learning advances in many practical ways, including expanded vocabulary and pragmatics.

7. Most children use one code, dialect, or language with their friends and another in school. Children who are adept at code-switching, or who are fluently bilingual, have a cognitive advantage.

8. Children of low SES are usually lower in linguistic skills, primarily because they hear less language at home. Parent and teacher expectations are crucial.

Teaching and Learning

9. The hidden curriculum may be more influential on children's learning than the formal curriculum. For example, some people believe elementary schools favor girls, although internationally gender similarities seem to outweigh gender differences.

10. International assessments are useful as comparisons. Reading is assessed with the PIRLS, math and science with the TIMSS, and practical intelligence with the PISA. Culture affects answers as well as learning: East Asian scores are high, Finland has improved, and the United States is middling.

11. In the United States, each state, each district, and sometimes each school retains significant control. This makes education a controversial topic in many communities. Most children attend their local public school, but some parents choose charter schools, others private schools, and still others opt for home schooling.

KEY TERMS

concrete operational thought (p. 300)
classification (p. 300)
seriation (p. 300)
automatization (p. 304)
knowledge base (p. 305)
control processes (p. 306)
English Language Learners (ELLs) (p. 308)
immersion (p. 308)
bilingual education (p. 308)
English as a Second Language (ESL) (p. 308)
hidden curriculum (p. 311)
National Assessment of Educational Progress (NAEP) (p. 316)

APPLICATIONS

1. Visit a local elementary school and look for the hidden curriculum. For example, do the children line up? Why or why not, when, and how? Does gender, age, ability, or talent affect the grouping of children or the selection of staff? What is on the walls? For everything you observe, speculate about the underlying assumptions.

2. Interview a 6- to 11-year-old child to find out what he or she knows *and understands* about mathematics. Relate both correct and incorrect responses to the logic of concrete operational thought and to the information-processing perspective.

3. What do you remember about how you learned to read? Compare your memories with those of two other people, one at least 10 years older and the other at least 5 years younger than you are. Can you draw any conclusions about effective reading instruction? If so, what are they? If not, why not?

4. Talk to two parents of primary school children. What do they think are the best and worst parts of their children's education? Ask specific questions and analyze the results.

Especially For ANSWERS

Response for Teachers (from p. 301): Here are two of the most obvious ways. (1) Use logic. Once children can grasp classification and class inclusion, they can understand cities within states, states within nations, and nations within continents. Organize your instruction to make logical categorization easier. (2) Make use of children's need for concrete and personal involvement. You might have the children learn first about their own location, then about the places where relatives and friends live, and finally about places beyond their personal experience (via books, photographs, videos, and guest speakers).

Response for Parents (from p. 308): Your son would understand your explanation, but you should take him along if you can do so without losing patience. You wouldn't ignore his need for food or medicine, so don't ignore his need for learning. While shopping, you can teach vocabulary (does he know pimientos, pepperoni, polenta?), categories (root vegetables, freshwater fish), and math (which size box of cereal is cheaper?). Explain in advance that you need him to help you find items and carry them and that he can choose only one item that you wouldn't normally buy. Seven-year-olds can understand rules, and they enjoy being helpful.

Response for School Administrators (from p. 316): The relationship reflects correlation, not causation. Wearing uniforms is more common when the culture of the school emphasizes achievement and study, with strict discipline in class and a policy of expelling disruptive students.

Observation Quiz ANSWERS

Answer to Observation Quiz (from p. 300) His hat, water bottle, and whistle. His caregivers try to protect him from the sun, dehydration, and predators.

Answer to Observation Quiz (from p. 309): Her posture is straight; her hands are folded; she is quiet, standing while her mother sits. All of this suggests that this scene is a frequent occurrence.

VISUALIZING DEVELOPMENT Education in Middle Childhood

Only 20 years ago, gender differences in education around the world were stark, with far fewer girls in school than boys. Now girls have almost caught up. However, many of today's children suffer from decades of past educational inequality: Recent data find that the best predictor of childhood health is an educated mother.

WORLDWIDE PRIMARY SCHOOL ENROLLMENT, 1978–2018

This graph shows net enrollment rate, which is the ratio of enrolled school-age children to the population of children who are the same school age. Progress toward university education and gender equity is evident.

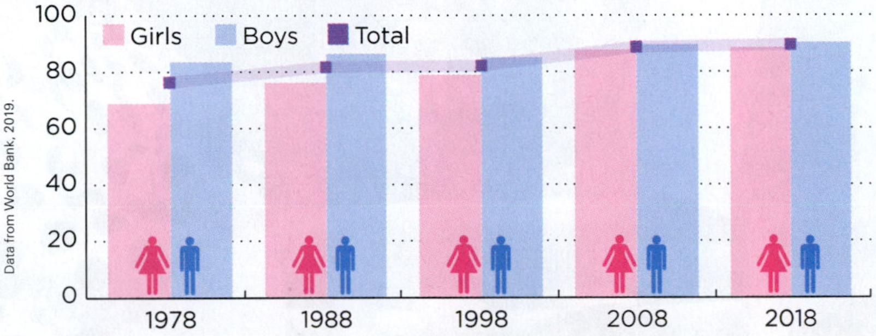

Worldwide concerns now focus less on the existence of school and more on its quality. International tests usually find the United States is middling. Improvements are evident, but many other nations have improved even more!

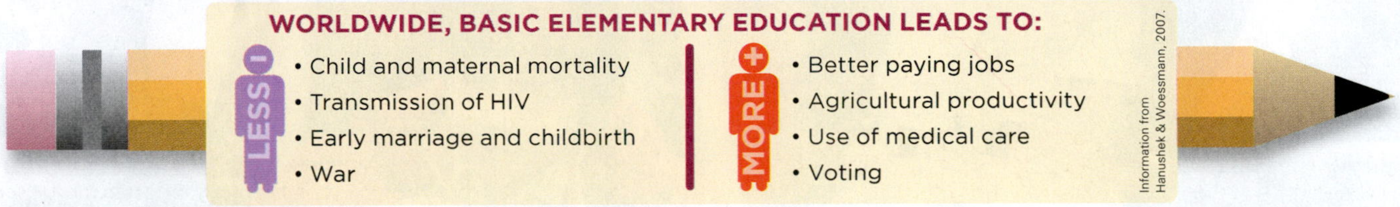

HOW U.S. FOURTH-GRADERS ARE DOING

Primary school enrollment is high in the United States, but not every student is learning, as these percentages from the National Assessment of Educational Progress (NAEP) show. While numbers are improving, less than half of fourth-graders are proficient in math and reading.

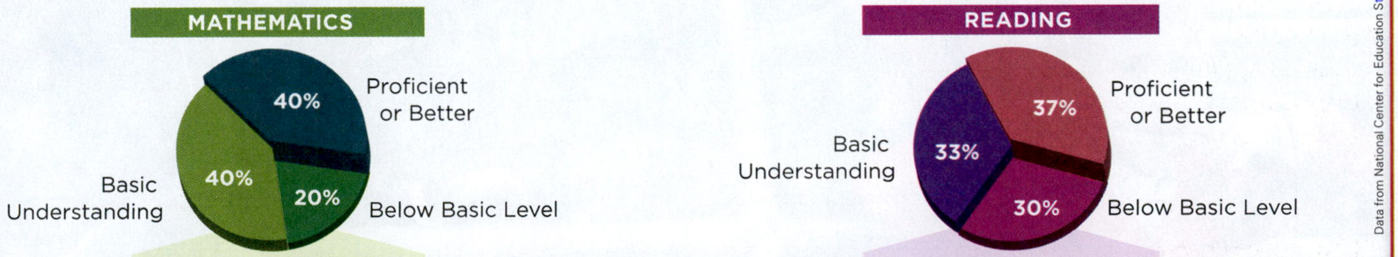

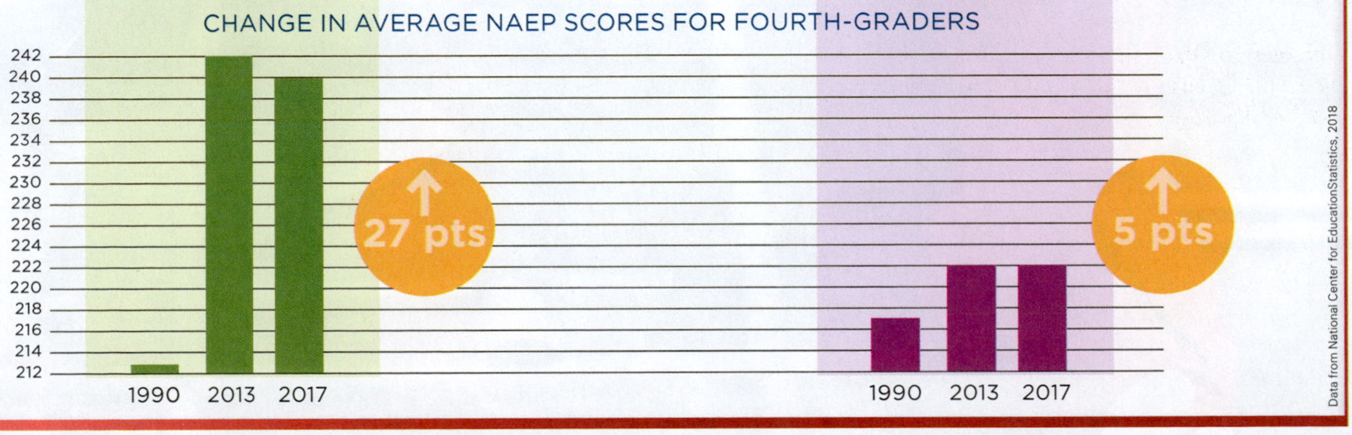

CHAPTER 13

Middle Childhood: The Social World

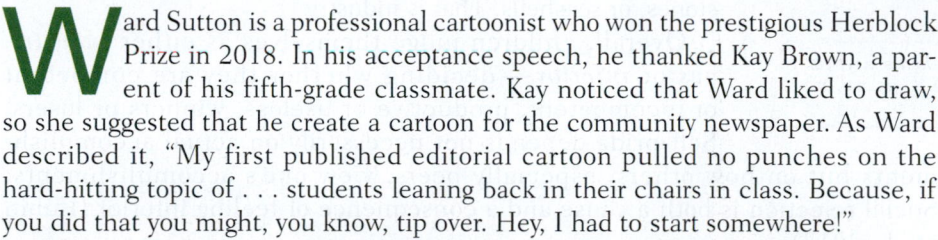

What Will You Know?

- What helps children thrive in difficult family or neighborhood conditions?
- Should parents marry, risking divorce, or not marry, risking separation?
- What can be done to stop a bully?

- **The Nature of the Child**
  - Industry and Inferiority
  - Parental Reactions
  - Self-Concept
  - Resilience and Stress
- **Families During Middle Childhood**
  - Shared and Nonshared Environments
  - A VIEW FROM SCIENCE: "I Always Dressed One in Blue Stuff . . ."
  - Function and Structure
  - Various Family Structures
  - Connecting Family Structure and Function
  - A CASE TO STUDY: How Hard Is It to Be a Kid?
  - Family Trouble
- **The Peer Group**
  - The Culture of Children
  - Friendships
  - Popular and Unpopular Children
  - Bullying
  - Children's Morality
  - OPPOSING PERSPECTIVES: Parents Versus Peers
- **CAREER ALERT: The Speech Therapist**
- **VISUALIZING DEVELOPMENT: Family Structures Around the World**

Ward Sutton is a professional cartoonist who won the prestigious Herblock Prize in 2018. In his acceptance speech, he thanked Kay Brown, a parent of his fifth-grade classmate. Kay noticed that Ward liked to draw, so she suggested that he create a cartoon for the community newspaper. As Ward described it, "My first published editorial cartoon pulled no punches on the hard-hitting topic of . . . students leaning back in their chairs in class. Because, if you did that you might, you know, tip over. Hey, I had to start somewhere!"

Ward and Kay are mentioned to open this chapter because their story illustrates the nature of 10-year-olds and the importance of the community that supports them. Ward's focus on the practical problems of fifth-graders—the tipping of chairs—is typical during middle childhood.

Later, larger issues become salient: Ward mentioned that his small Colorado town protected freedom of speech. But children do not see such issues. However, they respond to caring adults. Every reader of this book can aspire to be Kay for some young Ward.

This chapter details the concerns of children—peers, bullies, family life—and also puts that in context, as communities offer support for the many problems of children.

The Nature of the Child

As explained in the previous chapter, steady growth, brain maturation, and intellectual advances make middle childhood a time for more independence (see At About This Time). One practical result is that children between ages 6 and 11 learn to care for themselves. They not only hold their own spoon but also make their own lunch, not only zip their own pants but also pack their own suitcases, not only walk to school but also organize games with friends. They venture outdoors alone.

Industry and Inferiority

Throughout the centuries and in every culture, school-age children have been industrious. They busily master whatever skills their culture values. Their mental and physical maturation, described in the previous chapter, makes such activity possible.

Left: altrendo images/Stoked/Media Bakery
Top: EdZbarzhyvetsky/Deposit Photos

AT ABOUT THIS TIME

Signs of Psychosocial Maturation Over the Years of Middle Childhood*
Children responsibly perform specific chores.
Children make decisions about a weekly allowance.
Children can tell time and have set times for various activities.
Children have homework, including some assignments over several days.
Children are punished less often than when they were younger.
Children try to conform to peers in clothes, language, and so on.
Children voice preferences about their after-school care, lessons, and activities.
Children are responsible for younger children, pets, and, in some places, work.
Children strive for independence from parents.
*Of course, culture is crucial. For example, giving a child an allowance is typical for middle-class children in developed nations since about 1960. It was rare, or completely absent, in earlier times and other places.

With regard to his fourth psychosocial crisis, **industry versus inferiority,** Erikson noted that the child "must forget past hopes and wishes, while his exuberant imagination is tamed and harnessed to the laws of impersonal things," becoming "ready to apply himself to given skills and tasks" (Erikson, 1993a, pp. 258, 259).

Simply trying new things, as in the previous stage of initiative versus guilt, is no longer sufficient. The goal is sustained activity that leads to accomplishments that make one proud.

Think of learning to read and learning to add, both of which are painstaking and tedious tasks. For instance, slowly sounding out "Jane has a dog" or writing "3 + 4 = 7" for the hundredth time is not exciting.

Yet school-age children are intrinsically motivated to read a page, finish a worksheet, memorize a spelling word, color a map, and so on. Similarly, they enjoy collecting, categorizing, and counting whatever they gather—perhaps stamps, stickers, stones, or seashells. That is industry.

Overall, children judge themselves as either *industrious* or *inferior*—deciding whether they are competent or incompetent, productive or useless, winners or losers. Self-pride depends not necessarily on actual accomplishments but on how others, especially peers, view one's accomplishments. Social rejection is both a cause and a consequence of feeling inferior (Rubin et al., 2013).

industry versus inferiority The fourth of Erikson's eight psychosocial crises, during which children attempt to master many skills, developing a sense of themselves as either industrious or inferior, competent or incompetent.

Parental Reactions

Did you pause a moment ago when you read that 6- to 11-year-olds can "venture outdoors alone"? Cohort and context changes can be dramatic. Recently in the United States, many parents do not allow their children outside without an adult—even to walk to a neighbor's house, much less to go to town with money in their pocket.

Same Situation, Far Apart: Helping at Home Virginia, in the United States *(left)*, and Sichuan, in China *(right)*, provide vastly different contexts for child development. Children everywhere help their families with household chores, as these two do, but gender expectations vary a great deal.

Universally, children in middle childhood become *capable* of doing things themselves that they once could not do, but parents react in diverse ways: Some 10-year-olds care for younger children, make dinner, and clean house while parents are away at work; some use power tools or drive tractors on the family farm. Others are closely supervised if they venture outside or even turn on the kitchen stove.

For all children, parents gradually grant more autonomy, which helps their children feel happy and capable (Yan et al., 2017). Consequently, time spent with parents decreases while time alone, and with friends, increases.

For example, one study of U.S. families found that 8-year-olds, on average, spent 95 minutes a day with their mothers, and 12-year-olds spent 70 minutes, almost half an hour less. This study found substantial variation by context and family structure (Lam et al., 2012).

Self-Concept

As children mature, they develop their *self-concept,* which is their idea about themselves, including their intelligence, personality, abilities, gender, and ethnic background. As you remember, in toddlerhood children discover that they are individuals, and in early childhood they develop a positive, global self-concept.

That rosy self-concept is modified in middle childhood. The self-concept gradually becomes more specific and logical, the result of increases in cognitive development and social awareness (Orth & Robins, 2014). Many factors affect self-concept, some enduring (genes, poverty), some from previous experiences (insecure attachment and inadequate parenting), and some specific (emotional difficulties, academic failures).

THINK CRITICALLY: When would a realistic, honest self-assessment be harmful?

Compared to Peers

Crucial during middle childhood is **social comparison**—comparing oneself to others (Lapan & Boseovski, 2017; Dweck, 2013). Ideally, social comparison helps school-age children value themselves for who they are, abandoning the fantasy self-evaluation of preschoolers.

social comparison The tendency to assess one's abilities, achievements, social status, and other attributes by measuring them against those of other people, especially one's peers.

The self-concept becomes more realistic. Children incorporate comparison to peers and become more specific when they judge their own competence. The usual result is still a positive self-concept, now grounded in reality (Thomaes et al., 2017).

Some children—especially those from minority ethnic or religious groups—become aware of social prejudices. Children also notice gender discrimination. Girls complain that they are not allowed to play tougher sports, and boys complain that teachers favor the girls (Brown et al., 2011).

Over the years of middle childhood, children who affirm pride in their gender and ethnicity are likely to develop healthy self-esteem (Corenblum, 2014). Transgender children particularly experience discrimination. For them, parental support is crucial, but parents themselves experience stress (Hidalgo & Chen, 2019). Overall, one way to develop the self-esteem of children who are in the minority within their community is to help the parents.

Especially when the outside world seems hostile, parents and schools (e.g., teaching about ethnic heroes, gender stars, immigration successes) make a difference (Hernández et al., 2017). Much of the research focuses on adolescents and African Americans, but the same influences affect every age and ethnic group. Developing self-acceptance and pride bolsters self-confidence more than alerting children to prejudice (Reynolds & Gonzales-Backen, 2017).

Christina Kilgour/Moment Select/Getty Images

Learning from Each Other Middle childhood is prime time for social comparison. Swinging is done standing, or on the belly, or twisted, or head down (as shown here) if someone else does it.

Pictorial Press Ltd/Alamy Stock Photo

Black Panther Mythical superheroes, and the perpetual battle between good and evil, are especially attractive to boys in middle childhood but resonate with people of all ages, genders, and ethnic groups. *Black Panther* was first a comic-book hero in 1966 and then became a 2018 movie that broke records for attendance and impact. It features not only African American heroes but also an army of strong women—busting stereotypes and generating self-esteem for many children.

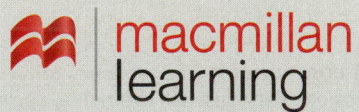

macmillan learning

Watch **VIDEO: Interview with Carol Dweck** to learn about how children's mindsets affect their intellectual development.

Culture and Self-Esteem Both academic and social competence are aided by realistic self-perception. That is beneficial. Unrealistically high self-esteem reduces effortful control (deliberately modifying one's impulses and emotions), and then reduced effortful control leads to lower achievement and increased aggression.

The same consequences occur if self-esteem is too low. Obviously, the goal then is to find a middle ground. This is not easy: Children may be too self-critical or not self-critical enough. Their self-control interacts with the reactions of their parents and culture. Cultures differ on what that middle ground is.

High self-esteem is neither universally valued nor criticized. Many cultures expect children to be modest. For example, Australians say that "tall poppies are cut down"; the Chinese say, "the nail that sticks up is hammered"; and the Japanese discourage social comparison aimed at making oneself feel superior. Self-esteem is moral issue. *Should* people believe that they are better than other people, as is typical in the United States but not in every nation? Answers vary.

One crucial component of self-concept has received considerable research attention (Dweck, 2013). As children become more self-aware, they benefit from praise for their process, not for their person—praise for *how* they learn, *how* they relate to others, and so on, not for static qualities such as intelligence and popularity. This encourages growth.

For example, children who fail a test are devastated if failure means that they are not smart. However, process-oriented children consider failure a "learning opportunity," a time to figure out how to study the next time.

The self-conscious emotions (pride, shame, guilt) first evident in early childhood may also develop during middle childhood. They guide social interaction, yet they can overcome a child's self-concept, leading to psychopathology (Muris & Meesters, 2014). Especially during middle childhood (less so in adolescence), school achievement is a crucial factor in developing self-esteem, and that affects later self-concept—as someone who is inferior or not.

In addition, the onset of concrete thinking in middle childhood leads children to notice material possessions. Objects that adults may find superficial (name-brand sunglasses, sock patterns) become important.

Insecure 10-year-olds might desperately want the latest jackets, smartphones, and so on. Or they may want something else that makes them seem special, such as lessons in African dance, or a brilliant light for their bicycle, or—as one of my daughters did—a bread-maker (used for weeks, discarded after years).

Resilience and Stress

In infancy and early childhood, children depend on their immediate families for food, learning, and life itself. In middle childhood, some children continue to benefit from supportive families, and others escape destructive families by finding their own niche in the larger world.

Surprisingly, some children seem unscathed by early experiences. They have been called "resilient" or even "invincible." Current thinking about resilience (see **Table 13.1**), with insights from dynamic-systems theory, emphasizes that no one is truly untouched by past history or current context, but some weather early storms and a few become stronger because of challenges (Masten, 2014; Luthar, 2015).

resilience The capacity to adapt well to significant adversity and to overcome serious stress.

Resilience has been defined as "a dynamic process encompassing positive adaptation within the context of significant adversity" (Luthar et al., 2000, p. 543) and

"the capacity of a dynamic system to adapt successfully to disturbances that threaten system function, viability, or development" (Masten, 2014, p. 10). Both of these researchers emphasize three parts of this definition:

- Resilience is *dynamic*. A person may be resilient at some periods but not others; the effects from one period reverberate as time goes on.
- Resilience is a *positive adaptation* to stress. For example, if parental rejection leads a child to a closer relationship with another adult, that is resilience.
- Adversity must be *significant*, a threat to development.

Cumulative Stress An important discovery is that stress accumulates over time, including minor disturbances (called "daily hassles"). A long string of hassles, day after day, takes a greater toll than an isolated major stress. Almost every child can withstand one trauma, but "the likelihood of problems increased as the number of risk factors increased" (Masten, 2014, p. 14).

The social context, especially supportive adults who do not blame the child, is crucial. A chilling example comes from the "child soldiers" in the 1991–2002 civil war in Sierra Leone (Betancourt et al., 2013). Children witnessed and often participated in murder, rape, and other traumas. When the war was over, 529 war-affected youth, then aged 10 to 17, were interviewed. Many were severely depressed, with crippling anxiety.

These war-damaged children were interviewed again two and six years later. Many had overcome their trauma and were functioning well. Recovery was likely for those who were in middle childhood, not adolescence, when the war occurred. If at least one caregiver survived, if their communities did not reject them, and if their daily routines were restored, the children usually regained emotional normality.

Family as a Buffer In England during World War II, many city children were sent to loving families in rural areas to escape the German bombs that were dropped every day. To the surprise of researchers, those children who stayed in London with their parents were more resilient, despite nights huddled in air-raid shelters, than those who were physically safe but without their parents (Freud & Burlingham, 1943).

Similar results were found in a longitudinal study of children exposed to a sudden, wide-ranging, terrifying wildfire in Australia. Almost all of the children suffered stress reactions at the time, but 20 years later the crucial factor was not proximity to the fire but whether or not it separated them from their mothers (McFarlane & Van Hooff, 2009).

Whenever war, or economic conditions, or immigration policies separate parents and children, developmentalists predict lifelong problems for the children. This is long evident in Holocaust survivors from World War II, refugees of African

TABLE 13.1

Dominant Ideas About Resilience, 1965 to Present

1965	All children have the same needs for healthy development.
1970	Some conditions or circumstances—such as "absent father," "teenage mother," "working mom," and "day care"—are harmful for every child.
1975	All children are *not* the same. Some children are resilient, coping easily with stressors that cause harm in other children.
1980	Nothing inevitably causes harm. Both maternal employment and preschool education, once thought to be risks, are often helpful.
1985	Factors beyond the family, both in the child (low birthweight, prenatal alcohol exposure, aggressive temperament) and in the community (poverty, violence), can be very risky for children.
1990	Risk–benefit analysis finds that some children are "invulnerable" to, or even benefit from, circumstances that destroy others.
1995	No child is invincible. Risks are always harmful—if not in education, then in emotions; if not immediately, then long term.
2000	Risk–benefit analysis involves the interplay among many biological, cognitive, and social factors.
2005	Focus on strengths, not risks. Assets in child (intelligence, personality), family (secure attachment, warmth), community (schools, after-school programs), and nation (income support, health care) must be nurtured.
2010	Strengths vary by culture and national values. Both universal ideals and local variations must be recognized and respected.
2015	Genes as well as cultural practices can be either strengths or weaknesses. Differential susceptibility: Identical stressors benefit one child and harm another.
2020	Resilience is seen more broadly as a characteristic of communities.

macmillan learning

VIDEO ACTIVITY: Child Soldiers and Child Peacemakers examines the state of child soldiers in the world and then explores how adolescent cognition impacts the decisions of five teenage peace activists.

Courtesy Unicef

civil wars, and children in Vietnam. Recently, the same consequences have been found in immigrant children in the United States, who suffer from many health problems, if their parents are not with them (Perreira & Pedroza, 2019). Some die.

For that reason, thousands of developmental scholars and dozens of professional societies have expressed their horror at the 2018 U.S. policy of separating children from their parents at the United States–Mexico border. For example, members of the Society for Developmental and Behavioral Pediatrics fear that "a generation of children will experience lifelong repercussions" from being forcefully separated from their parents. Their statement reads:

> Children and parents belong together. Children who are separated from their primary caregivers may experience toxic stress and a disruption of attachment that can have severe emotional, behavioral and physical implications.
>
> *[Society for Developmental and Behavioral Pediatrics, 2018]*

Cognitive Coping Obviously, these examples are extreme, but the general finding appears in many studies. Disasters take a toll, but resilience is possible. Factors in the child (especially problem-solving ability), in the family (consistency and care), and in the community (good schools and welcoming religious institutions) all help children recover (Masten, 2014).

The child's interpretation of events is crucial (Lagattuta, 2014). Cortisol increases in low-income children *if* they interpret events connected to their family's poverty as a personal threat and *if* the family lacks order and routines (thus increasing daily hassles) (Coe et al., 2018). If low-SES children do not feel personally to blame, and if their family is not chaotic, they may be resilient.

In general, children's interpretations of family situations (poverty, divorce, and so on) determine how they are affected. Think of people you know: Some adults from low-SES families did not feel deprived. Thus, poverty may not have damaged them.

Some children consider the family they were born into a temporary hardship; they look forward to the day when they can leave childhood behind. If they also have personal strengths, such as problem-solving abilities and intellectual openness, they may shine in adulthood—evident in the United States in thousands of success stories, from Abraham Lincoln to Oprah Winfrey.

One final example: Many children of immigrants in the United States are translators for their parents, who speak little English. If those children feel burdened by their role as language brokers, that increases their depression. But, if they feel they are making a positive contribution to their family well-being, they themselves benefit (Weisskirch, 2017a).

THINK CRITICALLY: Is there any harm in having the oldest child take care of the younger ones? Why or why not?

Bernd Jonkmanns / laif / Redux

Naftali Hilger /laif / Redux

Same Situation, Far Apart: Praying Hands Differences are obvious between the northern Indian girls entering their Hindu school *(left)* and the West African boy in a Christian church *(right),* even in their clothes and hand positions. But underlying similarities are more important. In every culture, many 8-year-olds are more devout than their elders. That is especially true if their community is under stress. Faith aids resilience.

WHAT HAVE YOU LEARNED?

1. How do Erikson's stages for preschool and school-age children differ?
2. Why is social comparison particularly powerful during middle childhood?
3. Why do cultures differ in how they value pride or modesty?
4. Why and when might minor stresses be more harmful than major stresses?
5. How might a child's interpretation of events help him or her cope with repeated stress?

Families During Middle Childhood

No one doubts that genes affect personality as well as ability, that peers are vital, and that schools and cultures influence what, and how much, children learn. At the same time, families are crucial.

Shared and Nonshared Environments

Many studies have found that children are much less affected by *shared environment* (influences that arise from being in the same environment, such as for two siblings living in one home, raised by their parents) than by *nonshared environment* (e.g., the distinct experiences and surroundings of two people). Even psychopathology, happiness, and sexual orientation (Burt, 2009; Långström et al., 2010; Bartels et al., 2013) can be attributed primarily to genes and nonshared environment.

Does that mean parents are merely caretakers, needed for basic care but inconsequential in daily restrictions, routines, and responses? No.

The analysis of shared and nonshared influences was correct, but the conclusion was based on a false assumption. Siblings raised together do *not* share the same environment. For example, moving to another town upsets a school-age child more than an infant; divorce harms boys more than girls; poverty may hurt preschoolers the most; and so on.

Differential susceptibility adds to the variation: One child might be more affected by parents than another (Pluess & Belsky, 2010). When siblings are raised together (experiencing the same family conditions), the mix of genes, age, and gender may lead one child to become antisocial, another to be pathologically anxious, and a third to be resilient (Beauchaine et al., 2009). Children differ, and parents do not treat each child the same, as A View from Science makes clear (see page 330).

monkeybusinessimages/iStock/Getty Images

Shared Environment? All three children live in the same home in Brooklyn, New York, with loving, middle-class parents. But, it is not hard to imagine that family life is quite different for the 9-year-old girl than for her sister, born a year later, or their little brother, age 3.

Observation Quiz Are significant gender differences evident here? (see answer, page 348)

Function and Structure

Family structure refers to the genetic and legal connections among related people. *Genetic* connections may be from parent to child, between cousins, between siblings, between grandparents and grandchildren, or more distantly, such as from great aunts, second cousins, and so on. *Legal* connections may be through marriage or adoption.

Family function is distinct from structure. It refers to how the people in a family actually care for one another. Some families function well; others are dysfunctional.

Function is more important than structure. Ideally, every family provides love and encouragement. For most people this comes from genetic relatives, so

family structure The legal and genetic relationships among relatives living in the same home. Possible structures include nuclear family, extended family, stepfamily, single-parent family, and many others.

family function The way a family works to meet the needs of its members. Children need families to provide basic material necessities, to encourage learning, to help them develop self-respect, to nurture friendships, and to foster harmony and stability.

A VIEW FROM SCIENCE

"I Always Dressed One in Blue Stuff . . ."

To separate the effects of genes and environment, many researchers have studied twins (McAdams et al., 2014). As you remember from Chapter 3, some twins are dizygotic, with only half of their genes in common, and some are monozygotic, identical in all their genes. Many scientists assumed that children growing up with the same parents would have the same nurture (shared environment).

Therefore, if dizygotic twins are less alike than monozygotic twins are, genes must be the reason. Further, if one monozygotic twin differs from his or her genetically identical twin who was raised by their parents in the same home, those differences must arise from the nonshared environment.

Logically, everyone is influenced by three forces: genes, shared environment (same home), and nonshared environment (different schools, friends, and so on). Many people were surprised when twin research discovered that almost everything could be attributed to genes and nonshared environment, with almost nothing left over for parents.

However, that conclusion is now tempered by another finding: Siblings raised in the same home may have quite different family experiences for reasons that are not genetic. A seminal study in this regard occurred with twins in England.

An expert team of scientists compared 1,000 sets of monozygotic twins reared by their biological parents (Caspi et al., 2004). Obviously, the pairs were identical in genes, sex, and age. The researchers asked the mothers to describe each twin. Descriptions ranged from very positive ("my ray of sunshine") to very negative ("I wish I never had her. . . . She's a cow, I hate her") (quoted in Caspi et al., 2004, p. 153). Some mothers noted personality differences between their twins. For example, one mother said:

> Susan can be very sweet. She loves babies . . . she can be insecure . . . she flutters and dances around. . . . There's not much between her ears. . . . She's exceptionally vain, more so than Ann. Ann loves any game involving a ball, very sporty, climbs trees, very much a tomboy. One is a serious tomboy and one's a serious girlie girl. Even when they were babies I always dressed one in blue stuff and one in pink stuff.
>
> *[quoted in Caspi et al., 2004, p. 156]*

Some mothers rejected one twin but not the other. In one case, one twin (Mike) weighed more and left the hospital before the other (Jeff):

> He was in the hospital and everyone was all "poor Jeff, poor Jeff" and I started thinking, "Well, what about me? I'm the one's just had twins. I'm the one's going through this, he's a seven-week-old baby and doesn't know a thing about it" . . . I sort of detached and plowed my emotions into Mike [Jeff's twin brother].
>
> *[quoted in Caspi et al., 2004, p. 156]*

This mother later blamed Jeff for favoring his father: "Jeff would do anything for Don but he wouldn't for me, and no matter what I did for either of them [Don or Jeff], it wouldn't be right" (quoted in Caspi et al., 2004, p. 157). She said Mike was much more lovable.

The researchers measured personality at age 5, including antisocial behavior as reported by kindergarten teachers. Then they measured each twin's personality two years later. They found that if a mother was more negative toward one of her twins, that twin *became* more antisocial, more likely to fight, steal, and hurt others at age 7 than at age 5, unlike the favored twin.

These researchers recognize that many other nonshared factors—peers, teachers, and so on—are significant. However, most developmental scientists now agree that parental influences are important. Especially when genes or neighborhood push a child toward unhealthy development, parental intervention can be crucial (Liu & Neiderhiser, 2017).

Genes are still powerful, of course, because "a given DNA sequence operating in different environments can generate different products in different amounts at the cellular and phenotypic levels" (Waldinger & Schulz, 2018). That expresses an underlying theme of this book, that human development is multifactorial and complex. It begins with genes (DNA), but a simple calculation of genetic and family influence is impossible.

The fact that parents sometimes treat each of a pair of monozygotic twins differently confirms that parents matter. This will surprise no one who has a brother or a sister. Children from the same family do not always experience their family in the same way.

structure and function overlap. For foster children and adopted children who share few distinct genes with their caregivers, family function is crucial (Flannery et al., 2017).

Everyone enters the world with unique genes and a particular prenatal environment. Then, differential susceptibility influences how family affects the person. Beyond that, people's needs differ depending on their age: Infants need responsive caregiving, teenagers need guidance, young adults need freedom, the aged need respect. What do school-age children need?

Especially for Scientists How would you determine whether or not parents treat all of their children the same? (see response, page 348)

The Needs of Children in Middle Childhood Ideally, families that function well for children aged 6 to 11 provide five things:

1. *Physical necessities.* In middle childhood, children can eat, dress, and wash themselves, but they need food, clothing, and shelter.
2. *Learning.* Families support, encourage, and guide schooling—connecting with teachers, checking homework, and so on.
3. *Self-respect.* Because children become self-critical and socially aware, families provide opportunities for success (in sports, the arts, and so on if academic success is difficult).
4. *Peer relationships.* Children need friends. Families choose friendly schools and neighborhoods, arrange play dates, and so on.
5. *Harmony and stability.* Families provide protective, predictable routines in a home that is a safe, peaceful haven. Conflict and chaos are destructive.

Harm from Instability The final item above may be especially significant in middle childhood: Children cherish safety and stability (Turner et al., 2012). Changes in caregivers (e.g., mother, stepmother, aunt, father), in residence, and in schools are difficult.

One study that focused on low-income children found that instability in early and middle childhood increased the rate of internalizing and externalizing problems, for boys as well as girls. Race made a difference: Harm was less apparent for African American children. The researchers suggested that grandparents and other relatives provided stability (Womack et al., 2018).

For all children, a well-functioning family can buffer the impact of change. Children in shelters whose mothers provide stability, affection, routines, and hope may be resilient.

A more benign example comes from children in military families. Enlisted parents tend to have higher incomes, better health care, and more education than many civilians. That is a benefit for the youngest children and the adults. But they have one major disadvantage: instability, which can disrupt schoolchildren.

For some children, parent deployment (which requires several disruptions in the child's home life) leads to higher rates of depression and aggression (Fairbank et al., 2018; Williamson et al., 2018).

On a broader level, children who are displaced because of storms, fire, war, and so on may suffer psychologically. They may try to comfort their parents, not telling them about their distress, but the data on health and achievement show that moving from place to place is highly stressful (Masten, 2014). All children must cope with some disruption: Some children learn to do it well, but ideally they do not need to.

Jose Luis Pelaez Inc/DigitalVision/Getty Images

Stay Home, Dad The rate of battle deaths for U.S. soldiers is lower for those deployed in Iraq and Afghanistan than for any previous conflict, thanks to modern medicine and armor. However, psychological harm from repeated returns and absences is increasing, especially for children.

Various Family Structures

A **nuclear family** is a family composed only of children and their parents (married or not). Usually the parents are the biological parents of the children, but other nuclear families are headed by adoptive parents, foster parents, stepparents, or same-sex couples, most of whom provide good care.

Rates of single-parenthood vary greatly worldwide (see Visualizing Development, page 349); about 31 percent of all U.S. 6- to 11-year-olds live in a **single-parent family.** Most are good caregivers. Some observers think that 31 percent is a low estimate, since more than half of all contemporary U.S. children will live in a single-parent family for at least a year before they reach age 18. However, as far as we can deduce, at any given moment most 6- to 11-year-olds are in nuclear families.

nuclear family A family that consists of a father, a mother, and their biological children under age 18.

single-parent family A family that consists of only one parent and his or her children.

extended family A family of relatives in addition to the nuclear family, usually three or more generations living in one household.

polygamous family A family consisting of one man, several wives, and their children.

Didn't Want to Marry This couple was happily cohabiting and strongly committed to each other but didn't wed until they learned that her health insurance would not cover them unless they were legally married. Twenty months after marriage, their son was born.

An **extended family** includes relatives in addition to parents and children. Usually the additional persons are grandparents. The crucial distinction for official tallies is who lives under the same roof. This measures family structure, not family function.

The distinction between one-parent, two-parent, and extended families is not as simple in practice as it is on the census. Many parents of young children live near, but not with, the grandparents, who provide meals, emotional support, money, and child care, functioning as an extended family. The opposite is true as well, especially in developing nations: Some extended families share a household but create separate living quarters for each set of parents and children.

In many nations, the **polygamous family** (one husband with two or more wives) is a legal family structure. Generally in polygamous families, income per child is reduced, and education, especially for the girls, is limited—in part because girls are expected to marry young. Polygamy is rare—and illegal—in the United States. Even in nations where it is allowed—most African and many Asian nations—polygamy is less common than it was 30 years ago.

Cohort Changes There are more single-parent households, more divorces and remarriages, and fewer children per family than in the past (see **Figure 13.1**). Specifics vary from decade to decade and nation to nation. That matters for children. In the United States, divorced, single-parent families were unusual in the 1960s, then more common, and now somewhat less common. Children are more likely to suffer when their family structure is unusual.

Connecting Family Structure and Function

How a family functions is more important for children than their family structure, although structure influences (but does not determine) function. Some structures increase the possibility that the five family functions mentioned earlier (physical necessities, learning, self-respect, friendship, and harmony/stability) will be fulfilled (see **Table 13.2**).

Two-Parent Families On average, nuclear families function best; children living with two married parents tend to learn more in school with fewer psychological problems. Why? Does this mean that parents should all marry and stay married? Not necessarily: Some benefits are correlates, not causes.

FIGURE 13.1

Possible Problems As the text makes clear, structure does not determine function, but raising children is more difficult as a single parent, in part because income is lower. African American families have at least one asset, however. They are more likely to have grandparents who are actively helping with child care.

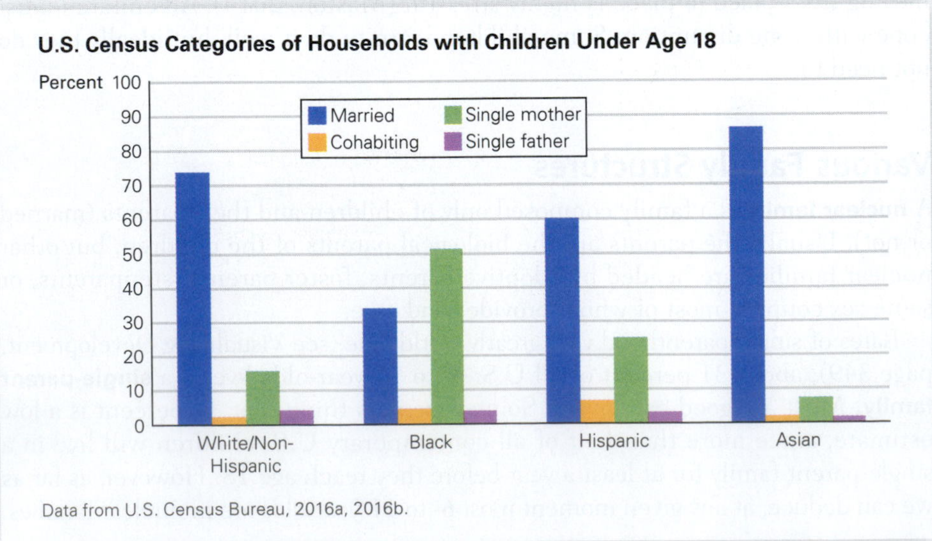

To understand that, remember the longitudinal life-span perspective. Education, earning potential, and emotional maturity increase the rate of marriage and parenthood and decrease the rate of divorce.

Thus, spouses tend to have personal assets *before* they marry and become parents, and those assets benefit the children when they arrive. The correlation between child success and married parents occurs partly because of who marries,

TABLE 13.2

Family Structures (percent of U.S. 6- to 11-year-olds in each type)*

Two-Parent Families (69%)

1. **Nuclear family** (56%). Named after the nucleus (the tightly connected core particles of an atom), the nuclear family consists of a man and a woman and their biological offspring under 18 years of age. In middle childhood, about half of all children live in nuclear families. About 10 percent of such families also include a grandparent, and often an aunt or uncle, living under the same roof. Those are *extended* families.
2. **Stepparent family** (9%). Divorced fathers usually remarry; divorced mothers remarry about half the time. If the stepparent family includes children born to two or more couples (such as children from the spouses' previous marriages and/or children of the new couple), that is a *blended* family.
3. **Adoptive family** (2%). Although as many as one-third of infertile couples adopt children, they usually adopt only one or two. Thus, only 2 percent of children are adopted, although the overall percentage of adoptive families is higher than that.
4. **Grandparents alone** (1%). Grandparents take on parenting for some children when biological parents are absent (dead, imprisoned, sick, addicted, etc.). That is a *skipped-generation* family.
5. **Two same-sex parents** (1%). Some two-parent families are headed by a same-sex couple. The children can be the biological children of one parent or the adoptive children of one or both parents.

Single-Parent Families (31%)

One-parent families are increasing, but they average fewer children than two-parent families. So, in middle childhood only 31 percent of children have a lone parent.

1. **Single mother—never married** (14%). In 2010, 41 percent of all U.S. births were to unmarried mothers; but when children are of school age, many such mothers have married. Thus, only about 14 percent of 6- to 11-year-olds, at any given moment, are in single-mother, never-married homes.
2. **Single mother—divorced, separated, or widowed** (12%). Although many marriages end in divorce (almost half in the United States, fewer in other nations), many divorcing couples have no children. Others remarry. Thus, only 12 percent of school-age children currently live with single, formerly married mothers.
3. **Single father** (4%). About 1 father in 25 has physical custody of his children and raises them without their mother or a new wife. This category increased at the start of the twenty-first century but has decreased since 2005.
4. **Grandparent alone** (1%). Sometimes a single grandparent (usually the grandmother) becomes the sole caregiving adult for a child.

More Than Two Adults (10%) [Also listed as two-parent or single-parent family]

1. **Extended family** (10%). Some children live with a grandparent and/or other relatives, as well as with one or both of their parents. This pattern is most common with infants but occurs in middle childhood as well.
2. **Polygamous family** (0%). In some nations (not the United States), men can legally have several wives. This family structure is more favored by adults than children. Everywhere, polyandry (one woman, several husbands) is rare.

*Less than 1 percent of children under age 12 live without any caregiving adult; they are not included in this table.

The percentages in this table are estimates, based on data in U.S. Census Bureau. (2013a). *America's families and living arrangements: 2012*. Washington, DC: U.S. Department of Commerce, Economics and Statistics Administration, U.S. Census Bureau. The category "extended family" in this table is higher than most published statistics, since some families do not tell official authorities about relatives living with them.

Middle American Family This photo seems to show a typical breakfast in Brunswick, Ohio — Cheerios for 1-year-old Carson, pancakes that 7-year-old Carter does not finish eating, and family photos crowded on the far table.

Observation Quiz What is unusual about this family? (see answer, page 348) ↑

not because of the wedding. These two factors — selection and income — explain some of the correlation between nuclear families and child well-being.

To the surprise of some outsiders, a large study comparing male–female and same-sex couples found that the major predictor of child well-being was not the parents' sexual orientation but their income and stability (Cenegy et al., 2018). Similar findings come from adoptive parents, grandparents raising children, and so on. A caregiver's emotional health and economic security benefit the children.

On average, married parents (of whatever gender identity and sexual orientation) are more likely to stay together than unmarried parents, and they become wealthier and healthier than either would alone. Further, seeing one's children day and night increases bonding. By contrast, single parenthood, especially after a bitter divorce, correlates with poor health and low income. Simply not seeing one parent very often increases internalizing and externalizing problems in children.

Contact tends to increase affection, health, and care. Recent data come from Russia, where economic and social pressures have led many single men to drink and despair, dying years earlier than married men. The reason is thought to be that the husband/father role leads men to take care of themselves and enables wives to protect their husband's health (Ashwin & Isupova, 2014).

Shared parenting also decreases the risk of maltreatment, because one parent is likely to protect their children if the other is abusive or neglectful. Having two involved parents makes it likely that someone will read to the children, check homework, invite friends over, buy clothes, and save for their education. Of course, having two married parents does not guarantee good care. One of my students wrote:

> My mother externalized her feelings with outbursts of rage, lashing out and breaking things, while my father internalized his feelings by withdrawing, being silent and looking the other way. One could say I was being raised by bipolar parents. Growing up, I would describe my mom as the Tasmanian devil and my father as the ostrich, with his head in the sand. . . . My mother disciplined with corporal punishment as well as with psychological control, while my father was permissive. What a pair.
>
> *[C., 2013]*

This student is now a single parent, having twice married, given birth, and divorced. She is one example of a general finding: The effects of childhood family function echo in adulthood, financially as well as psychologically.

Single Fathers Generally, fathers who do not live with their children become less involved every year. When the children reach age 18, fathers are no longer legally responsible, and many divorced or unmarried fathers no longer pay for education or other expenses. This is harsh in today's economy: Emerging adults usually need substantial funds before they can become self-sufficient adults (Goldfarb, 2014).

When a father is the single parent, he suffers the same problems as single mothers — too much to do and not enough money to do it. Single parents of both sexes tend to seek a new spouse, in part to help with parenthood. This does not usually work out as planned (Booth & Dunn, 2014).

Courts and social workers are increasingly recommending joint physical custody of children after a divorce. In general, when both parents are directly involved in caregiving, children of divorce are healthier, physically and emotionally, than when only one parent has custody (Baude et al., 2016; Braver & Votruba, 2018).

Randy Griffith/The Tribune-Democrat via AP Images

commerceandculturestock/Moment Select/Getty Images

Fortunate Boys This single father *(left)* in Pennsylvania takes his three sons to the playground almost every day, and this nuclear family *(right)* in Mali invests time and money in their only child's education. All four boys have loving fathers. Does family function make family structure irrelevant?

Stepfamilies may benefit the adults but not the children. Remarried adults whose household income is comparable to that of nuclear parents contribute less, on average, to children from their first marriage or to stepchildren (Turley & Desmond, 2011). For many reasons, the bond between stepparents and stepchildren is fragile.

Harmony is difficult in stepfamilies (Martin-Uzzi & Duval-Tsioles, 2013). Often the child's loyalty to both biological parents is challenged by ongoing disputes between them. A solid parental alliance is elusive when it includes three adults—two of whom disliked each other enough to divorce, plus another adult who is a newcomer to the child.

Children themselves impede the functioning of their new family structure. They often are angry or sad and they act out, fighting with friends, failing in school, refusing to follow household rules, harming themselves (with cutting, accidents, eating disorders, and so on). Added to that, disputes between half-siblings and stepsiblings are common. Remember, however, that structure affects function but does not determine it. Some stepparent families are troubled, but others function well for everyone (van Eeden-Moorefield & Pasley, 2013).

Single-Parent Families On average, the single-parent structure functions less well for children because single parents have less income, time, and stability. Most fill many roles—including wage earner, daughter or son (single parents often depend on their own parents), and lover (many seek a new partner). If they are depressed (and many are), that makes it worse. Neesha, in A Case to Study, is an example (see page 336).

All of these are generalities. Structure affects function, but many parents and communities overcome structural burdens. Contrary to the averages, thousands of nuclear families are destructive, thousands of stepparents provide excellent care, and thousands of single-parent families are wonderful.

Culture is always influential. In contrast to data from the United States, a study in the slums of Mumbai, India, found rates of psychological disorders among school-age children *higher* in nuclear families than in extended families, presumably because grandparents, aunts, and uncles provided more care and stability in that city than two parents alone (Patil et al., 2013). Single parents are much less common in India and in most other nations than in the United States, but in this study as in every nation, on average, children in such families are more likely to have emotional or academic problems.

macmillan learning

Check out the **Data Connections activity Family Structure in the United States and Around the World.**

Macmillan Archive/Danny Goldfield

Don't Judge We know this is a mother and her child, but structure and function could be wonderful or terrible. These two could be half of a nuclear family, or a single mother with one adoptive child, or part of four other family structures. That does not matter as much as family function: If this scene is typical, with both enjoying physical closeness in the great outdoors, this family functions well.

A CASE TO STUDY

How Hard Is It to Be a Kid?

Neesha's fourth-grade teacher referred her to the school guidance team because Neesha often fell asleep in class, was late 51 days, and was absent 15 days. Testing found Neesha at the seventh-grade level in reading and writing and at the fifth-grade level in math. Since achievement was not Neesha's problem, something psychosocial must be amiss.

The counselor spoke to Neesha's mother, Tanya, a single parent who was depressed and worried about paying the rent on a tiny apartment where she had moved when Neesha's father left three years earlier. He lived with his girlfriend, now with a new baby as well. Tanya said she had no problems with Neesha, who was "more like a little mother than a kid," unlike her 15-year-old son, Tyrone, who suffered from fetal alcohol effects and whose behavior worsened when his father left.

Tyrone was recently beaten up badly as part of a gang initiation, a group he considered "like a family." He was currently in juvenile detention, after being arrested for stealing bicycle parts. Note the nonshared environment here: Although the siblings grew up together and their father left them both, 12-year-old Tyrone became rebellious whereas 7-year-old Neesha became parentified, "a little mother."

The school counselor also spoke with Neesha.

> Neesha volunteered that she worried a lot about things and that sometimes when she worries she has a hard time falling asleep. . . . she got in trouble for being late so many times, but it was hard to wake up. Her mom was sleeping late because she was working more nights cleaning offices. . . . Neesha said she got so far behind that she just gave up. She was also having problems with the other girls in the class, who were starting to tease her about sleeping in class and not doing her work. She said they called her names like "Sleepy" and "Dummy." She said that at first it made her very sad, and then it made her very mad. That's when she started to hit them to make them stop.
>
> *[Wilmshurst, 2011, pp. 152–153]*

Neesha is coping with poverty, a depressed mother, an absent father, a delinquent brother, and classmate bullying. She seemed resilient—her achievement scores are impressive—but shortly after Neesha was interviewed,

> The school principal received a call from Neesha's mother, who asked that her daughter not be sent home from school because she was going to kill herself. She was holding a loaded gun in her hand and she had to do it, because she was not going to make this month's rent. She could not take it any longer, but she did not want Neesha to come home and find her dead. . . . While the guidance counselor continued to keep the mother talking, the school contacted the police, who apprehended [the] mom while she was talking on her cell phone. . . . The loaded gun was on her lap. . . . The mother was taken to the local psychiatric facility.
>
> *[Wilmshurst, 2011, pp. 154–155]*

Whether Neesha's resilience will continue depends on her ability to find support beyond her family. Perhaps the school counselor will help:

> When asked if she would like to meet with the school psychologist once in a while, just to talk about her worries, Neesha said she would like that very much. After she left the office, she turned and thanked the psychologist for working with her, and added, "You know, sometimes it's hard being a kid."
>
> *[Wilmshurst, 2011, p. 154]*

THINK CRITICALLY: Can you describe a situation in which having a single parent would be better for a child than having two parents?

Family Trouble

All of the generalities just explained are averages; many families find their own way to function well, overcoming structural problems. However, no matter what ethnicity, culture, or structure, two factors inevitably undercut family function: low income and high conflict. If a family has one of these, they often have the other, because financial stress increases conflict and vice versa.

Wealth and Poverty Family income affects function and structure. Marriage rates fall in times of economic recession, and divorce increases with unemployment. Low SES correlates with many other problems, and "risk factors pile up in the lives of some children, particularly among the most disadvantaged" (Masten, 2014, p. 95).

Several scholars have developed the *family-stress model,* which holds that any risk factor (such as poverty, divorce, single parenthood, unemployment) damages a family if, and only if, it increases stress on the parents, who become less patient and responsive to the children (Masarik & Conger, 2017). This is true for families of all types, ethnicities, and nations (Emmen et al., 2013).

Reaction to wealth may also cause difficulty (Luthar et al., 2018). Children in high-income families are more likely to have developmental problems in adulthood than children of middle-SES parents. Wealthy parents may be anxious about maintaining their status, which makes them pressure their children to excel. That may create externalizing and internalizing problems in middle childhood that lead to drug abuse, delinquency, and poor academic performance.

No one contends that family poverty is better than affluence for children. However, developmental scholars believe the crucial factor with SES is how economic pressures affect the ability of the parents and the community to provide children the attention and guidance they need (Roubinov & Boyce, 2017).

Nations that subsidize single parents (e.g., Austria and Iceland) tax wealthy adults at higher rates and have greater economic diversity within schools, which generally have smaller achievement gaps between low- and high-SES children. Of course, explanations for national differences in the impact of SES on children's achievement abound; not everyone agrees that national economic policies are the crucial factor.

Nonetheless, the score gap between schools with high- and low-income children is larger in the United States than in other nations (M. O. Martin et al., 2016) (see **Figure 13.2**), and the number of children living with only one parent is a possible reason. How the nation reacts to single parents may be pivotal: Research in Norway finds that the connection between low family income and children's emotional problems is smaller than in other nations because of the "buffering effect of the social safety net," including high-quality early education (Bøe et al., 2018).

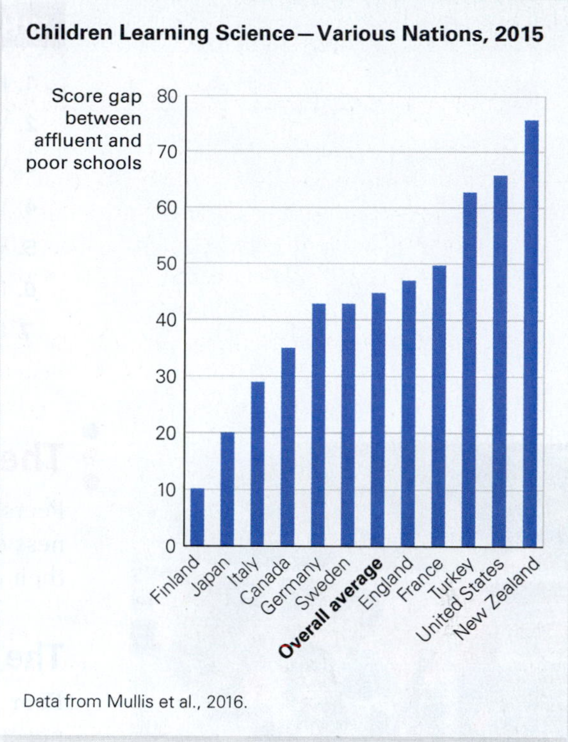

FIGURE 13.2

Families and Schools This graph shows the score gap in fourth-grade science on the 2015 TIMSS between children in schools where more than 25 percent of the children are from affluent homes compared to children in schools where more than 25 percent are poor. Generally, the nations with the largest gaps are also the nations with the most schools at one or the other end of the spectrum and the fewest in between. For example, only 23 percent of the children in the United States attended schools that were neither rich nor poor, compared to 37 percent of the children in Japan.

Conflict Every researcher agrees that family conflict harms children, especially when adults fight about child rearing. Such fights are more common in stepfamilies, divorced families, and extended families, but nuclear families are not immune. Children suffer not only if they are abused, physically or emotionally, but also if they merely witness their parents' abuse of each other or of their other children. Fights between siblings can be harmful, too (Turner et al., 2012).

Might families with feuding parents and hostile siblings have genes that affect the children, even those who are not directly mistreated? If that is so, the correlation between witnessing fights and personally suffering is deceptive: It is caused by a third variable.

This hypothesis was tested in a longitudinal study of conflict in the families of 867 adult twins (388 monozygotic and 479 dizygotic), with both twins married and having an adolescent child (Schermerhorn et al., 2011). Both parents were asked independently about marital conflict. Each teenager was compared to his or her cousin, who was the child of his or her parent's twin.

Thus, this study had data from 5,202 individuals—one-third of them adult twins, one-third of them spouses of twins, and one-third of them adolescents who were genetically linked to another adolescent. Adolescents whose parent was a monozygotic twin had one-fourth of their genes in common with their cousin; those whose parent was a dizygotic twin had one-eighth of the same genes. This enabled the researchers to compare the effects of genes versus family harmony.

Although genes had some effect, witnessing conflict itself was powerful, increasing externalizing problems in the boys and internalizing problems in the girls. Quiet disagreements didn't do much harm, but open conflict (e.g., yelling heard by the children) and divorce did (Schermerhorn et al., 2011). That leads to an obvious conclusion: Parents should not fight in front of their children.

WHAT HAVE YOU LEARNED?

1. How might siblings raised together not share the same family environment?
2. What is the difference between family structure and family function?
3. Why is a harmonious, stable home particularly important during middle childhood?
4. What are the advantages for children in a nuclear family structure?
5. Why might the single-parent structure function less well than two-parent structures?
6. How are family structure and family function affected by culture?
7. Using the family-stress model, explain how family income affects family function.

E.Hanazaki Photography/Moment/Getty Images

No Toys Many boys in middle childhood are happiest playing outside with equipment designed for work. This wheelbarrow is perfect, especially because at any moment the pusher might tip it.

child culture The idea that each group of children has games, sayings, clothing styles, and superstitions that are not common among adults, just as every culture has distinct values, behaviors, and beliefs.

The Peer Group

Peers become increasingly important in middle childhood. With their new awareness of reality (concrete operational thought), children become painfully aware of their classmates' opinions, judgments, and accomplishments.

The Culture of Children

Peer relationships, unlike adult–child relationships, involve partners who negotiate, compromise, share, and defend themselves as equals. Consequently, children learn lessons from one another that grown-ups cannot teach (Rubin et al., 2013).

Child culture includes the customs, rules, and rituals that are passed down to younger children from slightly older ones. The child's goal is to join the culture and thus be part of the peer group. Jump-rope rhymes, insults, and superstitions are examples.

For instance, "Ring around the rosy/Pocketful of posies/Ashes, ashes/We all fall down" may have originated as children coped with the Black Death, which killed half the population of Europe in the fourteenth century. (*Rosy* may be short for *rosary*, used by Roman Catholics for prayer.) Children have passed down that rhyme for centuries, laughing together with no thought of sudden death.

Throughout the world, child culture may be at odds with adult culture. Many children reject clothes that parents buy as too loose, too tight, too long, too short, or wrong in color, style, brand, decoration, or some other aspect that adults might not notice. If their schools are multiethnic, children may choose friends from other groups, even though their parents have no such friends.

Appearance is important for child culture, but more important is independence from adults. Classmates pity those (especially boys) whose parents kiss them ("mama's boy"), tease children who please the teachers ("teacher's pet," "suck-up"), and despise those who betray children to adults ("tattletale," "grasser," "snitch," "rat"). Keeping secrets from parents and teachers is a moral mandate.

Because they value independence, children may gravitate toward friends who defy authority, sometimes harmlessly (passing a note in class), sometimes not (shoplifting, smoking). This is part of the nature of children, who often do what their parents do not want them to do, and it is in the nature of parents to be upset when that happens. This is easier to criticize in other cultures and centuries, as in the following example.

In 1922, the magazine *Good Housekeeping* published an article titled "Aren't you glad you are not your grandmother?" In it, a daughter quotes letters from her dead grandmother that she found in the attic. One describes an incident that occurred when that daughter's father—also long dead—was a boy and snuck out of his house to play with other boys:

> When the door was left unlocked for a moment, out he ran in his little velvet suit. We did not miss him for a while because we thought he was doing his Latin Prose, and then some wealthy ladies . . . saw him literally in the gutter, groping in the mud for a marble. . . . Horace's father was white with emotion when he heard of it. He went out, brought Horace in, gave him another whipping, and, saying that since he acted like a runaway dog he should be treated like one, he went out, bought a dog-collar and a chain, and chained Horace to the post of his little bed. He was there all the afternoon, crying so you could hear nothing else in all the house. . . . I went many times up to the hall before his door and knelt there stretching out my arms to my darling child, the tears flooding down my cheeks. But, of course, I could not open the door and go in to him, to interfere with his punishment.
>
> *[Fisher, 1922, p. 8]*

The author is grateful that mothers now (in 1922!) know more than did nineteenth-century parents with their "ignorance of child-life" (Fisher, 1922, p. 15). This raises the question: What ignorance of child-life do we have today? If I knew, that would not be ignorance, but this text makes me humble; each new generation develops a child culture that may teach their elders.

Johnny Hawkins/CartoonStock

"Oh yeah? Well, my vocabulary is bigger than your vocabulary!"

Better Than Children of all genders, ethnic groups, religions, nations, and family structures think they are better than children of other groups. They can learn not to blurt out insults, but a deeper understanding of the diversity of human experience and abilities requires maturation.

Friendships

Teachers sometimes separate friends, but that may be a mistake. Developmentalists find that children help each other learn both academic and social skills (Bagwell & Schmidt, 2011). The loyalty of children to their friends may work for their benefit or harm (Rubin et al., 2013).

Both aspects of friendship are expressed by these two Mexican American children.

> *Yolanda:*
>
> There's one friend . . . she's always been with me, in bad or good . . . She's always telling me, "Keep on going and your dreams are gonna come true."
>
> *Paul:*
>
> I think right now about going Christian, right? Just going Christian, trying to do good, you know? Stay away from drugs, everything. And every time it seems like I think about that, I think about the homeboys. And it's a trip because a lot of the homeboys are my family, too, you know?
>
> *[quoted in Nieto, 2000, pp. 220, 249]*

Yolanda later went to college; Paul went to jail. This is echoed by other children. Many aspects of adult personality are influenced by the personalities of childhood friends (Wrzus & Neyer 2016). Indeed, quite apart from a child's family, school, and IQ, a study found that the intelligence of a best friend in sixth grade affected intelligence at age 15 (Meldrum et al., 2018).

Again, this can work to benefit children or not. As one study concludes, if low-achievers "select[ed] similarly low-achieving students as friends, this may dampen their academic achievement over time" (Laninga-Wijnen et al., 2019, p. 347).

Friendships become more intense and intimate over the years of middle childhood, as social cognition and effortful control advance. Six-year-olds may befriend anyone of the same sex and age who will play with them. By age 10, children demand more. They choose carefully, share secrets, expect loyalty, change friends less often, are upset when they lose a friend, find it harder to make new ones.

THINK CRITICALLY: Do adults also choose friends who agree with them or whose background is similar to their own?

Popular and Unpopular Children

In the United States, two types of popular children and three types of unpopular children have become apparent in middle childhood (Cillessen & Marks, 2011). First, at every age, children who are friendly and cooperative are well-liked and popular. By the end of middle childhood, as status becomes important, another avenue to popularity begins: Some popular children are also aggressive (Shi & Xie, 2012).

As for the three types of unpopular children, some are *neglected,* not rejected; ignored, not shunned. The other two types are actively rejected, either **aggressive-rejected,** disliked because they are antagonistic and confrontational, or **withdrawn-rejected,** disliked because they are timid and anxious.

aggressive-rejected A type of childhood rejection, when other children do not want to be friends with a child because of their antagonistic, confrontational behavior.

withdrawn-rejected A type of childhood rejection, when other children do not want to be friends with a child because of their timid, withdrawn, and anxious behavior.

Both aggressive-rejected and withdrawn-rejected children often misinterpret social situations, lack emotional regulation, and experience mistreatment at home. Each of these problems causes rejection, and the rejection itself makes it worse for the child (Stenseng et al., 2015). If they do not learn when to assert themselves and when to be quiet, they may become bullies and victims.

Whether a particular child is popular or not depends on cultural norms, which may change over time. This is illustrated by research on shyness in China. Shyness was admired in 1990 but less so in 2010, with age and region both influential (Chen et al., 1992; Chen et al., 2019; Zhang & Eggum-Wilkens, 2018). Culture, cohort, and context matter.

Now consider bullying, once quite acceptable ("boys will be boys!") but now seen as destructive, not only for victims but for bystanders and bullies as well.

macmillan learning

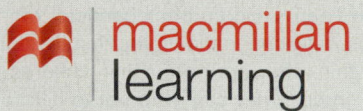

VIDEO: Bullying: Interview with Nikki Crick explores the causes and repercussions of the different types of bullying.

Bullying

Bullying is defined as repeated, systematic attacks intended to harm those who are unable or unlikely to defend themselves. It occurs in every nation, in every community, in every kind of school (religious/secular, public/private, progressive/traditional, large/medium/small), and perhaps in every child. As one girl said, "There's a little bit of bully in everyone" (Guerra et al., 2011, p. 303).

bullying Repeated, systematic efforts to inflict harm on other people through physical, verbal, or social attack on a weaker person.

Bullying is of four types:

- *Physical* (hitting, pinching, shoving, or kicking)
- *Verbal* (teasing, taunting, or name-calling)
- *Relational* (destroying peer acceptance)
- *Cyberbullying* (using electronic means to harm another)

Who Suffers More? Physical bullying is typically the target of antibullying laws and policies, because it is easier to spot than relational bullying. But being rejected from the group, especially with gossip and lies, may be more devastating to the victim and harder to stop. It may be easier for the boy to overcome victimization than for the girl.

The first three types are common in primary school and begin in preschool. Cyberbullying is more common later on and is discussed in Chapter 15.

Victims Almost every child experiences an isolated attack or is called a derogatory name at some point. Victims of bullying, however, endure shameful experiences again and again—pushed and kicked for no reason, called names, forced to do degrading things, and so on—with no defense. Victims tend to be "cautious, sensitive, quiet . . . lonely and abandoned at school. As a rule, they do not have a single good friend in their class" (Olweus, 1999, p. 15).

Even having a friend who is also a victim helps. Such friends may not be able to provide physical protection, but they provide psychological defense—reassuring victims that the bully is mean, stupid, racist, or whatever (Schacter & Juvonen, 2018). That is crucial, because the worst harm is loss of self-respect.

Although it is often thought that victims are particularly unattractive or odd, this is not necessarily the case. Victims are chosen because of their emotional vulnerability and social isolation, not their appearance. Children who are new to a school, or whose background and therefore home culture are unlike that of their peers, or whose clothes indicate poverty, are especially vulnerable. When bullying is pervasive, almost any trait can become an excuse to exclude a vulnerable child.

As one boy said,

> You can get bullied because you are weak or annoying or because you are different. Kids with big ears get bullied. Dorks get bullied. You can also get bullied because you think too much of yourself and try to show off. Teacher's pet gets bullied. If you say the right answer too many times in class you can get bullied. There are lots of popular groups who bully each other and other groups, but you can get bullied within your group too. If you do not want to get bullied, you have to stay under the radar, but then you might feel sad because no one pays attention to you.
>
> *[quoted in Guerra et al., 2011, p. 306]*

Remember the three types of unpopular children? *Neglected* children are not victimized; they are ignored, "under the radar." *Rejected* children fit into the bully network. Withdrawn-rejected children are likely victims; they are isolated, depressed, and friendless. Aggressive-rejected children may be **bully-victims** (or *provocative victims*), with neither friends nor sympathizers (Kochel et al., 2015). They suffer because they strike back ineffectively, which increases the bullying.

Bullies Unlike bully-victims, most bullies are *not* rejected. Many are proud, pleased with themselves, with friends who admire them and classmates who fear them (Guerra et al., 2011). Some are quite popular, with bullying being a form of social dominance and authority (Pellegrini et al., 2011).

The link between bullying and popularity has long been apparent during early adolescence (Pouwels et al., 2016), but bullies are already "quite popular in middle childhood." What changes from age 6 to age 12 is that bullies become skilled at avoiding adult awareness, at picking rejected and defenseless victims, and at using nonphysical methods—which avoid adult punishment (Pouwels et al., 2017).

Boys are bullies more often than girls, typically attacking smaller, weaker boys. Girl bullies usually use words to demean shyer, more soft-spoken girls. Young boys sometimes bully girls, but by puberty (about age 11), boys who bully girls are not admired (Veenstra et al., 2010), although sexual teasing is. Especially in the final years of middle childhood, boys who are thought to be gay become targets, with suicide attempts in adolescence one consequence (Hong & Garbarino, 2012).

Causes and Consequences of Bullying Bullying may begin early in life. Most toddlers try to dominate other children (and perhaps their parents) at

CHAPTER APP 13

Daisy Chain

RELATED TOPIC: Bullying

IOS: http://tinyurl.com/y6ywppow

Narrated by actress Kate Winslet, Daisy Chain is an interactive story about a girl's experience with bullying. Children can listen and peruse the picture book (if purchased) as Winslet reads, or they can play along with the interactive story on the device as it's read to them. A percentage of the proceeds from app-related merchandise (sold through an in-app store and protected by a parent gate) goes to anti-bullying organizations.

bully-victim Someone who attacks others and who is attacked as well. (Also called *provocative victims* because they do things that elicit bullying.)

Especially for Parents of an Accused Bully Another parent has told you that your child is a bully. Your child denies it and explains that the other child doesn't mind being teased. What should you do? (see response, page 348)

Danny Shanahan/The New Yorker Collection/The Cartoon Bank

"What'll it be, Tyler—your lunch money or heaps of verbal abuse?"

He Needs a Friend Boys and girls tend to use different bullying tactics, but friendship is protective for everyone. Note the ratio here: The bully has a friend, but the victim does not.

some point. When they hit, kick, and so on, their parents, teachers, and peers usually teach them to find other ways to interact.

However, if home life is chaotic, if discipline is ineffectual, if siblings are hostile, or if attachment is insecure, children do not learn how to express their frustration. Instead, vulnerable young children develop externalizing and internalizing problems, becoming bullies or victims (Turner et al., 2012).

By middle childhood, bullying is not the outburst of a frustrated child but an attempt to gain status. That makes it a social action: Bullies rarely attack victims when the two of them are alone. Instead, a bully might engage in a schoolyard fight, with onlookers who are more likely to cheer the victor than stop the fight; or a bully might utter an insult that provokes laughter in all except the target. By the end of middle childhood, bullies choose victims who are rejected by other children.

Siblings matter. Some brothers and sisters defend each other; children are protected if bullies fear that an older sibling will retaliate. On the other hand, if children are bullied by peers in school *and* by siblings at home, they are four times more likely to develop serious psychological disorders by age 18 (Dantchev et al., 2018).

Bullies and victims risk impaired social understanding, lower school achievement, and relationship difficulties, with higher rates of mental illness in adulthood (Copeland et al., 2013; Ttofi et al., 2014). Many victims become depressed; many bullies become increasingly cruel and have higher rates of imprisonment and death (Willoughby et al., 2014).

THINK CRITICALLY: The text says that both former bullies and former victims suffer in adulthood. Which would you rather be, and why?

The damage goes even further: In schools with high rates of bullying, *all* of the children are less likely to focus on academics and more likely to concentrate on the social dynamics of the classroom—hoping to avoid becoming the next victim.

Can Bullying Be Stopped? We know what does *not* work: simply increasing students' awareness of bullying, instituting zero tolerance for fighting, or putting bullies together in a therapy group or a classroom. This last measure tends to make daily life easier for teachers, but it increases aggression.

Since one cause of bullying is poor parent–child interaction, alerting parents may "create even more problems for the child, for the parents, and for their relationship" (Rubin et al., 2013, p. 267). This does not mean that parents should be kept ignorant, but it does mean that parents need help in understanding how to break the bully-victim connection (Nocentini et al., 2019).

Power to Peers Bullying is a way some children gain respect. If, instead, the school gives training and special shirts to bystanders, they can gain status by befriending victims. That seems to work in this school in Bensalem, Pennsylvania.

AP Images/JACQUELINE LARMA

To decrease bullying, the entire school should be involved (Juvonen & Graham, 2014). A Spanish concept, *convivencia,* describes a culture of cooperation and positive relationships within a community. Convivencia has been applied specifically to schools. When teachers are supportive and protective, and when friendships and cooperation among all students is encouraged, bullying decreases (Zych et al., 2017).

Bystanders are crucial: If they do not intervene—or worse, if they watch and laugh—bullying flourishes. Some children who are neither bullies nor victims feel troubled but also feel fearful and powerless (Thornberg & Jungert, 2013). However, if they empathize with victims and refuse to admire bullies, aggression is reduced.

Appreciation of human differences is not innate (remember, children seek friends who are similar to them), so adults need to encourage multicultural sensitivity. Then peers are more effective than teachers at halting bullying (Palmer & Abbott, 2018). As they mature during middle childhood, children become more socially aware, which creates a conflict—they are more aware of how someone's actions might hurt a child but also more aware of the possible harm to themselves if they befriend a bullied child. This raises the final question related to peers in middle childhood—moral development.

Children's Morality

Some moral values seem inborn. Babies prefer a puppet who is helpful to other puppets over a mean puppet, and young children believe that desired objects (cookies, stickers, candy) should be shared equally. The ideas of fairness, kindness, and equality are present in the minds of children (Rizzo & Killen, 2016; Van de Vondervoort & Hamlin, 2016).

However, the young child's idea of morality is quite limited. Middle childhood is prime time for moral education. These are:

> years of eager, lively searching on the part of children . . . as they try to understand things, to figure them out, but also to weigh the rights and wrongs. . . . This is the time for growth of the moral imagination, fueled constantly by the willingness, the eagerness of children to put themselves in the shoes of others.
>
> *[Coles, 1997, p. 99]*

Many lines of research have shown that children develop their own morality, guided by peers, parents, and culture (Jambon & Smetana, 2014). Children's growing interest in moral issues is guided by three forces: (1) child culture, (2) empathy, and (3) education.

Moral Rules of Child Culture First, when child culture conflicts with adult morality, children often align themselves with peers. A child might lie to protect a friend, for instance. Friendship itself has a hostile side: Many close friends (especially girls) resist other children who want to join their play (Rubin et al., 2013). Boys are particularly likely to protect a bully if he is a friend.

Three moral imperatives of child culture in middle childhood are:

- Defend your friends.
- Don't tell adults about children's misbehavior.
- Conform to peer standards of dress, talk, and behavior.

These three can explain both apparent boredom and overt defiance as well as standards of dress that mystify adults (such as jeans so loose that they fall off or so tight that they impede digestion—both styles worn by my children, who grew up in different cohorts). Given what is known about middle childhood, it is no surprise that children do not echo adult morality.

Part of child culture is that as children become more aware of their peers, they may reject other children who are outsiders as well as stay quiet about their own problems. When teachers ask, "Who threw that spitball?" or parents ask, "How did you get that bruise?" children may be mum.

Empathy The second factor, empathy, is key. As middle childhood advances, children become more socially perceptive and more able to learn about other people (Weissberg et al., 2016).

The authors of a study of 7-year-olds "conclude that moral *competence* may be a universal human characteristic, but that it takes a situation with specific demand characteristics to translate this competence into actual prosocial performance" (van Ijzendoorn et al., 2010, p. 1). Here, diversity in schools and neighborhoods can be helpful. Empathy is not an abstract idea as much as recognizing the basic humanity of other people. In order to achieve that, knowing a child from another group helps children understand.

THINK CRITICALLY: If one of your moral values differs from that of your spouse, your parents, or your community, should you still try to teach it to your children? Why or why not?

Universal Morality Remarkable? Not really. By the end of middle childhood, many children are eager to express their moral convictions, especially with a friend. Chaim Ifrah and Shai Reef believe that welcoming refugees is part of being a patriotic Canadian and a devout Jew, so they brought a welcoming sign to the Toronto airport where Syrian refugees (mostly Muslim) will soon deplane.

Steve Russell/Toronto Star/Getty Images

OPPOSING PERSPECTIVES

Parents Versus Peers

The fact that children place prime value on being accepted by peers sometimes results in a conflict between the moral values of society and the actions of children. Sometimes a child does something that the parents think their child would never do. This is not a time to argue, or despair; it is a time to teach. This is illustrated by another memory that Ward Sutton (who opened this chapter) told in 2018 at his acceptance speech.

> In the summer of 1974, I was seven years old.
>
> There was a kid living in my neighborhood. . . .
>
> For some reason this kid had built up animosity towards a family down the block. He started telling my friend Steve and me that this family had done all sorts of bad things, like hiding razor blades in the apples they gave out to trick-or-treaters at Halloween.
>
> Fake news for seven year olds . . . target people who had done absolutely nothing wrong.
>
> Steve became convinced of the conspiracy theory and fell in line, and then the two of them told me they were starting a club and I couldn't join unless I went along with them. . . .
>
> We snuck behind the family's house in the woods out back. We threw some rocks at the house and when there was no response we realized the family was not home. Then we escalated things, finding bricks, smashing windows, breaking in and vandalizing the home.
>
> I was a shy, introverted kid who never would have ever done anything like this on my own. But once I was swayed to join in, it was like a switch had been flipped and any sense of right or wrong was thrown by the wayside. Suddenly the unthinkable was okay. . . .
>
> Then the family came home. We ran. Police arrived. Steve was caught. I lied. To my parents. To everyone. Said I didn't know anything about it. Steve confessed, and eventually I did, too. As terrible as it all was, the worst of it was the fact that I had lied. My mother wouldn't speak to me for what felt like an eternity. . . .
>
> My father brought me back to the house to apologize to the family face-to-face. I begged him not to make me do it. . . . I expected them to be angry with me, but they weren't. They were gracious, and mostly puzzled at what could have possibly possessed me to do something like this. . . .
>
> I couldn't even explain why I had done it.
>
> As you might imagine, this episode was hugely formative for me. It awakened my moral compass and informed what I would create going forward. . . .
>
> I've never spoken of it publicly until today. For the longest time, I wished I could live that day all over again, and that someone could have talked some sense into me: "Stop and think about what you're doing."

Sutton's cartoons are often ethical comments on world affairs. He says he draws them because he hopes people will smile, and then stop and think.

Moral Education Finally, cognitive development might affect moral development, at least according to Piaget (1932/2013b) and then Kohlberg (1963), who described three levels of moral reasoning and two stages at each level, with parallels to Piaget's stages of cognition.

preconventional moral reasoning Kohlberg's first level of moral reasoning, emphasizing rewards and punishments.

conventional moral reasoning Kohlberg's second level of moral reasoning, emphasizing social rules.

postconventional moral reasoning Kohlberg's third level of moral reasoning, emphasizing moral principles.

- **Preconventional moral reasoning** is similar to preoperational thought in that it is egocentric, with children most interested in their own personal pleasure or avoiding punishment.
- **Conventional moral reasoning** parallels concrete operational thought in that it relates to current, observable practices: Children watch what their parents, teachers, and friends do and try to follow suit.
- **Postconventional moral reasoning** is similar to formal operational thought because it uses abstractions, going beyond what is concretely observed, willing to question "what is" in order to decide "what should be."

According to Kohlberg, intellectual maturation advances moral thinking. During middle childhood, children's answers shift from being primarily preconventional to being more conventional: Concrete thought and peer experiences help children move past preconventional to conventional. Postconventional reasoning is not usually present until adolescence or adulthood, if then.

Kohlberg posed moral dilemmas to school-age boys (and eventually girls, teenagers, and adults). The most famous example of these dilemmas involves a poor man named Heinz, whose wife was dying. He could not pay for the only drug

that could cure his wife, a drug that a local druggist sold for 10 times what it cost to make.

> Heinz went to everyone he knew to borrow the money, but he could only get together about half of what it cost. He told the druggist that his wife was dying and asked him to sell it cheaper or let him pay later. But the druggist said "no." The husband got desperate and broke into the man's store to steal the drug for his wife. Should the husband have done that? Why?
>
> *[Kohlberg, 1963, p. 19]*

Kohlberg's assessment of morality depends not on what a person answers, but why an answer is chosen. For instance, suppose a child says that Heinz should steal the drug. That itself does not indicate the level of morality. The reason could be that Heinz needs his wife to care for him (preconventional), or that people will blame him if he lets his wife die (conventional), or that the value of a human life is greater than the law (postconventional).

Or suppose another child says Heinz should not steal. Again, the reason is crucial. If it is that he will go to jail, that is preconventional; if it is that business owners will blame him, that is conventional; if it is that no one should deprive anyone else of their livelihood, that is postconventional.

Kohlberg has been criticized for not appreciating cultural or gender differences. For example, loyalty to family overrides other values in some cultures, so some people might avoid postconventional actions that hurt their family. Also, Kohlberg's original participants were all boys, which may have led him to discount female values of nurturance and relationships (Gilligan, 1982).

Overall, Kohlberg seemed to value rational principles more than individual needs, unlike other scholars of moral development who consider emotions more influential than logic (Haidt, 2013). Regarding global warming, for instance, the facts about the world's temperature rising by a degree over a decade is less compelling for children in middle childhood than the tragedy of the stranded polar bear cub on a melting ice flow.

Teaching Morality Fortunately, children enjoy thinking about and discussing moral values, and then peers help one another advance in moral behavior. Children may be more ethical than adults (once they understand moral equity, they complain when adults are not fair), and they are better at stopping a bully than adults are, because a bully is more likely to listen to other children than to adults.

Since bullies tend to be low on empathy, they need peers to teach them when their actions are not admired. During middle childhood, morality can be scaffolded just as cognitive skills are, with mentors—peers or adults—using moral dilemmas to advance moral understanding while they also advance the underlying moral skills of empathy and emotional regulation (Hinnant et al., 2013).

A detailed examination of the effect of peers on morality began with an update on one of Piaget's moral issues: whether punishment should seek *retribution* (hurting the transgressor) or *restitution* (restoring what was lost). Piaget found that children advance from retribution to restitution between ages 8 and 10 (Piaget, 1932/2013b), which many ethicists consider a moral advance (Claessen, 2017).

To learn how this occurs, researchers asked 133 9-year-olds:

> Late one afternoon there was a boy who was playing with a ball on his own in the garden. His dad saw him playing with it and asked him not to play with it so near the house because it might break a window. The boy didn't really listen to his dad, and carried on playing near the house. Then suddenly, the ball bounced up high and broke the window in the boy's room. His dad heard the noise and came to see what had happened. The father wonders what would be the fairest way to punish the boy. He thinks of two punishments. The first is to say: "Now, you didn't do as

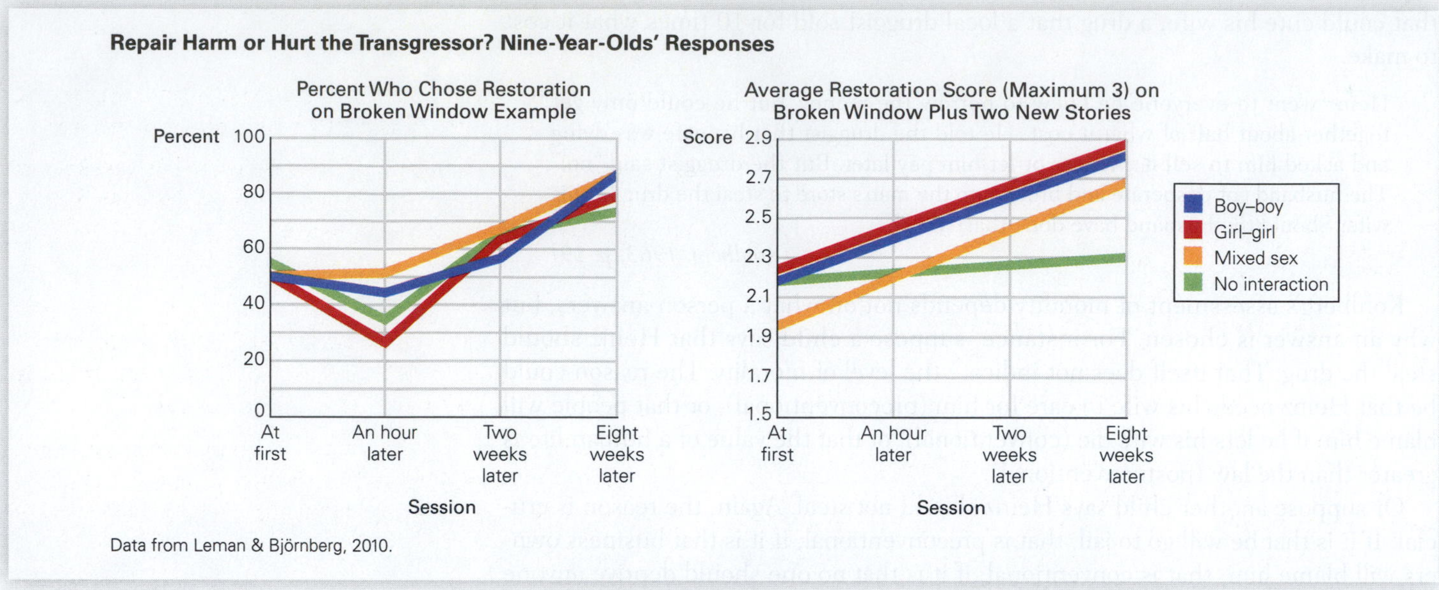

FIGURE 13.3

Benefits of Time and Talking The graph on the left shows that most children, immediately after their initial punitive response, became even more likely to seek punishment rather than to repair damage. However, after some time and reflection, they affirmed the response that Piaget would consider more mature. The graph on the right indicates that children who had talked about the broken window example moved toward restorative justice even in examples that they had not heard before, which was not true for those who had not talked about the first story.

> I asked. You will have to pay for the window to be mended, and I am going to take the money from your pocket money." The second is to say: "Now, you didn't do as I asked. As a punishment you have to go to your room and stay there for the rest of the evening." Which of these punishments do you think is the fairest?
>
> *[Leman & Björnberg, 2010, p. 962]*

The children were split almost equally in their answers. Then, 24 pairs were formed of children who had opposite views. Each pair was asked to discuss the issue, trying to reach agreement. (The other children did not discuss it.) Six pairs were boy–boy, six were boy–girl with the boy favoring restitution, six were boy–girl with the girl favoring restitution, and six were girl–girl.

The conversations typically took only five minutes, and the retribution side was more often chosen. Piaget would consider that a moral backslide, since more restitution than retribution advocates switched. However, two weeks and eight weeks later all of the children were queried again, and their responses changed toward the restitution thinking (see **Figure 13.3**). This advance occurred even for the children who merely thought about the dilemma again, but children who had discussed it with another child were particularly likely to decide that restitution was better.

The main conclusion from this study was that "conversation on a topic may stimulate a process of individual reflection that triggers developmental advances" (Leman & Björnberg, 2010, p. 969). Parents and teachers take note: Raising moral issues and letting children talk about them may advance morality—not immediately, but soon.

WHAT HAVE YOU LEARNED?

1. How does the culture of children differ from the culture of adults?
2. What are the different kinds of popular and unpopular children?
3. What do victims and bullies have in common?
4. How might bullying be reduced?
5. What three forces affect moral development during middle childhood?
6. What are the main criticisms of Kohlberg's theory of moral development?
7. What role do adults play in the development of morality in children?

SUMMARY

The Nature of the Child

1. All theories of development acknowledge that school-age children become more independent and capable in many ways. Erikson emphasized industry, when children busily strive to master various tasks.

2. Children develop their self-concept during middle childhood, basing it on a more realistic assessment of their competence than they had in earlier years. Cultures differ in their evaluation of high self-esteem.

3. Both daily hassles and major stresses take a toll on children, with accumulated stresses more likely to impair development than any single event on its own. Resilience is aided by the child's interpretation of the situation and the availability of supportive adults, peers, and institutions.

Families During Middle Childhood

4. Families influence children in many ways, as do genes and peers. Although most siblings share a childhood home and parents, each sibling experiences different (nonshared) circumstances within the family.

5. The five functions of a supportive family are to satisfy children's physical needs; to encourage learning; to support friendships; to protect self-respect; and to provide a safe, stable, and harmonious home.

6. The most common family structure worldwide is the nuclear family, usually with other relatives nearby and supportive. Two-parent families include adoptive, same-sex, grandparent, and stepfamilies, each of which sometimes functions well for children. However, each of these also has vulnerabilities.

7. Single-parent families have higher rates of change, and that stresses children. On average, such families have less income, which may cause stress. Nonetheless, some single parents function well.

8. Income affects family function for two-parent families as well as single-parent households. Poor children are at greater risk for emotional, behavioral, and academic problems because the stresses that often accompany poverty hinder effective parenting.

9. No matter what the family SES, instability and conflict are harmful. Children suffer even when the conflict does not involve them directly but their parents or siblings fight.

The Peer Group

10. Peers teach crucial social skills during middle childhood. Each cohort of children has a culture, passed down from slightly older children. Close friends are wanted and needed.

11. Popular children may be cooperative and easy to get along with or may be competitive and aggressive. Unpopular children may be neglected, aggressive, or withdrawn, sometimes becoming victims of bullying.

12. Bullying is common among school-age children. Both bullies and victims have difficulty with social cognition; their interpretation of the normal give-and-take of childhood is impaired.

13. Bullies themselves may be admired, which makes their behavior more difficult to stop. Overall, a multifaceted, long-term, whole-school approach—with parents, teachers, and bystanders working together—seems to be the best way to halt bullying.

14. School-age children seek to differentiate right from wrong as moral development increases over middle childhood. Peer values, cultural standards, empathy, and education all affect their personal morality.

15. Kohlberg described three levels of moral reasoning, each related to cognitive maturity. His description has been criticized for ignoring cultural and gender differences.

16. When values conflict, children often choose loyalty to peers over adult standards of behavior. When children discuss moral issues with other children, they develop more thoughtful answers to moral questions.

KEY TERMS

industry versus inferiority (p. 324)
social comparison (p. 325)
resilience (p. 326)
family structure (p. 329)
family function (p. 329)
nuclear family (p. 331)
single-parent family (p. 331)
extended family (p. 332)
polygamous family (p. 332)
child culture (p. 338)
aggressive-rejected (p. 340)
withdrawn-rejected (p. 340)
bullying (p. 340)
bully-victim (p. 341)
preconventional moral reasoning (p. 344)
conventional moral reasoning (p. 344)
postconventional moral reasoning (p. 344)

APPLICATIONS

1. Go someplace where many school-age children congregate (such as a schoolyard, a park, or a community center) and use naturalistic observation for at least half an hour. Describe what popular, average, withdrawn, and rejected children do. Note at least one potential conflict. Describe the sequence and the outcome.

2. Focusing on verbal bullying, describe at least two times when someone said something hurtful to you and two times when you said something that might have been hurtful to someone else. What are the differences between the two types of situations?

3. How would your childhood have been different if your family structure had been different, such as if you had (or had not) lived with your grandparents, if your parents had (or had not) gotten divorced, if you had (or had not) been adopted, if you had lived with one parent (or two), if your parents were both the same sex (or not)? Avoid blanket statements: Appreciate that every structure has advantages and disadvantages.

Especially For ANSWERS

Response for Scientists (from p. 330): Proof is very difficult when human interaction is the subject of investigation, since random assignment is impossible. Ideally, researchers would find identical twins being raised together and would then observe the parents' behavior over the years.

Response for Parents of an Accused Bully (from p. 341): The future is ominous if the charges are true. Your child's denial is a sign that there is a problem. (An innocent child would be worried about the misperception instead of categorically denying that any problem exists.) You might ask the teacher what the school is doing about bullying. Family counseling might help. Because bullies often have friends who egg them on, you may need to monitor your child's friendships and perhaps befriend the victim. Talk about the situation with your child. Ignoring the situation might lead to heartache later on.

Observation Quiz ANSWERS

Answer to Observation Quiz (from p. 329) Both parents are women. The evidence shows that families with same-sex parents are similar in many ways to families with opposite-sex parents, and children in such families develop well.

Answer to Observation Quiz (from p. 334) Did you notice that the two males are first, and that the father carries the boy? Everyone should notice gender, ethnic, and age differences, but interpretation of such differences is not straightforward. This scene may or may not reflect male–female roles.

CAREER ALERT The Speech Therapist

Teachers for children with special needs are in demand in the United States, as at least one of every six schoolchildren has a difference that affects that child's ability to learn. The most common of these differences are language disorders. Teachers who specialize in speech and reading, and who themselves are bilingual, are especially needed.

In the United States, there are about 130,000 speech pathologists. Most of them are certified by the American Speech, Language, and Hearing Association; half of them work in schools, but relatively few are fluent in the languages spoken by those children who do not hear English at home. The current annual salary is, on average, about $70,000, with marked variation from one state to another. The labor market for speech specialists is growing faster than for almost any other profession.

Many children with special needs have comorbid conditions, which means they have been diagnosed with multiple problems. For example, almost all children on the autism spectrum have speech problems. The need for speech pathologists is also evident for adults, who may have impairments from childhood or new problems as a result of strokes or injuries.

In the United States and many other nations, public funds pay for the diagnosis and treatment of speech disorders. However, most people with such problems never receive help—in part because parents and teachers may not recognize the problem, and most people do not know that language difficulties can be reduced with treatment.

Many children with speech problems can overcome them completely; adults with language impairment can almost always be helped, although usually some problems remain. Hearing loss is very common in late adulthood and usually impairs speech, but few adults realize it. Again, recognition is crucial.

There are dozens of reasons a person might have difficulty with language (Brookshire & McNeil 2015). Fortunately, therapists do not need to know the cause in order to help. Instead, they are experts in the many ways to remedy impaired articulation, speech, voice, and other aspects of language.

When people use language more effectively, self-esteem, academic competence, and social relationships improve. As a result, speech therapists sometimes gain much more than money: They experience the joy of knowing that they have changed someone's entire life.

VISUALIZING DEVELOPMENT Family Structures Around the World

Children fare best when both parents actively care for them every day. This is most likely to occur if the parents are married, although there are many exceptions. Many developmentalists focus on the rate of single parenthood, shown on this map. Single parents often raise children well, especially with support from their families, friends, and communities.

RATES OF SINGLE PARENTHOOD

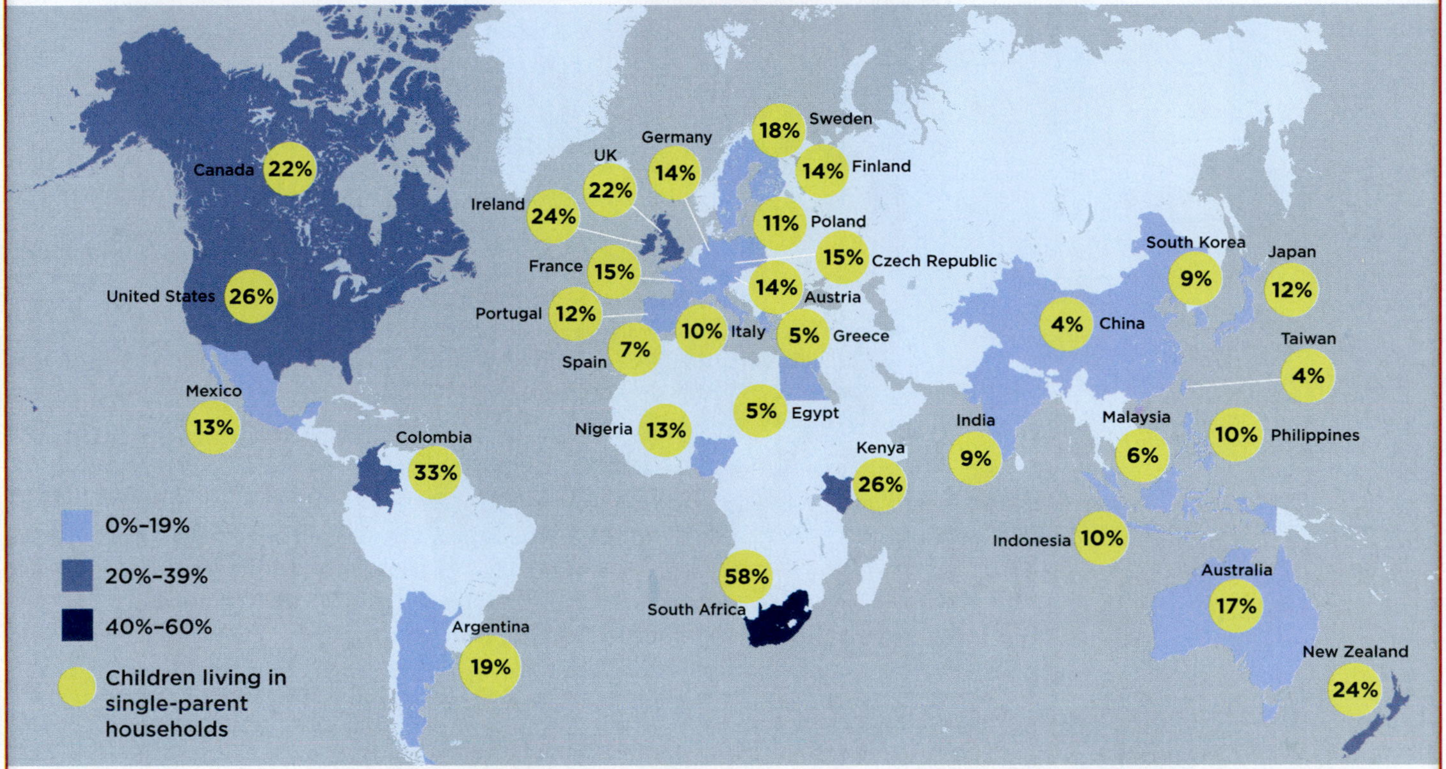

Data from Wilcox, 2011; OECD, 2011.

LIVING ARRANGEMENTS OF U.S. 0- TO 18-YEAR-OLDS

Note that, while fewer children live with their two married biological parents from birth to age 18, it is not that more children are living in stepfamilies but that more individuals have decided to raise children on their own. Another shift is evident: Single parents once were almost always mothers, but now some are single fathers.

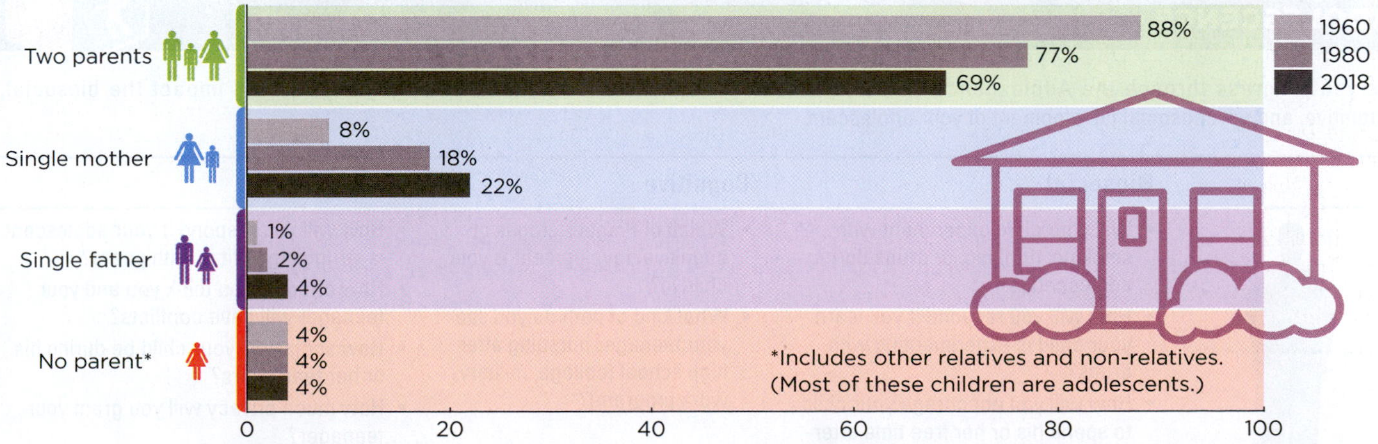

Information from Pew Research Center, December 17, 2015; U.S. Census Bureau, November, 2018.

APPLICATION TO DEVELOPING LIVES PARENTING SIMULATION
ADOLESCENCE

As you progress through the Adolescence simulation module, how you answer the following questions will impact the biosocial, cognitive, and psychosocial development of your adolescent.

	Biosocial	Cognitive	Psychosocial
	• Will your child experiment with smoking, drinking, or drugs during adolescence? • How will you respond if you learn your child is experimenting with drugs? • How will you encourage your child to spend his or her free time after school (sports, part-time job)?	• Which of Piaget's stages of cognitive development is your child in? • What kind of path do you see your teenager pursuing after high school (college, military, work program)?	• How will you respond if your adolescent is struggling to fit in with peers? • How often do you think you and your teenager will have conflicts? • How social will your child be during his or her teen years? • How much privacy will you grant your teenager? • How will you respond when your teenager starts dating?

CHAPTERS 14 • 15 • 16

PART V

Adolescence

A century ago, puberty began at age 15 or so. Soon after that age, most girls married and most boys found work. It is said that "adolescence begins with biology and ends with culture." If so, then a hundred years ago, adolescence lasted a few months.

Now, adolescence lasts for years. Puberty starts at age 10 or so, and adult responsibilities may be avoided for decades. Indeed, a few observers describe a *Peter Pan syndrome*—men who "won't grow up," too self-absorbed to love and care for anyone else (Kiley, 1983; Snow, 2015). That is unfair to men and to teenagers, but even at age 18, almost no adolescent is ready for all of the responsibilities of adulthood. If high school seniors want marriage, parenthood, and a lifelong career, they should wait at least a few years.

In the next three chapters (covering ages 11 to 18), we begin with biology (Chapter 14), consider cognition (Chapter 15), and then discuss culture (Chapter 16). Adolescence attracts the worst fears of adults, including parents, teachers, police officers, and social workers, yet children look forward to these years and some adults wish they were young again.

Developmental researchers avoid both these extremes. Instead, they consider adolescence to be one interval in a long process, with patterns and events that can push a teenager toward early death or a happy life. Understanding the possibilities and pitfalls described in these chapters will help us all make this a fulfilling, not devastating, time of life.

Left: Richard Bailey/Corbis/Getty Images
Right: Pixel-Shot/Shutterstock.com

CHAPTER 14

Adolescence: Biosocial Development

What Will You Know?

1. How can you predict when puberty will begin for a particular child?
2. Why do many teenagers ignore their nutritional needs?
3. What makes teenage sex often a problem instead of a joy?

- **Puberty Begins**
  - Sequence
  - Unseen Beginnings
  - Brain Growth
  - INSIDE THE BRAIN: Lopsided Growth
  - When Will Puberty Begin?
  - A VIEW FROM SCIENCE: Stress and Puberty
  - Too Early, Too Late
- **Growth and Nutrition**
  - Growing Bigger and Stronger
  - Diet Deficiencies
  - Eating Disorders
- **Sexual Maturation**
  - Sexual Characteristics
  - Sexual Activity
  - Sexual Problems in Adolescence
- **VISUALIZING DEVELOPMENT: Satisfied with Your Body?**

I overheard a conversation among three teenagers, including my daughter Rachel, all of them past their awkward years and now becoming beautiful. They were discussing the imperfections of their bodies. One spoke of her fat stomach (what stomach? I could not see it), another of her long neck (hidden by her silky, shoulder-length hair). Rachel complained about her fingers and her feet!

The reality that boys and girls become men and women is no shock to any adult. But for teenagers, heightened self-awareness often triggers surprise or even horror, joy, and despair at the details of their growth. Like these three, adolescents pay attention to each part of their bodies. Girls bond as they discuss their flaws; boys more often boast. Yet almost all are both self-focused and social, needing each other.

This chapter describes the biosocial specifics of growing bodies and emerging sexuality. It all begins with hormones, but other invisible changes may be even more potent—such as the timing of neurological maturation that did not yet allow these three teens to realize that minor imperfections are insignificant.

Puberty Begins

Puberty refers to the years of rapid physical growth and sexual maturation that end childhood, producing a person of adult size, shape, and sexuality. Puberty begins with a cascade of hormones that produce external growth and internal changes, including heightened emotions and sexual desires.

Sequence

The process typically starts sometime between ages 8 and 14. Most biological growth ends about four years after the first signs appear, although some individuals (especially boys) add height, weight, and muscle until age 20 or so.

For girls, the observable changes of puberty usually begin with nipple growth. Soon a few pubic hairs are visible, followed by a peak growth spurt, widening of the hips, the first menstrual period (**menarche**), a full pubic-hair pattern, and breast maturation. The average age of menarche in the United States is about

Left: Stephen Simpson/Divine Images/Media Bakery. Licensed Material is being used for illustrative purposes only; any person depicted in the licensed Material is a model.
Top: Pixel-Shot/Shutterstock.com

macmillan learning

VIDEO: The Timing of Puberty depicts the usual sequence of physical development for adolescents.

12 years, 4 months (Biro et al., 2013). Other nations are earlier or later, for genetic and nutritional reasons (Brix et al., 2019).

For boys, the usual sequence is growth of the testes, initial pubic-hair growth, growth of the penis, first ejaculation of seminal fluid (**spermarche**), appearance of facial hair, a peak growth spurt, deepening of the voice, and final pubic-hair growth. The typical age of spermarche is 13 years, almost a year later than menarche.

Unseen Beginnings

The changes just listed are visible, but the entire process begins with an invisible event—a marked increase in hormones.

Hormone production is regulated deep within the brain, where biochemical signals from the hypothalamus signal another brain structure, the **pituitary.** The pituitary produces hormones that stimulate the **adrenal glands,** located above the kidneys at either side of the lower back. The adrenal glands produce more hormones. Many hormones that regulate puberty follow this route, known as the **HPA (hypothalamus–pituitary–adrenal) axis.**

Sex Hormones Late in childhood, the pituitary activates not only the adrenal glands—the HPA axis—but also the **gonads,** or sex glands (ovaries in females; testes, or testicles, in males), following another sequence called the **HPG (hypothalamus–pituitary–gonad) axis.**

One hormone in particular, GnRH (gonadotropin-releasing hormone), causes the gonads to enlarge and dramatically increase their production of sex hormones, chiefly **estradiol** in girls and **testosterone** in boys. These hormones affect the body's shape and function, and they produce additional hormones that regulate stress and immunity. Throughout adolescence, hormone levels correlate with physiological changes, brain restructuring, and self-reported developments (Goddings et al., 2012; Vijayakumar et al., 2018).

Estrogens (including estradiol) are female hormones, and *androgens* (including testosterone) are male hormones, although each sex has some of both. The ovaries produce high levels of estrogens, and the testes produce dramatic increases in androgens. This "surge of hormones" affects bodies, brains, and behavior before visible signs of puberty, "well before the teens" (Peper & Dahl, 2013, p. 134).

The activated gonads soon produce mature ova or sperm that are released in menarche or spermarche, respectively. Conception is possible, although peak fertility occurs four to six years later. This is crucial information for teenagers who are sexually active: Some mistakenly believe they cannot become pregnant because they once had sex without protection. A few years later that same one-time carelessness may lead to pregnancy.

Probably because of sex differences in hormones, adolescent males are almost twice as likely as females to develop schizophrenia, and females are more than twice as likely to become severely depressed. Of course, the increase in hormones does not render the social context irrelevant.

For everyone, one psychological effect of estrogen and testosterone is new interest in sexuality. When puberty starts, most children become interested in the other gender (who used to be avoided or disparaged), and some find themselves attracted to members of the same sex, again an unanticipated surprise. Reactions to sexual interest can cause joy or depression, depending more on social circumstances than on hormones.

Usually the object of a young adolescent's first attraction is safely unattainable—a film star, a popular singer, a teacher—but by mid-adolescence, fantasies may

puberty The time between the first onrush of hormones and full adult physical development. Puberty usually lasts three to five years. Many more years are required to achieve psychosocial maturity.

menarche A girl's first menstrual period, signaling that she has begun ovulation. Pregnancy is biologically possible, but ovulation and menstruation are often irregular for years after menarche.

spermarche A boy's first ejaculation of sperm. Erections can occur as early as infancy, but ejaculation signals sperm production. Spermarche may occur during sleep (in a "wet dream") or via direct stimulation.

pituitary A gland in the brain that responds to a signal from the hypothalamus by producing many hormones, including those that regulate growth and sexual maturation.

adrenal glands Two glands, located above the kidneys, that respond to the pituitary, producing hormones.

HPA (hypothalamus–pituitary–adrenal) axis A sequence of hormone production originating in the hypothalamus and moving to the pituitary and then to the adrenal glands.

gonads The paired sex glands (ovaries in females, testicles in males). The gonads produce hormones and mature gametes.

HPG (hypothalamus–pituitary–gonad) axis A sequence of hormone production originating in the hypothalamus and moving to the pituitary and then to the gonads.

estradiol A sex hormone, considered the chief estrogen. Females produce much more estradiol than males do.

testosterone A sex hormone, the best known of the androgens (male hormones); secreted in far greater amounts by males than by females.

Pixelchrome Inc/DigitalVision/Getty Images

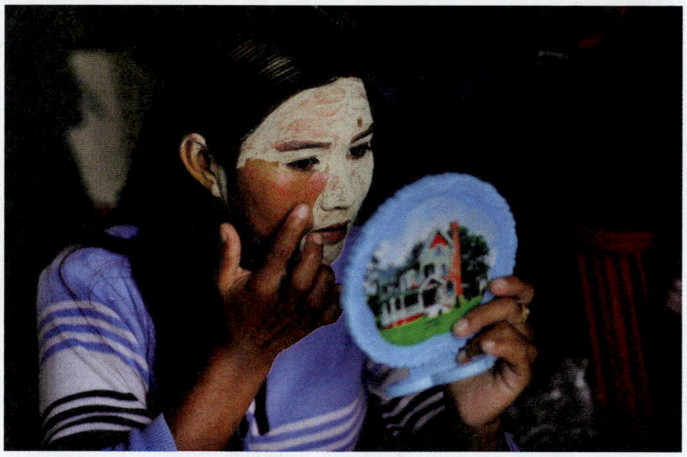

Timothy Allen/Photolibrary/Getty Images

Do They See Beauty? Both young women—the Mexican 15-year-old preparing for her Quinceañara and the Malaysian teen applying a rice facial mask—look wistful, even worried. They are typical of teenage girls everywhere, who do not realize how lovely they are.

settle on another young person. Hormones also direct adolescents toward typical sexual roles because of ancient evolutionary patterns (Sisk, 2016).

Although emotional surges, nurturant impulses, and lustful urges arise with hormones, remember that body, brain, and behavior always interact. Sexual thoughts themselves can *cause* physiological and neurological processes, not just result from them. As you just read, cortisol levels rise in puberty, and that makes adolescents quick to react with passion, fury, or ecstasy (Goddings et al., 2012; Klein & Romeo, 2013). Then those emotions, in turn, increase levels of various hormones. Bodies, brains, and behavior all affect one another.

For example, if adults react to a young person's emerging breasts or beards, these reactions evoke adolescent thoughts and frustrations, which then raise hormone levels, propel physiological development, and trigger more emotions. Because of hormones, emotions are more likely to be expressed during adolescence (with shouts and tears), and that affects everyone's next reactions. Thus, the internal and external changes of puberty are cyclical and reciprocal, each affecting the other.

circadian rhythm A day–night cycle of biological activity that occurs approximately every 24 hours.

Body Rhythms Because of hormones, the brain of every living creature responds to environmental changes over the hours, days, and seasons. For example, time of year affects body weight and height: Children gain weight more rapidly in winter and grow taller more quickly in summer.

Another example is seasonal affective disorder (SAD), when people develop symptoms of depression in winter. Those are seasonal changes, but many *biorhythms* are on a 24-hour cycle called the **circadian rhythm.** (*Circadian* means "about a day.") Puberty interacts with biorhythms.

For most people, daylight awakens the brain. That's why people experiencing jet lag are urged to take an early-morning walk. But at puberty, night may be more energizing, making some teens wide awake and hungry at midnight but half asleep, with no appetite or energy, all morning. Teenagers become "night owls" more than "early birds" (Gariépy et al., 2018).

In addition to circadian changes at puberty, some individuals (especially males) are naturally more alert in the evening than in the morning, a trait called *eveningness*. To some extent, this is genetic: 15 genes differ in people who are natural larks or night owls (Hu et al., 2016). Puberty plus eveningness increases risk (drugs, sex, delinquency), in part because teenagers are awake when adults are asleep. If they must wake up in the morning, many teenagers are sleep deprived (Roenneberg et al., 2012).

Steve Smeltzer/Cartoonstock.com

"I've diligently spent the last eight hours saving an entire colony of elves from a pack of vicious dragons and your only concern is that it is 2 am?"

Priorities! Parents and adolescents do not understand each other's goals.

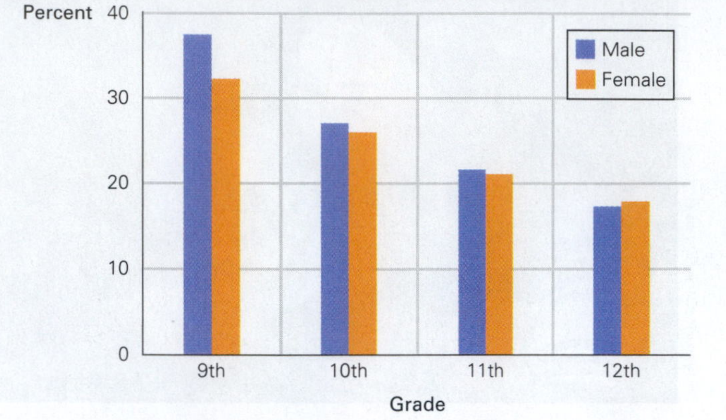

Data from MMWR, June 15, 2018.

FIGURE 14.1

Sleepyheads Three of every four high school seniors are sleep deprived. Even if they go to sleep at midnight, as many do, they must get up before 8 A.M., as almost all do. Then they are tired all day.

Observation Quiz As you see, the problems are worse for the girls. Why is that? (see answer, page 374) ↑

Added to the circadian sleep debt, "the blue spectrum light from TV, computer, and personal-device screens may have particularly strong effects on the human circadian system" (Peper & Dahl, 2013, p. 137). Watching late-night TV, working on a computer, or texting friends at 10 P.M. interferes with sleepiness. As a result, many adolescents find early bedtime and early rising almost impossible.

Schools that provide each student a tablet for homework warn against bedroom use. However, the powerful adolescent urge to stay in touch with friends results in sleeping next to their smartphones—and then sleeping in class. Another problem is video games and action movies, which can cut into sleep time and make class time slow and boring.

Sleep deprivation and irregular sleep schedules increase several dangers, including insomnia, nightmares, mood disorders (depression, conduct disorder, anxiety), and falling asleep while driving. Adolescents are particularly vulnerable to all of these, and sleepiness makes the situation worse (see **Figure 14.1**). In addition, sleepy students do not learn as well as well-rested ones.

Oblivious to adolescent biorhythms, some parents set early curfews or stay awake until their child comes home at night. They might drag their teenager out of bed for school—the same child who, a decade earlier, was commanded to stay in bed until dawn.

Some municipalities also fight adolescent biology. In 2014, Baltimore implemented a law that requires everyone under age 14 to be home by 9 P.M. and 14- to 16-year-olds to be off the streets by 10 P.M. on school nights and 11 P.M. on weekends. This too lightly assumes that home is a happy, safe place where teenagers go to sleep early, and it restricts the teen's ability to socialize or study with friends.

One study compared graduation rates and absenteeism in 29 high schools, across seven states, before and after they started school later than 8:30 A.M. Graduation rates increased from 79 to 88 percent, and average daily attendance rose from 90 to 94 percent (McKeever & Clark, 2017).

Many high schools, however, remain stuck in schedules set before the hazards of sleep deprivation were known. Although "the science is there; the will to change is not" (Snider, 2012, p. 25).

In August 2014, the American Academy of Pediatrics concluded that high schools should not begin until 8:30 or 9 A.M., because adolescent sleep deprivation causes a cascade of intellectual, behavioral, and health problems. The doctors noted that 43 percent of high schools in the United States start *before* 8 A.M.

Most developmentalists, pediatricians, and education researchers wonder why adult traditions are preserved while adolescent learning is ignored. There is good news here, however. As the evidence accumulates, schools are postponing their start times, and teenagers are learning more (Lo et al., 2018).

CHAPTER APP 14

Sleep Cycle

RELATED TOPIC:
Circadian rhythms and sleep

IOS:
https://tinyurl.com/y36gvtum

ANDROID:
https://tinyurl.com/pgj2jyk

Sleep Cycle allows users to track their sleep patterns and get analysis that helps ensure a good night's sleep. Sleep Cycle uses a wake-up phase (30 minutes by default) that ends at one's desired alarm time. During this phase, Sleep Cycle monitors body signals to wake users softly, when they are in the lightest possible sleep state.

Brain Growth

A more ominous example of the disconnect between what science tells us and what adolescents do concerns cars, guns, sex, and drugs, all of which result in injury and even death. A chilling example comes from teenage driving (legal at age 16 in most U.S. localities). Per mile driven, teenage drivers are three times more likely to die in a motor-vehicle crash than drivers over age 20 (Insurance Institute for Highway Safety, 2018).

Sequence of Changes Many aspects of adolescent body growth are uneven. One breast, one foot, or one ear may be bigger than the other—embarrassing, but harmless. However, the usual sequence of brain maturation, propelled by hormones that activate the limbic system at puberty, can lead to danger.

To be specific, the prefrontal cortex matures steadily, advancing gradually as time goes on. Because of that executive function, long-term planning, postponing gratification, and thinking flexibly are better in adults than in young adolescents. The limbic system, however, is affected more by hormones (the HPG axis) than by time, and thus grows dramatically in early adolescence.

Pubertal hormones target the amygdala directly (Romeo, 2013). Therefore, instinctual and emotional areas of the adolescent brain develop ahead of the reflective, analytic areas. Thus, puberty means emotional rushes, unchecked by caution. Powerful sensations—loud music, speeding cars, strong drugs—become compelling. Adolescents brag about being wasted, smashed, out of their minds—all conditions that adults try to avoid.

Immediate impulses thwart long-term planning and reflection. My friend said to his neighbor, who had given his son a red convertible for high school graduation, "Why didn't you just give him a loaded gun?" The mother of the 20-year-old who killed 20 first-graders and 7 adults in 2012 in Newtown, Connecticut, did just that. He killed her.

Sadly, that is not an isolated example. Guns, including those never used in hunting or target practice, are increasingly available to adolescents who may kill other adolescents.

It is not that the prefrontal cortex shuts down. Actually, it continues to develop throughout adolescence and beyond. Maturation doesn't stop, but the emotional hot spots of the brain zoom ahead. This was seen in a study of 886 adolescents (ages 9 to 16) and their parents (average age 44) in Hong Kong and England. All participants were asked questions to assess executive function. The adolescents were less accurate but notably quicker; their limbic systems race ahead while their prefrontal cortexes slowly matured (Ellefson et al., 2017).

When stress, arousal, passion, sensory bombardment, drug intoxication, or deprivation is extreme, the adolescent brain is flooded with impulses that overwhelm the cortex. Adults try to keep their thoughts straight, but adolescents may prefer such flooding. Many teenagers choose to spend a night without sleep, to eat nothing all day, to exercise in pain, to play music at deafening loudness, to drink until they black out.

A common example comes from reading and sending text messages while driving. Teenagers know that this is illegal almost everywhere, but the "ping" of a text message evokes emotions that compel attention. In one survey of U.S. high school seniors who had driven a car in the past month, 39 percent had texted while driving (MMWR, June 15, 2018).

When Will Puberty Begin?

Typically, pubertal hormones accelerate sometime between ages 8 and 14, and visible signs of puberty appear a year later. That six-year range is too great for many parents, teachers, and children, who want to know exactly when a given child will begin puberty. Fortunately, if a child's genes, gender, body fat, and stress level are known, prediction within a year or two is possible.

Genes and Gender Genetic sex differences have a marked effect. In height, the average pubescent girl is about two years ahead of the average boy. Sex affects sequence as well. The female height spurt occurs *before* menarche; the male increase in height occurs *after* spermarche.

PeopleImages/DigitalVision/E+/Getty Images

Fawkes, Not Fake Bonfires, fireworks, burning effigies, and—shown here—sparklers are waved in memory of Guy Fawkes, who tried to burn down the British Parliament and kill the king in 1605. In theory, Guy Fawkes Night celebrates his capture; in fact, it is a time for rebellion.

Especially for Health Practitioners How might you encourage adolescents to seek treatment for STIs? (see response, page 373)

THINK CRITICALLY: Given the nature of adolescent brain development, how should society respond to adolescent thoughts and actions?

INSIDE THE BRAIN

Lopsided Growth

Instead of beginning this box in the usual way, with data from neuroscience, we begin with one teenage boy and his father.

Laurence Steinberg is a noted expert on adolescence (e.g., Steinberg, 2014, 2015). He is also a father.

> When my son, Benjamin, was 14, he and three of his friends decided to sneak out of the house where they were spending the night and visit one of their girlfriends at around two in the morning. When they arrived at the girl's house, they positioned themselves under her bedroom window, threw pebbles against her windowpanes, and tried to scale the side of the house. Modern technology, unfortunately, has made it harder to play Romeo these days. The boys set off the house's burglar alarm, which activated a siren and simultaneously sent a direct notification to the local police station, which dispatched a patrol car. When the siren went off, the boys ran down the street and right smack into the police car, which was heading to the girl's home. Instead of stopping and explaining their activity, Ben and his friends scattered and ran off in different directions through the neighborhood. One of the boys was caught by the police and taken back to his home, where his parents were awakened and the boy questioned.
>
> I found out about this affair the following morning, when the girl's mother called our home to tell us what Ben had done. . . . After his near brush with the local police, Ben had returned to the house out of which he had snuck, where he slept soundly until I awakened him with an angry telephone call, telling him to gather his clothes and wait for me in front of his friend's house. On our drive home, after delivering a long lecture about what he had done and about the dangers of running from armed police in the dark when they believe they may have interrupted a burglary, I paused.
>
> "What were you thinking?" I asked.
>
> "That's the problem, Dad," Ben replied, "I wasn't."
>
> *[Steinberg, 2004, pp. 51, 52]*

Steinberg's son was right: When emotions are intense, especially when friends are nearby, cortisol floods the brain, causing the prefrontal cortex to shut down. This shutdown is not reflected in questionnaires that require teenagers to respond to paper-and-pencil questions regarding hypothetical dilemmas. On those tests, most teenagers think carefully and answer correctly.

In fact, when strong emotions are not activated, teenagers may be more logical than adults (Casey & Caudle, 2013). They remember facts that they have learned in biology or health class about sex and drugs. They know exactly how HIV is transmitted and how alcohol affects the brain. However,

> the prospect of visiting a hypothetical girl from class cannot possibly carry the excitement about the possibility of surprising someone you have a crush on with a visit in the middle of the night. It is easier to put on a hypothetical condom during an act of hypothetical sex than it is to put on a real one when one is in the throes of passion. It is easier to just say no to a hypothetical beer than it is to a cold frosty one on a summer night."
>
> *[Steinberg, 2004, p. 53]*

Ben reached adulthood safely. Other teenagers, with less cautious police or less diligent parents, do not. Brain immaturity makes teenagers vulnerable to social pressures and stresses, which typically bombard young people today (Casey & Caudle, 2013).

Brain scans confirm that emotional control, revealed by fMRI studies, is not fully developed until adulthood, because the prefrontal cortex is limited in connections and engagement (Luna et al., 2013; Hartley & Somerville, 2015) (see **Figure 14.2**).

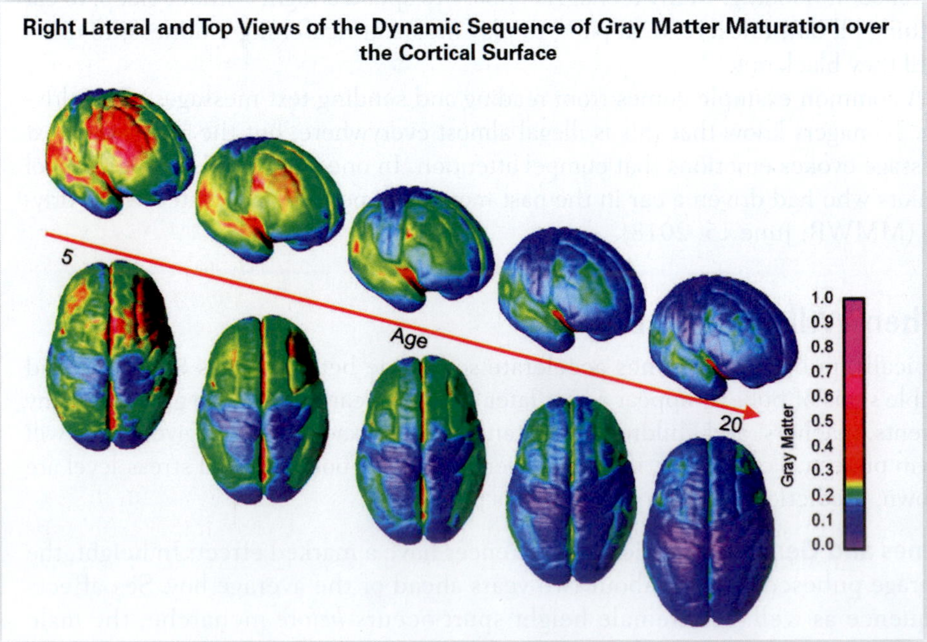

FIGURE 14.2

Same People, But Not the Same Brain These brain scans are part of a longitudinal study that repeatedly compared the proportion of gray matter from childhood through adolescence. (Gray matter refers to the cell bodies of neurons, which are less prominent with age.) Gray matter is reduced as white matter increases, in part because pruning during the teen years (the last two pairs of images here) allows intellectual connections to build. As the authors of one study that included this chart explained, teenagers may look "like an adult, but cognitively they are not there yet" (Powell, 2006, p. 865).

Longitudinal research finds that heightened arousal occurs in the brain's reward centers — specifically the nucleus accumbens, a region of the ventral striatum that is connected to the limbic system — when an adolescent's brain is compared to his or her brain in childhood or adulthood (Braams et al., 2015).

Teens seek excitement and pleasure, especially the social pleasure of a peer's admiration (Galván, 2013). In fact, when other teens are watching, they find it thrilling to take dramatic risks that produce social acclaim, risks they would not dare take alone (Albert et al., 2013). Interestingly, the same reward regions of the brain that are highly activated when peers are watching show decreased activation when the adolescent's mother is nearby (Telzer et al., 2015).

The research on adolescent brain development confirms two insights regarding adolescent growth in general (Goddings et al., 2019). First, physiological changes triggered by puberty are dramatic, unlike those of either childhood or adulthood. Second, the social context matters — the body and brain of humans respond not only to hormones and physical maturation but also to the friends and family members nearby.

Therefore, unlike height, for hormonal and sexual changes, girls are less than a year ahead of boys. Indeed, a recent study of thousands of Danish teenagers found that the boys took about four years from the beginning to the end of puberty, while the girls took five years. This means that by age 15 the two genders were about equal in development (Brix et al., 2019).

Thus, a short sixth-grade boy with sexual fantasies about the taller girls in his class is neither perverted nor precocious; his hormones are simply ahead of his height. It also means that, by the last years of high school, most adolescents have romantic relationships with other students in their grade.

Overall, about two-thirds of the variation in age of puberty is genetic — not only in the genes associated with the XX or XY chromosomes but also in the genes common in families and ethnic groups (Dvornyk & Waqar-ul-Haq, 2012; Biro et al., 2013). If both of a child's parents were early or late to reach puberty, the child will likely be early or late as well. Genetic influences on puberty have been proven again and again (Howard, 2018).

On average, African Americans reach puberty about seven months before European or Hispanic Americans; Chinese Americans average several months later. These are crude generalities: Remember that genetic differences within each group are greater than differences between groups.

Vicky Kasala/DigitalVision/Getty Images

Fully Grown These 14- to 17-year-old soccer players are in high school, probably already at their adult height since girls typically mature before boys. We can be glad that U.S. law (Title IX) now mandates equal sports funding for both sexes, so all students can also experience the joys of teamwork, competition, and body strength. Adolescent and young-adult athletes are at their peak in power and reaction time — although they need to learn strategy and self-acceptance.

Observation Quiz Do you see any sign that these girls are not yet comfortable with their new size and shape? (see answer, page 374) ↑

Body Fat and Chemicals Another influence on the onset of puberty is body fat, which itself is partly genetic and partly cultural. Body fat is clearly associated with earlier puberty for girls. The effects are more variable for boys: Being overweight seems to accelerate puberty, but being obese slows it down (Reinehr & Roth, 2019). The reasons probably involve hormones: For boys, body fat may interfere with expression of male hormones.

In some nations, inadequate food delays growth of every kind; but in developed nations, poor eating habits can result in overweight and, thus, early puberty. This is suggested by a study which found that girls who regularly drank several sugar-sweetened beverages each day were likely to experience earlier menarche (Carwile et al., 2015).

Malnutrition explains why youths reach puberty later in some parts of Africa, while their genetic relatives in North America mature much earlier. For example, girls in northern Ghana reach menarche more than a year later (almost age 14) than African American girls in the United States (just past 12).

Ghanaian girls in rural areas — where malnutrition is more common — are behind those in urban areas (Ameade & Garti, 2016). A more dramatic example arises from sixteenth-century Europe, where puberty is thought to have begun several years later than it does today.

Both the Same? Yes, they are former U.S. presidents. But what a difference 150 years makes! James Madison *(left)* was the fourth president of the United States, was popular and respected, and at 5 feet, 4 inches tall weighed about 100 pounds. Barack Obama *(right)*, the 44th president, was 6 feet, 1 inch tall, and Donald Trump (#45) is said to be 6 feet, 3 inches tall. Lincoln (#16) was tallest of all—6 feet, 4 inches—which then was a reason to mock his appearance.

In recent centuries puberty has begun at younger and younger ages. This is an example of what is called the **secular trend,** which is earlier or greater growth as nutrition and medicine improved.

secular trend The long-term upward or downward direction of a certain set of statistical measurements, as opposed to a smaller, shorter cyclical variation. As an example, over the past two centuries, because of improved nutrition and medical care, children have tended to reach their adult height earlier and their adult height has increased.

One curious bit of evidence of the secular trend is in the height of U.S. presidents. James Madison, the fourth president, was shortest at 5 feet, 4 inches; recent presidents have been much taller. Obama was 6 feet, 1 inch and Trump is said to be 6 feet, 3 inches, although some sources say he is not quite that tall.

The secular trend has stopped in most nations because childhood nutrition allows everyone to attain their genetic potential. Young men no longer look down at their short fathers, or girls at their mothers, unless their parents were born in nations where hunger was common. Future presidents will not be taller than those in the recent past.

Some scientists suspect that precocious (before age 8) or delayed (after age 14) puberty may be caused by hormones in the food supply. Cattle are fed steroids to increase bulk and milk production, and hundreds of chemicals and hormones are used to produce most of the food that children consume. All of these substances *might* affect appetite, body fat, and sex hormones, with effects at puberty (Bourguignon et al., 2016).

Especially for Parents Worried About Early Puberty Suppose your cousin's 9-year-old daughter has just had her first period, and your cousin blames hormones in the food supply for this "precocious" puberty. Should you change your young daughter's diet? (see response, page 373)

Stress Stress hastens puberty, especially if a child's parents are sick, drug-addicted, or divorced, or if the neighborhood is violent and impoverished. One study of sexually abused girls found that they began puberty as much as a year earlier than they otherwise would have, a result attributed not only to stress but also to the hormones activated by sexual contact (Noll et al., 2017).

Particularly for girls who are genetically sensitive, puberty comes early if their family interaction is stressful but late if their family is supportive (Ellis et al., 2011b; James et al., 2012). Developmentalists have known for decades that puberty is influenced by genes, hormones, and body fat. The effect of stress is a newer discovery (see A View from Science).

Too Early, Too Late

For a society's health, early puberty is problematic: It increases the rate of emotional and behavioral problems (Dimler & Natsuaki, 2015). Medical professionals are also concerned with trends toward earlier puberty because it is linked to

A VIEW FROM SCIENCE

Stress and Puberty

Emotional stress, particularly when it has a sexual component, precipitates puberty. This is not always the case, because differential susceptibility means that some young people are more affected by family stress than others, and girls seem more affected than boys. But, many lines of research agree that stress is one factor that can lead to early maturation (Ellis & Del Giudice, 2019).

For example, a large longitudinal study in England compared girls whose biological father lived at home with girls whose father was absent. Typically, in that community, when the father was absent, the mother was stressed. Often there were other men at home. The daughters were more likely to be depressed and reached menarche earlier, on average, than the other girls (Culpin et al., 2015).

The connection between sexual stress and early puberty occurs in developing nations as well as developed ones. For example, in Peru, if a girl was physically and sexually abused, she was much more likely (odds ratio 1.56) to have her first period before age 11 than if she had not been abused (Barrios et al., 2015).

Hypothetically, the connection between stress and early puberty could be indirect. For example, perhaps children in dysfunctional families eat worse and watch more TV and that makes them overweight, which correlates with early menarche. Or, perhaps they inherit genes for early puberty from their distressed mothers, and those genes led the mothers to become pregnant too young, creating a stressful family environment.

Either obesity or genes *could* cause early puberty, and then stress would be a by-product, not a cause. Plausible hypothesis—but *not* correct.

Many longitudinal studies show a direct link between stress and onset of puberty. For example, one longitudinal study of 756 children found that parents who demanded respect, who often spanked, and who rarely hugged their babies, had daughters who reached puberty earlier than other girls in the same study (Belsky et al., 2007). Perhaps harsh parenting increases cortisol, which precipitates puberty.

A follow-up of the same girls at age 15, controlling for genetic differences, found that harsh treatment in childhood increased sexual problems (more sex partners, pregnancies, sexually transmitted infections) but *not* other risks (drugs, crime) (Belsky et al., 2010). This suggests that stress triggers earlier increases of sex hormones but not generalized rebellion. The direct impact of stress on puberty seems proven.

Why would higher cortisol accelerate puberty? The opposite effect—delayed puberty—makes more sense. In such a scenario, stressed teens would still look and act childlike, which might evoke adult protection rather than lust or anger.

Protection is especially needed in conflict-ridden or stressed single-parent homes, yet such homes produce earlier puberty and less parental nurturance. Is this a biological mistake? Not according to evolutionary theory:

> Maturing quickly and breeding promiscuously would enhance reproductive fitness more than would delaying development, mating cautiously, and investing heavily in parenting. The latter strategy, in contrast, would make biological sense, for virtually the same reproductive-fitness-enhancing reasons, under conditions of contextual support and nurturance.
>
> [*Belsky et al., 2010, p. 121*]

In other words, thousands of years ago, when harsh conditions threatened survival of the species, adolescents needed to reproduce early and often, lest the entire community become extinct.

By contrast, in peaceful times with plentiful food, puberty could occur later, allowing children to postpone maturity and enjoy extra years of nurturance. Genes evolved to respond differently to war and peace.

Of course, this evolutionary benefit no longer applies. Today, early sexual activity and reproduction are more destructive than protective of communities. However, since the genome has been shaped over millennia, a puberty-starting allele that responds to social conditions will respond in the twenty-first century as it did thousands of years ago.

This idea complements the current behavioral genetic understanding of differential susceptibility (Harkness, 2014). Because of genetic protections, for some girls, family stress may speed up ovulation.

later health problems, including breast cancer, diabetes, and stroke (Day et al., 2015). Late puberty may also signify health problems, including sickle cell anemia (Alexandre-Heymann et al., 2019).

However, for most adolescents, these links between puberty, stress, and health are irrelevant. Only one aspect of timing matters: their friends' schedules. No one wants to be too early or too late.

Girls Think about the early-maturing girl. If she has visible breasts at age 10, the boys her age tease her; they are unnerved by the sexual creature in their midst.

Radius Images/Corbis

Ancient Rivals or New Friends? One of the best qualities of adolescents is that they identify more with their generation than their ethnic group, here Turk and German. Do the expressions of these 13-year-olds convey respect or hostility? Impossible to be sure, but given that they are both about mid-puberty (face shape, height, shoulder size), and both in the same school, they may become friends.

She must fit her developing body into a school chair designed for smaller children; she might hide her breasts in large T-shirts and bulky sweaters; she might refuse to undress for gym. Early-maturing girls tend to have lower self-esteem, more depression, and poorer body image than do other girls (Galvao et al., 2014; Compian et al., 2009).

Some early-maturing girls have older boyfriends, who are attracted to their womanly shape and girlish innocence. Having an older boyfriend bestows status among young adolescents, but it also promotes drug and alcohol use (Mrug et al., 2014). Early-maturing girls enter abusive relationships more often than other girls do. Is that because their social judgment is immature?

Boys For girls, early maturation is more harmful than helpful no matter when they were born, but for boys cohort matters. Early-maturing boys who were born around 1930 often became leaders in high school and earned more money as adults (Jones, 1965; Taga et al., 2006). Since about 1960, however, the risks associated with early male maturation have outweighed the benefits.

In the twenty-first century, early-maturing boys are more aggressive, lawbreaking, and alcohol-abusing than the average boy (Mendle et al., 2012). Although most of the research on the effects of puberty on male delinquency has been on U.S. boys, similar findings come from elsewhere, including a large study in China (Sun et al., 2016).

It is not hard to figure out why. A boy with rapidly increasing testosterone, whose body looks more like a man than a child, whose brain is more affected by emotions than logic, and who seeks approval from peers more than adults, is likely to trouble parents, schools, and the police.

Late puberty may also be difficult, especially for boys (Benoit et al., 2013). Slow-developing boys tend to be more anxious, depressed, and afraid of sex. Girls are less attracted to them, coaches less often want them on their teams, peers bully or tease them. If a 14-year-old boy still looks childish, he may react in ways (clowning, fighting, isolating) that are not healthy for him.

Ethnic Differences The specific impact of early puberty varies by both gender and culture. For instance, one study found that, in contrast to European Americans, early-maturing African American girls were not depressed, but early-maturing African American boys were (Hamlat et al., 2014a, 2014b). Another study found that Mexican American boys thought less of themselves as pubertal changes continued, except in one domain—their relationships with girls (Harris et al., 2017)

European research found that early-maturing Swedish girls were likely to encounter problems with boys and early drug abuse, but similar Slovak girls were not, presumably because parents and social norms kept Slovak girls under tight control (Skoog & Stattin, 2014).

Social context also matters in the United States. Early-maturing Mexican American boys were likely to experience trouble (with police and with peers) if their neighborhoods had few Mexican Americans, but not if they lived in ethnic enclaves (R. White et al., 2013). On their home turf they were perceived as leaders, not troublemakers. They responded accordingly.

Puberty that is late by world norms, at age 14 or so, is not troubling if one's friends are late as well. However, if students in the same large high school have diverse ethnic and genetic roots, the fact that some look like tall children and others like grown adults may create tension. Contextual factors interact with biological ones. The overall conclusion: Peers, parents, and communities make off-time puberty insignificant or a major problem.

WHAT HAVE YOU LEARNED?

1. What are the first visible signs of puberty?
2. What body parts of a teenage boy or girl are the last to reach full growth?
3. How do hormones affect the physical and psychological aspects of puberty?
4. Why do adolescents experience sudden, intense emotions?
5. How does the circadian rhythm affect adolescents?
6. What are the consequences of sleep deprivation?
7. What are the sex differences in the growth spurt?
8. What are the ethnic and cultural differences in the timing of puberty?
9. How are girls affected by early puberty?
10. How are boys affected by off-time puberty?

Growth and Nutrition

Puberty entails transformation of every body part, with each change affecting all of the others. Here, we discuss biological growth and the nutrition that fuels that growth. Then we will focus on sexual maturation.

Growing Bigger and Stronger

The first set of changes is called the **growth spurt**—a sudden, uneven jump in size that turns children into adults. Growth proceeds from the extremities to the core (the opposite of the earlier proximodistal growth). Thus, fingers and toes lengthen before hands and feet, hands and feet before arms and legs, arms and legs before the torso. Because the torso is the last body part to grow, many pubescent children are temporarily big-footed, long-legged, and short-waisted.

growth spurt The relatively sudden and rapid physical growth that occurs during puberty. Each body part increases in size on a schedule: Weight usually precedes height, and growth of the limbs precedes growth of the torso.

Sequence: Weight, Height, Muscles As the growth spurt begins, children eat more and gain weight. Exactly when, where, and how much weight they gain depends on heredity, hormones, diet, exercise, and whether they are boys or girls. By age 17, the average girl's body has twice as much body fat as the average boy. Of course, genes and exercise influence body shape; gender and maturation are far from the only influences on body composition.

A height spurt follows the weight spurt; a year or two later, a muscle spurt occurs. Thus, the pudginess and clumsiness of early puberty are usually gone by late adolescence. Keep in mind, however, that puberty may dislodge the usual relationship between height and weight. A child may be eating too much or too little, but that may not be apparent in conventional measures of BMI (Golden et al., 2012).

In the years after puberty, all of the muscles grow. Arm muscles develop particularly in boys, doubling in strength from ages 8 to 18. Other muscles are gender-neutral. For instance, both sexes run faster with each year of adolescence, with boys not much faster than girls (unless the girls choose to slow down) (see **Figure 14.3**).

Muscles are heavier than fat, so merely comparing weight and height, as BMI does, may make it seem as if a strong adolescent is overweight—but that may be inaccurate. Consider athletic activity. If

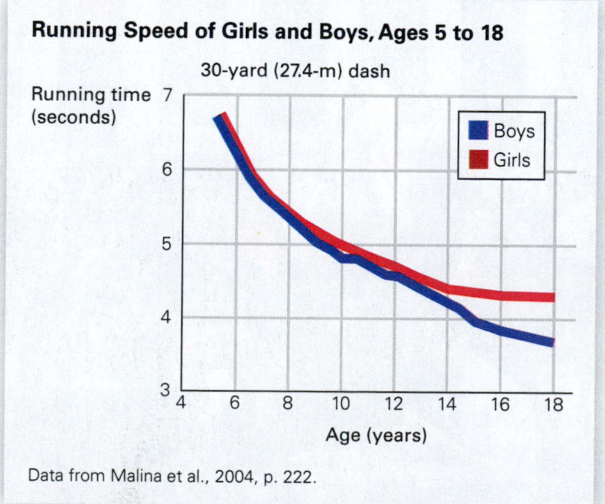

FIGURE 14.3
Little Difference Both sexes develop longer and stronger legs during puberty.

a particular teenage boy is among the 35 percent who are physically active at least an hour every day, he can have a BMI above 25 (technically overweight) and still be in good physical shape. The same applies to girls: 18 percent of them are active every day (MMWR, June 15, 2018).

Organ Growth Lungs triple in weight; consequently, adolescents breathe more deeply and slowly. The heart (another muscle) doubles in size as the heartbeat slows, decreasing the pulse rate while increasing blood pressure. Consequently, endurance improves: Some teenagers run for miles or dance for hours. Red blood cells increase, dramatically so in boys, which aids oxygen transport during intense exercise.

Both weight and height increase *before* muscles and internal organs: To protect immature muscles and organs, athletic training and weight lifting should be tailored to an adolescent's size the previous year. Sports injuries are the most common school accidents, and they increase at puberty. One reason is that the height spurt precedes increases in bone mass, making young adolescents particularly vulnerable to fractures.

The other relevant factor is stress—both in competition and in personal life—that accompanies puberty. As stress increases, so does injury, with the average athlete experiencing at least one injury every year. Training should not only be adjusted to the developing body but should also include ways to decrease emotional stress via meditation, mindfulness, deep breathing, and so on (Ivarsson et al., 2017).

One organ system, the lymphoid system (which includes the tonsils and adenoids), *decreases* in size, so teenagers are less susceptible to respiratory ailments. Mild asthma, for example, often switches off at puberty—half as many teenagers as younger children are asthmatic (MMWR, June 8, 2012). In addition, teenagers have fewer colds and allergies than younger children. This reduction in susceptibility is aided by growth of the larynx, which also deepens the voice, dramatically noticeable in boys.

Another organ system, the skin, becomes oilier, sweatier, smellier, and more prone to acne—which itself is an early sign of puberty (Brix et al., 2019). Hair also changes, becoming coarser and darker. New hair grows under arms, on faces, and over genitals (pubic hair, from the same Latin root as *puberty*).

Next Stop: Masterpieces of the Fifteenth Century These British teens eat chips and soda before they enter the National Gallery in London. Twenty-first century fast food is causing an epidemic of diet deficiencies and disordered eating among youth in every nation.

Robert Alexander/Archive Photos/Getty Images

Diet Deficiencies

All of the changes of puberty depend on adequate nourishment, yet many adolescents do not eat well. Teenagers often skip breakfast, binge at midnight, guzzle down unhealthy energy drinks, and munch on salty, processed snacks. One reason for their eating patterns is that their hormones affect the circadian rhythm of their appetites; another reason is that their drive for independence compels them to avoid family dinners, refusing to eat what their mothers say they should.

In 2017, only 14 percent of U.S. high school seniors ate the recommended three or more servings of vegetables a day (MMWR, June 15, 2018). That is even less than when they were sophomores (17 percent).

Deficiencies of iron, calcium, zinc, and other minerals are especially common during adolescence. Because menstruation depletes iron, anemia is more common among adolescent girls than among any other age or sex group. This is true everywhere, especially in South

Asia and sub-Saharan Africa, where teenage girls rarely eat iron-rich meat and green vegetables.

Boys everywhere may also be iron-deficient, especially if they engage in physical labor or intensive sports: Muscles need iron for growth and strength. Yet, in developed as well as developing nations, adolescents spurn iron-rich foods in favor of chips, sweets, and fries.

Similarly, although the daily recommended intake of calcium for adolescents is 1,300 milligrams, the average U.S. teen consumes less than 500 milligrams a day. About half of adult bone mass is acquired from ages 10 to 20, which means that many contemporary teenagers will develop osteoporosis (fragile bones), a major cause of disability, injury, and death in late adulthood, especially for women.

One reason for calcium deficiency is that milk drinking has declined. In 1961, most North American children drank at least 24 ounces (about three-fourths of a liter) of milk each day, providing almost all (about 900 milligrams) of their daily calcium requirement. Fifty years later, only 8 percent of high school students drank that much milk, and 27 percent (more girls than boys) drank no milk at all in the previous week (MMWR, June 15, 2018).

The decline of milk drinking is one reason for the prevalent deficiency in vitamin D. Skipping breakfast and avoiding dairy products are common for adolescents of every group, particularly African Americans, affecting later health (Van Horn et al., 2011). Some are lactose-intolerant (milk is difficult to digest), but they could choose cheese or yogurt. Instead, many choose soda and chips.

Body Image One reason for poor nutrition among teenagers is anxiety about **body image**—that is, the perception of how one's body looks. As one book on body image begins, each person's body "feels, conceives, imagines, represents, evaluates, loves, hates, and manipulates itself" (Cuzzolaro & Fassino, 2018, p. v). This is true lifelong, but since every part of the body changes dramatically in adolescence, the body image must change too.

body image A person's idea of how his or her body looks.

Most teenagers tend to focus on and exaggerate imperfections in their bodies (as did the three girls in the anecdote that opens this chapter). They often focus on size and shape. More than half of U.S. high school girls are trying to lose weight, yet only one-sixth are actually overweight or obese (MMWR, June 15, 2018).

One problem is that almost no one has a body like those in magazines, movies, and television programs that are marketed to teenagers (Bell & Dittmar, 2011). Closely related are the social media outlets that almost every teenager consults. The emphasis is strongly on appearance, which increases body dissatisfaction (de Vries et al., 2014).

Unhappiness with appearance—especially with weight for girls—is documented worldwide, including in South Korea, China, Australia, and Greece (Kim & Kim, 2009; Chen & Jackson, 2009; Murray et al., 2018; Argyrides & Kkeli, 2015). Many teenagers try to change their bodies: New diets, drugs, or intensive exercise are tried by almost every adolescent. Some seek surgery, to reduce breasts, remove fat, or change facial appearance (McGrath & Mukerji, 2000).

Bingeing, Cutting, Starving Stardom Both Demi Lovato *(left)* and Zayn Malik *(right)* are world-famous stars, with best-selling albums and international tours. Demi starred in *Camp Rock* (a Disney film) and now has a highly successful musical career; Zayn was integral to One Direction (a leading "boy band" from England). Yet, both suffered serious eating disorders while millions of fans adored them, a sobering lesson for us all.

Jon Kopaloff/FilmMagic/Getty Images

James Devaney/GC Images/Getty Images

Eating Disorders

Dissatisfaction with body image can be dangerous, even deadly. Many teenagers, mostly girls, eat erratically or ingest drugs (especially diet pills) to lose weight; others, mostly boys, take steroids to increase muscle mass. [**Life-Span Link:** Teenage drug use is discussed in Chapter 16.]

Eating disorders are rare in childhood but increase dramatically at puberty, accompanied by distorted body image, food obsession, and depression. (See Visualizing Development, page 375.) Many adolescents switch from obsessive dieting to overeating to overexercising and back again. Although girls are most vulnerable, boys are at risk too, especially those who aspire to be pop stars or who train to be wrestlers.

When distorted body image and excessive dieting result in severe weight loss, that indicates **anorexia nervosa**. Less than 1 in 100 adolescent girls develop anorexia, but those who do dramatically restrict their calorie intake and have a destructive, distorted attitude about their bodies. Their BMI may fall below 17 in cases of mild anorexia or 15 in extreme cases, but clinicians must be alert to any sudden weight loss or weight that is "less than that minimally expected" (American Psychiatric Association, 2013).

anorexia nervosa An eating disorder characterized by distorted body image, severe calorie restriction, and intense fear of weight gain. Affected individuals voluntarily undereat or binge and purge, depriving their vital organs of nutrition. Anorexia can be fatal.

bulimia nervosa An eating disorder characterized by binge eating and subsequent purging, usually by induced vomiting and/or use of laxatives.

About three times as common as anorexia is **bulimia nervosa.** Sufferers overeat compulsively, consuming thousands of calories within an hour or two, and then purge through vomiting or laxatives. Most are close to typical in weight and therefore unlikely to starve. However, they risk serious health problems, including damage to their gastrointestinal system and cardiac arrest from electrolyte imbalance (Mehler, 2018).

binge eating disorder An eating disorder common in adolescence, which involves compulsive overeating.

A disorder that is newly recognized in DSM-5 is **binge eating disorder**. Some adolescents periodically and compulsively overeat, quickly consuming large amounts of ice cream, cake, or snack food until their stomachs hurt. When bingeing becomes a disorder, overeating is typically done in private, at least weekly for several months. The sufferer does not purge (hence this is not bulimia) but feels out of control, distressed, and depressed.

Life-Span Causes and Consequences From a life-span perspective, teenage eating disorders are not limited to adolescence, even though this is the usual age when first signs appear. The origins occur much earlier in family eating patterns if parents do not help their children eat sensibly—when they are hungry, without food being a punishment or a reward. Indeed, the origin could be at conception, since a genetic vulnerability is suspected.

For all eating disorders, family function (not structure) is crucial (Tetzlaff & Hilbert, 2014). During the teen years, many parents are oblivious to eating disorders. They might have given up trying to get their child to eat breakfast before school or to join the family for dinner. They delay getting the help that their children need (Thomson et al., 2014).

Some adolescents with eating disorders die before midlife, especially of heart conditions, and others recover (Mehler, 2018). The chance of recovery is better if diagnosis and treatment occur during early adolescence (not adulthood) and if hospitalization is brief (Meczekalski et al., 2013; Errichiello et al., 2016).

WHAT HAVE YOU LEARNED?

1. What is the pattern of growth in adolescent bodies?
2. What complications result from the sequence of growth (weight/height/muscles)?
3. Why are many teenagers deficient in iron and calcium?
4. Why are many adolescents unhappy with their appearance?
5. What are the differences among the three eating disorders explained here?

Sexual Maturation

Sexuality is multidimensional, complicated, and variable—not unlike human development overall. Here, we consider biological changes at puberty and some cohort variations. Other aspects of adolescent sexuality and gender identity are discussed in Chapter 16.

Sexual Characteristics

The body characteristics that are directly involved in conception and pregnancy are called **primary sex characteristics.** During puberty, every primary sex organ (the ovaries, the uterus, the penis, and the testes) increases dramatically in size and matures in function. Reproduction becomes possible.

primary sex characteristics The parts of the body that are directly involved in reproduction, including the vagina, uterus, ovaries, testicles, and penis.

At the same time that maturation of the primary sex characteristics occurs, secondary sex characteristics develop. **Secondary sex characteristics** are bodily features that do not directly affect reproduction (hence they are secondary) but that signify masculinity or femininity.

secondary sex characteristics Physical traits that are not directly involved in reproduction but that indicate sexual maturity, such as a man's beard and a woman's breasts.

One secondary characteristic is body shape. Young boys and girls have similar shapes, but at puberty males widen at the shoulders and grow about 5 inches taller than females, while girls widen at the hips and develop breasts. Those female curves are often considered signs of womanhood, but neither breasts nor wide hips are required for conception; thus, they are secondary, not primary, sex characteristics.

The pattern of hair growth at the scalp line (widow's peak), the prominence of the larynx (Adam's apple), and several other anatomical features differ for men and women; all are secondary sex characteristics.

Facial and body hair increases in both sexes, affected by sex hormones as well as genes. Girls often pluck or wax any facial hair they see and shave their legs, while boys may proudly grow sideburns, soul patches, chinstraps, moustaches, and so on—with specifics dependent on culture and cohort. Hair on the head is cut and styled to be spikey, flat, curled, long, short, or shaved. Hair is far more than a growth characteristic; it is a display of sexuality, a mark of independence.

Steve Coleman/OJO Images/Getty Images

Everywhere Glancing, staring, and—when emotions are overwhelming—averting one's eyes are part of the universal language of love. Although the rate of intercourse among teenagers is lower than it was, passion is expressed in simple words, touches, and, as shown here, the eyes on a cold day.

Secondary sex characteristics are important psychologically, if not biologically. Breasts are an obvious example. Many adolescent girls buy "minimizer," "maximizer," "training," or "shaping" bras in the hope that their breasts will conform to an idealized body image.

During the same years, many overweight boys are horrified to notice swelling around their nipples—a temporary result of the erratic hormones of early puberty. If a boy's breast growth is very disturbing, tamoxifen or plastic surgery can reduce the swelling, although many doctors prefer to let time deal with the problem (Morcos & Kizy, 2012).

Sexual Activity

Primary and secondary sex characteristics such as menarche, spermarche, hair, and body shape are not the only evidence of sex hormones. Fantasizing, flirting, hand-holding, staring, standing, sitting, walking, displaying, and touching are all done in particular ways to reflect sexuality. As already explained, hormones trigger sexual thoughts, but the culture shapes thoughts into enjoyable fantasies, shameful obsessions, frightening impulses, or actual contact (see **Figure 14.4**).

Masturbation is common in both sexes, for instance, but culture determines attitudes, from private sin to mutual pleasure (Driemeyer et al., 2016). Caressing, oral sex, nipple stimulation, and kissing are all taboo in some cultures, expected in others.

macmillan learning

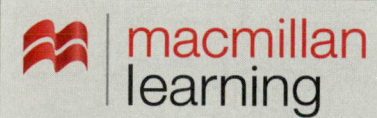

VIDEO: Romantic Relationships in Adolescence explores teens' attitudes and assumptions about romance and sexuality.

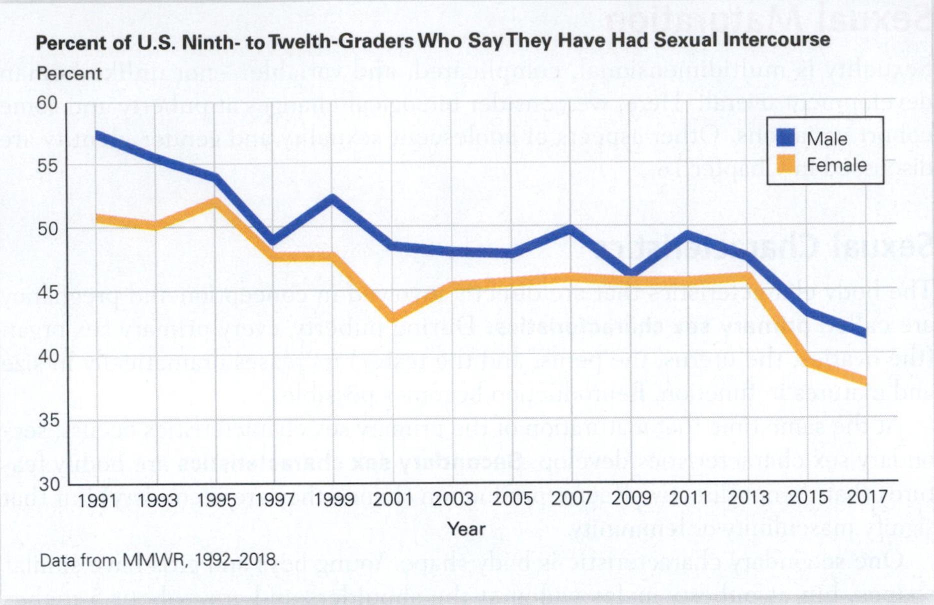

FIGURE 14.4

Boys and Girls Together Boys tend to be somewhat more sexually experienced than girls during the high school years, but since the Youth Risk Behavior Survey began in 1991, the overall trend has been toward equality in rates of sexual activity.

The distinction between early and later sexual experience during adolescence may be significant. A detailed longitudinal study in Finland found that depressed and rebellious 13-year-olds were more likely to use drugs and have sex (Kaltiala-Heino et al., 2015). That had flipped by age 19, when those who had experienced intercourse were less likely to be depressed (Savioja et al., 2015).

Emotions regarding sexual experience, like the rest of puberty, are strongly influenced by social norms that indicate what is expected at what age. Recently in the United States, one study found that girls who have sex early in adolescence are likely to be depressed, but those who have sex as older adolescents tend to be quite happy (Golden et al., 2016). Of course, much depends on the specific social context, whether a girl feels shamed or proud of her sexuality.

Indeed, everyone is influenced by hormones and society, biology and culture. All adolescents have sexual interests that they did not previously have (biology), and this propels teenagers in some nations to do things that teenagers in other nations would never do (culture).

Social norms regarding male–female differences are powerful. Traditionally, males were thought to have stronger sexual urges than females, which is why adolescent boys were supposed to "make the first move," from asking for a date to trying for a kiss. Then, girls were supposed to slow down the boys' advances. This was called the *double standard,* in that behaviors of boys and girls were held to different standards.

Many adolescents still expect boys and girls to approach heterosexual interactions differently, with boys more insistent and girls more hesitant. As one teen girl explained, "that's just how it is" (Tolman et al., 2016).

Nonetheless, many lines of research find that the double standard is less powerful than it once was, not only because of greater freedom for girls but also because many teens question the male–female binary. Interestingly, same-sex couples also find that the double standard is decreasing. A study in Italy found that lesbians experience patterns similar to those of gay males, and both are becoming more similar to straight youth (La Fauci, 2018).

"I think I'll be more relaxed once my secondary sex characteristics kick in."

Brain Before Body Hormones affect thoughts, but visible signs reveal maturation.

Over the past two decades in the United States, every gender, ethnic, and age group is *less* sexually active than the previous cohort. Between 1993 and 2017, intercourse experience among African American high school students decreased 42 percent (to 46 percent); among European Americans, down 18 percent (to 39 percent); and among Latinos, down 27 percent (to 41 percent) (MMWR, June 15, 2018).

Many reasons for the trends have been suggested: sex education, fear of HIV/AIDS, awareness of the hazards of pregnancy, more female education, less intimacy. To explore these hypotheses, more research is needed.

Worldwide, however, a universal experience (increasing hormones) that produces another universal experience (growth of primary and secondary sex characteristics) is powerfully shaped by cohort, gender, culture, and, especially in the United States, their friends (van de Bongardt et al., 2015).

Check out the **Data Connections activity Sexual Behaviors of U.S. High School Students,** which examines how sexually active teens really are.

Sexual Problems in Adolescence

Sexual interest and interaction are part of adolescence; healthy adult relationships are more likely to develop when adolescent impulses are not haunted by shame and fear. Teenagers are neither depraved nor degenerate in experiencing sexual urges. Before focusing on the hazards, we should note that several "problems" are less troubling now than in earlier decades. Here are three specifics:

- *Teen births have decreased.* In the United States, the 2017 rate of births to teenage mothers was less than half the rate 10 years earlier, with the biggest drop among Hispanic teens (Martin et al., 2018). (The 2017 rate was the lowest in 50 years.) Similar declines are evident in other nations. The most dramatic results are from China, where the 2015 teen pregnancy rate was about one-tenth the rate 50 years ago (reducing the 2015 world population by about 1 billion).
- *The use of "protection" has risen.* Contraception, particularly condom use among adolescent boys, has increased markedly in most nations since 1990. The U.S. Youth Risk Behavior Survey found that 61 percent of sexually active high school boys used a condom during their most recent intercourse (MMWR, June 15, 2018).
- *The teen abortion rate is down.* In the United States, the teen abortion rate has declined every year since abortion became legal. The rate today is about half that of 20 years earlier.

These are positive trends, but many aspects of adolescent sexual activity remain problematic.

Sex Too Soon Sex can, of course, be thrilling and affirming, a bonding experience. However, compared to a century ago, adolescent sexual activity—especially if it results in birth—is more hazardous. Five circumstances have changed:

1. Earlier puberty results in earlier fertility, and sex before age 15 correlates with depression, drug abuse, and lifelong problems (Kastbom et al., 2015).
2. If a teenager has a baby, she usually has no reliable partner to help. A century ago, teenage mothers were often married; now, almost all are unwed.
3. Raising a child has become more complex and expensive, and family helpers are scarce: Most young grandmothers are employed.
4. Sexually transmitted infections (STIs) are more common and dangerous. The rate of all STIs increased markedly over the past decade, with notable increases from 2016 to 2017 (Centers for Disease Control and Prevention, 2018).
5. Abortion has become illegal in the some U.S. states, so if a young teenager becomes pregnant, her future education and family formation are changed lifelong.

Especially for Parents Worried About Their Teenager's Risk-Taking You remember the risky things you did at the same age, and you are alarmed by the possibility that your child will follow in your footsteps. What should you do? (see response, page 374)

As you read, teen births are declining, as are teen abortions. However, the U.S. rate of adolescent pregnancy is the highest of any developed nation (true among every ethnic group). If a pregnant girl is under 16 (most are not), she is more likely than older pregnant teenagers to experience complications—including spontaneous abortion, high blood pressure, stillbirth, preterm birth, and low birthweight. This is true worldwide, in wealthy as well as low-income nations (Ganchimeg et al., 2014). She is more likely to drop out of high school.

There are many reasons for these hazards besides age. Poverty and lack of education correlate with teen pregnancy and with every problem just listed. Sadly, some of the problems begin with family life: Mothers who themselves had teenage births are more likely to have daughters who do the same (Liu et al., 2018). One reason for the frequency of complications is that younger pregnant teenagers are frequently undernourished and often postpone prenatal care.

Although some people imagine that the baby will benefit when an adolescent mother lives with her own mother, the opposite seems more accurate. Problems begin in infancy, with teenagers living with their mothers less likely to breast-feed their infants than teen mothers living on their own (Pilkauskas, 2014). [**Life-Span Link:** Attachment types and the importance of early attachment were discussed in Chapter 7.]

Even if sexually active adolescents avoid pregnancy, early intercourse increases psychosocial problems. A study of 3,923 adult women in the United States found that those who *voluntarily* had sex before age 16 were more likely to divorce later on, whether or not they became pregnant or later married their first sexual partner. The same study found that adolescents of any age whose first sexual experience was unwanted (either "really didn't want it" or "had mixed feelings about it") were also more likely to later experience divorce (Paik, 2011).

Forced sex is much worse, of course, as now explained.

child sexual abuse Any erotic activity that arouses an adult and excites, shames, or confuses a child, whether or not the victim protests and whether or not genital contact is involved.

Sexual Abuse

Abuse harms development lifelong. **Child sexual abuse** is defined as any sexual activity (including fondling and photographing) between a juvenile and an adult. Age 18 is the usual demarcation between adult and child (although legal age varies by state). Girls are particularly vulnerable, although boys are also at risk.

Although sexual abuse of young children gathers most headlines, young adolescents are, by far, the most frequent victims. The rate of sexual abuse increases at puberty, a particularly sensitive time because many young adolescents are confused about their own sexual urges and identity (Graber et al., 2010). Virtually every adolescent problem, including pregnancy, drug abuse, eating disorders, and suicide, is more frequent in adolescents who are sexually abused.

This is true worldwide. Although solid numbers are unknown for obvious reasons, it is apparent that millions of girls in their early teens are forced into marriage or prostitution each year. Adolescent girls are common victims of sex trafficking, not only because their youth makes them more alluring but also because their immaturity makes them more vulnerable (McClain & Garrity, 2011). Some believe they are helping their families by earning money to support them; others are literally sold by their families (Montgomery, 2015).

It is virtually impossible to know how common child sexual abuse is. The problem begins with the definition: Would you consider it sexual abuse when a 14-year-old marries a man chosen by her parents? What about a 16-year-old who has sex with her 19-year-old boyfriend? Estimates of the number of children being trafficked for sex in the United States range from 1,000 to 336,000—hardly definitive (Miller-Perrin & Wurtele, 2017).

When U.S.-born children suffer sexual abuse, they are usually not trafficked but instead are abused in their own homes. Typically, the victims are young

JEFF KOWALSKY/AFP/Getty Images

You, Too? Millions were shocked to learn that Larry Nassar, a physician for gymnasts training for the Olympics and at Michigan State University, sexually abused more than 150 young women. Among the victims was Kaylee Lorenz, shown here addressing Nassar in court. Nassar was convicted of multiple counts of sexual assault and sentenced to 40 to 175 years in prison, but his victims wonder why no one stopped him. The president of Michigan State University resigned in disgrace; many others are still in office.

adolescents who are not allowed friendships and romances that teach them how to develop a healthy and satisfying life. Sometimes the abuser is a biological parent, but more often it is a stepparent, older sibling, or uncle.

Young people who are sexually exploited tend to fear sex and to devalue themselves lifelong, with higher rates of virtually every developmental problem. They have much higher rates of repeated abuse, both as adolescents and as adults (Pittenger et al., 2018). Another developmental consequence is the birth of unwanted babies, who often become mistreated themselves (Noll et al., 2018).

Our discussion of sexual abuse focuses on girls because they are the most common victims. However, teenage boys may be sexually abused as well, a direct attack on their fledgling identity as men (Dorais, 2009). Disclosure of past abuse is particularly difficult for men, which makes reliable statistics difficult (Collin-Vézina et al., 2015).

Remember that perpetrators of all kinds of abuse are often people known to the child. After puberty, although sometimes abusers are parents, coaches, or other authorities, often they are other teenagers. In the most recent U.S. Youth Risk Behavior Survey of high school students, 15 percent of the girls and 4 percent of the boys said that they had been kissed, touched, or forced to have sex within a dating relationship when they did not want to (MMWR, June 15, 2018). Sex education is discussed in Chapter 16; obviously teenagers have much to learn.

Kevin Winter/Getty Images Entertainment/Getty Images

Could It Happen to You? Lady Gaga sang "Til It Happens to You" at the 2016 Academy Awards, holding hands with fellow victims of sexual assault. As explained in the film *The Hunting Ground,* unwanted sexual comments and actions have been part of the college experience for decades, but now thousands of victims say, "No more."

Sexually Transmitted Infections Unlike teen pregnancy and sexual abuse, the other major problem of teenage sex shows no signs of abating. A **sexually transmitted infection (STI)** (sometimes called a sexually transmitted disease [STD]) is any infection transmitted through sexual contact. Worldwide, sexually active teenagers have higher rates of the most common STIs—gonorrhea, genital herpes, and chlamydia—than do sexually active people of any other age group.

sexually transmitted infection (STI) A disease spread by sexual contact, including syphilis, gonorrhea, genital herpes, chlamydia, and HIV.

In the United States, half of all new STIs occur in people ages 15 to 25, even though this age group has less than one-fourth of the sexually active people (Satterwhite et al., 2013). Rates are particularly high among sexually active adolescents, ages 15 to 19.

Biology provides one reason: Pubescent girls are particularly likely to catch an STI compared to fully developed women, probably because adult women have more vaginal secretions that reduce infections. Further, if symptoms appear, teens are less likely to alert their partners or seek treatment unless pain requires it.

A survey of adolescents in a U.S. pediatric emergency department found that half of the teenagers (average age 15) were sexually active and 20 percent of those had an STI—although that was not usually the reason they came for medical help (Miller et al., 2015).

There are hundreds of STIs. *Chlamydia* is the most frequently reported one; it often begins without symptoms, yet it can cause permanent infertility.

Worse is *human papillomavirus (HPV),* which has no immediate consequences but increases the risk of "serious, life-threatening cancer" in both sexes (MMWR, July 25, 2014, p. 622). Immunization before first intercourse has reduced the rate of HPV, with half of all teenage girls receiving the recommended three doses (two if they start the series before age 15). Over the past decade, precancerous lesions are reduced in 18- to 24-year-olds but not in 30- to 64-year-olds (too old to have been immunized) (McClung et al., 2019).

National variations in laws and rates of STIs are large. Rates among U.S. teenagers are higher than those in any other medically advanced nation but lower than rates in some developing nations. HIV rates are not declining, despite increased awareness.

From a developmental perspective, *congenital syphilis,* which results in a newborn with lifelong disabilities (and sometimes early death), is the most frightening

macmillan learning

The **Data Connections activity Major Sexually Transmitted Infections: Some Basics** offers more information about the causes, symptoms, and rates of various STIs.

STI of all, because the infant suffers. In 2017, the rate of congenital syphilis in the United States was double the rate in 2014. Fortunately this STI is still rare, but it is completely avoidable if the mother gets early prenatal care. Thus, the increase is an alarming indication that national health care is missing the most vulnerable people.

Once again, it is apparent that a universal experience (the biology of puberty) varies remarkably depending on national and family context. As we stated earlier, adolescence begins with biology and ends with culture. You will see more examples of this in the next chapter.

WHAT HAVE YOU LEARNED?

1. What are examples of the difference between primary and secondary sex characteristics?
2. Why are there fewer problems caused by adolescent sexuality now than a few decades ago?
3. What is problematic regarding adolescent pregnancy?
4. What are the effects of child sexual abuse?
5. Among sexually active people, why do adolescents have more STIs than adults?
6. What are three ways to prevent STIs among teenagers?

SUMMARY

Puberty Begins

1. Puberty refers to the time when a child's body becomes an adult one. Even before the teenage years, biochemical signals from the hypothalamus to the pituitary gland to the adrenal glands (the HPA axis) increase production of testosterone, estrogen, and various other hormones that cause the body to grow rapidly and become capable of reproduction.

2. Some emotional reactions, such as quick mood shifts, are directly caused by hormones, as are thoughts about sex. The reactions of others to adolescents and the adolescents' own reactions to the physical changes they are undergoing also trigger emotional responses, which, in turn, affect hormones.

3. Hormones regulate all of the body rhythms of life, by day, by season, and by year. Changes in these rhythms in adolescence often result in sleep deprivation, partly because the natural circadian rhythm makes teenagers wide awake at night. Sleep deprivation causes numerous health and learning problems.

4. Various parts of the brain mature during puberty and in the following decade. The regions dedicated to emotional arousal (including the amygdala) mature before those that regulate and rationalize emotional expression (the prefrontal cortex).

5. Puberty typically begins anytime from about age 8 to about age 14. The young person's sex, genetic background, body fat, and level of stress all contribute to this variation in timing.

6. Girls generally begin and end puberty before boys do, although the time gap in sexual maturity is much shorter than the two-year gap in peak height.

Growth and Nutrition

7. The growth spurt is an acceleration of growth in every part of the body. Peak weight usually precedes peak height, which is then followed by peak muscle growth. This sequence makes adolescents particularly vulnerable to injuries. The lungs and the heart also increase in size and capacity.

8. All of the changes of puberty depend on adequate nourishment, yet adolescents do not always make healthy food choices. One reason for poor nutrition is the desire to lose (or, less often, gain) weight because of anxiety about body image.

9. Many adolescents eat too much of the wrong foods or too little food overall. Deficiencies of iron, vitamin D, and calcium are common, affecting bone growth and overall development. The precursors of serious eating disorders are evident in adolescence.

Sexual Maturation

10. Male–female differences in bodies and behavior become apparent at puberty. The maturation of primary sex characteristics means that by age 13 or so, after experiencing menarche or spermarche, teenagers are capable of reproducing, although peak fertility is several years later.

11. Secondary sex characteristics are not directly involved in reproduction but signify that the child is becoming a man or a woman. Body shape, breasts, voice, body hair, and numerous other features differentiate males from females. Sexual activity is influenced more by culture than by physiology.

12. In the twenty-first century, teenage sexual behavior has changed for the better in several ways. Hormones and growth may cause sexual thoughts and behaviors at younger ages, but teen pregnancy is far less common, condom use has increased, and the average age of first intercourse has risen.

13. Among the problems that adolescents still face is the urge to become sexually active before their bodies and minds are ready. Giving birth before age 16 takes a physical toll on a growing girl; it also puts her baby at risk of physical and psychological problems.

14. Sexual abuse is more likely to occur in early adolescence than at other ages. Girls are more often the victims than boys are. The perpetrators are often family members or close friends of the family or, for older adolescents, other teenagers. Rates of child sexual abuse are declining in the United States, but globalization has increased international sex trafficking.

15. Untreated STIs at any age can lead to infertility and even death. Rates among sexually active teenagers are rising for many reasons, with HIV/AIDS not yet halted. Immunization to prevent HPV is decreasing rates of vaginal cancer in adulthood.

KEY TERMS

puberty (p. 353)
menarche (p. 353)
spermarche (p. 354)
pituitary (p. 354)
adrenal glands (p. 354)
HPA (hypothalamus–pituitary–adrenal) axis (p. 354)
gonads (p. 354)
HPG (hypothalamus–pituitary–gonad) axis (p. 354)
estradiol (p. 354)
testosterone (p. 354)
circadian rhythm (p. 355)
secular trend (p. 360)
growth spurt (p. 363)
body image (p. 365)
anorexia nervosa (p. 366)
bulimia nervosa (p. 366)
binge eating disorder (p. 366)
primary sex characteristics (p. 367)
secondary sex characteristics (p. 367)
child sexual abuse (p. 370)
sexually transmitted infection (STI) (p. 371)

APPLICATIONS

1. Visit a fifth-, sixth-, or seventh-grade class. Note variations in the size and maturity of the students. Do you see any patterns related to gender, ethnicity, body fat, or self-confidence?

2. Interview two to four of your friends who are in their late teens or early 20s about their memories of menarche or spermarche, including their memories of others' reactions. Do their comments indicate that these events are or are not emotionally troubling for young people?

3. Talk with someone who became a teenage parent. Were there any problems with the pregnancy, the birth, or the first years of parenthood? Would the person recommend teen parenthood? What would have been different had the baby been born three years earlier or three years later?

4. Adult reactions to puberty can be reassuring or frightening. Interview two or three people about how adults prepared for, encouraged, or troubled their development. Compare that with your own experience.

Especially For ANSWERS

Response for Health Practitioners (from p. 357): Many adolescents are intensely concerned about privacy and fearful of adult interference. This means that your first task is to convince the teenagers that you are nonjudgmental and that everything is confidential.

Response for Parents Worried About Early Puberty (from p. 360): Probably not. If she is overweight, her diet should change, but the hormone hypothesis is speculative. Genes are the main factor; she shares only one-eighth of her genes with her cousin.

Response for Parents Worried About Their Teenager's Risk-Taking (from p. 369): You are right to be concerned, but you cannot keep your child locked up for the next decade or so. Since you know that some rebellion and irrationality are likely, try to minimize them by not boasting about your own youthful exploits, by reacting sternly to minor infractions to nip worse behavior in the bud, and by making allies of your child's teachers and the parents of your child's friends.

Observation Quiz ANSWERS

Answer to Observation Quiz (from p. 356): Girls tend to spend more time studying, talking to friends, and getting ready in the morning. Other data show that many girls get less than 7 hours of sleep per night.

Answer to Observation Quiz (from p. 359): Look at their legs. The shortest is standing tall; the tallest is bending her knees.

VISUALIZING DEVELOPMENT SATISFIED WITH YOUR BODY?

Probably not, if you are a teenager. At every age, accepting who you are—not just ethnicity and gender, but also body shape, size, and strength—correlates with emotional health. During the adolescent years, when everyone's body changes dramatically, body dissatisfaction rises. As you see, this is particularly true for girls—but if the measure were satisfaction with muscles, more boys would be noted as unhappy.

BODY DISSATISFACTION CORRELATES WITH...

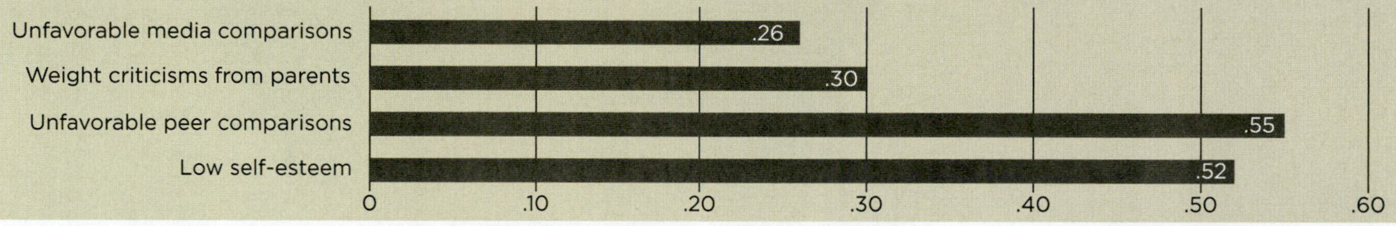

Data from Van Vonderen & Kinnally, 2012.

GENDER DIFFERENCES IN BODY DISSATISFACTION

Females of all ages tend to be dissatisfied with their bodies, but the biggest leap in dissatisfaction occurs when girls transition from early to mid-adolescence (Makinen et al., 2012).

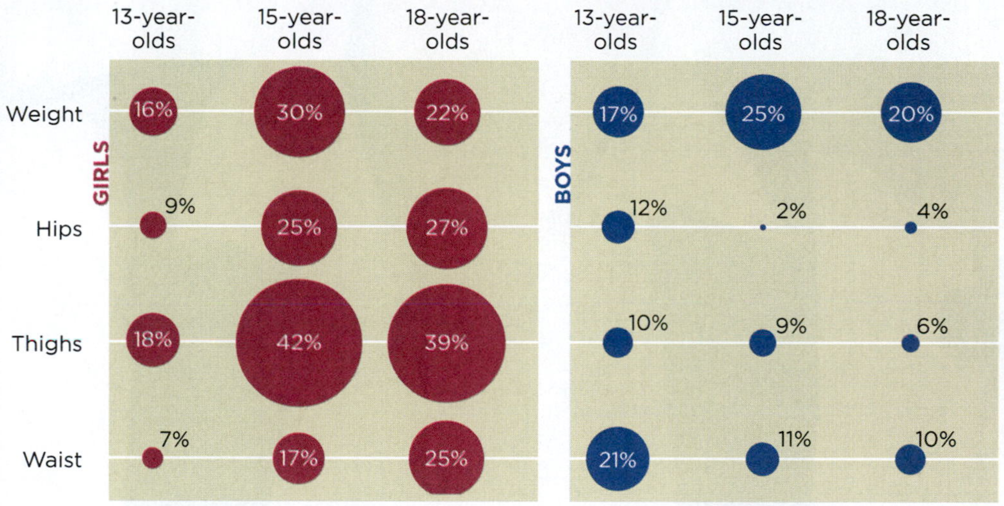

Data from Weinshenker, 2014; Rosenblum & Lewis, 1999.

SOCIAL MEDIA AND BODY DISSATISFACTION
• The more time teenage girls spend on social media, the higher their body dissatisfaction.
• 86% of teens say that social network sites hurt their body confidence.
(Information from Proud2Bme, 2012; Tiggemann & Stater, 2014)

NUTRITION AND EXERCISE

High school students are told, at home and at school, to eat their vegetables and not care about their looks. But they listen more to their peers and follow social norms. Fortunately, some eventually learn that, no matter what their body type, good nutrition and adequate exercise make a person feel more attractive, energetic, and happy.

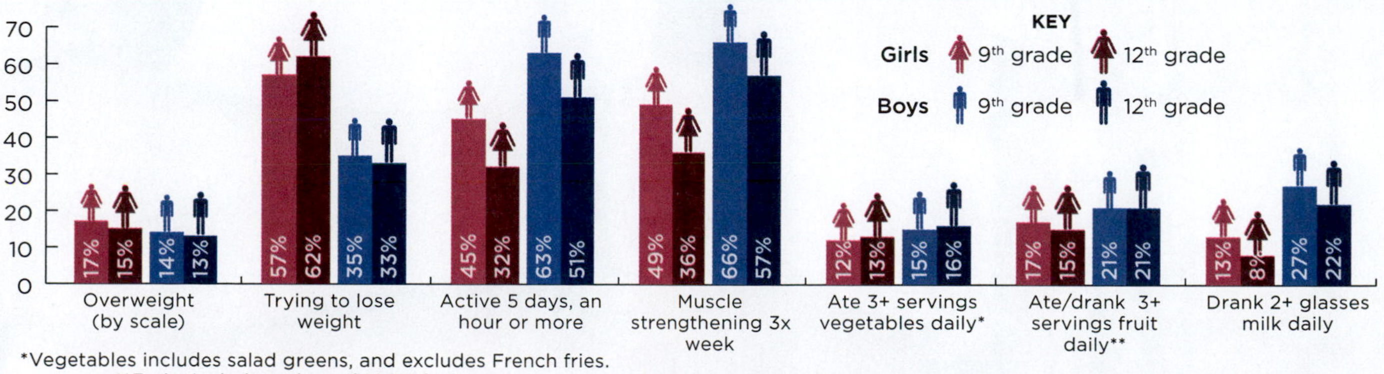

*Vegetables includes salad greens, and excludes French fries.
**Fruits include a glass of 100% fruit juice.

Data from MMWR, June 15, 2018.

CHAPTER 15

Adolescence: Cognitive Development

What Will You Know?

1. Why are young adolescents often egocentric?
2. Why does emotion sometimes overwhelm reason?
3. Is cyberbullying worse than direct bullying?
4. What kind of school is best for teenagers?

- **Logic and Self**
  - Egocentrism
  - Formal Operational Thought
- **Two Modes of Thinking**
  - Intuitive and Analytic Processing
  - A CASE TO STUDY: Biting the Policeman
  - INSIDE THE BRAIN: Stop and Think? No!
  - Better Thinking
- **Technology and Cognition**
  - Digital Natives
  - Technology in Schools
  - Sexual Abuse?
  - Computer Addiction
  - Cyber Danger
- **Secondary Education**
  - Definitions and Facts
  - Middle School
  - High School
  - OPPOSING PERSPECTIVES: High-Stakes Testing
  - Variability
- **VISUALIZING DEVELOPMENT: How Many Adolescents Are in School?**

On March 15, 2019, thousands of adolescents in almost 100 nations left their classrooms to gather in the streets. Their inspiration was a lone 16-year-old who skipped school on Fridays during the fall of 2018 to stand in front of the Swedish parliament to protest adult inaction on climate change.

News media worldwide reported on this event, often with students' own words. For example, the BBC (March 15, 2019) interviewed student protesters from a dozen towns in England. In Brighton, a 13-year-old girl said:

> They're messing up our future and we're the ones who are going to have to clean it up, so I think it's important that we come and tell them about it. The school haven't let us go, they say there's consequences but it's more important than school attendance to come here and protest.

Her friend said:

> I really don't care what consequences they give us, it's more important that we fight for our future. This is the world we're going to have to live in.

A 16-year-old boy in Birmingham said:

> We are at the point that in 12 to 20 years the effects of climate change are going to be irreversible. The only way to change it is through the younger generation because the older generation don't really care.

And a 15-year-old in Stockport was torn:

> I tried to come to the last protest but my school said no. My head of year said no this time but I think it is more important to come. I think I'm going to get into trouble though.

That protest stopped public transportation in Manchester, prompting one adult to say

> it's disappointing that they've chosen to disrupt Metrolink—which, ironically, is one of the greenest and most sustainable ways to travel across Greater Manchester.

Left: AE Pictures Inc./DigitalVision/Getty Images
Top: Pixel-Shot/Shutterstock.com

Dinendra Haria/SOPA Images/Sipa USA (Sipa via AP Images)

Ferocious Earthlings It's hard not to admire the passion of adolescent cognition, not only on climate change, but also on drugs, religion, patriotism, sex, and many other issues. Admiration does not always mean agreement, but that's why adolescents and adults need each other.

Observation Quiz What is the meaning of the four symbols on the bottom of the ferocious poster? (see answer, page 400) ↑

Five thousand miles away, in Missoula, Montana, students spoke again about the need for adolescents to act because the adults were oblivious. The U.S. reporters tried to put the protest into a political context (O'Brien, 2019). In response to such a question, one senior boy noted "a generation gap between the politicians of today and the politicians of the future."

A 15-year-old in Indiana said:

> This is not a Republican issue; this is not a Democrat issue. This is a human rights issue . . . I don't want to live in a world where the future is unclear. I have big plans for myself . . . People generally perceive it as us kids, we're just whining . . . Unfortunately, adults haven't done enough for us to make this future clear for me and for my peers. So we're taking it into our own hands.
>
> *[Fallahi, quoted in Van Dongen, 2019]*

These quotations begin this chapter on adolescent cognition because they illustrate how adolescents think—sometimes illogically (the public transportation disruption), sometimes considering adults clueless ("they don't really care"), sometimes exaggerating their importance (the young can reverse climate change). Yet, they are still influenced by the schools that the adults create ("consequences," "get into trouble") and the opinions adults might have ("whining").

None of this is surprising. Cognition reflects generation and culture. In the United States, reporters see climate change as a political issue; in England, adults see the young as misguided; developmental scientists think about the effects on human health worldwide (Watts et al., 2018; Sadana et al., 2019).

This chapter attempts to avoid these adult conclusions. Instead, we describe the facts of adolescent cognition, a mix of egocentrism and abstraction, of emotions and analysis.

We also explore the myriad structures of the schools that educate adolescents. What should the "consequences" be when adolescent thought leads to ditching school? Do the students quoted above illustrate hopeful priorities, or exaggerated self-importance? You draw your own conclusions.

Logic and Self

Brain maturation, additional years of schooling, moral challenges, increased independence, and intense conversations all occur between ages 11 and 18. These aspects of adolescents' development propel cognitive growth, beginning with intense focus on oneself and moving toward impressive rational thought.

Egocentrism

During puberty, young people center on themselves, in part because maturation of the brain and body heightens self-consciousness. Young adolescents grapple with conflicting feelings about their parents and friends, examine details of their physical changes, and think deeply (but not always realistically) about the future.

adolescent egocentrism A characteristic of adolescent thinking that leads young people (ages 10 to 13) to focus on themselves to the exclusion of others.

Adolescent egocentrism—that is, adolescents thinking intensely about themselves and about what others think of them—was first described by David Elkind (1967). He found that, egocentrically, adolescents regard themselves as much more unique, special, admired, or hated than other people consider them to be. Egocentric adolescents have trouble understanding others' points of view.

For example, few girls are attracted to boys with pimples and braces, but one boy's eagerness to be seen as growing up kept him from realizing this. According to his older sister:

> Now in the 8th grade, my brother has this idea that all the girls are looking at him in school. He got his first pimple about three months ago. I told him to wash it

with my face soap but he refused, saying, "Not until I go to school to show it off." He called the dentist, begging him to approve his braces now instead of waiting for a year. The perfect gifts for him have changed from action figures to a bottle of cologne, a chain, and a fitted baseball hat like the rappers wear.

[adapted from E., personal communication]

Egocentrism sometimes leads adolescents to interpret everyone else's behavior as if it were a judgment on them. A stranger's frown or a teacher's critique can make a teenager conclude that "No one likes me," and then deduce that "I am unlovable" or even "I can't leave the house." More positive casual reactions—a smile from a sales clerk or an extra-big hug from a younger brother—could lead to "I am great" or "Everyone loves me."

Acute self-consciousness about physical appearance may be more prevalent between ages 10 and 14 than at any other time, in part because adolescents notice changes in their body that do not exactly conform to social norms and ideals (Guzman & Nishina, 2014). Adolescents also instigate changes that they think other teenagers will admire.

For example, piercings, shaved heads, tattoos, and torn jeans—all contrary to the wishes of most parents—signify connection to youth culture, and wearing suits and ties, or dresses and pearls, would attract unwelcome attention from other youth. If you observe groups of adolescents waiting in line for a midnight show or clustering near their high school, you will see appearance that may seem rebellious to adults but that conforms to teen culture.

Because adolescents are focused on their own perspectives, their emotions may not be grounded in reality. A study of 1,310 Dutch and Belgian adolescents found that egocentrism was strong. For many of these teenagers, self-esteem and loneliness were closely tied to their *perception* of how others saw them, not to their actual popularity or acceptance among their peers. Gradually, after about age 15, some gained more perspective on what others actually thought. Then they became less depressed (Vanhalst et al., 2013).

Dianne Avery Photography/Moment/Getty Images

Three California Girls Who takes selfies? Anyone with a smartphone can, but teenagers do so more than any other age group. Egocentrism is also evident in details of dress and grooming. All three of these girls, from Thousand Oaks, California, appear to spend many hours on their makeup and their hair, which they have likely grown for years.

Rumination Egocentrism is one reason for **rumination,** which is thinking obsessively about self-focused concerns. Some adolescents go over their problems via phone, text, conversation, social media, and private, quiet self-talk (as when they lie in bed, unable to sleep), thinking about each nuance of everything they have done, are doing, might do, and should have done if only they had thought quickly enough. For girls, particularly, rumination in early adolescence is likely to lead to depression later on (Krause et al., 2018).

rumination Repeatedly thinking and talking about past experiences; can contribute to depression.

Others act impulsively without any rumination at all, blurting out words that they later regret and taking risks that they later realize were foolish, sometimes only when injury or arrest makes it clear that they were wrong. This is particularly common in boys, whose egocentrism leads them astray (Hill et al., 2012).

Gender differences should not be exaggerated, however. As found in both of the studies just cited, most adolescents of every gender do both, zigzagging from too much to too little thinking.

The Imaginary Audience Egocentrism creates an **imaginary audience** in the minds of many adolescents. They believe that they are at center stage, with all eyes on them, and they imagine how others might react to their appearance and behavior.

imaginary audience The other people who, in an adolescent's egocentric belief, are watching and taking note of his or her appearance, ideas, and behavior. This belief makes many teenagers very self-conscious.

One woman remembers:

When I was 14 and in the 8th grade, I received an award at the end-of-year school assembly. Walking across the stage, I lost my footing and stumbled in front of the entire student body. To be clear, this was not falling flat on one's face, spraining an ankle, or knocking over the school principal—it was a small misstep noticeable only to those in the audience who were paying close attention. As I rushed off the

> stage, my heart pounded with embarrassment and self-consciousness, and weeks of speculation about the consequence of this missed step were set into motion. There were tears and loss of sleep. Did my friends notice? Would they stop wanting to hang out with me? Would a reputation for clumsiness follow me to high school?
>
> *[Somerville, 2013, p. 121]*

This woman became an expert on the adolescent brain. She remembered from personal experience that "adolescents are hyperaware of others' evaluations and feel they are under constant scrutiny by an imaginary audience" (Somerville, 2013, p. 124).

personal fable An aspect of adolescent egocentrism characterized by an adolescent's belief that his or her thoughts, feelings, and experiences are unique, more wonderful, or more awful than anyone else's.

invincibility fable An adolescent's egocentric conviction that he or she cannot be overcome or even harmed by anything that might defeat a normal mortal, such as unprotected sex, drug abuse, or high-speed driving.

THINK CRITICALLY: How should you judge the validity of the idea of adolescent egocentrism?

formal operational thought In Piaget's theory, the fourth and final stage of cognitive development, characterized by more systematic logical thinking and by the ability to understand and systematically manipulate abstract concepts.

Fables Egocentrism also leads naturally to a **personal fable**, the belief that one is unique, destined to have a heroic, fabled, even legendary life. Some 12-year-olds plan to be star players in the NBA, or to become billionaires, or to cure cancer. The personal fable can extend to their entire generation, as found with some of the students quoted in the beginning of this chapter who said that *they* understood climate change and that adults did not care.

Some adolescents believe they may be destined to die an early, tragic death. For them, statistics about harm in later decades from STIs, junk food, vaping, or other actions seem irrelevant. One of my young students said, "That's just a statistic," dismissing its possible application to him.

Adolescents markedly overestimate the chance that they will soon die. One study found that teens estimate a 1 in 5 chance that they will die before age 20, when in fact the odds are less than 1 in 1,000. Even those most at risk of early death (urban African American males) survive at least to age 20 more than 99 times in 100.

Sadly, if adolescents think that they will die young, they might risk jail, HIV, drug addiction, and so on (Haynie et al., 2014). If they know someone who dies, the teenage response is fatalistic ("his number was up"), unaware that a self-fulfilling prophecy nailed the coffin.

The personal fable may coexist with the **invincibility fable**, the idea that death will not occur unless it is destined. This is another reason why some adolescents believe that fast driving, unprotected sex, or addictive drugs will spare them. Believing that one is invincible removes any impulse to control one's behavior, because personal control is neither needed nor possible (Lin, 2016).

Similarly, teens post comments on Snapchat, Instagram, Facebook, and so on, and they expect others to understand, laugh, admire, or sympathize. Their imaginary audience is other teenagers, not parents, teachers, college admission officers, or future employers, all of whom might have another interpretation (boyd, 2014).

Examination of the correlates of aggression among teen motorcycle gangs in Indonesia found a "strong and invulnerable against any possible danger while riding [a] motorcycle." That encouraged reckless driving (Saudi et al., 2018, p. 308). However, their sense of personal uniqueness did not correlate with aggression. Although adolescent egocentrism can be dangerous, it also has positive effects, giving young people confidence that they need (Hill et al., 2012).

Oblivious? When you see a teenager with purple hair or a nose ring, or riding a bicycle and reading, do you think he or she does not imagine what others think?

Lelia Valduga/Moment/Getty Images

Formal Operational Thought

Piaget described a shift in early adolescence to **formal operational thought**. Adolescents move past concrete operational thinking and consider abstractions, including "assumptions that have no necessary relation to reality" (Piaget, 1950/2001, p. 163). Is Piaget correct? Many educators think so. They adjust the curriculum between primary and secondary school, reflecting a shift from concrete thought to formal, logical thought. Here are three examples:

- *Math.* Younger children multiply real numbers, such as $4 \times 3 \times 8$; adolescents multiply unreal numbers, such as $(2x)(3y)$ or even $(25xy^2)(-3zy^3)$.

- *Social studies.* Younger children study other cultures by considering daily life—drinking goat's milk or building an igloo, for instance. Adolescents consider the effect of GNP (gross national product) and TFR (total fertility rate) on global politics.
- *Science.* Younger students grow carrots and feed gerbils; adolescents study invisible particles and distant galaxies.

Piaget's Experiments Piaget and his colleagues devised a number of tasks to assess formal operational thought (Inhelder & Piaget, 1958/2013b). In these tasks, "in contrast to concrete operational children, formal operational adolescents imagine all possible determinants . . . [and] systematically vary the factors one by one, observe the results correctly, keep track of the results, and draw the appropriate conclusions" (P. Miller, 2011, p. 57).

One of their experiments (diagrammed in **Figure 15.1**) required balancing a scale by hooking weights onto the scale's arms. To master this task, a person must recognize the reciprocal interaction between distance from the center and heaviness of the weight.

Balancing was not understood by the 3- to 5-year-olds. By age 7, children balanced the scale by putting the same amount of weight on each arm, but they didn't realize that the distance from the center mattered. By age 10, children experimented with the weights, using trial and error, not logic.

Finally, by about age 13 or 14, some children hypothesized about reciprocity. They realized that a heavy weight close to the center can be counterbalanced with a light weight far from the center on the other side (Piaget & Inhelder, 1972).

Hypothetical-Deductive Reasoning One hallmark of formal operational thought is the capacity to think of possibility, not just reality. "Here and now" is

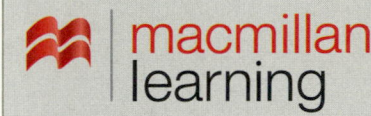

macmillan learning

VIDEO ACTIVITY: The Balance Scale Task shows children of various ages completing the task and gives you an opportunity to try it as well.

FIGURE 15.1

How to Balance a Scale Piaget's balance-scale test of formal reasoning, as it is attempted by *(a)* a 4-year-old, *(b)* a 7-year-old, *(c)* a 10-year-old, and *(d)* a 14-year-old. The key to balancing the scale is to make weight times distance from the center equal on both sides of the center; the realization of that principle is evidence of formal operational thought.

only one of many possibilities, including "there and then," "long, long ago," "not yet," and "never." As Piaget said:

> The adolescent . . . thinks beyond the present and forms theories about everything, delighting especially in considerations of that which is not.
>
> [Piaget, 1950/2001, p. 163]

hypothetical thought Reasoning that includes propositions and possibilities that may not reflect reality.

Adolescents are therefore primed to engage in **hypothetical thought**, reasoning about *if–then* propositions. Consider the following question (adapted from De Neys & Van Gelder, 2009):

> If all mammals can walk,
> And whales are mammals,
> Can whales walk?

Children answer "No!" They know that whales swim, not walk; the logic escapes them. Some adolescents answer "Yes." They understand the conditional *if*, and therefore they can use logic to interpret the phrase "if all mammals."

> *Possibility* no longer appears merely as an extension of an empirical situation or of action actually performed. Instead, it is *reality* that is now secondary to *possibility*.
>
> [Inhelder & Piaget, 1958/2013b, p. 251; emphasis in original]

Hypothetical thought transforms perceptions, not necessarily for the better. Adolescents might criticize everything from their mother's spaghetti (it's not *al dente*) to the Gregorian calendar (it's not the Chinese or Jewish one). They criticize what *is* because of their hypothetical thinking about what might be and their growing awareness of other families and cultures (Moshman, 2011).

Especially for Natural Scientists
Some ideas that were once universally accepted, such as the belief that the sun moved around Earth, have been disproved. Is it a failure of inductive or deductive reasoning that leads to false conclusions? (see response, page 400)

deductive reasoning Reasoning from a general statement, premise, or principle, through logical steps, to figure out (deduce) specifics. (Also called *top-down reasoning*.)

inductive reasoning Reasoning from one or more specific experiences or facts to reach (induce) a general conclusion. (Also called *bottom-up reasoning*.)

In developing the capacity to think hypothetically, by age 14 or so adolescents become more capable of **deductive reasoning**, or *top-down reasoning*, which begins with an abstract idea or premise and then uses logic to draw specific conclusions. In the example above, "if all mammals can walk" is a premise.

By contrast, **inductive reasoning**, or *bottom-up reasoning*, predominates when younger children accumulate facts and experiences to aid their thinking. Since they know whales cannot walk, that knowledge trumps the logic.

In essence, a child's reasoning goes like this: "This creature waddles and quacks. Ducks waddle and quack. Therefore, this must be a duck." This is inductive: It progresses from particulars ("waddles" and "quacks") to a general conclusion ("a duck"). By contrast, deduction progresses from the general to the specific: "If it's a duck, it will waddle and quack."

WHAT HAVE YOU LEARNED?

1. How does adolescent egocentrism differ from early-childhood egocentrism?
2. What perceptions arise from belief in the imaginary audience?
3. Why are the personal fable and the invincibility fable called "fables"?
4. What are the practical implications of adolescent cognition?
5. What are the advantages of using inductive rather than deductive reasoning?

Two Modes of Thinking

Piaget emphasized the sequence of thought, not only from egocentric to formal but throughout all four stages. Another group of scholars disagrees, especially when describing adolescent cognition. They suggest that thinking does not develop in

sequence but in parallel, with two processes that are not tightly coordinated within the brain (Baker et al., 2015).

To be specific, advanced logic in adolescence (formal operational thought) is counterbalanced by the increasing power of intuition. Thus, thinking occurs in two ways, called **dual processing** (see **Figure 15.2**).

The thinking described by the first half of each pair is easier and quicker, preferred in everyday life. Sometimes, however, circumstances necessitate the second mode, when deeper thought is demanded. The discrepancy between the maturation of the limbic system and the prefrontal cortex reflects this duality. [**Life-Span Link:** Timing differences in brain maturation are discussed in Chapter 14.]

To some extent, both modes of thinking reflect inborn temperament. Most children who are impulsive by nature learn to regulate their reactions in childhood, but a dual-processing perspective suggests that this regulation may break down during adolescence (Henderson et al., 2015).

Dual Processing

System 1	System 2
Intuitive	Analytic
Hot	Cold
Implicit	Explicit
Creative	Factual
Gist	Specific
Experiential	Rational
Qualitative	Quantitative
Contextualized	Decontextualized

FIGURE 15.2

Two Modes Each pair describes two modes of thought. Although researchers who use each pair differ in what they emphasize, all see two contrasting ways to think.

dual processing The notion that two networks exist within the human brain, one for emotional processing of stimuli and one for analytical reasoning.

intuitive thought Thought that arises from an emotion or a hunch, beyond rational explanation, and is influenced by past experiences and cultural assumptions.

analytic thought Thought that results from analysis, such as a systematic ranking of pros and cons, risks and consequences, possibilities and facts. Analytic thought depends on logic and rationality.

Intuitive and Analytic Processing

In describing these two processes of adolescent cognition, we use the terms *intuitive* and *analytic,* defined as follows:

- **Intuitive thought** begins with a belief, assumption, or general rule (called a *heuristic*) rather than logic. Intuition is quick and powerful; it feels "right."
- **Analytic thought** is the formal, logical, hypothetical-deductive thinking described by Piaget. It involves rational analysis of many factors whose interactions must be calculated, as in the scale-balancing problem.

When the two modes of thinking conflict, people of all ages sometimes use one and sometimes the other. We are all "predictably irrational" at times (Ariely, 2010), but since adolescent brains are increasingly myelinated, thought occurs with lightning speed. That may make them "fast and furious" intuitive thinkers, unlike their teachers and parents, who have time for slower, analytic thinking. The result is that "people who interact with adolescents often are frustrated by the mercurial quality of their decisions" (Hartley & Somerville, 2015, p. 112).

To test yourself on intuitive and analytic thinking, answer the following:

1. A bat and a ball cost $1.10 in total. The bat costs $1 more than the ball. How much does the ball cost?
2. If it takes 5 minutes for 5 machines to make 5 widgets, how long would it take 100 machines to make 100 widgets?
3. In a lake, there is a patch of lily pads. Every day the patch doubles in size. If it takes 48 days for the patch to cover the entire lake, how long would it take for the patch to cover half the lake?

[*From Gervais & Norenzayan, 2012, p. 494*]

Answers are on page 385. Quick, intuitive responses may be wrong.

Paul Klaczynski conducted dozens of studies comparing the thinking of children, young adolescents, and older adolescents (usually 9-, 12-, and 15-year-olds, respectively) (Klaczynski, 2001, 2011; Klaczynski et al., 2009). Variation was evident at every age.

Klaczynski reports that almost every adolescent is analytical and logical on some problems but not on others, with some passing the same questions that

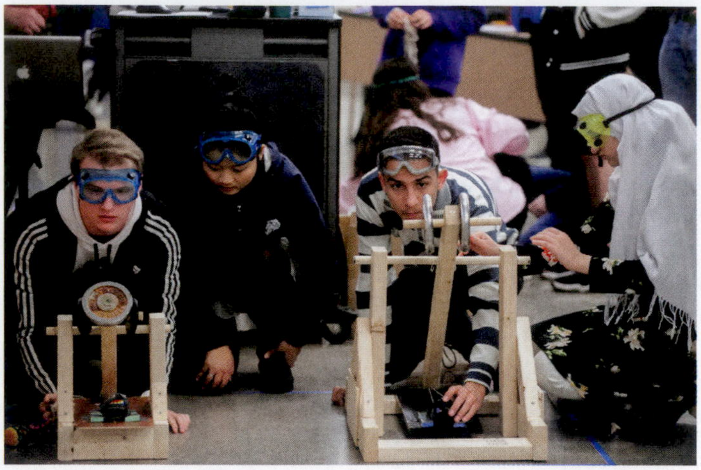

Bac Totrong/Daily News via AP Images

Fire Your Trebuchet! Denis Mujanovic, Anna Dim, Ahmed Kamaludeen, and Ghaden Asad are all high school students participating in the Western Kentucky Physics Olympics. Here they compete with their carefully designed trebuchets, a kind of catapult related to the slingshot.

THINK CRITICALLY: When might an emotional response be better than an analytic one?

others fail. As they grow older, adolescents sometimes gain in logic and sometimes regress, with the social context and training in statistics becoming major influences on cognition (Klaczynski & Felmban, 2014).

Interestingly, as adolescents become more aware of structural, social reasons affecting the phenomena they see, they also become more influenced by social stereotypes. For the stereotype that obese people are less competent that thinner people, adolescents actually regress, with younger children outperforming them (Felmban & Klaczynski, 2019).

Thus, neither age nor intelligence alone necessarily makes a person more logical. Even though the adolescent mind is capable of logic, sometimes "social variables are better predictors . . . than cognitive abilities" (Klaczynski & Felmban, 2014, pp. 103–104). (See A Case to Study.)

Preferring Emotions Why not use formal operational thinking? Adolescents learn the scientific method in school, so they know the importance of empirical evidence and deductive reasoning. But they do not always think like scientists. Why?

Dozens of experiments and extensive theorizing have found some answers (Albert & Steinberg, 2011; Blakemore, 2018). Essentially, logic is more difficult than intuition: It requires questioning ideas that are comforting and familiar, and it might lead to conclusions that are not accepted by one's peers. Once people of any age reach an emotional conclusion (sometimes called a "gut feeling"), they resist changing their minds. Prejudice is not seen as prejudice; people develop reasons to support their feelings.

A CASE TO STUDY

Biting the Policeman

Both suspicion of authority and awareness of context advance reasoning, but both also complicate simple issues and lead to impulsive but destructive actions. Indeed, suspicion of authority may propel adolescents to respond illogically.

One day my student, herself only 18 years old, was with her younger cousin. A police officer stopped them and asked why the cousin was not in school. He patted down the boy and asked for identification. That cousin was visiting from another state; he did not have an ID.

My student cited a U.S. Supreme Court case that said the officer did not have authority to "stop and frisk." He angrily grabbed her cousin; she bit the officer's hand and was arrested.

After she spent weeks in jail, she finally was brought before a judge. Perhaps those weeks, plus a meeting with her public defender, caused her analytic mind to activate. She had written an apology to the officer, which she read out loud in court. The officer did not press charges.

I appeared in court on her behalf; the judge released her to me. She was shivering; the first thing I did was put a warm coat on her. I found it ironic that the judge listened to me but that the justice system did not understand the developmental cognition of my student.

This was dual processing. In her education, my student had gained a formal understanding of the laws regarding police authority. However, there was a disconnect between her analysis and her emotions. She was still impulsive, intuitively defending her cousin in a way that an adult would not.

It is easy to conclude that more mature thought processes are wiser. The judge thought that I understood things that my student did not. Certainly she should not have bitten the officer. But it also is true that the entire incident shows that the authorities did not understand the adolescent mind.

My student's childhood experiences primed her to act as she did. It was unwise at the moment, but she had learned in childhood that family members must be protected. In the heat of the moment, she reacted emotionally.

She is not alone in that. Probably most readers of the book can think of something they did in adolescence that arose from emotions, and that, with the wisdom of time and maturity, they wish they had not done.

Answers	Intuitive	Analytic
1.	10 cents	5 cents
2.	100 minutes	5 minutes
3.	24 days	47 days

The correct answer is the analytic one, but few adolescents take the time to figure it out.

Better Thinking

A developmental approach finds gains and losses at every age, which suggests that adolescent thinking is sometimes good. For example, why do teenagers risk addiction by using drugs, or risk HIV/AIDS by not using a condom? Of course, drug use is foolish and condom use is wise. But perhaps we should not blame teenage irrationality and impulsivity for those actions.

Perhaps adolescents are rational, but their priorities differ from those of adults. Parents want healthy, long-lived children, so they blame faulty reasoning when adolescents risk their lives. Judges want law-abiding citizens, so they punish those who break the law.

Adolescents, however, value social acceptance and friendship, which are important for humans lifelong. During adolescence, hormones and brains are more attuned to social support than to long-term consequences (Blakemore, 2018). Teenagers are attuned to exploring new adventures and people, leaving their childhood social circle. Thus, instead of blaming their choices on foolish ignorance, we might consider it evidence of another value system (Hartley & Somerville, 2015).

A young person might be a thrilled passenger in a speeding car if many friends are there and an admired peer is driving. Similarly, a 15-year-old who is offered a cigarette might rationally choose peer acceptance and possible romance over the distant risk of cancer. Think of teenagers who want to be "cool" or "bad." Will they say "No, thank you, I promised my mother I would not smoke"?

Furthermore, the systematic, analytic thought that Piaget described is slow and costly, not fast and frugal, wasting precious time when a young person wants to act. Adolescents do not want to take time to weigh alternatives and think of the future. Some risks are taken impulsively, and that is not always bad.

Indeed, some experts suggest that the adolescent impulse to take risks, respond to peers, and explore new ideas is essential for development and beneficial for the larger society (Ernst, 2016). It may be that adolescent thinking is "adaptive and rational if one considers that a key developmental goal of this period of life is to mature into an independent adult in the context of a social world that is unstable and changing" (Blakemore, 2018, p. 116).

Societies need some people who question assumptions, and adolescents question everything. As social circumstances change, traditions need reexamination, lest old customs ossify and societies die. (See Inside the Brain.)

CHAPTER APP 15

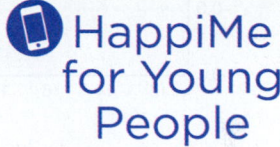

HappiMe for Young People

IOS:
https://tinyurl.com/y32tsywa

RELATED TOPIC:
Adolescent cognition

This free mindfulness app teaches its teen users to "Learn, Recognize, Deal with Your Emotions, and Replace" to encourage positive thinking. It illustrates three distinct characters in the brain that teens learn to recognize in their thought patterns. Users also create audio playlists of positive thoughts, play the Swipe game to identify negative thoughts, listen to mindfulness and visualization exercises, and find mental health resources (mostly U.K.-based).

INSIDE THE BRAIN

Stop and Think? No!

You already know from Chapter 14 that brain growth is uneven in adolescence, with the limbic system advancing ahead of the prefrontal cortex. As you see, this is directly relevant to the discussion of dual processing, since emotions (intuitive thought) arise from the limbic system while analysis is rooted in the prefrontal cortex.

This is evident in many ways in the adolescent brain. One phenomenon that has been much studied lifelong is *delay discounting,* which is the tendency of people of all ages to seek immediate rewards rather than gaining larger rewards after a delay. This is seen when young children eat one marshmallow immediately rather than waiting 15 minutes for two marshmallows (as described in Chapter 10), and it will be evident again when adults do not save for their retirement.

Research on the adolescent brain finds that the *ventral striatum,* the part of the brain that analyzes rewards, matures gradually during puberty, as does connectivity between the *amygdala* (as you remember, the hotbed of emotions) and the *prefrontal cortex.*

Adolescents differ from adults in neurological maturation and connectivity, and that correlates with the ability to delay rewards (Anandakumar et al., 2018). In other words,

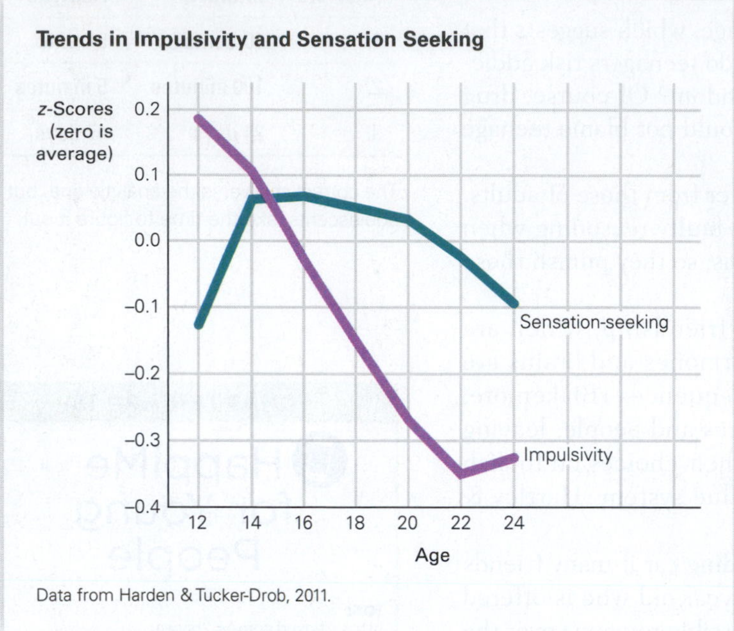

FIGURE 15.3

Look Before You Leap As you can see, adolescents become less impulsive as they mature, but they still enjoy the thrill of a new sensation.

the balance between intuitive and analytic thinking is directly related to connection between various parts of the brain.

Now we consider another aspect of coordination between and among the various parts of the brain. In one study, more than 7,000 adolescents, beginning at age 12 and ending at age 24, were repeatedly queried about their ideas, activities, and plans.

The results were "consistent with neurobiological research indicating that cortical regions involved in impulse control and planning continue to mature through early adulthood [and that] subcortical regions that respond to emotional novelty and reward are more responsive in middle adolescence than in either children or adults" (Harden & Tucker-Drob, 2011, p. 743).

Specifically, this longitudinal survey traced sensation seeking (e.g., "I enjoy new and exciting experiences") from early adolescence to the mid-20s. Increases were notable from ages 12 to 14 (see **Figure 15.3**).

Sensation seeking leads to intuitive thinking, direct from the gut to the brain. The researchers also studied impulsivity, as indicated by agreement with statements such as "I often get in a jam because I do things without thinking." Impulsive action declines as analytic thinking increases.

In this study, sensation seeking increased rapidly at puberty, and both sensation seeking and impulsivity slowly declined with maturation. However, trajectories varied from one person to another, and the two traits, sensation seeking and impulsivity, did not necessarily correlate. Thus, biology (the HPA axis) may not always link to experience (the prefrontal cortex) (Harden & Tucker-Drob, 2011). Both affect behavior: Risky sex correlates with both sensation seeking and impulsivity (Charnigo et al., 2013), but each has an independent impact.

The fact that each is independent is crucial. Another study found, as expected, that sensation seeking reached a peak in adolescence but did not lead to impulsive actions if the young person had strong cognitive control of their impulses (Khurana et al., 2018). A third study, mapping changes in the brain from ages 8 to 22, found that flexibility in information processing (the readiness to switch from considering the positive to negative aspects of an experience and then back again) led to better thinking (Medaglia et al., 2018).

In other words, destructive behavior is far from inevitable as the brain reorganizes in adolescence. A young person might appreciate an exquisite sunset, a sumptuous meal, a delicate rose—all because of the heightened sensation-seeking aspects of the human brain.

WHAT HAVE YOU LEARNED?

1. When might intuition and analysis lead to contrasting conclusions?
2. What mode of thinking—intuitive or analytic—do most people prefer, and why?
3. How might intuitive thinking increase risk taking?
4. How does egocentrism account for the clashing priorities of parents and adolescents?
5. When is intuitive thinking better than analytic thinking?

Technology and Cognition

A revolutionary change in the thinking of adolescents has centered on technology. Almost every adolescent worldwide now has Internet access, and in many nations, most adolescents own several technological devices, from smartwatches to large-screen computers. No doubt this affects how teenagers think and learn, but exactly how is not certain. As you will see, researchers disagree.

Jessica Rinaldi/The Boston Globe via Getty Images

Software Engineers? Not yet. But the Boston nonprofit Resilient Coders teaches minority adolescents the skills of coding. This organization hopes that they will break the unwritten code that keeps few people like Lawrence Edmonson and Anne Demosthene (shown here) from becoming digital engineers.

Digital Natives

There is no disagreement that technology is widespread and has changed the adolescent experience. Adults over age 50 grew up without the Internet, instant messaging, social media, blogs, cell phones, smartphones, MP3 players, tablets, 3-D printers, or digital cameras. Until 2006, only students at a few highly selective colleges could join Facebook.

In contrast, today's teenagers are called *digital natives,* although if that implies that they know everything about digital communication, it is a misnomer (boyd, 2014). Adolescents have been networking, texting, and clicking for definitions, directions, and data all their lives. Their smartphones are always within reach; some teens text hundreds of times a day.

Some psychologists suggest that this is not really new. Connection to peers has always been important to teenagers. In earlier generations, adults predicted that the automobile, or the shopping mall, or rock and roll music would lead their children astray. Now some fear that technology undercuts learning to compute, to spell, to write. Not a new fear!

Others praise the Internet for fostering social connections. Teens who formerly felt isolated, such as those with Down syndrome, or who are LGBTQ, or deaf, or simply at odds with their neighbors, now can find peers.

For some adolescents, the Internet is their only source of information about health and sex. Public health workers and therapists have found that text messaging is an effective way to combat adolescent depression and increase good health practices (Topooco et al., 2018). Most secondary students check facts, read explanations, view videos, and thus grasp concepts that they would not have understood without technology.

A decade ago, psychologists worried about a digital divide between the rich and the poor, who could not afford computers. Now, as costs tumble, adolescents of every ethnic and economic group have smartphones that they use primarily to connect with friends. In contrast to a decade ago, African American and Latinx teenagers are more likely than European American teens to say they are online "almost constantly" (34 percent, 32 percent, 19 percent, respectively) (Lenhart, 2015, p. 2).

Technology in Schools

In general, educators accept—even welcome—students' facility with technology. In most high schools, teachers use laptops, smartphones, smart boards, and so on as tools for learning. In some districts, students are *required* to take at least one class completely online. There are "virtual" schools in which students earn all of their credits via the Internet, never entering a school building, and some districts give everyone a tablet instead of a textbook.

However, another digital divide seems evident, between high school teachers who use technology to engage students and those who do not. A key variable is what the teachers believe about learning (Li et al., 2018).

When teachers are student-centered—encouraging discussion, critical thinking, and active engagement—they are more likely to use technology. On the other hand, traditional teachers use technology as an alternative to writing on the board, using PowerPoint, for instance, but not really changing their methods.

macmillan learning

Watch **VIDEO: The Impact of Media on Adolescent Development** to learn more about how digital technology affects cognition during adolescence.

For decades, developmentalists have recognized that instruction, practice, discussion, and experience within the zone of proximal development advance adolescent thought. Technology may speed up the process. Does it also subvert some kinds of learning? Does it encourage rapid shifts of attention, multitasking without reflection, and visual learning instead of invisible analysis (Greenfield, 2009)?

Might the Internet may be dangerous for adolescent health, not only interfering with sleep and physical exercise, but also with cognition? Adolescents may be particularly vulnerable to scams, advertisements, and disproven treatments (Keselman et al., 2019). It is crucial that high school classes emphasize critical thinking and evidence (primary sources in history, data in the sciences) to help adolescent process what they read online.

A major concern is that adolescents need to activate their analytic minds to evaluate what they see. Adults make the same mistake, believing "fake news" because they saw it on the Internet (Mihailidis & Viotty, 2017). Teachers can guide critical thinking about sources.

As Chapter 1 explains, science depends on evidence, not opinion, yet all humans (especially adolescents) find it easier to avoid formal operational thought. As two scholars point out regarding politically controversial topics (e.g., climate change, vaccination, evolution), students sometimes think that if the Internet contains contrary opinions, then they can ignore evidence (Plutzer & Hannah, 2018)!

Sexual Abuse?

Parents worry about sexual abuse via the Internet. The facts are reassuring: Although predators lurk online, most teens never encounter them, and digital natives delete and ignore distasteful messages. Sexual abuse is a serious problem, but if sexual abuse is defined as a perverted older stranger taking technological advantage of an innocent teen, it is "extremely rare" (Mitchell et al., 2013, p. 1226).

Between 2000 and 2010, the number of teenagers online rose dramatically, but the rate of teenagers who say that someone online tried to get them to talk about sex declined from 10 percent in 2000 to 1 percent in 2010. Those 1 percent were almost always solicited by another young person whom the teenager knew in person—a Facebook friend, for instance (Mitchell et al., 2013). Teenagers are actually more suspicious of strangers than they were!

Of course, abuse can be devastating. Ten years out of high school, adolescent bullies and victims—online or offline, sexual or otherwise—are less likely to have graduated from high school or college and less likely to have good jobs or any job at all (Sigurdson et al., 2014). Parents and teachers should be concerned more about teens who victimize each other than about strangers who lurk online.

Sexual abuse is one of the main reasons that more than half of all parents restrict their 13- to 17-year-olds' technology use. More than 90 percent of parents discuss online behavior and appropriate Web sites with their teenagers, and "nearly half (48%) of parents know the password to their teen's email account, while 43% know the password to their teen's cell phone and 35% know the password to at least one of their teen's social media accounts" (Anderson, 2016, p. 3).

Virtually all teenagers use social media, and those in romantic relationships usually flirt online. Texting—hundreds of times a day—is common among adolescent lovers. But almost all romantic relationships begin in person: Only 6 percent of 13- to 17-year-olds have *ever* had a romance that began online. If a relationship makes them uncomfortable, they block the sender or unfriend that person (Lenhart et al., 2015).

Although teenagers enjoy staying in touch with their dating partners via the Internet, when the relationship ends, it may turn ugly. Of those who have quit

"What's the matter, sweetie? You haven't touched your food or your phone."

Marty Bucella/cartoonstock.com

Why? For teenagers, it is more unusual to forgo texting than to forgo eating. Why is that?

a romance, 15 percent report being threatened online (Lenhart et al., 2015). Sexually, socially, and cognitively, the Internet is neither cause nor cure of adolescent problems.

Computer Addiction

One possible problem arises when social media, chat rooms, message boards, video games, and Internet gambling undercut active play, schoolwork, and friendship (Tang et al., 2014). When does computer use become addictive?

One study found that one-fourth of adolescents use video games as an escape, and one-fifth had "done poorly on a school assignment or test" because of time spent on video games. The heaviest users got lower school grades and had more physical fights than did the average users (Gentile, 2011).

Using criteria for addiction developed by psychiatrists for other addictions (gambling, drugs, and so on), an estimated 3 percent of U.S. adolescents suffer from Internet addiction, almost always with other disorders as well (Jorgenson et al., 2016). This rate is low according to research in other nations, with rates of 15 percent in Turkey, 12 percent in India, and 22 percent in Hong Kong (Şaşmaz et al., 2014; Yadav et al., 2013; Shek & Yu, 2016).

Reviewing international research, one team reports addiction rates from 0 to 26 percent. That wide range results more from varying definitions and methodology than from actual differences between nations (Y-H. Lee et al., 2015). Accurate science regarding Internet addiction is hard to establish.

Remember that correlation is not causation. Might low school achievement, depression, aggression, and so on lead to video game playing and social media obsession rather than vice versa? Do adults pathologize normal teen behavior?

Concern has focused on China, which has widespread use of computers and cell phones among adolescents. One Chinese study found a correlation between family neglect, abuse, and cell phone addiction (Sun et al., 2019). Some rehabilitation centers for youth with addiction to technology are strict—perhaps even abusive—in keeping teenagers from Internet use (Bax, 2014).

Similarly, Korean researchers found a correlation between excessive use of the Internet, parental addiction, and domestic violence (Kim et al., 2018). Cause and consequence are always unclear in correlational studies: Excessive technology use may be a symptom, not a cause, of family dysfunction.

Obviously, parents, teachers, and scientists have not yet settled on the appropriate response to adolescents and social media. The psychiatrists who wrote the DSM-5, after careful consideration of the evidence, did *not* include Internet use as an addiction. Instead, they wrote that further study was needed.

The danger is in our human instinct to take the easier route, and to avoid analysis. That can lead us astray, a tendency exploited by the beep of the new text message (which causes a conditioned response) and the targeted advertising on social media (which pushes exactly the unchallenged opinions and psychic profile of each person). As one critic notes:

> Our habitual and automatic responses save us valuable effort, energy, and time. The willpower required to make decisions with the prefrontal cortex, deciding how we're going to tie our shoe, or open the door anew each time, would paralyze us from ever living life.... stuck giving full attention to routine tasks, and drain our ability to concentrate and learn new things.
>
> *[Hendlin, 2018]*

Of course, learning new things is exactly what adolescent cognition should allow. However, the immaturity of the prefrontal cortex makes computer addiction and intellectual distortion particularly insidious in adolescence.

THINK CRITICALLY: The older people are, the more likely they are to be critical of social media. Is that wisdom or ignorance? Why?

Cyber Danger

cyberbullying Bullying that occurs when one person spreads insults or rumors about another by means of social media posts, e-mails, text messages, or cell phone videos.

Now we consider an Internet use that everyone agrees is harmful: **cyberbullying**. Electronic devices can be used to harass someone with rumors, lies, embarrassing truths, or threats, all from the safe distance of the private computer.

It is much easier to harm someone from a distance than directly. That is why guns kill more people than knives, why drones and bombs kill more people than face-to-face battle once did, and why cyberbullying is new threat.

Cyberbullies are usually already bullies or victims or both, with bully-victims especially likely to engage in, and suffer from, cyberbullying. Some leading researchers warn against exaggerating the power of cyberbullying, which they contend should be considered as another form of bullying, perhaps more powerful, but subject to the same pressures and protections (Olweus & Limber, 2018). [**Life-Span Link:** Bullying is discussed in Chapter 13.]

Worst in Adolescence

Although technology does not create bullies, it deepens the harm because it is a weapon that reaches a large audience, and because social acceptance is so crucial to adolescents (Giumetti & Kowalski, 2015). That lets cyberbullying echo after only one incident, unlike most bullying, which by definition is repeated (Underwood & Ehrenreich, 2017).

Texted and posted rumors and insults can instantly reach thousands, day and night, with shame magnified by the imaginary audience. Photos and videos of someone drunk, naked, or crying can be easily sent to dozens of others, who may send it further or post it on public sites for thousands to see. Since young adolescents act quickly without reflection, cyberbullying is particularly prevalent and thoughtlessly cruel between ages 11 and 14.

Cyberbullying is most damaging when the self-concept is fragile, when sexual impulses are new, and when impulsive thoughts precede analytic ones—all of which characterize many young adolescents. Particular concern has been raised regarding the racial and ethnic prejudices that are expressed online (Seaton & Iida, 2019; Tynes et al., 2018).

The most serious consequence of online insults is deep depression, added to the typical rise in depression at puberty. In extreme cases, cyberbullying may trigger suicide attempts (Hinduja & Patchin, 2018; Bonanno & Hymel, 2013; Geoffroy et al., 2016).

The school climate is a powerful antidote (Guo, 2016). When adolescents consider school a good place to be—with supportive teachers, friendly classmates, opportunities for growth (clubs, sports, theater, music), and the like—those with high self-esteem are less likely to engage in cyberbullying. They disapprove of it and stop it by blocking bullies and deleting messages. However, when the school climate is negative, those with high self-esteem may become bullies themselves (Gendron et al., 2011).

Parenting practices make a difference. Cyberbullying as well as addictive behaviors increase when parents are too strict or too permissive. As found in our earlier discussion of parental styles, authoritative parents seem to decrease an adolescent's need to engage in destructive use of technology (Zurcher et al., 2018).

sexting Sending sexual content, particularly photos or videos, via cell phones or social media.

Spencer Grant/Alamy Stock Photo

Consequences Unknown Few adolescents think about the consequences of their impulsive rage, responses, or retorts on social media or in text messages. This educator at a community center tries to explain that victims can be devastated—rarely suicidal but often depressed.

Sexting

The vulnerability of adolescence was tragically evident in the suicide of a California 15-year-old, Audrie Pott (Sulek, 2013). At a weekend sleepover, Audrie and her friends found alcohol. She got so drunk that she blacked out. The next Monday, three boys in her school bragged that they had had sex with her, showing pictures on their cell phones to classmates. The next weekend, Audrie hanged herself. Only then did her parents and teachers learn what had happened.

A related aspect of this tragedy will not surprise adolescents: **sexting**, as sending sexual photographs or texts is called. Adults may consider sexting dangerous and pornographic; teens usually do not (Erreygers et al., 2017).

Sexting is common, with frequency depending on peer culture. In a large Los Angeles high school, about half of the students knew someone who sexted. Compared to the half who knew no sexting peers, those who knew someone else often themselves sent and received sexts (twice and 13 times more likely, respectively). Sexting correlated with sexual experiences, especially oral sex (7 times more likely) and sex without a condom (5 times more likely) (Rice et al., 2018).

Sexting is a problem not only because it may increase unsafe sex but also because a jilted teen might resend a naked photo of a former lover. That is called *revenge porn,* and it is especially common among adolescents — who tend to act quickly and emotionally, not slowly and thoughtfully.

Another problem is that a sent image may not be appreciated by the recipient. Remember that body image formation is crucial during early adolescence. Many teens have distorted self-concepts and unrealistic fantasies. Teens are particularly vulnerable to shame and depression about how they look online.

Other Hazards The hazards of adolescent egocentrism, and of intuitive rather than analytic cognition, are obvious not only in sexting but also in technology use overall. Messages are sent in an instant, with no second thoughts. Troubled adolescents can connect with others who share their prejudices and self-destructive compulsions, such as anorexia, gun use, racism, or cutting.

The danger of technology lies not in the equipment but in the mind. As with many adolescent concerns (puberty, sexuality, body image, motivation), cognition and many other factors "shape, mediate, and/or modify effects" of technology (Oakes, 2009, p. 1142).

One careful observer claims that, instead of being *native* users of technology, many teenagers are *naive* users — believing they have privacy settings that they do not have, trusting sites that are markedly biased, believing news that is fake, misunderstanding how to search for and verify information (boyd, 2014). Educators can help with all of this — but only if they themselves understand technology and teens.

Teens are intuitive, impulsive, and egocentric, often unaware of the impact of what they send and overestimating the validity of what they read. Adults should know better.

WHAT HAVE YOU LEARNED?

1. What benefits come from adolescents' use of technology?
2. Why is adult fear of online adult predators exaggerated?
3. How do video games affect student learning?
4. Who is most apt and least apt to be involved in cyberbullying?
5. Why might sexting be a problem?
6. How might the term *digital native* be misleading?

Secondary Education

What does our knowledge of adolescent thought imply about school? Educators, developmentalists, political leaders, and parents wonder exactly which curricula and school structures are best for 11- to 18-year-olds. There are dozens of options: academic or practical skills, single-sex or coed, competitive or cooperative, large or small, public or private, and more.

To complicate matters, adolescents are far from a homogeneous group. As a result,

> some youth thrive at school—enjoying and benefiting from most of their experiences there; others muddle along and cope as best they can with the stress and demands of the moment; and still others find school an alienating and unpleasant place to be.
>
> *[Eccles & Roeser, 2011, p. 225]*

Given all of these variations, no school structure or pedagogy is best for everyone. Various scientists, nations, schools, and teachers try many strategies, some based on opposite but logical hypotheses. To begin to analyze this complexity, we present definitions, facts, issues, and possibilities.

Definitions and Facts

Each year of school advances human potential, a fact recognized by leaders and scholars in every nation and discipline. As you have read, adolescents are capable of deep and wide-ranging thought, no longer limited by concrete experience; yet they are often egocentric and impulsive. Quality matters: A year can propel thinking forward or can have little impact (Hanushek & Woessmann, 2010).

secondary education Literally, the period after primary education (elementary or grade school) and before tertiary education (college). It usually occurs from about ages 12 to 18, although there is some variation by school and by nation.

Secondary education—traditionally grades 7 through 12—denotes the school years after elementary or grade school (known as *primary education*) and before college or university (known as *tertiary education*). Adults are healthier and wealthier if they complete primary education, learning to read and write, and then continue on through secondary and tertiary education.

Partly because political leaders recognize that educated adults advance national wealth and health, every nation is increasing the number of students in secondary schools (see Visualizing Development on page 401). Education is compulsory until at least age 12 almost everywhere, and new high schools and colleges open daily in developing nations. The two most populous countries, China and India, are characterized by massive growth in education.

In many nations, two levels of secondary education are provided. Traditionally, secondary education was divided into junior high (usually grades 7 and 8) and senior high (usually grades 9 through 12). As the average age of puberty declined, **middle schools** were created for grades 5 or 6 through 8. This makes sense because, as you have learned, the pubescent 12-year-old is a quite different human being, cognitively as well as in many other ways, from the 17-year-old.

middle school A school for children in the grades between elementary school and high school. Middle school usually begins with grade 6 and ends with grade 8.

Middle School

Adjusting to middle school is bound to be stressful, as teachers, classmates, and expectations all change. Developmentalists agree that "teaching is likely to be particularly complex for middle school teachers because it happens amidst a critical period of cognitive, socio-emotional, and biological development of students who confront heightened social pressures from peers and gradual decline of parental oversight" (Ladd & Sorensen, 2017).

Regarding learning, "researchers and theorists commonly view early adolescence as an especially sensitive developmental period" (McGill et al., 2012, p. 1003). Yet many developmentalists find middle schools to be "developmentally regressive" (Eccles & Roeser, 2010, p. 13), which means learning goes backward.

THINK CRITICALLY: Would there be less bullying if more schools were multiethnic?

Increasing Behavioral Problems For many middle school students, academic achievement slows down and behavioral problems increase. Puberty itself is part of the problem. At least for other animals studied, especially when they are under stress, learning is reduced at puberty (McCormick et al., 2010). When school achievement decreases, that is both a sign and a cause of psychological as well as academic problems (Rahman et al., 2018).

The biological and psychological stresses of puberty are not the only reason learning suffers in early adolescence. Cognition matters, too: How much new middle school students like their school affects how much they learn (Riglin et al., 2013). This applies to students of every ethnic group, with declines in academics particularly steep for young adolescents of ethnic minorities, as they become more aware of low social expectations for them (Dotterer et al., 2009; McGill et al., 2012; Hayes et al., 2015).

Even if there were no discrimination in the larger society, students have reasons to dislike middle school. Bullying is common, particularly in the first year (Baly et al., 2014). Parents are less involved than in primary school, partly because students want more independence. It is psychologically healthy for adolescents to push their parents away, but the lack of parental support also increases risk.

Teacher support also decreases. Unlike teachers in primary school, where each classroom had one teacher, middle school teachers have hundreds of students. Teachers become impersonal and distant, not the personally engaging adults that young adolescents need (Meece & Eccles, 2010).

Signs of a future high school dropout, among them chronic absenteeism, appear in middle school (Ladd & Sorensen, 2017). Those students most at risk are low-SES boys from minority ethnic groups, yet almost no middle school has male guidance counselors or teachers who are African American or Latinx. Given their egocentric and intuitive thinking, many young adolescents need role models of successful, educated men (Morris & Morris, 2013).

Hill Street Studios/Blend Images/Newscom

More Like Him Needed In 2014 in the United States, half of the public school students were tallied as non-White and non-Hispanic, and half were male. Meanwhile, only 17 percent of teachers are non-White and non-Hispanic, and only 24 percent are male. This Gardena, California, high school teacher is a welcome exception in two other ways—he rarely sits behind his desk, and he uses gestures as well as his voice to explain.

Finding Acclaim To pinpoint the developmental mismatch between students' needs and the middle school context, note that just when egocentrism leads young people to feelings of shame, or fantasies of stardom (the imaginary audience), schools may require them to change rooms, teachers, and classmates every 40 minutes or so. That limits friendship and acclaim.

Especially for Teachers You are stumped by a question that one of your students asks. What do you do? (see response, page 400)

Recognition for academic excellence is rare, because middle school teachers grade more harshly than their primary school counterparts. Effort without accomplishment is not recognized, and achievement that was previously "outstanding" is now only average. Acclaim for after-school activities is also elusive, because many art, drama, dance, and other programs put adolescents of all ages together, and 11- to 13-year-olds are not as skilled as older adolescents.

When athletic teams become competitive, those with fragile egos protect themselves by not trying out. If sports require public showers, that is another reason for students in early puberty to avoid them: They do not feel at ease with their changing bodies, and they fear comments from their peers.

There is a positive correlation between physical activity, involvement in sports teams, and academic achievement in middle school (Rasberry et al., 2011; Im et al., 2016). Is this a cause or a consequence of sports? Ironically, some schools require good grades to join teams: Especially for boys, those who most need athletic engagement may be excluded.

As noted in the discussion of the brain, peer acceptance is more cherished at puberty than at any other time. Physical appearance—from eyebrows to foot size—suddenly becomes significant. Status symbols (e.g., gang colors, trendy sunglasses, a brand-name jacket) take on new meaning. Expensive clothes are coveted.

Sexual conquests are flaunted, girls may be seen as conquests, LGBTQ students may feel rejected. Consequently, many middle school students have no psychic energy left for homework.

entity theory of intelligence An approach to understanding intelligence that sees ability as innate, a fixed quantity present at birth; those who hold this view do not believe that effort enhances achievement.

incremental theory of intelligence An approach to understanding intelligence that holds that intelligence can be directly increased by effort; those who subscribe to this view believe they can master whatever they seek to learn if they pay attention, participate in class, study, complete their homework, and so on.

Coping with Middle School One way middle school students avoid feelings of failure in academics is to quit trying. Then they can blame a low grade on their choice ("I didn't study") rather than on their ability. Pivotal is how they think of their potential.

Educators write about a "fixed mindset" versus a "growth mindset." The same idea is described by psychologists as the **entity theory of intelligence** (i.e., ability is innate, a fixed quantity present at birth) and the **incremental theory of intelligence** (i.e., intelligence can increase if individuals work to master whatever they seek to understand) (Dweck, 1999).

If students hold the entity theory, they conclude that nothing they do can improve their academic skill. If they think they are "born stupid" at math, or language, or whatever, they mask their self-assessment by claiming not to study, try, or care. Thus, the entity belief relieves stress, but it also reduces learning.

By contrast, if adolescents adopt the incremental theory, they will pay attention, participate in class, study, complete their homework, and learn. That is also called *mastery motivation,* an example of intrinsic motivation. [**Life-Span Link:** Intrinsic and extrinsic motivation are discussed in Chapter 10.]

This is not hypothetical. In the first year of middle school, students with entity beliefs do not achieve much, whereas those with mastery motivation improve academically. This is found in many nations (e.g., Diseth et al., 2014; Zhao & Wang, 2014; Burnette et al., 2013).

Middle school is also a time when children learn how to cope with challenges, both academic and social. Coping style—solving problems rather than blaming oneself—is crucial (Monti et al., 2017). Of course, this is apparent at other ages as well. We discuss this here because the relationship between self-concept, motivation, and achievement is particularly fragile during middle childhood, as the brain reorganizes itself.

Believing that skills can be mastered and that effort pays off is crucial for learning social skills (Dweck, 2013). Students want friends, but some are convinced that no one likes them. That self-perception may lead to social avoidance and a downward spiral of feelings of rejection (Zimmer-Gembeck, 2016). Middle schools need to be organized so that friendships are encouraged and competition (which assumes winners and losers, a fixed mindset assumption) discouraged.

Observation Quiz Although the philosophy and strategy of these two schools are quite different, both share one aspect of the hidden curriculum. What is it? (see answer, page 400) ↓

High School

Many of the patterns and problems of middle school continue in high school. However, once the sudden growth and unfamiliar sexual impulses of puberty

Marmaduke St. John/Alamy Stock Photo

Carlos Osorio/Toronto Star/Getty Images

Now Learn This Educators and parents disagree among themselves about how and what middle school children need to learn. Accordingly, some parents send their children to a school where biology is taught via dissecting a squid *(left)*, others where obedience is taught via white shirts and lining up *(right)*.

are less novel, adolescents are better able to cope with school. Moreover, teachers and parents allow them more autonomy, and that encourages more self-motivation.

Added to that is cognitive maturation. When adolescents are better able to think abstractly, analytically, hypothetically, and logically (all formal operational thought), they can respond to the usual pedagogy of high school. Of course, ideally schools would also allow subjective, emotional, intuitive, and experiential thinking, helping students use both modes of thought.

The College-Bound From a developmental perspective, the fact that high schools emphasize formal thinking makes sense, since many older adolescents are capable of abstract logic. In several nations, attempts are under way to raise standards so that all high school graduates will be ready for college, where analysis is required.

A mantra in the United States is "college for all." This is intended to encourage low achievers to aspire for tertiary education, although some authors believe the effect may be the opposite (Carlson, 2016).

One result of the emphasis on college is that more students take classes that are assessed by externally scored exams, either the IB (International Baccalaureate) or the AP (Advanced Placement). Such classes have high standards and satisfy some college requirements if the student scores well.

With the class of 2017, more students than ever participate and succeed in AP. To be specific, more than 1.17 million students in the class of 2017 took 3.98 million AP Exams in public high schools nationwide, up from 1.14 million students in 2016 and 691,437 in the class of 2007. When it comes to performance, 711,518 students scored 3 or higher on at least one AP Exam in 2017, compared to 423,067 in 2007.

Other indicators of increasing standards are greater requirements for an academic diploma and restrictions on vocational or general diplomas. Most U.S. schools require two years of math beyond algebra, two years of laboratory science, three years of history, four years of English, and two years of a language other than English.

In addition to mandated courses, most U.S. public high school students are required to pass a **high-stakes test** in order to graduate. (Any exam for which the consequences of failing are severe is called "high-stakes.") A decade ago, no state required exit exams; in 2019, there are 12 states (including some with the most students, Florida, Texas, and New York) that do. Increased testing is evident in every state, but it is controversial, as Opposing Perspectives explains on the following page.

Alternatives to College In the United States, a sizable minority (about 30 percent) of high school graduates do not enter college, and many who enroll do not graduate (as discussed in Chapter 18). Even 10 years after the usual age for high school graduation, only 47 percent of U.S. young adults have earned any postsecondary degree. Rates are higher in some nations, lower in others.

These sobering statistics underlie another debate among educators. Should students be encouraged to "dream big" early in high school, aspiring for tertiary learning? This suggestion originates from studies that find a correlation between dreaming big in early adolescence and going to college years later (Domina et al., 2011a, 2011b).

Others suggest that college is a "fairy tale dream" that may lead to low self-esteem (Rosenbaum, 2011). If adolescents fail in AP classes, will they feel bored, stupid, and disengaged? If they then enter the job market, will they be ill-prepared because their education never gave them the practical and teamwork skills required?

Some high schools encourage college more than others. For example, high-achieving students in two major cities in neighboring states (Albuquerque, New Mexico and Fort Worth, Texas) had markedly different college enrollment rates (83 percent compared to 58 percent) (Center for Education Policy, 2012).

Will & Deni McIntyre/Getty Images

Melanie Stetson Freeman/The Christian Science Monitor/Getty Images

Same Situation, Far Apart: How to Learn Although developmental psychologists find that adolescents learn best when they are actively engaged with ideas, most teenagers are easier to control when they are taking tests (*top,* Winston-Salem, North Carolina, United States) or reciting scripture (*bottom,* Kabul, Afghanistan).

high-stakes test An evaluation that is critical in determining success or failure. If a single test determines whether a student will graduate or be promoted, it is a high-stakes test.

OPPOSING PERSPECTIVES

High-Stakes Testing

Secondary students in the United States take many more tests than they did even a decade ago. This includes many high-stakes tests—not only tests to earn a high school diploma but also tests to get into college (the SAT and ACT, achievement and aptitude) and tests to earn college credits (the AP and IB) while in high school.

High-stakes tests have become part of the culture, necessary to pass third, fifth, and eighth grades, and even to enter special kindergarten classes. Further, the 2016 federal education reform, the Every Student Succeeds Act (ESSA), requires standardized testing from the third grade on.

Tests also have high stakes for teachers, who may earn extra pay or lose their job based on how their students score, and for schools, which gain resources or are shuttered because of test scores. Entire school systems are rated on test scores. This is said to be one reason that widespread cheating on high-stakes tests occurred in Atlanta beginning in 2009 (Severson & Blinder, 2014).

Opposing perspectives on testing are voiced in many schools, parent groups, and state legislatures. In 2013, Alabama dropped its high-stakes test for graduation. In that same year Pennsylvania instituted such a test, but its opponents have postponed implementation of the requirement. A 2007 law in Texas required 15 tests for graduation; in 2013, Texas law reduced that to four tests (Rich, 2013).

A leading critic calls testing a *charade* that fools politicians and parents into thinking that students are learning (Koretz, 2017). On the other hand, tests are credited with narrowing the gap between African American and European American students, because measuring basic skills has increased teacher skill and expectations (Loeb & Byun, 2019).

Overall, high school graduation rates in the United States have increased every year for the past decade, reaching 85 percent in 2017 after four years in high school. Rates of students who take five years to graduate, or who drop out, are also reduced (see **Figure 15.4**). Some say that increased tests and higher standards are part of the reason, but others contend that the high-stakes tests discourage some students while making graduation too easy for those who are adept at test-taking (Hyslop, 2014).

Students who fail high-stakes tests are often those with intellectual disabilities, one-third of whom do not graduate (Samuels, 2013). Rates of not passing increase for those who attend schools in low-income neighborhoods, or whose first language is not English.

Some argue that the tests punish these students, when the real culprit is the school, the community, or the entire nation. Passing graduation exit exams does not correlate with excellence in college, but failing them increases the risk of harm—including prison later on (Baker & Lang, 2013).

Ironically, in the same decade during which U.S. schools are raising requirements, many East Asian nations, including China, Singapore, and Japan (all with high scores on international tests), have moved in the opposite direction. Particularly in Singapore, national high-stakes tests are being phased out, and local autonomy is increasing (Hargreaves, 2012).

International data support both sides of this controversy. One nation whose children generally score well is South Korea, where high-stakes tests have resulted in extensive studying. Many South Korean parents hire tutors to teach their children after school and on weekends to improve their test scores (Lee & Shouse, 2011). Almost all South Korean students graduate from high school, and most attend college.

On the opposite side of the globe, students in Finland also score well on international tests but have no national tests until

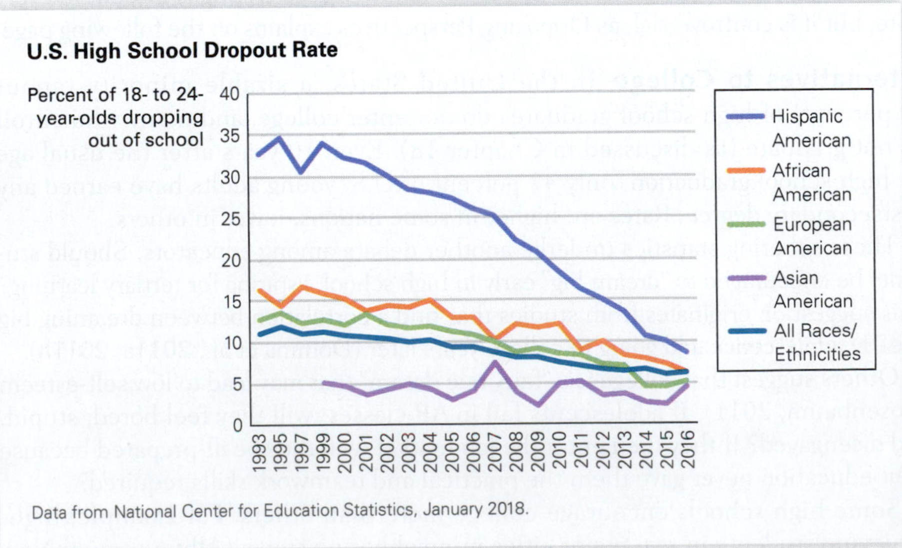

FIGURE 15.4
Mostly Good News This depicts wonderful improvements in high school graduation rates, especially among Hispanic youth, who drop out only half as often as they did 20 years ago. However, since high school graduation is increasingly necessary for lifetime success, even the rates shown here may not have kept pace with the changing needs of the economy. Future health, income, and happiness for anyone who drops out may be in jeopardy.

the end of high school. Nor do they spend much time on homework or after-school education. A Finnish expert proudly states that "schoolteachers teach in order to help their students learn, not to pass tests" (Sahlberg, 2011, p. 26).

A team who attempts to find merit and harm in high-stakes testing notes that every test is flawed, and every assessment can do harm as well as good (Loeb & Byum, 2019). The crucial question is whether the test measures what it is supposed to measure, and whether it is used to help teachers or punish them.

The most recent international data, from the TIMSS and the PIRLS (described in Chapter 12) and the PISA (described in this chapter), show that little has changed over the past decade, which suggests that U.S. high school students have neither benefited nor suffered from testing.

The critique of testing is part of the larger critique of the biases and benefits of aptitude and achievement tests, with opposite opinions expressed by experts (Sackett & Kuncel, 2018; Singer & Braun, 2018; Hagopian, 2014).

Should a national education curriculum prepare some students not for college, but for jobs, with training and practical experience to ease the transition to adult employment? Germany is one nation with such a curriculum (Ludwig-Mayerhofer et al., 2019). The United States is not.

That may be why, despite a thriving economy, Germany has relatively low rates of secondary degree attainment. In many other nations, students in vocational education have a higher employment rate than students in the academic track, but over a lifetime, their earnings are less (Hanushek et al., 2017). Which would you rather have at age 40—a steady and secure job or a high salary?

Overall, the data present a dilemma for educators. Suggesting that a student should *not* go to college may be racist, classist, sexist, or worse. On the other hand, many students who begin college do not graduate, so they lose time and gain debt when they could have advanced in a vocation. Everyone agrees that adolescents need to be educated for life as well as for employment, but it is difficult to decide what that means.

Especially for High School Teachers You are much more interested in the nuances and controversies than in the basic facts of your subject, but you know that your students will take high-stakes tests on the basics and that their scores will have a major impact on their futures. What should you do? (see response, page 400)

The PISA One international test, the PISA (mentioned in Chapter 12), was designed to measure high school students' ability to apply what they have learned. The PISA is taken by 15-year-olds, an age when almost all students are still in school but when many will soon stop formal education. The questions are supposed to be practical, measuring knowledge that adults might need. Recently the emphasis has been on science and analysis (OECD, 2016).

For example, among the 2012 math questions is this one:

> Chris has just received her car driving license and wants to buy her first car. The table below shows the details of four cars she finds at a local car dealer.
>
> What car's engine capacity is the smallest?
>
> A. Alpha B. Bolte C. Castel D. Dezal

Model	Alpha	Bolte	Castel	Dezal
Year	2003	2000	2001	1999
Advertised price (zeds)	4800	4450	4250	3990
Distance travelled (kilometers)	105 000	115 000	128 000	109 000
Engine capacity (liters)	1.79	1.796	1.82	1.783

For that and the other questions on the PISA, the calculations are quite simple—most 10-year-olds can do them; no calculus, calculators, or complex formulas required. However, almost half of the 15-year-olds worldwide got that question wrong. (The answer is D.) One problem is decimals: Some students do not remember how to interpret them when a practical question, not an academic one, is asked. Even in Singapore and Hong Kong, one out of five 15-year-olds got this question wrong. Another problem is that distance traveled, year, and price are irrelevant, yet many students are distracted by them.

Overall, U.S. students score lower on the PISA compared to those in many other nations, including Canada, the nation most similar to the United States in ethnicity and location. Compared to peers in other nations, the 2015 results rank U.S. 15-year-olds 25th out of 72.

Some 2015 results were not surprising (China, Japan, Korea, and Singapore were all high), but some were unexpected (high scores for Finland, Vietnam, and Estonia). Among the lowest results were Peru, Indonesia, and the Dominican Republic. The results reflect the educational systems more than geography, since low-scoring Indonesia is close to Singapore.

International analysis finds that the following items correlate with high achievement of high school students on the PISA. The standards were first articulated two decades ago (OECD, 2010, p. 4), but they continue to apply.

- Leaders, parents, and citizens value education overall, with individualized approaches to learning so that all students learn what they need.
- Standards are high and clear, so every student knows what he or she must do, with a "focus on the acquisition of complex, higher-order thinking skills."
- Teachers and administrators are valued, and they are given "considerable discretion . . . in determining content" and sufficient salary as well as time for collaboration.
- Learning is prioritized "across the entire system," with high-quality teachers assigned to the most challenging schools.

THINK CRITICALLY: Is it more important to prepare high school students for jobs or for college?

The PISA and international comparisons of high school students note that students who are immigrants and who are from low-income families do less well. Researchers caution that variations within nations affect results, so comparing one nation to another may be unfair. However, comparing students within nations is illuminating. Generally, girls do less well in science than boys, but this is less true in the United States than in most other nations. However, low-income students in general do especially poorly in the United States.

That is also true for college attendance. In the United States, girls are actually more likely than boys to enroll in college (the reverse was true a few decades ago), but low-income students are likely to avoid college. These differences are not based on potential. Students who are capable of college work, at least as measured on IQ tests, drop out of high school and college almost as often as those who are less capable.

Persistence, engagement, and motivation seem more crucial than intellectual ability alone (Duckworth, 2016; Tough, 2012). Not surprisingly, a school culture based on mastery, not competition, fosters learning (Park et al., 2018). As in middle school, the incremental (effort-based) theory of education may be crucial.

What Do They Need to Learn? Jesse Olascoaga and José Perez assemble a desk as part of a class in Trade Tech High School in Vista, California. Are they mastering skills that will lead to a good job? Much depends on what else they are learning. It may be collaboration and pride in work well done, in which case this is useful education.

San Diego Union-Tribune/ZUMA Press/Vista/CA/USA/Newscom

Variability

Adolescents themselves vary: Some are thoughtful, some are impulsive, some are ready for analytic challenges, some are egocentric, some will thrive in college, others would wither. All of them, however, need personal encouragement.

A study of student emotional and academic engagement from fifth grade to eighth grade found that, as expected, the overall average was a slow and steady decline of engagement. However, a distinctive group (about 18 percent) remained highly engaged throughout while another distinctive group (about 5 percent) experienced precipitous disengagement year by year (Li & Lerner, 2011).

The engaged middle schoolers are likely to do well in high school and college, and the disengaged are likely to drop out. However, some of those disengaged students are late bloomers who could succeed in college if given time and encouragement. Thus, schools and teachers need a variety of approaches to reach every adolescent.

What are the general conclusions for this chapter? The cognitive skills that boost national economic development and personal happiness are creativity, flexibility, relationship building, and analytic ability. Whether or not an adolescent is college-bound, those skills are exactly what the adolescent mind can develop—with proper education and guidance.

Every cognitive theorist and researcher believes that adolescents' logical, social, and creative potential is not always realized, but that it can be. Does that belief end this chapter on a hopeful note?

WHAT HAVE YOU LEARNED?

1. What characteristics of middle schools make them more difficult for students than elementary schools?
2. Why does puberty affect a person's ability to learn?
3. How do beliefs about intelligence affect motivation and learning?
4. What are the advantages and disadvantages of high-stakes testing?
5. What are the problems with Advanced Placement classes and tests?
6. Should high schools prepare everyone for college? Why or why not?
7. How does the PISA differ from other international tests?

SUMMARY

Logic and Self

1. Cognition in early adolescence may be egocentric, a kind of self-centered thinking. Adolescent egocentrism gives rise to the personal fable, the invincibility fable, and the imaginary audience.

2. Formal operational thought is Piaget's term for the last of his four periods of cognitive development. He tested and demonstrated formal operational thought with various problems that students in a high school science or math class might encounter.

3. Piaget realized that adolescents are no longer earthbound and concrete in their thinking; they imagine the possible, the probable, and even the impossible. They develop hypotheses and explore, using deductive reasoning.

Two Modes of Thinking

4. Many cognitive theories describe two types of thinking during adolescence. One set of names for these two types is intuitive and analytic. Both become more forceful during adolescence, but intuitive, emotional thinking matures before analytic, logical thought.

5. Few teenagers always use logic, although they are capable of doing so. Emotional, intuitive thinking is quicker and more satisfying (and sometimes better) than analytic thought.

6. Neurological as well as survey research finds that adolescent thinking is characterized by more rapid development of the limbic system and slower development of the prefrontal cortex. Peers further increase emotional impulses, so adolescents may make choices that their parents believe to be foolish.

Technology and Cognition

7. Adolescents use technology, particularly the Internet, more than people of any other age. They reap educational benefits, and many teachers welcome the accessibility of information and the research advances made possible by the Internet. Social connections are encouraged as well.

8. However, technology can be destructive. Some adolescents are addicted to video games; some use smartphones and instant messages for cyberbullying; some find like-minded peers to support eating disorders and other pathologies; some engage in sexting.

Secondary Education

9. Achievement in secondary education—after primary education (grade school) and before tertiary education (college)—correlates with the health and wealth of individuals and nations.

10. In middle school, many students struggle both socially and academically. One reason may be that middle schools are not structured to accommodate egocentrism or intuitive thinking. Students' beliefs about the nature of intelligence—entity or incremental—affects their learning.

11. Education in high school emphasizes formal operational thinking. In the United States, the demand for more accountability has led to an increase in the requirements for graduation and to more Advanced Placement (AP) classes and high-stakes testing.

12. A sizable number of high school students do not graduate or go on to college, and many more leave college without a degree. Current high school education in the United States may not meet their needs. In some other nations, educators pay substantial attention to vocational education in high school so that students are job-ready when they graduate.

13. The PISA test, taken by many 15-year-olds in 50 nations, measures how well students can apply the knowledge they have been taught. Students in the United States have particular difficulty with such tests.

KEY TERMS

adolescent egocentrism (p. 378)
rumination (p. 379)
imaginary audience (p. 379)
personal fable (p. 380)
invincibility fable (p. 380)
formal operational thought (p. 380)
hypothetical thought (p. 382)
deductive reasoning (p.382)
inductive reasoning (p. 382)
dual processing (p. 383)
intuitive thought (p. 383)
analytic thought (p. 383)
cyberbullying (p. 390)
sexting (p. 390)
secondary education (p. 392)
middle school (p. 392)
entity theory of intelligence (p. 394)
incremental theory of intelligence (p. 394)
high-stakes test (p. 395)

APPLICATIONS

1. Describe a time when you overestimated how much other people were thinking about you. How was your mistake similar to and different from adolescent egocentrism?

2. Talk to a teenager about politics, families, school, religion, or any other topic that might reveal the way he or she thinks. Do you hear any adolescent egocentrism? Intuitive thinking? Systematic thought? Flexibility? Cite examples.

3. Think of a life-changing decision you have made. How did logic and emotion interact? What would have changed if you had given the matter more thought—or less?

4. Describe what happened and what you thought in the first year you attended a middle school or a high school. What made it better or worse than later years in that school?

Especially For ANSWERS

Response for Natural Scientists (from p. 382): Probably both. Our false assumptions are not logically tested because we do not realize that they might need testing.

Response for Teachers (from p. 393): Praise the student by saying, "What a great question!" Egos are fragile, so it's best to always validate the question. Seek student engagement, perhaps asking whether any classmates know the answer, or by telling the student to discover the answer online, or saying you will find out. Whatever you do, don't fake it; if students lose faith in your credibility, you may lose them completely.

Response for High School Teachers (from p. 397): It would be nice to follow your instincts, but the appropriate response depends partly on pressures within the school and on the expectations of parents and the administration. A comforting fact is that adolescents can think about and learn almost anything if they feel a personal connection to it. Look for ways to teach the facts your students need for the tests as the foundation for the exciting and innovative topics you want to teach. Everyone will learn more, and the tests will be less intimidating to your students.

Observation Quiz ANSWERS

Answer to Observation Quiz (from p. 378) The first three you can probably guess: Climate change advocates speak of saving the planet, of scientific evidence, and of animals losing their habitat. Extra credit if you know the fourth: "XR" stands for Extinction Rebellion, a group that started with young people in England and has since spread to other nations.

Answer to Observation Quiz (from p. 394) Both are single-sex. What does that teach these students?

VISUALIZING DEVELOPMENT How Many Adolescents Are in School?

Attendance in secondary school is a psychosocial topic as much as a cognitive one. Whether or not an adolescent is in school reflects every aspect of the social context, including national policies, family support, peer pressures, employment prospects, and other economic concerns. Rates of violence, delinquency, poverty, and births to girls younger than 17 increase as school attendance decreases.

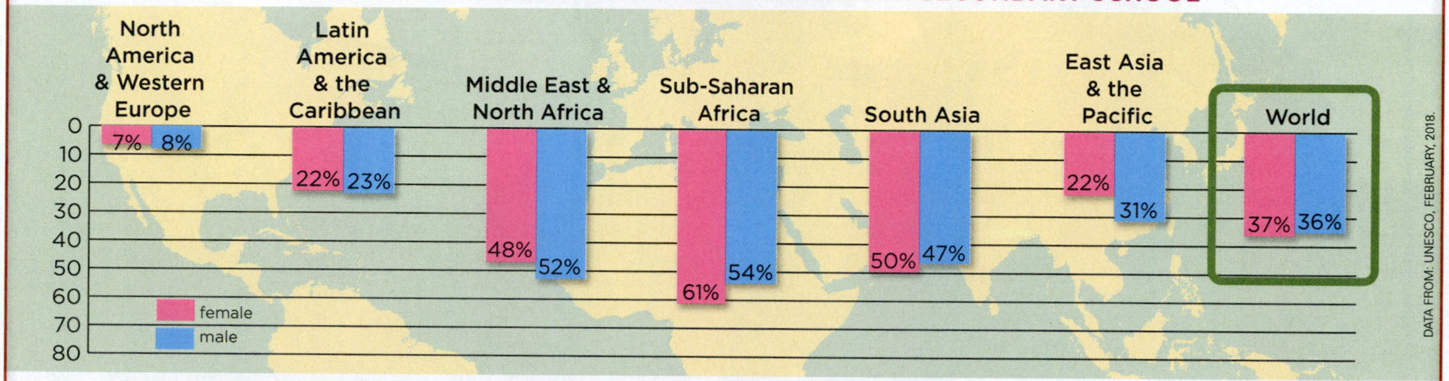

*In some nations, some students do not graduate because they go directly into the job market. For example, Germany has an extensive apprenticeship program.

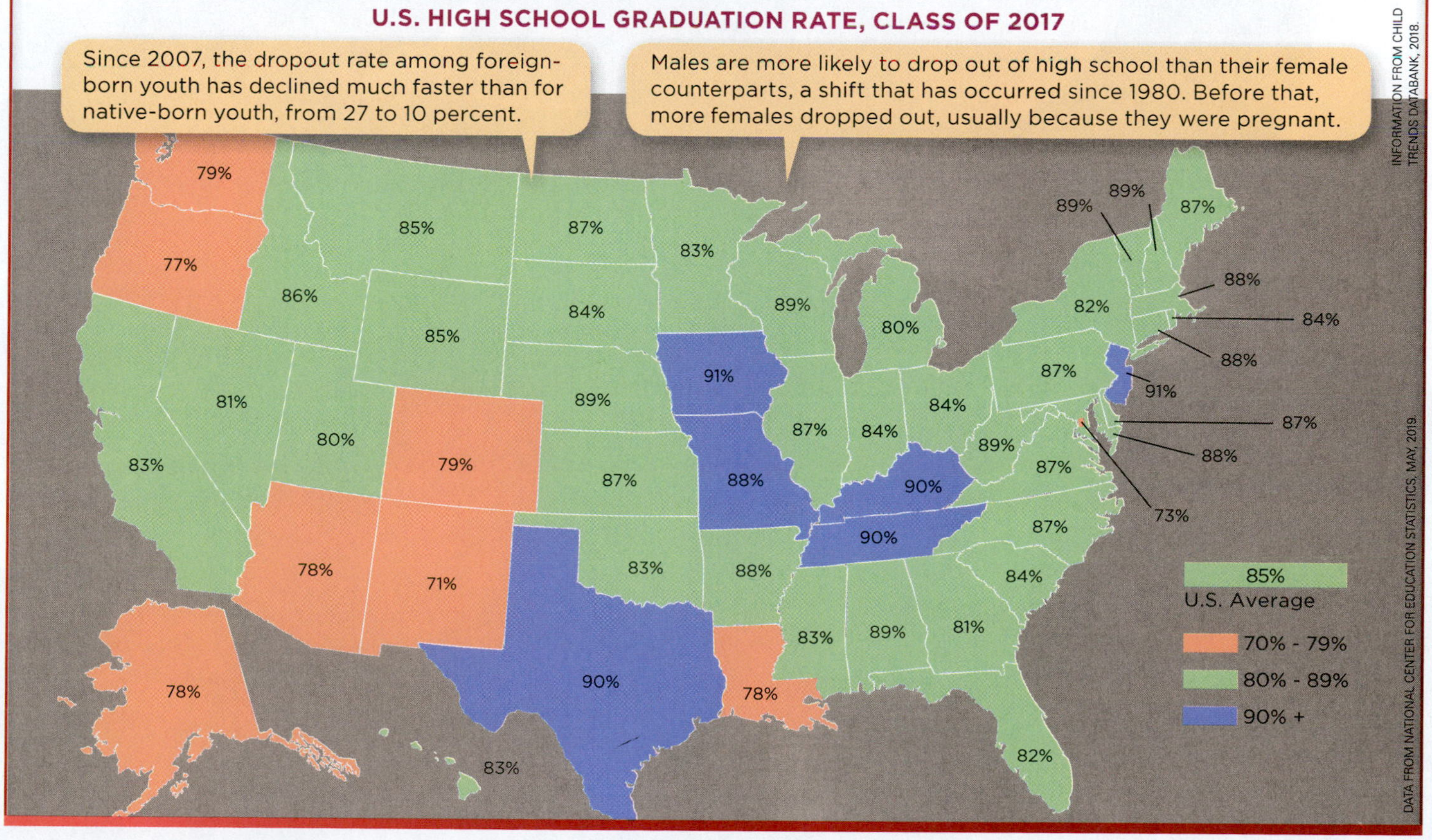

U.S. HIGH SCHOOL GRADUATION RATE, CLASS OF 2017
Since 2007, the dropout rate among foreign-born youth has declined much faster than for native-born youth, from 27 to 10 percent.
Males are more likely to drop out of high school than their female counterparts, a shift that has occurred since 1980. Before that, more females dropped out, usually because they were pregnant.
85% U.S. Average
70% - 79%
80% - 89%
90% +
INFORMATION FROM CHILD TRENDS DATABANK, 2018.
DATA FROM NATIONAL CENTER FOR EDUCATION STATISTICS, MAY, 2019.

CHAPTER 16

Adolescence: Psychosocial Development

What Will You Know?

1. Why might a teenager be into sports one year and into books the next?
2. Should parents back off when their teenager disputes every rule, wish, or suggestion they make?
3. Should we worry more about teen suicide or juvenile delinquency?
4. Why are adolescents forbidden to drink and smoke while adults are free to do so?

- **Identity**
  - Not Yet Achieved
  - Arenas of Identity Formation
- **Close Relationships**
  - Family
  - A VIEW FROM SCIENCE: Teens and Genes
  - Peer Power
  - A CASE TO STUDY: The Naiveté of Your Author
  - Learning About Sex
- **Sadness and Anger**
  - Depression
  - Delinquency and Defiance
  - INSIDE THE BRAIN: Impulses, Rewards, and Reflection
- **Drug Use and Abuse**
  - Age Trends
  - Harm from Drugs
  - OPPOSING PERSPECTIVES: E-Cigarettes: Path to Addiction or Health?
  - Preventing Drug Abuse: What Works?
- **CAREER ALERT: The Teacher**
- **VISUALIZING DEVELOPMENT: Adolescent Bullying**

It's not easy being a teenager, as the two previous chapters make clear, but neither is it easy being the parent of one. Sometimes I was too lenient. For example, once one of my daughters came home late. I was worried and angry but did not think about punishing her until she asked, "How long am I grounded?"

And sometimes I was too strict. For years, I insisted that my children wash the dinner dishes—until they told me, again and again, that none of their friends had such mean mothers.

At times, I reacted emotionally, not rationally. When our children were infants, my husband and I decided how we would deal with adolescent problems. We were ready to be firm, united, and consistent regarding illicit drugs, unsafe sex, and serious lawbreaking. More than a decade later, none of those issues appeared.

Instead, their clothing, neatness, and homework made us impatient, bewildered, inconsistent. My husband said, "I knew they would become adolescents. I didn't know we would become parents of adolescents."

This chapter is about adolescents' psychosocial development, including relationships with friends, parents, and the larger society. It begins with identity and ends with drugs, both of which may seem to be a personal choice but actually are strongly affected by social norms. I now understand that my children's actions and my reactions were influenced by our history (I washed family dishes) and by current norms (their friends did not).

Identity

Psychosocial development during adolescence is often understood as a search for a consistent understanding of oneself. Self-expression and self-concept become increasingly important at puberty. Each young person wants to know, "Who am I?"

According to Erik Erikson, life's fifth psychosocial crisis is **identity versus role confusion:** Working through the complexities of finding one's own identity is the primary task of adolescence (Erikson, 1968/1994).

Erikson believed that this crisis is resolved with **identity achievement**, when adolescents have reconsidered the goals and values of their parents and culture,

Left: Marc Romanelli/Tetra images/Getty Images
Top: Pixel-Shot/Shutterstock.com

No Role Confusion These are high school students in Junior ROTC training camp. For many youths who cannot afford college, the military offers a temporary identity—complete with haircut, uniform, and comrades.

accepting some and discarding others, while forging their own identity. This requires combining emotional separation from childhood and ongoing trust in parents, a difficult task in any nation (Sugimura et al., 2018).

Identity achievement entails neither wholesale rejection nor unquestioning acceptance of social norms. Teenagers maintain continuity with the past so that they can move toward the future, establishing their own identity. Simply following parental footsteps does not work, because the social context of each generation differs.

Not Yet Achieved

Over the past half-century, major psychosocial shifts have lengthened the duration of adolescence and made identity achievement more complex (Côté & Levine, 2015). How adolescents go about their search for identity also varies depending on genes, the social context, and whether their family encourages discussion (Markovitch et al., 2017).

Erikson argued that identity was a psychosocial need for every adolescent. Some react to the emotional stress of this crisis with actions that seem pathological. An expert warns against diagnosing adolescents by adult standards of mental illness and thus misunderstanding that the identity search is a time-limited condition (Côté, 2018).

One developmental scholar provided a useful expansion of Erikson's description of adolescence. James Marcia outlined four ways in which young people cope with their identity crisis: (1) role confusion, (2) foreclosure, (3) moratorium, and finally (4) achievement (Marcia, 1966; Kroger & Marcia, 2011).

Role confusion is the opposite of achievement. It is characterized by lack of commitment to any goals or values.

Identity **foreclosure** occurs when, in order to avoid the confusion of sorting through all the nuances of who they are and what they believe, young people lump traditional roles and values together, to be swallowed whole or rejected totally. They might follow every custom from their parents or culture, never exploring alternatives.

Some do the opposite, foreclosing on an oppositional, *negative identity*—rejecting all their elders' values and routines, again without thoughtful questioning. Foreclosure is comfortable but limiting. It is only a temporary shelter (Meeus, 2011).

A more mature shelter is **moratorium**, a time-out that includes exploration, either in breadth (trying many things) or in depth (following one path but with only tentative commitment). Finally, achievement is attained in adulthood, explained in Chapter 19.

identity versus role confusion Erikson's term for the fifth stage of development, in which the person tries to figure out "Who am I?" but is confused as to which of many possible roles to adopt.

identity achievement Erikson's term for the attainment of identity, or the point at which a person understands who he or she is as a unique individual, in accord with past experiences and future plans.

role confusion A situation in which an adolescent does not seem to know or care what his or her identity is. (Sometimes called *identity diffusion* or *role diffusion*.)

foreclosure Erikson's term for premature identity formation, which occurs when an adolescent adopts his or her parents' or society's roles and values wholesale, without questioning or analysis.

moratorium An adolescent's choice of a socially acceptable way to postpone making identity-achievement decisions. Going to college is a common example.

Arenas of Identity Formation

Erikson (1968/1994) highlighted four aspects of identity: religious, political, vocational, and sexual. Terminology and timing have changed, yet adolescents still seek identity in all of these domains.

Here we describe the process in three of Erikson's original four domains (religious, political, and gender) and in another domain that is crucial today—ethnic identity. (Vocational identity is discussed in Chapter 19.)

Religious Identity Most adolescents question some aspects of their faith, but their *religious identity* is similar to that of their parents. Few reject their religion if they have been raised in it, especially if they have a good relationship with their parents (Kim-Spoon et al., 2012).

Most of the research has been on Christian youth in Western nations. However, a recent study of mostly Buddhist young people in Japan confirmed that adolescents in every nation seek to establish their own religious beliefs and practices (Sugimura et al., 2019).

Some adolescents become more devout. A Muslim girl might start to wear a headscarf, a Catholic boy might study for the priesthood, a Baptist teenager might join a Pentecostal youth group, all surprising their parents.

The more common pattern is in the opposite direction: Attendance at places of worship gradually decreases (Lopez et al., 2011). Adolescents question "organized religion" because it seems to be a package of beliefs and rituals. They reexamine each part of the package, seeking their own way to be spiritual yet open (Saroglou, 2012).

ARMEND NIMANI/AFP/Getty Images

Jim West/The Image Works

Same Situation, Far Apart: Religious Identity Awesome devotion is characteristic of adolescents, whether devotion is to a sport, a person, a music group, or—as shown here—a religion. This boy *(left)* praying on a Kosovo street is part of a dangerous protest against the town's refusal to allow building another mosque. This girl *(right)* is at a stadium rally for young Christians in Michigan, declaring her faith for all to see. While adults see differences between the two religions, both teens share not only piety but also twenty-first-century clothing. Her T-shirt is a recent innovation, and on his jersey is Messi 10, for a soccer star born in Argentina.

Political Identity Parents also influence their children's *political identity*. In the twenty-first century, more U.S. adults identify as nonpartisan (38 percent) than Republican (26 percent), or Democrat (26 percent), or any other party (5 percent) (Pew Research Center, March 14, 2019). Their teenage children reflect their views, some boasting that they vote for the person, not the party, or that they do not care about politics, echoing their parents without realizing it.

Some proudly vote at age 18—an event that is much more likely if they are living at home and their parents are voting than if they have already left home. Just like other aspects of political involvement, voting is a social activity (Hart & Van Goethem, 2017).

In general, adolescents' interest in politics is predicted by their parents' involvement and by current events (Stattin et al., 2017). Adolescents tend to be more liberal than their elders, especially on social issues (LGBTQ rights, reproduction, the environment), but major political shifts do not usually occur until later (P. Taylor, 2014).

Ethnic Identity Related to political identity is *ethnic identity,* a topic not discussed by Erikson. In the United States and Canada, about half of all current adolescents are of African, Asian, Latinx, or Native American (Aboriginal in Canada) heritage. Many of them also have ancestors of another ethnic group. Those census categories are too broad; teenagers must forge a personal ethnic identity that is more specific.

Hispanic youth, for instance, must figure out how having grandparents from Mexico, Peru, Cuba, and/or California, Texas, or New York affects them. Many Latinx individuals (some identifying as *Chicano*) also have ancestors from Spain, Africa, Germany, and/or indigenous groups such as the Maya or Inca.

Unlike African American parents, who often prepare their children for possible prejudice, few White parents discuss race and ethnicity with their children (Loyd & Gaither, 2018). Thus, when most White children move past concrete operational thought, they need to figure out ethnic identity without parental help. For every adolescent, of every background, peers help sort through stereotypes, resistance, and finally achievement (Santos et al., 2017).

Establishing a solid ethnic identity is especially difficult for adolescents who are multiracial, or immigrants, or adopted by parents of another background. Interestingly, biracial youth tend to identify with the minority ethnic group. If they are not accepted by that group, they may be depressed (Nishina et al., 2018). Every adolescent seeks identity.

macmillan learning

VIDEO ACTIVITY: Adolescence Around the World: Rites of Passage presents a comparison of adolescent initiation customs in industrialized and developing societies.

THINK CRITICALLY: Since identity is formed lifelong, is your current identity different from what it was five years ago?

The Opposite Sex? Every cohort of adolescents rebels against the conventions of the older generations. Earlier generations of boys grew their hair long. A decade later, some girls shaved their heads. Now many teenagers do not see male and female as opposites, choosing instead a nonbinary approach to gender expression.

In general, pride in ethnic identity correlates with academic achievement and overall well-being, but the relationship is "complex and nuanced" (Miller-Cotto & Byrnes, 2016, p. 67). Interestingly, a strong ethnic identity in early adolescence correlates with intergroup contact later on (Meeus, 2017). It seems that once adolescents are secure in their, they can befriend people of other ethnic groups. In the twenty-first century, ethnic identity continues to develop.

Gender Identity As you remember, *sex* refers to certain physical and genetic traits assigned at birth, whereas *gender* refers to the cultural and social genetic factors that differentiate males, females, and nonbinary individuals. A half-century ago, psychoanalytic theorists did not understand this distinction. They assumed that adolescents needed to adopt male or female roles (Erikson, 1968/1994; A. Freud, 1958/2000).

Thus, adolescence was once time for "gender intensification," when people increasingly identified as one or the other of two opposites, male or female. No longer (Priess et al., 2009). Erikson's term *sexual identity* has been replaced by **gender identity,** which is much more varied than the old dichotomy assumed.

gender identity A person's acceptance of the roles and behaviors that society associates with the biological categories of male and female.

Many adolescents use analytic, hypothetical thinking to question gender expression. This may trouble their elders, who have traditional expectations. One mother thought she was guiding her daughter into a proper female role when she suggested that her daughter's skirt was too tight. Her daughter replied, "Don't slut-shame me."

The speed and specifics of changing gender roles vary dramatically by culture and cohort. A new term, *cisgender,* refers to people whose gender identity is the same as their natal sex. The existence of the term is evidence of the complexity of sex and gender. Interestingly, adolescent boys more than girls express anti-gay attitudes, probably because boys experience stronger pressures to conform to traditional, heterosexual, male identity (Horn, 2019).

As more young people identify as lesbian, gay, bisexual, transgender, or queer (those who reject existing terms related to sexual orientation or gender identity), heterosexual adolescents distinguish between policy and their personal attitudes. They tend to endorse equal rights, even when they, personally, are unwilling to have a friend who is LGBTQ (Horn, 2019).

Identity and Depression All adolescents are vulnerable to feelings of depression and anxiety as they try to sort out their identity. This is true for religious, political, and ethnic identity, but it is particularly apparent regarding gender identity.

Among Western psychiatrists in former decades, people who had "a strong and persistent cross-gender identification" were said to have *gender identity disorder,* a serious diagnosis according to DSM-IV. However, the DSM-5 instead describes *gender dysphoria,* when people are distressed at the gender that was assigned to them at birth.

This is more than a change in terminology. A "disorder" means something is amiss with the individual, no matter how he or she feels about it, whereas "dysphoria" means the problem is in the distress, which can be mitigated by social conditions, by cognitive framing, or by becoming the other gender. As with all aspects of the identity crisis, self-definition and then acceptance is the psychosocial need.

WHAT HAVE YOU LEARNED?

1. What is Erikson's fifth psychosocial crisis, and how is it resolved?
2. How does identity foreclosure differ from identity moratorium?
3. What role do parents play in adolescent religious and political identity?
4. How does ethnic identity affect self-esteem and achievement?
5. What assumptions about gender identity did most adults hold 50 years ago?
6. What is the difference between gender identity disorder and gender dysphoria?

Close Relationships

The focus on adolescent identity may make it seem as if teenagers are intensely individualized, unaffected by the social environment surrounding them. However, the opposite is more accurate. Parents, peers, grandparents, siblings, teachers, and cultures shape adolescent lives (Seaton et al., 2017).

Family

Family relationships affect identity, expectations, and daily life. Parents shift from providing direct guidance to being available, but close parent–child relationships continue (E. Chen et al., 2017).

Siblings also become influential, as role models and confidants as well as more directly by bullying or protecting each other (Gallagher et al., 2018; Aizpitarte et al., 2019). This is especially important if the environment and genetic tendencies push teens toward negative behavior (see A View from Science).

Peers do not replace parents; they supplement them. A longitudinal study of all middle school students in one community (almost 800 of them) found that three-fourths had healthy relationships with their parents *and* peers. That protected them from serious problems during adolescence and early adulthood (Dishion et al., 2019).

A VIEW FROM SCIENCE

Teens and Genes

Sometimes observers imagine that the biology of adolescence, with puberty and the drive for autonomy, is so strong that family influences fade. But, as already explained in Chapter 1, nature and nurture always interact. Thus, we need to avoid attributing teenage rebellion to the child, or to the parents, or to society. All of these matter.

Developmentalists try to connect molecular genetics with practical programs that allow individuals to help each other. A leading researcher, Gene Brody, has done that. He warns of overreliance on genetic analysis, even as he lauds genetic research (Brody, 2017).

Brody's lifelong work has been to help African American boys in rural Georgia, a "resource-poor" social context. He developed an intervention for parents and their 11-year-old sons in this area.

Brody was not positive that the intervention would succeed, so he randomly assigned half of a group of 611 parent–son pairs to a control group, with no special intervention. The other half were taught in small groups, with seven two-hour sessions designed to foster healthy parent–child relationships (Brody et al., 2009).

Leaders of those sessions were energetic and creative, and they were good role models: Most were African American men who had grown up in the same communities as the boys.

Parents and sons were taught separately for an hour and then brought together. Teaching was active, with discussion and role-playing. In designing the classes, Brody benefited from earlier research by other scientists. He knew that learning depends on carefully structured social interaction.

The parents learned:

- The importance of being nurturing and involved
- The importance of conveying racial pride
- How monitoring benefits adolescents
- Why clear norms and expectations reduce substance use
- How to talk about sex

The 11-year-olds learned:

- The importance of household rules
- Adaptive behaviors when encountering racism
- The need to plan for the future
- The differences between them and peers who use alcohol

After the first hour, parents and sons were engaged in games and exercises designed to improve family communication and cohesion. Three years after the intervention, both the experimental and control groups were reassessed regarding sex and alcohol/drug activity.

The initial results were disappointing. The intervention decreased early sex, drinking, and smoking, but not by much. Apparently, the social context of rural Georgia was more powerful for those teenage boys than the intervention.

Then, four years after the study began, research was published that the short allele of the 5-HTTLPR gene heightened risks of depression, delinquency, and other problems. Might this apply to these African American teenagers?

Brody tracked down his original groups, now 16 years old. He convinced them to donate saliva to be analyzed for the 5-HTTLPR allele. As **Figure 16.1** shows, the training had a definitive effect on those who were genetically vulnerable. Encouraged, the researchers continued to follow those boys. Benefits continued, at least until age 20 (E. Chen et al., 2017).

How could 14 or fewer hours of parent–son training, at age 11, affect vulnerable adolescents for a decade, despite toxic influences of the environment? Apparently, those seven sessions gave insights, instilled habits, and made connections that affected parent/child relationships.

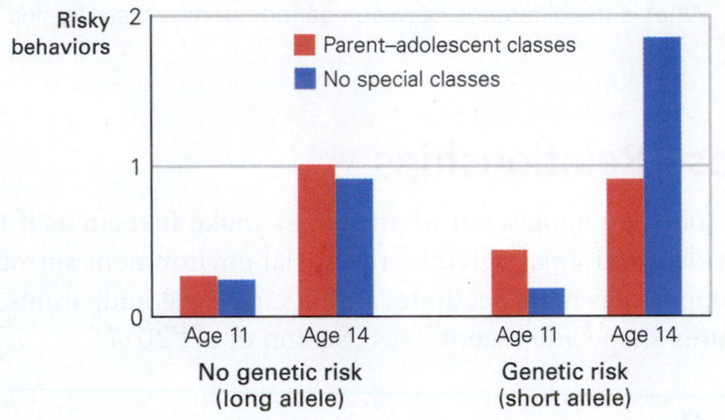

Data from Brody et al., 2009.

FIGURE 16.1

Not Yet The risk score was a simple one point for each of the following: had drunk alcohol, had smoked marijuana, had had sex. As shown, most of the 11-year-olds had done none of these. By age 14, most had done one (usually had drunk beer or wine)—except for those at genetic risk who did not have the seven-session training. Some of them had done all three, and many had done at least two. As you see, for those youths without genetic risk, the usual parenting was no better or worse than the parenting that benefited from the special classes: The average 14-year-old in either group had tried only one risky behavior. But for those at genetic risk, the special program made a decided difference.

Family Conflict The fact that families are influential does not mean that family life is peaceful. Disputes are common when biology, cognition, and culture all push for adolescent independence, while parents want to provide control and protection. Each generation tends to misjudge the other. Adolescents are quick to judge parents as disrespectful; parents worry that adolescents are pressured by peers to rebel.

THINK CRITICALLY: When do parents forbid an activity that they should approve of, or ignore a behavior that should alarm them?

All close relationships include conflict. The peace that results from neglect is destructive. Indeed, some developmentalists think that conflict is a useful step toward understanding and emotional growth (Branje, 2018).

Authors of research on mothers and their adolescents suggest that "although too much anger may be harmful . . . some expression of anger may be adaptive" (Hofer et al., 2013, p. 276). In this study, as well as generally, the parent–child relationship usually improved with time as both parties adjust to the adolescent's increasing independence.

Crucial is that caregivers avoid extremes of strictness or leniency but instead maintain support while increasing autonomy (Yeager et al., 2018). As a review of dozens of studies expressed it: "parent–adolescent conflict might signal the need for families to adapt and change . . . to accommodate adolescents' increasing needs for independence and egalitarianism" (Weymouth et al., 2016, p. 107).

Closeness Within the Family

Several specific aspects of parent–child relationships have been studied. Specifically:

1. Communication (Do family members talk openly and honestly?)
2. Support (Do family members rely on each other?)
3. Connectedness (How emotionally close are family members?)
4. Control (Do parents allow independence?)

No social scientist doubts that the first two, communication and support, are crucial. Patterns from childhood continue, ideally buffering the turbulence of adolescence. Regarding the next two, connectedness and control, consequences vary and observers differ in what they see. How do you react to this example, written by one of my students?

> I got pregnant when I was sixteen years old, and if it weren't for the support of my parents, I would probably not have my son. And if they hadn't taken care of him, I wouldn't have been able to finish high school or attend college. My parents also helped me overcome the shame that I felt when . . . my aunts, uncles, and especially my grandparents found out that I was pregnant.
>
> [I., *personal communication*]

Barbara Smaller/The New Yorker Collection/Cartoonbank.com.

"So I blame you for everything—whose fault is that?"

Not My Fault Humans always find it easier to blame someone else, but this is particularly true when teenage girls talk to their mothers.

My student's boyfriend is no longer part of her life. She is grateful that she still lives with her parents, who care for her son. However, did motherhood make her dependent on her parents, preventing her from establishing her own identity? Why didn't her parents monitor her romantic relationship, or at least explain contraception? Is this the best or the worst of parent–adolescent relationships?

One issue here is **parental monitoring**—that is, parental knowledge about each child's whereabouts, activities, and companions. Many studies have shown that when parental knowledge arises from a warm, supportive relationship, adolescents usually become confident, well-educated adults, avoiding drugs and risky sex.

parental monitoring Parents' ongoing awareness of what their children are doing, where, and with whom.

However, if parents are cold and punitive, monitoring may lead to rebellion. If mothers are too controlling, adolescents are likely to become depressed and anxious; if fathers are too controlling, adolescents may develop substance abuse disorders (Eun et al., 2018).

There is a "dynamic interplay between parent and child behaviors," which affects the results of monitoring. Teenagers choose what to reveal (Abar et al., 2014, p. 2177). They are more likely to lie if their parents are controlling and cold (Lushin et al., 2017).

macmillan learning

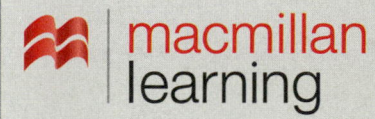

VIDEO: Parenting in Adolescence examines how family structure can help or hinder parent–teen relationships.

Cultural Expectations for Parents of Teenagers

Several researchers have compared parent–child relationships in various cultures: Everywhere, parent–child communication and encouragement reduce teenage depression, suicide, and low self-esteem, and increase motivation and achievement. However, details of expectations, interactions, and behavior vary by culture (Brown & Bakken, 2011).

Parent–child conflict is less evident in cultures that stress **familism**, the belief that family members should sacrifice personal freedom and success to care for one another. For example, most refugee youth (Palestinian, Syrian, Iraqi) in Jordan agree that parents have the right to decide their children's hairstyles, clothes, and music—contrary to what most U.S. teenagers believe (Smetana et al., 2016).

familism The belief that family members should support one another, sacrificing individual freedom and success, if necessary, in order to preserve family unity and protect the family from outside forces

In many traditional cultures, teens do not tell their parents whatever they have done that might earn disapproval. By contrast, some U.S. adolescents deliberately provoke an argument by advocating marijuana legalization, LGBTQ acceptance, citizenship for immigrants, or abortion access, especially if they personally are not affected by those policies.

EyesWideOpen/Getty Images

More Familiar Than Foreign? Even in cultures with strong and traditional family influence, teenagers choose to be with peers whenever they can. These boys play at Cherai Beach in India.

Observation Quiz What evidence do you see that traditional norms remain in this culture? (see answer, page 426)

Cultural variations in parent–child interaction are evident not only between nations but also within U.S. ethnic groups. This is illustrated by a longitudinal study of Mexican American adolescents (Wheeler et al., 2017). Unlike their more Americanized peers, those who strongly endorsed familism were more obedient to their parents and were less likely to quit school, join gangs, or carry a weapon.

Personality also matters, with differential susceptibility. Impulsive, fearful, or adventurous adolescents take *more* risks than average *unless* their family is supportive, in which case they are *less* likely to break the law than the average adolescent (Rioux et al., 2016).

This contrast is evident in academic achievement as well. A longitudinal study found that when parents are relatively harsh at puberty, fewer students who are capable of college actually enroll. Gender matters in exactly what they do instead of gaining more education: Boys are likely to break the law; girls to become pregnant (Hentges & Wang, 2018).

Peer Power

Peers are also crucial. They help each other navigate the physical changes of puberty, the intellectual challenges of high school, and the social challenges of leaving childhood. They also share emotions, and by so doing become closer friends (von Salisch, 2018).

Peers and Parents Peers do not negate the need for parental support: Healthy relationships with parents during childhood enhance later friendships and foster reciprocal romances (Flynn et al., 2017). However, parents alone are not enough.

For example, in one experiment, children and adolescents had to give a speech, with or without their parents present. For 9-year-olds, their parents' presence relieved stress, as indicated by lower levels of cortisol, as well as by visible signs. For 15-year-olds, however, the parents' presence was no help (Hostinar et al., 2015).

Other research confirms that parental buffering of stress is less effective in adolescence than it was earlier in childhood. Peers may or may not be able to reduce stress. Sometimes, when friends help with speech preparation for instance, stress increases (Doom et al., 2017).

peer pressure Encouragement to conform to one's friends or contemporaries in behavior, dress, and attitude; usually considered a negative force, as when adolescent peers encourage one another to defy adult authority.

THINK CRITICALLY: Why is peer pressure thought to be much more sinister than it actually is?

Peer pressure refers to someone being pushed by their friends to do something that they would not do alone. Peer pressure is especially strong in early adolescence, when adults seem clueless about biological and social stresses. Some teenagers are more susceptible to peer pressure than others. Gender is one factor. Boys influence other boys more than girls influence other girls (McCoy et al., 2019).

Adults warn children against peer pressure, but they should be more nuanced. Sometimes having friends is beneficial: Peers pressure each other to study, to apply to college, to plan for their future.

The Immediacy of Peers Given the areas of the brain that are quickest to myelinate and mature in adolescence, it is not surprising that the most influential peers are those nearby at the moment. This was found in a study in which all eleventh-graders in several public schools in Los Angeles were offered a free online SAT prep course (worth $200) that they could take if they signed up on a paper distributed by the organizers (Bursztyn & Jensen, 2015).

In this study, students were *not* allowed to talk before deciding whether or not to accept the offer. So, they did not know that, although all of the papers had identical, detailed descriptions of the SAT program, one word differed in who would learn of their decision—either no other students or only the students in that particular class.

The two versions were:

- *Your decision to sign up for the course will be kept completely private from everyone, except the other students in the room.*
- *Your decision to sign up for the course will be kept completely private from everyone, including the other students in the room.*

It mattered whether students thought their classmates would learn of their decision: The honors students were *more* likely to sign up, and the non-honors students *less* likely when they thought their classmates would know what they did.

To make sure this was a peer effect, not just divergent motivation and ability between honors and non-honors students, the researchers compared students who took exactly two honors classes and several non-honors classes. There were 107 such students, some who happened to be in their honors class when they decided whether or not to sign up for SAT prep and some who happened to be in their non-honors class.

When the decisions of those two-honors students were kept totally private, acceptance rates were similar (72 and 79 percent) no matter which class students were in at the moment. But, if students thought their classmates might know their decision, imagined peer pressure affected them. When sitting with other students in an honors class, 97 percent signed up for the SAT program. Of those sitting in a non-honors class, only 54 percent signed up (Bursztyn & Jensen, 2015).

Especially for Parents of a Teenager Your 13-year-old comes home after a sleepover at a friend's house with a new, weird hairstyle—perhaps cut or colored in a bizarre manner. What do you say and do? (see response, page 426)

Selecting Friends Peers *can* lead one another into trouble. A study of substance misuse and delinquency among twins found that—even controlling for genes and environment—when one twin became a delinquent, the other was more likely to do so (Laursen et al., 2017).

A CASE TO STUDY

The Naiveté of Your Author

Adults are sometimes unaware of adolescents' desire for respect from their classmates. I did not recognize this with my own children:

- Our oldest daughter wore the same pair of jeans in tenth grade, day after day. She washed them each night by hand, and I put them in the dryer early each morning. [Circadian rhythm—I was asleep hours before she was, and awake hours earlier.] My husband was bewildered. "Is this some weird female ritual?" he asked. Years later, our daughter explained that she was afraid that if she wore different pants each day, her classmates would think she cared about her clothes, which would prompt them to criticize her choices. To avoid that imaginary audience, she wore only one pair of jeans.
- Our second daughter, at 16, pierced her ears for the third time. I asked if this meant she would do drugs; she laughed at my foolishness. Only later did I notice that many of her friends also had multiple holes in their ear lobes.
- At age 15, our third daughter was diagnosed with cancer. My husband and I weighed opinions from four physicians, each explaining treatment that would minimize the risk of death. She had other priorities: "I don't care what you choose, as long as I keep my hair." (Now her health is good; her hair grew back.)
- Our youngest, in sixth grade, refused to wear her jacket (it was new; she had chosen it), even in midwinter. Years later she told me why—she wanted her classmates to think she was tough.

In retrospect, I am amazed that I was unaware of the power of peers, a stronger immediate influence than self-acceptance, personal choice, long life, or even a warm body.

Matthew Staver/Bloomberg via Getty Images

Everyday Danger After cousins Alex and Arthur, here ages 16 and 20, followed family wishes to shovel snow around their Denver, Colorado, home, they followed their inner risk impulses and jumped from the roof. Not every young man can afford the expense of motocross or hang gliding, but almost every one of them leaps into risks that few 40-year-olds would dare.

deviancy training Destructive peer support in which one person shows another how to rebel against authority or social norms.

Collectively, peers provide **deviancy training**, whereby one person shows another how to resist social norms (Van Ryzin & Dishion, 2013; Dishion et al., 2001). However, innocent teens are not corrupted by deviants. Adolescents choose their friends and models—not always wisely, but never randomly.

A developmental progression can be traced: The combination of "problem behavior, school marginalization, and low academic performance" at age 11 leads to gang involvement two years later, deviancy training two years after that, and violent behavior at age 18 or 19 (Dishion et al., 2010, p. 603).

Friends not only teach each other, they encourage each other. This is shown in *coercive joining*, when two people join together in making derogatory comments about a third person. A pair of teenagers may compete in who can make the most pointed criticisms. Coercive joining at age 12 predicts antisocial violence at age 21 (Dishion et al., 2019).

This cascade is not inevitable; adults need to connect with 12-year-olds instead of blaming their friends. Young adolescents who have healthy relationships with their parents are less likely to use drugs or to be convicted of violent crimes later on (Dishion et al., 2019).

Teachers are crucial as well: If young adolescents are mildly disruptive (e.g., they don't follow directions), they are not necessarily headed for trouble. However, if their teachers are sarcastic, demeaning, and rigid, teenagers are more likely to select other troubled students as friends and become more defiant themselves (Shin & Ryan, 2017).

To further understand the impact of peers, two concepts are helpful: *selection* and *facilitation*. Teenagers *select* friends with similar values and interests, abandoning former friends with other interests. Then, friends *facilitate* destructive or constructive behaviors.

It is easier to do wrong ("Let's all skip school on Friday") or right ("Let's study together for the chem exam") with friends. Peer facilitation helps adolescents do things they are unlikely to do alone. This provides an important clue for adults who want to halt destructive patterns in adolescents. Grouping troubled adolescents together might make all of them worse, not better (Lochman et al., 2015).

Thus, adolescents select and facilitate, choose and are chosen. Happy, energetic, and successful teens have close friends who themselves are high achievers, with no major emotional problems.

The opposite also holds: Those who are drug users, sexually active, and alienated from school choose compatible friends. In general, peers provide opportunity, companionship, and encouragement for what young adolescents already might do.

Research on teenage alcohol abuse finds that selection *precedes* peer pressure (Osgood et al., 2013). Similarly, with early sexual activity, selection was the crucial peer influence on behavior (van de Bongardt et al., 2015).

Selection and facilitation are evident lifelong, but the balance between the two shifts. Early adolescence is a time of selection; facilitation is more evident in later adolescence. In emerging adulthood, after age 18 or so, selection becomes important again, as young adults abandon some high school friends and establish new ones (Samek et al., 2016).

Romantic Partners Selection is obvious in romance. Adolescents choose and are chosen by romantic partners, and then they influence each other on almost everything—sex, music, work, play, education, food, and so on. Even small things matter: If one gets a new jacket, or tattoo, or sunglasses, the other might too.

Teens' first romances typically occur in high school, with girls having a steady partner more often than boys. Exclusive commitment is the ideal, but the fluidity and rapidity of the selection process mitigate against permanency.

macmillan learning

VIDEO: Romantic Relationships in Adolescence explores teens' attitudes and assumptions about romance and sexuality.

Cheating, flirting, switching, and disloyalty are rife. Breakups are common, as are unreciprocated crushes. Emotions range from exhilaration to despair, leading to impulsive sex, cruel revenge, and deep depression.

Peer support is vital: Friends help adolescents cope with ups and downs. They also make sexual intercourse either more likely or less likely. Their peers' actual experience is not as influential as the perception of their peers' activity. Thus, friends influence each other by talking about what they are doing: The one who brags is more influential than the one who stays quiet.

Consequently, although young teens are especially vulnerable to sexual abuse, teen romances are not necessarily harmful. Chapter 14 discusses many potential problems with early sexual experience, and Chapter 15 explains harm in sexting. But most online connections between romantic partners are benign—more bonding than destructive, more voluntary than coerced (Englander, 2015; Burén & Lunde, 2018).

Further, most peer relationships are asexual. Most teenagers have platonic friends of all genders (Kreager et al., 2016), and they have romances that do not include intercourse. For specifics of romance, peer norms vary from group to group, school to school, city to city, nation to nation. For instance, twice as many high school students in Cleveland as in San Francisco say they have had intercourse (46 percent versus 22 percent) (MMWR, June 15, 2018).

Hero Images/Getty Images

Hang Loose? Are these two dating couples or a group of friends at the basketball court? Notice who has the ball and who does not want to show her face.

Same-Sex Romances Some adolescents are attracted to peers of the same sex. **Sexual orientation** refers to the direction of a person's erotic desires. One meaning of *orient* is "to turn toward"; thus, sexual orientation refers to whether a person is attracted to (turned on by) people of the other sex, the same sex, or both sexes. Sexual orientation can be strong, weak, overt, secret, or unconscious.

sexual orientation A term that refers to whether a person is sexually and romantically attracted to others of the same sex, the opposite sex, or both sexes.

Obviously, culture and cohort are powerful (Bailey et al., 2016) (see **Figure 16.2**). Some cultures accept youth who are gay, lesbian, bisexual, or transgender (the census in India gives people three choices: male, female, or Hijra [transgender]). Other cultures criminalize LGBTQ youth (38 of the 53 African nations), even killing them (Uganda).

Worldwide, many gay and lesbian teens date the other sex to hide their orientation; this deception puts them at risk for binge drinking, suicidal thoughts, and drug use. Those hazards are less common in cultures where same-sex partnerships are accepted, especially when parents affirm their offspring's sexuality.

At least in the United States, adolescents have similar difficulties and strengths whether they are gay or straight. Nonsexual friendships with peers of whatever orientation decrease loneliness and increase resilience (Van Harmelen et al., 2017). However, LGBTQ youth have a higher risk of depression and anxiety, for reasons from every level of Bronfenbrenner's ecological-systems approach (Mustanski et al., 2014). [**Life-SpanLink:** Ecological systems are described in Chapter 1.]

Bullying also targets sexual-minority adolescents. Interestingly, at puberty and in high school, bullying generally decreases for heterosexual youth but increases for LGBTQ youth (Sterzing et al., 2018).

As with gender identity, sexual orientation is surprisingly fluid during adolescence. In one study, 10 percent of sexually active teenagers had had

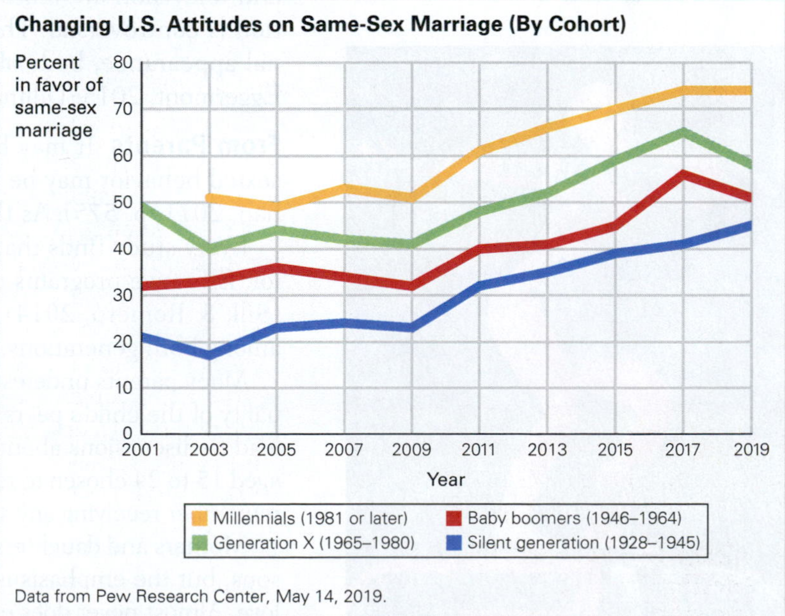

FIGURE 16.2
Young and Old Everyone knows that attitudes about same-sex relationships are changing. Less well-known is that cohort differences are greater than the shift over the first decade of the twenty-first century.

macmillan learning

Check out the **Data Connections activity Sexual Behaviors of U.S. High School Students,** which examines how sexually active teens really are.

same-sex partners, but many of those 10 percent nonetheless identified as heterosexual (Pathela & Schillinger, 2010). In that study, those most at risk of abusive relationships and sexually transmitted infections had partners of both sexes, a correlation also found in other studies (e.g., Russell et al., 2014).

Learning About Sex

Many adolescents have strong sexual urges but minimal logic about pregnancy, disease, lust, and love. Millions of teenagers worry that they are oversexed, undersexed, or deviant, unaware that thousands, maybe millions, of others have the same sexual needs. Gay, lesbian, and transgender teenagers may be especially troubled.

In 2010, several LGBTQ youth, aged 13 to 15, killed themselves, prompting 50,000 adults to post "It gets better" videos. They said that sexual orientation and gender identity becomes less burdensome in adulthood, a message that young people need to learn (Garrett, 2018).

Indeed, every young person has much to learn. As one observer wrote, adolescents "seem to waffle their way through sexually relevant encounters driven both by the allure of reward and the fear of negative consequences" (Wagner, 2011, p. 193). Where do they learn it?

From the Media Many adolescents learn about sex from the media. The Internet is a common source, particularly regarding sexually transmitted infections (Simon & Daneback, 2013). Unfortunately, Web sites are often frightening (pictures of diseased organs), mesmerizing (pornography), or misleading (offering false information).

Media consumption peaks in early adolescence. Television programs that attract teen audiences include sexual content almost seven times per hour (Steinberg & Monahan, 2011). That content is deceptive: Almost never does a character develop an STI, deal with an unwanted pregnancy, or mention (much less use) a condom.

Adolescents with intense exposure to sex in music, print, social media, film, and television are more often sexually active, but the direction of this correlation is controversial. The media may reinforce, but not cause, a focus on external appearance, body objectification, and thus sexual activity (Vandenbosch & Eggermont, 2015; Dillman Carpentier & Stevens, 2018).

Laura Cavanaugh/Getty Images

To Be a Woman Here Miley Cyrus performs for thousands of fans in Brooklyn, New York. Does pop culture make it difficult for teenagers of all genders to reconcile their own sexual impulses with the images of their culture?

From Parents It may be that "the most important influences on adolescents' sexual behavior may be closer to home than to Hollywood" (Steinberg & Monahan, 2011, p. 575). As that quote implies, sex education begins at home.

Every study finds that parental communication influences adolescents' behavior. Effective programs of sex education explicitly require parental participation (Silk & Romero, 2014). However, embarrassment and ignorance are common among both generations.

Many parents underestimate their own child's sexual activity while fearing the sexuality of the child's peers and the media (Elliott, 2012). However, those fears do not lead to discussions about sex, love, and life. According to a survey of young women aged 15 to 24 chosen to represent the U.S. population, only 25 percent of adolescents remember receiving any sex education from either parent (Vanderberg et al., 2016).

Mothers and daughters more often have detailed conversations than do fathers and sons, but the emphasis is on avoiding pregnancy and diseases, not on pleasure and love. Almost never does either generation share personal details (Coffelt, 2017).

From Peers Especially when parents are silent, forbidding, or vague, adolescent sexual behavior is strongly influenced by peers. Boys learn about sex from other boys (Henry et al., 2012), and girls learn from other girls, with the strongest influence being what peers say they have done, not something abstract (Choukas-Bradley et al., 2014).

Partners also teach each other. However, their lessons are more about pleasure than consequences: Few U.S. adolescent couples decide together *before* they have sex how they will prevent pregnancy and disease, and what they will do if their efforts fail.

When adolescents were asked with whom they discussed sexual issues, friends were the most common confidants, then parents, and last of all dating partners. Indeed, only half of the them had *ever* discussed specifics of sexual expression with a partner (Widman et al., 2014).

From Educators Sex education from teachers varies dramatically by school and by nation. The curriculum for middle schools in most European nations includes information about masturbation, same-sex romance, oral and anal sex, and uses and failure rates of methods of contraception. Those subjects are rarely covered in U.S. classes, even in high school.

Rates of teenage pregnancy in most European nations are less than half of those in the United States. Obviously, curriculum is part of the larger culture, and cultural differences regarding sex are vast, but sex education in schools is part of the reason.

Within the United States, the timing and content of sex education vary by state and by community. Some high schools provide comprehensive education, free condoms, and medical treatment; others provide nothing. Some school systems begin sex education in primary school; others wait until senior year of high school.

One controversy has been whether schools should teach that abstinence is the only acceptable strategy. Of course, abstaining from sex (including oral and anal sex) prevents STIs and avoids pregnancy, so some adults favor it.

But longitudinal data comparing students who had abstinence-only education with those who had comprehensive sex education, showed no difference in group averages for onset of sexual activity. Indeed, abstinence-only programs increase the rate of teen pregnancy and sexually transmitted infections, since students in those programs do not learn about preventive measures (Santelli et al., 2017; Fox et al., 2019).

Legislative support for abstinence-only education is an example of the problem described in Chapter 1: Opinions may ignore evidence (Hall et al., 2016).

Some adults present disease facts and morals to adolescents, yet teen behavior is driven by peer norms and emotions. Sexual behavior does not spring from the prefrontal cortex! Consequently, effective sex education must engage emotions and peer support (Suleiman & Brindis, 2014).

Most educators and developmentalists want sex education to begin early and to be medically accurate (Hall et al., 2016; Lindberg et al., 2016). Most parents, including those who are evangelical Christians, want schools to teach children to make responsible as well as fulfilling choices about sex (Dent & Maloney, 2017). Yet many schools do not do so.

Laugh and Learn Emotions are as crucial as facts in sex education.

Especially for Sex Educators Suppose adults in your community never talk to their children about sex or puberty. Is that a mistake? (see response, page 426)

THINK CRITICALLY: Why has sex education become a political issue?

WHAT HAVE YOU LEARNED?

1. Why do parents and adolescents often bicker?
2. How do parent–adolescent relationships change over time?
3. When is parental monitoring a sign of a healthy parent–adolescent relationship?
4. How do the influences of peers and parents differ for adolescents?
5. Why do many adults misunderstand the role of peer pressure?
6. How does culture affect sexual orientation?
7. From whom do adolescents usually learn about sex?
8. Why do some schools teach abstinence-only sex education?

CHAPTER APP 16

My3 - Support Network

RELATED TOPIC:
Suicidal ideation among adolescents

IOS:
https://tinyurl.com/yyzlpmqo

ANDROID:
https://tinyurl.com/qgsd6qb

My3—Support Network is a crisis support app for people who experience suicidal thoughts. Users choose three trusted people from their contacts list to place on the app (911 and the National Suicide Hotline are automatically listed). Users also create their own safety plan, listing warning signs, coping strategies, distractions, and their "reason to live." A resources page links users to organizations that address specific needs, such as suicide attempt survivors, LGBTQ youth, and more.

Sadness and Anger

Adolescence can be a wonderful time. Nonetheless, troubles plague about 20 percent of youths. For instance, one specific survey of more than 10,000 13- to 17-year-olds in the United States found that 23 percent had a psychological disorder in the past month (Kessler et al., 2012).

Most disorders are *comorbid*, with several problems occurring at once. Some are temporary—not too serious and soon outgrown. Parents and peers can help a sad or angry child regulate emotions, or they can push a teenager toward deep despair or life in prison.

Sadness and anger may become intense, chronic, even deadly. To provide the support that adolescents need, adults need to understand the when normal moodiness becomes pathological.

Depression

The general emotional trend from early childhood to early adolescence is toward less confidence and higher rates of depression. Then, gradually, self-esteem increases. A dip in self-esteem at puberty is found for children of every ethnicity and gender (Fredricks & Eccles, 2002; Greene & Way, 2005; Kutob et al., 2010; Zeiders et al., 2013b), with notable individual differences.

Some families expect high achievement from every adolescent, and then teens are quick to criticize themselves and everyone else when any sign of failure appears (Bleys et al., 2016). Perfectionism is considered to be one cause of teenage eating disorders, and high-SES girls are particularly vulnerable (Wade et al., 2019).

Generally, self-esteem tends to be higher in boys than in girls, higher in African Americans than in European Americans, who themselves have higher self-esteem than Latinx and Asian Americans. All studies find notable variability, and these trends are not universal. The immediate social context—in the school, the family, and the community—is crucial.

major depression Feelings of hopelessness, lethargy, and worthlessness that last two weeks or more.

For example, for immigrant Latinx youth with strong familism, ethnic pride is higher than for most other groups, and many increase in self-esteem over the years of adolescence. When compared to the high rates of depression among European American girls, the Latina rise in self-esteem from about age 16 is particularly notable (Zeiders et al., 2013b).

The likely reason is that family and cultural norms are protective. Latinas with high familism become increasingly helpful at home, which makes their parents appreciative and them proud, unlike other U.S. teenage girls.

Every subgroup is affected by current conditions, which may particularly affect today's Latinas. If adolescents of any gender or ethnicity have relatives who fear deportation, those teens experience sleep disturbances, lower school achievement, and other symptoms of depression, a major concern of developmentalists (Gulbas et al., 2016; Suárez-Orozco, 2017).

Sibling Rivalry? No! This Latina 15-year-old is a role model for her 11-year-old sister, evident here as she helps with homework.

Bruce Laurance/The Image Bank/Getty Images

Major Depressive Disorder Some adolescents sink into **major depression**, a deep sadness and hopelessness that disrupts all normal, regular activities. The causes predate adolescence, but puberty—with physical and emotional turbulence—pushes some vulnerable children, especially girls, into despair.

The rate of serious depression more than doubles during this time to an estimated 15 percent, affecting about 1 in 5 girls and 1 in 10 boys. This gender difference occurs for many reasons, biological and cultural. One study found that the short allele of the serotonin transporter promoter gene (5-HTTLPR) increased the rate of depression among girls everywhere but increased depression among boys only if they lived in low-SES communities (Uddin et al., 2010).

Why does neighborhood affect boys more than girls? Perhaps hormones depress females everywhere, but cultures protect boys unless jobs, successful adult men,

and encouragement within their community are scarce?

Suicide Serious, distressing thoughts about killing oneself (called **suicidal ideation**) are most common at about age 15. More than one-third (41 percent) of U.S. high school girls felt so hopeless that they stopped doing some usual activities for two weeks or more in the previous year (an indication of depression), and nearly one-fourth (22 percent) thought seriously about suicide. For boys the rates were 21 and 12 percent (MMWR, June 15, 2018).

Suicidal Ideation and Parasuicide Among U.S. High School Students

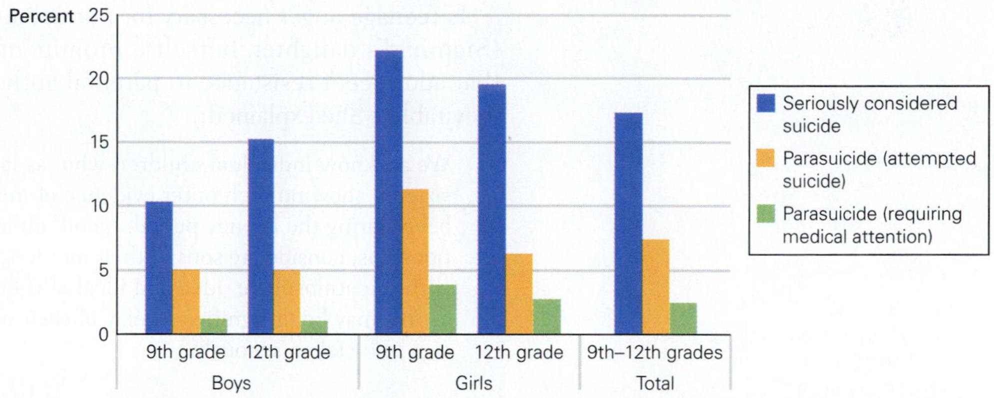

Data from MMWR, June 15, 2018.

FIGURE 16.3

Sad Thoughts Completed suicide is rare in adolescence, but serious thoughts about killing oneself are frequent. Depression and parasuicide are more common in girls than in boys, but rates are high even in boys. There are three reasons to suspect that the rates for boys are underestimates: Boys tend to be less aware of their emotions than girls are; boys consider it unmanly to try to kill themselves and to fail; and completed suicide is also higher in males than in females.

Observation Quiz Does thinking seriously about suicide increase or decrease during high school? (see answer, page 426) ↑

Suicidal ideation can lead to **parasuicide**, also called *attempted suicide* or *failed suicide.* Parasuicide includes any deliberate self-harm that could have been lethal.

Parasuicide is the preferred term because "failed" suicide implies that to die is to succeed (!). "Attempt" is likewise misleading because, especially in adolescence, the difference between attempt and completion may be luck and treatment, not intent.

As you see in **Figure 16.3**, parasuicide can be divided according to instances that require medical attention (surgery, pumped stomach, etc.) and those that do not, but any parasuicide is a warning. Among U.S. twelfth-graders in 2017, 9 percent of the girls and 6 percent of the boys attempted suicide in the previous year (MMWR, June 15, 2018).

Although suicidal ideation during adolescence is common, completed suicides are not. In the United States in 2016, the rate of completed suicide for White teenagers, aged 15 to 19 (in school or not), was about 5 per 100,000, or 0.005 percent. The rate for non-White teenagers is about half that. The rate for adults aged 20 or older is three times the teen rate. Keep this statistic in mind if someone claims that adolescent suicide is "epidemic." It is not.

Of course, even one teen suicide is a tragedy, and it is particularly poignant when the media tells details with a photo of the fresh-faced young person. That itself causes for teen depression. All manner of adolescent self-harm (parasuicide, cutting, extreme dieting), and deep sadness seem to be increasing; teen media use is a correlate (Twenge et al., 2018).

For example, teen suicide rates increased by almost a third after the release of a Netflix program "Thirteen Reasons Why," which depicted a girl slitting her wrists (Bridge et al., 2019). A chief executive of Netflix said, "no one has to watch it." Whether he is naïve, cynical, or cruel is a matter of opinion.

Because they are more emotional and egocentric than logical and analytical, adolescents are particularly affected when they read of someone else's suicide. That explains **cluster suicides,** which are several suicides within a group over a brief span of time.

suicidal ideation Thinking about suicide, usually with some serious emotional and intellectual or cognitive overtones.

parasuicide Any potentially lethal action against the self that does not result in death. (Also called *attempted suicide* or *failed suicide.*)

If you or someone you know needs help, **call 1-800-273-8255** for the National Suicide Prevention Lifeline. You can also **text HOME to 741-741** for free, 24-hour support from the Crisis Text Line.

cluster suicides Several suicides committed by members of a group within a brief period.

Delinquency and Defiance

Like low self-esteem and suicidal ideation, bouts of anger are common in adolescence. In fact, a moody adolescent could be both depressed and angry: Externalizing and internalizing behavior are closely connected during these years. This may explain suicide in jail: Teenagers jailed for assault (externalizing) are higher suicide risks (internalizing) than adult prisoners (Ruch et al., 2019).

Externalizing actions are obvious. Many adolescents slam doors, curse parents, and tell friends exactly how badly other teenagers (or siblings or teachers) have behaved. Some —particularly boys—"act out" by breaking laws. They steal, damage property, or injure others.

Is teenage anger necessary for normal development? That is what Anna Freud (Sigmund's daughter, herself a prominent psychoanalyst) thought. She wrote that adolescent resistance to parental authority was "welcome . . . beneficial . . . inevitable." She explained:

> We all know individual children who, as late as the ages of fourteen, fifteen or sixteen, show no such outer evidence of inner unrest. They remain, as they have been during the latency period, "good" children, wrapped up in their family relationships, considerate sons of their mothers, submissive to their fathers, in accord with the atmosphere, idea and ideal of their childhood background. Convenient as this may be, it signifies a delay of their normal development and is, as such, a sign to be taken seriously.
>
> *[A. Freud, 1958/2000, p. 37]*

However, most contemporary psychologists, teachers, and parents like well-behaved, considerate teenagers, who often become happy adults. A 30-year longitudinal study found that adults who had never been arrested usually earned degrees, "held high-status jobs, and expressed optimism about their own futures" (Moffitt, 2003, p. 61). Thus, teenage acting out, while not unusual, is not essential for healthy development.

Breaking the Law Both the *prevalence* (how widespread) and the *incidence* (how frequent) of criminal actions are higher during adolescence than earlier or later. Arrest statistics in every nation reflect this fact, with 30 percent of African American males and 22 percent of European American males being arrested at least once before age 18 (Brame et al., 2014).

Many more broke the law but were not caught, or were caught but not arrested. Self-reports suggest that most adolescents (male or female) are law-breakers before age 20. One reason is that many behaviors that are legal for adults—buying cigarettes, having intercourse, skipping school—are illegal for adolescents.

Arrest rates are higher for youth of minority ethnic groups and boys are three times as likely as girls to be caught, arrested, and convicted. Does this reflect prejudice (Marotta & Voisin, 2017)? Some studies find that female aggression typically targets family and friends. Parents hesitate to call the police to arrest their daughters.

False Confessions Determining accurate gender, ethnic, and income differences in actual lawbreaking, not just in arrests, is complex. Self-reports may be biased. For instance, research in the Netherlands found that when teenagers

In Every Nation Everywhere, older adolescents are most likely to protest against government authority. Adolescents in Alabama *(left)* celebrate the 50-year anniversary of the historic Selma-to-Montgomery march across the Pettus Bridge. In that historic movement, most of those beaten and killed were under age 25. In the fall of 2014, thousands of students in Hong Kong *(right)* led pro-democracy protests, which began peacefully but led, days later, to violent confrontations, shown here as they began.

who were interrogated by the police were asked later if they had any police contact, a third said no (van Batenburg-Eddes et al., 2012).

The opposite is also likely. In the United States, about 20 percent of confessions are false, with higher rates among teenagers. Why? Brain immaturity makes young people ignore long-term consequences, and prioritize protecting family members, defending friends, and pleasing adults—including the police (Feld, 2013; Steinberg, 2009).

One dramatic case involved 13-year-old Tyler Edmonds, who confessed to killing his brother-in-law. He was sentenced to life in prison. He then said that he confessed falsely to protect his 26-year-old sister, whom he admired. His conviction was overturned—after he spent four years behind bars (Malloy et al., 2014).

The researchers who cited Tyler's case interviewed 194 boys, aged 14 to 17, all convicted of serious crimes. More than one-third (35 percent) said they had confessed falsely to a crime (not necessarily the one for which they were serving time). False confessions were more likely after two hours of intense interrogation—the adolescents wanted it to stop; acting on impulse, they said they were guilty (Malloy et al., 2014). And the police believed them.

Jim Weber/ZUMA Press/Memphis/TN/U.S./Newscom

Change Their Uniforms Juvenile offenders wear prison orange—easy to spot should they try to escape—as they listen to an ex-offender, Tony Allen, who grew up on the rough streets of Chicago. When this photo was taken, he earned $5 million a year as a basketball player for the Memphis Grizzlies. If an adolescent-limited offender is imprisoned, talks like this have little effect unless at least two of the following four factors are also present: a supportive family, a dedicated teacher, a strong religious community, and a circle of friends and neighbors who encourage another path.

adolescence-limited offender
A person whose criminal activity stops by age 21.

life-course-persistent offender
A person whose criminal activity typically begins in early adolescence and continues throughout life; a career criminal.

A Criminal Career? Many researchers distinguish between two kinds of teenage lawbreakers (Monahan et al., 2013; Levey et al., 2019), as first proposed by Terri Moffitt (2001, 2003). Both types are usually arrested for the first time in adolescence and for similar crimes, but their future diverges.

1. Most juvenile delinquents are **adolescence-limited offenders**, whose criminal activity stops by age 21. They break the law with their friends, facilitated by their chosen antisocial peers.
2. Some delinquents are **life-course-persistent offenders**, who become career criminals. Their lawbreaking is more often done alone than as part of a gang, and the cause is neurological impairment (either inborn or caused by early experiences), evident in learning disabilities.

During adolescence, the criminal records of both types may be similar. However, if adolescence-limited delinquents can be protected from various snares (quitting school, entering prison, drug addiction), they outgrow their criminal behavior.

Causes of Delinquency The best way to reduce adolescent crime is to notice early behavior that predicts lawbreaking and to change patterns *before* puberty. Strong and protective social relationships, emotional regulation, and moral values from childhood keep many teenagers from jail.

Adolescent crime in the United States and many other nations has decreased in the past 20 years. Only half as many juveniles under age 18 are currently arrested for murder as compared to 1990. There are many possible explanations:

- fewer high school dropouts (more education means less crime);
- wiser judges (more community service than prison);
- better policing (arrests for misdemeanors are up, which may warn parents);
- smaller families (parents attend more to each of 2 children than each of 12);
- better contraception (unwanted children often become delinquents);
- stricter drug laws (binge drinking and crack-cocaine use increase crime);
- more immigrants (who are more law-abiding); and
- less lead in the blood (lead poisoning reduces brain functioning).

Nonetheless, adolescents remain more likely to break the law than adults, perhaps because of their brains as well as because of the social context. (See Inside the Brain.)

INSIDE THE BRAIN

Impulses, Rewards, and Reflection

For almost every crime, in almost every nation, the arrest rate for 15- to 17-year-olds is twice that for those over 18 (exceptions are fraud, forgery, and embezzlement).

What is wrong with those teenagers? Perhaps the problem is in the brain, not the environment.

The limbic system is activated by puberty while the prefrontal cortex is "developmentally constrained," maturing more gradually (Hartley & Somerville, 2015, p. 109). Thus, adolescents are swayed by their intuition instead of by analysis.

Many studies confirm that adolescents show "heightened activity in the striatum, both when anticipating rewards and when receiving rewards" (Crone et al., 2016, p. 360). In choosing between a small but guaranteed reward and a large possible reward, adolescent brains show more activity for the larger reward than the brains of children or adults.

This means that when teenagers weigh the possible results of a particular action, their brains make them more inclined to imagine success than to fear failure. Whether this makes them brave and bold, or foolish and careless, is a matter of opinion, but there is no doubt that neurological circuits tip the balance toward action. Nor is there any doubt that the reward circuits in the brain are powerfully activated in adolescence (Cao et al., 2019).

The joy of suddenly possessing a coveted jacket, or of joining a group of peers who are beating up a disrespectful stranger, is immediate. Later, if reflection occurs as the teen sits in jail, then another problem appears: According to one review, "incarcerated juveniles are at a four times higher risk of suicide than adolescents in general population" (Joshi & Billick, 2017, p. 141).

A related aspect of adolescent brains is that peer acclaim or rejection is deeply felt, with activation throughout the limbic system as well as other subcortical areas. This may help explain another aspect of adolescent crime: It often occurs in groups, whereas most adult crime is a loner's game.

Thus, neurological sensitivity may explain why teens readily follow impulses that promise social approval from friends and shun experiences that might bring rejection. In experiments in which adults and adolescents, alone or with peers, play video games in which taking risks might lead to crashes or gaining points, adolescents are much more likely than adults are to risk crashing, especially when they are with peers.

When they are with their mothers, not their peers, teenagers are cautious in such simulations. However, as the connection between two brain regions (the anterior insula and the ventral striatum) increases in adolescence, risk taking when the mother is absent increases, especially if the family relationship is not supportive (Guassi Moreira & Telzer, 2018).

There are other notable differences in brain activity (specifically in the ventral striatum) between adolescents and adults. When with other adults, adult brains signal more caution (inhibition) than when alone—opposite to the adolescent brain with peers (Albert et al., 2013) (see **Figure 16.4**).

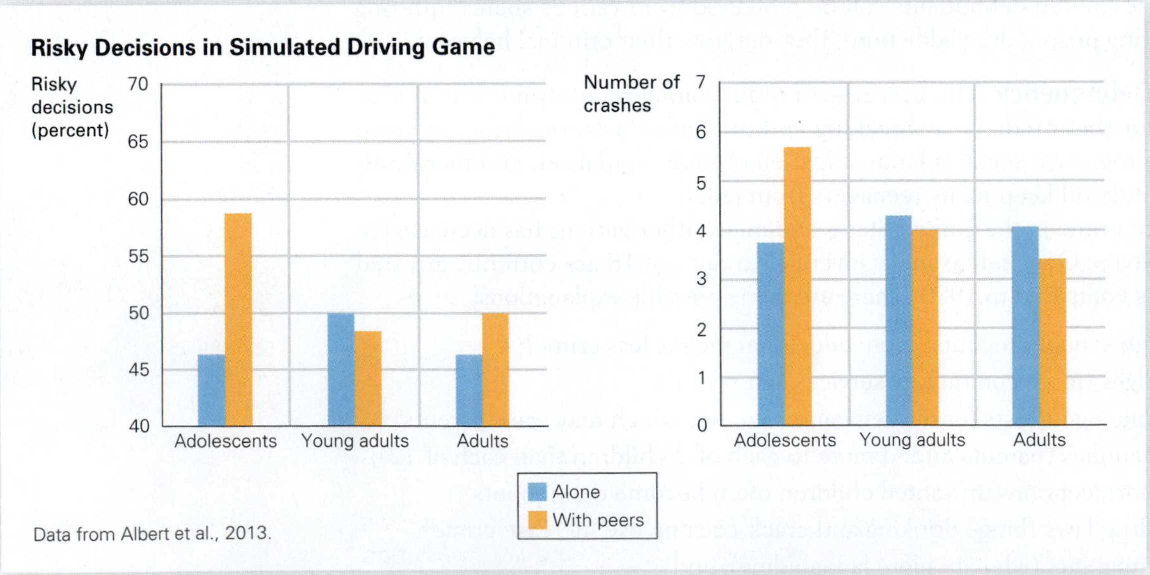

FIGURE 16.4

Losing Is Winning In this game, risk taking led to more crashes and fewer points. As you see, adolescents were strongly influenced by the presence of peers—so much so that they lost points that they would have kept if they had played alone. In fact, sometimes they laughed when they crashed instead of bemoaning their loss. Note the contrast with emerging adults, who were more likely to take risks when alone.

This peer influence is apparent in both sexes but is stronger in boys—particularly when they are with other boys (de Boer et al., 2017). This may explain why adolescent boys use drugs, get arrested, and die accidentally twice as often as girls.

Teenage drivers like to fill (or overfill) cars with teen passengers who will admire them for speeding, for passing trucks on blind curves, for racing through railroad crossings when the warning lights are flashing, and so on. Fatal accidents are much more likely if the driver and the passengers are adolescents.

The accident rate in adolescence is aided by a third brain change in adolescence. Compared to children, there is a substantial increase in myelination between the emotional and action parts of the brain. This increase in white matter means rapid responses. As a result, adolescents act before slower-thinking adults can stop them (Hartley & Somerville, 2015).

Thus, don't blame teen crashes, juvenile delinquency, or drug use on inexperience; blame it on the brain. Some states now prohibit teen drivers from transporting other teenagers, reducing deaths and banning one source of adolescent excitement. States that allow marijuana always prohibit it before age 18. Some judges hesitate to give life sentences to adolescents.

Teens advocate for some laws, such as those that protect the environment; they do not advocate for laws that restrict drug use, driver's licenses, or gun purchases based on age. Now that you understand the teenage brain, perhaps you will.

WHAT HAVE YOU LEARNED?

1. What is the difference between adolescent sadness and clinical depression?
2. Why do many adults think adolescent suicide is more common than it is?
3. Why are there gender differences in adolescent depression and arrest?
4. Why are cluster suicides more common in adolescence than in later life?
5. What are the similarities between life-course-persistent and adolescence-limited offenders?

Drug Use and Abuse

Most teenagers try *psychoactive drugs,* that is, drugs that activate the brain. Brain changes in the reward system lead directly to increases in drug abuse, such as binge drinking (Morales et al., 2018). Hormonal surges, the brain's reward centers, and cognitive immaturity make adolescents particularly attracted to the sensations produced by psychoactive drugs. But their immature bodies and brains make drug use especially toxic to the brain.

Moreover, every psychoactive drug excites the limbic system and interferes with the prefrontal cortex. Because of these neurological reactions, drug users are more emotional (varying from euphoria to terror, from paranoia to rage) than they would otherwise be. They are less reflective. The rate of every hazard—including car crashes, unsafe sex, and suicide—is higher when teens use psychoactive drugs.

JASON LEE/Reuters

A Man Now This boy in Tibet is proud to be a smoker—in many Asian nations, smoking is considered manly.

Age Trends

Adolescence is a sensitive time for experimentation with psychoactive drugs. Use increases from about ages 10 to 25 and then decreases when adult responsibilities and experiences make drugs less attractive.

Alcohol and cigarettes use before age 15 are especially worrisome, because early use escalates. That makes depression, sexual abuse, bullying, and later addiction more likely.

One drug follows another pattern—*inhalants* (fumes from aerosol containers, glue, cleaning fluid, etc.). Sadly, the youngest adolescents are most likely to try inhalants, because inhalants are easy to get (hardware stores, drug stores, and supermarkets stock them). Cognitive immaturity means that few pubescent

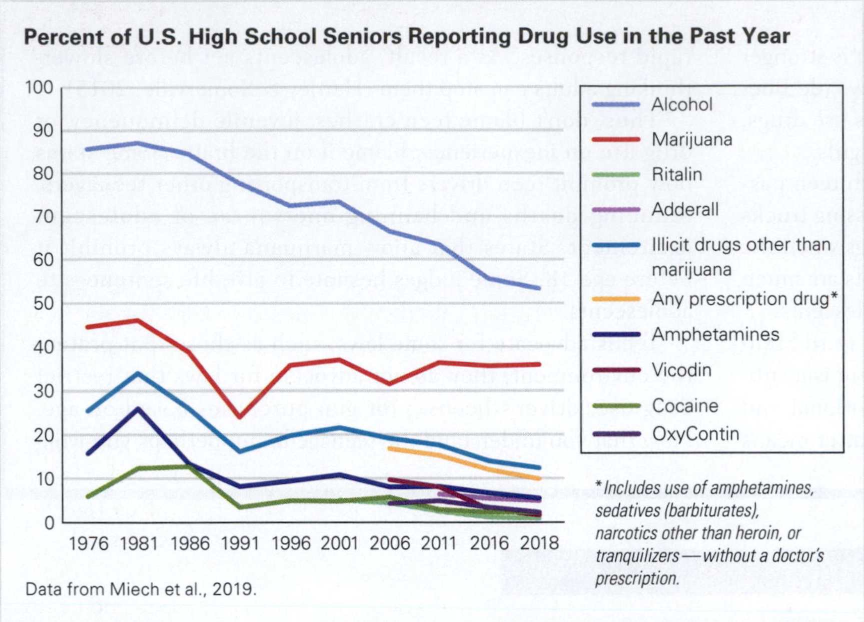

FIGURE 16.5

Rise and Fall By asking the same questions year after year, the Monitoring the Future study shows notable historical effects. It is encouraging that something in society, not in the adolescent, makes drug use increase and decrease and that the most recent data show a continued decline in the drug most commonly abused—alcohol.

Especially for Parents Who Drink Socially You have heard that parents should allow their children to drink at home to teach them to drink responsibly and not get drunk elsewhere. Is that wise? (see response, page 426)

children understand the risks—brain damage and even death (Nguyen et al., 2016).

Cohort differences are evident for every drug, even from one year to the next. Legalization of marijuana, stores selling electronic cigarettes in many flavors, hundreds of deaths from opioids—these are three examples of changes in the psychoactive drug scene over the past few years.

Adolescent drug use in the United States has declined since 1976 (see **Figure 16.5**) with one major exception: vaping. Perception of risk, not availability, reduces use, since most high school students have always said that they could easily get alcohol, cigarettes, and marijuana if they wanted to (Miech et al., 2016).

Availability is notable for e-cigarettes. Although most states prohibit adolescent purchase, teens can buy them from at least 116 Internet vendors with no problem (Nikitin et al., 2016). Vaping is common among teenagers. Should adults worry about that? (See Opposing Perspectives.)

Harm from Drugs

Drug use before maturity is particularly likely to harm growth and risk addiction. However, few adolescents know when they or their friends move past use (experimenting) to abuse (experiencing harm).

Each drug is harmful in a particular way. *Tobacco* impairs digestion and nutrition, slowing down growth. Since internal organs mature after the height spurt, smoking teenagers who appear to be full-grown may damage their developing hearts, lungs, brains, and reproductive systems.

Alcohol is the most frequently abused drug in North America. Heavy drinking impairs memory and self-control by damaging the hippocampus and the prefrontal cortex, perhaps distorting the reward circuits of the brain lifelong (Guerri & Pascual, 2010).

Ironically, many antidrug parents condone adolescent drinking. For instance, a careful longitudinal study in Australia found that parents who provided alcohol to their teenagers thought they were teaching responsible drinking, but instead they were increasing binge drinking and substance use disorder six years later (Mattick et al., 2018).

Marijuana seems harmless to many people (especially teenagers), partly because users are more relaxed than aggressive. Yet adolescents who regularly smoke marijuana are more likely to drop out of school, become teenage parents, be depressed, and later be unemployed—although that evidence comes from years when marijuana was illegal.

In the next few years, we will learn more. Canada legalized marijuana for adults in the summer of 2018. Canadian health researchers hope that, once the brain is mature, benefits outweigh risks (Lake & Kerr, 2017). Marijuana is illegal in Canada for those under 18, although some doctors wish 21 were the cutoff (Rankin, 2017).

Any age restriction encourages younger adolescents to covet drugs used by older youth, which creates a major problem. This was evident when New Zealand lowered the age for legal purchase of alcohol from 20 to 18. Hospital admissions for intoxication, car crashes, and injuries from assault increased, not only for 18- to 19-year-olds but also for 16- to 17-year-olds (Kypri et al., 2006, 2014).

OPPOSING PERSPECTIVES

E-Cigarettes: Path to Addiction or Health?

Electronic cigarettes (called e-cigs) are less damaging to the lungs than conventional cigarettes, because they deliver the drugs by vapor. Smokers with asthma heart disease, or lung cancer benefit from vaping if it reduces their smoking of combustible cigarettes (Veldheer et al., 2019).

E-cigs are not harmless. They deliver fewer harmful chemicals than combustible cigarettes (Goniewicz et al., 2017), but one by-product is benzene, a known carcinogen (Pankow et al., 2017). Most e-cigs also contain nicotine, sometimes said to be more addictive than heroin.

Developmentalists fear that e-cigarettes make smoking more acceptable. E-cigs are illegal for people under age 18 (in some states, under 21), but they are marketed in kid-friendly flavors, they can be placed for a fee in Hollywood films, and they are permitted in public places where cigarettes are banned.

Teenagers who try e-cigs are likely to smoke tobacco later (Miech et al., 2017b). Is that because e-cigs open a door or because those adolescents would be smokers no matter what? The American Pediatric Association warns that e-cigs will harm the next generation of children and adolescents (Jenssen & Walley, 2019). Maybe so; maybe not.

The opposing perspective come from one company (JUUL), that designed a sleek e-cig gadget that looks like a USB drive, and advertised on Twitter, Instagram, and YouTube. Sales approach a billion dollars per year. They argue that good business practices and clever advertising has made them successful without harming the youth (Huang et al., 2019).

They say that their products are healthier than cigarettes, that people should make their own choices, and that the fear of adolescent vaping is exaggerated—part of the irrational fear that everything teenagers do is trouble.

Teenagers themselves, by the millions, use e-cigarettes, with use skyrocketing (see **Figure 16.6**). Adults with chronic diseases, especially former smokers with chronic obstructive pulmonary disease (COPD), often use e-cigarettes (Kruse et al., 2017). Addiction counselors report that e-cigs reduce smoking (Rohsenow et al., 2018).

Yet most public health doctors advise against them, and pediatricians worry that fetal and infant lungs suffer if the mother uses e-cigs (Carlsen et al., 2018). With rats, vaping decreases birthweight, which increases risks for early death and brain damage (Orzabal et al., 2019).

The evidence says caution, but as seen many times in adolescence, caution is scarce during the teen years. The opposing perspectives are apparent: Which perspective is yours?

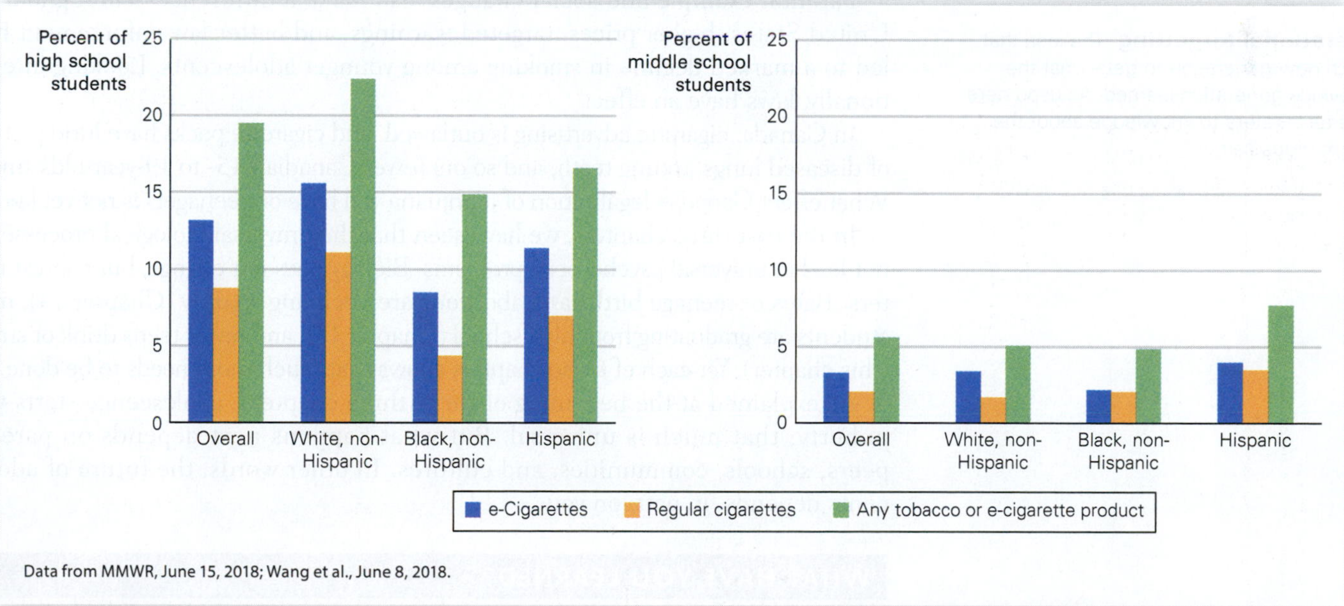

FIGURE 16.6

Getting Better The fact that more than one in five high school students (that's 3 million people) used tobacco—even though purchase of any kind is illegal—in the past month is troubling. This means that more that 3 million students are at risk for addiction and poor health. The surprise (not shown) is that all of these rates are lower than a year earlier. Is that because laws are stricter or teenagers are getting wiser?

Pat Vasquez-Cunningham/Albuquerque Journal/ZUMAPRESS.com/Alamy Images

Telling Their Story Erika Pohl and her mother Brenda reflect on a documentary in which Erika had a leading role—as a teenager addicted to opioids who managed to get clean. Both hope "never again." That is true for about half of teenage addicts; the film was created to improve those odds.

THINK CRITICALLY: Might the fear of adolescent drug use be foolish, if most adolescents use drugs whether or not they are forbidden?

generational forgetting The idea that each new generation forgets what the previous generation learned. As used here, the term refers to knowledge about the harm drugs can do.

Preventing Drug Abuse: What Works?

Remember that most adolescents think they are exceptions, sometimes feeling invincible, sometimes fearing social disapproval, but almost never realistic about potential addiction. Instead, some get a thrill from breaking the law, and some use stimulants to improve cognition or other drugs to relieve stress. They do not see that over time stress and depression increase, and achievement decreases (McCabe et al., 2017; Bagot, 2017).

With harmful drugs, as with many other aspects of life, people of each generation prefer to learn things for themselves. A common phenomenon is **generational forgetting**, that each new cohort forgets what the previous cohort learned.

Mistrust of the older generation along with a loyalty to one's peers leads not only to generational forgetting but also to a backlash. When adults forbid something, that is a reason to try it, especially if adults exaggerate the dangers. If a friend passes out from drug use, adolescents may be slow to get medical help—a dangerous hesitancy.

Some antidrug curricula and advertisements make drugs seem exciting. Antismoking announcements produced by cigarette companies (such as a clean-cut young person advising viewers to think before they smoke) actually increase use (Strasburger et al., 2009).

By contrast, massive ad campaigns by public health advocates in Florida and California cut adolescent smoking almost in half, in part because the publicity appealed to the young. Teenagers respond to graphic images. In one example:

> A young man walks up to a convenience store counter and asks for a pack of cigarettes. He throws some money on the counter, but the cashier says "that's not enough." So the young man pulls out a pair of pliers, wrenches out one of his teeth, and hands it over. . . . A voiceover asks: "What's a pack of smokes cost? Your teeth."
>
> *[Krisberg, 2014]*

Parental example and social changes also make a difference. Throughout the United States, higher prices, targeted warnings, and better law enforcement have led to a marked decline in smoking among younger adolescents. Looking internationally, laws have an effect.

In Canada, cigarette advertising is outlawed, and cigarette packs have lurid pictures of diseased lungs, rotting teeth, and so on; fewer Canadian 15- to 19-year-olds smoke. What effect Canada's legalization of marijuana will have on teenagers is not yet known.

In the past three chapters, we have seen that the universal biological processes do not lead to universal psychosocial problems. Biology does not change, but context matters. Rates of teenage births and abortions are declining sharply (Chapter 14), more students are graduating from high school (Chapter 15), and fewer teens drink or smoke (this chapter). Yet each of these chapters shows that much more needs to be done.

As explained at the beginning of these three chapters, adolescence starts with puberty; that much is universal. But what happens next depends on parents, peers, schools, communities, and cultures. In other words, the future of adolescents depends, in part, on you.

WHAT HAVE YOU LEARNED?

1. Why are psychoactive drugs particularly attractive in adolescence?
2. Why are psychoactive drugs particularly destructive in adolescence?
3. What specific harm occurs with tobacco products?
4. How has adolescent drug use changed in the past decade?
5. What methods to reduce adolescent drug use are successful?

SUMMARY

Identity

1. Adolescence is a time for self-discovery. According to Erikson, adolescents seek their own identity, sorting through the traditions and values of their families and cultures.

2. Many young adolescents foreclose on their options without exploring possibilities, and many experience role confusion. Identity achievement takes longer for contemporary adolescents than it did a half-century ago when Erikson first described it.

3. Identity achievement occurs in many domains, including religion, politics, vocation, and gender. Each of these domains remains important over the life span, but timing, contexts, and often terminology have changed since Erikson and Marcia first described them. Achieving vocational and gender identity is particularly difficult.

Close Relationships

4. Parents continue to influence their growing children, despite bickering over minor issues. Ideally, communication and warmth remain high, while parental control decreases and adolescents develop autonomy.

5. There are cultural differences in the timing of conflicts and in the benefits of parental monitoring. Too much parental control is harmful, as is neglect. Respect for adolescents is crucial.

6. Peers and peer pressure can be beneficial or harmful, depending on who the peers are. Adolescents select their friends, who then facilitate constructive and/or destructive behavior. Peer approval is particularly potent during adolescence.

7. Adolescents experience diverse sexual needs and may be involved in short-term or long-term romances, depending in part on their peer group. Contemporary teenagers are less likely to have intercourse than was true a decade ago.

8. Some youths are sexually attracted to people of the same sex. Social acceptance of same-sex relationships is increasing, but in some communities and nations, gay, lesbian, bisexual, and transgender youth are bullied, rejected, or worse.

9. Many adolescents learn about sex from peers and the media—sources that are not comprehensive. Ideally, parents are the best teachers on topics about sex, but many are silent or naive.

10. Some nations provide comprehensive sex education beginning in the early grades, and most U.S. parents want schools to teach adolescents about sex. Abstinence-only education is not effective at slowing down the age of sexual activity, and it may increase STIs.

Sadness and Anger

11. Almost all young adolescents become more self-conscious and self-critical than they were as children. A few become chronically sad and depressed.

12. Many adolescents (especially girls) think about suicide, and some attempt it. Few adolescents actually kill themselves; most who do so are boys.

13. At least in Western societies, almost all adolescents become more independent and angry as part of growing up, although most still respect their parents. Breaking the law and bursts of anger are common; boys are more likely to be arrested for violent offenses than are girls.

14. Adolescence-limited delinquents should be prevented from hurting themselves or others; life-course-persistent offenders may become career criminals. Early intervention—before the first arrest—is crucial to prevent serious delinquency.

Drug Use and Abuse

15. Most adolescents experiment with drugs, which may temporarily reduce stress and increase peer connections but soon add to stress and social problems. Almost every adolescent tries alcohol, and many use e-cigarettes and marijuana. Both are technically illegal for those under 18 but are readily available to teenagers.

16. All psychoactive drugs are particularly harmful in adolescence, as they affect the developing brain and threaten the already shaky impulse control. Prevention and moderation of adolescent drug use and abuse are possible. Price, perception, and parents have an effect.

KEY TERMS

identity versus role confusion (p. 404)
identity achievement (p. 404)
role confusion (p. 404)
foreclosure (p. 404)
moratorium (p. 404)
gender identity (p. 406)
parental monitoring (p. 409)
familism (p. 409)
peer pressure (p. 410)
deviancy training (p. 412)
sexual orientation (p. 413)
major depression (p. 416)
suicidal ideation (p. 417)
parasuicide (p. 417)
cluster suicides (p. 417)
adolescence-limited offender (p. 419)
life-course-persistent offender (p. 419)
generational forgetting (p. 424)

APPLICATIONS

1. Locate a news article about a teenager who committed suicide. Were there warning signs that were ignored? Does the report inadvertently encourage cluster suicides?

2. Research suggests that most adolescents have broken the law but that few have been arrested or incarcerated. Ask 10 of your fellow students whether they broke the law when they were under 18 and, if so, how often, in what ways, and with what consequences. (Assure them of confidentiality; remind them that drug use, breaking curfew, and skipping school were illegal.) Do you see any evidence of gender or ethnic differences? What additional research needs to be done?

3. Cultures vary in expectations for drug use. Interview three people from different backgrounds (not necessarily from different nations; each SES, generation, or religion has different standards) about their culture's drug use, including reasons for what is allowed and when. (Legal drugs should be included in your study.)

Especially For ANSWERS

Response for Parents of a Teenager (from p. 411): Remember: Communicate, do not control. Let your child talk about the meaning of the hairstyle. Remind yourself that a hairstyle in itself is harmless. Don't say, "What will people think?" or "Are you on drugs?" or anything that might give your child a reason to stop communicating.

Response for Sex Educators (from p. 415): Yes, but forgive them. Ideally, parents should talk to their children about sex, presenting honest information and listening to children's concerns. However, many parents find it very difficult to do so because they feel embarrassed and ignorant. You might schedule separate sessions for adults over 30, for emerging adults, and for adolescents.

Response for Parents Who Drink Socially (from p. 422): No. Alcohol is particularly harmful for young brains. It is best to drink only when your children are not around. Children who are encouraged to drink with their parents are more likely to drink when no adults are present. It is true that adolescents are rebellious, and they may drink even if you forbid it. But if you allow alcohol, they might rebel with other drugs.

Observation Quiz ANSWERS

Answer to Observation Quiz (from p. 410): The girls are only observers, keeping a respectful distance. The boys compete in a game that tests agility and reaction time.

Answer to Observation Quiz (from p. 417): Both. It increases for boys but decreases for girls.

CAREER ALERT The Teacher

Many people who study human development hope to become teachers, for good reason. Teachers can make a huge impact on a child's life. Every adult probably remembers a teacher or two whose interest and insight still affects them.

The need is great, and the demand huge. According to the U.S. Bureau of Labor Statistics' Occupational Outlook Handbook, in 2016 there were 1,500,000 elementary school teachers and 1,008,000 secondary school teachers. But every year, more than 100,000 teachers leave the profession—some retire, some quit, some die. They need to be replaced.

Depending on the local school district, an aspiring teacher can qualify with a bachelor's degree in almost any field. Courses in education can be taken while teaching. Better would be a master's degree in education, ideally with on-the-job training with excellent teachers.

Many specialties within the teaching profession are chronically understaffed. In the United States, those trained to teach math, science, a non-English language, or children with special needs will be hired—as long as they are willing to live outside their home community.

Those interested in teaching probably already know that the salary is not that great, but the benefits are adequate, and teaching children can be immensely satisfying as well as challenging. Further, teachers have more vacation days than most professions, and the workday may seem short since most school days end by 3 P.M.

However, good teachers spend as much time preparing and planning as they do in direct teaching. Further, the work is exhausting, physically and emotionally. Teachers become painfully aware that some students have serious problems that teaching cannot solve: abusive or neglectful parents, learning differences, severe poverty, chronic depression.

The greatest openings in the profession are in areas that require special training. Novices may hope to teach high school English or to teach third grade in an affluent suburb. But such jobs are taken by teachers who have seniority; they are unlikely to be filled by new recruits.

Instead, aspiring teachers are most likely to be hired in areas of greatest need: math teachers in cities, teachers who specialize in autism, bilingual teachers, speech teachers who can relate with children and parents of many backgrounds, middle school science teachers.

Some of my students want to be teachers. I encourage them, warning that this profession is more difficult that it may seem. As one leading educator wrote: "teaching is not rocket science—it is much harder than that" (Sahlberg, 2015, p. 133).

VISUALIZING DEVELOPMENT ADOLESCENT BULLYING

Bullying is defined as repeated attempts to hurt someone else, physically or socially. It can take many forms. For younger children, it was often physical—hitting, shoving, fighting. That is less common among adolescents, who can hurt each other with words or exclusion. Among teenagers, not being invited to a party can be hurtful and is common—as teenagers develop dominance hierarchies and need peer support. The best protection is to have one or more close friends, and adults who encourage whatever talents the child has.

THE NATURE OF SCHOOL BULLYING

When bullying takes place at school, about two-thirds of it occurs in hallways, schoolyards, bathrooms, cafeterias, or buses. A full one-third occurs in classrooms, while teachers are present. An estimated 30% of school bullying goes unreported.

FEATURES OF SCHOOL ANTI-BULLYING PROGRAMS

- Increased supervision of students
- A school climate that encourages friendship
- Teachers who promote empathy
- School-wide implementation of anti-bullying policies
- Cooperation among school staff, parents, and professionals across disciplines
- Identification of risk factors for bullying

Success varies, with some programs having no effect. But overall, a good program can reduce bullying by 25% or more.

Data from McCallion & Feder, 2013

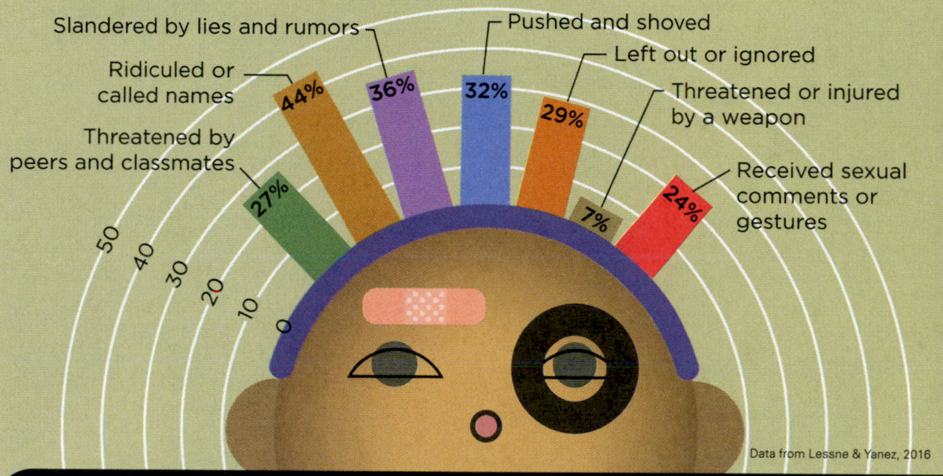

Data from Lessne & Yanez, 2016

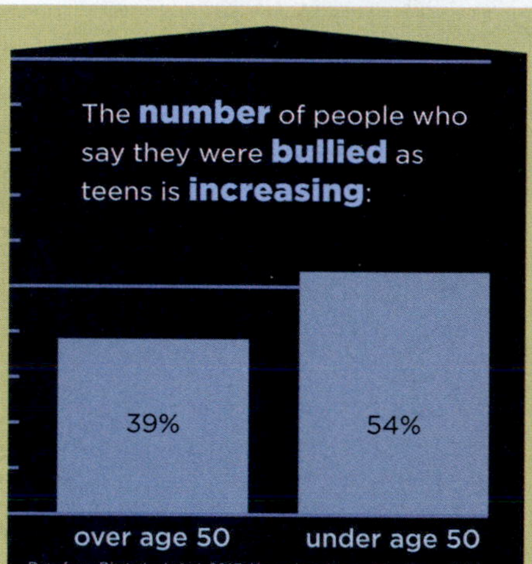

Data from Ditch the Label, 2017; Harris Insights and Analytics, 2014, National Foundation For Educational Research, 2010

CYBERBULLYING

Cyberbullying (discussed in Chapter 15) takes place via e-mail, text messages, Web sites and apps, instant messaging, chat rooms, or posted videos or photos. About 60% of boys and girls have been cyberbullied, but girls are more often the targets of online rumor-spreading or nonconsensual explicit messages (Anderson, 2018).

WHY DO TEENS CYBERBULLY?

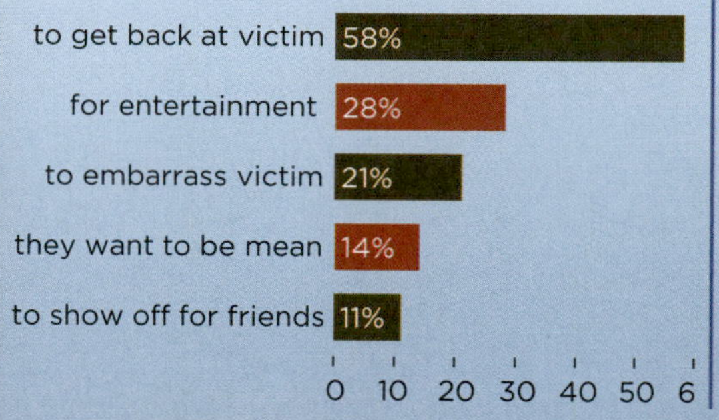

SOCIAL MEDIA AND CYBERBULLYING

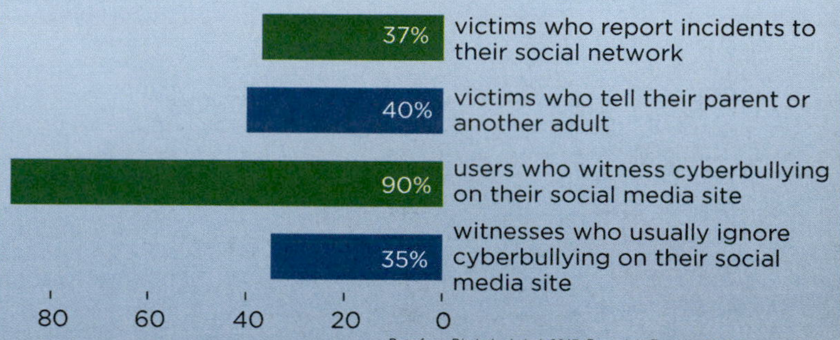

Data from Ditch the Label, 2017; Enough Is Enough, 2017; Duggan, 2017

CHAPTERS 17 • 18 • 19

PART VI

Emerging Adulthood

For most of human history, three roles signified adulthood: employee, spouse, and parent. In the nineteenth century, many women in the United States had their first baby by age 20 and married a year or so before that. Their husbands were usually young men who started working full time several years earlier, to prove that they could support a wife.

Those adult roles were more important than higher education. In 1940, less than one-fourth of all U.S. residents completed high school, and only about 4 percent (mostly rich, White men) graduated from college (U.S. Department of Commerce, 1975). Part-time employment (paper boy, babysitter) was common; dating was expected; high school graduation was an achievement.

In the last part of the twentieth century, several demographic revolutions changed life for everyone. No longer do 18- to 25-year-olds rush toward adult roles. Instead, they linger between adolescence and adulthood, gaining education and experience, not careers, spouses, and children.

The next trio of chapters describes this time between childhood and adulthood, between growing up and being "a grown-up," as children call adults. During emerging adulthood, learning and exploring continue. We now describe what people do as they hover on the edge of adulthood.

Left: Peathegee Inc/Blend Images/Getty Images
Right: RapidEye/iStock/E+/Getty Images

CHAPTER 17

Emerging Adulthood: Biosocial Development

What Will You Know?

1. Why are emerging adults quite healthy, even though they may avoid doctors?
2. What has changed in the sexual activity of emerging adults?
3. Why do people risk their lives unnecessarily?

- **Biological Universals**
  - A New Stage
  - Body Systems
  - A View from Science: Universal or WEIRD?
  - Health and Sickness
  - Capacity for Recovery
  - Examples of Load and Balancing
  - Appearance
- **Sexual Activity**
  - Births
  - Universal Sex Drives
  - Opposing Perspectives: Premarital Sex
- **Taking Risks**
  - Who Are the Risk Takers?
  - Benefits of Risk Taking
  - A Case to Study: A Hero for Millions
- **VISUALIZING DEVELOPMENT: Highlights in the Journey to Adulthood**

I thought I was an emerging-adult pioneer, yet I still followed many traditional norms.

As a young woman, filled with energy and hope to change society, I was happy to earn college degrees (transferring, as many emerging adults do) and then to be hired to teach in a public middle school.

I did not like that the school was all boys, or that the 14 seventh-grade home rooms were tracked (mine, 7-14, was the lowest one). But I paid rent on my own city apartment, a fourth-floor walkup, and had a boyfriend and a job. I was grateful that times were changing: A few decades earlier, no woman would have been allowed to teach in junior high and no parent would have allowed a daughter to live alone.

My problem was limited experience. I was surprised that some of my students could not read, that some were bullied because their clothes were torn, and that some were afraid of me. When I walked up to remonstrate one miscreant, he cringed and covered his face with his arm, expecting to be hit.

I set about to learn what I needed to know, by tutoring a nonreader after school, by asking my parents to donate a clothes voucher to the bullied boy, by visiting the homes of many of my students to meet their parents (surprised to see me, but very hospitable). It did not occur to me that I was not only filled with energy but also taking a risk, riding on rickety elevators in public housing in the evening to arrive at a student's home unannounced.

I was married that February, a wedding scheduled to coincide with a school holiday (President's Day). Soon I became pregnant, and, since the Board of Education did not allow visibly pregnant teachers, I left when that year was over and entered a Ph.D. program.

As I recollect it now, I see that my energy, strength, marriage, and pregnancy were all traditional for young adults. There were glimmers of a new stage, but emerging adulthood had not yet come full force.

I took risks, and I sought more education and independence than my foremothers had, but I imagine that current young people will consider my version of those emerging-adult characteristics quite tame.

Left: Tempura/E+/Getty Images
Top: RapidEye/iStock/E+/Getty Images

FRANCK FIFE/AFP/Getty Images

What a Body Can Do Here at age 27, Tobin Heath leaps to celebrate her goal at the soccer World Cup Final in Vancouver, her most recent of seven years of star performances. All young adults can have moments when their bodies and minds crescendo to new heights.

emerging adulthood The period of life between the ages of 18 and 25. Emerging adulthood is now widely thought of as a distinct developmental stage.

WEIRD An acronym that refers to people from Western, Educated, Industrialized, Rich Democracies, in other words, to North American college students, not necessarily the rest of humanity.

Biological Universals

Certain biosocial characteristics have always been present in young adults. Bodies are ready for hard work and reproduction, and young adults welcome physical challenges that older adults would fear. Biologically, the years from ages 18 to 25 have always been prime time for high energy, hard physical work, and safe reproduction.

A New Stage

However, the fact that young adults can carry rocks, plow fields, or produce babies is no longer admired. If a contemporary young couple left high school to marry, build a home, till a field, and produce babies year after year, neighbors would be appalled, not approving.

Societies, families, and young adults expect more education, later marriage, and fewer births than the norm a few decades ago. The term **emerging adulthood** was coined by Jeffrey Arnett. He was a college professor in Missouri who listened to his own students and concluded that they were neither adolescents nor adults.

As a good researcher, he also queried young adults elsewhere in the United States, he read published research about "youth" or "late adolescence," and he thought about his own life. Arnett decided that a new stage, requiring a new label, had appeared, and he proposed "a new conception of development for the period from the late teens through the twenties, with a focus on ages 18–25" (Arnett, 2000, p. 469). Many others agreed.

Thousands of scientists now study emerging adults. But some remain skeptical. Research is ongoing. Between 2015 and 2019, more than 40,000 scholarly articles regarding emerging adulthood have been published. The validity of this stage is the topic of A View from Science on page 433, with some suggesting that it applies only to **WEIRD** adults.

Body Systems

As has been true for thousands of years, every body system—digestive, respiratory, circulatory, musculoskeletal, and sexual-reproductive—functions optimally in emerging adulthood. The rapid and sometimes unsettling changes of adolescence are over: Emerging adults are at their peak of fertility and strength.

To be specific, maximum height is usually reached by age 16 for girls and age 18 for boys, with final touches in size and shape evident in emerging adulthood. A few late-maturing boys gain another inch or two by age 21.

By age 22, women have developed adult breasts and hips, and men have reached full shoulder width and upper-arm strength. During emerging adulthood, muscles grow, bones strengthen, and shape changes, with males gaining more arm muscle and females more fat (Whitbourne & Whitbourne, 2014).

Maximum strength soon follows, dependent on exercise. When people are actively training, emerging adults are at peak performance in most sports, especially when power, not endurance, is the measure (Allen & Hopkins, 2015). For everyone, muscles that are regularly used are quite strong. People aged 18 to 25 are best able to race up a flight of stairs, to lift a heavy load, or to grip an object with maximum force.

Even with exercise, strength gradually decreases after emerging adulthood, with some muscles weakening more quickly than others. Back and leg muscles shrink faster than the arm muscles, for instance.

Few adults notice such differences, but sports fans do, and athletes are aware of how their own bodies function with age.

A VIEW FROM SCIENCE

Universal or WEIRD?

Some ask whether emerging adulthood is evident only for youth who can afford to postpone work and family commitments (Munson et al., 2013). It might describe some North American college students, but not humans overall.

Critics note that conclusions based on American college students may apply only to those who are WEIRD—from Western, Educated, Industrialized, and Rich Democracies (Henrich et al., 2010). Most of the world's people never attend college, are poor (even low-SES Americans are rich by global measures), and live in nations without regular, fair elections. WEIRD people are not typical of the world's nearly 8 billion people.

The Canadian professor who developed the acronym WEIRD wrote, "many psychologists . . . tend to think of cross-cultural research as a nuisance, necessary only to confirm the universality of their findings (which are usually based on WEIRD undergraduates)" (Henrich, 2015, p. 86).

This possibility is particularly provocative for scholars of human development. As you remember from Chapter 1, developmentalists seek to be multicultural and multicontextual.

Many are troubled that, as one leading researcher expressed it, "the WEIRD group represents maximally 5% of the world's population, but probably more than 90% of the researchers and scientists producing the knowledge that is represented in our textbooks work with participants from that particular context" (Keller, quoted in Armstrong, 2018).

Perhaps WEIRD young adults are unlike most others. Might "emerging adulthood"—when young adults become autonomous and independent, postponing marriage, parenthood, and work commitments, forging a future untethered by parents—be a WEIRD anomaly?

That is a question worth asking. Many scientists seek to answer it. The evidence suggests that this stage indeed describes many contemporary young adults, Western or not. As expected, developmental variations are found, but the overall trends seem apparent among youth of all national and ethnic backgrounds (Murray & Arnett, 2019; Boisvert & Poulin, 2017).

One example comes from a study that found a personality shift between adolescence and adulthood among youth in 62 nations (Bleidorn et al., 2013). That study found age variations. Emerging adulthood ended when full-time employment began, sometimes at age 20 or earlier (Pakistan, Malaysia, and Zimbabwe) and sometimes past age 25 (the Netherlands, Canada, and the United States).

Further confirmation that emerging adulthood is appearing in every nation, not just the WEIRD ones, comes from statistics on age of marriage. A century ago, most women married in their teens. That is now unusual in all but the very poorest nations.

Data on childbearing, college attendance, and career commitment show similar worldwide trends. This leads most scholars to believe that although emerging adulthood was first recognized in Missouri, it is now evident worldwide.

For instance, baseball players over age 30 still hit home runs but no longer try to steal bases; swimmers age faster than golfers; basketball players improve in aim—especially at a distance—but are less likely to step instantly to grab the ball as it falls from the hoop.

Health and Sickness

In a large U.S. survey, 96 percent of 18- to 24-year-olds rated their health as good, very good, or excellent. Only 3.9 percent rated it fair or poor, a significant improvement over the past two decades, and better than older adults (National Center for Health Statistics, 2018). Very few emerging adults report any limitations on their activities due to chronic health conditions (see **Table 17.1**).

Nonetheless, some emerging adults already have signs of poor health. A study of biological aging found that some people age three times faster than others, with about half of the difference between fast and slow aging evident by age 26 (Belsky et al., 2015). As a result, by the mid-30s, some people have bodies like those in their 20s and some like those in their 40s.

If getting an annual medical checkup were the way to stay healthy, then most emerging adults would be sick: They avoid doctors.

The average 18- to 25-year-old in the United States sees a health professional once a year, and that includes those who are pregnant or injured. In 2016, about

TABLE 17.1

U.S. Deaths from the Top Two Causes (Heart Disease and Cancer)

Age Group	Annual Rate per 100,000
15–24	6
25–34	16
35–44	60
45–54	176
55–64	470
65–74	961
75–84	2,119
85+	5,494

Data from National Center for Health Statistics, 2018.

CHAPTER APP 17

First Aid: American Red Cross

IOS:
https://tinyurl.com/yxvza9r6

ANDROID:
https://tinyurl.com/7p8x9jq

RELEVANT TOPIC:
Physical health in emerging adulthood

The official American Red Cross First Aid app offers quick access to expert advice for everyday emergencies. With videos, interactive quizzes, safety tips, and simple step-by-step instructions—including Spanish-language translation—users are guided through everyday first aid scenarios. 9-1-1 can be dialed in one click.

one in every four emerging adults never saw a health professional, either in an office or a hospital (National Center for Health Statistics, 2017). This compares with about eight medical visits per year for the typical adult over age 65 (who are less often injured and never pregnant).

Similarly, although the Centers for Disease Control and Prevention recommends the flu shot each year for everyone over 6 months of age, less than one-third of those aged 18 to 45 comply (National Center for Health Statistics, 2017). Their reasons? It's not guaranteed, and it takes time (ignoring the time saved by *not* getting the flu).

Capacity for Recovery

As you read, about half of the difference between fast and slow aging is already evident by age 26, but many people are unaware that their bodies are aging. To appreciate the long trajectory of emerging adult health, we need to understand *organ reserve, homeostasis,* and *allostatic load.*

organ reserve The capacity of organs to allow the body to cope with stress, via extra, unused functioning ability.

Organ Reserve

Organ reserve is the extra power that each organ can employ when needed. This reserve capacity shrinks each year of adulthood so that by old age, a strain—shoveling snow, catching the flu, minor surgery—can overwhelm the body.

In emerging adulthood, organ reserve allows speedy recovery. A 20-year-old can stay awake all night, or take drugs that disrupt body function, and still get up the next day, seemingly unharmed. The reason is that organ reserve has been activated, and the body has recovered.

It is not only the reserve capacity of the organs themselves but also the cells' metabolic reserve—the "functional resilience of a biochemical network" (Atamna et al., 2018, p. 177)—that protects all of the organs.

Organ reserve is thought to be crucial when emerging adults undergo surgery or radiation for serious health problems, such as cancer (Ahles et al., 2012). Typically, because of organ reserve, emerging-adult bodies and brains recover much more quickly from various stresses than is true for older adults.

homeostasis The adjustment of all of the body's systems to keep physiological functions in a state of equilibrium. As the body ages, it takes longer for these homeostatic adjustments to occur, so it becomes harder for older bodies to adapt to stress.

Homeostasis

Closely related to organ reserve is **homeostasis**—a balance between various body reactions that keeps every physical function in sync with every other. For example, if the air temperature rises, people sweat, move slowly, and thirst for cold drinks—three aspects of body functioning that cool them. Homeostasis is rapid in early adulthood, partly because of organ reserve.

The next time you read about a rash of heat-wave deaths (e.g., California and Arizona in 2017, Québec in 2018), note the age of the victims. As aging makes homeostasis slow down, the body dissipates heat less efficiently. The demands may temporarily overwhelm the heart, kidneys, or other organs, causing death before recovery occurs. Even middle-aged adults are less protected from temperature changes—or any other stress on the body—than emerging adults (Larose et al., 2013).

Heat-wave deaths seem to be increasing in recent years, in part because of climate change, in part because more people are living in cities (which radiate the heat), and in part because more people live to be very old, when homeostasis does not work as well to cool down the body (Guo et al., 2017). Young bodies, fortunately, survive temperature changes much better.

Of course, at every age, external efforts to aid homeostasis may be needed. For example, a study of heat stroke during a long race found that if runners who collapsed with high body temperature were immersed immediately in ice water, recovery occurred before organ failure (Demartini et al., 2015).

Allostasis Also related to organ reserve is **allostasis,** a dynamic body adjustment that gradually changes overall physiology. The main difference between homeostasis and allostasis is time: Homeostasis requires an immediate response from body systems, whereas allostasis refers to long-term adjustment. Both draw on organ reserve.

Allostasis depends on the biological circumstances of every earlier time of life, beginning at conception. The process continues, with early-adulthood conditions affecting later life, evident in a measure called **allostatic load.** Although organ reserve usually protects emerging adults, the effects of lack of sleep, drug use, inactivity, unhealthy eating, and so on accumulate. Some organ reserve is depleted to maintain health, gradually adding to allostatic load.

allostasis A dynamic body adjustment, related to homeostasis, that affects overall physiology over time. The main difference is that homeostasis requires an immediate response, whereas allostasis requires adjustment in the longer term.

allostatic load The stresses of basic body systems that burden overall functioning, such as hypertension.

Examples of Load and Balancing

Every habit in emerging adulthood affects later health. An accumulation of poor habits can cause *metabolic syndrome,* a collection of factors that, together, make illness more likely.

A Good Night's Sleep Consider sleep. One night's poor sleep makes a person tired the next day—that is homeostasis, the body's way to maintain equilibrium. But if poor sleep quality is typical every day, then appetite, mood, and activity adjust (more, down, less) to achieve homeostasis, while allostatic load rises and organ reserve declines (see **Figure 17.1**).

By mid- and late adulthood, years of inadequate sleep impair overall health (McEwen & Karatsoreos, 2015; Carroll et al., 2014). Sleep is directly biological, but the quality of sleep is affected by many social and psychological factors. For example, some researchers find that emerging adults who experience ethnic or racial discrimination get poorer quality sleep, and that affects their health (Hope et al., 2015).

Other research finds that emerging adults are particularly likely to engage in habits that impair their sleep. One such habit is drug use, especially alcohol, and another is bedtime media use (computer games, smartphones). Those correlate with anxiety, depression, and insomnia (Brunborg et al., 2011).

FIGURE 17.1
Don't Set the Alarm? Every emerging adult sometimes sleeps too little and is tired the next day—that is homeostasis. But years of poor sleep habits reduce years of life—a bad bargain. That is allostatic load.

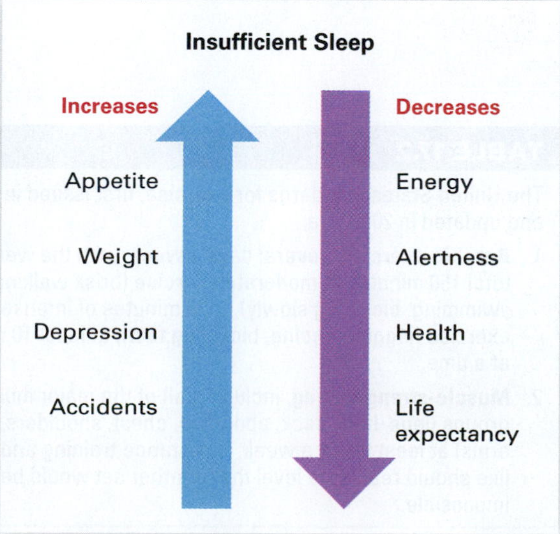

Exercise A second example is physical activity, which protects against serious illness lifelong, even if a person smokes and overeats. Exercise reduces blood pressure, strengthens the heart and lungs, and makes depression, osteoporosis, diabetes, arthritis, dementia (now called *major neurocognitive disorder*), and some cancers less likely. Health benefits are substantial for men and women, old and young, former sports stars and those who never joined an athletic team.

By contrast, sitting for long hours correlates with almost every chronic illness. Every movement—gardening, light housework, walking up the stairs or to the bus—helps. Walking briskly for 30 minutes a day, five days a week, is good; more intense exercise (swimming, jogging, bicycling, and the like) is better; and adding muscle-strengthening exercise is best.

After a few minutes of exertion, the heart beats faster and breathing becomes heavier—these are homeostatic responses. Because of organ reserve, such temporary stresses on the body in early adulthood are no problem.

If a young adult develops a regular exercise habit, over time, homeostasis adjusts and allows the person to exercise longer and harder. That decreases allostatic load by reducing the health risks that otherwise

Matt Cardy/Getty Images News/Getty Images

See the Sweat This is "hot yoga," a 90-minute class in London with 26 positions and 2 breathing exercises, in 105°F (40.5°C) heat. Homeostasis allows young adults to stretch their muscles more easily in an overly heated room.

Observation Quiz Who is unlikely to choose hot yoga? (see answer, page 450) ↑

increase, as evident in blood analysis and body fat. Metabolic syndrome does not appear in middle age for those who developed healthy patterns decades earlier.

One longitudinal study, CARDIA (Coronary Artery Risk Development in Adulthood) began with thousands of healthy 18- to 30-year-olds. They were queried about their exercise habits. Their strength, endurance, and many blood and body fat markers were measured.

Many (3,154) were reexamined decades later. Compared to the most fit, those who were the least fit at the first assessment (more than 400 of them) were four times more likely to have diabetes and high blood pressure in middle age. The repeated demands of homeostasis had affected organ reserve and allostatic load.

To be specific, problems for the least fit CARDIA participants began but were unnoticed (except in blood work) when they were emerging adults. Organ reserve allowed them to function quite well for the moment. Nonetheless, allostatic load increased (Camhi et al., 2013). By age 65, a disproportionate number had died.

Regarding most emerging adults, there is good news. They are quite active, getting aerobic exercise by climbing stairs, jogging to the store, joining intramural college and company athletic teams, playing at local parks, biking, hiking, swimming, and so on. In the United States, emerging adults walk more and drive less than older adults.

Not only are emerging adults the most active age group, they have improved over the past decades. Fully 62 percent met the standard for aerobic exercise and 33 percent met the standard for muscle-strengthening in 2016. Indeed, 31 percent meet both standards, compared to only 18 percent of middle-aged adults (National Center for Health and Human Services, 2017) (see **Table 17.2**).

In general, more activity is better, with 300 or even 450 minutes (not 150) a weekly goal. The upper limit, when no more health benefits occur, is not known, and anything is better than zero. (It is possible to overuse one particular set of muscles, especially when neglecting another set.)

For everyone, movement should be part of daily life, walking or biking (not driving), climbing stairs (not taking elevators), stretching while making the bed, squatting and standing while gardening, and the like. Labor-saving devices may also be disability-promoting devices!

The U.S. Office of Disease Prevention and Health Promotion's 2016 restatement of activity goals gives an example of an emerging adult, a college student named Anita.

> Anita plays league basketball (vigorous-intensity activity) 4 days each week for 90 minutes each day. She wants to reduce her risk of injury from doing too much of one kind of activity (this is called an overuse injury). Anita starts out by cutting back her basketball playing to 3 days each week. She begins to bicycle to and from campus (30 minutes each way) instead of driving her car. She also joins a yoga class that meets twice each week. Eventually, Anita is bicycling 3 days each week to and from campus in addition to playing basketball. Her yoga class helps her to build and maintain strength and flexibility.

What is interesting about this case is that Anita did not realize at first that her intense basketball for 360 minutes a week was not enough. At the end of her readjustment, Anita has 450 minutes of aerobic exercise and is using all of the muscle groups in yoga. She finally is a shining example of a healthy person.

Past generations quit exercising when marriage, parenthood, and career became more demanding. Young adults today, aware

TABLE 17.2

The United States standards for exercise, first issued in 2008 and updated in 2016, are:

1. **Aerobic exercise,** several days a week, with the weekly total 150 minutes of moderate exercise (brisk walking, swimming, bicycling slowly) or 75 minutes of intense exercise (jogging, racing, bicycling fast), at least 10 minutes at a time.
2. **Muscle-strengthening,** including all of the major muscle groups (legs, hips, back, abdomen, chest, shoulders, and arms) at least twice a week. Resistance training and the like should reach the level that another set would be almost impossible.

of this tendency, can choose friends and communities that support, rather than preclude, staying active. Two factors encourage activity:

1. *Friendship*. People exercise more if their friends do so, too. Social networks typically shrink with age, and with leaving college. For that reason, emerging adults need to maintain, or begin, friendships that include movement, especially when they leave college. They might meet a friend for a jog instead of a beer or play tennis instead of going to a movie.
2. *Communities*. Some neighborhoods have walking and biking paths, safe fields and parks, and subsidized pools and gyms. Most colleges provide these amenities, which increases the exercise of students.

Kevin Foy/Alamy Stock Photo

Fastest Increase Obesity rates are rising faster in China than in any other nation as new American restaurants open every day. McDonald's and Starbucks each have about 5,000 outlets in China, with students particularly likely customers.

When emerging adults seek their first independent living place, they need to look for more than low rent and a working kitchen. They need to seek a neighborhood with trees and sidewalks, where they will walk often.

Health experts cite extensive research showing that community design, safety, and neighbor friendliness promotes walking and biking, reducing obesity, hypertension, and depression (Nehme et al., 2016; Yu & Lippert, 2016). Most students probably think they are active enough, walking to class and so on. But like Anita, using all of the muscle groups in a variety of activities is best, and here many people fall short.

Eating the Right Amount Diet is the third example of finding a healthy balance that will sustain life. How much a person eats on a given day is affected by dozens of physiological and psychological factors. An empty stomach triggers hormones, stomach pains, low blood sugar, and so on, all signaling that it is time to eat.

If an empty stomach is occasional, the cascade of homeostatic reactions makes a person suddenly realize at 6 P.M. that they haven't eaten since breakfast. Dinner becomes a priority; the body signals that food is needed. Again, the social context, such as what food is available and whether other people are also eating, affects consumption.

An example of the importance of context is that many college students find that living away from home increases weight. The idea that weight gain is large and inevitable (the "freshman fifteen") is false, but it is true that many college students change eating habits and gain some weight (de Vos et al., 2015; Fedewa et al., 2014).

Whether this is beneficial or not depends on weight before college began. For body weight, there is a homeostatic **set point,** or settling point, that makes people eat when hungry and stop eating when full. Further, many mechanisms of the body work to keep people well nourished (Augustine et al., 2018).

set point A particular body weight that an individual's homeostatic processes strive to maintain.

Scientists are impressed with the many physiological measures that keep mammals at a healthy weight: Blood chemistry, hormones, stomach grumbling, mental alertness, and circadian rhythm are all part of this homeostatic system.

Extreme dieting or overeating may alter the set point: Eating disorders such as anorexia, bulimia, and obesity sometimes worsen in early adulthood, although more often the odd eating habits of adolescents become more rational. [**Life-Span Link:** Eating disorders are discussed in detail in Chapter 14; specifics of weight loss are discussed in Chapter 20.]

The **body mass index (BMI)**—the ratio between weight and height (see **Table 17.3**)—is used to determine whether a person is below, at, or above

body mass index (BMI) The ratio of a person's weight in kilograms divided by height in meters squared.

TABLE 17.3

BMI	Weight Status
Below 18.5	Underweight
18.5–24.9	Normal or healthy weight
25.0–29.9	Overweight
30.0 and above	Obese

Calculate BMI by dividing weight in pounds (lb.) by height in inches (in.) squared and multiplying by a conversion factor of 703.

Example: Weight = 150 lb., Height = 5 ft, 5 in. (65 in.)

Calculation: $[150 \div (65)^2] \times 703 = 24.96$

normal weight. A BMI below 18 is a symptom of anorexia, between 20 and 25 indicates a normal weight, above 25 is considered overweight, and 30 or more is called obese.

About half of all emerging U.S. adults are within the normal BMI range, as are less than one-third of adults aged 25 to 65. Fortunately, once emerging adults become independent, they can change childhood eating patterns. Some do. As a generation, U.S. young adults consume more water, organic foods, and nonmeat diets than do older adults, becoming more fit than their parents were at the same age.

Not all is well, however. Emerging adults are also most likely to drink sugar-sweetened soda, juice, and energy drinks. Men, especially those who are emerging adults and who live in the southern states, have the highest rates of soda consumption (Kumar et al., 2014). A habit of drinking water is likely to protect health lifelong.

Particular nutritional hazards await young adults who are immigrants or children of immigrants now in the United States. Many seek to prove that they are good citizens and as American as anyone whose ancestors immigrated a hundred years ago. One way they do this is to "eat American," avoiding curry, hot peppers, or wasabi—each of which has been discovered to have health benefits. Instead they tend to choose fast foods, which are high in fat, sugar, and salt.

Probably for that reason, although older immigrants overall are healthier than the American average, their young-adult offspring have significantly higher rates of obesity and diabetes than their elders, particularly if their origin is in Africa or South Asia (Oza-Frank & Narayan, 2010).

No matter what their ancestry, today's emerging adults are heavier than past cohorts. As they age, they gain weight—about a pound a year, according to the CARDIA study. Specifics of diet matter: CARDIA found that fast foods, high-fat diets, and diet soda each had independent effects, with the cumulative allostatic load affecting every indication of poor health (Duffey et al., 2012).

Over the years, allostasis is evident. If a person over- or undereats day after day, the body adjusts: Appetite increases or decreases accordingly. But that repeated homeostasis eventually increases allostatic load, as measured by body fat, factors in the blood, hypertension, and so on.

A heavy allostatic load makes a person vulnerable to diabetes, heart disease, stroke, and more—all the result of physiological adjustment (allostasis) to daily overeating (Sterling, 2012). At the opposite extreme, allostasis allows people with anorexia to feel energetic, not hungry, but the burden on their body eventually kills them.

Most young people learn to eat well, but some do not, making "emerging adulthood . . . a critical risk period in the development and prevention of disordered eating" (Goldschmidt et al., 2016, p. 480). The deadly consequences come later.

The natural, homeostatic drive to eat enough and not too much can also be short-circuited by manufactured food. Chips and cookies are developed, packaged, and advertised to disrupt the normal appetite: That's why it is hard to eat just one potato chip and why people binge on high-fat ice cream, not broccoli.

Emerging adults enjoy socializing: They typically have more friends and acquaintances at this age than later in life. That has many benefits, of course, but a healthy diet is not one of them. If you think of the food offered at the most recent party you attended, you can understand why.

Long-Term Effects on the Body Measures of health are usually biological, but a developmental perspective urges us to think about awareness and attitudes as well as physiological indicators. This is particularly important in emerging adulthood, because patterns are set in early adulthood that affect health later on.

For example, young CARDIA adults were rarely obese, but if they sometimes felt their eating was out of control and had dieted, they were—25 years later—more often obese (Yoon et al., 2018). A young person who thinks their sports activities keep them in top shape may need to rethink their overall exercise strategy, as evident for Anita.

The importance of the psyche to physical health suggests an explanation for long-term effects of childhood poverty, racial discrimination, and maltreatment. Those problems affect all functions of the body, impairing health in middle age even if the childhood problems stopped decades ago (Duncan, 2018; Widom et al., 2015a). Some of this is directly biological, but much is psychological. Sleep, for instance, is influenced by anxiety and depression as much as specifics of light and sound.

Lars Zahner/EyeEm/Getty Images

Fix the Face It may surprise older men and women of every age that this young man in Germany is not alone in his skincare regimen. Most young men in every developed nation care about their appearance, and many use facial cleansers, creams, and serums if they think it helps.

Appearance

Partly because of their overall health, strength, and activity, most emerging adults look vital and attractive. The oily hair, pimpled faces, and awkward limbs of adolescence are gone, and the wrinkles and hair loss of middle adulthood have not yet appeared.

Body shape is often ideal; the gradual accumulation of unwanted fat comes over the later decades, and, as already mentioned, many young adults exercise regularly. As you remember, self-esteem falls in adolescence, especially for pubescent girls concerned about their weight, but then "individuals stop becoming more dissatisfied with their bodies as they enter emerging adulthood" (Nelson et al., 2018).

The organ that protects people from the elements, the skin, becomes clear and taut (Whitbourne & Whitbourne, 2014). The attractiveness of young skin is one reason that newly prominent fashion models, popular singers, and film stars tend to be in their early 20s, looking fresh and glamorous.

Most emerging adults value appearance more than older adults do, and this perceived importance may be problematic. Many spend time and money, and endure pain, to improve their looks. A study of college students (average age 19.5) who viewed a reality show depicting plastic surgery found that most students—male and female, of many ethnicities—rated the show positively.

Comments included: "I was amazed at how quickly and easily they turned her into a gorgeous young lady" and "It seemed like the story of an ugly duckling turning into a swan" (Markey & Markey, 2012, p. 212). Students who noted the shallowness of superficial appearance, the cost, or the pain were a decided minority.

Emerging adults spend more money on clothes, shoes, cosmetics, skin and hair care products, and so on than adults of any other age. They get eyebrows, teeth, and nails professionally changed. When they exercise, their main reason is to maintain—or attain—fit, slender, attractive bodies, unlike older adults, whose main exercise motive is health. New students in college, no matter what their ethnicity, usually care a great deal about looking good (Gillen & Lefkowitz, 2012).

Before criticizing this focus on looks, think about the underlying reasons. Appearance is connected to sexual drives, and appearance attracts sexual interest. Since society functions best if young adults find partners, it benefits the community if young adults care about appearance.

Furthermore, employment is a prime concern for emerging adults. Attractiveness (in clothing, body, and face) correlates with whether or not a person is interviewed, as well as with better jobs and higher pay. Of course, what is attractive to one person may not be attractive to another: Differences in the perception of attractiveness arising from unconscious ethnic prejudice affects employment decisions (Maddox & Perry, 2018).

The same may be true for gender expression and sexual orientation. It is illegal to consider such differences in hiring, promoting, and so on, yet individuals give clues regarding such factors, and those signs (e.g., "Does she wear a skirt or pants?") influence the employment process. The genders of the interviewer, the applicant, the boss, and the coworkers matter.

This is true internationally. Interestingly, for everyone, the perception of unfair treatment is a more powerful force on employee satisfaction than the actual discrimination (Triana et al., 2018).

Apart from gender, appearance itself may be pivotal. In one study, fictitious applications were sent on Facebook to real job openings. The résumés were identical, but some photos were attractive, some not. Attractive applicants were called for an interview 38 percent more often than applicants with the same qualifications but a less attractive face (Baert, 2018).

More than for men, women's faces and bodies affect dating and hiring (Fikkan & Rothblum, 2012; A. Morgan et al., 2012). Gradually over the years of adulthood, prospective mates and employers become less interested in appearance (Sprecher et al., 2018).

It is not surprising that emerging adults try to look their best. Usually they succeed.

Same Situation, Far Apart: The Bride and Groom Weddings everywhere involve special gowns and apparel—notice the gloves in Bali *(bottom)* and the headpiece in Malaysia *(top)*. They also involve families. In many places, the ceremony includes the new couple promising to care for their parents—a contrast to the U.S. custom of a father giving away his daughter to the groom.

Rozikassim Photography/Moment Select/Getty Images

© Ingetje Tadros/The Image Bank/Getty Images

WHAT HAVE YOU LEARNED?

1. How and why has emerging adulthood become a distinct stage?
2. Why is maximum physical strength usually attained in emerging adulthood?
3. How does organ reserve protect against heart attacks?
4. How are homeostasis and allostasis apparent in the human need for food?
5. Why are people more attractive during emerging adulthood than at other times of life?

Sexual Activity

As already mentioned, the sexual-reproductive system is quick and strong during emerging adulthood: Orgasms are frequent, the sex drive is powerful, erotic responses are joyful, fertility is optimal, miscarriage is less common, and serious birth complications are unusual.

Births

Historically, most people married before age 20, had their first child within two years, and often had a second and third child before age 25; that is what their bodies did and their culture expected.

That has changed dramatically. Since 1980 in the United States, the birth rate among emerging adults has decreased virtually every year, continuing at least through 2018. Data are usually presented by age of the mother, but the same trends are evident for men. For men aged 20 to 25, the annual rate of fatherhood in 1980 was 92 per 1,000 males; in 2015 it was 52.

Not until over age 30 does the birth rate rise for either sex. Interestingly, although still unusual, the rate of births to unmarried women over age 35 is rising. Apparently, more women are deciding against marriage but for motherhood!

Universal Sex Drives

What has not changed for emerging adults are hormones, impulses, and fertility potential. Fertility still peaks in late adolescence and early adulthood. But society and emerging adults prefer births in the

OPPOSING PERSPECTIVES

Premarital Sex

In earlier decades, premarital sex was taboo, especially for women.

For example, in about 1960, according to a national sample of adults in the United States, only 7 percent believed that premarital sex was acceptable for women, and only 12 percent believed it was acceptable for men (Reiss, 1964). Rates were slightly higher if a couple were engaged (17 and 20 percent), but always people of both genders were more restrictive of women than men.

Cultures developed many ways to counter the sexual urges of adolescents and emerging adults, such as diligent chaperoning and single-sex schools. If an unmarried woman became pregnant, she and the young man were forced to marry in a *shotgun wedding,* so called because the girl's father would shoot the young man if he refused to marry the pregnant girl.

"You'd better ask your grandparents about that, son—my generation is very uncomfortable talking about abstinence."

All of this has changed. The United States in 2018 has only four all-male and 27 all-female colleges. The shotgun wedding "is rapidly becoming a relic" of another era (Jayson, 2014), evidence of a cohort change. In most nations, if an unmarried woman becomes pregnant, neither she nor the man feel compelled to marry.

The advent of effective contraception allowed a sexual revolution, welcomed by many young adults who, unlike earlier cohorts, no longer consider premarital sex a moral issue. For example, a survey of college students found that 85 percent agreed that "Any kind of consensual sex is okay as long as both persons freely agree to it" (England & Bearak, 2014, p. 1331).

When cohorts are compared, approval of premarital sex declines as age increases, an example of a negative correlation. Sexual behavior often elicits strong opinions, typically formed when people first experienced sexual urges (Sprecher et al., 2013). This is true for premarital sex, extramarital sex, single parenthood, and much more.

In another specific example, support for sexual activity between adults of the same sex declines markedly in each older cohort, and if that couple decides to marry, again disapproval increases with every generation. For instance, most adults (71 percent) aged 18 to 36 approve of such marriages; those over age 71 do not (41 percent) (Masci et al., 2017).

This makes it easy to see why there are opposing perspectives on premarital sex. People disagree as to what needs to change. Attitudes or behavior? In emerging adults, their parents, or their grandparents?

Your own opinion is strongly influenced by your cohort: Ask your parents and their parents. Read novels written 100 years ago. And then ask yourself if you are glad to come of age today rather than in former times.

late 20s or early 30s. Biology and social preferences clash, which could cause a decade or more of sexual frustration or unwanted births.

Medical research has found a solution: contraception. Young adults may be sexually active, but the world's 2015 birth rate for women aged 20 to 24 is one-third lower than it was in 1960. In the United States, it is two-thirds lower (United Nations, 2017).

Relatively few emerging adults *never* want children; they just don't want them soon. This was dramatically evident in a study of young men who were diagnosed with cancer (Nahata et al., 2019).

Thanks to organ reserve and modern medicine, almost all emerging adults survive cancer treatment, but about half become infertile. These young men did not want to be fathers yet, but almost all wanted to preserve the potential for fatherhood someday. Most did, via freezing some sperm.

The Double Standard In all of the surveys, adults condone more sexual activity among young men than among young women. This *sexual double standard* was once particularly apparent regarding premarital sex, for good reason: If premarital sex meant premarital pregnancy, and if unmarried fathers were less committed to their children, those children suffered. Social disapproval led to labels for them ("illegitimate," "bastard") that seem shocking in today's era.

The double standard was unfair to girls, especially because in a committed relationship the man was likely to believe that he could have a sexual relationship. But, the man was likely to think less of his future wife if she allowed it (Sprecher et al., 2013).

Even today, many people believe that women don't want sex as much as men do. Young adult men are supposed to make the first move and to brag about "scoring." The double standard has not disappeared, but it is changing rapidly, particularly for premarital sex (with notable national differences) (Bordin & Sperb, 2013) (see **Figure 17.2**).

In other examples that indicate the enduring double standard, much more research has gone into contraception for women than for men. Women tend to underreport their casual sexual activity, and men tend to overreport (England & Bearak, 2014). And finally, women are more likely than men to regret participating in casual sex, especially if they themselves hold the double standard (Kaestle & Evans 2018; Wesche et al., 2018).

Sexually Transmitted Infections The same innovations that brought sex without pregnancy have also created problems for many emerging adults. One is that the rate of sexually transmitted infections (STIs) is rising among unmarried people in their 20s.

Globally, improvements in transportation and the adventure seeking of emerging adults have led to the spread of STIs. To be specific, during the same years that contraception improved, travel became far easier and cheaper, and this means that an STI caught in one place quickly spreads.

Most emerging adults voluntarily engage in sex, which makes them unlikely victims of sex-trafficking, who suffer involuntarily (Russell, 2018). However, the more sexual partners a person has, the more STIs spread.

This proliferation is particularly tragic with HIV/AIDS, which medical researchers now believe existed occasionally and locally for a hundred years. Its prevalence initially followed the tracks of one railroad line in Africa, because that was the only form of transportation that a young person might take.

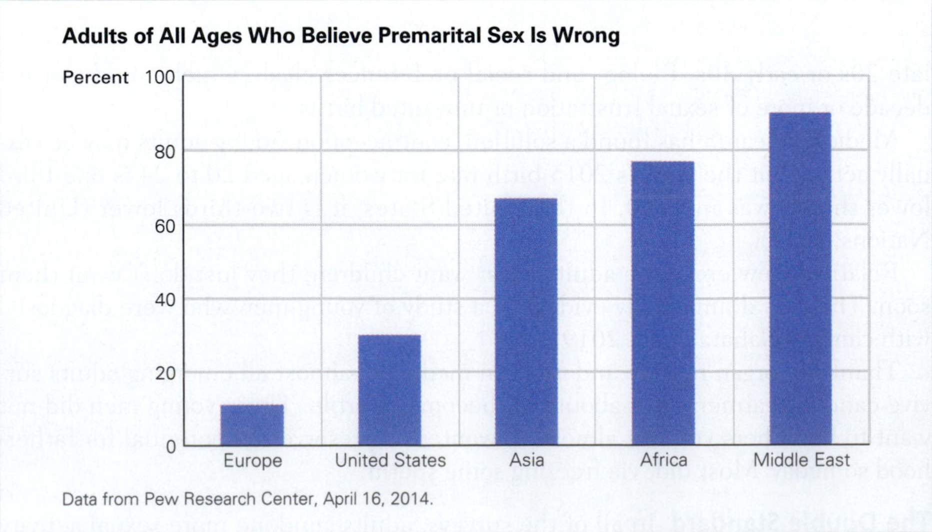

FIGURE 17.2
Everybody Is Doing It? Cultural variation regarding sex before marriage, evident in this figure, illustrates a paradox: Sex is essential for community survival, yet attitudes about who, how, when, and why are diametrically opposite from one place, one era, and even one person to another.

However, within the past 40 years, primarily because of air travel and the sexual activities of young adults, HIV has become a worldwide epidemic, with victims in every nation (Fan et al., 2014). Young adults are the prime STI *vectors* (those who spread disease) as well as the most common new victims.

Organ reserve and medical treatment almost always prevent death in emerging adulthood, but that requires young adults to see a doctor. As you remember, emerging adults hesitate to contact the medical establishment. Many STIs are symptomless at first, and many people try to treat symptoms on their own—passing the infection along.

The lack of prevention and early treatment for STIs is tragic for four reasons:

1. Sexual infections spread when the carriers are unaware of them.
2. If a person with an STI has sex with several people, spread is rapid and the attempt to trace back to partners may miss someone.
3. Untreated STIs increase infertility, disease, and death later in life, including for diseases that may seem unrelated, such as cancer and tuberculosis.
4. STIs infect people who never imagined that they would be harmed.

Vasyl Shevchenko/AP Images

Ashamed to Use a Condom? This public health effort attempts to remove the stigma, in order to reduce STIs and unwanted babies.

Observation Quiz Where is this? (see answer, page 450) ↑

The best-known example comes from South Africa, where customs have resulted in millions of wives, sexually faithful to their husbands, with STIs. Because of inadequate care, and the man's unwillingness to acknowledge his own infection, women transmitted HIV to their newborns, causing another generation of deaths (United Nations, 2004).

Indeed, many aspects of culture in South Africa combined to make that nation the world leader in the rate of HIV/AIDS cases, with young married women especially vulnerable. In recent years, treatment has increased, and the rate of new infections has slowed. An estimated 8 million South Africans carry the virus, including more than one-fourth of all pregnant women (Barron et al., 2013).

HIV is a tragic example, but new problems have appeared. *Congenital syphilis,* which results in a newborn with lifelong disabilities and sometimes an early death, has increased every year in the United States since 2012.

In 2017, the U.S. rate of congenital syphilis was double the rate in 2014 (Centers for Disease Control, 2018). Fortunately, this STI is still rare, but it is completely avoidable if the mother gets early prenatal care. Thus, the increase is an alarming indication that the most vulnerable Americans lack health care.

In the United States, increasing rates of STIs are especially evident among emerging-adult men. Both poverty and pride keep them away from medical care. This is particularly true for homeless youth, who have many barriers that prevent good health care (Caccamo et al., 2017).

Another recent problem is *human papilloma virus* (*HPV*). Most sexually active emerging adults are infected, but they do not know it until warts appear on their genitals (which could be years after HPV infection) or—in the worst cases—women are diagnosed with cervical cancer, or adults of any gender are diagnosed with anal, oral, or other cancers.

Prevention includes inoculation at age 11 or 12, a measure that is resisted by some parents who hope their child will have sex with only one, uninfected, person. In other nations, notably Australia, high rates of vaccination for the past decade have already substantially reduced cancer deaths (Patel et al., 2018).

Especially for Nurses When should you suspect that a patient has an untreated STI? (see response, page 450)

Unwanted Pregnancy The second problem with the sexual activities of young adults is unwanted pregnancy, which leads either to abortion or to birth of an unwanted child. Effective contraception requires planning—contrary to the idea that passion is spontaneous.

Moreover, cost is an issue. The most effective methods of contraception are automatic and long-acting (implants, intrauterine devices), with a failure rate of once in a hundred years (Winner et al., 2012), but they require anticipation of a sexual future, seeing a doctor, and an initial cost.

A study in Finland offered free, long-acting contraception. The result: increased use in young women and fewer abortions (Gyllenberg et al., 2018). However, to make contraception free for all emerging adults would require a massive cultural shift among older adults, who remember when fear of unmarried conception kept marriage rates high and single women abstinent.

A study in the United States discovered a connection between financial pressure and lack of contraception. For emerging adults, the link between the two was much stronger than for women over age 30 (Lyons et al., 2019). Apparently, more mature women, even when money is tight, consider the long-term costs of an unwanted conception and find free gynecological care.

WHAT HAVE YOU LEARNED?

1. What has changed, and what has not changed, in sexual activity among young adults?
2. Why are STIs more common currently than 50 years ago?
3. Why do nations differ in their rates of HIV?
4. Why is prevention of HPV more common in Australia than in the United States?
5. Why is unwanted pregnancy still common in the United States?

Taking Risks

The spread of sexual diseases is one example of a generalization first expressed in Chapter 1: Every behavior and every age entails gains and losses. One human behavior is taking risks.

Who Are the Risk Takers?

Some emerging adults bravely, or foolishly, take risks—a behavior that is gender- and age-related, as well as genetic and hormonal. Those who are genetically impulsive *and* male *and* emerging adults are most likely to be brave and foolish.

In one study, 10- to 30-year-olds judged "how good or bad an idea is it to . . ." do various risky things (such as riding a bicycle down the stairs or taking pills at a party) (Shulman & Cauffman, 2014). The participants had only two seconds to make a snap judgment on a sliding scale from 0 to 100. For instance, the bicycle-riding could be rated at 70 (somewhat bad idea) and the pills at 99 (very bad idea). There also were items that were not risky at all (eating a sandwich).

Risky items were rated more favorably (closer to a good idea) every year from ages 10 to 20 and then less favorably (closer to a bad idea) every year from ages 20 to 30. More of the older respondents had done the risky things (the average

Who and Where? Knowing the attraction to danger of emerging-adult men makes it easy to guess who—a 19-year-old male. But where is harder—that dangerous leap into the ocean could be occurring in many nations. This one is taking place in the Indian Ocean in Sri Lanka.

stuart dunn/Alamy Stock Photo

15- to 17-year-old had done four of the items; the average 20- to 25-year-old had done seven), but that did not affect their judgment.

For example, whether or not a person had taken pills at a party was not related to whether or not they thought that was very risky. Instead, the crucial factor was maturation. Every year past age 20 increased the likelihood that a person would consider various behaviors as risky, whether or not they personally had done them.

Benefits of Risk Taking

Of course, sometimes taking a risk is beneficial. For instance, an emerging adult's willingness to take chances may lead to enrolling in college, moving to a new place, joining a sports team, finding a new job, enlisting in the military, or volunteering for work in a poor nation or troubled neighborhood. Emerging adults do these more than older adults, and societies benefit.

I once taught a college course in Sing Sing Correctional Facility, a maximum-security prison for serious criminals. More than half of my students had sentences that ended with "life," such as "25 years to life." That sentence meant that the inmate could not be paroled until serving at least 25 years, and maybe never.

My course was social psychology, and I required my students to write essays using their personal experiences to illustrate concepts in the course. I was struck by how many of them had committed their crimes when they were emerging adults. Moreover, several of them did not write about what they had done wrong but about what they had done right.

Jimmy, for instance, had run into a burning building and rescued a child. He was commended in the local paper. He was a risk taker: That landed him in prison but also enabled him to save that child.

Extreme Sports Most young adults do not end up in prison, of course. Instead they take risks that society accepts, such as joining the military or traveling to unfamiliar lands. Particularly common are recreational activities that have elements of risk and challenge.

Emerging adults climb mountains with perpendicular cliffs, surf in oceans with 20-foot waves, run in pain, play past exhaustion, and so on. An attraction to danger has always been characteristic of humans at this age, causing what demographers call an *accident bump* in early adulthood. Thousands of soldiers over the centuries volunteer to fight, and often died, against foes they never knew.

Observation Quiz What signs of caution are evident? (see answer, page 450)

Getting High Rock climbing is one way to enjoy the thrills of emerging adulthood. The impulse to do so is universal, illustrated with two examples here: a limestone cliff called "the Egg" in Yangshuo, Guangxi Zhuang, China *(left)*, and an Art of Motion festival in Santorini, Greece *(right)*.

Henn Photography/Cultura/Getty Images

Handout/Predrag Vuckovic/Red Bull via Getty Images

THINK CRITICALLY: In 40 of the 50 U.S. states, the highest salary for a public employee is not paid to the governor or the college president but to the football coach. Is that how it should be?

New extreme sports—skydiving, bungee jumping, pond swooping, parkour, potholing (in caves), waterfall kayaking, shark-diving, jet skiing, and ziplining hundreds of feet above the ground—attract thousands of emerging adults.

Many doctors try to mitigate the risks of each sport, and equipment is designed to protect the skull or the spine in a fall (Denq & Delasobera, 2018). However, broken ankles, twisted muscles, and dislocated shoulders are common—and many young adults with crutches proudly explain how that injury occurred.

Popular college sports entail physical risks. Football not only injures the body (star players often are on the disabled list) but also the brain, with lifelong effects. Concussions increase the risk of severe brain damage and disease (Vos et al., 2018). College football players were compared with matched athletes who were stars of track and field. Brains of the former were significantly impaired (Adler et al., 2018).

Why, then, would any college promote that sport? Because emerging adults want it. Large stadiums, tailgate parties, cheerleaders, mascots, homecoming weekends, and so on are integral to college life on many campuses.

Apparently, college students enjoy taking risks, and they enjoy watching others take risks. Think of who watches which television programs, who admires

A CASE TO STUDY

A Hero for Millions

The fact that extreme sports are age-related is evident in Travis Pastrana, "an extreme sports renaissance man—a pro adrenaline junkie/daredevil/speed demon—whatever you want to call him" (Giblin, 2014). Several accidents almost killed him.

Pastrana won the 2006 X Games motocross competition at age 22 with a double backflip, because, he explained, "I've been healthy and able to train at my fullest, and a lot of guys have had major crashes this year" (quoted in Higgins, 2006, p. D-7).

Four years later, Pastrana set a new record for leaping through big air in an automobile, as he drove over the ocean from a ramp on the California shoreline to a barge more than 250 feet out. He crashed into a barrier on the boat but emerged, seemingly ecstatic and unhurt, to the thunderous cheers of thousands of other young adults on the shore (Roberts, 2010).

In 2011, a broken foot and ankle made Pastrana temporarily halt extreme sports—but soon he returned to the acclaim of his cohort, winning races rife with flips and other hazards. In 2013, after some more serious injuries, he said he was "still a couple of surgeries away" from racing on a motorcycle, so he turned to NASCAR auto racing.

In 2014, at age 30 and after becoming a husband and a father (twice), he quit NASCAR. He said his most hazardous race days are over, which is similar to many emerging adults who with marriage and maturity become less likely to engage in risk taking.

However, in July 2018, at age 34, Pastrana executed three more stunning jumps on his motorcycle: one 143 feet over 52 crushed cars, one 192 feet over 16 Greyhound buses, and the final one 149 feet so high in the air that he was higher than the fountains outside Caesars Palace, a famous Las Vegas hotel.

Those three jumps had been executed in 1967 by Evel Knieval, a man who made a career of daredevil stunts. He was a hero to Pastrana.

Does that suggest that Pastrana is still an emerging adult, years past the time when he should have been an adult? Not quite. His deference to Evel may be evidence that he respects the past, a trait more typical of adults than emerging adults.

© Gene Blevins/ZUMA Wire

A Role Model, But... Travis Pastrana came out of retirement to follow his idol, Evel Knievel, who also wore white attempting the same three jumps. Three major differences: a better helmet, a better motorcycle, and success.

daredevils like Evel Knievel or Travis Pastrana, and who takes a pill that someone else gave them.

Dangerous Risks As you see, risk taking is often destructive. Although their bodies are strong and their reactions quick, emerging adults nonetheless have more serious accidents than do people of any other age (see **Figure 17.3**). The low rate of disease between ages 18 and 25 is counterbalanced by a high rate of violent death.

THINK CRITICALLY: Why are college students more likely to abuse drugs than emerging adults who are not in college?

Risks that are more common in emerging adulthood than any other time include unprotected sex with a new partner, driving without a seat belt, carrying a loaded gun, abusing drugs, and addictive gambling—all done partly for a rush of adrenaline (Cosgrave, 2010). In the United States, the peak age for serious crime is 19; for unintended pregnancy, 18 to 19; for automobile driver death, 21 (Shulman & Cauffman, 2014).

In 2016 in the United States, of the 20- to 24-year-olds who died, fewer than 4 percent were victims of cancer, although that was the leading disease cause. For the other deaths, risk taking was almost always implicated.

To be specific, of the 21,763 U.S. deaths in 2016 of 20- to 24-year-olds, accidents killed 45 percent, suicide 17 percent, and homicide 15 percent (Heron, 2018). Males were three times more likely to die than females, but emerging-adult females also die of these causes far more often than at any other age. Rates of all of these rise in late adolescence and peak in the early 20s (Heron, 2018).

Fatal accidents, homicide, and suicide result in more deaths in emerging adulthood than all other causes *combined*. This is true even in nations with high rates of infectious diseases and malnutrition. The contrast between sudden violent deaths and slower disease deaths is most stark in nations with good medical care.

In the United States, 77 percent of all emerging-adult deaths are from those three violent causes. Disease deaths are low because research continues to find cures for cancer, sepsis, heart disease, and so on—but research on guns, poisons, and depression lags behind. Is that because older adults accept those deaths but not the ones that become more common in middle age and late adulthood?

Drug Abuse By definition, **drug abuse** occurs whenever a drug (legal or illegal, prescribed or not) is used in a harmful way, damaging a person's physical,

drug abuse A condition of harmful drug dependence in which the absence of the given drug in the individual's system produces a drive—physiological, psychological, or both—to ingest more of the drug.

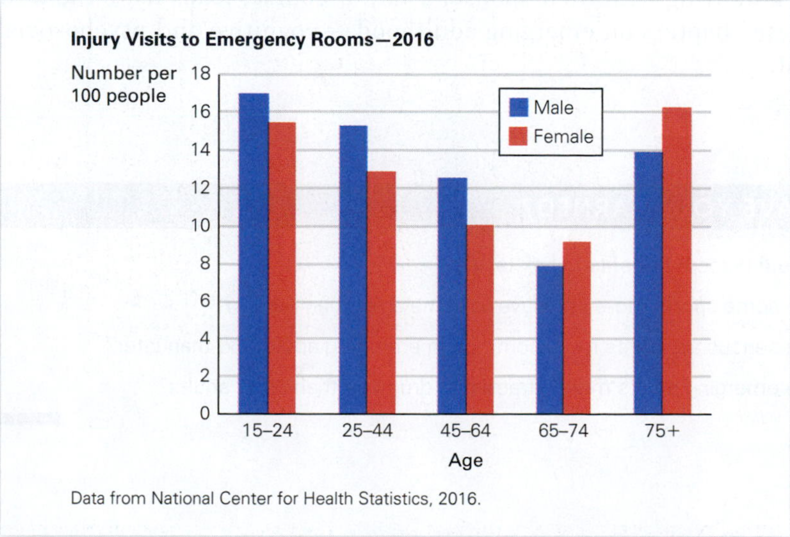

FIGURE 17.3
Safe at Age 70? Two reasons for the major age differences: more risk taking (young) and impaired balance (old).

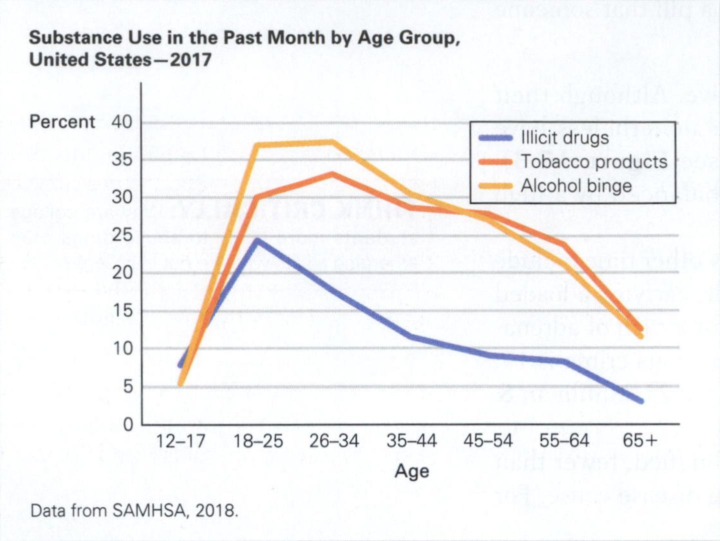

FIGURE 17.4

Too Old for That As you can see, emerging adults are the biggest substance abusers, but illegal drug use drops much faster than does cigarette use or binge drinking.

macmillan learning

VIDEO: College Binge Drinking shows college students engaging in (and rationalizing) this risky behavior.

Andrew Burton/Getty Images

What the F— Happened? That's what 30-year-old Reggie Colby asks. He says he had a happy childhood, tried heroin at age 18, married and dropped out of college, joined the army, and became addicted after an injury in Afghanistan. Since then he has been dishonorably discharged, divorced, and estranged from his daughter. Now he is sheltered by an overpass in Camden, New Jersey, two days after serving time in jail for stealing food. "What happened?" is the right question. Did the stress of emerging adulthood have anything to do with it?

cognitive, or psychosocial well-being. The interaction between age and drug abuse illustrates the nature of emerging adults, who seem attracted rather than repulsed by the potential for harm and arrest in buying, carrying, and using a forbidden drug.

Illegal drug use peaks at about age 20 and declines sharply with age (see **Figure 17.4**). Addiction to legal drugs (no arrest imminent) has a much slower quit rate, probably because thrill is not part of the addiction.

Quitting any addiction is difficult, but when emerging adulthood is over, the process eases a bit. Long-term consequences (illness, loss of family, unemployment, poverty) seem more significant, and the thrill is gone.

In adulthood, drugs are used to stop pain and unpleasant emotions more than to promote joy and excitement. For that reason, abstinence becomes more common—a source of pride not embarrassment—after emerging adulthood (Heyman, 2013).

Men tend to take more risks and use more drugs, but especially in the United States, young women are also vulnerable. A nationwide study found that 24 percent of women aged 18 to 25 had binged on alcohol in the past month (for women a binge is defined as four or more drinks on one occasion).

That emerging-adult rate was higher than the rate for either younger or older women (MMWR, January 11, 2013). Moreover, those 24 percent *averaged* four binge episodes per month and six drinks per occasion, both more than older female bingers. Rates rose with income.

Many colleges restrict alcohol on campus, not only for legal reasons but to decrease property destruction and sexual assault (which tends to occur when both parties have been drinking or drugging [Zinzow & Thompson, 2015]). Colleges have only limited success, however, because local bars and national fraternities resist (McMurtrie, 2014).

Of course, the basic problem is the students themselves, who encourage each other to drink. Students at residential colleges use alcohol and drugs far more than young adults the same age who live with their parents or who are married and living with their spouse. That, of course, leads us to the next topics of these chapters on emerging adulthood—cognitive and psychosocial development.

WHAT HAVE YOU LEARNED?

1. What are the social benefits of risk taking?
2. Why are some sports more attractive at some ages than others?
3. Why are serious accidents more common in emerging adulthood than later?
4. Why are emerging adults more attracted to drug use than older adults?

SUMMARY

Biological Universals

1. Young adults usually have strong and healthy bodies. However, the social world in which they live has changed, so a new stage, emerging adulthood, has appeared.

2. Full growth and strength characterize emerging adulthood. Most emerging adults are quite healthy, although they rarely see a doctor.

3. Health habits in emerging adulthood affect later health. The body adjusts to various stresses, which are usually unnoticed at first, because of organ reserve and homeostasis.

4. Over time, the insults and adjustments of emerging adulthood may accumulate, causing a heavy allostatic load. That makes it more likely that an older adult will develop a serious illness. The rate of aging varies, dependent on habits.

5. All aspects of development adjust and protect the developing body. This is true for sleep, exercise, and diet. For the most part, emerging adults keep active and avoid harmful diets.

6. Most emerging adults look attractive, as their shape is good, skin is clear, and they use many products to enhance their appearance. Appearance is a factor in sexual attraction and in employment, both particularly important during these years.

Sexual Activity

7. The sexual-reproductive system reaches a peak during these years, but most current emerging adults postpone childbearing. Since sexual urges are strong, many emerging adults are sexually active but use effective contraception.

8. However, rates of sexually transmitted infections are increasing in this age group. The reasons include more partners and frequent travel: The consequences may be infertility and transmission to family members, especially partners and children.

9. The other result of sexual activity among emerging adults is unwanted pregnancy. This occurs more often in the United States than in other nations, in part because many emerging adults avoid health care and effective contraception.

Taking Risks

10. Willingness to take risks is characteristic of emerging adults. This allows positive behaviors, such as entering college, meeting new people, volunteering for difficult tasks, and finding new jobs.

11. Risk taking can also be harmful. It increases unprotected sex, fatal accidents, suicide, and homicide. Death from those causes is by far the leading cause of fatalities during these years.

12. Extreme sports are attractive to some emerging adults, who find the risk of serious injury thrilling. The same impulses can lead to drug abuse, which peaks in emerging adulthood, especially among college students.

KEY TERMS

emerging adulthood (p. 432)
WEIRD (p. 432)
organ reserve (p. 434)
homeostasis (p. 434)
allostasis (p. 435)
allostatic load (p. 435)
set point (p. 437)
body mass index (p. 437)
drug abuse (p. 447)

APPLICATIONS

1. Describe an incident during your emerging adulthood when taking a risk could have led to disaster. What were your feelings at the time? What would you do if you knew that a child of yours was about to do the same thing?

2. Read a biography or autobiography that includes information about the person's thinking from adolescence through adulthood. How did personal experiences, education, and maturation affect the person's thinking?

3. Statistics on cohort and culture in students and in colleges are fascinating, but only a few are reported here. Compare your nation, state, or province with another. Analyze the data and discuss causes and implications of differences.

4. Talk to three people you would expect to have contrasting views on love and marriage (differences in age, gender, upbringing, experience, and religion might affect attitudes). Ask each of them the same questions, and then compare their answers.

Especially For ANSWERS

Response for Nurses (from p. 443): Always. In this context, "suspect" refers to a healthy skepticism, not to prejudice or disapproval. Your attitude should be professional rather than judgmental, but be aware that education, gender, self-confidence, and income do not necessarily mean that a given patient is free of an STI.

Observation Quiz ANSWERS

Answer to Observation Quiz (from p. 436) Almost never do men, or non-whites, or people over age 30, choose this, as evident in this photo. London is now very diverse, as are most U.S. cities.

Answer to Observation Quiz (from p. 443) Kyiv, in Ukraine. As evident in the globalization of emerging adulthood, the same challenges are everywhere.

Answer to Observation Quiz (from p. 445) Ropes. But note that neither young adult wears a helmet and that the climber's ropes are not that protective. Even the rope keeping the observers from falling in Greece seems symbolic—which explains why an official stands in front of the rope.

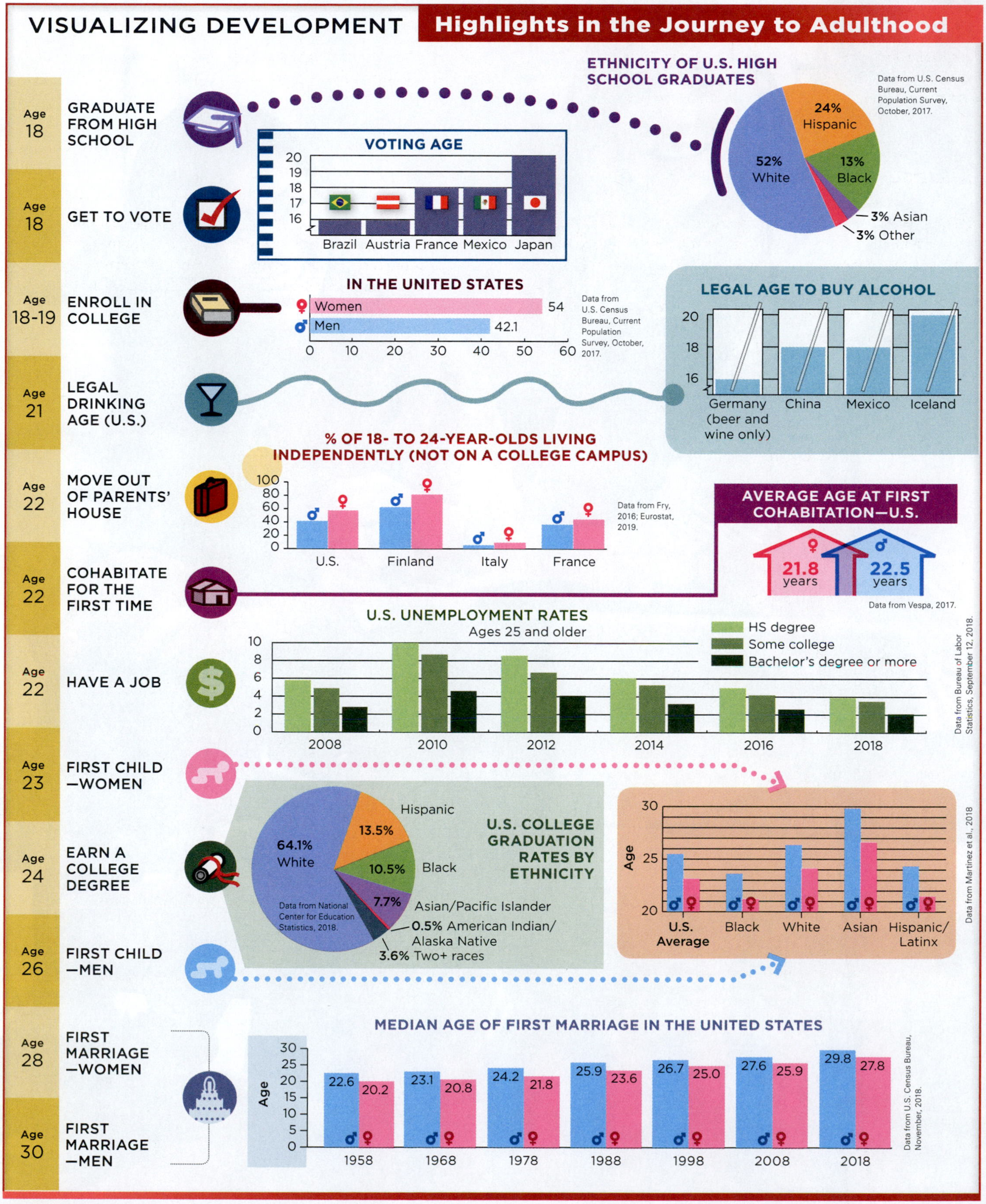
VISUALIZING DEVELOPMENT
Highlights in the Journey to Adulthood
Age 18
GRADUATE FROM HIGH SCHOOL
ETHNICITY OF U.S. HIGH SCHOOL GRADUATES
52% White
24% Hispanic
13% Black
3% Asian
3% Other
Data from U.S. Census Bureau, Current Population Survey, October, 2017.
Age 18
GET TO VOTE
VOTING AGE
20
19
18
17
16
Brazil
Austria
France
Mexico
Japan
Age 18-19
ENROLL IN COLLEGE
IN THE UNITED STATES
Women 54
Men 42.1
0 10 20 30 40 50 60
Data from U.S. Census Bureau, Current Population Survey, October, 2017.
Age 21
LEGAL DRINKING AGE (U.S.)
LEGAL AGE TO BUY ALCOHOL
20
18
16
Germany (beer and wine only)
China
Mexico
Iceland
Age 22
MOVE OUT OF PARENTS' HOUSE
% OF 18- TO 24-YEAR-OLDS LIVING INDEPENDENTLY (NOT ON A COLLEGE CAMPUS)
100
80
60
40
20
0
U.S.
Finland
Italy
France
Data from Fry, 2016; Eurostat, 2019.
Age 22
COHABITATE FOR THE FIRST TIME
AVERAGE AGE AT FIRST COHABITATION—U.S.
21.8 years
22.5 years
Data from Vespa, 2017.
Age 22
HAVE A JOB
U.S. UNEMPLOYMENT RATES
Ages 25 and older
HS degree
Some college
Bachelor's degree or more
10
8
6
4
2
0
2008
2010
2012
2014
2016
2018
Data from Bureau of Labor Statistics, September 12, 2018.
Age 23
FIRST CHILD —WOMEN
Age 24
EARN A COLLEGE DEGREE
U.S. COLLEGE GRADUATION RATES BY ETHNICITY
64.1% White
13.5% Hispanic
10.5% Black
7.7% Asian/Pacific Islander
0.5% American Indian/Alaska Native
3.6% Two+ races
Data from National Center for Education Statistics, 2018.
Age
30
25
20
U.S. Average
Black
White
Asian
Hispanic/Latinx
Data from Martinez et al., 2018
Age 26
FIRST CHILD —MEN
Age 28
FIRST MARRIAGE —WOMEN
Age 30
FIRST MARRIAGE —MEN
MEDIAN AGE OF FIRST MARRIAGE IN THE UNITED STATES
Age
30
25
20
15
10
5
0
22.6 20.2
23.1 20.8
24.2 21.8
25.9 23.6
26.7 25.0
27.6 25.9
29.8 27.8
1958
1968
1978
1988
1998
2008
2018
Data from U.S. Census Bureau, November, 2018.

CHAPTER

18

Emerging Adulthood: Cognitive Development

What Will You Know?

1. How is adult thinking different from that of adolescents?
2. Are adults more moral or more religious than adolescents?
3. How does college affect a person's thinking processes?

- **A New Level of Thinking**
  - Postformal Thought
  - INSIDE THE BRAIN: A New Stage?
  - Dialectical Thought
- **Ethics and Religion**
  - Doing the Right Thing
  - Faith and Practice
- **Cognitive Growth and Higher Education**
  - Health and Wealth
  - A VIEW FROM SCIENCE: Women and College
  - College and Cognition
  - A CASE TO STUDY: Generation to Generation
  - Improving the College Experience
  - Technology in College
  - Why Learn?
- **VISUALIZING DEVELOPMENT: Why Study?**

On the bench outside my grandson's class sat a small boy, alone. He told me that another boy said he liked a particular presidential candidate, and this small boy knew that the candidate "hated Mexicans." Since he himself was Mexican American, he got into a fight with that other boy. The teacher had sent him to the hall. He seemed quite proud of himself.

I could have explained why fighting is bad, or praised him for his political opinions, or praised the teacher, or told him about my Mexican friend. Instead, I just nodded. I did not take sides.

In this incident, I thought as an adult. Cognition in adulthood considers many perspectives, combining emotions and logic, the personal and the political. Compared to children, who are quick to judge, adults weigh values, interests, and strategies.

Developmentalists themselves use many approaches to analyze adult cognition.

- The *stage approach* describes a new shift in the characteristics of thought.
- The *psychometric approach* analyzes intelligence longitudinally via various tests.
- The *information-processing approach* studies neurological encoding, storage, and retrieval.

Each of these approaches includes adults from ages 18 to 100, and each has merit. These approaches are neither exclusive nor confined to any particular chronological period. To make it easier to study, each of the three chapters on adult cognition (Chapters 18, 21, and 24) emphasizes one of these approaches.

This chapter focuses on the idea that emerging adults begin to think at a higher stage than adolescents, a stage that continues throughout adulthood. Chapter 21 takes the psychometric approach, charting the ups and downs of thinking over the decades. Chapter 24 explains how information processing changes over adulthood and, thus, how changes in the brain and the senses affect cognition. Each of these chapters includes adults at many ages, because adult cognition does not follow chronological cutoffs.

Each chapter also includes specific topics that are particularly relevant at a certain period. For example, college education is discussed in this chapter; learning on the job is discussed in Chapter 21; severe cognitive loss (formerly called dementia) is discussed in Chapter 24.

Left: AJ_Watt/E+/Getty Images
Top: RapidEye/iStock/E+/Getty Images

But remember that adulthood has no strict age cutoffs. Some college students are age 70; people of every age learn from their work; severe neurocognitive disorders can begin at age 30.

I hope that all adults are long past the preoperational egocentrism of that small boy who reacted with fisticuffs to a political opinion of another child. Since I think like an adult, I was able to hold my tongue and also to question myself, as adults often do. Should I have done more than nod?

macmillan learning

VIDEO ACTIVITY: Brain Development: Emerging Adulthood shows the changes that occur in a person's brain between ages 18 and 25.

A New Level of Thinking

The perspective on adult cognition that we take in this chapter is the stage approach, reflecting the idea that adults can think at a level higher than adolescent thought. For this perspective, we are grateful to Piaget, who changed our understanding of cognitive development.

Piaget recognized that maturation does not simply add knowledge; it allows a leap forward at each stage, from sensorimotor to preoperational (because of symbolic thought), from preoperational to concrete, and then from concrete to formal (each with new logic).

Postformal Thought

Although *formal operational* thought was Piaget's final stage, many cognitive psychologists find that post-adolescent thinking is a cut above that.

postformal thought A proposed adult stage of cognitive development, following Piaget's four stages, that goes beyond adolescent thinking by being more practical, more flexible, and more dialectical (i.e., more capable of combining contradictory elements into a comprehensive whole).

They describe a fifth stage, called **postformal thought,** a "type of logical, adaptive problem-solving that is a step more complex than scientific formal-level Piagetian tasks" (Sinnott, 2014, p. 3). In postformal cognition, "thinking needs to be integrated with emotional and pragmatic aspects, rather than only dealing with the purely abstract" (Labouvie-Vief, 2015, p. 89).

As they integrate emotion and pragmatics, postformal thinkers are flexible, with a "more complex, nuanced, and paradoxical" thinking (Gidley, 2016). They consider all aspects of a situation, anticipating and dealing with problems rather than denying, avoiding, or procrastinating. As a result, postformal thought is practical and creative (Kallio, 2011; Su, 2011; Gidley, 2016).

Observation Quiz Where is this? (see answer, page 476) ↓

Learning About Health Hundreds of health professionals offer free medical care at this Buddhist temple, likely employing postformal thought as they identify problems and risks and recommend strategies for promoting health. One of the professionals is Daniel Garcia, shown here with the clipboard.

MARCUS YAM/LOS ANGELES Times/Getty Images

Rejecting Stereotypes Not every adult reaches postformal thought, nor does every postformal thinker always think with the flexibility and complexity that characterizes this fifth stage. However, postformal thought allows movement past simplistic ideas, shedding stereotypes (Chang & Chiou, 2014).

That is one conclusion from an experiment that involved voters in South Florida (Broockman & Kalla, 2016). Canvassers sought to reduce *transphobia* (fear regarding transgender people), a common prejudice that follows naturally from childish stereotypes. They designed a field study based on what had been learned in laboratory studies (Flores et al., 2018).

The study began with the public list of registered voters. Half of the names and addresses were allocated to the experimental group and the other half to the control group. Canvassers rang the doorbells of the voters, asking the experimental half to talk about a time when they had been marginalized because of some characteristic (ethnicity, age, religion, and so on).

The voters were then asked how their experiences and emotions might apply to transgender people. Canvassers were

INSIDE THE BRAIN

A New Stage?

Piaget himself never used the term *postformal,* and developmentalists debate whether cognition in adulthood merits consideration as a "stage." No brain areas accelerate cognitive growth in adulthood, as happens with the language areas at about age 2, when sensorimotor thought becomes preoperational thought. But one meaning of a cognitive stage is that the brain advances significantly. By that definition, adulthood is a new stage.

One developmental scholar wrote:

> we hypothesize that there exists, after the formal thinking stage, a fifth stage of post-formal thinking, as Piaget had already studied its basic forms and would have concluded the same thing, had he the time to do so.
>
> [*Lemieux, 2012, p. 404*]

Several scholars criticize Piaget because he did not recognize the limits of formal operational thinking. As one wrote:

> [S]ince about 1980, a number of researchers offered critiques of the implication that cognitive growth abated in adolescence. Instead, a number of proposals appeared that, though independent, converged on an extension of Piaget's theory. These extensions proposed that thinking needs to be integrated with emotional and pragmatic aspects, rather than only dealing with the purely abstract.
>
> [*Labouvie-Vief, 2015, p. 89*]

How does postformal cognition relate to the human brain? As described in Chapter 14, the prefrontal cortex is not fully mature until the early 20s, and new dendrites form throughout life. It is now apparent that thinking changes as the brain matures (Lemieux, 2012), with brain development affected by experiences more than by time alone (Sinnott, 2014). Adult brains benefit from better neurological connections and greater experience of the social world (Grayson & Fair, 2017).

It is not that new brain areas appear. Instead, the areas already developed increase in their connections (Colver & Dovey-Pearce, 2018). Of great interest, developmentally, is the link between emotional sensitivity and creativity (He et al., 2018). A creative adolescent might have an idea that is wildly out of touch with the emotions of other people; adults are less likely to make that mistake.

Stronger links form between one part of the brain and another. A single event might activate multiple brain areas. Adults are better able to connect emotions and reason, and to connect emotional sensitivity with creative thought, because the neurological links are tighter.

Thus, adult brains are not as quick to activate the action neurons as adolescent brains are: An adult might lose at a video game that requires fast decisions. However, in adulthood, more regions of the brain react to a single event, and longer fibers connect one area with another (Liu et al., 2018). Adults move toward wisdom, a trait that is beyond most adolescents.

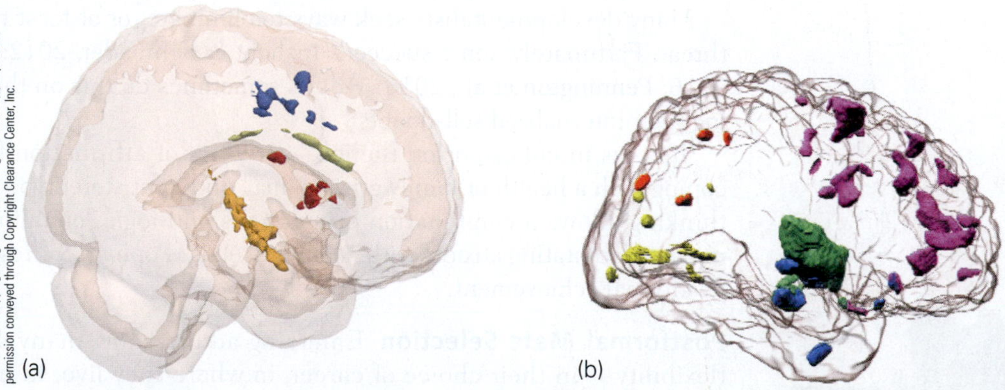

Thinking Away from Home Both brain scans show maturation during emerging adulthood. *(a)* Entering a residential college means experiencing new foods, new friends, and new neurons. A longitudinal study of 18-year-old students at the beginning and end of their first year in college (Dartmouth) found increases in the brain areas that integrate emotion and cognition—namely, the cingulate (blue and yellow), caudate (red), and insula (orange). Researchers also studied one-year changes in the brains of students over age 25 at the same college and found no dramatic growth. *(b)* Shown here are the areas of one person's brain that changed from age 14 to age 25. The frontal cortex (purple) demonstrated many changes in particular parts, as did the areas for processing speech (green and blue)—a crucial aspect of emerging-adult learning. Areas for visual processing (yellow) showed minimal change.

Researchers now know that brains mature in many ways between adolescence and adulthood; scientists are not yet sure of the cognitive implications.

instructed to listen respectfully and to facilitate "deep processing" of the information, which means to encourage reflection, not snap answers.

The other half of the voters, in the control group, experienced the same conditions, except that their canvassers focused on climate change and recycling. Three days, three weeks, and three months later both groups answered a questionnaire that they did not know was related to their encounter with a canvasser.

The answers on the questionnaires showed that those who had a brief conversation about transgender concerns become somewhat more positive over time toward trans people, especially if the canvassers had identified themselves as transgender. The control group did not change their opinion. The scientists believe that the crucial difference was cognitive.

Personally, I harbor many stereotypes; it gives me joy when I recognize and discard them. One of the intellectual benefits of teaching and parenting is to recognize, with the help of my students and children, that complex, postformal thinking is needed.

For example, when I taught social psychology in Sing Sing Correctional Facility, every week another stereotype about convicted criminals was dispelled. I learned that many had done admirable acts as well as some harmful ones, that all were eager to learn, and that they were fiercely protective of me. Teaching in prison was an intellectual joy as well as a challenge, because of postformal thinking.

stereotype threat The thought in a person's mind that one's appearance or behavior will be misread to confirm another person's oversimplified, prejudiced attitudes.

THINK CRITICALLY: What imagined criticisms impair your own achievement, and how can you overcome this?

Stereotype Threat Unfortunately, it is difficult to recognize one's own stereotypes. One of the most pernicious is **stereotype threat,** arising in people who worry that other people might judge them as stupid, lazy, oversexed, or worse because of their ethnicity, sex, age, or appearance. In other words, the stereotype is that other people hold a stereotype! Stereotype threat arises from an imagined and envisioned idea, a "threat in the air" (Steele, 1997).

Then the *possibility* of being stereotyped arouses emotions and hijacks memory, disrupting cognition. Most of the research on stereotype threat has been on students in schools and colleges who do not perform as well when their worries about other people's stereotypes are activated.

Many developmentalists seek ways to eliminate, or at least reduce, stereotype threat. Fortunately, some succeed (Inzlicht & Schmader, 2012; S. Spencer et al., 2016; Pennington et al., 2016). Adults sometimes do this on their own, confronting their internalized self-doubts.

Success in college or on the job—or years of affirmation from a partner, or coping with a health or family crisis—may undercut stereotype threat. Postformal thinking allows a combination of emotions and logic, enabling some people to replace debilitating anxiety with cognitive focus (Popham & Hess, 2015). That is a postformal achievement.

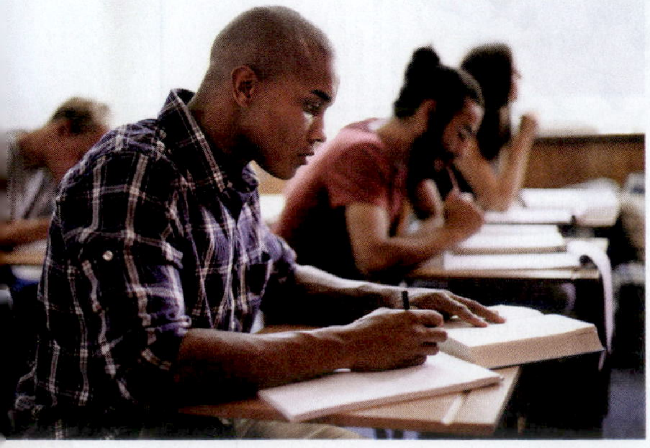

Anxiety? Does thinking about taking a test make this man anxious, and does that undercut his performance? If so, that is stereotype threat.

Postformal Mate Selection Emerging adults show many signs of cognitive flexibility—in their choice of career, in where they live, in how they dress, in what they eat. Their choices do not duplicate what their parents did but instead reflect their childhood while moving beyond it.

A major example relates to romance. As described in Chapter 17, emerging adults today tend to marry much later than their parents did. Increasingly, they cross ethnic or religious lines in choosing a partner. Thus, couple by couple, adult thinking is not determined by childhood culture, parental example, or traditional norms.

To be specific, in 2017, 18 percent of all newlyweds were from different racial or ethnic groups. That is six times the rate 50 years earlier (U.S. Census Bureau, 2018). Those statistics underestimate the rate of intermarriage, because the U.S. Census lumps together all Hispanics, all Blacks, all Asians, and all Europeans, ignoring the fact that intermarriages might be with one spouse who has Italian heritage and the other, Swedish or Mexican/Puerto Rican, or Pakistani/

Japanese. None of those three are included in the 18 percent of marriages that are interethnic.

The people most likely to intermarry have attended college, where they have been encouraged to think for themselves and thus reach postformal cognition. The people least likely to approve of intermarriage are older, less-educated adults (Livingston & Brown, 2017).

Cross-ethnic relationships are not the only sign of postformal thinking. One expert suggests that "every marriage is a cross-cultural experience" (Gottman & Gottman, 2017, p. 19), in that partners need to coordinate their values.

Finding a common ground may be easier with postformal thought, which may be one reason that the older newlyweds are, the less likely they are to divorce. Indeed, every close companionship, with friends and co-workers as well as relatives, benefits from an adult's ability to combine emotion and logic, in order to be good companions.

Dialectical Thought

Cross-cultural research suggests that adult thought, at its best, becomes **dialectical thought,** which may be the most advanced cognitive process (Basseches, 1984, 1989; Riegel, 1975). The word *dialectic* refers to the philosophical concept, developed by Hegel two centuries ago, that every idea or truth bears within itself the opposite idea or truth.

To use the words of philosophers, each idea, or **thesis,** implies an opposing idea, or **antithesis.** Dialectical thought involves considering both of these poles simultaneously and then forging them into a **synthesis**—that is, a new idea that integrates the original and its opposite. Note that the synthesis is not a compromise: It is a new concept that transforms both original ideas (Lemieux, 2012).

For example, many young children idolize their parents (thesis), and many adolescents are highly critical of their parents (antithesis). Ideally, adults appreciate their parents and forgive their shortcomings, which they attribute to their parents' background, historical conditions, and age. Thus, with postformal thinking, adults gain a more nuanced respect for their parents (synthesis).

Dynamic Systems Thinking dynamically, as first described regarding systems in Chapter 1, means that each new synthesis deepens and refines the thesis and antithesis that initiated it, with "cognitive development as the dance of adaptive transformation" (Sinnott, 2009, p. 103).

Thus, dialectical thinking involves ongoing integration of beliefs and experiences with all the contradictions and inconsistencies of daily life. Change throughout the life span is multidirectional and often unexpected—a dynamic, dialectical process. Insight may require a "dialectic between routine and creative cognition" in that the thinker needs to combine new and old thought (Ohlsson, 2018).

Many scholars who study adult thinking recognize that conflict between opposing ideas is a catalyst for cognitive growth:

- Piaget thought conflict between new and old schemas caused disequilibrium that led to new thinking.
- Erikson described two opposites at each stage (intimacy versus isolation, generativity versus stagnation) causing a psychosocial "crisis" that required a synthesis to allow forward movement.
- Baltes noted that "the occurrence and effective mastery of crises and conflicts represent not only risks, but also opportunities for new development" (Baltes et al., 1998, p. 1041).

New demands, roles, responsibilities, and conflicts become learning opportunities. Students might take a class in an unfamiliar subject; young adults might leave their childhood home and move to another town or nation; employees might apply

dialectical thought The most advanced cognitive process, characterized by the ability to consider a thesis and its antithesis simultaneously and thus to arrive at a synthesis. Dialectical thought makes possible an ongoing awareness of pros and cons, advantages and disadvantages, possibilities and limitations.

thesis A proposition or statement of belief; the first stage of the process of dialectical thinking.

antithesis A proposition or statement of belief that opposes the thesis; the second stage of the process of dialectical thinking.

synthesis A new idea that integrates the thesis and its antithesis, thus representing a new and more comprehensive level of truth; the third stage of the process of dialectical thinking.

Especially for Someone Who Has to Make an Important Decision Which is better, to go with your gut feelings or to consider pros and cons as objectively as you can? (see response, page 476)

"I CAN'T WAIT TILL
I'M OLD ENOUGH TO HOLD MY NOSE AND VOTE."

Leo Cullum/Cartoon Collections

Ideal Versus Real One indication of adult cognition is the ability to accept some imperfections in oneself, one's family, and one's nation.

THINK CRITICALLY: Can you see dialectical thinking when you remember what you believed as a child?

for an uncertain promotion; a parent might need to try a new approach when a baby keeps crying, or a young child keeps lying, or a teenager flaunts a prohibition.

In such situations, when comfortable old ideas and routines are ineffective, dialectical thinkers find a new synthesis, thus gaining insight. New challenges promote learning.

A "Broken" Marriage Now consider an example of dialectical thought familiar to many: the end of a love affair. A nondialectical thinker might believe that each person has stable, enduring, independent traits. Faced with a troubled romance, then, a nondialectical thinker concludes that one partner (or the other) is at fault, or perhaps the relationship was a mistake from the beginning because the two were a bad match.

By contrast, dialectical thinkers see people and relationships as constantly evolving; time and social interaction changes both partners. Therefore, a romance becomes troubled, not because the partners are fundamentally incompatible, or because one or the other is fatally flawed, but because they have not adapted to the changes in the other.

As a dialectical thinker assesses it, marriages do not "break"; relationships do not "fail." Instead, relationships either grow as circumstances change or they stagnate as people move apart. Partners who think dialectically can move from the initial thesis ("I love you because you are perfect") to the antithesis ("I hate you—you are selfish") to a new synthesis ("Neither of us is perfect, but together we can grow").

A dialectic perspective not only encourages adults to work together on their relationships but also helps them cope if they break up. Many adults feel guilty after divorce, switching from blaming their partner to blaming themselves (Kiiski et al., 2013; Leonoff, 2015). They need a synthesis to move forward.

Ideally, adults achieve a dialectical understanding, seeing divorce as an opportunity to look at themselves more closely and make necessary changes. They move from the thesis ("My partner was bad") and antithesis ("I was bad") to synthesis ("We have learned from this").

Similar problems occur in emerging adults whose parents divorced. Children tend to blame one parent and idealize the other, an interpretation that impairs their ability to develop partnerships of their own. Worse is blaming themselves, as children sometimes do. Hopefully adults whose parents have divorced move beyond those childish thoughts (Shanholtz et al., 2019).

Combining the Facts and Emotions Adult thinkers realize that purely objective, logical thinking is maladaptive when navigating the complexities and commitments of adult life. Emotional sensitivity is needed for productive families, workplaces, and neighborhoods. Subjective feelings and individual experiences must be taken into account because objective reasoning alone is limited, rigid, and impractical.

Yet subjective thinking is also limited. Truly mature thought involves an interaction between abstract, objective forms of processing and expressive, subjective forms.

If people do not reach this synthesis of intellect and emotion, behavioral extremes (such as those that lead to binge eating, anorexia, obesity, addiction, and violence) and cognitive extremes (such as believing that one is the best or the worst person on Earth) are common. Those are typical of the egocentrism of adolescence—and of some adults. By contrast, dialectical thinkers balance personal experience with knowledge.

As an example of such balance, an emerging adult student of mine wrote:

> Unfortunately, alcoholism runs in my family. . . . I have seen it tear apart not only my uncle but my family also. . . . I have gotten sick from drinking, and it was the most horrifying night of my life. I know that I didn't have alcohol poisoning or anything, but I drank too quickly and was getting sick. All of these images flooded my head about how I didn't want to ever end up the way my uncle was. From that point on, whenever I have touched alcohol, it has been with extreme caution. . . . When I am old and gray, the last thing I want to be thinking about is where my next beer will come from or how I'll need a liver transplant.
>
> *[Laura, personal communication]*

Laura's thinking about alcohol is postformal in that it combines knowledge (e.g., of alcohol poisoning) with emotions (images flooding her head). Note that she is cautious, not abstinent; she has both objective awareness of her genetic potential and subjective experience of wanting to be part of the crowd.

She combines both modes of thought to reach a conclusion that works for her. She does not need searing personal experiences (becoming an uncontrollable drinker and reaching despair). If she did, she would need to go to the other extreme (avoiding even one sip).

This development of postformal thought regarding alcohol is seen in most U.S. adults over time. Those in their early 20s are more likely than people of any other age to abuse alcohol and other drugs—perhaps with periods of swearing off drugs, only to begin again.

With personal experience and learning from others (social norms), cognitive maturity allows most adults to drink occasionally and moderately by age 30. Some, for both genetic and social reasons, have become addicts and must stop completely, but most adults can drink a glass or two on occasion because they have moved past the extremes of bingeing and abstinence of their younger selves. They have achieved a new synthesis.

Dialectical Reasoning Lifelong Remember that adults achieve postformal thought and dialectical reasoning not simply because of maturation, but also because of experience. To illustrate that even the best-educated adults sometimes fail to use postformal thought, consider this example.

One of the leading scholars of adult cognition is Jan Sinnott, a professor and past editor of the *Journal of Adult Development*. She describes the first course she taught:

> I did not think in a postformal way. . . . Teaching was good for passing information from the informed to the uninformed. . . . I decided to create a course in the psychology of aging . . . with a fellow graduate student. Being compulsive graduate students had paid off in our careers so far, so my colleague and I continued on that path. Articles and books and photocopies began to take over my house. And having found all this information, we seem to have unconsciously sworn to use all of it. . . .
>
> Each class day, my colleague and I would arrive with reams of notes and articles and lecture, lecture, lecture. Rapidly! . . .
>
> The discussion of death and dying came close to the end of the term (naturally). As I gave my usual jam-packed lecture, the sound of note taking was intense. But toward the end of the class . . . an extremely capable student burst into tears and said she had to drop the class. . . . Unknown to me, she had been the caretaker of an older relative who had just died in the past few days. She had not said anything about this significant experience when we lectured on caretaking. . . . How could she? . . . We never stopped talking. "I wish I could tell people what it's really like," she said.
>
> *[Sinnott, 2008, pp. 54–55]*

Sinnott changed her lesson plan. In the next class, she asked that student to share her experiences.

> In the end, the students agreed that this was a class when they . . . synthesized material and analyzed research and theory critically.
>
> [*Sinnott, 2008, p. 56*]

Sinnott still lectures and gives multiple-choice exams, but she also realizes the impact of the personal story. She combines analysis and emotion; she includes the personal experiences of the students. Her teaching became postformal, dialectical, and responsive.

Culture and Dialectics Several researchers have compared cognition in East Asian and North American adults, focusing on dialectical thought. It may be that ancient Greek philosophy led Europeans and Americans to use analytic, absolutist logic—to take sides in a battle between right and wrong, good and evil—whereas Confucianism, Buddhism, and Taoism led the Chinese and other Asians to seek compromise, the "Middle Way."

Others peg such thought to agriculture: Rice cultivation required cooperation from everyone, so group harmony was essential to the culture (Talhelm et al., 2014).

For whatever reason, people from Asian cultures tend to think holistically, about the whole rather than the parts, seeking the synthesis because "in place of logic, the Chinese developed a dialectic" (Nisbett et al., 2001, p. 294). One example is in judging emotions: Westerners are more likely to pay close attention to facial expressions, and Asians are more likely to consider the context, such as surrounding circumstances (Matsumoto et al., 2012).

This may leave people of Asian descent open to more possibilities and make them less likely to conclude that one answer is the only correct one. A study of Chinese Canadians, some of them born in China and others born in Canada, found that the Chinese-born Canadians were more likely to consider many perspectives, and thus they were less opinionated and decisive (Li et al., 2014).

Of course, too much can be made of the distinction between Eastern and Western thought. Individuals in every culture vary in how they approach problems. It is stereotyping to think that Asians are quieter and more cooperative (Okazaki, 2018). But divergent, dialectical thinking seems advanced compared to narrow, dogmatic thought. Some cultures encourage such thinking more than others.

Working Together Seeing advantages and disadvantages in every course of action—weighing personal and political consequences—is characteristic of dialectical thought but not of the "fast and furious" thinking that some people prefer.

Consider this problem:

> Every card in a pack has a letter on one side and a number on the other. Imagine that you are presented with the following four cards, each of which has something on the back. Turn over only those cards that will confirm or disconfirm this proposition: *If a card has a vowel on one side, then it always has an even number on the other side.*
>
> E 7 K 4
>
> Which cards must be turned over?

The difficulty of this puzzle is "notorious in the literature of human reasoning" (Moshman, 2011, p. 50). Fewer than 10 percent of college students solve it when working independently. Almost everyone wants to turn over the E and the 4—and almost everyone is mistaken.

However, when groups of college students, who had guessed wrong individually, had a chance to discuss the problem together, 75 percent got it right: They avoided the 4 card (even if it has a consonant on the other side, the statement could still be true) and selected the E and the 7 cards (if the 7 has a vowel on the other side, the proposition is proved false) (Moshman, 2011).

As in this example, adults can think things through and change their minds after listening. Can you remember when you thought one thing that is opposite to what you now think? Why did you change your mind? It was probably a combination of logic and social experience. That was cognitive flexibility, leading to a new thought, a synthesis.

WHAT HAVE YOU LEARNED?

1. Why did scholars choose the term *postformal* to describe the fifth stage of cognition?
2. How does postformal thinking differ from typical adolescent thought?
3. What is the relationship between thesis, antithesis, and synthesis?
4. Why does the term *broken home* indicate a lack of dialectical thought?
5. How does the combination of subjective and objective thinking represent dialectical thought?
6. How does listening to opposing opinions demonstrate cognitive flexibility?

Ethics and Religion

As explained in earlier chapters, in infancy and early childhood children spontaneously help others. They believe in their parents' religion and ethics. In middle childhood, prosocial and antisocial behaviors are evident. Then, in adolescence, teenagers use abstract reasoning to espouse moral principles, sometimes contrary to their parents.

Finally, in adulthood, with maturation and experience, adults increasingly apply moral values and think about spiritual concerns. They no longer have the luxury of debating abstractions: They must make choices for themselves.

Doing the Right Thing

In adulthood, ethics no longer are just abstract principles but are guides to relationships, child-rearing, financial decisions, religious principles, and so on. Four studies comparing adults of several ages find that, over the years of adulthood, people become less interested in their own financial gain and more interested in the welfare of others (Freund & Blanchard-Fields, 2014).

Does that mean that adults become more moral with age? Your answer reflects your own idea of morality.

Defining Issues One scholar who has devoted his life to the study of moral development wrote decades ago:

> Dramatic and extensive changes occur in young adulthood (the 20s and 30s) in the basic problem-solving strategies used to deal with ethical issues. . . . These changes are linked to fundamental reconceptualizations in how the person understands society and his or her stake in it.
>
> [Rest, 1993, p. 201]

Defining Issues Test (DIT) A series of questions developed by James Rest and designed to assess respondents' level of moral development by having them rank possible solutions to moral dilemmas.

Rest developed a measure of moral reasoning called the **Defining Issues Test (DIT)**, which presents moral situations. The person must choose priorities. For example, in one DIT dilemma, a news reporter must decide whether to publish some old personal information that will damage a political candidate. Respondents rank their priorities from personal benefits ("credit for investigative reporting") to higher goals ("serving society").

The DIT continues to be used in thousands of studies, in almost every nation. It seems that the DIT correlates with how a person functions in their profession, whether they engage in political action, and how they live (Moreira et al., 2018; Han et al., 2019).

Rest wrote that college education may propel a shift in moral reasoning. This is especially likely if coursework includes extensive discussion of ethics or if the student's future profession (such as law, business, or medicine) requires ethical decisions. Students in those curricula often are taught ethical guidelines (Kalshoven & Taylor, 2018; Shapiro & Stefkovich, 2016; Carrese et al., 2015).

The DIT has been used to measure moral thought. Another measure is the National Study of Youth and Religion (NSYR), which asks about volunteering to help other people. Both have been used extensively on college campuses, because instructors hope to advance moral activity in adulthood.

Listening to Other Perspectives One way to deepen ethical and religious thought is to learn about perspectives that are not one's own. Just as with the odd/even cards above, listening and discussing can help clarify ideas in adulthood.

For instance, in one course for business students in Arkansas, students studied five major "wisdom traditions." Almost all of the students identified as Christian, most knew something about Judaism, and almost no one knew much about Buddhism, Hinduism, or Islam.

Instructors asked the students to write, and rewrite, a "personal mission statement" as one indication of learning in the course (Herzog et al., 2016). Here are two of the final statements:

> [My mission is] being an authentic, genuine and reliable leader that others can admire, look up to and aspire to be. Establish and create a work environment that is welcoming and accepting of all people who come from different backgrounds, experiences and walks of life. Challenge myself to seek opportunities to try or learn something new as often as possible. Vow to surround myself with individuals different from myself, ask questions and search for answers in order to cultivate growth.

Praise God? Rituals and ceremonies are remarkably diverse. Some worshipers kiss the ground five times a day, or reach for heaven seven times (as these women do in London, England *[left]*). Some worshipers shout "Amen," while others pray quietly (like these students at Zion Bible College in Massachusetts *[right]*). Nonetheless, as people everywhere grow older, they seem to believe in something greater than themselves.

Dan Kitwood/Getty Images

Melanie Stetson Freeman/The Christian Science Monitor via Getty Images

Another wrote:

> I was very interested in the idea of learning more about the world religions and how they hold power over the hearts and minds of so many people. In doing so I had hoped to strengthen my own beliefs as well. I feel as though I have accomplished both of these initiatives. Learning from the many speakers we have had has been incredibly insightful. The Buddhist monk was especially interesting to me. His illustration of Logic and reason as a sort of salvation from the world was incredible. While I disagree with him in this it was an amazing experience to hear from him about his beliefs.

By the end of the course many students thought in the adult mode, welcoming ideas that they did not know before. Their scores on the NSYR were higher than those of a control group. Many reaffirmed their own religious beliefs: Postformal thinking is more likely to deepen thought than supplant it.

Faith and Practice

The study of five faiths by the students in Arkansas raises a question. What happens to religious beliefs from ages 18 to 65? Does mature thought and an understanding of ethics follow religious convictions?

There is a paradox here: From adolescence to adulthood, people are *less* likely to attend religious services (Pew Research Center, June 13, 2018) but *more* likely to see themselves as having moral values (Barry et al., 2012). They think they are at least as spiritual as they were when younger (Smith & Snell, 2009). Maturation may move adults past the doctrinaire religion of childhood to a more flexible, dialectical, postformal faith.

Stages of Religious Development To describe this process, James Fowler (1981, 1986) developed a now-classic sequence of six stages of faith, building on the work of Piaget and Kohlberg. Remember that both of those men developed stage theories, as children moved from self-focused to more social, logical thought.

Before any thought occurs, according to Fowler, a person is at "zero," when religion simply reflects children's relationship with their parents. Then thought begins.

- *Stage one: Intuitive-projective faith.* Faith is magical, illogical, imaginative, and filled with fantasy, especially about the power of God and the mysteries of birth and death. It is typical of children ages 3 to 7.
- *Stage two: Mythic-literal faith.* Individuals take the myths and stories of religion literally, believing simplistically in the power of symbols. God is seen as rewarding those who follow divine laws and punishing others. Stage two is typical from ages 7 to 11, but it also characterizes some adults. Fowler cites a woman who says extra prayers at every opportunity, to put them "in the bank."
- *Stage three: Synthetic-conventional faith.* This is a conformist stage. Faith is conventional, reflecting concern about other people and favoring "what feels right" over what makes intellectual sense. Fowler quotes a man whose personal rules include "being truthful with my family. Not trying to cheat them out of anything. . . . I'm not saying that God or anybody else set my rules. I really don't know. It's what I feel is right."
- *Stage four: Individual-reflective faith.* Faith is characterized by intellectual detachment from the values of the culture and from the approval of other people. College may be a springboard to stage four, as young people learn to question the authority of parents, professors, and others and to rely instead on their own understanding of the world. Faith becomes an active commitment.

macmillan learning

The **Data Connections activity Religious Identity: Young Adults Versus Older Cohorts** further explores the religious behaviors and beliefs of U.S. adults.

- *Stage five: Conjunctive faith.* Faith incorporates both powerful emotional ideas (such as the power of prayer and the love of God) and rational conscious values (such as the worth of life compared with that of property). People are willing to accept contradictions (obviously a postformal manner of thinking). Fowler says that this perspective is seldom achieved before middle age.
- *Stage six: Universalizing faith.* People at this stage have a powerful vision of universal compassion, justice, and love that compels them to live their lives in a way that others may think is either saintly or foolish. A transforming experience is often the gateway to stage six, as happened to Moses, Muhammad, the Buddha, and Saul/Paul of Tarsus, as well as more recently to Mohandas Gandhi, Martin Luther King Jr., and Mother Teresa.

As you know, these seven named people were compelled by their religious faith to act ethically. This is true for others as well, but not for most of us: Few people reach stage six, according to Fowler. Notice the parallels between religious convictions and Kohlberg's stages, from magical, self-centered thinking (preconventional), to a more social stage (conventional), and finally a universal one (postconventional).

Interpreting religious development is even more complicated than interpreting moral development. Judging someone's faith at a lower stage might offend a believer who, for instance, thinks that a literal understanding of religion is correct (Fowler's stage two).

Similar problems appear in Kohlberg's stages: Some adults believe that everyone should prioritize their own welfare (Kohlberg's stage two) or that family loyalty trumps universal concerns (conventional over postconventional).

Adding to the difficulty with interpretation is what adults themselves say. People who consider themselves unaffiliated with any particular religion (see **Figure 18.1**), including those who say they are atheists or agnostics, nonetheless pray, believe in God, and consider themselves quite moral. Sometimes faith seems to foster ethical values, but sometimes—especially at the earlier stages of development—it impedes them (Thomas, 2018).

Deciding whether religion makes people more ethical or less so is a matter of interpretation, which depends partly on the perspective of the person doing the interpreting. Indeed, as postformal thinkers understand, perspective is crucial for every judgment regarding the cognitive maturity of moral and religious convictions.

FIGURE 18.1

Explain This The trends are clear, but the reasons are not. Are older adults wiser, or more traditional? Many of the unaffiliated younger adults pray often and believe in God—does that make their lack of religious identity foolish or profound?

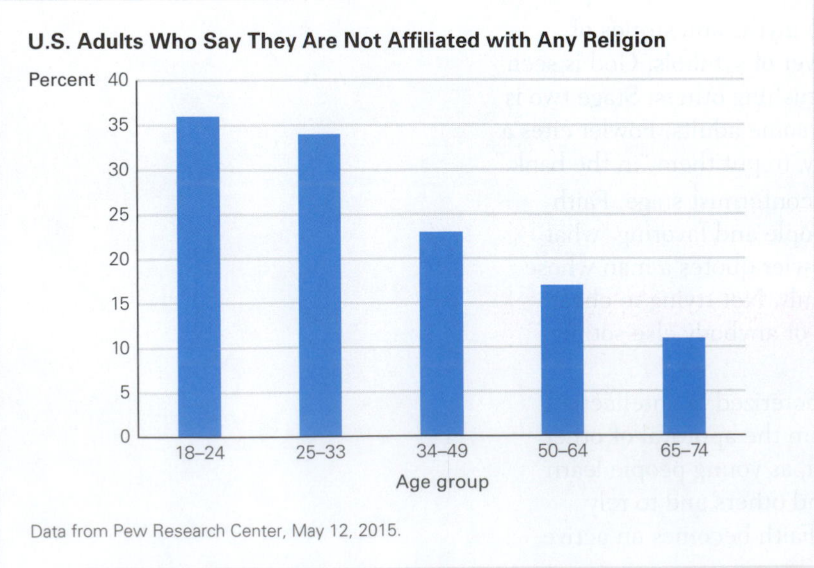

Moral Foundations The importance of the perspective of the interpreter is apparent in the work of another prominent theorist of moral development. Jonathan Haidt has studied morals in many religions and cultures, internationally as well as among groups within the United States.

He wrote many scenarios to uncover which moral principles were important to people. Here are three of them:

- A family dog is killed by a car and the family cooks the carcass and eats it for dinner.
- A brother and sister on vacation in a distant land where no one knows them, using excellent contraception, have intercourse.
- Someone drinks water from a glass that has a dead, sterilized cockroach in it.

Each of these was highly offensive to most adults, who tried to explain their reactions based on logic. In fact, their reactions revealed their deep moral values. Haidt believes that adults have five moral foundations:

1. Care for others; harm no one.
2. Promote freedom; avoid oppression.
3. Be fair; do not cheat.
4. Seek purity; avoid contamination.
5. Respect authority; do not break religious rules.

The importance of these five varies from nation to nation, with #4, for instance, much stronger in India and #2 much stronger in the United States. The emphasis on each of the five is influenced by the doctrines of each religion and by the values of each political party.

If one group prioritizes the first two and another group the last two, then each group will interpret the middle one, fairness, differently. This may explain why people of different religious, political, or cultural backgrounds consider each other immoral; they prioritize differently (Haidt, 2013).

For instance, in 2019 a law was passed in the Netherlands forbidding covering one's face in any public building, including schools and hospitals. The reason was said to be protection of the public (avoiding harm #1) from masked bandits, but the regulation made no exception for devout Muslim women (who wear a burka in order to avoid contamination #4 and #5) or skiers (who wear a balaclava in subzero temperatures—personal freedom #2). No wonder the law was considered immoral by some but fair (#3) by others.

Adult Thinking and Moral Development Haidt and his colleagues applied dialectical thinking to their model of moral development. Knowing that people tend to seek proof, not valid critiques, of their beliefs (called *confirmation bias*) and that social learning makes people reluctant to criticize others directly, Haidt offered a thousand dollars to anyone who would "demonstrate the existence of an additional foundation, or show that any of the current five foundations should be merged or eliminated" (quoted in Graham et al., 2013, p. 99). The offer was open for two years.

No one won, but three people came close enough to be awarded $500, and "many critics have stepped forward and volunteered to criticize MFT [moral foundations theory] for free" (Graham et al., 2013, p. 99). It is apparent that individuals can see moral questions from quite different perspectives.

That may be evidence of adult dialectical cognition, in that, as one scholar explains it: "The evolved human brain has provided humans with cognitive capacity that is so flexible and creative that every conceivable moral principle generates opposition and counter principles" (Kendler, 2002, p. 503).

Quantitative research does not allow us to conclude that morality increases and faith deepens over adulthood. However, some qualitative research does.

Evidence for moral growth and religious insight abounds in biographical and autobiographical literature. Most people probably know someone (or might *be* that

WHAT HAVE YOU LEARNED?

1. Why do adults make more decisions involving morality than adolescents do?
2. How does education affect moral development?
3. How are Fowler's stages of faith similar to Kohlberg's and Piaget's stages?
4. How difficult is it to reach the highest level of religious development?
5. Why do people disagree about moral issues, according to Haidt?

someone) who had a narrow, shallow outlook on the world at age 18 and then developed a broader, deeper perspective, with more empathy, after adolescence.

Cognitive Growth and Higher Education

Many readers of this textbook have a personal interest in the final topic of this chapter, the relationship between college, cognition, and later life.

Health and Wealth

Education improves health and wealth. The data on virtually every physical condition, and every indicator of material success, show college graduates are ahead of high school graduates, who themselves are ahead of those without a high school diploma.

Long-Term Benefits In the United States, each additional level of education correlates with everything from happy marriages to strong teeth, from spacious homes to long lives, from healthy children to working digestive systems (U.S. Department of Health and Human Services, 2018). Similar findings come from other nations, with and without national health insurance (Maskileyson, 2014). Particularly when the educated person is a woman, the rest of the community also benefits, in health and wealth.

Longitudinal data find that, on average, investing in college education returns the initial expense more than five times. That means if students spend a nickel now, they get a quarter back in a few decades, or if a degree costs $200,000, over a lifetime the return is $1 million.

massification The idea that establishing institutions of higher learning and encouraging college enrollment can benefit everyone (the masses).

Massification The idea that college might benefit everyone (the masses) has led to the goal of **massification,** that college should be available for all. The United States was the first major nation to embrace massification, beginning with federal legislation to establish land-grant colleges in every state. (Iowa was the first, in 1864.)

In the twenty-first century, every state has a publicly supported university, and most have a network of community colleges, four-year colleges, and graduate programs. California had the most: 146 public colleges as of 2019.

One result is that the United States led the world throughout the twentieth century in the percentage of college graduates, many of whom are now in their prime earning years. The United States is one of the wealthiest nations (perhaps the wealthiest?), which can be traced to the growth of universities (Brint, 2019).

That international distinction is no longer. Twelve nations have a higher rate of emerging adults who earn college degrees than does the United States (OECD, 2018). Some other nations have much higher college attendance compared to 50 years ago (e.g., Canada, Finland, Israel, England). A rapid increase in educated citizens is evident in many developing nations, because leaders have created and funded thousands of new colleges and universities (see **Figure 18.2**).

One result is greater economic development in nations that once were poor. In 1995, China had about a thousand colleges with 6 million students. In 2016, China had about 2,600 colleges (400 of them private) with 30 million students (Normile, 2018). China is no longer considered a poor nation.

And Millions More When few U.S. colleges enrolled African Americans, many historically black colleges (HBCs) educated millions of young adults, benefiting the entire society. This is graduation day at Howard University, chartered by U.S. Congress in 1867.

Cheriss May/NurPhoto via Getty Images

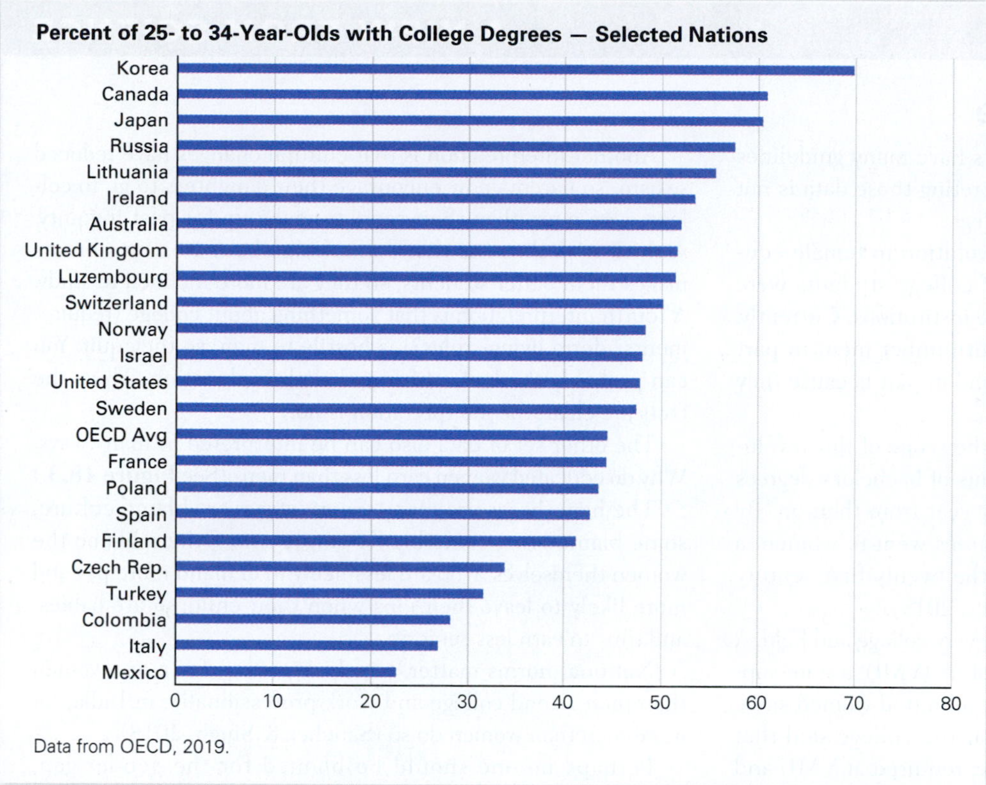

FIGURE 18.2

Too Many or Not Enough? Adults in every nation debate whether almost everyone needs to graduate from college. Does your opinion depend on your national origin?

Dropping Out of College The benefits of college are most evident for those who earn a degree. But in the United States, about half of those who enroll in college leave before graduating. Quit rates are highest for low-SES African American, Latinx, and Native American students.

This might be an example of what is termed the *Matthew effect*, the idea that the rich get richer but the poor stay poor. Parental SES is the strongest predictor of whether or not someone will earn a college degree. Money (not grades) is the major reason that many college students drop out before graduation (McKinney & Burridge, 2015).

Most nations counter this problem by investing public funds directly in colleges, which are free for qualified emerging adults. The United States uses that strategy to some extent, but the main U.S. strategy is to provide tuition assistance to some students and to offer loans to everyone.

Two-thirds of adults who attended some college must pay back college loans. The interest on those loans is high, as is the default rate—about 10 percent (Friedman, 2019). Students at for-profit colleges are more likely to obtain loans and to default, perhaps because those colleges have the lowest graduation and employment rates.

For many emerging adults, paying back loans is a major burden. Some analysts question whether the debt burden on students, the cost to taxpayers, and the profits to lending institutions are a good investment, especially since those students who borrow the most are not necessarily those most likely to graduate or find jobs (Herzog, 2018; Zhan et al., 2018).

The burden of debt falls particularly heavily on students from minority groups or whose parents never attended college, exactly the ones the program is supposed to help. Paying back loans causes anxiety and sometimes disappearance: Adults move without a forwarding address, change their name, or even leave the country, all of which makes getting a good job more difficult.

A VIEW FROM SCIENCE

Women and College

As you know from Chapter 1, scientists have many guidelines that ensure valid data. However, interpreting those data is not simple. Consider data on women in college.

The first set of numbers show a revolution in female education. In 1970, at least two-thirds of college students were male, often educated in exclusively male institutions. Currently, at every level of education, women outnumber men, in part because males are less likely to enroll and in part because they are more likely to quit before graduation.

Data from the United States reveal the scope of this revolution. In 1950, 24 percent of the recipients of bachelor's degrees were female. Proportions shifted every year from then on. By 2000, 57 percent of the bachelor's degrees went to women, a ratio that has continued every year of the twenty-first century (National Center for Education Statistics, 2019).

Women are now enrolled in virtually every college and field. A historic example is Virginia Military Institute (VMI), a state-supported military academy that had never admitted women since its founding in 1839. Administrators at the college said that females could not do the physical tasks required at VMI, and alumni said no woman would want to be an army officer.

However, in 1997, the U.S. Supreme Court ruled (7-1) that VMI, as a public institution, could not discriminate based on gender. In 2018, 11 percent (about 185) of the VMI students were female.

Why do more women than men earn college degrees?

One suggestion from the previous chapter is contraception. In 1950, sexually active women soon became mothers: Caring for babies made college very difficult.

Another interpretation is that cultural changes have reduced sexism, so parents now encourage their daughters to go to college even more than their sons, to make up for past inequity. A third hypothesis is that something about women's brains makes them better students, so they are more inclined to study. A fourth interpretation is that something about college (requirements? dorm living? rules?) is hostile to men, so they quit. You can probably think of a fifth and sixth explanation. Thus, the facts are clear; the interpretation is not.

The other set of data also can be interpreted in many ways. Why do educated women earn less than men? (See **Figure 18.3**.)

The hypotheses are many. Some observers blame culture, some blame laws, some blame employers. Others blame the women themselves, who are less likely to demand more pay and more likely to leave their jobs when their children are babies, and thus to earn less seniority.

National norms matter, too. In Vietnam, far more women than men attend college and work professionally; in India, far more men than women do so (Sánchez & Singh, 2018).

Perhaps no one should be blamed for the gender gap, because income is not the best indicator of employment equality. Women may choose lower pay in order to do work they love. They become teachers, not corporate executives; they become nurses, not computer systems experts.

In 2018, the United States Department of Education reported on annual salaries of 25- to 29-year-olds, employed full time, who earned a bachelor's degree in various fields. (Some students in every field had advanced degrees; these data focused on their first degree.) Gender differences in pay were smaller than differences by profession. Workers in STEM fields (science, technology, engineering, math) earned an average of $60,000; in non-STEM fields, $45,490.

When specifics are further tallied, the lowest annual salary was early-childhood education ($35,940) and the highest was computer engineering ($78,080). By far, most early-childhood teachers are women; most computer programmers are men, but that may be by choice.

Perhaps when people of any gender choose to be teachers, they believe that helping children discover and grow is valuable in itself. Do most teachers wish they had chosen to be digital analysts?

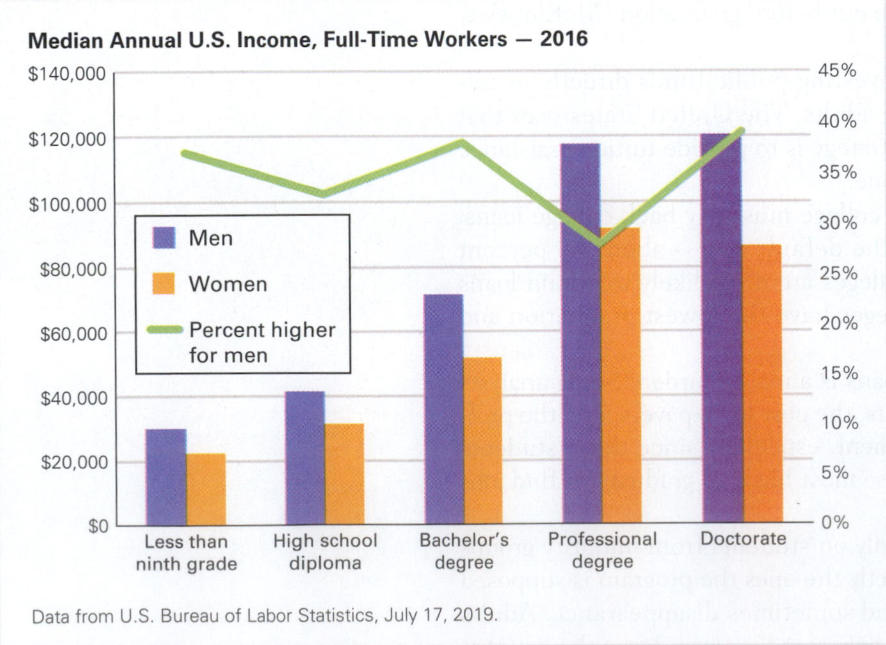

FIGURE 18.3

Inequality or Choice? Women earn much less at every level of education. Is that because social norms are stacked against them, or because women make less materialistic choices?

One example, hopefully unusual, is a young American woman who fled to Berlin to escape dunning phone calls about the $50,000 she owes. She says:

> I have this shame on the part of my parents because I really did not want this for them. When I thought about going to college, this is not what I had in mind. I really thought that they were going to be so proud of me. I was the first child in my family . . . to graduate college. But . . . we weren't thinking about the debt when we were signing up for school. And sometimes I think living in New York City and going to a private university maybe wasn't the best idea. I could have gone somewhere else. . . .
>
> I don't have the money to pay for loans. I need to eat and live and not be a slave to this debt. But I'm scared. When I look back, I wonder what I could have done differently.
>
> [*Vanessa, quoted in Coggin, 2016*]

It is easy to see the need for postformal thinking in this young woman and her parents. Her emotional reaction ("I thought they were going to be so proud") overwhelmed practical, future thoughts.

College and Cognition

For developmentalists interested in cognition, the crucial question about college education is not about wealth, health, rates, expense, or even graduation. Instead, developmentalists wonder whether college advances critical thinking and postformal thought. The answer seems to be yes.

Before 2000 Let us begin with the classic work of William Perry (1981, 1970/1998). After repeatedly questioning students at Harvard, Perry described students' thinking through nine levels of complexity over the four years that led to a bachelor's degree. In that study, thinking became more reflective and expansive with each year of college.

In the first year, students had a simplistic either/or dualism (right or wrong, success or failure) understanding of knowledge. Most 18-year-olds thought in absolutes. Answers to questions were yes or no, the future led to success or failure, and professors needed to teach the right answers.

As they moved through college, Perry's subjects no longer believed in absolutes. Instead, they recognized that many perspectives are possible and that almost nothing is, totally and forever, right or wrong. Thinking was more dialectical.

At first that was unsettling, but by their senior year students moved past their uncertainty. They had become critical thinkers, adapting a perspective yet remaining flexible. Perry reported that many aspects of the college experience caused this progression: Peers, professors, books, and class discussion all stimulated new questions and thoughts.

Similar conclusions were drawn from many other studies. According to one comprehensive review:

> Compared to freshmen, seniors have better oral and written communication skills, are better abstract reasoners or critical thinkers, are more skilled at using reason and evidence to address ill-structured problems for which there are no verifiably correct answers, have greater intellectual flexibility in that they are better able to understand more than one side of a complex issue, and can develop more sophisticated abstract frameworks to deal with complexity.
>
> [*Pascarella & Terenzini, 1991, p. 155*]

Note that many of these abilities characterize postformal thinking.

Current Contexts But wait. You probably noticed that this research occurred decades ago. Do those conclusions still hold? Many recent books question the

© Celia Peterson/arabianEye/Corbis

Culture and Cohort Ideally, college brings together people of many backgrounds who learn from each other. This scene from a college library in the United Arab Emirates would not have happened a few decades ago. The dress of these three suggests that culture still matters, but education is recognized worldwide as benefiting every young person in every nation.

Especially for Those Considering Studying Abroad Given the effects of college, would it be better for a student to study abroad in the first year or last year of a college education? (see response, page 476)

value of college. Notable is a twenty-first-century longitudinal study of a cross section of U.S. college students (Arum & Roksa, 2011). The authors concluded that current college students advance in critical thinking, analysis, and communication only half as much as students did two decades ago. They found that 45 percent of the students did not advance at all in their first two years of college.

College students today study less and avoid classes that require much reading or writing. They avoid courses in English, history, and philosophy where serious reading, writing, and critical thinking are required. Even in those classes, professors require less.

A follow-up study found that students who did more socializing than studying tended to be unemployed or underemployed. College did not give them the skills or self-discipline that they needed for adult success (Arum & Roksa, 2014).

Some other observers blame the wider culture for forcing colleges to follow a corporate model, with students as customers who need to be satisfied rather than youth who need to be challenged (Deresiewicz, 2014). Customers, apparently, demand costly dormitories and sports facilities; they do not choose colleges that require extensive reading, research, and writing.

Another problem of current college students is "unprecedented levels of distress," with increasing suicide and self-harm (Liu et al., 2018). Compared to a generation ago, today's college students may be more anxious and depressed, not only at high-pressure Ivy League schools but in smaller, less urban, religious schools as well.

For example, Franciscan University in Steubenville, Ohio, reported a 231-percent increase in visits to the college's counseling center over a five-year period (2008–2013). They reported that about one-third of the students could be diagnosed as anxious or depressed, with about 10 percent of those severely disturbed. Students in their senior year had the highest rates (Beiter et al., 2015).

Another indicator of trouble is the use of drugs, specifically Adderall and Ritalin, taken to enhance cognition and to allow all-night studying before an exam. Some say drug taking in college is "as common as coffee," although that probably is an exaggeration (Partridge et al., 2011).

FIGURE 18.4

Blue Is Higher Except . . . Since blue is for emerging adults and red is for adults of all ages (including emerging ones), it is no surprise that massification has produced higher scores among the young adults than the old ones. Trouble appears when young adults score about the same as older ones.

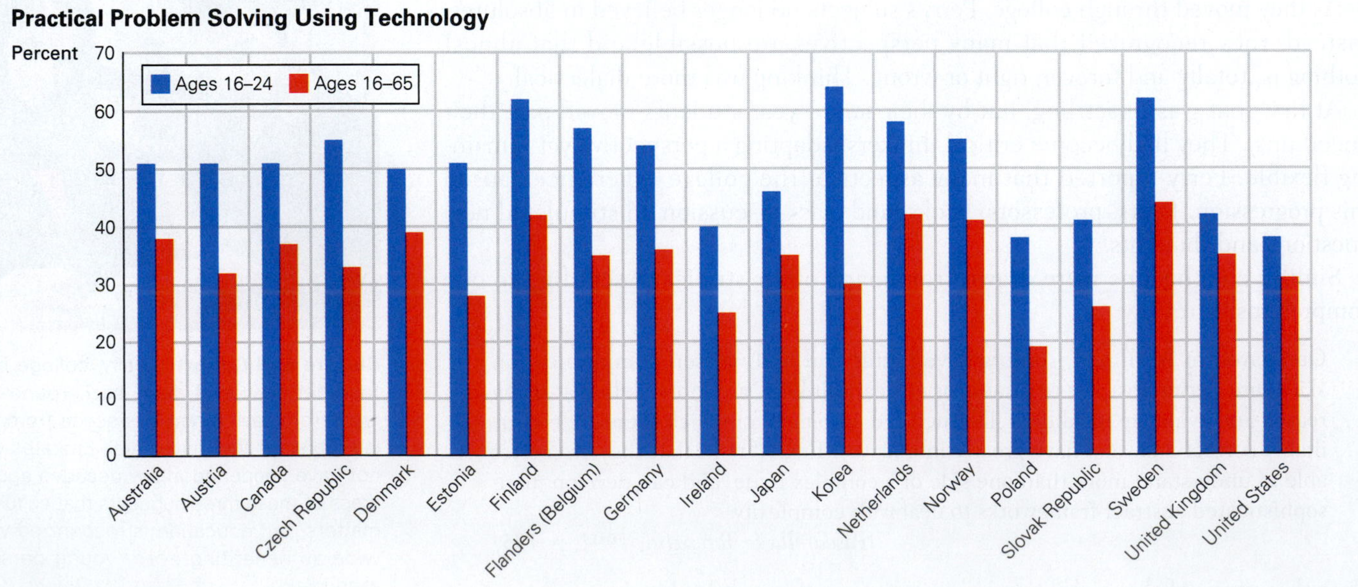

Data from OECD, 2013.

However, even some use may be too much, because "smart drugs" help cognition very little or not at all—contrary to what students believe (Ilieva & Farah, 2013). Belief itself is motivating. Thus, drug-using students might study harder, crediting the drug instead of their false belief, while harming their health.

College for All? The phrase "college for all" has become a mantra among many political leaders, parents, and high school graduates themselves. Often high schools are measured by how many of their graduates go on to college. However, might college become a frustrating and expensive experience (Gelbgiser, 2018; Ovink, 2017)?

Many critics of American education wonder whether massification is misguided. Might the economic benefits of college occur not from college itself but from the fact that children from wealthier families are more likely to go to college, graduate, and find good jobs?

Now is time for some dialectical thinking. The traditional thesis is that college benefits everyone. The antithesis is that it benefits no one. But there is a new synthesis. When the relationship between family background and adult success is carefully examined, those from low-SES homes who, against the odds, earn a college degree benefit even more from that degree than those from wealthier backgrounds (Brand & Xie, 2010; Karlson, 2019).

Parents who never went to college may underestimate the advantages of a college education for their children. (See A Case to Study.) Fifty years ago, the income gap between college graduates and others was much less than it is now (Pew Research Center, February 11, 2014). As a result, many parents and grandparents knew people who earned good salaries despite never going to college.

If students flock to the least expensive colleges (for-profit ones), they are also less likely gain the benefits of a college education, including advanced cognition and better jobs. Thus, the synthesis is that the benefits of college depend on both the student and the institution: Not all colleges deliver the same experience (Gelbgiser, 2018).

A CASE TO STUDY

Generation to Generation

One young man said:

> People always ask me, why don't you go to college. My dad, he never went. You work, you pay your bills, you help with the rent. My priority right now is to be responsible, to know how adult life works. It might go bad for me, or it might go good. It's going to be hard. . . . I'm scared we'll wake up some day and say "We don't got nothing to eat."
>
> *[Maldonado, quoted in Healy, 2017]*

His thinking is not unusual for young men like him. Students from families with little money are not only unlikely to be able to pay for college, they are unlikely to have role models who went to college or to have friends, teachers, and relatives who pave the way for high school seniors.

Giovanni Maldonado's father may be unaware of admission criteria, application deadlines, early admission, scholarship opportunities, and much more that some parents obsess about. GPA, SAT, AP, IB, and FAFSA are household acronyms to some, unknown to others. Giovanni's father learned decades ago that a good man pays the bills, month by month, and he has passed that lesson on to his son.

When Giovanni worries "we don't got nothing to eat," he is reflecting financial stress that he learned at home. As mentioned in Chapter 1, food insecurity is a common cause of shame as well as fear. Many low-income people live paycheck to paycheck: The term breadwinner began because putting food on the table was a crucial concern; financing education that had no immediate economic benefits seemed to be a luxury.

No wonder Giovanni does not think college is worth it. If he does enroll, he is likely to be discouraged. His grammar suggests that he will need remedial, noncredit writing courses, and then he will need more than four years (assuming full-time attendance) to complete his degree. Poverty impedes planning, future investment, and analysis (Haushofer & Fehr, 2014), so it is cruel as well as foolish to blame Giovanni for his decision.

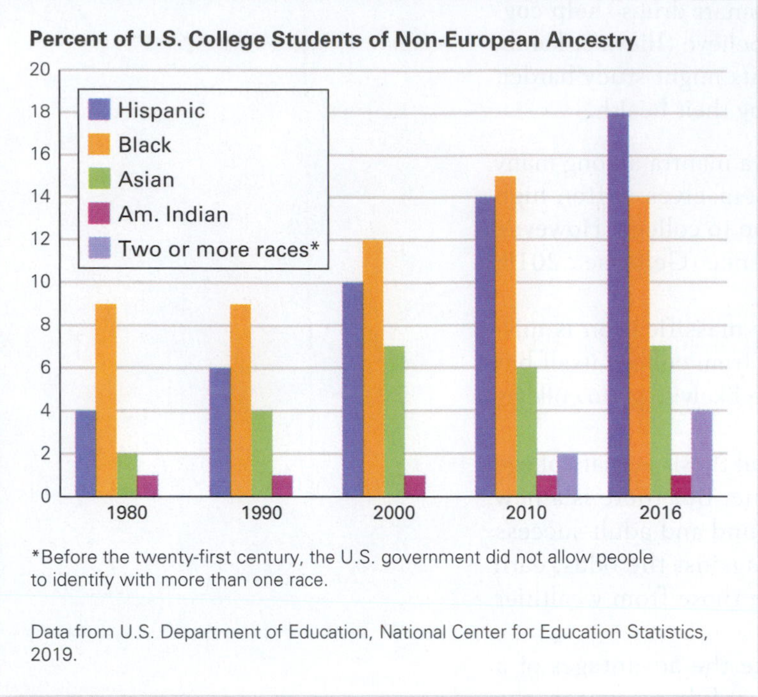

FIGURE 18.5

Increasing Diversity Note that the total proportion of "minority" students has increased from 16 percent to 44 percent. This makes it likely that all emerging adults will have personal experience with peers of other backgrounds, which may help them throughout their future lives. Most college students in the United States, now and in prior years, are European American.

Observation Quiz Which group has experienced the largest increase? (see answer, page 476) ↑

Especially for High School Teachers One of your brightest students doesn't want to go to college. She would rather keep waiting tables in a restaurant where she makes good money in tips. What do you say? (see response, page 476)

Choosing to Avoid College In some ways, it is better to avoid college than to enroll and then leave. Some students arrive with poor academic skills, no role models, and with work and family obligations that do not allow adequate, quiet time to study, or opportunity to develop the relationships with other students that may be crucial for the college experience (Choi, 2018).

But not attending college may reduce later health, income, and cognition. Many adults who started working instead of college after high school discover years later that they want a college degree.

Of the almost 20 million students in tertiary education in 2016, 40 percent are over age 24 and 16 percent are over age 35. Most are employed and are part-time students, but even among full-time students, 24 percent are age 25 or older (Snyder et al., 2018). That suggests that some adults wish they had earned a degree in emerging adulthood.

Improving the College Experience

The ideal synthesis of the hopes and fears about college is a better college experience for everyone. The challenge is to keep what works in higher education, while incorporating innovations.

Benefits of Diversity One innovation that has been welcomed by colleges is an increase in the number of students from ethnic groups who traditionally were excluded. You already learned that colleges are expanding in developing nations. Similarly, in the United States, more minority students are attending, and graduating from, college (see **Figure 18.5**).

This increase presumably helps students from economic and ethnic minorities, but advances cognition for everyone. One catalyst for learning is honest conversations with people from other backgrounds and perspectives. That is what colleges do at their best, when they encourage students to express opinions that they might not say at work or with their families. A comprehensive study of 48 colleges found that having conversations with people of other backgrounds advanced thought (Bowman, 2013).

Among the current problems of the United States is the political divide between those who identify as liberals and those who identify as conservatives. Those groups not only vote for opposite policies, they listen to opposite radio and television programs, read different books and newspapers, are targeted by filtered social media, and so on. To combat this, colleges can include diverse perspectives and mutual respect.

Sometimes college students are portrayed as radicals, with extreme left or right views. But most are middling, with only 4 percent of incoming first-year students considering themselves "far left" and only 2 percent considering themselves "far right." The most common response to the question "How would you characterize your political views?" was Middle-of-the-road (41 percent) (Stolzenberg et al., 2018, p. 35).

The diversity within colleges advances the cognition of today's emerging adults, who are much more accepting of differences than earlier generations were. Many studies have found that diversity of every kind *can* lead to intellectual challenge and deeper thought, with benefits lasting for years after graduation (Pascarella et al., 2014). Current U.S. college students raise issues that adults did not recognize, such as the #MeToo movement (sexual harassment), Black Lives Matter (unjust policing), and the Dreamers (immigration policies).

The result is often student protests against college policies set decades ago and clashes between student groups, faculty, and administrators. Nonetheless, the fact that people with divergent views might hear each other, and reflect on views other than their own, is a benefit of diversity. Remember the dialectical: Opposites can lead to a new synthesis.

As we know from our study of adult cognition, simply having a diverse student body does not guarantee intellectual growth. Instead, intellectual expansion comes from honest conversations among people of varied backgrounds and perspectives (Pascarella et al., 2014).

Colleges that make use of their diversity—via curriculum, assignments, discussions, cooperative education, learning communities, residence halls, and so on—stretch students' understanding, not only of other people but also of themselves (Harper & Yeung, 2013; Shim & Perez, 2018).

AP Images/Charles Rex Arbogast

Love Thy Neighbor This is Larycia Hawkins, a tenured professor at a Christian college (Wheaton) who in 2017 wore a hijab during Advent to express respect for Muslims, because "we worship the same God." The result: demonstrations of support by many Wheaton students and several bouts of theological questioning by the president of the college, himself a Wheaton graduate (1988). She either was fired or chose to leave (depending on who reports). Nonetheless, every Wheaton student had to think more deeply about the relationship between Christianity and Islam.

Technology in College

Almost every college classroom now has a computer and a video screen. Most college instructors incorporate technology in their classes, with PowerPoint presentations or Google Slides, video clips, and online grade reports. Almost every college student now has a smartphone, most have a tablet or laptop computer, every college library has Internet access to aid research and learning, and textbooks (including this one) have extensive, interactive, technological aids.

Most colleges and universities offer some classes completely online, with students doing all of their homework and reading on their computers when they wish, and with tests and final grades sent through the Internet. Online courses are particularly attractive to students in rural areas far from colleges, or those unable to leave home because they have young children or mobility issues, or those serving in the armed forces far from their home college.

MOOCs: Pros and Cons As with diversity, using technology to increase learning requires deliberate effort. An illustrative example is the **massive open online course (MOOC),** in which thousands of students enroll. Students in MOOCs often live in places where few rigorous or specialized classes are accessible. The first MOOC offered by Massachusetts Institute of Technology (MIT) and Harvard enrolled 155,000 students from 194 nations, including 13,044 from India (Breslow et al., 2013).

massive open online course (MOOC)
A course that is offered solely online for college credit. Typically, tuition is very low, and thousands of students enroll.

Some data from the MOOCs have been disappointing. Only 4 percent of the students in that first MOOC completed the course. MOOCs are most successful if students are highly motivated, adept at computer use, and have the needed prerequisites (Reich, 2015). Completion rates have risen in later courses, but the dropout rate is almost always over 80 percent.

In theory, a MOOC saves instructional costs, because a professor sets up the lessons but provides no individualized attention. However, it seems that college education "is not a spectator sport" (Koedinger, 2015). Active personalized engagement is needed.

The potential for education of millions of students who could not attend conventional classes is exciting, so many people are trying to figure out when and how MOOCs can work. One crucial variable is the involvement of the teacher (Gregori et al., 2018). Another crucial variable is the preparation and motivation of the students (Tsai et al., 2018).

This would not surprise anyone who understands adult cognitive development. Students learn best in MOOCs if they have another classmate, a local expert, or a teacher as a personal guide. This is true for all kinds of college learning: Technology can enhance education, but it does not substitute for it.

Imaginechina via AP Images/cdsb

Learning from Peers and Computers College students often learn via computer, allowing more education in nations where relatively few elders are professors. This is true here, in Chengu, China. But note: Computer education works best with other learners nearby.

CHAPTER APP 18

SimpleMind Pro+ Mind Mapping

IOS:
https://tinyurl.com/yylpswka

ANDROID:
https://tinyurl.com/yxznp5hh

RELEVANT TOPIC: College and cognition

This brainstorming app aims to help college students maximize their efficiency and focus on their studies. Through organizational charts and unique layouts for mind maps, users capture their ideas, clarify thinking, and manage complex information. Users can even add media to their mind maps.

The Flipped Classroom Another way to combine technology and traditional learning is called the *flipped class,* in which students are required to watch videos and practice problems on their computers before class. Then class time is used for discussion, with the professor prodding and encouraging but not lecturing. From a developmental perspective, it seems that flipped classrooms combine insights from two developmental theorists, Piaget and Skinner. This is an example of a thesis and an antithesis leading to a new synthesis. As two professors wrote:

> The flipped classroom is a new pedagogical method, which employs asynchronous video lectures and practice problems as homework, and active, group-based problem solving activities in the classroom. It represents a unique combination of learning theories once thought to be incompatible—active, problem-based learning activities founded upon a constructivist ideology [Piaget] and instructional lectures derived from direct instruction methods founded upon behaviorist principles.
>
> *[Bishop & Verleger, 2013]*

In general, students prefer flipped classes and learn more in them. One detailed study found that the number of students earning D, F, or W (withdraw without a grade) in an introductory course in networking was 49 percent before the flipped classroom and only 7 percent when the same class was flipped (Nwosisi et al., 2016).

Active Learning As evident in all of these innovations, instructors seek engaged learners, not passive students. Many professors still lecture, but they include more student involvement. An exposition of how this is done begins with a quote from a Canadian satirist, Stephen Leacock:

> Most people tire of the lecture in ten minutes; clever people can do it in five. Sensible people never go to lectures at all.
>
> *[quoted in Chaudhury, 2011, p. 13]*

College instructors are well aware of the criticism implied by Leacock. Professors used to be "a sage on the stage," that is, an expert who lectures from the front of the room. Instead, more instructors seek to be "a guide on the side." Pedagogy has changed: more projects, teamwork, technology, and discussion.

Particularly in human development, *service learning* (when students apply their knowledge to helping people) can help make classroom learning more important and relevant. However, as with other methods of active learning, the design of service learning matters. Active involvement of the professor is needed (Gerholz et al., 2018).

Unlike Their Parents Both photos show large, urban colleges in the United States (California and New York), with advantages that older college generations did not have: wireless Internet (in use by all three students in the left photo) and classmates from 50 nations (evident in the right photo).

Kevork Djansezian/Getty Images News/Getty Images

Melanie Stetson Freeman/The Christian Science Monitor via Getty Images

Why Learn?

To conclude this chapter, we need to raise a question: Why is learning and cognition important for adults?

Underlying our entire discussion of college, indeed our entire discussion of adult cognition, is the assumption that adults benefit from combining the practical and the theoretical, the emotional and the analytic, thinking that characterizes adult thought at its best. Not everyone agrees with that assumption (Heimlich, 2011).

Many adults (55 percent) who have never attended college believe that "acquiring specific skills and knowledge" is the most important reason to go to college. For them, success is a high-paying job. Students who endorse that perspective seek a degree in computer systems or the health professions (doctor, nurse, therapist), because those are areas in increasing demand and higher pay.

Other students consider college as a moratorium, a way to postpone the responsibilities of adulthood. They seek social comfort, not cognitive challenge.

By contrast, many college graduates (56 percent) believe that the main purpose of higher education is "personal and intellectual growth." Professors hope to foster critical thinking and analysis, the postformal cognition that began this chapter. Critical thinking, however, requires all of us, textbook authors as well as professors and students, to ask what this academic endeavor is all about!

WHAT HAVE YOU LEARNED?

1. What are the economic benefits of college?
2. How might student loans be harmful for adult development?
3. How does cognitive development compare between current students and those in college several decades ago?
4. What are the problems with the idea of "college for all"?
5. How can diversity among students advance cognitive development?
6. What are the benefits and problems of MOOCs?

SUMMARY

A New Level of Thinking

1. Piaget thought the highest level of thinking was his fourth stage, formal operational, which began in adolescence and continued through all of adult life. Many scientists believe he was mistaken, in that he did not realize that more advanced cognition was possible.

2. In adulthood the complex and conflicting demands of daily life may produce a new, advanced cognitive perspective. Postformal thinking combines the practical and analytical in a flexible manner.

3. Stereotypes may be useful in childhood but need to be abandoned in adulthood. The flexibility of postformal thought helps people shed stereotypes and defend against stereotype threat.

4. Contemporary marriage patterns are an example of adults' ability to reject earlier stereotypes. Emerging adults tend to postpone marriage, and they are more likely to marry across ethnic lines than was true for their parents.

5. Dialectical thinking synthesizes complexities and contradictions. Instead of seeking absolute, immutable truths, dialectical thought recognizes that people and situations are dynamic and ever-changing.

6. Dialectical thinking can apply to many adult experiences, from surviving a romantic breakup to drinking in moderation. The ability to synthesize emotions and rational analysis is particularly useful in responding to social understanding and actions, because each relationship requires complex and flexible responses.

7. Dialectical thought may be more typical in Asian cultures than in Western ones. However, working together and considering many perspectives is useful for everyone, as many adults from every culture do.

Ethics and Religion

8. Thinking about questions of morality, faith, and ethics advance in adulthood. Specific moral opinions are strongly influenced by culture and context, but adults generally become less self-centered as they mature.

9. In many academic fields, coursework is designed to raise ethical issues. Progress can be measured with the Defining Issues Test, which requires people to prioritize conflicting moral values.

10. Adults tend to identify less with a particular religion but nonetheless consider themselves quite moral and spiritual. According to

Fowler, with experience and maturation, religious faith also moves beyond culture-bound concepts toward universal principles.

11. Jonathan Haidt has studied moral thinking, finding five foundations that are influenced by religion and culture. Most adults have strong convictions that are not necessarily logical.

Cognitive Growth and Higher Education

12. Research over the past several decades indicates that college graduates are wealthier and healthier than those who never went to college. That makes college education is a worthwhile investment. However, benefits come with earned degrees, and many students drop out of college with huge debts but without a degree.

13. Traditionally, college education advanced reading, thinking and communication skills. That may be less true currently, in that reading and writing requirements are less demanding. Many students do not seem to advance cognitively in their first years of college.

14. Many colleges seek to improve instruction. Diversity (ethnic, SES, political) is increasing in colleges, and that can expand awareness of other perspectives. Colleges can foster discussions that encourage dialectical thought,

15. Technology can improve instruction and allow MOOCs and flipped classes, both of which have potential but need to be carefully crafted. Personal engagement still seems to be a catalyst for cognitive growth.

KEY TERMS

postformal thought (p. 454)
stereotype threat (p. 456)
dialectical thought (p. 457)
thesis (p. 457)
antithesis (p. 457)
synthesis (p. 457)
Defining Issues Test (DIT) (p. 462)
massification (p. 466)
massive open online course (MOOC) (p. 473)

APPLICATIONS

1. Read a biography or an autobiography that includes information about the person's thinking from age 18 to age 60, paying particular attention to practical, flexible, or dialectical thought. How did personal experiences, education, and ideas affect the person's thinking?

2. Some ethical principles are thought to be universal, respected by people of every culture. Think of one such idea and analyze whether it is accepted by each of the world's major religions.

3. Statistics on changes in students and in colleges are fascinating, but only a few are reported here. Compare your nation, state, or province with another. Analyze the data and discuss causes and implications of differences.

4. One way to assess cognitive development during college is to study yourself or your classmates, comparing thoughts and decisions at the beginning and end of college. Since case studies are provocative but not definitive, identify some hypotheses that you might examine and explain how you would do so.

Especially For ANSWERS

Response for Someone Who Has to Make an Important Decision (from p. 457): Both are necessary. Mature thinking requires a combination of emotions and logic. To make sure you use both, take your time (don't act on your first impulse) and talk with people you trust. Ultimately, you will have to live with your decision, so do not ignore either intuitive or logical thought.

Response for Those Considering Studying Abroad (from p. 470): Since one result of college is that students become more open to other perspectives while developing their commitment to their own values, foreign study might be most beneficial after several years of college. If they study abroad too early, some students might be either too narrowly patriotic (they are not yet open) or too quick to reject everything about their national heritage (they have not yet developed their own commitments).

Response for High School Teachers (from p. 472): Even more than ability, motivation is crucial for college success, so don't insist that she attend college immediately. Since your student has money and a steady job (prime goals for today's college-bound youth), she may not realize what she would be missing. Ask her what she hopes for, in work and in lifestyle, over the decades ahead.

Observation Quiz ANSWERS

Answer to Observation Quiz (from p. 454): Los Angeles, California. Garcia is an undergraduate at the University of California at Los Angeles. Clues—ethnic diversity and the temple's architecture.

Answer to Observation Quiz (from p. 472) Hispanic, from 4 percent to 18 percent. If you guessed two or more races, you might be right, but that was not tallied before 2010.

VISUALIZING DEVELOPMENT Why Study?

From a life-span perspective, college graduation is a good investment, for individuals (they become healthier and wealthier) and for nations (national income rises). However, when the effort and cost of higher education depend on immediate choices made by students and families, as in the United States, many decide it is not worth it, as illustrated by the number of people who earn Bachelor's degrees.

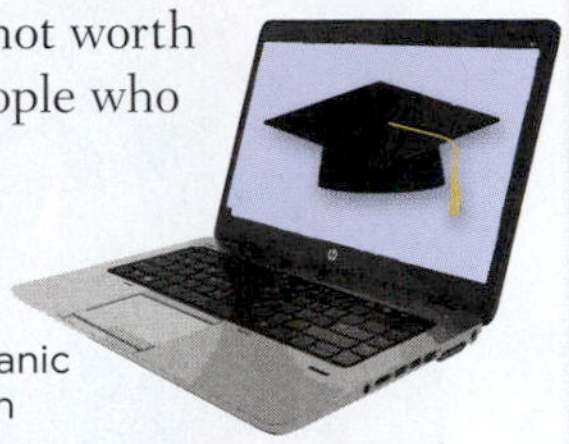

CURRENT COLLEGE ENROLLMENT AMONG U.S. 18- TO 24-YEAR-OLDS

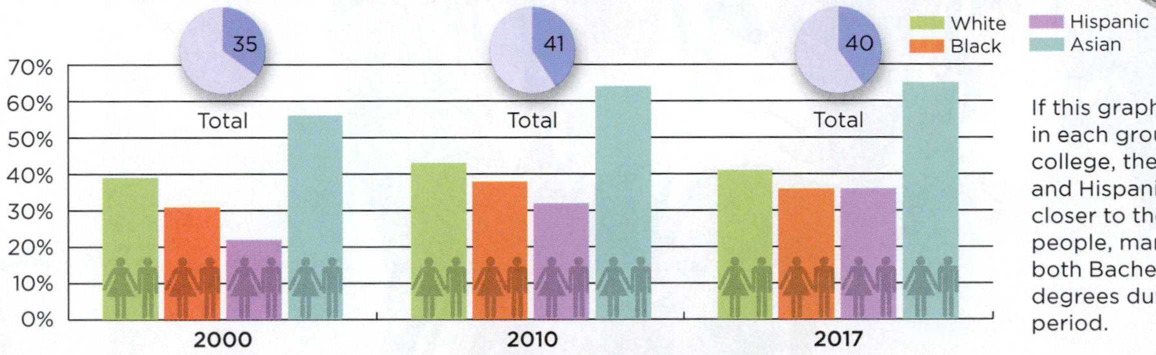

Data from: National Center for Education Statistics, February, 2019.

If this graph showed how many in each group *ever* attended college, the numbers for Black and Hispanic people would be closer to the numbers for Asian people, many of whom earn both Bachelor's and advanced degrees during this six-year period.

HIGHEST LEVEL OF EDUCATION ATTAINED BY U.S. ADULTS

The percentage of U.S. residents with high school and college diplomas is increasing as more of the oldest cohort (often without degrees) dies and the youngest cohorts aim for college. The data below are for people ages 25 and older. In 1968, half of them reached high school age when education past eighth grade was a luxury, expected for those who were rich, native-born, and white, not for the general population.

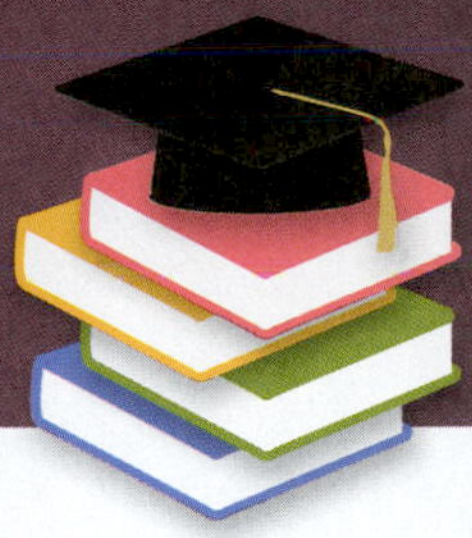

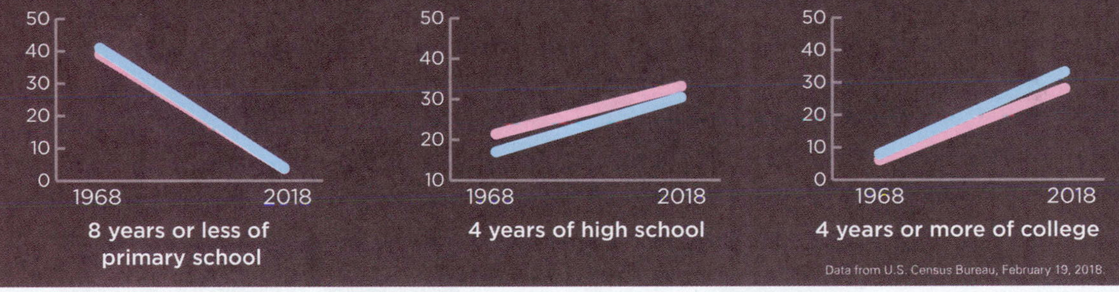

Data from U.S. Census Bureau, February 19, 2018.

INCOME IMPACT

Over an average of 40 years of employment, someone who completes at least a Master's degree earns 1.5 million dollars more than someone who leaves school in eleventh grade. That translates into more than $200,000 for each year of education from twelfth grade to a Master's. The earnings gap is even wider than those numbers indicate because this chart includes only adults who have jobs, yet finding work is more difficult for those with less education.

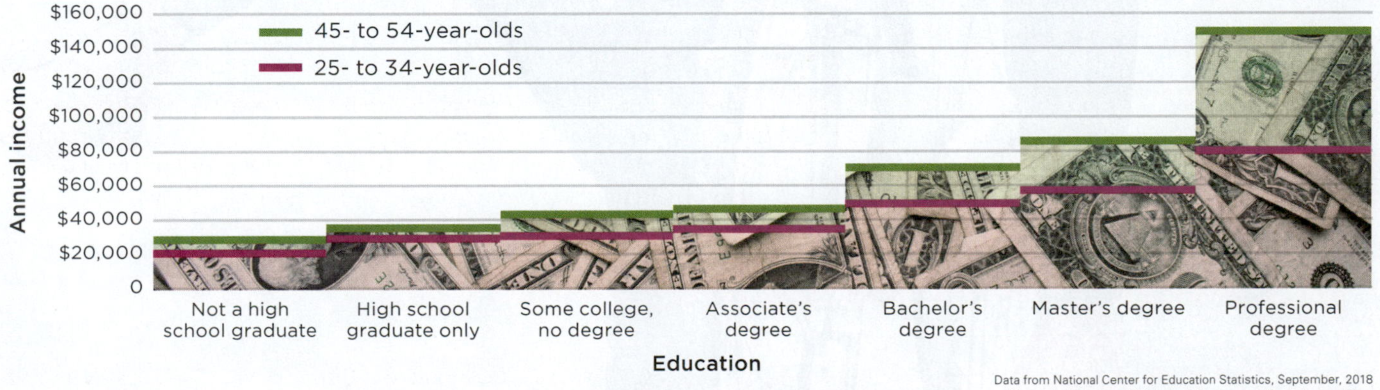

Data from National Center for Education Statistics, September, 2018
Photo: Jupiterimages/Thinkstock/Photos.com/Getty Images Plus.

Emerging Adulthood: Psychosocial Development

CHAPTER 19

What Will You Know?

1. How did the recent economic recession affect emerging adults?
2. How is a family more than a collection of individuals?
3. In spouse abuse, is it better for partners to be counseled or to separate?

- **Identity Achievement**
  - Moratoria
  - Ethnic Identity
  - Vocational Identity
- **Identity and Intimacy**
  - Emerging Adults and Their Parents
  - Friendship
- **Romantic Partners**
  - The Dimensions of Love
  - A CASE TO STUDY: My Students, My Daughters, and Me
  - Cohabitation
  - OPPOSING PERSPECTIVES: Making Divorce More Likely?
  - Concluding Hopes
- **CAREER ALERT: The Career Counselor**
- **VISUALIZING DEVELOPMENT: Marital Status in the United States**

It used to be that people would "settle down" after high school, as adulthood began at age 18 and that meant getting serious. My husband and I expected that for our daughters.

In high school, our youngest daughter did not care much about her studies. We thought the problem was too much TV, so we hid the television. She searched and found it. In desperation, my husband cut the wire (he reconnected it later). Our daughter's English teacher said that he had seen many like her, and they eventually settled down. We waited.

She chose a small college in a semirural community; we hoped that social context would stabilize her. Wrong. She still experimented and explored, as emerging adults do. In her first college year, she tutored refugees and got a part-time job at a chain restaurant. After that, she transferred to another college where she joined the crew team (which meant rising at dawn), majored in economics (as no one in our family ever had), spent a semester in a nation none of us had visited (Spain), and—to our happy surprise—graduated with honors.

But she was still unsettled. After graduation, she lived in three places within a few years, was an intern at one company, a temporary employee at another, and unemployed for several months. She skipped some family gatherings to be with friends. However, since age 25, she has had one job, lived in one neighborhood, and is warmly supportive of the family! In retrospect, I see emerging adulthood in her and in many other 18- to 25-year-olds.

This chapter describes that period, with evidence of exploration—in ethnic identity, in family relationships, in personality—and eventual commitment to one adult life.

Identity Achievement

Identity exploration begins in adolescence (as explained in Chapter 16), but identity achievement does not usually arrive until age 25 or later. As one team explains: "identity development in the areas of love, work, and worldviews is a central task of the third decade of life" (Padilla-Walker & Nelson, 2017, p. 5).

Left: pixelfit/E+/Getty Images
Top: RapidEye/iStock/E+/Getty Images

JUNG YEON-JE/AFP/Getty Images

Grown Up Now? In Korean tradition, age 19 signifies adulthood, when people can drink alcohol and, in modern times, vote. In 2011, administrators invited 100 19-year-olds to a public Coming of Age ceremony, shown here, continuing a tradition that began centuries before. Emerging adults are torn between old and new. For example, in many nations, coming of age ceremonies are exclusive to one gender, but here young men and women participate.

Moratoria

A defining feature of emerging adulthood is postponing commitment, which makes this "the period of life that offers the most opportunities for identity exploration" (Luyckx et al., 2013, p. 703). Two aspects of identity formation are particularly salient in current times: ethnic identity and vocational identity. Often political and sexual identity are connected with those two, and thus they are discussed in this section.

As explained in Chapter 16, the identity crisis sometimes causes confusion or foreclosure (see **Table 19.1**). A more mature response is a moratorium, postponing identity achievement and avoiding marriage and parenthood while exploring possibilities. Our current culture offers many moratoria: attending college; joining the military; taking on religious mission work; various internships in government, academe, and industry. All moratoria reduce the pressure to achieve identity, and all may be seen either as "floundering haphazardly" or as "sagely avoiding foreclosure and premature commitment in a treacherous job market" (Konstam, 2015, p. 95). Emerging adults do what is required (as student, soldier, missionary, or whatever), which explains why a moratorium is more mature than role confusion. But a moratorium avoids commitment.

Ethnic Identity

Identity achievement requires an interaction between the individual and the historical context. This is particularly evident in ethnic identity, which is "not a matter of one's idiosyncratic self-perception but rather, profoundly shaped by

TABLE 19.1

Erikson's Eight Stages of Development

Stage	Virtue / Pathology	Possible in Emerging Adulthood If Not Successfully Resolved
Trust vs. mistrust	Hope / withdrawal	Suspicious of others, making close relationships difficult
Autonomy vs. shame and doubt	Will / compulsion	Obsessively driven, single-minded, not socially responsive
Initiative vs. guilt	Purpose / inhibition	Fearful, regretful (e.g., very homesick in college)
Industry vs. inferiority	Competence / inertia	Self-critical of any endeavor, procrastinating, perfectionistic
Identity vs. role diffusion	Fidelity / repudiation	Uncertain and negative about values, lifestyle, friendships
Intimacy vs. isolation	Love / exclusivity	Anxious about close relationships, jealous, lonely
Generativity vs. stagnation	Care / rejection	[In the future] Fear of failure
Integrity vs. despair	Wisdom / disdain	[In the future] No "mindfulness," no life plan

Information from Erikson, 1982/1998.

one's social context, including one's social role and place in society" (Seaton et al., 2017, p. 683).

That makes ethnic identity tied to political identity, as explained in Chapter 16. Exploration and gradual commitment to a certain ethnic identity is particularly notable in the first two years of college.

Changing Self-Definition It may seem from a distance that each emerging adult has one, and only one, ethnic identity. Currently, however, most American young adults combine many threads to forge their own self-definition.

Some identify as being of two or more races (still uncommon, but rates have doubled over the past decade), but almost everyone claims several ancestors who pull in divergent directions; almost everyone is also buffeted by current identity issues, with immigration debates, Black Lives Matter, and so on to incorporate in identity.

Ethnic identity is affected by a person's stage in life as well. For example, in San Diego, the same people (age 14 at the start and age 37 at the end) were repeatedly asked about their ethnic identity (What do you call yourself?) (Feliciano & Rumbaut, 2019).

Few chose pan-ethnic terms (Asian, Latino, etc.) to identify themselves. Especially in adolescence, many used specific heritage terms (Cambodian, Mexican, and so on), with a trend toward American (hyphenated or not) as time went on. For example, one identified as Vietnamese in high school but in adulthood said he was American.

> I wouldn't identify myself as Vietnamese. . . Physically from a phenotype perspective, I don't look typical American. . . most people when they think of Americans they think of just White. But living in San Diego, you see a multicultural group of people. . .

In this study, the relationship of ethnic self-identity to how outsiders see them differed for those who appear White and those who appear Black. The white-appearing ones deliberately included their immigrant roots, such as Mexican-American: None of them simply said they were American.

The African-American-appearing ones did not always identify as Black during adolescence but did later, in part because of the larger community. One example of a woman with a Filipina mother and Black father said she was Black-Filipina. She added:

> . . . if it was up to me, actually, I'd just say, I'm American [but] I know what they're asking. . . I don't want to be rude about it.

Those who were of Mexican heritage were particularly likely to assert that in adulthood. As one said:

> For me it's very important to label me Mexican-American because I wanna show people . . . two sides. I wanna show my parents that, hey, I made it. And I'm proud of being Mexican. And . . ., I wanna show . . . conservatives . . . I'm an immigrant that came to this country and I succeeded and I don't take advantage of the system.

This and every similar study finds that ethnic identity is not a private, personal choice but a community one, with differences depending on education (more education led to more specificity), family, and national politics. The impact of those influences is not the same on every individual, even those with the same origin.

As development continues from adolescence through adulthood, ethnic identity is "complex and varied" (Feliciano & Rumbaut, 2018, p. 42). Historical conditions as well as maturation have an effect.

CHAPTER APP 19

Countable

IOS:
https://tinyurl.com/jeh8m6y

ANDROID:
https://tinyurl.com/y8rb3q5b

RELEVANT TOPIC:
Political choices in emerging adulthood

This app informs users of pending U.S. federal legislation (and soon, state and local legislation) with succinct, non-partisan, sourced writeups that include pro and con arguments. Countable also enables users to give instant feedback on pending bills and see how their representatives voted.

Kevin Winter/Getty Images Entertainment/Getty Images

What Are You? Many emerging adults refuse to identify as a single ethnicity or sexual orientation. That may be why Halsey, a proudly bisexual singer–songwriter of Irish, Italian, Hungarian, and African American heritage, is a superstar for many of her generation. Among her many record-breaking accomplishments, her album *Badlands* sold 115,000 copies in the first week after its release. She was born in 1994; here she is 24.

Dreamers and Adoptees Establishing ethnic identity is especially difficult for two particular groups of emerging adults within the United States.

About 2 million emerging adults are called *Dreamers*—unauthorized immigrants to the United States who came as children and who now seek higher education (some states allow them in-state tuition at public colleges, some do not), employment, and family creation. They want to become responsible U.S. citizens, but they are prevented from doing so.

Legally, about half earned a two-year stay of deportation. They had to apply, pay $495, and meet five criteria, set by the Obama administration:

1. Under age 31 in 2012;
2. Entered the United States before age 16;
3. Lived continuously in the United States for at least five years;
4. Never convicted of a felony or serious misdemeanor; and
5. Graduated from a U.S. high school or served in the armed forces.

Successful applicants were promised another two years if they reapplied, paid another $495, and continued to obey the law. The Trump administration later attempted to reverse Dreamer status. The U.S. Congress and judges resisted. As of April 2019, the future status of the Dreamers was unknown.

What *is* known is that many have a new identity—Dreamer. They are unlike either their age-mates still living in their original nation or other emerging adults who are citizens of the United States. Instead, many have taken on an activist political identity (de la Torre & Germano, 2014; DeAngelo et al., 2016). From a developmental psychology perspective, this is what young adults need to do: Embracing an identity resolves uncertainty and allows movement toward adulthood.

Another large group (estimated at 300,000) of emerging adults were adopted internationally and raised in the United States, usually by parents of another ethnicity. They are citizens, but they must reconcile many identities: racial, ethnic, national, immigrant, and adoptee (Pinderhughes & Rosnati, 2015; Godon-Decoteau et al., 2018).

Ideally, they develop a multifaceted identity, appreciating all of the genetic and cultural influences on them (Ferrari et al., 2015). Their success at that complex task, with affirmation or rejection from both their adoptive and original cultures, affects their entire lives—enriching them or undermining their later development.

Everyone Else Dreamers and adoptees have complex identities to establish, but every emerging adult must establish an ethnic and political identity. Almost never are all four grandparents from the same geographical region, with the same political opinions and religion.

This identity struggle affects all emerging adults, who struggle with aspects of themselves even as they think other people are less troubled. My students were bewildered when I told them that I do not consider myself Anglo or Caucasian, because my ancestors were not from England (Anglo) or Eastern Russia (the Caucasus). That matters to me, but not to other people: Each person's ethnic identity journey is his or her own.

For all people, becoming proud of their particular heritage correlates with healthy psychosocial development. On the other hand, too much sensitivity about ethnicity can increase awareness of discrimination, making the emerging adult vulnerable to stereotype threat. Ethnic identity is said to be a "double-edged sword," making this aspect of identity critical for self-concept (Yip, 2018).

Political Choices As already evident with the Dreamers, political choices are crucial to the self-definition of many emerging adults. In former times, growing up in a particular community established political identity. People identified as a Democrat or a Republican because that was the party of their parents, their classmates, their church. That is less true today.

For the first time in the past 70 years of U.S. history, in 2008 millions of young adults voted for a candidate for president (Obama) whom their grandparents did not support. That age divide continues: In 2016, only about one-third of 18- to 29-year-olds voted for Trump, as did slightly more than half of voters over age 45, a 16-percent gap.

This was not true for earlier cohorts. In the 2000 presidential contest, when both candidates were quite similar in ethnicity, gender, and age, the difference between older and younger voters was only 2 percent.

Of course, there are many plausible explanations, but one is that the younger generation are more accepting of ethnic and gender diversity, in part because they are likely to have friends who are unlike them in their various identities. (Specifics of sexual identity and partnership formation are discussed later in this chapter.)

For all kinds of diversity, emerging adults are more welcoming than older adults. For example, in the United States, almost three-fourths of people under age 30 believe more diversity is needed, compared to only about half of those over age 50. Similar age trends are evident in other nations (Poushter et al., 2019).

Vocational Identity

Establishing a vocational identity is considered part of growing up, not only by developmental psychologists influenced by Erikson but also by emerging adults themselves. As explained in Chapter 18, many go to college to prepare for a good job.

Help from Adults Vocational identity may be elusive for emerging adults. Most employees find their jobs via personal contacts, who alert them to openings, provide recommendations, and so on. Since the job market is changing rapidly, the older generation is of limited use to young adults. Parents usually know only their own job and employer, not labor-market projections.

One result is that many emerging adults have a limited understanding of which jobs would make them happy or even what to look for, other than income and benefits. Some use John Holland's description (1997) of six possible interests (see **Figure 19.1**). However, even if they earn a degree (most don't, as you saw in Chapter 18) and know what they want (again, most don't), they still may be unable to find the work they hope for (Konstam, 2015).

An added problem is finding a well-paying job. Financial independence has traditionally been considered a marker of adulthood. Yet because the recent recession hit emerging

FIGURE 19.1
Happy at Work John Holland's six-part diagram helps job seekers realize that income and benefits are not the only goals of employment. Workers have healthier hearts and minds if their job fits their personal preferences.

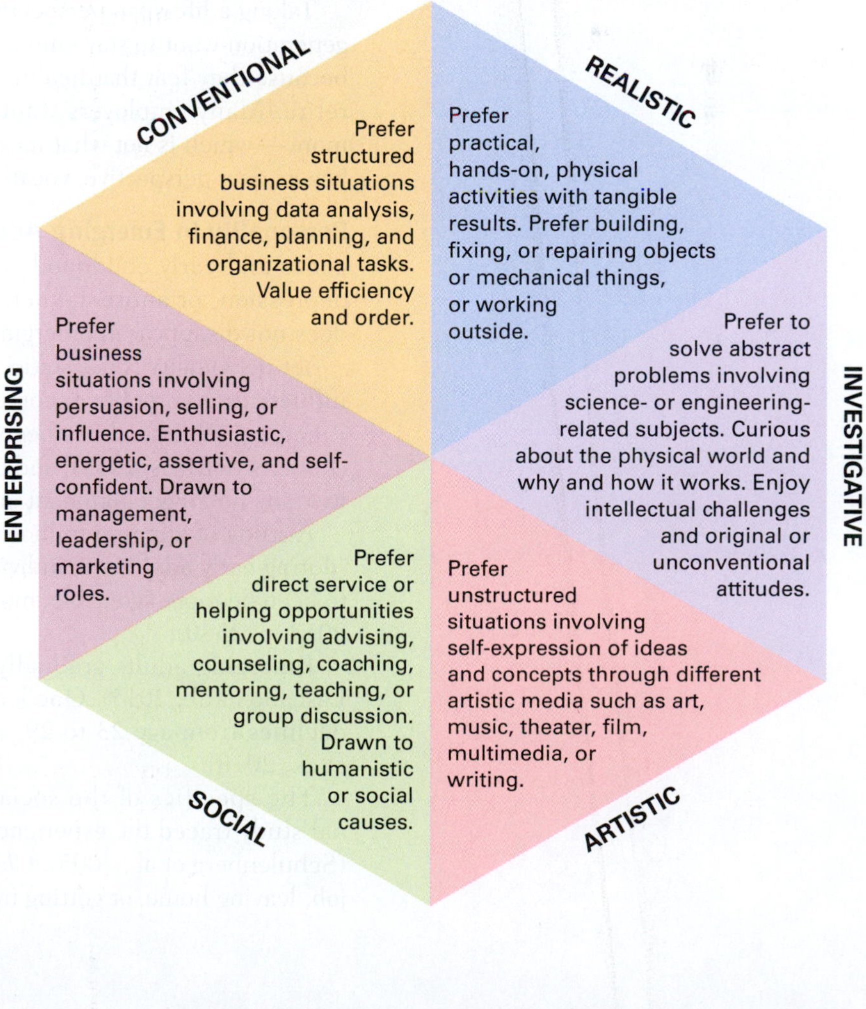
CONVENTIONAL
Prefer structured business situations involving data analysis, finance, planning, and organizational tasks. Value efficiency and order.
REALISTIC
Prefer practical, hands-on, physical activities with tangible results. Prefer building, fixing, or repairing objects or mechanical things, or working outside.
INVESTIGATIVE
Prefer to solve abstract problems involving science- or engineering-related subjects. Curious about the physical world and why and how it works. Enjoy intellectual challenges and original or unconventional attitudes.
ARTISTIC
Prefer unstructured situations involving self-expression of ideas and concepts through different artistic media such as art, music, theater, film, multimedia, or writing.
SOCIAL
Prefer direct service or helping opportunities involving advising, counseling, coaching, mentoring, teaching, or group discussion. Drawn to humanistic or social causes.
ENTERPRISING
Prefer business situations involving persuasion, selling, or influence. Enthusiastic, energetic, assertive, and self-confident. Drawn to management, leadership, or marketing roles.

Clive Goddard/cartoonstock.com

Ordinary Workers Most children and adolescents want to be sports heroes, star entertainers, billionaires, or world leaders—yet fewer than one in 1 million succeed in doing so.

adults hardest, most emerging adults depended on their parents for financial support in an uncertain job market (Bea & Yi, 2019).

To make vocational identity even harder, many young adults consider their job part of who they are. As one psychologist wrote:

> [C]areer choices faced by individuals inevitably raise the question of the meaning that they intend to give their lives. To choose their work or sector in which they want to evolve is also to consider the purpose of their existence, the priorities (physical, spiritual, social, aesthetic, etc.) that they want to give, the choices that they wish to operate, the overall style of life that they wish to give themselves.
>
> *[Bernaud, 2014, p. 36]*

Thus, for many younger adults, vocational identity is not just about finding a job; it is about deciding what kind of person they want to be and then becoming that person. Many do stop-gap work in the *gig economy,* which includes all of the temporary, episodic, or independent jobs that are not part of a regular contract, with minimum hourly wage and health benefits. They drive cars for hire, tutor children, sell items online, act as social media "influencers," and much more.

If they are hired for more traditional jobs, they quit more often than older workers do. Between ages 18 and 25, the average U.S. worker has held seven jobs, with the college-educated changing jobs more than the high school graduate (U.S. Bureau of Labor Statistics, 2018).

Many emerging adults avoid the demands of a 9-to-5 job; they do not want to climb, rung by rung, up a career ladder. Some have little choice: Employers save money by hiring temporary or contract-based workers, and older adults are less likely to retire. This is obvious in higher education: Many colleges have more part-time instructors than tenured faculty.

Taking a life-span perspective suggests a generational clash. Many in the older generation want to stay employed, partly to support their adult children and partly because they fear that health and housing expenses will become too steep if they retire. Many employers want workers who will stay on the job for decades or more—which is not what most emerging adults want. Thus, because each cohort has its own perspective, vocational identity for the young is difficult to attain.

Personality in Emerging Adulthood As adult identity is gradually established, genes and early childhood continue to have an impact. If self-doubt, anxiety, depression, or antisocial behavior characterizes childhood and adolescence, it does not disappear in emerging adulthood.

Yet personality is not static, and each emerging adult combines genes, parental influences, and political contexts in a specific way to form an adult personality. Emerging adulthood has been called the "crucible for personality development" (Roberts & Davis, 2016), and the result is usually positive, with negative personality traits no longer dominant and positive ones strengthened.

A study of almost a million adolescents and adults from 62 nations found that "during early adulthood, individuals from different cultures across the world tend to become more agreeable, more conscientious, and less neurotic" (Bleidorn et al., 2013, p. 2530).

Emerging adults gradually feel more in control of their own lives (Vargas Lascano et al., 2015). One longitudinal study found that self-criticism gradually declines from age 23 to 29, which improves mental health later on (Michaeli et al., 2018).

The specifics of the social context make a difference. Another longitudinal study traced the experiences of 3,912 U.S. high school seniors for five years (Schulenberg et al., 2005). *Chosen* transitions (such as entering college, starting a job, leaving home, or getting married) tended to increase well-being.

In that study, those who went to college away from home, and thus learned to live independently, showed the largest gains. Those who became single parents showed the least. Even the latter, however, tended to be happier than they had been in high school (see **Figure 19.2**).

Another longitudinal study found that most young adults relied on parental financial help for years, even after college was over. Financial help meant less stress and eventually more independence, from age 18 to 27 (Bea & Yi, 2019).

Those (about one-fourth) who were totally independent, financially, tended to fare worse at age 27 than those with substantial assistance. The conclusion of this study is that family support is not a barrier to independence but more often the opposite—a helpful launching pad toward adulthood (Bea & Yi, 2019).

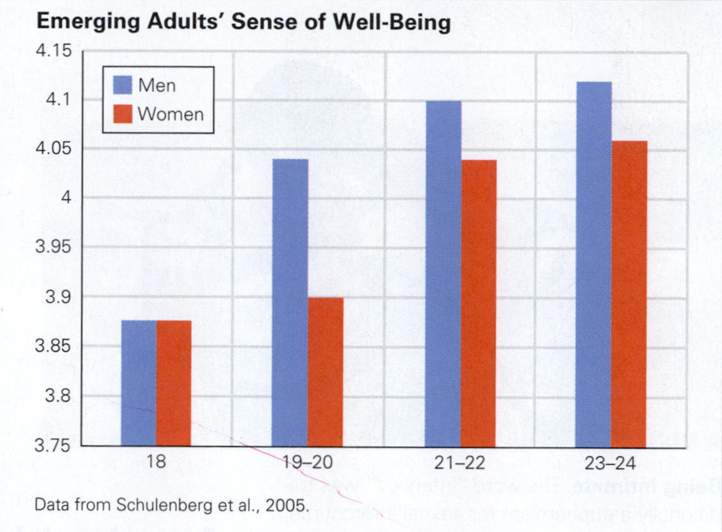

FIGURE 19.2

Worthy People This graph shows a steady, although small, rise in young adults' sense of well-being from age 18 to age 24, as measured by respondents' ratings of statements such as "I feel I am a person of worth." The ratings ranged from 1 (complete disagreement) to 5 (complete agreement). The average rating was actually quite high at age 18, and it increased steadily over the years of emerging adulthood.

Observation Quiz It looks as if well-being more than doubled between age 18 and the early 20s. Is that right? (see answer, page 502) ↑

WHAT HAVE YOU LEARNED?

1. How does a moratorium differ from identity achievement?
2. Why is ethnic identity particularly complicated in the United States?
3. How does vocational identity differ among emerging adults and older adults?
4. How does personality change, and not change, with age?

Identity and Intimacy

In Erikson's theory, after achieving identity, people experience the crisis of **intimacy versus isolation.** He explains:

> The young adult, emerging from the search for and the insistence on identity, is eager and willing to fuse his identity with others. He is ready for intimacy, that is, the capacity to commit himself to concrete affiliations and partnerships and to develop the ethical strength to abide by such commitments, even though they call for significant sacrifices and compromises.
>
> *[Erikson, 1993a, p. 263]*

intimacy versus isolation The sixth of Erikson's eight stages of development. Adults seek someone with whom to share their lives in an enduring and self-sacrificing commitment. Without such commitment, they risk profound aloneness and isolation.

Other theorists have different words for the same human need: *affiliation, affection, interdependence, communion, belonging, love.* But all developmentalists agree that social connections are pivotal lifelong (Padilla-Walker et al., 2017). In adulthood, intimacy progresses from attraction to connection to commitment. Each relationship demands vulnerability and compromise, shattering the isolation caused by too much self-protection.

The social context may be particularly influential in emerging adulthood, a period called the "frontier" of efforts to prevent problems and foster positive growth (Schwartz & Petrova, 2019). Individual differences matter, but the trend is toward more social connections, with family relationships maintained and friendships established. That benefits emerging adults (Jorgensen & Nelson, 2018).

Wave/Cultura Images/Media Bakery

chee gin tan/E+/Getty Images

Being Intimate The word "intimacy" was traditionally a euphemism for sexual intercourse, but to developmentalists it is much more than that. Look closely at these two couples, one in Spain *(left)* and one in Malaysia *(right)*. Whether or not they are having sex does not matter: They are intimate in their touching, emotions, and even clothing.

Emerging Adults and Their Parents

It is hard to overestimate the importance of the family during any time of the life span. Although a family is composed of individuals who identify as members of that family, it is much more than just the persons who belong to it. In the dynamic synergy of a well-functioning family, children grow, adults find support, and everyone is part of a unit that gives meaning to life.

Parents may now be more important during emerging adulthood than they were in past history. Two experts in human development write, "with delays in marriage, more Americans choosing to remain single, and high divorce rates, a tie to a parent may be the most important bond in a young adult's life" (Fingerman & Furstenberg, 2012).

linked lives Lives in which the success, health, and well-being of each family member are connected to those of other members, including those of another generation, as in the relationship between parents and children.

All members of each family have **linked lives;** that is, the experiences and needs of family members at every stage of life are affected by everyone else (Elder, 1998; Macmillan & Copher, 2005; Settersten, 2015). In earlier chapters you read that children suffer when their parents fight, that family financial stress troubles everyone, that siblings can be role models for good or for ill.

The concept of linked lives highlights the need for awareness of intersectionality—that ethnicity, income, and gender affect family function (Wong, 2018). This is more evident today than ever, in that young adults less often establish their own families and more often depend on their families of origin. Further, since family size is smaller, parents have fewer children and thus are more able to invest in their young-adult offspring.

Many emerging adults still live at home, though the percentage varies from nation to nation. Almost all unmarried young adults in Italy and Japan live with their parents, as do an increasing number in the United States. Those who are living with their parents, especially the "boomerang" group who came back to their parents' home because they lost jobs or partnerships, are often depressed. However, those who have never left, who are now employed and planning to leave, are sometimes quite happy (Copp et al., 2015).

The crucial test of linked lives is not who lives together but who supports whom. When young adults have their own residence, many see their parents several times a week and phone or text them often (Fingerman et al., 2012b). That is a sign of family closeness, as support is mutual.

Attitudes are affected by parents, who themselves are affected by their young-adult children (Padilla-Walker et al., 2018), benefitting both generations. For example, religious values and practices reflect parental faith, although they rarely duplicate it. Religious values foster mental health, reflecting past and current family ties (Haney & Rollock, 2018).

A detailed Dutch study found substantial agreement between parents and their adult children on contentious issues: cohabitation, same-sex partnerships, and divorce. Generational differences appeared, with the young more accepting of diversity than the old; but when parents were compared with their own children (not young adults in general), "intergenerational congruence" was apparent (Bucx et al., 2010, p. 131).

Support from Parents At least according to legend, in former years children left the family home at age 18 or so, and parents were no longer responsible for them. The term *empty nest* came from the idea that children, like little birds, established their own lives because they were able to fly away without parental help. That may no longer be the case.

It certainly is not the case financially. Parents of all income levels in the United States provide substantial help to their adult children, for many reasons (Padilla-Walker et al., 2012). A major reason is that the parents' generation has more income. On average, households with the highest average income are headed by someone aged 45 to 54 (U.S. Census Bureau, 2019).

This harks back to the concept of linked lives. In nations such as the United States, where neither college nor preschool education is free, family financial help may be crucial for the emerging adult's later financial and personal success (Bea & Yi, 2019).

About half of all emerging adults in the United States receive cash from their parents, in addition to tuition, medical care, food, and other material support. Most are also given substantial gifts of time, such as help with laundry, moving, household repairs, and, if the young adult becomes a parent, free child care. Earning a college degree or raising small children is almost impossible without family help.

Financial support is less essential in many European nations, where college tuition is free or less expensive, where early-childhood education is considered a public right, and where housing and health care are less costly. Accordingly, parents in Europe usually spend less on their adult children.

However, European parents support their adult children in many other ways—the urge to support grown children is universal; specifics depend on family resources and national policies (Brandt & Deindl, 2013).

In cultures with arranged marriages, parents provide practical support (such as child care) and emotional encouragement, and they may also protect their grown child if the chosen marriage is a disaster. For instance, if the husband severely beats the wife, if the wife refuses sex, if the husband never works or the wife never cooks, then the parents intervene. Again, parents respond to the expectations of their culture: They intervene differently in, say, Cambodia, than they might in, say, Colorado.

Too Little or Too Much? A major question everywhere is how much family support is needed. One example is children in foster care. Because of laws established decades ago, at age 18, these young people are considered adults, able to take their place in society. Given all that is now known, this is far too young (Avery & Freundlich, 2009); few 18-year-olds can manage life on their own.

Financially, some help is available for former foster children (food stamps, college scholarships), but emotional support and encouragement are still needed. Without that, former foster children are at risk of almost every problem.

The emotional needs of foster children were evident in Sweden in a study of 65 young adults, aged 18 to 26, who once were in foster care (Höjer & Sjöblom, 2014). Although they were supported well financially, the former foster children had more problems of every kind, such as arrest, early parenthood, and mental illness.

By contrast, some parents keep their adult children too dependent. One example is the so-called **helicopter parent,** hovering over the emerging-adult child,

"This property comes complete with grown-up children left behind by the vendors."

Grizelda via CartoonStock

No Thanks Even living with one's own children is problematic.

Especially for Family Therapists More emerging-adult children today live with their parents than ever before, yet you have learned that families often function better when young adults live on their own. What would you advise? (see response, page 502)

helicopter parents The label used for parents who hover (like a helicopter) over their emerging-adult children. The term is pejorative, but parental involvement is sometimes helpful.

Who Needs It? Is Sophia grateful that her mother is making her bed as she moves into her freshman dorm at Saint Joseph's College in Maine? Your answer may be influenced by whether you identify with the mother or the daughter.

snowplow parents Parents who try to remove any impediments in the way of their children. This term is pejorative; it implies that parents do not allow children to learn how to overcome obstacles on their own.

ready to swoop down if any problem arises (Fingerman et al., 2012a). This can occur at college or in the workplace: Parents sometimes complain about a bad performance review from a work supervisor of their adult child (Karl & Peluchette, 2016).

Even worse may be the so-called **snowplow parents,** who try to clear every obstacle in the path of their children. This erupted in a major U.S. scandal in 2019, when some parents paid to have college applications distorted to make their children seem more capable and talented than was the case (Coleman, 2019).

The basic problem is that young people begin adulthood later, and older adults live longer, lengthening the time for possible support from the parents. What should that support be? Doing laundry? Baking cookies? Editing papers? Paying bills?

All of this may keep young adults dependent, not learning from their mistakes, but may aid development. One factor is the parents' relationship. If parents fight between themselves and then one parent intrudes in the life of the emerging adult to compensate for the poor marital relationship, that is particularly harmful to the child (Kumar & Mattanah, 2018). On the other hand, mutual care and support is beneficial for the entire family, as the life of each person is linked to the others.

One mother explains that her son doesn't come home from college as often as she would like, but when he does, he brings bags of dirty laundry that she washes and

> I always send him back with some food and maybe a little bit of money as well. . . . I just feel that he is my baby, and I feel as though I am still providing for him, if I at least know he is eating right and has enough money.
>
> [*quoted in Hendry & Kloep, 2011, p. 84*]

Cultural norms matter, too. In mainstream American culture, unsolicited parental advice is not welcome. One mother says her tongue is scarred from biting it so much.

Yet among many cultures (including some American subcultures), parents advise their grown children about everything from clothing styles to marriage partners—they would consider themselves remiss not to do so. Americanized emerging adults might say that is hostile and intrusive, whereas their parents might consider that reaction from their adult children to be selfish and rude.

Given the reality that emerging adults are not yet mature, and the lifelong need for family support, it may be that parental involvement of all kinds benefits the children. Too much parental protection hinders growth, but too much criticism of helicopter parents may undercut family relationships, and may result in loneliness and isolation in both generations rather than self-reliant young adults.

Most emerging adults find a balance: Only about 20 percent of them disclose personal as well as routine information about their lives to their parents. In general, some distance is better, but individuals vary by culture and personality (Son & Padilla-Walker, 2019). Family lives are linked, but time, place, and family interaction determine when chains are restrictive and when support is beneficial.

Friendship

Friends are another important source of support for emerging adults. Lifelong friends increase our understanding of our experiences via *self-expansion*

(Aron et al., 2013); they enlarge our understanding as we absorb their experiences and ideas.

Friends in Emerging Adulthood Since fewer emerging adults today are married and have children, their social world can, and usually does, include friends who provide needed companionship and critical support. Unlike relatives, friends are selected for their ability to be loyal, trustworthy, supportive, and enjoyable — a mutual choice, not an obligatory one.

Thus, friends understand and comfort each other when romance turns sour, and they provide useful information about everything from which college to attend to which socks to wear. For example, many young adolescents are depressed about how their bodies appear. Interviews with 26-year-olds found that negative body image lifted in late adolescence and early adulthood, primarily because of friends who reassured them about their bodies (Gattario & Frisén, 2019).

People tend to make more friends during emerging adulthood than at any later period. They often use social media to extend and deepen friendships that begin face-to-face, becoming more aware of the day-to-day tribulations and celebrations of their friends.

Some older adults originally feared that increasing Internet use would diminish the number or quality of friendships. That fear has been proven false.

Internet users tend to have more face-to-face friends, to know more about political and social events, and to advance in learning, all examples of self-expansion. Internet use is neither a boon nor a burden to emerging adults; the benefit or harm depends on the person (Castellacci & Tveito, 2018; Hood et al., 2017; Blank & Lutz, 2018).

Friendship patterns change with maturation. Young adults want many friends, and they work to gather them — befriending classmates; attending parties; speaking to strangers at concerts, on elevators, in parks, and so on. At about age 30, a switch begins, when quality becomes more important than quantity (Carmichael et al., 2015). Consequently, some friendships from early adulthood fade away, but others deepen. Social media helps with both processes.

There is a paradox here. Not only do young adults, on average, have more friends and acquaintances than adults of other ages, they also have more loneliness. Only adults over age 80 have higher rates of loneliness (Luhmann & Hawkley, 2016).

This leads us back to Erikson, who notes that each ongoing relationship demands some personal sacrifice, including vulnerability that brings deeper

THINK CRITICALLY: Can a person with many friends also be lonely?

Luis Santana/ZUMA Press/Tampa/Florida/U.S./Newscom

xPACIFICA/The Image Bank/Getty Images

Same Situation, Far Apart: Good Friends Together These smiling emerging adults show that friendship matters everywhere. Culture matters, too. Would the eight Florida college students celebrating a 21st birthday at a Tex-Mex restaurant *(left)* be willing to switch places with the two Tibetan workers *(right)*?

self-understanding and shatters the isolation of too much self-protection. To establish intimacy, the young adult must

> face the fear of ego loss in situations which call for self-abandon: in the solidarity of close affiliations [and] sexual unions, in close friendship and in physical combat, in experiences of inspiration by teachers and of intuition from the recesses of the self. The avoidance of such experiences . . . may lead to a deep sense of isolation and consequent self-absorption.
>
> *[Erikson, 1993a, pp. 163–164]*

Gender and Friendship It is a mistake to imagine that men and women have opposite friendship needs. All humans seek intimacy throughout their lives. Claiming that men are from Mars and women are from Venus ignores reality: People are from Earth (Hyde, 2007).

Nonetheless, for cultural and biological reasons, some sex differences are traditional. A meta-analysis of 37 studies (Hall, 2011) found that men shared activities and interests. They talked about external matters—sports, work, politics, cars. They were less likely to tell other men of their failures, emotional problems, and relationship dilemmas; if they did, they expected practical advice, not sympathy.

Women's friendships were typically more intimate and emotional. They expected to share secrets with their friends and engage in self-disclosing talk, including difficulties with their health, romances, sex life, and relatives. Women reveal their weaknesses and problems and receive an attentive and sympathetic ear, a shoulder to cry on.

Physical touch showed sex differences as well. Men rarely touched each other except in aggressive activities, such as competitive athletics or military combat. The butt-slapping or body-slamming immediately after a sports victory, or the sobbing in a buddy's arms in the aftermath of a battlefield loss, are less likely in everyday life. Many women routinely hug friends in greeting or farewell; men might fist bump or hand slap.

Especially for Young Men Why would you want at least one close friend who is a woman? (see response, page 502)

Male–Female Friendships The gender differences above may now be less apparent, since gender divisions are changing. As already noted, gender differences are cultural, not biological. One difference is apparent: Male–female friendships are no longer rare. Some male–female friendships are platonic and some include sex (called "friends with benefits") (Weger et al., 2019). Neither is a hookup (sex without friendship) or a romance (a couple in love).

Same-sex and cross-sex friendships develop among people of every sexual orientation. One study of friendships included 25,185 adults, 1,361 who were sexual minorities (Gillespie et al., 2015). The number of friends was quite similar among people of every sexual orientation and gender identity.

As earlier research on heterosexual adults had reported, most people had at least three same-sex friendships and at least two of the other sex. Gay men under age 30 tended to have the highest number of cross-sex friends, perhaps because their cross-sex friendships avoided the sexual tension that heterosexual cross-sex friendships might entail.

In this study, participants were asked how many friends they could discuss sex with, celebrate their birthdays with, or call if in trouble late at night. Not surprisingly, all groups thought of more people to celebrate birthdays with than to talk about sex with. Generally, the number of friends to call when in trouble was between the other two numbers (see **Figure 19.3**).

In this study, the *number* of friends did not correlate with life satisfaction, but the *quality* of friendship did (Gillespie et al., 2015). Everyone benefits from good friends.

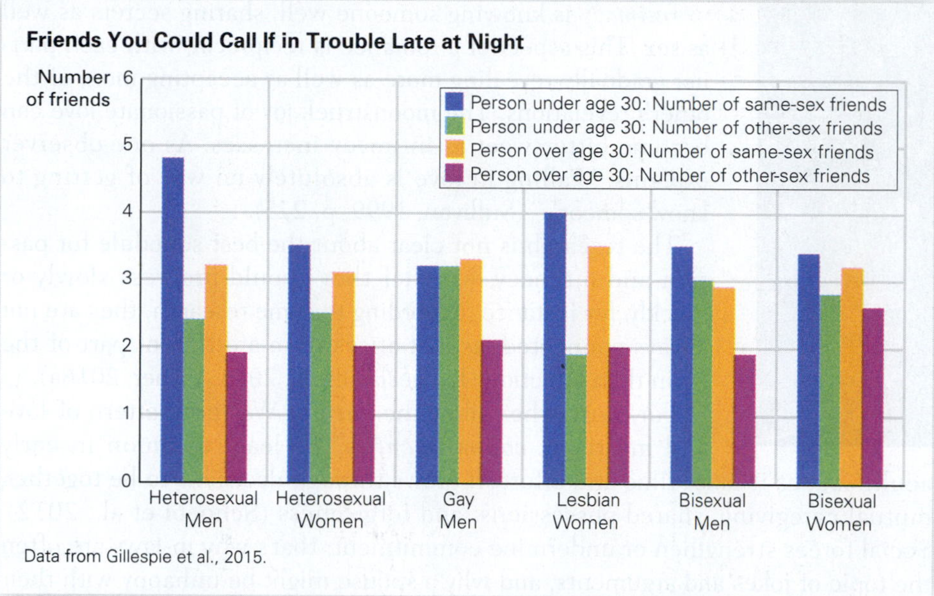

Data from Gillespie et al., 2015.

FIGURE 19.3

Same, Yet Different The authors of this study were struck by how similar the friendship patterns of sexual minority and majority people were. As you see, the one noticeable trend is age, not sexuality. People over 30 reported fewer friends overall, and fewer other-sex friends in particular, from an average of 2.6 to an average of 2.1.

WHAT HAVE YOU LEARNED?

1. How does the idea of linked lives apply to emerging adults?
2. What kinds of support do parents provide their grown children?
3. What are the advantages and disadvantages of having a "helicopter parent"?
4. What special difficulties occur for emerging adults who were foster children?
5. How are friendships different for young adults and older adults?
6. How does sexual orientation affect friendship?

Romantic Partners

"Falling in love" is a common experience for emerging adults. But exactly what that means is affected by many particulars—personality, age, cohort, and gender among them.

The Dimensions of Love

"Love" itself has many manifestations. In a classic analysis, Robert Sternberg (1988) described three distinct aspects of love: passion, intimacy, and commitment. The presence or absence of these three gives rise to seven different forms of love (see **Table 19.2**).

Early in a relationship, *passion* is evident in falling in love, an intense physical, cognitive, and emotional onslaught characterized by excitement, ecstasy, and euphoria. The entire body and mind, hormones and neurons, are activated; the person is obsessed (Sanz Cruces et al., 2015).

Passionate love is difficult to measure. In fact, 33 scales attempt to measure it; each of these is distinct, although overlap is also common (Hatfield et al., 2012).

TABLE 19.2

Sternberg's Seven Forms of Love

Present in the Relationship?			
Form of Love	**Passion**	**Intimacy**	**Commitment**
Liking	No	Yes	No
Infatuation	Yes	No	No
Empty love	No	No	Yes
Romantic love	Yes	Yes	No
Fatuous love	Yes	No	Yes
Companionate love	No	Yes	Yes
Consummate love	Yes	Yes	Yes

Information from Sternberg, 1988.

Postponing Parenthood? A challenge for many adults is how to combine work and family. Most postpone parenthood, but Shaun Creeden took another path. Here he holds his infant son, Dean, at his graduation from New York University.

Intimacy is knowing someone well, sharing secrets as well as sex. This aspect of a romance is reciprocal, with each partner gradually revealing more as well as accepting more of the other's revelations. The moonstruck joy of passionate love can become bittersweet as intimacy increases. As one observer explains, "Falling in love is absolutely no way of getting to know someone" (Sullivan, 1999, p. 225).

The research is not clear about the best schedule for passion and intimacy, whether they should progress slowly or quickly, for instance. According to some research, they are not always connected, as lust arises from a different part of the brain than affection (Langeslag et al., 2013; Fisher, 2016a).

For those who follow the current Western pattern of love and marriage, *commitment* is the least common in early adulthood, as it takes time and effort. It grows through decisions to be together, mutual caregiving, shared possessions, and forgiveness (Schoebi et al., 2012). Social forces strengthen or undermine commitment; that's why in-laws are often the topic of jokes and arguments, and why a spouse might be unhappy with their mate's close friends.

Commitment is powerfully influenced by culture. When cultures endorse arranged marriages, commitment occurs early on, before passion or intimacy. A study of husbands and wives in arranged marriages reports that the commitment by both partners to make the marriage work led to love, not vice versa. One husband said:

> Perhaps I could say that love involves commitment or [that] marriage is a commitment to love. From the beginning I was committed to love [my wife]. Sometimes I have been challenged to keep the commitment or just challenged to love her, but I do my best to be a loving husband. Loving her is usually easy but sometimes not.
>
> [*quoted in Epstein et al., 2013, pp. 352–353*]

Couples are affected by whether or not their friends and acquaintances endorse the value of committed relationships. An odd correlation was found in Sweden: Couples who lived in detached houses (with yards between them) broke up more often than did couples living in attached dwellings (such as apartments). Perhaps "single-family housing might have deleterious effects on couple stability due to the isolating lack of social support for couples staying together" (Lauster, 2008, p. 901). In other words, suburban couples may be too far from their neighbors to receive encouraging and helpful advice when conflicts arise.

When children are born, passion may fade for both partners, but commitment increases. This may be one reason why most sexually active young adults try to avoid pregnancy unless they believe their partner is a lifelong mate. **[Life-Span Link:** The relationship of parenthood to marital satisfaction is discussed in Chapter 22.]

The Ideal and the Real In Europe in the Middle Ages, love, passion, and marriage were considered to be distinct phenomena. Currently, however, the Western ideal of consummate love includes all three components: passion, intimacy, and commitment.

For developmental reasons, this ideal is difficult to achieve. Passion seems to be sparked by unfamiliarity, uncertainty, and risk, all of which are diminished by the familiarity and security that contribute to intimacy and by the time needed for commitment.

In short, with time, passion may fade, intimacy may grow and stabilize, and commitment may deepen. This pattern occurs for all types of couples—married,

unmarried, and remarried; gay, lesbian, and straight; young, middle-aged, and old; in arranged, guided, and self-initiated relationships. In this chapter we focus on the young, many of whom shy away from commitment. The reason may be that they are trying to coordinate their identity with that of a life partner—not an easy task (Shulman & Connolly, 2013).

Thus far on the subject of finding a partner, we have described the universal drives of young adults—drives that have been part of the human species for thousands of years. It seems that love is a universal emotion, and thus passion, intimacy, and commitment have been built into every culture.

Hookups As already mentioned, a **hookup** is a sexual interaction between partners who do not know each other well, perhaps having met just a few hours before. The phrase, and the experience, arose from emerging adults, first on college campuses in the United States, with scholars describing a new *hookup culture*. When such a relationship occurred in prior generations, it was either prostitution or illicit, as in a "fling" or a "dirty secret." No longer.

hookup A sexual encounter between two people who are not in a romantic relationship. Neither intimacy nor commitment is expected.

Hookups are more common among first-year college students than among those about to graduate, perhaps because older students want partners. Thus, a hookup is considered a temporary act and does not diminish the desire to enter a committed relationship sometime in the future (James-Kangal et al., 2018). As one student put it, "if you hook up with somebody it probably is just a hookup and nothing is going to come of it" (quoted in Bogle, 2008, p. 38).

The desire for physical sex without emotional commitment is stronger in young men than in young women, either for hormonal (testosterone) or cultural (women want committed fathers if children are born) reasons. In a U.S. survey of 18- to 24-year-olds who had completed at least one year of college, 56 percent of the men but only 31 percent of the women said they had had a hookup (Monto & Carey, 2014).

As contraception, employment, and college education have changed women's lives, this "guy" pattern includes more females. The hookup rates for women are about twice as high in the twenty-first century as they were late in the twentieth century, although men's rates did not increase as much (Monto & Carey, 2014). Nonetheless, women are less likely to hook up and less happy when they do.

Indeed, some of the current college awareness of date rape and sexual assault may be fueled by women's reluctance to be involved in casual sex and men's assumption that their dates share their sexual desires. Of course, this topic is complicated by many old myths and falsehoods. Three of those misleading myths: (1) Men can't control themselves; (2) women want sex even when they don't admit it; and (3) rape is an attack by a stranger, or involving a woman who is drugged, not an aggressive act between acquaintances (Deming et al., 2013).

The ideal sexual interaction during emerging adulthood is obviously a complex topic, one that cannot be described in a few paragraphs here. However, as has been apparent many times in this text, the body and the psyche function together, so the hope that sex can occur with no psychic consequences is an illusion (Fisher, 2016b). The hookup is not merely a physical activity.

Interestingly, emerging adults of both sexes who want a serious relationship with someone recognize this. They are likely to begin their courtship with covert glances, spoken pleasantries, direct gazing, casual touch, more serious talk, and more—all before beginning sexual interaction (Fisher, 2016b).

Although most U.S. emerging adults find premarital sex acceptable, only about 5 percent consider extramarital sex sometimes OK. That extramarital approval rate is similar in men and women and is actually slightly lower than 20 years ago (Monto & Carey, 2014).

Just Friends? This photo was taken in a public park in Isfala, Iran. Given that context, these two are probably more than friends.

Observation Quiz What indicates that this is romance, not mere friendship? (see answer, page 502) ↑

choice overload Having so many possibilities that a thoughtful choice becomes difficult. This is particularly apparent when social networking and other technology make many potential romantic partners available.

Finding Each Other and Living Together One major innovation of the current cohort of emerging adults is the use of social networks, as the online connections between dozens or hundreds of people are called. Virtually all emerging adults have smartphones and social-networking accounts, and some of them use this technology many times each day to keep in touch with others. Use increased rapidly from 2010 on, but this rise has now stopped—in part because use is near universal (Hitlin, 2018).

Many young adults seeking romance join one or more matchmaking Web sites that provide dozens of potential partners to meet and evaluate. Often physical attraction is the gateway to a relationship. Intimacy and then commitment require much more.

The large number of possible partners whom young adults find—the thousands of fellow students at most colleges or the hundreds of suggestions that matchmaking sites provide—causes a potential problem, **choice overload,** when too many options are available. Choice overload makes some people unable to choose, and it increases second thoughts after a selection is made (Chernev et al., 2015).

Choice overload has been proven with many consumer goods (jams, chocolates, pens, restaurants), but it applies to mate selection as well. Having many complex options that require weighing present and future advantages and disadvantages (trade-offs are inevitable in partner selection) may be overwhelming and lead to poor decisions (Lee & Chiou, 2016). One solution provided by some Internet dating sites is to allow the program to do the filtering, selecting possible mates based on mutual interests and background.

Because Internet dating sites offer a plethora of choices, overload makes people who choose to meet someone in person wonder whether they should have chosen someone else, or whether the computer algorithm missed a good match (Tong et al., 2016; D'Angelo & Toma, 2016). Fortunately, most people overcome this liability.

Changing Historical Patterns Love, romance, and lasting commitment all remain of primary importance for emerging adults. Nonetheless, a defining characteristic of emerging adults is that they marry later, in part because marriage is no longer what it once was—a legal and religious arrangement that was the exclusive avenue for sexual expression, the only legitimate prelude to childbearing, and a lifelong source of intimacy and support. Now, sex almost always begins before marriage, and almost as many babies are born to unmarried people as to married couples.

Further evidence for this cultural shift is found in U.S. statistics:

- Less than half of all adults aged 18 to 65 are married and living with their spouse.
- Only one-fifth of all emerging adults marry before age 25.
- The divorce rate is almost half the marriage rate, primarily because fewer people marry, and those who divorce are more likely to marry again as well as divorce again.
- Women having their first baby under age 30 are more often unmarried than married.

[U.S. Census Bureau, 2018]

Especially for Social Scientists Suppose your 25-year-old Canadian friend, never married, says, "Look at the statistics. If I marry now, there is a 50/50 chance I will get divorced." What three statistical facts allow you to insist, "Your odds of divorce are much lower"? (see response, page 502)

Such statistics make some people fear that marriage is a dying institution. However, few developmentalists hold that assessment. They believe that emerging adults are postponing, not abandoning, marriage. The efforts that gay and lesbian couples made to achieve marriage equality, the backlash in "defense of marriage," and then the 400,000 gay and lesbian couples who wed suggest the power of the institution.

What does seem to have occurred, however, is a change in the relationship between love and marriage. Three distinct patterns were evident in former centuries.

- In about one-third of the world's families, love did not lead to marriage because parents arranged matches that joined two families together.
- In roughly another one-third, adolescents met only a select group (single-sex schools keep them from unsuitable mates). Some then decided to marry, and young men asked the young women's fathers for "her hand in marriage." Parents supervised interactions and then bestowed their blessing. (When parents disapproved, young people separated reluctantly or eloped—neither of which occurs often today.)
- A third pattern involves what were called *love marriages,* which distinguishes them from the first two. Young people met thousands of others, sometimes falling in love and having sex, but they did not expect to marry until they were able to be independent, both financially and emotionally.

Jena Cumbo Photography

How to Find Your Soul Mate Tiago and Mariela met on a dating site for people with tattoos, connected on Skype, moved in together, and soon were engaged to marry.

The "one-third" suggested for each of the first two types is a rough approximation. In former times, nearly all marriages were of the first type, and the rest were of the second type.

Currently, the practice in developing nations often blends these two types. For example, in modern India most brides believe they have a choice, but one source says that two-thirds of Indian brides meet their husband for the first time on their wedding day (Allendorf & Pandian, 2016).

The final pattern is relatively new (although familiar to most readers of this book) but is becoming the most common one. The choices of the young couple tilt toward personal qualities observable at the moment—appearance, hygiene, sexuality, a sense of humor—and not to qualities that parents value, such as religion, ethnicity, and evidence of long-term stability. (See A Case to Study.)

This is true worldwide. In parts of India, love marriages have become more popular than arranged marriages, but marrying someone of a higher or lower caste is still much more troubling to the parents than to the emerging adults (Allendorf, 2013).

A CASE TO STUDY

My Students, My Daughters, and Me

I was married late for my cohort (at age 25) to a man my parents never met until we were very much a couple. I had children late for my cohort (two by age 30 and another two by age 40).

Of my four children, only one is married—and she and her husband decided to marry so they could both have health insurance. My other three daughters are older than I was when I married, and they are still single. I am proud of all four; they are admirable women working in professions that I respect. But sometimes I wonder why they did not marry.

Few of my young college students have children, and even fewer of them are currently married. I pay close attention to their thoughts about love and marriage. Emerging adult Kerri wrote:

> All young girls have their perfect guy in mind, their Prince Charming. For me he will be tall, dark, and handsome. He will be well educated and have a career with a strong future . . . a great personality, and the same sense of humor as I do. I'm not sure I can do much to ensure that I meet my soul mate. I believe that is what is implied by the term *soul mate;* you will meet them no matter what you do. Part of me is hoping this is true, but another part tells me the idea of soul mates is just a fable.
>
> [Personal communication]

Kerri's classmate Chelsea, also an emerging adult, wrote:

> I dreamt of being married. The husband didn't matter specifically, as long as he was rich and famous and I had a long, off-the-shoulder wedding dress. Thankfully, my views since then have changed. . . . I have a fantastic boyfriend of almost two years who I could see myself marrying, as we are extremely compatible. Although we are different, we have mastered . . . communication and compromise. . . . I think I will be able to cope with the trials and tribulations life brings.
>
> [Personal communication]

Neither of these students is naive. Kerri uses the words *Prince Charming* and *fable* to express her awareness that her ideas are childish, and Chelsea seems to have moved beyond her "long, off-the-shoulder wedding dress."

My students reflect the attitudes of most emerging-adult women, as found in a study that asked college students to reflect on the media portrayal of love and their own attitudes (Koontz et al., 2019). For example, one wrote:

You'd like to have a perfect marriage. Your husband is the prince and you are the princess. But I think realistically no. Because it's more important that my husband just treats me right. Not necessarily have to [sic] treat me like a princess. . . . as long as you love each other and respect each other and you trust each other and he makes me laugh. To me that means more than whether he treats me like I'm Cinderella . . . as I grow older, the realistic side of it comes out more which is probably a good thing.

[*Personal communication*]

I wish every young adult well. As a scientist, I read about divorce and the pain of separation; I do not want that for my children or my students. They are wise to be wary of marriage.

But as a mother, I wish that all of my daughters would have loving partners, committed to them for life. When my daughters were babies, I imagined them in homes with lawns, picket fences, children, a dog, and a cat. Ridiculous. Foolish. Not logical. Bad for the planet.

Even worse, I sometimes blame myself. Did I promote female independence too much, forgetting to highlight my happy marriage? Certainly my daughters are not unlike millions of their peers, and like most of my students, influenced by their context as I was. My postformal mind makes me realize that their attitudes and practices may be better in the twenty-first century than mine are. Still . . .

For Western emerging adults, love is considered a prerequisite for marriage, according to a survey of 14,121 individuals of many ethnic groups and sexual orientations (Meier et al., 2009). They were asked to rate from 1 to 10 the importance of money, racial background, long-term commitment, love, and faithfulness for a successful marriage or a serious, committed relationship. Faithfulness was the most important of all (rated 10 by 89 percent), and love was almost as high (rated 10 by 86 percent). By contrast, most thought being from the same race was not important (57 percent rated it 1, 2, or 3).

Cohabitation

The fact that marriage is often postponed, and that sex sometimes occurs without commitment, does not mean that emerging adults do not hope for a committed romantic partnership. In fact, having a steady partner is still sought. This makes sense for human development: Young adults in romantic relationships tend to be happier and healthier than their lonely peers.

cohabitation An arrangement in which a couple lives together in a committed romantic relationship but are not formally married.

What has changed is the rise of **cohabitation,** living with an unmarried partner. Cohabitation was relatively unusual 50 years ago: Only 1 in 9 marriages in 1970 began with cohabitation. Now cohabitation is the norm (see **Figure 19.4**). About three of every four couples cohabit before marriage (Rosenfeld & Roesler, 2019).

Cohabitation rates vary from nation to nation. Almost everyone in Canada and Europe cohabits at some point. Many people in Sweden, France, Jamaica,

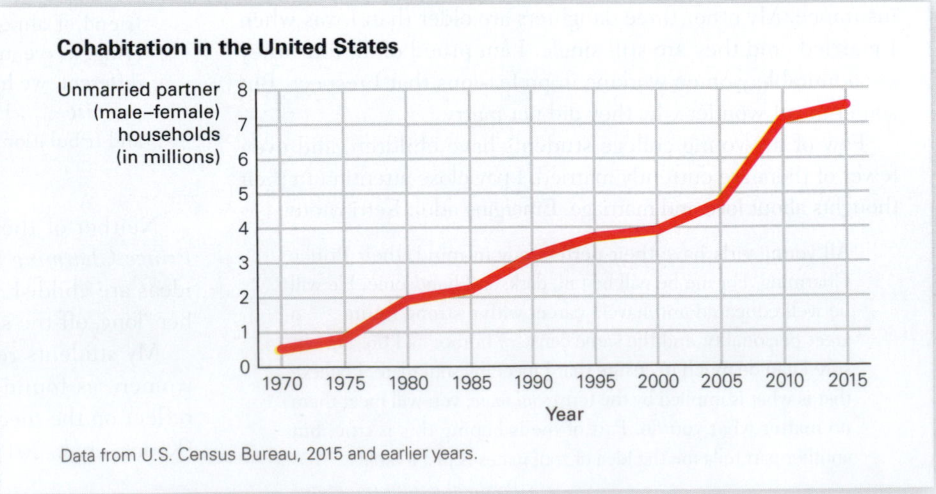

FIGURE 19.4

More Together, Fewer Married As you see, the number of cohabiting male–female households in the United States has increased dramatically over the past decades. These numbers are an underestimate: Couples do not always tell the U.S. Census that they are living together, nor are cohabiters counted within their parents' households. Same-sex couples (not tallied until 2000) are also not included here.

OPPOSING PERSPECTIVES

Making Divorce More Likely?

Many emerging adults consider cohabitation to be a wise choice, a prelude to marriage, a way for people to make sure they are compatible before tying the knot and thus reducing the chance of divorce. However, research suggests otherwise.

Contrary to widespread belief, living together before marriage does not prevent problems after a wedding. There is a short-term benefit, in that divorce in the first year after marriage is lower in couples who have lived together. After that, however, rates of divorce rise in couples who have previously cohabited, especially if they have lived with someone other than the person they eventually married (Rosenfeld & Roesler, 2019).

Some emerging adults want to avoid customs and institutions. They believe that cohabitation allows a couple to have the advantages of marriage without the legal and institutional trappings.

But cohabitation is unlike marriage in many ways. Cohabiters are less likely to pool their money, less likely to have close relationships with their parents or their partner's parents, less likely to take care of their partner's health, more likely to commit crimes, and more likely to break up (Forrest, 2014; Guzzo, 2014; Hamplová et al., 2014).

Particularly problematic is *churning,* when couples live together, then break up, and then come back together. Churning relationships have high rates of verbal and physical abuse (Halpern-Meekin et al., 2013) (see **Figure 19.5**). Cohabitation is fertile ground for churning because the partners are less committed to each other than if they were married, but they cannot slow down their relationship as easily as if they were not living together.

Although research suggests many problems with cohabitation, most emerging adults do it, and most of their grandparents did not. Of course, humans tend to justify whatever they do. In this case, cohabiting adults typically think they have found intimacy without the restrictions of marriage. Are they fooling themselves?

If so, gay and lesbian couples may be fooling themselves as well. When same-sex couples were finally allowed to marry in the United States, about 400,000 couples did so—many of whom had been cohabiting for decades. They thought marriage was better than cohabitation. Interestingly, most of them married to express their love and commitment, exactly the reasons that other-sex couples marry. There are many legal advantages for married couples, especially if one partner gets sick or dies, but that is not the usual reason for marriage.

Most researchers thought that cohabitation would reduce the rates of divorce, because people would know that they really wanted to marry their partners. When researchers analyzed the data, they were surprised to find that they were mistaken (Rosenfeld & Roesler, 2019). Now, most emerging adults choose to live together instead of marrying. Are they mistaken as well?

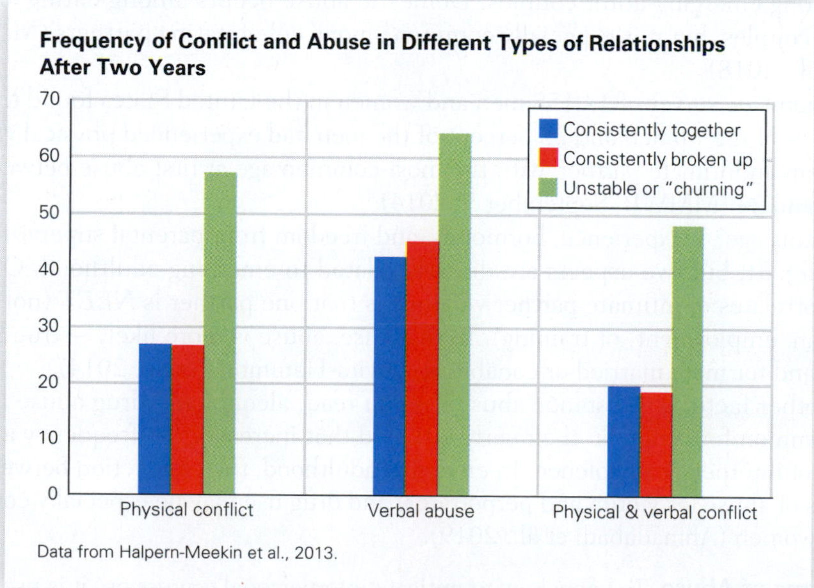

FIGURE 19.5

Love You, Love You Not In a random sample of unmarried emerging adults (half men, half from two-parent homes, two-thirds European American, all from Toledo, Ohio) who had had a serious dating or cohabiting relationship in the past two years, some (15 percent) had broken up and not reunited, some (41 percent) had been together without breaking up, and some (44 percent) were churners, defined as having broken up and gotten together again with their partner. As you see, young-adult relationships are often problematic, but churning correlates with the stormiest relationships, with half of churners fighting both physically and verbally.

macmillan learning

Data Connections activity Technology and Romance: Trends for U.S. Adults examines how emerging adults find romantic partners.

and Puerto Rico live with a partner for decades, sometimes all their lives, never marrying.

Although marriage rates are down and cohabitation is up in every demographic group, education increases the chance of marriage and marital childbearing. Cohabiting couples without college degrees have children about five times as often as couples the same age who have graduated from college (Lundberg et al., 2016).

The reason is not that college graduates know something that others do not. Instead, they are more likely to have a steady, well-paying job, which often is considered a requirement for marriage. Some young women who cannot find a suitable mate decide that they would rather have a child than an unemployable husband.

In some nations—including Japan, Ireland, and Italy—cohabitation is not yet the norm, although it is becoming increasingly common. For example, Spain was once a nation where cohabitation was unusual; now one-third of all couples in Spain live together before they marry, a pattern that has become accepted and preferred (Dominguez-Folgueras & Castro-Martin, 2013).

The meaning and consequences of cohabitation and marriage vary from couple to couple no matter what their education level or sexual orientation. However, one definite advantage and one clear disadvantage have been found in study after study.

The advantage is economic: People save money by living together, so cohabitation is better financially than living alone. This is a reason given by many couples who struggle to pay the rent (Sassler & Miller, 2017). The disadvantage occurs if children are born: Cohabiting partners have lower incomes than married partners and are less committed to child rearing, and their children are less likely to excel in school, graduate, and go to college (Manning, 2015).

Some of these differences relate to the economic status of the parents, since families with little money are more likely to cohabit, and their children have reduced well-being because of it. In addition, however, marriage seems to increase the partners' commitment to each other and to their children.

Intimate Partner Violence Now we turn to a problem that is particularly common among emerging-adult couples. Domestic abuse occurs among dating and married couples, but it is especially common among cohabitating partners (Manning et al., 2018).

A nationwide survey of 14,155 men and women in the United States found that 32 percent of the women and 28 percent of the men had experienced physical violence from an intimate partner, with the most common age at first abuse between ages 18 and 24 (MMWR, September 5, 2014).

Why this age? Inexperience, hormones, and freedom from parental supervision all play a part, but two aspects are directly related to emerging adulthood. One of the correlates of intimate partner violence is that one partner is *NEET* (not in education, employment, or training). In that case, abuse is more likely—true for women and for men, married or cohabiting (Alvira-Hammond et al., 2014).

The other factor is substance abuse. As you read, alcohol and drug abuse are more common for people in their early 20s, and that increases the frequency and severity of interpersonal violence. In emerging adulthood, the connection between all forms of abuse (as victim and perpetrator) and drug use may be especially common in women (Ahmadabadi et al., 2019).

Two Forms of Abuse To know how to mitigate interpersonal aggression, it is useful to distinguish two types: (1) situational couple violence and (2) intimate terrorism. Each has distinct causes, patterns, and means of prevention (Johnson, 2008).

situational couple violence Fighting between romantic partners that is brought on more by the situation than by the deep personality problems of the individuals. Both partners are typically victims and abusers.

Situational couple violence occurs when both partners fight—with words, slaps, and exclusion (leaving home, refusing sex, and so on)—and yet both partners are sometimes caring and affectionate. The *situation* brings out the anger, and then the partners abuse each other. This is the most common form of domestic conflict, with women at least as active in situational violence as men.

Situational couple violence can be reduced with maturation and counseling; both partners need to learn how to interact without violence. Often the roots are in the culture, not primarily in the individuals, which makes it possible for adults who love each other to learn how to overcome the culture of violence. Both partners are distressed, which makes it easier to help them (Sader et al., 2018).

Intimate terrorism is more violent, more demeaning, and more likely to lead to serious harm. Usually intimate terrorism involves a male abuser and female victim, although the sex roles can be reversed (Dutton, 2012). (See **Figure 19.6**.)

intimate terrorism A violent and demeaning form of abuse in a romantic relationship, in which the victim (usually female) is frightened to fight back, seek help, or withdraw. In this case, the victim is in danger of physical as well as psychological harm.

Terrorism is dangerous to the victim and to anyone who intervenes. It is also difficult to treat because the terrorist gets some satisfaction from abuse, and the victim often submits and apologizes. A sign of intimate terrorism is extreme jealousy and social isolation, which makes it hard for outsiders to know what is happening, much less to stop it. With intimate terrorism, the victim must be immediately separated from the abuser, relocated to a safe place, and given help to restore independence.

This is a useful distinction, because it helps to know when protection (including police, safe houses, prison) is needed and when counseling of both partners is advised. Of course, to some extent interpersonal violence is a continuum (Love et al., 2018). Some couples need to learn how to keep from insulting and criticizing each other; at the other extreme, guns need to be taken away from people who might harm their families. (About half of all female homicides are the result of interpersonal violence, usually with guns.)

The scientist who originally distinguished these two forms of intimate partner abuse says it is a mistake to ask a cross section of people about their current relationship, since those most severely abused will not, or cannot, answer honestly. However, when asking about ex-spouses, many people admit to being victims of intimate terrorism (W. Johnson et al., 2015).

Traditionally, women, not men, were asked whether they experienced spousal abuse. It was assumed that females were victims and males were abusers. It is true that more women are seriously injured or killed by male lovers than vice versa—evident in every hospital emergency room or police summary. However, when the definition of abuse includes threats, insults, and slaps as well as physical battering, women are *more* likely to be abusers than men are.

This was one finding in a study of the effect of witnessing domestic abuse as a child. Such girls were more likely to become abusive to their partners in emerging

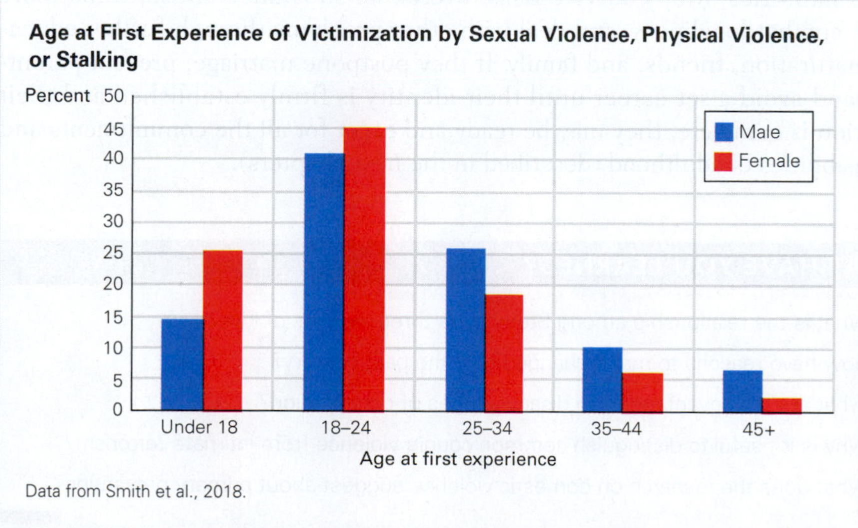

FIGURE 19.6

When Did It Begin? These data are from the U.S. Centers for Disease Control and Prevention, a reputable source. As you see, when victims are asked when the first incident of sexual violence, physical violence, or stalking occurred, emerging adulthood is the most likely time. For a sizable minority, the first incidence occurred before age 18 (especially for females) or after age 25 (especially for men). Almost never does intimate partner violence begin after age 45 (although victimization, once started, often continues). Not shown here are other data from this report, which shows that, over their lifetime, about a third of all adults have been victimized in some way (raped, physically abused, threatened, stalked). Rates are similar for both women (36 percent) and men (34 percent), although more women sought medical, legal, or psychological help in recovery than men did (25 percent of all women versus 11 percent of all men).

adulthood than the boys were (Kaufman-Parks et al., 2018). That fact may help fathers be more respectful of their wives. One man said, after his young daughter witnessed a violent argument, "I really had to stand back and just check myself on that because do I want my little Doodlebug growing up and seeing that and thinking it's okay for her man to treat her that way" (Merchant & Whiting, 2018).

The original, mistaken male-abuser/female-victim assumption occurred because men are physically stronger, thus causing more injury. Moreover, men are reluctant to admit that they are victims, and outsiders are less likely to believe them.

Likewise, same-sex couples hesitate to publicly acknowledge conflict, although in domestic violence and most other aspects of relationships, they are very similar to heterosexual couples (Kurdek, 2006; Stults et al., 2019).

Social scientists have identified numerous causes of domestic violence, including youth, poverty, personality (such as poor impulse control), mental illness (such as antisocial disorders), and substance use disorder. Developmentalists note that many children who are harshly punished or sexually abused, or who witness domestic assault, grow up to become abusers or victims themselves.

Just as we now know it is a mistake to assume that women are victims and men are perpetrators, it is also a mistake to think that interpersonal violence happens only in established relationships. A study of college students in dating relationships found that about 20 percent had experienced interpersonal violence, with the same predictors as for those in marriages, specifically childhood experiences and current alcohol use (Paat & Markham, 2019).

Knowing causes points toward primary prevention. Halting child maltreatment, for instance, averts some later abuse. For tertiary prevention, all medical professionals need to recognize the signs (such as depression, anger, bruises, silence) of intimate partner violence, a preventable health problem (Collett & Bennett, 2015).

Concluding Hopes

Asking people about their lives, and encouraging them to talk to each other, is good advice for every problem in emerging adulthood. In Chapter 17, risk taking is reduced when people talk about the implications of what they do. In Chapter 18, listening to the experiences and beliefs of others, particularly in college classes, advances postformal thought. In this chapter, we emphasized the benefits of having friends and lovers who expand one's mind.

Fortunately, most emerging adults, like humans of all ages, have strengths as well as liabilities. Many survive risks, overcome substance abuse, think more deeply, combat loneliness, and deal with other problems through further education, maturation, friends, and family. If they postpone marriage, prevent parenthood, and avoid a set career until their identity is firmly established and their education is complete, they may be ready and eager for all the commitments and responsibilities of adulthood (described in the next chapters).

WHAT HAVE YOU LEARNED?

1. What is the relationship among Sternberg's three aspects of love?
2. How have reasons to marry changed over the past century?
3. What are the advantages and disadvantages of cohabitation?
4. Why is it useful to distinguish common couple violence from intimate terrorism?
5. What does the research on domestic violence suggest about primary prevention?

SUMMARY

Identity Achievement

1. For today's youth, the identity crisis continues into adulthood. In multiethnic nations, ethnic identity becomes important but difficult to achieve, and it requires complex psychosocial adjustment.

2. Vocational identity requires knowing what career one will have. Few young adults are certain about their career goals. Many societies offer some moratoria on identity achievement (such as college) that allow postponement of vocational identity.

3. Current economic circumstances make vocational identity particularly difficult. Many adults of all ages switch jobs, with turnover particularly quick in emerging adulthood. Most short-term jobs are not connected to the young person's skills or ambitions.

4. Personality can change in early adulthood. Genes and childhood influences are always factors, but many people improve their personal characteristics once they are able to make their own choices.

Identity and Intimacy

5. Family support is needed lifelong. Family members have linked lives, always affected by one another and often helping those older and younger.

6. In most nations, emerging adults and their parents are closely connected. Sometimes this means living in the same household, but even when it does not, complete separation of the two generations is unusual.

7. Especially in nations with less public support for young adults, parents often pay college costs, provide free child care, and contribute in other ways to their young-adult children's welfare. Parental financial and emotional support for emerging-adult children usually is helpful, but too much may impede independence.

8. Friendships are needed at every age, particularly in emerging adulthood. Close friendships typically include some other-sex as well as same-sex friends, with few differences found for adults of various sexual orientations. Women may exchange more confidences and physical affection with their friends than men do.

Romantic Partners

9. Romantic love is complex, involving passion, intimacy, and commitment. In some nations, commitment is crucial and parents arrange marriages with that in mind. Among emerging adults in developed nations, passion is more important but does not necessarily lead to marriage.

10. Many emerging adults use social networking and matchmaking sites on the Internet to expand and deepen their friendship circles and mating options. This has advantages and disadvantages.

11. Cohabitation is increasingly common, with marked national variations. This arrangement does not necessarily improve marital happiness or stability.

12. Marriages work best if couples are able to communicate well. Conflict is part of many intimate relationships.

13. Spousal abuse is common worldwide. In situational couple violence, both partners need to learn how to love each other. In other cases (intimate terrorism), the abused spouse needs to leave the abuser and be protected.

KEY TERMS

intimacy versus isolation (p. 485)
linked lives (p. 486)
helicopter parents (p. 487)
snowplow parents (p. 488)
hookup (p. 493)
choice overload (p. 494)
cohabitation (p. 496)
situational couple violence (p. 498)
intimate terrorism (p. 499)

APPLICATIONS

1. Talk to three people you would expect to have contrasting views on love and marriage (differences in age, gender, upbringing, experience, and religion affect attitudes). Ask each the same questions, and then compare their answers.

2. Vocational identity is fluid in early adulthood. Talk with several people over age 30 about their work history. Are they doing what they expected they would be doing when they were younger? Are they settled in their vocation and job? Pay attention to their age when they decided on their jobs. Was age 25 a turning point?

Especially For ANSWERS

Response for Family Therapists (from p. 487): Remember that family function is more important than family structure. Sharing a home can work out well if contentious issues—like sexual privacy, money, and household chores—are clarified before resentments arise. You might offer a three-session preparation package to explore assumptions and guidelines.

Response for Young Men (from p. 490): Not for sex! Women friends are particularly responsive to deep conversations about family relationships, personal weaknesses, and emotional confusion. But women friends might be offended by sexual advances, bragging, or advice giving. Save these for a future romance.

Response for Social Scientists (from p. 494): First, Canada's divorce rate is not as high as that of the United States. Second, the divorce rate in the United States comes from dividing the number of divorces by the number of marriages. Because some people are married and divorced many times, that minority drives up the ratio and skews the average. (In the United States, only one first marriage in three—not one in two—ends in divorce.) Finally, teenage marriages are especially likely to end: Older brides and grooms are less likely to divorce. The odds of your friend getting divorced are about one in five.

Observation Quiz ANSWERS

Answer to Observation Quiz (from p. 485): No. Read the caption and the scale on the *y*-axis. Well-being rose, on average, about 4 percent—a significant rise, but not a dramatic one.

Answer to Observation Quiz (from p. 494): Note body position, hands, and her facial expression.

CAREER ALERT The Career Counselor

We need more career counselors! Job growth in this occupation is above average, and so is annual income: 13 percent above and $56,000 a year, according to the Occupational Outlook Handbook (United States Bureau of Labor Statistics, 2019).

This occupation is both challenging and satisfying: Helping people find the right work for them benefits individuals, families, and communities. Studying human development is a good first step, so you are already on your way! After earning a Bachelor's degree, a Master's in counseling is recommended.

As you know from Erikson, vocational identity is crucial, and work is central to development. Emerging adults often change jobs (every year, on average), sometimes because they expected the job to be temporary (e.g., summer work as a waitress, lifeguard, or office assistant). But many employment shifts occur because young adults are unaware of job availability or of their own skills and values. Education improves job fit and satisfaction (Ilies et al., 2019), but which education for which job?

Many adults have not found the best employment for them. They take jobs that are available; they consult friends and family. They may discover that they hate their work, or an economic shift may put them out of work. Even if they are doing work they enjoy, people may be happier with another employer, or self-employment, or somewhere else. Career counseling needed!

This vocation is especially vital today for at least six reasons:

- Most current vocations did not exist a generation ago, making past sources of job information (parents and teachers) less reliable.
- Adult lives change over time, obviously for veterans, for parents with new babies or growing children, and for immigrants, but also for everyone else.
- The economy is shifting, with startups, closed factories, relocated corporations, and emerging markets.
- Long-term unemployment is one of the worst problems of adulthood, destroying personal happiness, as well as families and communities.
- Major groups—women, minorities, people with disabilities—who were once shut out of productive work now can be vital workers in today's economy.
- Adults who enjoy their work, with co-workers, challenges, and hours that make each day a good one, achieve a fulfilling, productive life.

This career alert follows the chapters on emerging adulthood because floundering is more common than flourishing during these years. Most high school graduates know that they need more education in order to be hired for the work they want, but few know what college courses, requirements, and vocational training satisfy the demands of the job market. Most employees find their work by chance, or through word of mouth, or by stumbling across something on the Internet. Fantasy conflicts with reality; rejection and discouragement are common. Everyone needs guidance by a wise and informed advisor.

A few decades ago, vocational counselors had a simple task. There were valid tests of skills and personality, and the counselor used those to match a person with a career. Holland's description of six general vocational areas (see page 543) was one of the best of these matching efforts.

Currently, however, a skilled counselor must do more than match. Vocational advisors still need to know the current and future job market, but they also must help each person recognize their particular skills and personality, values and aspirations (Rothausen & Henderson, 2019).

Career counselors motivate and guide, helping with searches and applications, role-playing for interviews, crafting résumés, suggesting additional education, gathering recommendations, encouraging applicants after rejection, analyzing offers after acceptance, negotiating benefits, and more.

Can you do this?

VISUALIZING DEVELOPMENT Marital Status in the United States

Adults seek committed partners, but do not always find them—age, cohort, and culture are always influential. Some choose to avoid marriage, more commonly in northern Europe and less commonly in North Africa than in the United States. As you see, in 2018, U.S. emerging adults were unlikely to marry, middle-aged adults had the highest rates of separation or divorce, and widows often chose to stay alone while widowers often remarried.

MARITAL STATUS IN THE UNITED STATES

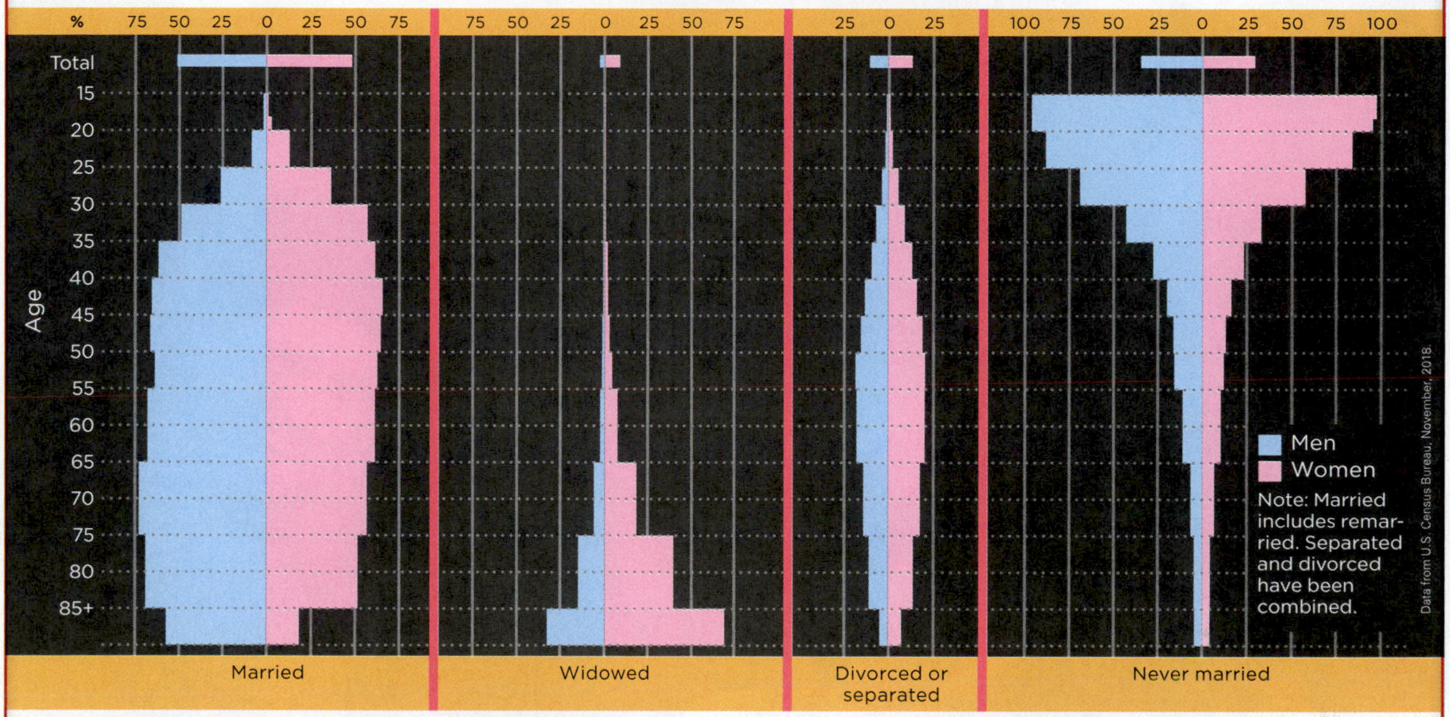

TOP REASONS FOR GETTING MARRIED, ACCORDING TO U.S. ADULTS

NEARLY HALF OF NEW MARRIAGES INVOLVE REMARRIAGES

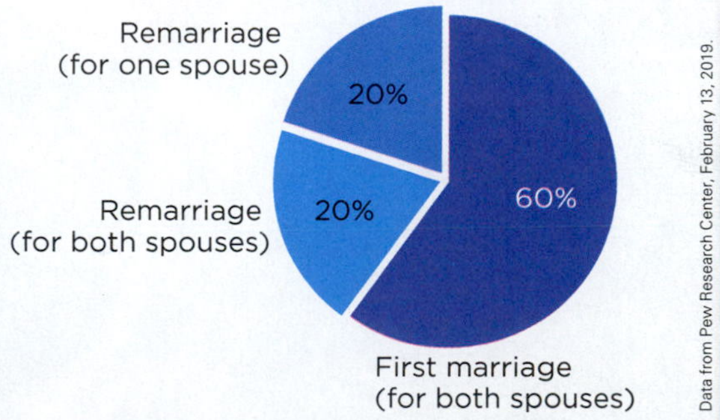

LIVING ARRANGEMENTS OF 25 TO 34 YEAR OLDS

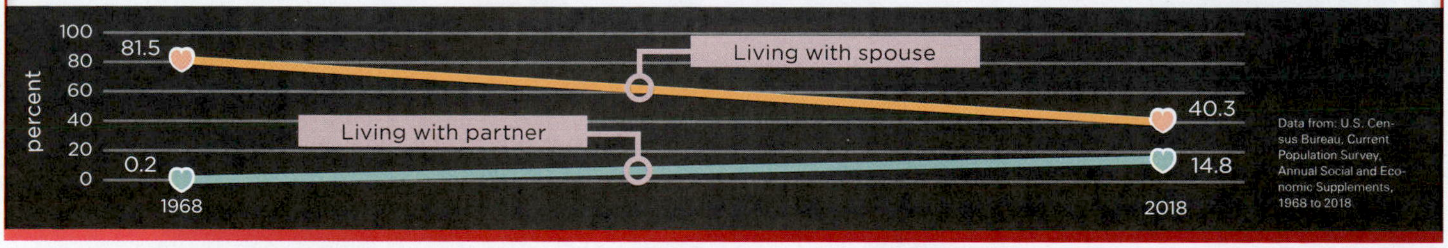

CHAPTERS 20 • 21 • 22

PART VII

Adulthood

We now begin the seventh part of this text. These three chapters cover 40 years (ages 25 to 65), when bodies mature, minds master new material, and people work productively.

Adulthood spans such a long period because no particular year is a logical divider. Adults of many ages marry; raise children; care for aging parents; are hired and fired; grow richer or poorer; experience births, deaths, weddings, divorces, illness, and recovery. Thus, adulthood is punctuated by joys and sorrows, which can occur at any time. Most days are neither happy nor sad; they are quite similar to the day before or the day after.

Although events are not programmed by age, they are not random: Adults build on their past—creating their own ecological niche—and prepare for their future. They choose their activities, communities, and habits.

Culture and context are crucial. Many U.S. adults choose marriage, but an increasing number of all ages choose cohabitation or partnerships that involve separate homes. Rates of marriage, singlehood, and divorce vary markedly not only by age but also by nation: The United States has one of the highest divorce rates in the world, but divorce is rare in Chile, Malta, and the Philippines, where it was illegal until recently.

Some experiences once thought to occur to almost every North American adult—midlife crisis, sandwich generation, and empty nest among them—are much less common than assumed. As you will see, adulthood is not what most people think, or thought, or will experience.

Left: Zing Images/DigitalVision/Getty Images
Right: iko/Shutterstock

CHAPTER 20

Adulthood: Biosocial Development

What Will You Know?

- When do people start to show their age?
- Should a woman bear children before age 30, 40, or 50?
- How can a person be vitally healthy *and* severely disabled?

- **Growing Older**
  - Senescence
  - INSIDE THE BRAIN: Neurons Forming in Adulthood
  - Outward Appearance
  - The Senses
- **The Sexual-Reproductive System**
  - Sexual Responsiveness
  - The Sexual-Reproductive System in Middle Age
- **Habits: Good and Bad**
  - Exercise
  - Drugs
  - Nutrition
  - Correlating Income and Health
- **VISUALIZING DEVELOPMENT: Adult Overweight Around the World**

Jenny was in her early 30s, a star student in my human development class. She told the class that she was divorced, raising her 7-year-old son, 10-year-old daughter, and two orphaned teenage nephews in a huge public housing complex in a south Bronx neighborhood infamous for guns, gangs, and drugs. She spoke enthusiastically about free activities for her children—public parks, museums, the zoo, Fresh Air camp. We were awed by her creativity, optimism, and energy.

A year later, Jenny came to my office to speak privately. She was about to graduate with honors and had found a job that would enable her family to leave their dangerous neighborhood. She sought my advice because she had recently discovered that she was pregnant. The father, Billy, was a married man who told her he would not leave his wife but would pay for an abortion. She loved him and feared he might end their relationship if she did not terminate the pregnancy.

I did not advise her; I listened intently. I learned that she thought she was too old to have another infant; that she was a carrier for sickle-cell anemia, which had complicated her other pregnancies; that her crowded apartment was no longer "babyproof"; that her son needed special care because he had a speech impediment; that she was not opposed to abortion. She was eager to get on with her adult life, and a baby would stop that.

After a long conversation, Jenny thanked me profusely for helping her reach a decision—although I had only asked questions, provided facts, and nodded. Then she surprised me.

"I'll have the baby. Men come and go, but children are always with you." I had thought her narrative was leading to the opposite conclusion, but she was planning her life, not mine.

Despite feeling too old, Jenny was relatively young. Nonetheless, she was a typical adult in many ways. Many worry about reproduction, genes, health, and aging.

This chapter explains some choices that people make about their bodies and their futures. First you will learn about physiological changes in strength, appearance, and body functioning, including changes in vision, hearing, and sexual responses, as well as ways to slow down aging. You will learn who ages quickly and who is likely to be strong and vital at age 65. At the end of this chapter, you will read how Jenny's adulthood progressed after she left my office.

Left: PhotoAlto/Frederic Cirou/PhotoAlto Agency RF Collections/Getty Images. Licensed Material is being used for illustrative purposes only; any person depicted in the licensed Material is a model.
Top: iko/Shutterstock

Just Keeping Rolling Along After four years in Iraq and two in Afghanistan, Jared McCallum sought new challenges. He hiked the Appalachian Trail (2,180 miles) and, on September 1, 2014, began rowing the Mississippi River. Here, on October 1, 2014, he is at Rock Island, Iowa.

Observation Quiz Is Jared closer age 30, 40, or 50 in this photo? (see answer, page 528) ↑

senescence The process of aging, whereby the body becomes less strong and efficient.

Growing Older

"Aging—we are all doing it," a subway poster proclaims. However, few of us realize it. Organ reserve, homeostasis, and allostasis (described in Chapter 17) allow declines to go unnoticed. Few adults under age 65 consider themselves old. Typically, 30- to 65-year-olds feel 5 to 10 years younger than their chronological age and think that "old" describes people significantly older than they themselves are.

Senescence

Most adults consider themselves strong, capable, and healthy. Economic analysis supports this perception: Adults ages 26 to 60 contribute more to society than those older or younger, supporting those not yet, or no longer, "in their prime" (Zagheni et al., 2015).

Genes are crucial. **Senescence,** as the aging process is called, is genetically coded for every species. Genes allow humans to live to age 80 or beyond. Some of us inherit genes that will allow us to live more than a century.

That is true for our species, but personal choices and the social context are more important than genes in allowing one individual to live twice as long and with more vitality than another. All agree that vast variation in aging is evident, and the cause is *not* primarily genetic.

People disagree as to what speeds up aging and whether economic constraints (poverty of the nation or individual) or personal habits (drug use, diet) are more crucial (Selita & Kovas, 2019; Robert & Labat-Robert, 2015; Rea et al., 2018). But all agree that, especially before old age, genes are not the major reason that some adults age more quickly than others.

The Experience of Aging Every organ, every body system, and indeed every neurotransmitter slows down with age. For that reason, in our culture, aging is often linked to disease and decline, but that link may be broken. Aging—everyone does it; impairment—many avoid it.

One example is breath. Because of homeostasis, the body naturally maintains a certain level of oxygen. Aging affects this; on average, oxygen dispersal into the bloodstream from the lungs drops about 4 percent per decade after age 20. Thus, older adults may become "winded" after running fast, or they may pause after climbing a long flight of stairs to "catch their breath." That is homeostatic.

However, the rate that organ reserve is depleted depends more on habits than age. Some people lose as little as 2 percent a decade, but those who are heavy smokers, who are obese, or who live in polluted cities lose up to 10 percent a decade. By age 60, they may need an oxygen mask to breathe, and some have trouble even with extra oxygen.

For U.S. adults aged 45 to 64, chronic breathing problems are the fourth most common cause of death (after heart failure, cancer, and accidents). It gets worse: After age 65, inability to breathe is the third most common cause of death, the result of lifestyle patterns that began 50 years before (National Center for Health Statistics, 2019).

But impairment need not occur. Adults can maintain their breathing by exercising regularly and avoiding pollutants, including cigarette smoke. If a smoker quits by age 30, lung functioning gradually improves. As a result, ex-smokers have stronger lungs at age 40 than they did at age 20. Indeed, an estimated 10 years of life is gained by stopping smoking (Jha et al., 2013).

This has practical applications. Suppose a 50-year-old who is winded when climbing several flights of stairs wants to run a marathon. That's possible—if the person spends a year or more doing practice runs, eating and sleeping well, not smoking, and so on. Like the muscles of the legs, the lungs can be strengthened with judicious exercise.

The word *judicious* refers to judgment. People judge how to protect their bodies. Improved functioning with age is not automatic—quite the opposite. The need for healthy eating and adequate exercise has been understood for decades and is discussed in detail later in this chapter.

More recently, however, sleep is increasingly seen as a crucial foundation, so we highlight it now. Adults need to get ample, sound sleep in order to function well (Spira, 2018). This may mean avoiding late-night television, abstaining from coffee or alcohol after dinner, or taking a shorter afternoon nap. All of that needs judgment.

For example, the "heterogeneity among naps, nappers, and napping" means that health and cognition sometimes benefit from naps and sometimes suffer (Spira, 2018, p. 357). Adults must figure out whether napping is best for them (Mantua & Spencer, 2017). Sleeping excessively and sleeping too little both seem to cause (not just correlate with) anxiety, depression, and many other problems—but this again varies from one person to another.

At least among women, poorer sleep is more likely among African Americans and Latinas, primarily because of health problems and financial stress, and among Asian Americans, primarily because of anxiety and depression (Matthews et al., 2019). However, anyone, at any age, can have problems sleeping too much or too little, waking up too often or lying in bed awake.

For all health habits, decision are crucial; without proper decisions, that marathon is impossible. In other words, the effects of aging in adulthood depend as much on the mind as on the body.

In the short term, people may combat the anxieties of life by smoking, eating junk food, or sitting rather than exercising, but that momentary homeostasis can lead to compromised body functioning with age. This explains why stress early in life impairs health later on.

Sylvain Grandadam/The Image Bank/Getty Images

Having Fun? Here are some of the 98,247 aspiring marathoners running on the Verrazano-Narrows Bridge from Staten Island to Brooklyn, New York, as part of a 26-mile race. Everyone should exercise and should figure out how to make that enjoyable to them. Some choose this.

The Brain with Age Like every other body part, the brain slows down. Neurons fire more slowly, and reaction time lengthens because messages from the axon of one neuron are not picked up as quickly by the dendrites of other neurons. New neurons and dendrites appear, but others atrophy.

For most adults, cognitive reserve, homeostasis, and allostasis protect the brain, and neurogenesis allows new learning. Adults may be slower, losing to a teenager at a video game, but their analysis is more comprehensive. This is one reason why judges, bishops, and world leaders are almost always at least 50 years old.

A balanced understanding of human biology requires that we temper this encouraging conclusion. For about 1 percent of all adults, brain loss is significant between ages 25 and 65, and compensation is inadequate. However, the cause is pathology, not normal aging (Schaie, 2005/2013). (More specifics of typical cognitive changes with age are discussed in the next chapter.)

Here we mention the biological factors that can cause severe brain loss before age 65:

- *Drug abuse.* Any psychoactive drug can harm the brain, especially alcohol abuse over decades, which can cause Wernicke-Korsakoff syndrome ("wet brain"), because vitamin B1 is depleted.
- *Poor circulation.* Everything that impairs blood flow—such as hypertension and cigarette smoking—impairs circulation in the brain and thus harms thinking (Sweeney et al., 2018).
- *Viruses.* Various membranes, called the *blood–brain barrier,* protect the brain from most viruses, but a few—including HIV and the prion that causes mad cow disease—cross that barrier and destroy neurons.

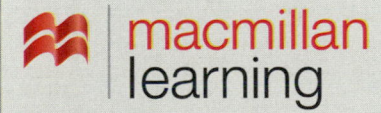

macmillan learning

VIDEO: Brain Development Animation: Middle Adulthood offers an animated look at how the brain changes with age.

Especially for Drivers A number of states have passed laws requiring hands-free technology for people who use cell phones while driving. Do these measures cut down on accidents? (see response, page 528)

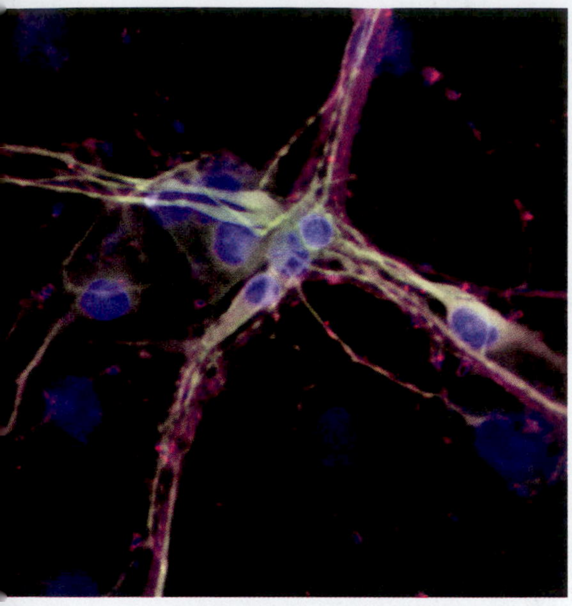

Neurons Growing Even in adulthood, dendrites grow (pale yellow in this picture). Here the cells are in a laboratory and the growth is cancerous, but we now know that healthy neurons develop many new connections in adulthood.

- *Genes.* About 1 in 1,000 persons inherits a dominant gene for Alzheimer's disease, and even fewer people inherit genes for other severe neurocognitive disorders. Genetic effects on the brain usually involve more than one gene, and they are also influenced by nurture, not just nature (Burlina, 2018).
- *Traumatic brain injury (TBI).* Brain damage can be caused by a blow, by an extremely loud noise, or by rapid acceleration or deceleration of the head. Causes are many—a concussion in a football game, whiplash in a car crash, a punch in an assault, an explosion in a war. None of these usually causes permanent damage, but all can lead to a devastating disease called *chronic traumatic encephalopathy* (CTE).

Brains continue to mature throughout adulthood. Regarding addiction and TBI, it is comforting to know that brains are designed to reestablish broken connections, compensating with other brain areas when neurons in one part are destroyed. This means that time, rest, and avoiding further toxins or concussions may be all that is needed for full recovery.

On the other hand, several causes of brain malfunction may cluster together. An adult with alcohol use disorder who is genetically vulnerable and is repeatedly hit on the head is likely to suffer irreversible brain damage. Time aids recovery, but some brain responses render neuronal connections worse as time goes on (Corps et al., 2015).

Barring these serious problems, age strengthens the connections between various parts of the brain. Adults are better able to understand how one aspect of life impacts another. This can happen on a global scale—adults can understand the connection between famine in South Sudan and electricity use in North Dakota—as well as on a more personal level.

The most dramatic evidence comes from stroke victims, whose brains can literally be restructured to learn new movements in adulthood. That same principle of plasticity, because of exercise and experience, applies to all brains in all adults (Sampaio-Baptista et al., 2018).

Gains? Brain growth? In adulthood? Yes! Myelination continues and dendrites grow. An adult who performs a particular action, time and time again, becomes better and quicker at it because of changes in the brain, a topic explored in the next chapter in the discussion of expertise. More detail about brain growth is provided in the following.

INSIDE THE BRAIN

Neurons Forming in Adulthood

It has long been known that brains slow down with age and that some parts of the brain shrink in size. It also has long been known that neurons are formed rapidly during prenatal development and that most of those neurons are eliminated by pruning, especially in infancy and in early adolescence. It was thought that brain growth and *neurogenesis* (the formation of neurons) stopped long before adulthood.

But in the past two decades, scientists learned that parts of the brain gain neurons during adulthood. Not only do dendrites form and pathways strengthen, but new neurons are born. One area that gains brain cells is the hippocampus, the brain structure that is most prominent in memory (Bergmann et al., 2015). That neurogenesis "appears to contribute significantly to hippocampal plasticity across the life span" (Kempermann et al., 2015).

The specific area of the hippocampus where new neurons settle is the *dentate gyrus,* a region activated in forming new memories and exploring new places. One conclusion of the new research is that the adult human brain is characterized by amazing plasticity (Kempermann et al., 2015).

This means that shrinkage of parts of the brain is accompanied by neurological expansion and reorganization between ages 25 and 65. Those new brain cells facilitate learning and memory (Lepousez et al., 2015).

Brain plasticity is evident lifelong, a finding now accepted by almost all scientists. But not everyone agrees that a significant number of new neurons are born in adulthood. One team of 19 scientists reported that the number of new neurons created after age 13 is so low as to be undetectable (Sorrells et al., 2018). That conclusion is contrary to the one found by another team of 12 scientists—that new neurons form even at age 79, although the rate of neurogenesis slows with age (Boldrini et al., 2018).

I mentioned the number of scientists in each of these two contradictory studies to highlight that this is not a controversy between an optimist and a pessimist; it is a dispute between two teams of careful scientists. For neuroscientists, this dispute is thrilling: They await new techniques to study the brain, to determine exactly what changes in adulthood.

For our purposes, however, it is evident that cognitive reserve, homeostasis, and allostasis protect the brain. New learning occurs during adulthood, perhaps because of neurogenesis but certainly because dendrites sprout to reach hundreds of other neurons as new situations demand it.

Outward Appearance

Knowing that aging of the vital internal organs is not usually devastating in adulthood is comforting: Bodies can function well at age 30 or age 60, if people take care of themselves.

However, few adults are comforted by the visible signs of aging. In an age-conscious society, few adults want to look older. As early as age 30, everyone does.

Skin and Hair The first visible signs of age are in the skin, which becomes dryer, rougher, and less regular in color. Collagen, the main component of the connective tissue of the body, decreases by about 1 percent per year starting at age 20. By age 30, the skin is thinner and less flexible, the cells just beneath the surface are more variable, and wrinkles become visible, particularly around the eyes.

Hormones and diet have an effect—fat slows down wrinkling—but aging is apparent in all four layers of the skin, with "looseness, withering, and wrinkling" particularly notable at about age 50 for women, as a result of lower estrogen during menopause (Piérard et al., 2015, p. 98).

Wrinkles are not the only sign of skin senescence. Especially on the face (the body part most exposed to sun, rain, heat, cold, and pollution), skin becomes less firm. Age spots, tiny blood vessels, and other imperfections appear. These are visible by age 40 in most people.

In addition, veins on the legs and wrists become more prominent, and toenails and fingernails become thicker (Whitbourne & Whitbourne, 2014). Changes in appearance are barely noticeable from one year to the next, but if you meet three typical sisters, ages 18, 28, and 38, their skin tells you who is older. By age 60, all faces have aged significantly—some much more than others. The smooth, taut, young face is gone.

Hair usually becomes gray and thinner, first at the temples by age 40 and then over the rest of the scalp. This change does not affect health, but since hair is a visible sign of aging, many adults spend substantial money and time on coloring, thickening, styling, and more.

Both men and women lose hair, but the pattern differs. Women's hair becomes thinner overall, whereas some men lose hair on the top of their heads but not on the sides. That is *male pattern baldness*. I saw a man wearing a T-shirt that read, "This is not a bald spot; it is a solar plate for a sex machine." It is true that male pattern baldness correlates with hormones; it also correlates with increased risk of prostate cancer (Zhou et al., 2016).

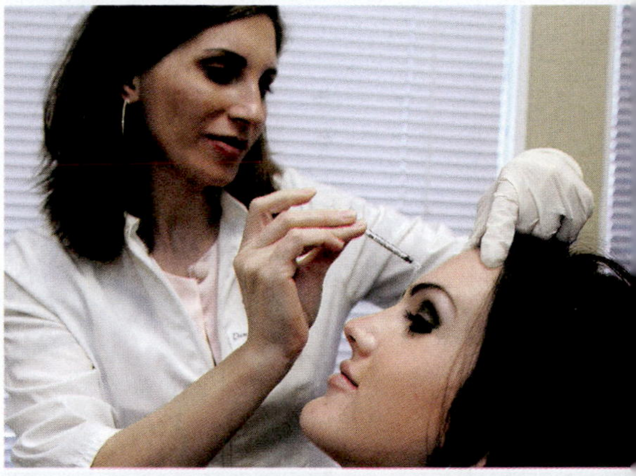

Orange County Register/ZUMAPRESS.com

Look Your Age? Jennifer Roe is used to getting Botox injections—she has been doing this since she was 21. She is among an estimated 16 million people in the United States who in 2017 turned to these injections, or more invasive cosmetic surgery, to mitigate the signs of aging.

Observation Quiz What is this woman's age? (see answer, page 528) ↑

THINK CRITICALLY: Is the saying "beauty is only skin deep" accurate?

Body hair (on the arms, legs, and pubic area) also becomes less dense over the 40 years of adulthood. An occasional thick, unwanted hair may appear on the chin, inside the nose, or in some other place. That has no known correlates with any disease, although it distresses many adults.

Shape and Agility The body changes shape between ages 25 and 65. A "middle-age spread" increases waist circumference; muscles weaken; fat settles on the abdomen, the upper arms, the buttocks, and the chin; people stoop slightly when they stand (Whitbourne & Whitbourne, 2014).

By late middle age, even if they stretch to their tallest, adults are shorter than they were, because back muscles, connective tissue, and bones lose density, making the vertebrae in the spine shrink. People lose about an inch (2 to 3 centimeters) of height by age 65, a loss in the trunk because cushioning between spinal disks is reduced. As torsos shrink, waists widen, hence the dreaded middle-age spread.

Muscles weaken; joints lose flexibility; stiffness is more evident; bending is harder; agility is reduced. Rising from sitting on the floor, twisting in a dance, or even walking "with a spring in your step" is more difficult. A strained back, neck, or other muscle may occur. All this depends on muscle use: Judicious, daily workouts allow yoga at age 80 (see Chapter 23).

The Senses

The senses become less acute with passage of time, although nurture always plays a role—as first explained with nearsightedness in Chapter 3. Each part of each organ is on a particular timetable.

Vision Some 30 distinct brain areas as well as at least a dozen aspects of the eye combine to allow sight. Peripheral vision (at the sides) narrows faster than frontal vision; some colors fade more than others; nearsightedness and farsightedness follow different paths.

Nearsightedness is particularly affected by age. It increases gradually in childhood and more rapidly in adolescence; then it stabilizes, reversing in midlife. Because of changes in the shape of the lens, nearsightedness is often reduced in the 50s while farsightedness (difficulty seeing close objects) increases.

This explains why 40-year-olds hold the newspaper much farther away than 20-year-olds do: Their near focus is blurry, but far focus is better (Aldwin & Gilmer, 2013). Adults who have never needed corrective lenses suddenly require reading glasses.

Other aspects of vision are also affected by age. It takes longer for the eyes to adjust to darkness (as when entering a dark theater after being in daylight) or to adjust to glare (as when headlights of an oncoming car cause temporary blindness) (Aldwin & Gilmer, 2013). Motion perception (how fast is that car approaching?) and contrast sensitivity (is that a bear, a tree, or a person?) slows down (Owsley, 2011). The lens of the eye thickens; brighter lighting is needed.

C Flanigan/Getty Images

Compensation All of the senses decline with age. Some people accept these losses as inevitable, becoming socially isolated and depressed. Instead, compensation is possible in two ways. One is to increase use of the other senses and abilities. Stevie Wonder illustrates this well—he relies on hearing and touch, which have enabled him to sell over 100 million records and win 25 Grammys. The other way is more direct: Many technological and medical interventions are available for every sensory loss.

Hearing Hearing is most acute at about age 10, again with specific intrapersonal variations. Gender is significant: Females lose less than males, on average. Sounds at high frequencies (a small child's voice) are lost earlier than sounds at low frequencies (a man's voice). Although some middle-aged people hear much better than others, everyone's hearing is less acute with age.

Actually, hearing is always limited: No one hears a conversation from 100 feet away; "shouting distance" is limited. Because deafness is rarely absolute, gradual losses are not noticed. *Presbycusis* (literally, "aging hearing") is rarely diagnosed until about age 60, although whispers become inaudible years earlier.

WHAT WILL YOU KNOW?

1. How can people improve the functions of their lungs?
2. What sleep patterns are unhealthy in adulthood?
3. What suggests that the aging process is not dependent solely on time and genes?
4. What aspects of appearance signify that a person is aging?
5. How does sight change with age?
6. Who is likely to experience hearing losses over time?

The Sexual-Reproductive System

One more set of changes needs to be discussed. Many adults worry about the aging of their sexual and reproductive system.

Sexual Responsiveness

Sexual arousal occurs more slowly, and orgasm takes longer with senescence. However, some say that sexual responsiveness improves with age. Could that be? Might familiarity with one's own body and with that of one's partner make slower response more often a pleasure than a problem?

A U.S. study of women aged 40 or older found that sexual activity decreased each decade but that sexual satisfaction did not (Trompeter et al., 2012). A British study of more than 2,000 adults in their 50s found that almost all of them were sexually active (94 percent of the men and 76 percent of the women) and, again, that most were quite satisfied with their sex lives (D. Lee et al., 2015).

Variability is evident. A study of 38,207 adults in the United States who had been in a committed relationship for more than three years found that about half (55 percent of the women and 43 percent of the men) were highly satisfied with their sex lives, but about one-third (27 percent of the women and 41 percent of the men) were not (Frederick et al., 2016). Interestingly, age was not a major factor, but variety of sex acts (including oral sex) and quality of sexual communication were.

Long-Lasting Joy In every nation and culture, many couples who have been together for decades continue to delight in their relationship. Talk shows and headline stories tend to focus on bitter divorces, ignoring couples like these who are clearly happy together.

Indeed, for some couples, physiological slowdowns are counterbalanced by reduced anxiety and better communication, as partners become more familiar with their own bodies and those of their mates and are willing to talk about it. Distress at slower responsiveness seems less connected to biology than to troubled interpersonal relationships and unrealistic fears and expectations (Burri & Spector, 2011; DeLamater, 2012).

Overall, research finds that some adults are sexually satisfied, even thrilled, with their sex lives, and some are unhappy. Although sexual satisfaction tends to be highest in the early months of a relationship, some long-married couples report that happiness with their sexual interactions is as good as or better than ever (Frederick et al., 2016).

Differences and Variations in Sexual Response Male/female differences could be biological or cultural. Wives sometimes said, "Not tonight, I have a headache," because they did not want to become pregnant with an unwanted baby, for whom they would provide exclusive care. No more.

Some experts say that, without the fear of pregnancy, women are as sexual as men. However, comparisons are difficult. If two people both say they are highly aroused sexually, does that mean that they are equally aroused, or is one person's "highly aroused" unlike another's?

Every large study finds a vast range of sexuality and sexual satisfaction, not only between men and women but between one individual and another. Some people are strongly heterosexual or homosexual, and others less so; some people are pansexual and others bisexual. Some adults are *asexual,* not interested or aroused by sex. This is apparent more in attitude than in biology (Brotto & Yule, 2011). On the other hand, some people think about sex almost all the time.

Arrest rates for sexual offenses are much higher in men than women, but very few people, male or female, ever commit a harmful sexual act (estimates vary widely), so arrest rates do not reflect typical sexuality. Further, correlation is not causation.

All adults, of varying sexualities, can be sexually aroused by pornography, which is legal unless children are depicted (Spape et al., 2014). Many choose not to look; some seem unable to stop looking. Viewing pornography is related to culture and age: Older men and women view less.

Are age differences caused by reduced sexual arousal, less computer expertise, or greater wisdom? Pornography interferes, at least temporarily, with rational thinking, acute hearing, and healthy relationships (Laier et al., 2014; Oliver et al., 2016).

Sexual arousal, orgasm, and, as we will soon see, fertility and menopause are all connected to senescence, but the effects, and even the occurrence, are strongly influenced by the mind (Pfaus et al., 2014). As many say: "The most important human sexual organ is between the . . . ears."

The brain and culture are particularly relevant for contraception. For example, most couples in India rely on female sterilization to control family size. An estimated half of all women are sterilized by age 30, but virtually no men in India have a vasectomy (Sunita & Desai, 2013).

In the United States, young women are rarely sterilized, but the most popular contraception is the birth control pill, which is almost never used for contraception in Japan (Matsumoto et al., 2011). In the United States, sterilization is common after age 35 and involves a fair number of men: 44 percent of sexually active women and 20 percent of older men are surgically infertile.

infertility The inability to conceive a child after trying for at least a year.

Seeking Pregnancy Rates of **infertility** (failure to conceive after one year of trying) vary from nation to nation, primarily because the rate increases when medical care is scarce. Worldwide, an estimate of *primary* infertility (never able to conceive naturally) is about 2 percent of all couples, and *secondary* infertility (inability to have a second child after a year of trying) is about 10 percent.

Both forms of infertility are usually kept secret from friends, as are the results of various tests. Some women do not even discuss it with their partners, although most do (Sormunen et al., 2018). In general, infertility, contraception, and miscarriage are not typically talked about. That adds to the problem for people with these experiences and for their friends and family.

Age matters. In the United States, about 12 percent of all adult couples do not conceive after one year of trying, partly because many postpone childbearing. Peak fertility is at about age 18.

If couples in their 40s try to conceive, about half fail (a 50 percent infertility rate) and the other half risk various complications. Of course, risk is not reality: In 2014 in the United States, 118,464 babies were born to women age 40 or older. Most of those babies become healthy, well-loved children.

Choosing Motherhood In 2018, U.S. Senator Tammy Duckworth, age 50, had her second baby via IVF and won the right to bring her infant daughter to the Senate floor. Next: Will the United States continue to be the only nation (except for New Guinea) without mandated paid family leave?

We need to put age and fertility into perspective. By far, most babies born in the United States have mothers aged 23 to 33, and only about 3 percent are born to women over 40. However, the age trends over the past two decades are dramatic: The teenage birth rate is half of what it was, and older women are the only ones whose birth rate is rising.

Age matters particularly for women, who are less likely to conceive in midlife. Ovulation stops at menopause. Age affects men as well. When couples are infertile, either or both partners may be the problem.

A common reason for male infertility is low sperm count. Conception is most likely if a man ejaculates more than 20 million sperm per milliliter of semen, two-thirds of them mobile and viable. Each sperm's journey to the ovum is aided by millions of fellow travelers.

Depending on a man's age, each day about 100 million sperm reach maturity after a developmental process that lasts about 75 days. Anything that impairs body functioning during those days (e.g., fever, radiation, drugs, time in a sauna, stress, pollution, alcohol, cigarettes) reduces sperm number, shape, and motility (activity), making conception less likely. Sedentary behavior, perhaps particularly watching television, correlates with lower sperm count (Gaskins et al., 2013).

As with men, women's fertility is affected by anything that impairs physical functioning—including disease, smoking, extreme dieting, and obesity. Many infertile women do not realize that they have contracted one specific disease that impairs conception—*pelvic inflammatory disease (PID)*. PID creates scar tissue that may block the fallopian tubes, preventing sperm from reaching an ovum (Brunham et al., 2015).

Fertility Treatments In the past 50 years, medical advances have solved about half of all fertility problems. Surgery can repair some problems directly, and *assisted reproductive technology* (*ART*) overcomes obstacles such as a low sperm count and blocked fallopian tubes. One ART procedure, in vitro fertilization (IVF), was explained in Chapter 3.

What was not discussed was the impact on the adults, who may be depressed if they are unable to have a baby. Infertility and subsequent fertility measures affect the psyche, not just the body. People may question their own morality (is parenthood selfish?) and their partner's wishes. Remember that communication is crucial for a satisfying adult sex life; this is especially true when ART is involved.

Photo by Lezlie Sterling/Sacramento Bee/Zuma Press

Barcroft/Getty Images

Remembering Younger Days When Chris McNulty was diagnosed with cancer, he and his wife decided to freeze his sperm so that they could later have children. He died, but his widow used his sperm five years after his death. Her twin sons, Kyle and Cole, are the result *(left)*. Bala Ram Devi Lohan and his wife, Rajo, wanted a child but had tried for 40 years without success. Finally, a donor egg and Bala Ram's sperm produced a zygote, which was implanted in Rajo's uterus. She gave birth to a 3-pound, 4-ounce girl, shown here with her happy parents, ages 70 and 72 *(right)*.

Some ART is morally acceptable to virtually everyone, especially when couples anticipate disease-related infertility. For example, many cancer patients freeze their ova. When the treatment is over, if they want a baby, their IVF success rate (about one-third of attempts) is similar to that for those who freeze their ova for reasons not related to cancer (Cardozo et al., 2015).

Some healthy young women freeze their ova for IVF years later because the age of the ova is a significant factor in success rates (Mac Dougall et al., 2013). When women over 40 have babies via IVF, most use donor ova (Hamilton et al., 2015).

ART has helped millions who thought they could never have a baby. The most dramatic example is with HIV-positive adults. Three decades ago, doctors recommended sterilization and predicted early death. Now, people with HIV can live happily for decades, using condoms for sex and taking antiviral drugs.

If an HIV-positive woman wants a child, drugs and a c-section almost always protect the fetus. If an HIV-positive man wants a child, his sperm can be collected, washed, and used in IVF to achieve conception. Indeed, conception for HIV-positive men can occur naturally with virus-suppressing drugs, but IVF is safer (Wu & Ho, 2015).

The Sexual-Reproductive System in Middle Age

During adulthood, the level of sex hormones circulating in the bloodstream declines—suddenly in women, gradually in men. Both sexes are affected by those changes, with some taking hormones to replace the hormones that are lost. That may be ill-advised—as you will see.

menopause The time in middle age, usually around age 50, when a woman's menstrual periods cease and the production of estrogen, progesterone, and testosterone drops. Strictly speaking, menopause is dated one year after a woman's last menstrual period, although many months before and after that date are menopausal.

Menopause For women, sometime between ages 42 and 58 (the average age is 51), ovulation and menstruation stop because of a marked drop in production of several hormones. This is **menopause.** The age of natural menopause is affected primarily by genes (17 have been identified) (D. Morris et al., 2011; Stolk et al., 2012) and normal aging but also by smoking (earlier menopause), exercise (later), and moderate alcohol consumption (later) (Taneri et al., 2016).

Menopause is connected to many physical reactions beyond the cessation of menstruation and ovulation. The symptoms include vaginal dryness and body temperature disturbances, including hot flashes (feeling hot), hot flushes (looking hot),

and cold sweats (feeling chilled). Those physical responses can be hardly noticeable, or they can be dramatic—interfering with sleep, which can make a woman tired and irritable.

The psychological effects of menopause also vary a great deal, with some women sad that they can no longer become pregnant and other women happy for the same reason. Anthropologist Margaret Mead famously said, "There is no more creative force in the world than the menopausal woman with zest." Some menopausal women are depressed, some are moody, and others are more energetic.

In the United States, about one in five women has a *hysterectomy* (surgical removal of the uterus), which may include removal of her ovaries (Morgan et al., 2018). If she was pre-menopausal, removal of the ovaries suddenly reduces estrogen and therefore causes menopausal symptoms.

Early menopause, surgical or not, correlates with various health problems later on, including heart disease, sleep difficulties, and frailty (Verschoor & Tamim, 2019). Female hormones protect health, which is one reason why hysterectomies are less common than 40 years ago. Many current hysterectomies are done laparoscopically, without major surgery, and keep the ovaries intact.

Hormone Replacement Toward the end of the twentieth century, millions of post-menopausal women used **hormone replacement therapy (HRT).** Some did so to alleviate symptoms of menopause, others to prevent osteoporosis (fragile bones), heart disease, strokes, or cognitive loss. Correlational studies found that these diseases occurred less often among women taking HRT.

hormone replacement therapy (HRT)
Taking hormones (in pills, patches, or injections) to compensate for hormone reduction. HRT is most common in women at menopause or after removal of the ovaries, but it is also used by men as their testosterone decreases. HRT has some medical uses but also carries health risks.

However, that correlation was misleading. In a multiyear study of thousands of women, half (the experimental group) took HRT and half (the control group) did not. The results were a shock: Taking estrogen and progesterone *increased* the risk of heart disease, stroke, and some types of cancer (U.S. Preventive Services Task Force, 2002).

The most dramatic difference was an increase in breast cancer, at the rate of 6 per year for 1,000 women taking HRT compared to 4 per 1,000 for women who did not take the hormone (Chlebowski et al., 2013). The women had been randomly assigned to the experimental or control group, which meant that the results were solid. The study was halted before its scheduled end because the researchers were convinced that the experimental group was at risk.

How could the previous research have been mistaken? In retrospect, scientists realized that simply comparing women who chose HRT with women who did not resulted in women with higher SES being compared with women of lower SES (who could not afford HRT). Benefits were the result of some women's education and health care, not of HRT.

Scientists agree that HRT has some beneficial uses: It relieves the symptoms of menopause, which some women find very troubling, psychologically as well as physically. It also decreases osteoporosis and may improve hearing. But HRT also has risks, the greatest of which is a slight increase in the chance of breast cancer.

Overall, experts now recognize the need for "individualized decision." For example, some studies show an increased incidence of heart disease; others show a decreased risk, with the key factors being genes, diet, and exercise, as well as when the woman took HRT (Keck & Taylor, 2018). Indeed, because of the wide variation in bodies and benefits, each person must make daily decisions about drugs, diet, and so on, guided by the research but not ruled by it.

Another study emphasizing the need for individualized decision included 872 women in 17 nations whose ovaries were surgically removed because they carried the BRAC1 gene, which increases the risk of ovarian cancer. If they were under age 45 when they took estrogen (but not progesterone) for symptoms of menopause, they did *not* have higher rates of breast cancer than similar women who did not take hormones (Kotsopoulos et al., 2018). Indeed, they may have been at less risk—but the data were not significant for that.

Andropause? Do men undergo anything like menopause? Some say yes, suggesting that the word *andropause* should be used to signify an age-related lower testosterone level, which reduces sexual desire, erections, and muscle mass (Samaras et al., 2012). Even with erection-inducing drugs such as Viagra and Levitra, sexual desire and speed of orgasm decline with age, as do many other physiological and cognitive functions.

andropause A term coined to signify a drop in testosterone levels in older men, which typically results in reduced sexual desire, erections, and muscle mass. (Also called *male menopause*.)

But most experts think that the term **andropause** (or *male menopause*) is misleading because it implies a sudden drop in reproductive ability or hormones. That does not occur in men, some of whom produce viable sperm at age 80 and older. Sexual inactivity and anxiety reduce testosterone—superficially similar to menopause but with a psychological, not physiological, cause. In addition, some medical conditions and treatments reduce testosterone.

To combat their hormonal decline, some men take HRT. Of course, their H is the hormone testosterone, not estrogen. The result seems to be less depression, more sexual desire, and leaner bodies. (Some women also take smaller amounts of testosterone to increase their sexual desire.)

Weighing of costs and benefits is again needed (Hackett, 2016). One recent study found that men who took testosterone for years had lower rates of cardiovascular disease and fewer deaths, but in the short term more deaths occurred than usual (Wallis et al., 2016).

One team found that older men were most likely to seek more testosterone when they were troubled by declining sexual desire and function, but the added hormones did not necessarily help (Rastrelli et al., 2019). Many scientists rightly call for more longitudinal randomized studies, a wise suggestion given the results from women's HRT.

WHAT HAVE YOU LEARNED?

1. How does sexual arousal change with age?
2. How does contraception vary from one culture to another?
3. How are male and female sexual behaviors similar and not similar?
4. What impairs fertility in men and in women?
5. What are the effects of menopause?
6. How do male changes in sexual behavior differ from female ones?
7. What are the consequences of HRT in women and in men?

Habits: Good and Bad

As you have seen, personal habits and attitudes are crucial for physiological aging. Allostatic load, described in Chapter 17, builds quickly or slowly, so some adults seem decrepit by age 50 while others seem youthful. Measured by 18 indicators of health and aging—as well as appearance in photographs—some 26- to 38-year-olds age three years per chronological year, and some age hardly at all (Belsky et al., 2015).

Exercise, nutrition, and drugs influence how long, how strong, and how full each adult life is. We describe the impact of each of these in turn.

Exercise

Many people have sought the secret sauce, the fountain of youth, the magic bullet that will slow, or stop, or even reverse the effects of senescence. Few realize that it has already been found. Thousands of scientists, studying every disease of aging, have found something that helps every condition—exercise.

Regular physical activity protects against serious illness even if a person overeats, smokes, or drinks (all discussed soon). Exercise reduces blood pressure, strengthens the heart and lungs, promotes digestion, and makes depression, diabetes, osteoporosis, strokes, arthritis, and several cancers less likely. Health benefits from exercise are substantial for men and women, old and young, former sports stars and those who never joined a team (Aldwin & Gilmer, 2013).

Bruce Eric Kaplan/The New Yorker Collection/Cartoonbank.com

"The fresh mountain air is starting to depress me."

Just Give Me the Usual Even bad habits feel comfortable—that's what makes them habits.

Moving the body protects both mental health and physical health. Surroundings are key. Neighborhoods high in walkability (paths, sidewalks, etc.) reduce time driving and watching television (Kozo et al., 2012). This relationship between the surroundings, movement, and health is causal, not merely correlational: Exercise strengthens the immune system (Davison et al., 2014). Moreover, active people feel energetic, which increases other good habits.

Exercise maintains flexibility and strength, evident in those who do yoga or swim laps in late adulthood. The same is true for internal muscles—the heart, the lungs, the digestive system.

By contrast, sitting for long hours correlates with almost every unhealthy condition, especially heart disease and diabetes. Even a little movement—gardening, light housework, walking up the stairs or to the bus—helps. Some research suggests that intensity is not necessary: Regular exercise is (Ross et al., 2015).

How Much and When? Unfortunately, exercise takes time and effort. It cannot be put in a pill and sold. Perhaps this is one reason why no corporation subsidizes research to understand and promote it. Consequently, scientists do not know exactly which exercise—and for how long—is best, nor how to get every adult to do it.

As one cardiologist said, "It's almost like we have something more powerful than any drug that we have for cardiovascular disease—physical activity—but we don't know how to dose it" (Ashley, quoted in Servick, 2015, p. 1307). For example, is it better to exercise a little every day than to exercise a lot on weekends?

Overweight people are sometimes healthier than trim ones. How can that be? The crucial difference is body fitness: Heavy people who exercise regularly reduce their risk for the diseases of aging, unlike those who are thinner but do not move much. A meta-analysis showed that physical activity reduced the risk of breast cancer, no matter how heavy the woman was (Pizot et al., 2016).

Ideally, exercise is varied—working on overall fitness and specific muscle groups—and is part of daily life, not something that occurs on vacation or in a particular season of the year. Unused muscles atrophy quickly—even a few weeks of bed rest weakens the legs.

The fibers for Type II muscles (the fast ones needed for forceful actions) are reduced much faster than Type I muscle fibers (for slower, more routine movement) (Nilwik et al., 2013). This means that as adults age, they become less able to win a 100-meter dash than a marathon, or less able to lift heavy rocks for a few minutes than to pick vegetables for hours.

CHAPTER APP 20

Couch to 5K

IOS:
https://tinyurl.com/yydkles4

ANDROID:
https://tinyurl.com/mhalrkl

RELEVANT TOPIC:
Health habits

As its name suggests, this app pledges to get users off of their couches and running a 5k run in a matter of nine weeks— no experience necessary. It tracks progress and logs workout routines via four coaches, each of whom provides audio cues to keep users motivated as the runs get more challenging. (**Note:** It is important to consult with a doctor before embarking on a new exercise routine.)

Historical Change Cohort changes are evident. Adults today do not move their legs, arms, or even hands as much as adults did a century ago, thanks to many modern devices, from the automobile to the TV remote. Fortunately, some adults fight the lazy comfort of modern life.

More than half (62 percent of those aged 18 to 44 and 53 percent of those aged 45 to 64) meet either the U.S. weekly goal of 150 minutes of moderate exercise *or* 75 minutes of intense exercise. That is much better than 20 years ago, when only 41 percent met either benchmark (National Center for Health Statistics, 2018).

Of course, it is better to meet both goals, and only 23 percent did so—with lower rates as adults grow older. That 23 percent is nonetheless a cohort improvement. In 1998, only 14 percent of adults met both goals (National Center for Health Statistics, 2018).

The aging of the adult body is most evident in sports that require strength, agility, and speed: Gymnasts, boxers, and basketball players are among the athletes whose bodies slow down in their 20s. These are physiological slowdowns: The intellectual and emotional gains of adulthood may compensate for physical changes; some 30-year-olds are more valuable teammates than younger athletes.

Although there is no pill that duplicates exercise, that does not stop people from trying to find one. As you saw, many older adult men take testosterone because it adds lean body mass. Many doctors are skeptical about the benefits, even though many pharmaceutical companies advertise "T" to make a man's body young again.

Drugs

Adults take many drugs, prescription and not, for medical uses and for personal enjoyment. As you will see, people differ as to the benefit and harm.

Medication Medication has improved health for many people, but many note that the profits of drug companies are among the highest in the United States. (In many other nations, medical drugs are much cheaper because they are regulated by the government.) The pharmacological industry argues that drug research is very expensive and that other countries benefit from the results but do not pay for the research.

In the past month in the United States, 37 percent of 18- to 44-year-olds and almost 70 percent of 45- to 64-year-olds took at least one prescription drug, according to surveys completed between 2011 and 2014. About 21 percent of adults took three or more prescription drugs in the past month. About half of those prescriptions were for chronic conditions (such as high blood pressure) and about half were for pain. Prescribed psychoactive drugs were also common: 9 percent of young adults and 17 percent of those aged 45 to 64 took antidepressants (Pratt et al., 2017).

Chip Somodevilla/Getty Images News/Getty Images

Almost Died Twice As a younger woman, U.S. Supreme Court Justice Sonia Sotomayor twice survived a loss of consciousness from her type 1 diabetes. Fortunately, her friends noticed her crisis. Now she has automatic monitoring and calibrated insulin, and she is expected to interpret the Constitution for 30 more years or so.

Over the past 50 years, prescription medication has cut the adult death rate in half and markedly reduced disability. Childhood diabetes (type 1), for instance, was once a death sentence; now diet and insulin allow diabetics to reach the highest levels of success, as Supreme Court Justice Sonia Sotomayor did. She began injecting herself at age 7; now she takes newer medication that is more precisely calibrated to her daily needs (Sotomayor, 2014).

There is no accurate tally of over-the-counter drugs, but almost every adult frequently takes vitamins, analgesics, laxatives, antihistamines, or some other medication. Advertisements for expensive drugs are common. One benefit of growing older might be wisdom regarding drug use: Adults tell each other what works, doctors adjust their prescribing, and each person knows his or her personal reactions to various drugs.

Nonmedical Drugs Most adults take drugs that affect their mood. Almost everyone drinks caffeinated soda and coffee, and a few take illegal drugs. Some improvement over adulthood is evident. Illegal drug abuse decreases markedly over adulthood—often before age 25 and almost always by age 40. Past data show reduced use of marijuana, although recent legal changes may affect adult use, and we need to analyze data for another decade to understand the effect.

New evidence on coffee is good news: We now know that the effect of coffee varies genetically, and adults learn how coffee affects them (Cornelis et al., 2015). For some, coffee does no harm but reduces various problems, including depression and type 2 diabetes (Palatini, 2015). For others, coffee disrupts nighttime sleep and undercuts daytime efficiency. Adults adjust accordingly.

Tobacco Always, culture and SES matter. This is shown dramatically in use of tobacco, considered the leading risk factor for many diseases. Rates are quite different depending on nation, SES, gender, and cohort.

In the United States, high-SES people are less likely to smoke. However, in poor nations, rates of smoking *increase* with income, because poor people cannot afford cigarettes. Traditionally in Asia, women rarely smoked, but as their incomes have risen, rates of smoking are increasing rapidly.

The World Health Organization calls tobacco "the single largest preventable cause of death and chronic disease in the world today," with 1 billion smoking-related deaths projected between 2010 and 2050, most in low-income nations where rates of abject poverty are declining. This is glaringly evident in Asia, where smoking rates have plateaued in nations that have had high incomes for decades (e.g., Japan, Singapore) but continue to increase in China (Yang et al., 2013).

Cigarette smoking in the United States also illustrates marked cohort and gender effects. During World War II (1941–1945), American soldiers (always men) were given free cigarettes. Then in 1964, the U.S. surgeon general first reported on the health risks of smoking, with many follow-up reports in the next few decades. As a result, many former soldiers quit.

Meanwhile, some women celebrated another historical happening, women's liberation, by smoking—encouraged by cigarette advertisements. (One brand launched in 1968, Virginia Slims, used the slogan "you've come a long way, baby.")

In the 1960s, more than half of U.S. adult men and more than a third of women smoked. Over the next decades, as research became clearer on smoking, cancer, heart disease, and secondhand smoke, both sexes had decreased smoking rates. Recent data show that only 19 percent of adult men (aged 25 to 65) and 15 percent of women are smokers. Rates peak at about age 30 and then decrease, indicating the advantages of maturation among adults (National Center for Health Statistics, 2018). By age 60, more adults are former smokers than current smokers.

The changes over the past decades are reflected in lung cancer deaths. A half-century ago in the United States, five times as many men as women died of lung cancer. More recently, rates are closer to equal, because "women who smoke like men die like men who smoke" (Schroeder, 2013, p. 389). In the past decades, adults of both sexes quit smoking and lung cancer was reduced by 500 percent—not primarily because of better medical care but because of wiser adults (see **Figure 20.1**).

Image Courtesy of The Advertising Archives

Wishful Thinking Would you like to be her, with a thin cigarette in your hand? If this was her usual appearance, she might now suffer from cancer and heart disease.

FIGURE 20.1

No More Cancer Sticks The rates of lung cancer deaths dropped dramatically about a decade after smoking rates decreased. Other age groups of adults show similar results, although improvements are not as dramatic for older adults because they learned too late about the damage done to their lungs. In another few decades we will know whether e-cigarettes reverse this trend.

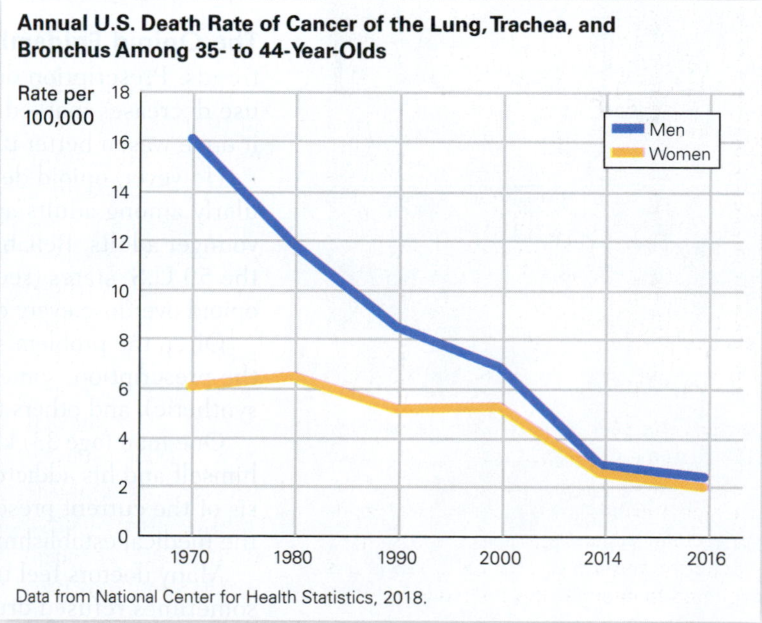

Not only cohort but also culture has a strong effect on both smoking and gender differences. Almost half of the adults of both sexes in Germany, Denmark, Poland, Holland, Switzerland, and Spain smoke. A joke in Europe is "if you want to stop smoking, go to America."

Alcohol The harm from cigarettes is dose-related: Each puff, each day, each breath of secondhand smoke makes cancer, heart disease, strokes, and emphysema more likely. No such linear harm results from drinking alcohol. In fact, some alcohol may be beneficial: Adults who drink wine, beer, or spirits *in moderation*—never more than two drinks a day—live longer than abstainers (Goel et al., 2018).

This may be a misleading correlation because some of those abstainers were formerly heavy drinkers, so their death rate reflects earlier damage done by alcohol (Chikritzhs et al., 2015; Knott et al., 2015). Whether or not moderation is beneficial is debatable, but everyone agrees that excessive drinking is harmful. Certainly abstainers should not be encouraged to start drinking (Goel et al., 2018).

Especially for Doctors and Nurses If you had to choose between recommending various screening tests and recommending various lifestyle changes to a 35-year-old, which would you do? (see answer, page 528)

Alcohol use disorder destroys brain cells, is a major cause of liver damage and several cancers, contributes to osteoporosis, decreases fertility, and accompanies many suicides, homicides, and accidents—all while wreaking havoc in families. Even moderate consumption is unhealthy if it leads to smoking, overeating, casual sex, or other destructive habits.

Alcohol abuse shows age, gender, cohort, and cultural differences. For example, the risk of accidental death while drunk is most common among young men: Law enforcement in the United States has cut their drunk-driving rate in half. However, middle-aged parents who abuse alcohol are more harmful to other people, because of their neglect and irrational rage (Blas & Kurup, 2010).

In the United States, about one in three adults under age 45 have gotten drunk in the past year, as have about one in five adults over age 45. Rates of alcohol abuse are higher among men than women, higher among European Americans than African or Hispanic Americans (National Center for Health Statistics, 2018).

THINK CRITICALLY: How would you apportion blame for drug addiction?

In general, low-income nations have more abstainers, more abusers, and fewer moderate drinkers than more affluent nations (Blas & Kurup, 2010). In developing nations, prevention and treatment strategies for alcohol use disorder have not been established, regulation is rare, and laws are lax (Bollyky, 2012). Thus, alcohol is particularly lethal to a community as national income falls.

The Opioid Epidemic Most of the data on adult use of drugs show positive trends. Prescription drugs reduce blood pressure and heart disease; illegal drug use decreases markedly after age 25; cigarette smoking is less than half of what it once was; a better understanding of alcohol abuse results in fewer abusers.

However, opioid deaths have increased every year of the past decade, particularly among adults aged 26 to 44, who are more often addicted than older or younger adults. Reliable data comparing 2015 to 2016 show an increase in 48 of the 50 U.S. states (see **Figure 20.2**). Nationwide, more than 100 people die of opioid overdose every day (Seth et al., 2018).

Often the problem starts with a prescribed pain medication. If the doctor stops the prescription, some people switch to heroin, others obtain *fentanyl* (an illegal synthetic), and others try desperate means to get prescribed drugs.

One man (age 33) killed four people when he robbed a drug store to get pills for himself and his addicted wife (age 30). The local attorney general said, "the genesis of the current prescription pill and heroin epidemic lies squarely at the feet of the medical establishment" (Spota, quoted in James, 2012).

Many doctors feel unjustly accused, and patients with severe, chronic pain are sometimes refused drugs that they need. Is the problem in the addicted people,

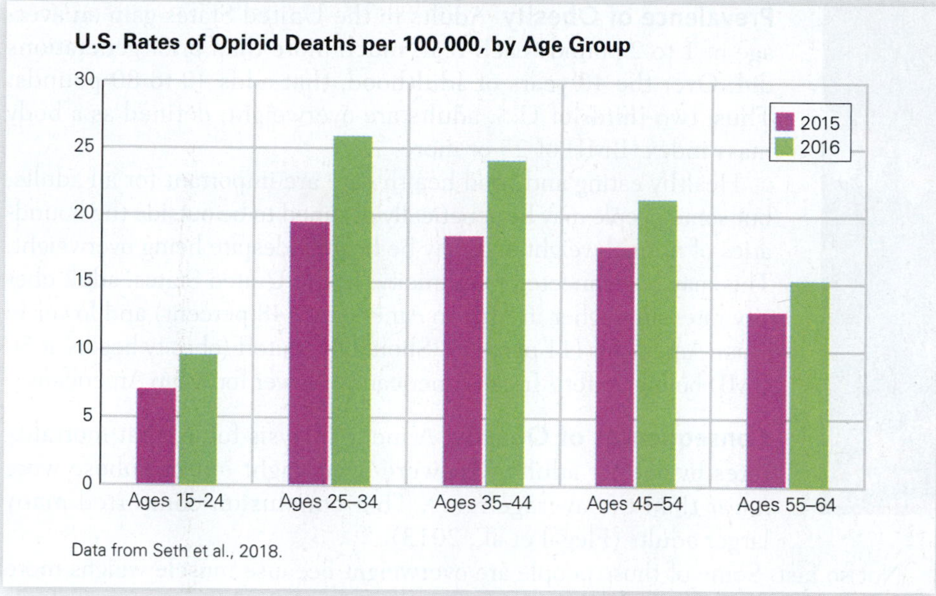

FIGURE 20.2

Bad News Which is most troubling: that rates of opioid deaths have more than tripled in a decade, that rates continue to rise, or that rates in middle age are almost three times the rates for emerging adults? These data are for 2016; high rates continue, although some data suggest that addiction deaths are no longer increasing.

the drug dealers, the doctor, the pharmaceutical companies, the community, or the culture? From a developmental perspective, blame is unproductive: We need accurate understanding, effective prevention, and successful treatment.

Pain may be alleviated in other ways. For example, one study compared sufferers of severe back, hip, or knee pain, half of whom were prescribed opioids (usually morphine or oxycodone) and half nonsteroidal anti-inflammatory drugs (NSAIDS). Other opioids or non-opioid drugs were dispensed if needed. Pain relief was no better for either half (Krebs et al., 2018).

Hope comes from data on other substances: Rates of alcohol abuse and cigarette smoking are much lower than a few decades ago because we better understand *how* to reduce those behaviors. Such measures combine laws, taxes, awareness, and norms to reduce adolescent use. If a young person is prevented from smoking or drinking excessively, then addiction "ages out" in adulthood. The major battle is won, because few adults begin to abuse those substances.

However, that does not apply to opioids. What stops drug abuse that *begins* in adulthood? At least we know how to reduce deaths: *Naloxone* (a medication that blocks the effects of opioids) is lifesaving if given to someone who has stopped breathing from an opioid overdose. Campaigns to make naloxone more readily available are succeeding. The hope is that a near-death experience will motivate an addict toward treatment.

But prevention should begin long before that. A clue may be in the geographic distribution of opioid addictions. Some states (New Hampshire, Ohio, West Virginia, Massachusetts) have death rates four times higher than in others (Iowa, Oregon, Texas, Hawaii). Some communities have much higher rates than others. Since local policies and norms make a difference, scientists must understand what they are.

John Shearer/Getty Images

Pain Killer "Never meant to cause you any pain," sang Prince in his classic song, "Purple Rain." But his own pain led to an opioid addiction and then to an accidental overdose of fentanyl, a synthetic opioid that is 50 times more powerful than heroin. His death at age 57 hurt us all.

Nutrition

Diet is increasingly important as adults grow older, because metabolism decreases by one-third between ages 20 and 60, and digestion becomes less efficient. This means that to stay healthy at the same weight, adults should eat less, add more vegetables, and move more as they grow older. That is not what happens.

John Normile/Getty Images News/Getty Images

Winners or Losers? Erik Booker, Miki Sudo, Joey Chestnut, and Sonya Thomas *(left to right)* compete in the annual chicken-wing eating contest in Buffalo, New York. Chestnut won by eating 205 wings in 12 minutes; Sudo was second with 170. The festival was attended by 70,000 people; the contest was part of the International Federation of Competitive Eating.

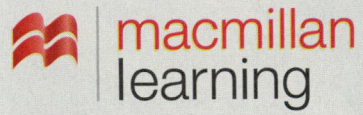

macmillan learning

Try the **Data Connections activity Body Mass Index** to see how BMI is determined.

Prevalence of Obesity Adults in the United States gain an average of 1 to 2 pounds each year, much more than prior generations did. Over the 40 years of adulthood, that adds 40 to 80 pounds. Thus, two-thirds of U.S. adults are overweight, defined as a body mass index (BMI) of 25 or more.

Healthy eating and good health care are important for all adults, but some people may be genetically destined to be outside the boundaries of normal weight and may be healthy despite being overweight. This may be connected to ethnicity: In the United States, adult obesity rates are higher in African Americans (48 percent) and lower in Asian Americans (11 percent). Should the cutoff (obesity begins at 30 BMI) be higher for African Americans or lower for Asian Americans?

Consequences of Obesity A meta-analysis found that mortality rates by age for adults who were overweight but not obese were *lower* than the average rates. That conclusion comforted many larger adults (Flegal et al., 2013).

Not so fast. Some of those people are overweight because muscle weighs more than fat, so their BMI is high while the fat content of their body is not. Excess body fat (no matter what the BMI) increases the risk of almost every chronic disease.

For example, diabetes causes eye, heart, and foot problems as well as early death. Type 1 diabetes is primarily genetic, but type 2 is only partly genetic. It may be triggered by overweight. The United States is the world leader in both obesity and diabetes.

The consequences of obesity are psychological as well as physical. Adults who are obese are targets of scorn and prejudice. They are less likely to be chosen as marriage partners, as employees, and even as friends. The stigma leads them to avoid medical checkups, to eat more, and to exercise less—impairing their health far more than their weight alone (Puhl & Heuer, 2010).

For the morbidly obese, surgery may be the best option. Each year, about 200,000 U.S. residents undergo bariatric surgery to restrict weight gain. The rate of complications is high: About 2 percent die during or soon after the operation, and about 10 percent need additional surgery. Patients have fewer complications if they lose weight in preparation for the surgery (Anderin et al., 2015). That could be an aspect of homeostasis—the body is getting ready to adjust to a better diet.

Despite the high rate of initial complications, such surgery saves lives because morbid obesity increases the likelihood of many diseases. The greatest benefits seem to occur for people with type 2 diabetes: 70 percent find that their diabetes disappears, usually not to return (Arterburn et al., 2013; Chen et al., 2016).

Correlating Income and Health

The relationship between ethnicity and various health behaviors may reflect income more than national origin. Thus, the fact that Asian Americans are less often overweight could be a consequence of another fact: Asian Americans tend to have more education and income than other Americans.

Worldwide, high-SES adults live longer, avoiding morbidity and disability more than their fellow citizens. Even in nations with universal health care, the poorest people have shorter lives on average.

SES protects health between nations as well as within them. For example, a baby born in 2015 in a high-income nation can expect to live to age 80; but if that baby happens to be born in a low-income nation, life expectancy is only 61 (see **Figure 20.3**). The extremes are separated by 33 years: Life expectancy in Hong Kong is 83; in the Central African Republic, it is 50 (United Nations, 2017).

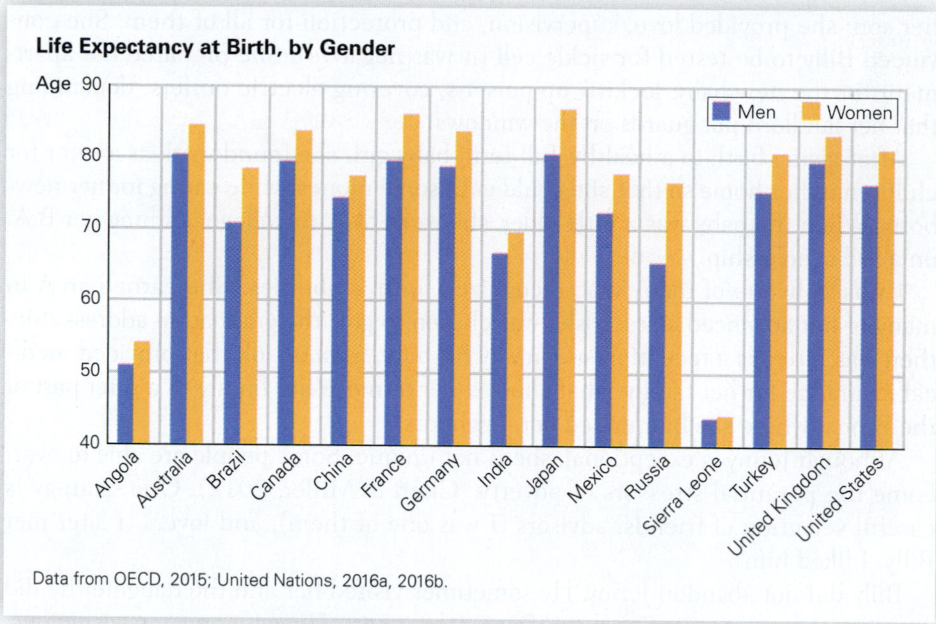

Data from OECD, 2015; United Nations, 2016a, 2016b.

FIGURE 20.3

More Widows Than Widowers Women live longer than men, but it matters where they live. The cause is probably both nature and nurture: Nature is that extra X chromosome, more estrogen, or less testosterone; nurture is that men have fewer social supports, suppress their emotions, and use more harmful drugs.

Within the United States, the overall risk of dying between ages 25 and 65 is about 15 percent, but for the poorest groups it is as high as 50 percent (e.g., Sioux men in South Dakota) and for the richest less than 2 percent (Asian American women in Connecticut) (Lewis & Burd-Sharps, 2010). Overall, the 10 million U.S. residents with the highest SES outlive the 10 million with the lowest SES by about 30 years on average (Lewis & Burd-Sharps, 2010).

Every health risk in the United States is more prevalent among those below the poverty line than among those above it. For example, the rate of cigarette smoking is 25 percent among poor Americans but only 14 percent among those who are not so poor (Jamal et al., 2018).

Without doubt, low SES harms human development in every way, evident in statistics on mortality, morbidity, disability, and vitality. Unfortunately, more often in the United States than in most nations, babies born poor are unlikely to escape their SES, as their education, health care, job prospects, and so on are all likely to work against them; they therefore enter adulthood already impaired. Is there any hope?

THINK CRITICALLY: Does SES protect health because of personal habits or social conditions?

Back to Jenny That question returns us to Jenny, whose story began this chapter. When I first met her, she was among the poorest 10 million people in the United States, living in a Bronx neighborhood known as "Gunsmoke Territory" because of its high homicide rate. She is also African American, and people of her ethnicity tend to have a higher allostatic load.

Her decision to have another baby—with no promise of marriage or of the father's support—made me fear that she would never escape from poverty. My fear was not prejudice: Lifelong poverty is the usual future for low-income mothers of four who have another child, out of wedlock, with a married man.

But those statistics do not reflect Jenny's intelligence, creativity, and attitude. She made the best of available government help. Her tuition was paid for with a Pell Grant; she lived in public housing; her children went to public schools; she found parks and museums where her children could play and learn.

Remember that Jenny was a star student. I saw that she applied everything she learned from my class, although much of it just confirmed what she already knew. She helped her children with their homework; she found speech therapy for her son; she provided love, supervision, and protection for all of them. She convinced Billy to be tested for sickle cell (it was negative). She prepared her apartment for the new baby, locking up poisons, covering electric outlets, demanding that her landlord put guards on the windows.

After giving birth to a healthy, full-term baby girl, she found work as a tutor for children in her home so that she could earn some money while caring for her newborn. When the baby was a little older, she went back to college, earning her B.A. on a full scholarship.

I was only one of many who recognized Jenny's abilities. She earned an A in many of her advanced classes; she was chosen to give the graduation address. She then was hired as a receptionist in a city hospital, a union job that provided medical insurance for her family. That allowed her to move her family to a safer part of the Bronx, where she befriended her neighbors.

Although Jenny is exceptional, she is not unique: Some people are able to overcome the potential stressors of poverty (Chen & Miller, 2012). One strategy is careful selection of friends, advisors (I was one of them), and lovers (I later met Billy; I liked him).

Billy did not abandon Jenny. He sometimes visited her and the daughter he did not want, providing emotional and financial support. His wife became suspicious, hired a private investigator, and then delivered an ultimatum: Stop seeing Jenny or obtain a divorce. He chose Jenny. Soon after that, they married and moved to Florida.

Jenny continues to do well, although, as a developmentalist would predict, Jenny could not completely escape the toll of her early life. For instance, she developed diabetes and must watch her diet carefully. But she bikes, swims, and gardens almost every day. She works full time in education, having earned a master's degree. That is one reason I know what she is doing: She took a graduate course that assigned an earlier edition of this book, and she phoned me to tell me so.

She and Billy seem happy together. I met the son who had a speech impediment: He earned a Ph.D. and is an assistant professor. Jenny's daughters are also college graduates.

This example might give the impression that escaping from poverty is easy; longitudinal data show that it is not. Most poor children do not thrive as Jenny's children did. For her two teenage nephews, Jenny's help came too late—they were lost to the streets of the South Bronx.

But the study of human development is not only about statistics and generalities. Each person is buffeted by all of the habits, conditions, and circumstances described in this chapter, but each makes choices that affect their future. Jenny chose well.

WHAT HAVE YOU LEARNED?

1. How much should an adult exercise?
2. Why do some experts think exercise is more important than weight?
3. What are the longitudinal changes in weight in the United States?
4. How does lung cancer reflect trends in cigarette smoking?
5. How do ethnicity, gender, and nationality affect smoking rates?
6. Who is most likely to suffer from opioid abuse?
7. Why would SES predict health, even in a nation with free public health care?

SUMMARY

Growing Older

1. Senescence causes a universal slowdown during adulthood, but aging does not necessarily mean impairment. Brains show evidence of growth as well as shrinkage: Plasticity is evident lifelong.

2. A person's appearance undergoes gradual but noticeable changes as middle age progresses, including more wrinkles, less hair, and more fat, particularly around the abdomen. People lose some height because of compression of the spine.

3. Senescence is apparent in the sense organs. Vision becomes less sharp with age. Nearsightedness decreases and farsightedness increases in midlife. Hearing also becomes less acute.

The Sexual-Reproductive System

4. Sexual responsiveness slows down with age, as does speed of recovery after orgasm. This is only a physical decline; many couples find that, overall, sexual relations improve with age, especially if the couple communicates well.

5. Fertility problems become more common with increased age, for many reasons. The most common reason for men is a reduced number of sperm, and for women it is either ovulation failure or blocked fallopian tubes. For both sexes, not only youth but also health—especially sexual health—correlates with fertility.

6. At menopause, as a woman's menstrual cycle stops, ovulation ceases and levels of estrogen are markedly reduced. This hormonal change produces various symptoms. Hormone replacement therapy was once common, but it increases the risk of breast cancer.

7. Hormone production declines in men, too, though not as suddenly as in women. Men produce viable sperm lifelong. Some men take extra testosterone, but hormone replacement therapy in men has health costs as well as benefits.

Habits: Good and Bad

8. Exercise is the key to good health, both physical and psychological. Adults in the United States are exercising more than they did a decade ago but less than they did a century ago.

9. North Americans are smoking far less than they once did, and rates of lung cancer and other diseases are falling, largely for that reason. Women cut down on smoking later than men did. In many nations, female smoking is increasing.

10. Moderate drinking of alcohol may be beneficial for heart health, but excessive drinking is a major health problem. Opioid addiction has led to more than 100 deaths per day in the United States. There is no consensus as to whether the blame should focus on individuals, doctors, or drug companies.

11. Good health habits include not gaining too much weight. Today's adults worldwide are faring worse than did previous generations on this metric. There is a worldwide "epidemic of obesity," as more people have access to abundant food and overeat as a result. That is one reason the rates of diabetes are rising.

12. Aging and health status can be greatly affected by SES. In general, those who have more education and money are more likely to live longer and avoid illness than their poorer counterparts. However, low SES does not inevitably lead to poor health, because genes and health habits are protective.

KEY TERMS

senescence (p. 508)
infertility (p. 514)
menopause (p. 516)
hormone replacement therapy (HRT) (p. 517)
andropause (p. 518)

APPLICATIONS

1. Guess the age of five adults you know, ideally of different ages. Then ask them how old they are. Analyze the clues you used for your guesses and the reactions to your question.

2. Find a speaker willing to come to your class who is an expert on weight loss, adult health, smoking, or drinking. Write a one-page proposal explaining why you think this speaker would be good and what topics he or she should address. Give this proposal to your instructor, with contact information for your speaker. The instructor will call the potential speakers, thank them for their willingness, and decide whether or not to actually invite them to speak.

3. Attend a gathering for people who want to stop a bad habit or start a good one, such as an open meeting of Alcoholics Anonymous or another 12-step program, an introductory session of Weight Watchers or Smoke Enders, or a meeting of prospective gym members. Report on who attended, what you learned, and what your reactions were.

Especially For ANSWERS

Response for Drivers (from p. 509): No. Car accidents occur when the mind is distracted, not the hands.

Response for Doctors and Nurses (from p. 522): Obviously, much depends on the specific patient. Overall, however, far more people develop a disease or die because of years of poor health habits than because of various illnesses not spotted early. With some exceptions, age 35 is too early to detect incipient cancers or circulatory problems, but it's prime time for stopping cigarette smoking, curbing alcohol abuse, and improving exercise and diet.

Observation Quiz ANSWERS

Answer to Observation Quiz (from p. 508): He is closer to 30—28 to be exact. Clues: He still has the strength, stamina, and risk-taking adventurousness of an emerging adult. Another clue is contextual and historical: His two years as a U.S. Marine in Afghanistan must have been recent when this photo was taken.

Answer to Observation Quiz (from p. 511): She is only 24 in this photo. The clue is her smooth skin.

VISUALIZING DEVELOPMENT Adult Overweight Around the World

A century ago, being overweight was a sign of affluence, as the poor were less likely to enjoy a calorie-rich diet and more likely to be engaged in physical labor. Today, that link is less clear. Overweight—defined as having a body mass index (BMI) over 25—is common across socioeconomic groups and across nations, and obesity (a BMI over 30) is a growing health threat worldwide.

OVERWEIGHT AND GDP

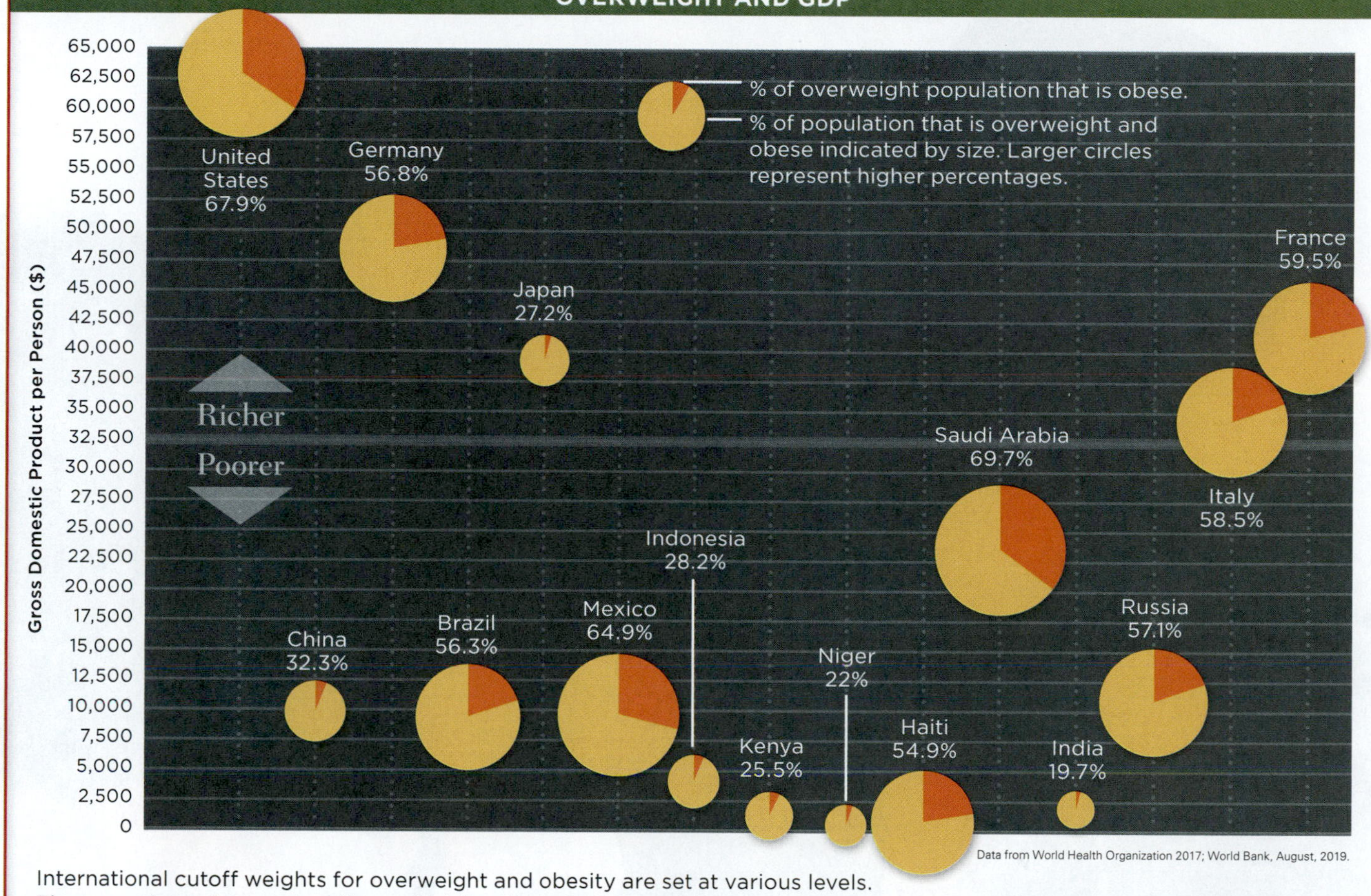

International cutoff weights for overweight and obesity are set at various levels. These numbers show proportions of adults whose BMI is over 25.

U.S. OBESITY RATES BY INCOME LEVEL AND ETHNICITY

While common wisdom holds that overweight and obesity correlate with income, recent data suggests that culture and gender may play a bigger role. Obesity tends to be less prevalent among wealthy U.S. women; for men, the patterns are less consistent.

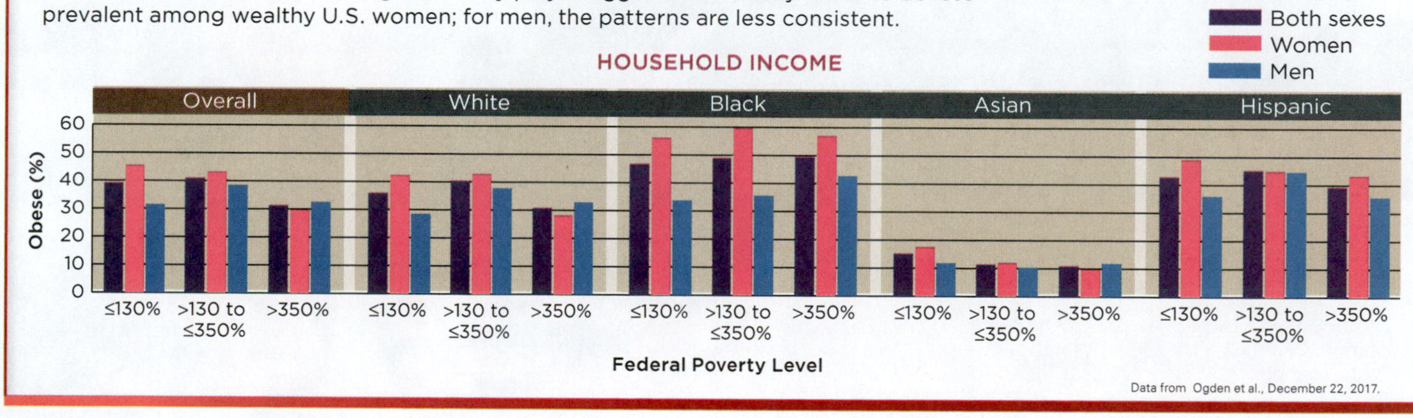

CHAPTER 21

Adulthood: Cognitive Development

What Will You Know?

1. Do people get smarter as they get older?
2. Are people who are high in analytic intelligence also high in practical intelligence?
3. Does stress make a person sick and confused?
4. Is everyone an expert at something?

- **Intelligence Changes During Adulthood?**
  - Inborn IQ
  - Age and IQ
  - Putting It All Together
- **Components of Intelligence: Many and Varied**
  - Two Clusters of Intelligence
  - Three Forms of Intelligence
- **Selective Gains and Losses**
  - Optimization with Compensation
  - Expert Cognition
  - A VIEW FROM SCIENCE: Who Wins in Soccer?
  - Expertise, Age, and Experience
  - A CASE TO STUDY: Parenting Expertise
- **VISUALIZING DEVELOPMENT: Media Use Among U.S. Adults**

One of my daughters, herself a professor, was on a committee that selected a new college president. She says that this new leader is improving the institution in many ways, although he came from outside academia.

"You must be glad they selected the one you wanted," I said.

"He's not the one I wanted. I didn't even want to interview him. Others on the committee outvoted me."

She was unimpressed with his paper résumé because she is a scholar and he had few publications. But she listened with an open mind during his interview and rethought her criteria.

This illustrates adult cognition. Adults have ideas based on their personal experience, but ideally they also listen to others. Everyone has areas of expertise. My daughter is proficient in analytic intelligence; she knows how to assess scholarship. But analytic intelligence in only one form of cognition; practical intelligence is another, and this new president, apparently, is adept at that.

This chapter explains the many facets of adult cognition. Some abilities improve with age; others do not. Each person gains skills and knowledge, and most adults advance in language and social understanding. That enables them to listen to each other. A well-functioning committee can choose a leader better than any one person.

Remember that scientists use many research strategies to explore cognitive development in adulthood. Chapter 18 described postformal thinking as well as the impact of college. Chapter 24 will take an information-processing perspective, highlighting processing abilities and describing neurocognitive disorders.

This chapter uses the psychometric approach (*metric* means "measure"; *psychometric* refers to the measurement of psychological characteristics) and considers various kinds of intelligence, including those that produce experts of one sort or another.

I am proud that my daughter realized that the new president could use his creative and practical intelligence to improve the school. He is smart and talented, albeit not in the metrics familiar to her (publications, citations). She listened to other people, who articulated their opinions well. They all were thinking as adults.

Left: Plan Shoot/Multi-bits/ImaZinS/Getty Images
Top: iko/Shutterstock

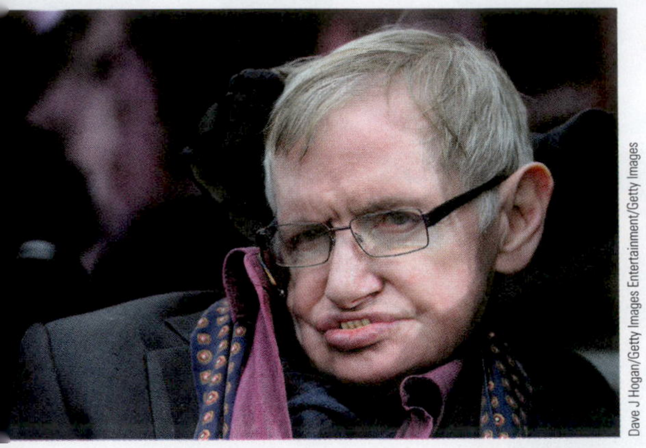
Dave J Hogan/Getty Images Entertainment/Getty Images

Talk and Think Stephen Hawking (1942–2018) wrote *A Brief History of Time,* which sold more than 10 million copies—an astounding number for a book about theoretical physics and cosmology. He also had ALS, diagnosed at age 21, which did not stop him from marriage (twice), fatherhood (thrice), and becoming a leading international scholar. Toward the end of his life, he could not talk but instead communicated with a muscle in his cheek—striking evidence that intellect cannot always be assessed via speech.

Intelligence Changes During Adulthood?

Many scientists and much of the general public believe that "intelligence" is some kind of physical thing, like a lump in the brain that some people have more of than others and that stays about the same size until old age shrinks everything. That belief has been called into question, as you will see.

Inborn IQ

In the twentieth century, most people who specialized in measuring intelligence assumed that intelligence was born into a person, in much the same way eye color was innate. Genetic instructions made that inborn intelligence grow until it reached full capacity at about age 18, when the rest of the body was grown.

Unequal intelligence was a fact of life, not to be affected by age or experience. As one scholar begins a book on intelligence:

> Homer and Shakespeare lived in very different times, more than two thousand years apart, but they both captured the same idea: we are not all equally intelligent. I suspect that anyone who has failed to notice this is somewhat out of touch with the species.
>
> [Hunt, 2011a, p. 1]

Intelligence was measured by IQ tests in childhood in order to predict later life, including higher education and longevity (Arden et al., 2016). When scientists tallied IQ scores measured at various ages, they found that IQ was fairly stable by age 20 or so (Plomin & Deary, 2015).

Some children were much smarter than others. They continued to be smart, usually graduating from college and succeeding in adulthood.

Measuring *g* One leading theoretician, Charles Spearman (1927), called that lump "*g*," for *general intelligence*. Although *g* cannot be measured directly, Spearman thought it could be inferred from various abilities, such as vocabulary, memory, and reasoning.

Therefore, Spearman proposed that general intelligence could be quantified by summarizing scores on a diverse mix of measures. The combination of abilities such as memory, vocabulary, and reasoning would reveal whether a person's intelligence was superior, average, below average, or, in the terms (no longer used) of a century ago, "genius," "mentally retarded," "imbecile," or "idiot." [**Life-Span Link:** See Chapter 11 for the theoretical distribution of IQ scores.]

The belief that there is a *g* continues to influence thinking on intelligence, as "*g* is one of the most thoroughly studied concepts in the behavioral sciences. Measures of intelligence are predictive of a wide range of educational, occupational, and life outcomes" (Geary, 2018, p. 1028).

Since *g* was thought to be inborn, many researchers searched for the genetic underpinnings of intellectual capacity. One recent effort, contending that "intelligence is highly heritable," examined the entire genome and found 1,016 genes linked to intelligence (Savage et al., 2018, p. 912).

Other researchers look elsewhere for the origins of *g*—perhaps prenatal brain development, experiences in infancy, or physical health. One leading scholar suggests that how well the mitochondria function is the crucial factor (Geary, 2019). However, no one has succeeded in finding any particular intelligence gene or in proving that a particular biological entity is *g*.

A counter movement from other researchers suggests that no inborn *g* exists. Some criticize the psychometric approach as "neglecting the roles of

emotion, motivation, stress, intuition, and creativity in cognitive development" (Zelazo, 2018, p. 44). As one scholar wrote: "Intelligent researchers will likely continue to disagree about *g*" (Gignac, 2016, p. 84).

Neuroscience and *g* Currently, many think that *g* arises from brain functioning. The size of a particular part of the adult midbrain (the *caudate nuclei*) correlates with adult IQ (Grazioplene et al., 2015). An attempt to integrate all of the neuroscience research on *g* suggests that no particular part of the brain is crucial. Instead, "network flexibility and dynamics are crucial for the diverse range of mental abilities underlying general intelligence" (Barbey, 2018, p. 15).

In other words, the hubs and interconnections of brain parts are crucial. An intelligent person has strong and flexible networks, which allows the brain to combine, say, social perception and statistical logic, or verbal proficiency and visual acuity. Details vary from person to person over the life span, but always

> *g* originates from individual differences in the system-wide topology and dynamics of the human brain. . . . the capacity to flexibly transition between network states provides the foundation for individual differences in *g*—supporting the rapid exchange of information across networks and capturing individual differences in cognitive processing at a global level.
>
> [Barbey, 2018, pp. 16, 18]

macmillan learning

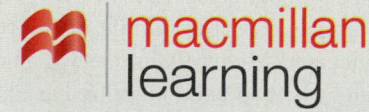

VIDEO ACTIVITY: Research Methods and Cognitive Aging explores how various research methods have been employed to study how intelligence changes with age.

Age and IQ

Although most psychometricians throughout the twentieth century assumed that intelligence could be measured and quantified via IQ tests, they disagreed about interpreting the data—especially about whether *g* rises or falls during adulthood.

Methodology was one reason for that disagreement. Consider the three methods used for studying human development that were introduced in Chapter 1: cross-sectional, longitudinal, and cross-sequential.

Cross-Sectional Declines For the first half of the twentieth century, psychologists thought that children gained intelligence each year, reaching a peak in late adolescence. For children, the number of questions answered correctly on an IQ test increased with age. So to keep the average at 100, testers consulted an age table that indicated how many correct answers an average child *of a particular age* would have.

Over the adult years, the number of correct answers held steady until middle age or later, when it slowly declined. Thus, psychologists believed that adults gradually became less intelligent over time. This was evident on IQ tests but not in daily life: Older adults were not stupid, but they were not geniuses either.

This belief was based on the best evidence available. For instance, the U.S. Army tested the aptitude of all draftees in World War I. When the scores of men of various ages were compared, it seemed apparent that intellectual ability reached its peak at about age 18, stayed at that level until the mid-20s, and then declined (Yerkes, 1923).

However, longitudinal research showed the opposite effect. People seem to gain intelligence over the years of adulthood, as explained in Opposing Perspectives.

Observation Quiz In addition to intellectual ability, what two aspects of this test situation might affect older men differently than younger men? (see answer, page 552) ↓

Smart Enough for the Trenches? These young men were drafted to fight in World War I. Younger men (about age 17 or 18) did better on the military's intelligence tests than slightly older ones did.

Time Life Pictures/The LIFE Picture Collection/Getty Images

OPPOSING PERSPECTIVES

Who Is Smarter, the College Student or the Retiree?

Whether intelligence increases or decreases with age is answered differently depending partly on the age of the person answering, whether that person is a "foolish whippersnapper" or a "doddering geezer"—both terms that demonstrate ageism in the young or old person who utters them. Scientists have evidence for both perspectives.

Shortly after the middle of the twentieth century, Nancy Bayley and Melita Oden (1955) analyzed the intelligence of adults who had been identified as child geniuses decades earlier. Bayley was an expert in intelligence testing. She knew that "invariable findings had indicated that most intellectual functions decrease after about 21 years of age" (Bayley, 1966, p. 117). Instead, she found that the IQ scores of these gifted individuals *increased* between ages 20 and 50.

Did their high childhood IQ protect them from age-related declines? To find out, Bayley retested a large group of adults who had been tested decades earlier as children. Their childhood intelligence varied, from way below average to way above, as would be expected in the general population. Their adult IQs varied as well, with most of the low ones still low and most of the high ones still high.

However, on this longitudinal study, many scored higher than their own IQ scores when they were children. Why did they gain, not lose, IQ during adulthood? The reason, Bayley suggested, is that cross-sectional research can be misleading because each cohort has unique life experiences. Longitudinal data are better.

That was welcome news for many scholars, who were growing older themselves. They were happy to realize that adults who were studied in the first part of the twentieth century often left school before eighth grade and had no technology to inform them of ideas, inventions, and innovations beyond their personal experience. It was unfair to compare the IQ scores of people who grew up decades earlier with those of contemporary 20-year-olds, almost all of whom attended high school.

Bruce Kaplan/CartoonStock

"I used to be innocent. Then I was naïve. Now I'm just dumb."

Powerful evidence that younger adults score higher because of more education, increased information, and better health, not because of age, comes from longitudinal research from many nations. Recent cohorts everywhere outscore previous ones. As you remember from Chapter 11, this is the *Flynn effect*.

However, longitudinal results might be inaccurate as well. Scholars note three reasons why people might seem smarter with age when really they were not:

1. Repeated testing provides practice, and that itself may improve scores.
2. Some participants move, or refuse retesting, or die. They tend to be the ones whose IQs are declining, while the more intelligent ones stay to be retested. That skews the study in favor of those who gain IQ.
3. Dramatic, unpredictable events (war, polio vaccine) and gradual changes (widespread computer use, nationwide cleaner air or chemicals in the food supply, changes in rates of drug addiction) make it hard to predict the future. This could produce IQ improvements or reductions, depending on specifics.

This possibility is suggested by data on longevity. The average life span of adults in the United States has declined slightly since 2015 (Murphy et al., 2018). The reason is said to be "deaths of despair"—for example, suicide, cirrhosis of the liver, fatal drug addiction, obesity (Muennig et al., 2018). The same psychological factors affect intelligence, so longitudinal studies may soon show declines.

New longitudinal data on the Flynn effect find that adults in developed nations are less likely to gain in IQ than adults were a few generations ago. In many nations, decline is already evident (Flynn & Shayer, 2018). Scandinavian nations were among the first to show the Flynn effect, and they now show declines.

Lower national IQ is less evident in developing nations, where past childhood deprivation experienced by older adults, and the recent benefits of better health and technology, favor the young. But Flynn himself worries that increased screen time, and the reduced cognitive challenges in many jobs, will soon reduce cognition in every nation (Flynn & Shayer, 2018).

Thus, whether a person of one age is smarter than another depends on how intelligence is measured and what the life experience of the person might be. People still hold opposing perspectives.

The Famous Seattle Study The best method to understand the effects of aging without the complications of historical change is to combine cross-sectional and longitudinal research, a strategy pioneered by a graduate student at the University of Washington in 1956.

To earn his Ph.D., K. Warner Schaie tested a cross section of 500 adults, aged 20 to 50, on five standard primary mental abilities Sternberg considered to be the foundation of intelligence: (1) verbal meaning (vocabulary), (2) spatial orientation, (3) inductive reasoning, (4) number ability, and (5) word fluency (rapid verbal associations). Cross-sectional scores showed age-related decline in all five abilities, as others had found before (Schaie, 1958).

Schaie decided to replicate the longitudinal gains that Bayley found (in Opposing Perspectives). He did more than that. He combined longitudinal and cross-sectional methods. Seven years later, he retested his initial participants and also tested a new group of people who were the same age that his earlier sample had been. Consequently, he could compare people not only to their own previous scores (longitudinal) but also to people currently as old as his original group had been when first tested, and others who were older or younger (cross-sectional).

Over his entire career, Schaie resisted and added a new group every seven years. Known as the **Seattle Longitudinal Study**, this was the first *cross-sequential* study of adult intelligence. Schaie confirmed and extended what others had found: Cross-sectional research shows declines, but longitudinal research shows improvement during adulthood (Schaie, 2005/2013). So, *g* varies more than others thought.

As **Figure 21.1** shows, Schaie found that each ability at each age has a distinct pattern. Men were initially better at number skills and women at verbal skills, but the two sexes grew closer over time. This reflected trends in the overall culture, which encouraged people of every gender to nurture all of their abilities.

The figure shows that some abilities increase over the years of adulthood. As many other scientists have found, vocabulary is particularly likely to increase. Schaie found that everyone declined by age 60 in at least one of their basic abilities, not until about age 70 did everyone decline from their earlier scores in all five skills.

Seattle Longitudinal Study The first cross-sequential study of adult intelligence. This study began in 1956 and is repeated every seven years.

Observation Quiz Which ability in which gender shows the steepest decline after age 60? (see answer, page 552)

FIGURE 21.1

Age Differences in Intellectual Abilities Cross-sectional data on intellectual abilities at various ages would show much steeper declines. Longitudinal research, in contrast, would show more notable rises. Because Schaie's research is cross-sequential, the trajectories it depicts are more revealing: None of the average scores for the five abilities at any age is above 55 or below 35, which means that the average older person still is able to function intellectually.

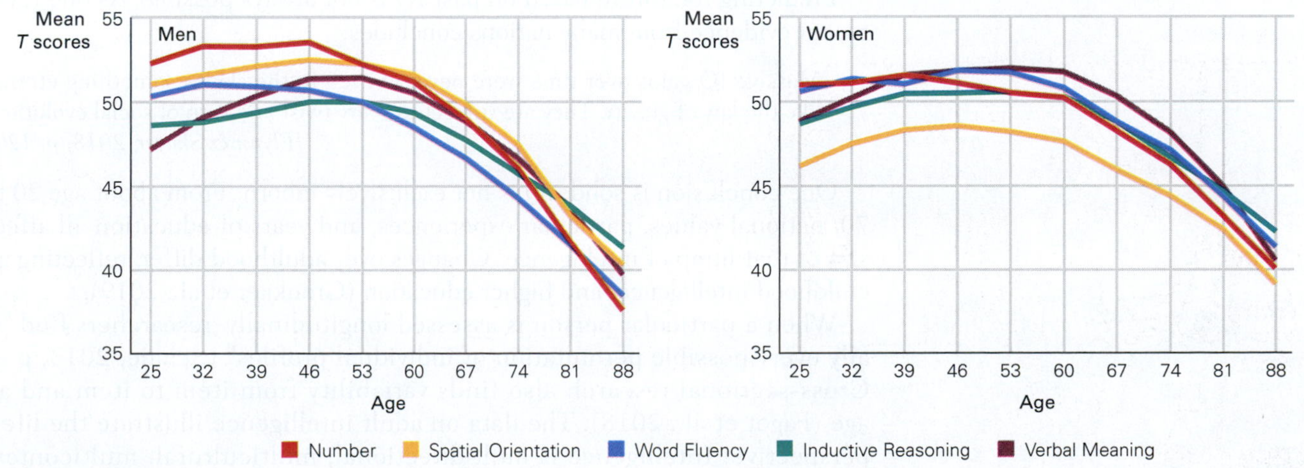

Data from Schaie, 2005, p. 116.

Especially for Older Brothers and Sisters If your younger siblings mock your ignorance of current TV shows and beat you at the latest video games, does that mean your intellect is fading? (see page 552)

Other researchers from many nations have found similar trends, although specifics differ. IQ scores typically increase, or are at least maintained, in adulthood, because performance on timed items declines but on verbal items increases (Salthouse, 2019). Individuals may show marked intellectual ups or downs. Some fade by middle age; others not until decades later (W. Johnson et al., 2014; Kremen et al., 2014).

Schaie discovered cohort changes that had been previously unrecognized. Each successive cohort (born at seven-year intervals from 1889 to 1973) scored higher in adulthood than did the previous generations in verbal memory and inductive reasoning. However, number ability (math) peaked for one cohort (those born in 1924) and fell in each later cohort until about 1970, when it stabilized (Schaie, 2005/2013).

Why this cohort (not age) decline in math? Probably education. The curriculum in schools changed: By the mid-twentieth century, reading, writing, and self-expression were emphasized, and math became less important. It also relates to the experience of adults. Scanners at stores, cash registers, and calculators on smartphones make math skills atrophy for current adults.

Other cohort effects include increases in female IQ, since many women entered the labor market. The reason? Jobs provide intellectual challenges. Overall, more decades of stable IQ for people of all genders before age-related decline (Schaie, 2005/2013). Older adults are now healthier, and that affects cognition.

Putting It All Together

Many studies using sophisticated designs and statistics have supplanted early cross-sectional, longitudinal, and cross-sequential studies. No study is perfect, because "no design can fully sanitize a study so as to solve the age-cohort-period identification problem" (Hertzog, 2010, p. 5). Cultures, eras, and individuals vary substantially regarding which cognitive abilities are nurtured and tested.

Longitudinal studies continue to show slight improvement in IQ over the decades of adulthood, with genes and experiences both significant. The fact that experience matters was proven, again, in a study of monozygotic twins, one who suffered a traumatic brain injury as a soldier and one who did not (Lyons et al., 2017). The ones with brain injury, decades after seemingly complete recovery, had lower average IQ than their identical twins.

Predicting the future based on past IQ is not always possible. As one review of recent evidence from many nations concludes:

> Massive IQ gains over time were never written in the sky as something eternal like the law of gravity. They are subject to every twist and turn of social evolution.
> *[Flynn & Shayer, 2018, p. 120]*

One conclusion is solid: IQ is not exclusively inborn. From about age 20 to age 70, national values, particular experiences, and years of education all affect the size of that lump of intelligence. Changes over adulthood differ, reflecting genes, childhood intelligence, and higher education (Grønkjær et al., 2019).

When a particular person is assessed longitudinally, researchers find "virtually every possible permutation of individual profiles" (Schaie, 2013, p. 497). Cross-sectional research also finds variability from item to item and age to age (Fagot et al., 2018). The data on adult intelligence illustrate the life-span perspective: Intelligence is multidirectional, multicultural, multicontextual, and plastic.

WHAT HAVE YOU LEARNED?

1. Many scientists have searched for the source of *g;* how successful have they been?
2. What does cross-sectional research on IQ throughout adulthood usually find?
3. What does longitudinal research on IQ throughout adulthood usually find?
4. How do historical changes affect the results of longitudinal research?
5. How does cross-sequential research control for cohort effects?
6. Why does IQ vary as much as it does?

Components of Intelligence: Many and Varied

Responding to all of these data, developmentalists seek patterns of cognitive gain and loss. It is mistaken to ask whether intelligence either increases or decreases with age; it does not move in lockstep. Individuals vary, as does each aspect of intelligence. For example, math slowdowns are usually apparent by age 40, but verbal ability usually keeps rising. Both of those patterns, however, depend on what the person does professionally.

We consider here only two proposals, one that posits two distinct abilities and the other, three. [**Life-Span Link:** There are many more formulations, notably Gardner's theory of nine intelligences, described in Chapter 11.]

Two Clusters of Intelligence

In the 1960s, a leading researcher, Raymond Cattell, teamed up with a promising graduate student, John Horn, to study intelligence tests. They concluded that adult intelligence is best understood by grouping various measures into two categories, which they called *fluid* and *crystallized*.

Fluid Intelligence As its name implies, **fluid intelligence** is like water, flowing to its own level no matter where it happens to be. Fluid intelligence is quick and flexible, enabling people to learn anything, even things that are unfamiliar and unconnected to what they already know. Curiosity, learning for the joy of it, solving abstract puzzles, and the thrill at discovery are marks of fluid intelligence.

fluid intelligence Those types of basic intelligence that make learning of all sorts quick and thorough. Abilities such as short-term memory, abstract thought, and speed of thinking are all usually considered part of fluid intelligence.

People who are high in fluid abilities are quick and flexible, drawing inferences, grasping relationships between concepts, with a large working memory. Questions that test fluid intelligence among Western adults might be:

What comes next in each of these two series?*

4 9 1 6 2 5 3
V X Z B D

Puzzles are often used to measure fluid intelligence, with bonus points for speedy solutions (as on many IQ tests). Immediate recall—of nonsense words, of numbers, of a sentence just read—is one indicator because working memory is crucial for fluid intelligence, especially in timed tests (Singh et al., 2018). However, whether working memory is the underlying cause for high fluid intelligence, or merely a correlate, is still questioned (Burgoyne et al., 2019).

*The correct answers are **6** and **F**. The clue is to think of multiplication (squares) and the alphabet: Some series are much more difficult to complete.

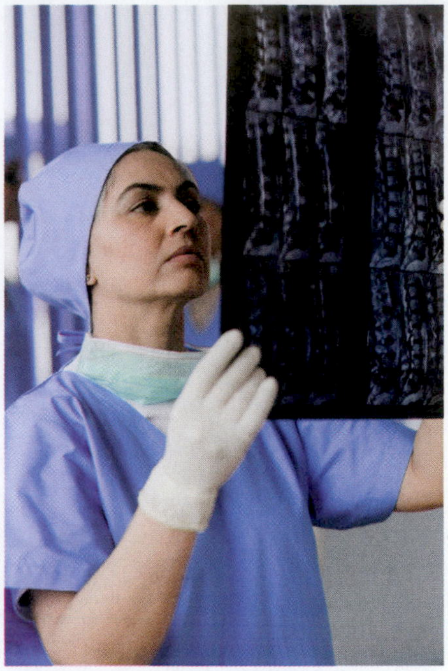

Photosindia com/AGE Fotostock

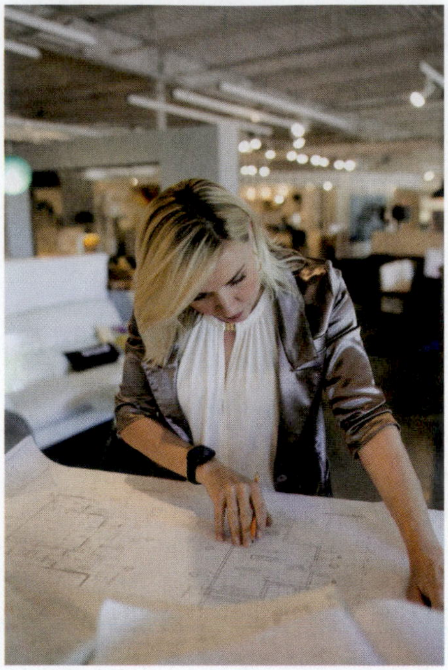

Hero Images/Getty Images

Think Before Acting Both of these adults need to combine fluid intelligence and crystallized intelligence, insight and intuition, logic and experience. One *(left)* is a surgeon, studying X-rays before picking up her scalpel. The other *(right)* appears to be an architect, using working memory and abstract reasoning.

Crystallized Intelligence The accumulation of facts, information, and knowledge as a result of education and experience is called **crystallized intelligence**. The size of a person's vocabulary, the knowledge of chemical formulas, and long-term memory for dates in history all indicate crystallized intelligence. Tests designed to measure this intelligence might include questions like these:

> What is the meaning of the word *eleemosynary*?
> Who was Descartes?
> Explain the difference between a tangent and a triangle.
> Why does the city of Peking no longer exist?

Although such questions seem to measure achievement more than aptitude, these two are connected, especially in adulthood. Intelligent adults read widely, think deeply, and remember what they learn—so their achievement reflects their aptitude. Crystallized intelligence is an outgrowth of fluid intelligence.

Thus someone who is high in fluid intelligence is likely to become high in crystallized intelligence. Neurological research finds that network connections in the brain underlie both kinds of intelligence (Barbey, 2018).

crystallized intelligence Those types of intellectual ability that reflect accumulated learning. Vocabulary and general information are examples. Some developmental psychologists think crystallized intelligence increases with age, while fluid intelligence declines.

Both Together Now To reflect the total picture of a person's intellectual aptitude, both fluid and crystallized intelligence must be measured. Scores on items measuring fluid intelligence decrease with age, whereas scores on items measuring crystallized intelligence increase.

This distinction is useful, not only for typically developing individuals but also for those with intellectual disability (I. Chen et al., 2017). They also show reduced fluid and increased crystallized intelligence over time.

For everyone, combining these two types of intelligence makes total IQ scores fairly steady from age 30 to age 70. Although brain slowdown begins at age 20 or so, it is rarely apparent until massive declines in fluid intelligence affect crystallized intelligence. Only then do overall IQ scores fall.

Three Forms of Intelligence

Robert Sternberg (1988, 2015) agrees that a single intelligence score is misleading. As first mentioned in Chapter 11 and alluded to in the opening anecdote of this chapter, Sternberg proposed three fundamental forms of intelligence: analytic, creative, and practical (see **Table 21.1**).

analytic intelligence A form of intelligence that involves such mental processes as abstract planning, strategy selection, focused attention, and information processing, as well as verbal and logical skills.

Analytic intelligence includes all of the mental processes that foster academic proficiency by making efficient learning, remembering, and thinking possible. Thus, it draws on abstract planning, strategy selection, focused attention, and information processing, as well as on verbal and logical skills.

Strengths in those areas of analytic intelligence are valuable in emerging adulthood, particularly in college and in graduate school. Multiple-choice tests and brief essays that call forth remembered information, with only one right answer, indicate analytic intelligence.

TABLE 21.1

Sternberg's Three Forms of Intelligence

	Analytic Intelligence	Creative Intelligence	Practical Intelligence
Mental processes	• Abstract planning • Strategizing • Focused attention • Verbal skills • Logic	• Imagination • Appreciation of the unexpected or unusual • Originality • Vision	• Adaptive actions • Understanding and assessing daily problems • Applied skills and knowledge
Valued for	• Analyzing • Learning and understanding • Remembering • Thinking	• Intellectual flexibility • Originality • Future hopes	• Adaptability • Concrete knowledge • Cooperation • Family interactions
Indicated by	• Multiple-choice tests • Brief essays • Recall of information	• Inventiveness • Innovation • Resourcefulness • Ingenuity	• Performance in real situations • Street smarts • Tacit intelligence

creative intelligence A form of intelligence that involves the capacity to be intellectually flexible and innovative.

practical intelligence The intellectual skills used in everyday problem solving. (Sometimes called *tacit intelligence*.)

Creative intelligence is flexible and innovative, divergent rather than convergent, valuing the unexpected, imaginative, and unusual rather than standard and conventional answers. Sternberg developed tests of creative intelligence that include writing a short story titled "The Octopus's Sneakers" or planning an advertising campaign for a new doorknob. Those with many novel ideas earn high scores.

Practical intelligence is adaptive. This capacity includes an accurate grasp of the expectations and needs of other people and understanding what skills are needed to meet whatever challenges appear. Then people who are high in practical intelligence can use their social insights and skills to accomplish whatever is needed.

Practical intelligence is sometimes called *tacit intelligence* because it is not obvious on tests (Cianciolo & Sternberg, 2018). Instead, it comes from "the school of hard knocks" and is sometimes called "street smarts," not "book smarts."

The Three Intelligences in Adulthood The benefits of practical intelligence are obvious when thinking about adults' cognition. Few adults need to define obscure words or deduce the next item in a number sequence (analytic intelligence), and few need to compose new music, restructure local government, or invent an innovative gadget (creative intelligence). Ideally, those few have found a niche for themselves and have found people with practical intelligence to implement their analytic or creative ideas.

By contrast, almost every adult needs practical intelligence to maintain a home; advance a career; manage money; sift information (from media, mail, the Internet, friends); decide what habits to maintain, stop, or begin; and address the emotional needs of lovers, relatives, neighbors, and colleagues.

Schaie found that scores on tests of practical intelligence were steadier than scores on other kinds of tests from age 20 to age 70. There was no notable decrement, in part because these skills are needed and therefore practiced throughout life (Schaie, 2005/2013).

Walter McBride/Getty Images Entertainment/Getty Images

Intelligence in Action Lin-Manuel Miranda created and starred in *Hamilton: An American Musical,* that has been the hottest ticket on Broadway for five years. His creative intelligence is obvious, but his analytic and practical intelligence are also part of his success.

Without practical intelligence, a solution found by analytic intelligence might fail because people resist academic brilliance as unrealistic and elite, as the term *ivory tower* implies. Some of the best examples come from the history of medicine.

For example, the idea that stomach ulcers were caused by bacteria was not believed until an Australian internist used his practical intelligence to convince people, specifically by drinking infectious broth that made him sick. (He then took an antibiotic.) Likewise, many successful cancer treatments were first tried by creative doctors but rejected by everyone else (Cornwall, 2013). Ideas that arise from creative or analytic intelligence are often rejected as ridiculous and weird rather than serious and sensible—until someone adds practical intelligence.

Imagine that you are a business manager, a school principal, a political leader, or a parent trying to change routine practices—perhaps for a good reason, because the old way was inefficient or destructive. If the new procedures are not compatible with the group's culture, and are misunderstood, then the workers, teachers, voters, or family members will misinterpret and resist. Without practical intelligence, innovation fails.

No abstract test can assess practical intelligence because context is crucial. For instance, with prospective employees, a hiring committee might describe an actual situation and ask how the applicant would handle it. Because practical intelligence is evident on the job, many professions have probationary periods, internships, and apprenticeships.

Consider the strengths and guard against the limitations of each type of intelligence. Choosing which intelligence to use takes wisdom, which Sternberg considers the fourth ingredient of successful intelligence. He wrote:

> One needs creativity to generate novel ideas, analytical intelligence to ascertain whether they are good ideas, practical intelligence to implement the ideas and persuade others of their value, and wisdom to ensure that the ideas help reach a common good.
>
> *[Sternberg, 2012, p. 21]*

[**Life-Span Link:** Wisdom is discussed in Chapter 24.]

Age and Culture Which kind of intelligence is most needed and valued depends partly on a person's age and partly on their national context. Analytic intelligence is usually valued in North American high schools and colleges, as students try to remember and analyze various ideas. Students who are considered "smart" usually have analytic intelligence, but that is not enough in adulthood.

Creative intelligence is prized if life circumstances change and new challenges arise; it is much more valued in some cultures and countries than in others. In times of social chaos and change, or in certain professions (such as the arts), creativity is a better predictor of accomplishment than is IQ.

However, creativity can be *too* innovative, causing creative people to be ignored, scorned, or, in some nations, killed. Many creative geniuses—Vincent Van Gogh and Igor Stravinsky, for example—were unrecognized in their lifetime.

Creative individuals are critical of tradition and therefore not always appreciated. Analytic individuals might be seen as absentminded, head-in-the-clouds dreamers. Practical intelligence might be most useful. Yet without wisdom, practical intelligence could be used for evil as well as for good.

Cultural differences are evident in every kind of cognition. Remember Gardner's nine intelligences? Currently in the United States, linguistic and mathematical intelligence are the core of most tests of aptitude and achievement. But in some other nations, the ability to dance (kinesthetic intelligence), or to grow herbs (naturalistic intelligence), or to pray (existential intelligence) might be essential.

THINK CRITICALLY: If an adult lived in another nation, would that person be smarter? And, because of that, would the adult live longer and healthier?

John M Lund Photography Inc/DigitalVision/Getty Images

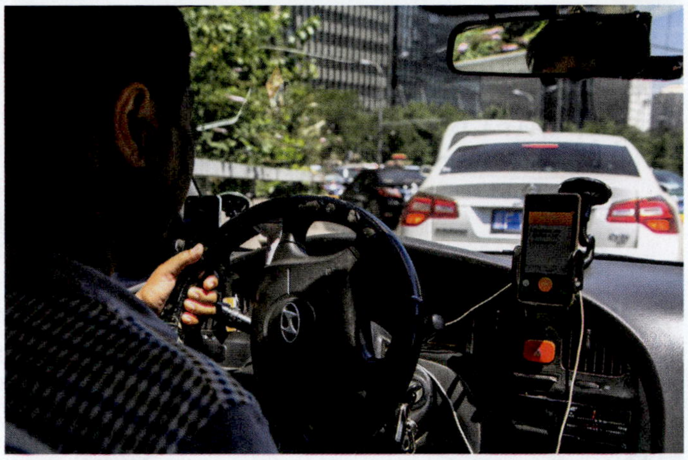

Zhang Peng/LightRocket/Getty Images

What Kind of Intelligence? Adult intelligence is difficult to assess because context is crucial. What kind of intelligence would you need to successfully herd camels in Saudi Arabia, or to drive a taxi using an app that connects you to customers in Beijing?

Worldwide, people in some nations seem extraordinarily adept at intrapersonal and interpersonal intelligence (India? Japan?).

Be careful with any definition of intelligence. Sternberg himself argues that distorted ideas of intelligence are likely to lead us astray (Sternberg, 2018). He cites environmental destruction, unregulated guns, and chemicals in food and water as examples of "smart" adults producing disaster.

Observation Quiz What signs of practical intelligence are apparent in the camel herder? (see answer, page 552) ↑

WHAT HAVE YOU LEARNED?

1. Why would a person prefer to have greater crystallized intelligence than fluid intelligence?
2. Why would a person prefer to have greater fluid intelligence than crystallized intelligence?
3. How might you convince your professors that you are smart, and what type of intelligence is that?
4. How might you convince your neighbors to compost their food scraps, and what type of intelligence does that involve?
5. What tests could measure creative intelligence?
6. Which intelligence do you think is undervalued in your community?

Selective Gains and Losses

Aging neurons, cultural pressures, historical conditions, and past education all affect adult cognition. None of these can be controlled directly by an individual. Nonetheless, adults make crucial choices about intellectual development, deciding how to develop their minds.

Optimization with Compensation

Paul and Margret Baltes (1990) developed a theory called **selective optimization with compensation** to describe the "general process of systematic functioning" (Baltes, 2003, p. 25), by which people maintain a balance in their lives as they grow older. They believe that people seek to *optimize* their development, *selecting* the best way to *compensate* for physical and cognitive losses, becoming more proficient at activities they want to perform well.

selective optimization with compensation The theory, developed by Paul and Margaret Baltes, that people try to maintain a balance in their lives by looking for the best way to compensate for physical and cognitive losses and to become more proficient in activities they can already do well.

Bradford Veley/Cartoonstock

What's the Point? This time, you write the caption! (Use creative intelligence.)

Selective optimization with compensation applies to every aspect of life, ranging from choosing friends to playing baseball. Each adult seeks to maximize gains and minimize losses, practicing some abilities and ignoring others.

Choices are critical, because any ability can be enhanced or diminished, depending on how, when, and why a person uses it. It is possible to "teach an old dog new tricks," but learning requires that adults *want* to learn those new tricks.

As Baltes and Baltes (1990) explain, selective optimization means that each adult selects certain aspects of intelligence to optimize and neglects the rest. If the ignored aspects happen to be the ones measured on intelligence tests, then IQ scores will fall, even if the adult's selection improves (optimizes) other aspects of intellect.

The brain is plastic over the entire life span. We develop new dendrites and activation sequences, adjusting to whatever we choose to learn (Karmiloff-Smith, 2010).

Multitasking One example of selective optimization is multitasking, which becomes harder with every passing decade. The problem is that focusing attention on one task is more difficult when two tasks are done simultaneously or when repeated switches are required from one task to another and back again. Actually, multitasking slows down everyone of every age, but it worsens after age 40 because the brain's switching slows down (Lin et al., 2016).

Cell phone use is an example. Many adults use cell phones when walking on the street, sitting in class, or cooking dinner at home. Yet each of those tasks involves more forgetfulness because of multitasking. That may be why those who use cell phones extensively are vulnerable to serious depression and anxiety (Coyne et al., 2019).

Problems became obvious when people drive cars while talking on a cell phone. That is dangerous for everyone but particularly for older drivers, because as the brain focuses on the conversation, the neurological shift needed to react to a darting pedestrian is slower.

Some jurisdictions require drivers to use hands-free phones, as if the distraction originates in the arms. These misguided laws have not reduced traffic accidents because the multitasking brain, not the arms, is the problem.

Some say that passenger conversation is as distracting as cell phone talk, but that is not true: Years of practice have taught adult passengers (though not young children) when to stop talking so that the driver can focus on the road. If passengers do not quiet down on their own, experienced drivers stop listening and replying because they know they must concentrate.

However, even knowing that concentration is needed may not be enough. In one experiment, older and younger drivers in a virtual car were instructed to follow a car that sometimes slowed down and sometimes speeded up. Periodically, they were asked to type three numbers (as if they were adjusting the radio) or they were asked a question (as if they were on a cell phone). Drivers of all ages sometimes drove over the median, but the older adults did so more often—and sometimes drove off the road (Wechsler et al., 2018).

This is why statements such as "I can't do everything at once" and "Don't rush me" are more often spoken by older adults than by teenagers. Adults compensate for slower thinking by selecting one task at a time. Resources within the brain are increasingly limited with age, but compensation may allow optimal functioning.

CHAPTER APP 21

Freedom

IOS:
https://tinyurl.com/y6y6o4u2

ANDROID:
https://tinyurl.com/y58wyjv9

RELEVANT TOPIC:
Multitasking and concentration in adulthood

This app and Web site blocker for Mac, Windows, Android, and iOS aims to help adults reclaim focus and productivity. Simply select distracting and time-consuming apps from a pre-made blocklist or create your own custom blocklist to temporarily block as many apps as you would like, at a specified time and/or for a certain length of time. Users report gaining an average of 2.5 hours of productive time each day.

One father tried to explain this concept to his son as follows:

I told my son: triage
Is the main art of aging.
At midlife, everything
Sings of it. In law
Or healing, learning or play,
Buying or selling—above all
In remembering—the rule is
Cut losses, let profits ring.
Specifics rise and fall
By selection.

[Hamill, 1991]

Expert Cognition

Another way to describe selective optimization is to say that everyone develops *expertise,* becoming a selective expert. Adults are not restrained, as most children and adolescents are, by the demand to do and learn everything: physics and poetry, basketball and baseball, handwriting and texting.

Instead, adults specialize in activities that are personally meaningful—anything from car repair to gourmet cooking, from illness diagnosis to fly fishing. As people develop expertise in some areas, they ignore others.

For example, in a well-functioning domestic partnership, each partner does certain tasks. Traditionally, wives prepared meals and husbands took care of the car. Currently, roles may be reversed and some tasks are shared, but it is rare for partners to each do the same tasks, alternating days instead of activities. People gravitate to what they do best or like most. For instance, one of my daughters does not mind rinsing dishes and putting them in the dishwasher, but she dislikes unloading the dishwasher and putting the dishes away. Her husband does that.

Those who live alone also are selective, doing what they prefer. For example, everyone watches only a few of the dozens of channels on television, deletes hundreds of unread emails every day, avoids some sports contests or concerts that others wait in line for hours to attend, or set their alarm to phone the minute that tickets are available to what they prefer.

Colin McConnell/Getty Images

ADEK BERRY/Getty Images

Same Situation, Far Apart: Don't Be Afraid The police officer in Toronto collecting slugs and the violinist in Jakarta collecting donations have both spent years refining their skills. Many adults would fear being that close to a murder victim or that close to thousands of rushing commuters, but both men have learned to practice their vocation no matter where they are. They are now experts: The cop discovered that two guns were used, and the musician earns more than $5 a day (the average for street musicians in Indonesia).

expert Someone with specialized skills and knowledge developed around a particular activity or area.

Defining Expertise An **expert**, as cognitive scientists define it, is not necessarily someone with rare and outstanding proficiency (Dall'Alba, 2018). Although sometimes the term *expert* connotes an extraordinary genius, to researchers it means more — and less — than that. Expertise is not innate, although it may begin with inherited abilities that are later developed (Hambrick et al., 2016).

Culture and context guide people in this process. Who mails letters and cards with distinctive and legible handwriting? Adults born 90 years ago. The reason: In childhood they practiced penmanship for hours, became experts in it, and maintained that expertise. Today's schools, and today's children, make other choices.

Few young adults mail handwritten letters, but virtually all read and text, unlike a century ago when many adults were illiterate. Indeed, some become experts at it: In 2014, one teen from Brazil took only 18 seconds to text "The razor-toothed piranhas of the genera *Serrasalmus* and *Pygocentrus* are the most ferocious freshwater fish in the world. In reality they seldom attack a human."

Whether such feats count as expertise is debatable, but it is evident that adults choose to specialize in some tasks while ignoring others. Expertise has become increasingly important as societies become more complex: Adults no longer do everything for themselves; they find experts to do it for them.

After time and effort, experts are transformed by knowledge, practice, and experience — they enter a higher league than most people. The quality, not just the quantity, of their cognition is advanced. Expert thought is (1) intuitive, (2) automatic, (3) strategic, and (4) flexible, as we now describe.

Intuitive Novices follow formal procedures and rules. Experts rely more on past experiences and immediate contexts; this makes their actions more intuitive and less stereotyped than those of the novice. The role of experience and intuition is evident, for example, during surgery. Outsiders might think medicine is straightforward, but experts understand the reality:

> Hospitals are filled with varieties of knives and poisons. Every time a medication is prescribed, there is potential for an unintended side effect. In surgery, collateral damage is inherent. External tissue must be cut to allow internal access so that a diseased organ may be removed, or some other manipulation may be performed to return the patient to better health.
>
> *[Dominguez, 2001, p. 287]2016*

Experts are usually unable to articulate reasons and criteria for their intuition, or why they know what they know (Greco, 2014). That is what makes the expert intuitive. When expert chefs are asked to describe how they conceived of their extraordinarily sumptuous dishes, they speak of sudden insight, not step-by-step analysis (Stierand & Dörfler, 2016).

Sometimes intuition is portrayed as opposed to logic and evidence and, therefore, as inferior. But that is not necessarily true (Wieten, 2018). Expert intuition incorporates past experience, seeming to seem to leap over logic — sometimes with excellent results, sometime not.

Automatic The complex action and skill required for many tasks become routine for experts, making it appear that most aspects of the task are performed instinctively. Experts process incoming information quickly, analyze it efficiently, and then act in well-rehearsed ways that make their efforts seem unconscious. In fact, some automatic actions are no longer accessible to the conscious mind.

For example, adults are much better at tying their shoelaces than children are (adults can do it in the dark, without thinking about their movements), but they are much worse at describing how they do it. When experts think, they engage in "automatic weighting" of various nonverbalized factors. The automatic aspect of

A VIEW FROM SCIENCE

Who Wins in Soccer?

One experiment that studied the relationship between expertise and intuition involved 486 college students who were asked to predict the winners of soccer games not yet played. The students who were avid fans (the experts) made better predictions when they had a few minutes of unconscious thought than when they had the same number of minutes to mull over their choice (see **Figure 21.2**). Those who didn't care much about soccer (the nonexperts) did worse overall, but they did especially poorly when they had time to use unconscious intuition (Dijksterhuis et al., 2009).

The details of this experiment are intriguing. For 20 seconds, all participants were shown a computer screen with four soon-to-be-played soccer matches and were asked to predict the winners. One-third of the predictions were made immediately, one-third were made after two minutes of conscious thought, and one-third were made after two minutes when *only* unconscious thought could occur—because people assigned to that group were required to calculate a series of mind-taxing math questions during those two minutes.

Nonexperts did no better than chance. They did worse after thinking about their answer, especially when the thought was unconscious. Perhaps the stress of doing math interfered.

By contrast, the predictions of the experts were not much better than those of the nonexperts when they guessed immediately, a little better when they had two minutes to think, and best of all after unconscious thought. Apparently, the experts' knowledge of soccer helped them most when they were thinking of something else.

This experiment has led to many follow-up studies, including in medicine, where intuition sometimes finds a diagnosis that a textbook would not. A recent meta-analysis cautioned against applying this finding too broadly: Medical knowledge, and thoughtful analysis, may lead to better conclusions than intuition (Vadillo et al., 2015). Hopefully, your doctor is expert enough to realize that.

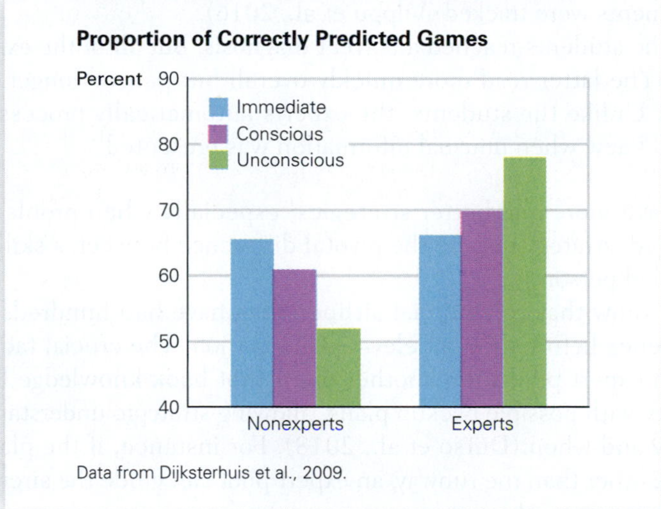

FIGURE 21.2

If You Don't Know, Don't Think! Undergraduates at the University of Amsterdam were asked to predict winners of four World Cup soccer matches in one of three conditions: (1) immediate—as soon as they saw the names of the nations that were competing in each of the contests, (2) conscious—after thinking for two minutes about their answers, and (3) unconscious—after two minutes of solving distracting math tasks. As you can see, the experts were better at predicting winners after unconscious processing, but the nonexperts became less accurate when they thought about their answers, either consciously or unconsciously.

expertise is particularly evident in medicine, when experienced specialists diagnose an illness within seconds, unlike the newly minted doctor (Norman et al., 2018).

Chess players have been studied intensely, in part because international rankings define levels of expertise. The general finding is that, although chess players show age-related decrements and slowdowns in general tests of cognition, age seems to have little effect on chess ability. This is particularly apparent for speedy recognition that the king was threatened: Older experts do that almost as quickly as younger adults (in a fraction of a second) despite steep, age-related declines on standard tests (Gobert & Charness, 2018).

If you are an experienced driver and try to teach someone else to drive, then you can see automaticity in action. Excellent drivers who are inexperienced instructors find it hard to recognize or verbalize things that have become automatic—such as anticipating the movements of pedestrians and cyclists on the far side of the road, or feeling the gears shift on an incline, or hearing the tires lose traction on a bit of sand. Yet such factors differentiate the expert from the novice.

This may explain why, despite powerful motivation, quicker reactions, and better vision, teenagers have three times the rate of fatal car accidents than adults over age 25 do. Sometimes teenage drivers deliberately take risks (speeding, running a red light, drinking, and so on), but often they simply misjudge and misperceive conditions that a more experienced driver would automatically notice.

The same gap between knowledge and instruction occurs when a computer expert tries to teach a novice what to do, as I know myself when my daughters try to help me with the finer points of Microsoft Excel. They are unable to verbalize what they know, although they are proficient when they work. It is much easier to click the mouse or do the keystroke oneself than to teach what has become automatic.

When something—such as an audience, a stressor, or too much conscious thought—interferes with automatic processing, the result may be clumsy performance. This is thought to be the problem when some experienced athletes "choke under pressure"—their automatic actions are hijacked. The most effective solution is not more thought but more automaticity, such as practicing a pre-performance routine that can be automatically accessed during a game (Gröpel & Mesagno, 2017).

In a final example, medical students and doctors were asked to diagnose a difficult case of cardiac failure and pulmonary embolus. They read details of the case while their eye movements were tracked (Vilppu et al., 2016).

Less than half of the students reached a correct diagnosis, but all of the experienced doctors did. The latter read more quickly overall but paused longer on particular sentences. Unlike the students, the experts automatically processed some information and knew when unusual information was presented.

Strategic Experts have more and better strategies, especially when problems are unexpected. Indeed, strategy may be the pivotal difference between a skilled person and an unskilled person.

It is reassuring to know that commercial airline pilots have had hundreds of hours of flight experience before they are elevated to that job. The crucial factor that differentiates an expert pilot from another one is not book knowledge but experienced familiarity with possible backup plans, allowing strategic understanding of which to apply and when (Durso et al., 2018). For instance, if the plane must land somewhere other than the runway, an expert pilot can guide the aircraft to a safety on a field, or even on the water.

A strategy used by expert team leaders in both the military and civilian arenas is ongoing communication, especially during slow times. Therefore, when stress builds, no team member misinterprets previously rehearsed plans, commands, and requirements. Expert teams include individuals from many backgrounds, but they all have learned to work together when need be (Sonesh et al., 2018).

The ability to plan ahead is evident in experts of many kinds. Writers, for instance, need to plan what they want to say before they begin putting words on paper (Kellogg, 2018). Likewise, you have witnessed the same phenomenon in expert professors: At the beginning of the semester they institute routines and policies, strategies that avoid problems later in the term. They also are able to change the plan on the fly if the class needs it, which leads to the final point.

Strategies need updating as situations change—and no chess game, or flight, or class is exactly like another. The monthly fire drill required by some schools, the standard lecture given by some professors, and the pat safety instructions read by airline attendants before takeoff become less effective over time.

I recently heard a flight attendant precede his standard talk with, "For those of you who have not ridden in an automobile since 1960, this is how you buckle a seat belt," a good strategy! In that preflight monologue, I listened.

The superior strategies of the expert permit selective optimization with compensation. In a detailed study of two music students, both of them pianists with many years of training, strategy was a crucial difference (McPherson et al., 2019). Before a practice session, the students were asked for their goals in the practice.

One student applied strategies that were consistent with her goal for the practice session, which was to learn a new étude. "It's a new étude, so I'm playing it slow. Trying to improve technique. Really slow practice, trying not to lift the fingers too high."

The other student had no apparent strategy. She said about practicing: "That's what I'm here to do, to achieve. That's it." The former student, after a semester, was rated in the top 5 percent in her playing; the latter was in the bottom 5 percent. A detailed description of these two emphasized the importance of planning ahead, and analyzing it afterward. That's strategy.

Flexible Finally, perhaps because they are intuitive, automatic, and strategic, experts are also flexible. That may be the most important of all. The expert artist, musician, chef, or scientist is creative and curious, deliberately experimenting and enjoying the unexpected (Csikszentmihalyi, 2013).

Remember Pavlov (Chapter 2)? He already had won the Nobel Prize when he noticed his dogs' reaction before they were fed. His expertise made him notice, then investigate, and eventually develop insights that opened a new perspective in psychology.

In the same way, experts in all walks of life adapt to individual cases and exceptions. An expert chef will adjust ingredients, temperature, technique, and timing as a dish develops, tasting to see whether a little more spice is needed, seldom following a recipe exactly.

Standards are high: Some cooks throw food in the garbage rather than serve a dish that many people would happily eat. Expert chess players, auto mechanics, and violinists are similarly aware of nuances that might escape the novice.

Travis Dove/The New York Times/Redux

Expertise Illustrated Vivian Howard is chef and creator of Chef and the Farmer, a North Carolina restaurant that gained rave reviews and national attention.

Observation Quiz What do you see that signifies an expert chef? (see answer, page 552) ↑

In the field of education, best practices for the educator now emphasize flexibility and strategy, as each group of students has distinct and often erroneous beliefs. It is not helpful to simply teach the right answers; flexibility requires matching the instruction to the individual students, discovering what learning is needed (Ford & Yore, 2012).

Flexibility includes knowing which particular skills are needed for expertise in each profession. For example, repeated practice is needed in typing, sports, and games, but in some other fields, practice can make the product stale rather than smooth.

Human survival may have depended on the brain's flexibility. Unlike our primate relatives, who share most genes with us, the "plasticity of evolved cognitive structures" allowed the expertise needed for humans to thrive (Winegard et al., 2018). Two remarkable human traits are the result of this neurological flexibility.

1. Humans adjusted to climate, each group developing the expertise needed for life in the Arctic, the desert, the islands, or the forests. Food, shelter, and child care are radically different in each of these places; each community has experts who teach the young what they need to know.
2. The survival of humanity depends on cooperative relationships with other humans, not only with family and neighbors but also with other nations. That requires another kind of expertise, the ability to adjust to a wide range of policies and practices.

macmillan learning

In **VIDEO: Expertise in Adulthood: An Expert Discusses His Work,** Kenneth Davis explains his research on how the neurotransmitter acetylcholine affects memory.

Expertise, Age, and Experience

The relationship between expertise and age is not straightforward (Krampe & Charness, 2018). One essential requirement for expertise is time, both hours of practice and years of maturity.

Some researchers think practice must be extensive, several hours a day for at least 10 years (Charness et al., 1996; Ericsson, 1996). We now know that each form of expertise has particular practice requirements. For example, in music, violinists need more practice to become proficient than singers do; in medicine, neurosurgeons need more practice than geriatric nurses; among political leaders, presidents need more preparation than school board members.

Of course, the latter of each of these pairs also benefit from years of practice, but they can become experts without years of learning. Circumstances, training, genes, ability, practice, and age all affect expertise, which means that experts in one specific field are often quite inexpert in other areas.

Examples from Various Professions An interesting example comes from perfumers: They need an acute sense of smell as they seek to develop new scents. Although the sense of smell typically declines with age, this is not so for perfumers. Experts outdid younger nonexperts: They had significantly developed those parts of the brain that were attuned to scents (Delon-Martin et al., 2013).

Expertise may counteract some effects of aging. As you read earlier in this chapter, the young have an advantage when speed is needed, but they are less adept at vocabulary and communication. This illustrates a general conclusion from research on cognitive plasticity: Experienced adults often use selective optimization with compensation, thus becoming expert. In many workplaces, the best employees may be the older, more experienced ones—if they want to do their best.

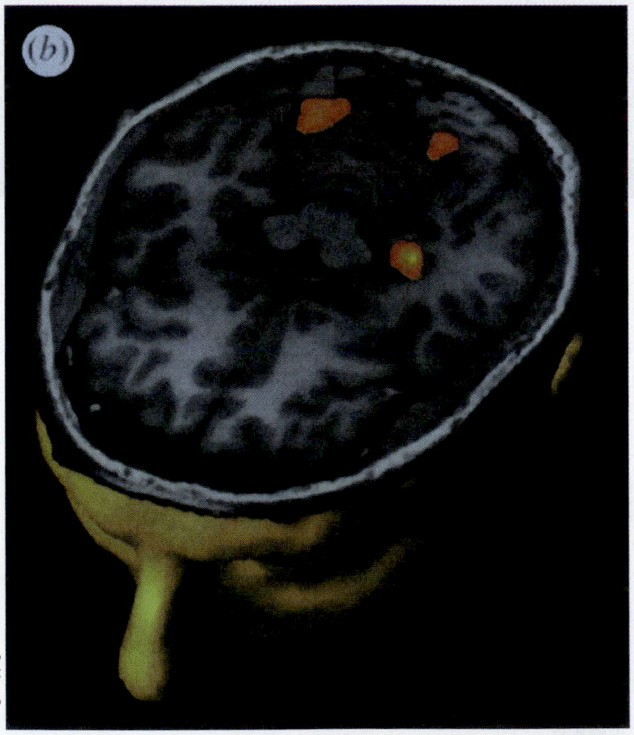

Red Means Go! The red shows the activated brain areas in London taxi drivers as they navigated the busy London streets. Not only were these areas more active than the same areas in the average person's brain, but they also had more dendrites. In addition, the longer a cabby had been driving, the more brain growth was evident. This research confirms plasticity, implying that we all could develop new skills, not only by remembering but also by engaging in activities that change the very structures of our brains.

The expertise of employees of various ages creates what is called the *management paradox:* Investing in teaching employees new skills and knowledge might make them more likely to be sought by other firms, so the investment pays off for the worker and for a rival, not for the employer who provided it. The solution to that paradox is not to withhold training, but to increase opportunities for promotion within the company to "keep the expert," as a study of 2,137 employees advocates (De Vos et al., 2017).

For many aspects of decision making, experience gives older adults an advantage. Losses in speed may require adjustment, of course. One pianist deliberately slowed down on some parts in order to make the fast parts seem faster. Expert chess players under 30 have a slight advantage in rapidly assessing moves, but adults over age 50 maintain steady expertise if they take a few moments more to think.

One final example of the relationship between age and job effectiveness comes from an occupation familiar to all of us: driving a taxi. This is not an easy job. In major cities, taxi drivers must find the best route (factoring in traffic, construction, time of day, and many other details) while knowing where new passengers are likely to be found and how to relate to customers, some of whom might want to talk, others not.

Research in England—where taxi drivers "have to learn the layout of 25,000 streets in London and the locations of thousands of places of interest, and pass stringent examinations" (Woollett et al., 2009, p. 1407)—found not only that the drivers became more expert with time but also that their brains adjusted to the need for particular knowledge. Some parts of their brains (areas dedicated to spatial representation) were more extensive and active than those of an average person (Woollett et al., 2009). On ordinary IQ tests, the taxi drivers' scores were average, but their expertise was apparent in navigating London.

Expert Women This discussion of expertise has focused so far on occupations (surgeons, musicians, taxi drivers) that once had far more male than female workers. In recent years, three important shifts have occurred that add to this topic.

First, more women are educated than before. As you learned in Chapter 18, in the United States and many other nations, women are more likely to attend college than men are. This has changed entire societies and millions of brains.

For example, the number of people who die in a disaster does not correlate with the strength of the disaster (the force of the hurricane, the earthquake, the terrorist attack) as much as with the number of educated women in the community.

This was found in a meta-analysis of 167 nations (Lutz et al., 2014). Educated women built safer houses, stockpiled supplies, cared for physical and mental health, heard and understood warnings on various devices. All of this required cognition, quite apart from other measures of adult success, such as income or education. (Lutz et al., 2014, p. 1061).

The second change is that more women are working in occupations traditionally reserved for men. Remember from Chapter 4 that Virginia Apgar, when she earned her M.D. in 1933, was told she could not be a surgeon because only men were surgeons. Fortunately for the survival of millions of newborns, she did not quit hospital medicine.

Today that sexist assumption has changed; half of the new M.D.s in the United States are women, including thousands of surgeons (see **Figure 21.3**). More generally, most college women expect to have careers, husbands, and children. Thus, occupational expertise is more gender-neutral.

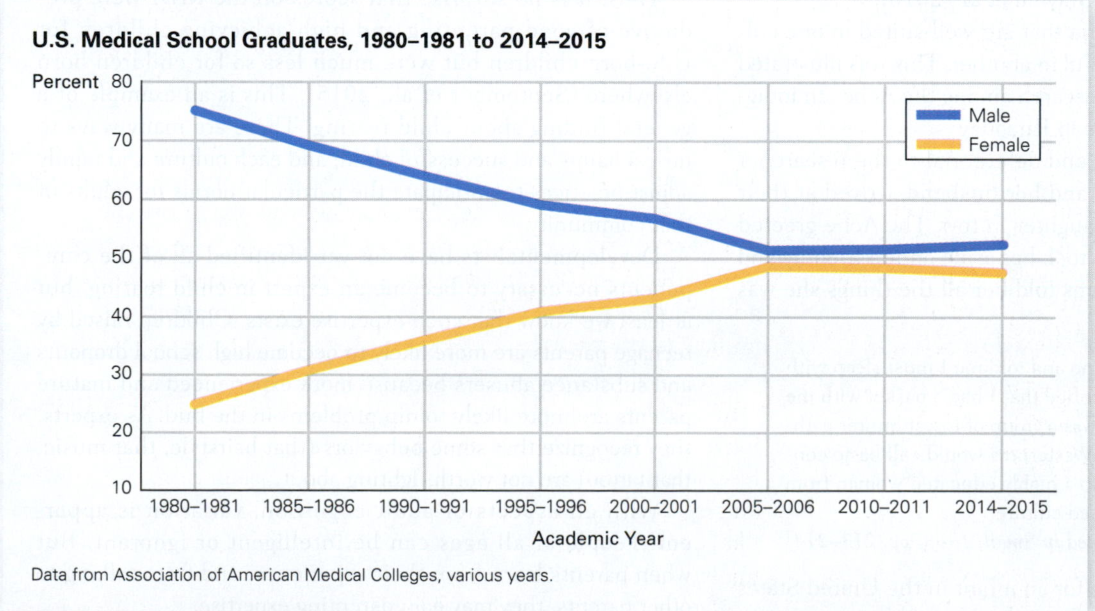

FIGURE 21.3

Expect a Woman Next time you hear "The doctor will see you now," the physician is as likely to be a woman as a man—unless the doctor is over age 40.

Especially for Prospective Parents
In terms of the intellectual challenge, what type of intelligence is most needed for effective parenthood? (see response, page 552)

The third major shift is that so called "women's work" has also become gender neutral. In earlier generations, women sometimes said they were "just a housewife," even though their domestic work included caring for the biological, cognitive, and psychosocial needs of several children. Recently, however, the importance of child care is increasingly recognized, and men as well as women do it.

The skill, flexibility, and strategies needed to raise a family are a manifestation of expertise. Here again, age matters. Although fertility and easy births are more common in the late teens, older parents tend to be more patient, with lower rates of child abuse as well as more successful offspring.

Of course, the mere passage of time does not make a person a better parent. However, an expert on the science of parenting concludes that, in general, as people gain in maturity and experience, "the more appropriate and optimal their parenting cognitions and practices are likely to be" (Bornstein, 2015, p. 91). (See A Case to Study.)

Raising a child teaches men as well as women how to become the intuitive, strategic, and flexible expert parent that children need. For this, the children themselves get some credit. As one of my first two daughters said to the next two, "You should be grateful to me. I broke them [my husband and me] in."

As with all aspects of adult cognition, variation is apparent, and age and gender do not guarantee intelligence. But experience, wisely understood, may help.

A CASE TO STUDY

Parenting Expertise

A team of North American experts have developed a test to measure intelligent parenting, called the KIDI (Knowledge of Infant Development). In the United States, high scores on the KIDI often correlate with intelligent baby care (e.g., Howard, 2010; McMillin et al., 2015; Graybill et al., 2016).

However, sometimes criteria that are well-suited in one cultural context might not be useful in another. This was illustrated by a social scientist who did research among the Ache, an indigenous tribe living in the jungle in Paraguay.

The Ache were respectful and deferential to the researcher on repeated visits. Then she and her husband arrived at their study site with their infant daughter in tow. The Ache greeted her in a whole new way. They took her aside and in friendly and intimate but no-nonsense terms told her all the things she was doing wrong as a mother. . . .

> This older woman sat with me and told me I must sleep with my daughter. They were horrified that I had a basket with me for her to sleep in. . . . here was a group of forest hunter-gatherers, people living in what Westerners would call basic conditions, giving instructions to a highly educated woman from a technologically sophisticated culture.
>
> *[Hurtado, quoted in Small, 1998, pp. 213–214]*

The intelligent way to care for an infant in the United States (a basket would allow easy transport and would protect against SIDS) was not intelligent for the expert Ache. For them, a baby who didn't sleep with her mother might be bitten by poisonous snakes or wild dogs, or kidnapped by strangers (that did happen among the Ache).

Thus, it is no surprise that scores on the KIDI were predictive of good parenting and high-achieving children for U.S.-born children but were much less so for children born elsewhere (September et al., 2015). This is an example of a general finding about child rearing: There are many ways to raise a happy and successful child, and each culture and family adjust practices to anticipate the particular norms for adults of that community.

Developmentalists have not yet identified all of the components necessary to become an expert in child rearing, but at least we know that such expertise exists. Children raised by teenage parents are more likely to become high school dropouts and substance abusers because more experienced and mature parents are more likely to nip problems in the bud. As experts, they recognize that some behaviors (that hairstyle, that music, that tattoo) are not worth fighting about.

With all aspects of adult cognition, variation is apparent! People of all ages can be intelligent or ignorant. But when parents learn from their experience, and from talking to other parents, they may gain parenting expertise.

WHAT HAVE YOU LEARNED?

1. At what age should a person begin selective optimization?
2. What selective optimization can you see in your parents?
3. In what domain are you an expert that most people are not?
4. How does automatic processing contribute to expertise?
5. Explain when intuition helps or diminishes ability.
6. In what occupations would age be an asset, and why?
7. In what occupations would age be a liability, and why?
8. What do parents learn from experience?

SUMMARY

Intelligence Changes During Adulthood?

1. It was traditionally assumed that intelligence was one general entity. From that assumption sprung the idea that intelligence in a measurable quantity, which Spearman called *g*.

2. Cross-sectional research found that IQ scores decreased over the years of adulthood. However, longitudinal research has found that the IQ of each adult tends to increase, particularly in vocabulary and general knowledge, until age 60 or so.

3. Cross-sectional research has found that the reason younger adults traditionally score higher than older adults on IQ tests is because of historical improvements in health and education. Some abilities tend to decline with age while others, such as vocabulary, increase.

Components of Intelligence: Many and Varied

4. As people age, fluid intelligence (which includes working memory and speedy thought) decreases while crystallized intelligence (which is based on accumulated knowledge) increases.

5. Because of rising crystallized intelligence and falling fluid intelligence, IQ scores may be quite stable during adulthood. Only in late adulthood does crystallized intelligence decline.

6. Sternberg proposed three fundamental forms of intelligence: analytic, creative, and practical. Most research finds that although analytic and creative abilities decline with age, practical intelligence may improve. In daily life, practical intelligence may be most important.

Selective Gains and Losses

7. As people grow older, they choose to focus on certain aspects of their lives, optimizing development in those areas and compensating for declines in others.

8. As applied to cognition, selective optimization with compensation means that people specialize in whatever intellectual skills they choose. Meanwhile, abilities that are not exercised may fade.

9. In addition to being more experienced, experts are better thinkers than novices for four reasons. They are more intuitive; their cognitive processes are automatic, often seeming to require little conscious thought; they use more and better strategies to perform whatever task is required; they are more flexible.

10. Expertise in adulthood is particularly apparent in the workplace. Experienced workers often outperform younger workers because they specialize, compensating for any losses that may appear. Experience and practice may be crucial, more so in some fields than others.

11. Raising children and responding well to the emotional complexities and unanticipated challenges of family life are now recognized and valued as expert work. Experience and maturation increase the likelihood of family expertise.

KEY TERMS

general intelligence (*g*) (p. 532)
Seattle Longitudinal Study (p. 535)
fluid intelligence (p. 537)
crystallized intelligence (p. 538)
analytic intelligence (p. 538)
creative intelligence (p. 539)
practical intelligence (p. 539)
selective optimization with compensation (p. 541)
expert (p. 544)

APPLICATIONS

1. The importance of context and culture is illustrated by the things that people think are basic knowledge. With a partner from the class, write four questions that you think are hard but fair as measures of general intelligence. Then give your test to your partner, and answer the four questions that your partner has prepared for you. What did you learn from the results?

2. Skill at video games is sometimes thought to reflect intelligence. Interview three or four people who play such games. What abilities do they think video games require? What do you think these games reflect in terms of experience, age, and motivation?

3. Some people mistakenly assume that almost any high school graduate can become a teacher, since most adults know the basic reading and math skills that elementary children need to learn. Describe aspects of expertise that experienced teachers need to master, with examples from your own experience.

Especially For ANSWERS

Response for Older Brothers and Sisters (from p. 536) No. While it is true that each new cohort might be smarter than the previous one in some ways, cross-sequential research suggests that you are smarter than you used to be. Knowing that might help you respond wisely—smiling quietly rather than insisting that you are superior.

Response for Prospective Parents (from p. 550): Because parenthood demands flexibility and patience, Sternberg's practical intelligence is probably most needed. Anything that involves finding a single correct answer, such as analytic intelligence or number ability, would not be much help.

Observation Quiz ANSWERS

Answer to Observation Quiz (from p. 533) Older adults might be more stressed by the proctors, and they might find it uncomfortable to sit on the floor while writing.

Answer to Observation Quiz (from p. 535) Spatial ability in men. But note that this ability was also highest overall at age 46. Not until about age 60 were both genders equal.

Answer to Observation Quiz (from p. 541) Both practical intelligence, evident in the clothes and staff of the camel herder, and the technology on the dash of the taxi-drivers.

Answer to Observation Quiz (from p. 547) At least nine things! Full apron, hair in bun (not in eyes), gas flame, tilt of pan, moving pan partly off to adjust heat, long handle on pan, the pan itself (durable, heat-conducting, expensive), constant stirring, and most important of all—intense concentration on the task.

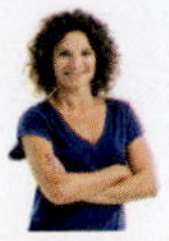

VISUALIZING DEVELOPMENT MEDIA USE AMONG U.S. ADULTS

While emerging adults are the biggest users of digital technology, older adults are also heavy adopters. Smart devices and social media sites can enable positive interactions with friends and relatives. However, some users worry about over-consuming and decide, for instance, to delete an app or avoid a certain platform for some time.

How Many U.S. Adults in Each Cohort...

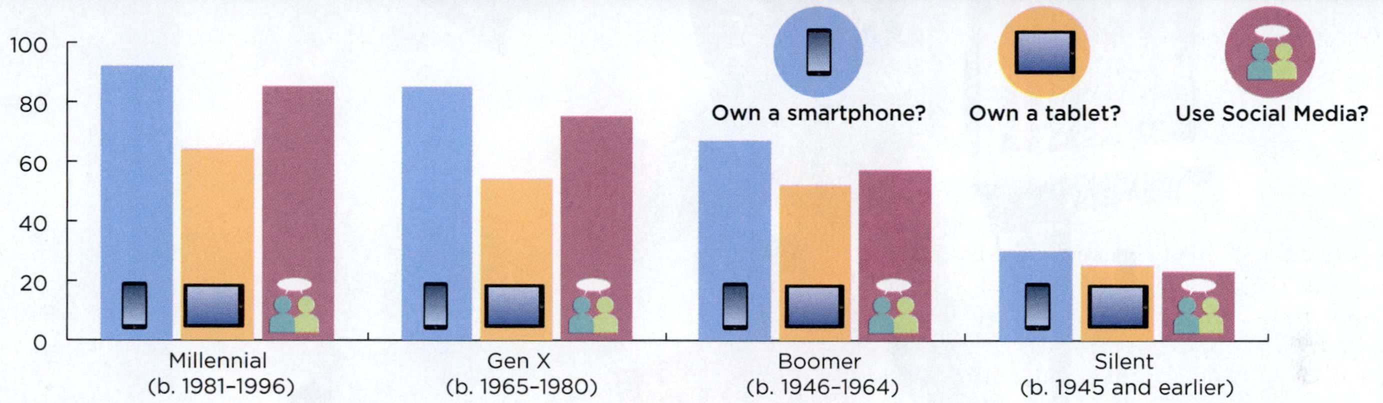

Data from Pew Research Center, May 2, 2018.

There are substantial age differences in social media use. About 90 percent of 18- to 29-year-olds use some form of social media, but that number falls to 37 percent among Americans 65 and older. As of 2019, Facebook continues to be the most widely used social media platform: Approximately 68% of U.S. adults are users. Other than YouTube, no other social media sites or apps are used by more than half of U.S. adults.

How Many U.S. Adults Use At Least One Social Media Site per Day?

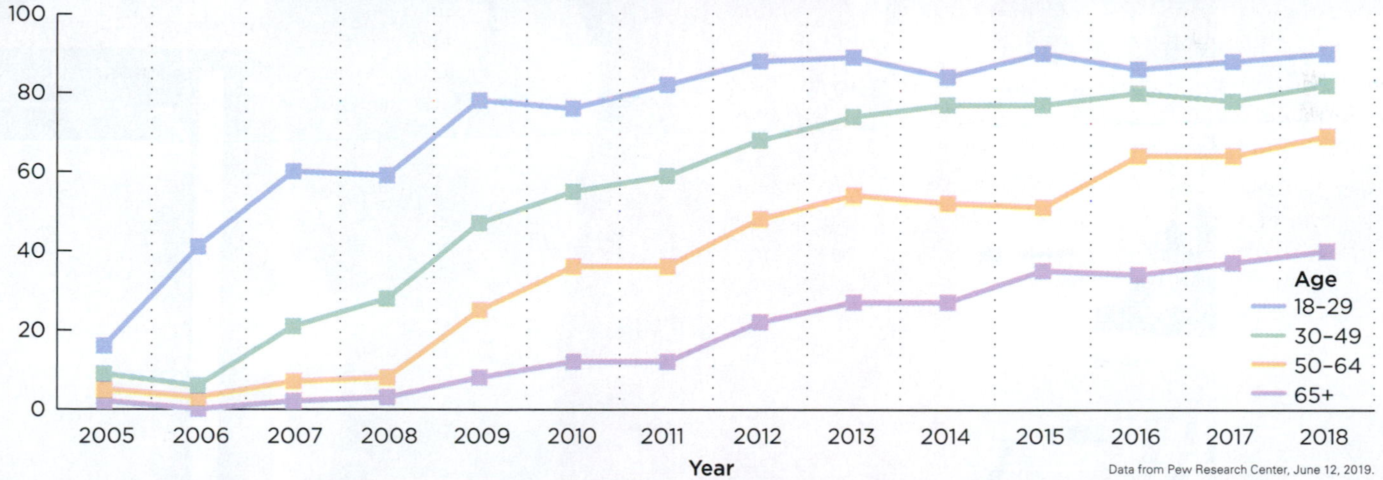

Data from Pew Research Center, June 12, 2019.

While social media has many positive uses, many adults are concerned about privacy and the information they see on social media sites: According to Pew Research Center, only 5 percent of social media users trust that information "a lot." Nevertheless, news and social media sites are the most common ways U.S. adults access news.

When asked twice a day for one week, where did online news consumers say they viewed news stories?

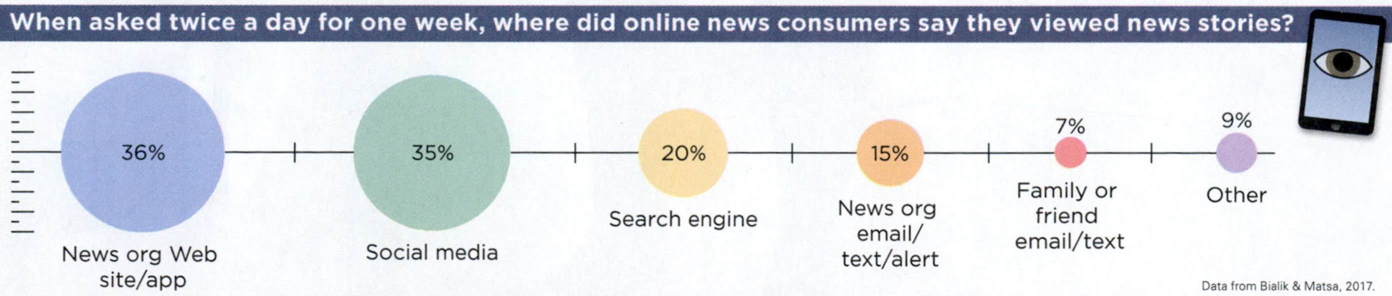

Data from Bialik & Matsa, 2017.

CHAPTER 22

Adulthood: Psychosocial Development

What Will You Know?

1. Does personality change from childhood to adulthood?
2. Why doesn't everyone get married?
3. Is being a parent work or joy?

- **Personality Development in Adulthood**
  - Erikson's Theory
  - Maslow's Theory of Personality
  - The Big Five
  - Common Themes
- **Intimacy: Connecting with Others**
  - Romantic Partners
  - A CASE TO STUDY: The Benefits of Marriage
  - Friends and Acquaintances
  - Family Bonds
- **Generativity: The Work of Adulthood**
  - Parenthood
  - A VIEW FROM SCIENCE: The Skipped-Generation Family
  - Caregiving
  - Employment
  - OPPOSING PERSPECTIVES: Accommodating Diversity
  - Finding the Balance
- **CAREER ALERT: The Physical Therapist**
- **VISUALIZING DEVELOPMENT: Family Connections**

"Your backpack is open."

I hear that several times a day from strangers on sidewalks, at street corners, in stores. "Thank you. I know," I reply.

My backpack is large, with three deep pockets. I like to zip it up halfway, leaving the top open so that I can see each section. Nothing visible is valuable, and nothing ever falls out when the backpack is strapped to my back, half-open.

Sometimes I thank those strangers; sometimes not. One time, as I was waiting for the subway, next to me sat a young boy, with his father on his other side. The man said,

"Your backpack is open."

"Thank you. I know."

"Do you want me to zip it for you?"

I smiled and shook my head.

"I know you must be tired and busy," he said. "My son could zip it for you."

He seemed upset, and the boy was looking at me, ready to zip. I gave up.

"OK."

The son zipped; the father was happy.

I thanked them both, as if I were grateful.

The merits of open backpacks can be argued either way, but this chapter begins with my backpack because it reveals three characteristics of adult development.

First, this chapter discusses personality: That man and I have quite different attitudes about things being closed. (I keep kitchen cabinets, closet doors, and jackets open, too.) One of the Big Five traits on which people differ is called *openness;* some people are very open (me), and others are troubled when they encounter such openness.

Unless people recognize personality differences, they will misunderstand each other. That father assumed that my backpack was open because I was tired, not because I liked it that way. That could have led to a disagreement, but I am high on another of the Big Five traits, *agreeableness.*

The second major topic of this chapter is human relationships. All members of this triad were quite social: Father and son were aligned, and I responded to social pressure.

Left: Cecilie_Arcurs/E+/Getty Images
Top: iko/Shutterstock

The final topic of this chapter is caregiving. Adults want to care for each other, yet each wants to be independent. I did not want anyone to zip up my backpack, but I recognized the father's need to take care of me. I decided that I would be caring for him by letting him care for me.

Personality Development in Adulthood

You already know that each human is genetically unique, in temperament and inclinations, and that parenting and culture shape personality. Then, in adulthood, personality traits continue, sometimes with notable shifts influenced by age and context (Dweck, 2017).

Erikson's Theory

As you remember, Erikson described eight stages of development. His first five stages begin in a particular chronological period. His adult stages are less age-based (see **Table 22.1**).

The three adult stages—*intimacy versus isolation, generativity versus stagnation,* and *integrity versus despair*—do not always appear in chronological sequence; they overlap, with many social and cultural factors influencing all three.

generativity versus stagnation The seventh of Erikson's eight stages of development. Adults seek to be productive in a caring way, often as parents. Generativity also occurs through art, caregiving, and employment.

Social influences are most evident in intimacy versus isolation. This stage begins in emerging adulthood, as explained in the Chapter 19 discussion of family, friends, and romance. It continues throughout adulthood.

TABLE 22.1

Erikson's Stages of Adulthood
Unlike Freud or other early theorists who thought adults simply worked through the legacy of their childhood, four of Erikson's eight psychosocial stages occur after puberty. His most famous book, *Childhood and Society* (1993a), devoted only two pages to each adult stage, but elaborations in later works have led to a much richer depiction (Hoare, 2002).
Identity Versus Role Confusion Although Erikson originally situated the identity crisis during adolescence, he realized that identity concerns could be lifelong. Identity combines values and traditions from childhood with the current social context. Since contexts keep evolving, many adults reassess all four types of identity (sexual/gender, vocational/work, religious/spiritual, and political/ethnic).
Intimacy Versus Isolation Adults seek intimacy—a close, reciprocal connection with another human being. Intimacy is mutual, not self-absorbed, which means that adults need to devote time and energy to one another. This process begins in emerging adulthood and continues lifelong. Isolation is especially likely when divorce or death disrupts established intimate relationships.
Generativity Versus Stagnation Adults need to care for the next generation, either by raising their own children or by mentoring, teaching, and helping others. Erikson's first description of this stage focused on parenthood, but later he included other ways to achieve generativity. Adults extend the legacy of their culture and their generation with ongoing care, creativity, and sacrifice.
Integrity Versus Despair When Erikson himself reached his 70s, he decided that integrity, with the goal of combating prejudice and helping all humanity, was too important to be left to the elderly. He also thought that each person's entire life could be directed toward connecting a personal journey with the historical and cultural purpose of human society, the ultimate achievement of integrity.

According to Erikson, after intimacy comes **generativity versus stagnation**, when adults seek to be productive in a caring way. Erikson wrote that a mature adult "needs to be needed" (1993a, p. 266). Without generativity, adults experience "a pervading sense of stagnation and personal impoverishment" (Erikson, 1993a, p. 267).

Generativity is often expressed by caring for the younger generation, but it occurs in ways other than child rearing. Meaningful employment, important creative production, and caregiving of other adults also are generative ways to avoid stagnation.

The final adult stage, *integrity versus despair,* is described in Chapter 25. However, although the drive to understand the whole of one's life is especially evident in late adulthood, it may come to the fore in midlife as well. Thus, Erikson's stages of adulthood may be evident at any age.

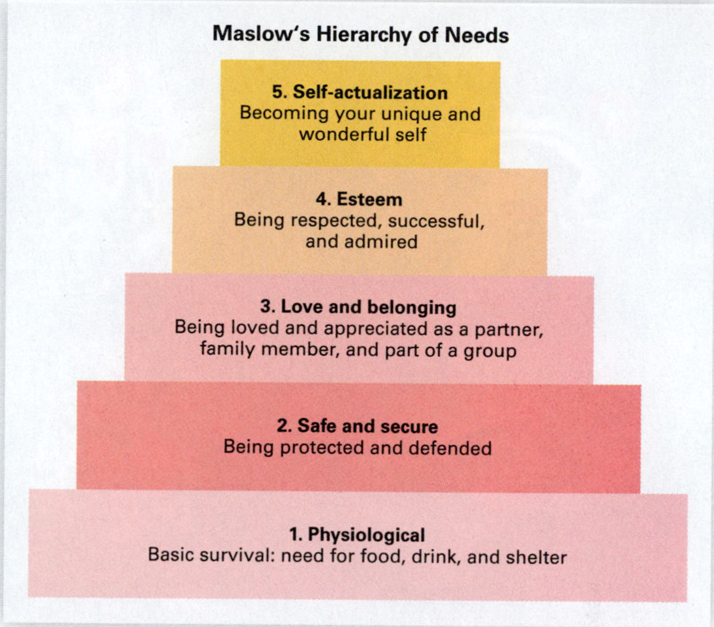

FIGURE 22.1
Moving Up, Not Looking Back Maslow's hierarchy is like a ladder: Once a person stands firmly on a higher rung, the lower rungs are no longer needed. Thus, someone who has arrived at step 4 might devalue safety (step 2) and be willing to risk personal safety to gain respect.

Maslow's Theory of Personality

Some scientists are convinced that there is something hopeful, unifying, and noble in humans. People seek love and then respect, and finally, if all goes well, they become truly themselves. This is the central idea of **humanism**, a theory developed by Abraham Maslow (1908–1970) and many others.

humanism A theory that stresses the potential of all humans, who have the same basic needs regardless of culture, gender, or background.

Maslow believed that all people—no matter what their culture, gender, or background—have the same basic needs. He arranged these needs in a hierarchy, often illustrated as a pyramid (see **Figure 22.1**):

1. Physiological: needing food, water, warmth, and air
2. Safety: feeling protected from injury and death
3. Love and belonging: having friends, family, and a community (often religious)
4. Esteem: being respected by the wider community as well as by oneself
5. Self-actualization: becoming truly oneself, fulfilling one's unique potential while appreciating all of life

This pyramid caught on almost immediately. It was one of the most "contagious ideas in behavioral science" because it seemed insightful about human psychology (Kenrick et al., 2010, p. 292).

Maslow did not believe that the five levels were connected to a particular stage or age, but he thought that lower needs must be met before higher needs can be. That makes it relevant for life-span development. At the highest level, when all four earlier needs have been satisfied, adults can be fully themselves—creative, spiritual, curious, appreciative of nature, respectful of everyone else.

Humanism is prominent among medical professionals because they recognize that illness and pain are connected to the psychological needs of the patient (Felicilda-Reynaldo & Smith, 2018; Jackson et al., 2014). As a medical team from the famed Mayo Clinic states,

> solely addressing physiological recovery in the ICU, without also placing focus on psychological recovery, is limiting and not sufficient for recovery of the entire patient—both body and mind
>
> (*Karnatovskaia et al., 2015, p. 210*).

Maybe Next Year Self-acceptance is a gradual process over the years of adulthood, aided by the appreciation of friends and family. At some point in adulthood, people shift from striving to fulfill their potential to accepting their limitations.

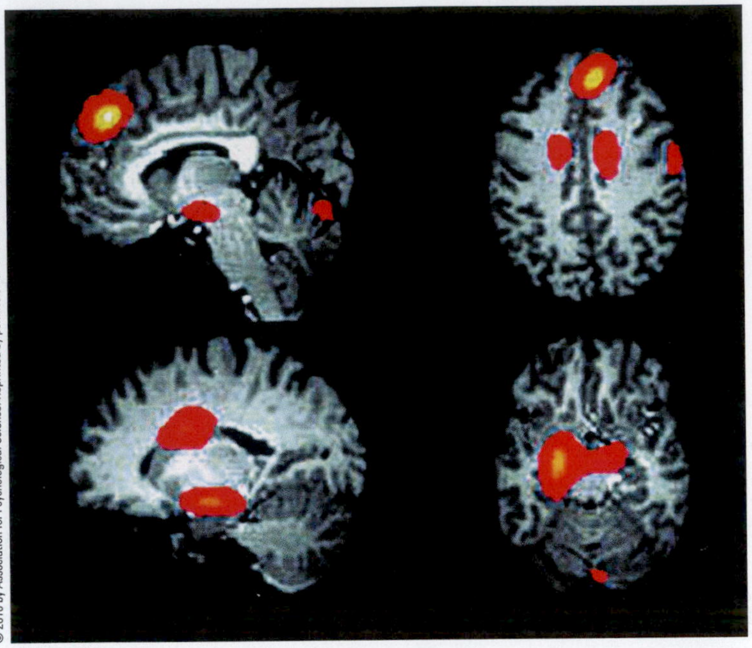

Active Brains, Active Personality The hypothesis that individual personality traits originate in the brain was tested by scientists who sought to find correlations between brain activity (shown in red) and personality traits. People who rated themselves high in four of the Big Five (conscientiousness, extroversion, agreeableness, neuroticism—but not openness) also had more activity in brain regions that are known to relate to those traits. Here are two side views *(left)* and a top and bottom view *(right)* of the brains of people high in neuroticism. Their brain regions known to be especially sensitive to stress, depression, threat, and punishment (yellow bullseyes) were more active than the same brain regions in people low in neuroticism (DeYoung et al., 2010).

Big Five The five basic clusters of personality traits that remain quite stable throughout adulthood: openness, conscientiousness, extroversion, agreeableness, and neuroticism.

The Big Five

Another theory of personality begins with the idea that people have five distinct clusters of characteristics, expressed in various ways over the decades of the life span. They are called the **Big Five**:

- *Openness:* imaginative, curious, artistic, creative, open to new experiences
- *Conscientiousness:* organized, deliberate, conforming, self-disciplined
- *Extroversion:* outgoing, assertive, active
- *Agreeableness:* kind, helpful, easygoing, generous
- *Neuroticism:* anxious, moody, self-punishing, critical

Each person is somewhere on a continuum on each of these five. The low end might be described, in the same order as above, with these five adjectives: *closed, careless, introverted, hard to please,* and *placid*.

According to this theory, adults choose vocations, hobbies, health habits, partners, and neighborhoods to reflect their personality. Those high in extroversion might work in sales, those high in openness might be artists, and so on. International research confirms that human personality traits (there are hundreds of them) can be grouped based on these five dimensions.

Age Changes When adults are followed longitudinally, stability of the Big Five is evident. Change is more likely in emerging adulthood or late adulthood than for 25- to 64-year-olds (Wagner et al., 2019).

The general age trend is positive, as people align with the norms of their community. Adults gradually become less neurotic and more conscientious. Similar trends are found in research on attachment over the life span. Anxious and avoidant attachment become less common, while secure attachment becomes more prominent (Fraley, 2019).

All theories find that people become more accepting of themselves and their community over the decades of adult life. People under the age of 30 "actively try to change their environment," moving away from home and finding new friends, changing their nurture. Later in life, context shapes traits, because once adults have chosen their vocation, family, and neighborhoods, they "change the self to fit the environment" (Kandler, 2012, p. 294).

Cultural Influences As in these examples, culture shapes personality. One team wrote, "personality may acculturate" (Güngör et al., 2013, p. 713). A study of well-being and self-esteem in 28 nations found that people are happiest if their personality traits match their social context. This has implications for immigrants, who might feel (and be) less appreciated when the personality values of their home culture clash with their new community.

For example, extroversion is valued in Canada and less so in Japan; consequently, Canadians and Japanese have a stronger sense of well-being if their personal ratings on extroversion (high or low) are consistent with their culture (Fulmer et al., 2010). Many people criticize immigrants for the very traits that are valued in their home cultures.

Especially for Immigrants and Children of Immigrants Poverty and persecution are the main reasons why some people leave their home for another country, but personality is also influential. Which of the Big Five personality traits do you think is most characteristic of immigrants? (see response, page 580)

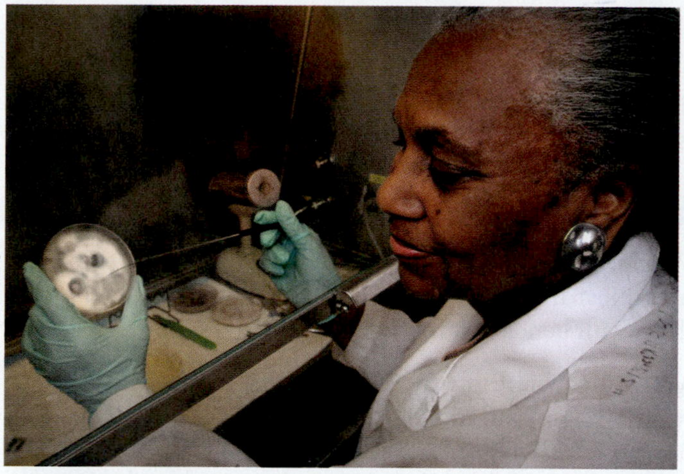

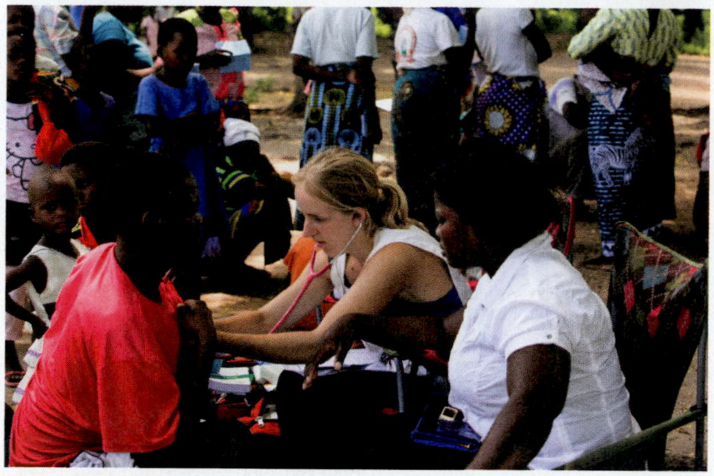

James Gathany/Science Source/Getty Images

Ashley Cooper pics/Alamy

Same Situation, Far Apart: Scientists at Work Most scientists are open-minded and conscientious (two of the Big Five personality traits), as both of these women are. Culture and social context are crucial, however. If the woman on the left was in Malawi, working for Doctors Without Borders in an open-air clinic with to fight malaria, as the woman on the right is doing, would she still be the happy and proud professional that she is? Or is she so accustomed to her North American laboratory, protected by gloves and a screen, that she could not adjust? The answer depends on personality, not intelligence.

Common Themes

Universal trends are more significant than cultural differences. Regarding the Big Five, adults who are low in neuroticism and high in agreeableness tend to be happier than the opposite. Personal experiences matter, affecting individuals everywhere more than nations anywhere. For example, people who personally experience a happy marriage become less neurotic over time; people in unhappy marriages become more neurotic (O'Meara & South, 2019).

As for universal human needs, every well-known theorist or scholar of adult personality echoes the same themes. Freud did it first: He said that a healthy adult is able to do two things: *lieben und arbeiten* (to love and to work).

Likewise, as you just read, Maslow considered love/belonging and then success/esteem to be steps in his hierarchy. Similarly, extroversion and conscientiousness are two of the Big Five, again suggesting that these are among the basic human attributes.

Other theorists call these two needs *affiliation/achievement*, or *emotional/instrumental*, or *communion/agency*. Every theory recognizes both; all adults seek to love and to work in ways that fit their personality, culture, and gender. In the rest of this chapter, to simplify and organize our discussion, we will use Erikson's terms, *intimacy* and *generativity*, each of which refers to a cluster of adult psychosocial development.

THINK CRITICALLY: Would your personality fit better in another culture?

WHAT HAVE YOU LEARNED?

1. What do all people strive for, according to Maslow?
2. What are the three needs of adults, according to Erikson?
3. What are the Big Five traits?
4. How are personality traits affected by age?
5. How does personality interact with culture?

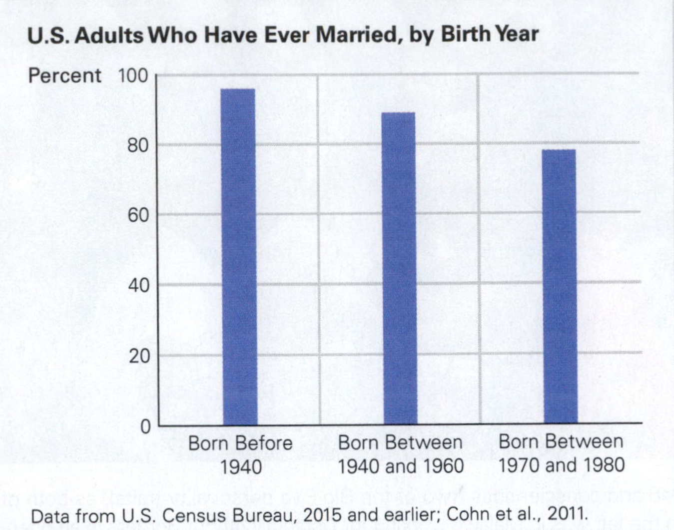

FIGURE 22.2
And Now? Not only are far fewer people marrying, but they also marry later, so it seemed misleading to include a bar for those born between 1980 and 2000. If we had, the rates would be under 50 percent. Most emerging adults are unmarried.

Intimacy: Connecting with Others

Humans are not meant to be loners. Decades of research finds that physical health and psychological well-being flourish if family and friends are supportive (Li & Zhang, 2015).

Romantic Partners

We begin with romance. Adults tend to be happiest and healthiest if they have a long-term partner, connected to them with bonds of affection and care.

Marriage Traditionally, the romantic bond was codified via marriage. You already read that most emerging adults postpone marriage, and they cohabit instead. That trend continues in adulthood and is evident worldwide. Despite marked cultural variations, age of marriage is increasing everywhere, as is the number of unmarried adults (Cherlin, 2018) (see **Figure 22.2**).

Nonetheless, worldwide, a satisfying marriage improves health, wealth, and happiness. Most adults continue to seek a partner, and marriage correlates with adult health and longevity everywhere.

Humans know this emotionally, although not always logically. Why else would millions of people advocate for same-sex marriage, or why would the opposition rally "in defense of marriage"? Why else would people whose marriages became so intolerable that they divorced nonetheless have a higher remarriage rate than the marriage rate for single adults of the same age? Not logical, but very human.

It was once thought that men benefited more from marriage than women (Bernard, 1982). However, that is no longer true.

A meta-analysis in the United States found no marked gender differences in marital happiness (J. B. Jackson et al., 2014). Early in a marriage, wives tended to be slightly more satisfied with the relationship than husbands, but this shifted by about the 15-year mark, with husbands slightly more satisfied. Both mates benefit.

In linked lives, spouses and partners usually adjust to each other's needs, allowing them to function better as a couple than they did as singles. A large survey of married heterosexual couples found that the man's average salary five years after their wedding was notably higher than for men at similar jobs who remained single. Also, their home was more comfortable, perhaps because the wife had worked to make it so (Kuperberg, 2012). That reflects gender norms, but both spouses should be credited with these improvements in their lives.

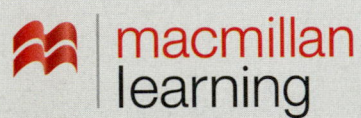

macmillan learning

VIDEO: Marriage in Adulthood features researcher Ronald Sabatelli and interviews of people discussing the joys and challenges of marriage.

THINK CRITICALLY: Is marriage a failed institution?

Nonmarital Romantic Relationships As explained in Chapter 19, romantic partnerships do not always mean marriage. Cohabitation is no longer the exclusive purview of young adults; cohabitation is increasing for adults of all ages.

A sizable number of adults have found a third way (neither marriage nor cohabitation) to meet their intimacy needs with a steady romantic partner. They *live apart together* (LAT). They have separate residences, but they function as a couple—sexually faithful, vacationing together, recognized as a couple by other people, and so on.

Some LAT couples *must* live apart because they have jobs in distant cities, but more often they could share a home but prefer not to. LAT is chosen more often as adults grow older: Most LAT couples under age 30 intend to cohabit or marry eventually, but most LAT couples over age 50 prefer to keep separate homes for years (Lewin, 2018).

Financial matters are a particular issue for LAT couples. Most married couples combine their wealth; many cohabiting couples do not (Hamplová et al., 2014). LAT couples struggle with this aspect of their relationship, with the women particularly wanting to pay their own way (Lyssens-Danneboom & Mortelmans, 2014).

Children often are a strong influence on adult decisions to marry, divorce, cohabit, or LAT. Cohabiters who have had children together are more likely to marry than those who have not, especially when the children start school. Likewise, married couples sometimes stay together for the children and sometimes do the opposite, as when one parent leaves a violent mate to protect the children.

As for LAT couples, many older parents maintain separate households. They do not want to upset their grown children (de Jong Gierveld & Merz, 2013). All of these illustrate linked lives.

Frank Baron/Camera Press/Guardian/Redux

One Love, Two Homes Their friends and family know that Jonathan and Diana are a couple, happy together day and night, year after year. But one detail distinguishes them from most couples: Each owns a house. They commute 10 miles and are living apart together—LAT.

Partnerships Over the Years Love is complex. Sternberg described romantic love as having three aspects: passion, intimacy, and commitment (Sternberg, 2004). Passion typically is strong at the beginning of a relationship; intimacy occurs when a couple shares secrets, possessions, and a bed; and commitment is expressed in promises—typically a wedding with vows of faithfulness. When all three occur together, that is *consummate love*—only sometimes attained.

A wealth of research on the decades of adulthood finds that, for most adults, mutual commitment is the most crucial of the three. People have a deep psychological need for someone who listens, understands, and shares their heartfelt goals. A happy relationship reduces health risks and increases longevity (Whisman et al., 2018).

The passage of time makes a difference. In general, establishing a new partnership tends to make both partners happy. For marriages, satisfaction is highest in the "honeymoon period." Then frustration with a partner increases as conflicts—even those not directly between the couple—arise. On the other hand, over the decades of a committed adult partnership, satisfaction is more likely to improve than not (Bell & Harsin, 2018).

Partnerships (heterosexual married couples, committed cohabiters, same-sex couples, and LAT couples) tend to be less happy when the first child is in infancy or toddlerhood and again when children reach puberty, but there are many exceptions. Sometimes child rearing increases satisfaction with the partnership (Umberson et al., 2010). Divorce risk rises in the first years of marriage, and then it falls.

Remember, however, that averages obscure differences of age, ethnicity, personality, and circumstances. In the United States, Asian Americans are least likely, and African Americans are most likely, to divorce.

Ethnic differences are partly cultural and partly economic. Any broad effort to promote marriage for everyone doomed to disappoint politicians, social workers, and individuals (Johnson, 2012). Variation in marriage and happiness is evident, as in A Case to Study.

AT ABOUT THIS TIME

Marital Happiness Over the Years

Interval After Wedding	Characterization
First 6 months	Honeymoon period—happiest of all.
6 months to 5 years	Happiness dips; divorce is more common now than later in marriage.
5 to 10 years	Happiness holds steady.
10 to 20 years	Happiness dips as children reach puberty.
20 to 30 years	Happiness rises when children leave the nest.
30 to 50 years	Happiness is high and steady, barring serious health problems.

Not Always These are trends, often masked by more pressing events. For example, some couples stay together because of the children; so for them, unlike most couples, the empty-nest stage becomes a time of conflict or divorce.

A CASE TO STUDY

The Benefits of Marriage

Marriage can be a benefit or a problem, depending on whom you ask. A study of long-term cohabiting and married adults in England found a great variety of responses. Consider two quotations from that study (quoted in Soulsby & Bennett, 2017).

Dave, age 45, had been married for seven years when he said:

> Being married is molding the person that I am and who I'm becoming. It's helping me fulfil dreams and ambitions and goals, . . . it's giving me a deeper meaning of love, it's given me a sense of achievement and a sense of encouragement.

Gina, age 50, had been married for 23 years, and she said:

> As a single person you do what you want, you live your life as you like, you do what you want. . . . When you get married, all of a sudden you've got washing to do, you've got to tidy up in case your mess is impinging on someone else, or theirs on you, you've got to think about eating at the same time. You've got someone else that you need to factor in, so your life changes completely.

Which of these two seems more valid to you? For this A Case to Study, the final case to be considered is your own.

Consider the relationship between your own parents. If they were married or in a stable cohabiting relationship, did they benefit from this? Did you? If they were never married, or if they married and divorced, would it have been better if they were legally wed and were still together? Consider, as in the quotations above, both perspectives.

Education and religion matter, too: College-educated couples are more likely to marry, and less likely to divorce, no matter what their ethnic background. Some unhappy couples stay married for religious reasons, and the result may be a long-lasting, troubled relationship, or, instead, a marriage that grows stronger every year.

empty nest The time in the lives of parents when their children have left the family home. This is often a happy time for everyone.

Contrary to outdated impressions, the **empty nest**—when parents are alone again after the children have left—is usually a time for improved relationships. Simply having time for each other, without crying babies, demanding children, or rebellious teenagers, improves intimacy. Partners can focus on their mates, doing together whatever they both enjoy.

Gay and Lesbian Couples Almost everything just described applies to gay and lesbian partners as well as to heterosexual ones. Some same-sex couples are faithful and supportive of each other; their emotional well-being thrives on their intimacy and commitment, which increases over the decades. Others are conflicted: Problems of finances, communication, and domestic abuse resemble those in heterosexual marriages.

John Moore/Getty Images News/Getty Images

A Dream Come True When Melissa Adams and Meagan Martin first committed to each other, they thought they could never marry, at least in their South Carolina home. On July 11, 2015, they celebrated their union, complete with flower girl, bridesmaids, Reverend Sidden, and all the legal documents.

As the U.S. Supreme Court acknowledged in 2013, love between partners is the crucial bond. Same-sex couples fight about money and children, just as heterosexual couples do. For every partnership, communication is crucial (Ogolsky & Gray, 2016).

The similarity of same-sex and other-sex couples surprised many researchers. For example, one study focused on alcohol abuse in romantic couples, same-sex as well as other-sex. The scientists expected that the stress of minority sexual orientation would increase alcohol use disorder. That was *not* what the data revealed. Instead, the crucial variable was whether the couple was married or not. For both same-sex and other-sex couples, excessive drinking was more common among cohabiters than among married couples (Reczek et al., 2014).

An increasing number of families headed by same-sex couples have children, some from a former marriage, some adopted, and some the biological child of one partner, conceived because the couple wanted a child. Again, the well-being of such children depends on the same factors that affect the children of other-sex couples.

Family income is probably the crucial factor. On average. same-sex couples have less money than other-sex couples (Cenegy et al., 2018). As you remember from earlier chapters, low SES increases a child's risk of physical, academic, and emotional problems. Economic stress decreases the parents' patience and joy with their children.

Another finding also relates to all partnerships: family connections. In a study of married gay couples in Iowa, one man said that he decided to marry because of his mother: "I had a partner that I lived with . . . And I think she, as much as she accepted him, it wasn't anything permanent in her eyes" (Ocobock, 2013, p. 196). In this study, most family members were supportive, but some were not—again eliciting deep emotional reactions.

In heterosexual marriages as well, in-laws usually welcome the new spouse. But when they do not, the partnership may be troubled. Family influences are hard to ignore, as there is both a premium and a penalty in relationships with in-laws (Danielsbacka et al., 2018).

Divorce and Remarriage Throughout this text, developmental events that seem isolated, personal, and transitory are shown to be interconnected and socially constructed, with enduring consequences. Family relationships are part of the microsystem, but the macrosystem, mesosystem, and exosystem all have an impact. Indeed, a study of many nations found that a couple's happiness and separation are powerfully influenced by national norms (Wiik et al., 2012).

Especially for Young Couples
Suppose you are one-half of a turbulent relationship in which moments of intimacy alternate with episodes of abuse. Should you break up? (see response, page 580)

Separation occurs because at least one partner believes that he or she would be happier without the other, a conclusion reached fairly often. In 1980 in the United States, half as many divorces occurred as marriages. Then, emerging adults in large numbers avoided marriage until they were older, and that itself reduced the divorce rate.

That has changed again: In the past decades, slightly more couples are marrying and slightly fewer divorcing, so the 2017 divorce rate is about 46 percent of the marriage rate.

Another change is in the age at which people divorce. Instead of being almost exclusively a young-adult experience, divorce of middle-aged or older couples is no longer rare (Stepler, 2017). To be specific, in 1990 the rate of divorce among those over 50 was only one-sixth the rate of those under 40, but in 2015 it was almost half the younger-adult rate.

Family problems from divorce arise not only with children (usually custodial parents become stricter and noncustodial parents become distant) but also with other relatives. The divorced adults' parents are often financially supportive but not emotionally supportive. Relationships with in-laws typically end when the couple splits, as do many relationships with married friends. No wonder divorce increases loneliness (van Tilburg et al., 2015).

Many divorced people find another partner. Initially, remarriage restores intimacy, health, and financial security. For fathers, bonds with stepchildren or with a new baby may replace strained relationships with the children who live with the former wife (Noël-Miller, 2013a). That helps the adult but not the children.

Divorce is never easy, but the negative consequences just explained are not inevitable. If divorce ends an abusive, destructive relationship (as it does about one-third of the time), it usually benefits at least one spouse (Amato, 2010). Such divorces lead to stronger and warmer mother–child and/or father–child relationships after the marital fights are over.

Surprised? Many brides and grooms hope to rescue and reform their partners, but they should know better. Changing another person's habits, values, or addictions is very difficult.

"But you knew I was addicted to bad men when you married me."

But note that most divorces occur not because one spouse is abusive but because the spouses no longer love each other. Ideally, parents then cooperate in child care, which benefits the children. This realization has transformed what psychologists recommend to divorcing parents: It is best if parents share custody, cooperating for the sake of the children, who live with each parent in turn (Braver & Votruba, 2018).

Shared physical custody helps grandparents as well. When mothers had sole custody, the maternal grandparents were often overburdened and the paternal grandparents rarely saw the children. That troubled all the grandparents.

social convoy Collectively, the family members, friends, acquaintances, and even strangers who move through the years of life with a person.

Luke Thompson

Fellow Travelers Here that phrase is not a metaphor for life's journey but a literal description of a good friend, Tom, carrying 30-year-old Kevan Chandler, from Fort Wayne, Indiana, as they view the Paris Opera House. Kevan was born with spinal muscular atrophy because both his parents are carriers of the recessive gene. He cannot walk, but three of his friends agreed to take him on a three-week backpacking adventure through Europe. The trip was funded by hundreds of people who read about Kevan's plans online.

Friends and Acquaintances

Each person is part of a **social convoy.** The term *convoy* originally referred to a group of travelers in hostile territory, such as the pioneers in ox-drawn wagons headed for California or soldiers marching across unfamiliar terrain. Individuals were strengthened by the convoy, sharing difficult conditions and defending one another.

As people move through life, their social convoy functions as those earlier convoys did. The current social convoy is a group of people who provide "a protective layer of social relations to guide, socialize, and encourage individuals as they move through life" (Antonucci et al., 2001, p. 572).

Sometimes a friend needs care and cannot reciprocate at the time, but it is understood that later the roles may be reversed. Friends provide practical help and useful advice when serious problems—death of a family member, personal illness, job loss—arise. They also offer companionship, information, and laughter in daily life.

Friends are a crucial part of the social convoy; they are chosen for the traits that make them reliable fellow travelers. Mutual loyalty and aid characterize friendship (Rawlins, 2016). An unbalanced friendship (one giving and the other taking) often ends because *both* parties are uncomfortable.

Friendships tend to improve over the decades of adulthood. As adults grow older, they tend to have fewer friends overall, but they keep their close friends and nurture those relationships (English & Carstensen, 2014). One of the benefits of friendship is that a person has someone to talk with about problems and joys. That itself increases happiness, especially when a friend celebrates accomplishments (Demir et al., 2017).

Although most friendships last for decades, conflicting health habits may end a relationship. For instance, a chain-smoker and a friend who quit smoking are likely to part ways. On the other hand, shared health problems can bind a friendship together. For example, overweight people become friends with other overweight people, and together their eating habits reinforce each other as both continue to gain weight (Powell et al., 2015).

Adults who have no close and positive friends suffer in both physical and mental health (Dunbar, 2018; Santini et al., 2015). This seems as true in poor nations as in rich ones: Universally, humans are healthier with social support and sicker when socially isolated.

Family Bonds

Beyond romance and friendship, family links span generations and endure over time. Childhood history influences people decades after they have left their childhood home, and adults connect with siblings, nieces and nephews, parents and grandparents. Even parental death does not stop parental influence (see Epilogue).

THINK CRITICALLY: Does the divorce rate indicate stronger or weaker family links?

Past and present family experiences affect adult motivation, fears, and desires. For example, going to museums, reading books, discussing current events, and other family practices influence adult habits and values and, thus, SES (Erola et al., 2016). Secure attachment and emotional support begin in early childhood; the benefits continue lifelong.

This does not mean that adults always do what their own parents did: Sometimes the opposite occurs. One of my students complained about her life as one of 16 children; she had only one child, and she said that was enough. As she explained this to the class, it seemed apparent that her choice was in reaction to her childhood.

Steve Skjold/Alamy Stock Photo

Picnic in Poland Like families everywhere, these four generations in Zawady (a village in central Poland) enjoy time together, eating, laughing, and supporting each other. At the end of the day, however, each adult generation has their own home if they can afford it. Particularly in emerging adulthood, family bonds are strong, but so it the desire for independence.

The power of family experiences was documented in data from all of the twins in Denmark. They married less often than single-born Danes, but if they wed, they were less likely to divorce. According to the researchers, twins may have their intimacy needs met by each other and therefore they are less likely to seek a spouse. But if they marry, they know how to maintain a close relationship (Petersen et al., 2011).

Parents and Their Adult Children A crucial part of family life for many adults is raising children. That is discussed soon as part of generativity. Here we focus on family bonds that meet adult intimacy needs, providing companionship, support, and affection for their parents as well as their grown children.

Do not confuse intimacy with residence. If income allows, most adults seek to establish their own households. A study of 7,578 adults in seven nations found that physical separation did not weaken family ties. Indeed, intergenerational relationships seem to be strengthened, not weakened, when adult children lived apart from their parents (Treas & Gubernskaya, 2012), because "the intergenerational support network is both durable and flexible" (Bucx et al., 2012, p. 101).

Considerable research has recently focused on "boomerang children," adults who live with their parents for a while. In the United States in 1980, only 11 percent of 25- to 34-year-olds lived with their parents for at least a few months. Every year since then, more young adults have lived with their parents, and more have lived with someone of another generation who is not a romantic partner (e.g., a grandparent, aunt, or nonrelative who rents a room).

To be specific, in 2016, one-third of U.S. 25- to 30-year-olds lived with adults not from their generation—that is, not a romantic partner, spouse, or a peer. In most cases, that older adult was a parent (Cohn & Passel, 2018). The reasons were primarily economic. Adults generally are happier and healthier when they and their parents are mutually supportive but have separate homes.

Fictive Kin Most adults maintain connections with brothers and sisters, sometimes traveling great distances to attend weddings, funerals, and holidays. The power of this link is apparent when we note that often, unlike friends, family members may be on opposite sides of a political or social divide. Even radically different views do not usually keep them apart.

Sometimes, however, adults avoid their blood relatives because they find them toxic—not because they disagree on politics but because their personal interactions are hostile. Such adults may become **fictive kin** in another family. They are introduced by a family member who says this person is "like a sister" or "my brother" and so on. Over time, the new family accepts them. They are

fictive kin People who become accepted as part of a family in which they are not genetically or legally members.

Strangers or Twins? Both. Aysha Lord *(left)* is a "genetic twin" to Peter Milburn *(right)*, a father of four who had a fatal blood cancer. He was saved by stem cells donated by a stranger—Aysha—whose cells were a perfect match.

not technically related (hence *fictive*), but they are treated like a family member (hence *kin*).

Fictive kin can be a lifeline for adults who are rejected by their original family (perhaps because of sexual orientation or gender identity), or are unable to visit family (perhaps because of prohibitive immigration policies), or who resist family practices (perhaps by stopping addiction, or by joining a religious group).

Fictive kin can be part of a community strategy to provide personal support. This has been documented among African Americans in the United States. When hostility and prejudice segregated and marginalized them, many African American neighbors became fictive kin. Adults were expected to guide and help each other, allowing survival and success (Glover et al., 2018).

The role of fictive kin reinforces a general theme: Adults benefit from kin, fictive or not.

WHAT HAVE YOU LEARNED?

1. What needs do long-term partners meet?
2. Why would people choose to live apart together (LAT)?
3. How do same-sex marriages compare to heterosexual marriages?
4. What are the consequences of divorce?
5. How does a social convoy aid development?
6. What roles do friends play in a person's life?
7. What is the usual relationship between adult children and their parents?
8. Why do people have fictive kin?

Generativity: The Work of Adulthood

Adults satisfy their need to be generative in many ways, especially through parenthood, caregiving, and employment.

Parenthood

Erikson thought that generativity often became manifest in "establishing and guiding the next generation" (Erikson, 1993a, p. 267). Traditionally, that meant raising one's own children.

Parenthood is never easy, but it is particularly difficult if a person is not ready for generativity and still struggles with intimacy or identity needs. Marital happiness may dip in the first year or two after a birth, because intimacy diminishes. Worse yet is having a baby as part of the search for identity—to prove manhood or womanhood to oneself.

Parenthood also requires reexamination of gender norms. Many emerging adults believe in gender equality—that men and women are equally suited for employment, housework, and child care. But with birth, breast-feeding, and infant care, they tilt toward believing that women and men differ in their roles and abilities (Endendijk et al., 2018).

That may mean joyous acceptance, or ongoing resentment—for her because she feels stuck with more baby care and housework than she expected, and for him because he feels excluded from the mother–infant bond. Not always, of course, but these emotions arise more from the day-to-day family interaction than from cultural sexism.

MoMo Productions/Taxi/Getty Images

Marka/Universal Images Group/Getty Images

More Dad . . . and Mom Worldwide, fathers are spending more time playing with their children—daughters as well as sons, as these two photos show. Does that mean that mothers spend less time with their children? No—the data show that mothers are spending more time as well.

Observation Quiz In what ways might these fathers differ from mothers? (see answer, page 580) ←

We know this because the data came from a large study in the Netherlands, where gender equity is a national value. Nonetheless, when Dutch adults become parents, they tend to take on more traditional gender roles.

This gender division is found despite another fact: Fathers are more involved with child care than they were a few generations ago, and mothers are far more likely to be employed. This does not mean that mothers do less child care. Indeed, the data suggest that mothers are more intensely involved with each child than they were a few generations ago.

The gender division of family labor remains (Frejka et al., 2018). On average, mothers provide child care, schedule doctor appointments, plan birthday parties, arrange play dates, choose schools and after-school activities, and so on more than fathers do.

What has changed is that there is more flexibility in roles. Each couple figures out what is best for them. The number of U.S. couples in which the father provides primary child care while the mother is the chief wage earner has almost tripled, from 3 percent in 2004 to 8 percent in 2012, and continues to grow (Young & Schieman, 2018).

Employed women are earning more money and have more responsibilities than a few decades ago, when they were relegated to subordinate roles—the secretary, not the boss; the nurse, not the doctor. Nonetheless, old patterns persist, especially in family life, prompting the concept of a "stalled revolution" (Scarborough et al., 2019; Chancer, 2019).

For example, one man became the primary caregiver for his infant and 2-year-old but wanted to earn a paycheck. He found a part-time job (as a schoolbus driver) that allowed him to bring his children along. He said:

> In the last generation it's changed so much . . . . it's almost like you're on ice that's breaking up. That's how I felt. Like I was on ice breaking up. You don't really know what or where the father role is. You kind of have to define it for yourself . . . I think that's what I've learned most from staying home with the kids . . . Does it emasculate me that my wife is making more money?
>
> *[Geoff, quoted in Doucet, 2015, p. 235]*

Another father in the same study opened a day-care business for his own children and several others. Neither of these men felt comfortable being solely caregivers; both felt they should contribute financially.

No matter who does what, adults find parenting an ongoing challenge. Just when they figure out how to care for their infants, or preschoolers, or schoolchildren, those children grow older, presenting new dilemmas. One exasperated

CHAPTER APP 22

Cozi Family Organizer

IOS: https://tinyurl.com/y5cynkkk

ANDROID: https://tinyurl.com/y4b4byu8

RELEVANT TOPIC: Sharing family labor

The Cozi Family Organizer app helps users manage everyday family life with a shared calendar, reminders, to-do lists, and grocery list. This free, easy-to-use app can be used on most mobile devices and computers; a premium ad-free version with additional features is available for a yearly fee.

macmillan learning

VIDEO: Interview with Jay Belsky explores how problematic parenting practices are transmitted (or not) from one generation to the next.

mother told her criticizing teenager, "Give me a break. I'm learning on the job, I've never been a mother of an adolescent before."

Exactly how the parents collaborate may change as the children have new needs. Both parents tend to reduce outside work or choose more flexible hours when raising children, but specifics depend on the age of the children. Mothers are more likely to scale back (working part time instead of full time) during infancy; fathers reduce work hours or choose more flexible schedules when the children are in elementary school (Young & Schieman, 2018).

Throughout, privacy and income rarely seem adequate, and almost every child encounters some difficulties—with reading or math, with talking too much or too little, with being clumsy at sports or having illegible handwriting, and so on. It is the nature of childhood that challenges come and go, so a second-grader with a problem might, with a different teacher or better friends, have a happy fourth-grade year. Meanwhile, parents worry.

Tampa Bay Times/Brendan Fitterer/The Image Works

Joy from Generativity Six smiling members of this family from New Port Richey, Florida, are typical in one way and not in another. Unusual is that all four sisters are adopted. Typical is that the parents get great joy from their daughters, as is evident from their wide smiles.

Adoptive Parents Every form of nonbiological parenting poses special challenges. The easiest form may be adoption, since those adults are legally connected to their children for life. Moreover, adopted children are much wanted, so the parents are willing to provide the intensive care that children need.

Current adoptions are usually "open," which means that the birth parents decided that someone else would be a better parent, but they still want some connection to the child. The child knows about this arrangement, which makes it easier for everyone than the former "closed" adoption, when children and birth parents felt abandoned.

Strong parent–child attachments are often evident, especially when children are adopted as infants. Sadly, some adopted children have spent their early years in an institution, never attached to anyone. DSM-5 recognizes *reactive attachment disorder,* when a young child cannot seem to form any attachments. This can occur with children who live with their biological parents, but it is particularly likely with children who have spent infancy in institutions or who experienced a series of placements before adoption.

As you remember, adolescence—the time when teenagers seek their own identity—can stress any family. This stage is particularly problematic for adoptive families because normal conflicts can cut deep (Grotevant et al., 2017). One college student who feels well loved and cared for by her adoptive parents explains:

> In attempts to upset my parents sometimes I would (foolishly) say that I wish I was given to another family, but I never really meant it. Still when I did meet my birth family I could definitely tell we were related—I fit in with them so well. I guess I have a very similar attitude and make the same faces as my birth mother! It really makes me consider nature to be very strong in personality.
>
> [*A., personal communication*]

Tensions increase if outsiders hold the mistaken notion that only biological parents are the "real" parents. Of course, no matter what the genetic or ethnic connection between parents and children, the *real* parents are those who provide generative care.

Many adoptive parents who adopt either internationally or inter-ethnically seek multiethnic family friends and teach their children about their heritage. Helping children develop pride in themselves is also part of generativity if the child has same-sex parents, or single parents, or immigrant parents. Each family type provides special strengths. Adults realize that; children may need to be told.

Stepparents Generativity is also required for stepparents. The average new stepchild is 9 years old. This means that the child already has habits, morals, and a distinct personality before the stepparent arrived.

Often stepchildren have lived with both biological parents and then with a single parent, a grandparent, other relatives, and/or a paid caregiver. Every living condition affects the child, thus adding to adjustment complications.

New living arrangements are always disruptive for children (Goodnight et al., 2013). The effects are cumulative; emotions erupt in adolescence if not before, especially if the child is coping with a new school, loss of friends, or puberty. Stepchildren may intensify their attachment to their birth parents, which may be upsetting to a stepparent who wants to parent the child.

Most children are loyal to their birth parents. Added to that, stepchildren are more likely to become sick or injured, or, if they are teenagers, pregnant, drunk, or arrested. That childish reaction to disruption is understandable; so is the resentment that stepparents feel.

Few adults—biological parents or not—can live up to the generative ideal, day after day. Some stepparents quit trying. Wrong again. Hopefully, the new couple feels happy with each other, and the stepparent is sufficiently mature to react to hostility with patience. But, as one stepmother said:

> The dynamic is too crazy and you're trying as a, you know, as a stepmom I felt like I didn't want to overstep my bounds but yet I didn't want to seem like I was aloof either. So it's really hard. It was really hard for me to find my place with the boys.
>
> *[quoted in Perry-Fraser & Fraser, 2018, p. 245]*

Foster Parents An estimated 437,465 children were officially in foster care in the United States in 2016, about half of them cared for by adults who were strangers to them (Child Welfare Information Gateway, 2018). Many others are unofficially in foster care, because someone other than their biological parent has taken them in.

This is the most difficult form of parenting of all, partly because foster children typically have emotional and behavioral needs that require intense involvement. Foster parents need to spend far more time and effort on each child than biological parents do, yet the social context tends to devalue their efforts (J. Smith et al., 2013).

Contrary to popular prejudice, adults become foster parents more often for psychosocial than financial reasons, part of the adult generativity impulse (Geiger et al., 2013). Official foster parents are paid, but they typically earn far less than a babysitter would, or than they themselves would in a conventional job.

Most children are in foster care for less than a year, as the goal is usually a reunion with the birth parent. Children may be moved back to the original family for reasons unrelated to the wishes, competence, or emotions of the foster parents or the children.

The average child entering the foster-care system is 6 years old (Child Welfare Information Gateway, 2018). Many spent their early years with their birth families and are attached to them. Such human bonding is normally beneficial, not only for the children but also for the adults.

However, if birth parents are so neglectful or abusive that their children are removed, the child's past insecure or disorganized attachment impedes acceptance of the foster parent. Most foster children have experienced long-standing maltreatment and have witnessed violence; they are understandably suspicious of any adult.

Given the realities of life for those half a million U.S. children in official foster care, and the millions more in other nations, it is sad but unsurprising that a review of longitudinal research concludes that many foster children develop serious problems, including less education, more arrests, and earlier death (Gypen et al., 2017). Generative adults needed!

Heather Charles/Chicago Tribune/MCT via Tribune News Service/Getty Images

Here's Your Baby But only for a few weeks. More than 70 babies have spent days or weeks with Becky O'Connell until being united with their adoptive parents. As with baby Alex, shown here, the hardest part is giving them up—but, at age 64, Becky is unlikely to become a mother herself.

Everybody Contributes A large four-generation family such as this one helps meet the human need for love and belonging, the middle level of Maslow's hierarchy. When social scientists trace who contributes what to whom, the results show that everyone does their part, but the flow is more down than up: Grandparents give more money and advice to younger generations than vice versa.

Your knowledge of human development leads us to understand something not recognized by usual practices: Barriers make it difficult for foster parents to develop a generative attachment to their children. Nonetheless, sometimes such attachments develop, especially if the child is kept with one loving foster parent.

When adolescents have been with a stable foster family for years, about half the time a healthy, mutual attachment develops, a marked contrast to the relationship with their biological parents (Joseph et al., 2014).

Grandparents As already mentioned, the empty-nest stage of a marriage, when children have finally grown up and started independent lives, is often a happy time for parents. Grown children are more often a source of pride than of stress.

A new opportunity for generativity, as well as a new source of stress, occurs if grandchildren appear. That event once occurred on average at age 40, but now, in developed nations, grandparenthood begins on average at about age 50. Since adults now live longer and in better health than they once did, the length of active grandparenting is as long as it was in earlier times (Margolis & Arpino, 2018).

Thus, most adults begin grandparenthood 15 years before the next stage of development, late adulthood, which begins at age 65. Most continue to be grandparents and sometimes great-grandparents for several decades, while they also look after members of the older generation, as discussed in detail in Chapter 25.

Especially when the grandchildren's parents are troubled or overwhelmed, grandparents worldwide believe that they must help raise their grandchildren. Specifics depend on policies, customs, gender, past parenting, and income of both adult generations, but for every adult the generative impulse extends to caring for the youngest generation (Price et al., 2019).

Don't make the mistake of thinking that involved grandparents share a residence with their grandchildren. Only about 5 percent of all grandparents do so, and usually the child's mother lives there, too, doing most of the child care. Co-residence is more often a sign of poverty than generativity and correlates with more problems in all three generations (Masfety et al., 2019).

Regarding co-residence, one study surprised the researchers (Black et al., 2002). They focused on young African American mothers who had young children, comparing those who lived with their mothers and those who did not.

The scientists were not surprised that the live-in grandparents did not fare as well as grandparents who lived nearby but not with their children. That finding had already been discovered and replicated. But given "the enthusiasm of policy-makers for three-generation households," the study authors expected that the younger generations would benefit.

Not so. The young women who had their own homes were less often depressed than those who lived with their mothers (Black et al., 2002). The children also fared better, cognitively and emotionally, when they lived only with their mothers but not their grandmothers.

Why? The researchers suggested possible reasons. Perhaps conflicts arose when the mother and grandmother disagreed about child care, or perhaps the grandmothers disrupted mother–child attachment (Black et al., 2002).

Other research finds that a grandmother who is employed is more likely to retire early if she has major responsibility for her grandchildren (Timonen, 2018).

Typically, the grandfather is also supportive, but not always. One grandmother reports:

> When my daughter divorced, they nearly lost the house to foreclosure, so I went on the loan and signed for them. But then again they nearly foreclosed, so my husband and I bought it. . . . I have to make the payment on my own house and most of the payment on my daughter's house, and that is hard. . . . I am hoping to get that money back from our daughter, to quell my husband's sense that the kids are all just taking and no one is ever giving back. He sometimes feels used and abused.
>
> *[quoted in Meyer, 2014, pp. 5–6]*

We should not focus on the intergenerational problems. In every nation, adults who are grandparents usually enjoy helping their children and connecting with grandchildren. Some grandmothers are rhapsodic and spiritual about their experience. As one writes:

> Not until my grandson was born did I realize that babies are actually miniature angels assigned to break through our knee-jerk habits of resistance and to remind us that love is the real reason we're here.
>
> *[Golden, 2010, p. 125]*

Caregiving

Child care is the most common form of generativity for adults, but caregiving can and does occur in many other ways as well. Indeed, "life begins with care and ends with care" (Talley & Montgomery, 2013, p. 3). Some caregiving requires meeting physical needs—feeding, cleaning, and so on—but much of it involves fulfilling psychological needs. Caregiving is part of generative adulthood.

A VIEW FROM SCIENCE

The Skipped-Generation Family

Some U.S. households (about 1 percent) are two-generation families because the middle generation is missing. That is a *skipped-generation family,* with all parenting work done by the grandparents. Skipped-generation families require every ounce of generativity that grandparents can muster, often at the expense of their own health and happiness. This family type sometimes is designated officially to provide kinship care (true for one-third of the foster children), and it may include formal adoption by the grandparents.

In general, skipped-generation families have several strikes against them. Both the grandparents and the grandchildren are sad about the missing middle generation. In addition, difficult grandchildren (such as drug-affected infants and rebellious school-age boys) are more likely to live with grandparents (Hayslip & Smith, 2013). Many grandparents are resilient, but the challenges are real.

But before concluding that grandparents suffer when they are responsible for grandchildren, consider China, where millions of grandparents outside the urban areas become full-time caregivers because members of the middle generation have jobs in the cities and are unable to take children with them. In this way, Chinese culture and policy harms families, but, surprisingly, it does not seem to harm the elders.

The Chinese parents who are employed far from their natal home typically send money and visit once a year, on a national holiday. Studies are contradictory regarding the welfare of the children, but those grandparents seem to have *better* physical and psychological health (Baker & Silverstein, 2012; Chen et al., 2011) than grandparents who are not caregivers.

Better health does not necessarily mean happiness, however. A recent study of skipped-generation families in China found that grandparents under age 70 who live with their grandchildren without the children's parents were less happy overall. Those over age 70 were happier—contrary to the expectation of the researchers (Wen et al., 2019).

This suggests that the social context is crucial: If grandparents are supported and appreciated by their children and the community, a skipped-generation family may benefit the grandparents. Much depends on attitudes, not simply caregiving itself.

A Peak Experience For many men, the best part of fatherhood is when their children become old enough to share interest in world events, sports, or, as shown here, climbing a mountain in Norway.

Observation Quiz Father and daughter are each doing something that typifies their care for one another. What is each of them doing? (see answer, page 580) ↑

kinkeeper Someone who becomes the gatherer and communications hub for their family.

sandwich generation The generation of middle-aged people who are supposedly "squeezed" by the needs of the younger and older members of their families.

Kinkeepers A prime example of caregiving is the **kinkeeper**, who gathers all the generations for holidays; spreads the word about illness, relocation, or accomplishments; and reminds family members of one another's birthdays and anniversaries.

Kinkeepers also chronicle the family's history and thereby connect family members, adding to satisfaction and belonging for all family members (Hendry & Ledbetter, 2017). Middle-aged adults allow families and societies "to engage and value the assets found in every generation" (Butts, 2017, p. vi). Mutual caregiving and shared information strengthens family bonds; wise kinkeepers keep those intergenerational channels open; everyone is generative (Hendry & Ledbetter, 2017).

Middle-aged adults have been called the **sandwich generation**, a term that evokes an image of a layer of filling pressed between two slices of bread. This analogy suggests that the middle generation is squeezed because they are expected to support their parents and their growing children. This sandwich metaphor is vivid but misleading (Gonyea, 2013).

Longitudinal data found "relatively few cases where middle-aged adults were in a 'sandwich generation' of simultaneously providing care for aged parents and children younger than 15" (Fingerman et al., 2012d, p. 200). Family members across the generations are especially significant for some adults, but that is more voluntary than obligatory. Moreover, caregiving is mutual, taking many forms

Far from being squeezed, middle-aged adults who provide some financial and emotional help to their adult children are *less* likely to be depressed than those adults whose children no longer relate to them. The research finds that family members continue to care for each other, less as a matter of obligation but more as a result of varied connections.

Emerging adults, depicted as squeezing their parents, often help their parents understand music, media, fashion, and technology—setting up their smartphones, sending digital photos, fixing computer glitches. They also are more cognizant of nutritional and medical discoveries and guidelines.

Caregiving on the other side of the supposed sandwich, from middle-aged adults to their elderly parents, is typically much less demanding than the metaphor implies. Most members of the over-60 generation are quite independent. Financial support is more likely to flow from them to their middle-aged children than vice versa. In the United States, if more care is needed, it is more often provided by a spouse, another elderly person, or a paid caregiver, than by a middle-aged child.

Employment

Besides parenthood and caregiving, the other major avenue for generativity is employment. A well-established specialty within the field of psychology focuses on the productivity of workers and companies.

You can read extensive research regarding many aspects of economic development, such as when and where telecommuting is beneficial, how to organize work teams and times, and almost every aspect of job conditions—lighting, wall colors, coffee breaks, and more. Details are not presented here. Instead we consider the personal details of human development and employment.

Lowered Expectations It was once realistic, a "secular trend," for adults to expect to be better off than their parents had been, but hard times have reduced the socioeconomic status of many adults.

Generativity and Work As is evident from many terms that describe healthy adult development—*generativity, success and esteem, instrumental,* and *achievement*—adults have many psychosocial needs that work can fill.

Employment meets these needs by allowing people to do the following:

- Develop and use their personal skills.
- Express their creative energy.

- Aid and advise coworkers, as mentor or friend.
- Support the education and health of their families.
- Contribute to the community by providing goods or services.

These facts highlight the distinction between the **extrinsic rewards of work** (the tangible benefits such as salary, health insurance, and pension) and the **intrinsic rewards of work** (the intangible gratifications of actually doing the job). Generativity is intrinsic. [**Life-Span Link:** Extrinsic and intrinsic motivation are introduced in Chapter 10.]

extrinsic rewards of work The tangible benefits, usually in salary, insurance, pension, and status, that come with employment.

intrinsic rewards of work The personal gratifications, such as pleasure in a job well done or friendships with coworkers, that accompany employment.

These two types of rewards may be negatively correlated, which means that employers may increase pay *instead* of creating working conditions that improve intrinsic rewards. That is a mistake, as intrinsic rewards correlate with worker satisfaction, worker effort, less burnout, and fewer workers who quit to find another job (Kuvaas et al., 2017).

There may be a developmental shift here. Prospective young workers compare pay, hours, and insurance (Kooij et al., 2011). However, as time goes on, the intrinsic rewards of work, especially relationships among coworkers, keep employees at the same job and working hard (Inceoglu et al., 2012).

The power of intrinsic rewards explains why older employees are, on average, less often absent or late and more committed to doing a good job than younger workers are (Rau & Adams, 2014). Because of seniority, they also have more control over what they do, as well as when and how they do it. That reduces strain and increases dedication.

Further, experienced workers are more likely to be mentors—people who help new workers navigate the job. Mentors benefit in many ways, gaining status and generativity—both intrinsic.

Surprisingly, absolute income (whether a person earns $30,000 or $40,000 or even $100,000 a year, for instance) matters less for job satisfaction than how a salary compares with others in their profession or neighborhood, or with their own salary a year or more earlier. That may explain why some executives make far more money than they need—they compare themselves with other corporate heads.

It is a human trait to react more strongly to personal losses than to personal gains, ignoring systemic losses unless they become personal (Kahneman, 2011). Consequently, salary cuts have emotional, not just financial, effects.

Apparently, resentment about work arises not directly from wages and benefits but from how wages are determined and whether people believe that their income or status might improve. If workers have a role in setting wages and they perceive that those wages are fair, they are more satisfied (Choshen-Hillel & Yaniv, 2011).

This explains a puzzle. Most Americans are troubled about the large salary disparity between the rich and the poor. However, relatively few consider this a major problem (Norton & Ariely, 2011). Why not?

One answer is that people believe that social mobility is possible—that they themselves will be able to earn more (Davidai & Gilovich, 2015). They also blame people who are poorer than they are, judging them lazy, or spendthrift, or worse. That is psychologically healthy, even if irrational.

Unemployment For adults of any age, unemployment—especially if it lasts more than a few weeks—is destructive of mental and physical health. Generative needs are unmet, which increases the rate of domestic abuse, substance use disorder, depression, and many other social and mental health problems (Wanberg, 2012). Recent studies

Michael Short/Bloomberg/Getty Images

Designed for People The Google headquarters in Mountain View, California, includes many places to relax and socialize, inside and outside. How much of Google's success came from emphasizing the intrinsic rewards of employment?

suggest that, in addition to the burden of unemployment, uncertainty about future income and work adds to family stress (Schneider et al., 2017).

A meta-analysis of research on eight stressful events found that losing a job was even worse for mental health than the death of a parent. The stress of past unemployment lingered after finding a job (Luhmann et al., 2012).

THINK CRITICALLY: Is the connection between employment and developmental health cause or correlation?

Developmentalists are particularly concerned when the economy, or the automization of labor, results in fewer jobs for millions of adults. Current unemployment of emerging adults—people who are NEET (Not in Education, Employment, or Training)—may harm that generation lifelong, a "grave concern." One careful study of thousands of NEETs in Great Britain found that they seek work but are stymied by the job market and by their own traits (Goldman-Mellor et al., 2016).

Unemployment is troubling at any age. Adults who are unemployed are 60 percent more likely to die than other people, especially if they are younger than 40 (Roelfs et al., 2011). They are twice as likely to be clinically depressed (Wanberg, 2012) and almost twice as likely to be addicted to drugs (Compton et al., 2014).

Worst may be job loss when adults have a partner and children. That causes a "cascade" of family stresses, harming every family member, with trouble reverberating within the family and adding new stresses and increasing problems for everyone (McKee-Ryan & Maitoza, 2018).

For example, job loss may change child-care arrangements, so children fight more and comply less, so parents punish more, so everyone sleeps less, so children are tired in school, so the teacher asks parents to come in, so the parent cannot focus on finding work. Family meals become erratic, with less fresh vegetables and sometimes less food overall, causing hunger, obesity, and health problems.

Unemployment can turn a happy, supportive family into a sad and destructive one. Family and friends are the best buffer against the psychological strain of losing a job, but that support also may be reduced when it is needed most (Crowe & Butterworth, 2016; McKee-Ryan & Maitoza, 2018).

The Changing Workplace Employment is changing in many ways that affect adult development. We focus here on only three—diversity among workers, job changes, and alternate schedules. Dramatic shifts have occurred in all three. We will use U.S. statistics to illustrate these shifts, but these phenomena occur worldwide.

FIGURE 22.3

Better or Worse? It depends on who you are. Ideally, everyone has a job.

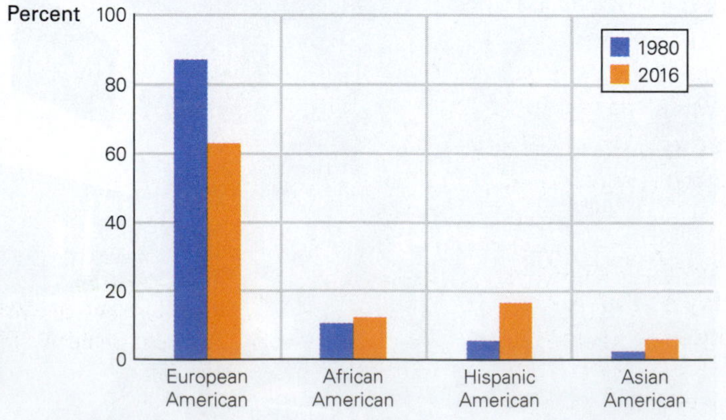

Data from Toossi, 2002, pp. 19–20, and U.S. Bureau of Labor Statistics, August, 2018.

As you can see from **Figure 22.3**, the workforce is becoming more diverse. Fifty years ago, the U.S. civilian labor force was 74 percent male and 89 percent non-Hispanic White. In 2017, 53 percent were male and 63 percent non-Hispanic White (15 percent were Hispanic who identified as White, 2 percent Hispanic who identified as Black, 13 percent African American, 6 percent Asian, 1 percent American Indian or Pacific Islander).

This shift is also notable within occupations. For example, in 1960, male nurses and female police officers were rare, perhaps 1 percent. Now 11 percent of registered nurses are men and 14 percent of police officers are women—still an unbalanced ratio, but a dramatic shift nonetheless (U.S. Bureau of Labor Statistics, 2016b). Job discrimination relating to gender and ethnicity still exists—but it is much less prevalent than it once was.

OPPOSING PERSPECTIVES

Accommodating Diversity

Accommodating the various sensitivities and needs of a diverse workforce requires far more than reconsidering the cafeteria menu and the holiday schedule. Private rooms for breast-feeding, revised uniform guidelines, new office design, and changing management practices may be necessary.

Many corporations and executives are trying to make the workplace a productive environment for everyone, with mixed results (Robinson, 2019). Exactly what is needed depends on the particular culture of the workers: Some are satisfied with conditions that others would reject.

To make the situation more complex, diversity is about more than ethnicity. Religious differences (holidays that were not in the calendar), age differences (especially boomers versus millennials), and gender disparities (e.g., in uniforms) are also concerns.

Now consider one example. Many New Zealand supervisors of European descent criticize Maori workers (descendent from Polynesians who had lived there several hundred years before the first Europeans) for "extending the leave they were given for attending a family or tribe *hui* (gathering or meeting) without notifying them. . . . If the reasons behind are not understood, such critical incidents may . . . easily lead to over-generalizations and stereotyping and finally to less employment of people who are labeled as 'unreliable'" (Podsiadlowski & Fox, 2011, p. 8).

What might those "reasons behind" be? For British New Zealanders, a funeral of a cousin might take a day. Employees from that culture resent that a Maori coworker might be gone much longer, appearing back at work a week or more later.

Yet, the Maori were expected by their families to stay for several days: It would be disrespectful to leave quickly. The cultural clash regarding work schedules and family obligations led to anger and rejection.

Less obvious examples occur daily, at every workplace. Certain words, policies, jokes, or mannerisms seem innocuous to one group but hostile to others.

- Women object to suggestive calendars or pictures hung in offices and to any comments that are gender-specific.
- Exchanging Christmas presents, as in the office "Secret Santa," may be troubling to those who are Jehovah's Witnesses or to those who are not Christian.
- Resentment may stir if a man calls a woman "honey" or if a supervisor creates a nickname for an employee with a hard-to-pronounce name.
- Comments about a celebrity of another race, gender identity, or sexual orientation may be heard as insults.

Researchers have begun to explore *micro-aggressions*—small things that go unnoticed by one person but seem aggressive to another (Sue, 2010). Mentioning "senior moments" or being "color-blind" or the "fairer sex" can be perceived as aggressive, even though the speaker believes they are benign.

The question "Where are you from?" may seem innocent, or even friendly, but it implies that someone is from elsewhere. This question may be micro-aggressive to a Hispanic American born in Puerto Rico or Texas, whose family members have been U.S. citizens for decades (Nadal et al., 2014). Micro-aggressions can affect anyone who feels different because of their ethnicity, age, gender identity, sexual orientation, religion, or anything else.

To create a workplace that respects diversity, mutual effort is needed. Not only must everyone learn about sensitivities and customs, but everyone also must communicate. When an innocent comment is heard as an insult, both parties need to be more aware.

These changes benefit millions of adults who would have been jobless in previous decades. They also require workers and employers to be sensitive to differences that they did not previously notice. Younger adults may have an advantage: A 25-year-old employee is not surprised to have a female boss or a coworker of another ethnicity. Since a goal of human development is for everyone to fulfill their potential, developmentalists welcome reduced discrimination at work. The next two changes are not as positive.

Changing Locations Today's workers change employers more often than did workers decades ago. Hiring and firing are common. Employers constantly downsize, reorganize, relocate, outsource, or merge. Loyalty between employee and employer, once assumed, now seems quaint.

Whether they originate from the workers or the employers, changes may increase corporate profits, worker benefits, and consumer choice. However, churning employment may harm development. Losing work friendships means

Especially for Entrepreneurs
Suppose you are starting a business. In what ways would middle-aged adults be helpful to you? (see response, page 580)

losing a source of social support. Bouts of employment and unemployment may be worse for older adults for several reasons.

1. Seniority brings higher salaries, more respect, and greater expertise; workers who leave a job they have had for years lose these advantages.
2. Many skills required for employment were not taught decades ago, so older workers are less likely to find a new job.
3. Workers believe that age discrimination is widespread. Even if this is a misperception, stereotype threat undercuts successful job searching.
4. Especially if a new job requires relocation, long-standing intimacy and generativity are reduced.

From a developmental and family perspective, this last factor is crucial. Imagine that you are a 50-year-old who has always lived in West Virginia and your employer goes out of business. You try to find work, but no one hires you, partly because unemployment in West Virginia is among the highest in the nation. Would you move a thousand miles to North Dakota, where the 2019 unemployment rate is less than half that of West Virginia (2.3 versus 5 percent)?

If you were unemployed and in debt, and a new job was guaranteed, you might. You would leave friends, community, and local culture, but at least you would have a paycheck.

But, would your family leave their homes, jobs, schools, places of worship, and friends to move with you? If not, you would be deprived of social support; but if they did, their food and housing would be expensive, their schools overcrowded, and their lives lonely. For you and your family, moving reduces intimacy—harmful for psychosocial development.

Such difficulties are magnified for immigrants, who make up about 15 percent of the U.S. adult workforce and 22 percent of Canada's. Many depend on other immigrants for housing, work, religion, and social connections (García Coll & Marks, 2012). That may meet some of their intimacy and generativity needs, but their relationships with their original family and friends are strained by distance. The climate, the food, and the language are not comforting.

These developmental needs are ignored by most business owners and by many workers themselves. However, intimacy and generativity are best satisfied by a thriving social network, and each neighborhood and workplace fosters that. When that is disrupted, psychological and physical health suffers. The myth of the rugged, self-sufficient individual may underlie the increasing rate of "deaths of despair" in middle-aged men when economic security is high (Knapp et al., 2019; Griffith et al., 2019).

Changing Schedules The standard workweek is 9 A.M. to 5 P.M., Monday through Friday. In the United States, about one-third of all workers have nonstandard schedules. Retail services (online and in-store) are increasingly available 24/7, which requires night and weekend employees. Many other parts of the economy (hospitals, police, hotels) need employees with nonstandard schedules. Employers, customers, and employees see many benefits.

It has long been recognized that varied schedules upset body rhythms, making adults vulnerable to physical illness as well as emotional problems (Cho, 2018; Schneider & Harknett, 2019). All mammals depend on circadian rhythm. When schedules vary, either with one person working varied hours or with different family members not having the same schedule, that undercuts the body systems and family systems that protect health.

Specific data find that, perhaps because of disrupted sleep, shift workers have higher rates of obesity, illness, and death. One detail: Women more often develop breast cancer if their work hours vary (Wegrzyn et al., 2017). Night work itself increases the risk of breast cancer (Cordina-Duverger et al., 2018). Rotating schedules are worse than steady night work.

Beyond health, the impact of varying schedules on family life is a major concern for developmentalists (Cho, 2018). Those who are most likely to have mandatory nonstandard schedules are parents of young children, exactly the people who need regular schedules, with time allowed in case of a sick child.

The focus is often on working mothers, but weekend work, especially with mandatory overtime, is also difficult for father–child relationships, because "normal rhythms of family life are impinged upon by irregular schedules" (Hook, 2012, p. 631). Couples who have less time together are more likely to divorce (Maume & Sebastian, 2012).

PAUL ROVERE/Fairfax Media/Getty Images

Happy Family Dad is a firefighter, and when this photo was taken he had been on call for two weeks because of bushfires near his home in Victoria, Australia. The scene here is idyllic, but often irregular schedules—typical of firefighters, nurses, police officers, and shift workers of all kinds—disrupt family life. Fortunately, this family may truly be as happy as they seem because of four factors: (1) wife and mother (Helen) keeps the family running smoothly; (2) the children are old enough to understand why their father's schedule is necessary; (3) communities are usually quite proud of their firefighters; and (4) perhaps most importantly, Dad volunteered for this assignment.

Choices about hours, overtime, and tasks increase job satisfaction. This is true no matter how experienced the workers are, what their occupation is, or where they live (Tuttle & Garr, 2012). For instance, a nationwide study of 53,851 nurses, ages 20 to 59, found that *required* overtime was one of the few factors that reduced job satisfaction in every cohort (Klaus et al., 2012). Apparently, although employment is often satisfying, working too long, not by choice, undercuts the psychological and physical benefits.

In theory, part-time work or self-employment allows adults to balance conflicting demands. But reality does not conform to the theory. In many nations, part-time work is underpaid and without benefits. Thus, workers avoid part-time employment if they can, making a choice that inadvertently undercuts their emotional well-being and family life. Self-employment also typically means more work for less money.

Similar problems occur with temporary work. Temporary employment is increasing. This makes sense for the employers: It provides a buffer against another recession, and it is cheaper to hire workers without full benefits. However, job uncertainty increases job dissatisfaction, which increases stress on families (Dawson et al., 2017). Again, the needs of employers and employees conflict.

A major concern has arisen for all working adults, a conflict between employment and family life. This difficulty was once thought to be a problem only for women, but men now also experience it. A balance between all aspects of adult life is needed for adults of every gender and family situation.

National policies make a difference. For example, virtually every nation except the United States mandates paid leave for new mothers, and about 20 nations allow paid leave for new fathers. Both of those make sense to developmentalists who support family life. However, no nation prioritizes a satisfying balance between employment and family life for every adult (Ollo-Lopez & Goñi-Legaz, 2017). The task of finding that balance rests with individuals.

Finding the Balance

As you see, adulthood is filled with opportunities and challenges. Adults choose their mates, their locations, and their lifestyles to express their personality. Extroverts surround themselves with many social activities, and introverts choose a quieter but no less rewarding life.

Adults have many ways to meet their intimacy needs, with partners of the same or other sex, with marriage or cohabiting, with friends and family, with their older parents or grown children. Ideally, they find some combination that results in solid social support. Similarly, generativity can focus on raising children, caring for others, or satisfying work, again with more choices and flexibility than in past decades.

In some ways, then, modern life allows adults to "have it all," to combine family and work in such a way that all needs are satisfied at once. However, some very articulate observers suggest that "having it all" is an illusion or, at best, a mistaken ideal achievable only by the very rich and very talented (Slaughter, 2012; Sotomayor, 2014; Kramer et al., 2019).

Compromises, trade-offs, and selective optimization with compensation may be essential to finding an appropriate work–family balance. Both halves of these two sources of generativity can bring joy, but both can bring stress—and often do. In general, adults—mates, family, and friends—help each other, together balancing intimacy and generativity needs.

Because personality is enduring and variable, opinions about the impact of modern life reflect personality as well as objective research. Some people are optimists—high in extroversion and agreeableness—and they tend to believe that adulthood is better now than it used to be.

Others are pessimists—high in neuroticism and low in openness—and they are likely to conclude that adults were better off before the rise of cohabitation, LAT, divorce, and economic stress. They may praise the time when most people married and stayed married, raising children on the man's steady salary from his 9-to-5 job with one stable employer. Were those days idyllic or destructive?

Data could be used to support both perspectives. For instance, in the United States, suicide is less common than it was 40 years ago, and crime is down (life is better); but the gap between rich and poor is increasing, as is the frequency of climate-related disasters (life is worse). Fewer people are marrying and fewer children are born: Is that evidence for improved adult lives or the opposite?

Every adult benefits from friends and family, caregiving responsibilities, and satisfying work. Whether this is easier or more difficult at this historical moment is debatable.

As you will read in the final set of chapters, there are many possible perspectives on life in late adulthood as well. Some view the last years of life with horror, while others consider them golden. The next trio of chapters will help you develop your own view, informed by empirical data, not prejudice.

WHAT HAVE YOU LEARNED?

1. How is generativity a distinct human need?
2. In what ways does parenthood satisfy the need to be generative?
3. Why might it be more difficult for parents to bond with nonbiological children?
4. What do kinkeepers do, and who becomes one?
5. What is the relationship between caregiving and generativity?
6. What is the relationship between the extrinsic and intrinsic rewards of work?
7. What are the advantages of greater ethnic diversity at work?
8. Why is changing jobs stressful?
9. How have innovations in work scheduling helped and harmed families?

SUMMARY

Personality Development in Adulthood

1. Erikson emphasized that people at every stage of life are influenced by their social context. The adulthood stages are much less age-based than the childhood stages because the need for intimacy and generativity are evident throughout adulthood.

2. Maslow and other humanists believe that people of all ethnic and national origins have the same basic needs. People first must have their physical needs met and then feel safe. Beyond that, love and respect are crucial. Finally, people can be truly themselves, becoming self-actualized.

3. Personality traits over the years of adulthood are quite stable, although many adults become closer to their culture's ideal. The Big Five personality traits—openness, conscientiousness, extroversion, agreeableness, and neuroticism—characterize personality at every age. Culture and context affect everyone.

Intimacy: Connecting with Others

4. Intimacy is a universal human need, satisfied in diverse ways with romantic partners, friends, and family. Variations are evident, by culture and cohort.

5. Marriage is no longer the only way to establish a romantic partnership. Although societies benefit if people marry and stay married, many adults prefer cohabitation or living apart together. Same-sex and other-sex relationships are similar in most ways.

6. Divorce sometimes may be the best way to end a conflicted relationship, but divorce is difficult for every partner and family member, not only immediately but for years before and after the decree.

7. Remarriage is common, especially for men. This solves some of the problems (particularly financial and social) of divorced adults, but the success of second marriages varies. Children add complications.

8. Friends are crucial for buffering stress and sharing secrets as well as for everyday companionship and guidance. This is true for both men and women, with younger adults having more friends but older adults preferring fewer, closer friends.

9. Family members have linked lives, continuing to affect one another as they all grow older. Parents and adult children are less likely to live together than in the twentieth century, but family members are still mutually supportive, emotionally and financially.

Generativity: The Work of Adulthood

10. Adults seek to be generative, successful, achieving, instrumental—all words used to describe a major psychosocial need that each adult meets in various ways.

11. Parenthood is a common expression of generativity. Wanted and planned-for biological children pose challenges. Other forms of parenthood are harder. Adoptive children, stepchildren, and especially foster children bring additional stresses.

12. Caregiving is more likely to flow from the older generations to the younger ones, so the "sandwich generation" metaphor is misleading. Many families have a kinkeeper, who aids generativity within the family.

13. Employment brings many rewards to adults, including intrinsic benefits such as pride and friendship. Changes in employment patterns—job switches, shift work, and the diversity of fellow workers—affect other aspects of adult development. Unemployment is particularly difficult for self-esteem, and it impacts everyone in the family.

14. Balancing work and family life, personal needs, and social involvement is a major task for adults. This is true for men as well as women, since both now function in both spheres.

15. Combining work demands, caregiving requirements, intimacy, and generativity is not easy; consequences are mixed. Some adults benefit from new patterns within the labor market and in the overall culture; others find that a happy balance is difficult.

KEY TERMS

generativity versus stagnation (p. 556)
humanism (p. 557)
Big Five (p. 558)
empty nest (p. 562)
social convoy (p. 564)
fictive kin (p. 565)
kinkeeper (p. 572)
sandwich generation (p. 572)
extrinsic rewards of work (p. 573)
intrinsic rewards of work (p. 573)

APPLICATIONS

1. Describe a relationship that you know of in which a middle-aged person and a younger adult learned from each other.

2. Did your parents' marital and employment status affect you? How would you have fared if they had chosen other marriage or work patterns?

3. Imagine becoming a foster parent or adoptive parent yourself. What do you see as the personal benefits and costs?

4. Ask several people how their personalities have changed in the past decade. The research suggests that changes are usually minor. Is that what you found?

Especially For ANSWERS

Response for Immigrants and Children of Immigrants (from p. 558): Extroversion and neuroticism, according to one study (Silventoinen et al., 2008). Because these traits decrease over adulthood, fewer older adults migrate.

Response for Young Couples (from p. 563): There is no simple answer, but you should bear in mind that while abuse usually decreases with age, breakups become more difficult with every year, especially if children are involved.

Response for Entrepreneurs (from p. 575): As employees and as customers. Middle-aged workers are steady, with few absences and good "people skills," and they like to work. In addition, household income is likely to be higher at about age 50 than at any other time, so middle-aged adults will probably be able to afford your products or services.

Observation Quiz ANSWERS

Answer to Observation Quiz (from p. 567) Mothers could have those facial expressions or use their arms that way—but fathers do it more often.

Answer to Observation Quiz (from p. 572) He carries the pack with supplies for both of them; she memorializes the hike with a selfie.

CAREER ALERT The Physical Therapist

Almost every adult will, at some point, need physical therapy. Bodies age, and with aging comes reduced physical ability. Moreover, dozens of diseases that affect strength and agility—such as diabetes, arthritis, osteoporosis, heart disease—are increasing, because people are living longer, but fewer exercise as part of their work or normal routine. Cars, riding lawnmowers, and robotic vacuum cleaners have replaced walking, pushing a mower, sweeping the floor.

Thus, for many reasons, physical therapists are among the fastest growing occupations in the United States today. The U.S. Bureau of Labor Statistics projects a 25-percent increase over the next 10 years in the number of PTs (physical therapists)—and that does not include the closely-related, also expanding, profession of occupational therapy.

Salaries are high—in 2016, the median annual salary was $85,400. Education requirements are also high: A physical therapist needs to know how to advise people with every kind of disability.

For instance, as you read in Chapter 1, I had very minor surgery (one toe kept sticking up, making it hard to wear dress shoes, so the bone needed to be realigned). The surgeon said it would be painful and that I should not walk much for weeks. I was defiant, discarding most of my pain medication and walking two days after the surgery.

I reluctantly followed the surgeon's advice to see a physical therapist. I expected the PT to laugh and tell me that this therapy was for legs, arms, and backs, not for toes. But instead she put special lotion on her hands and massaged my toes and taught me six exercises to do every day. When I told her that I was amazed that she knew exercises for a toe, she explained that she was taught what to do for every part of the body and added, "Your toe is connected to the rest of you."

I realized that she knew about my whole body, and everything that might affect my ability to do whatever I wanted to do with it. A worthy profession indeed.

VISUALIZING DEVELOPMENT Family Connections

There are many ways to depict family living arrangements, and all of them lead to the same conclusions. Generally, family members remain connected to each other lifelong. Burdensome caregiving is not the norm.

LIVING ARRANGEMENTS, YOUNG AND OLD, UNITED STATES

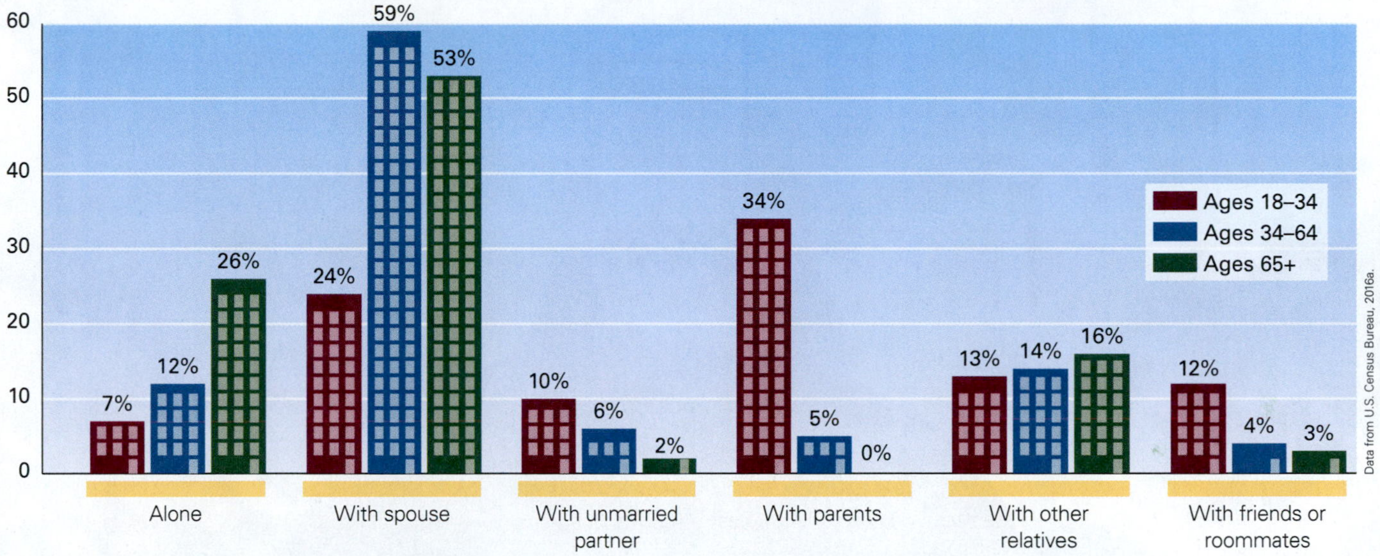

Most families have only one generation of adults, but when two generations are present, parents are more often helping adult children than the reverse.

U.S. FAMILIES WITH ONLY ONE GENERATION OF ADULTS (OVER AGE 18)

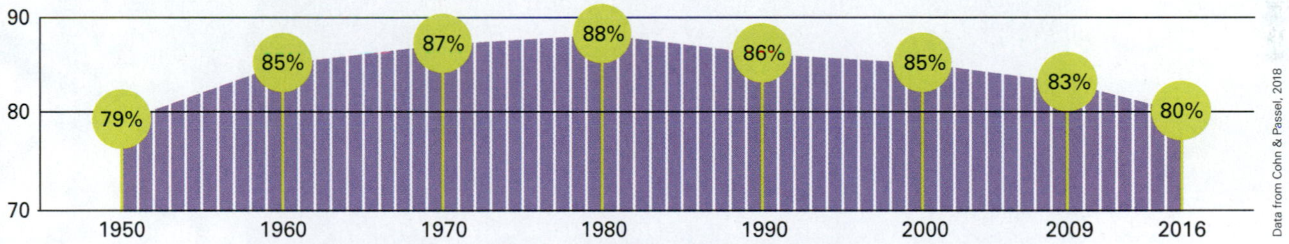

As you see, there are only slightly more two-adult generation families in the United States today than 30 years ago. What *has* changed, however, is that those extra adults are usually adult children, not aged parents. So, what percentage of adults live with other generations of adults over age 18?

ADULTS LIVING WITH OTHER GENERATIONS

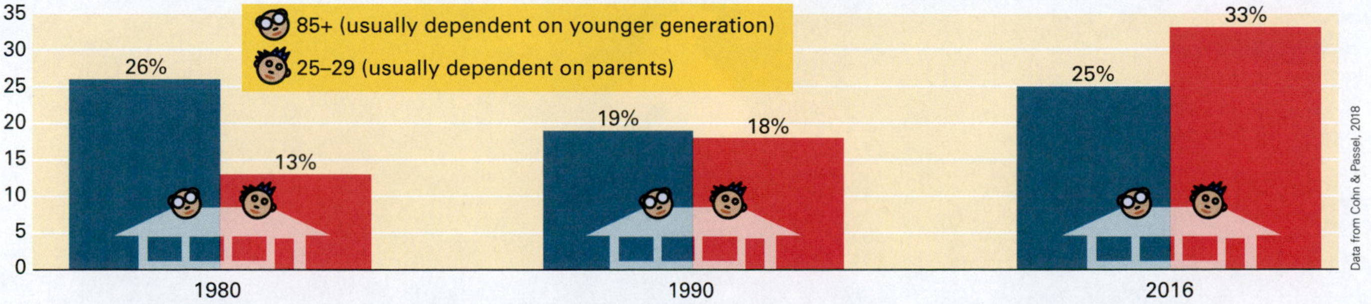

Currently about one-fourth of younger adults and about one-third of the oldest-old are living with the middle generation. Thus, despite the hype of intergenerational living, this is not the norm.

CHAPTERS 23•24•25

PART VIII

Late Adulthood

What emotions do you expect when you read about late adulthood? Sadness, fear, depression, resignation, sympathy, sorrow? Expect instead surprise and joy. You will learn that most older adults are active, alert, and self-sufficient; that dramatic loss of memory and logic ("senility") is unusual; and that many are independent and happy.

This does not mean that you should anticipate mindless contentment. Earlier personality and social connections continue; the complexities of life are evident. Joy is mixed with sorrow. Poverty, loneliness, and chronic illness are difficult. However, most older adults — most of the time — overcome such difficulties.

If you doubt this, you are not alone. Late adulthood, more than any other part of life, is a magnet for misinformation. Ageism may be worse than other *-isms* because everyone experiences it if they live long enough, but almost no one is well prepared for it.

Left: Maskot/Getty Images
Right: Image Source/Divine Images/Media Bakery

Late Adulthood: Biosocial Development

CHAPTER 23

What Will You Know?

- How is ageism like racism?
- Can people slow down the aging process?
- Why would anyone want to live to 100?

- **Prejudice and Predictions**
  - The Special Harm
  - A VIEW FROM SCIENCE: I'm Not Like Those Other Old People
  - Demography and Ageism
- **Adjusting to Changes**
  - Microsystem Compensation: Sex
  - A CASE TO STUDY: Sex Among Older Adults
  - Macrosystem Compensation: Driving
  - Exosystem Compensation: The Senses
  - Primary and Secondary Aging
- **Theories of Aging**
  - Wear and Tear
  - It's All Genetic
  - Aging of the Cells
- **VISUALIZING DEVELOPMENT: Elders Behind the Wheel**

I took Asa, age 1, to the playground. One mother, watching her son, warned that the sandbox would soon be crowded because the children from a nearby day-care center were coming. I asked questions, and to my delight she explained details of the center's curriculum, staffing, scheduling, and tuition, as if she assumed I was Asa's mother, weighing my future options.

Soon I realized that she was merely being polite, because a girl too young to be graciously ageist glanced at me and asked, "Is that your grandchild?"

I nodded.

"Where is the mother?" was her next question.

Later that afternoon came the final blow. As I opened the gate for a middle-aged man, he said, "Thank you, young lady." I don't think I look old, but no one would imagine I was young. That "young lady" was benevolent, but it made me realize that my pleasure at the first woman's words was a sign of my own self-deceptive prejudice.

Now we begin our study of the last phase of life, from age 65 or so until death. This chapter starts by exploring the prejudices that surround aging. We describe biosocial changes—and what can be done to mitigate them. Then we provide a perspective on diseases, an exploration of the causes of aging, and what can be done to slow them down.

This is not a medical textbook, but various ailments that are common in the elderly—insomnia, heart disease, diabetes, osteoporosis, arthritis, erectile dysfunction, poor vision, deafness, hypertension, pneumonia, influenza, and accidental death—are all described in context, as examples of primary or secondary aging, selective optimization, the compression of morbidity, acute or chronic illness, and so on.

We also describe some of the advantages of the later years. One of them is that all of these ailments can be avoided or mitigated. For everyone, most of the body functions well, allowing exercise, interests, and joy.

Prejudice and Predictions

ageism A prejudice whereby people are categorized and judged solely on the basis of their chronological age.

Prejudice about late adulthood is common among people of all ages. That is **ageism**, which "shares parallels with other prejudices, such as racism and sexism. Like any form of bias, ageism effectively reduces individuals to broad, stereotypical categories" (North, 2015).

Because it is part of the culture, ageism is particularly hard to combat. That was a conclusion of a program that attempted to dislodge ageism from the implicit thoughts of children (Babcock et al., 2018).

The Special Harm

Ageism is likely to become a *self-fulfilling prophecy,* a prediction that comes true because people believe it. There are three harmful consequences:

- If older people are treated as frail and confused, they become less independent.
- If the norms for younger adults are taken as universal, people try to make older adults fit them.
- If older people themselves think that their age makes them feeble, they may stop self-care, avoid social interaction, or ignore early, treatable symptoms of disease.

THINK CRITICALLY: Why do many people contemplate aging with sorrow rather than joy?

Every *-ism* is destructive, but ageism is distinctly harmful. One reason is that its victims are unprepared, without decades of recognizing and counteracting it. Another reason is that both perpetrators and victims of ageism may think it is benevolent (Kagan, 2018).

For example, describing someone as a "sweet old lady" who "still has all her marbles" is ageist. The third reason is that the aged themselves may avoid the company of other older people, thus removing the social experiences that could benefit them all. (My mother did that, as described in A View from Science.)

Finally, some truth is mixed in with the stereotype. That makes it harder to recognize. Accordingly, we begin with three examples: sleep, exercise, and elderspeak.

Sleep Inadequate sleep contributes to illness. Many problems that appear in late adulthood—restless legs, muscle pain, breathing difficulties, snoring—interfere with sleep. Then disturbed and inadequate sleep makes these and every other problem worse and may cause major depression (D. Patel et al., 2018). The origin of the problem may be ageism, if elders and doctors expect the same sleep patterns in adults no matter what their age.

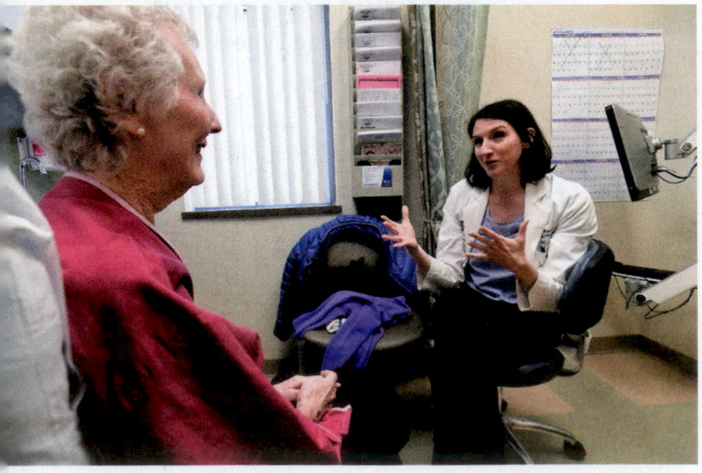

Explaining Her Cancer Dr. Magnuson is a specialist in geriatric oncology, so she knows how to explain treatment options to Nancy Simpson. The elderly are quite capable of making informed decisions, as long as their doctors do not oversimplify or use elderspeak.

AP Images/Adrian Kraus

Instead, sleep (and everything else) changes with age. Only babies should "sleep like a baby." The circadian rhythm that shifts at adolescence shifts again, in the other direction, in late adulthood. Elders are often sleepy in the early evening and up before dawn. It is also typical for elders to wake often during the night and to nap every day (Gulia & Kumar, 2018).

How much sleep a person needs varies, not only from one person to another and from one age to another, with the old needing less sleep (unless they are sick) than the young (D. Patel et al., 2018). If elders do not realize this, they may lie in bed at dawn, awake and frustrated for hours.

Many elders complain of *insomnia,* which, according to DSM-5, is defined as being distressed with their sleep. They may self-medicate by drinking alcohol at bedtime, which increases nighttime falls, disturbing dreams, and early waking. In other words, because normal changes make them distressed, that causes insomnia, which they treat with alcohol, and that causes real sleep disturbances.

A VIEW FROM SCIENCE

I'm Not Like Those Other Old People

My mother, in her 80s, was reluctant to enter an assisted-living apartment. She told me that she did not want to live there because too many of the people were old. Her attitude was not unusual: Many older people believe that "they" are old, but "I" am younger (Weiss & Lang, 2012).

Asked how old they feel, most 80-year-olds lop a decade or more off their age (Pew Research Center, June 29, 2009). Think of the logical lapse here. If *most* 80-year-olds feel how they imagine the average 70-year-old feels, then that feeling is, in fact, typical of 80-year-olds. Thus, 80-year-olds have a stereotype of 80-year-olds, and they believe it does not apply to them.

This same phenomenon is apparent for every aspect of functioning in late adulthood. One study asked people to estimate trajectories over the life span of six cognitive functions and four social ones (Riediger et al., 2014). People of all age groups estimated that most people would decline, usually by age 60 and clearly by age 80. That is accurate: Many declines occur.

However, on every measure, older people were most likely to estimate that their own functioning was better than that of the average older person (see **Table 23.1**). This was particularly true for memory, speed, and making new friends—the three abilities most often stereotyped as dropping markedly with age. Again, they share a cultural stereotype then reject it when it applies to them.

In an ageist culture, for older people to feel younger than others of their chronological age is understandable, even healthy. As one commentator noted, "feeling youthful is more strongly predictive of health than any other factors including commonly noted ones like chronological age, gender, marital status and socioeconomic status" (Barrett, 2012, p. 3). Self-perception is crucial. Another study found that:

> Perceptions are a strong predictor of psychological wellbeing in later life . . . [and] older adults with negative self-perceptions of aging also have greater levels of disability, ill health, worse physical function and a higher risk of mortality over time.
>
> *[Robertson et al., 2016, p. 71]*

Before deciding that it is foolish as well as ageist for older adults to feel younger than their years, remember that self-perceived age correlates with health and happiness (Kotter-Grühn et al., 2016). This is true lifelong, although it takes different forms. Emerging adults are more likely to say they feel older than they actually are, and for them that indicates maturity.

Apparently, people at every age have stereotypes of what that age entails, and many want to escape the stereotype. Thus, it may be good that older people believe that they are younger than they are. Ageism regarding other old people is harmful, but worse may be ageism about oneself.

My mother entered that assisted-living home and was quite happy. She did many of the same things she had always done—not the things she associated with old age.

TABLE 23.1

How Do You Compare to Other People Your Age?

	9-Year-Olds	13- to 15-Year-Olds	21- to 26-Year-Olds	70- to 76-Year-Olds
Memory	Better	Same	Worse	Better
Cognitive speed	Same	Worse	Worse	Better
Mental math	Better	Same	Worse	Better
Concentration	Same	Same	Worse	Better
New friends	Same	Worse	Worse	Better
Self-assertion	Better	Same	Same	Better

Information from Riediger et al., 2014.

Not Like the Others People in this study thought that most young adults were quite competent in these six areas and that most older people were not. That is accurate, according to laboratory research. However, when evaluating themselves, most emerging adults thought their peers were better, and most older adults thought their peers were worse.

THINK CRITICALLY: How do you compare to other people your age?

Doctors may make the same mistake. If a patient complains about sleep, they might prescribe

> drugs that are commonly used to manage insomnia, such as benzodiazepines and non-benzodiazepines, [which] can lead to several residual side-effects like drug dependence, tolerance, rebound insomnia, muscle relaxation, hallucinations, depression, and amnesia . . .
>
> [Gulia & Kumar, 2018, p. 161]

Instead, everyone of every age is advised to practice good *sleep hygiene*. That includes, several hours before bedtime, (1) turning off television and other screens, (2) exercising, and (3) avoiding substances (alcohol, caffeine, nicotine, hard-to-digest foods) that might interfere with sleep. Bodies adjust to patterns, so regular exercise, set bedtimes, routine meditation and relaxation practices, and a midday nap may all be part of a healthy lifestyle.

Less Exercise or More? One of the proven ways to help elders sleep at night is to exercise during the day, but every decade of adulthood is marked by less exercise (see **Figure 23.1**).

How is this the result of ageism? One reason why older adults do not exercise is that some younger people still tell elders to sit down instead of walk (Franco et al., 2015). And elders obey.

Social encouragement and companionship are crucial. However, most exercise activities are styled for the young; traditional dancing assumes a balanced sex ratio; many yoga, aerobics, and other classes are paced and designed for people in their 20s: Pickup basketball games are rough and rapid; jogging attire is styled for younger bodies.

Added to the problems caused by the ageism of the culture is self-imposed ageism. Instead of stretching and pushing, an older adult might choose comfort—reducing range of motion while impairing circulation and digestion. If balance is decreased, elders might reduce walking instead of getting better shoes, a cane, or whatever.

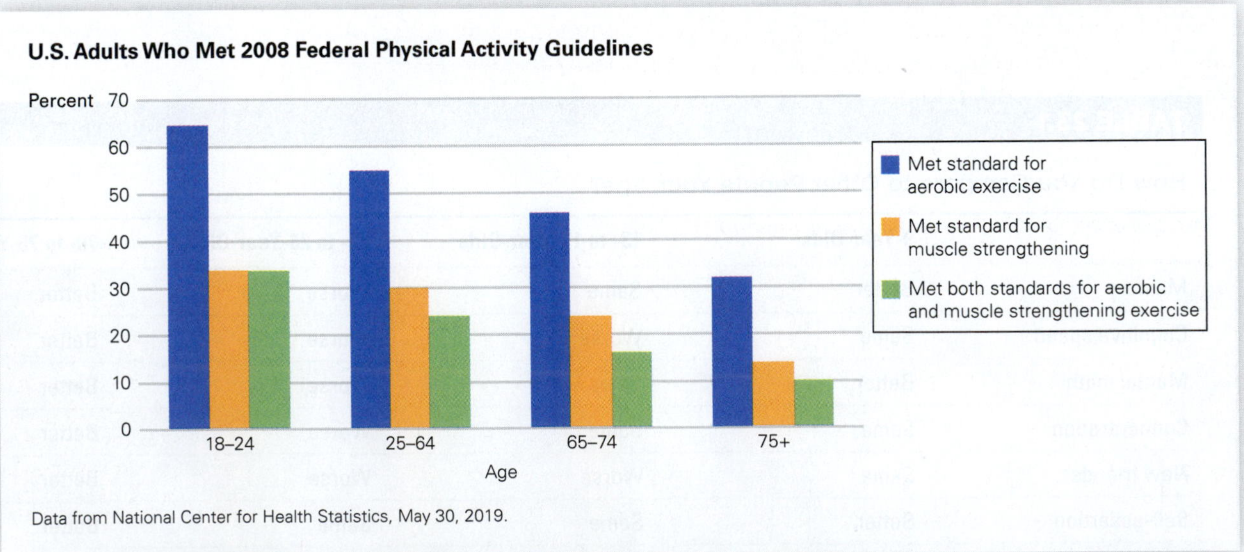

FIGURE 23.1

Worse and Worse As people grow older, they should exercise more, because exercise is the best defense against all ailments of age. Unfortunately, the opposite is true: Twice as many of the oldest do not exercise compared to the youngest. These data are from the United States, where the standards for aerobic exercise and weight-bearing exercise are defined by minutes spent per week. Elders could meet the standards even if they walk more slowly, but most of them simply stop.

Overall, ageism shortens life: Lack of exercise may be a crucial reason (Westerhof et al., 2014). Recovery from illness and surgery is faster when people are active, but health professionals may think they are showing respect for the aged when they do things for them (Kagan, 2018).

Talk and Prejudice Many people think they are compassionate when they talk about the elderly as if they were children ("so cute," "second childhood"), address an older person with "honey" or "dear," or use a nickname instead of a surname ("Billy," not "Mr. White"). When they speak to the an older person, some people use simple and short sentences, slower talk, higher pitch, louder volume, and frequent repetition, a combination called **elderspeak** that is similar to baby talk.

elderspeak A condescending way of speaking to older adults that resembles baby talk, with simple and short sentences, exaggerated emphasis, repetition, and a slower rate and a higher pitch than used in normal speech.

The reality that leads to elderspeak is that about 1 in every 12 people over age 65 is deaf or almost deaf (National Center for Health Statistics, 2018). But that rate of 8 percent doesn't justify yelling at anyone or talking loudly at the other 92 percent over age 65.

Most elders, including those with some hearing loss, can hear well if a person talks normally while facing them so that lip movements and facial expressions are visible. If an older person is really among those 8 percent, the solution is to help them get a good hearing aid, not to shout.

Especially for Young Adults Should you always speak louder and slower when talking to a senior citizen? (see response, page 608)

Elderspeak, then, is rooted in ageism. Ironically, many aspects of elderspeak *reduce* communication (Kemper, 2015). Higher frequencies are harder to hear, stretching out words makes comprehension worse, shouting causes anxiety, and simplified vocabulary reduces the precision of language. The result is not only less communication; elderspeak reduces comprehension.

Destructive Protection Younger adults' experiences and the media discourage the elderly from leaving home. For example, whenever an older person is robbed, raped, or assaulted, sensational headlines add to fear and consequently promote ageism. In fact, street crime more frequently targets young adults, not old ones (see **Figure 23.2**).

The homicide rate (the most reliable indicator of violent crime, since reluctance to report is not an issue) of those over age 65 is less than one-tenth the rate for those in their 20s. To protect our relatives, perhaps we should insist that our

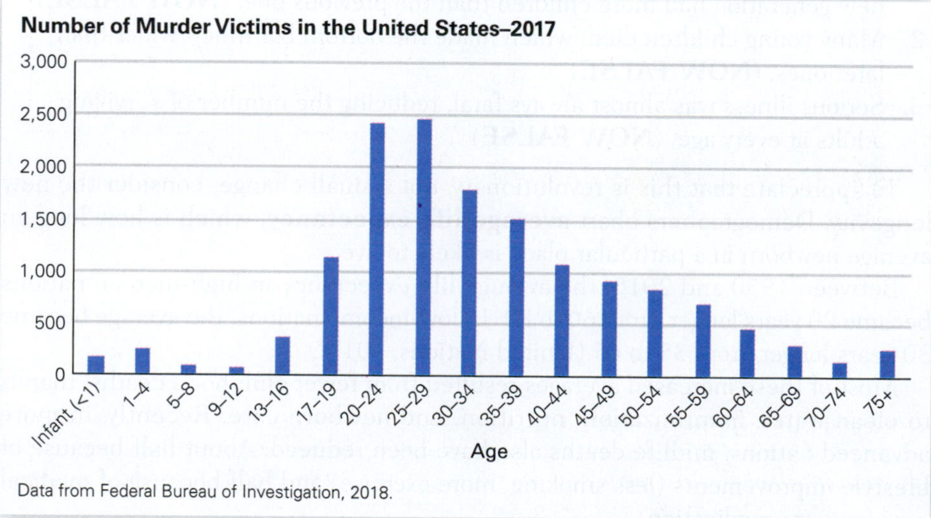

Data from Federal Bureau of Investigation, 2018.

FIGURE 23.2

Victims of Crime As people grow older, they are less likely to be crime victims. This is true for murder (shown here) and is also reported in personal interviews. Respondents were asked whether they had been the victim of a violent crime—assault, sexual assault, rape, or robbery—in the past several months. This approach yields more accurate results than official crime statistics because many crimes are never reported to the police.

young adults never leave the house alone—a ridiculous suggestion that makes it obvious why telling older adults to stay home is ageist.

Although advertisements induce younger adults to buy medical-alert devices for older relatives, it might be better to go biking with them. Lest you think that bikes are only for children, a study of five nations (Germany, Italy, Finland, Hungary, and the Netherlands) found that 15 percent of Europeans *older than* 75 ride their bicycles *every day* (Tacken & van Lamoen, 2005).

In the United States, few elders ride bikes, partly because communities are not designed for elderly bike riders. Protected bike paths are scarce, and many bikes are designed for speed, not stability. Laws requiring bike helmets often apply only to children—another example of ageism.

Demography and Ageism

Demography is the science that describes populations, including by cohort, age, gender, or region. How could numbers be prejudiced? Yes. Data are objective, but emphasis and interpretation are not.

demographic shift A shift in the proportions of the populations of various ages.

The Demographic Shift Two hundred years ago, there were 20 times more children under age 15 than people over age 64. In a massive **demographic shift**, the proportion of children has been reduced and the proportion of elders has increased. Now there are only three times as many children as elders, and the trend continues. In the future, those under 15 are projected to be less numerous than those over age 65.

Evidence for the demographic shift can be found in many statistics. As recently as half a century ago, only 5 percent of the world's population was over age 65; now 9 percent are. In many nations, the older population is much larger—15 percent in the United States, 16 percent in Canada, 22 percent in Italy, and 26 percent in Japan. Only 11 percent of the population of Japan are under age 15 (United Nations, 2017) (see **Figure 23.3**).

Demographers often depict the age structure of a population as a series of stacked bars—one bar for each age group, with the youngest at the bottom and the oldest at the top. Always, the shape was a *demographic pyramid*. Like a wedding cake, it was wide at the base, with each higher level narrower than the one beneath it. There were three reasons, none of which is true today.

1. More babies were born than the replacement rate of one per adult, so each new generation had more children than the previous one. (**NOW FALSE**)
2. Many young children died, which made the bottom bar much wider than later ones. (**NOW FALSE**)
3. Serious illness was almost always fatal, reducing the number of surviving adults at every age. (**NOW FALSE**)

To appreciate that this is revolutionary, not a small change, consider the new longevity. Demographers chart **average life expectancy**, which is how long an average newborn in a particular place is likely to live.

average life expectancy The number of years the average newborn in a particular population group is likely to live.

Between 1950 and 2015, the average life expectancy in high-income nations became 20 years longer, from 60 to 80. In low-income nations, the average became 30 years longer, from 35 to 65 (United Nations, 2017).

Most of these increased averages resulted from fewer childhood deaths, thanks to clean water, immunization, nutrition, and newborn care. Recently, in more advanced nations, midlife deaths also have been reduced: About half because of lifestyle improvements (less smoking, more exercise) and half because of medical care (surgery, medication).

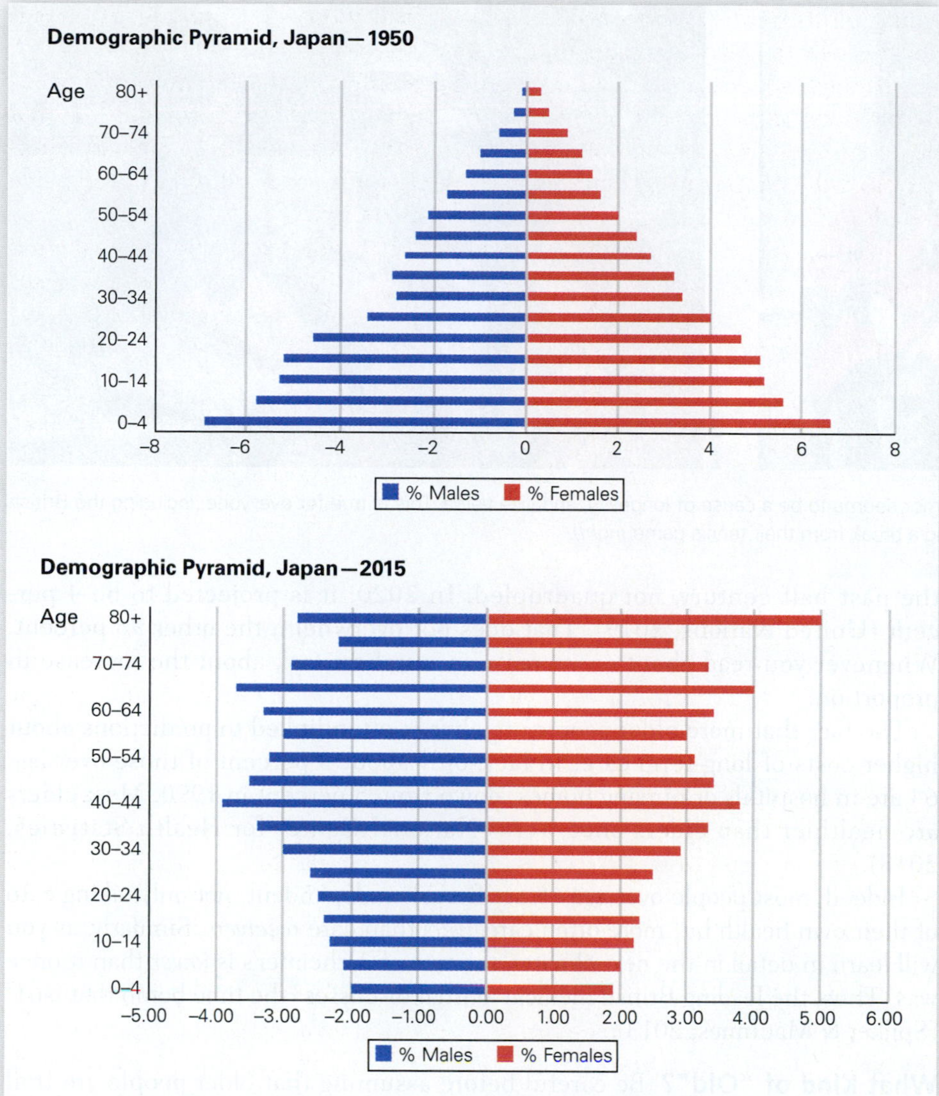

Data from National Institute of Population and Social Security Research, August, 2019.

FIGURE 23.3

Not Yet Square But certainly not a pyramid. Changes in birth rates worldwide are already making the shape of the population square in some nations, evident in Japan for those under age 25. If trends continue, Japan will be a rectangle in 50 years!

Of course, improvements in average life expectancy are not inevitable. In the United States, opioid and gun deaths have slightly reduced average life expectancy every year since 2015. However, once a U.S. resident reaches age 60, that person is projected to live to 83, five years longer than was the case in 1950.

Statistics That Frighten All the data just presented are objective. So how can this reflect prejudice? Unfortunately, demographic data are sometimes reported in ways not designed convey objective reality but instead to raise subjective fear.

For instance, have you heard that people over age 80 are the fastest-growing age group, four times larger than 50 years ago, and thus we are about to be hit with a time bomb that will drag everyone down? Or, that more and more people suffer from Alzheimer's disease, a major burden to their family? Both statistics are objectively true; both statements are misleading.

Yes, there are more old people alive. But the overall population has also grown. The *proportion* of U.S. residents age 80 and older has doubled over

Tim Graham/Getty Images News/Getty Images

Mark J. Barrett/Alamy

Same Situation, Far Apart: Keep Smiling Good humor seems to be a cause of longevity, and vice versa. This is true for everyone, including the British men on Founder's Day *(left)* and the two women taking a break from their tennis game *(right)*.

the past half century, not quadrupled. In 2020, it is projected to be 4 percent (United Nations, 2019). That does not overwhelm the other 96 percent. Whenever you read about an increase in numbers, ask about the increase in proportion.

The fact that more older people are alive is often linked to predictions about higher costs of long-term care. In fact, only about 3 percent of those over age 64 are in hospitals or nursing homes, down from 5 percent in 1990. Most elders are healthier than elders once were (National Center for Health Statistics, 2018).

Indeed, most people over age 65 are fiercely independent, not only taking care of their own health but more often care*givers* than care *receivers*. Similarly, as you will learn in detail in the next chapter, the rate of Alzheimer's is *lower* than it once was. Thus, the leading British medical journal discusses "the time bomb that isn't" (Spijker & MacInnes, 2013).

What Kind of "Old"? Be careful before assuming that older people are frail and feeble. Most are not.

It is important to distinguish between the *young-old*, the *old-old*, and the *oldest-old*.

young-old Healthy, vigorous, financially secure older adults (generally, those aged 65 to 75) who are well integrated into the lives of their families and communities.

old-old Older adults (generally, those over age 75) who suffer from physical, mental, or social deficits.

oldest-old Elderly adults (generally, those over age 85) who are dependent on others for almost everything, requiring supportive services such as nursing homes and hospital stays.

- The **young-old** are the largest group of older adults. They are healthy, active, and independent. Few people notice them or realize their age.
- The **old-old** suffer losses in body, mind, or social support, but they care for themselves.
- The **oldest-old** are dependent, needing help. They are a small group, easy to notice.

If you think most older people are among the oldest-old, ask yourself how many of your relatives (aunts, uncles, parents, grandparents, etc.) are over age 65? How many of them are now in nursing homes?

When I ask my students, the proportion in nursing homes is about 2 percent. Then they say that, in their families, people take care of the old, unlike in other families. In that my students reflect one of the findings about humans everywhere: We all tend to believe that we are a little better than most other people.

Objective data find that less than 10 percent of those over age 64 are the oldest-old, dependent on other people for basic care. That minority are most often cared for at home by relatives, typically by a spouse who is elderly, too.

This is not to deny that many of the elderly suffer from various health conditions, or that the rates of hospital admission increase with age. Nor does it minimize the real burdens on caregivers when an elderly relative is actually frail, sick, and confused.

However, most health conditions are managed with medication, and U.S. data find that when the elderly are admitted to a hospital, two-thirds are discharged after one night. In 2016, only 4.7 percent of the hospitalized population over age 64 spent two or more nights in a hospital, a rate about 25 percent lower than a decade ago (5.8 percent) (National Center for Health Statistics, 2018).

The other misleading idea is that the older a person is, the more sick, dependent, and lonely he are. In fact, chronological age is an imperfect predictor. The "oldest-old" could be age 60, or 80, or 100. The "young-old" could also be 60, or 80, or 100.

Can someone who has lived for a century possibly be "healthy, active, and independent"? Yes. Those who study centenarians find that many are quite happy and require no special care from other people (Jopp & Rott, 2006; Paúl et al., 2013).

Disease, disability, and depression may eventually set in; studies disagree about how common these problems are past age 100. One large study of 1,253 centenarians in five nations found that a third were considered frail, in that they had four or five of the following: weight loss, fatigue, weakness, slow walking speed, and low level of physical activity. But a third of them had only two or one of these, or none at all (Herr et al., 2018). Obviously, if someone who is 100 years old walks slow and feels tired but has not lost weight, energy, or strength, then that person is doing quite well.

Indeed, centenarians may have fewer physical and mental health problems than younger people. For example, in Sweden, where medical care (including medicine) is free, centenarians were less likely to take antidepressants than those who were aged 80 or so (Wastesson et al., 2012). They were not necessarily anti-drug—they were more likely to take pain medication, often for arthritis.

In the United States, more than half of those who live past 100 show no cognitive impairment (Ailshire et al., 2015). Could centenarians be happier than octogenarians, as the Swedish data suggest? That is not known.

What is known is that centenarians tend to be upbeat about life. Why? They have lived through a devastating worldwide depression; World War II (which included the Holocaust and the atom bomb); racism and sexism far greater than today; and, in the United States, no Social Security or Medicare. No wonder they consider themselves fortunate.

John Phillips/Getty Images

Is She Old Yet? Maggie Smith began her acting career in Shakespeare's *Twelfth Night* at age 17, and she has appeared every year since then in films, television, and on stage. Many people have watched her work as Professor Minerva McGonagall in eight Harry Potter movies and as Violet Crawley in the TV series and movie *Downton Abbey*. She is still acting, making her a young-old person.

Observation Quiz How old is she? (see answer, page 608) ↑

WHAT HAVE YOU LEARNED?

1. How are ageism, racism, and sexism similar and different?
2. Is there any harm in being especially kind to people who are old?
3. How is elderspeak like baby talk?
4. How does ageism affect insomnia?
5. Why don't the elderly exercise as much as the young?
6. How is the demographic pyramid changing?
7. Why are statistics about the aging population misleading?
8. How do the oldest-old differ from the young-old?

Hot or Cold? The weather is chilly and the beach is lonely, but it is evident that this senior couple is enjoying the moment. Physical attraction and intimacy continue into later adulthood, despite what younger people might think.

Adjusting to Changes

Ageism distorts reality, but senescence is real. As bodies age, it may be time to counteract, compensate, control, or celebrate. Selective compensation with optimization (explained in Chapter 21) becomes increasingly important on many levels—the microsystem, macrosystem, and exosystem. To illustrate, we now explain three examples: sexual intercourse, driving, and the senses. Each involves all three levels, but here we emphasize one level for each.

Microsystem Compensation: Sex

Physiological sexual responses slow down with age. Many people become widows or widowers and do not seek another partner, but even for the married, the frequency of intercourse decreases and arousal and orgasm are slower.

The best data on over 6,000 U.S. residents found that middle-aged (age 44–59) people had intercourse twice as often as older (age 57–72) people did, down from six to three times a month for the men and from five to two times for the women (Karraker et al., 2011). (Fewer of the older women had partners.)

However, sexual activity is remarkably varied among the old. For example, a European study of almost 3,000 older adults (age 60 and up, all of whom had a partner) in four nations found that about a fourth had no intercourse in the past month, and another fourth said they had intercourse at least every week (N. Fischer et al., 2018).

In that study, the researchers expected age and cultural differences between adults in nations with different cultural norms about sex (Norway, Denmark, Belgium, and Portugal). Instead they found similar rates as well as similar reasons offered for more or less sexual activity.

Although health (of oneself for the men and of one's partner for the women) was significant in every nation, even more important was attitude. Those who thought sex was good for overall well-being were more likely to be sexually active—no matter what their nationality or age (N. Fischer et al., 2018).

Beyond more variation among couples than among nations, the other surprise is that sexual satisfaction often increases after middle age (Heiman et al., 2011). The explanation for that paradox is that many older adults reject the ageist idea that *sexual activity* means *intercourse*. For many of the elderly, kissing, caressing, cuddling, sex talk, and fantasizing are more important than coitus.

This was confirmed by a study of more than 7,000 people in England (Tetley et al., 2018). Many stressed the importance of a loving relationship. One man in his 80s, when asked about intercourse, replied:

> Now too old but my wife and I sleep in the same bed, and kiss and cuddle each other before settling down to sleep. We enjoy each other's company.

Another man used the word *sex* to mean intercourse, but then he said:

> I don't feel that sex is the most important thing in a relationship. Commitment and care are more, or as, important.

And a woman said:

> The act of sex does not make you 'happy' but having a loving partner does.

A five-nation study (United States, Germany, Japan, Brazil, Spain) found that kissing and hugging, not intercourse, predicted happiness in long-lasting romances (Heiman et al., 2011). Is that optimization, compensation, or both?

The following in-depth study provides some clues.

A CASE TO STUDY

Sex Among Older Adults

Two researchers wanted to study sexual activity among the elderly, but they rejected the usual ways of studying sex. They feared that laboratory measures of sexual arousal might be calibrated on young bodies and that questions about sex might be offensive or misinterpreted (Lodge & Umberson, 2012).

Accordingly, they used a method called *grounded theory.* They found 17 couples, aged 50 to 86, most married for decades, and interviewed each person privately, transcribing all 34 interviews. They read and reread the transcripts, line by line, and identified topics that came up repeatedly. They then tallied all of the topics and sorted the results by age and gender.

From their intensive study, the researchers concluded that sexual activity was more a social construction than a biological event. They reported that everyone said that intercourse was less frequent with age, including four couples for whom intercourse stopped completely because of the husband's health. Despite that, more of the respondents said that their sex life had improved than said it had deteriorated (44 percent compared to 30 percent).

Surprisingly, the middle-aged couples, who were more likely to have intercourse, were also more likely to be among the 30 percent who said that their sex lives had deteriorated. The older couples usually said that their sex lives were better than before.

The middle-aged husbands and wives had different concerns. The men were troubled by difficulty maintaining an erection, and the women were worried that they were less attractive. The solution for several middle-aged couples was for the man to take Viagra, typically at the woman's suggestion.

One woman said:

> All of a sudden, we didn't have sex after I got skinny. And I couldn't figure that out . . . I look really good now and we're not having sex. It turns out that he was going through a major physical thing at that point and just had lost his sex drive. It didn't have anything to do with me, but I thought it did. I went through years thinking it was my fault. So, [I said] let's go make sure it's your fault [laughs] or let's find out what the problem is instead of me just assuming the blame.
>
> *[Irene, quoted in Lodge & Umberson, 2012, p. 435]*

The researchers believe that "images of masculine sexuality are premised on high, almost uncontrollable levels of penis-driven sexual desire," while the cultural ideals for women emphasize female passivity and yet "implore women to be both desirable and receptive to men's sexual desires and impulses," deeming "older women and their bodies unattractive" (p. 430).

Thus, when people in middle age first realize that aging has changed their sexual interactions, their distress takes a gender-specific form. Men are distressed that their erections are slower and weaker, and women are distressed that their bodies are less youthful. Middle-aged men and women attempt to reverse aging, through drugs, hormones, lubricants, diet, hairstyles, clothes, and so on.

A few years later, this study found that couples over age 70 often realized that the young idea of good sex (which many still thought of as intercourse) was not relevant to them. Instead, they *compensated* for physical changes by *optimizing* their relationship in other ways. As one man (who still equated the word *sex* with intercourse) said:

> I think the intimacy is a lot stronger even though the sex is bad. Probably more often now we do things like holding hands and wanting to be close to each other or touch each other. It's probably more important now than sex is.
>
> *[Jim, quoted in Lodge & Umberson, 2012, p. 438]*

A woman said that her marriage improved because

> we have more opportunities and more motivation. [Sex] was wonderful. It got thwarted, with . . . the medication he is on. And he hasn't been functional since. The doctors just said that it is going to be this way, so we have learned to accept that. But we have also learned long before that there are more ways than one to share your love.
>
> *[Helen, quoted in Lodge & Umberson, 2012, p. 437]*

The researchers note that their conclusions may not be accurate in the future. This cohort grew up with the social construction that men were rapacious and women had to be demure but attractive. Both sexes were taught when they were young that sexual desire stopped before old age. It was considered deviant ("dirty old man") or ridiculous ("Does she think she is a teenager?") if an older adult still felt sexy.

Now the culture says that older people should be sexually active, but these participants needed time and experience to know what that entailed. They were loving, sexy, and active, although not as they were as newlyweds.

This view helps us understand how older people adapt, sexually, to divorce or the death of a partner. Since the sex drive varies from person to person, some elders prefer to stay single and alone, some no longer seek intercourse, some cohabit, some begin LAT (living apart together) with a new partner, and some remarry. Each older person selects whether and how to be sexual.

Should She Drive? Queen Elizabeth II was 91 years old when this photo was taken. She is the only person in the United Kingdom who is not required to have a driver's license, but her driving is usually limited to her private estates.

Neither the old myth that no elder is sexually active, nor the new myth that all older people have strong sexual drives, is accepted by elderly people themselves. All individuals select, optimize, and compensate in their own way. Of course, with every aspect of development, individual adjustment is only part of the process. The social context makes some actions difficult, which leads to the next topic.

Macrosystem Compensation: Driving

A life-span perspective reminds us that "aging is a process, socially constructed as a problem" (Cruikshank, 2009, p. 7). The process is biological, but society creates the problem. Selective optimization with compensation is needed by each community, not just by each individual. One example is driving.

The Biological Process With age, driving safely is more difficult. The elderly compensate: They drive more slowly, less often, and when there is more daylight and less traffic (Molnar et al., 2018).

Relying solely on each person to decide when, how, and whether to drive is foolhardy, however. Driving is a source of pride and independence; the elderly do not want to quit, and families and communities are reluctant to stop them. This was evident in 2019 in England, as reported by one physician:

> On 17 January the Duke of Edinburgh was driving his Land Rover when it was in a collision with another car. One of three passengers in the other car was injured, and the duke's car flipped over. The duke, 97, was reportedly left bruised and bewildered. Two days later he was seen driving another Land Rover with no seatbelt and was spoken to by police.
>
> *[Oliver, 2019]*

Spoken to! More needs to be done, but what?

Because they are cautious and drive less, elderly drivers have fewer accidents than 20-year-olds (see Visualizing Development, page 609). They see teenagers speeding, ignoring stop signs, using cell phones, driving after drinking. They conclude that they are better drivers than those "young whippersnappers."

By comparing themselves to younger drivers, few older drivers notice their losses. Nonetheless, per mile driven, they are more likely to have accidents, more likely to hit pedestrians (whom they did not see), and more likely to be fatally injured themselves when accidents occur.

Concerns focus on physiological losses: Hearing and vision are not as acute, reaction time is slower, grip strength is reduced, head-turning is more difficult. However, cognitive losses—quick reactions, estimates of speed of other vehicles, lapses of attention—impair the sequence of visual-motor activity more than the directly physiological problems. That also needs to be assessed in measuring risk (Sun et al., 2018).

What the Community Can Do So far we have detailed the losses that impair driving, but this section is about the macrosystem, not the biosystem. There are many ways that societies can compensate for all those age-related reductions in driving ability. Often, however, they do not. For instance, many jurisdictions renew licenses by mail, even at age 80. If an older adult causes a crash, the individual is blamed, not the department of motor vehicles.

Retesting may not solve the problem. Often retesting is merely answering multiple-choice questions about road rules and reading letters on a well-lit chart while looking straight ahead. Anyone who fails should have stopped driving long ago, but proficiency does not guarantee competence.

There are many solutions that local jurisdictions could adopt. Current technology allows simulated driving via a computer and video screen, with the prospective driver seated with a steering wheel, accelerator, and brakes. The results of this test could allow some older adults to renew their licenses and some to have their licenses revoked. Elders would realize that they are less proficient than they thought.

Driving simulators are especially useful if an older adult has had a stroke or if there are signs of neurological impairment. Some elders are nonetheless competent drivers and some not: Age is a poor predictor, and medical doctors are not the best judges (Vardaki et al., 2016). Individuals may be even worse at self-assessment: An on-road analysis of older drivers found that some overestimated their competence and some underestimated it (Broberg & Willstrand, 2014).

Axel Heimken/picture-alliance/dpa/AP Images

And on Icy Curves . . . Everywhere in the world, the elderly want to keep driving. Some nations require extensive training for license renewals. This is a special safety class for elderly drivers in Germany.

THINK CRITICALLY: How do drivers decide whether their driving is impaired?

Beyond requiring accurate retesting, macrosystem compensation can take many other forms. Larger-print signs before highway exits, mirrors that replace the need to turn the neck, illuminated side streets and driveways, non-glaring headlights and hazard flashers, and warnings of ice or fog ahead would all reduce accidents. Well-designed cars, roads, signs, lights, and guardrails, as well as appropriate laws and enforcement, also allow selective optimization.

Education geared to the issues faced by older drivers could make a difference. For example, elderly drivers are particularly likely to benefit from proper use of GPS devices to tell them when to turn and where, but many do not know how to use such measures—relying instead on memory or paper instructions (Thomas et al., 2018).

The community could provide other ways to reduce accidents. Free and efficient public transportation would keep elderly drivers off the road, and better sidewalks and pedestrian crossings would save their lives. Ironically, the pedestrians most likely to be killed by older drivers are themselves over age 70, yet communities do virtually nothing to protect them (Musselwhite, 2018). Instead, stoplights are timed for speedy walkers, school-crossing guards protect children, and bicycle helmets are required only for the young. Why?

Exosystem Compensation: The Senses

Every sense becomes slower and less sharp with each passing decade. We focus here on the two most crucial for thought and behavior, vision and audition; but similar losses and exosystem compensation apply to touch, pain, taste (particularly for sour and bitter), and smell.

Of course, sensory losses can be seen as problems of the individual, as already described in Chapter 20. Here we focus on the exosystem, which can ameliorate every sensory loss.

Vision Only 10 percent of people of either sex over age 65 see well without glasses (see **Table 23.2**). Several eye diseases increase with age, specifically cataracts, glaucoma, and macular degeneration. Each of these can cause blurry vision and eventual blindness, but each can be treated and, if discovered early, damage can be prevented. The culture's provision of health care is one aspect of the exosystem that affects vision in late adulthood.

TABLE 23.2

Common Vision Impairments Among the Elderly
• *Cataracts.* As early as age 50, about 10 percent of adults have cataracts, a thickening of the lens, causing vision to become cloudy, opaque, and distorted. By age 70, 30 percent have cataracts, which can be removed in outpatient surgery and replaced with an artificial lens.
• *Glaucoma.* About 1 percent of those in their 70s and 10 percent of those in their 90s have glaucoma, a buildup of fluid within the eye that damages the optic nerve. Early stages have no symptoms. Without treatment, glaucoma causes blindness, but the damage can be prevented. Testing is crucial, particularly for African Americans and people with diabetes, since the first signs of glaucoma may occur for them as early as age 40.
• *Macular degeneration.* About 4 percent of those in their 60s and about 12 percent of those over age 80 have a deterioration of the retina, called macular degeneration. An early warning occurs when vision is spotty (e.g., some letters missing when reading). Again, early treatment—in this case, medication—can restore some vision, but without treatment, blindness occurs about five years after macular degeneration starts.

CHAPTER APP 23

Magnifying Glass with light

IOS:
https://tinyurl.com/y3ptjyss

RELEVANT TOPIC:
Vision in late adulthood

This free app helps users with imperfect eyesight zoom in on and brighten text, making screen reading much easier. The app is also useful for reading small print on restaurant menus, mailings, and even keypads.

Beyond treatment with medication, many inventions, from eyeglasses (first invented in the thirteenth century) to tiny video cameras worn on the forehead that connect directly to the brain, improve sight. Changing the environment—brighter lights, halogen streetlights, newspapers with larger and darker print—make a difference.

For those with severe vision loss, dogs, canes, and audio devices allow mobility and cognition. The exosystem matters: The availability of such implements depends on the nation—they are free in some countries, rare in others.

Hearing Everyone loses some hearing with age. Of all people in the United States over age 65, 36 percent report some trouble hearing, and 8 percent say that they are virtually deaf (U.S. Department of Health and Human Services, 2018). Men are twice as likely to have hearing loss as women. High frequencies—the voice of a small child—are lost especially quickly.

The exosystem, again, may be crucial. A dramatic improvement in the ability of people with severe hearing loss to enjoy concerts, plays, museums, and so on results from a *hearing loop*, a small device in a room that enables people with hearing aids to hear the words or music without the distracting clatter. Installing a loop requires a change in the exosystem. David Myers, himself now hearing-impaired, explains:

> In the United States, most hearing assistance in public places ignores the human factor. Picture someone with hearing loss struggling to hear a lecture or a movie. Instead of a simple button push that transforms their hearing aids into in-the-ear speakers, the person typically must take the initiative to locate, check out, wear, and return a conspicuous FM or infrared receiver and headset that delivers generic sound. When I asked at my local seven-screen theater how often these assistive units get used, the unsurprising answer was only "once per month per theater." Although satisfying Americans With Disabilities Act requirements (for one such unit for every 50 seats), they nearly all sit gathering dust. Given these two alternative technologies—one compatible with hearing aids and the other not—it should not take a human factors psychologist (someone who designs technology with the real human user in mind) to understand which technology people are more likely to use and love.
>
> *[Myers, 2019, pp. 29–30]*

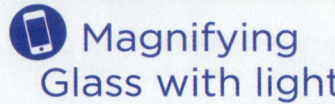

universal design The creation of settings and equipment that can be used by everyone, whether or not they are able-bodied and sensory-acute.

Michael Kamber/The New York Times/Redux

Looped In? This sign indicates that a hearing loop is installed in this New York City subway booth, enabling most people with hearing aids and cochlear implants to receive important messages and to communicate with transit personnel. Frequent riders of public transit, however, complain that the public address system malfunctions, the elevators are often broken, and the signs do not always reflect reality.

Universal Design Disability advocates want designers and engineers to think of **universal design**, which is planning environments and equipment that can be used by everyone, whether or not they are able-bodied and sensory-acute. Many disabilities would disappear with better design. That would be a change in the exosystem. At the moment, just about everything, from houses to fashionable shoes, is designed for adults with no impairments.

Look around at the built environment (stores, streets, colleges, and homes); notice the print on medicine bottles; listen to the public address systems in train stations; ask why most homes have entry stairs and narrow bathrooms, why most buses and cars require a big step up to enter, why smelling remains the usual way to detect a gas leak.

Then, look for signs that indicate accessibility or hearing loop availability. How accurate are those signs? Are elevators working, curb cuts smooth, ramps visible? Universal design is needed everywhere, particularly crucial in education. People cannot learn if their senses cannot access, process, and communicate information (Murawski & Scott, 2019).

Thus, sensory loss is part of aging, but it need not lead to morbidity. However, without compensation, any disability, especially deafness and blindness, leads to isolation, inactivity, and reduced cognition. The blame is aimed at individuals, but the exosystem is at fault.

Primary and Secondary Aging

To further understand how people and communities can adjust to the changes of aging bodies, we need to distinguish between **primary aging**, those age-related changes that occur to everyone as they grow older, and **secondary aging**, those changes that only people with particular genes, habits, and environments experience.

primary aging The universal and irreversible physical changes that occur to all living creatures as they grow older.

secondary aging The specific physical illnesses or conditions that become more common with aging but are caused by health habits, genes, and other influences that vary from person to person.

The speed of primary aging can be slowed with exercise, a healthy diet, and low pollution, but time does not stop. Primary aging makes compensation more important. However, secondary aging is the reason for most age-related illnesses and disabilities.

For example, with age, the lungs take in and expel less air with each breath, so blood oxygen is reduced. That is primary aging. However, most older adults take in sufficient oxygen to maintain life unless secondary aging, such as from years of smoking or breathing polluted air, have damaged the lungs. In that case, *chronic obstructive pulmonary disease (COPD)* is may cause death, as it did in 2016 for 131,002 people over age 65 in the United States.

Similarly, with age, healing of all kinds slows down and the immune system becomes less efficient. A cut takes longer to heal, and a cold takes longer to shake.

Because of slower healing, if accidents happen—falls, crashes, fires, poisonings—young bodies are likely to recover, but 53,000 people in the United States over age 65 died accidentally in 2016. That is secondary aging, because whether or not an older person has an accident depends on the context and the person, more than on age. Then primary aging makes that accident more lethal.

The Flu Because of primary aging, medical intervention affects the old differently than the young. For this reason, drugs, surgeries, and so on that have been validated on young adults may be less effective on the elderly.

Consider flu (influenza). The particular strains that circulate differ slightly each year, so the vaccine is redesigned annually to fight whatever strains are predicted. This is why North Americans are advised to get another flu shot every fall for the following winter. (Timing, and the composition of the vaccine, differs in other parts of the world.)

Annual immunization is particularly recommended for those over age 65, because about 90 percent of flu fatalities occur in that age group. Primary aging reduces the immune system, making flu more likely, even when the person is vaccinated. In other words, the vaccine is simultaneously less powerful but more necessary for the elderly (Smetana et al., 2018). But, almost everyone who dies from flu does so because of a weakness caused by secondary aging. The flu then pushes them over the edge.

There is an added complication. Immunity resulting from vaccines for some (but not all) viruses fades over time, so an older person who was immunized years ago might need a new dose. According to some experts, this is particularly important for the flu (Cohen, 2019). Here you can see benefits of the exosystem in the United States, which designs the vaccine to be stronger for the old and makes it free for those on Medicare.

Compression of Morbidity The relation of primary and secondary aging is helpful in understanding **compression of morbidity**, which is the reduction (compression) of sickness before death (Fries et al., 2011). Secondary aging may produce poor health for years before death. In that case, a person experiences a long period of morbidity (no compression).

compression of morbidity A shortening of the time a person spends ill or infirm, accomplished by postponing illness.

Ideally, in contrast, a person is in good health for decades after age 65, and then, within a few days or months, primary aging reaches the point when the entire body shuts down and death occurs fairly soon. Years of frailty are avoided.

Antony Dickson/South China Morning Post via Getty Images

Touch Your Toes? This woman can even put both feet behind her neck. Although everyone loses some flexibility with age, daily practice is crucial. Tao Porchon-Lynch has taught yoga for a half-century. At age 99, shown here, she can balance on one leg in tree pose, stretch her hamstrings in downward dog, and then relieve any remaining stress in cobra pose.

osteoporosis A disease whose symptoms are low bone mass and deterioration of bone tissue, which leads to increasingly fragile bones and greater risk of fracture.

In this way, morbidity can be compressed (shortened) even as mortality is postponed. This has certainly happened with some diseases. For instance, unlike 30 years ago, most people diagnosed today with cancer, diabetes, or a heart condition continue to be vital for decades. The World Health Organization and many experts recognize that disability is the result of person–environment interaction, so changing the environment limits disability (as with universal design).

An Example: Osteoporosis Primary and secondary aging, as well as compression of morbidity, are apparent with **osteoporosis** (fragile bones). Primary aging makes bones more porous as cells that build bone (*osteoblasts*) are outnumbered by cells that reabsorb bone (*osteoclasts*).

Peak bone buildup occurs at about age 30, and from then on everyone loses more bone than they gain. The rate of loss varies by genes and gender. Osteoporosis is particularly common in women with European ancestry, although it can occur in men and people of any background.

All that is primary aging; age always produces some breakdown of bone. However, secondary aging may be crucial. Lack of exercise, too much alcohol, and being underweight all decrease bone density.

The result of this combination of primary and secondary aging can be deadly, not just disabling. A fall that would have merely bruised a young person may break a hip or fracture a spine. Neither of those is lethal but either may impede movement and start a dangerous cascade. People who move less risk heart conditions, digestive problems, and many other complications.

A fall that breaks a major bone leads to death for 10 percent of elderly victims, and it increases morbidity for the other 90 percent. According to the Centers for Disease Control and Prevention, a broken hip is "a leading cause of morbidity and excess mortality among older adults" (MMWR, March 31, 2000). In the twentieth century, half of the people with broken hips never walked again; their immobility caused their other body systems to deteriorate.

Note the 2000 date above. Twelve years later, a report concludes: "In the 21st century, osteoporosis, a disease once considered an inevitable consequence of aging, is both diagnosable and treatable" (Black et al., 2012, p. 2051).

How was this compression of morbidity achieved? Early diagnosis via a bone density test (not available a few decades ago) detects bone weakening long before the first fracture. Screening is now recommended in middle age for everyone at high risk (with family history) and routinely for women at age 65. Prevention includes weight-bearing, muscle-strengthening exercise and a diet with sufficient calcium and vitamin D (Kemmler et al., 2015). In addition, a dozen drug treatments reduce bone loss (Tu et al., 2018).

The 44 million people over age 50 in the United States who have weak bones need not experience the disabling breaks that those with osteoporosis once did. That is compression of morbidity.

Further, those who have weakened or broken hips can have surgery for hip replacement, which is one of the most common, cost-effective ways to improve the quality of later life, reducing morbidity although not necessarily mortality from other causes (Schwartsmann et al., 2015). A regimen of physical therapy and movement allows recovery after a hip replacement: It benefits everyone (primary), but only some people do it (secondary).

Osteoporosis is just one example. For almost every condition, morbidity can be compressed, although many people do not realize it. The first line of defense is exercise, diet, reduced stress, and reduced toxins in the air, water, and food. Those measures can begin in childhood, and, as discussed in Chapter 20, should be part of every adult's life.

The second line is screening, family history, and various medical measures. For example, coronary bypass surgery occurs *before* a heart attack, mastectomy occurs *before* breast cancer, hypertension medication begins *before* a stroke, and so on.

No medical intervention, especially ones that anticipate future illness, is without risk, so none should occur unless screening reveals that someone is at high risk of serious illness and death. Ironically, one current danger is unnecessary treatment!

An example is prostate cancer. About one in eight older men are diagnosed with it (about the same incidence as women diagnosed with breast cancer). The best treatment varies, dependent not only on the specifics of the cancer but also on the emotions of the person.

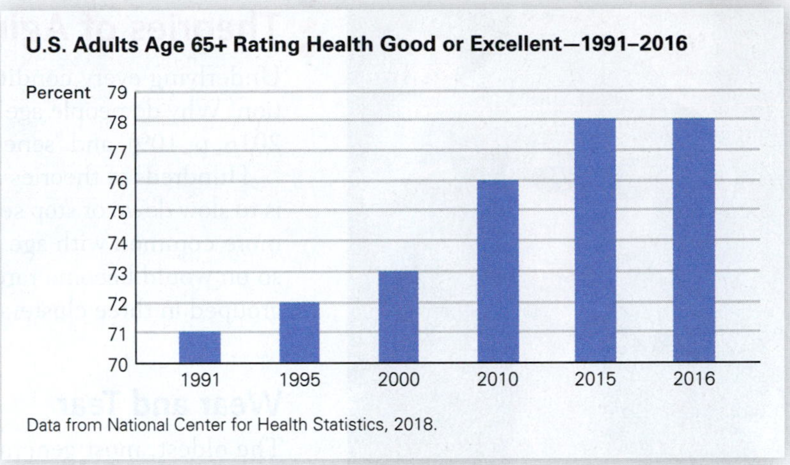

FIGURE 23.4

Feeling Better Note the percentages on the left—this is not a dramatic improvement, but it is true that more older adults are feeling that their health is pretty good. Overall, if you know someone who often complains about their many physical complaints, remember that they are in the minority. Three of every four elders says their health is good or excellent.

Longitudinal studies find that for some the best prostate cancer strategy is "watchful waiting"; for others surgery reduces the risk of death (Egger et al., 2018; Bill-Axelson et al., 2018). Treatment depends not only on the cancer itself, but also on the patient's attitudes.

Some men want aggressive treatment, because they worry that their local cancer will spread. Others would rather wait than endure the aftereffects of surgery, which include urinary and sexual problems. As one review states, the patient's quality of life is "becoming even more important to allow for informed treatment decision-making" (Ansman et al., 2018, p. 401).

Thus, compression of morbidity is accomplished by two parallel tracks: Medical care and the patient's attitude. Note that 78 percent of adults over age 65 considered their health good or excellent in 2016, even though most had one or more serious chronic conditions. That is an improvement (see **Figure 23.4**). It is also a sign of increasing compression of morbidity.

The goal is clear: not merely to add years to life but to add life to years, via health habits, early treatment, and so on. Data from many nations show that there is no set age when people become frail. Primary aging is a fact of living, but compression of morbidity is possible with compensation and optimization.

WHAT HAVE YOU LEARNED?

1. How is it possible for older adults to have satisfying sex lives?
2. How can the independence of older drivers continue while reducing the risk of accidents?
3. How does vision change with age?
4. How does hearing change with age?
5. How does selective optimization apply to decreases in the senses?
6. What are the differences between primary and secondary aging?
7. How would researchers know whether compression of morbidity is occurring?
8. Why might falls be a serious health problem in old age?
9. How is compression of morbidity good for society as well as the individual?

Donna Ward/Getty Images

Looking Good Here is Cher at age 69, still with skin that looks much younger. How a person ages depends partly on genes and partly on lifelong skin care and nutrition.

wear-and-tear theory A view of aging as a process by which the human body wears out because of the passage of time and exposure to environmental stressors.

calorie restriction The practice of limiting dietary energy intake (while consuming sufficient quantities of vitamins, minerals, and other important nutrients) for the purpose of improving health and slowing down the aging process.

www.CartoonStock.com

"If you give up alcohol, cigarettes, sex, red meat, cakes and chocolate, and don't get too excited, you can enjoy life for a few more years yet."

Find the Joy Most elders are happier than when they were younger. They appreciate nature, other people, and life itself, and are less often dependent on food, drugs, or possessions.

Theories of Aging

Underlying every condition and disease just mentioned is a fundamental question: Why do people age? Many scientists say that "aging is modifiable" (Kennedy, 2016, p. 109), and "senescence is not inevitable" (Jones & Vaupel, 2017, p. 965).

Hundreds of theories and thousands of scientists theorize about aging. The goal is to slow down or stop senescence. If we can do that, then all diseases that become more common with age —most cancers, most heart diseases, most strokes, and so on would become rare. What are the theories that explain aging? They can be grouped in three clusters: wear and tear, genetic adaptation, and cellular aging.

Wear and Tear

The oldest, most general theory of aging is known as the **wear-and-tear theory**. The idea is that the body wears out after years of use. Organ reserve and repair processes may be exhausted as the decades pass.

This theory arose from evidence that some body parts suffer from overuse. Three examples are well known: (1) Anyone who puts repeated stress on elbows, shoulders, or knees may have chronically painful joints by middle age; (2) people who inhale asbestos or smoke cigarettes damage their lungs; (3) athletes in football, ice hockey, or boxing who suffer repeated blows to the head destroy brain connections.

Jobs That Wear Workers Out One recent application of this theory focuses on occupation. Workers who do manual labor become old more rapidly than workers in managerial occupations. Thus, 65-year-old construction workers show many more signs of aging than stock market analysts.

An analysis of U.S. data found that manual workers were 50 percent more likely to die in a given year than other workers (D. Cutler et al., 2011). A careful study found that ongoing physical labor—specifically heavy lifting, crouching, or standing for hours each day—speeds up aging because of wear and tear (Ravesteijn et al., 2018).

Not only physical strain, but also weather, harmful food, drugs, pollution, and radiation may wear down the body. For instance, skin cancer is caused partly by extensive sun exposure, clogged arteries are caused partly by too much animal fat, and some cancerous tumors result from excessive pollution and radiation.

Every older person's hands and face are wrinkled, often with discolorations known as "age spots." By contrast, the skin on the torso may be smooth and clear, even at age 80. That's evidence of wear and tear from exposure to sun, wind, and cold.

Eating Less An astonishing finding from lower animals suggests an application of wear and tear. If an adult reduced digestion, metabolism, and so on by eating 1,800 calories a day instead of the usual 3,000, would reduced body activity slow down aging? The answer seems to be yes.

Calorie restriction—a drastic reduction in calories consumed—increases the life span in many organisms, from fruit flies to monkeys. Extensive research on mice finds that specifics of genes and diet matter, but also that many creatures live twice as long as average if their diet is restricted (Rizza et al., 2014).

Regarding humans, thousands of members of the Calorie Restriction Society voluntarily undereat (Roth & Polotsky, 2012). They give up some things that many people cherish, not just cake and hot dogs but also a strong sex drive and high energy. As a result, they have lower blood pressure, fewer strokes, less cancer, and almost no diabetes.

In several places (e.g., Okinawa, Denmark, and Norway), wartime occupation forced severe calorie reduction for almost everyone. People ate local vegetables and not much else, and disease deaths were markedly lower (Fontana et al., 2011).

Similar results were reported from Cuba, as already mentioned. Because the United States led an embargo, Cuba experienced food and gas shortages from 1991 to 1995. People walked more, ate homegrown fruits and vegetables, and lost weight. They had much less heart disease and diabetes, and they lived longer (Franco et al., 2013).

But in all of these nations, once more food was available, people ate more, gained weight, and died earlier. Consequently, many researchers seek the benefits of calorie restriction without the diet that few people choose. Drugs to accomplish this have not succeeded.

However, one strategy seems to work, **intermittent fasting**, in which people periodically fast but eat normally most of the time. Several versions work: Two of the seven days per week, or every other day, or for 14 to 20 hours each day. Intermittent fasting results in lower blood pressure, less obesity, and better metabolism, not only because the digestive system is less active but also because some other physiological responses increase to protect against temporary starvation (Mani et al., 2018). That is, again, selective compensation with optimization.

The benefits of intermittent fasting are similar to the benefits of calorie restriction, but this strategy is more palatable to most people. For example, one study entailed four comparison groups, about 35 healthy but overweight women in each group. One group reduced daily calories by 20 percent (the usual weight-loss diet), one reduced weekly calories by 20 percent but were allowed to eat more on some days and less on others, one group fasted (75 percent fewer calories, as in classic calorie restriction) two days a week and then ate without restriction on the other five days, and the final group was the experimental control—no special diet.

The results: Weight loss was about the same for all three groups with restricted calories (Schübel et al., 2018). However, the women preferred the two-day fasting version.

Fasting is not recommended for people under age 18, or for pregnant or lactating women, or for the elderly who have certain health problems, including diabetes. But even those with diabetes, with medical supervision, may be helped by intermittent fasting (Grajower & Horne, 2019).

One remarkable study involved 11 people with type 2 diabetes (Taylor, 2019). They had been told they needed to eat regularly and not skimp on quantity, and they were also told they had a lifelong impairment with "major risk to eyesight, feet, heart and brain."

Remember that most people choose comfort over diet restriction. Not so for these people. They took daily medication, they watched their diet, and they knew they risked blindness and amputation. No wonder that, when they were offered medically supervised fasting, they were motivated to try it. With intensive advice and encouragement from a nurse, they restricted their eating and lost 15 pounds, stopped medication, and then were guided in keeping the weight off. The happy result: remission of diabetes (Taylor, 2019).

Such results are encouraging to those who would slow down aging. However, most scientists reject wear and tear as a general theory. They point out that bodies sometime need activity: Exercise benefits hearts and lungs; tai chi improves balance; weight training increases muscle mass; sexual activity stimulates the sexual-reproductive system; dietary fiber aids digestion; intermittent fasting succeeds partly because it activates some parts of body functioning while halting others.

A surprising study of 55- to 79-year-olds who bicycled over 100 miles per week (they enjoyed the exercise and the scenery!) found very little age-based deterioration of the muscles. Indeed, on most measures those older bikers had much stronger legs than the average 30-year-old (Pollock et al., 2018). Thus, wear and tear fails as an overall theory of aging, although some specific applications succeed.

THINK CRITICALLY: Do people want the comforts of daily life—driving and eating—more than longer lives?

intermittent fasting A pattern of eating that include periods of restricted eating interspersed with usual consumption. The most popular pattern is two days per week eating less than 750 calories and five days of normal eating, all while drinking plenty of water.

Kyodo/AP Images

World's Record for Centenarians Can you sprint 100 meters in less than 30 seconds? Almost until his death in 2019, this man, Hidekichi Miyazaki, could. Maybe you need more practice. Hidekichi had been running for 105 years!

It's All Genetic

A second cluster of theories focuses on genes—both genes of the entire species and genes that vary from one person to another.

maximum life span The oldest possible age to which members of a species can live under ideal circumstances. For humans, that age is approximately 122 years.

Maximum and Average Every species has, genetically, a **maximum life span**, defined as the oldest possible age that members of that species can attain (Wolf, 2010). For rats that is 4 years; rabbits, 13; tigers, 26; house cats, 30; brown bats, 34; brown bears, 37; chimpanzees, 55; Indian elephants, 70; finback whales, 80; lake sturgeon, 150; giant tortoises, 180.

The oldest well-documented human life ended at age 122, when Jeanne Calment died in southern France in 1997. That is several years longer than the previous record or the age that other very old people have attained. Some researchers consider that implausible and suggest that Calment actually died in her 70s, her identity taken by her daughter, Yvonne, in order to escape serious debt (Zak, 2019).

Be that as it may, it is certain that no one has yet been proven to have outlived her, despite documented birth dates for over a billion people who have died since then. This suggests that the maximum is not more than 122 (Medford & Vaupel, 2019).

It is apparent that genes affect aging lifelong, from how long the fetus stays in the womb to the details of graying or loss of hair. Remember puberty: It begins with genes that direct the pituitary to make growth and sexual hormones, and then every organ is affected. The same may occur for aging and, eventually, for death.

Further evidence for the role of genes comes from a genetic disorder called Hutchinson-Gilford syndrome (or *progeria*). It causes children to stop growing at about age 5 and begin to look old, with wrinkled skin and balding heads in childhood. They die in their teens of diseases typically found in people five times their age.

Other genes promote a long and healthy life. People who reach age 100 usually have alleles that other people do not (Tindale et al., 2019). Jeanne Calment had the DR1 allele, common in centenarians, not in the general population.

Many other longevity genes have been identified (Santos-Lozano et al., 2016). Sometimes the crucial factor is in a particular allele.

For the Apoe gene, about 80 percent of the population have allele 3, about 12 percent have allele 2, and about 8 percent have allele 4, with proportions varying slightly based on ethnic ancestry (González et al., 2018). Those with Apoe4 are more likely to suffer from heart disease and neurocognitive disorders; and those with Apoe2 are protected from those ailments.

GUILLAUME SOUVANT/Getty Images

Still Together At age 104 in 2016, the Lamolie twins are twice fortunate to be alive. The first time was at birth, when Paulette *(left)* weighed 3 pounds and Simone *(right)* weighed 2 pounds. The second is genetic—their shared genes must include some for longevity.

As a result, when the genes of people over age 85 are assessed, up to 16 percent have Apoe2 and only about 4 percent have allele 4. because of the genes that increased the death rate for Apoe4 and reduced it for Apoe2. Allele 3 seems neither lethal nor protective, so its frequency remains at about 80 percent (McKay et al., 2011).

Almost every disease is partly genetic, which is one reason why disease rates vary among people with ancestors from particular parts of the world. For example, many scientists search for the genes that increase the risk for diabetes. Genetic-wide research (called GWAS), which looks at the entire genome, has found more than 100 such genes (Visscher et al., 2017). Many of those genes are more common in some groups than in others.

For example, for genetic reasons, people with Asian ancestors tend to develop diabetes at younger ages and lower weights than Europeans. In China, Han people have higher rates than other Chinese people (L. Wang et al., 2017; Hsu et al.,

2015). In the United States, African Americans are particularly likely to develop diabetes (Layton et al., 2018).

Current researchers in the genes of aging focus more on epigenetic factors than on genes alone because, as you remember from Chapter 3, genes alone do not determine anything; they depend on methylation to be expressed or stifled. That is true for the genes of aging.

As a theory of aging, looking at genes makes sense. However, the danger is that focusing on genes may distract people from other causes of disease and death. They might think that fate, not secondary aging, is the reason for aging.

That might discourage them from stopping smoking, exercising more, improving their diet. It might discourage public officials from securing clean water, or better health care, or nutritious food for everyone. Since nature and nurture always interact, genes alone do not cause the diseases and other signs of old age.

THINK CRITICALLY: For the benefit of the species as a whole, why would genes promote aging?

That is especially apparent in the United States. In 2015, average life expectancy at birth was 80 (77 for men, 82 for women), eight years more than half a century ago. However, the average has fallen between 2015 and 2019 because of more "deaths of despair" in middle age, specifically from opioid addiction, suicide, alcohol, and extreme obesity (Gaydosh et al., 2019). Those are private and public health problems, not genetic ones.

Aging of the Cells

The third cluster of theories examines **cellular aging**, focusing on molecules and cells. Remember, cells duplicate many times over the life span. Minor copying errors — repetitions and deletions of triplets — accumulate. Early in life, the immune system repairs such errors, but eventually the immune system itself becomes less adept.

cellular aging The cumulative effect of stress and toxins, causing cellular damage first and eventually the death of cells.

Hayflick limit The number of times a human cell is capable of dividing into two new cells. The limit for most human cells is approximately 50 divisions, an indication that the life span is limited by our genetic program.

In general, when the organism can no longer repair cellular errors, senescence occurs. This process is first apparent in the skin, an organ that replaces itself often, particularly if damage occurs (such as peeling skin with sunburn). Cuts take a little longer to heal, and scarring becomes more obvious. Cellular aging also occurs inside the body; the aging immune system is increasingly unable to control abnormal cells.

Cellular aging, with some cells out of normal control, is a major cause of all forms of cancer (Martincorena & Campbell, 2015). Before age 40, biological mechanisms keep cancer cells from reproducing and metastasizing. The annual cancer death rate for U.S. adults under age 40 is less than 1 in 10,000.

However, once the childbearing years are over, and thus the human species no longer needs people to reproduce, cancer cells duplicate unchecked. In the United States in 2016, more than 1 in every 100 adults over age 65 died of cancer. Cancer is the second cause of death for the elderly, not far behind the first (heart disease) (National Center for Health Statistics, 2018).

Even without cancer, cells eventually lose the ability to replicate normally. This point is referred to as the **Hayflick limit**, named after the scientist who discovered it. Hayflick believes that aging is caused primarily by a natural loss of molecular fidelity — that is, by inevitable errors in transcription as each cell reproduces itself. He believes that aging is natural, built into our cells (Hayflick, 2004). There are dozens of cellular changes with age, from the seemingly insignificant mitochondria to the obviously crucial stem cells (López-Otín et al., 2013).

Old Caterpillars? No, these are young chromosomes, stained to show the glowing white telomeres at the ends.

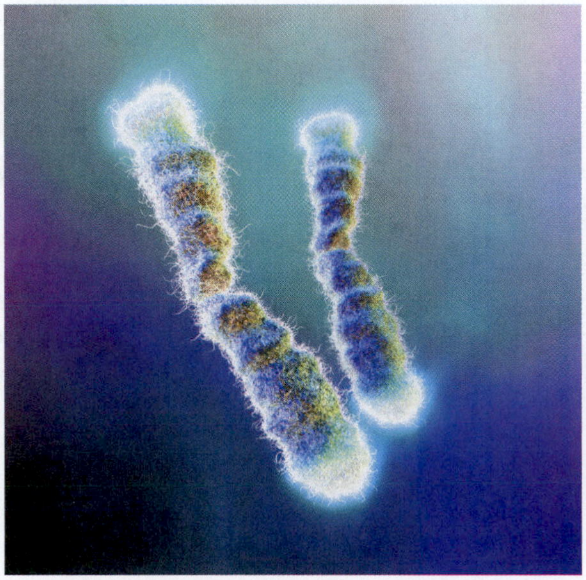

Hybrid Medical/Science Source

telomeres The area of the tips of each chromosome that is reduced a tiny amount as time passes. By the end of life, the telomeres are very short.

One particular cell change that has been studied in connection with aging involves the **telomeres**, material at the end of each chromosome that becomes shorter over time. Telomeres are longer in children (except those with progeria) and shorter in old adults. Eventually, at the Hayflick limit, the telomere is gone, duplication stops, and the creature dies.

Researchers note that bodies make a substance called *telemerase* that protects telomeres allowing cells can continue to duplicate. Other substances (particularly mitochondria) also aid the cells and prolong cell function. On the other hand, some molecules (called *free radicals*) attack cells, creating what is called *oxidative stress,* impairing the cells' ability to function.

The more researchers consider the role of cells in aging, the more complex the process seems to be. For example, opinions are changing about free radicals. As one review explains:

> A few decades ago, the belief regarding free radicals and oxidative stress was that they were completely undesired and dangerous for the human body. . . . Today, this demonizing view has mellowed down and it is known that oxidative stress is part of the innate human immune system, and that free radicals are also related to defence mechanisms, but also used as cell mediators, pathway signalling, cell differentiation, proliferation and migration.
>
> [*Carocho et al., 2019*]

Scientists continue to confirm, however, that the more stress people experience from childhood on, the shorter their telomeres are in late adulthood and the sooner they will die. Stress shortens telomeres, even in childhood, as evident in the institutionalized children of Romania described in several early chapters (Drury et al., 2012).

By late adulthood, telomeres are longer in women than in men, and longer in European Americans than in African Americans (Aviv, 2011). There are many possible causes, but cellular-aging theorists focus on the consequences: Women outlive men, and European Americans outlive African Americans, at least until age 80.

This discussion of theories of aging has mentioned cognitive and social influences many times. Perhaps especially in late adulthood, biology is intertwined with cognitive and psychosocial development. Certainly ageism and demography affect every aspect of life after age 65. This chapter, then, provides an introduction to the next two.

Especially for Biologists What are some immediate practical uses for research on the causes of aging? (see response, page 608)

WHAT HAVE YOU LEARNED?

1. Why is the wear-and-tear theory of aging no longer considered accurate?
2. Why do relatively few people use calorie restriction to slow down aging?
3. What evidence supports the genetic theory of aging?
4. Why is the average life span much lower than the maximum?
5. How does the Hayflick limit relate to aging?
6. How can immune system failure cause aging?

SUMMARY

Prejudice and Predictions

1. Stereotypes about the elderly are prevalent in the culture, evident in the assumptions and behaviors of both the young and the old. That prejudice is called ageism, and it can lead to self-fulfilling prophecies regarding health and well-being. Elderspeak is one example.

2. The demographic shift describes the changing size of various age groups, as fewer babies are born and more people live long lives. What once was a pyramid is becoming a rectangle.

3. Statistics about the elderly are sometimes presented in ways to alarm younger people. Currently, about 14 percent of people in the U.S. population are elderly, with 90 percent of them self-sufficient and productive, more often caregivers than care receivers.

4. Gerontologists sometimes distinguish among the young-old, the old-old, and the oldest-old, according to each group's relative degree of dependency. Only 10 percent of those over age 65 are dependent (they are the oldest-old), and only 3 percent of the elderly are in nursing homes or hospitals.

Adjusting to Changes

5. Compensation for senescence can occur at every level of the ecological system. Regarding the microsystem, frequency of intercourse is not the best measure of sexual activity among older couples, some of whom say their sexual interactions improve with age.

6. An older person's ability to drive safely depends on the interaction between the biological effects of aging and the macrosystem. For example, determining who should be licenced to drive is one way to keep able elders on the road, and impaired elders off it.

7. Exosystem compensation for sensory decline is crucial. Vision losses are common and critical: Many elders have cataracts, glaucoma, or macular degeneration. Hearing also declines: Most older men are significantly hard-of-hearing. All these declines affect many aspects of functioning and all can be remediated by better technology, construction, and universal design.

8. Primary aging happens to everyone, reducing organ reserve in the body and brain. Secondary aging depends on the individual's past health habits, as well as on the social context. Compensation is possible and brings many benefits, including compression of morbidity.

9. Both the flu and osteoporosis illustrate the distinction between primary and secondary aging. With age, everyone's immune system declines and bones weaken, but whether this causes serious impairment depends on secondary factors. Understanding that has dramatically reduced deaths from flu and broken hips.

Theories of Aging

10. Hundreds of theories address the causes of aging. Wear-and-tear theory suggests that living wears out the body; it applies to some parts of the body but not to overall aging. Calorie restriction and intermittent fasting can be seen as promising applications of this theory.

11. Genes of every species allow a maximum life span, which is far longer than the life span of the average person. Thus, aging is partly genetic but also dependent on many non-genetic factors.

12. Genes may allow humans to survive through the reproductive years but then become seriously ill and inevitably die. Some individuals have genes or alleles that lead to long life; others to shorter lives. Nonetheless, genes never act alone.

13. Cellular theories of aging include the idea that the processes of DNA duplication and repair are affected by aging, making repair of errors more difficult. Cancer is an example of cellular measures that no longer control the errors the result from repeated duplication of cells.

14. Cells stop duplicating at a certain point, called the Hayflick limit. This stoppage seems to occur when the telomeres shorten and then disappear.

KEY TERMS

ageism (p. 586)
elderspeak (p. 589)
demographic shift (p. 590)
average life expectancy (p. 590)
young-old (p. 592)
old-old (p. 592)
oldest-old (p. 592)
universal design (p. 598)
primary aging (p. 599)
secondary aging (p. 599)
compression of morbidity (p. 599)
osteoporosis (p. 600)
wear-and-tear theory (p. 602)
calorie restriction (p. 602)
intermittent fasting (p. 603)
maximum life span (p. 604)
cellular aging (p. 605)
Hayflick limit (p. 605)
telomeres (p. 606)

APPLICATIONS

1. Write down the degree of independence of all your relatives over age 65, such as grandparents and great-grandparents, great aunts and great uncles, and so on. What percent are in nursing homes? How and why is that percent higher or lower than the national average?

2. Compensating for sensory losses is difficult because it involves learning new habits. To better understand the experience, reduce your hearing or vision for a day by wearing earplugs or dark glasses that let in only bright lights. (Use caution and common sense: Don't drive a car while wearing earplugs or cross streets while wearing dark glasses.) Report on your emotions, the responses of others, and your conclusions.

3. Ask five people of various ages whether they want to live to age 100, and record their responses. Would they be willing to eat half as much, exercise much more, experience weekly dialysis, or undergo other procedures in order to extend life? Analyze the responses.

Especially For ANSWERS

Response for Young Adults (from p. 589): No. Some seniors hear well, and they would resent it.

Response for Biologists (from p. 606): Although ageism and ambivalence limit the funding of research on the causes of aging, the applications include prevention of AIDS, cancer, neurocognitive disorders, and physical damage from pollution—all urgent social priorities.

Observation Quiz ANSWER

Answer to Observation Quiz (from p. 593): She was born in 1932. When this picture was taken, she was 83.

VISUALIZING DEVELOPMENT Elders Behind the Wheel

Older people often reduce or change their driving habits in order to compensate for their slowing reaction time, avoiding nighttime, bad weather, and long distances. Many states have initiated restrictions, including requiring older drivers to renew their licenses in person, to make sure they stay safe. Consequently, their crash rate is low overall, but not when measured by the rate per miles driven.

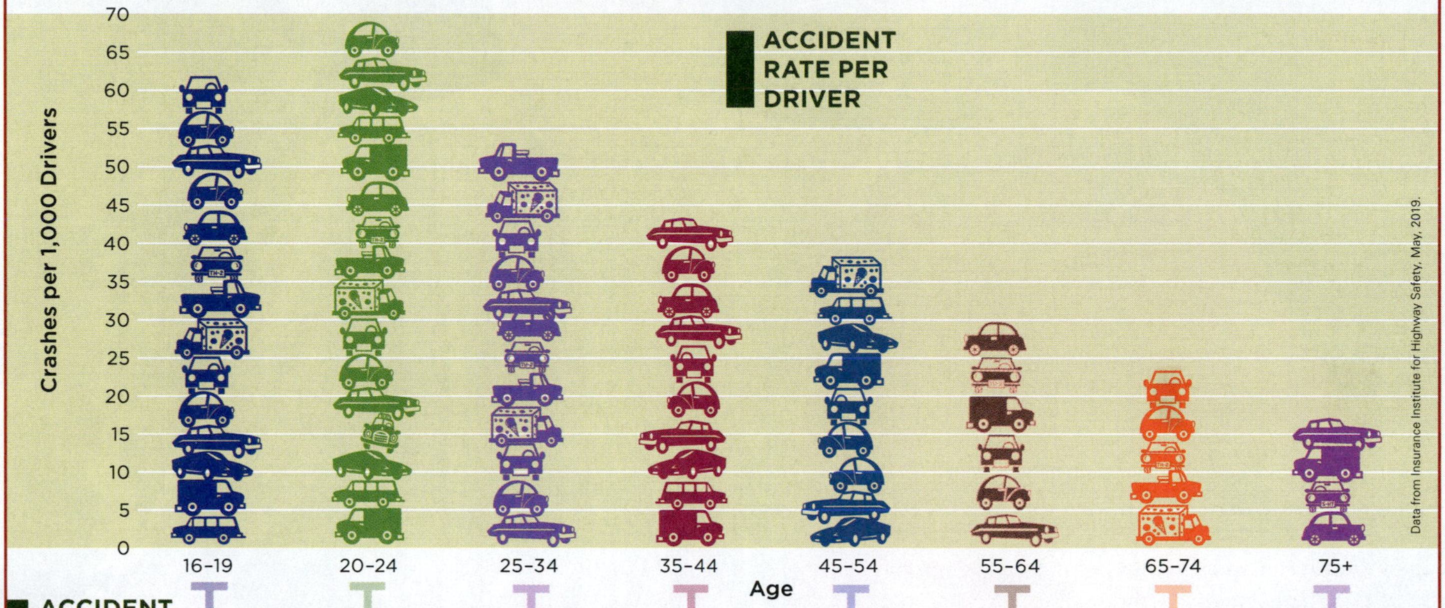

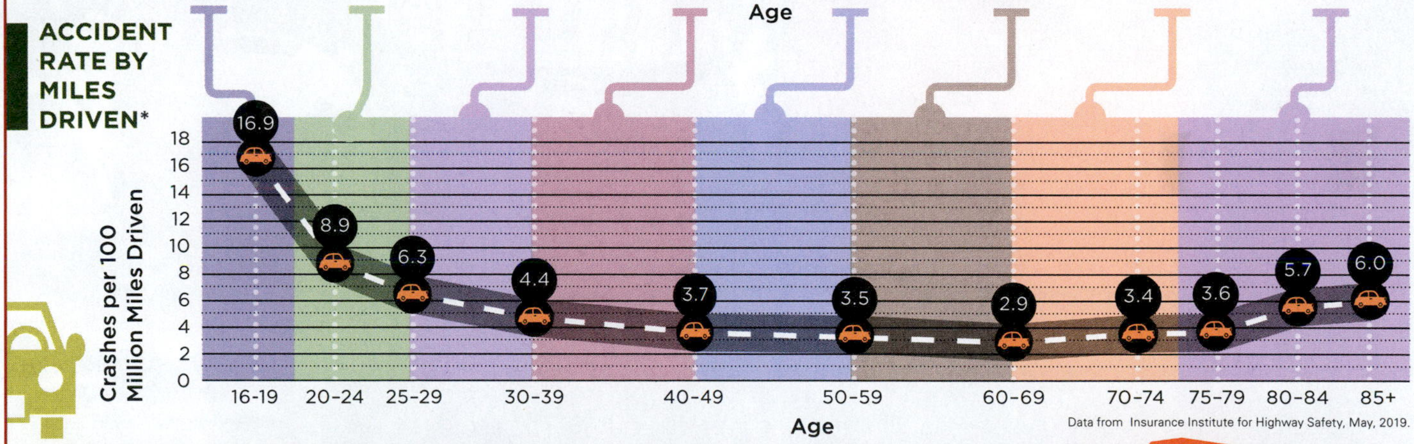

*Although their crash rate per miles driven is higher than that of younger adults, older people tend to drive in city conditions, which have higher crash rates than freeway or highway driving. Thus, the elevated crash rates for older drivers per mile traveled may be inflated due to where they drive.

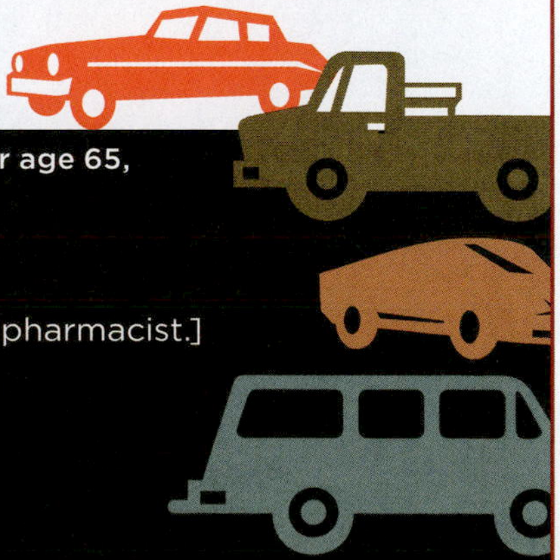

SELF-CHECK Humans of all ages tend to overestimate their abilities. Especially after age 65, adults who want to drive need to answer six questions:

1. Is your vision fading? [Ask your optometrist if any visual losses affect driving.]
2. Do your medications affect reaction time or alertness? [Ask both doctor and pharmacist.]
3. Do your physical limitations affect neck-turning, foot-pushing, wheel-turning?
4. Do you get lost more easily now than in earlier years?
5. Do other drivers honk at you? [Don't just get angry; consider the reason.]
6. Have you had any minor accidents? [Even a scrape or a fender bender signifies something.]

If your answers are all "no," review them with someone who will be honest with you. Some of the elderly are very safe drivers, whereas others can be a risk to themselves and to those around them. Before you step on the accelerator, make sure you are one of the safe ones.

Late Adulthood: Cognitive Development

CHAPTER 24

What Will You Know?

- Does the brain grow or shrink in old age?
- What kinds of memory are least apt to fade in old age, and what kinds are the most apt to fade?
- What is the difference between these four terms: *Alzheimer's disease, senility, dementia,* and *neurocognitive disorders*?
- What cognitive gains occur in late adulthood?

- **The Brain During Late Adulthood**
  - Ongoing Development
  - OPPOSING PERSPECTIVES: Slower Thinking
- **Step-by-Step Processing**
  - Input
  - Memory
  - Control Processes
  - Output
- **Neurocognitive Disorders**
  - Mild Cognitive Impairment
  - The Ageism of Words
  - Prevalence of NCDs
  - The Many Neurocognitive Disorders
  - Preventing Impairment
  - Reversible Neurocognitive Disorder?
  - A CASE TO STUDY: The More You Know . . .
- **New Cognitive Development**
  - Erikson and Maslow
  - Aesthetic Sense and Creativity
  - Wisdom
- **VISUALIZING DEVELOPMENT: Global Prevalence of Major NCD**

"Being blind is not lethal," says my friend Diana.

"It is not life threatening, like cancer or heart disease," she told me as she tapped her white-tipped cane on the sidewalk, holding on to my arm.

I was stunned. I have watched her over the past two decades losing more and more of her sight. Is she trying to make me feel better? Or trying to make herself feel better?

I once thought being blind meant total darkness, but that is true for only 15 percent of those who are legally blind. The rest see some light and shapes. However, even with corrective lenses, their vision is so poor that seeing something a foot away is like someone with normal corrected vision seeing it more than 20 feet away.

Diana is legally blind. She gave away hundreds of books because she can no longer read them; she does not recognize anyone until they touch her shoulder and speak; she asks me to fill her teacup because she, laughingly, fears making a mess.

As a child, I was asked whether I would rather be blind or deaf. I said deaf. Diana made me realize that this was a false choice. The crucial question, from an information-processing perspective, relates to perception, not sensation; and perception is in the brain, not the sense organs.

Diana is a psychotherapist, paid by clients who talk about their troubles and hear her wise responses. She told me years ago that she sometimes saw double—two faces of her patients rather than one. That was a distressing sign that her vision was fading. But she also said it was not an impediment: She concentrates on the words, the tone, the silences of her clients, not on how many faces she sees.

This chapter is about the information-processing approach to cognitive development. As you remember, our senses convey information to our brains, where we process it, activate the prefrontal cortex, and respond. You will read that memory and the senses convey information.

All of the senses become less acute with age, and it is better to see and hear well, but the crucial question is whether or not the brain can coordinate past experiences and current sensations to produce cogent responses. That is what Diana does.

Some people compensate for sensory losses. Diana relies on her cane, her voice-sensitive phone, and her friends. She uses her other senses: listening to books on tape, touching clothes to decide what to wear, smelling food to identify it. She ventures out in the daytime, because she remembers where to go and strangers help her find the right subway, or store, or restaurant.

Left: Uwe Umstätter/Westend 61/Media Bakery
Top: Image Source/Divine Images/Media Bakery

Compensation and independence are easier for her than for most blind people, because she can afford to hire a Pilates instructor who comes to her home four days a week, and a personal assistant who opens her mail, writes checks, cooks, and accompanies her when she goes out at night.

She processes information well. She not only helps her clients, but she also writes witty and profound articles online. (An assistant helps her edit and send.)

As you will read in this chapter, some of the elderly suffer from major neurocognitive disorders, but even they still experience pleasure, curiosity, and happiness. And some of the very old become wise. Diana is one of them.

The Brain During Adulthood

As you know, the brain develops rapidly from the first days of life throughout childhood and adolescence, with the prefrontal cortex finally reaching full maturation at about age 25. Chapter 20 explained that new neurons appear during adulthood and that severe problems (chronic alcohol abuse, repeated blows to the head, and so on) can do lasting damage to the brain.

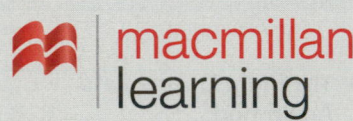

macmillan learning

VIDEO: Brain Development Animation: Late Adulthood shows gray matter loss in the normal aging brain.

Ongoing Development

Those protective and destructive factors continue in later adulthood. An information-processing approach to adult development emphasizes that the brain continues to form neurons and dendrites.

Shrinkage and slowdown, already noted in Chapter 20, continue. The rate accelerates, and the problems mentioned earlier accumulate. By age 80, the average adult brain does not process information as it did at age 30, or even at age 60. Losses are apparent, especially for speed, but also for memory and logic (Salthouse, 2019). Fortunately, as you will now see, in some ways the brain functions as well as it ever did! In some ways, better (Spreng & Turner, 2019).

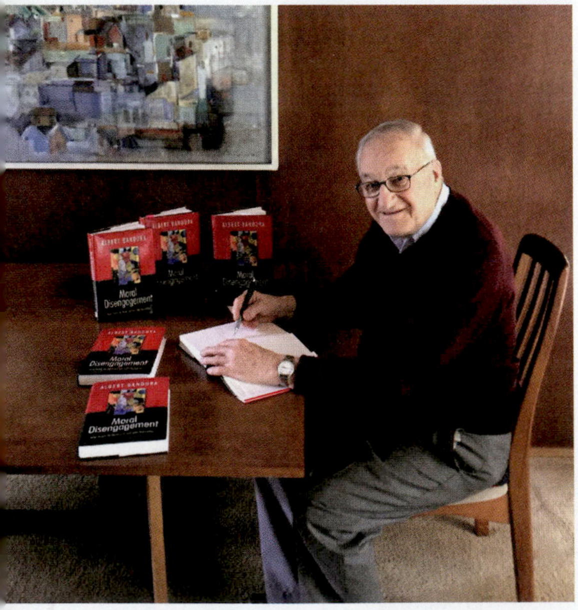

David Maxfield

Still Thinking New dendrites can lead to new ideas. Albert Bandura was a young scholar when he developed social learning theory to explain why preschoolers attacked a doll with a hammer. Here, at age 90, he signs copies of his most recent book that explains his theory of moral disengagement, in hopes that we can develop a more compassionate, humane society.

New Cells The fact that new neurons appear in the adult brain is one of the most surprising discoveries of the past few decades. Debate continues about the rate and significance of this growth, but it is known that these neurons are located in two specific parts of the brain: the hippocampus (memory) and the olfactory (smell) cortex (Boldrini et al., 2018; Choi & Goldstein, 2018).

Those areas are particularly crucial for brain health in late adulthood. Failing memory is the classic sign of a neurocognitive disorder, and lost sense of smell is often the first sign of severe brain disease. Thus, new neurons in those areas may be a defense against reduced information processing in late adulthood.

Dendrites Sprouting Dendrite growth is also variable and crucial. In adult brains, dendrites grow with new experiences as well as with antidepressants (M. Levy et al., 2018). New dendrites are evidence of lifelong plasticity. Thus, "neuroimaging results have recast our framework around cognitive aging from one of decline to one emphasizing plasticity" (Gutchess, 2014).

An intriguing age-related correlation is found between depression and aging. With age, fewer adults experience episodes of major depression. For example, in 2019, the National Institute of Mental Health reported incidence of major depressive events at various ages: 13 percent for ages 18 to 25; 8 percent for ages 25 to 49; 5 percent for ages 50+.

Other research from many nations also finds that people are less depressed, less anxious, and happier overall as they age (Jorm, 2000; Machado et al., 2019). The neurological evidence of major depression suggests that dendrite growth in the adult brain reduces depression.

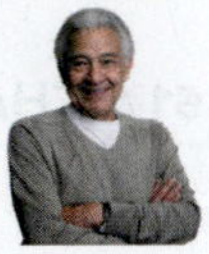

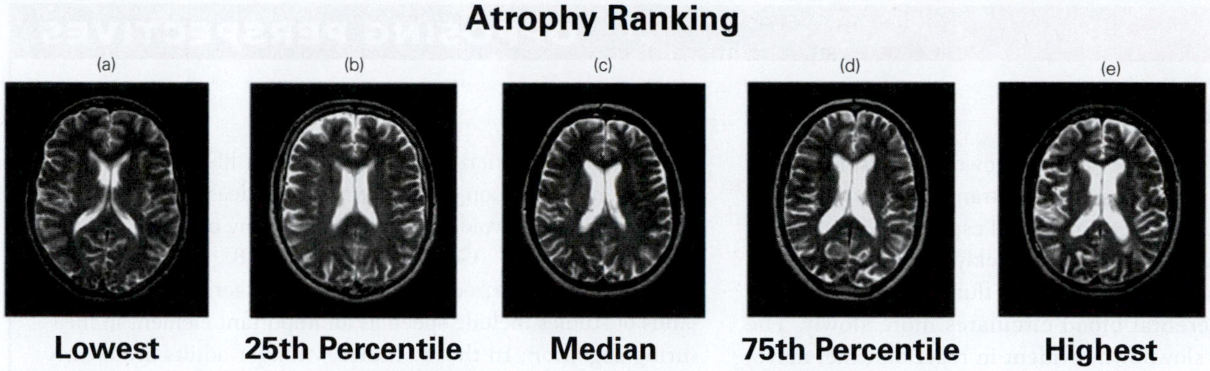

Not All Average A team of neuroscientists in Scotland (Farrell et al., 2009) published these images of the brains of healthy 65- to 70-year-olds. The images show normal brain loss (the white areas) from the lowest (5th percentile) to the highest (95th percentile). Some atrophy is inevitable (even younger brains atrophy), but few elders are merely average.

Brain Shrinkage During the same years of life in which neurons and dendrites increase, thousands of other neurons die and brains shrink. Specifically, during every decade from ages 20 to 80 and beyond, the volume of *gray matter* (crucial for processing new experiences) is reduced as the cortex thins. *White matter* (mostly myelin) generally is reduced as well. However, white matter also increases in an odd way: Bright white spots appear on MRIs after age 50 or so. Both of these neurological events (shrinkage and white spots) correlate with cognitive loss in late adulthood.

Brain shrinkage is variable, however. Every study of cognition over the decades of early, middle, and late adulthood shows substantial variation from culture to culture, person to person, and brain region to brain region. The hippocampus is one area that has been the target of intense study as new brain-imaging techniques have become available.

The hippocampus has many distinct parts, each affected in a particular way with age. Two parts of the hippocampus (CA1 and CA2) show reduced volume over every decade of adulthood, with an accelerating pace of decline in later adulthood. One part (CA3) was reduced over most of adulthood but then stabilized in the later years. Finally, one (the *subiculum,* which itself has four parts) seemed not to shrink at all (Daugherty et al., 2016).

What makes the brain change over time? An evolutionary perspective finds that over thousands of years the human brain has changed in response to social circumstances (Kempermann, 2016). When agriculture began (widely believed to be approximately 10,000 years ago), the prefrontal cortex expanded: Adults needed more planning, remembering, and strategizing than was previously necessary, because living in stable communities and towns required laws, markets, and labor specialization. As one scholar suggests:

> Moving actively in a changing world and dealing with novelty and complexity regulate adult neurogenesis. New neurons might thus provide the cognitive adaptability to conquer ecological niches rich with challenging stimuli.
>
> [Kempermann, 2012, p. 727]

As best we know, this process is ongoing. The average brains of twenty-first-century adults may differ from the average brains of nineteenth-century adults because of the increasing challenges of the modern world. On an individual level as well, brains may adapt to the specific experiences of a person. Plasticity is evident in brains lifelong (Pauwels et al., 2018).

OPPOSING PERSPECTIVES

Slower Thinking

Now let us drill down on the effect of slower processing. Senescence reduces the production of neurotransmitters—including glutamate, acetylcholine, serotonin, and especially dopamine—that allow a nerve impulse to jump quickly across the synaptic gap from one neuron to another. Neural fluid decreases, myelination thins, and cerebral blood circulates more slowly. The result is an overall slowdown, evident in reaction time, movement, speech, and thought.

This severely affects thinking because speed is crucial for many aspects of cognition. In fact, some experts believe that processing speed is a basic element of the *g* mentioned in Chapter 21—an ability that underlies all other aspects of intelligence (Schubert et al., 2017).

Is speed really basic to cognition? Our language connects the two. A smart person is said to be a *quick* thinker; the opposite is said of someone who is a *slow* learner. The notion that slow thinking produces cognitive losses and overall impairment is evident in many studies. Researchers have studied the connection between walking speed and intellectual sharpness and found that the slower gait predicts cognitive impairment and brain disease (Montero-Odasso et al., 2017).

Indeed, slower thinking correlates with every kind of physical disability (Sugimoto et al., 2018; Hackett et al., 2018). Walks slow? Talks slow? Oh no—thinks slow!

There is another perspective, however. Speed may not always be ideal. A fable credited to Aesop, an enslaved Greek storyteller who lived 2,600 years ago, describes a race between a tortoise and a hare. The rabbit lost: Slow and steady won the race.

Many people criticize the pace of current life, with fast food, flashy trends that soon disappear, popular ideas. Business leaders are advised to avoid "chasing 'bright shiny objects'. . . flavor of the day novelties" (Gorbatov & Lane, 2018).

If speed is prioritized, accuracy may be sacrificed. Yet, thousands of studies include speed as an important element in measuring cognition: In those studies, younger adults are clearly superior to older ones. However, age-related differences are less apparent, or even absent, when older adults are granted as much time as they wish (Cappelletti et al., 2014).

Lifelong, brains adjust to whatever demands are put on them. Older adults have automatized some tasks, and they sometimes use old assumptions (e.g., about gender, drugs, medicine) rather than readjusting their thoughts. It takes them longer to learn new skills, think new thoughts, and adjust to new realities. They may reduce the bottleneck of too many demands at once by allowing some neurons to fire automatically.

In practical terms, if two challenging tasks are presented at once, an older adult may ignore one to concentrate on the other (Bercovitz & Pagnini, 2016). This can impair them when multiple quick thoughts are required simultaneously, when participating in a discussion with several people, or when driving a car on a city street.

Suppose that a child asks Grandpa about dinosaurs while he is reading the paper, or that a child asks Grandma which bus to take while she is getting dressed. A wise Grandpa puts down the newspaper and then answers. Grandma first dresses and then thinks about transportation (avoiding mismatched shoes). Slow, methodical thinking may be best.

Selective Losses This is not to deny that the brain shrinks. That has been evident for decades, and newer methods of brain analysis confirm it. As already mentioned with the hippocampus, loss and shrinkage is selective. The prefrontal cortex continues to grow over adulthood, but there is less "brain activity in the default mode network (DMN), the fronto-parietal control network (FPCN), as well as their inter-networks connections" (Lou et al., 2019, p. 341).

Connections between brain areas are particularly disturbed from the occipital and temporal lobes—the parts of the brain that specialize in seeing and hearing. This means that over the years of adulthood, people are slower to process what they see and hear. Is this a cause or a result of sensory loss? Probably both. If an individual has difficulty seeing or hearing, that person will have less dendritic growth and fewer connections in the occipital and temporal lobes.

Changes in brain structures with age not only include less activation of those lobes but also more bilateral activation in the prefrontal lobe. Some tasks that make younger adult brains activate only one area on one side of the frontal lobe are likely to activate more parts on both sides of the aging brain. Why do older adults use more parts of their brains, including both hemispheres, to solve problems? Perhaps to compensate for loss in each single part: More brain power is needed A recent review finds that changes in brain activation with age can be "adaptive and maladaptive," in that "engaging prior knowledge . . . can both hinder and support performance" (Spreng & Turner, 2019, p. 529). (See Opposing Perspectives on page 614.)

WHAT HAVE YOU LEARNED?

1. What is encouraging and discouraging about the formation of new neurons in adulthood?
2. What new challenges does historical change present to adults?
3. Why is multitasking particularly difficult in late adulthood?
4. The fact that more parts of the prefrontal cortex are used in later adulthood can be interpreted optimistically or pessimistically. What are both interpretations?

Step-by-Step Processing

The information-processing perspective not only highlights brain processes, as we have just discussed, but also considers every step of thinking, from input (sensing), to memory (storage), to control processes (programming), and finally to output.

Input

The first step in information processing is input. As you remember from Chapter 5, sensation precedes perception, which precedes comprehension. Then, as Chapters 20 and 23 explained, all of the senses become less sharp with age. That limits input, because in order to be perceived, information must cross the *sensory threshold*—the divide between what is sensed and what is not. Small sensory losses—not noticed by the person or family but inevitable with age—impair cognition.

Such small losses are unnoticed because the brain automatically fills in missed sights and sounds, not always accurately. Elders miss some information. For example, they are less accurate at knowing where someone is looking or what their facial expression means (Hughes & Devine, 2015; Granger et al., 2016).

One study of visual information processing began with point-light walkers, (people who walk in the dark with lights on their hands, feet, elbows, knees, and so on). Only the lights, not the person, are visible. Older adults are less accurate at judging the movements and emotions of those point-light walkers, particularly when the walkers express anger (stamping feet and so on) or sadness (slower movement) (Spencer et al., 2016).

Similarly, small hearing losses make a difference. The cognition and the hearing of almost 2,000 adults (average age 77) was repeatedly tested (Lin et al., 2013). Between the start of the study and 11 years later, the average cognitive scores of the adults with hearing loss (who were often unaware of it) were down 7 percent; those with no hearing impairment were down 5 percent.

That 2-percent difference seems small, but statistically it was highly significant (.004). Greater hearing losses correlated with greater cognitive declines (Lin et al., 2013). Many other researchers likewise find that small input losses have a notable effect on output. This conclusion is reached when the people who are

Observation Quiz Beyond conversation, what do you see that predicts cognition? (see answer, page 632) ↓

Doug McKinlay/Lonely Planet Images/Getty Images

Keeping Alert These three men on a park bench in Malta are doing more than engaging in conversation; they are keeping their minds active through socialization and the discussion of current events and politics.

studied have good overall health and no sign of brain disease. Of course, it is not surprising that intelligence is impaired when a person has a neurocognitive disorder, but it is remarkable that, even with brain health, hearing can reduce cognition (Loughrey et al., 2018).

There is an important qualifier here. Although every study of each sense in isolation finds significant input loss with age, one recent study found no loss in perception of emotion when the emotion was genuine (not produced by an actor, as in some standardized tests) and when participants could use three input sources (seeing facial expressions, hearing words, listening to tone) (Wieck & Kunzmann, 2017).

In other words, input from each sense is reduced, but using all of the senses together may allow normal information-processing in late adulthood. No wonder elders prefer to talk face-to-face instead of via email, or to feel a reassuring touch with words of comfort and gestures of sorrow instead of receiving a condolence card.

Memory

After input, the second step is processing what has been sensed. Stereotype threat may impede this: Simply knowing that they are taking a memory test might make older adults anxious, consequently feeling years older and remembering less (Hughes et al., 2013). This is not inevitable: The impact of stereotype threat varies depending on circumstances, which sometimes evoke an elder's best processing efforts (Hess et al., 2019).

In general, the more complex a memory task is (such as in *associative memory,* connecting one idea with another), the more likely stereotype threat will undercut ability (Brubaker & Naveh-Benjamin, 2018). [**Life-Span Link**: Stereotype threat is discussed in Chapter 18.] The entire topic of memory is complex, because psychologists now realize that memory is not one function but many. One recent book describes 14 distinct types of memory (Slotnick, 2017). Every type of memory may originate in a distinct brain region, and each may have a specific pattern of loss that is affected by emotions as well as age.

Some age-related losses are typical, such as the "tip-of-the-tongue" experience, (knowing something but not quite able to find the words). Others are pathological, such as failure to recognize one's own adult child. For everyone, stress reduces memory. People who feel that others are judging them, or who have experienced a recent stress, remember less than they do in more relaxed circumstances (James et al., 2018; Shields et al., 2017).

In general, *explicit memory* (such as the ability to recall something verbally without clues) fades faster than *implicit memory* (the ability to recognize someone or something as familiar, or to perform a habitual action). Both are affected by age (Ward et al., 2013; Fraundorf et al., 2019).

The distinction between implicit and explicit memory is evident in what the oldest-old can and cannot do. It is harder to remember names than actions. Old-old people may still swim, bike, and drive even if they cannot name both U.S. senators from their state.

One particular memory deficit is *source amnesia*—forgetting the origin of a fact, idea, or snippet of conversation. Source amnesia is particularly problematic currently, with the Internet, many channels of television, and many printed sources bombarding the mind.

In practical terms, source amnesia means that elders might believe fake news, a rumor, or a political advertisement because they forget that the information came from a biased source. Compensation requires deliberate attention to the reason behind a message before accepting a con artist's promises or the politics of a TV ad. However, elders are less likely than younger adults to analyze, or even notice, who said what and why (Devitt & Schacter, 2016).

Another crucial type of memory is called *prospective memory*—remembering to do something in the future (to take a pill, to meet someone for lunch, to buy milk). Prospective memory also fades notably with age. This loss becomes dangerous if, for instance, a person cooking dinner forgets to turn off the stove, or if a driver is in the far lane of the highway when the exit appears.

The crucial aspect of prospective memory seems to be the ability to shift the mind quickly from one task to another: Older adults get immersed in one thought and have trouble changing gears (Schnitzspahn et al., 2013). For that reason, many elders follow routine sequences (brush teeth, take medicine, get the paper) and set an alarm to remind them to leave for a doctor's appointment. That is compensation.

William Haefeli/The New Yorker Collection/The Cartoon Bank

"I'm not losing my memory. I'm living in the now."

More broadly, impaired prospective memory is evident if a person must anticipate demands and experiences that have never been experienced before. "Proactive cognitive control," which requires sustained attention to possibilities that have not yet occurred, is increasingly difficult with age (Lamichhane et al., 2018).

Thus far we have focused on what elders do not remember. But some things are remembered well. Vocabulary is one example: Cross-sectional, longitudinal, and cross-sequential studies all show that vocabulary increases over most of adulthood. Even at age 90, elders score higher on word recognition than 20- to 40-year-olds (Salthouse, 2019). Older people remember words and languages that they learned decades ago, and they continually learn new words and phrases.

For example, the words *Internet, smartphone, email,* and *fax* appeared long after today's elders were young. With repeated hearing, most very old people understand and use these words. This demonstrates that they have learned in middle and late adulthood.

Especially for Students If you want to remember something that you learn in class for the rest of your life, what should you do? (see response, page 632)

Older adults are not usually confused by a word's meaning, but they may have difficulty recalling a word on command, a task that requires explicit memory. Control strategies are particularly useful in that case: Allowing time ("It will come to me"), reducing stress (deep and slow breathing), and using clues (remembering the first letter, remembering when that word was used) compensate.

Another crucial element is past experience. Thus, the current cohort of the elderly is more proficient in vocabulary than earlier generations of older adults were, probably because words—in the media and in social interaction—are increasingly important in daily life (Hartshorne & Germine, 2015).

Control Processes

We have already alluded to the next step in information processing: *control processes*. Many scholars believe that impaired control is the underlying reason that cognition is impaired in late adulthood. Control processes include selective attention, strategic judgment, and then appropriate action—the so-called *executive function* of the brain. Some of this was already evident in the previous section on memory. For example, remembering the first letter of a word or associating a new name with someone else who has the same name are control processes.

Inadequate control processes may explain why many older adults have extensive vocabularies (measured by written tests) but limited fluency (when they write or

Daniel Acker/Bloomberg/Getty Images

Active in the Community One the best ways for the elderly to stay mentally active is to be active in their neighborhoods. Registering new voters, as this man is doing, benefits the community while also helping seniors to maintain their control processes.

ecological validity The idea that cognition should be measured in settings that are as realistic as possible and that the abilities measured should be those needed in real life.

macmillan learning

VIDEO: Old Age: Thinking and Moving at the Same Time features a research study demonstrating how older brains are quite adaptable.

talk), why they are much better at recognition than recall, why tip-of-the-tongue forgetfulness is common, and why spelling is poorer than pronunciation.

Output

The final step in information processing is output. Scientists usually measure output through use of standardized tests of mental ability. As already noted, if older adults think their memory is being tested, that alone may impair them (Hughes et al., 2013). Even without stereotype threat, output on cognitive tests may not reflect ability.

Since abstract thinking and processing speed are the aspects of cognition that fade most with age, is there a better way to measure output in late adulthood? Perhaps ability should be measured in everyday tasks and circumstances, not as laboratory tests assess it. To test and measure in everyday settings is to seek **ecological validity**, to assess ability in the contexts and modes that it actually is used. This may be particularly important when measuring cognition in the elderly.

For example, because of changes in their circadian rhythm, older adults are at their best in the early morning, when adolescents are half asleep. If a study were to compare 85-year-olds and 15-year-olds, both tested at 7 A.M., the teenagers would be at a disadvantage. The opposite would occur with a test at 7 P.M.

Similarly, if intellectual ability were to be assessed via a timed test, then faster thinkers (usually young) would score higher than slower thinkers (usually old), although the slower ones might be accurate if they had a few more seconds to think. Context matters, too: Who feels stressed if the tests occur on a college campus?

Indeed, age differences in prospective memory are readily apparent in laboratory tests but disappear in some naturalistic settings, a phenomenon called the *age-prospective memory-paradox* (Schnitzspahn et al., 2011). Motivation seems to be crucial; elders are less likely to forget whatever they believe is important—phoning a child to say "happy birthday," for instance.

Similarly, as already noted, older adults are not as accurate as younger adults when tested on the ability to read emotions by looking at someone's face or listening to someone's voice. But seeing and hearing are less acute with age, so that may not be the best way to measure empathy in older adults. Accordingly, a team decided to measure empathy when visual contact was impossible.

Their study included a hundred couples who had been together for years, and all participants were repeatedly asked to indicate their own emotions (how happy, enthusiastic, balanced, content, angry, downcast, disappointed, nervous they were) and to guess the emotions of their partner at that moment. Technology helped: The participants were beeped at various times and indicated their answers on a smartphone that they kept with them. Sometimes they happened to be with their partner, sometimes not.

When the partner was present, accuracy was higher for the younger couples, presumably because they could see and hear their mate. But when the partner was absent, the older participants were as good as the younger ones (see **Figure 24.1**). The researchers asked a question of those who read this study.

> [Could you] predict a social partner's feelings when that person is absent? Your judgment would probably be better than chance, and although many abilities deteriorate with aging, this particular ability may remain reliable throughout your life.
>
> *[Rauers et al., 2013, p. 2215]*

Ecological Validity Awareness of the need for ecological validity has helped scientists restructure research on memory, trying to avoid time pressures and abstractions. Restructured studies find fewer deficits than originally thought. However, any test may overestimate or underestimate ability. For instance, what is an accurate test of long-term memory? Many older people recount in vivid detail some events that occurred decades ago. That is impressive . . . if the memories are accurate.

Unfortunately, "there is no objective way to evaluate the degree of ecological validity . . . because ecological validity is a subjective concept" (Salthouse, 2010, p. 77). It is impossible to be totally objective in assessing memory; memory and tests of memory always have a subjective component.

The final ecological question is, "What is memory for?" Older adults usually think they remember well enough. Fear of memory loss is more typical at age 60 than at age 80, even though actual memory loss increases with age.

Watch out for ageism in assessing the everyday cognition of the elderly. In daily life, output is usually verbal. If the timbre and speed of a person's speech sounds old, ageism might cause listeners to dismiss the content without realizing that the substance may be profound. Then, if elders realize that what they say is ignored, they talk less. Output is diminished because it is devalued.

In work contexts as well, elders sometimes feel stereotyped if younger workers think their elders lack strength, health, or technological knowledge. That may be inaccurate. Feeling stereotyped at work reduces motivation and work effort, a self-fulfilling prophecy (von Hippel et al., 2019).

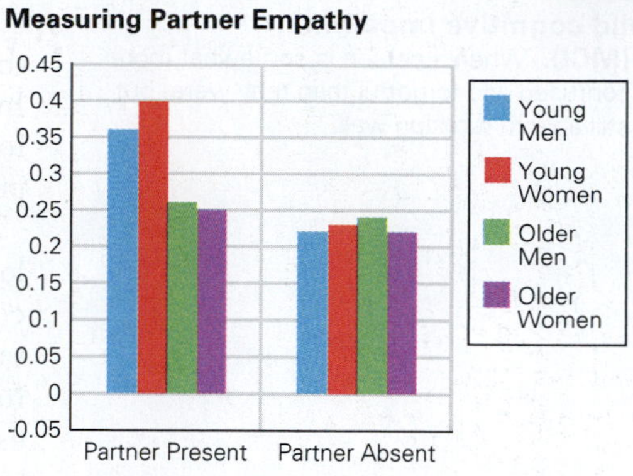

Data from Rauers et al., 2013.

FIGURE 24.1

Always on My Mind When they were together, younger partners were more accurate than older ones at knowing their partner's emotions, but older partners were as good as younger ones when they were apart. This study used "smartphone experience sampling," buzzing both partners simultaneously to ask how they and their partner felt. Interestingly, differences were found with age but not length of relationship—5, 10, 20, or 30 years of togetherness did not necessarily increase empathy when apart, but men who were in their 70s were better at absent mood assessment than men in their 20s.

WHAT HAVE YOU LEARNED?

1. How does sensory loss affect cognition?
2. Which kinds of things are harder to remember with age?
3. Why do some elderly people resist learning strategies for memory retrieval?
4. How might output be affected by the aging process?
5. What needs to be considered in ecologically valid measurement of adult intelligence?
6. What would be an ecologically valid test of cognition in late adulthood?

Neurocognitive Disorders

Although most older people think and remember quite well, the rate of those who experience serious cognitive decline increases with age. Severe decline results from a **neurocognitive disorder (NCD)**.

neurocognitive disorder (NCD) Any of a number of brain diseases that affect a person's ability to remember, analyze, plan, or interact with other people.

Mild Cognitive Impairment

Before describing the many manifestations of NCDs, we need to reiterate that most older people are cognitively quite capable. It is ageist to jump to the conclusion that every memory loss is a sign of serious problems. We all forget our keys, can't think of a name, need reminders of our dentist appointments. Usually we pay little attention to such problems, but if the person who forgets the keys or the appointment is over 70, everyone (including the forgetful person) might assume the worst. That is a mistake.

mild cognitive impairment (MCI). When a person is somewhat more confused and forgetful than they were, but still able to function well.

Many older people experience **mild cognitive impairment (MCI)** which is more than the usual, occasional forgetfulness but far short of a neurocognitive disorder. In this mild version, a person needs to write down appointments, set alarms, wait for a name to come to mind, and so on. Stress and worry make it worse, so other people should be more reassuring than accusatory.

Many measures can reverse MCI, or at least halt the decline. Exercise, weight loss, and social engagement are all antidotes. Hypertension and diabetes can be controlled with medication and diet, and that also reduces the likelihood of mild impairment becoming a serious disorder. Especially if a person is at genetic risk for Alzheimer's disease, smoking cigarettes speeds up the decline, so quitting is essential.

Various preventive measures are estimated to halt about a third of incipient brain diseases (Berkowitz et al., 2018). Mild impairment *sometimes,* not usually, proceeds to a neurocognitive disorder.

The Ageism of Words

The rate of neurocognitive disorders increases with every decade after age 60, a fact that is distorted and exaggerated by ageism. Since fear and stress make the problems worse, we need to use words carefully.

Senile simply means "old." If the word *senility* is used to mean "severe mental impairment," that would imply that old age always brings intellectual failure—an ageist myth. *Dementia* (used in DSM-IV) was a more precise term than *senility* for irreversible, pathological loss of brain functioning, but people once thought that dementia occurs because a demon possessed the person. Obviously, the word *dementia* has harmful connotations.

The DSM-5 now categorizes neurocognitive disorders as either *major* (previously called *dementia*) or *mild* (as in *mild cognitive impairment*). For DSM-5, a mild NCD is the first step toward a serious one. But remember that some mild impairments disappear or stabilize, so not all people who experience mild cognitive impairment are on their way toward severe problems.

Diagnosis is complicated. The line between typical age-related changes, mild disorder, and major disorder is not clear; symptoms vary depending on the specifics of both brain loss and context. Many scientists seek biological indicators (called *biomarkers,* such as in the blood or cerebrospinal fluid) or brain indicators (as on brain scans) that predict major memory loss, but so far none is certain, in timing, in severity, or in behavior.

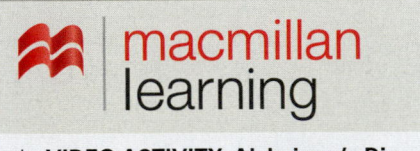

macmillan learning

In **VIDEO ACTIVITY: Alzheimer's Disease,** experts and family members discuss the progression of the disease.

Prevalence of NCDs

How many people suffer from neurocognitive disorders in their older years? When the general public is asked, the answer may be "almost everyone, if they live long enough." People speak about their own older relative who seems cognitively intact with the same surprise and awe that they might speak of a rainbow. However, every study of the frequency of major NCDs finds much lower rates, from about 5 to 10 percent of the older population (see Visualizing Development, page 633).

The World Health Organization (2019) estimates that 50 million people are affected worldwide, 60 percent of them in low-income nations. That is about 9 percent of the world's population over age 65, (less than 1 percent of the total population), with rates lowest in the very poor nations where most people die before age 60. Neurocognitive disorders are the most common cause of *morbidity* (the inability to function normally because of a disease or condition) and the second most common cause of death (Global Burden of Disease Neurological Disorders Collaborator Group, 2017).

Rates vary markedly from one nation to another. First, as public health measures improve longevity, rates of major NCD rise. This is happening in China, where only 4 million people had a serious NCD in 1990, compared to 9 million in 2010 and 15 million projected in 2020 (K. Chan et al., 2013). Rates are higher in Chinese rural areas than in cities, perhaps because of better urban education and health care (Jia et al., 2014).

That highlights the second trend, which is apparent in the wealthiest nations. As better medical and personal interventions make people healthier overall, the rate (not the number) of people with neurocognitive disorders is reduced.

In England and Wales, the rate of major NCD for people over age 65 was 8.3 percent in 1991 but only 6.5 percent in 2011 (Matthews et al., 2013). Sweden had a similar decline (Qiu et al., 2013), and the U.S. rate has declined since 2000 (Sullivan et al., 2018).

As noted in the previous chapter, as more people live to age 90 or so, the *number* of people who have a major neurocognitive disorder increases. But, as people learn more about healthy living and reduce the rate of obesity, high blood pressure, cigarette smoking, and other habits, the *rate* of NCDs decreases.

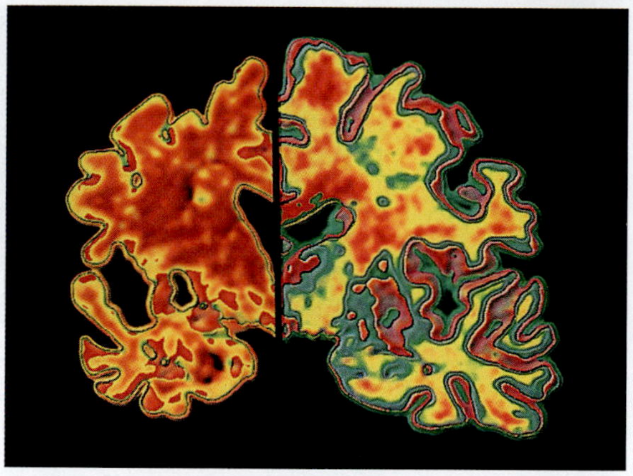

A. Pasieka/SPL/Science Source

The Alzheimer's Brain This computer graphic shows a vertical slice through a brain ravaged by Alzheimer's disease *(left)* compared with a similar slice of a normal brain *(right)*. The diseased brain is shrunken because neurons have degenerated. The red indicates plaques and tangles.

Alzheimer's disease (AD) The most common cause of major NCD, characterized by gradual deterioration of memory and personality and marked by the formation of plaques of beta-amyloid protein and tangles of tau in the brain.

plaques Clumps of a protein called beta-amyloid, found in brain tissue surrounding the neurons.

tangles Twisted masses of threads made of a protein called tau within the neurons of the brain.

The Many Neurocognitive Disorders

As more is learned, it has become apparent that there are more than a hundred types of brain disease, each beginning in a distinct part of the brain and having particular symptoms. One mistaken belief was that a person with a good memory could not be experiencing a neurocognitive disorder, an idea that prevented diagnosis and treatment. To avoid that mistake, we describe some of these disorders now.

Alzheimer's Disease In the past century, millions of people in every large nation have been diagnosed with **Alzheimer's disease (AD)** (now formally referred to as *major NCD due to Alzheimer's disease*). Severe and worsening memory loss is the main symptom, but diagnosis was not definitive until an autopsy found extensive plaques and tangles in the cerebral cortex (see **Table 24.1**).

Plaques are clumps of a protein called *beta-amyloid* in tissues surrounding the neurons; **tangles** are twisted masses of threads made of a protein called *tau* within the neurons. A normal brain contains some beta-amyloid and some tau, but these plaques and tangles proliferate in brains with AD, especially in the hippocampus. Forgetfulness is the dominant symptom, from momentary lapses to—after years of progressive disease—forgetting the names and faces of one's own children.

Alzheimer's disease is partly genetic. If it develops in middle age, the affected person either has trisomy-21 (Down syndrome) or has inherited one of three genes: amyloid precursor protein (APP), presenilin 1, or presenilin 2. The disease progresses quickly for these people, reaching the last phase within three to five years.

TABLE 24.1

Stages of Alzheimer's Disease
Stage 1. People in the first stage forget recent events or new information, particularly names and places. For example, they might forget the name of a famous film star or how to get home from a familiar place. This first stage is similar to mild cognitive impairment—even experts cannot always tell the difference. In retrospect, it seems clear that President Ronald Reagan had early AD while in office, but no doctor diagnosed it.
Stage 2. Generalized confusion develops, with deficits in concentration and short-term memory. Speech becomes aimless and repetitious, vocabulary is limited, words get mixed up. Personality traits are not curbed by rational thought. For example, suspicious people may decide that others have stolen the things that they themselves have mislaid.
Stage 3. Memory loss becomes dangerous. Although people at stage 3 can care for themselves, they might leave a lit stove or hot iron on or might forget whether they took essential medicine and thus take it twice—or not at all.
Stage 4. At this stage, full-time care is needed. People cannot communicate well. They might not recognize their closest loved ones.
Stage 5. Finally, people with AD become unresponsive. Identity and personality have disappeared. When former president Ronald Reagan was at this stage, a longtime friend who visited him was asked, "Did he recognize you?" The friend answered, "Worse than that—I didn't recognize him." Death comes 10 to 15 years after the first signs appear.

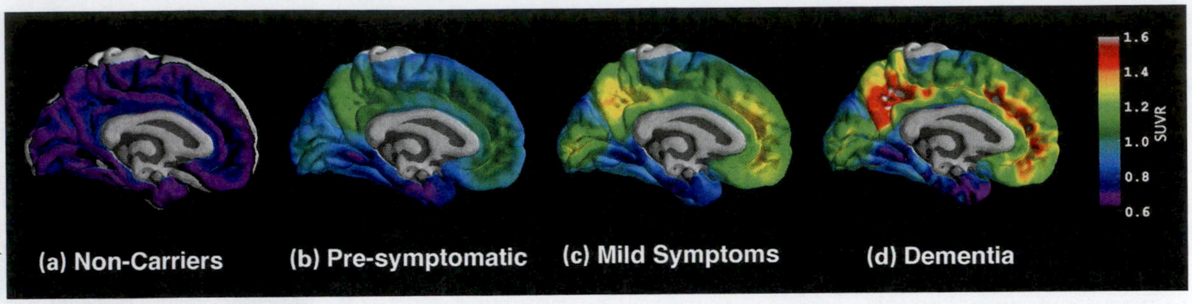

Tammie Benzinger, MD, PhD, Tyler Blazey, Washington University School of Medicine in St. Louis, MO

Hopeful Brains Even the brain without symptoms *(a)* might eventually develop Alzheimer's disease, but people with a certain dominant gene definitely will. They have no symptoms in early adulthood *(b)*, some symptoms in middle adulthood *(c)*, and stage-five Alzheimer's disease *(d)* before old age. Research finds early brain markers (such as those shown here) that predict the disease. This is not always accurate, but it may soon lead to early treatment that halts AD, not only in those who are genetically vulnerable but in everyone.

Most cases begin much later, at age 75 or so. Many genes have some impact, including SORL1 and APOE4 (allele 4 of the APOE gene). People who inherit one copy of APOE4 (as about one-fifth of all U.S. residents do) have about a 50/50 chance of developing AD, with women more at risk than men (Altmann et al., 2014). Those who inherit two copies almost always develop the disorder if they live long enough.

vascular disease Formerly called *vascular* or *multi-infarct dementia,* vascular disease is characterized by sporadic, and progressive, loss of intellectual functioning caused by repeated infarcts, or temporary obstructions of blood vessels, which prevent sufficient blood from reaching the brain.

frontotemporal NCDs Deterioration of the amygdala and frontal lobes that may be the cause of 15 percent of all major neurocognitive disorders. (Also called *frontotemporal lobar degeneration.*)

Vascular Disease The second most common cause of neurocognitive disorder is a *stroke* (a temporary obstruction of a blood vessel in the brain) or a series of strokes, called *transient ischemic attacks* (*TIAs,* or *ministrokes*). The interruption in blood flow reduces oxygen, destroying part of the brain. Symptoms (blurred vision, weak or paralyzed limbs, slurred speech, and mental confusion) suddenly appear.

In a TIA, symptoms may vanish quickly, unnoticed. However, unless recognized and prevented, another TIA is likely, eventually causing **vascular disease**, commonly referred to as *vascular* or *multi-infarct dementia* (Kalaria, 2018) (see **Figure 24.2**). This is evident in many aspects of dendrite formation and brain functioning. The behavior impairment is reduced executive functioning, which means that poor decisions and uncontrolled impulses are as prevalent as memory problems.

Vascular disease correlates with the APOE4 allele, as well as other genetic precursors (Vinters et al., 2018). For some of the elderly, vascular disease is caused by surgery that requires general anesthesia. They suffer a ministroke, which damages their brains, especially when their cognitive reserve is depleted.

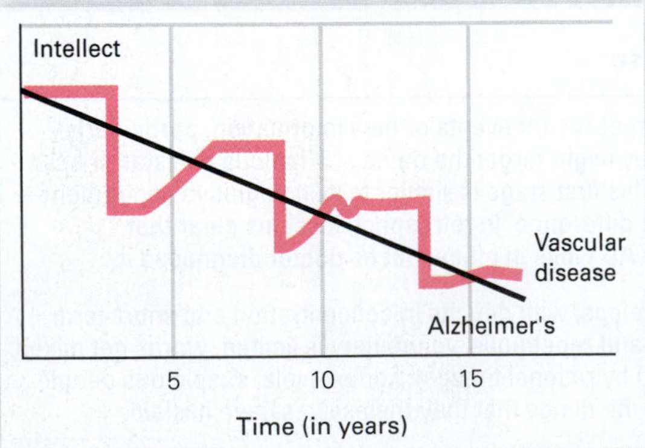

FIGURE 24.2
The Progression of Alzheimer's Disease and Vascular Disease Cognitive decline is apparent in both Alzheimer's disease and vascular disease. However, the pattern of decline for each disease is different. Individuals with Alzheimer's show steady, gradual decline, while those with vascular disease get suddenly much worse, improve somewhat, and then experience another serious loss.

Frontotemporal Disorders Several types of neurocognitive disorders affect the frontal lobes and thus are called **frontotemporal NCDs**, or *frontotemporal lobar degeneration.* (Pick disease is the most common form.) These disorders cause perhaps 15 percent of all cases of NCDs in the United States.

In frontotemporal NCDs, parts of the brain that regulate emotions and social behavior (especially the amygdala and prefrontal cortex) deteriorate. Emotional and personality changes are the main symptoms (Seelaar et al., 2011). A loving mother with a frontotemporal NCD might reject her children, or a formerly astute businessman might invest in a hare-brained scheme. As you can imagine, caregivers of people with this disorder are more stressed, and less supported, than caregivers of people with Alzheimer's (Nowaskie et al., 2019).

Frontotemporal NCDs tend to occur before age 70, unlike Alzheimer's or vascular disease. Part of the problem is that diagnosis is more difficult because the symptoms appear at younger ages (the 60s more than the 80s) and the primary symptom is not memory loss. These disorders more often occur in men than women, so often a wife will wonder why her husband is no longer loving and caring—but no doctor notices the problem.

One wife, Ruth French, was furious because her husband

> threw away tax documents, got a ticket for trying to pass an ambulance and bought stock in companies that were obviously in trouble. Once a good cook, he burned every pot in the house. He became withdrawn and silent, and no longer spoke to his wife over dinner. That same failure to communicate got him fired from his job.
>
> [D. Grady, 2012, p. A1]

Finally, he was diagnosed with a frontotemporal NCD. Ruth asked him to forgive her fury. It is not clear that he understood either her anger or her apology.

There are many forms and causes of frontotemporal NCDs—including a dozen or so alleles. All usually progress rapidly, leading to death in about five years.

Other Disorders Many other brain diseases begin with impaired motor control (shaking when picking up a cup of coffee, falling when trying to walk), not with impaired thinking. The most common of these is **Parkinson's disease**, the cause of about 3 percent of all cases of NCDs.

Parkinson's disease A chronic, progressive disease that is characterized by muscle tremor and rigidity and sometimes major neurocognitive disorder; caused by reduced dopamine production in the brain.

Lewy body disease A form of major neurocognitive disorder characterized by an increase in Lewy body cells in the brain. Symptoms include visual hallucinations, momentary loss of attention, falling, and fainting.

Parkinson's disease starts with rigidity or tremor of the muscles as dopamine-producing neurons degenerate, affecting movement long before cognition (Jankovic, 2018). Middle-aged adults with Parkinson's disease usually have sufficient cognitive reserve to avoid major intellectual loss, although about one-third have mild cognitive decline, sometimes in advance of more obvious symptoms (Darweesh et al., 2017).

Age matters. If someone over age 65 develops Parkinson's, cognitive problems are likely to emerge within a few years. No matter what age a person is when Parkinson's begins, if they live 10 years or more, major neurocognitive impairment occurs (Pahwa & Lyons, 2013).

Another 3 percent of people with NCD in the United States suffer from **Lewy body disease**: excessive deposits of a particular kind of protein in their brains. Lewy bodies are also present in Parkinson's disease, but in Lewy body disease they are more numerous and dispersed throughout the brain, interfering with communication between neurons.

The main symptom is loss of inhibition: A person might gamble or become hypersexual. In many ways, Lewy body symptoms are similar to Parkinson's, but brain impairments are more comprehensive and begin sooner (Walker et al., 2019).

Some other types of NCDs begin in middle age or even earlier, caused by Huntington's disease, multiple sclerosis, a severe head injury, or the last stages of syphilis, AIDS, or *bovine spongiform encephalopathy* (*BSE*, or *mad cow disease*). Repeated blows to the head (traumatic brain injury), even without concussions, can cause *chronic traumatic encephalopathy* (*CTE*), which first causes memory loss and emotional changes. Differentiating CTE from other forms of neurocognitive disorder is complex, but one thing is certain: Many people suffer from brain disorders, and Alzheimer's is only one of them (Smith et al., 2019).

Although the rate of systemic brain disease increases dramatically with every decade after age 60, brain disease can occur at any age, as revealed by the autopsies of a number of young professional athletes. For them, prevention includes better helmets and fewer head and body blows. Already, tackling is avoided in football practice.

Jason Kempin/Getty Images Entertainment/Getty Images

Why? Many people wonder why actor and comedian Robin Williams committed suicide at age 63. One explanation: He was in the early stages of a serious neurocognitive disorder. Williams was diagnosed with Parkinson's disease a few months before he died, but an autopsy revealed Lewy body disease, whose symptoms include loss of inhibition, severe anxiety, tremors, and difficulty reasoning.

Jim West/Alamy

Kostas Tsironis/Bloomberg/Getty Images

Exercise for Elders In every nation, those who exercise have healthier hearts, lungs, brains, and lives than those who do not. Two contrasting examples are the exercise class in a Michigan Senior Center led by Diane Evans (foreground) and the stepper machine on a beach in Greece.

Observation Quiz Both are beneficial, but neither is ideal. Why not? (see answer, page 632) ↑

Preventing Impairment

Severe brain damage cannot be reversed, although the rate of decline and some of the symptoms can be treated. However, education, exercise, and good health not only ameliorate mild losses but may prevent worse ones (Kivipelto et al., 2018). That seems to be the reason why rates of NCD are declining in the United States and elsewhere.

Because brain plasticity is lifelong, exercise that improves blood circulation not only prevents cognitive loss but also builds capacity and repairs damage. The benefits of exercise have been repeatedly cited in this text. Now we simply reiterate that physical exercise—even more than good nutrition and mental exercise—prevents, postpones, and slows cognitive loss of all kinds.

Avoiding specific pathogens is critical. For example, beef can be tested to ensure that it does not have BSE, condoms can protect against HIV/AIDS, sprays, screens, and bed nets can protect against Zika.

Thousands of scientists have sought to halt the production of beta-amyloid, with some success in mice but not yet in humans. A current goal is to diagnose Alzheimer's disease 10 or 15 years before the first outward signs in order to prevent brain damage. That is one reason for the interest in mild cognitive impairment.

Older people who have notable, but not severe, memory loss sometimes, but not always, progress to major problems. If it were known why some mild losses do not lead to major ones, prevention might be possible.

Professionals are hopeful. Earlier diagnosis seems possible; many drug and lifestyle treatments are under review. Hope comes from other public health victories mentioned in earlier chapters: unwanted pregnancies, underweight newborns, wasted and stunted children, polluted water, polio, measles, smallpox, heart disease, breast cancer, and many other conditions. The average life span is twice what it was: The cognitive diseases of late adulthood are the next public health challenge.

Most research focuses on people who are clearly experiencing a neurocognitive disorder. Yet, it is much easier to prevent cognitive problems than to reverse brain destruction that has already occurred. The case for better and earlier research is clear. As one team stressed:

> Diversifying and exploring new treatment ideas is essential, as these diseases are inherently complex and not terribly well understood. . . . interventions can be started prior to neuronal loss, which likely would result in the highest chance for success.
>
> *[Baker & Petersen, 2018, p. 1214]*

Reversible Neurocognitive Disorder?

Care improves when everyone knows what disease is undermining intellectual capacity. Accurate diagnosis is even more crucial when memory problems do *not* arise from a neurocognitive disorder. Brain diseases destroy parts of the brain, but some people are thought to be permanently "losing their minds" when a reversible condition is at fault.

Depression The most common reversible condition that is mistaken for major NCD is depression. Typically, older people tend to be quite happy; frequent sadness or anxiety is not normal. Ongoing, untreated depression increases the risk of major NCD (Gao et al., 2013).

Ironically, people with untreated anxiety or depression may exaggerate minor memory losses or refuse to talk. Quite the opposite reaction occurs with early Alzheimer's disease, when victims are often surprised that they cannot answer questions, or with Lewy body disease or frontotemporal NCDs, when people talk too much without thinking. Talking, or lack of it, provides an important clue.

Specifics provide other clues. People with neurocognitive loss might forget what they just said, heard, or did because current brain activity is impaired, but they might repeatedly describe details of something that happened long ago. The opposite may be true for emotional disorders, when memory of the past is impaired but short-term memory is not.

Malnutrition Malnutrition and dehydration can also cause symptoms that seem like brain disease. The aging digestive system is less efficient but needs more nutrients and fewer calories. This requires new habits, less fast food, and more grocery money (which many do not have).

Some elderly people deliberately drink less to avoid frequent urination, yet inadequate fluid in the body impedes cell health. Since homeostasis slows with age, older people may not recognize and remedy their hunger and thirst and thus may inadvertently impair their cognition.

Beyond the need to drink water and eat vegetables, several specific vitamins in food may stave off cognitive impairment. Among the suggested foods are those containing antioxidants (vitamins C, A, E) and vitamin B_{12}. Homocysteine (from animal fat) needs to be avoided, since high levels correlate with major NCD (Whalley et al., 2014). Psychoactive drugs, especially alcohol, cause confusion and hallucinations at much lower doses than in the young.

Obviously, any food that increases the risk of heart disease and stroke also increases the risk of vascular disease. In addition, some prescribed drugs destroy nutrients, although specifics require more research.

Indeed, well-controlled longitudinal research on the relationship between particular aspects of nutrition and NCD still needs to be done (Coley et al., 2015; Vlachos & Scarmeas, 2019). It is known, however, that people who already suffer from NCD tend to choose unhealthy foods or forget to eat, hastening their mental deterioration.

It is also known that alcohol abuse interferes with nutrition, directly (reducing eating and hydration) and indirectly (blocking vitamin absorption). Tobacco, in cigarettes or pipes, may be worse. Ironically, although chronic smoking clearly harms cognition in the elderly (Conti et al., 2019), most quit programs are aimed at the young.

Polypharmacy At home as well as in the hospital, most elderly people take numerous drugs—not only prescribed medications but also over-the-counter preparations and herbal remedies—a situation known as **polypharmacy**. Excessive reliance on drugs can occur on doctor's orders as well as via patient ignorance.

The rate of polypharmacy is increasing in the United States. For instance, the number of people over age 65 who took *five* drugs or more was 13 percent in 1988. By 2015 that number had tripled to 39 percent (National Center for Health Statistics, 2018).

Unfortunately, recommended doses of many drugs are determined primarily by clinical trials with younger adults, for whom homeostasis usually eliminates excess medication. When homeostasis slows down, excess lingers. In addition, most trials to test the safety of a new drug exclude people who have more than one disease. This means that drugs are not tested on the people who will use them most.

The average elderly person in the United States sees a physician eight times a year (National Center for Health Statistics, 2018). Typically, each doctor follows *clinical practice guidelines,* which are recommendations for one specific condition. A *prescribing cascade* (when many interacting drugs are prescribed) may occur. Each drug may be beneficial when it is the only drug prescribed, but the more drugs a person takes, the less effective any one is (Fried & Mecca, 2019).

polypharmacy A situation in which elderly people are prescribed several medications. The various side effects and interactions of those medications can result in dementia symptoms.

CHAPTER APP 24

Medisafe

IOS:
https://tinyurl.com/y3x7fk75

ANDROID:
https://tinyurl.com/96fvedt

RELEVANT TOPIC:
Polypharmacy

This free app reminds users when it's time to take medication and when they are running low on a prescription. (A "Medifriend" can be designated by the user to receive these reminders as well.) A drug interaction checker notifies users if they have been prescribed medications that aren't supposed to be taken together.

In one disturbing case, a doctor prescribed medication to raise his patient's blood pressure, and another doctor, noting the raised blood pressure, prescribed a drug to lower it (McLendon & Shelton, 2011–2012). Usually, doctors ask patients what medications they are taking and why, which could prevent such an error. However, people who are sick and confused may not give accurate responses.

A related problem is that people of every age forget when to take which drugs (before, during, or after meals? after dinner or at bedtime?) (Bosworth & Ayotte, 2009). Short-term memory loss makes this worse, and poverty cuts down on pill purchases.

Even when medications are taken as prescribed and the right dose reaches the bloodstream, drug interactions can cause confusion and memory loss. Cognitive side effects can occur with almost any drug, but they are especially prevalent with drugs intended to reduce anxiety and depression.

THINK CRITICALLY: Who should decide what drugs a person should take—doctor, family, or the person him- or herself?

The solution seems simple: Discontinue drugs. However, that may increase disease and hasten cognitive decline. One expert warns of polypharmacy but adds that "underuse of medications in older adults can have comparable adverse effects on quality of life" (Miller, 2011–2012, p. 21).

For instance, untreated diabetes and hypertension cause cognitive loss. Lack of drug treatment for those conditions may be one reason why low-income elders experience more illness, more cognitive impairment, and earlier death than do high-income elders: They may not be able to afford good medical care or life-saving drugs.

Another health condition that markedly increases the rate of NCD is *sleep apnea*—when someone wakes up repeatedly at night because breathing slows down. Medical treatment can remedy the problem, but many of the most vulnerable people do not have good medical care (Mansukhani et al., 2019).

Misdiagnosis The rate of misdiagnosis of NCDs is perhaps as high as one-third of all cases. A false positive leads to needless drugs and anxiety, but a false negative delays treatment that would stall or prevent devastation to the individual and family. Brain scans, blood analysis, and cerebral fluid measurements reduce misdiagnosis, but those require expert and expensive interpretation.

Currently, many efforts are under way to provide a cost-effective diagnosis of Alzheimer's and other NCDs before death, but none are yet definitive (Leuzy et al., 2018; Cilento et al., 2018). Misdiagnosis rates have been reduced but are far from zero. Ideally diagnosis begins with behavior, recognizable by family members and the people themselves. Unfortunately, fear slows down recognition, and ageism distorts it.

Yamaguchi Haruyoshi/Corbis News/Getty Images

Comfort and Conversation A cuddly seal robot, PARO, responds to petting with 12 tactile senses, encouraging touch and eye contact. Designed and used in Japan, which has the highest proportion of elders in the world, here PARO is a companion in a nursing home. Critics complain that humans should interact with humans; advocates ask critics whether they also think teddy bears should be removed from children.

One indicator of incipient NCD is vulnerability to financial scams. A study of almost a thousand elders found that those most likely to fall for deceptive sales pitches, and who were intrigued by risky investments, were, years later, likely to develop Alzheimer's (Boyle et al., 2019).

Another study began when physicians referred their patients who might be in the early stages of Alzheimer's for a PET scan (paid for by the researchers). One-third of the patients did not, in fact, have the disease. They simply were aging normally but had been taking medication that they did not need. The doctors adjusted their treatment plans based on the results (De Wilde et al., 2018).

An additional problem that is sometimes mistaken for NCD is *terminal decline*, the drop in cognitive abilities that often happens in the months before death. The entire body—heart, lungs, digestive system, and so on—often slows down in the final months of life; the brain does, too. It is impossible to predict, years in advance, when terminal decline will occur, but this suggests that diagnosis of brain disease when every organ is failing is pointless.

A CASE TO STUDY

The More You Know . . .

In the years after she was diagnosed with vascular disease, Dr. Gerda Saunders dedicated her memoir:

> for you, whether you or someone you love has dementia, or you're a medical professional, or a person searching for your own self after a huge life change, or someone just plain curious, who—like me—feels that the more you know, the better you are able to love.
>
> *[Saunders, 2019]*

Saunders was an English professor at the University of Utah. Her first inkling that something was wrong with her brain came as she was teaching.

> Forebodings that not all was well started to cloud my class time. I would lose the thread of a discussion, or forget the point toward which I had intended to steer the students' thinking. Often the name of a novel or author I used to know as well as my children's names would not come to mind. Not infrequently, a student would remind me during the last moments of class that I had failed to distribute notes or an assignment.
>
> *[Saunders, 2019]*

She arranged to teach fewer classes, soon only one per year. Instead, she took on more administrative duties. But when she chaired a meeting, she suddenly panicked. She looked at her planned agenda and her eyes lit on "Introductions," so she asked all of those in attendance to introduce themselves. But "as the words left my mouth I remembered with horror that we had already gone around the table."

Someone said "we all have too much on our plates," and everyone nodded sympathetically. But Saunders concluded that she had "committed the cardinal sin of academia, not thinking accurately on my feet." As the months went by, her friends excused her lapses as senior moments, and her two grown children said that they also forgot things sometimes. She joined them in denying that anything was wrong.

Finally, four years after her initial "forebodings," she consulted a doctor, who sent her to a neurologist and a neuropsychologist. After dozens of tests, the conclusion was clear: White lesions in her brain halted connections between one thought and another. After initially resisting the diagnosis, she resigned and began taking medication to slow down the decline.

Saunders began to write about her experiences, recalling details of her childhood in South Africa and checking her memories with her five siblings (they said her memories were close to their own). She pondered about memory, about selfhood, about when and how a person should die.

One day she had frightening hallucinations, but she realized that she had forgotten to take her medicine that day. She wished she could always blame her problems on lack of medication, but her increasing dementia was making many tasks impossible. For example, she habitually drove neighbors who needed a lift to buy groceries:

Two years after her diagnosis, she

> Took Bob and Bea grocery shopping. [Been taking them since their son Bobbie took away Bob's keys after his stroke last year]. When we were done, I could not find my keys. The car doors were unlocked, the keys were in the ignition. Returning home, I forgot to stop at Bob and Bea's and pulled into my driveway instead. Last time I took the old people shopping I did not notice the traffic light changing until Bea reminded me to go. She is eighty-six.
>
> *[Saunders, 2019]*

Saunders stopped driving and, after burning some dinner, she stopped cooking. But she did not stop writing. Many people with major neurocognitive disorder continue to do whatever they valued most: Some play music, some do yoga, and, like Saunders, some write. What next?

Eventually, Saunders plans a "death trip" to the Netherlands, where she is legally allowed physician-assisted suicide because her ancestors were Dutch. But that is years hence. Dementia is robbing her memory but not her love for her husband and children. She wants to live "As long as I mean something to my children, and as long as I can be a 'warm body' who can hold a grandchild, and I find comfort in that, and the grandchild finds comfort in that" (Saunders quoted in Schulzke, 2017).

Thus, people with a neurocognitive disorder are another of the "all kinds of people" explained in Chapter 1. In some ways each person is unique, and in other ways all people are alike. Those whose brains no longer function as well as they did nonetheless may enjoy their friends, their family, their work, and their lives.

A study of 30,064 nursing home residents, already impaired, found that most of them functioned quite well cognitively before experiencing a notable drop in the months before dying (Hülür et al., 2019). The only group who did not experience terminal decline were those who already suffered from a severe neurocognitive disorder. Their intellectual losses continued, but the rate did not accelerate in the final months.

WHAT HAVE YOU LEARNED?

1. How does changing terminology reflect changing attitudes?
2. What changes in the prevalence of neurocognitive disorders have occurred in recent years?
3. How relevant are genes in Alzheimer's disease?
4. How does the progression of Alzheimer's differ from that of vascular disease?
5. In what ways are frontotemporal NCDs worse than Alzheimer's disease?
6. Why is Lewy body disease sometimes mistaken for Parkinson's disease?
7. What conditions affect the rate of NCD?
8. What is the relationship between depression, anxiety, and neurocognitive disorders?
9. Why is polypharmacy particularly common among the elderly?

New Cognitive Development

Remember that the life-span perspective holds that gains as well as losses occur during every period. Are there cognitive gains in late adulthood? Yes, according to many developmentalists.

Erikson and Maslow

Both Erik Erikson and Abraham Maslow were particularly interested in the elderly, interviewing older people to understand their thoughts. Erikson's final book, *Vital Involvement in Old Age* (Erikson et al., 1986/1994), written when he was in his 90s, was based on responses from other 90-year-olds—the cohort who had been studied since they were babies in Berkeley, California.

Erikson found that in old age many people gained interest in the arts, in children, and in human experience as a whole. He observed that elders are "social witnesses," aware of the interdependence of the generations as well as of all human experience. His eighth stage, *integrity versus despair*, marks the time when life comes together in a "resynthesis of all the resilience and toughness of the basic strengths already developed" (Erikson et al., 1986/1994, p. 40).

Maslow maintained that older adults are more likely than younger people to reach what he originally thought was the highest stage of development, **self-actualization**. Remember that Maslow rejected an age-based sequence of life, refusing to confine self-actualization to the old. However, Maslow also believed that life experience helps people move forward, so more of the old reach the final stage.

self-actualization The final stage in Maslow's hierarchy of needs, characterized by aesthetic, creative, philosophical, and spiritual understanding.

The stage of self-actualization is characterized by aesthetic, creative, philosophical, and spiritual understanding (Maslow, 1954/1997). A self-actualized person might have a deeper spirituality than ever; might be especially appreciative of nature; or might see the humor in many aspects of life, laughing often.

This seems characteristic of many of the elderly. Studies of centenarians find that they often have a deep spiritual grounding and a surprising sense of humor—surprising, that is, to anyone who thinks that people with limited sight, poor hearing, and aching bodies have nothing to laugh about.

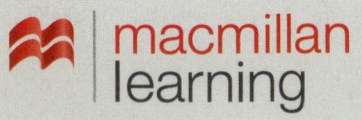

macmillan learning

In **VIDEO: Portrait of Aging: Bill, Age 99,** one man shares his secret to longevity.

Aesthetic Sense and Creativity

Robert Butler was a geriatrician who popularized the study of aging in the United States. He coined the word *ageism* and wrote a book titled *Why Survive: Being Old in America,* first published in 1975. Partly because his grandparents were crucial

in his life, Butler understood that the elderly can contribute to their families and communities.

Butler explained that "old age can be a time of emotional sensory awareness and enjoyment" (Butler et al., 1998, p. 65). Older adults learn new skills and take up new activities. For example, some of the elderly begin gardening, bird-watching, sculpting, painting, or making music, each of which requires new learning.

Elderly Artists Many well-known artists continue to work in late adulthood, sometimes producing their best work. Michelangelo painted the awe-inspiring frescoes in the Sistine Chapel at age 75; Verdi composed the opera *Falstaff* when he was 80; Frank Lloyd Wright completed the design of the Guggenheim Museum when he was 91.

In a study of extraordinarily creative people, very few felt that their ability, their goals, or the quality of their work had been much impaired by age. The leader of that study observed, "in their seventies, eighties, and nineties, they may lack the fiery ambition of earlier years, but they are just as focused, efficient, and committed as before . . . perhaps more so" (Csikszentmihalyi, 2013, p. 207).

But an older artist does not need to be extraordinarily talented. Some of the elderly learn to play an instrument, and many enjoy singing. In China, people gather spontaneously in public parks to sing together. The groups are intergenerational—with a disproportionate number of elderly (Wei, 2013).

Music and singing are often used to reduce anxiety in those who suffer from neurocognitive impairment, because the ability to appreciate music is preserved in the brain when other functions fail. The evidence is clear: Music, the visual arts, and creative work of all kinds help the mind, the mood, and overall well-being (Charise & Eginton, 2018).

One particular method that is often used to deepen elderly cognition is the **life review.** In that method, elders provide an account of their personal lifelong journey by writing or telling their story. They want others to know their history, not only their personal experiences but also those of their family, cohort, or ethnic group. According to Robert Butler:

> We have been taught that this nostalgia represents living in the past and a preoccupation with self and that it is generally boring, meaningless, and time-consuming. Yet as a natural healing process it represents one of the underlying human capacities on which all psychotherapy depends. The life review should be recognized as a necessary and healthy process in daily life as well as a useful tool in the mental health care of older people.
>
> *[Butler et al., 1998, p. 91]*

Hundreds of developmentalists, following Butler's lead, have guided elderly people in self-review. Sometimes the elderly write down their thoughts, and sometimes they simply tell their story, responding to questions from the listener.

The result is almost always positive, especially for the person who tells the story. For instance, half of a group of 202 elderly people in a study in the Netherlands were randomly assigned to a life-review process. For them, depression and anxiety were markedly reduced compared to the control group (Korte et al., 2012). A study of elders in the United States also found that telling their story helped them see a purpose in life—just what Erikson would hope (Robinson & Murphy-Nugen, 2018).

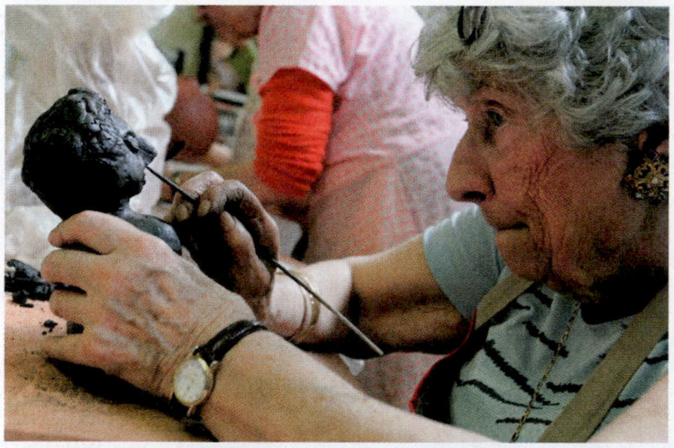

Pierre Bessard / REA/ Redux

Jim West / Alamy Stock Photo

Exercise and the Mind Creative activity may improve the intellect, especially when it involves social activity. Both the woman in a French ceramics class *(top),* subsidized by the government for residents of Grenoble over age 60, and the men in the Fourth of July Parade in Amherst, New Hampshire (*bottom*), are doing what every senior should do—engaging in creative work with other people. Finger dexterity and lung capacity are, in general, impaired with age, but that does not stop these two, nor should it. Everyone has abilities that remain strong in late adulthood, despite the ageism of stereotypes.

Sean Caffrey/Getty Images

Long Past Warring Many of the oldest men in Mali, like this imam, are revered. Unfortunately, Mali has experienced violent civil wars and two national coups in recent years, perhaps because 75 percent of the male population are under age 30 and less than 2 percent are over age 70. In 2019, the British newspaper *The Guardian* described Mali as the most dangerous nation in the world.

Wisdom

It is possible that "older adults . . . understand who they are in a newly emerging stage of life, and discovering the wisdom that they have to offer" (Bateson, 2011, p. 9). A massive international survey of 26 nations from every corner of the world found that most people everywhere agree that wisdom is a characteristic of the elderly (Löckenhoff et al., 2009).

Contrary to these wishes and opinions, most objective research finds that wisdom does not necessarily increase with age. Starting at age 25 or so, some adults of every age are wise, but most, even at age 80, are not. However, what is clear is that wisdom builds over time.

People who are open to new experiences in early adulthood, and who cope well with stress in middle age, are more likely to be wise in late adulthood. As one study concludes, "a balance between personality adjustment and growth, aided by social support and competence during the formative years, might be required to promote wisdom development throughout life" (Ardelt et al., 2018, p. 1514).

An underlying quandary is that a universal definition of wisdom is elusive: Each culture and each cohort have their own concepts, with fools sometimes seeming wise (as happens in Shakespearean drama) and those who are supposed to be wise sometimes acting foolishly (provide your own examples). Older and younger adults differ in how they make decisions; one interpretation of these differences is that the older adults are wiser, but not every younger adult would agree.

Several factors just mentioned, including self-reflective honesty (as in integrity), perspective on past living (the life review), and the ability to put aside one's personal needs (as in self-actualization), are considered part of wisdom.

If this is true, the elderly may have an advantage in developing wisdom, particularly if they have (1) dedicated their lives to the "understanding of life," (2) learned from their experiences, and (3) become more mature and integrated. That may be why popes and U.S. Supreme Court justices are usually quite old.

As two psychologists explain:

> Wisdom is one domain in which some older individuals excel. . . . [They have] a combination of psychosocial characteristics and life history factors, including openness to experience, generativity, cognitive style, contact with excellent mentors, and some exposure to structured and critical life experiences.
>
> *[Baltes & Smith, 2008, p. 60]*

A review of personality development during adulthood found that some people became wiser but not everyone did (Reitz & Staudinger, 2017). This returns us to a theme of this chapter that continues in the next: Late adulthood is a time of marked variation.

Especially for Caregivers of the Elderly How much of your care should be physical, how much social, and how much psychological? (see answer, page 632)

WHAT HAVE YOU LEARNED?

1. What do Erikson and Maslow say about cognitive development in late adulthood?
2. What happens with creative ability as people grow older?
3. What is the special role of music in old age?
4. Who benefits from a life review?
5. Why are scientists hesitant to say that wisdom comes from old age?

SUMMARY

The Brain During Late Adulthood

1. The human brain continues to add cells and grow dendrites as people age. It also becomes smaller and slower. The effects of senescence are apparent not only in motor skills (such as speed of walking) but also in cognitive skills (such as how quickly an older adult remembers a name).

2. Remarkable plasticity is also apparent, with wide variation from person to person in the rate and specifics of brain slowdown. In general, older adults use more of their brains, not less, to do various tasks, and they prefer doing one task at a time instead of multitasking.

3. Some parts of the brain are more likely to shrink than others. Fortunately, areas of the prefrontal cortex are likely to maintain activity, sometimes with several areas working at once.

Step-by-Step Processing

4. The senses become less acute with age, making it difficult for older people to register stimuli. Small losses are not easily noticed, but all of the senses need to be maintained if possible.

5. There are many types of memory, each with a distinct trajectory. Source memory and prospective memory are less accurate in elders, but memory for semantics, emotions, and values is better. Implicit memory may be maintained when explicit memory fades. Verbal memory—especially for recognition, not recall—may increase.

6. In daily life, most of the elderly are not seriously handicapped by cognitive difficulties. The need for ecologically valid, real-life measures of cognition, and the harm from ageist stereotypes, is increasingly apparent to developmental scientists.

Neurocognitive Disorders

7. Neurocognitive disorders (NCDs) are characterized by cognitive loss of varying degrees. The many NCDs differ, as do individuals and families who suffer from them, but early diagnosis seems helpful.

8. All of the traditional forms of NCDs increase with each decade of late adulthood, so the number of people with these problems is expected to increase as more people worldwide survive past age 65. On the other hand, rates of NCDs are decreasing in developed nations, including the United States.

9. Mild cognitive impairment is far more common than severe brain disease. It is particularly crucial for elders to maintain or increase preventative measures, especially exercise, diet, and good sleep habits.

10. The most common cause of cognitive loss among the elderly in the United States is Alzheimer's disease, an incurable ailment that worsens over time, as plaques and tangles increase.

11. Also common is vascular disease (also called multi-infarct dementia). This results from a series of mini-strokes (transient ischemic attacks, or TIAs) that occur when impairment of blood circulation destroys portions of brain tissue.

12. Other NCDs, including frontotemporal NCDs and Lewy body disease, also become more common with age. Parkinson's disease reduces muscle control and also causes neurocognitive problems, particularly in the elderly.

13. Several forms of NCDs are common before age 65. Among them is serious injury to the head, as sometimes occurs in tackle football and ice hockey, or domestic abuse, or war. Also evident before age 65 are NCDs caused by HIV/AIDS and mad cow disease.

14. An NCD may be mistakenly diagnosed when the individual is suffering from a reversible problem. Malnutrition, depression, drug addiction, and polypharmacy are among the reasons that an older person might be cognitively impaired. These symptoms can disappear if the problem is recognized and treated.

15. Accurate and early diagnosis is essential for the best treatment and prevention. Brain diseases (Alzheimer's and vascular disease) cannot be reversed. But the onset can be delayed, and the progression slowed.

New Cognitive Development

16. Many people become more interested and adept in creative endeavors, as well as more philosophical, as they grow older. The life review is a personal reflection that many older people undertake, remembering earlier experiences, putting their entire lives into perspective, and achieving integrity or self-actualization.

17. Wisdom does not necessarily increase as a result of age, but some elderly people are unusually wise or insightful. Learning from experience can occur at any age.

KEY TERMS

ecological validity (p. 618)
neurocognitive disorder (NCD) (p. 619)
mild cognitive impairment (MCI) (p. 620)
Alzheimer's disease (AD) (p. 621)
plaques (p. 621)
tangles (p. 621)
vascular disease (p. 622)
frontotemporal NCDs (p. 622)
Parkinson's disease (p. 623)
Lewy body disease (p. 623)
polypharmacy (p. 625)
self-actualization (p. 628)

APPLICATIONS

1. At all ages, memory is selective. People forget much more than they remember. Choose someone—a sibling, a former classmate, or a current friend—who went through some public event that you did, too. Sit down together, write separate lists of all details that each of you remembers about the event, and then compare your accounts. What insight does this exercise give you into the kinds of things adults remember and forget?

2. Many factors affect intellectual sharpness. Think of an occasion when you felt inept and an occasion when you felt smart. How did the contexts of the two experiences differ? How might those differences affect the performance of elderly and young adults who go to a university laboratory for testing?

3. Visit someone in a hospital. Note all of the elements in the environment—such as noise, lights, schedules, and personnel—that might cause an elderly patient to feel confused.

Especially For ANSWERS

Response for Students (from p. 617): Review it several times over the next days and weeks, and you will probably remember it in fifty years, with a little review.

Response for Caregivers (from p. 630) Ideally, the person does most of the physical care themselves, and the caregiver listens and talks.

Observation Quiz ANSWERS

Answer to Observation Quiz (from p. 615): Friendship is protective at every age. In addition, being outside in daylight, wearing appropriate clothing (note the hats and shoes), and simply experiencing fresh air and greenery are all correlates of a healthy mind and body. (Look also at the chapter-opening photo on p. 610.)

Answer to Observation Quiz (from p. 624) Neither photo depicts exercise that is likely to become an enjoyable routine. The teacher is not facing the class, so she may not know when someone cannot follow her pose, and the beach exerciser is unlikely to return every day, because exercise machines are often symbols of good intentions that do not last longer than a few days.

VISUALIZING DEVELOPMENT Global Prevalence of Major NCD

The map below shows the number of people ages 60 and over in each world region, and the percentage of those people who have a major neurocognitive disorder. Population data come from the United Nations, where skilled statisticians compile data on all 193 member nations. Therefore, the numbers are quite accurate. Prevalence data come from *The Lancet*, a highly respected British medical journal, and are as accurate as possible. However, those numbers are affected by cultural variations, not only in definition and diagnosis, but also in survival rates. Thus, a low percentage of people living with major NCD is not necessarily a sign of regional health. Comparisons between regions may be unfair, but one conclusion is clear: Nowhere in the world are more than 8 percent of the elderly suffering from severe brain disease.

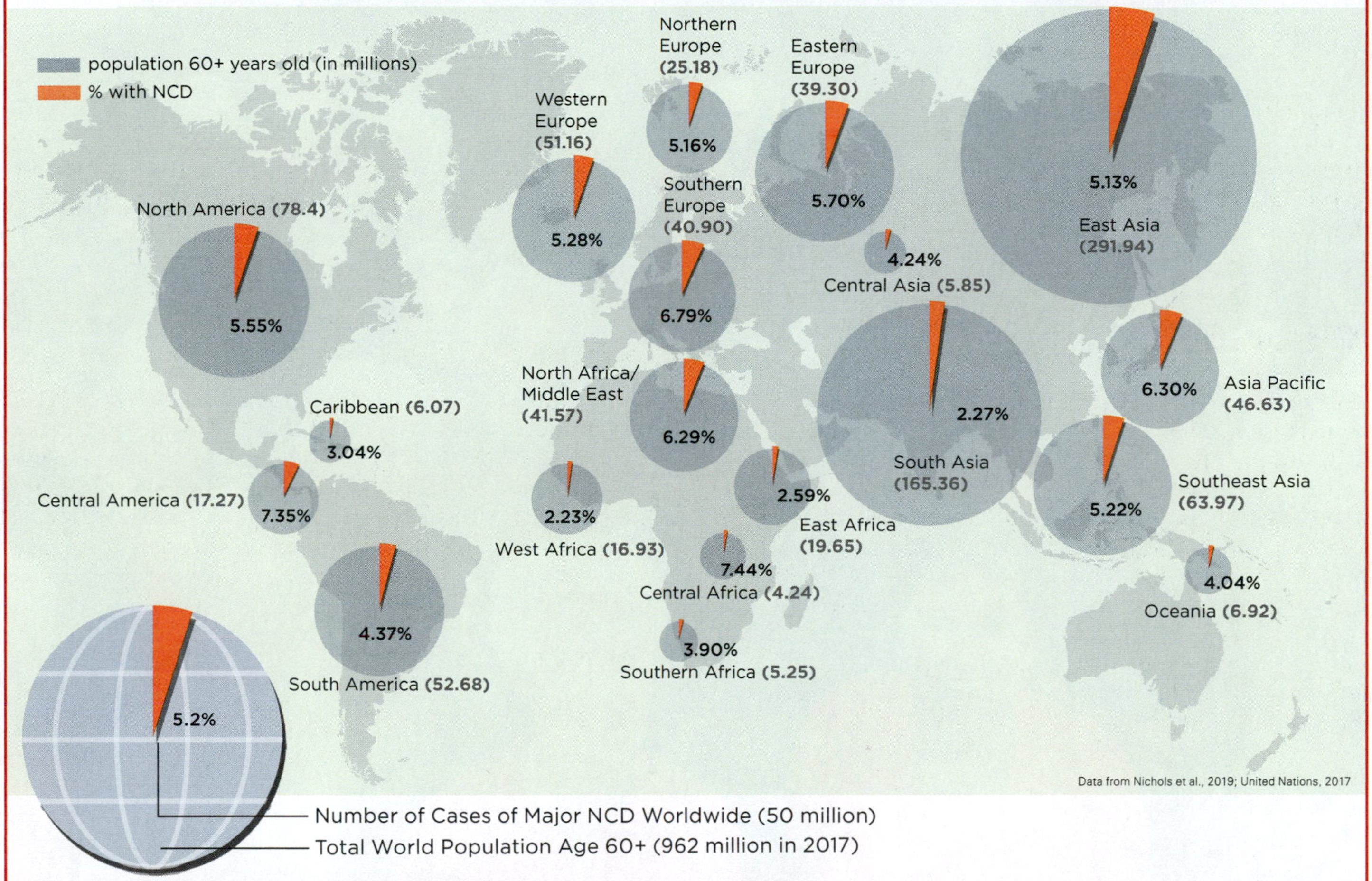

HEALTH CARE COSTS ASSOCIATED WITH MAJOR NCD

Alzheimer's disease and other major neurocognitive disorders are among the costliest chronic diseases to society: Individuals with a major NCD have more hospital and skilled nursing facility stays and home health care visits than other older people. However, the human cost may be greater than these estimates: Many family members spend substantial time caring for people with a major NCD, but often that time is not calculated until the disorder is severe.

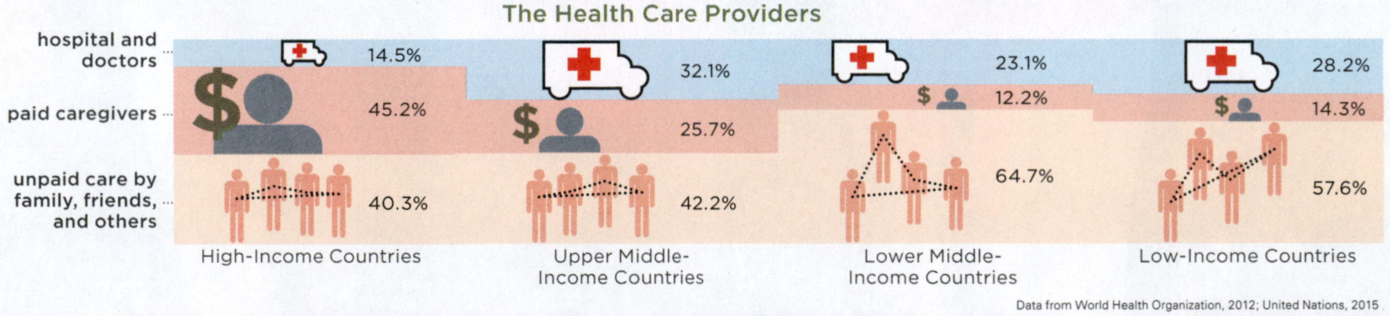

CHAPTER 25

Late Adulthood: Psychosocial Development

What Will You Know?

- Do older people become sadder or happier?
- Do the elderly want to move to a distant, warm place?
- Is home care better than nursing-home care?

- **Theories of Late Adulthood**
  - Self Theories
  - A CASE TO STUDY: Saving Old Newspapers
  - Stratification Theories
- **Activities in Late Adulthood**
  - Working
  - Home Sweet Home
  - Religious Involvement
  - Political Activity
  - Friends and Relatives
- **The Frail Elderly**
  - Activities of Daily Life
  - Preventing Frailty
  - Cognitive Failure
  - Caring for the Frail Elderly
  - A CASE TO STUDY: A Trusted Sister
  - Long-Term Care
- **CAREER ALERT: The Developmental Scientist**
- **VISUALIZING DEVELOPMENT: Living Independently After Age 65**

Almost every week I walk through a park with my friend Doris, a 90-year-old widow. Many people greet her by name, including men playing cards on a park table and a woman who owns a nearby hotel. Doris is an icon for street performers, including Colin, who plays his piano (on wheels) on sunny days, and Tic and Tac, who are middle-aged African American twins who do astonishing tumbling tricks with audience participation. The police watch the cardplayers carefully because they suspect drug dealing, and they ticketed Colin for not having a permit.

Doris organized a protest. She got Community Board 2 (she has been reappointed by the City Council every two years since 1964) to pass a resolution supporting entertainment in the park. The city withdrew the ticket, and the Parks Department revised its policy.

We walk slowly, not only because Doris has a walker, but because she greets babies, birds, and animals. Squirrels scamper to grab peanuts from her hand, sometimes pigeons perch on her arm. Tourists photograph her; the local press admires her (Google "Doris Diether").

Doris dresses well, appropriate for each season. One hot August day I was surprised that she wore a long-sleeved blouse. She proudly told me why: Her arm was scratched because two pigeons fought over the same spot. She tells me about her grandmother from Finland, her two marriages, her journalist days as a dance critic, her efforts to style her very white hair.

We often stop at a mailbox to drop in a timely greeting card: I have become one of hundreds on her list. Colorful envelopes arrive in my box—green for St. Patrick's Day, orange for Halloween, gray for Thanksgiving, red for July 4th, and multicolored for my birthday. She sends 426 Christmas cards; she orders stamps from a post office catalog.

Usually friends have much in common, but Doris is not like me. I have four children; she has none. I never send cards, feed squirrels, or protect pianists (although Doris did get me to help Colin). We belong to opposing political parties. Often she is the lone "nay" vote on Community Board resolutions.

How did we become friends? Twelve years ago, Doris had knee surgery. She asked for volunteers to push her wheelchair to her many meetings, appointments, and social engagements. Many people did so; I offered to take her once a week.

Ira Berger / Alamy Stock Photo

Not a Puppet One park regular is a puppeteer, Ricky Syers, who entertains hundreds of tourists with an array of puppets. He recently made a puppet of Doris, one more bit of evidence that the real Doris is beloved by many—and not controlled by anyone.

Soon she could walk, but she wanted me to keep coming. I bring her the Sunday paper (she pays me back, with cash and a wrapped piece of chocolate); I watch for cars when we cross the street; I lift her walker down the two stairs from her front door. I have grown to enjoy her anecdotes, her memories, her attitudes.

Eight years ago, Doris had surgery for a broken hip. The hospital soon put her in a private room because her younger roommate complained that Doris had too many visitors. Among them were park regulars, our state senator, and a man who credits her for his victory over his landlord. He avoided eviction: Doris is an expert on zoning and rent laws.

Two years ago, another fracture occurred. Medicare paid for six weeks of physical therapy. When the six weeks were over, her therapist joked, "Don't break a bone again just to get me back." She laughed; he is yet another friend. She was happy to see him again when she recently scraped her leg.

Doris defies stereotyping, which makes her an illustration of the theme of this chapter. Each older person is unique, not just one of millions. Some are frail, lonely, and vulnerable. But even the very old, with several disabilities, may be like Doris—active, involved, and beloved. I hope to be like her someday.

Theories of Late Adulthood

Some elderly people run marathons and lead nations; others no longer walk or talk. Social scientists theorize about this diversity.

Self Theories

Certain theories of late adulthood can be called **self theories;** they focus on individuals, especially each person's self-concept and challenges to identity. One study found that as people grow older, they feel that they are closer to their "authentic self" (Seto & Schlegel, 2018). That particular study was limited in size and age span, but other studies point in the same direction.

self theories Theories of late adulthood that emphasize the core self, or the search to maintain one's integrity and identity.

Elders who feel more in control of their own life also are happier and healthier. One study followed over a thousand people ages 40 to 85 for 15 years. Reduced sense of control correlated with more loneliness and more dependence later on (Drewelies et al., 2017).

The Self and Aging Ideally, people become more truly themselves with age. That is what Anna Quindlen found:

> It's odd when I think of the arc of my life from child to young woman to aging adult. First I was who I was, then I didn't know who I was, then I invented someone and became her, then I began to like what I'd invented, and finally I was what I was again. It turned out I wasn't alone in that particular progression.
>
> [*Quindlen, 2012, p. ix*]

Of course, one person's self-reflection on the "arc of life" should not be taken as a general truth. However, substantial research on both cognitive and personality traits find fluctuation earlier in life and then stability in late adulthood (Briley & Tucker-Drob, 2017). Thus, older people themselves think they are becoming more themselves (Cook, 2018).

For the oldest-old who suffer from numerous disabilities, maintaining independence is crucial for the self because it signifies resilience (Hayman et al., 2017). Many authors contend that the sense of self is multifaceted, including a moral sense ("I am kind to others"), a sensory sense ("I enjoy jazz"), an interactive self ("I am a wife"), and an autobiographical self ("I graduated from college") (Gallagher, 2013; Neisser, 1988). All of these are evident in older adults.

Even those with neurocognitive disorders seek to preserve the self when memory and health disappear (Strohminger & Nichols, 2015; Tippett et al., 2018). People can be clearly impaired by Alzheimer's and still appreciate flowers, or ice cream, or music as they always did.

Integrity The most comprehensive self theory came from Erik Erikson. His eighth and final stage of development, **integrity versus despair,** requires adults to integrate their unique experiences with their community concerns (Erikson et al., 1986/1994). The word *integrity* is often used to mean honesty, but it also means a feeling of being whole, not scattered, comfortable with oneself. The virtue of old age, said Erikson, is wisdom, which implies a broad perspective.

integrity versus despair The final stage of Erik Erikson's developmental sequence, in which older adults seek to integrate their unique experiences with their vision of community.

As an example of integrity, many older people are proud of their personal history. They glorify their past, boasting about bad experiences such as skipping school, taking drugs, escaping arrest, or being beaten with a belt. Feeling pride at having overcome past problems may explain an interesting finding: Several studies report that depression is more common in middle age than in late adulthood. A sense of mastery is protective of the self (Nicolaisen et al., 2017; Blanchflower & Oswald, 2017).

This may be particularly true for the current cohort of U.S. women aged 65 and older. Women generally are less likely to reach such overwhelming despair that they take their own lives, but this is particularly true in late adulthood. In 2016, older women died by suicide about half as often as women aged 45 to 64 (5.3 compared to 9.9 per 100,000) (National Center for Health Statistics, 2018).

As Erikson explained it, self-glorifying memories and self-acceptance counteract despair, because "time is now short, too short for the attempt to start another life" (Erikson, 1993a, p. 269). For every stage, the tension between the two opposing aspects (here integrity versus despair) propels growth. In this final stage,

> life brings many, quite realistic reasons for experiencing despair: aspects of a past we fervently wish had been different; aspects of the present that cause unremitting pain; aspects of a future that are uncertain and frightening. And, of course, there remains inescapable death, that one aspect of the future which is both wholly certain and wholly unknowable. Thus, some despair must be acknowledged and integrated as a component of old age.
>
> [*Erikson et al., 1994, p. 72*]

Integration of death and the self is the crucial accomplishment of Erikson's eighth stage. The life review (explained in Chapter 24) and acceptance of death (explained in the Epilogue) are crucial aspects of the integrity envisioned by Erikson (Zimmermann, 2012).

Self theory may explain why many of the elderly strive to maintain childhood cultural and religious practices. For instance, grandparents may painstakingly teach a grandchild a language that is rarely spoken, or they may encourage the child to repeat traditional rituals and prayers. In cultures that emphasize newness, elders worry that their traditional values will be lost and thus that they themselves will disappear.

As Erikson wrote, the older person

> knows that an individual life is the accidental coincidence of but one life cycle with but one segment of history and that for him all human integrity stands or falls with the one style of integrity of which he partakes. . . . In such a final consolation, death loses its sting.
>
> [*Erikson, 1993a, p. 268*]

Holding On to the Self Most older people consider their personalities and attitudes quite stable over their life span, even as they acknowledge physical changes of their bodies and lapses in their minds (Klein, 2012).

Always Himself Leading nonviolent protest is a sign of lifelong integrity for John Lewis. In his early 20s, he was beaten and arrested dozens of times as he sought civil rights for African Americans. At age 23, he spoke at the 1963 March on Washington, when Martin Luther King, Jr. proclaimed his dream. In this photo, at age 73, he is at the unveiling of a stamp commemorating that march 50 years earlier. Lewis was elected to represent Georgia in the U.S. Congress in 1986 and has been reelected 15 times. At age 76, he led a sit-in on the Congressional floor, asking the leadership to allow discussion and a vote on a bill to require background checks for gun ownership. He has not succeeded . . . yet.

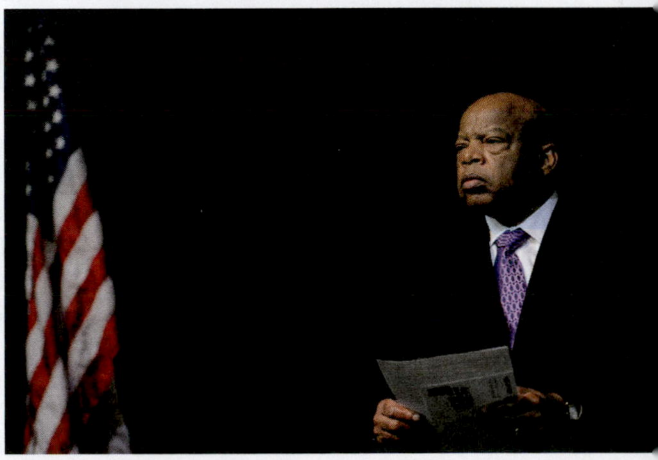

Riccardo S. Savi/Getty Images

Jim Wilkes/ZUMA Press/Toronto/Newscom

Trash or Treasure? Tryphona Flood, threatened with eviction, admitted she's a hoarder and got help from Megan Tolen, shown here discussing what in this four-room apartment can be discarded. Flood sits on the only spot of her bed that is not covered with stuff. This photo was taken midway through a three-year effort to clean out the apartment—the clutter was worse a year earlier.

One 103-year-old woman, wrinkled, shrunken, and severely crippled by arthritis, displayed a photo of herself as a beautiful young woman. She said, "My core has stayed the same. Everything else has changed" (quoted in Troll & Skaff, 1997, p. 166).

Many older people refuse to move from drafty and dangerous dwellings into safer apartments, because leaving old places means abandoning personal history. They keep objects and papers that a younger person would throw away, a habit now labeled **compulsive hoarding.**

Hoarding may seem irrational, but it may signify an attempt to maintain the self (see A Case to Study). Likewise, elders may refuse surgery, chemotherapy, or medicine because they fear anything that might distort their thinking or emotions: They want to be themselves, even if it shortens their life.

Socioemotional Selectivity Theory Another self theory is **socioemotional selectivity theory** (Carstensen, 1993), which is the idea that older people select familiar social contacts who reinforce their generativity, pride, and joy. As socioemotional theory would predict, when people believe that their future time is limited, they think about the meaning of life and decide that they should appreciate family and old friends, thus furthering their happiness.

An outgrowth of both socioemotional selectivity and selective optimization is known as the **positivity effect.** The elderly perceive, prefer, and remember positive images, memories, and experiences more than negative ones (Reed et al., 2014; Carstensen & DeLiema, 2018). Unpleasant experiences are ignored, forgotten, or reinterpreted.

The sense of self is crucial, not only for happiness but also for survival. A study of centenarians found that social and personal beliefs were at least as important for a long life as biology. Believing that one can still do things oneself—and that other people recognize one's individuality—is life-sustaining (Yorgason et al., 2018).

compulsive hoarding The urge to accumulate and hold on to familiar objects and possessions, sometimes to the point of their becoming health and/or safety hazards. This impulse tends to increase with age.

socioemotional selectivity theory The theory that older people prioritize regulation of their own emotions and seek familiar social contacts who reinforce generativity, pride, and joy.

positivity effect The tendency for elderly people to perceive, prefer, and remember positive images and experiences more than negative ones.

THINK CRITICALLY: Does the positivity effect avoid reality?

Stratification Theories

Self theories focus on the individual, specifically how each person's unique and positive perceptions help them cope with age. This contrasts with another set of theories called **stratification theories,** which emphasize social forces that position each person in a social stratum or level. That positioning creates disadvantages for some and advantages for others.

Stratification begins in the womb, as "individuals are born into a society that is already stratified—that is, differentiated—along key dimensions, including sex, race, and SES" (Lynch & Brown, 2011, p. 107). Indeed, stratification affects the prenatal environment, so some newborns already suffer from being born to a disadvantaged mother.

Stratification can arise from gender, ethnicity, immigration history, income, or age. Intersectionality is evident. Each of types of stratification can occur with other types, creating double, triple, or quadruple jeopardy.

stratification theories Theories which emphasize that social forces, particularly those related to a person's social stratum or social category, limit individual choices and affect a person's ability to function in late adulthood because past stratification continues to limit life in various ways.

Gender Stratification Older women are typically financially disadvantaged. Many of them spent years as unpaid caregivers, and when they had jobs, their earnings were low. They are also more often victims of benevolent ageism ("sweet old lady") than men are ("dirty old man").

Why do adult children urge their widow mothers more than their widower fathers to live with them? Is that sexist? It is not logical, as men are more likely to experience a sudden health crisis, and thus living alone is more dangerous for them.

A CASE TO STUDY

Saving Old Newspapers

My friend Doris (in the opening anecdote) keeps old newspaper clippings, records (many of which she recently sold to a music collector), and many other things. She has accumulated these possessions over the 40 years she has lived in a small apartment, about 200 square feet in total, with almost every surface covered.

To her, all of her saved items are meaningful; she sometimes offers them to libraries and other institutions. She lives alone, with two cats. Do you remember that she sends hundreds of greeting cards? She also receives hundreds, displayed all around her small space and only taken down when each holiday is over. Is that a problem?

A social worker might label that *compulsive hoarding,* which until recently was not considered a disorder. Many elderly hoarders grew up during the Great Depression and World War II. Saving, rationing, and reusing meant survival and patriotism, and homes typically had attics or basements with space for old magazines, clothes, toys, and knickknacks. Sayings like "a penny saved is a penny earned" were passed down as wisdom from one generation to the next.

Saving is no longer admired; pennies on the street are rarely picked up. Unlike all previous editions, the fifth edition of the DSM classifies hoarding as a psychological disorder (American Psychiatric Association, 2013, pp. 247–251). In the twenty-first century, expiration dates are stamped on food and drugs; electronics, from computers to televisions, are designed to become obsolete quickly.

Is saving old objects a sign of mental illness? Perhaps the elderly are expressing values formed decades ago. As an expression of the self, hoarding may bring emotional satisfaction (Frost et al., 2015), the same joy a younger person might get from buying the latest smartphone.

Self theory might suggest that keeping possessions is part of self-expression. The elderly seek to maintain childhood mores, lifelong habits, and past history. Faded photographs and chipped china may help them do that.

However, there is evidence that hoarding correlates with social isolation and many physical and psychological problems (Roane et al., 2017). In today's smaller dwellings, there is no space for extra possessions. A hoarder cannot have friends over for visits (no room) and may be embarrassed for anyone to see his or her home (at least Doris lets me in; she asks me to change the cats' water).

Because stacks of old papers and junk can attract dirt, mold, and small insects (not to mention pose a fire hazard), I thought of offering to help Doris get rid of her stuff. But then I realized that would be too painful for both of us.

I understand the general conclusions from the research: Hoarding may signify pathology, including social isolation that worsens over time. But to me, Doris's stacks of papers are part of her maintenance of identity, not hoarding. My view may be distorted; everyone sometimes ignores evidence when it applies to people they love. Have I lost my scientific mind?

Gender stratification may harm males in another way, however. Boys are taught to be stoic, repressing emotions. Later in life, they avoid medical attention, thus shortening their lives (Hamm et al., 2017). Males die more often than females at every age, yet in 2016 in the United States about twice as many men as women never saw a doctor (19 percent versus 10 percent) (National Center for Health Statistics, 2018).

Thus, all older people are affected adversely by gender stratification. One final example: Young women typically marry men who are a few years older and then outlive them by several years. A few decades ago, married women relied on their husbands to manage money, and men relied on their wives for cooking, laundry, health care, and so on, making each dependent on the other.

Partly because of past gender stratification, when one spouse of a long-married couple dies, the other is more vulnerable to death compared to other people of the same age, health, and SES. If the survivor is a man (the case about one-fourth of the time), he is even more likely to die before his time than a widow is (Boyle et al., 2011).

Ethnic and Income Stratification For many reasons, people of minority ethnicity are more often poor than those of majority ethnicity. A child who is born into a poor family is likely to be poor lifelong. Thus, both income and ethnic

AP Images/Wang zhide - Imaginechina

Twice Fortunate Ageism takes many forms. Some cultures are youth-oriented and devalue the old, while others are the opposite. These twin sisters are lucky to be alive: They were born in rural China in 1905, a period when most female twins died. When this photo was taken, they were age 103, and fortunate again, venerated because they have lived so long.

stratification keep some people at the bottom of the social hierarchy. For example, racial and income discrimination reduce quality of education, health of neighborhoods, wages earned—and the effects of past poverty accumulate and spread, affecting the current lives of older adults who were poor decades ago.

Consider one detailed example: home ownership, a source of financial security for many seniors. Fifty years ago, stratification prevented many young-adult African Americans from buying homes. They rented instead, which did not build housing equity. They could not obtain a reverse mortgage, which provides an additional income for elders who own a home.

About forty years ago, new laws reduced housing discrimination, which meant that many middle-aged African Americans bought homes. However, at that point, mortgages had high interest rates but were easy to obtain. Thus, the foreclosure crisis that began in 2007 fell particularly hard on African Americans, whose homes were "under water"—more money owed than the houses were worth.

Of course, the causes of the housing crisis went far beyond past ethnic discrimination. Nonetheless, some suggest that this is a new example of an old story: past stratification causing late life poverty (Forrest, 2018; Saegert et al., 2011).

A related problem for the poorest elderly, White as well as Black, is that few had long-lasting jobs that qualified for Social Security benefits or pensions. Thus, they lack an important source of income for many middle-class older Americans. Further, people who were poor decades ago could not save for late adulthood (Haushofer & Fehr, 2014). No matter what ethnicity, income stratification weighs heavily on the low-income oldest-old: They cannot afford being alive after age 80.

disengagement theory The view that aging makes a person's social sphere increasingly narrow, resulting in role relinquishment, withdrawal, and passivity.

activity theory The view that elderly people want and need to remain active in a variety of social spheres—with relatives, friends, and community groups—and become withdrawn only unwillingly, as a result of ageism.

Age Stratification Ageism and age segregation also affect every older person. Even middle-SES men who had good jobs and benefits find that income builds with seniority and then drops: Retirement pensions are significantly lower than peak earnings.

For everyone, health care costs increase with age. Medicare does not pay for all medical expenses. The various drugs and devices that have led to better lives are least likely to be covered by medical plans that were developed a few decades ago.

The most controversial version of age stratification is **disengagement theory** (Cumming & Henry, 1961), which holds that as people age, four significant changes occur: (1) Traditional roles become unavailable; (2) the social circle shrinks; (3) coworkers stop relying on elders; and (4) adult children turn away to focus on their own children. Meanwhile, older people become less mobile and less able to engage in social interaction.

According to this theory, disengagement is a mutual process, chosen by both adult generations. Thus, younger adults disengage from the old, who themselves disengage, withdrawing from life's action.

Resisting Jeopardy These men and women in Beijing, China, are gathering at dawn for a prayer meeting. Like many of the elderly who identify with a particular ethnic group, their community is a powerful antidote to the harm of stratification.

Richard Ellis/Alamy Stock Photo

Disengagement theory provoked a storm of protest. Many gerontologists insisted that older people need and want new involvements. They proposed an opposing theory, **activity theory,** that the elderly seek to remain active. According to activity theory, if the elders disengage, they do so unwillingly and suffer because of it (Kelly, 1993; Rosow, 1985).

The evidence supports activity theory. Most studies of the elderly find that being active correlates with happiness, intelligence, and health. Disengagement is more likely among those low in SES, another harmful outcome of past economic stratification (Clarke et al., 2011).

Double and Triple Jeopardy? Every form of stereotyping makes it more difficult for people to break free from social institutions that assign them to a particular path. The results are cumulative over the entire life span, severely harming those who suffer several forms of discrimination.

The idea of *intersectionality*, explained in Chapter 1, may apply. One scholar contends, "[W]omen . . . are much more likely to live in households that fall below the federal poverty line. Black and Hispanic women are particularly vulnerable" (Jackson et al., 2011, p. 93).

But not everyone agrees. In fact, one scholar suggests that older African American women in the United States have the best mental health of all. He does not think that "stratification systems such as gender, race and class" result in high risk for older adults. Instead, "multiple minority statuses affect mental health in paradoxical ways . . . that refute triple jeopardy approaches" (Rosenfield, 2012, p. 791).

Overall, past stratification might buffer the problems of old age. Might those who were stratified in adulthood develop coping strategies, such as being able to laugh at problems and establishing strong social bonds that improve late adulthood? That would reverse the effect of stratification.

Indeed, immigrant elders generally are happier with their lives than nonimmigrants, a phenomenon called the *happiness paradox* (Calvo et al., 2019). As you see, stratification theories may not describe the actual experience of many elders.

Especially for Social Scientists The various social science disciplines tend to favor different theories of aging. Can you tell which theories would be more acceptable to psychologists and which to sociologists? (see response, page 658)

WHAT HAVE YOU LEARNED?

1. How does Erikson's use of the word *integrity* differ from its usual meaning?
2. How does hoarding relate to self theory?
3. Is there any harm in older people striving to become themselves?
4. Which type of stratification is most burdensome: economic, ethnic, or gender?
5. How can disengagement be mutual?
6. If activity theory is correct, what does that suggest older adults should do?
7. What is the evidence for and against stratification theory?

Activities in Late Adulthood

As you have read, most elders are active and independent. That might surprise emerging adults, who see few gray hairs at sports events, political rallies, job sites, or midnight concerts. Ageism leads young people to imagine older people sitting quietly at home. This is not so, especially for the current cohort of elders. Large-scale research finds that, if anything, elders are more socially engaged than younger generations (Ang, 2019).

Working

A significant proportion of the elderly continue working, because work provides social support and status. Others retire from full-time, paid employment but remain productive in other ways.

Paid Work The employment rate for older workers has risen since 2005 (see **Figure 25.1**), largely because workers want or need to keep earning money. Pensions—federal as well as private—are less secure than they once were, and many investments have not worked out well. Health care expenses are costly, especially in the United States.

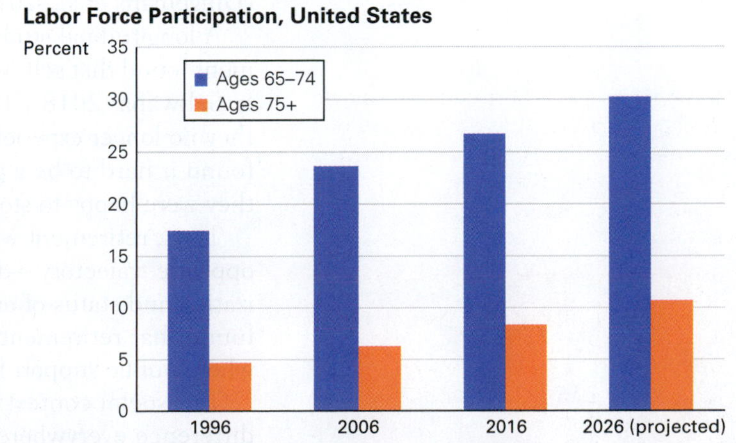

Data from U.S. Bureau of Labor Statistics, January 18, 2019.

FIGURE 25.1

Not Ready to Quit An increasing number of elders are still in the labor force. Why? Do they enjoy the work? Do they need the money? Are they healthier than previous cohorts? Has age discrimination been reduced? Or do more older people enjoy the status and friendships of employment?

J.D. Pooley/Getty Images

The Best New Hire Clayton Fackler, age 72, is shown here at his new job, a cashier at a Wal-Mart in Bowling Green, Ohio. He is among thousands of elderly people hired by that corporation, in part because retired seniors are reliable workers. They are also more willing than younger adults to work for minimum wage at part-time hours—a boon for employers but not for young adults.

That is one reason why some people keep working past age 62 (the age at which many people claim Social Security and pensions). Surprisingly, increasing rates of employment over time are particularly apparent in older women, who are twice as likely to be employed as older women were 20 years ago. (For women aged 75 to 79, the rate increased from 5 percent to 10 percent.)

Adequate income is a crucial predictor of health and happiness in late adulthood. Nonunionized, low-wage workers (who need the income) and professionals (who welcome the status) are especially likely to stay employed in their 60s (Komp et al., 2010).

Retirement The United States is one of the few developed nations that does not mandate a particular age for retirement (except in some occupations, such as firefighters and airplane pilots). Many older adults continue working until they believe that their retirement income is adequate, or until health concerns prompt them to quit.

Family connections also matter, as linked lives (first described in Chapter 19) continue. Generally, fathers tend to work a little longer than other men, perhaps because they want income to support their adult children.

Mothers, on average, tend to retire a little earlier than other women, perhaps because they become caregivers (Hank & Korbmacher, 2013). Many women leave full-time jobs in order to provide care for grandchildren (Hochman & Lewin-Epstein, 2013).

Some retirees work part time or become self-employed, with small businesses or consulting work. Some employers provide *bridge* jobs, enabling older workers to transition from full employment. Crafting an employment bridge, or consulting work, is an option that is more available to highly educated, long-term employees; thus, SES continues to stratify older people (Calvo et al., 2018).

Employment in late adulthood varies markedly, with many older workers convinced that age discrimination is common. In some occupations, physical ability is crucial and expertise is minimal: In those occupations, older workers are rarely hired and often fired. In other jobs, the experience and reliability of older workers (who are less often absent, late, or hungover) make them particularly valuable (Dingemans et al., 2016; James et al., 2011).

A longitudinal study of older adults in the Netherlands before and after retirement found that self-esteem decreased in the five years *before* retirement (Bleidorn & Schwaba, 2018). Then, for many, self-esteem rose after retirement because they no longer experienced work–family conflicts: Apparently many older workers found it hard to be a good worker, spouse, and grandparent simultaneously, and they were happy to stop working.

Thus, retirement was a relief for many—but not everyone. Some followed the opposite trajectory—decreasing in self-esteem—presumably because the socialization and status of employment were lost. Note that this study, which generally found that retirement increased happiness, was of workers in the Netherlands, where public support for retirees is extensive.

The social context (particularly culture, pensions, and health care) makes a difference everywhere in how older adults feel about retirement. For those reasons, retirement often increases self-esteem in many nations of Europe and North America but decreases it in many Asian nations (Mukku et al., 2018).

THINK CRITICALLY: Can you think of another definition of volunteering that would increase the rate for elderly adults?

Volunteer Work Volunteering provides some of the benefits of paid employment (generativity, social connections). Longitudinal as well as cross-sectional research finds a strong link between volunteering, health, and well-being, especially for older adults (Russell et al., 2019; Kahana et al., 2013; Tabassum et al., 2016). A *regular* volunteer commitment to a social-service organization, religious institution, or community group is best.

One meta-analysis found that volunteering cuts the death rate in half. Even when various confounds (such as marital status and health before volunteering) were taken into account, being a volunteer correlated with a longer and healthier life (Okun et al., 2013).

In one project, older people interested in "active retirement" attended a two-hour session that explained the benefits of volunteering, the importance of planning and initiative, and various ways to find an activity that suited one's values and preferences. They were given a list of nearby volunteer opportunities (Warner et al., 2014).

Six weeks later, the rate of volunteering among the attendees had doubled. Some began volunteering for the first time. Many who already had been volunteers increased their commitment.

Sadly, without encouragement, many elders do not volunteer. Data from the United States found that only 24 percent of those over age 64 volunteered for any organization even once in 2015 (U.S. Bureau of Labor Statistics, February 25, 2016) (see **Figure 25.2**).

Overall, people are more likely to volunteer if they are married, employed, and middle-aged. About half of all volunteers did so because someone in the organization asked them— which should alert everyone who wants to know how to help elders and organizations.

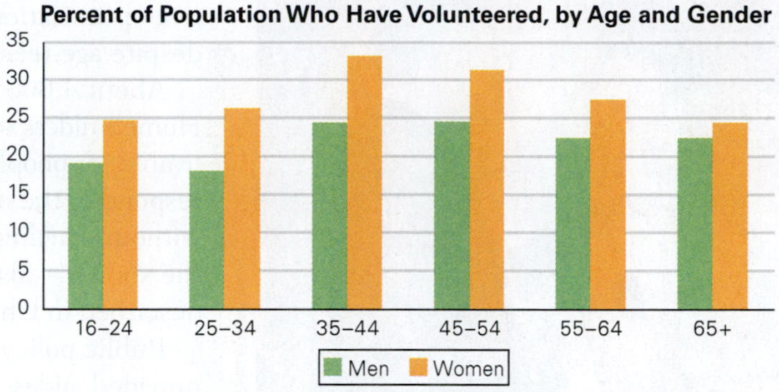

FIGURE 25.2

Official Volunteers As you can see, older adults volunteer less often than do middle-aged adults, according to official statistics. However, this counts people who volunteer for organizations—schools, churches, social service groups, and so on. Not counted is help given to friends, family members, neighbors, and even strangers. If that were counted, would elders have higher rates than everyone else?

Observation Quiz When is the gender gap least evident? (see answer, page 658)

Home Sweet Home

One of the favorite activities of many retirees is caring for their own homes and personal needs. Typically, all adults do more housework and meal preparation (less fast food, more fresh ingredients) after retirement (Luengo-Prado & Sevilla, 2012). They go to fewer restaurants, stores, and parties, because they like to stay put.

Older adults do yard work, redecorate, build shelves, hang pictures, rearrange furniture. One study found that husbands did much more housework and yard work when they retired. Surprising, although husbands helped more around the house, their wives did not reduce their work. Apparently, couples find more things to do when they have more time to do them (Leopold & Skopek, 2015b).

Gardening is popular: More than half of the elderly in the United States do it. Growing flowers, herbs, and vegetables is productive because it involves creativity, exercise, and social interaction (Schupp & Sharp, 2012; Miller et al., 2018).

Aging in Place In keeping up with household tasks and maintaining property, almost all older people—about 90 percent, even when they are frail—prefer to **age in place** rather than move. That means they like to stay in their own homes.

age in place To remain in the same home and community in later life, adjusting but not leaving when health fades.

The preference for aging in place is evident in state statistics. Of the 50 states, Florida has the largest percentage of people over age 65, many of whom moved there not only for the climate but also because they already knew people there. The next three states highest in proportion of population over age 65 are Maine, West Virginia, and Pennsylvania, all places where older people have aged in place.

Fortunately, aging in place has become easier. One successful project sent a team (a nurse, occupational therapist, and handyman) to vulnerable aged adults, who then became better able to take care of themselves at home, avoiding nursing

NicolasMcComber/E+/Getty Images

Imagining the Future Couples like this one in Quebec, Canada, often build new homes with modifications in their current neighborhoods so that they can age in place for 20 or more years. Note that the younger man in this photo (the architect) is pleased to show them a model of their new home—no stairs and fewer bedrooms.

homes and hospitals (Szanton et al., 2015). Elders themselves use selective optimization with compensation as they envision staying in their homes despite age-related problems (Fiske et al., 2015).

About 4,000 consultants are now certified by the National Association of Homebuilders to advise about *universal design,* which includes making a home livable for people who find it hard to reach the top shelves, to climb stairs, to respond to the doorbell. Non-design aspects of housing—such as bright lights without dangling cords, carpets affixed to the floor, and seats and grab bars in the shower—also allow aging in place. [**Life-Span Link:** Universal design is described in Chapter 23.]

Public policy affects all of the elderly. Laws reduce rents; transportation is provided; aides, therapists, and meal services come to homes. Doris (opening anecdote) tells me that none of these public policies works as well in practice as in pronouncements. Nonetheless, she—and many others—could not age in place without them.

NORCs Some homes have become part of a **naturally occurring retirement community (NORC).** A NORC develops when young adults move into a new suburb or large building and then stay for decades. People in NORCs may live alone after children leave and partners die. They enjoy home repair, housework, and gardening, partly because their lifelong neighbors notice the new curtains, the polished door, the blooming rose bush.

If low-income elders are in a NORC within a high-crime neighborhood, they and their neighbors sometimes form a protective social network. NORCs can be granted public money to replace after-school karate with senior centers, or piano teachers with visiting nurses, if that is what the community needs (Greenfield et al., 2012; Vladeck & Altman, 2015).

naturally occurring retirement community (NORC) A neighborhood or apartment complex whose population is mostly retired people who moved to the location as younger adults and never left.

Religious Involvement

The old-old attend fewer religious services than do the young-old, but faith and praying increase over the life span. For example, two-thirds of Americans over age 65 pray every day, as do only about one-third of those in their 20s (Pew Research Center, November 3, 2015). Many elders study religious texts.

The psychological construct of *attachment* has been applied to late-life religious activity. Remember that attachment was described Chapter 7: Some babies are securely attached to their caregivers and some are not. In late adulthood, attachment can describe a person's relationship with God (Granqvist & Kirkpatrick, 2013).

One study found that elders who feel securely attached to God (e.g., "When I talk to God, I know he listens to me") are more likely to be optimistic, accepting their faults but also feeling good about themselves (Bradshaw & Kent, 2018). Another study found that prayer itself does not seem to promote a sense of well-being. However, if prayer is part of a personal attachment to God, it benefits the old (Bradshaw & Kent, 2018).

Religious activity correlates with physical and emotional health in late adulthood. Developmentalists have several explanations:

1. Religious prohibitions encourage good habits (e.g., less drug use).
2. Faith communities promote caring relationships.
3. Beliefs give meaning for life and death, thus reducing stress.

Religious identity and institutions are especially important for older members of minority groups, who often identify more strongly with their religious heritage than with their national or ethnic background. A nearby house of worship, with familiar words, music, and rituals, is one reason that elders prefer to age in place.

macmillan learning

Many of the older adults in **VIDEO: Active and Healthy Aging: The Importance of Community** frequent senior centers for continual social contact, and some benefit from volunteering.

Especially for Religious Leaders
Why might the elderly have strong faith but poor church attendance? (see response, page 658)

Immigrants bring their religion with them. About one-third of all U.S. Catholics are immigrants or children of immigrants, as are most U.S. Hindus and Buddhists and many U.S. Muslims (Pew Research Center, May 12, 2015). Although the average congregant in these newer groups is younger than the average member of traditional U.S. Christian or Jewish groups, in every religious group the elderly members tend to be most devout.

Ana Fernandez / SOPA Images/Sipa USA via AP Images

Legacy and Politics Older adults are sometimes stereotyped as caring only for their own political issues, such as Social Security. In fact, many care about the future world, as evident here. These elders organized their protest on the same day in 2019 that thousands of teenagers marched for the climate.

Political Activity

It is easy to assume that elders are not political activists. Few turn out for rallies, and only about 2 percent are active in political campaigns. By other measures, however, the elderly are very political. More than any other age group, they write letters to their representatives, identify with a political party, and vote.

In addition, they keep up with the news. The Pew Research Center periodically asks a cross section of U.S. residents questions about current events and civic understanding. The elderly usually best the young. For example, 73 percent of elders (65 and older) but only half as many (38 percent) of young adults (ages 18 to 29) knew that the vice president casts the deciding vote if the U.S. Senate is split 50/50 (as it was in 2017 for Secretary of Education Betsy DeVos's confirmation) (Pew Research Center, June 13, 2018).

Many government policies affect the elderly, especially those regarding housing, pensions, prescription drugs, and medical costs. However, members of this age group do not necessarily vote their own economic interests or vote as a bloc. Instead they are divided on most national issues, including global warming, military conflicts, and public education.

Friends and Relatives

Companions are particularly important during old age. As socioemotional theory predicts, the size of the social circle shrinks, but close relationships are crucial. Bonds formed over the years allow people to share triumphs and tragedies with others who understand and appreciate them. Siblings, old friends, and spouses are ideal convoy members.

Long-Term Partnerships For most of the current cohort of elders, their spouse is the central convoy member, a buffer against the problems of old age. Even more than other social contacts, a spouse is protective of health and well-being (Wong & Waite, 2015).

Mutual interaction is crucial: Each healthy and happy partner improves the other's well-being (Ruthig et al., 2012). A lifetime of shared experiences—living together, raising children, and dealing with financial and emotional crises—brings partners closer.

Older couples have learned how to disagree, considering conflicts to be discussions rather than fights. I know one example personally. Irma and Bill are proud parents of two adults, devoted grandparents, and informed about current events. They seem happily married, and they cooperate admirably when caring for their grandsons.

However, they vote for opposing candidates. Irma explained: "We sit together on the fence, seeing both perspectives, and then, when we vote, Bill and I fall on opposite sides." I can predict, long before the discussion, who will fall on which side, but for them, the discussion is productive. Their long-term affection avoids the polarization common among U.S. voters who don't know each other.

Older couples often find patterns of interaction that work for them. One study found that older husbands were generally satisfied with their marriages because

AP Images/Bloomington Herald-Times, ChrisHowell

VIKTOR DRACHEV/AFP/Getty Images

A Lover's Kiss Ralph Young awakens Ruth *(left)* with a kiss each day, as he has for most of the 78 years of their marriage. Here they are both 99, sharing a room in their Indiana residence, "more in love than ever." Half a world away, in Ukraine *(right),* more kisses occur, with 70 newly married couples and one couple celebrating their golden anniversary. Developmental data suggest that now, several years after these photos, the two old couples are more likely to be happily married than the 70 young ones.

their wives took good care of them, and wives were satisfied because enjoyed taking care of their husbands (Carr et al., 2014). This may seem sexist to younger people, but both partners may be content with their interaction.

A couple together can achieve selective optimization with compensation. For example, I know a couple in their early 90s. His memory is fading; her legs are so weak that she has difficulty getting out of bed. If either had been alone, he or she would need extensive care. However, the husband helps the wife move, and she keeps track of what needs to be done: Together they need minimal outside help.

Intergenerational Relationships Since the average couple now has fewer children, the *beanpole family*, with multiple generations but with only a few members at each level, is becoming more common (see **Figure 25.3**). Some children have no cousins, brothers, or sisters but have a dozen older relatives. The result may be stronger connections across generations.

filial responsibility The obligation of adult children to care for their aging parents.

As you remember, *familism* prompts family caregiving. One norm is **filial responsibility,** the obligation of adult children to care for their aging parents. As a cultural ideal, filial responsibility is strongest in Asia, but in practice, Asians may be less likely to care for elderly parents than those in Western cultures (Kim et al., 2015).

Another norm that is strong among many grandparents is that the older generation should help the younger ones. When the government provides assistance for the aged (housing, pensions, and so on), the generations are *more* involved with each other, not less (Herlofson & Hagestad, 2012).

Similarly, in nations where governments provide early-childhood education, grandmothers are more likely to provide occasional child care. In nations where the government does not provide care, fewer grandmothers provide care, but those who do are likely to do so intensely (Price et al., 2018).

As you also remember, older adults do not want to move in with younger generations, doing so only if poverty or frailty require it. This is true not only in the United States but worldwide, including in nations with a tradition of adult children caring for elder parents.

Every generation values independence. But that does not mean that they do not affect each other's lives. Family links continue to be maintained in the twenty-first century as they have always been (Berger, 2019; Timonen, 2018). Generally, financial assistance and help with daily life is more likely to flow from older generations to younger ones, although much depends on specific family dynamics.

MOELLER
Grampa says it's what they used to use for social networking!

Moeller, M/Cartoonstock

Universal Needs Hurray for grandparents who recognize that every generation needs to connect—even though the hayride, the soda fountain, and the balcony of the movie theater have all been replaced.

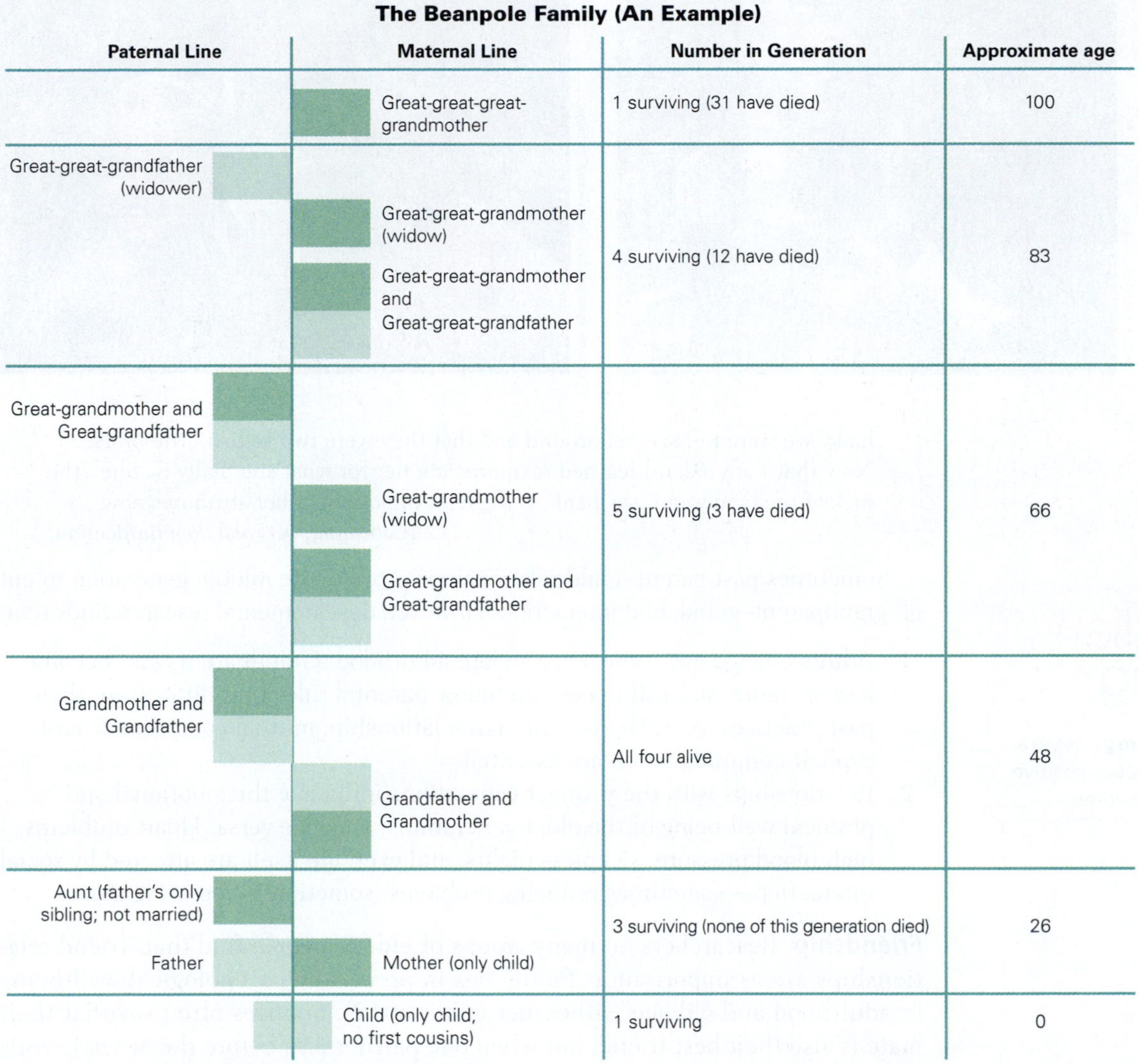
The Beanpole Family (An Example)
Paternal Line
Maternal Line
Number in Generation
Approximate age
Great-great-great-grandmother
1 surviving (31 have died)
100
Great-great-grandfather (widower)
Great-great-grandmother (widow)
Great-great-grandmother and Great-great-grandfather
4 surviving (12 have died)
83
Great-grandmother and Great-grandfather
Great-grandmother (widow)
Great-grandmother and Great-grandfather
5 surviving (3 have died)
66
Grandmother and Grandfather
Grandfather and Grandmother
All four alive
48
Aunt (father's only sibling; not married)
Father
Mother (only child)
3 surviving (none of this generation died)
26
Child (only child; no first cousins)
1 surviving
0

FIGURE 25.3

Many Households, Few Members The traditional nuclear family consists of two parents and their children living together. Today, as couples have fewer children, the beanpole family is becoming more common. This kind of family has many generations, each typically living in its own household, with only a few members in each generation. In this example, the child has zero relatives in his generation, but 17 elder relatives!

Grandparents and Great-Grandparents Eighty-five percent of U.S. elders currently older than 65 are grandparents. (The rate was lower in previous cohorts because the birth rate fell during the 1930s, and it is expected to be lower again.) Almost all grandparents provide some caregiving and gifts, unless the middle generation does not allow it (Berger, 2019).

As with parents and children, specifics of the grandparent–grandchild relationship depend on culture, personality, and age. Grandparents typically are active caregivers of the youngest children; they provide material support for the school-age children; and they offer advice and encouragement while acting as a role model for the older grandchildren.

One of my college students realized this when she wrote:

> Brian and Brianna are twins and are turning 13 years old this coming June. Over the spring break my family celebrated my grandmother's 80th birthday and I overheard the twins' talking about how important it was for them to still have grandma around because she was the only one who would give them money if they really wanted something their mom wasn't able to give them. . . . I lashed out . . . how

Same Situation, Far Apart: Happy Grandfathers No matter where they are, grandparents and grandchildren often enjoy each other partly because conflict is less likely, as grandparents are usually not as strict as parents are. Indeed, Sam Levinson quipped, "The reason grandparents and grandchild get along so well is that they have a common enemy."

Floresco Productions/Fuse/Corbis

Atlantide Phototravel/Corbis Documentary/Getty Images

> lucky we were to have her around and that they were two selfish little brats. . . . Now that I am older, I learned to appreciate her for what she really is. She's the rock of the family and "the bank" is the least important of her attributes now.
>
> [*Giovanna, personal communication*]

Sometimes past parent–child relationships provoke the middle generation to cut off grandparent–grandchild interaction. However, developmental research finds that:

1. Adults change over time, even in late adulthood. Grandparents can become less, or more, strict, if needed to follow parental rules that differ from their past practices. As with every human relationship, mutual compromise and explicit communication are essential.
2. Relationships with the younger generations influence the emotional and physical well-being of the older generations, and vice versa. Heart problems, high blood pressure, sleepless nights, and even life itself are affected by social interaction—sometimes reducing problems, sometimes increasing them.

macmillan learning

In **VIDEO: Grandparenting,** several individuals discuss their close, positive attachments to their grandchildren.

Friendship Researchers on many groups of elderly people find that "friend relationships are as important as family ties in predicting psychological well-being in adulthood and old age" (Blieszner et al., 2019). Spouses often say that their mate is also their best friend, but when one partner dies before the other, friends are more crucial than other relatives. Ideally, elders have both.

Nonetheless, the friendship circle shrinks every decade of adult life. Elders are healthiest if some family friends (a favorite cousin, for instance) are among their close friends, yet worse health correlates with a lack of nonfamily friends (Shiovitz-Ezra & Litwin, 2015). Older adults are more likely to keep longtime friends than find new ones (Wrzus & Neyer, 2016), which is another reason why they like to age in place.

WHAT HAVE YOU LEARNED?

1. Why would a person want to keep working in late adulthood?
2. How does retirement affect the health of people who have worked all their lives?
3. Who is more likely to volunteer and why?
4. What are the benefits and liabilities for elders who want to age in place?
5. How does religion affect the well-being of the aged?
6. How does the political activity of older and younger adults differ?
7. What is the usual relationship between older adults who have been partners for decades?
8. Who benefits most from relationships between older adults and their grown children?
9. Why do older people tend to have fewer friends as they age?

The Frail Elderly

Remember the diversity of development in late adulthood? As you just read, most aging adults are active in many venues, enjoying supportive friends and family. But that is not true for everyone.

Now we turn to the **frail elderly**—those who are infirm, inactive, seriously disabled. Most frail elders have several infirmities (taking many medications is a predictor), but some have no diagnosed illness.

frail elderly People over age 65, and often over age 85, who are physically infirm, very ill, or cognitively disabled. Low energy is a key characteristic.

Frailty is defined by low energy. One sign is weight loss (especially in men); another is extreme fatigue (especially in women); and a third is difficulty walking (everyone). Before death, about one-third of the elderly experience at least a year of frailty.

Activities of Daily Life

One way to measure frailty, according to insurance standards and medical professionals, is by assessing a person's ability to maintain self-care. Gerontologists often assess five physical **activities of daily life (ADLs):** eating, dressing, bathing, toileting, and moving (transferring) from a bed to a chair.

activities of daily life (ADLs) Typically identified as five tasks of self-care that are important to independent living: eating, bathing, toileting, dressing, and transferring from a bed to a chair. The inability to perform any of these tasks is a sign of frailty.

instrumental activities of daily life (IADLs) Actions (for example, paying bills and car maintenance) that are important to independent living and that require some intellectual competence and forethought. The ability to perform these tasks may be even more critical to self-sufficiency than ADL ability.

In part because mortality increases if a person cannot do the ADLs, a mnemonic that is sometimes used is DEATH [dressing, eating, ambulating (moving), toileting, hygiene (bathing)]. Sometimes additional ADLs are included, such as brushing teeth, walking 50 feet, and putting on shoes.

If a person cannot perform one or more of the ADLs, it may be a temporary problem that is common after a major illness. The ADLs are dynamic: Most people who have difficulty with an ADL are able to recover (Dyer et al., 2016).

Recovery is especially likely if someone teaches people how to recover—for instance, to don shoes without needing to reach way down, or to get out of bed without pain or risking a fall. Physical therapists show ways to accomplish self-care, recommend specialized equipment, and teach exercises that increase the range of motion to make tasks easier.

More important than ADLs may be the **instrumental activities of daily life (IADLs),** which require intellectual competence and forethought. Difficulty with IADLs often precede problems with ADLs since planning and problem solving help frail elders maintain self-care.

IADLs vary from culture to culture. In developed nations, IADLs may include interpreting the labels on medicine bottles, preparing nutritious meals, filling out tax forms, keeping track of investments and expenses, scheduling doctor appointments, planning a route home, or using a computer, a cell phone, or a microwave (see **Table 25.1**). In some nations, feeding one's animals, following religious rituals, and keeping the home clean, warm, and dry are IADLs.

Better or Worse? It depends. The advantage of having a motorized wheelchair is that a person can stay engaged in life, even on the streets of Beijing, as shown here. The disadvantage is that riding may replace walking—but that is up to the person. This man might be on his way to strength training at the gym, and if he gets there safely and regularly, his electric wheelchair can add years to his life.

WANG ZHAO/Getty Images

Preventing Frailty

The ideal is to prevent frailty, with an elder healthy and self-sufficient one day and dead the next, never frail. Instead, almost every older person eventually has difficulty with ADLs or IADLs.

Prevention depends on everyone realizing that disability is dynamic rather than static. Self-sufficiency is protected and extended if individuals, families, and the larger community all do their part. We focus on two examples: first an ADL (mobility) and second a cognitive one (an IADL).

TABLE 25.1

Instrumental Activities of Daily Life in Twenty-first-century United States

Domain	Exemplar Task
Managing medical care	Keeping current on checkups, including teeth, ears, and eyes Assessing supplements as good, worthless, or harmful
Food preparation	Evaluating nutritional information on food labels Preparing and storing food to prevent spoilage
Transportation	Comparing costs of car, taxi, bus, and train Determining quick and safe walking routes
Communication	Knowing when, whether, and how to use landline, cell, texting, postal mail, e-mail Programming speed dial for friends, emergencies
Maintaining household	Following instructions for operating an appliance Keeping safety devices (fire extinguishers, CO_2 alarms) active
Managing one's finances	Budgeting future expenses (housing, utilities, etc.) Completing timely income tax returns Avoiding costly scams, unread magazines

Muscle Weakness The preeminent symptom of frailty is weakness. To some extent, that is everyone's problem: Muscles weaken with age, a condition called *sarcopenia*. In fact, muscle mass at age 90 averages only half of what it was at age 30, with much of that loss occurring in late adulthood (McLean & Kiel, 2015).

Bones and balance are impaired as well. Thus, elderly people are more likely than younger people to fall, and they are more likely to break a bone when doing so. As mentioned in Chapter 23, osteoporosis (weak bones) is a common problem in old age, and broken bones—particularly the hip bone—cause immobility and morbidity, which sometimes lead to death.

Mobility is crucial for ADLs and IADLs. Fortunately immobility can be prevented. Some measures target bones directly: Drugs, diet, exercise, and replacement of hips, shoulders, knees, and so on are all common. Older people can choose to strengthen bones and balance, and other people can encourage such actions. However, often the opposite happens. Elders move less because they fear falling, and the social context encourages passivity.

Don't Laugh One of the impediments to life and health is the notion that people who exercise must look young and attractive. This man is wise and brave, as well as admirably balanced.

Melanie Stetson Freeman/The Christian Science Monitor/Getty Images

For example, caregiving relatives might think they are benevolent if they bring meals, buy a portable toilet, and get a remote control for a large bedroom TV. The community may not provide affordable and accessible housing, and may not build smooth sidewalks. The TV news may highlight violent crime, further immobilizing the old.

Instead, individuals, families, and communities need to prioritize active lives. A person could exercise daily, walking with family members on pathways built to be safe and pleasant. A physical therapist—paid by the individual, the family, or the government—could prescribe exercises and equipment (a walker? a cane? special shoes?) that keep an elder moving.

Extensive research has found again and again that lack of exercise leads to lower quality of life, increasing both

ADLs and IADLs. On the other hand, exercise improves life and health, whether a person ages in place or moves to a senior residence. Even the oldest-old who suffer neurocognitive disorders and live in long-term care facilities benefit from exercise (Traynor et al., 2018).

Cognitive Failure

All three—the elder, the family, and the community—could prevent or at least postpone frailty, not only by improving mobility but also by protecting the mind.

Consider this example.

> A 70-year-old Hispanic man came to his family doctor following a visit to his family in Colombia, where he had appeared to be disoriented (he said he believed he was in the United States, and he did not recognize places that were known to be familiar to him) and he was very agitated, especially at night. An interview with the patient and a family member revealed a history that had progressed over the past six years, at least, of gradual worsening cognitive deficit, which that family had interpreted as part of normal aging. Recently his symptoms had included difficulty operating simple appliances, misplacement of items, and difficulty finding words, with the latter attributed to his having learned English in his late 20s. . . . [His] family had been very protective and increasingly had compensated for his cognitive problems.
>
> . . . He had a lapse of more than five years without proper control of his medical problems [hypertension and diabetes] because of difficulty gaining access to medical care. . . .
>
> Based on the medical history, a cognitive exam . . . and a magnetic resonance imaging of the brain . . . the diagnosis of moderate Alzheimer's disease was made. Treatment with ChEI [cholinesterase inhibitors] was started. . . . His family noted that his apathy improved and that he was feeling more connected with the environment.
>
> *[Griffith & Lopez, 2009, p. 39]*

Both the community (those five years without treatment for hypertension and diabetes) and the family (making excuses, protecting him) contributed to major neurocognitive disorder that could have been prevented or at least delayed.

Note that the man himself did not safeguard his health, and his family allowed his neglect. They helped him arrange his Colombia trip, which was the worst thing they could do, since change of routine and locale are particularly disorienting to the elderly.

Caring for the Frail Elderly

Prevention is best, but it is not always sufficient. Some problems, such as major neurocognitive disorder or severe heart failure, can be postponed but not eliminated. Caregivers themselves are usually elderly, and they often have poor health, limited strength, and failing immune systems. Thus, an aging parent who cares for the other parent needs help from the adult children long before a crisis.

Caregiving is especially difficult when IADLs are failing. If an elder cannot perform an ADL, they know they need help. But if an elder cannot do an IADL, they might not realize it. For example, they might insist that they can file their taxes, and become angry if the Internal Revenue Service finds fault.

Filial Responsibility? There are marked cultural differences in norms and practices regarding care for the frail elderly, with some cultures expecting that family will do it and others that the government should provide care.

Now that families are smaller and many daughters and daughters-in-law are employed, a given couple may have several older relatives but no siblings to share the burden of care. Fortunately, most elderly relatives care for themselves. Those

DEA/G. SIOEN/Getty Images

Never Frail This man is playing the recorder at an Easter celebration in Arachova, a mountain town in Greece.

Observation Quiz It is impossible to be sure, but from what you see and know there are seven clues that this man will never be frail. How many can you name? (see answer, page 658) ↑

CHAPTER APP 25

Caring Bridge

IOS:
https://tinyurl.com/y2ntba95

RELEVANT TOPIC:
Caring for the frail elderly

This caregiver app enables users and their loved ones to stay in touch and arrange for care—especially useful to those facing procedures and rehabilitation and to older adults living alone. Multiple caregivers and family members can share updates and encouragement, including via a guest book with room for journal entries, medical updates, photos, stories, and tributes.

Denise Hager, Catchlight Visual Services/Alamy stockphoto

A Fortunate Man Henk Huisman gets care from his wife, Ria, who is happy to provide it. One reason is that this couple has three daughters, all of whom also help. Another reason may be that they live in the Netherlands, which provides extensive public assistance for everyone over age 65.

who not only provide self-care but also believe that they are not dependent on their children are less likely to become frail (Elliot et al., 2018).

Most of the elderly are cared for by their husbands and wives, who are elderly themselves. This is not always for the best: Many caregiving spouses feel they cannot leave their partner alone, becoming homebound and isolated from their friends and family, who visit less often and help even less. As one review explains:

> Spousal caregivers report more emotional, physical, and financial burden when compared with other caregivers, such as those who care for their elderly parents. They experience greater isolation and less help.
>
> *[Glauber & Day, 2018, p. 537]*

Whenever a person "does not want to be a burden," that can lead to not asking for needed care. Some older men, particularly, are fiercely independent, refusing help from family, doctors, and technology (such as walkers and hearing aids). That shortens their lives, as well as the lives of their wives (Hamm et al., 2017).

Adult siblings may also fight over who provides care and how. In general, in North America, brothers expect their sisters to care for dependent elders, which can reactivate long-standing resentments. The decision to move a parent to a care facility is a contentious one.

Ironically, few family caregivers know how to care for a frail elder, so the caregiver burden is often overwhelming, "a chronic stressor" (Glauber & Day, 2018, p. 538).

The Role of the Government There is no worldwide consensus about the role of the government in senior care. In northern European nations, most elder care is provided through a social safety net of senior day-care centers, senior homes, and skilled nurses. In African cultures, families are fully responsible for the aged. Daughters in North America and sons in Asia are assumed to be primary caregivers, but the government is involved if that is needed.

Even in ideal circumstances, family members disagree with each other and with formal caregivers about appropriate nutrition, medical help, and dependence. One family member may insist that an elderly person *never* enter a nursing home, and that insistence may create family conflict.

In the United States, governments do not intervene unless a crisis arises. This troubles developmentalists, who study "change over time." From a life-span perspective, caregiver exhaustion and elder abuse are predictable and preventable.

integrated care Care of frail elders that combines the caregiving strengths of everyone—family, medical professionals, social workers, and the elders themselves.

The ideal is **integrated care,** in which professionals and family members cooperate to provide good individualized care, whether at a long-term care facility, at the elder's home, or at someone else's home (Lopez-Hartmann et al., 2012). Just as a physical therapist knows which specific exercises and movements improve mobility, a professional can evaluate an impaired elder and figure out which tasks are best done by a relative, which by the frail person themselves, and which by a medical professional.

Multidisciplinary teams are needed because frail elders need medical, social, and financial care, yet need to do as much of their own care as possible (Pollina et al., 2017). Integrated care eases some of the burden of caregiving, since the emotional stress is reduced when a professional explains what is needed and who can do it.

In one study, a year after a professional planned and coordinated care, family caregivers improved in their overall attitude and quality of life. They spent the same amount of time in caregiving before and after professional help, but their tasks changed, with more time spent on household tasks (e.g., meal preparation and cleanup) and less on direct care (Janse et al., 2014).

Professionals also know what is needed for elders to care for themselves. For example, a pill container can be locked but then opened when an alarm indicates that it is time to take the medicine. That avoids both over- and undermedication, and thus fosters more independence. Similarly, a large-screen video hookup can allow an older person to age in place while the caregiver lives elsewhere, visiting in person when necessary. This screen can be activated day and night, enabling more freedom for both the elder and the caregiver, with companionship whenever desired.

Elder Abuse As you see, caregiving can lead to resentment and social isolation. That may increase rates of depression, sickness, and abuse (of either the frail person or the caregiver). Abuse is likely if:

- the *caregiver* suffers from emotional problems or substance abuse;
- the *care receiver* is frail, confused, and demanding;
- the *care location* is isolated, where visitors are few.

Each of these factors increases the risk, and each of them is apparent before abuse begins (Chen & Dong, 2017). Ironically, although relatives are less able to cope with difficult patients than professionals are, they typically provide round-the-clock care. Those most vulnerable to abuse are older women who live with their caregivers and who suffer from neurocognitive problems as well as medical ones (Lachs & Pillemer, 2015).

Ideally, when one person becomes the caregiver, other family members provide respite care. Instead they may avoid visiting. If they suspect abuse, they may accuse the abuser, but they often keep "family secrets," avoiding outsiders.

Some caregivers overmedicate, lock doors, and use physical restraints, all of which may be abusive. That may lead to inadequate feeding, medical neglect, or rough treatment. Obvious abuse is less likely in nursing homes and hospitals, not only because laws forbid it but also because workers are not alone and are not expected to work 24/7.

That statement may raise questions in your mind, because publicity is likely to occur when an instance of abuse occurs in a hospital or long-term care facility. However, most instances of abuse occur within families and are never reported.

International research finds that elder abuse occurs everywhere. A meta-analysis estimated the prevalence at 16 percent (Yon et al., 2017). That number may be too high or too low because accurate incidence data and intervention are complicated by definitions. If an elder feels abused but a caregiver disagrees, who is right?

Long-Term Care

Although more than 90 percent of elders are independent and live in the community at any given moment, about 10 percent need some institutional care. Nursing-home and rehabilitation stays are often for less than a month after a few days in a hospital. However, some elders need specialized institutional care for more than a year, and a very few—the oldest and least capable—stay for 10 years or more. Variations in such care are vast.

Nursing Homes The trend in the United States and elsewhere is away from nursing homes and toward aging in place. Currently, residents of nursing homes tend to be the very old—at least age 85—with significant cognitive decline and several medical problems (Moore et al., 2012). They also are disproportionately widows (because men are usually married or remarried and die before their wives), with no capable descendants.

The skill of the staff, especially of the aides who provide frequent personal care, is crucial: Such simple tasks as helping a frail person out of bed can be done either clumsily and painfully or skillfully and patiently. Currently, however, many

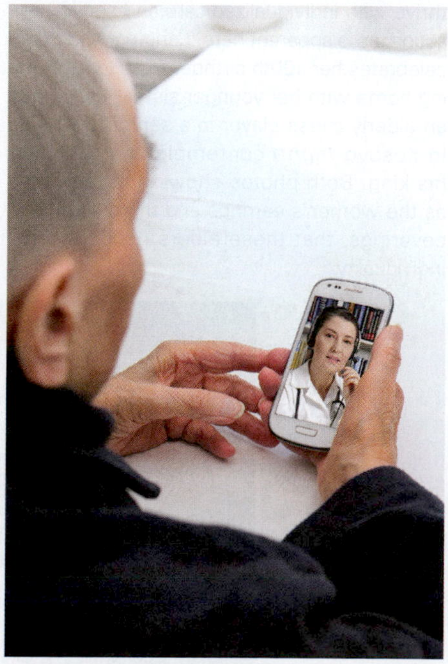
Anja Schaefer/Alamy Stock Photo

Always There This elderly man can simply push one button to speak with his doctor.

A CASE TO STUDY

A Trusted Sister

Most elder abuse is not physical, and some of the elderly are quiet, or lose weight, or accuse others for reasons other than abuse. Often elder abuse is financial, yet bankers, lawyers, and investment advisors are not trained to recognize it or obligated to respond and notify anyone.

Generally, abuse cases do not reach the courts unless the abuse is ongoing and extreme. Professionals and relatives alike hesitate to spot and then question a family caregiver who spends the Social Security check, disrespects the elder, or does not comply with the elder's demands. At what point is this abuse? Typically, abuse begins gradually and continues unnoticed for years. Political and legal definitions and remedies are not clear-cut (Dong & Simon, 2011).

Consider this example.

> A sister [Mrs. Watson] made large withdrawals from her elderly brother's bank account. The victim, Mr Clark, was admitted to hospital after a serious fall. He had cognitive impairment and subsequently his mental capacity deteriorated. His sister began to look after his finances. Mrs Watson claimed that Mr Clark intended for her to have the money which she withdrew, describing it as her 'slush fund'. The Judge noted that Mr Clark was suffering from dementia and therefore was vulnerable, he trusted his sister but she had betrayed his trust, and she did not show remorse or appreciate that her actions were wrong, but acted out of greed rather than need. Mrs Watson was sentenced to ten months under house arrest followed by one year of probation. The Judge took into account that she had no prior criminal record, was unlikely to reoffend, and had provided personal care to her brother before he was admitted to hospital.
>
> [Matthews, 2018, p. 75]

As you see, the judge and the sister disagree as to whether this was greed, not need. Is a courtroom the best place to decide such a case? Developmental scientists are working to define elder abuse (S. Han et al., 2019).

However, a recent review by the U.S. Preventive Services Task Force reported "no valid, reliable screening tools in the primary care setting to identify abuse of older or vulnerable adults without recognized signs and symptoms of abuse" (U.S. Preventive Services Task Force, 2018, p. 1681).

In other words, although financial and emotional abuse is far more common among elders than bruises and broken limbs, there is no good method to decide whether abuse has occurred. This is a challenge for future scientists, including some who are reading this book!

front-line workers have little training, low pay, and too many patients—and almost half leave each year (Golant, 2011).

Currently in the United States, many aides in nursing homes are immigrants, some with a limited understanding of the language or background of the residents. One group who frequently work in nursing home are those from Africa, which has a tradition of respect for the aged. Immigrants from Africa tend to have trouble finding other jobs, so working as an aide is a good first step, but they often leave that job within a few years (Covington-Ward, 2017).

In North America, good nursing-home care is available for those who can afford it and know what to look for. Some nursing homes provide individualized, humane care, allowing residents to decide what to eat, where to walk, whether to have a pet. Some excellent nonprofit homes are subsidized by religious organizations.

Same Situation, Far Apart: Diversity Continues No matter where they live, elders thrive with individualized care and social interaction, as is apparent here. Lenore Walker *(left)* celebrates her 100th birthday in a Florida nursing home with her younger sister nearby, and an elderly chess player in a senior residence in Kosovo *(right)* contemplates protecting his king. Both photos show, in details such as the women's earrings and the men's head coverings, that these elders maintain their individuality.

Taylor Jones © The Palm Beach Post/ZUMAPRESS.com/ZUMA Press Inc / Alamy

VALDRIN XHEMAJ/Newscom/European Pressphoto Agency/ PRISTINA/KOSOVO/Serbia

Good care encourages independence, individual choice, and privacy. This is called "person-centered care" and is now a goal of most nursing homes (Simmons & Rahman, 2014). As with day care for young children, continuity of care is crucial: A high rate of staff turnover is a bad sign.

At every age, relationships with other people are crucial: If the residents have the same caregivers year after year, that improves well-being. A nationwide survey of nursing-home residents found that almost all thought it was very important that every effort be made to provide continuity of care.

Quality care is much more labor-intensive and expensive than most people realize. Variations are dramatic, primarily because of the cost of personnel. According to John Hancock Life & Health Insurance Company in 2015, the cost of a year in a private room at a nursing home was $200,750 in Alaska and $56,575 in Louisiana. (Most people think that Medicare, Medicaid, or long-term insurance covers the entire cost—a gross misconception.)

Especially for Those Uncertain About Future Careers Would you like to work in a nursing home? (see response, page 658)

Alternative Care An ageist stereotype is that older people are either completely capable of self-care or completely dependent on others. In actuality, everyone is on a continuum, capable of some self-care and yet needing some help.

Once that is understood, a range of options can be envisioned. Recall the study cited in Chapter 24 that found that major NCD is less common in England than it used to be. That study also found that the percentage of people with neurocognitive disorders in nursing homes has risen (from 56 percent in 1991 to 65 percent in 2011) primarily because of a rise in the number of oldest-old women in such places (Matthews et al., 2013).

This means that more British elderly who need some care are now in the community. This is good news for the elderly, for developmentalists, and for the economy, because aging in place, assisted living, and other options cost less and have individualized care.

The number of assisted-living facilities has increased as the number of nursing homes has decreased. Typically, assisted-living residences provide private apartments for each person and allow pets and furnishings as in a traditional home.

The "assisted" aspects vary, often one daily communal meal, special transportation and activities, household cleaning, and medical assistance, such as supervision of pill-taking and blood pressure or diabetes monitoring, with a nurse, doctor, and ambulance if needed. In the United States, these assistances incur additional expenses. As the number of assisted-living places increases, a concern arises about the lack of oversight (Han et al., 2017). As with nursing homes, quality varies a great deal.

Douglas C. Pizac/AP Images

STR/Getty Images

Many Possibilities This couple in Wyoming *(left)* sold their Georgia house and now live in this RV, and this Cuban woman *(right)* continues to live in her familiar home. Ideally, all of the elderly have a range of choices—and when that is true, almost no one needs nursing-home care.

Assisted-living facilities range from group homes for three or four elderly people to large apartments or townhouse developments for hundreds. Almost every state, province, or nation has its own standards for assisted-living facilities, but many such places are unlicensed. Some regions of the world (e.g., northern Europe) have many assisted-living options, while others (e.g., sub-Saharan Africa) have almost none.

The first step in figuring out the best care—a step that should be taken long before a person needs to move to a nursing facility—is to invite a public health nurse to the home to assess needs. As one advocate of personalized care wrote:

> In the home, nurses sit around all kinds of kitchen tables, on rickety wooden chairs and sleek bar stools, experiencing firsthand the diverse ways people live, care and connect. Interactions with family, friends and neighbours are generally frequent—and in some cases, noticeably absent.
>
> *[Sharkey & Lefebre, 2017, p. 11]*

Overall, the emphasis in living arrangements is on selective optimization with compensation. Elders need settings that allow them to be safe, social, respected, and as independent as possible. Housing solutions vary depending not only on ADLs and IADLs but also on the elder's personality and social network of family and friends. (The photo on page 634 shows one of the best.)

We close with a wonderful example of family care and nursing-home care at their best. A young adult named Rob related that his 98-year-old great-grandmother "began to fail. We . . . thought, well, maybe she is growing old" (quoted in Adler, 1995, p. 242). All three younger generations decided that she should move to a nearby nursing home, leaving the place she had lived for decades. She reluctantly agreed.

Fortunately, this nursing home did not assume that decline is always a sign of "final failing" (Rob's phrase). The doctors discovered that her pacemaker was not working properly. Rob tells what happened next:

> We were very concerned to have her undergo surgery at her age, but we finally agreed. . . . Soon she was back to being herself, a strong, spirited, energetic, independent woman. It was the pacemaker that was wearing out, not Great-grandmother.
>
> *[quoted in Adler, 1995, p. 242]*

This story contains a lesson repeated throughout this book. Whenever a toddler does not talk, a preschooler grabs a toy, a teenager gets drunk, an emerging adult takes risks, an adult seeks divorce, or an older person becomes frail, it is easy to conclude that it is normal. Indeed, each of these possible problems is common at the ages mentioned and may be appropriate and acceptable for some individuals. But none should simply be accepted without question. Each should also alert others to encourage talking, sharing, moderation, caution, communication, or self-care. The life-span perspective holds that, at every age, people can be "strong, spirited, and energetic."

WHAT HAVE YOU LEARNED?

1. What factors make an older person frail?
2. What are the basic differences between ADLs and IADLs?
3. Why might IADLs be more important than ADLs in deciding whether a person needs care?
4. How is cognitive decline related to prevention of frailty?
5. What three factors increase the likelihood of elder abuse?
6. What are the advantages and disadvantages of assisted living for the elderly?
7. What factors distinguish a good nursing home from a bad one?

SUMMARY

Theories of Late Adulthood

1. Self theories hold that adults make personal choices in ways that allow them to become fully themselves. One such theory arises from Erikson's last stage, integrity versus despair, in which individuals seek integrity that connects them to the human community.

2. Compulsive hoarding can be understood as an effort to hold onto the self, keeping objects from the past that others might consider worthless.

3. Stratification theories maintain that social forces—such as ageism, racism, and sexism—limit personal choices throughout the life span, keeping people on a particular level or stratum of society.

4. Age stratification can be blamed for the disengagement of older adults. Activity theory counters disengagement theory, stressing that older people need to be active.

5. In late adulthood, some aspects of stratification theory seem apt, but others do not.

Activities in Late Adulthood

6. At every age, employment can provide social and personal satisfaction as well as needed income. Retirement may be welcomed because it enables other activities.

7. Some elderly people perform volunteer work and are active politically—writing letters, voting, staying informed. Many also value religious beliefs and practices.

8. Most of the elderly want to age in place. Many engage in home improvement.

9. Older adults in long-standing marriages tend to be satisfied with their relationships and to safeguard each other's health. As a result, married elders tend to live longer, happier, and healthier lives than unmarried ones.

10. Friends and other relatives are important for health and happiness lifelong. The social circle shrinks, but it may become deeper.

11. Relationships with adult children and grandchildren are usually mutually supportive, although conflicts arise as well. Financial support usually flows down the generational ladder.

The Frail Elderly

12. Most elderly people are self-sufficient, but some eventually become frail. They need help, either with physical tasks (ADLs such as eating and bathing) or with instrumental ones (IADLs such as completing income taxes).

13. Care of the frail elderly is usually undertaken by adult children or by spouses, who are often elderly themselves. Most families have a strong sense of filial responsibility.

14. Elder abuse is a problem worldwide. It occurs because of a combination of caregiver characteristics, care receiver characteristics, and reluctance to get help when needed. Abuse can be financial, physical, or emotional.

15. Nursing homes, assisted living, and professional home care are of varying quality and availability. Good care for the frail elderly is personalized, combining professional and family support while recognizing diversity in needs and personality.

KEY TERMS

self theories (p. 636)
integrity versus despair (p. 637)
compulsive hoarding (p. 638)
socioemotional selectivity theory (p. 638)
positivity effect (p. 638)
stratification theories (p. 638)
disengagement theory (p. 640)
activity theory (p. 640)
age in place (p. 643)
naturally occurring retirement community (NORC) (p. 644)
filial responsibility (p. 646)
frail elderly (p. 649)
activities of daily life (ADLs) (p. 649)
instrumental activities of daily life (IADLs) (p. 649)
integrated care (p. 652)

APPLICATIONS

1. Political attitudes vary by family and by generation. Interview several generations within the same family about issues of national and local importance, such as education, immigration, climate, or LGBTQ family member. How do you explain the similarities and differences between the generations? What is more influential: experience, SES, heritage, or age?

2. People of different ages, cultures, and experiences vary in their values regarding family caregiving, including the need for safety, privacy, independence, and professional help. Find four people whose backgrounds (age, ethnicity, SES) differ. Ask their opinions and analyze the results.

3. A major expense for many older people is health care, both routine and catastrophic. Government payment for health care expenses (hospitals, drugs, and preventive care) varies widely from nation to nation. Compare two nations, your own and one other, on specifics of coverage and on data that indicate the health of the elderly (rates of longevity, diseases, etc.).

4. Visit a nursing home or assisted-living residence in your community. Record details about the physical setting, the social interactions of the residents, and the activities of the staff. Would you like to work or live in this place? Why or why not?

Especially For ANSWERS

Response for Social Scientists (from p. 641): In general, psychologists favor self theories, and sociologists favor stratification theories. Of course, each discipline respects the other, but each believes that its perspective is more honest and accurate.

Response for Religious Leaders (from p. 644): There are many possible answers, including the specifics of getting to church (transportation, stairs), physical comfort in church (acoustics, temperature), and content (unfamiliar hymns and language).

Response for Those Uncertain About Future Careers (from p. 655): Why not? The demand for good workers will obviously increase as the population ages, and the working conditions are likely to improve. An important problem is that the quality of nursing homes varies, so you need to make sure you work in one whose policies incorporate the view that the elderly can be quite capable, social, and independent.

Observation Quiz ANSWERS

Answer to Observation Quiz (from p. 643): Late adulthood. The hard question is why that is the case.

Answer to Observation Quiz (from p. 651): He has an activity that he enjoys (recorder playing), he walks regularly (that walking stick), he breathes unpolluted air (mountain town), he is religious (it is Easter, so he is probably Greek Orthodox), his community values him (he was chosen to play), he is male (men are more likely to die quickly), and he has a healthy diet (the Mediterranean diet—with lots of fish, vegetables, and olive oil, the healthiest diet we know). Of course, we cannot be certain, but chances are this man has many more healthy years.

CAREER ALERT The Developmental Scientist

The need for developmental scientists is apparent: Much more must be learned about "how and why people—all kinds of people—change over time." Would-be researchers must become scholars who know what has already been studied—earning at least a master's degree. Leaders in developmental science almost always need a Ph.D. as well.

Often scholars need further study as they work as "post-docs," researching and writing after their doctoral degree under the direction of a leading scientist at a major university. Sometimes they work in government offices such as the Centers for Disease Control or the Bureau of Labor Statistics. Sometimes they teach developmental psychology at colleges, universities, or community centers.

Learning how to design valid research is an important beginning. Beyond the basics described in Chapter 1, many details of valid research have been developed. For example, to achieve multicultural understanding, a scholar often lives in another culture, absorbing its practices and values.

In research within that culture, words and phrases of questionnaires are typically translated by a bilingual native speaker and then back-translated by someone else. Back translation requires someone who is fluent in both languages to read the translated text and restore it to English (or whatever the first language was) to make sure the translation conveys the original meaning.

Then, in a pilot study, the questionnaire is administered to people who are similar to those who will take it in the full study. They interpret the questions, raise concerns, and suggest whether a particular question is misleading or whether the entire direction of the study is off the mark. Experts in statistics are consulted to suggest the proper analysis, as well as to advise how many participants are needed. The scientists who undertake the research must read published studies, consult colleagues, and work together.

In many instances, study participants do not know the goal of the research: They are said to be "blind" to the experimenter's goal. This deception prevents conscious or unconscious efforts to either validate or undermine the study. An ethical mandate is that any deception must be explained to the participants after their involvement.

Scientists may need to be "blind," as well: They do not directly interact with the participants of the study so that they cannot inadvertently clue responses. The entire endeavor requires many people to design, implement, and interpret the research. This is where novice scientists are crucial. Depending on the particulars, novices may do most of the hard work of implementing the design.

All of this is expensive: Some of the work of the scientist is to convince other people (foundations, government, private philanthropists) to support a particular study.

Another necessity is knowledge of statistics. There are many ways to analyze numbers and verbal responses to ensure that results which seem conclusive are really so. Those who wish to be developmental scientists study statistics for at least a semester—more often a year or longer. Some statistical measures are shown in Table 1.4 on page 19, but there are many more.

Once a study is completed and analyzed and its conclusions are drawn, but before it is published, the written report is subject to peer review. This means that other scientists (peers) who are not involved in the study read the unpublished report, make suggestions, and, finally, determine whether it is sufficiently well designed, honest, and clear for publication.

If students are preparing to become developmental scientists, they are likely to take courses in which they summarize and critique published studies so that they are ready to be peer reviewers. In order to earn a Ph.D., a student must undertake innovative research and write the results, usually in a thesis that is at least 100 pages long—more often double or triple that.

Most important of all is that the scientists follow ethical guidelines, always protecting the participants. This is so crucial that some mandates are explained at the end of Chapter 1 because everyone, scientist or not, must understand it.

Some who study this textbook will become developmental scientists, always ethical but going far beyond the basics explained here. Some of the work is tedious, some of the course requirements seem irrelevant, and some results of the research are discouraging. However, for those who choose this career, the joy of new discovery seems well worth the effort, and the potential reward—a better life for thousands of people who benefit from the research—makes all of the work worthwhile. Go for it!

VISUALIZING DEVELOPMENT Living Independently After Age 65

Most people who reach age 65 not only survive a decade or more, but also live independently.

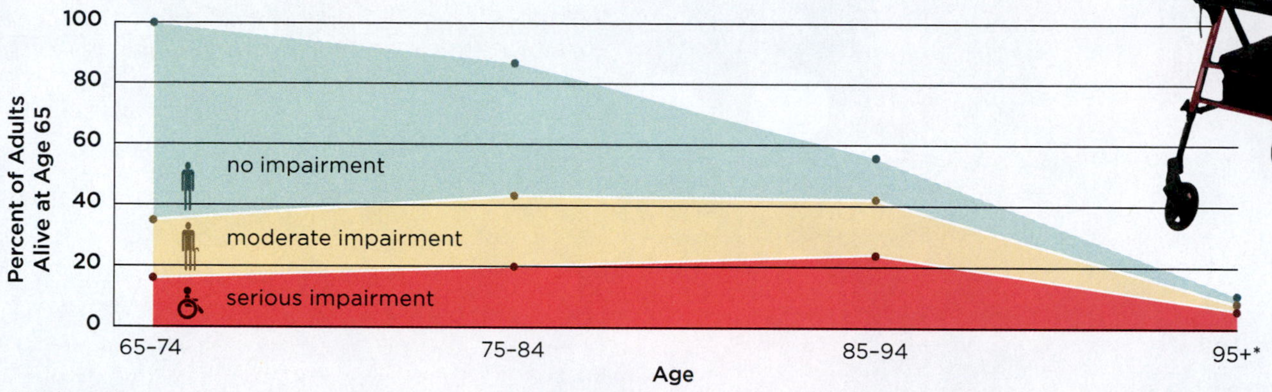

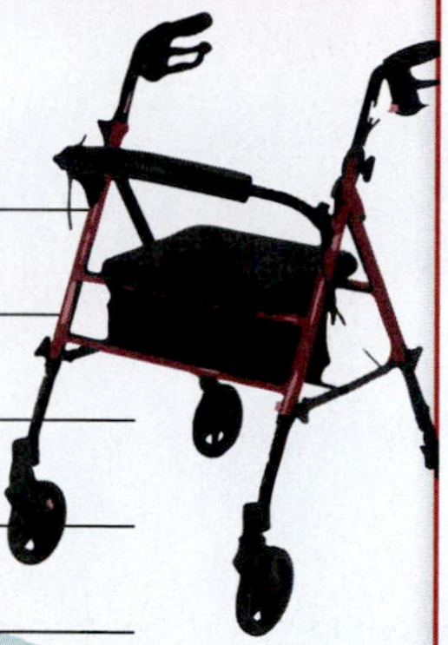

*With each year after 95, some survivors are still self-sufficient!

AGE 65

Of 100 people, in the next decade: Most will care for all their basic needs. But, 35 will become unable to take care of at least one instrumental activity of daily living (IADL) like household chores or taking care of finances, or one activity of daily living (ADL) like bathing, dressing, or getting in and out of bed. And 16 are so impaired that they need extensive care. 87 will survive another decade.

AGE 75

Of the 87 people who survived, in the next decade: About half will not need help caring for their basic needs. But 43 will become unable to take care of at least one IADL or ADL. And half of these 43 become so impaired that they require extensive care. 56 will survive another decade.

AGE 85

Of the 56 people who survived, in the next decade: Most need help. 42 will be unable to take care of at least one IADL or ADL. And 24 of them become so impaired that they require extensive care. Only 11 will survive another decade.

AGE 95

Of the 11 people who survived, in the next decade: Those who reach 95 live for about four more years, on average. Most need some help, and about half require extensive care.

Data from Arias et al., 2017.

WITH WHOM? WHERE?

As you see, there are many ways to depict life after 65, but the overall conclusion is the same: Most older people function well, especially if they are in a relationship with a partner who provides emotional and practical support, in the community where they have always lived. It is also true that over age 85, most people need some help.

LIVING ARRANGEMENTS OF PERSONS 65+

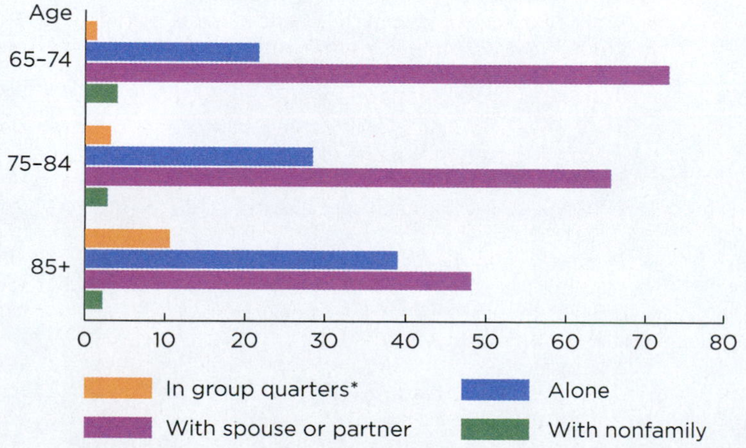

*Include nursing homes, assisted living, and other health care facilities

Data from Roberts et al., 2018.

PERSONS 65+ AS A PERCENTAGE OF TOTAL POPULATION

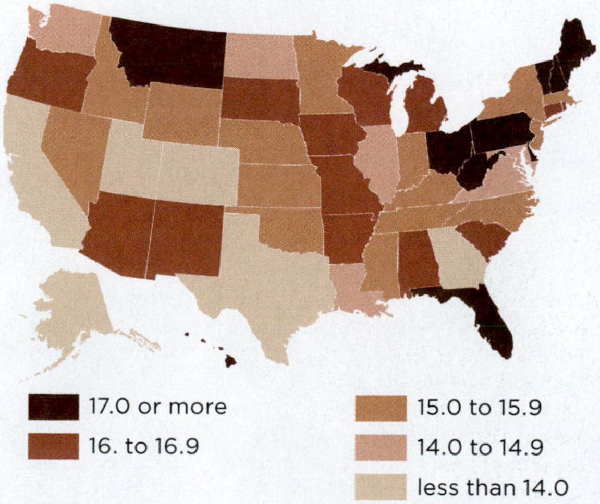

Data from U.S. Census Bureau, October 30, 2018.

EPILOGUE

Death and Dying

What Will You Know?

1. Why is death a topic of hope, not despair?
2. What is the difference between a good death and a bad one?
3. How does mourning help with grief?

- **Death and Hope**
  - Cultures, Epochs, and Death
  - Understanding Death Throughout the Life Span
  - Near-Death Experiences
- **Choices in Dying**
  - A Good Death
  - Better Ways to Die
  - Ethical Issues
  - A CASE TO STUDY: What is Your Intention?
  - OPPOSING PERSPECTIVES: The "Right to Die"?
  - Advance Directives
- **Affirmation of Life**
  - Grief
  - Mourning
  - Placing Blame and Seeking Meaning
  - Diversity of Reactions

"When is Pappy going to die?" asked a 4-year-old when he was in the car with Pappy (his grandfather), his grandmother, and his parents. Those three adults answered, "A lot of years"; "Not for a long, long time"; "We hope he never does."

That quieted the boy for a while. He had his birthday a week before and was acutely aware of time passing. He was no longer 3; he now had a new number, 4. That evening he asked his parents, "What is Pappy's last number?" And then, "What is my last number?"

The answer came after a pause. "We don't know" (Sekeres, 2013).

This chapter explores what we know and do not know about death. We know that everyone will have a "last number" and that Pappy's number is likely to come sooner than the boy's. We also know that humans, everywhere and for hundreds of thousands of years, have thought about death, burying the dead, and hoping for longer and better lives because of those who have gone before.

You will read about long-lasting cultural variations in death and bereavement. You will also ponder new ethical dilemmas, such as deciding when death occurs and what can be done to stop or postpone dying, or to make a good death more likely.

Ultimately, you will learn that "those who think dialectically [remember Chapter 18] work through the contradictions of a loss, and go on to experience significant growth following a traumatic event" (Tedeschi et al., 2017). There is *hope* in death, *choice* in dying, and *affirmation* in mourning, as each of the three main sections of this Epilogue describe.

Death and Hope

A multicultural life-span perspective reveals that reactions to death are filtered through many cultural prisms, affected by historical changes and regional variations as well as by the age of both the dying and the bereaved.

One emotion is constant, however: hope. It appears in many ways: hope for life after death, hope that the world is better because someone lived, hope that death occurred for a reason, hope that survivors rededicate themselves to whatever they deem meaningful in life. Immortality of some kind seems evident as people think about death (Robben, 2018).

Left: Pascal Deloche / Godong/Getty Images

TABLE EP.1

How Death Has Changed in the Past 100 Years

Death occurs later. A century ago, the average life span worldwide was less than 40 years (47 in the rapidly industrializing United States). Half of the world's babies died before age 5. Now newborns are expected to live to age 72 (79 in the United States); in many nations, centenarians are the fastest-growing age group.
Dying takes longer. In the early 1900s, death was usually fast and unstoppable. Once the brain, the heart, or any other vital organ failed, the rest of the body quickly followed. Now death can often be postponed through medical technology: Hearts can beat for years after the brain stops functioning, respirators can replace lungs, and dialysis does the work of failing kidneys.
Death often occurs in hospitals. For most of our ancestors, death occurred at home, with family nearby. Now most deaths occur in hospitals or other institutions, with the dying surrounded by medical personnel and machines.
Causes have changed. People of all ages once usually died of infectious diseases (tuberculosis, typhoid, smallpox), or, for many women and most infants, in childbirth. Now disease deaths before age 50 are rare, and in developed nations most newborns (99 percent) and their mothers (99.99 percent) live.
And after death . . . People once knew about life after death. Some believed in heaven and hell; others, in reincarnation; others, in the spirit world. Prayers were repeated—some on behalf of the souls of the deceased, some for remembrance, some to the dead asking for protection. Believers were certain that their prayers were heard. People now are aware of cultural and religious diversity; many raise doubts that never occurred to their ancestors.

Cultures, Epochs, and Death

Many people in developed nations have never witnessed someone die. This was not always the case (see **Table EP.1**). If someone reached age 50 in 1900 in the United States and had had 20 high school classmates, at least six of those fellow students would have already died. The survivors would have visited and reassured their dying friends at home, promising to see them in heaven.

People today are less sure about heaven but still have hope. We begin by describing traditional responses when familiarity with death was common.

Ancient Times Paleontologists have evidence from 120,000 years ago that the Neanderthals buried their dead with tools, bowls, or jewelry, signifying belief in an afterlife (Stiner, 2017). The date is controversial: Burial with objects could have begun earlier, but it is certain that long ago death was an occasion for hope, mourning, and remembrance.

Two Western civilizations with written records—Egypt and Greece—had elaborate death rituals millennia ago. The ancient Egyptians built magnificent pyramids, refined mummification, and scripted instructions (called the *Book of the Dead*) to help the soul (*ka*), personality (*ba*), and shadow (*akh*) reunite after death so that the dead could protect the living (Taylor, 2010).

Another set of beliefs came from the ancient Greeks. Again, continuity between life and death was evident, with hope for this world and the next. The fate of a dead person depended on his or her life. A few would have a blissful afterlife, a few were condemned to torture in Hades, and most would enter a shadow world until they were reincarnated.

Ancient Chinese, Mayan, Indian, and African cultures also had rituals about death, and they venerated ancestors as still connected to the living in some way (Hill & Hageman, 2016). That gave survivors hope for themselves. Everywhere:

- Actions during life were thought to affect destiny after death.
- An afterlife was assumed.
- Mourners said prayers and made offerings to prevent the spirit of the dead from haunting and hurting them, and to gain blessing and strength from the ancestors.

Conversation Who is talking here? Unless you are an Egyptologist, you would not guess that this depicts a dead man conversing with the gods of the Underworld. Note that the deceased is relatively young and does not seem afraid—both typical for people in ancient Egypt.

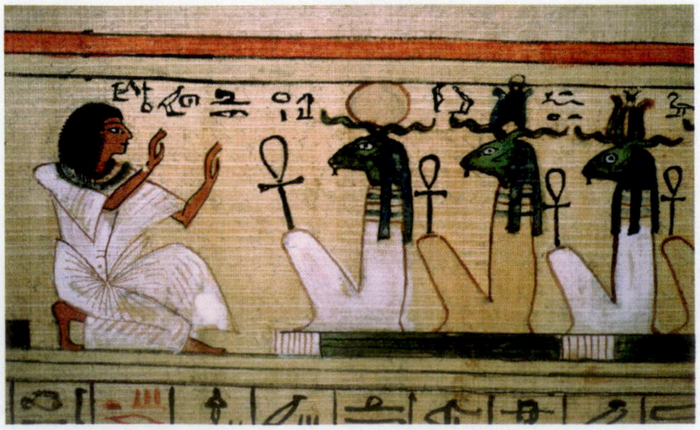

HIP/Art Resource, NY

Contemporary Beliefs Now consider contemporary beliefs. Diversity of customs and beliefs is apparent, yet common themes are also evident. It is now recognized that connections between the living and the dead continue, so each person and each community memorializes the dead in a way to help the survivors live on (Klass & Steffen, 2017).

This is evident in beliefs in life after death. Heaven? Purgatory? Hell? Rebirth and reincarnation? Continued presence on Earth as a spirit? Despite such differences, in all cultures and religions, death brings communities together, affirming sacrifice, continuity, and compassion. An international study of 890 people from four Asian cultures and 695 people from

North America found that most (including many of the 295 who said they were not religious) believed in life after death (Nichols et al., 2018).

Understanding Death Throughout the Life Span

Thoughts about death—as about everything else—are influenced by each person's age, cognitive maturation, and past experiences. Here are some of the specifics.

Death in Childhood Some adults think children are oblivious to death; others believe children should participate in funerals and other rituals, just as adults do. You know from your study of childhood cognition that neither view is completely correct.

Children are affected by the attitudes of others. They may be upset if they see grown-ups cry or if grown-ups keep them away from death rituals for someone they loved. Thus, adults should neither ignore the child's emotions nor expect mature reactions. Because the limbic system matures more rapidly than the prefrontal cortex, children may seem happy one day and morbidly depressed the next.

Johan Ordoñez/AFP/Getty Images

Sorrow All Around When a 5-day-old baby died in Santa Rosa, Guatemala, the entire neighborhood mourned. Symbols and a procession help with grief: The coffin is white to indicate that the infant was without sin and will therefore be in heaven.

Observation Quiz Beyond the coffin, do you see any other signs of ritual? (see answer, page 682) ↑

Young children who themselves are terminally ill typically fear that death means being abandoned (Wolchik et al., 2008). Consequently, parents should stay with a dying child—holding, reading, singing, and sleeping. A frequent and caring presence is more important than logic.

By school age, many children seek independence. Parents and professionals can be too solicitous; older children do not want to be babied if they are dying or if someone else is dying. They want facts and a role in "management of illness and treatment decisions" (Varga & Paletti, 2013, p. 27).

Adults always need to listen to children, avoiding lies or platitudes (Stevenson, 2017). Children who lose a friend, a relative, or a pet might, or might not, seem sad, lonely, or angry. If a child is told that Grandma is sleeping, that God wanted a sibling in heaven, or that Grandpa went on a trip, there are two possibilities, neither of them good.

(1) The first is that the child believes the explanation and insists on waking up Grandma, complaining to God, or phoning Grandpa to say, "Come home."

(2) The second is worse. If adults lie, the child may conclude that death is so terrifying to adults that they cannot be trusted to talk about it.

As children become concrete operational thinkers, they seek facts, such as exactly how a person died and where that person is now. They want something to do: bring flowers, repeat a prayer, write a letter. Interestingly, older children are better able to understand that death is a biological event and that the dead cannot come back to life. But simultaneously they also are more likely to accept a religious/spiritual understanding. They see no contradiction in that (Harris, 2018).

Death in Adolescence and Emerging Adulthood Remember that adolescent emotions are powerful and erratic, changing quickly. Adolescents may be self-absorbed, philosophical, analytic, or distraught—or all four at different moments. Self-expression is part of the search for identity; death of a loved one does not put an end to that search. Some adolescents use social media to write to the dead person or to vent their grief—an effective way to express their personal identity concerns (Balk & Varga, 2017).

"Live fast, die young, and leave a good-looking corpse" is advice often attributed to actor James Dean, who died in a car crash at age 24. At what stage would a person be most likely to agree? Emerging adulthood, of course (see **Figure EP.1**).

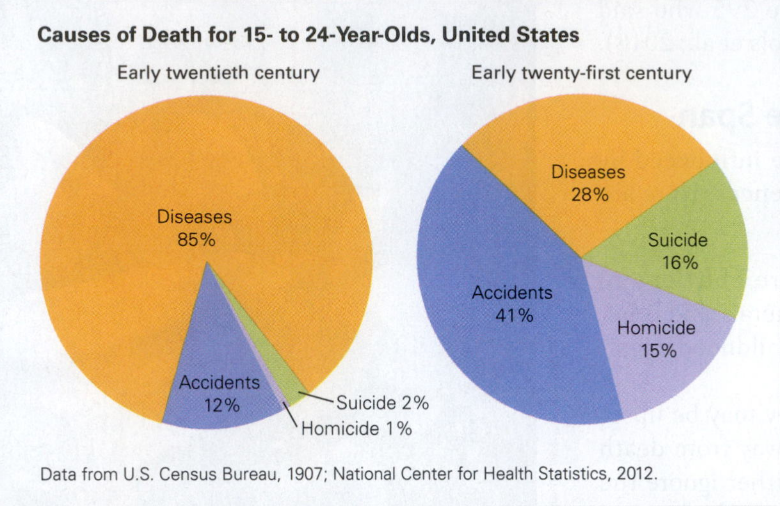

FIGURE EP.1
Typhoid Versus Driving into a Tree In 1905, most young adults in the united states who died were victims of diseases, usually infectious ones like tuberculosis and typhoid. In 2012, almost three times more died violently (accidents, homicide, and suicide) than died of all diseases combined.

Observation Quiz Which cause of death shows the greatest change over the past century? (see answer, page 682) ↑

terror management theory The idea that people adopt cultural values and moral principles in order to cope with their fear of death. This system of beliefs protects individuals from anxiety about their mortality and bolsters their self-esteem.

Terror management theory explains some illogical responses to death. The idea is that people who fear death become more defensive of their own culture, more ageist, and more likely to take risks (Burke et al., 2010). They manage their terror by defying death. Terror management is particularly evident among college students and seems to disappear when people are middle-aged or older (Maxfield et al., 2007).

Terror management may explain an illogical action by some adolescents in Florida who suffer from asthma. Compared to high school students without asthma, they are *more* likely to use tobacco products (28 percent versus 24 percent). That includes higher rates of smoking cigarettes and cigars, which they know are harmful for their lungs (Reid et al., 2018).

Death in Adulthood When adults become responsible for work and family, attitudes shift. Death is not romanticized. Many adults quit addictive drugs, start wearing seat belts, and adopt other death-avoiding behaviors when they reach age 30 or so.

Adults who are dying may be less concerned about themselves than about the other people they will leave, especially children. It helps if they write a letter to the child to be opened at some age—such as 18—so they know that their love and care will continue after they die.

Many adults seek comfort in religious values. That helps many but not everyone. Research finds that religious beliefs sometimes increase death anxiety, although they usually decrease it (Jong et al., 2017). Variation occurs partly because religions differ in attitudes about death.

To defend against their own fears, adults do not accept the death of others. When Dylan Thomas was about age 30, he wrote to his dying father: "Do not go gentle into that good night/Rage, rage against the dying of the light" (Thomas, 2003, p. 239). Adults also do not accept their own death. A woman diagnosed at age 42 with a rare and almost always fatal cancer (*sarcoma*) wrote:

> I hate stories about people dying of cancer, no matter how graceful, noble, or beautiful. . . . I refuse to accept I am dying; I prefer denial, anger, even desperation.
>
> *[Robson, 2010, pp. 19, 27]*

Adult reactions depend partly on the age of the deceased. Millions of people mourned Heath Ledger, Prince, and Whitney Houston (ages 28, 57, and 48, respectively). Equally talented entertainers who die at age 80 or 90 are less mourned.

Logically, adults should work to change social factors that increase the risk of mortality—such as air pollution, junk food, and unsafe cars. Instead, many react more strongly to rare causes of death, such as anthrax and avalanches. They particularly fear deaths beyond their control.

For example, people fear travel by plane more than by car. In fact, flying is safer: In 2017 in the entire world, only 399 people were killed in airplane accidents; but in the United States alone, 40,100 were killed by motor vehicles, according to the National Safety Council.

Ironically, after four airplanes were hijacked by terrorists on September 11, 2001, many North Americans drove long distances because they were afraid to fly. In the next few months, 2,300 more U.S. residents died in car crashes than usual (Blalock et al., 2009). Not logical, but certainly very human.

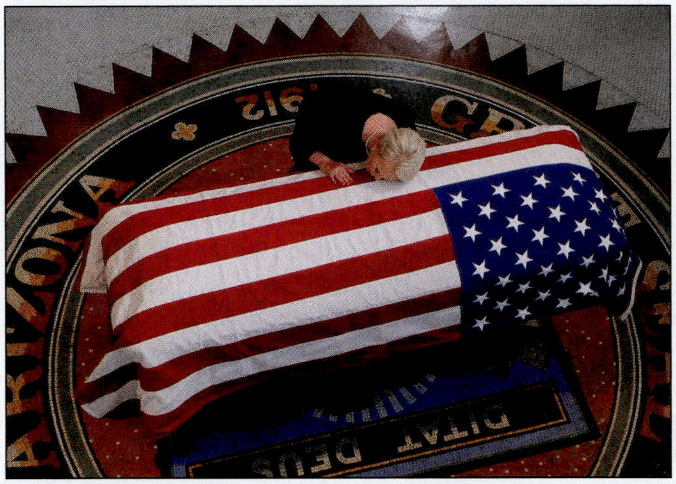

Ross D. Franklin/Getty Images

Scott Olson/Getty Images

Bot on August 31, 2018 Every culture mourns the dead, but variations are vast. Two famous Americans died at the end of August 2018. Senator John McCain lay in state at the U.S. capitol in Washington D.C., with his widow kissing his flag-draped casket. The Queen of Soul, Aretha Franklin, lay in a flower-covered casket in a Detroit church, as thousands cried while Ariana Grande sang Franklin's hit song, "(You Make Me Feel Like) A Natural Woman."

Death in Late Adulthood In late adulthood, attitudes shift again. Anxiety decreases; hope rises (De Raedt et al., 2013).

Some older people remain happy when they are terminally ill. Many developmentalists believe that one sign of mental health among older adults is acceptance of mortality, which increases concern for others. Some elders engage in *legacy work,* trying to leave something meaningful for later generations (Lattanzi-Licht, 2013).

As evidence of this attitude change, older people seek to reconcile with estranged family members and tie up loose ends. Do not be troubled when elders allocate heirlooms, discuss end-of-life wishes, or buy a burial plot: All of those actions are developmentally appropriate.

Acceptance of death does not mean that the elderly give up on living; rather, their priorities shift. In an intriguing series of studies (Carstensen, 2011), people were presented with the following scenario:

> Imagine that in carrying out the activities of everyday life, you find that you have half an hour of free time, with no pressing commitments. You have decided that you'd like to spend this time with another person. Assuming that the following three persons are available to you, whom would you want to spend that time with?
>
> - A member of your immediate family
> - The author of a book you have just read
> - An acquaintance with whom you seem to have much in common

Older adults, more than younger ones, choose the family member (see **Figure EP.2**). The researchers explain that family becomes more important when death seems near.

FIGURE EP.2

Turning to Family as Death Approaches Both young and old people diagnosed with cancer (one-fourth of whom died within five years) more often preferred to spend a free half-hour with a family member rather than with an interesting person whom they did not know well.

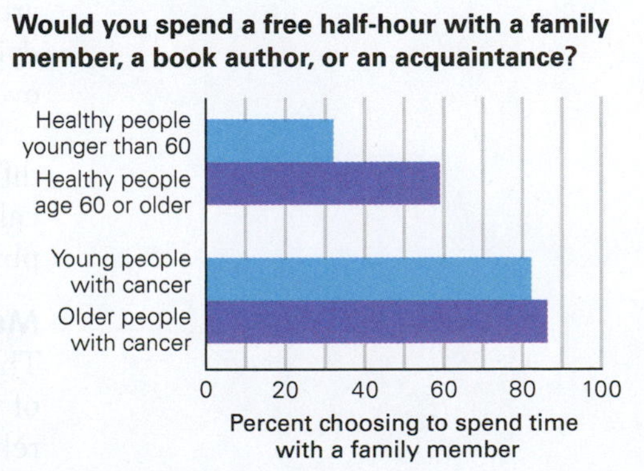

Data from Pinquart & Silbereisen, 2006.

Near-Death Experiences

At every age, coming close to death may be an occasion for hope. This is most obvious in what is called a *near-death experience,* in which a person almost dies. Survivors sometimes report having left the body and moved toward a bright light while feeling peace and joy. The following classic report is typical:

> I was in a coma for approximately a week. . . . I felt as though I were lifted right up, just as though I didn't have a physical body at all. A brilliant white light appeared. . . . The most wonderful feelings came over me—feelings of peace, tranquility, a vanishing of all worries.
>
> *[quoted in Moody, 1975, p. 56]*

THINK CRITICALLY: When a person is almost dead, might thoughts occur that are not limited by the neuronal connections in the brain?

Near-death experiences often include religious elements (angels seen, celestial music heard). Survivors often become more spiritual, less materialistic.

A reviewer of near-death experiences is struck by their endorsement of religious beliefs. In every culture, "all varieties of the dying experience" move people toward the same realizations: (1) the limitations of social status, (2) the insignificance of material possessions, and (3) the narrowness of self-centeredness (Greyson, 2009).

In fact, people who have merely heard about near-death experiences from other people tend to have some of the same emotions, feeling more spiritual and less materialistic (Tassell-Matamua et al., 2017). That brings us back to a general theme. Thinking about death can make people more hopeful about the future—their own and that of others.

WHAT HAVE YOU LEARNED?

1. In ancient cultures, how did people deal with death?
2. What are the common themes in religious understanding about death?
3. How do children respond to death?
4. Why might fear of death lead to more risk taking?
5. How does being closer to one's own death affect a person's attitudes?
6. In what ways do people change after a near-death experience?

Choices in Dying

Do you recoil at the heading "Choices in Dying"? If so, you may be living in the wrong century. Every twenty-first-century death involves choices, beginning with risks taken or avoided, habits sustained, and specific measures to postpone or hasten death.

A Good Death

People everywhere hope for a good death, one that is:

- At the end of a long life
- Peaceful
- Quick
- In familiar surroundings
- With family and friends present
- Without pain, confusion, or discomfort

Many would add that *control over circumstances* and *acceptance of the outcome* are also characteristic of a good death, but cultures and individuals differ. Some dying individuals willingly cede control to doctors or caregivers, and others fight every sign that death is near.

A review finds that family, medical personnel, and the dying person emphasize different aspects of "a good death" (Meier et al., 2016). One issue is psychological and spiritual well-being, which is important for many patients but less so for physicians.

Medical Care In some ways, modern medicine makes a good death more likely. The first item on the list has become the norm: Death usually occurs at the end of a long life. Younger people still get sick, but surgery, drugs, radiation, and rehabilitation typically mean that the ill enter a hospital and then return home. If young people die, their death is typically quick (a fatal accident or suicide) and without pain, although painful for their loved ones.

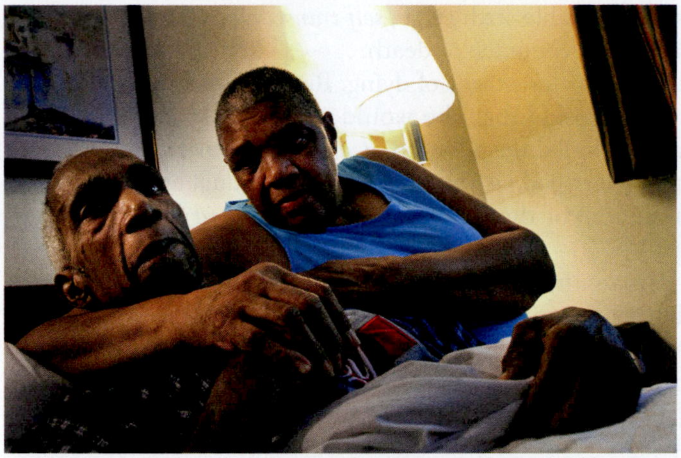

Jerry Wolford/Polaris/Newscom

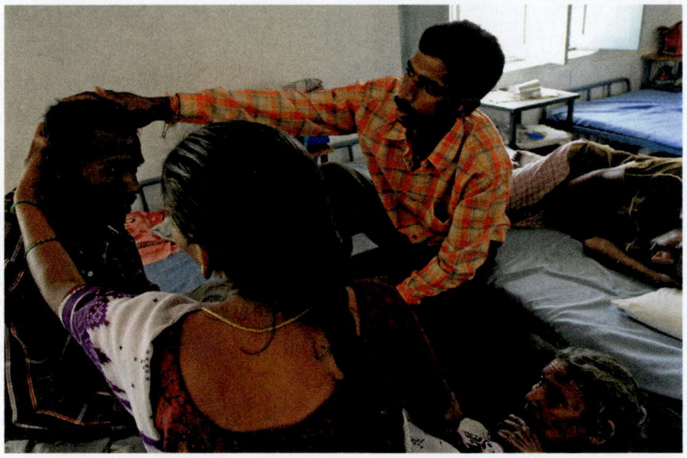

Chris Stowers/Panos Pictures

Same Situation, Far Apart: As It Should Be Dying individuals and their families benefit from physical touch and suffer from medical practices (gowns, tubes, isolation) that restrict movement and prevent contact. A good death is likely for these two patients—a husband with his wife in their renovated hotel/hospital room in North Carolina *(left)*, and a man with his family in a Catholic hospice in Andhra Pradesh, India *(right)*.

In other ways, however, medical advances make a bad death more likely. When a cure is impossible, physical and emotional comfort deteriorate. Nurses and doctors are slower to respond to a bell, explain less when they come, and use medical measures that increase pain. Hospitals may exclude visitors when a person is about to die; patients may become delirious or unconscious.

Although people want to die at home, most deaths in developed nations occur in hospitals. Even in England, where one published goal of public medicine is a good death, half of the deaths occur in hospitals, one-fourth in *care homes* (called *nursing homes* in the United States), and only one-fourth at home (Bone et al., 2018).

The underlying problem may be the medical care profession, which is so focused on lifesaving that dying is resisted (Lee, 2019). Medical staff members are taught about drugs, surgeries, and so on to heal the body; they may ignore the emotions of the patients or those who love them. They do not know what one pastor said: "Cancer is a family disease; dying is not a solo experience."

macmillan learning

VIDEO: End of Life: Interview with Laura Rothenberg features a young woman with a terminal illness discussing her feelings about death.

Stages of Dying Emotions were the focus of Elisabeth Kübler-Ross (1975, 1997). In about 1960, she asked the administrator of a large hospital for permission to speak with dying patients. He told her that no one was dying! Eventually, she found a few terminally ill patients who wanted very much to talk.

From ongoing interviews, Kübler-Ross identified reactions of dying people. She divided their emotions into five stages.

1. Denial ("I am not really dying.")
2. Anger ("I blame my doctors, or my family, or my God.")
3. Bargaining ("I will be good from now on if I can live.")
4. Depression ("I don't care; nothing matters anymore.")
5. Acceptance ("I accept my death as part of life.")

Especially for Relatives of a Person Who Is Dying Why would a healthy person want the attention of hospice caregivers? (see response, page 682)

Another set of stages of dying is based on Maslow's hierarchy (Zalenski & Raspa, 2006):

1. Physiological needs (freedom from pain)
2. Safety (no abandonment)
3. Love and acceptance (from close family and friends)
4. Respect (from caregivers)
5. Self-actualization (appreciating one's unique past and present)

Maslow later suggested a possible sixth stage, *self-transcendence* (Koltko-Rivera, 2006), which emphasizes the acceptance of death.

Other researchers have *not* found stages of dying. Remember the woman dying of sarcoma, cited earlier? She said that she would never *accept* death and that Kübler-Ross should have included desperation as a stage. Kübler-Ross said that her stages have been misunderstood, as "our grief is as individual as our lives. . . . Not everyone goes through all of them or goes in a prescribed order" (Kübler-Ross & Kessler, 2005, p. 7).

Nevertheless, both lists remind caregivers that each dying person has strong emotions and needs that may be unlike that same person's emotions and needs a few days or weeks earlier. These emotions may differ from those of the person's doctors and loved ones, who themselves have varied emotions. A good death recognizes dynamic changes in everyone's thoughts.

Telling the Truth Many wise contemporary physicians stress honest conversations (Gawande, 2014; Kalanithi, 2016). Knowing the truth allows the dying to choose appropriate care (including addictive painkillers, music or prayers that are personal to the individual, favorite foods, visits from distant relatives, and so on (Lundquist et al., 2011).

This ideal is difficult, because patients misunderstand, symptoms change, priorities shift. Some dying people do *not* want the whole truth, some want every possible medical intervention, some do *not* want visitors, some do *not* want to hear music that comforts someone else. Ideally, conversation among all concerned is interactive, occurring over weeks and months (Cripe & Frankel, 2017).

hospice An institution or program in which terminally ill patients receive palliative care to reduce suffering; family and friends of the dying are helped as well.

THINK CRITICALLY: What are the possible reasons that fewer people in hospice are from non-European backgrounds?

Better Ways to Die

Several practices have become more prevalent since the contrast between a good death and the usual hospital death has become clear. The hospice and palliative care are examples.

Hospice In London in the 1950s, Cecily Saunders opened the first modern **hospice,** where terminally ill people could spend their last days in comfort. Since then, thousands of hospices have opened in many nations, and hundreds of thousands of caregivers bring hospice care to dying people in hospitals and in homes.

Two principles characterize hospice care:

- Each patient's autonomy is respected. For example, pain medication is readily available, not on a schedule or set dosage.
- Family members and friends are counseled before the death, taught to provide care, and guided in mourning afterward. Death is thought to happen to a family, not just to an individual.

Hospice allows measures that hospitals may forbid: acupuncture, special foods, flexible schedules, visitors at midnight, excursions outside, massage, aromatic oils, religious rituals, and so on (Doka, 2013). Comfort takes precedence over cure, but that reduces stress and may extend life. Curative treatments are also allowed, although paying for them is complex. Some (about 16 percent) U.S. hospice patients are discharged alive, having gotten better unexpectedly.

Unfortunately, hospice does not reach everyone (see **Table EP.2**). It is more common in England than in

TABLE EP.2

Barriers to Entering Hospice Care

- Hospice patients must be terminally ill, with death anticipated within six months, but predictions are difficult. For example, in one study of noncancer patients, physician predictions were 90 percent accurate for those who died within a week but only 13 percent accurate when death was predicted in three to six weeks (usually the patients died sooner) (Brandt et al., 2006). Other research confirms that "death is highly unpredictable" (Einav et al., 2018, p. 1462).
- Patients and caregivers must accept death. Traditionally, entering a hospice meant the end of curative treatment (chemotherapy, dialysis, and so on). This is no longer true. Now treatment can continue. Many hospice patients survive for months, and some are discharged alive (Salpeter et al., 2012).
- Hospice care is costly. Skilled workers—doctors, nurses, psychologists, social workers, clergy, music therapists, and so on—provide individualized care day and night.
- Availability varies. Hospice care is more common in England than in mainland Europe and is a luxury in poor nations. In the United States, western states have more hospices than midwestern states do. Even in one region (northern California) and among clients of one insurance company (Kaiser), the likelihood that people with terminal cancer will enter hospice depends on exactly where they live (Keating et al., 2006).

mainland Europe, more common in the western part of the United States than the Southeast, and rare in poor nations.

Everywhere, hospice care correlates with higher income. Only recently have Medicare and Medicaid covered some hospice care, but if a person chooses hospice, payment for curative care stops, and room and board expenses are not covered. Thus, a poor person seeking hospice care must live at home and must agree that a cure is no longer possible.

Ethnic differences are apparent. For example, African Americans choose hospice about half as often as European Americans do. They are more likely to seek aggressive hospital care—which, ironically, means more pain and distress. One team suggests that African American churches should explain the spiritual benefits of hospice (Townsend et al., 2017).

Some private insurance policies pay for hospice *only* if a doctor certifies that the patient has less than six months to live, a judgment doctors are reluctant to render. One sad consequence: Hospice care usually begins within two weeks of death—too late for ideal personalized care (see **Figure EP.3**).

Where Death Occurs in the United States—2016

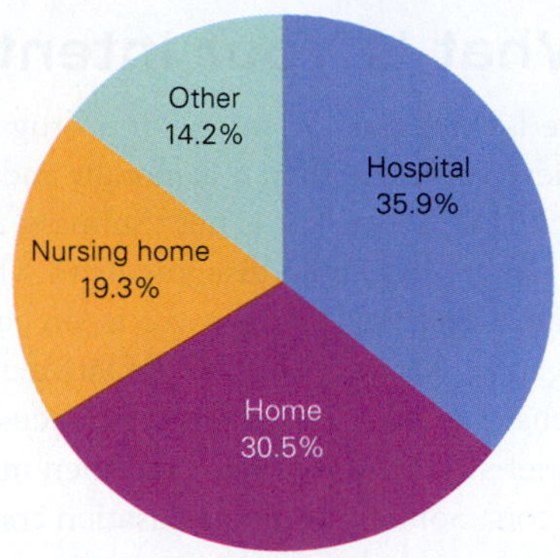

Data from Centers for Disease Control and Prevention, July 3, 2018.

FIGURE EP.3

Not with Family Almost everyone prefers to die at home, yet most people die in an institution, surrounded by medical personnel and high-tech equipment, not by the soft voices and gentle touch of loved ones. The "other" category is even worse, as it includes most lethal accidents or homicides. But don't be too saddened by this chart—improvement is possible. Twenty years ago, the proportion of home deaths was notably lower.

Palliative Care In 2006 the American Medical Association approved a new specialty, **palliative care,** which focuses on relieving pain and suffering. Palliative measures are not only for the dying; every patient may benefit. Palliative-care doctors prescribe powerful drugs and procedures that make patients comfortable, and they can treat nonlethal symptoms, such as rashes, muscle soreness, and nausea, with salves, foods, exercise, and meditation.

The need for skilled palliative care is obvious when one considers pain relief. Doctors have become very cautious in prescribing addictive opioids, yet high doses may be needed if someone has progressive cancer, or other painful conditions. Morphine and other opiates have a **double effect:** They relieve pain (a positive effect), but slow down respiration (a negative effect).

Painkillers that reduce both pain and breathing are allowed by law, ethics, and medical practice. Indeed, almost any medical measure has several effects. Surgery itself is removes or repairs something harmful, but causes pain, infection, and sometimes death.

Heavy sedation is sometimes used to stop suffering. However, sedation may delay death more than extend life, since an unconscious patient cannot think or feel. Is being unconscious, with no chance of recovery, worse than death itself?

palliative care Medical treatment designed primarily to provide physical and emotional comfort to the dying patient and guidance to his or her loved ones.

double effect When an action (such as administering opiates) has both a positive effect (relieving a terminally ill person's pain) and a negative effect (hastening death by suppressing respiration).

Ethical Issues

As you see, medical successes create new dilemmas. Death is no longer the natural outcome of age and disease; when and how death occurs involves human choices. (See A Case to Study.)

Deciding When Death Occurs One difficult ethical decision is deciding when a person is dead. This used to be simple: A person was dead when the heart stopped beating and the lungs no longer took in air. Now stopped hearts are restarted, breathing continues with respirators, feeding tubes provide calories, drugs fight pneumonia. At what point, if ever, should those interventions stop?

Almost every life-threatening condition results in treatments started, stopped, or avoided, with death postponed, prevented, or welcomed. This has fostered impassioned moral arguments, between nations (evidenced by radically different laws) and within them.

Religious advisers, doctors, and lawyers disagree with colleagues within their respective professions; family members have opposite opinions; and people within each group diverge. For example, outsiders might imagine that all Roman

A CASE TO STUDY

What Is Your Intention?

The law focuses on intent: If a drug or surgery is intended to relieve suffering, then it is morally and legally justifiable if death occurs. Otherwise, it is not (Sulmasy, 2018).

However, people disagree as to whether a drug, or surgery, or any other medical measure is, on balance, more positive than negative. About half of all palliative care physicians have been accused of killing a patient. The accusation usually comes from a grief-stricken loved one, and then medical facts exonerate the doctors. Sometimes the accusation comes from another medical person, and judgment become more complicated.

Consider a court case. A man with terminal cancer was terrified of future pain and loss of control, so his doctor gave him a drug that he could take if he reached the point where he could not bear living. That man told another doctor, who accused the first doctor of breaking the law as well as defying medical ethics. The first doctor argued that this was double effect: He was relieving the "existential suffering" of the patient (a positive effect), knowing that death might be the result (the negative effect). The first court found him guilty, but he appealed and was exonerated.

This troubled many others. One wrote:

> The offer to provide the drug was described as a palliative treatment in that it gave reassurance and comfort to the patient. Double effect reasoning was extended in this instance to encompass potentially facilitating a patient's death. This extension further muddies the murky double effect reasoning waters . . .
>
> *[Duckett, 2018, p. 33]*

Catholic leaders share the same views, but that is far from the truth (Bedford et al., 2017).

THINK CRITICALLY: At what point, if ever, should intervention stop to allow death?

Evidence of Death Historically, death was determined by listening to a person's chest: No heartbeat meant death. To make sure, a feather was put to the person's nose to indicate respiration—a person who had no heartbeat and did not exhale was pronounced dead. Very rarely, but widely publicized when it happened, death was declared when the person was still alive.

Modern medicine has changed that: Hearts and lungs need not function on their own. Many life-support measures and medical interventions circumvent the organ failures that once caused death. Checking breathing with feathers is a curiosity that, thankfully, is never used today.

But how do we know that a person is dead? In the late 1970s, a group of Harvard physicians concluded that death occurred when brain waves ceased, a definition now used worldwide (Wijdicks et al., 2010). Current criteria involve several tests of brain functioning (see **Table EP.3**). However, people are still uneasy about the declaration of death (Lewis & Greer, 2017).

When is someone in a *permanent* vegetative state (and thus will never be able to think) and when are they merely in a coma? Is a person with an unresponsive brain unable to ever breathe again without a respirator dead? Does "ever" mean 10 or 20 years hence?

Few laypeople understand all of the tests that determine brain death, and even doctors using brain scans struggle with the ethical and practical problems of deciding when a person is brain dead and when they are merely "locked in"

TABLE EP.3

Dead or Not? Yes, No, and Maybe
Brain death: Prolonged cessation of all brain activity with complete absence of voluntary movements; no spontaneous breathing; no response to pain, noise, and other stimuli. Brain waves have ceased; the electroencephalogram is flat; *the person is dead.*
Locked-in syndrome: The person cannot move, except for the eyes, but normal brain waves are still apparent; *the person is not dead.*
Coma: A state of deep unconsciousness from which the person cannot be aroused. Some people awaken spontaneously from a coma; others enter a vegetative state; *the person is not yet dead.*
Vegetative state: A state of deep unconsciousness in which all cognitive functions are absent, although eyes may open, sounds may be emitted, and breathing may continue; *the person is not yet dead.* The vegetative state can be *transient, persistent,* or *permanent.* No one has ever recovered after two years; most who recover (about 15 percent) improve within three weeks. After sufficient time has elapsed, the person may, effectively, be dead, although exactly how many days that requires has not yet been determined.

and might someday become able to respond to life (Underwood, 2014, October 31; Fins & Bernat, 2018).

Family members may cling to hope long after medical experts are convinced that recovery is impossible. Beyond the cost and psychic distress of this divide, people who want to donate their organs after death cannot do so if too much time elapses between brain death and donation. On the other hand, doctors may hasten to declare death if a dying person has a beating heart that could save another person (Teresi, 2012).

Euthanasia Ethical dilemmas are particularly apparent with *euthanasia* (sometimes called *mercy-killing*). There are two kinds of euthanasia.

In **passive euthanasia**, a person near death is allowed to die. The person's medical chart may include a **DNR (do not resuscitate) order**, instructing medical staff not to restore breathing or restart the heart if breathing or pulsating stops. A more detailed version is the **POLST (physician-ordered life-sustaining treatment)**, which describes when antibiotics, feeding tubes, and so on should be used.

Passive euthanasia is legal everywhere, but many emergency personnel automatically start artificial respiration and stimulate hearts. POLSTs are not always followed as the doctor intended, and they raise additional ethical questions (Moore et al., 2016). Passive euthanasia may be contrary to patient wishes, but more often the opposite occurs: Some patients want to die in peace, but medical measures prolong life.

Active euthanasia is deliberate action to cause death, such as turning off a respirator or giving a lethal drug. Some physicians accept active euthanasia when three conditions occur: (1) Suffering cannot be relieved, (2) the illness is incurable, and (3) the patient wants to die. Active euthanasia is legal in the Netherlands, Belgium, Luxembourg, Switzerland, Colombia, and Canada (each nation has different requirements) and illegal (but rarely prosecuted) elsewhere.

In every nation, some physicians would never perform active euthanasia (even in nations in which it is legal); but others have done so (even in nations where it is illegal). Acceptance of active euthanasia seems to be increasing among physicians. For example, in 1999 and again in 2015, hundreds of doctors in Finland were given the following situation:

> A 60-year-old male patient is suffering from prostatic cancer with metastases. Metastases in the thoracic spine led to total paraparesis [paralysis of the legs] 1 month earlier. There is no hope for a cure. The patient is well aware of the situation. He has totally lost his will to live. When you are together with him alone, he asks for a sufficient dose of morphine to "get away". You have denied the overdose, explaining that it is against your ethical principles. During the following days, you notice that the patient asks you to double his morphine dose because of unbearable pain. You suppose that increasing the dose in such a way would lead to the patient's death.

The doctors were asked, anonymously, what they would do. Most declined to give the deadly dose, but the percentage of those who would double the morphine increased over the 16 years, from 25 percent to 34 percent. Interestingly, rates were higher among older men than younger women (Piili et al., 2018).

Physician Help with Death Between passive and active euthanasia is another option: A doctor may provide the means for patients to end their own lives in

passive euthanasia When a seriously ill person is allowed to die naturally, without active attempts to prolong life.

DNR (do not resuscitate) order A written order from a physician (sometimes initiated by a patient's advance directive or by a health care proxy's request) that no attempt should be made to revive a patient if he or she suffers cardiac or respiratory arrest.

POLST (physician-ordered life-sustaining treatment) This is an order from a doctor regarding end of life care. It advises nurses and other medical staff which treatments (e.g., feeding, antibiotics, respirators) should be used and which not. It is similar to a living will, but it is written for medical professionals and thus is more specific.

active euthanasia When someone does something that hastens another person's death, with the intention of ending that person's suffering.

AP Images/Rich Pedroncelli

Too Late for Her When Brittany Maynard was diagnosed with progressive brain cancer that would render her unable to function before killing her, she moved from her native California to establish residence in Oregon so that she could die with dignity. A year later, the California Senate Health Committee debated a similar law, with Brittany's photo on a desk. They approved the law, 5–2.

physician-assisted suicide A form of active euthanasia in which a doctor provides the means for someone to end his or her own life, usually by prescribing lethal drugs.

advance directives Any description of what a person wants to happen as they die and after death. This can include medical measures, visitors, funeral arrangements, cremation, and so on.

physician-assisted suicide, typically by prescribing lethal medication that a patient can choose to take when they are ready to die. Oregon was the first U.S. state to legalize this practice, asserting that such deaths are "death with dignity," not suicide. This practice is now legal in Washington state, Montana, Vermont, and California.

The Oregon law requires the following:

- The dying person must be an Oregon resident, over age 17.
- The dying person must request the lethal drugs three times, twice spoken and once in writing.
- Fifteen days must elapse between the first request and the prescription.
- Two physicians must confirm that the person is terminally ill, has less than six months to live, and is competent (i.e., not mentally impaired or depressed).

Even if all of this occurs, approval is not automatic. Only about one-third of the initial requests are granted.

Opposite opinions are deeply held. Some people believe that suicide can be noble. Buddhist monks publicly burned themselves to death to advocate Tibetan independence from China; one individual's suicide set off the Arab Spring; one terminally ill woman (Brittany Maynard) pleading to die changed the laws of California. (She moved to Oregon to die before the law changed.) Everywhere, some people die for the honor of their nation, their family, or themselves.

Personality and religion affect acceptance of physician-assisted suicide. The practice is anathema in Islamic nations; in North America, people who are devout Christians often are strongly opposed (Bulmer et al., 2017).

Pain: Physical and Psychological The Netherlands has permitted active euthanasia since 1980. The patient must be clear and aware in making the request, and the goal is to halt "unbearable suffering" (Buiting et al., 2009). Dutch physicians first try to make the suffering bearable via medication.

The Netherlands' law was revised in 2002 to allow euthanasia not only when a person is terminally ill but also when a person is chronically ill and in pain. A qualitative analysis found that Dutch physicians considered "unbearable suffering" to include "fatigue, pain, decline, negative feelings, loss of self, fear of future suffering, dependency, loss of autonomy, being worn out, being a burden, loneliness, loss of all that makes life worth living, hopelessness, pointlessness and being tired of living" (Dees et al., 2011, p. 727). Too extensive?

Oregon residents also request lethal drugs primarily for psychological, not physiological, pain (see **Table EP.4**). That raises additional ethical questions, as Opposing Perspectives explains. Is there a clear divide between physical and psychological pain?

TABLE EP.4

Oregon Residents' Reasons for Requesting Physician Assistance in Dying, 2018

Percent of Patients Giving Reason (most had several reasons)	
Less able to enjoy life	91
Loss of autonomy	92
Loss of dignity	67
Burden on others	54
Loss of control over body	37
Pain	26
Financial implications of treatment	5

Data from Oregon Public Health Division, 2019, p. 6.

Advance Directives

Recognizing that people differ, many professionals hope everyone has **advance directives**, which specify desired medical treatment, where and how death occurs, what should happen to the body (cremation or burial, traditional or "green"), and details of the funeral or memorial. The legality of such directives varies by jurisdiction: Sometimes a lawyer must ensure that documents are legal; sometimes a written request, signed and witnessed, is adequate.

OPPOSING PERSPECTIVES

The "Right to Die"?

Some legal scholars believe that people have a right to choose their death, but others believe that the right to life forbids the right to die (Wicks, 2012). Indeed, some people fear that legalizing euthanasia or physician-assisted suicide creates a slippery slope, leading toward ending life for people who are disabled, poor, or non-White.

The data refute that concern. In Oregon and elsewhere, the oldest-old, the poor, and those of non-European heritage are *less* likely to use fatal prescriptions. In Oregon, almost everyone who chose "death with dignity" was European American (96 percent), had health insurance, was educated (73 percent had some college), and had lived a long life (see **Figure EP.4**). Most died at home, with friends or family.

The number of Dutch people (again tilted toward those with higher SES) choosing euthanasia is increasing. Is this a slippery slope? Some people think so; others think it shows that people welcome a choice about dying.

Addressing the slippery-slope argument, a cancer specialist writes:

> To be forced to continue living a life that one deems intolerable when there are doctors who are willing either to end one's life or to assist one in ending one's own life, is an unspeakable violation of an individual's freedom to live—and to die—as he or she sees fit. Those who would deny patients a legal right to euthanasia or assisted suicide typically appeal to two arguments: a "slippery slope" argument, and an argument about the dangers of abuse. Both are scare tactics, the rhetorical force of which exceeds their logical strength.
>
> [*Benatar, 2011, p. 206*]

Not everyone agrees with that doctor. Might deciding to die be a sign of depression? Should physicians consult with a psychiatrist rather than prescribe lethal drugs (Finlay & George, 2011)? Declining ability to enjoy life was cited by 91 percent of Oregonians who requested physician-assisted suicide in 2018 (see **Table EP.4**). Is that sanity or depression?

Might acceptance of death be mentally healthy in the old but not in the young? If only those over age 64 were allowed the right to die, that would exclude 22 percent of Oregonians who opted to die with dignity. Might they consider age-based restrictions an example of reverse ageism, in that an age cutoff assumes that the young are not capable of choice, but that life matters less for the old?

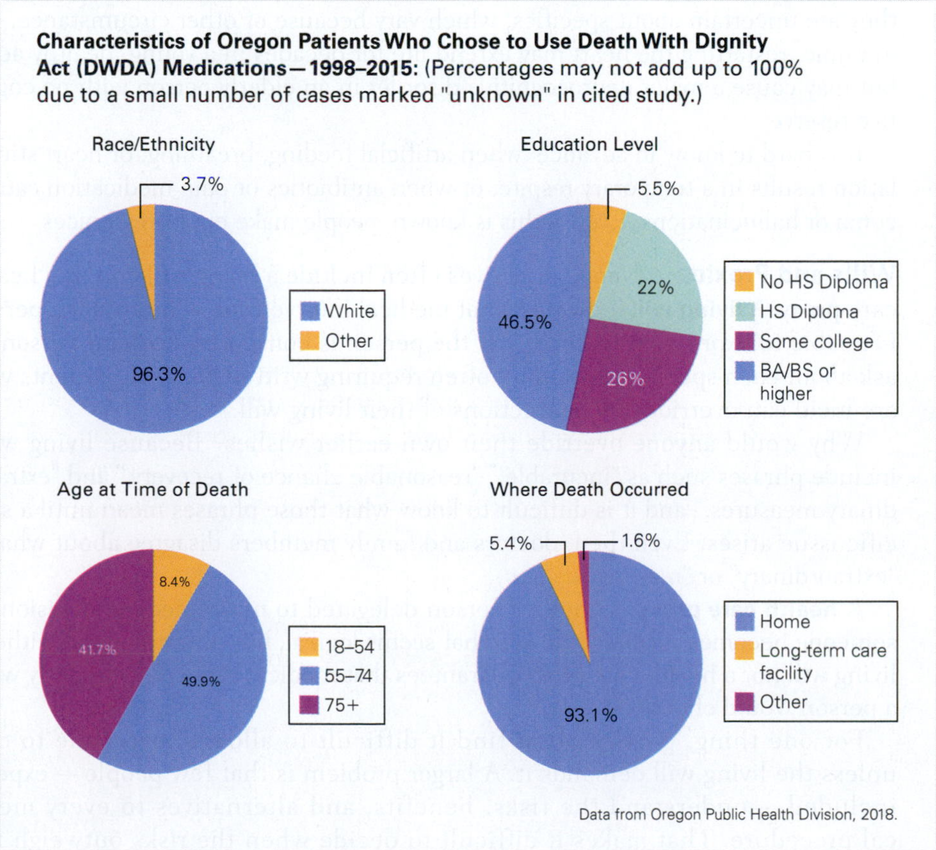

FIGURE EP.4

Death with Dignity? The data do not suggest that people of low SES are unfairly pushed to die. Quite the opposite—people who choose physician-assisted suicide tend to be among the better-educated, more affluent citizens.

In 2018, 240 Oregonians obtained lethal prescriptions, and 158 of them legally used those drugs to die. Most of the others died naturally, but some were alive in January 2019, keeping the drugs for possible future use (in the past, about 10 percent used their prescriptions the year after obtaining them). These numbers have increased every year: Only 16 died with physician assistance in 1998.

An increase is also evident in the Netherlands, where some form of euthanasia accounted for about 1 in 50 deaths when the law was first in place but 1 in 30 deaths in 2014. Some might interpret these data as evidence of a slippery slope; others see it as proof that the law is useful, allowing both the 3.3 percent and the 96.6 percent to die as they wish.

There is another argument against physician-assisted-suicide: It may distract from care for the dying. One doctor wrote:

> We still need to deal with the problem that confronts most dying patients: how to get optimal symptom relief, and how to avoid the hospital and stay at home in the final weeks. Legalizing euthanasia and PAS is really a sideshow in end-of-life care—championed by the few for the few, extensively covered by the media, but not targeted to improve the care for most dying patients who still suffer.
>
> *[Emanuel, 2017].*

Could a law designed to allow death with dignity actually undercut death with dignity?

A position statement from the International Association of Hospice and Palliative Care says:

> [N]o country or state should consider the legalization of euthanasia or PAS until it ensures universal access to palliative care services and to appropriate medications, including opioids for pain and dyspnea.
>
> *[De Lima et al., 2017, p. 8]*

Since no state or nation has "universal access to palliative care," by that standard, no nation is ready to offer physician-assisted suicide. A contrary opinion is evident in Canada, where its Supreme Court unanimously approved physician-assisted suicide after the Canadian Medical Association withdrew their objection to it (Attaran, 2015).

Most jurisdictions recognize the dilemma: Doctors are almost never prosecuted for helping with death as long as it is done privately and quietly. Opposing perspectives, and opposite choices, are evident.

Many people approve of personal choice and advance directives in theory, but they are uncertain about specifics, which vary because of other circumstance. For example, restarting the heart may extend life for decades in a young, healthy adult but may cause a major neurocognitive disorder in an elderly person with no cognitive reserve.

THINK CRITICALLY: Why would someone take all of the steps to obtain a lethal prescription and then not use it?

It is hard to know in advance: when artificial feeding, breathing, or heart stimulation results in a temporary respite, or when antibiotics or pain medication causes coma or hallucinations. Even if this is known, people make opposite choices.

Wills and Proxies Advance directives often include a living will and/or a health care proxy. A **living will** indicates what medical intervention is desired if a person is unable to express preferences. (If the person is conscious, hospital personnel ask about each specific procedure, often requiring written consent. Patients who are lucid can override any instructions of their living will.)

living will A document that indicates what medical intervention an individual prefers if he or she is not conscious when a decision is to be expressed. For example, some do not want mechanical breathing.

Why would anyone override their own earlier wishes? Because living wills include phrases such as "incurable," "reasonable chance of recovery," and "extraordinary measures," and it is difficult to know what those phrases mean until a specific issue arises. Even then, doctors and family members disagree about what is "extraordinary" or "reasonable."

A **health care proxy** is another person delegated to make medical decisions if someone becomes unable to do so. That seems logical, but unfortunately neither a living will nor a health care proxy guarantees that medical care will be exactly what a person would choose.

health care proxy A person chosen to make medical decisions if a patient is unable to do so, as when in a coma.

For one thing, proxies often find it difficult to allow a loved one to die, unless the living will demands it. A larger problem is that few people—experts included—understand the risks, benefits, and alternatives to every medical procedure. That makes it difficult to decide when the risks outweigh the benefits.

Medical professionals know that advance directives are not simple. As one couple wrote:

> Working within the reality of mortality, coming to death is then an inevitable part of life, an event to be lived rather than a problem to be solved. Ideally, we would live the end of our life from the same values that have given meaning to the story of our life up to that time. But in a medical crisis, there is little time, language, or ritual to guide patients and families in conceptualizing or expressing their values and goals.
>
> *[Farber & Farber, 2014, p. 109]*

Especially for People Without Advance Directives Why do very few young adults have advance directives? (see response, page 682)

WHAT HAVE YOU LEARNED?

1. What is a good death?
2. What are Kübler-Ross's five stages of dying, and why doesn't everyone agree with them?
3. What determines whether or not a person will receive hospice care?
4. Why is the double effect legal, even though it speeds death?
5. How is it determined that death has occurred?
6. What is the difference between passive and active euthanasia?
7. What are the four prerequisites of "death with dignity" in Oregon?
8. Why would a person who has a living will also need a health care proxy?

Affirmation of Life

Human relationships are life sustaining, but all adults lose someone they love. Grief and mourning are part of living.

Grief

Grief is the powerful sorrow felt after a profound loss, especially when a loved one dies. Grief is deep and personal, an anguish that can overtake daily life.

Normal Grief Grief is normal, even when it includes odd actions and thoughts. The specifics vary from person to person, but uncontrollable sobbing, sleeplessness, and irrational and delusional thoughts are common (Doka, 2016).

Sheryl Sandberg described her grief a year after her husband died:

> I was swallowed up in the deep fog of grief—what I think of as the void. An emptiness that fills your heart, your lungs, constricts your ability to think, or even to breathe.
>
> *[Sandberg & UC Berkeley, 2016, 05:07–05:19]*

Joan Didion remembers her reaction after her husband's sudden death. She refused the offers of her friends to come stay with her:

> Grief has no distance. Grief comes in waves, paroxysms, sudden apprehensions that weaken the knees and blind the eyes and obliterate the dailiness of life. . . . I see now that my insistence on spending that first night alone was more complicated than it seemed, a primitive instinct. . . . There was a level on which I believed that what had happened remained reversible. . . . I needed to be alone so that he could come back.
>
> *[Didion, 2005, pp. 27, 32, 33]*

macmillan learning

VIDEO: Bereavement: Grief in Early and Late Adulthood presents the views of a young-adult daughter and middle-aged mother on the death of the mother's brother, to whom they were both close.

grief The deep sorrow that people feel at the death of another. Grief is personal and unpredictable.

Why Flags? This couple expresses their grief after a mass shooting at the Pulse nightclub by bringing flowers to a memorial at the Phillips Center for Performing Arts in Orlando, Florida. Some mourners bring candles and flags, and others join marches and protests. Grief is expressed in many ways—some simple, some complicated.

complicated grief A type of grief that impedes a person's future life, usually because the person clings to sorrow or is buffeted by contradictory emotions.

absent grief When mourners do not grieve, either because other people do not allow expressions of grief or because the mourners do not allow themselves to feel sadness.

disenfranchised grief A situation in which certain people, although they are bereaved, are prevented from mourning publicly by cultural customs or social restrictions.

incomplete grief When circumstances, such as a police investigation or an autopsy, interfere with the process of grieving.

When a loved one dies, loneliness, denial, anger, and sorrow come in sudden torrents. Many people want some time alone, yet everyone also needs to be with other people, because other people are a reminder that life continues. Grief typically hits hardest in the first week, but unexpected rushes can occur months or years later.

Complicated Grief Sometimes grief festers, becoming what is called **complicated grief**, impeding life over a long period. The DSM-IV had a "bereavement exclusion," stating that major depression could not be diagnosed within two months of a death, but DSM-5 changed that. Major depression can begin soon after someone dies (LeBlanc et al., 2019).

Depression may begin with **absent grief**, when a bereaved person does not seem to grieve. This is a common first reaction, but ongoing unexpressed grief can trigger physical or psychological symptoms, such as trouble breathing, panic attacks, or crippling sorrow.

Another kind of complicated grief is **disenfranchised grief**, which is "not merely unnoticed, forgotten, or hidden; it is socially disallowed and unsupported" (Corr & Corr, 2013b, p. 135). Some people experience deep grief but are forbidden by social norms to express it.

For instance, often only a current spouse or close blood relative is legally allowed to decide on funeral arrangements, disposal of the body, and other matters. This made sense when all family members were close, but it may now result in "gagged grief and beleaguered bereavement" (Green & Grant, 2008, p. 275).

Sometimes a long-time but unmarried partner is excluded, especially when the partner is of the same sex (Curtin & Garrison, 2018). Relatives, especially those who live far away, may not know who are the deceased person's friends. Thus, some mourners are disenfranchised—not informed about the funeral, unable to grieve with fellow mourners.

Incomplete Grief Grief is a process, usually intense at first, diminishing over time, and eventually reaching closure. Customs such as viewing the dead, or throwing dirt on the grave, or scattering ashes, all allow expression and then closure. However, many circumstances can interfere, creating **incomplete grief**.

Traumatic death is always unexpected, and then denial, anger, and depression undercut the emotions of grief (Kauffman, 2013). Murders and suicides often trigger police, judges, and the press, so mourners who need time to grieve instead must answer questions. An autopsy may prevent grief if someone believes that the body will rise or that the soul remains in the body.

Inability to recover a body, as with soldiers who are missing in action or with victims of a major flood or fire, may prevent grief from being expressed and thereby hinder completion. That explains why, after the destruction of the World Trade Center on 9/11, when DNA identified a fragment of bone, families often had a funeral and burial to allow grieving.

In natural or human-caused disasters such as hurricanes and wars, incomplete grief is common, because survival—food, shelter, medical care—takes precedence. In the days and weeks after disasters, the death rate of causes not directly attributable to the trauma increases, as people suffer from the indifference of others and of their own diminished self-care.

The reality that grief is a process suggests that other people should not try to cut it short or prescribe its course. No one should tell parents who lost a newborn, "You never knew that baby; you can have another," or pet owners "It was only a cat," or those with aged relatives "It was time for them to die." These phrases may ring true for some mourners, but not for all. Grief has its own expressions and boundaries; others should not decide what is appropriate (Doka, 2016).

People who live and work where no one knows their personal lives may lack customs to help them grieve. The laws of some nations—China, Chile, and Spain, for example—mandate paid bereavement leave, but this is not true in the United States (Meagher, 2013).

Indeed, for workers at large corporations or students in universities, grief may become "an unwelcome intrusion (or violent intercession) into the normal efficient running of everyday life" (Anderson, 2001, p. 141).

Many college professors (me included) wish that students would not miss classes or delay assignments because of a death. I may be wrong. My rationale is that people should move past intense grief. However, incomplete grief impedes recovery.

Hector Retamal/AFP/Getty Images

Did These People Survive? This scene that occurred days after Hurricane Maria devastated Puerto Rico is tragic for reasons that are not visible. Because disaster takes attention away from the needs of daily life, according to the Puerto Rican government, 2,975 people died because of the hurricane and its effects, which unfolded over months.

Mourning

Grief splinters people into jumbled pieces, making them vulnerable. Mourning reassembles them, making them whole again and able to rejoin the larger community. To be more specific, **mourning** is the public and ritualistic expression of bereavement, the ceremonies and behaviors that a religion or culture prescribes to honor the dead and allow recovery in the living.

mourning The ceremonies and behaviors that a religion or culture prescribes for people to express their grief after a death.

How Mourning Helps Mourning customs are a buffer between normal and complicated grief. That is needed because the grief-stricken are vulnerable to irrational thoughts and self-destructive acts. Some eat too little or drink too much; some forget caution as they drive or even as they walk across the street. Physical and mental health dips in the recently bereaved; the rate of suicide increases.

Sometimes death continues to affect people years later. The death of a child is particularly hard on the parents, who need each other but, in the irrationality of grief, may blame each other. Years after the loss of a child, illness and death rates of parents rise (Brooten et al., 2018).

A large study in Sweden found that adults whose brother or sister died years ago had higher death rates in adulthood. This was true no matter how the sibling died, but if suicide was the cause, adult survivors were three times more likely to die by suicide than were other Swedes of the same age and background (Rostila et al., 2013).

Similarly, after the suicide of a celebrity, rates rise for ordinary people. This alerts us that shared mourning is especially important when suicide occurs.

Survivors tend to blame themselves, feel angry at the deceased, or consider following the example. Outsiders may stay away after a suicide because they do not know what to say. All of this adds difficulty to expressions of grief and rituals of mourning, yet both are especially crucial.

Many customs are designed to help people move from grief toward reaffirmation. For example, eulogies emphasize the dead person's good qualities; people who did not personally know the deceased attend wakes, funerals, or memorial services to comfort the survivors.

Public expression of grief channels and contains private grief. Examples include the Jewish custom of sitting Shiva at home for a week and then walking around the block to signify a return to life, or the three days of active sorrow among some Muslim groups, or the 10 days of ceremonies beginning at the next full moon

David Larsen/africanpictures.net/The Image Works

Sonny Tumbelaka/AFP/Getty Images

Same Situation, Far Apart: Gateway to Heaven or Final Rest? Many differences are obvious between a Roman Catholic burial in Mbongolwane, South Africa *(left)*, and a Hindu cremation procession in Bali, Indonesia *(right)*. The Africans believe that the soul goes to heaven; the Indonesians believe that the body returns to the elements. In both places, however, friends and neighbors gather to honor the dead and comfort their relatives.

following a Hindu death. In many cultures, the continuity of life is symbolized by flowers, or ashes, or long-lasting candle flames, or a baby named after a dead person. Many cultures set a day aside each year to honor the dead.

One example of cultural differences compares individualistic cultures (e.g., the United States and Western Europe) and community cultures (e.g., most Asian and African cultures). In an individualistic culture, the person is memorized, and mourners take action—with gravestones, black armbands, and so on to remember that particular person. A photo is framed and placed where everyone can see it.

By contrast, Asians see people as interdependent. Therefore, mourning is a family and group event, when a dead person joins the ancestors, reflecting continuity over the generations (Valentine, 2017). A family area is designated for all the ancestors.

The Western practice of building a memorial, dedicating a plaque, or naming a location for a dead person is antithetical to some Eastern cultures. Indeed, some Asian cultures believe that the spirit should be allowed to rest in peace, and thus all possessions, signs, and other evidence of a particular dead person are removed after proper prayers.

This created a cultural clash when terrorist bombs in Bali killed 38 Indonesians and 164 foreigners (mostly Australian and British). The Indonesians prayed intensely and then destroyed all reminders; the Australians raised money to build a memorial (de Jonge, 2011). Indonesian officials posed many obstacles to prevent construction; the Australians were frustrated; the memorial was never built. Neither group understood the deep emotions of the other.

Growth After Death In recent decades, many people everywhere have become less religiously devout, and mourning practices are now less ritualized. Has death become a source of despair, not hope? Maybe not. People worldwide become more spiritual when confronted with death (Lattanzi-Licht, 2013).

If the dead person was a public figure, mourners may include thousands, even millions. They express their sorrow to one another, stare at photos, and listen to music that reminds them of the dead person, weeping as they watch funerals on television. Mourners often pledge to affirm the best of the deceased, forgetting any criticisms that they might have had in the past.

Some observers suggest that mourning can lead people to *post-traumatic growth* (the opposite of post-traumatic stress disorder, or PTSD) (Tedeschi et al., 2017). As you remember, Kübler-Ross found that reactions to death eventually lead to acceptance. Finding meaning may be crucial to the reaffirmation that follows grief. In some cases, this search starts with preserving memories: Displaying photographs and personal effects and telling anecdotes about the deceased person are central to many memorial services in the United States.

Organizations that are devoted to combating a particular problem (such as breast cancer or AIDS) find their most dedicated donors, demonstrators, and advocates among people who have lost a loved one to that specific danger. That also explains why, when someone dies, survivors often designate a charity that is connected to the deceased. Then mourners contribute, hoping the death has led to good.

Placing Blame and Seeking Meaning

A common impulse after death is for the survivors to assess blame—for medical measures not taken, for laws not enforced, for unhealthy habits not changed. The bereaved sometimes blame the dead person, sometimes themselves, and sometimes others.

The medical establishment is often blamed. In November 2011, Michael Jackson's personal doctor, Conrad Murray, was found guilty and jailed for prescribing the drugs that led to the singer's death. Many fans and family members cheered at the verdict; Murray was one of the few who blamed Jackson, not himself.

In 2018, the doctor who prescribed painkillers to Prince was fined $30,000, but he was not prosecuted because he was not the source of the illegal drugs that killed Prince. Many of Prince's friends knew about his addiction: They blamed themselves and each other.

For public tragedies, nations accuse one another. Blame is not rational or proportional to guilt. For instance, outrage at the assassination of Archduke Francis Ferdinand of Austria by a Serbian terrorist in 1914 provoked a conflict between Austria and Serbia—soon joined by a dozen other nations—that led to the four years and 16 million deaths of World War I.

When death occurs from a major disaster, survivors often seek to honor the memory of the dead. Many people believe that Israel would not have been created without the Holocaust, or that same-sex marriage would not have been be legalized if the AIDS epidemic had not occurred.

Mourners often resolve to bring those responsible to justice. Blame can land on many people with responses that some praise and others criticize.

For example, after 17 people died in a gun massacre at a high school in Parkland, Florida, surviving students accused adults of not curbing the National Rifle Association (NRA), and they successfully persuaded major companies to discontinue discounts for NRA members. Florida enacted a law to raise the age for gun purchase to 21 and to require a wait period before a person can buy a gun (the NRA opposed that law). School districts nationwide considered arming teachers.

The search for blame in Parkland included:

- the school resource officer who stayed outside during the shooting,
- the mental health workers who did not hospitalize the gunman,
- the design of the school classrooms that made killing easier,
- the specifics of gun manufacture (e.g., assault weapons, bump stocks),
- the sheriff,
- the FBI,
- the school superintendent (who was almost fired),
- the Republican president (Trump),
- the former Democratic president (Obama).

John Moore/Getty Images

The Human Touch Benetha Coleman fights Ebola in this treatment center by taking temperatures, washing bodies, and drawing blood, but she also comforts those with symptoms. Why would anyone risk working here? Benetha has recovered from Ebola, and, like many survivors of a disaster, she wants to help others who suffer.

THINK CRITICALLY: Do you think current wars are fueled by a misguided impulse to assign blame?

Andrew Lichtenstein/Polaris Images/Newscom

Childish Response? The survivors of the high school shooting in Parkland, Florida, sparked a nationwide protest against the National Rifle Association and the lawmakers and corporations who support it. Are these protestors in Washington, D.C., naive? People on both sides of the gun control debate believe so.

Humans seek to blame someone—and the response may not be logical. The students who became spokespeople for gun laws were both lauded and derided.

Ideally, counselors, politicians, and clergy can steer grief-stricken survivors toward beneficial ends. That may have happened in 2015, when a gunman killed nine people in a prayer group at Emanuel African Methodist Episcopal Church in Charleston, South Carolina. Some people noted that the killer identified with the Confederate soldiers who fought in the U.S. Civil War.

Within a month, the state Senate voted to remove the Confederate flag from the center of Charleston, and major retailers stopped selling that flag. The church members chose forgiveness.

Those church members may have had the right idea. When homicides occur, some family members want revenge, and others forgive. More generally, some people forgive the dead for past misdeeds rather than blaming them, a practice more likely to lead to psychological well-being (Gassin, 2017).

Diversity of Reactions

The specifics of bereavement vary. No particular reaction is necessarily best. Culture matters. For example, mourners who keep the dead person's possessions, talk to the deceased, and frequently review memories are notably *less* well adjusted than other mourners 18 months after the death if they live in the United States, but they are *better* adjusted if they live in China (Lalande & Bonanno, 2006).

Past experiences affect bereavement. Children who lost their parents might be more distraught decades later when someone else dies. Past attachment also matters (Kosminsky, 2017). Older adults who were securely attached as children are likely to experience normal grief; those whose attachment was insecure-avoidant are likely to have absent grief; and those who were insecure-resistant may become stuck, focusing on blame, unable to reaffirm their own lives.

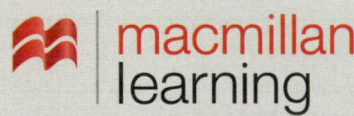

macmillan learning

In **VIDEO: Bereavement and Grief: Late Adulthood,** people discuss their experiences with the loss of beloved family members and friends—and all agree that these losses have been very difficult experiences.

continuing bonds The ongoing attachment and connection that the living have with the dead. Currently, continuing bonds are considered common and often beneficial.

Continuing Bonds

Reaffirmation does not mean forgetting; **continuing bonds** are evident years after death (Klass & Steffen, 2017; M. Stroebe et al., 2012). Such bonds are memories and connections that link the living and the dead. They may help or hinder ongoing life, depending on past relationship to the dead person and on the circumstances of death. Often survivors write letters or talk to the deceased person, or consider events—a sunrise, a butterfly, a rainstorm—as messages of comfort.

Bereavement theory once held an "unquestioned assumption" that mourners should grieve and then move on, accepting that the dead person is gone forever (Neimeyer, 2017). It was thought that if this progression did not take place, pathological grief could result, with the person either not grieving enough (absent grief) or grieving too long (incomplete grief).

But now a much wider variety of reactions are recognized. Continuing bonds are not only normal but, as one researcher notes, the "centrality of relations between the living and the dead" is helpful to the mourner and to everyone else (Neimeyer, 2017).

A bereaved person *might or might not* want to visit the grave, light a candle, cherish a memento, pray, or sob. Mourners may want time alone or may want company. Those who have been taught to bear grief stoically may be distressed if a friend advises them to cry but they cannot. Conversely, those whose cultures expect loud wailing may resent being told to hush.

AP Photo/The Daily News, Todd Maisel, Pool

She Didn't Forget Eleven years after planes crashed into the World Trade Center, the field in Pennsylvania, and the Pentagon, killing 2,977 innocent people, several memorial ceremonies were held. Alice Watkins attended one of them to remember a friend who died. Are continuing bonds an expression of our connection to heritage and history, or a sign that some people are stuck in the past?

Don't Assume

Assumptions arising from one culture or religion might be inaccurate; people's reactions about death and hope vary for many reasons. One example came from a 13-year-old girl who refused to leave home after her

17-year-old brother was shot dead on his way to school. The therapist was supposed to get her to go to school again.

> It would have been easy to assume that she was afraid of dying on the street, and to arrange for a friend to accompany her on her way to school. But careful listening revealed the real reason she stayed home: She worried that her depressed mother might kill herself if she were left alone.
>
> [Crenshaw, 2013]

To help the daughter, the mother had to be helped.

No matter what fears arise, what rituals are followed, or what grief entails, mourning gives the living a deeper appreciation of themselves and others. In fact, a theme frequently sounded by those who work with the dying and the bereaved is that death leads to a greater appreciation of life, especially of the value of intimate, caring relationships.

It is fitting to end this Epilogue, and this book, with a reminder of the creative work of living. As first described in Chapter 1, the study of human development is a science, with topics to be researched, understood, and explained.

But the process of living is an art as well as a science, with strands of love and sorrow woven into each person's unique tapestry. Death, when it leads to hope; dying, when it is accepted; and grief, when it fosters affirmation—all add meaning to birth, growth, development, and love.

WHAT WILL YOU KNOW?

1. What is grief, and what are some of its signs?
2. What are some of the complications of grief?
3. What are the differences among grief, mourning, and bereavement?
4. If a person still feels a loss six months after a death, is that pathological?
5. How can other people help someone who is grieving?

SUMMARY

Death and Hope

1. In ancient times, death connected the living, the dead, and the spirit world. People respected the dead and tried to live their lives so that their own death and afterlife would be good.

2. Every modern religion includes rituals and beliefs about death. These vary a great deal, but all bring hope to the living and strengthen the community.

3. Death has various meanings, depending partly on the age of the person involved. For example, young children want companionship; older children want to know specifics of death.

4. Terror management theory finds that some emerging adults cope with death anxiety by defiantly doing whatever is risky. In adulthood, people tend to worry about leaving something undone or abandoning family members; older adults are more accepting of death.

Choices in Dying

5. A death that is painless and that comes at the end of a long life may be more possible currently than a century ago. However, other aspects of a good death—quick, at home, surrounded by loved ones—are less likely than in earlier times.

6. The emotions of people who are dying change over time. Some may move from denial to acceptance, although stages of dying are much more variable than originally proposed. Honest conversation helps many, but not all, dying persons.

7. Hospice caregivers meet the biological and psychological needs of terminally ill people and their families. Comfort is prioritized over cure, especially when attempts to cure prolong suffering and keep families away.

8. Palliative care relieves pain and suffering. This is now an important part of care in most hospitals and every hospice.

9. Drugs that reduce pain may decrease breathing, producing a double effect. That is legal everywhere. However, euthanasia and physician-assisted suicide are controversial. Several nations and U.S. states allow some forms of these; most do not.

10. Since 1980, death has been defined as occurring when brain waves stop. Many measures now prolong life when no conscious thinking occurs.

11. Advance directives, such as a living will and a health care proxy, are recommended for everyone. However, no one can anticipate the specifics of possible interventions. Family members as well as professionals and nations often disagree.

Affirmation of Life

12. Grief is overwhelming sorrow. It may be irrational and complicated, absent, disenfranchised, or incomplete.

13. Mourning rituals channel human grief, helping people move to affirm life. Specifics vary by culture and cohort. Everywhere, bereavement is a community experience, not borne by the individual alone.

14. Continuing bonds with the deceased are no longer thought to be pathological. Past attachment history affects how a person responds to death.

KEY TERMS

- terror management theory (p. 664)
- hospice (p. 668)
- palliative care (p. 669)
- double effect (p. 669)
- passive euthanasia (p. 671)
- DNR (do not resuscitate) order (p. 671)
- POLST (physician-ordered life-sustaining treatment) (p. 671)
- active euthanasia (p. 671)
- physician-assisted suicide (p. 672)
- advance directives (p. 672)
- living will (p. 674)
- health care proxy (p. 674)
- grief (p. 675)
- complicated grief (p. 676)
- absent grief (p. 676)
- disenfranchised grief (p. 676)
- incomplete grief (p. 676)
- mourning (p. 677)
- continuing bonds (p. 680)

APPLICATIONS

1. The text recommends that everyone should have a health care proxy and a living will. Ask 10 people if they have these, and why or why not. Analyze the reasons—including your own.

2. Find quotes about death in *Bartlett's Familiar Quotations* or a similar collection that includes many centuries and cultures. Do you see any historical or cultural patterns of acceptance, denial, or fear?

3. People of varying ages have different attitudes toward death. Ask someone younger than 20, someone between 20 and 60, and someone over 60 what thoughts they have about their own death. What differences do you find?

Especially For ANSWERS

Response for Relatives of a Person Who Is Dying (from p. 667): Death affects the entire family, including children and grandchildren. I learned this myself when my mother was dying. A hospice nurse not only administered my mother's pain medication (which made it easier for me to be with her) but also counseled me. At the nurse's suggestion, I asked for forgiveness. My mother indicated that there was nothing to forgive. We both felt a peace that would have eluded us without hospice care.

Response for People Without Advance Directives (from p. 675): Young adults tend to avoid thinking realistically about their own deaths. This attitude is emotional, not rational. The actual task of preparing the documents is easy (the forms can be downloaded; no lawyer is needed). Young adults have no trouble doing other future-oriented things, such as getting a tetanus shot or enrolling in a pension plan.

Observation Quiz ANSWERS

Answer to Observation Quiz (from p. 663): The chief mourners are wearing white (unlike the others) and the grandmother has red roses—a luxury often reserved for weddings and funerals.

Answer to Observation Quiz (from p. 664): Homicide, which is 15 times more common. The question the chart does not answer: Why?

More About Research Methods

APPENDIX

This appendix explains how to learn about any topic. It is crucial that you distinguish valid conclusions from wishful thinking. Such learning begins with your personal experience.

Make It Personal

Think about your life, observe your behavior, and watch the people around you. Pay careful attention to details of expression, emotion, and behavior. The more you see, the more fascinated, curious, and reflective you will become. Ask questions and listen carefully and respectfully to what other people say regarding development.

Whenever you ask specific questions as part of an assignment, remember that observing ethical standards (see Chapter 1) comes first. *Before* you interview anyone, inform the person of your purpose and assure him or her of confidentiality. Promise not to identify the person in your report (use a pseudonym) and do not repeat any personal details that emerge in the interview to anyone (friends or strangers). Your instructor will provide further ethical guidance. If you might publish what you've learned, get in touch with your college's Institutional Review Board (IRB).

Read the Research

No matter how deeply you think about your own experiences, and no matter how intently you listen to others whose background is unlike yours, you also need to read scholarly published work in order to fully understand any topic that interests you. Be skeptical about magazine or newspaper reports; some are bound to be simplified, exaggerated, or biased.

Professional Journals and Books

Part of the process of science is that conclusions are not considered solid until they are corroborated in many studies, which means that you should consult several sources on any topic. Five journals in human development are:

- *Developmental Psychology* (published by the American Psychological Association)
- *Child Development* (Society for Research in Child Development)
- *Developmental Review* (Elsevier)
- *Human Development* (Karger)
- *Developmental Science* (Wiley)

These journals differ in the types of articles and studies they publish, but all are well respected and peer-reviewed, which means that other scholars review each article submitted and recommend that it be accepted, rejected, or revised. Every article includes references to other recent work.

Also look at journals that specialize in longer reviews from the perspective of a researcher.

- *Child Development Perspectives* (from Society for Research in Child Development)
- *Perspectives on Psychological Science* (This is published by the Association for Psychological Science. APS publishes several excellent journals, none specifically on development but every issue has at least one article that is directly relevant.)

Beyond these seven are literally thousands of other professional journals, each with a particular perspective or topic, including many in sociology, family studies, economics, and so on. To judge them, look for journals that are peer-reviewed. Also consider the following details: the background of the author (research funded by corporations tends to favor their products); the nature of the publisher (professional organizations, as in the first two journals above, protect their reputations); and how long the journal has been published (the volume number tells you that). Some interesting work does not meet these criteria, so you be careful before believing what you read.

Many *books* cover some aspect of development. Single-author books are likely to present only one viewpoint. That view may be insightful, but it is limited. You might consult a *handbook,* which is a book that includes many authors and many topics. One good handbook in development, now in its seventh edition (a sign that past scholars have found it useful) is:

- *Handbook of Child Psychology and Developmental Science* (7th ed.), edited by Richard M. Lerner, 2015, Hoboken, NJ: Wiley.
- Another set of handbooks—*Handbook of the Biology of Aging, Handbook of the Psychology of Aging,* and *Handbook of Aging and the Social Sciences*—is now in its eighth edition, published by Academic Press in 2016.

Both of these handbooks are updated about every five years, so a new edition might be out soon. Check on it, and use the newest one. Dozens of other good handbooks are available, many of which focus on a particular age, perspective, or topic.

The Internet

The *Internet* is a mixed blessing, useful to every novice and experienced researcher but dangerous as well. Every library worldwide and most homes in North America, Western Europe, and East Asia have computers that provide access to journals and other information. If you're doing research in a library, ask for help from the librarians; many of them can guide you in the most effective ways to conduct online searches. In addition, other students, friends, and even strangers can be helpful.

Virtually everything is on the Internet, not only massive national and international statistics but also accounts of very personal experiences. Photos, charts, quizzes, ongoing experiments, newspapers from around the world, videos, and much more are available at a click. Every journal has a Web site, with tables of contents, abstracts, and sometimes full texts. (An abstract gives the key findings; for the full text, you may need to consult the library's copy of the print version.)

Unfortunately, you can spend many frustrating hours sifting through information that is useless, trash, or tangential. *Directories* (which list general topics or areas and then move you step by step in the direction you choose) and *search engines* (which give you all the sites that use a particular word or words) can help you select appropriate information. Each directory or search engine provides somewhat different lists; none provides only the most comprehensive and accurate sites. Sometimes organizations pay, or find other ways, to make their links appear first, even though they are biased. With experience and help, you will find quality on the Internet, but you will also encounter some junk no matter how experienced you are.

Anybody can put anything online, regardless of its truth or fairness, so you need a very critical eye. Make sure you have several divergent sources for every "fact" you find; consider who provided the information and why. Every controversial issue has sites that forcefully advocate opposite viewpoints, sometimes with biased statistics and narrow perspectives.

Here are four Internet sites that are quite reliable:

- *embryo.soad.umich.edu* The Multidimensional Human Embryo. Presents MRI images of a human embryo at various stages of development, accompanied by brief explanations.
- *childdevelopmentinfo.com* Child Development Institute. A useful site, with links and articles on child development and information on common childhood psychological disorders.
- *eric.ed.gov* Education Resources Information Center (ERIC). Provides links to many education-related sites and includes brief descriptions of each.
- *www.cdc.gov/nchs/hus.htm* The National Center for Health Statistics issues an annual report on health trends, called *Health, United States*.

Every source—you, your interviewees, journals, books, and the Internet—is helpful. Do not depend on any particular one. Avoid plagiarism and prejudice by citing every source and noting objectivity, validity, and credibility. Your own analysis, opinions, words, and conclusions are crucial, backed up by science.

Additional Terms and Concepts

As emphasized throughout the text, the study of development is a science. Social scientists spend years in graduate school, studying methods and statistics. Chapter 1 touches on some of these matters (observation and experiments; correlation and statistical significance; independent and dependent variables; experimental and control groups; cross-sectional, longitudinal, and cross-sequential research), but there is much more. A few additional aspects of research are presented here to help you evaluate research wherever you find it.

Who Participates?

The entire group of people about whom a scientist wants to learn is called a **population.** Generally, a research population is quite large—not usually the world's entire population of more than 7 billion, but perhaps all of the 3,785,235 babies born in the United States in 2018.

The particular individuals who are studied in a specific research project are called the **participants.** They are used as a **sample** of the larger group. Ideally, the participants are a **representative sample,** that is, a sample that reflects the population. Every peer-reviewed, published study reports details on the sample.

Selection of the sample is crucial. People who volunteer, or people who have telephones, or people who have some particular condition are not a *random sample;* in a random sample, everyone in a particular population is equally likely to be selected. To avoid *selection bias,* some studies are *prospective,* beginning with an entire cluster of people (for instance, every baby born on a particular day) and then tracing the development of some particular characteristic.

population The entire group of individuals who are of particular concern in a scientific study, such as all the children of the world or all newborns who weigh less than 3 pounds.

participants The people who are studied in a research project. Participants is the term now used in psychology; other disciplines still call these people "subjects."

sample A group of individuals drawn from a specified population. A sample might be the low-birthweight babies born in four particular hospitals that are representative of all hospitals.

representative sample A group of research participants who reflect the relevant characteristics of the larger population whose attributes are under study.

For example, prospective studies find the antecedents of heart disease, or child abuse, or high school dropout rates—all of which are much harder to find if the study is *retrospective,* beginning with those who had heart attacks, experienced abuse, or left school. Thus, although retrospective research finds that most high school dropouts say they disliked school, prospective research finds that some who like school still decide to drop out and then later say they hated school, while others dislike school but stay to graduate. Prospective research discovers how many students are in these last two categories; retrospective research on people who have already dropped out does not.

Research Design

Every researcher begins not only by formulating a hypothesis but also by learning what other scientists have discovered about the topic in question and what methods might be useful and ethical in designing research. Often they include measures to prevent inadvertently finding only the results they expect. For example, the people who actually gather the data may not know the purpose of the research. Scientists say that these data gatherers are **blind** to the hypothesized outcome. Participants are sometimes "blind" as well, because otherwise they might, for instance, respond the way they think they should.

blind The condition of data gatherers (and sometimes participants, as well) who are deliberately kept ignorant of the purpose of the research so that they cannot unintentionally bias the results.

Another crucial aspect of research design is to define exactly what is to be studied. Researchers establish an **operational definition** of whatever phenomenon they will be examining, defining each variable by describing specific, observable behavior. This is essential in quantitative research, but it is also useful in qualitative research.

operational definition A description of the specific, observable behavior that will constitute the variable that is to be studied, so that any reader will know whether that behavior occurred or not. Operational definitions may be arbitrary (e.g., an IQ score at or above 130 is operationally defined as "gifted"), but they must be precise.

For example, if a researcher wants to know when babies begin to walk, does walking include steps taken while holding on? Is one unsteady step enough? Some parents say yes, but the usual operational definition of *walking* is "takes at least three steps without holding on." This operational definition allows comparisons worldwide, making it possible to discover, for example, that well-fed African babies tend to walk earlier than well-fed European babies.

When emotions or personality traits are studied, operational definitions are difficult to formulate but crucial for interpretation of results. How should *aggression* or *sharing* or *shyness* be defined? Lack of an operational definition leads to contradictory results. For instance, critics report that infant day care makes children more aggressive, but advocates report that it makes them less passive. In this case, both may be seeing the same behavior but defining it differently. For any scientist, operational definitions are crucial, and studies usually include descriptions of how they measured attitudes or behavior.

Reporting Results

You already know that results should be reported in sufficient detail so that another scientist can analyze the conclusions and replicate the research. Various methods, populations, and research designs may produce divergent conclusions. For that reason, handbooks, some journals, and some articles are called *reviews:* They summarize past research. Often, when studies are similar in operational definitions and methods, the review is a **meta-analysis,** which combines the findings of many studies to present an overall conclusion.

meta-analysis A technique of combining results of many studies to come to an overall conclusion. Meta-analysis is powerful, in that small samples can be added together to lead to significant conclusions, although variations from study to study sometimes make combining them impossible.

Table 1.4 (p. 19) describes some other statistical measures. One of them is *statistical significance,* which indicates whether or not a particular result could have occurred by chance.

A crucial statistic is **effect size,** a way of measuring how much impact one variable has on another. Effect size ranges from 0 (no effect) to 1 (total transformation, never found in actual studies). Effect size may be particularly important when the sample size is large, because a large sample often leads to highly "significant" results (results that are unlikely to have occurred by chance) that have only a tiny effect on the variable of interest.

effect size A way of indicating statistically how much of an impact the independent variable in an experiment had on the dependent variable.

Hundreds of statistical measures are used by developmentalists. Often the same data can be presented in many ways: Some scientists examine statistical analysis intently before they accept conclusions as valid. A specific example involved methods to improve students' writing ability between grades 4 and 12. A meta-analysis found that many methods of writing instruction have a significant impact, but effect size is much larger for some methods (teaching strategies and summarizing) than for others (prewriting exercises and studying models). For teachers, this statistic is crucial, for they want to know what has a big effect, not merely what is better than chance (significant).

Numerous articles published in the past decade are meta-analyses that combine similar studies to search for general trends. Often effect sizes are also reported, which is especially helpful for meta-analyses since standard calculations almost always find some significance if the number of participants is in the thousands.

An added problem is the "file drawer" problem—that studies without significant results tend to be filed away rather than published. Thus, an accurate effect size may be much smaller than the published meta-analysis finds, or may be nonexistent. For this reason, replication is an important step.

Overall, then, designing and conducting valid research is complex yet crucial. Remember that with your own opinions: As this appendix advises, it is good to "make it personal," but do not stop there.

GLOSSARY

A

accommodation The restructuring of old ideas to include new experiences.

activities of daily life (ADLs) Typically identified as five tasks of self-care that are important to independent living: eating, bathing, toileting, dressing, and transferring from a bed to a chair. The inability to perform any of these tasks is a sign of frailty.

activity theory The view that elderly people want and need to remain active in a variety of social spheres—with relatives, friends, and community groups—and become withdrawn only unwillingly, as a result of ageism.

adolescence-limited offender A person whose criminal activity stops by age 21.

adolescent egocentrism A characteristic of adolescent thinking that leads young people (ages 10 to 13) to focus on themselves to the exclusion of others.

adrenal glands Two glands, located above the kidneys, that respond to the pituitary, producing hormones.

age in place To remain in the same home and community in later life, adjusting but not leaving when health fades.

age of viability The age (about 22 weeks after conception) at which a fetus might survive outside the mother's uterus if specialized medical care is available.

ageism A prejudice whereby people are categorized and judged solely on the basis of their chronological age.

aggressive-rejected A type of childhood rejection, when other children do not want to be friends with a child because of their antagonistic, confrontational behavior.

allele A variation that makes a gene different in some way from other genes for the same characteristics. Many genes never vary; others have several possible alleles.

allocare Literally, "other-care"; the care of children by people other than the biological parents.

allostasis A dynamic body adjustment, related to homeostasis, that affects overall physiology over time. The main difference is that homeostasis requires an immediate response, whereas allostasis requires longer-term adjustment.

allostatic load The stresses of basic body systems that burden overall functioning, such as hypertension.

Alzheimer's disease (AD) The most common cause of major NCD, characterized by gradual deterioration of memory and personality and marked by the formation of plaques of beta-amyloid protein and tangles of tau in the brain.

analytic intelligence A form of intelligence that involves such mental processes as abstract planning, strategy selection, focused attention, and information processing, as well as verbal and logical skills.

analytic thought Thought that results from analysis, such as a systematic ranking of pros and cons, risks and consequences, possibilities and facts. Analytic thought depends on logic and rationality.

andropause A term coined to signify a drop in testosterone levels in older men, which typically results in reduced sexual desire, erections, and muscle mass. (Also called *male menopause*.)

animism The belief that natural objects and phenomena are alive, moving around, and having sensations and abilities that are human-like.

anorexia nervosa An eating disorder characterized by distorted body image, severe calorie restriction, and intense fear of weight gain. Affected individuals voluntarily undereat or binge and purge, depriving their vital organs of nutrition. Anorexia can be fatal.

anoxia A lack of oxygen that, if prolonged, can cause brain damage or death.

antipathy Feelings of dislike or even hatred for another person.

antisocial behavior Actions that are deliberately hurtful or destructive to another person.

antithesis A proposition or statement of belief that opposes the thesis; the second stage of the process of dialectical thinking.

Apgar scale A quick assessment of a newborn's health, from 0 to 10. Below 5 is an emergency—a neonatal pediatrician is summoned immediately. Most babies are at 7, 8, or 9—almost never a perfect 10.

apprenticeship in thinking Vygotsky's term for how cognition is stimulated and developed in people by more skilled members of society.

assimilation The reinterpretation of new experiences to fit into old ideas.

asthma A chronic disease of the respiratory system in which inflammation narrows the airways from the nose and mouth to the lungs, causing difficulty in breathing. Signs and symptoms include wheezing, shortness of breath, chest tightness, and coughing.

attachment According to Ainsworth, "an affectional tie" that an infant forms with a caregiver—a tie that binds them together in space and endures over time.

attention-deficit/hyperactivity disorder (ADHD) A condition characterized by a persistent pattern of inattention and/or by hyperactive or impulsive behaviors; ADHD interferes with a person's functioning or development.

authoritarian parenting An approach to child rearing that is characterized by high behavioral standards, strict punishment of misconduct, and little communication from child to parent.

authoritative parenting An approach to child rearing in which the parents set limits and enforce rules but are flexible and listen to their children.

autism spectrum disorder (ASD) A developmental disorder marked by difficulty with social communication and interaction — including difficulty seeing things from another person's point of view—and restricted, repetitive patterns of behavior, interests, or activities.

automatization A process in which repetition of a sequence of thoughts and actions makes the sequence routine so that it no longer requires conscious thought.

autonomy versus shame and doubt Erikson's second crisis of psychosocial development. Toddlers either succeed or fail in gaining a sense of self-rule over their actions and their bodies.

average life expectancy The number of years the average newborn in a particular population group is likely to live.

axon A fiber that extends from a neuron and transmits electrochemical impulses from that neuron to the dendrites of other neurons.

B

babbling An infant's repetition of certain syllables, such as *ba-ba-ba,* that begins when babies are between 6 and 9 months old.

bed-sharing When two or more people sleep in the same bed.

behavioral teratogens Agents and conditions that can harm the prenatal brain, impairing the future child's intellectual and emotional functioning.

behaviorism A grand theory of human development that studies observable behavior. Behaviorism is also called *learning theory* because it describes the laws and processes by which behavior is learned.

Big Five The five basic clusters of personality traits that remain quite stable throughout adulthood: openness, conscientiousness, extroversion, agreeableness, and neuroticism.

bilingual education A strategy in which school subjects are taught in both the learner's original language and the second (majority) language.

binge eating disorder An eating disorder common in adolescence, which involves compulsive overeating.

binocular vision The ability to focus the two eyes in a coordinated manner in order to see one image.

body image A person's idea of how his or her body looks.

body mass index (BMI) The ratio of a person's weight in kilograms divided by height in meters squared.

Brazelton Neonatal Behavioral Assessment Scale (NBAS) A test that is often administered to newborns which measures responsiveness and records 46 behaviors, including 20 reflexes.

bulimia nervosa An eating disorder characterized by binge eating and subsequent purging, usually by induced vomiting and/or use of laxatives.

bullying Repeated, systematic efforts to inflict harm on other people through physical, verbal, or social attack on a weaker person.

bullying aggression Unprovoked, repeated physical or verbal attack, especially on victims who are unlikely to defend themselves.

bully-victim Someone who attacks others and who is attacked as well. (Also called *provocative victims* because they do things that elicit bullying.)

C

calorie restriction The practice of limiting dietary energy intake (while consuming sufficient quantities of vitamins, minerals, and other important nutrients) for the purpose of improving health and slowing down the aging process.

carrier A person whose genotype includes a gene that is not expressed in the phenotype. The carried gene occurs in half of the carrier's gametes and thus is passed on to half of the carrier's children. If such a gene is inherited from both parents, the characteristic appears in the phenotype.

cellular aging The cumulative effect of stress and toxins, causing cellular damage first and eventually the death of cells.

centration A characteristic of preoperational thought in which a young child focuses (centers) on one idea, excluding all others.

cephalocaudal Growth and development that occurs from the head down.

cerebral palsy A disorder that results from damage to the brain's motor centers. People with cerebral palsy have difficulty with muscle control, so their speech and/or body movements are impaired.

cesarean section (c-section) A surgical birth in which incisions through the mother's abdomen and uterus allow the fetus to be removed quickly instead of being delivered through the vagina. (Also called simply *section.*)

child abuse Deliberate action that is harmful to a child's physical, emotional, or sexual well-being.

child culture The idea that each group of children has games, sayings, clothing styles, and superstitions that are not common among adults, just as every culture has distinct values, behaviors, and beliefs.

child maltreatment Intentional harm to or avoidable endangerment of anyone under 18 years of age.

child neglect Failure to meet a child's basic physical, educational, or emotional needs.

child sexual abuse Any erotic activity that arouses an adult and excites, shames, or confuses a child, whether or not the victim protests and whether or not genital contact is involved.

childhood obesity In a child, having a BMI above the 95th percentile, according to the U.S. Centers for Disease Control's 1980 standards for children of a given age.

childhood overweight In a child, having a BMI above the 85th percentile, according to the U.S. Centers for Disease Control's 1980 standards for children of a given age.

choice overload Having so many possibilities that a thoughtful choice becomes difficult. This is particularly apparent when social networking and other technology make many potential romantic partners available.

chromosome One of the 46 molecules of DNA (in 23 pairs) that virtually every cell of the human body contains and that, together, contain all the genes. Other species have more or fewer chromosomes.

chronosystem In Bronfenbrenner's ecological approach, the impact of historical conditions (wars, inventions, policies) on the development of people who live in that era.

circadian rhythm A day–night cycle of biological activity that occurs approximately every 24 hours.

classical conditioning The learning process in which a meaningful stimulus (such as the smell of food to a hungry animal) is connected with a neutral stimulus (such as the sound of a tone) that had no special meaning before conditioning. (Also called *respondent conditioning.*)

classification The logical principle that things can be organized into groups (or categories or classes) according to some characteristic that they have in common.

cluster suicides Several suicides committed by members of a group within a brief period.

cognitive equilibrium In cognitive theory, a state of mental balance in which people are not confused because they can use their existing thought processes to understand current experiences and ideas.

cognitive theory A grand theory of human development that focuses on changes in how people think over time. According to this theory, our thoughts shape our attitudes, beliefs, and behaviors.

cohabitation An arrangement in which a couple lives together in a committed romantic relationship but are not formally married.

cohort People born within the same historical period who therefore move through life together, experiencing the same events, technologies, and cultural shifts at the same ages. For example, the effect of the Internet varies depending on what cohort a person belongs to.

comorbid Refers to the presence of two or more unrelated disease conditions at the same time in the same person.

compression of morbidity A shortening of the time a person spends ill or infirm, accomplished by postponing illness.

compulsive hoarding The urge to accumulate and hold on to familiar objects and possessions, sometimes to the point of their becoming health and/or safety hazards. This impulse tends to increase with age.

concrete operational thought Piaget's term for the ability to reason logically about direct experiences and perceptions.

conservation The principle that the amount of a substance remains the same (i.e., is conserved) even when its appearance changes.

control processes Mechanisms (including selective attention, metacognition, and emotional regulation) that combine memory, processing speed, and knowledge to regulate the analysis and flow of information within the information-processing system. (Also called *executive processes*.)

conventional moral reasoning Kohlberg's second level of moral reasoning, emphasizing social rules.

corporal punishment Disciplinary techniques that hurt the body (*corpus*) of someone, from spanking to serious harm, including death.

corpus callosum A long, thick band of nerve fibers that connects the left and right hemispheres of the brain and allows communication between them.

correlation A number between +1.0 and –1.0 that indicates the relationship between two variables, expressed in terms of the likelihood that one variable will (or will not) change when the other variable does (or does not). A correlation indicates that two variables are somehow related, NOT that one variable causes the other to occur.

cortisol The primary stress hormone; fluctuations in the body's cortisol level affect human emotions.

co-sleeping A custom in which parents and their children (usually infants) sleep together in the same room.

couvade Symptoms of pregnancy and birth experienced by fathers.

creative intelligence A form of intelligence that involves the capacity to be intellectually flexible and innovative.

critical period A crucial time when certain events (either biological or social) must occur in order for development to proceed normally.

cross-sectional research Research that compares people who differ in age but are similar in other important characteristics.

cross-sequential research Research that begins by comparing people of different ages (a cross-sectional approach) and then follows those people over the years (a longitudinal approach). (Also called *cohort-sequential research* or *time-sequential research*.)

crystallized intelligence Those types of intellectual ability that reflect accumulated learning. Vocabulary and general information are examples. Some developmental psychologists think crystallized intelligence increases with age, while fluid intelligence declines.

culture A system of shared beliefs, norms, behaviors, and expectations that persist over time and guide behavior and assumptions.

cyberbullying Bullying that occurs when one person spreads insults or rumors about another by means of social media posts, e-mails, text messages, or cell phone videos.

D

deductive reasoning Reasoning from a general statement, premise, or principle, through logical steps, to figure out (deduce) specifics. (Also called *top-down reasoning*.)

Defining Issues Test (DIT) A series of questions developed by James Rest and designed to assess respondents' level of moral development by having them rank possible solutions to moral dilemmas.

demographic shift A shift in the proportions of the populations of various ages.

dendrite A fiber that extends from a neuron and receives electrochemical impulses transmitted from other neurons via their axons.

deoxyribonucleic acid (DNA) The chemical composition of the molecules that contain the genes, which are the chemical instructions for cells to manufacture various proteins.

dependent variable In an experiment, the variable that may change as a result of whatever new condition or situation the experimenter adds. In other words, the dependent variable *depends* on the independent variable.

developmental psychopathology The field that uses insights into typical development to understand and remediate developmental disorders.

developmental theory A group of ideas, assumptions, and generalizations that interpret and illuminate the thousands of observations that have been made about human growth.

deviancy training Destructive peer support in which one person shows another how to rebel against authority or social norms.

dialectical thought The most advanced cognitive process, characterized by the ability to consider a thesis and its antithesis simultaneously and thus to arrive at a synthesis. Dialectical thought makes possible an ongoing awareness of pros and cons, advantages and disadvantages, possibilities and limitations.

difference-equals-deficit error The mistaken belief that unusual behavior or conditions are necessarily inferior.

differential susceptibility The idea that people vary in how sensitive they are to particular experiences, either because of their genes or because of past events. The same experience might harm some people and help others. (Also called *differential sensitivity*.)

disengagement theory The view that aging makes a person's social sphere increasingly narrow, resulting in role relinquishment, withdrawal, and passivity.

disorganized attachment A type of attachment that is marked by an infant's inconsistent reactions to the caregiver's departure and return.

distal parenting Caregiving practices that involve remaining distant from the baby, providing toys, food, and face-to-face communication with minimal holding and touching.

dizygotic (DZ) twins Twins who are formed when two separate ova are fertilized by two separate sperm at roughly the same time. (Also called *fraternal* twins.)

dominant Reflected in the phenotype. Dominant genes have more influence on traits than recessive genes.

doula A woman who helps with the birth process. Traditionally in Latin America, a doula was the only professional who attended childbirth. Now doulas are likely to arrive at the woman's home during early labor and later work alongside a hospital's staff.

Down syndrome A condition in which a person has 47 chromosomes instead of the usual 46, with 3 rather than 2 chromosomes at the 21st site. People with Down syndrome typically have distinctive characteristics, including unusual facial features, heart abnormalities, and language difficulties. (Also called *trisomy-21*.)

drug abuse A condition of harmful drug dependence in which the absence of the given drug in the individual's system produces a drive—physiological, psychological, or both—to ingest more of the drug.

dual processing The notion that two networks exist within the human brain, one for emotional processing of stimuli and one for analytical reasoning.

dynamic-systems approach A view of human development as an ongoing, ever-changing interaction between the physical, cognitive, and psychosocial influences. This approach recognizes that development is never static.

dyscalculia Unusual difficulty with math, probably originating from a distinct part of the brain.

dyslexia Unusual difficulty with reading; thought to be the result of some neurological underdevelopment.

E

eclectic perspective The approach taken by most developmentalists, in which they apply aspects of each of the various theories of development rather than adhering exclusively to one theory.

ecological validity The idea that cognition should be measured in settings that are as realistic as possible and that the abilities measured should be those needed in real life.

ecological-systems approach A perspective on human development that considers all of the influences from the various contexts of development. (Later renamed *bioecological theory*.)

effortful control The ability to regulate one's emotions and actions through effort, not simply through natural inclination.

egocentrism Piaget's term for children's tendency to think about the world entirely from their own personal perspective.

elderspeak A condescending way of speaking to older adults that resembles baby talk, with simple and short sentences, exaggerated emphasis, repetition, and a slower rate and a higher pitch than used in normal speech.

embryo The name for a developing human organism from about the third week through the eighth week after conception.

embryonic period The stage of prenatal development from approximately the third week through the eighth week after conception, during which the basic forms of all body structures, including internal organs, develop.

emerging adulthood The period of life between the ages of 18 and 25. Emerging adulthood is now widely thought of as a distinct developmental stage.

emotional regulation The ability to control when and how emotions are expressed.

empathy The ability to understand the emotions and concerns of another person, especially when they differ from one's own.

empirical evidence Evidence that is based on data, i.e., that is demonstrated, not assumed.

empty nest The time in the lives of parents when their children have left the family home. This is often a happy time for everyone.

English Language Learners (ELLs) Children in the United States whose proficiency in English is low—usually below a cutoff score on an oral or written test. Many children who speak a non-English language at home are also capable in English; they are *not* ELLs.

entity theory of intelligence An approach to understanding intelligence that sees ability as innate, a fixed quantity present at birth; those who hold this view do not believe that effort enhances achievement.

epigenetics The study of how environmental factors affect genes and genetic expression—enhancing, halting, shaping, or altering the expression of genes.

equifinality A basic principle of developmental psychopathology which holds that one symptom can have many causes.

English as a Second Language (ESL) A U.S. approach to teaching English that gathers all of the non-English speakers together and provides intense instruction in English. Students' first languages are never used; the goal is to prepare students for regular classes in English.

estradiol A sex hormone, considered the chief estrogen. Females produce much more estradiol than males do.

ethnic group People whose ancestors were born in the same part of the world, often sharing language, culture, and religion.

evolutionary theory When used in human development, the idea that many current human emotions and impulses are a legacy from thousands of years ago.

executive function A combination of memory, inhibition, and cognitive flexibility that allows better thinking, so people can anticipate, strategize, and plan behavior.

exosystem In Bronfenbrenner's ecological approach, the community institutions that affect the immediate contexts, such as churches and temples, schools and colleges, hospitals and courts.

experience-dependent growth Brain functions that depend on particular, variable experiences and therefore may or may not develop in a particular infant.

experience-expectant growth Brain functions that require certain basic common experiences (which an infant can be expected to have) in order to develop normally.

experiment A research method in which the researcher seeks to discover what causes what. One variable (called the *independent variable*) is added. Then the scientist observes and records the effect on the other variable (called the *dependent variable*).

expert Someone with specialized skills and knowledge developed around a particular activity or area.

extended family A family of relatives in addition to the nuclear family, usually three or more generations living in one household.

extremely low birthweight (ELBW) A body weight at birth of less than 1,000 grams (2 pounds, 3 ounces).

extrinsic motivation A drive, or reason to pursue a goal, that arises from the wish to have external rewards, perhaps by earning money or praise.

extrinsic rewards of work The tangible benefits, usually in salary, insurance, pension, and status, that come with employment.

F

false positive The result of a laboratory test that reports something as true when in fact it is not true. This can occur for pregnancy tests, when a woman might not be pregnant even though the test says she is, or during pregnancy, when a problem is reported that actually does not exist.

familism The belief that family members should support one another, sacrificing individual freedom and success, if necessary, in order to preserve family unity and protect the family from outside forces

family function The way a family works to meet the needs of its members. Children need families to provide basic material necessities, to encourage learning, to help them develop self-respect, to nurture friendships, and to foster harmony and stability.

family structure The legal and genetic relationships among relatives living in the same home. Possible structures include nuclear family, extended family, stepfamily, single-parent family, and many others.

fast-mapping The speedy and sometimes imprecise way in which children learn new words by tentatively placing them in mental categories according to their perceived meaning.

fetal alcohol syndrome (FAS) A cluster of birth defects, including abnormal facial characteristics, slow physical growth, and reduced intellectual ability, that may occur in the fetus of a woman who drinks alcohol while pregnant.

fetal period The stage of prenatal development from the ninth week after conception until birth, during which the fetus gains about 7 pounds (more than 3,000 grams) and organs become more mature, gradually able to function on their own.

fetus The name for a developing human organism from the start of the ninth week after conception until birth.

fictive kin People who become accepted as part of a family in which they are not genetically or legally members.

filial responsibility The obligation of adult children to care for their aging parents.

fine motor skills Physical abilities involving small body movements, especially of the hands and fingers, such as drawing and picking up a coin. (The word *fine* here means "small.")

fluid intelligence Those types of basic intelligence that make learning of all sorts quick and thorough. Abilities such as short-term memory, abstract thought, and speed of thinking are all usually considered part of fluid intelligence.

Flynn effect The rise in average IQ scores that has occurred over the decades in many nations.

focus on appearance A characteristic of preoperational thought in which a young child ignores all attributes that are not apparent.

foreclosure Erikson's term for premature identity formation, which occurs when an adolescent adopts his or her parents' or society's roles and values wholesale, without questioning or analysis.

formal operational thought In Piaget's theory, the fourth and final stage of cognitive development, characterized by more systematic logical thinking and by the ability to understand and systematically manipulate abstract concepts.

foster care A legal, publicly supported system in which a maltreated child is removed from the parents' custody and entrusted to another adult or family, who is reimbursed for expenses incurred in meeting the child's needs.

fragile X syndrome A genetic disorder in which part of the X chromosome seems to be attached to the rest of it by a very thin string of molecules. The cause is a single gene that has more than 200 repetitions of one triplet.

frail elderly People over age 65, and often over age 85, who are physically infirm, very ill, or cognitively disabled. Low energy is a key characteristic.

frontotemporal NCDs Deterioration of the amygdala and frontal lobes that may be the cause of 15 percent of all major neurocognitive disorders. (Also called *frontotemporal lobar degeneration.*)

G

gamete A reproductive cell. These sperm (for males) and ova (for females) each contain 23 chromosomes, so the zygote will contain 46 chromosomes, in 23 pairs.

gender differences Differences in male and female roles, behaviors, clothes, and so on that arise from society, not biology.

gender identity A person's acceptance of the roles and behaviors that society associates with the biological categories of male and female.

gender schema A child's cognitive concept or general belief about male and female differences.

gene A small section of a chromosome; the basic unit for the transmission of heredity. A gene consists of a string of chemicals that provide instructions for the cell to manufacture certain proteins.

general intelligence (*g*) The idea of *g* assumes that intelligence is one basic trait, underlying all cognitive abilities. According to this concept, people have varying levels of this general ability.

generational forgetting The idea that each new generation forgets what the previous generation learned. As used here, the term refers to knowledge about the harm drugs can do.

generativity versus stagnation The seventh of Erikson's eight stages of development. Adults seek to be productive in a caring way, often as parents. Generativity also occurs through art, caregiving, and employment.

genome The full set of genes that are the instructions to make an individual member of a certain species.

genotype An organism's entire genetic inheritance, or genetic potential.

germinal period The first two weeks of prenatal development after conception, characterized by rapid cell division and the beginning of cell differentiation.

gonads The paired sex glands (ovaries in females, testicles in males). The gonads produce hormones and mature gametes.

grammar All of the methods—word order, verb forms, and so on—that languages use to communicate meaning, apart from the words themselves.

gross motor skills Physical abilities involving large body movements, such as walking and jumping. (The word *gross* here means "big.")

growth spurt The relatively sudden and rapid physical growth that occurs during puberty. Each body part increases in size on a schedule: Weight usually precedes height, and growth of the limbs precedes growth of the torso.

guided participation The process by which people learn from others who guide their experiences and explorations.

H

Hayflick limit The number of times a human cell is capable of dividing into two new cells. The limit for most human cells is approximately 50 divisions, an indication that the life span is limited by our genetic program.

Head Start A federally funded early-childhood intervention program for low-income children of preschool age.

head-sparing A biological mechanism that protects the brain when malnutrition disrupts body growth. The brain is the last part of the body to be damaged by malnutrition.

helicopter parents The label used for parents who hover (like a helicopter) over their emerging-adult children. The term is pejorative, but parental involvement is sometimes helpful.

heritability A statistic that indicates what percentage of the variation in a particular trait within a particular population, in a particular context and era, can be traced to genes.

heterozygous Referring to two genes of one pair that differ in some way. Typically one allele has only a few base pairs that differ from the other member of the pair.

hidden curriculum The unofficial, unstated, or implicit patterns within a school that influence what children learn. For instance, teacher background, organization of the play space, and tracking are all part of the hidden curriculum—not formally prescribed, but instructive to the children.

high-stakes test An evaluation that is critical in determining success or failure. If a single test determines whether a student will graduate or be promoted, it is a high-stakes test.

holophrase A single word that is used to express a complete, meaningful thought.

homeostasis The adjustment of all of the body's systems to keep physiological functions in a state of equilibrium. As the body ages, it takes longer for these homeostatic adjustments to occur, so it becomes harder for older bodies to adapt to stress.

homozygous Referring to two genes of one pair that are exactly the same in every letter of their code. Most gene pairs are homozygous.

hookup A sexual encounter between two people who are not in a romantic relationship. Neither intimacy nor commitment is expected.

hormone replacement therapy (HRT) Taking hormones (in pills, patches, or injections) to compensate for hormone reduction. HRT is most common in women at menopause or after removal of the ovaries, but it is also used by men as their testosterone decreases. HRT has some medical uses but also carries health risks.

HPA (hypothalamus–pituitary–adrenal) axis A sequence of hormone production originating in the hypothalamus and moving to the pituitary and then to the adrenal glands.

HPG (hypothalamus–pituitary–gonad) axis A sequence of hormone production originating in the hypothalamus and moving to the pituitary and then to the gonads.

Human Genome Project An international effort to map the complete human genetic code. This effort was essentially completed in 2001, though analysis is ongoing.

humanism A theory that stresses the potential of all humans, who have the same basic needs regardless of culture, gender, or background.

hypothesis A specific prediction that can be tested. Hypotheses that turn out to be false are as meaningful as those that are confirmed.

hypothetical thought Reasoning that includes propositions and possibilities that may not reflect reality.

I

identity achievement Erikson's term for the attainment of identity, or the point at which people understand who they are as unique individuals, in accord with past experiences and future plans.

identity versus role confusion Erikson's term for the fifth stage of development, in which the person tries to figure out "Who am I?" but is confused as to which of many possible roles to adopt.

imaginary audience The other people who, in an adolescent's egocentric belief, are watching and taking note of his or her appearance, ideas, and behavior. This belief makes many teenagers very self-conscious.

immersion A strategy in which instruction in all school subjects occurs in the second (usually the majority) language that a child is learning.

immigrant paradox The surprising, paradoxical fact that low-SES immigrant women tend to have fewer birth complications than native-born peers with higher incomes.

immunization A process that stimulates the body's immune system by causing production of antibodies to defend against attack by a particular contagious disease. Creation of antibodies may be accomplished either naturally (by having the disease), by injection, by drops that are swallowed, or by a nasal spray.

impulse control The ability to postpone or deny the immediate response to an idea or behavior.

in vitro fertilization (IVF) Fertilization that takes place outside a woman's body (as in a glass laboratory dish). The procedure involves mixing sperm with ova that have been surgically removed from the woman's ovary. If a zygote is produced, it is inserted into a woman's uterus, where it may implant and develop into a baby.

incremental theory of intelligence An approach to understanding intelligence that holds that intelligence can be directly increased by effort; those who subscribe to this view believe they can master whatever they seek to learn if they pay attention, participate in class, study, complete their homework, and so on.

independent variable In an experiment, the variable that is introduced to see what effect it has on the dependent variable. (Also called *experimental variable*.)

individual education plan (IEP) A document that specifies educational goals and plans for a child with special needs.

induction A disciplinary technique in which the parent tries to get the child to understand why a certain behavior was wrong. Listening, not lecturing, is crucial.

inductive reasoning Reasoning from one or more specific experiences or facts to reach (induce) a general conclusion. (Also called *bottom-up reasoning*.)

industry versus inferiority The fourth of Erikson's eight psychosocial crises, during which children attempt to master many skills, developing a sense of themselves as either industrious or inferior, competent or incompetent.

infertility The inability to conceive a child after trying for at least a year.

information-processing theory A perspective that compares human thinking processes, by analogy, to computer analysis of data, including sensory input, connections, stored memories, and output.

initiative versus guilt Erikson's third psychosocial crisis, in which young children undertake new skills and activities and feel guilty when they do not succeed at them.

injury control/harm reduction Practices that are aimed at anticipating, controlling, and preventing dangerous activities; these practices reflect the beliefs that accidents are not random and that injuries can be made less harmful if proper controls are in place.

insecure-avoidant attachment A pattern of attachment in which an infant avoids connection with the caregiver, as when the infant seems not to care about the caregiver's presence, departure, or return.

insecure-resistant/ambivalent attachment A pattern of attachment in which an infant's anxiety and uncertainty are evident, as when the infant becomes very upset at separation from the caregiver and both resists and seeks contact on reunion.

instrumental activities of daily life (IADLs) Actions (for example, paying bills and car maintenance) that are important to independent living and that require some intellectual competence and forethought. The ability to perform these tasks may be even more critical to self-sufficiency than ADL ability.

instrumental aggression Hurtful behavior that is intended to get something that another person has.

integrated care Care of frail elders that combines the caregiving strengths of everyone—family, medical professionals, social workers, and the elders themselves.

integrity versus despair The final stage of Erik Erikson's developmental sequence, in which older adults seek to integrate their unique experiences with their vision of community.

intermittent fasting A pattern of eating that include periods of restricted eating interspersed with usual consumption. The most popular pattern is two days per week eating less than 750 calories and five days of normal eating, all while drinking plenty of water.

intersectionality The idea that the various identities need to be combined. This is especially important in determining if discrimination occurs.

intimacy versus isolation The sixth of Erikson's eight stages of development. Adults seek someone with whom to share their lives in an enduring and self-sacrificing commitment. Without such commitment, they risk profound aloneness and isolation.

intimate terrorism A violent and demeaning form of abuse in a romantic relationship, in which the victim (usually female) is frightened to fight back, seek help, or withdraw. In this case, the victim is in danger of physical as well as psychological harm.

intrinsic motivation A drive, or reason to pursue a goal, that comes from inside a person, such as the joy of reading a good book.

intrinsic rewards of work The personal gratifications, such as pleasure in a job well done or friendships with coworkers, that accompany employment.

intuitive thought Thought that arises from an emotion or a hunch, beyond rational explanation, and is influenced by past experiences and cultural assumptions.

invincibility fable An adolescent's egocentric conviction that they cannot be overcome or even harmed by anything that might defeat a normal mortal, such as unprotected sex, drug abuse, or high-speed driving.

irreversibility A characteristic of preoperational thought in which a young child thinks that nothing can be undone. A thing cannot be restored to the way it was before a change occurred.

K

kangaroo care A form of newborn care in which mothers (and sometimes fathers) rest their babies on their naked chests, like kangaroo mothers that carry their immature newborns in a pouch on their abdomen.

kinkeeper Someone who becomes the gatherer and communications hub for their family.

kinship care A form of foster care in which a relative of a maltreated child, usually a grandparent, becomes the approved caregiver.

knowledge base A body of knowledge in a particular area that makes it easier to master new information in that area.

L

language acquisition device (LAD) Chomsky's term for a hypothesized mental structure that enables humans to learn language, including the basic aspects of grammar, vocabulary, and intonation.

lateralization Literally, sidedness, referring to the specialization in certain functions by each side of the brain, with one side dominant for each activity. The left side of the brain controls the right side of the body, and vice versa.

least restrictive environment (LRE) A legal requirement that children with special needs be assigned to the most general educational context in which they can be expected to learn.

Lewy body disease A form of major neurocognitive disorder characterized by an increase in Lewy body cells in the brain. Symptoms include visual hallucinations, momentary loss of attention, falling, and fainting.

life-course-persistent offender A person whose criminal activity typically begins in early adolescence and continues throughout life; a career criminal.

life-span perspective An approach to the study of human development that takes into account all phases of life, not just childhood or adulthood.

linked lives Lives in which the success, health, and well-being of each family member are connected to those of other members, including those of another generation, as in the relationship between parents and children.

"little scientist" The stage-five toddler (age 12 to 18 months) who experiments without anticipating the results, using trial and error in active and creative exploration.

longitudinal research Research in which the same individuals are followed over time, as their development is repeatedly assessed.

low birthweight (LBW) A body weight at birth of less than 2,500 grams (5½ pounds).

M

macrosystem In Bronfenbrenner's ecological approach, the overarching national or cultural policies and customs that affect the more immediate systems, such as the effect of the national economy on local hospitals (an exosystem) or on families (a microsystem)

major depression Feelings of hopelessness, lethargy, and worthlessness that last two weeks or more.

massification The idea that establishing institutions of higher learning and encouraging college enrollment can benefit everyone (the masses).

massive open online course (MOOC) A course that is offered solely online for college credit. Typically, tuition is very low, and thousands of students enroll.

maximum life span The oldest possible age to which members of a species can live under ideal circumstances. For humans, that age is approximately 122 years.

mean length of utterance (MLU) The average number of words in a typical sentence (called utterance because children may not talk in complete sentences). MLU is often used to measure language development.

menarche A girl's first menstrual period, signaling that she has begun ovulation. Pregnancy is biologically possible, but ovulation and menstruation are often irregular for years after menarche.

menopause The time in middle age, usually around age 50, when a woman's menstrual periods cease and the production of estrogen, progesterone, and testosterone drops. Strictly speaking, menopause is dated one year after a woman's last menstrual period, although many months before and after that date are menopausal.

mesosystem In Bronfenbrenner's ecological approach, a connection between one system and another, such as parent–teacher conferences (connecting home and school) or workplace schedules (connecting family and job).

meta-analysis Combining the results of many studies, each of which may have small, and limited samples, to reach a general conclusion.

microbiome All the microbes (bacteria, viruses, and so on) with all their genes in a community; here, the millions of microbes of the human body.

microsystem In Bronfenbrenner's ecological approach, the immediate social contexts that directly affect each person, such as family, peer group, work team.

middle school A school for children in the grades between elementary school and high school. Middle school usually begins with grade 6 and ends with grade 8.

mild cognitive impairment (MCI). When a person is somewhat more confused and forgetful than they were, but still able to function well.

modeling The central process of social learning, by which a person observes the actions of others and then copies them.

monozygotic (MZ) twins Twins who originate from one zygote that splits apart very early in development. (Also called *identical twins.*) Other monozygotic multiple births (such as triplets and quadruplets) can occur as well.

Montessori schools Schools that offer early-childhood education based on the philosophy of Maria Montessori, which emphasizes careful work and tasks that each young child can do.

moratorium An adolescent's choice of a socially acceptable way to postpone making identity-achievement decisions. Going to college is a common example.

motor skill The learned abilities to move some part of the body, in actions ranging from a large leap to a flicker of the eyelid. (The word *motor* here refers to movement of muscles.)

multifinality A basic principle of developmental psychopathology which holds that one cause can have many (multiple) final manifestations.

multiple intelligences The idea that human intelligence is composed of a varied set of abilities rather than a single, all-encompassing one.

myelin The coating on axons that speeds transmission of signals from one neuron to another.

myelination The process by which axons become coated with myelin, a fatty substance that speeds the transmission of nerve impulses from neuron to neuron.

N

naming explosion A sudden increase in an infant's vocabulary, especially in the number of nouns, that begins at about 18 months of age.

National Assessment of Educational Progress (NAEP) An ongoing and nationally representative measure of U.S. children's achievement in reading, mathematics, and other subjects over time; nicknamed "the Nation's Report Card."

naturally occurring retirement community (NORC) A neighborhood or apartment complex whose population is mostly retired people who moved to the location as younger adults and never left.

nature The genetic influences on a person.

neglectful/uninvolved parenting An approach to child rearing in which the parents seem indifferent toward their children, not knowing or caring about their children's lives.

neurocognitive disorder (NCD) Any of a number of brain diseases that affect a person's ability to remember, analyze, plan, or interact with other people.

neurodiversity The idea that each person has neurological strengths and weaknesses that should be appreciated, in much the same way diverse cultures and ethnicities are welcomed. Neurodiversity seems particularly relevant for children with disorders on the autism spectrum.

nuclear family A family that consists of a father, a mother, and their biological children under age 18.

nurture The non-genetic influences on each developing person, which is everything from the mother's nutrition while pregnant to the national culture.

O

object permanence The realization that objects (including people) still exist when they can no longer be seen, touched, or heard.

Oedipus complex The unconscious desire of young boys to replace their fathers and win their mothers' exclusive love.

oldest-old Elderly adults (generally, those over age 85) who are dependent on others for almost everything, requiring supportive services such as nursing homes and hospital stays.

old-old Older adults (generally, those over age 75) who suffer from physical, mental, or social deficits.

operant conditioning The learning process by which a particular action is followed by something desired (which makes the person or animal more likely to repeat the action) or by something unwanted (which makes the action less likely to be repeated). (Also called *instrumental conditioning.*)

organ reserve The capacity of organs to allow the body to cope with stress, via extra, unused functioning ability.

osteoporosis A disease whose symptoms are low bone mass and deterioration of bone tissue, which leads to increasingly fragile bones and greater risk of fracture.

overimitation When a person imitates an action that is not a relevant part of the behavior to be learned. Overimitation is common among 2- to 6-year-olds when they imitate adult actions that are irrelevant and inefficient.

overregularization The application of rules of grammar even when exceptions occur, making the language seem more "regular" than it actually is.

oxytocin The primary bonding hormone, evident lifelong but particularly high at birth and in lactation.

P

parasuicide Any potentially lethal action against the self that does not result in death. (Also called *attempted suicide* or *failed suicide.*)

parental monitoring Parents' ongoing awareness of what their children are doing, where, and with whom.

parent–infant bond The strong, loving connection that forms as parents hold, examine, and feed their newborn.

Parkinson's disease A chronic, progressive disease that is characterized by muscle tremor and rigidity and sometimes major neurocognitive disorder; caused by reduced dopamine production in the brain.

peer pressure Encouragement to conform to one's friends or contemporaries in behavior, dress, and attitude; usually considered a negative force, as when adolescent peers encourage one another to defy authority.

percentile A point on a ranking scale of 0 to 100. The 50th percentile is the midpoint; half of the people in the population being studied rank higher and half rank lower.

perception When the brain is conscious of a sensation or idea. Perception sometimes combines several senses and ideas: You might suddenly perceive that your mother is angry because of her face and voice and your past experience of her anger.

permanency planning An effort by child-welfare authorities to find a long-term living situation that will provide stability and support for a maltreated child. A goal is to avoid repeated changes of caregiver or school, which can be particularly harmful to the child.

permissive parenting An approach to child rearing that is characterized by high nurturance and communication but little discipline, guidance, or control.

perseverate To stay stuck, or persevere, in one thought or action for a long time. The ability to be flexible, switching from one task to another, is beyond most young children.

personal fable An aspect of adolescent egocentrism characterized by an adolescent's belief that his or her thoughts, feelings, and experiences are unique, more wonderful, or more awful than anyone else's.

phallic stage Freud's third stage of development, when the penis becomes the focus of concern and pleasure.

phenotype The characteristics of a person, including appearance, personality, intelligence, and all other traits.

pituitary A gland in the brain that responds to a signal from the hypothalamus by producing many hormones, including those that regulate growth and sexual maturation.

plaques Clumps of a protein called beta-amyloid, found in brain tissue surrounding the neurons.

plasticity The concept that suggests that abilities, personality, neurons, and so on are moldable, not immutable.

polygamous family A family consisting of one man, several wives, and their children.

polypharmacy A situation in which elderly people are prescribed several medications. The various side effects and interactions of those medications can result in dementia symptoms.

positivity effect The tendency for elderly people to perceive, prefer, and remember positive images and experiences more than negative ones.

postconventional moral reasoning Kohlberg's third level of moral reasoning, emphasizing moral principles.

postformal thought A proposed adult stage of cognitive development, following Piaget's four stages, that goes beyond adolescent thinking by being more practical, more flexible, and more dialectical (i.e., more capable of combining contradictory elements into a comprehensive whole).

postpartum depression A new mother's feelings of inadequacy and sadness in the days and weeks after giving birth.

post-traumatic stress disorder (PTSD) An anxiety disorder that develops as a delayed reaction to exposure to actual or threatened death, serious injury, or sexual violence. Its symptoms may include flashbacks to the event, hyperactivity and hypervigilance, displaced anger, sleeplessness, nightmares, sudden terror or anxiety, and confusion between fantasy and reality.

practical intelligence The intellectual skills used in everyday problem solving. (Sometimes called *tacit intelligence*.)

pragmatics The practical use of language that includes the ability to adjust language communication according to audience and context.

preconventional moral reasoning Kohlberg's first level of moral reasoning, emphasizing rewards and punishments.

preoperational intelligence Piaget's term for cognitive development between the ages of about 2 and 6; it includes language and imagination (which involve symbolic thought), but logical, operational thinking is not yet possible.

preterm A birth that occurs two or more weeks before the full 38 weeks of the typical pregnancy—that is, at 36 or fewer weeks after conception.

primary aging The universal and irreversible physical changes that occur to all living creatures as they grow older.

primary circular reactions The first of three types of feedback loops in sensorimotor intelligence, this one involving the infant's own body. The infant senses motion, sucking, noise, and other stimuli and tries to understand them.

primary prevention Actions that change overall background conditions to prevent some unwanted event or circumstance, such as injury, disease, or abuse.

primary sex characteristics The parts of the body that are directly involved in reproduction, including the vagina, uterus, ovaries, testicles, and penis.

private speech The internal dialogue that occurs when people talk to themselves (either silently or out loud).

prosocial behavior Actions that are helpful and kind but that are of no obvious benefit to the person doing them.

protein-calorie malnutrition A condition in which a person does not consume sufficient food of any kind. This deprivation can result in several illnesses, severe weight loss, and even death.

proximal parenting Caregiving practices that involve being physically close to the baby, with frequent holding and touching.

proximodistal Growth or development that occurs from the center or core in an outward direction.

psychological control A disciplinary technique that involves threatening to withdraw love and support, using a child's feelings of guilt and gratitude to the parents.

puberty The time between the first onrush of hormones and full adult physical development. Puberty usually lasts three to five years. Many more years are required to achieve psychosocial maturity.

Q

qualitative research Research that considers qualities instead of quantities, and hence includes narratives and other aspects of development that express individuality.

quantitative research Research that provides data that can be expressed with numbers, such as ranks or scales.

R

race Categorizing people based on inherited traits. Anthropologists and biologists no longer think race is a valid biological concept, although it is a powerful social construction.

reaction time The time it takes to respond to a stimulus, either physically (with a reflexive movement such as an eyeblink) or cognitively (with a thought).

reactive aggression An impulsive retaliation for another person's intentional or accidental hurtful action.

recessive Hidden, not dominant. Recessive genes are carried in the genotype and are not evident in the phenotype, except in special circumstances.

reflex An unlearned, involuntary action or movement in response to a stimulus. A reflex occurs without conscious thought.

Reggio Emilia A program of early childhood education that originated in the town of Reggio Emilia, Italy, and that encourages each child's creativity in a carefully designed setting.

reinforcement When a behavior is followed by something desired, such as food for a hungry animal or a welcoming smile for a lonely person.

relational aggression Nonphysical acts, such as insults or social rejection, aimed at harming the social connection between the victim and other people.

REM (rapid eye movement) sleep A stage of sleep characterized by flickering eyes behind closed lids, dreaming, and rapid brain waves.

replication Repeating a study, usually using different participants but similar or identical procedures and measures.

reported maltreatment Harm or endangerment about which someone has notified the authorities.

resilience The capacity to adapt well to significant adversity and to overcome serious stress.

response to intervention (RTI) An educational strategy intended to help children who demonstrate below-average achievement in early grades, using special intervention.

role confusion A situation in which an adolescent does not seem to know or care what his or her identity is. (Sometimes called *identity diffusion* or *role diffusion*.)

rough-and-tumble Play that seems to be rough, as in play wrestling or chasing, but in which there is no intent to harm.

rumination Repeatedly thinking and talking about past experiences; can contribute to depression.

S

sandwich generation The generation of middle-aged people who are supposedly "squeezed" by the needs of the younger and older members of their families.

scaffolding Temporary support that is tailored to a learner's needs and abilities and aimed at helping the learner master the next task in a given learning process.

science of human development The science that seeks to understand how and why people of all ages and circumstances change or remain the same over time.

scientific method A way to answer questions beginning with hypotheses that are then tested with empirical research before drawing conclusions.

scientific observation A method of testing a hypothesis by systematically watching and recording participants' behavior, in a natural setting, in a laboratory, or in archival data.

Seattle Longitudinal Study The first cross-sequential study of adult intelligence. This study began in 1956 and is repeated every seven years.

secondary aging The specific physical illnesses or conditions that become more common with aging but are caused by health habits, genes, and other influences that vary from person to person.

secondary circular reactions The second of three types of feedback loops in sensorimotor intelligence, this one involving people and objects. Infants respond to other people, to toys, and to any other object that they can touch or move.

secondary education Literally, the period after primary education (elementary or grade school) and before tertiary education (college). It usually occurs from about ages 12 to 18, although there is some variation by school and by nation.

secondary prevention Actions that avert harm in a high-risk situation, such as holding a child's hand when crossing the street.

secondary sex characteristics Physical traits that are not directly involved in reproduction but that indicate sexual maturity, such as a man's beard and a woman's breasts.

secular trend The long-term upward or downward direction of a certain set of statistical measurements, as opposed to a smaller, shorter cyclical variation. As an example, over the past two centuries, because of improved nutrition and medical care, children have tended to reach their adult height earlier and their adult height has increased.

secure attachment A relationship in which an infant obtains both comfort and confidence from the presence of his or her caregiver.

selective adaptation The process by which living creatures (including people) adjust to their environment. Genes that enhance survival and reproductive ability are selected, over the generations, to become more prevalent.

selective optimization with compensation The theory, developed by Paul and Margaret Baltes, that people try to maintain a balance in their lives by looking for the best way to compensate for physical and cognitive losses and to become more proficient in activities they can already do well.

self theories Theories of late adulthood that emphasize the core self, or the search to maintain one's integrity and identity.

self-actualization The final stage in Maslow's hierarchy of needs, characterized by aesthetic, creative, philosophical, and spiritual understanding.

self-awareness A person's realization that they are a distinct individual whose body, mind, and actions are separate from those of other people.

self-concept A person's understanding of who they are, in relation to self-esteem, appearance, personality, and various traits.

senescence The process of aging, whereby the body becomes less strong and efficient.

sensation The response of a sensory organ (eyes, ears, skin, tongue, nose) when it detects a stimulus.

sensitive period A time when a certain development is most likely to occur. For example, early childhood is considered a sensitive period for language learning.

sensorimotor intelligence Piaget's term for the way infants think—by using their senses and motor skills—during the first period of cognitive development.

separation anxiety An infant's distress when a familiar caregiver leaves; most obvious between 9 and 14 months.

seriation The concept that things can be arranged in a logical series, such as the number sequence or the alphabet.

set point A particular body weight that an individual's homeostatic processes strive to maintain.

sex differences Biological differences between males and females, in organs, hormones, and body shape.

sexting Sending sexual content, particularly photos or videos, via cell phones or social media.

sexual orientation A term that refers to whether a person is sexually and romantically attracted to others of the same sex, the opposite sex, or both sexes.

sexually transmitted infection (STI) A disease spread by sexual contact, including syphilis, gonorrhea, genital herpes, chlamydia, and HIV.

shaken baby syndrome A life-threatening injury that occurs when an infant is forcefully shaken back and forth, a motion that ruptures blood vessels in the brain and breaks neural connections.

single-parent family A family that consists of only one parent and his or her children.

situational couple violence Fighting between romantic partners that is brought on more by the situation than by the deep personality problems of the individuals. Both partners are typically victims and abusers.

small for gestational age (SGA) A term for a baby whose birthweight is significantly lower than expected, given the time since conception. For example, a 5-pound (2,265-gram) newborn is considered SGA if born on time but not SGA if born two months early. (Also called *small-for-dates.*)

snowplow parents Parents who try to remove any impediments in the way of their children. This term is pejorative; it implies that parents do not allow children to learn how to overcome obstacles on their own.

social comparison The tendency to assess one's abilities, achievements, social status, and other attributes by measuring them against those of other people, especially one's peers.

social construction An idea that is built on shared perceptions, not on objective reality. Many age-related terms (such as *childhood, adolescence, yuppie,* and *senior citizen*) are social constructions, connected to biological traits but strongly influenced by social assumptions.

social convoy Collectively, the family members, friends, acquaintances, and even strangers who move through the years of life with a person.

social learning theory An extension of behaviorism that emphasizes the influence that other people have over a person's behavior. Even without specific reinforcement, every individual learns many things through observation and imitation of other people. (Also called *observational learning.*)

social mediation Human interaction that expands and advances understanding, often through words that one person uses to explain something to another.

social referencing Seeking information about how to react to an unfamiliar or ambiguous object or event by observing someone else's expressions and reactions. That other person becomes a social reference.

social smile A smile evoked by a human face, normally first evident in infants about 6 weeks after birth.

sociocultural theory A newer theory which holds that development results from the dynamic interaction of each person with the surrounding social and cultural forces.

sociodramatic play Pretend play in which children act out various roles and themes in plots or roles that they create.

socioeconomic status (SES) A person's position in society as determined by income, occupation, education, and place of residence. (Sometimes called *social class.*)

socioemotional selectivity theory The theory that older people prioritize regulation of their own emotions and seek familiar social contacts who reinforce generativity, pride, and joy.

specific learning disorder A marked deficit in a particular area of learning that is not caused by an apparent physical disability, by an intellectual disability, or by an unusually stressful home environment.

spermarche A boy's first ejaculation of sperm. Erections can occur as early as infancy, but ejaculation signals sperm production. Spermarche may occur during sleep (in a "wet dream") or via direct stimulation.

static reasoning A characteristic of preoperational thought in which a young child thinks that nothing changes. Whatever is now has always been and always will be.

stem cells Cells from which any other specialized type of cell can form.

stereotype threat The thought in a person's mind that one's appearance or behavior will be misread to confirm another person's oversimplified, prejudiced attitudes.

still-face technique An experimental practice in which an adult keeps his or her face unmoving and expressionless in face-to-face interaction with an infant.

stranger wariness An infant's expression of concern—a quiet stare while clinging to a familiar person, or a look of fear—when a stranger appears.

stratification theories Theories which emphasize that social forces, particularly those related to a person's social stratum or social category, limit individual choices and affect a person's ability to function in late adulthood because past stratification continues to limit life in various ways.

stunting The failure of children to grow to a normal height for their age due to severe and chronic malnutrition.

substantiated maltreatment Harm or endangerment that has been reported, investigated, and verified.

sudden infant death syndrome (SIDS) A situation in which a seemingly healthy infant, usually between 2 and 6 months old, suddenly stops breathing and dies unexpectedly while asleep.

suicidal ideation Thinking about suicide, usually with some serious emotional and intellectual or cognitive overtones.

superego In psychoanalytic theory, the judgmental part of the personality that internalizes the moral standards of the parents.

survey A research method in which information is collected from a large number of people by interviews, written questionnaires, or some other means.

symbolic thought A major accomplishment of preoperational intelligence that allows a child to think symbolically, including understanding that words can refer to things not seen and that an item, such as a flag, can symbolize something else (in this case, a country).

synapse The intersection between the axon of one neuron and the dendrites of other neurons.

synchrony A coordinated, rapid, and smooth exchange of responses between a caregiver and an infant.

synthesis A new idea that integrates the thesis and its antithesis, thus representing a new and more comprehensive level of truth; the third stage of the process of dialectical thinking.

T

tangles Twisted masses of threads made of a protein called tau within the neurons of the brain.

telomeres The area of the tips of each chromosome that is reduced a tiny amount as time passes. By the end of life, the telomeres are very short.

temperament Inborn differences between one person and another in emotions, activity, and self-regulation. It is measured by the person's typical responses to the environment.

teratogen An agent or condition, including viruses, drugs, and chemicals, that can impair prenatal development and result in birth defects or even death.

tertiary circular reactions The third of three types of feedback loops in sensorimotor intelligence, this one involving active exploration and experimentation. Infants explore a range of new activities, varying their responses as a way of learning about the world.

tertiary prevention Actions, such as immediate and effective medical treatment, that are taken after an adverse event (such as illness or injury) and that reduce harm.

testosterone A sex hormone, the best known of the androgens (male hormones); secreted in far greater amounts by males than by females.

theory of mind A person's theory of what other people might be thinking. In order to have a theory of mind, children must realize that other people are not necessarily thinking the same thoughts that they themselves are. That realization seldom occurs before age 4.

theory-theory The idea that children attempt to explain everything they see and hear by constructing theories.

thesis A proposition or statement of belief; the first stage of the process of dialectical thinking.

threshold effect In prenatal development, when a teratogen is relatively harmless in small doses but becomes harmful once exposure reaches a certain level (the threshold).

time-out A disciplinary technique in which a person is separated from other people and activities for a specified time.

transient exuberance The great but temporary increase in the number of dendrites that develop in an infant's brain during the first two years of life.

trust versus mistrust Erikson's first crisis of psychosocial development. Infants learn basic trust if the world is a secure place where their basic needs (for food, comfort, attention, and so on) are met.

23rd pair The chromosome pair that, in humans, determines sex. The other 22 pairs are autosomes, inherited equally by males and females.

U

universal design The creation of settings and equipment that can be used by everyone, whether or not they are able-bodied and sensory-acute.

V

vascular disease Formerly called *vascular* or *multi-infarct dementia,* vascular disease is characterized by sporadic, and progressive, loss of intellectual functioning caused by repeated infarcts, or temporary obstructions of blood vessels, which prevent sufficient blood from reaching the brain.

very low birthweight (VLBW) A body weight at birth of less than 1,500 grams (3 pounds, 5 ounces).

W

Waldorf schools An early-childhood education program that emphasizes creativity, social understanding, and emotional growth. It originated in Germany with Rudolf Steiner, and now is used in thousands of schools throughout the world.

wasting The tendency for children to be severely underweight for their age as a result of malnutrition.

wear-and-tear theory A view of aging as a process by which the human body wears out because of the passage of time and exposure to environmental stressors.

WEIRD An acronym that refers to people from Western, Educated, Industrialized, Rich Democracies, in other words, to North American college students, not necessarily the rest of humanity.

withdrawn-rejected A type of childhood rejection, when other children do not want to be friends with a child because of their timid, withdrawn, and anxious behavior.

working model In cognitive theory, a set of assumptions that the individual uses to organize perceptions and experiences. For example, a person might assume that other people are trustworthy and be surprised by an incident in which this working model of human behavior is erroneous.

X

X-linked A gene carried on the X chromosome. If a male inherits an X-linked recessive trait from his mother, he expresses that trait because the Y from his father has no counteracting gene. Females are more likely to be carriers of X-linked traits but are less likely to express them.

XX A 23rd chromosome pair that consists of two X-shaped chromosomes, one each from the mother and the father. XX zygotes become females.

XY A 23rd chromosome pair that consists of an X-shaped chromosome from the mother and a Y-shaped chromosome from the father. XY zygotes become males.

Y

young-old Healthy, vigorous, financially secure older adults (generally, those aged 65 to 75) who are well integrated into the lives of their families and communities.

Z

zone of proximal development (ZPD) In sociocultural theory, a metaphorical area, or "zone," surrounding a learner that includes all of the skills, knowledge, and concepts that the person is close ("proximal") to acquiring but cannot yet master without help.

zygote The single cell formed from the union of two gametes, a sperm and an ovum.

REFERENCES

Aarnoudse-Moens, Cornelieke S. H.; Smidts, Diana P.; Oosterlaan, Jaap; Duivenvoorden, Hugo J. & Weisglas-Kuperus, Nynke. (2009). Executive function in very preterm children at early school age. *Journal of Abnormal Child Psychology*, 37(7), 981–993.

Abar, Caitlin C.; Jackson, Kristina M. & Wood, Mark. (2014). Reciprocal relations between perceived parental knowledge and adolescent substance use and delinquency: The moderating role of parent–teen relationship quality. *Developmental Psychology*, 50(9), 2176–2187.

Abraham, Eyal & Feldman, Ruth. (2018). The neurobiology of human allomaternal care; implications for fathering, coparenting, and children's social development. *Physiology & Behavior*, 193, 25–34.

Abramovitch, Amitai; Anholt, Gideon; Raveh-Gottfried, Sagi; Hamo, Naama & Abramowitz, Jonathan. (2018). Meta-analysis of intelligence quotient (IQ) in obsessive-compulsive disorder. *Neuropsychology Review*, 28(1), 111–120.

Accardo, Pasquale. (2006). Who's training whom? *The Journal of Pediatrics*, 149(2), 151–152.

Acharya, Arnab; Lalwani, Tanya; Dutta, Rahul; Knoll Rajaratnam, Julie; Ruducha, Jenny; Varkey, Leila Caleb, . . . Bernson, Jeff. (2015). Evaluating a large-scale community-based intervention to improve pregnancy and newborn health among the rural poor in India. *American Journal of Public Health*, 105(1), 144–152.

Acharya, Kartikey; Leuthner, Stephen; Clark, Reese; Nghiem-Rao, Tuyet-Hang; Spitzer, Alan & Lagatta, Joanne. (2017). Major anomalies and birth-weight influence NICU interventions and mortality in infants with trisomy 13 or 18. *Journal of Perinatology*, 37(4), 420–426.

Acuto, Michele & Parnell, Susan. (2016). Leave no city behind. *Science*, 352(6288), 873.

Adamson, Lauren B. & Bakeman, Roger. (2006). Development of displaced speech in early mother-child conversations. *Child Development*, 77(1), 186–200.

Adamson, Lauren B.; Bakeman, Roger; Deckner, Deborah F. & Nelson, P. Brooke. (2014). From interactions to conversations: The development of joint engagement during early childhood. *Child Development*, 85(3), 941–955.

Addati, Laura; Cassirer, Naomi & Gilchrist, Katherine. (2014). *Maternity and paternity at work: Law and practice across the world*. Geneva: International Labour Office.

Adler, Caleb; DelBello, Melissa, P; Weber, Wade; Williams, Miranda; Duran, Luis Rodrigo Patino; Fleck, David, . . . Divine, Jon. (2018). MRI evidence of neuropathic changes in former college football players. *Clinical Journal of Sport Medicine*, 28(2), 100–105.

Adler, Lynn Peters. (1995). *Centenarians: The bonus years*. Santa Fe, NM: Health Press.

Adolph, Karen E. & Franchak, John M. (2017). The development of motor behavior. *WIREs*, 8(1/2), e1430.

Adolph, Karen E. & Robinson, Scott. (2013). The road to walking: What learning to walk tells us about development. In Philip D. Zelazo (Ed.), *The Oxford handbook of developmental psychology* (Vol. 1, pp. 402–447). New York, NY: Oxford University Press.

Adolph, Karen E. & Tamis-LeMonda, Catherine S. (2014). The costs and benefits of development: The transition from crawling to walking. *Child Development Perspectives*, 8(4), 187–192.

Aggarwal, Bharat B. & Yost, Debora. (2011). *Healing spices: How to use 50 everyday and exotic spices to boost health and beat disease*. New York, NY: Sterling.

Ahler, Douglas J. & Sood, Gaurav. (2018). The parties in our heads: Misperceptions about party composition and their consequences. *The Journal of Politics*, 80(3), 964–981.

Ahles, Tim A.; Root, James C. & Ryan, Elizabeth L. (2012). Cancer- and cancer treatment-associated cognitive change: An update on the state of the science. *Journal of Clinical Oncology*, 30(30), 3675–3686.

Ahmadabadi, Zohre; Najman, Jackob M.; Williams, Gail M.; Clavarino, Alexandra M.; d'Abbs, Peter & Smirnov, Andrew. (2019). Intimate partner violence in emerging adulthood and subsequent substance use disorders: Findings from a longitudinal study. *Addiction*, 114(7), 1264–1273.

Ailshire, Jennifer A.; Beltrán-Sánchez, Hiram & Crimmins, Eileen M. (2015). Becoming centenarians: Disease and functioning trajectories of older U.S. adults as they survive to 100. *The Journal of Gerontology Series A*, 70(2), 193–201.

Ainsworth, Mary D. Salter. (1967). *Infancy in Uganda: Infant care and the growth of love*. Baltimore, MD: Johns Hopkins Press.

Ainsworth, Mary D. Salter. (1973). The development of infant-mother attachment. In Bettye M. Caldwell & Henry N. Ricciuti (Eds.), *Child development and social policy* (pp. 1–94). Chicago, IL: University of Chicago Press.

Aizer, Anna & Currie, Janet. (2014). The intergenerational transmission of inequality: Maternal disadvantage and health at birth. *Science*, 344(6186), 856–861.

Aizpitarte, Alazne; Atherton, Olivia E.; Zheng, Lucy R.; Alonso-Arbiol, Itziar & Robins, Richard W. (2019). Developmental precursors of relational aggression from late childhood through adolescence. *Child Development*, 90(1), 117–126.

Akhtar, Nameera & Jaswal, Vikram K. (2013). Deficit or difference? Interpreting diverse developmental paths: An introduction to the special section. *Developmental Psychology*, 49(1), 1–3.

Aksglaede, Lise; Link, Katarina; Giwercman, Aleksander; Jørgensen, Niels; Skakkebæk, Niels E. & Juul, Anders. (2013). 47, XXY Klinefelter syndrome: Clinical characteristics and age-specific recommendations for medical management. *American Journal of Medical Genetics Part C: Seminars in Medical Genetics*, 163(1), 55–63.

Al Otaiba, Stephanie; Baker, Kristi; Lan, Patrick; Allor, Jill; Rivas, Brenna; Yovanoff, Paul & Kamata, Akihito. (2019). Elementary teacher's knowledge of response to intervention implementation: A preliminary factor analysis. *Annals of Dyslexia*, 69(1), 34–53.

Al Otaiba, Stephanie; Wanzek, Jeanne & Yovanoff, Paul. (2015). Response to intervention. *European Scientific Journal*, 1, 260–264.

Al-Hashim, Aqeela H.; Blaser, Susan; Raybaud, Charles & MacGregor, Daune. (2016). Corpus callosum abnormalities: Neuroradiological and clinical correlations. *Developmental Medicine & Child Neurology*, 58(5), 475–484.

Al-Namlah, Abdulrahman S.; Meins, Elizabeth & Fernyhough, Charles. (2012). Self-regulatory private speech relates to children's recall and organization of autobiographical memories. *Early Childhood Research Quarterly*, 27(3), 441–446.

Al-Sayes, Fatin; Gari, Mamdooh; Qusti, Safaa; Bagatian, Nadiah & Abuzenadah, Adel. (2011). Prevalence of iron deficiency and iron deficiency anemia among females at university stage. *Journal of Medical Laboratory and Diagnosis*, 2(1), 5–11.

Albert, Dustin; Chein, Jason & Steinberg, Laurence. (2013). The teenage brain: Peer influences on adolescent decision making. *Current Directions in Psychological Science*, 22(2), 114–120.

Albert, Dustin & Steinberg, Laurence. (2011). Judgment and decision making in adolescence. *Journal of Research on Adolescence*, 21(1), 211–224.

Aldwin, Carolyn M. & Gilmer, Diane Fox. (2013). *Health, illness, and optimal aging: Biological and psychosocial perspectives* (2nd ed.). New York, NY: Springer.

Alegre, Alberto. (2011). Parenting styles and children's emotional intelligence: What do we know? *The Family Journal*, 19(1), 56–62.

Alesi, Marianha; Bianco, Antonino; Padulo, Johnny; Vella, Francesco Paolo; Petrucci, Marco; Paoli, Antonio, . . . Pepi, Annamaria. (2014). Motor and cognitive development: The role of karate. *Muscle, Ligaments and Tendons Journal*, 4(2), 114–120.

Alexander, Karl L.; Entwisle, Doris R. & Olson, Linda Steffel. (2014). *The long shadow: Family background, disadvantaged urban youth, and the transition to adulthood*. New York, NY: Russell Sage Foundation.

Alexandre-Heymann, Laure; Dubert, Marie; Diallo, Dapa A.; Diop, Saliou; Tolo, Aissata;

Belinga, Suzanne, . . . Ranque, Brigitte. (2019). Prevalence and correlates of growth failure in young African patients with sickle cell disease. *British Journal of Haematology, 184*(2), 253–262.

Allen, Sian & Hopkins, Will. (2015). Age of peak competitive performance of elite athletes: A systematic review. *Sports Medicine, 45*(10), 1431–1441.

Allendorf, Keera. (2013). Schemas of marital change: From arranged marriages to eloping for love. *Journal of Marriage and Family, 75*(2), 453–469.

Allendorf, Keera & Pandian, Roshan K. (2016). The decline of arranged marriage? Marital change and continuity in India. *Population and Development Review, 42*(3), 435–464.

Allport, Gordon. (1954). *The nature of prejudice*. Cambridge, MA: Addison-Wesley.

Alper, Meryl. (2013). Developmentally appropriate New Media Literacies: Supporting cultural competencies and social skills in early childhood education. *Journal of Early Childhood Literacy, 13*(2), 175–196.

Altmann, Andre; Tian, Lu; Henderson, Victor W. & Greicius, Michael D. (2014). Sex modifies the *APOE*-related risk of developing Alzheimer disease. *Annals of Neurology, 75*(4), 563–573.

Alvarado, Louis; Muller, Martin; Eaton, Melissa & Thompson, Melissa Emery. (2018). Steroid hormone reactivity in fathers watching their children compete. *Human Nature,* 29(3), 268–282.

Alvira-Hammond, Marta; Longmore, Monica A.; Manning, Wendy D. & Giordano, Peggy C. (2014). Gainful activity and intimate partner aggression in emerging adulthood. *Emerging Adulthood, 2*(2), 116–127.

Amato, Michael S.; Magzamen, Sheryl; Imm, Pamela; Havlena, Jeffrey A.; Anderson, Henry A.; Kanarek, Marty S. & Moore, Colleen F. (2013). Early lead exposure (<3 years old) prospectively predicts fourth grade school suspension in Milwaukee, Wisconsin (USA). *Environmental Research, 126*, 60–65.

Amato, Paul R. (2010). Research on divorce: Continuing trends and new developments. *Journal of Marriage and Family*, 72(3), 650–666.

Ameade, Evans Paul Kwame & Garti, Helene Akpene. (2016). Age at menarche and factors that influence it: A study among female university students in Tamale, northern Ghana. *PLoS ONE, 11*(5), e0155310.

American Academy of Pediatrics. (2014). *Caring for your baby and young child, birth to age 5* (6th ed.). New York, NY: Bantam.

American Academy of Pediatrics. (2016). Media and young minds. *Pediatrics, 138*(5).

American Academy of Pediatrics. (2018, May 1). Children and media tips from the American Academy of Pediatrics [Press release]. Itasca, IL: American Academy of Pediatrics.

American Psychiatric Association. (2013). *Diagnostic and statistical manual of mental disorders: DSM-5* (5th ed.). Washington, DC: American Psychiatric Association.

Amin, Avnika; Bednarczyk, Robert; Ray, Cara; Melchiori, Kala; Graham, Jesse; Huntsinger, Jeffrey & Omer, Saad. (2017). Association of moral values with vaccine hesitancy. *Nature Human Behaviour, 1*(12), 873–880.

Anandakumar, Jeya; Mills, Kathryn L.; Earl, Eric A.; Irwin, Lourdes; Miranda-Dominguez, Oscar; Demeter, Damion V., . . . Fair, Damien A. (2018). Individual differences in functional brain connectivity predict temporal discounting preference in the transition to adolescence. *Developmental Cognitive Neuroscience, 34*, 101–113.

Anderin, Claes; Gustafsson, Ulf O.; Heijbel, Niklas & Thorell, Anders. (2015). Weight loss before bariatric surgery and postoperative complications: Data from the Scandinavian Obesity Registry (SOReg). *Annals of Surgery, 261*(5), 909–913.

Anderson, Craig A.; Shibuya, Akiko; Ihori, Nobuko; Swing, Edward L.; Bushman, Brad J.; Sakamoto, Akira, . . . Saleem, Muniba. (2010). Violent video game effects on aggression, empathy, and prosocial behavior in Eastern and Western countries: A meta-analytic review. *Psychological Bulletin, 136*(2), 151–173.

Anderson, Daniel R. & Hanson, Katherine G. (2016). Screen media and parent–child interactions. In Rachel Barr & Deborah Nichols Linebarger (Eds.), *Media exposure during infancy and early childhood: The effects of content and context on learning and development* (pp. 173–194). Cham, Switzerland: Springer.

Anderson, Michael. (2001). 'You have to get inside the person' or making grief private: Image and metaphor in the therapeutic reconstruction of bereavement. In Jenny Hockey, et al. (Eds.), *Grief, mourning, and death ritual* (pp. 135–143). Buckingham, UK: Open University Press.

Anderson, Monica. (2016, January 7). *Parents, teens and digital monitoring. Numbers, Facts and Trends Shaping the World*. Washington, DC: Pew Research Center.

Anderson, Monica. (2018, September 27). *A majority of teens have experienced some form of cyberbullying*. Washington, DC: Pew Research Center.

Andreas, Nicholas J. ; Kampmann, Beate & Le-Doare, Kirsty Mehring. (2015). Human breast milk: A review on its composition and bioactivity. *Early Human Development, 91*(11), 629–635.

Ang, Shannon. (2019). Life course social connectedness: Age-cohort trends in social participation. *Advances in Life Course Research, 39*, 13–22.

Ansado, Jennyfer; Collins, Louis; Fonov, Vladimir; Garon, Mathieu; Alexandrov, Lubomir; Karama, Sherif, . . . Beauchamp, Miriam H. (2015). A new template to study callosal growth shows specific growth in anterior and posterior regions of the corpus callosum in early childhood. *European Journal of Neuroscience, 42*(1), 1675–1684.

Ansmann, Lena; Winter, Nicola; Ernstmann, Nicole; Heidenreich, Axel; Weissbach, Lothar & Herden, Jan. (2018). Health-related quality of life in active surveillance and radical prostatectomy for low-risk prostate cancer: A prospective observational study (HAROW — Hormonal therapy, Active Surveillance, Radiation, Operation, Watchful Waiting). *BJU International, 122*(3), 401–410.

Antonucci, Toni C.; Akiyama, Hiroko & Merline, Alicia. (2001). Dynamics of social relationships in midlife. In Margie E. Lachman (Ed.), *Handbook of midlife development* (pp. 571–598). New York, NY: Wiley.

Ardelt, Monika; Gerlach, Kathryn R. & Vaillant, George E. (2018). Early and midlife predictors of wisdom and subjective well-being in old age. *The Journals of Gerontology Series B: Psychological Sciences and Social Sciences*, 73(8), 1514–1525.

Arden, Rosalind; Luciano, Michelle; Deary, Ian J.; Reynolds, Chandra A.; Pedersen, Nancy L.; Plassman, Brenda L., . . . Visscher, Peter M. (2016). The association between intelligence and lifespan is mostly genetic. *International Journal of Epidemiology, 45*(1), 178–185.

Areba, Eunice M.; Eisenberg, Marla E. & McMorris, Barbara J. (2018). Relationships between family structure, adolescent health status and substance use: Does ethnicity matter? *Journal of Community Psychology, 46*(1), 44–57.

Argyrides, Marios & Kkeli, Natalie. (2015). Predictive factors of disordered eating and body image satisfaction in Cyprus. *International Journal of Eating Disorders, 48*(4), 431–435.

Arias, Elizabeth; Heron, Melonie & Xu, Jiaquan. (2017, April 11). *United States life tables, 2013. National Vital Statistics Report, 66*(3). Hyattsville, MD: National Center for Health Statistics.

Ariely, Dan. (2010). *Predictably Irrational: The hidden forces that shape our decisions* (Revised and Expanded ed.). New York, NY: Harper Perennial.

Armstrong, Kim. (2018). The WEIRD science of culture, values, and behavior [Web log post]. Association for Psychological Science.

Arnett, Jeffrey Jensen. (2000). Emerging adulthood: A theory of development from the late teens through the twenties. *American Psychologist*, 55(5), 469–480.

Arnheim, Norman & Calabrese, Peter. (2016). Germline stem cell competition, mutation hot spots, genetic disorders, and older fathers. *Annual Review of Genomics and Human Genetics, 17*, 219–243.

Aron, Arthur; Lewandowski, Gary W.; Mashek, Debra & Aron, Elaine N. (2013). The self-expansion model of motivation and cognition in close relationships. In Jeffry A. Simpson & Lorne Campbell (Eds.), *The Oxford handbook of close relationships* (pp. 90–115). New York, NY: Oxford University Press.

Arshad, S. Hasan; Karmaus, Wilfried; Zhang, Hongmei & Holloway, John W. (2017). Multigenerational cohorts in patients with asthma and allergy. *Journal of Allergy and Clinical Immunology, 139*(2), 415–421.

Arterburn, David E.; Bogart, Andy; Sherwood, Nancy E.; Sidney, Stephen; Coleman, Karen J.; Haneuse, Sebastien, . . . Selby, Joe. (2013). A multisite study of long-term remission and relapse of type 2 diabetes mellitus following gastric bypass. *Obesity Surgery*, *23*(1), 93–102.

Arum, Richard & Roksa, Josipa. (2011). *Academically adrift: Limited learning on college campuses*. Chicago, IL: University of Chicago Press.

Arum, Richard & Roksa, Josipa. (2014). *Aspiring adults adrift: Tentative transitions of college graduates*. Chicago, IL: University of Chicago Press.

Ashraf, Quamrul & Galor, Oded. (2013). The 'Out of Africa' hypothesis, human genetic diversity, and comparative economic development. *American Economic Review*, *103*(1), 1–46.

Ashwin, Sarah & Isupova, Olga. (2014). "Behind every great man . . . ": The male marriage wage premium examined qualitatively. *Journal of Marriage and Family*, *76*(1), 37–55.

Aslin, Richard N. (2012). Language development: Revisiting Eimas et al.'s /ba/ and /pa/ study. In Alan M. Slater & Paul C. Quinn (Eds.), *Developmental psychology: Revisiting the classic studies* (pp. 191–203). Thousand Oaks, CA: Sage.

Association of American Medical Colleges. (2013). *Enrollment, graduates, and MD/PhD data: Table 27, Total graduates by U.S. medical school and sex, 2009–2013*. Washington, DC: Association of American Medical Colleges.

Association of American Medical Colleges. (2014). *Table 1: Medical students, selected years, 1965–2013. The state of women in academic medicine: The pipeline and pathways to leadership, 2013–2014*. Washington, DC: Association of American Medical Colleges.

Association of American Medical Colleges. (2015, November 25). *Table B-2.2: Total graduates by U.S. medical school and sex, 2010–2011 through 2014–2015. FACTS: Applicants, matriculants, enrollment, graduates, M.D.-Ph.D., and residency applicants data*. Washington, DC: Association of American Medical Colleges.

Astington, Janet W.; Harris, Paul L. & Olson, David R. (Eds.). (1988). *Developing theories of mind*. New York, NY: Cambridge University Press.

Atamna, Hani; Tenore, Alfred; Lui, Forshing & Dhahbi, Joseph M. (2018). Organ reserve, excess metabolic capacity, and aging. *Biogerontology*, *19*(2), 171–184.

Attaran, Amir. (2015). Unanimity on death with dignity — Legalizing physician-assisted dying in Canada. *New England Journal of Medicine*, *372*, 2080–2082.

Atzaba-Poria, Naama; Deater-Deckard, Kirby & Bell, Martha Ann. (2017). Mother-child interaction: Links between mother and child frontal electroencephalograph asymmetry and negative behavior. *Child Development*, *88*(2), 544–554.

Atzil, Shir; Hendler, Talma & Feldman, Ruth. (2014). The brain basis of social synchrony. *Social Cognitive and Affective Neuroscience*, *9*(8), 1193–1202.

Aud, Susan; Hussar, William; Planty, Michael; Snyder, Thomas; Bianco, Kevin; Fox, Mary Ann, . . . Drake, Lauren. (2010). *The condition of education 2010*. Washington, DC: National Center for Education Statistics, Institute of Education Sciences, U.S. Department of Education.

Augustine, Vineet; Gokce, Sertan Kutal & Oka, Yuki. (2018). Peripheral and central nutrient sensing underlying appetite regulation. *Trends in Neurosciences*, *41*(8), 526–539.

Aunola, Kaisa; Tolvanen, Asko; Viljaranta, Jaana & Nurmi, Jari-Erik. (2013). Psychological control in daily parent–child interactions increases children's negative emotions. *Journal of Family Psychology*, *27*(3), 453–462.

Austin, Makeda K.; Chen, Edith; Ross, Kharah M.; Mcewen, Lisa M.; Maclsaac, Julia L.; Kobor, Michael S. & Miller, Gregory E. (2018). Early-life socioeconomic disadvantage, not current, predicts accelerated epigenetic aging of monocytes. *Psychoneuroendocrinology*, *97*, 131–134.

Avery, Rosemary J. & Freundlich, Madelyn. (2009). You're all grown up now: Termination of foster care support at age 18. *Journal of Adolescence*, *32*(2), 247–257.

Aviv, Abraham. (2011). Leukocyte telomere dynamics, human aging and life span. In Edward J. Masoro & Steven N. Austad (Eds.), *Handbook of the biology of aging* (7th ed., pp. 163–176). San Diego, CA: Academic Press.

Ayoub, Mona; Briley, Daniel A.; Grotzinger, Andrew; Patterson, Megan W.; Engelhardt, Laura E.; Tackett, Jennifer L., . . . Tucker-Drob, Elliot M. (2018). Genetic and environmental associations between child personality and parenting. *Social Psychological and Personality Science*, (In Press).

Ayyanathan, Kasirajan (Ed.). (2014). *Specific gene expression and epigenetics: The interplay between the genome and its environment*. Oakville, Canada: Apple Academic Press.

Azrin, Nathan H. & Foxx, Richard M. (1974). *Toilet training in less than a day*. New York, NY: Simon & Schuster.

Babadjouni, Robin M.; Hodis, Drew M.; Radwanski, Ryan; Durazo, Ramon; Patel, Arati; Liu, Qinghai & Mack, William J. (2017). Clinical effects of air pollution on the central nervous system; A review. *Journal of Clinical Neuroscience*, *43*, 16–24.

Babchishin, Lyzon K.; Weegar, Kelly & Romano, Elisa. (2013). Early child care effects on later behavioral outcomes using a Canadian nation-wide sample. *Journal of Educational and Developmental Psychology*, *3*(2), 15–29.

Babcock, Renée L.; Malonebeach, Eileen E. & Salomon, Hannah M. (2018). A quantitative and qualitative evaluation of the impact of an intergenerational program on children's biases toward older adults. *Journal of Intergenerational Relationships*, *16*(1/2), 123–138.

Bachman, Heather J.; Votruba-Drzal, Elizabeth; El Nokali, Nermeen E. & Castle Heatly, Melissa. (2015). Opportunities for learning math in elementary school: Implications for SES disparities in procedural and conceptual math skills. *American Educational Research Journal*, *52*(5), 894–923.

Baert, Stijn. (2018). Facebook profile picture appearance affects recruiters' first hiring decisions. *New Media & Society*, *20*(3), 1220–1239.

Bagchi, Debasis (Ed.). (2019). *Global perspectives on childhood obesity: Current status, consequences and prevention* (2nd ed.). San Diego, CA: Academic Press.

Bagot, Kara. (2017). Making the grade: Adolescent prescription stimulant use. *Journal of the American Academy of Child & Adolescent Psychiatry*, *56*(3), 189–190.

Bagwell, Catherine L. & Schmidt, Michelle E. (2011). *Friendships in childhood & adolescence*. New York, NY: Guilford Press.

Bailey, J. Michael; Vasey, Paul L.; Diamond, Lisa M.; Breedlove, S. Marc; Vilain, Eric & Epprecht, Marc. (2016). Sexual orientation, controversy, and science. *Psychological Science in the Public Interest*, *17*(2), 45–101.

Baillargeon, Renée & DeVos, Julie. (1991). Object permanence in young infants: Further evidence. *Child Development*, *62*(6), 1227–1246.

Baio, Jon; Wiggins, Lisa; Christensen, Deborah L.; Maenner, Matthew J.; Daniels, Julie; Warren, Zachary, . . . Dowling, Nicole F. (2018, April 27). *Prevalence of autism spectrum disorder among children aged 8 years — Autism and Developmental Disabilities Monitoring Network, 11 Sites, United States, 2014. Morbidity and Mortality Weekly Report*, *67*(SS-6), 1–23.

Baker, Darren J. & Petersen, Ronald C. (2018). Cellular senescence in brain aging and neurodegenerative diseases: Evidence and perspectives. *The Journal of Clinical Investigation*, *128*(4), 1208–1216.

Baker, Jeffrey P. (2000). Immunization and the American way: 4 childhood vaccines. *American Journal of Public Health*, *90*(2), 199–207.

Baker, Lindsey A. & Silverstein, Merril. (2012). The wellbeing of grandparents caring for grandchildren in rural China and the United States. In Sara Arber & Virpi Timonen (Eds.), *Contemporary grandparenting: Changing family relationships in global contexts* (pp. 51–70). Chicago, IL: Policy Press.

Baker, Olesya & Lang, Kevin. (2013). *The effect of high school exit exams on graduation, employment, wages and incarceration*. Cambridge, MA: National Bureau of Economic Research.

Baker, Simon T. E.; Lubman, Dan I.; Yücel, Murat; Allen, Nicholas B.; Whittle, Sarah; Fulcher, Ben D., . . . Fornito, Alex. (2015). Developmental changes in brain network hub connectivity in late adolescence. *Journal of Neuroscience*, *35*(24), 9078–9087.

Balk, David & Varga, Mary Alice. (2017). Continuing bonds and social media in the lives of bereaved college students. In Dennis Klass & Edith Maria Steffen (Eds.), *Continuing bonds in bereavement: New directions for research and practice*. New York, NY: Routledge.

Ball, Helen L. & Volpe, Lane E. (2013). Sudden infant death syndrome (SIDS) risk reduction and infant sleep location — Moving the discussion forward. *Social Science & Medicine*, *79*(1), 84–91.

Baltes, Paul B. (2003). On the incomplete architecture of human ontogeny: Selection, optimization and compensation as foundation of developmental theory. In Ursula M. Staudinger & Ulman Lindenberger (Eds.), *Understanding human development: Dialogues with lifespan psychology* (pp. 17–43). Boston, MA: Kluwer Academic Publishers.

Baltes, Paul B. & Baltes, Margret M. (1990). Psychological perspectives on successful aging: The model of selective optimization with compensation. In Paul B. Baltes & Margret M. Baltes (Eds.), *Successful aging: Perspectives from the behavioral sciences* (pp. 1–34). New York, NY: Cambridge University Press.

Baltes, Paul B.; Lindenberger, Ulman & Staudinger, Ursula M. (1998). Life-span theory in developmental psychology. In William Damon (Ed.), *Handbook of child psychology* (5th ed., Vol. 1, pp. 1029–1144). New York, NY: Wiley.

Baltes, Paul B.; Lindenberger, Ulman & Staudinger, Ursula M. (2006). Life span theory in developmental psychology. In William Damon & Richard M. Lerner (Eds.), *Handbook of child psychology* (6th ed., Vol. 1, pp. 569–664). Hoboken, NJ: Wiley.

Baltes, Paul B. & Smith, Jacqui. (2008). The fascination of wisdom: Its nature, ontogeny, and function. *Perspectives on Psychological Science*, 3(1), 56–64.

Baly, Michael W.; Cornell, Dewey G. & Lovegrove, Peter. (2014). A longitudinal investigation of self- and peer reports of bullying victimization across middle school. *Psychology in the Schools*, *51*(3), 217–240.

Bancks, Michael P.; Kershaw, Kiarri; Carson, April P.; Gordon-Larsen, Penny; Schreiner, Pamela J. & Carnethon, Mercedes R. (2017). Association of modifiable risk factors in young adulthood with racial disparity in incident type 2 diabetes during middle adulthood. *JAMA*, *318*(24), 2457–2465.

Bandura, Albert. (1986). *Social foundations of thought and action: A social cognitive theory*. Englewood Cliffs, NJ: Prentice-Hall.

Bandura, Albert. (1997). The anatomy of stages of change. *American Journal of Health Promotion*, *12*(1), 8–10.

Bandura, Albert. (2006). Toward a psychology of human agency. *Perspectives on Psychological Science*, *1*(2), 164–180.

Bandura, Albert. (2016). *Moral disengagement: How people do harm and live with themselves*. New York, NY: Worth.

Banks, James R. & Andrews, Timothy. (2015). Outcomes of childhood asthma to the age of 50 years. *Pediatrics*, *136*(Suppl. 3).

Bannon, Michael J.; Johnson, Magen M.; Michelhaugh, Sharon K.; Hartley, Zachary J.; Halter, Steven D.; David, James A., . . . Schmidt, Carl J. (2014). A molecular profile of cocaine abuse includes the differential expression of genes that regulate transcription, chromatin, and dopamine cell phenotype. *Neuropsychopharmacology*, *39*(9), 2191–2199.

Baranowski, Tom & Taveras, Elsie M. (2018). Childhood obesity prevention: Changing the focus. *Childhood Obesity*, *14*(1), 1–3.

Barber, Brian K. (Ed.). (2002). *Intrusive parenting: How psychological control affects children and adolescents*. Washington, DC: American Psychological Association.

Barber, Sarah J. & Mather, Mara. (2014). Stereotype threat in older adults: When and why does it occur and who is most affected? In Paul Verhaeghen & Christopher Hertzog (Eds.), *The Oxford handbook of emotion, social cognition, and problem solving in adulthood*. New York, NY: Oxford University Press.

Barbey, Aron K. (2018). Network neuroscience theory of human intelligence. *Trends in Cognitive Sciences*, *22*(1), 8–20.

Barnes, J. C. & Motz, Ryan. (2018). Reducing racial inequalities in adulthood arrest by reducing inequalities in school discipline: Evidence from the school-to-prison pipeline. *Developmental Psychology*, *54*(12), 2328–2340.

Barnett, W. Steven; Carolan, Megan E.; Squires, James H.; Brown, Kirsty Clarke & Horowitz, Michelle. (2015). *The state of preschool 2014: State preschool yearbook*. New Brunswick, NJ: National Institute for Early Education Research.

Barnett, W. Steven; Weisenfeld, G. G.; Brown, Kirsty; Squires, Jim & Horowitz, Michelle. (2016, July 29). *Implementing 15 essential elements for high quality: A state and local policy scan*. New Brunswick, NJ: National Institute for Early Education Research.

Baron-Cohen, Simon; Tager-Flusberg, Helen & Lombardo, Michael (Eds.). (2013). *Understanding other minds: Perspectives from developmental social neuroscience* (3rd ed.). New York, NY: Oxford University Press.

Barone, Joseph. (2015). *It's not your fault!: Strategies for solving toilet training and bedwetting problems*. New Brunswick, NJ: Rutgers University Press.

Barr, Rachel. (2013). Memory constraints on infant learning from picture books, television, and touchscreens. *Child Development Perspectives*, 7(4), 205–210.

Barrett, Anne E. (2012). Feeling young—A prescription for growing older? *Aging Today*, 33, 3–4.

Barrios, Yasmin V.; Sanchez, Sixto E.; Nicolaidis, Christina; Garcia, Pedro J.; Gelaye, Bizu; Zhong, Qiuyue & Williams, Michelle A. (2015). Childhood abuse and early menarche among Peruvian women. *Journal of Adolescent Health*, 56(2), 197–202.

Barron, Peter; Pillay, Yogan; Doherty, Tanya; Sherman, Gayle; Jackson, Debra; Bhardwaj, Sanjana, . . . Goga, Ameena. (2013). Eliminating mother-to-child HIV transmission in South Africa. *Bulletin of the World Health Organization*, *91*(1), 70–74.

Barry, Carolyn McNamara; Padilla-Walker, Laura M. & Nelson, Larry J. (2012). The role of mothers and media on emerging adults' religious faith and practices by way of internalization of prosocial values. *Journal of Adult Development*, *19*(2), 66–78.

Bartels, Meike; Cacioppo, John T.; van Beijsterveldt, Toos C. E. M. & Boomsma, Dorret I. (2013). Exploring the association between well-being and psychopathology in adolescents. *Behavior Genetics*, *43*(3), 177–190.

Basseches, Michael. (1984). *Dialectical thinking and adult development*. Norwood, NJ: Ablex.

Basseches, Michael. (1989). Dialectical thinking as an organized whole: Comments on Irwin and Kramer. In Michael L. Commons, et al. (Eds.), *Adult development* (Vol. 1, pp. 161–178). New York, NY: Praeger.

Bassok, Daphna; Latham, Scott & Rorem, Anna. (2016). Is kindergarten the new first grade? *AERA Open*, 2(1).

Bateson, Mary Catherine. (2011). *Composing a further life: The age of active wisdom*. New York, NY: Vintage Books.

Bateson, Patrick & Martin, Paul. (2013). *Play, playfulness, creativity and innovation*. New York, NY: Cambridge University Press.

Bathory, Eleanor & Tomopoulos, Suzy. (2017). Sleep regulation, physiology and development, sleep duration and patterns, and sleep hygiene in infants, toddlers, and preschool-age children. *Current Problems in Pediatric and Adolescent Health Care*, 47(2), 29–42.

Baude, Amandine; Pearson, Jessica & Drapeau, Sylvie. (2016). Child adjustment in joint physical custody versus sole custody: A meta-analytic review. *Journal of Divorce & Remarriage*, 57(5), 338–360.

Bauer, Clemens C. C.; José-Luis, Díaz; Concha, Luis & Barrios, Fernando A. (2014). Sustained attention to spontaneous thumb sensations activates brain somatosensory and other proprioceptive areas. *Brain and Cognition*, *87*, 86–96.

Bauer, Patricia J.; San Souci, Priscilla & Pathman, Thanujeni. (2010). Infant memory. *Wiley Interdisciplinary Reviews: Cognitive Science*, *1*(2), 267–277.

Baumrind, Diana. (1967). Child care practices anteceding three patterns of preschool behavior. *Genetic Psychology Monographs*, 75(1), 43–88.

Baumrind, Diana. (1971). Current patterns of parental authority. *Developmental Psychology*, *4*(1, Pt. 2), 1–103.

Bax, Trent. (2014). *Youth and Internet addiction in China*. New York, NY: Routledge.

Bayley, Nancy. (1966). Learning in adulthood: The role of intelligence. In Herbert J. Klausmeier & Chester W. Harris (Eds.), *Analyses of concept learning* (pp. 117–138). New York, NY: Academic Press.

Bayley, Nancy & Oden, Melita H. (1955). The maintenance of intellectual ability in gifted adults. *The Journal of Gerontology Series B: Psychological Sciences and Social Sciences*, *10*(1), 91–107.

BBC News. (2019, February 15). Schools' climate strike: 'Why we skipped school to protest'.

Bea, Megan Doherty & Yi, Youngmin. (2019). Leaving the financial nest: Connecting young adults' financial independence to financial security. *Journal of Marriage and Family*, 81(2), 397–414.

Beal, Susan. (1988). Sleeping position and sudden infant death syndrome. *The Medical Journal of Australia*, *149*(10), 562.

Beauchaine, Theodore P.; Klein, Daniel N.; Crowell, Sheila E.; Derbidge, Christina & Gatzke-Kopp, Lisa. (2009). Multifinality in the development of personality disorders: A Biology × Sex × Environment interaction model of antisocial and borderline traits. *Development and Psychopathology, 21*(3), 735–770.

Beck, Melinda. (2009, May 26). How's your baby? Recalling the Apgar score's namesake. *Wall Street Journal*, p. D1.

Becker, Derek R.; McClelland, Megan M.; Loprinzi, Paul & Trost, Stewart G. (2014). Physical activity, self-regulation, and early academic achievement in preschool children. *Early Education and Development*, 25(1), 56–70.

Bedford, Elliott Louis; Blaire, Stephen; Carney, John G.; Hamel, Ron; Mindling, J. Daniel & Sullivan, M. C. (2017). Advance care planning, palliative care, and end-of-life care. *The National Catholic Bioethics Quarterly*, 17(3), 489–501.

Bee, Margaret; Shiroor, Anushree & Hill, Zelee. (2018). Neonatal care practices in sub-Saharan Africa: A systematic review of quantitative and qualitative data. *Journal of Health, Population and Nutrition*, 37(1).

Beebe, Beatrice; Messinger, Daniel; Bahrick, Lorraine E.; Margolis, Amy; Buck, Karen A. & Chen, Henian. (2016). A systems view of mother–infant face-to-face communication. *Developmental Psychology*, 52(4), 556–571.

Beilin, Lawrence & Huang, Rae-Chi. (2008). Childhood obesity, hypertension, the metabolic syndrome and adult cardiovascular disease. *Clinical and Experimental Pharmacology and Physiology*, 35(4), 409–411.

Beiter, R.; Nash, R.; Mccrady, M.; Rhoades, D.; Linscomb, M.; Clarahan, M. & Sammut, S. (2015). The prevalence and correlates of depression, anxiety, and stress in a sample of college students. *Journal of Affective Disorders*, 173, 90–96.

Beitsch, Rebecca. (2018, July 12). The U.S. targeted breastfeeding abroad. Here at home, it's another story. [Web log post]. PEW Charitable Trusts.

Bell, Beth T. & Dittmar, Helga. (2011). Does media type matter? The role of identification in adolescent girls' media consumption and the impact of different thin-ideal media on body image. *Sex Roles*, 65(7/8), 478–490.

Bell, Georgie; Hiscock, Harriet; Tobin, Sherryn; Cook, Fallon & Sung, Valerie. (2018). Behavioral outcomes of infant colic in toddlerhood: A longitudinal study. *The Journal of Pediatrics*, 201, 154–159.

Bell, Linda G. & Harsin, Amanda. (2018). A prospective longitudinal study of marriage from midlife to later life. *Couple and Family Psychology*, 7(1), 12–21.

Bell, Martha Ann & Calkins, Susan D. (2011). Attentional control and emotion regulation in early development. In Michael I. Posner (Ed.), *Cognitive neuroscience of attention* (2nd ed., pp. 322–330). New York, NY: Guilford Press.

Bellinger, David C. (2016). Lead contamination in Flint — An abject failure to protect public health. *New England Journal of Medicine*, 374(12), 1101–1103.

Belsky, Daniel W.; Caspi, Avshalom; Houts, Renate; Cohen, Harvey J.; Corcoran, David L.; Danese, Andrea, . . . Moffitt, Terrie E. (2015). Quantification of biological aging in young adults. *Proceedings of the National Academy of Sciences of the United States of America, 112*(30), E4104–E4110.

Belsky, Jay; Bakermans-Kranenburg, Marian J. & van IJzendoorn, Marinus H. (2007). For better and for worse: Differential susceptibility to environmental influences. *Current Directions in Psychological Science*, 16(6), 300–304.

Belsky, Jay; Steinberg, Laurence; Houts, Renate M. & Halpern-Felsher, Bonnie L. (2010). The development of reproductive strategy in females: Early maternal harshness → earlier menarche → increased sexual risk taking. *Developmental Psychology*, 46(1), 120–128.

Bem, Sandra L. (1981). Gender schema theory: A cognitive account of sex typing. *Psychological Review*, 88(4), 354–364.

Benatar, David. (2011). A legal right to die: Responding to slippery slope and abuse arguments. *Current Oncology, 18*(5), 206–207.

Bender, Heather L.; Allen, Joseph P.; McElhaney, Kathleen Boykin; Antonishak, Jill; Moore, Cynthia M.; Kelly, Heather O'Beirne & Davis, Steven M. (2007). Use of harsh physical discipline and developmental outcomes in adolescence. *Development and Psychopathology*, 19(1), 227–242.

Benigno, Joann P.; Byrd, Dana L.; McNamara, Joseph P. H.; Berg, W. Keith & Farrar, M. Jeffrey. (2011). Talking through transitions: Microgenetic changes in preschoolers' private speech and executive functioning. *Child Language Teaching and Therapy*, 27(3), 269–285.

Benn, Peter. (2016). Prenatal diagnosis of chromosomal abnormalities through chorionic villus sampling and amniocentesis. In Aubrey Milunsky & Jeff M. Milunsky (Eds.), *Genetic disorders and the fetus: Diagnosis, prevention, and treatment* (7th ed., pp. 178–266). Hoboken, NJ: Wiley-Blackwell.

Bennett, Craig M. & Baird, Abigail A. (2006). Anatomical changes in the emerging adult brain: A voxel-based morphometry study. *Human Brain Mapping*, 27(9), 766–777.

Benoit, Amelie; Lacourse, Eric & Claes, Michel. (2013). Pubertal timing and depressive symptoms in late adolescence: The moderating role of individual, peer, and parental factors. *Development and Psychopathology*, 25(2), 455–471.

Bentley, Gillian R. & Mascie-Taylor, C. G. Nicholas. (2000). Introduction. In Gillian R. Bentley & C. G. Nicholas Mascie-Taylor (Eds.), *Infertility in the modern world: Present and future prospects* (pp. 1–13). New York, NY: Cambridge University Press.

Bercovitz, Katherine & Pagnini, Francesco. (2016). Mindfulness as an opportunity to narrow the grey digital divide. In Daniela Villani, et al. (Eds.), *Integrating technology in positive psychology practice* (pp. 214–228). Hershey, PA: IGI Global.

Berg, Jeremy. (2018). Imagine a world without facts. *Science*, 362(6413), 379.

Bergelson, Elika & Swingley, Daniel. (2018). Young infants' word comprehension given an unfamiliar talker or altered pronunciations. *Child Development*, 89(5), 1567–1576.

Berger, Kathleen S. (1980). *The developing person* (1st ed.). New York, NY: Worth.

Berger, Kathleen S. (2019). *Grandmothering: Building strong ties with every generation*. Lanham, MD: Rowman & Littlefield.

Bergmann, Olaf; Spalding, Kirsty L. & Frisén, Jonas. (2015). Adult neurogenesis in humans. *Cold Spring Harbor Perspectives in Biology*, 7, a018994.

Berken, Jonathan A.; Gracco, Vincent L. & Klein, Denise. (2017). Early bilingualism, language attainment, and brain development. *Neuropsychologia*, 98, 220–227.

Berko, Jean. (1958). The child's learning of English morphology. *Word, 14*, 150–177.

Berkowitz, C.; Mosconi, L.; Rahman, A.; Scheyer, O.; Hristov, H. & Isaacson, Richard. (2018). Clinical application of APOE in Alzheimer's prevention: A precision medicine approach. *The Journal of Prevention of Alzheimer's Disease*, 5(4), 245–252.

Berkowitz, Talia; Schaeffer, Marjorie W.; Maloney, Erin A.; Peterson, Lori; Gregor, Courtney; Levine, Susan C. & Beilock, Sian L. (2015). Math at home adds up to achievement in school. *Science*, 350(6257), 196–198.

Berlin, Lisa J.; Martoccio, Tiffany L. & Jones Harden, Brenda. (2018). Improving early head start's impacts on parenting through attachment-based intervention: A randomized controlled trial. *Developmental Psychology*, 54(12), 2316–2327.

Bernard, Jessie S. (1982). *The future of marriage* (Revised ed.). New Haven, CT: Yale University Press.

Bernard, Kristin; Lind, Teresa & Dozier, Mary. (2014). Neurobiological consequences of neglect and abuse. In Jill E. Korbin & Richard D. Krugman (Eds.), *Handbook of child maltreatment* (pp. 205–223). New York, NY: Springer.

Bernaud, Jean-Luc. (2014). Career counseling and life meaning: A new perspective of life designing for research and applications. In Fabio A. Di & J- L. Bernaud (Eds.), *The Construction of the Identity in 21st century: A Festschrift for Jean Guichard* (pp. 29–40). New York, NY: Nova Science.

Betancourt, Theresa S.; McBain, Ryan; Newnham, Elizabeth A. & Brennan, Robert T. (2013). Trajectories of internalizing problems in war-affected Sierra Leonean youth: Examining conflict and postconflict factors. *Child Development*, 84(2), 455–470.

Bettelheim, Bruno. (1972). *The empty fortress: Infantile autism and the birth of the self*. New York, NY: Free Press.

Bhatia, Tej K. & Ritchie, William C. (Eds.). (2013). *The handbook of bilingualism and multilingualism* (2nd ed.). Malden, MA: Wiley-Blackwell.

Bialik, Kristen & Matsa, Katerina Eva. (2017, October 4). *Key trends in social and digital news media. Fact Tank.* Washington, DC: Pew Research Center.

Bialystok, Ellen. (2017). The bilingual adaptation: How minds accommodate experience. *Psychological Bulletin, 143*(3), 233–262.

Bialystok, Ellen. (2018). Bilingualism and executive function: What's the connection? In David Miller, et al. (Eds.), *Bilingual cognition and language: The state of the science across its subfields* (pp. 283–306). Amsterdam, the Netherlands: John Benjamins.

Bick, Johanna; Palmwood, Erin N.; Zajac, Lindsay; Simons, Robert & Dozier, Mary. (2019). Early parenting intervention and adverse family environments affect neural function in middle childhood. *Biological Psychiatry, 85*(4), 326–335.

Biemiller, Andrew. (2009). Parent/caregiver narrative: Vocabulary development (0–60 Months). In Linda M. Phillips (Ed.), *Handbook of language and literacy development: A roadmap from 0–60* (Online ed.). London, ON: Canadian Language and Literacy Research Network.

Biffen, Stevie C.; Warton, Christopher M. R.; Lindinger, Nadine M.; Randall, Steven R.; Lewis, Catherine E.; Molteno, Christopher D., . . . Meintjes, Ernesta M. (2018). Reductions in corpus callosum volume partially mediate effects of prenatal alcohol exposure on IQ. *Frontiers in Neuroanatomy, 11*(132).

Bill-Axelson, Anna; Holmberg, Lars; Garmo, Hans; Taari, Kimmo; Busch, Christer; Nordling, Stig, . . . Johansson, Jan-Erik. (2018). Radical prostatectomy or watchful waiting in prostate cancer — 29-year follow-up. *New England Journal of Medicine, 379*(24), 2319–2329.

Biro, Frank M.; Greenspan, Louise C.; Galvez, Maida P.; Pinney, Susan M.; Teitelbaum, Susan; Windham, Gayle C., . . . Wolff, Mary S. (2013). Onset of breast development in a longitudinal cohort. *Pediatrics, 132*(6), 1019–1027.

Bjorklund, David F. (2018). A metatheory for cognitive development (or "Piaget is dead" revisited). *Child Development, 89*(6), 2288–2302.

Bjorklund, David F. & Ellis, Bruce J. (2014). Children, childhood, and development in evolutionary perspective. *Developmental Review, 34*(3), 225–264.

Bjorklund, David F. & Sellers, Patrick D. (2014). Memory development in evolutionary perspective. In Patricia Bauer & Robyn Fivush (Eds.), *The Wiley handbook on the development of children's memory* (Vol. 1, pp. 126–150). Malden, MA: Wiley.

Black, Dennis M.; Bauer, Douglas C.; Schwartz, Ann V.; Cummings, Steven R. & Rosen, Clifford J. (2012). Continuing bisphosphonate treatment for osteoporosis — for whom and for how long? *New England Journal of Medicine, 366*, 2051–2053.

Black, Maureen M.; Papas, Mia A.; Hussey, Jon M.; Hunter, Wanda; Dubowitz, Howard; Kotch, Jonathan B., . . . Schneider, Mary. (2002). Behavior and development of preschool children born to adolescent mothers: Risk and 3-generation households. *Pediatrics, 109*(4), 573–580.

Blair, Clancy. (2016). Developmental science and executive function. *Current Directions in Psychological Science, 25*(1), 3–7.

Blair, Clancy & Raver, C. Cybele. (2015). School readiness and self-regulation: A developmental psychobiological approach. *Annual Review of Psychology, 66*, 711–731.

Blaise, Jean G. (2018). The effects of high-stakes accountability measures on students with limited English proficiency. *Urban Education*, 53(9), 1154–1181.

Blakemore, Sarah-Jayne. (2018). Avoiding social risk in adolescence. *Current Directions in Psychological Science*, 27(2), 116–122.

Blalock, Garrick; Kadiyali, Vrinda & Simon, Daniel H. (2009). Driving fatalities after 9/11: A hidden cost of terrorism. *Applied Economics, 41*(14), 1717–1729.

Blanchflower, David G. & Oswald, Andrew. (2017). *Do humans suffer a psychological low in midlife? Two approaches (with and without controls) in seven data sets. NBER Working Paper*. Cambridge, MA: National Bureau of Economic Research. Working Paper No. 23724.

Blandon, Alysia Y.; Calkins, Susan D. & Keane, Susan P. (2010). Predicting emotional and social competence during early childhood from toddler risk and maternal behavior. *Development and Psychopathology*, 22(1), 119–132.

Blank, Grant & Lutz, Christoph. (2018). Benefits and harms from Internet use: A differentiated analysis of Great Britain. *New Media & Society*, 20(2), 618–640.

Blas, Erik & Kurup, Anand Sivasankara (Eds.). (2010). *Equity, social determinants, and public health programmes*. Geneva, Switzerland: World Health Organization.

Bleidorn, Wiebke; Klimstra, Theo A.; Denissen, Jaap J. A.; Rentfrow, Peter J.; Potter, Jeff & Gosling, Samuel D. (2013). Personality maturation around the world: A cross-cultural examination of social-investment theory. *Psychological Science*, 24(12), 2530–2540.

Bleidorn, Wiebke & Schwaba, Ted. (2018). Retirement is associated with change in self-esteem. *Psychology and Aging*, 33(4), 586–594.

Bleys, Dries; Soenens, Bart; Boone, Liesbet; Claes, Stephan; Vliegen, Nicole & Luyten, Patrick. (2016). The role of intergenerational similarity and parenting in adolescent self-criticism: An actor–partner interdependence model. *Journal of Adolescence, 49*, 68–76.

Blieszner, Rosemary; Ogletree, Aaron M. & Adams, Rebecca G. (2019). Friendship in later life: A research agenda. *Innovation in Aging, 3*(1).

Blomqvist, Ylva Thernström; Nyqvist, Kerstin Hedberg; Rubertsson, Christine & Funkquist, Eva-Lotta. (2017). Parents need support to find ways to optimise their own sleep without seeing their preterm infant's sleeping patterns as a problem. *Acta Paediatrica, 106*(2), 223–228.

Blurton-Jones, Nicholas G. (1976). Rough-and-tumble play among nursery school children. In Jerome S. Bruner, et al. (Eds.), *Play: Its role in development and evolution* (pp. 352–363). New York, NY: Basic Books.

Bodner-Adler, Barbara; Kimberger, Oliver; Griebaum, Julia; Husslein, Peter & Bodner, Klaus. (2017). A ten-year study of midwife-led care at an Austrian tertiary care center: A retrospective analysis with special consideration of perineal trauma. *BMC Pregnancy and Childbirth, 17*, 357–371.

Bøe, Tormod; Serlachius, Anna; Sivertsen, Børge; Petrie, Keith & Hysing, Mari. (2018). Cumulative effects of negative life events and family stress on children's mental health: The Bergen Child Study. *Social Psychiatry and Psychiatric Epidemiology*, 53(1), 1–9.

Boerma, Ties; Ronsmans, Carine; Melesse, Dessalegn Y.; Barros, Aluisio J. D.; Barros, Fernando C.; Juan, Liang, . . . Temmerman, Marleen. (2018). Global epidemiology of use of and disparities in caesarean sections. *The Lancet*, 392(10155), 1341–1348.

Bögels, Susan M.; Knappe, Susanne & Clark, Lee Anna. (2013). Adult separation anxiety disorder in *DSM-5*. *Clinical Psychology Review*, 33(5), 663–674.

Bogle, Kathleen A. (2008). *Hooking up: Sex, dating, and relationships on campus*. New York, NY: New York University Press.

Bohannon, John. (2015). Many psychology papers fail replication test. *Science, 349*(6251), 910–911.

Bohlen, Tabata M.; Silveira, Marina A.; Zampieri, Thais T.; Frazão, Renata & Donato, Jose. (2016). Fatness rather than leptin sensitivity determines the timing of puberty in female mice. *Molecular and Cellular Endocrinology, 423*, 11–21.

Bohn, Manuel & Köymen, Bahar. (2018). Common ground and development. *Child Development Perspectives, 12*(2), 104–108.

Boisvert, Stéphanie & Poulin, François. (2017). Navigating in and out of romantic relationships from adolescence to emerging adulthood: Distinct patterns and their correlates at age 25. *Emerging Adulthood*, 5(3), 216–223.

Boldrini, Maura; Fulmore, Camille A.; Tartt, Alexandria N.; Simeon, Laika R.; Pavlova, Ina; Poposka, Verica, . . . Mann, John. (2018). Human hippocampal neurogenesis persists throughout aging. *Cell Stem Cell, 22*(4), 589–599.e585.

Bolk, Jenny; Padilla, Nelly; Forsman, Lea; Broström, Lina; Hellgren, Kerstin & Åden, Ulrika. (2018). Visual–motor integration and fine motor skills at 6½ years of age and associations with neonatal brain volumes in children born extremely preterm in Sweden: A population-based cohort study. *BMJ Open, 8*(2), e020478.

Bollyky, Thomas J. (2012). Developing symptoms: Noncommunicable diseases go global. *Foreign Affairs, 91*(3), 134–144.

Bonanno, Rina A. & Hymel, Shelley. (2013). Cyber bullying and internalizing difficulties: Above and beyond the impact of traditional forms of bullying. *Journal of Youth and Adolescence, 42*(5), 685–697.

Bone, Anna E.; Gomes, Barbara; Etkind, Simon N.; Verne, Julia; Murtagh, Fliss Em; Evans, Catherine J. & Higginson, Irene J. (2018). What is the impact of population ageing on the future provision of end-of-life care? Population-based projections of place of death. *Palliative Medicine, 32*(2), 329–336.

Bonora, Massimo; Wieckowski, Mariusz R.; Sinclair, David A.; Kroemer, Guido; Pinton, Paolo & Galluzzi, Lorenzo. (2019). Targeting mitochondria for cardiovascular disorders: Therapeutic potential and obstacles. *Nature Reviews Cardiology, 16*, 33–55.

Booth, Alan & Dunn, Judy (Eds.). (2014). *Stepfamilies: Who benefits? Who does not?* New York, NY: Routledge.

Bordini, Gabriela Sagebin & Sperb, Tania Mara. (2013). Sexual double standard: A review of the literature between 2001 and 2010. *Sexuality & Culture, 17*(4), 686–704.

Borke, Jörn; Lamm, Bettina; Eickhorst, Andreas & Keller, Heidi. (2007). Father-infant interaction, paternal ideas about early child care, and their consequences for the development of children's self-recognition. *Journal of Genetic Psychology, 168*(4), 365–379.

Bornstein, Marc H. (2015). Children's parents. In Richard M. Lerner (Ed.), *Handbook of child psychology and developmental science* (7th ed., Vol. 4, pp. 55–132). New York, NY: Wiley.

Bornstein, Marc H.; Mortimer, Jeylan T.; Lutfey, Karen & Bradley, Robert. (2011). Theories and processes in life-span socialization. In Karen L. Fingerman, et al. (Eds.), *Handbook of life-span development* (pp. 27–56). New York, NY: Springer.

Bornstein, Marc H. & Putnick, Diane L. (2016). Mothers' and fathers' parenting practices with their daughters and sons in low- and middle-income countries. *Monographs of the Society for Research in Child Development, 81*(1), 60–77.

Bornstein, Marc H.; Putnick, Diane L.; Bradley, Robert H.; Deater-Deckard, Kirby & Lansford, Jennifer E. (2016). Gender in low- and middle-income countries: Introduction. *Monographs of the Society for Research in Child Development, 81*(1), 7–23.

Bosworth, Hayden B. & Ayotte, Brian J. (2009). The role of cognitive and social function in an applied setting: Medication adherence as an example. In Hayden B. Bosworth & Christopher Hertzog (Eds.), *Aging and cognition: Research methodologies and empirical advances* (pp. 219–239). Washington, DC: American Psychological Association.

Boundy, Ellen O.; Dastjerdi, Roya; Spiegelman, Donna; Fawzi, Wafaie W.; Missmer, Stacey A.; Lieberman, Ellice, . . . Chan, Grace J. (2016). Kangaroo mother care and neonatal outcomes: A meta-analysis. *Pediatrics, 137*(1), e20152238.

Bourguignon, Jean-Pierre; Juul, Anders; Franssen, Delphine; Fudvoye, Julie; Pinson, Anneline & Parent, Anne-Simone. (2016). Contribution of the endocrine perspective in the evaluation of endocrine disrupting chemical effects: The case study of pubertal timing. *Hormone Research in Paediatrics, 86*(4), 221–232.

Bouter, Lex M. (2015). Commentary: Perverse incentives or rotten apples? *Accountability in Research, 22*(3), 148–161.

Bowlby, John. (1983). *Attachment* (2nd ed.). New York, NY: Basic Books.

Bowman, Nicholas A. (2013). How much diversity is enough? The curvilinear relationship between college diversity interactions and first-year student outcomes. *Research in Higher Education, 54*(8), 874–894.

boyd, danah. (2014). *It's complicated: The social lives of networked teens*. New Haven, CT: Yale University Press.

Boyd, Wendy; Walker, Susan & Thorpe, Karen. (2013). Choosing work and care: Four Australian women negotiating return to paid work in the first year of motherhood. *Contemporary Issues in Early Childhood, 14*(2), 168–178.

Boyle, J., Paul; Feng, M., Zhiqiang & Raab, M., Gillian. (2011). Does widowhood increase mortality risk?: Testing for selection effects by comparing causes of spousal death. *Epidemiology, 22*(1), 1–5.

Boyle, Patricia A.; Yu, Lei; Schneider, Julie A.; Wilson, Robert S. & Bennett, David A. (2019). Scam awareness related to incident Alzheimer dementia and mild cognitive impairment: A prospective cohort study. *Annals of Internal Medicine, 70*(10), 702–709.

Braams, Barbara R.; van Duijvenvoorde, Anna C. K.; Peper, Jiska S. & Crone, Eveline A. (2015). Longitudinal changes in adolescent risk-taking: A comprehensive study of neural responses to rewards, pubertal development, and risk-taking behavior. *The Journal of Neuroscience*, 35(18), 7226–7238.

Bracken, Bruce A. & Crawford, Elizabeth. (2010). Basic concepts in early childhood educational standards: A 50-state review. *Early Childhood Education Journal*, 37(5), 421–430.

Bradley, Rachel & Slade, Pauline. (2011). A review of mental health problems in fathers following the birth of a child. *Journal of Reproductive and Infant Psychology*, 29(1), 19–42.

Bradshaw, Matt & Kent, Blake Victor. (2018). Prayer, attachment to God, and changes in psychological well-being in later life. *Journal of Aging and Health*, 30(5), 667–691.

Braithwaite, David W.; Tian, Jing & Siegler, Robert S. (2018). Do children understand fraction addition? *Developmental Science, 21*(4), e12601.

Brame, Robert; Bushway, Shawn D.; Paternoster, Ray & Turner, Michael G. (2014). Demographic patterns of cumulative arrest prevalence by ages 18 and 23. *Crime & Delinquency*, 60(3), 471–486.

Brand, Jennie E. & Xie, Yu. (2010). Who benefits most from college?: Evidence for negative selection in heterogeneous economic returns to higher education. *American Sociological Review*, 75(2), 273–302.

Brandone, Amanda C.; Horwitz, Suzanne R.; Aslin, Richard N. & Wellman, Henry M. (2014). Infants' goal anticipation during failed and successful reaching actions. *Developmental Science, 17*(1), 23–34.

Brandt, Hella E.; Ooms, Marcel E.; Ribbe, Miel W.; van der Wal, Gerrit & Deliens, Luc. (2006). Predicted survival vs. actual survival in terminally ill noncancer patients in Dutch nursing homes. *Journal of Pain and Symptom Management, 32*(6), 560–566.

Brandt, Martina & Deindl, Christian. (2013). Intergenerational transfers to adult children in Europe: Do social policies matter? *Journal of Marriage and Family, 75*(1), 235–251.

Branje, Susan. (2018). Development of parent–adolescent relationships: Conflict interactions as a mechanism of change. *Child Development Perspectives, 12*(3), 171–176.

Braun, Katharina. (2011). The prefrontal-limbic system: Development, neuroanatomy, function, and implications for socioemotional development. *Clinics in Perinatology*, 38(4), 685–702.

Braver, Sanford L. & Votruba, Ashley M. (2018). Does joint physical custody "cause" children's better outcomes? *Journal of Divorce & Remarriage, 59*(5), 452–468.

Brazelton, T. Berry & Sparrow, Joshua D. (2006). *Touchpoints, birth to 3: Your child's emotional and behavioral development* (2nd ed.). Cambridge, MA: Da Capo Press.

Bremner, J. Gavin; Slater, Alan M. & Johnson, Scott P. (2015). Perception of object persistence: The origins of object permanence in infancy. *Child Development Perspectives, 9*(1), 7–13.

Bremner, J. Gavin & Wachs, Theodore D. (Eds.). (2010). *The Wiley-Blackwell handbook of infant development* (2nd ed.). Malden, MA: Wiley-Blackwell.

Brennan, Arthur; Ayers, Susan; Ahmed, Hafez & Marshall-Lucette, Sylvie. (2007). A critical review of the Couvade syndrome: The pregnant male. *Journal of Reproductive and Infant Psychology*, 25(3), 173–189.

Breslow, Lori; Pritchard, David E.; Deboer, Jennifer; Stump, Glenda S.; Ho, Andrew D. & Seaton, Daniel T. (2013). Studying learning in the worldwide classroom research into edX's first MOOC. *Research and Practice in Assessment*, 8(1), 13–25.

Bridge, Jeffrey A.; Greenhouse, Joel B.; Ruch, Donna; Stevens, Jack; Ackerman, John; Sheftall, Arielle H., . . . Campo, John V. (2019). Association between the release of Netflix's *13 Reasons Why* and suicide rates in the United States: An interrupted times series analysis. *Journal of the American Academy of Child & Adolescent Psychiatry*, (In Press).

Bridgers, Sophie; Buchsbaum, Daphna; Seiver, Elizabeth; Griffiths, Thomas L. & Gopnik, Alison. (2016). Children's causal inferences from conflicting testimony and observations. *Developmental Psychology*, 52(1), 9–18.

Bridgett, David J.; Burt, Nicole M.; Edwards, Erin S. & Deater-Deckard, Kirby. (2015). Intergenerational transmission of self-regulation: A multidisciplinary review and integrative conceptual framework. *Psychological Bulletin, 141*(3), 602–654.

Briley, Daniel A. & Tucker-Drob, Elliot M. (2017). Comparing the developmental genetics of cognition and personality over the life span. *Journal of Personality, 85*(1), 51–64.

Brinkman, Sally A.; Johnson, Sarah E.; Codde, James P.; Hart, Michael B.; Straton, Judith A.; Mittinty, Murthy N. & Silburn, Sven R. (2016). Efficacy of infant simulator programmes to prevent teenage pregnancy: A school-based cluster randomised controlled trial in Western Australia. *The Lancet,* 388(10057), 2264–2271.

Brint, Steven. (2019). *Two cheers for higher education why American universities are stronger than ever—and how to meet the challenges they face.* Princeton, New Jersey: Princeton University Press.

Brix, Nis; Ernst, Andreas; Lauridsen, Lea Lykke Braskhoj; Parner, Erik; Stovring, Henrik; Olsen, Jorn, . . . Ramlau-Hansen, Cecilia Høst. (2019). Timing of puberty in boys and girls: A population-based study. *Paediatric and Perinatal Epidemiology,* 33(1), 70–78.

Broberg, Thomas & Willstrand, Tania Dukic. (2014). Safe mobility for elderly drivers—Considerations based on expert and self-assessment. *Accident Analysis & Prevention, 66,* 104–113.

Brodsky, Michael C. (2016). *Pediatric neuro-ophthalmology* (3rd ed.). New York, NY: Springer.

Brody, Gene H. (2017). Using genetically informed prevention trials to test gene × environment hypotheses. In Patrick H. Tolan & Bennett L. Leventhal (Eds.), *Gene-environment transactions in developmental psychopathology: The role in intervention research* (pp. 211–233). Cham, Switzerland: Springer.

Brody, Gene H.; Beach, Steven R. H.; Philibert, Robert A.; Chen, Yi-fu & Murry, Velma McBride. (2009). Prevention effects moderate the association of 5-HTTLPR and youth risk behavior initiation: Gene × environment hypotheses tested via a randomized prevention design. *Child Development, 80*(3), 645–661.

Brody, Jane E. (2013, February 26). Too many pills in pregnancy. *New York Times.*

Broekhuizen, Martine L.; Aken, Marcel A. G.; Dubas, Judith S. & Leseman, Paul P. M. (2018). Child care quality and Dutch 2- and 3-year-olds' socio-emotional outcomes: Does the amount of care matter? *Infant and Child Development,* 27(1), e2043.

Bronfenbrenner, Urie & Morris, Pamela A. (2006). The bioecological model of human development. In William Damon & Richard M. Lerner (Eds.), *Handbook of child psychology* (6th ed., Vol. 1, pp. 793–828). Hoboken, NJ: Wiley.

Broockman, David & Kalla, Joshua. (2016). Durably reducing transphobia: A field experiment on door-to-door canvassing. *Science,* 352(6282), 220–204.

Brooks-Gunn, J. & Furstenberg, Frank F. (1986). The children of adolescent mothers: Physical, academic, and psychological outcomes. *Developmental Review, 6*(3), 224–251.

Brookshire, Robert H. & McNeil, Malcolm R. (2015). *Introduction to neurogenic communication disorders* (8th ed.). St. Louis, MO: Mosby.

Brooten, Dorothy; Youngblut, Joanne M.; Caicedo, Carmen; Del Moral, Teresa; Cantwell, G. Patricia & Totapally, Balagangadhar. (2018). Parents' acute illnesses, hospitalizations, and medication changes during the difficult first year after infant or child NICU/PICU death. *American Journal of Hospice and Palliative Medicine,* 35(1), 75–82.

Broström, Stig. (2017). A dynamic learning concept in early years' education: A possible way to prevent schoolification. *International Journal of Early Years Education, 25*(1), 3–15.

Brotto, Lori A. & Yule, Morag A. (2011). Physiological and subjective sexual arousal in self-identified asexual women. *Archives of Sexual Behavior, 40*(4), 699–712.

Brouwer, Rachel M.; van Soelen, Inge L. C.; Swagerman, Suzanne C.; Schnack, Hugo G.; Ehli, Erik A.; Kahn, René S., . . . Boomsma, Dorret I. (2014). Genetic associations between intelligence and cortical thickness emerge at the start of puberty. *Human Brain Mapping,* 35(8), 3760–3773.

Brown, B. Bradford & Bakken, Jeremy P. (2011). Parenting and peer relationships: Reinvigorating research on family–peer linkages in adolescence. *Journal of Research on Adolescence, 21*(1), 153–165.

Brown, Christia Spears; Alabi, Basirat O.; Huynh, Virginia W. & Masten, Carrie L. (2011). Ethnicity and gender in late childhood and early adolescence: Group identity and awareness of bias. *Developmental Psychology, 47*(2), 463–471.

Brown, Steven D. & Lent, Robert W. (2016). Vocational psychology: Agency, equity, and well-being. *Annual Review of Psychology,* 67, 541–565.

Brownell, Celia A.; Svetlova, Margarita; Anderson, Ranita; Nichols, Sara R. & Drummond, Jesse. (2013). Socialization of early prosocial behavior: Parents' talk about emotions is associated with sharing and helping in toddlers. *Infancy, 18*(1), 91–119.

Brubaker, Matthew S. & Naveh-Benjamin, Moshe. (2018). The effects of stereotype threat on the associative memory deficit of older adults. *Psychology and Aging,* 33(1), 17–29.

Bruder, Gerard E.; Stewart, Jonathan W. & Mcgrath, Patrick J. (2017). Right brain, left brain in depressive disorders: Clinical and theoretical implications of behavioral, electrophysiological and neuroimaging findings. *Neuroscience and Biobehavioral Reviews,* 78, 178–191.

Brummelman, Eddie; Nelemans, Stefanie A.; Thomaes, Sander & Orobio De Castro, Bram. (2017). When parents' praise inflates, children's self-esteem deflates. *Child Development,* 88(6), 1799–1809.

Brunborg, Geir Scott; Mentzoni, Rune Aune; Molde, Helge; Myrseth, Helga; Skouverøe, Knut Joachim Mår; Bjorvatn, Bjørn & Pallesen, Ståle. (2011). The relationship between media use in the bedroom, sleep habits and symptoms of insomnia. *Journal of Sleep Research,* 20(4), 569–575.

Brunham, Robert C.; Gottlieb, Sami L. & Paavonen, Jorma. (2015). Pelvic inflammatory disease. *New England Journal of Medicine,* 372, 2039–2048.

Bucx, Freek; Raaijmakers, Quinten & van Wel, Frits. (2010). Life course stage in young adulthood and intergenerational congruence in family attitudes. *Journal of Marriage and Family,* 72(1), 117–134.

Bucx, Freek; van Wel, Frits & Knijn, Trudie. (2012). Life course status and exchanges of support between young adults and parents. *Journal of Marriage and Family,* 74(1), 101–115.

Budiman, Abby & Lopez, Mark Hugo. (2017, October 17). *Amid decline in international adoptions to U.S., boys outnumber girls for the first time. Fact Tank.* Washington, DC: Pew Research Center.

Bueno, Clarissa & Menna-Barreto, Luiz. (2016). Environmental factors influencing biological rhythms in newborns: From neonatal intensive care units to home. *Sleep Science,* 9(4), 295–300.

Buiting, Hilde; van Delden, Johannes; Onwuteaka-Philpsen, Bregje; Rietjens, Judith; Rurup, Mette; van Tol, Donald, . . . van der Heide, Agnes. (2009). Reporting of euthanasia and physician-assisted suicide in the Netherlands: Descriptive study. *BMC Medical Ethics, 10*(18).

Bulmer, Maria; Böhnke, Jan R. & Lewis, Gary J. (2017). Predicting moral sentiment towards physician-assisted suicide: The role of religion, conservatism, authoritarianism, and Big Five personality. *Personality and Individual Differences, 105,* 244–251.

Bulpitt, Christopher J.; Beckett, Nigel; Peters, Ruth; Staessen, Jan A.; Wang, Ji-Guang; Comsa, Marius, . . . Rajkumar, Chakravarthi. (2013). Does white coat hypertension require treatment over age 80? Results of the hypertension in the very elderly trial ambulatory blood pressure side project. *Hypertension, 61*(1), 89–94.

Burchinal, Margaret R.; Lowe Vandell, Deborah & Belsky, Jay. (2014). Is the prediction of adolescent outcomes from early child care moderated by later maternal sensitivity? Results from the NICHD study of early child care and youth development. *Developmental Psychology,* 50(2), 542–553.

Burén, Jonas & Lunde, Carolina. (2018). Sexting among adolescents: A nuanced and gendered online challenge for young people. *Computers in Human Behavior,* 85, 210–217.

Burgoyne, Alexander P.; Hambrick, David Z. & Altmann, Erik M. (2019). Is working memory capacity a causal factor in fluid intelligence? *Psychonomic Bulletin & Review,* (In Press).

Burke, Brian L.; Martens, Andy & Faucher, Erik H. (2010). Two decades of terror management theory: A meta-analysis of mortality salience research. *Personality and Social Psychology Review, 14*(2), 155–195.

Burlina, Alessandro P. (Ed.). (2018). *Neurometabolic hereditary diseases of adults*. Cham, Switzerland: Springer.

Burnette, Jeni L.; O'Boyle, Ernest H.; VanEpps, Eric M.; Pollack, Jeffrey M. & Finkel, Eli J. (2013). Mind-sets matter: A meta-analytic review of implicit theories and self-regulation. *Psychological Bulletin, 139*(3), 655–701.

Burri, Andrea & Spector, Timothy. (2011). Recent and lifelong sexual dysfunction in a female UK population sample: Prevalence and risk factors. *Journal of Sexual Medicine, 8*(9), 2420–2430.

Bursztyn, Leonardo & Jensen, Robert. (2015). How does peer pressure affect educational investments? *Quarterly Journal of Economics, 130*(3), 1329–1367.

Burt, S. Alexandra. (2009). Rethinking environmental contributions to child and adolescent psychopathology: A meta-analysis of shared environmental influences. *Psychological Bulletin, 135*(4), 608–637.

Buss, David M. (2015). *Evolutionary psychology: The new science of the mind* (5th ed.). New York, NY: Routledge.

Buss, Kristin A.; Jaffee, Sara; Wadsworth, Martha E. & Kliewer, Wendy. (2018). Impact of psychophysiological stress-response systems on psychological development: Moving beyond the single biomarker approach. *Developmental Psychology, 54*(9), 1601–1605.

Butler, Ashley M. & Titus, Courtney. (2015). Systematic review of engagement in culturally adapted parent training for disruptive behavior. *Journal of Early Intervention, 37*(4), 300–318.

Butler, Robert N.; Lewis, Myrna I. & Sunderland, Trey. (1998). *Aging and mental health: Positive psychosocial and biomedical approaches* (5th ed.). Boston, MA: Allyn & Bacon.

Butterworth, Brian & Kovas, Yulia. (2013). Understanding neurocognitive developmental disorders can improve education for all. *Science, 340*(6130), 300–305.

Butterworth, Brian; Varma, Sashank & Laurillard, Diana. (2011). Dyscalculia: From brain to education. *Science, 332*(6033), 1049–1053.

Butts, Donna. (2017). Foreword. In Matthew Kaplan, et al. (Eds.), *Intergenerational pathways to a sustainable society* (pp. v–vii). New York: NY: Springer.

Byard, Roger W. (2014). "Shaken baby syndrome" and forensic pathology: An uneasy interface. *Forensic Science, Medicine, and Pathology, 10*(2), 239–241.

Byers-Heinlein, Krista; Burns, Tracey C. & Werker, Janet F. (2010). The roots of bilingualism in newborns. *Psychological Science, 21*(3), 343–348.

Cabrera, Natasha. (2015). Why do fathers matter for children's development? In Susan M. McHale, et al. (Eds.), *Gender and Couple Relationships* (pp. 161–168). New York, NY: Springer.

Caccamo, Alexandra; Kachur, Rachel & Williams, Samantha. (2017). Narrative review: Sexually transmitted diseases and homeless youth—What do we know about sexually transmitted disease prevalence and risk? *Sexually Transmitted Diseases, 44*(8), 466–476.

Cacioppo, Stephanie; Capitanio, John P. & Cacioppo, John T. (2014). Toward a neurology of loneliness. *Psychological Bulletin, 140*(6), 1464–1504.

Calarco, Jessica McCrory. (2014). The inconsistent curriculum: Cultural tool kits and student interpretations of ambiguous expectations. *Social Psychology Quarterly, 77*(2), 185–209.

Calkins, Susan D. & Keane, Susan P. (2009). Developmental origins of early antisocial behavior. *Development and Psychopathology, 21*(4), 1095–1109.

Callaghan, Tara. (2013). Symbols and symbolic thought. In Philip D. Zelazo (Ed.), *The Oxford handbook of developmental psychology* (Vol. 1). New York, NY: Oxford University Press.

Calvo, Esteban; Madero-Cabib, Ignacio & Staudinger, Ursula M. (2018). Retirement sequences of older Americans: Moderately destandardized and highly stratified across gender, class, and race. *The Gerontologist, 58*(6), 1166–1176.

Calvo, Rocío; Carr, Dawn C. & Matz-Costa, Christina. (2019). Expanding the happiness paradox: Ethnoracial disparities in life satisfaction among older immigrants in the United States. *Journal of Aging and Health, 31*(2), 231–255.

Camhi, Sarah M.; Katzmarzyk, Peter T.; Broyles, Stephanie; Church, Timothy S.; Hankinson, Arlene L.; Carnethon, Mercedes R., . . . Lewis, Cora E. (2013). Association of metabolic risk with longitudinal physical activity and fitness: Coronary artery risk development in young adults (CARDIA). *Metabolic Syndrome and Related Disorders, 11*(3), 195–204.

Campbell, Frances; Conti, Gabriella; Heckman, James J.; Moon, Seong H.; Pinto, Rodrigo; Pungello, Elizabeth & Pan, Yi. (2014). Early childhood investments substantially boost adult health. *Science, 343*(6178), 1478–1485.

Campbell, Frances A.; Pungello, Elizabeth P.; Miller-Johnson, Shari; Burchinal, Margaret & Ramey, Craig T. (2001). The development of cognitive and academic abilities: Growth curves from an early childhood educational experiment. *Developmental Psychology, 37*(2), 231–242.

Campo, Juan Eduardo. (2015). Muslim ways of death: Between the prescribed and the performed. In Kathleen Garces-Foley (Ed.), *Death and religion in a changing world*. New York, NY: Routledge.

Cao, Zhipeng; Bennett, Marc; Orr, Catherine; Icke, Ilknur; Banaschewski, Tobias; Barker, Gareth J., . . . Whelan, Robert. (2019). Mapping adolescent reward anticipation, receipt, and prediction error during the monetary incentive delay task. *Human Brain Mapping, 40*(1), 262–283.

Cappelletti, Marinella; Didino, Daniele; Stoianov, Ivilin & Zorzi, Marco. (2014). Number skills are maintained in healthy ageing. *Cognitive Psychology, 69*, 25–45.

Cardozo, Eden R.; Thomson, Alexcis P.; Karmon, Anatte E.; Dickinson, Kristy A.; Wright, Diane L. & Sabatini, Mary E. (2015). Ovarian stimulation and in-vitro fertilization outcomes of cancer patients undergoing fertility preservation compared to age matched controls: A 17-year experience. *Journal of Assisted Reproduction and Genetics, 32*(4), 587–596.

Carey, Nessa. (2012). *The epigenetics revolution: How modern biology is rewriting our understanding of genetics, disease, and inheritance*. New York, NY: Columbia University Press.

Carlsen, Karin C. Lødrup; Skjerven, Håvard O. & Carlsen, Kai-Håkon. (2018). The toxicity of e-cigarettes and children's respiratory health. *Paediatric Respiratory Reviews*, (In Press).

Carlson, Deven; Cowen, Joshua M. & Fleming, David J. (2013). Life after vouchers: What happens to students who leave private schools for the traditional public sector? *Educational Evaluation and Policy Analysis, 35*(2), 179–199.

Carlson, Robert G.; Nahhas, Ramzi W.; Martins, Silvia S. & Daniulaityte, Raminta. (2016). Predictors of transition to heroin use among initially non-opioid dependent illicit pharmaceutical opioid users: A natural history study. *Drug & Alcohol Dependence, 160*, 127–134.

Carlson, Scott. (2016, May 1). Should everyone go to college?: For poor kids, 'College for all' isn't the mantra it was meant to be. *Chronicle of Higher Education*.

Carlson, Stephanie M.; Koenig, Melissa A. & Harms, Madeline B. (2013). Theory of mind. *Wiley Interdisciplinary Reviews: Cognitive Science, 4*(4), 391–402.

Carmichael, Cheryl L.; Reis, Harry T. & Duberstein, Paul R. (2015). In your 20s it's quantity, in your 30s it's quality: The prognostic value of social activity across 30 years of adulthood. *Psychology and Aging, 30*(1), 95–105.

Carocho, Márcio; Ferreira, Isabel C. F. R.; Morales, Patricia & Soković, Marina. (2019). Antioxidants and prooxidants: Effects on health and aging. *Oxidative Medicine and Cellular Longevity, 2019*(1472708).

Carr, Deborah; Freedman, Vicki A.; Cornman, Jennifer C. & Schwarz, Norbert. (2014). Happy marriage, happy life? Marital quality and subjective well-being in later life. *Journal of Marriage and Family, 76*(5), 930–948.

Carra, Cecilia; Lavelli, Manuela; Keller, Heidi & Kärtner, Joscha. (2013). Parenting infants: Socialization goals and behaviors of Italian mothers and immigrant mothers from West Africa. *Journal of Cross-Cultural Psychology, 44*(8), 1304–1320.

Carrese, Joseph A.; Malek, Soleymani, Janet; Watson, J., Katie; Lehmann, B., Lisa; Green, H., Michael; Mccullough, J., Laurence, . . . Doukas, J., David. (2015). The essential role of medical ethics education in achieving professionalism: The Romanell report. *Academic Medicine, 90*(6), 744–752.

Carroll, Linda J.; Cassidy, David; Cancelliere, Carol; Côté, Pierre; Hincapié, Cesar A.; Kristman, Vicki L., . . . Hartvigsen, Jan. (2014). Systematic review of the prognosis after mild traumatic brain injury in adults: Cognitive, psychiatric, and mortality outcomes: Results of the international collaboration on mild traumatic brain injury prognosis. *Archives of Physical Medicine and Rehabilitation, 95*(3, Suppl.), S152–S173.

Carson, Valerie; Tremblay, Mark S.; Spence, John C.; Timmons, Brian W. & Janssen, Ian. (2013). The Canadian Sedentary Behaviour Guidelines for the Early Years (zero to four years of age) and screen time among children from Kingston, Ontario. *Paediatrics & Child Health, 18*(1), 25–28.

Carstensen, Laura L. (1993). Motivation for social contact across the life span. In Janis E. Jacobs (Ed.), *Developmental perspectives on motivation: Nebraska Symposium on Motivation (1992)* (pp. 209–254). Lincoln, NE: University of Nebraska.

Carstensen, Laura L. (2011). *A long bright future: Happiness, health, and financial security in an age of increased longevity*. New York, NY: PublicAffairs.

Carstensen, Laura L. & DeLiema, Marguerite. (2018). The positivity effect: A negativity bias in youth fades with age. *Current Opinion in Behavioral Sciences, 19*, 7–12.

Caruso, Federica. (2013). Embedding early childhood education and care in the socio-cultural context: The case of Italy. In Jan Georgeson & Jane Payler (Eds.), *International perspectives on early childhood education and care*. New York, NY: Open University Press.

Carwile, Jenny L.; Willett, Walter C.; Spiegelman, Donna; Hertzmark, Ellen; Rich-Edwards, Janet W.; Frazier, A. Lindsay & Michels, Karin B. (2015). Sugar-sweetened beverage consumption and age at menarche in a prospective study of US girls. *Human Reproduction, 30*(3), 675–683.

Casey, B. J. & Caudle, Kristina. (2013). The teenage brain: Self control. *Current Directions in Psychological Science, 22*(2), 82–87.

Caspi, Avshalom; Moffitt, Terrie E.; Morgan, Julia; Rutter, Michael; Taylor, Alan; Arseneault, Louise, . . . Polo-Tomas, Monica. (2004). Maternal expressed emotion predicts children's antisocial behavior problems: Using monozygotic-twin differences to identify environmental effects on behavioral development. *Developmental Psychology, 40*(2), 149–161.

Cassina, Matteo; Cagnoli, Giulia A.; Zuccarello, Daniela; Gianantonio, Elena Di & Clementi, Maurizio. (2017). Human teratogens and genetic phenocopies. Understanding pathogenesis through human genes mutation. *European Journal of Medical Genetics, 60*(1), 22–31.

Castellacci, Fulvio & Tveito, Vegard. (2018). Internet use and well-being: A survey and a theoretical framework. *Research Policy, 47*(1), 308–325.

Cavalari, Rachel N. S. & Donovick, Peter J. (2014). Agenesis of the corpus callosum: Symptoms consistent with developmental disability in two siblings. *Neurocase: The Neural Basis of Cognition, 21*(1), 95–102.

Ceballo, Rosario; Maurizi, Laura K.; Suarez, Gloria A. & Aretakis, Maria T. (2014). Gift and sacrifice: Parental involvement in Latino adolescents' education. *Cultural Diversity and Ethnic Minority Psychology, 20*(1), 116–127.

Cecil, Kim M.; Brubaker, Christopher J.; Adler, Caleb M.; Dietrich, Kim N.; Altaye, Mekibib; Egelhoff, John C., . . . Lanphear, Bruce P. (2008). Decreased brain volume in adults with childhood lead exposure. *PloS Medicine, 5*(5), 741–750.

Cenegy, Laura Freeman; Denney, Justin T. & Kimbro, Rachel Tolbert. (2018). Family diversity and child health: Where do same-sex couple families fit. *Journal of Marriage and Family, 80*(1), 198–218.

Center for Education Policy. (2012). *SDP strategic performance indicator: The high school effect on college-going. The SDP College-Going Diagnostic Strategic Performance Indicators*. Cambridge, MA: Harvard University, Center for Education Policy Research.

Center for Education Policy. (2013). *SDP college-going diagnostic: The school district of Philadelphia*. Cambridge, MA: Harvard University, Center for Education Policy Research.

Centers for Disease Control and Prevention. (Updated 2018, August 1). Breastfeeding rates: Results.

Centers for Disease Control and Prevention. (2017, November 21). Birth defects: Facts about cleft lip and cleft palate.

Centers for Disease Control and Prevention. (2018). *Sexually transmitted disease surveillance 2017*. Atlanta, GA: U.S. Department of Health and Human Services.

Centers for Disease Control and Prevention. (2018, June 14). Adolescent and school health: Youth risk behavior surveillance — United States, 2017 supplementary tables 203-221: Physical activity.

Centers for Disease Control and Prevention. (2018, June 29). *Blood lead levels (μg/dl) among U.S. children < 72 months of age, by state, year, and blood lead level (bll) group. CDC's National Surveillance Data (2012–2016)*. Atlanta, GA: U.S. Department of Health and Human Services.

Centers for Disease Control and Prevention. (2018, October 15). Sexually transmitted disease surveillance 2017.

Centers for Disease Control and Prevention. (2019, April 12). Statistics overview: HIV surveillance report.

Centers for Disease Control and Prevention. (2019, June 17). Measles cases and outbreaks.

Centers for Disease Control and Prevention. (2019, June 21). Hemophilia: Data & statistics on hemophilia.

Centers for Disease Control and Prevention. (2019, March 21). Hearing loss in children: Data and statistics about hearing loss in children.

Centers for Disease Control and Prevention. (2019, May 30). Diabetes: Type 2 diabetes.

Centers for Disease Control and Prevention, National Center for Health Statistics. (2018, July 3). Underlying cause of death, 1999–2017 on CDC WONDER Online Database. CDC WONDER.

Cesana-Arlotti, Nicoló; Martín, Ana; Téglás, Ernö; Vorobyova, Liza; Cetnarski, Ryszard & Bonatti, Luca L. (2018). Precursors of logical reasoning in preverbal human infants. *Science, 359*(6381), 1263–1266.

Cespedes, Elizabeth M.; McDonald, Julia; Haines, Jess; Bottino, Clement J.; Schmidt, Marie Evans & Taveras, Elsie M. (2013). Obesity-related behaviors of US- and non-US-born parents and children in low-income households. *Journal of Developmental & Behavioral Pediatrics, 34*(8), 541–548.

Champagne, Frances A. & Curley, James P. (2010). Maternal care as a modulating influence on infant development. In Mark S. Blumberg, et al. (Eds.), *Oxford handbook of developmental behavioral neuroscience* (pp. 323–341). New York, NY: Oxford University Press.

Chan, Kit Yee; Wang, Wei; Wu, Jing Jing; Liu, Li; Theodoratou, Evropi; Car, Josip, . . . Rudan, Igor. (2013). Epidemiology of Alzheimer's disease and other forms of dementia in China, 1990–2010: A systematic review and analysis. *The Lancet, 381*(9882), 2016–2023.

Chancer, Lynn S. (2019). *After the rise and stall of American feminism: Taking back a revolution*. Redwood City, CA: Stanford University Press.

Chang, Alicia; Sandhofer, Catherine M. & Brown, Christia S. (2011). Gender biases in early number exposure to preschool-aged children. *Journal of Language and Social Psychology, 30*(4), 440–450.

Chang, Yevvon Yi-Chi & Chiou, Wen-Bin. (2014). Diversity beliefs and postformal thinking in late adolescence: A cognitive basis of multicultural literacy. *Asia Pacific Education Review, 15*(4), 585–592.

Charise, Andrea & Eginton, Margaret L. (2018). Humanistic perspectives: Arts and the aging mind. In Matthew Rizzo, et al. (Eds.), *The Wiley handbook on the aging mind and brain*. Hoboken, NJ: Wiley.

Charness, Neil; Krampe, Ralf & Mayr, Ulrich. (1996). The role of practice and coaching in entrepreneurial skill domains: An international comparison of life-span chess skill acquisition. In Karl Anders Ericsson (Ed.), *The road to excellence: The acquisition of expert performance in the arts and sciences, sports, and games* (pp. 51–80). Hillsdale, NJ: Erlbaum.

Charnigo, Richard; Noar, Seth M.; Garnett, Christopher; Crosby, Richard; Palmgreen, Philip & Zimmerman, Rick S. (2013). Sensation seeking and impulsivity: Combined associations with risky sexual behavior in a large sample of young adults. *The Journal of Sex Research, 50*(5), 480–488.

Chartier, Karen G.; Scott, Denise M.; Wall, Tamara L.; Covault, Jonathan; Karriker-Jaffe, Katherine J.; Mills, Britain A., . . . Arroyo, Judith A. (2014). Framing ethnic variations in alcohol outcomes from biological pathways to neighborhood context. *Alcoholism: Clinical and Experimental Research, 38*(3), 611–618.

Chaudhury, S. Raj. (2011). The lecture. In William Buskist & James E. Groccia (Eds.), *Evidence-based teaching: New directions for teaching and learning* (pp. 13–20). New York, NY: Wiley.

Chen, Edith; Brody, Gene H. & Miller, Gregory E. (2017). Childhood close family relationships and health. *American Psychologist, 72*(6), 555–566.

Chen, Edith & Miller, Gregory E. (2012). "Shift-and-persist" strategies: Why low socioeconomic status isn't always bad for health. *Perspectives on Psychological Science*, 7(2), 135–158.

Chen, Feinian; Mair, Christine A.; Bao, Luoman & Yang, Yang Claire. (2015). Race/ethnic differentials in the health consequences of caring for grandchildren for grandparents. *The Journals of Gerontology Series B: Psychological Sciences and Social Sciences*, 70(5), 793–803.

Chen, Hong & Jackson, Todd. (2009). Predictors of changes in weight esteem among mainland Chinese adolescents: A longitudinal analysis. *Developmental Psychology*, 45(6), 1618–1629.

Chen, Irit; Lifshitz, Hefziba & Vakil, Eli. (2017). Crystallized and fluid intelligence of adolescents and adults with intellectual disability and with typical development: Impaired, stable or compensatory trajectories? *Grant Medical Journals*, 2(5), 104–115.

Chen, Mu-Hong; Lan, Wen-Hsuan; Bai, Ya-Mei; Huang, Kai-Lin; Su, Tung-Ping; Tsai, Shih-Jen, . . . Hsu, Ju-Wei. (2016). Influence of relative age on diagnosis and treatment of Attention-deficit hyperactivity disorder in Taiwanese children. *The Journal of Pediatrics*, 172, 162–167.e161.

Chen, M. Keith & Rohla, Ryne. (2018). The effect of partisanship and political advertising on close family ties. *Science*, *360*(6392), 1020–1024.

Chen, Ruijia & Dong, XinQi. (2017). Risk factors of elder abuse. In XinQi Dong (Ed.), *Elder abuse: Research, practice and policy* (pp. 93–107). New York, NY: Springer.

Chen, Xinyin; Cen, Guozhen; Li, Dan & He, Yunfeng. (2005). Social functioning and adjustment in Chinese children: The imprint of historical time. *Child Development*, 76(1), 182–195.

Chen, Xinyin; Fu, Rui; Li, Dan & Liu, Junsheng. (2019). Developmental trajectories of shyness-sensitivity from middle childhood to early adolescence in China: Contributions of peer preference and mutual friendship. *Journal of Abnormal Child Psychology*, 47(7), 1197–1209.

Chen, Xinyin; Rubin, Kenneth H. & Sun, Yuerong. (1992). Social reputation and peer relationships in Chinese and Canadian children: A cross-cultural study. *Child Development*, *63*(6), 1336–1343.

Chen, Xinyin; Wang, Li & Wang, Zhengyan. (2009). Shyness-sensitivity and social, school, and psychological adjustment in rural migrant and urban children in China. *Child Development*, *80*(5), 1499–1513.

Chen, Xinyin; Yang, Fan & Wang, Li. (2013). Relations between shyness-sensitivity and internalizing problems in Chinese children: Moderating effects of academic achievement. *Journal of Abnormal Child Psychology*, *41*(5), 825–836.

Chen, Yijun; Corsino, Leonor; Shantavasinkul, Prapimporn Chattranukulchai; Grant, John; Portenier, Dana; Ding, Laura & Torquati, Alfonso. (2016). Gastric bypass surgery leads to long-term remission or improvement of type 2 diabetes and significant decrease of microvascular and macrovascular complications. *Annals of Surgery*, *263*(6), 1138–1142.

Chen, Yalin; Loehr, Janeen D. & Campbell, Jamie I. D. (2019). Does the min-counting strategy for simple addition become automatized in educated adults? A behavioural and ERP study of the size congruency effect. *Neuropsychologia*, *124*, 311–321.

Cheng, Diana; Kettinger, Laurie; Uduhiri, Kelechi & Hurt, Lee. (2011). Alcohol consumption during pregnancy: Prevalence and provider assessment. *Obstetrics & Gynecology*, *117*(2), 212–217.

Cherlin, Andrew. (2018). How inequality drives family formation. In Naomi R. Cahn, June Carbone, Laurie Fields DeRose & W. Bradford Wilcox (Eds.), *Unequal family lives: Causes and consequences in Europe and the Americas* (pp. 69–82). New York, NY: Cambridge University Press.

Chernev, Alexander; Böckenholt, Ulf & Goodman, Joseph. (2015). Choice overload: A conceptual review and meta-analysis. *Journal of Consumer Psychology*, 25(2), 333–358.

Cherng, Hua-Yu Sebastian & Liu, Jia-Lin. (2017). Academic social support and student expectations: The case of second-generation Asian Americans. *Asian American Journal of Psychology*, 8(1), 16–30.

Cheslack-Postava, Keely; Liu, Kayuet & Bearman, Peter S. (2011). Closely spaced pregnancies are associated with increased odds of autism in California sibling births. *Pediatrics*, *127*(2), 246–253.

Chikritzhs, Tanya; Stockwell, Tim; Naimi, Timothy; Andreasson, Sven; Dangardt, Frida & Liang, Wenbin. (2015). Has the leaning tower of presumed health benefits from 'moderate' alcohol use finally collapsed? *Addiction*, *110*(5), 726–727.

Child Trends Data Bank. (2015, March). *Lead poisoning: Indicators on children and youth*. Bethesda, MD: Child Trends.

Child Welfare Information Gateway. (2018). *Foster care statistics, 2016*. Washington, DC: U.S. Department of Health and Human Services, Children's Bureau.

Chlebowski, Rowan T.; Manson, JoAnn E.; Anderson, Garnet L.; Cauley, Jane A.; Aragaki, Aaron K.; Stefanick, Marcia L., . . . Prentice, Ross L. (2013). Estrogen plus progestin and breast cancer incidence and mortality in the Women's Health Initiative observational study. *Journal of the National Cancer Institute*, *105*(8), 526–535.

Cho, Youngmin. (2018). The effects of nonstandard work schedules on workers' health: A mediating role of work-to-family conflict. *International Journal of Social Welfare*, 27(1), 74–87.

Choe, Daniel E.; Lane, Jonathan D.; Grabell, Adam S. & Olson, Sheryl L. (2013a). Developmental precursors of young school-age children's hostile attribution bias. *Developmental Psychology*, 49(12), 2245–2256.

Choe, Daniel E.; Olson, Sheryl L. & Sameroff, Arnold J. (2013b). The interplay of externalizing problems and physical and inductive discipline during childhood. *Developmental Psychology*, *49*(11), 2029–2039.

Choi, Hyunkyung; Van Riper, Marcia & Thoyre, Suzanne. (2012). Decision making following a prenatal diagnosis of Down syndrome: An integrative review. *Journal of Midwifery & Women's Health*, 57(2), 156–164.

Choi, Rhea & Goldstein, Bradley J. (2018). Olfactory epithelium: Cells, clinical disorders, and insights from an adult stem cell niche. *Laryngoscope Investigative Otolaryngology*, 3(1), 35–42.

Choi, Yool. (2018). Student employment and persistence: Evidence of effect heterogeneity of student employment on college dropout. *Research in Higher Education*, 59(1), 88–107.

Chomsky, Noam. (1968). *Language and mind*. New York, NY: Harcourt Brace & World.

Chomsky, Noam. (1980). *Rules and representations*. New York, NY: Columbia University Press.

Chong, Jessica X.; Buckingham, Kati J.; Jhangiani, Shalini N.; Boehm, Corinne; Sobreira, Nara; Smith, Joshua D., . . . Bamshad, Michael J. (2015). The genetic basis of Mendelian phenotypes: Discoveries, challenges, and opportunities. *American Journal of Human Genetics*, *97*(2), 199–215.

Choshen-Hillel, Shoham & Yaniv, Ilan. (2011). Agency and the construction of social preference: Between inequality aversion and prosocial behavior. *Journal of Personality and Social Psychology*, *101*(6), 1253–1261.

Choudhury, Ananyo; Aron, Shaun; Sengupta, Dhriti; Hazelhurst, Scott & Ramsay, Michèle. (2018). African genetic diversity provides novel insights into evolutionary history and local adaptations. *Human Molecular Genetics*, 27(R2), R209–R218.

Choukas-Bradley, Sophia; Giletta, Matteo; Widman, Laura; Cohen, Geoffrey L. & Prinstein, Mitchell J. (2014). Experimentally measured susceptibility to peer influence and adolescent sexual behavior trajectories: A preliminary study. *Developmental Psychology*, 50(9), 2221–2227.

Christakis, Dimitri A.; Ramirez, Julian S. Benedikt; Ferguson, Susan M.; Ravinder, Shilpa & Ramirez, Jan-Marino. (2018). How early media exposure may affect cognitive function: A review of results from observations in humans and experiments in mice. *Proceedings of the National Academy of Sciences of the United States of America*, *115*(40), 9851–9858.

Christakis, Erika. (2016). *The importance of being little: What preschoolers really need from grownups*. New York, NY: Viking.

Christian, Cindy W. & Block, Robert. (2009). Abusive head trauma in infants and children. *Pediatrics*, *123*(5), 1409–1411.

Christian, Kimberly M.; Song, Hongjun & Ming, Guo-Li. (2018). A previously undetected pathology of Zika virus infection. *Nature Medicine*, 24(3), 258–259.

Christoforides, Michael; Spanoudis, George & Demetriou, Andreas. (2016).

Coping with logical fallacies: A developmental training program for learning to reason. *Child Development*, 87(6), 1856–1876.

Chronicle of Higher Education. (2010). *Almanac of higher education 2010–2011*. Washington, DC: Chronicle of Higher Education.

Chu, Shuyuan; Chen, Qian; Chen, Yan; Bao, Yixiao; Wu, Min & Zhang, Jun. (2017). Cesarean section without medical indication and risk of childhood asthma, and attenuation by breastfeeding. *PLoS ONE*, *12*(9), e0184920.

Cianciolo, Anna T. & Sternberg, Robert J. (2018). Practical intelligence and tacit knowledge: An ecological view of expertise. In K. Anders Ericsson, et al. (Eds.), *The Cambridge handbook of expertise and expert performance* (pp. 770–792). New York, NY: Cambridge University Press.

Cicchetti, Dante. (2013a). Annual research review: Resilient functioning in maltreated children—past, present, and future perspectives. *Journal of Child Psychology and Psychiatry*, 54(4), 402–422.

Cicchetti, Dante. (2013b). An overview of developmental psychopathology. In Philip D. Zelazo (Ed.), *The Oxford handbook of developmental psychology* (Vol. 2, pp. 455–480). New York, NY: Oxford University Press.

Cicchetti, Dante. (2016). Socioemotional, personality, and biological development: Illustrations from a multilevel developmental psychopathology perspective on child maltreatment. *Annual Review of Psychology*, 67, 187–211.

Cicconi, Megan. (2014). Vygotsky meets technology: A reinvention of collaboration in the early childhood mathematics classroom. *Early Childhood Education Journal*, *42*(1), 57–65.

Cierpka, Manfred & Cierpka, Astrid. (2016). Developmentally appropriate vs. persistent defiant and aggressive behavior. In Manfred Cierpka (Ed.), *Regulatory disorders in infants*. Cham, Switzerland: Springer.

Cilento, Eugene M.; Jin, Lorrain; Stewart, Tessandra; Shi, Min; Sheng, Lifu & Zhang, Jing. (2018). Mass spectrometry: A platform for biomarker discovery and validation for Alzheimer's and Parkinson's diseases. *Journal of Neurochemistry*, (In Press).

Cillessen, Antonius H. N. & Marks, Peter E. L. (2011). Conceptualizing and measuring popularity. In Antonius H. N. Cillessen, et al. (Eds.), *Popularity in the peer system* (pp. 25–56). New York, NY: Guilford Press.

Claessen, Jacques. (2017). *Forgiveness in criminal law through incorporating restorative mediation*. Oisterwijk, the Netherlands: Wolf Legal Publishers.

Clark, Caron A. C.; Fang, Hua; Espy, Kimberly A.; Filipek, Pauline A.; Juranek, Jenifer; Bangert, Barbara, . . . Taylor, H. Gerry. (2013). Relation of neural structure to persistently low academic achievement: A longitudinal study of children with differing birth weights. *Neuropsychology*, 27(3), 364–377.

Clark, Lee Anna; Cuthbert, Bruce; Lewis-Fernández, Roberto; Narrow, William E. & Reed, Geoffrey M. (2017). Three approaches to understanding and classifying mental disorder: ICD-11, *DSM-5*, and the National Institute of Mental Health's Research Domain Criteria (RDoC). *Psychological Science in the Public Interest*, *18*(2), 72–145.

Clarke, Philippa; Marshall, Victor; House, James & Lantz, Paula. (2011). The social structuring of mental health over the adult life course: Advancing theory in the sociology of aging. *Social Forces*, 89(4), 1287–1313.

Coe, Jesse L.; Davies, Patrick T. & Sturge-Apple, Melissa L. (2018). Family instability and young children's school adjustment: Callousness and negative internal representations as mediators. *Child Development*, 89(4), 1193–1208.

Coffelt, Tina A. (2017). Deciding to reveal sexual information and sexuality education in mother-daughter relationships. *Sex Education*, *17*(5), 571–587.

Coggin, Alexander. (January 17, 2016). Debt dodgers: Meet the Americans who moved to Europe and went AWOL on their student loans. *Vice*.

Cohen, Jon. (2014). Saving lives without new drugs. *Science*, *346*(6212), 911.

Cohen, Jon. (2018). What now for human genome editing? *Science*, 362(6419), 1090–1092.

Cohen, Jon. (2019). Moratorium for germline editing splits biologists. *Science*, 363(6432), 1130–1131.

Cohen, Jon. (2019, April 19). Waning immunity. *Science*, 364(6437), 224–227.

Cohen, Joel E. & Malin, Martin B. (Eds.). (2010). *International perspectives on the goals of universal basic and secondary education*. New York, NY: Routledge.

Cohn, D'Vera & Passel, Jeffrey S. (2018, April 5). *A record 64 million Americans live in multigenerational households. Fact Tank*. Washington, DC: Pew Research Center.

Cohn, D'Vera; Passel, Jeffrey S.; Wang, Wendy & Livingston, Gretchen. (2011, December 14). *Barely half of U.S. adults are married—A record low: New marriages down 5% from 2009 to 2010*. Washington, DC: Pew Research Center.

Colaco, Marc; Johnson, Kelly; Schneider, Dona & Barone, Joseph. (2013). Toilet training method is not related to dysfunctional voiding. *Clinical Pediatrics*, 52(1), 49–53.

Cole, Pamela M. & Hollenstein, Tom. (2018). *Emotion regulation: A matter of time*. New York, NY: Routledge.

Coleman, Patrick A. (2019, March 22). Snowplow parenting isn't just morally repulsive, it's bad for kids [Web log post]. Fatherly.

Coleman-Jensen, Alisha; Rabbitt, Matthew P.; Gregory, Christian & Singh, Anita. (2015). *Household food security in the United States in 2014*. Washington, DC: U.S. Department of Agriculture, Economic Research Service. ERR–194.

Coles, Robert. (1997). *The moral intelligence of children: How to raise a moral child*. New York, NY: Random House.

Coley, Nicola; Vaurs, Charlotte & Andrieu, Sandrine. (2015). Nutrition and cognition in aging adults. *Clinics in Geriatric Medicine*, *31*(3), 453–464.

Coley, Rebekah Levine; Votruba-Drzal, Elizabeth; Miller, Portia L. & Koury, Amanda S. (2013). Timing, extent, and type of child care and children's behavioral functioning in kindergarten. *Developmental Psychology*, *49*(10), 1859–1873.

Collett, DeShana & Bennett, Tamara. (2015). Putting intimate partner violence on your radar. *Journal of the American Academy of Physician Assistants*, 28(10), 24–28.

Collin-Vézina, Delphine; De La Sablonnière-Griffin, Mireille; Palmer, Andrea M. & Milne, Lise. (2015). A preliminary mapping of individual, relational, and social factors that impede disclosure of childhood sexual abuse. *Child Abuse & Neglect*, *43*, 123–134.

Colson, Eve R.; Willinger, Marian; Rybin, Denis; Heeren, Timothy; Smith, Lauren A.; Lister, George & Corwin, Michael J. (2013). Trends and factors associated with infant bed sharing, 1993–2010: The National Infant Sleep Position study. *JAMA Pediatrics*, *167*(11), 1032–1037.

Colver, Allan & Dovey-Pearce, Gail. (2018). The anatomical, hormonal and neurochemical changes that occur during brain development in adolescents and young adults. In Albert C. Hergenroeder & Constance M. Wiemann (Eds.), *Health care transition* (pp. 15–19). Cham, Switzerland: Springer.

Committee on Health Care for Underserved Women. (2014). *Health disparities in rural women—Committee opinion number 586 (replaces committee opinion number 429, March 2009): Reaffirmed 2018*. Washington, DC: American College of Obstetricians and Gynecologists.

Compian, Laura J.; Gowen, L. Kris & Hayward, Chris. (2009). The interactive effects of puberty and peer victimization on weight concerns and depression symptoms among early adolescent girls. *Journal of Early Adolescence*, 29(3), 357–375.

Compton, Wilson M.; Gfroerer, Joe; Conway, Kevin P. & Finger, Matthew S. (2014). Unemployment and substance outcomes in the United States 2002–2010. *Drug & Alcohol Dependence*, *142*, 350–353.

Confer, Jaime C.; Easton, Judith A.; Fleischman, Diana S.; Goetz, Cari D.; Lewis, David M. G.; Perilloux, Carin & Buss, David M. (2010). Evolutionary psychology: Controversies, questions, prospects, and limitations. *American Psychologist*, 65(2), 110–126.

Conti, Aldo Alberto; McLean, L.; Tolomeo, Serenella; Steele, J. Douglas & Baldacchino, Alex M. (2019). Chronic tobacco smoking and neuropsychological impairments: A systematic review and meta-analysis. *Neuroscience & Biobehavioral Reviews*, 96, 143–154.

Cook, Peta S. (2018). Continuity, change and possibility in older age: Identity and ageing-as-discovery. *Journal of Sociology*, 54(2), 178–190.

Coon, Carleton S. (1962). *The origin of races*. New York, NY: Knopf.

Coovadia, Hoosen M. & Wittenberg, Dankwart F. (Eds.). (2004). *Paediatrics and child* *health: A manual for health professionals in developing countries* (5th ed.). New York, NY: Oxford University Press.

Copeland, William E.; Wolke, Dieter; Angold, Adrian & Costell, E. Jane. (2013). Adult psychiatric outcomes of bullying and being bullied by peers in childhood and adolescence. *JAMA Psychiatry, 70*(4), 419–426.

Coplan, Robert J. & Weeks, Murray. (2009). Shy and soft-spoken: Shyness, pragmatic language, and socio-emotional adjustment in early childhood. *Infant and Child Development, 18*(3), 238–254.

Copp, Jennifer E.; Giordano, Peggy C.; Longmore, Monica A. & Manning, Wendy D. (2015). Living with parents and emerging adults' depressive symptoms. *Journal of Family Issues*, (In Press).

Corballis, Michael C. (2011). *The recursive mind: The origins of human language, thought, and civilization*. Princeton, NJ: Princeton University Press.

Cordina-Duverger, Emilie; Menegaux, Florence; Popa, Alexandru; Rabstein, Sylvia; Harth, Volker; Pesch, Beate, . . . Guénel, Pascal. (2018). Night shift work and breast cancer: A pooled analysis of population-based case–control studies with complete work history. *European Journal of Epidemiology*, 33(4), 369–379.

Corenblum, Barry. (2014). Relationships between racial–ethnic identity, self-esteem and in-group attitudes among First Nation children. *Journal of Youth and Adolescence, 43*(3), 387–404.

Cornelis, Marilyn C.; Byrne, E. M.; Esko, T.; Nalls, M. A.; Ganna, A.; Paynter, N., . . . Wojczynski, M. K. (2015). Genome-wide meta-analysis identifies six novel loci associated with habitual coffee consumption. *Molecular Psychiatry, 20*(5), 647–656.

Cornwall, Claudia. (2013). *Catching cancer: The quest for its viral and bacterial causes*. Lanham, MD: Rowman & Littlefield.

Corps, Kara N.; Roth, Theodore L. & McGavern, Dorian B. (2015). Inflammation and neuroprotection in traumatic brain injury. *JAMA Neurology, 72*(3), 355–362.

Corr, Charles A. & Corr, Donna M. (2013b). Historical and contemporary perspectives on loss, grief, and mourning. In David Meagher & David E. Balk (Eds.), *Handbook of thanatology: The essential body of knowledge for the study of death, dying, and bereavement* (2nd ed., pp. 135–148). New York, NY: Routledge.

Cosgrave, James F. (2010). Embedded addiction: The social production of gambling knowledge and the development of gambling markets. *Canadian Journal of Sociology, 35*(1), 113–134.

Costa, Albert & Sebastián-Gallés, Núria. (2014). How does the bilingual experience sculpt the brain? *Nature Reviews Neuroscience, 15*(5), 336–345.

Costa, Albert; Vives, Marc–Lluís & Corey, Joanna D. (2017). On language processing shaping decision making. *Current Directions in Psychological Science, 26*(2), 146–151.

Côté, James E. (2018). The enduring usefulness of Erikson's concept of the identity crisis in the 21st century: An analysis of student mental health concerns. *Identity, 18*(4), 251–263.

Côté, James E. & Levine, Charles. (2015). *Identity formation, youth, and development: A simplified approach*. New York, NY: Psychology Press.

Council on Communications and Media. (2011). Policy statement—Children, adolescents, obesity, and the media. *Pediatrics, 128*(1), 201–208.

Couzin-Frankel, Jennifer. (2013a). Return of unexpected DNA results urged. *Science, 339*(6127), 1507–1508.

Couzin-Frankel, Jennifer. (2013b). How does fetal environment influence later health? *Science, 340*(6137), 1160–1161.

Couzin-Frankel, Jennifer. (2016). A cancer legacy. *Science, 351*(6272), 440–443.

Couzin-Frankel, Jennifer. (2017). Fateful imprints. *Science, 355*(6321), 122–125.

Couzin-Frankel, Jennifer. (2018). Toxin or treatment? *Science, 362*(6412), 278–282.

Covington-Ward, Yolanda. (2017). African immigrants in low-wage direct health care: Motivations, job satisfaction, and occupational mobility. *Journal of Immigrant and Minority Health, 19*(3), 709–715.

Cowell, Jason M.; Lee, Kang; Malcolm-Smith, Susan; Selcuk, Bilge; Zhou, Xinyue & Decety, Jean. (2017). The development of generosity and moral cognition across five cultures. *Developmental Science, 20*(4), e12403.

Cowen, Joshua M.; Fleming, David J.; Witte, John F.; Wolf, Patrick J. & Kisida, Brian. (2013). School vouchers and student attainment: Evidence from a state-mandated study of Milwaukee's parental choice program. *Policy Studies Journal, 41*(1), 147–168.

Coyne, Sarah M.; Stockdale, Laura & Summers, Kjersti. (2019). Problematic cell phone use, depression, anxiety, and self-regulation: Evidence from a three year longitudinal study from adolescence to emerging adulthood. *Computers in Human Behavior, 96*, 78–84.

Craig, Stephanie G.; Davies, Gregory; Schibuk, Larry; Weiss, Margaret D. & Hechtman, Lily. (2015). Long-term effects of stimulant treatment for ADHD: What can we tell our patients? *Current Developmental Disorders Reports, 2*(1), 1–9.

Crain, William C. (2011). *Theories of development: Concepts and applications* (6th ed.). Boston, MA: Prentice–Hall.

Cree, Robyn A.; Bitsko, Rebecca H.; Robinson, Lara R.; Holbrook, Joseph R.; Danielson, Melissa L.; Smith, Camille, . . . Peacock, Georgina. (2018). *Health care, family, and community factors associated with mental, behavioral, and developmental disorders and poverty among children aged 2–8 years — United States, 2016*. 67(50), 1377–1383. Atlanta, GA: Centers for Disease Control and Prevention.

Crenshaw, David A. (2013). The family, larger systems, and traumatic death. In David K. Meagher & David E. Balk (Eds.), *Handbook of thanatology: The essential body of knowledge for the study of death, dying, and bereavement* (2nd ed., pp. 305–309). New York, NY: Routledge.

Crenshaw, Kimberle. (1989). Demarginalizing the intersection of race and sex: A Black feminist critique of antidiscrimination doctrine, feminist theory and antiracist politics. *University of Chicago Legal Forum*, 139–167.

Cripe, Larry D. & Frankel, Richard M. (2017). Dying from cancer: Communication, empathy, and the clinical imagination. *Journal of Patient Experience, 4*(2), 69–73.

Crnic, Keith A.; Neece, Cameron L.; McIntyre, Laura Lee; Blacher, Jan & Baker, Bruce L. (2017). Intellectual disability and developmental risk: Promoting intervention to improve child and family well-being. *Child Development, 88*(2), 436–445.

Crone, Eveline A.; van Duijvenvoorde, Anna C. K. & Peper, Jiska S. (2016). Annual research review: Neural contributions to risk-taking in adolescence—developmental changes and individual differences. *Journal of Child Psychology and Psychiatry, 57*(3), 353–368.

Crosnoe, Robert; Purtell, Kelly M.; Davis-Kean, Pamela; Ansari, Arya & Benner, Aprile D. (2016). The selection of children from low-income families into preschool. *Developmental Psychology, 52*(4), 599–612.

Crossley, Nicolas A.; Mechelli, Andrea; Scott, Jessica; Carletti, Francesco; Fox, Peter T.; McGuire, Philip & Bullmore, Edward T. (2014). The hubs of the human connectome are generally implicated in the anatomy of brain disorders. *Brain, 137*(8), 2382–2395.

Crowe, Laura & Butterworth, Peter. (2016). The role of financial hardship, mastery and social support in the association between employment status and depression: Results from an Australian longitudinal cohort study. *BMJ Open, 6*, e009834.

Cruikshank, Margaret. (2009). *Learning to be old: Gender, culture, and aging* (2nd ed.). Lanham, MD: Rowman & Littlefield.

Csikszentmihalyi, Mihaly. (2013). *Creativity: Flow and the psychology of discovery and invention*. New York, NY: Harper Perennial.

Culpin, Iryna; Heron, Jon; Araya, Ricardo & Joinson, Carol. (2015). Early childhood father absence and depressive symptoms in adolescent girls from a UK cohort: The mediating role of early menarche. *Journal of Abnormal Child Psychology, 43*(5), 921–931.

Cumming, Elaine & Henry, William Earl. (1961). *Growing old: The process of disengagement*. New York, NY: Basic Books.

Cunningham, F. Gary; Leveno, Kenneth; Bloom, Steven; Spong, Catherine Y.; Dashe, Jodi; Hoffman, Barbara, . . . Sheffield, Jeanne S. (2014). *Williams obstetrics* (24th ed.). New York, NY: McGraw-Hill Education.

Currie, Janet & Widom, Cathy S. (2010). Long-term consequences of child abuse and neglect on adult economic well-being. *Child Maltreatment, 15*(2), 111–120.

Curry, Andrew. (2018, November 5). How can you eat dairy if you lack the gene for digesting it? Fermented milk may be key, ancient Mongolian study suggests. *Science*.

Curtin, Nancy & Garrison, Mary. (2018). "She was more than a friend": Clinical intervention strategies for effectively addressing disenfranchised grief issues for same-sex couples. *Journal of Gay & Lesbian Social Services, 30*(3), 261–281.

Cutler, David M.; Lleras-Muney, Adriana & Vogl, Tom. (2011). Socioeconomic status and health: Dimensions and mechanisms. In Sherry Glied & Peter C. Smith (Eds.), *The Oxford handbook of health economics*. New York, NY: Oxford University Press.

Cutuli, J. J.; Ahumada, Sandra M.; Herbers, Janette E.; Lafavor, Theresa L.; Masten, Ann S. & Oberg, Charles N. (2017). Adversity and children experiencing family homelessness: Implications for health. *Journal of Children and Poverty*, 23(1), 41–55.

Cuzzolaro, Massimo & Fassino, Secondo (Eds.). (2018). *Body image, eating, and weight: A guide to assessment, treatment, and prevention*. Cham, Switzerland: Springer.

D'Angelo, Jonathan D. & Toma, Catalina L. (2016). There are plenty of fish in the sea: The effects of choice overload and reversibility on online daters' satisfaction with selected partners. *Media Psychology*, (In Press).

Dabbagh, Alya; Laws, Rebecca L.; Steulet, Claudia; Dumolard, Laure; Mulders, Mick N.; Kretsinger, Katrina, . . . Goodson, James L. (2018, November 30). *Progress toward regional measles elimination — Worldwide, 2000–2017. Morbidity and Mortality Weekly Report, 67*(47), 1323–1329: Centers for Disease Control and Prevention.

Dahmen, Brigitte; Puetz, Vanessa B.; Scharke, Wolfgang; Von Polier, Georg G.; Herpertz-Dahlmann, Beate & Konrad, Kerstin. (2018). Effects of early-life adversity on hippocampal structures and associated HPA axis functions. *Developmental Neuroscience, 40*(1), 13–22.

Daley, Tamara C.; Whaley, Shannon E.; Sigman, Marian D.; Espinosa, Michael P. & Neumann, Charlotte. (2003). IQ on the rise: The Flynn Effect in rural Kenyan children. *Psychological Science, 14*(3), 215–219.

Dall'Alba, Gloria. (2018). Reframing expertise and its development: A lifeworld perspective. In K. Anders Ericsson, et al. (Eds.), *The Cambridge handbook of expertise and expert performance* (pp. 33–39). New York, NY: Cambridge University Press.

Daly, Jeanette M.; Gaskill, Kathryn J. & Jogerst, Gerald J. (2011). Essential data elements for reporters of elder abuse. *Journal of Elder Abuse & Neglect*, 23(3), 234–245.

Damasio, Antonio R. (2012). *Self comes to mind: Constructing the conscious brain*. New York, NY: Vintage.

Damasio, Antonio R. (2018). *The strange order of things: Life, feeling, and the making of cultures*. New York, NY: Pantheon.

Danielsbacka, Mirkka; Tanskanen, Antti & Rotkirch, Anna. (2018). The "kinship penalty": Parenthood and in-law conflict in contemporary Finland. *Evolutionary Psychological Science, 4*(1), 71–82.

Dantchev, Slava; Zammit, Stanley & Wolke, Dieter. (2018). Sibling bullying in middle childhood and psychotic disorder at 18 years: A prospective cohort study. *Psychological Medicine*, 48(14), 2321–2328.

Dar-Nimrod, Ilan & Heine, Steven J. (2011). Genetic essentialism: On the deceptive determinism of DNA. *Psychological Bulletin, 137*(5), 800–818.

Darweesh, Sirwan K. L.; Wolters, Frank J.; Postuma, Ronald B.; Stricker, Bruno H.; Hofman, Albert; Koudstaal, Peter J., . . . Ikram, M. Arfan. (2017). Association between poor cognitive functioning and risk of incident parkinsonism: The Rotterdam study. *JAMA Neurology*, 74(12), 1431–1438.

Darwin, Charles. (1859). *On the origin of species by means of natural selection*. London, UK: J. Murray.

Darwin, Zoe; Galdas, Paul; Hinchliff, Sharron; Littlewood, Elizabeth; McMillan, Dean; McGowan, Linda & Gilbody, Simon. (2017). Fathers' views and experiences of their own mental health during pregnancy and the first postnatal year: A qualitative interview study of men participating in the UK Born and Bred in Yorkshire (BaBY) cohort. *BMC Pregnancy and Childbirth, 17*(45).

Dasgupta, Rajib; Sinha, Dipa & Yumnam, Veda. (2016). Rapid survey of wasting and stunting in children: What's new, what's old and what's the buzz? *Indian Pediatrics*, 53(1), 47–49.

Daugherty, Ana M.; Bender, Andrew R.; Raz, Naftali & Ofen, Noa. (2016). Age differences in hippocampal subfield volumes from childhood to late adulthood. *Hippocampus*, 26(2), 220–228.

Daum, Moritz M.; Ulber, Julia & Gredebäck, Gustaf. (2013). The development of pointing perception in infancy: Effects of communicative signals on covert shifts of attention. *Developmental Psychology*, 49(10), 1898–1908.

Davidai, Shai & Gilovich, Thomas. (2015). Building a more mobile America: One income quintile at a time. *Perspectives on Psychological Science, 10*(1), 60–71.

Davis, Corey S.; Green, Traci C.; Hernandez-Delgado, Hector & Lieberman, Amy Judd. (2018). Status of US state laws mandating timely reporting of nonfatal overdose. *American Journal of Public Health, 108*(9), 1159–1161.

Davison, Glen; Kehaya, Corinna & Jones, Arwel Wyn. (2014). Nutritional and physical activity interventions to improve immunity. *American Journal of Lifestyle Medicine*.

Dawson, Chris; Veliziotis, Michail & Hopkins, Benjamin. (2017). Temporary employment, job satisfaction and subjective well-being. *Economic and Industrial Democracy*, 38(1), 69–98.

Day, Felix R.; Elks, Cathy E.; Murray, Anna; Ong, Ken K. & Perry, John R. B. (2015). Puberty timing associated with diabetes, cardiovascular disease and also diverse health outcomes in men and women: The UK Biobank study. *Scientific Reports*, 5(11208).

Dayanim, Shoshana & Namy, Laura L. (2015). Infants learn baby signs from video. *Child Development, 86*(3), 800–811.

De Boeck, Paul & Jeon, Minjeong. (2018). Perceived crisis and reforms: Issues, explanations, and remedies. *Psychological Bulletin, 144*(7), 757–777.

de Boer, Anouk; Peeters, Margot & Koning, Ina. (2017). An experimental study of risk taking behavior among adolescents: A closer look at peer and sex influences. *Journal of Early Adolescence*, 37(8), 1125–1141.

de Hoog, Marieke L. A.; Kleinman, Ken P.; Gillman, Matthew W.; Vrijkotte, Tanja G. M.; van Eijsden, Manon & Taveras, Elsie M. (2014). Racial/ethnic and immigrant differences in early childhood diet quality. *Public Health Nutrition, 17*(6), 1308–1317.

de Jong Gierveld, Jenny & Merz, Eva-Maria. (2013). Parents' partnership decision making after divorce or widowhood: The role of (step)children. *Journal of Marriage and Family*, 75(5), 1098–1113.

de Jonge, Ank; Geerts, C. C.; van der Goes, Birgit Y.; Mol, Ben W.; Buitendijk, S. E. & Nijhuis, Jan. (2015). Perinatal mortality and morbidity up to 28 days after birth among 743,070 low-risk planned home and hospital births: A cohort study based on three merged national perinatal databases. *BJOG, 122*(5), 720–728.

de Jonge, Huub. (2011). Purification and remembrance: Eastern and Western ways to deal with the Bali bombing. In Peter Jan Margry & Cristina Sánchez-Carretero (Eds.), *Grassroots memorials: The politics of memorializing traumatic death* (pp. 262–284). New York, NY: Berghahn Books.

de la Torre, Pedro & Germano, Roy. (2014). Out of the shadows: DREAMer identity in the immigrant youth movement. *Latino Studies, 12*(3), 449–467.

De Lima, Liliana; Woodruff, Roger; Pettus, Katherine; Downing, Julia; Buitrago, Rosa; Munyoro, Esther, . . . Radbruch, Lukas. (2017). International Association for Hospice and Palliative Care position statement: Euthanasia and physician-assisted suicide. *Journal of Palliative Medicine, 20*(1), 8–14.

De Neys, Wim & Van Gelder, Elke. (2009). Logic and belief across the lifespan: The rise and fall of belief inhibition during syllogistic reasoning. *Developmental Science, 12*(1), 123–130.

de Oliveira Cardoso, Caroline; Dias, Natália; Senger, Joana; Colling, Ana Paula Cervi; Seabra, Alessandra Gotuzo & Fonseca, Rochele Paz. (2018). Neuropsychological stimulation of executive functions in children with typical development: A systematic review. *Applied Neuropsychology: Child*, 7(1), 61–81.

De Raedt, Rudi; Koster, Ernst H. W. & Ryckewaert, Ruben. (2013). Aging and attentional bias for death related and general threat-related information: Less avoidance in older as compared with middle-aged adults. *The Journals of Gerontology Series B: Psychological Sciences and Social Sciences, 68*(1), 41–48.

De Vos, Ans; Forrier, Anneleen; Van Der Heijden, Beatrice & De Cuyper, Nele. (2017). Keep the expert! Occupational expertise, perceived employability and job search. *Career Development International, 22*(3), 318–332.

de Vos, Paul; Hanck, Christoph; Neisingh, Marjolein; Prak, Dennis; Groen, Henk & Faas, Marijke M. (2015). Weight gain in freshman college students and perceived health. *Preventive Medicine Reports, 2*, 229–234.

de Vries, Dian A.; Peter, Jochen; Nikken, Peter & de Graaf, Hanneke. (2014). The effect of social network site use on appearance investment and desire for cosmetic surgery among adolescent boys and girls. *Sex Roles, 71*(9/10), 283–295.

de Vrieze, Jop. (2018). The metawars. *Science, 361*(6408), 1184–1188.

De Wilde, Arno; Van Der Flier, Wiesje M.; Pelkmans, Wiesje; Bouwman, Femke; Verwer, Jurre; Groot, Colin, . . . Scheltens, Philip. (2018). Association of amyloid positron emission tomography with changes in diagnosis and patient treatment in an unselected memory clinic cohort: The abide project. *JAMA Neurology, 75*(9), 1062–1070.

Dean, Angela J.; Walters, Julie & Hall, Anthony. (2010). A systematic review of interventions to enhance medication adherence in children and adolescents with chronic illness. *Archives of Disease in Childhood, 95*(9), 717–723.

Deangelo, Linda; Schuster, Maximilian T. & Stebleton, Michael J. (2016). California DREAMers: Activism, identity, and empowerment among undocumented college students. *Journal of Diversity in Higher Education, 9*(3), 216–230.

Dearing, Eric; Wimer, Christopher; Simpkins, Sandra D.; Lund, Terese; Bouffard, Suzanne M.; Caronongan, Pia, . . . Weiss, Heather. (2009). Do neighborhood and home contexts help explain why low-income children miss opportunities to participate in activities outside of school? *Developmental Psychology, 45*(6), 1545–1562.

Dearing, Eric & Zachrisson, Henrik D. (2017). Concern over internal, external, and incidence validity in studies of child-care quantity and externalizing behavior problems. *Child Development Perspectives, 11*(2), 133–138.

Deater-Deckard, Kirby & Lansford, Jennifer E. (2016). Daughters' and sons' exposure to childrearing discipline and violence in low- and middle-income countries. *Monographs of the Society for Research in Child Development, 81*(1), 78–103.

Dees, Marianne K.; Vernooij-Dassen, Myrra J.; Dekkers, Wim J.; Vissers, Kris C. & van Weel, Chris. (2011). 'Unbearable suffering': A qualitative study on the perspectives of patients who request assistance in dying. *Journal of Medical Ethics, 37*(12), 727–734.

Dehaene-Lambertz, Ghislaine. (2017). The human infant brain: A neural architecture able to learn language. *Psychonomic Bulletin & Review, 24*(1), 48–55.

Deighton, Jessica; Humphrey, Neil; Belsky, Jay; Boehnke, Jan; Vostanis, Panos & Patalay, Praveetha. (2018). Longitudinal pathways between mental health difficulties and academic performance during middle childhood and early adolescence. *British Journal of Developmental Psychology, 36*(1), 110–126.

DeLamater, John. (2012). Sexual expression in later life: A review and synthesis. *The Journal of Sex Research, 49*(2/3), 125–141.

Delaunay-El Allam, Maryse; Soussignan, Robert; Patris, Bruno; Marlier, Luc & Schaal, Benoist. (2010). Long-lasting memory for an odor acquired at the mother's breast. *Developmental Science, 13*(6), 849–863.

Delon-Martin, Chantal; Plailly, Jane; Fonlupt, Pierre; Veyrac, Alexandra & Roye, Jean-Pierre. (2013). Perfumers' expertise induces structural reorganization in olfactory brain regions. *NeuroImage, 68*, 55–62.

Demartini, Julie K.; Casa, Douglas; Stearns, Rebecca; Belval, Luke; Crago, Arthur; Davis, Rob & Jardine, John. (2015). Effectiveness of cold water immersion in the treatment of exertional heat stroke at the Falmouth Road Race. *Medicine & Science in Sports & Exercise, 47*(2), 240–245.

Deming, Michelle E.; Covan, Eleanor Krassen; Swan, Suzanne C. & Billings, Deborah L. (2013). Exploring rape myths, gendered norms, group processing, and the social context of rape among college women a qualitative analysis. *Violence Against Women, 19*(4), 465–485.

Demir, Melikşah; Haynes, Andrew & Potts, Shannon K. (2017). My friends are my estate: Friendship experiences mediate the relationship between perceived responses to capitalization attempts and happiness. *Journal of Happiness Studies, 18*(4), 1161–1190.

Denq, William & Delasobera, B. Elizabeth. (2018). Adaptive extreme sports: A clinical guide. In Arthur Jason De Luigi (Ed.), *Adaptive sports medicine* (pp. 343–357). Cham, Switzerland: Springer.

Dent, Lauren & Maloney, Patricia. (2017). Evangelical Christian parents' attitudes towards abstinence-based sex education: "I want my kids to have great sex!". *Sex Education, 17*(2), 149–164.

Derek M. Griffith, Marino A. Bruce, Roland J. Thorpe, Jr., (Eds.). (2019). Men's Health Equity: A Handbook. New York: Routledge.

Deresiewicz, William. (2014). *Excellent sheep: The miseducation of the American elite and the way to a meaningful life.* New York, NY: Free Press.

Desai, Rishi J.; Hernandez-Diaz, Sonia; Bateman, Brian T. & Huybrechts, Krista F. (2014). Increase in prescription opioid use during pregnancy among Medicaid-enrolled women. *Obstetrics & Gynecology, 123*(5), 997–1002.

Devine, Rory T. & Hughes, Claire. (2014). Relations between false belief understanding and executive function in early childhood: A meta-analysis. *Child Development, 85*(5), 1777–1794.

Devitt, Aleea L. & Schacter, Daniel L. (2016). False memories with age: Neural and cognitive underpinnings. *Neuropsychologia, 91*, 346–359.

Dewan, Michael C.; Rattani, Abbas; Mekary, Rania; Glancz, Laurence J.; Yunusa, Ismaeel; Baticulon, Ronnie E., . . . Warf, Benjamin C. (2018). Global hydrocephalus epidemiology and incidence: Systematic review and meta-analysis. *Journal of Neurosurgery, 130*(4), 1039–1408.

Dey, Matthew; Houseman, Susan & Polivka, Anne. (2016). *Manufacturers' outsourcing to temporary help services: A research update.* Washington, DC: U.S. Department of Labor.

DeYoung, Colin G.; Hirsh, Jacob B.; Shane, Matthew S.; Papademetris, Xenophon; Rajeevan, Nallakkandi & Gray, Jeremy R. (2010). Testing predictions from personality neuroscience. *Psychological Science, 21*(6), 820–828.

Diamond, Adele. (2012). Activities and programs that improve children's executive functions. *Current Directions in Psychological Science, 21*(5), 335–341.

Diamond, Adele. (2016). Why improving and assessing executive functions early in life is critical. In James Alan Griffin, et al. (Eds.), *Executive function in preschool-age children: Integrating measurement, neurodevelopment, and translational research* (pp. 11–43). Washington, DC: American Psychological Association.

Diamond, Adele & Lee, Kathleen. (2011). Interventions shown to aid executive function development in children 4 to 12 years old. *Science, 333*(6045), 959–964.

Diamond, Marian C. (1988). *Enriching heredity: The impact of the environment on the anatomy of the brain.* New York, NY: Free Press.

Didion, Joan. (2005). *The year of magical thinking.* New York, NY: Knopf.

Diener, Ed & Seligman, Martin E. P. (2018). Beyond money: Progress on an economy of well-being. *Perspectives on Psychological Science, 13*(2), 171–175.

Diener, Ed; Seligman, Martin E. P.; Choi, Hyewon & Oishi, Shigehiro. (2018). Happiest people revisited. *Perspectives on Psychological Science, 13*(2), 176–184.

Digest of Education Statistics. (2016, February). *Table 205.10. Private elementary and secondary school enrollment and private enrollment as a percentage of total enrollment in public and private schools, by region and grade level: Selected years, fall 1995 through fall 2013.* Washington, DC: National Center for Education Statistics.

Dijksterhuis, Ap. (2018). Reflection on the professor-priming replication report. *Perspectives on Psychological Science, 13*(2), 295–296.

Dijksterhuis, Ap; Bos, Maarten W.; van der Leij, Andries & van Baaren, Rick B. (2009). Predicting soccer matches after unconscious and conscious thought as a function of expertise. *Psychological Science, 20*(11), 1381–1387.

Dijksterhuis, Ap & van Knippenberg, Ad. (1998). The relation between perception and behavior, or how to win a game of Trivial Pursuit.

Journal of Personality and Social Psychology, 74(4), 865–877.

Dillman Carpentier, Francesca & Stevens, Elise. (2018). Sex in the media, sex on the mind: Linking television use, sexual permissiveness, and sexual concept accessibility in memory. *Sexuality & Culture*, 22(1), 22–38.

Dimler, Laura M. & Natsuaki, Misaki N. (2015). The effects of pubertal timing on externalizing behaviors in adolescence and early adulthood: A meta-analytic review. *Journal of Adolescence*, 45, 160–170.

Dingemans, Ellen; Henkens, Kène & van Solinge, Hanna. (2016). Access to bridge employment: Who finds and who does not find work after retirement? *The Gerontologist*, 56(4), 630–640.

Dinh, Michael M.; Bein, Kendall; Roncal, Susan; Byrne, Christopher M.; Petchell, Jeffrey & Brennan, Jeffrey. (2013). Redefining the golden hour for severe head injury in an urban setting: The effect of prehospital arrival times on patient outcomes. *Injury*, 44(5), 606–610.

Diseth, Åge; Meland, Eivind & Breidablik, Hans J. (2014). Self-beliefs among students: Grade level and gender differences in self-esteem, self-efficacy and implicit theories of intelligence. *Learning and Individual Differences*, 35.

Dishion, Thomas J.; Mun, Chung; Ha, Thao & Tein, Jenn-Yun. (2019). Observed family and friendship dynamics in adolescence: A latent profile approach to identifying "mesosystem" adaptation for intervention tailoring. *Prevention Science*, 20(1), 41–55.

Dishion, Thomas J.; Poulin, François & Burraston, Bert. (2001). Peer group dynamics associated with iatrogenic effects in group interventions with high-risk young adolescents. In Douglas W. Nangle & Cynthia A. Erdley (Eds.), *The role of friendship in psychological adjustment* (pp. 79–92). San Francisco, CA: Jossey-Bass.

Dishion, Thomas J.; Véronneau, Marie-Hélène & Myers, Michael W. (2010). Cascading peer dynamics underlying the progression from problem behavior to violence in early to late adolescence. *Development and Psychopathology*, 22(3), 603–619.

Ditch the Label. (2017). *The annual bullying survey 2017*. Los Angeles, CA: Ditch the Label.

Dix, Theodore & Yan, Ni. (2014). Mothers' depressive symptoms and infant negative emotionality in the prediction of child adjustment at age 3: Testing the maternal reactivity and child vulnerability hypotheses. *Development and Psychopathology*, 26(1), 111–124.

Doka, Kenneth J. (2013). Historical and contemporary perspectives on dying. In David K. Meagher & David E. Balk (Eds.), *Handbook of thanatology: The essential body of knowledge for the study of death, dying, and bereavement* (2nd ed., pp. 17–23). New York, NY: Routledge.

Doka, Kenneth J. (2016). *Grief is a journey: Finding your path through loss*. New York, NY: Atria.

Domina, Thurston; Conley, AnneMarie & Farkas, George. (2011a). The case for dreaming big. *Sociology of Education*, 84(2), 118–121.

Domina, Thurston; Conley, AnneMarie & Farkas, George. (2011b). The link between educational expectations and effort in the college-for-all era. *Sociology of Education*, 84(2), 93–112.

Dominguez, Cynthia O. (2001). Expertise in laparoscopic surgery: Anticipation and affordances. In Eduardo Salas & Gary A. Klein (Eds.), *Linking expertise and naturalistic decision making* (pp. 287–301). Mahwah, NJ: Erlbaum.

Dominguez-Folgueras, Marta & Castro-Martin, Teresa. (2013). Cohabitation in Spain: No longer a marginal path to family formation. *Journal of Marriage and Family*, 75(2), 422–437.

Dong, XinQi & Simon, Melissa A. (2011). Enhancing national policy and programs to address elder abuse. *JAMA*, 305(23), 2460–2461.

Doom, Jenalee R.; Doyle, Colleen M. & Gunnar, Megan R. (2017). Social stress buffering by friends in childhood and adolescence: Effects on HPA and oxytocin activity. *Social Neuroscience*, 12(1), 8–21.

Dorais, Michel. (2009). *Don't tell: The sexual abuse of boys* (2nd ed.). Montreal, Canada: McGill-Queen's University Press.

Doraiswamy, P. Murali. (2012). Silent cerebrovascular events and Alzheimer's disease: An overlooked opportunity for prevention? *American Journal of Psychiatry*, 169(3), 251–254.

Dorn, Lorah D. & Biro, Frank M. (2011). Puberty and its measurement: A decade in review. *Journal of Research on Adolescence*, 21(1), 180–195.

Dotterer, Aryn M.; McHale, Susan M. & Crouter, Ann C. (2009). The development and correlates of academic interests from childhood through adolescence. *Journal of Educational Psychology*, 101(2), 509–519.

Doucet, Andrea. (2015). Parental responsibilities: Dilemmas of measurement and gender equality. *Journal of Marriage and Family*, 77(1), 224–242.

Dougherty, Rachel. (2019). *Secret engineer: How Emily Roebling built the Brooklyn Bridge*. New York, NY: Roaring Brook.

Dow-Edwards, Diana & Silva, Lindsay. (2017). Endocannabinoids in brain plasticity: Cortical maturation, HPA axis function and behavior. *Brain Research*, 1654(Part B), 157–164.

Downing, Katherine L.; Hinkley, Trina; Salmon, Jo; Hnatiuk, Jill A. & Hesketh, Kylie D. (2017). Do the correlates of screen time and sedentary time differ in preschool children? *BMC Public Health*, 17(285).

Drake, Patrick; Driscoll, Anne K. & Mathews, T. J. (2018). *Cigarette smoking during pregnancy: United States, 2016*. Hyattsville, MD: National Center for Health Statistics. NCHS Data Brief No. 305.

Drewelies, Johanna; Wagner, Jenny; Tesch-Römer, Clemens; Heckhausen, Jutta & Gerstorf, Denis. (2017). Perceived control across the second half of life: The role of physical health and social integration. *Psychology and Aging*, 32(1), 76–92.

Driemeyer, Wiebke; Janssen, Erick; Wiltfang, Jens & Elmerstig, Eva. (2016). Masturbation experiences of Swedish senior high school students: Gender differences and similarities. *The Journal of Sex Research*, (In Press).

Drover, James; Hoffman, Dennis R.; Castañeda, Yolanda S.; Morale, Sarah E. & Birch, Eileen E. (2009). Three randomized controlled trials of early long-chain polyunsaturated fatty acid supplementation on means-end problem solving in 9-month-olds. *Child Development*, 80(5), 1376–1384.

Drury, Stacy S.; Gleason, Mary M.; Smyke, Anna T.; Theall, Katherine; De Vivo, Immaculata; Wong, Jason Y. Y., . . . Nelson, Charles A. (2012). Telomere length and early severe social deprivation: Linking early adversity and cellular aging. *Molecular Psychiatry*, 17, 719–727.

Duckett, Stephen. (2018). Knowing, anticipating, even facilitating but still not intending: Another challenge to double effect reasoning. *Journal of Bioethical Inquiry*, 15(1), 33–37.

Duckworth, Angela L. (2016). *Grit: The power of passion and perseverance*. New York, NY: Scribner.

Duckworth, Angela L. & Kern, Margaret L. (2011). A meta-analysis of the convergent validity of self-control measures. *Journal of Research in Personality*, 45(3), 259–268.

Duffey, Kiyah J.; Steffen, Lyn M.; Van Horn, Linda; Jacobs, David R. & Popkin, Barry M. (2012). Dietary patterns matter: Diet beverages and cardiometab olic risks in the longitudinal Coronary Artery Risk Development in Young Adults (CARDIA) Study. *American Journal of Clinical Nutrition*, 95(4), 909–915.

Dugas, Lara R.; Fuller, Miles; Gilbert, Jack & Layden, Brian T. (2016). The obese gut microbiome across the epidemiologic transition. *Emerging Themes in Epidemiology*, 13(1).

Duggan, Maeve. (2017, July 11). *Online harassment 2017. Internet & Technology*. Washington, DC: Pew Research Center.

Duh, Shinchieh; Paik, Jae H.; Miller, Patricia H.; Gluck, Stephanie C.; Li, Hui & Himelfarb, Igor. (2016). Theory of mind and executive function in Chinese preschool children. *Developmental Psychology*, 52(4), 582–591.

Dumas, A.; Simmat-Durand, L. & Lejeune, C. (2014). Pregnancy and substance use in France: A literature review. *Journal de Gynécologie Obstétrique et Biologie de la Reproduction*, 43(9), 649–656.

Dunbar, R. I. M. (2018). The anatomy of friendship. *Trends in Cognitive Sciences*, 22(1), 32–51.

Duncan, Dustin T. & Kawachi, Ichiro (Eds.). (2018). *Neighborhoods and health* (2nd ed.). New York, NY: Oxford University Press.

Duncan, Greg J. & Magnuson, Katherine. (2013). Investing in preschool programs. *Journal of Economic Perspectives*, 27(2), 109–132.

Dunn, Erin C.; Nishimi, Kristen; Powers, Abigail & Bradley, Bekh. (2017). Is developmental timing of trauma exposure associated with depressive and post-traumatic stress disorder symptoms in adulthood? *Journal of Psychiatric Research*, 84, 119–127.

Dunn, Kristy & Bremner, J. Gavin. (2017). Investigating looking and social looking measures as an index of infant violation of expectation. *Developmental Science, 20*(6), e12452.

Dunning, David. (2011). *Social motivation*. New York, NY: Psychology Press.

DuPont, Robert L. & Lieberman, Jeffrey A. (2014). Young brains on drugs. *Science, 344*(6184), 557.

Duran, Chelsea A. K.; Cottone, Elizabeth; Ruzek, Erik A.; Mashburn, Andrew J. & Grissmer, David W. (2018). Family stress processes and children's self-regulation. *Child Development,* (In Press).

Durso, Francis T.; Dattel, Andrew R. & Pop, Vlad L. (2018). Expertise and transportation. In K. Anders Ericsson, et al. (Eds.), *The Cambridge handbook of expertise and expert performance* (2nd ed., pp. 356–371). New York, NY: Cambridge University Press.

Dutton, Donald G. (2012). The case against the role of gender in intimate partner violence. *Aggression and Violent Behavior, 17*(1), 99–104.

Dvornyk, Volodymyr & Waqar-ul-Haq. (2012). Genetics of age at menarche: A systematic review. *Human Reproduction Update, 18*(2), 198–210.

Dweck, Carol S. (1999). *Self-theories: Their role in motivation, personality, and development*. Philadelphia, PA: Psychology Press.

Dweck, Carol S. (2013). Social development. In Philip D. Zelazo (Ed.), *The Oxford handbook of developmental psychology* (Vol. 2, pp. 167–190). New York, NY: Oxford University Press.

Dweck, Carol S. (2017). From needs to goals and representations: Foundations for a unified theory of motivation, personality, and development. *Psychological Review, 124*(6), 689–719.

Dyer, Nazly; Owen, Margaret T. & Caughy, Margaret O'Brien. (2014). Ethnic differences in profiles of mother–child interactions and relations to emerging school readiness in African American and Latin American children. *Parenting, 14*(3/4), 175–194.

Dyer, Suzanne M.; Crotty, Maria; Fairhall, Nicola; Magaziner, Jay; Beaupre, Lauren A.; Cameron, Ian D. & Sherrington, Catherine. (2016). A critical review of the long-term disability outcomes following hip fracture. *BMC Geriatrics*, 16, 158.

Eagly, Alice H. & Wood, Wendy. (2013). The nature–nurture debates: 25 years of challenges in understanding the psychology of gender. *Perspectives on Psychological Science, 8*(3), 340–357.

Eccles, Jacquelynne S. & Roeser, Robert W. (2010). An ecological view of schools and development. In Judith L. Meece & Jacquelynne S. Eccles (Eds.), *Handbook of research on schools, schooling, and human development* (pp. 6–22). New York, NY: Routledge.

Eccles, Jacquelynne S. & Roeser, Robert W. (2011). Schools as developmental contexts during adolescence. *Journal of Research on Adolescence, 21*(1), 225–241.

Egger, Sam J.; Calopedos, Ross J.; O'Connell, Dianne L.; Chambers, Suzanne K.; Woo, Henry H. & Smith, David P. (2018). Long-term psychological and quality-of-life effects of active surveillance and watchful waiting after diagnosis of low-risk localised prostate cancer. *European Urology, 73*(6), 859–867.

Eggum, Natalie D.; Eisenberg, Nancy; Kao, Karen; Spinrad, Tracy L.; Bolnick, Rebecca; Hofer, Claire, . . . Fabricius, William V. (2011). Emotion understanding, theory of mind, and prosocial orientation: Relations over time in early childhood. *The Journal of Positive Psychology, 6*(1), 4–16.

Ehrenberg, Rachel. (2016). GMOs under scrutiny. *Science News, 189*(3), 22–27.

Ehrlich, Sara Z. & Blum-Kulka, Shoshana. (2014). 'Now I said that Danny becomes Danny again': A multifaceted view of kindergarten children's peer argumentative discourse. In Asta Cekaite, et al. (Eds.), *Children's peer talk: Learning from each other* (pp. 23–41). New York, NY: Cambridge University Press.

Eichhorst, Werner; Rodríguez-Planas, Núria; Schmidl, Ricarda & Zimmermann, Klaus F. (2012). *A roadmap to vocational education and training systems around the world*. Bonn, Germany: Institute for the Study of Labor.

Einav, Liran; Finkelstein, Amy; Mullainathan, Sendhil & Obermeyer, Ziad. (2018). Predictive modeling of U.S. health care spending in late life. *Science, 360*(6396), 1462–1465.

Eisenberg, Nancy; Hofer, Claire; Sulik, Michael J. & Spinrad, Tracy L. (2014). Self-regulation, effortful control, and their socioemotional correlates. In James J. Gross (Ed.), *Handbook of emotion regulation* (2nd ed., pp. 157–172). New York, NY: Guilford Press.

Eisenberg, Nancy & Zhou, Qing. (2016). Conceptions of executive function and regulation: When and to what degree do they overlap? In James A. Griffin, et al. (Eds.), *Executive function in preschool-age children: Integrating measurement, neurodevelopment, and translational research* (pp. 115–136). Washington, DC: American Psychological Association.

El-Sheikh, Mona & Kelly, Ryan J. (2017). Family functioning and children's sleep. *Child Development Perspectives, 11*(4), 264–269.

Elder, Glen H. (1998). The life course as developmental theory. *Child Development, 69*(1), 1–12.

Elkind, David. (1967). Egocentrism in adolescence. *Child Development*, 38(4), 1025–1034.

Elkind, David. (2007). *The power of play: How spontaneous, imaginative activities lead to happier, healthier children*. Cambridge, MA: Da Capo Press.

Ellefson, Michelle R.; Ng, Florrie Fei-Yin; Wang, Qian & Hughes, Claire. (2017). Efficiency of executive function: A two-generation cross-cultural comparison of samples from Hong Kong and the United Kingdom. *Psychological Science*, 28(5), 555–566.

Elliot, Ari J.; Mooney, Christopher J.; Infurna, Frank J. & Chapman, Benjamin P. (2018). Perceived control and frailty: The role of affect and perceived health. *Psychology and Aging*, 33(3), 473–481.

Elliott, Sinikka. (2012). *Not my kid: What parents believe about the sex lives of their teenagers*. New York, NY: New York University Press.

Ellis, Bruce J. & Boyce, W. Thomas. (2008). Biological sensitivity to context. *Current Directions in Psychological Science, 17*(3), 183–187.

Ellis, Bruce J.; Boyce, W. Thomas; Belsky, Jay; Bakermans-kranenburg, Marian J. & Van Ijzendoorn, Marinus H. (2011a). Differential susceptibility to the environment: An evolutionary–neurodevelopmental theory. *Development and Psychopathology, 23*(1), 7–28.

Ellis, Bruce J. & Del Giudice, Marco. (2019). Developmental adaptation to stress: An evolutionary perspective. *Annual Review of Psychology, 70*(1), 111–139.

Ellis, Bruce J.; Shirtcliff, Elizabeth A.; Boyce, W. Thomas; Deardorff, Julianna & Essex, Marilyn J. (2011b). Quality of early family relationships and the timing and tempo of puberty: Effects depend on biological sensitivity to context. *Development and Psychopathology, 23*(1), 85–99.

Ellison, Christopher G.; Musick, Marc A. & Holden, George W. (2011). Does conservative Protestantism moderate the association between corporal punishment and child outcomes? *Journal of Marriage and Family*, 73(5), 946–961.

Emanuel, Ezekiel J. (2017). Euthanasia and physician-assisted suicide: Focus on the data. *Medical Journal of Australia*, *206*(8), 1–2e1.

Emery, Carolyn A. (2018). Injury prevention in kids' adventure and extreme sports: future directions. *Research in Sports Medicine*, 26(Suppl.1), 199–211.

Emmen, Rosanneke A. G.; Malda, Maike; Mesman, Judi; van IJzendoorn, Marinus H.; Prevoo, Mariëlle J. L. & Yeniad, Nihal. (2013). Socioeconomic status and parenting in ethnic minority families: Testing a minority family stress model. *Journal of Family Psychology*, 27(6), 896–904.

Endendijk, Joyce J.; Derks, Belle & Mesman, Judi. (2018). Does parenthood change implicit gender-role stereotypes and behaviors? *Journal of Marriage and Family*, *80*(1), 61–79.

Engelberts, Adèle C. & de Jonge, Guustaaf Adolf. (1990). Choice of sleeping position for infants: Possible association with cot death. *Archives of Disease in Childhood, 65*(4), 462–467.

England, Paula & Bearak, Jonathan. (2014). The sexual double standard and gender differences in attitudes toward casual sex among U.S. university students. *Demographic Research, 30*(46), 1327–1338.

Englander, Elizabeth. (2015). Coerced sexting and revenge porn among teens. *Bullying, Teen Aggression & Social Media, 1*(2), 19–21.

English, Tammy & Carstensen, Laura L. (2014). Selective narrowing of social networks across adulthood is associated with improved emotional experience in daily life. *International Journal of Behavioral Development*, 38(2), 195–202.

Ennis, Linda Rose. (2015). *Intensive mothering: The cultural contradictions of modern motherhood.* Toronto: Demeter Press.

Enough Is Enough. (2017). *Cyberbullying statistics.* Great Falls, VA: Enough Is Enough.

Enserink, Martin. (2011). Can this DNA sleuth help catch criminals? *Science, 331*(6019), 838–840.

Epps, Chad & Holt, Lynn. (2011). The genetic basis of addiction and relevant cellular mechanisms. *International Anesthesiology Clinics, 49*(1), 3–14.

Epstein, Robert; Pandit, Mayuri & Thakar, Mansi. (2013). How love emerges in arranged marriages: Two cross-cultural studies. *Journal of Comparative Family Studies, 44*(3), 341–360.

Erickson, Anders C.; Ostry, Aleck; Chan, Hing Man & Arbour, Laura. (2016). Air pollution, neighbourhood and maternal-level factors modify the effect of smoking on birth weight: A multilevel analysis in British Columbia, Canada. *BMC Public Health, 16*(1).

Ericsson, K. Anders. (1996). The acquisition of expert performance: An introduction to some of the issues. In Karl Anders Ericsson (Ed.), *The road to excellence: The acquisition of expert performance in the arts and sciences, sports, and games* (pp. 1–50). Hillsdale, NJ: Erlbaum.

Erikson, Erik H. (1968). *Identity: Youth and crisis.* New York, NY: Norton.

Erikson, Erik H. (1982). *The life cycle completed: A review.* New York, NY: Norton.

Erikson, Erik H. (1993a). *Childhood and society* (2nd ed.). New York, NY: Norton.

Erikson, Erik H. (1993b). *Gandhi's truth: On the origins of militant nonviolence.* New York, NY: Norton.

Erikson, Erik H. (1994). *Identity: Youth and crisis.* New York, NY: Norton.

Erikson, Erik H. (1998). *The life cycle completed.* New York, NY: Norton.

Erikson, Erik H.; Erikson, Joan M. & Kivnick, Helen Q. (1986). *Vital involvement in old age.* New York, NY: Norton.

Erikson, Erik H.; Erikson, Joan M. & Kivnick, Helen Q. (1994). *Vital involvement in old age.* New York, NY: Norton.

Ernst, Monique. (2016). A tribute to the adolescent brain. *Neuroscience & Biobehavioral Reviews, 70*, 334–338.

Erola, Jani; Jalonen, Sanni & Lehti, Hannu. (2016). Parental education, class and income over early life course and children's achievement. *Research in Social Stratification and Mobility, 44*, 33–43.

Erreygers, Sara; Vandebosch, Heidi; Vranjes, Ivana; Baillien, Elfi & De Witte, Hans. (2017). Nice or naughty? The role of emotions and digital media use in explaining adolescents' online prosocial and antisocial behavior. *Media Psychology, 20*(3), 374–400.

Errichiello, Luca; Iodice, Davide; Bruzzese, Dario; Gherghi, Marco & Senatore, Ignazio. (2016). Prognostic factors and outcome in anorexia nervosa: A follow-up study. *Eating and Weight Disorders, 21*(1), 73–82.

Esposito, Gianluca; Setoh, Peipei & Bornstein, Marc H. (2015). Beyond practices and values: Toward a physio-bioecological analysis of sleeping arrangements in early infancy. *Frontiers in Psychology, 6*, 264.

Espy, Kimberly Andrews. (2016). *Monographs of the society for research in child development: The changing nature of executive control in preschool, 81*(4), 1–179.

Espy, K. A.; Clark, C. A. C.; Garza, J. P.; Nelson, J. M.; James, T. D. & Choi, H.-J. (2016). Executive control in preschoolers: New models, new results, new implications. *Monographs of the Society for Research in Child Development, 81*(4), 111–128.

Eun, John; Paksarian, Diana; He, Jian-Ping & Merikangas, Kathleen R. (2018). Parenting style and mental disorders in a nationally representative sample of US adolescents. *Social Psychiatry and Psychiatric Epidemiology, 53*(1), 11–20.

European Society of Human Reproduction and Embryology. (2018, July 3). More than 8 million babies born from IVF since the world's first in 1978: European IVF pregnancy rates now steady at around 36 percent, according to ESHRE monitoring. *ScienceDaily.*

Evans, Angela D.; Xu, Fen & Lee, Kang. (2011). When all signs point to you: Lies told in the face of evidence. *Developmental Psychology, 47*(1), 39–49.

Evans, Gary W. & Kim, Pilyoung. (2013). Childhood poverty, chronic stress, self-regulation, and coping. *Child Development Perspectives, 7*(1), 43–48.

Evans, M. D. R.; Kelley, Jonathan; Sikora, Joanna & Treiman, Donald J. (2010). Family scholarly culture and educational success: Books and schooling in 27 nations. *Research in Social Stratification and Mobility, 28*(2), 171–197.

Everett, Caleb. (2017). *Numbers and the making of us: Counting and the course of human cultures.* Cambridge, MA: Harvard University Press.

Eyer, Diane E. (1992). *Mother-infant bonding: A scientific fiction.* New Haven, CT: Yale University Press.

Fadjukoff, Päivi & Kroger, Jane. (2016). Identity development in adulthood: Introduction. *Identity, 16*(1), 1–7.

Fagot, Delphine; Mella, Nathalie; Borella, Erika; Ghisletta, Paolo; Lecerf, Thierry & De Ribaupierre, Anik. (2018). Intra-individual variability from a lifespan perspective: A comparison of latency and accuracy measures. *Journal of Intelligence, 6*(1).

Fairbank, John; Briggs, Ernestine; Lee, Robert; Corry, Nida; Pflieger, Jacqueline; Gerrity, Ellen, . . . Murphy, Robert. (2018). Mental health of children of deployed and nondeployed US military service members: The millennium cohort family study. *Journal of Developmental & Behavioral Pediatrics, 39*(9), 683–692.

Fairhurst, Merle T.; Löken, Line & Grossmann, Tobias. (2014). Physiological and behavioral responses reveal 9-month-old infants' sensitivity to pleasant touch. *Psychological Science, 25*(5), 1124–1131.

Fan, Hung; Conner, Ross F. & Villarreal, Luis P. (2014). *AIDS: Science and society* (7th ed.). Burlington, MA: Jones & Bartlett Learning.

Farber, Stu & Farber, Annalu. (2014). It ain't easy: Making life and death decisions before the crisis. In Leah Rogne & Susana Lauraine McCune (Eds.), *Advance care planning: Communicating about matters of life and death* (pp. 109–122). New York, NY: Springer.

Fareed, Mohd; Anwar, Malik Azeem & Afzal, Mohammad. (2015). Prevalence and gene frequency of color vision impairments among children of six populations from North Indian region. *Genes & Diseases, 2*(2), 211–218.

Fast, Anne A. & Olson, Kristina R. (2018). Gender development in transgender preschool children. *Child Development, 89*(2), 620–637.

Federal Bureau of Investigation. (2018). Expanded homicide data table 2: Murder victims by age, sex, race, and ethnicity, 2017. Crime in the United States, 2017.

Fedewa, Michael V.; Das, Bhibha M.; Evans, Ellen M. & Dishman, Rod K. (2014). Change in weight and adiposity in college students: A systematic review and meta-analysis: A systematic review and meta-analysis. *American Journal of Preventive Medicine, 47*(5), 641–652.

Feeley, Nancy; Sherrard, Kathyrn; Waitzer, Elana & Boisvert, Linda. (2013). The father at the bedside: Patterns of involvement in the NICU. *Journal of Perinatal & Neonatal Nursing, 27*(1), 72–80.

Feld, Barry C. (2013). *Kids, cops, and confessions: Inside the interrogation room.* New York, NY: New York University Press.

Feliciano, Cynthia & Rumbaut, Rubén G. (2018). Varieties of ethnic self-identities: Children of immigrants in middle adulthood. *RSF: The Russell Sage Foundation Journal of the Social Sciences, 4*(5), 26–46.

Feliciano, Cynthia & Rumbaut, Rubén G. (2019). The evolution of ethnic identity from adolescence to middle adulthood: The case of the immigrant second generation. *Emerging Adulthood, 7*(2), 85–96.

Felicilda-Reynaldo, Rhea & Smith, Lucretia. (2018). Needs based frameworks. In Rose Utley, et al. (Eds.), *Frameworks for advanced nursing practice and research: Philosophies, theories, models, and taxonomies* (pp. 157–172). New York, NY: Springer.

Felmban, Wejdan S. & Klaczynski, Paul A. (2019). Adolescents' base rate judgments, metastrategic understanding, and stereotype endorsement. *Journal of Experimental Child Psychology, 178*, 60–85.

Ferguson, Christopher J. (2013). Spanking, corporal punishment and negative long-term outcomes: A meta-analytic review of longitudinal studies. *Clinical Psychology Review, 33*(1), 196–208.

Ferguson, Christopher J. & Kilburn, John. (2009). The public health risks of media violence: A meta-analytic review. *The Journal of Pediatrics, 154*(5), 759–763.

Ferguson, Christopher J. & Kilburn, John. (2010). Much ado about nothing: The misestimation and overinterpretation of violent video game effects in Eastern and Western nations—Comment on Anderson et al. (2010). *Psychological Bulletin, 136*(2), 174–178.

Fernando, Dulini; Cohen, Laurie & Duberley, Joanne. (2018). What helps? Women engineers' accounts of staying on. *Human Resource Management Journal, 28*(3), 479–495.

Ferrari, Laura; Rosnati, Rosa; Manzi, Claudia & Benet-Martínez, Verònica. (2015). Ethnic identity, bicultural identity integration, and psychological well-being among transracial adoptees: A longitudinal study. *New Directions for Child and Adolescent Development, 2015*(150), 63–76.

Ferrari, Marco & Quaresima, Valentina. (2012). A brief review on the history of human functional near-infrared spectroscopy (fNIRS) development and fields of application. *NeuroImage, 63*(2), 921–935.

Fields, R. Douglas. (2014). Myelin—More than insulation. *Science, 344*(6181), 264–266.

Fikkan, Janna L. & Rothblum, Esther D. (2012). Is fat a feminist issue? Exploring the gendered nature of weight bias. *Sex Roles, 66*(9-10), 575–592.

Filippa, Manuela; Kuhn, Pierre & Westrup, Björn (Eds.). (2017). *Early vocal contact and preterm infant brain development: Bridging the gaps between research and practice*. Cham, Switzerland: Springer.

Finer, Lawrence B. & Zolna, Mia R. (2016). Declines in unintended pregnancy in the United States, 2008–2011. *New England Journal of Medicine, 374*, 843–852.

Fingerman, Karen L.; Berg, Cynthia; Smith, Jacqui & Antonucci, Toni C. (2011). *Handbook of lifespan development*. New York, NY: Springer.

Fingerman, Karen L.; Cheng, Yen-Pi; Birditt, Kira & Zarit, Steven. (2012a). Only as happy as the least happy child: Multiple grown children's problems and successes and middle-aged parents' well-being. *The Journals of Gerontology Series B: Psychological Sciences and Social Sciences, 67B*(2), 184–193.

Fingerman, Karen L.; Cheng, Yen-Pi; Tighe, Lauren; Birditt, Kira S. & Zarit, Steve. (2012b). Relationships between young adults and their parents. In Alan Booth, et al. (Eds.), *Early adulthood in family context* (pp. 59–85). New York, NY: Springer.

Fingerman, Karen L.; Cheng, Yen-Pi; Wesselmann, Eric D.; Zarit, Steven; Furstenberg, Frank & Birditt, Kira S. (2012c). Helicopter parents and landing pad kids: Intense parental support of grown children. *Journal of Marriage and Family, 74*(4), 880–896.

Fingerman, Karen L. & Furstenberg, Frank F. (2012, May 30). You can go home again. *New York Times*.

Fingerman, Karen L.; Pillemer, Karl A.; Silverstein, Merril & Suitor, J. Jill. (2012d). The baby boomers' intergenerational relationships. *The Gerontologist, 52*(2), 199–209.

Finlay, Ilora G. & George, R. (2011). Legal physician-assisted suicide in Oregon and the Netherlands: Evidence concerning the impact on patients in vulnerable groups—Another perspective on Oregon's data. *Journal of Medical Ethics, 37*(3), 171–174.

Finn, Amy S.; Kraft, Matthew A.; West, Martin R.; Leonard, Julia A.; Bish, Crystal E.; Martin, Rebecca E., . . . Gabrieli, John D. E. (2014). Cognitive skills, student achievement tests, and schools. *Psychological Science, 25*(3), 736–744.

Fins, Joseph J. & Bernat, James L. (2018). Ethical, palliative, and policy considerations in disorders of consciousness. *Archives of Physical Medicine and Rehabilitation, 99*(9), 1927–1931.

Fischer, Henry; Raghunath, Silvia; Durfee, Josh & Ritchie, Natalie. (2018). The effectiveness of text message support for weight loss to reduce diabetes risk. *Diabetes, 67*(Suppl. 1).

Fischer, Nantje; Træen, Bente & Hald, Gert Martin. (2018). Predicting partnered sexual activity among older adults in four European countries: The role of attitudes, health, and relationship factors. *Sexual and Relationship Therapy*, (In Press).

Fischetti, Mark & Armstrong, Zan. (2017). The baby spike. *Scientific American, 317*(1), 76.

Fiset, Sylvain & Plourde, Vickie. (2013). Object permanence in domestic dogs (*Canis lupus familiaris*) and gray wolves (*Canis lupus*). *Journal of Comparative Psychology, 127*(2), 115–127.

Fisher, Dorothy Canfield. (1922). *What grandmother did not know*. Boston: Pilgrim Press.

Fisher, Helen E. (2016a). *Anatomy of love: A natural history of mating, marriage, and why we stray*. New York, NY: Norton.

Fisher, Helen E. (2016b). Broken hearts: The nature and risks of romantic rejection. In Alan Booth, et al. (Eds.), *Romance and sex in adolescence and emerging adulthood* (pp. 3–28). New York, NY: Routledge.

Fiske, Amy; Lutz, Julie; Ciliberti, Caroline M.; Clegg-Kraynok, Megan M.; Gould, Christine E.; Stahl, Sarah T. & Nazem, Sarra. (2015). Mental health and aging. In James E. Maddux & Barbara A. Winstead (Eds.), *Psychopathology: Foundations for a contemporary understanding* (4th ed., pp. 341–362). New York, NY: Routledge.

Flanagan, Constance A. (2013). *Teenage citizens: The political theories of the young*. Cambridge, MA: Harvard University Press.

Flannery, Jessica E.; Beauchamp, Kathryn G. & Fisher, Philip A. (2017). The role of social buffering on chronic disruptions in quality of care: Evidence from caregiver-based interventions in foster children. *Social Neuroscience, 12*(1), 86–91.

Flegal, Katherine M.; Kit, Brian K.; Orpana, Heather & Graubard, Barry I. (2013). Association of all-cause mortality with overweight and obesity using standard body mass index categories: A systematic review and meta-analysis. *JAMA, 309*(1), 71–82.

Fleming, Peter; Pease, Anna & Blair, Peter. (2015). Bed-sharing and unexpected infant deaths: What is the relationship? *Paediatric Respiratory Reviews, 16*(1), 62–67.

Fletcher, Erica N.; Whitaker, Robert C.; Marino, Alexis J. & Anderson, Sarah E. (2014). Screen time at home and school among low-income children attending Head Start. *Child Indicators Research, 7*(2), 421–436.

Fletcher, Richard; St. George, Jennifer & Freeman, Emily. (2013). Rough and tumble play quality: Theoretical foundations for a new measure of father–child interaction. *Early Child Development and Care, 183*(6), 746–759.

Flores, Andrew R.; Haider-Markel, Donald P.; Lewis, Daniel C.; Miller, Patrick R.; Tadlock, Barry L. & Taylor, Jami K. (2018). Transgender prejudice reduction and opinions on transgender rights: Results from a mediation analysis on experimental data. *Research & Politics, 5*(1).

Flynn, Heather Kohler; Felmlee, Diane H. & Conger, Rand D. (2017). The social context of adolescent friendships: Parents, peers, and romantic partners. *Youth & Society, 49*(5), 679–705.

Flynn, James & Shayer, Michael. (2018). IQ decline and Piaget: Does the rot start at the top? *Intelligence, 66*(112–121).

Fontana, Luigi; Colman, Ricki J.; Holloszy, John O. & Weindruch, Richard. (2011). Calorie restriction in nonhuman and human primates. In J. Masoro Edward & N. Austad Steven (Eds.), *Handbook of the biology of aging* (7th ed., pp. 447–461). San Diego, CA: Academic Press.

Fontenot, Kayla; Semega, Jessica & Kollar, Melissa. (2018). *Income and poverty in the United States: 2017. Current Population Reports*. Washington, DC: U.S. Census Bureau. P60-263.

Forbes, Deborah. (2012). The global influence of the Reggio Emilia Inspiration. In Robert Kelly (Ed.), *Educating for creativity: A global conversation* (pp. 161–172). Calgary, Canada: Brush Education.

Forbes, Thomas A. & Gallo, Vittorio. (2017). All wrapped up: Environmental effects on myelination. *Trends in Neurosciences, 40*(9), 572–587.

Ford, Carole L. & Yore, Larry D. (2012). Toward convergence of critical thinking, metacognition, and reflection: Illustrations from natural and social sciences, teacher education, and classroom practice. In Anat Zohar & Yehudit Judy Dori (Eds.), *Metacognition in Science Education* (pp. 251–271). New York, NY: Springer.

Foreman, Kyle J.; Marquez, Neal; Dolgert, Andrew; Fukutaki, Kai; Fullman, Nancy; Mcgaughey, Madeline, . . . Murray, Christopher J. L. (2018). Forecasting life expectancy, years of life lost, and all-cause and cause-specific mortality for 250 causes of death: Reference and alternative scenarios for 2016–40 for 195 countries and territories. *The Lancet, 392*(10159), 2052–2090.

Forestell, Catherine A. & Mennella, Julie A. (2017). The relationship between infant facial expressions and food acceptance. *Current Nutrition Reports, 6*(2), 141–147.

Forget-Dubois, Nadine; Dionne, Ginette; Lemelin, Jean-Pascal; Pérusse, Daniel; Tremblay, Richard E. & Boivin, Michel. (2009). Early child language mediates the relation between home environment and school readiness. *Child Development, 80*(3), 736–749.

Forrest, Ray. (2018). Housing wealth, social structures and changing narratives. *International Journal of Urban Sciences*, (In Press).

Forrest, Walter. (2014). Cohabitation, relationship quality, and desistance from crime. *Journal of Marriage and Family*, 76(3), 539–556.

Fortin, Andrée; Doucet, Martin & Damant, Dominique. (2011). Children's appraisals as mediators of the relationship between domestic violence and child adjustment. *Violence and Victims*, 26(3), 377–392.

Foster, Eugene A.; Jobling, Mark A.; Taylor, P. G.; Donnelly, Peter; de Knijff, Peter; Mieremet, Rene, . . . Tyler-Smith, C. (1998). Jefferson fathered slave's last child. *Nature*, 396(6706), 27–28.

Foulkes, Lucy & Blakemore, Sarah-Jayne. (2018). Studying individual differences in human adolescent brain development. *Nature Neuroscience*, *21*, 315–323.

Fowler, James W. (1981). *Stages of faith: The psychology of human development and the quest for meaning*. San Francisco, CA: Harper & Row.

Fowler, James W. (1986). Faith and the structuring of meaning. In Craig Dykstra & Sharon Parks (Eds.), *Faith development and Fowler* (pp. 15–42). Birmingham, AL: Religious Education Press.

Fox, Ashley; Himmelstein, Georgia; Khalid, Hina & Howell, Elizabeth A. (2019). Funding for abstinence-only education and adolescent pregnancy prevention: Does state ideology affect outcomes? *American Journal of Public Health*, e1–e8.

Fox, Molly; Thayer, Zaneta M.; Ramos, Isabel F.; Meskal, Sarah J. & Wadhwa, Pathik D. (2018). Prenatal and postnatal mother-to-child transmission of acculturation's health effects in Hispanic Americans. *Journal of Women's Health*, 27(8), 154–1063.

Fox, Nathan A.; Henderson, Heather A.; Marshall, Peter J.; Nichols, Kate E. & Ghera, Melissa M. (2005). Behavioral inhibition: Linking biology and behavior within a developmental framework. *Annual Review of Psychology*, 56, 235–262.

Fox, Nathan A.; Henderson, Heather A.; Rubin, Kenneth H.; Calkins, Susan D. & Schmidt, Louis A. (2001). Continuity and discontinuity of behavioral inhibition and exuberance: Psychophysiological and behavioral influences across the first four years of life. *Child Development*, 72(1), 1–21.

Fox, Nathan A.; Reeb-Sutherland, Bethany C. & Degnan, Kathryn A. (2013). Personality and emotional development. In Philip D. Zelazo (Ed.), *The Oxford handbook of developmental psychology* (Vol. 2, pp. 15–44). New York, NY: Oxford University Press.

Fraley, R. Chris. (2019). Attachment in adulthood: Recent developments, emerging debates, and future directions. *Annual Review of Psychology*, 70, 401–422.

Franco, Manuel; Bilal, Usama; Orduñez, Pedro; Benet, Mikhail; Alain, Morejón; Benjamín, Caballero, . . . Cooper, Richard S. (2013). Population-wide weight loss and regain in relation to diabetes burden and cardiovascular mortality in Cuba 1980–2010: Repeated cross sectional surveys and ecological comparison of secular trends. *BMJ*, 346(7903), f1515.

Franco, Marcia R.; Tong, Allison; Howard, Kirsten; Sherrington, Catherine; Ferreira, Paulo H.; Pinto, Rafael Z. & Ferreira, Manuela L. (2015). Older people's perspectives on participation in physical activity: A systematic review and thematic synthesis of qualitative literature. *British Journal of Sports Medicine*, 49, 1268–1276.

Frankenburg, William K.; Dodds, Josiah; Archer, Philip; Shapiro, Howard & Bresnick, Beverly. (1992). The Denver II: A major revision and restandardization of the Denver Developmental Screening Test. *Pediatrics*, 89(1), 91–97.

Fraundorf, Scott H.; Hourihan, Kathleen L.; Peters, Rachel A. & Benjamin, Aaron S. (2019). Aging and recognition memory: A meta-analysis. *Psychological Bulletin*, *145*(4), 339–371.

Frayer, David W. (2017). Talking hyoids and talking Neanderthals. In Assaf Marom & Erella Hovers (Eds.), *Human Paleontology and Prehistory: Contributions in Honor of Yoel Rak* (pp. 233–237). Switzerland: Springer.

Frazier, A. Lindsay; Camargo, Carlos A.; Malspeis, Susan; Willett, Walter C. & Young, Michael C. (2014). Prospective study of peripregnancy consumption of peanuts or tree nuts by mothers and the risk of peanut or tree nut allergy in their offspring. *JAMA Pediatrics*, *168*(2), 156–162.

Frederick, David A.; Lever, Janet; Gillespie, Brian Joseph & Garcia, Justin R. (2016). What keeps passion alive? Sexual satisfaction is associated with sexual communication, mood setting, sexual variety, oral sex, orgasm, and sex frequency in a national U.S. study. *The Journal of Sex Research*, (In Press).

Fredricks, Jennifer A. & Eccles, Jacquelynne S. (2002). Children's competence and value beliefs from childhood through adolescence: Growth trajectories in two male-sex-typed domains. *Developmental Psychology*, 38(4), 519–533.

Freeman, Joan. (2010). *Gifted lives: What happens when gifted children grow up?* New York, NY: Routledge.

Frejka, Tomas; Goldscheider, Frances & Lappegård, Trude. (2018). The two-part gender revolution, women's second shift and changing cohort fertility. *Comparative Population Studies*, 43, 99–130.

Freud, Anna. (1958). Adolescence. *Psychoanalytic Study of the Child*, *13*, 255–278.

Freud, Anna. (2000). Adolescence. In James B. McCarthy (Ed.), *Adolescent development and psychopathology* (pp. 29–52). Lanham, MD: University Press of America.

Freud, Anna & Burlingham, Dorothy T. (1943). *War and children*. New York, NY: Medical War Books.

Freud, Sigmund. (1935). *A general introduction to psychoanalysis*. New York, NY: Liveright.

Freud, Sigmund. (1938). *The basic writings of Sigmund Freud*. New York, NY: Modern Library.

Freud, Sigmund. (1989). *Introductory lectures on psycho-analysis*. New York, NY: Liveright.

Freud, Sigmund. (1995). *The basic writings of Sigmund Freud*. New York, NY: Modern Library.

Freud, Sigmund. (2001). An outline of psychoanalysis. In, *The standard edition of the complete psychological works of Sigmund Freud* (Vol. 23). London, UK: Vintage.

Freund, Alexandra M. & Blanchard-Fields, Fredda. (2014). Age-related differences in altruism across adulthood: Making personal financial gain versus contributing to the public good. *Developmental Psychology*, 50(4), 1125–1136.

Fried, Terri R. & Mecca, Marcia C. (2019). Medication appropriateness in vulnerable older adults: Healthy skepticism of appropriate polypharmacy. *Journal of the American Geriatrics Society*, 67(6), 1123–1127.

Friedman, Naomi P. & Miyake, Akira. (2017). Unity and diversity of executive functions: Individual differences as a window on cognitive structure. *Cortex*, 86, 186–204.

Friedman, Zack. (2019). Student loan debt statistics in 2019: A $1.5 trillion crisis. *Forbes*.

Friedmann, Naama & Rusou, Dana. (2015). Critical period for first language: The crucial role of language input during the first year of life. *Current Opinion in Neurobiology*, 35, 27–34.

Friend, Stephen H. & Schadt, Eric E. (2014). Clues from the resilient. *Science*, *344*(6187), 970–972.

Frost, Randy O.; Steketee, Gail; Tolin, David F.; Sinopoli, Nicole & Ruby, Dylan. (2015). Motives for acquiring and saving in hoarding disorder, OCD, and community controls. *Journal of Obsessive-Compulsive and Related Disorders*, 4, 54–59.

Fry, Douglas P. (2014). Environment of evolutionary adaptedness, rough-and-tumble play, and the selection of restraint in human aggression. In Darcia Narvaez, et al. (Eds.), *Ancestral landscapes in human evolution: Culture, childrearing and social wellbeing* (pp. 169–188). New York, NY: Oxford University Press.

Fry, Richard. (2016, May 24). *For first time in modern era, living with parents edges out other living arrangements for 18- to 34-year-olds*. Washington, DC: Pew Research Center.

Fryar, Cheryl D.; Carroll, Margaret D. & Ogden, Cynthia L. (2018). *Prevalence of overweight, obesity, and severe obesity among children and adolescents aged 2–19 years: United States, 1963–1965 through 2015–2016. Health E-Stats*. Hyattsville, MD: National Center for Health Statistics.

Fujiwara, Takeo; Weisman, Omri; Ochi, Manami; Shirai, Kokoro; Matsumoto, Kenji; Noguchi, Emiko & Feldman, Ruth. (2019). Genetic and peripheral markers of the oxytocin system and parental care jointly support the cross-generational transmission of bonding across three generations. *Psychoneuroendocrinology*, *102*, 172–181.

Fuligni, Allison Sidle; Howes, Carollee; Huang, Yiching; Hong, Sandra Soliday & Lara-Cinisomo, SaNdraluz. (2012). Activity settings and daily routines in preschool classrooms: Diverse experiences in early learning settings for low-income children. *Early Childhood Research Quarterly*, 27(2), 198–209.

Fuller, Bruce & García Coll, Cynthia. (2010). Learning from Latinos: Contexts, families, and child development in motion. *Developmental Psychology*, *46*(3), 559–565.

Fulmer, C. Ashley; Gelfand, Micheke J.; Kruglanski, Arie W.; Kim-Prieto, Chu; Diener, Ed; Pierro, Antonio & Higgins, E. Tory. (2010). On "feeling right" in cultural contexts: How person-culture match affects self-esteem and subjective well-being. *Psychological Science*, *21*(11), 1563–1569.

Fury, Gail; Carlson, Elizabeth A. & Sroufe, Alan. (1997). Children's representations of attachment relationships in family drawings. *Child Development*, 68(6), 1154–1164.

Fusaro, Maria & Harris, Paul L. (2013). Dax gets the nod: Toddlers detect and use social cues to evaluate testimony. *Developmental Psychology*, *49*(3), 514–522.

Gabrieli, John D. E. (2009). Dyslexia: A new synergy between education and cognitive neuroscience. *Science*, *325*(5938), 280–283.

Galak, Jeff; Givi, Julian & Williams, Elanor F. (2016). Why certain gifts are great to give but not to get: A framework for understanding errors in gift giving. *Current Directions in Psychological Science*, 25(6), 380–385.

Galanello, Renzo & Origa, Raffaella. (2010). Beta-thalassemia. *Orphanet Journal of Rare Diseases*, 5(11).

Galasso, Vincenzo; Profeta, Paola; Pronzato, Chiara & Billari, Francesco. (2017). Information and women's intentions: Experimental evidence about child care. *European Journal of Population*, 33(1), 109–128.

Gallagher, Annabella; Updegraff, Kimberly; Padilla, Jenny & McHale, Susan M. (2018). Longitudinal associations between sibling relational aggression and adolescent adjustment. *Journal of Youth and Adolescence*, *47*(10), 2100–2113.

Gallagher, Shaun. (2013). A pattern theory of self. *Frontiers in Human Neuroscience*, 7(443).

Gallup. (2017, August). *Time to play: A study on children's free time—how it is spent, prioritized and valued*. Washington, DC: Gallup.

Galván, Adriana. (2013). The teenage brain: Sensitivity to rewards. *Current Directions in Psychological Science*, 22(2), 88–93.

Galvao, Tais F.; Silva, Marcus T.; Zimmermann, Ivan R.; Souza, Kathiaja M.; Martins, Silvia S. & Pereira, Mauricio G. (2014). Pubertal timing in girls and depression: A systematic review. *Journal of Affective Disorders*, *155*, 13–19.

Gambaro, Ludovica; Stewart, Kitty & Waldfogel, Jane (Eds.). (2014). *An equal start?: Providing quality early education and care for disadvantaged children*. Chicago, IL: Policy Press.

Ganapathy, Thilagavathy. (2014). Couvade syndrome among 1st time expectant fathers. *Muller Journal of Medical Science Research*, 5(1), 43–47.

Ganchimeg, Togoobaatar; Ota, Erika; Morisaki, Naho; Laopaiboon, Malinee; Lumbiganon, P.; Zhang, Jun, . . . Mori, Rintaro. (2014). Pregnancy and childbirth outcomes among adolescent mothers: A World Health Organization multicountry study. *BJOG*, *121*(Suppl. 1), 40–48.

Gao, Wei; Lin, Weili; Grewen, Karen & Gilmore, John H. (2017). Functional connectivity of the infant human brain: Plastic and modifiable. *Neuroscientist*, *23*(2), 169–184.

Gao, Yuan; Huang, Changquan; Zhao, Kexiang; Ma, Louyan; Qiu, Xuan; Zhang, Lei, . . . Xiao, Qian. (2013). Depression as a risk factor for dementia and mild cognitive impairment: A meta-analysis of longitudinal studies. *International Journal of Geriatric Psychiatry*, 28(5), 441–449.

García Coll, Cynthia T. & Marks, Amy K. (2012). *The immigrant paradox in children and adolescents: Is becoming American a developmental risk?* Washington, DC: American Psychological Association.

Gardner, Howard. (1983). *Frames of mind: The theory of multiple intelligences*. New York, NY: Basic Books.

Gardner, Howard. (1999). Are there additional intelligences? The case for naturalist, spiritual, and existential intelligences. In Jeffrey Kane (Ed.), *Education, information, and transformation: Essays on learning and thinking* (pp. 111–131). Upper Saddle River, NJ: Merrill.

Gardner, Howard. (2006). *Multiple intelligences: New horizons in theory and practice*. New York, NY: Basic Books.

Gardner, Howard. (2011). *Frames of mind: The theory of multiple intelligences*. New York, NY: Basic Books.

Gardner, Howard & Moran, Seana. (2006). The science of multiple intelligences theory: A response to Lynn Waterhouse. *Educational Psychologist*, *41*(4), 227–232.

Gardner, Paula & Hudson, Bettie L. (1996). *Advance report of final mortality statistics, 1993. Monthly Vital Statistics Report*, *44*(7, Suppl.). Hyattsville, MD: National Center for Health Statistics.

Gariépy, Geneviève; Riehm, Kira E.; Whitehead, Ross D.; Doré, Isabelle & Elgar, Frank J. (2018). Teenage night owls or early birds? Chronotype and the mental health of adolescents. *Journal of Sleep Research*, e12723.

Garrett, Mallory. (2018). "It Gets Better" media campaign and gay youth suicide. In Chuck Stewart (Ed.), *Lesbian, gay, bisexual, and transgender Americans at risk: Problems and solutions* (pp. 119–128). New York, NY: Praeger.

Garthus-Niegel, Susan; Ayers, Susan; Martini, Julia; von Soest, Tilmann & Eberhard-Gran, Malin. (2017). The impact of postpartum post-traumatic stress disorder symptoms on child development: A population-based, 2-year follow-up study. *Psychological Medicine*, *47*(1), 161–170.

Gaskins, Audrey Jane; Mendiola, Jaime; Afeiche, Myriam; Jørgensen, Niels; Swan, Shanna H. & Chavarro, Jorge E. (2013). Physical activity and television watching in relation to semen quality in young men. *British Journal of Sports Medicine*, *49*(4), 265–270.

Gassin, Elizabeth A. (2017). Forgiveness and continuing bonds. In Dennis Klass & Edith Maria Steffen (Eds.), *Continuing bonds in bereavement: New directions for research and practice*. New York, NY: Routledge.

Gattario, Kristina Holmqvist & Frisén, Ann. (2019). From negative to positive body image: Men's and women's journeys from early adolescence to emerging adulthood. *Body Image*, 28, 53–65.

Gawande, Atul. (2014). *Being mortal: Medicine and what matters in the end*. New York, NY: Metropolitan Books.

Gaydosh, Lauren; Hummer, Robert A.; Hargrove, Taylor W.; Halpern, Carolyn T.; Hussey, Jon M.; Whitsel, Eric A., . . . Harris, Kathleen Mullan. (2019). The depths of despair among US adults entering midlife. *American Journal of Public Health*, *109*(5), 774–780.

Ge, Xinting; Shi, Yonggang; Li, Junning; Zhang, Zhonghe; Lin, Xiangtao; Zhan, Jinfeng, . . . Liu, Shuwei. (2015). Development of the human fetal hippocampal formation during early second trimester. *NeuroImage*, *119*, 33–43.

Geary, David C. (2018). Efficiency of mitochondrial functioning as the fundamental biological mechanism of general intelligence (g). *Psychological Review*, *125*(6), 1028–1050.

Geiger, Jennifer Mullins; Hayes, Megan J. & Lietz, Cynthia A. (2013). Should I stay or should I go? A mixed methods study examining the factors influencing foster parents' decisions to continue or discontinue providing foster care. *Children and Youth Services Review*, 35(9), 1356–1365.

Gelbgiser, Dafna. (2018). College for all, degrees for few: For-profit colleges and socioeconomic differences in degree attainment. *Social Forces*, *96*(4), 1785–1824.

Gellert, Anna S. & Elbro, Carsten. (2017). Does a dynamic test of phonological awareness predict early reading difficulties? A longitudinal study from kindergarten through grade 1. *Journal of Learning Disabilities*, 50(3), 227–237.

Gendron, Brian P.; Williams, Kirk R. & Guerra, Nancy G. (2011). An analysis of bullying among students within schools: Estimating the effects of individual normative beliefs, self-esteem, and school climate. *Journal of School Violence*, *10*(2), 150–164.

Gentile, Douglas A. (2011). The multiple dimensions of video game effects. *Child Development Perspectives*, 5(2), 75–81.

Geoffroy, Marie-Claude; Boivin, Michel; Arseneault, Louise; Turecki, Gustavo; Vitaro, Frank; Brendgen, Mara, . . . Côté, Sylvana M. (2016). Associations between peer victimization and suicidal ideation and suicide attempt during adolescence: Results from a prospective population-based birth cohort. *Journal of the American Academy of Child and Adolescent Psychiatry*, 55(2), 99–105.

Georgeson, Jan & Payler, Jane (Eds.). (2013). *International perspectives on early childhood education and care*. New York, NY: Open University Press.

Gergely, György & Csibra, Gergely. (2013). Natural pedagogy. In Mahzarin R. Banaji & Susan A. Gelman (Eds.), *Navigating the social world: What infants, children, and other species can teach us*. New York, NY: Oxford University Press.

Gerholz, Karl-Heinz; Liszt, Verena & Klingsieck, Katrin B. (2018). Effects of learning design patterns in service learning courses. *Active Learning in Higher Education*, *19*(1), 47–59.

Gernhardt, Ariane; Keller, Heidi & Rübeling, Hartmut. (2016). Children's family drawings as expressions of attachment representations across cultures: Possibilities and limitations. *Child Development*, *87*(4), 1069–1078.

Gershoff, Elizabeth T.; Lansford, Jennifer E.; Sexton, Holly R.; Davis-Kean, Pamela & Sameroff, Arnold J. (2012). Longitudinal links between spanking and children's externalizing behaviors in a national sample of White, Black, Hispanic, and Asian American families. *Child Development*, *83*(3), 838–843.

Gershoff, Elizabeth T.; Purtell, Kelly M. & Holas, Igor. (2015). *Corporal punishment in U.S. public schools: Legal precedents, current practices, and future policy*. New York, NY: Springer.

Gervais, Will M. & Norenzayan, Ara. (2012). Analytic thinking promotes religious disbelief. *Science*, *336*(6080), 493–496.

Gibbons, Ann. (2012). An evolutionary theory of dentistry. *Science*, *336*(6084), 973–975.

Giblin, Chris. (2014). Travis Pastrana makes comeback for Red Bull's inaugural straight rhythm competition. *Men's Fitness*.

Gibson-Davis, Christina & Rackin, Heather. (2014). Marriage or carriage? Trends in union context and birth type by education. *Journal of Marriage and Family*, *76*(3), 506–519.

Gidley, Jennifer M. (2016). *Postformal education: A philosophy for complex futures*. Cham, Switzerland: Springer.

Gignac, Gilles E. (2016). On the evaluation of competing theories: A reply to van der Maas and Kan. *Intelligence*, *57*, 84–86.

Gilbert, Daniel T.; King, Gary; Pettigrew, Stephen & Wilson, Timothy D. (2016). Comment on "Estimating the reproducibility of psychological science". *Science*, *351*(6277), 1037-b.

Gilchrist, Julie & Parker, Erin M. (2014, May 16). *Racial/ethnic disparities in fatal unintentional drowning among persons aged ≤29 years — United States, 1999–2010. Morbidity and Mortality Weekly Report*, *63*(19), 421–426. Atlanta, GA: U.S. Department of Health and Human Services, Centers for Disease Control and Prevention.

Gillen, Meghan M. & Lefkowitz, Eva S. (2012). Gender and racial/ethnic differences in body image development among college students. *Body Image*, *9*(1), 126–130.

Gillespie, Brian Joseph; Frederick, David; Harari, Lexi & Grov, Christian. (2015). Homophily, close friendship, and life satisfaction among gay, lesbian, heterosexual, and bisexual men and women. *PLoS ONE*, *10*(6), e0128900.

Gilligan, Carol. (1982). *In a different voice: Psychological theory and women's development*. Cambridge, MA: Harvard University Press.

Gillon, Raanan. (2015). Defending the four principles approach as a good basis for good medical practice and therefore for good medical ethics. *Journal of Medical Ethics*, *41*(1), 111–116.

Gilmore, John H.; Knickmeyer, Rebecca C. & Gao, Wei. (2018). Imaging structural and functional brain development in early childhood. *Nature Reviews Neuroscience*, *19*, 123–137.

Giumetti, Gary W. & Kowalski, Robin M. (2015). Cyberbullying matters: Examining the incremental impact of cyberbullying on outcomes over and above traditional bullying in North America. In Raúl Navarro, et al. (Eds.), *Cyberbullying across the globe: Gender, family, and mental health* (pp. 117–130). New York, NY: Springer.

Glance, Laurent G.; Dick, Andrew W.; Glantz, Christopher; Wissler, Richard N.; Qian, Feng; Marroquin, Bridget M., . . . Kellermann, Arthur L. (2014). Rates of major obstetrical complications vary almost fivefold among US hospitals. *Health Affairs*, *33*(8), 1330–1336.

Glauber, Rebecca & Day, Melissa D. (2018). Gender, spousal caregiving, and depression: Does paid work matter? *Journal of Marriage and Family*, *80*(2), 537–554.

Glenberg, Arthur M.; Witt, Jessica K. & Metcalfe, Janet. (2013). From the revolution to embodiment: 25 years of cognitive psychology. *Perspectives on Psychological Science*, *8*(5), 573–585.

Glenn, Dana E.; Demir-Lira, Özlem Ece; Gibson, Dominic J.; Congdon, Eliza L. & Levine, Susan C. (2018). Resilience in mathematics after early brain injury: The roles of parental input and early plasticity. *Developmental Cognitive Neuroscience*, *30*, 304–313.

Global Burden of Disease Neurological Disorders Collaborator Group. (2017). Global, regional, and national burden of neurological disorders during 1990–2015: A systematic analysis for the Global Burden of Disease Study 2015. *The Lancet Neurology*, *16*(11), 877–897.

Glover, Crystal Polite; Jenkins, Toby S. & Troutman, Stephanie. (2018). *Culture, community, and educational success: Reimagining the invisible knapsack*. Lanham, MD: Lexington.

Gobet, Fernand & Charness, Neil. (2018). Expertise in chess. In K. Anders Ericsson, Robert R. Hoffman, Aaron Kozbelt & A. Mark Williams (Eds.), *The Cambridge handbook of expertise and expert performance* (pp. 597–615). New York, NY: Cambridge University Press.

Goddings, Anne-Lise & Giedd, Jay N. (2014). Structural brain development during childhood and adolescence. In Michael S. Gazzaniga & George R. Mangun (Eds.), *The cognitive neurosciences* (5th ed., pp. 15–22). Cambridge, MA: MIT Press.

Goddings, Anne-Lise; Heyes, Stephanie Burnett; Bird, Geoffrey; Viner, Russell M. & Blakemore, Sarah-Jayne. (2012). The relationship between puberty and social emotion processing. *Developmental Science*, *15*(6), 801–811.

Godinet, Meripa T.; Li, Fenfang & Berg, Teresa. (2014). Early childhood maltreatment and trajectories of behavioral problems: Exploring gender and racial differences. *Child Abuse & Neglect*, *38*(3), 544–556.

Godon-Decoteau, Danielle; Ramsey, Patricia G. & Suyemoto, Karen L. (2018). Korean transracial and international adoptees: Ethnic identity and sense of belonging and exclusion in relation to birth and adoptive groups. *Identity*, *18*(3), 178–194.

Goel, Sunny; Sharma, Abhishek & Garg, Aakash. (2018). Effect of alcohol consumption on cardiovascular health. *Current Cardiology Reports*, *20*(4).

Goesling, Brian; Colman, Silvie; Trenholm, Christopher; Terzian, Mary & Moore, Kristin. (2014). Programs to reduce teen pregnancy, sexually transmitted infections, and associated sexual risk behaviors: A systematic review. *Journal of Adolescent Health*, *54*(5), 499–507.

Gogtay, Nitin; Giedd, Jay N.; Lusk, Leslie; Hayashi, Kiralee M.; Greenstein, Deanna; Vaituzis, A. Catherine, . . . Ungerleider, Leslie G. (2004). Dynamic mapping of human cortical development during childhood through early adulthood. *Proceedings of the National Academy of Sciences of the United States of America*, *101*(21), 8174–8179.

Golant, Stephen M. (2011). The changing residential environments of older people. In Robert H. Binstock & Linda K. George (Eds.), *Handbook of aging and the social sciences* (7th ed., pp. 207–220). San Diego, CA: Academic Press.

Golden, Marita. (2010). Angel baby. In Barbara Graham (Ed.), *Eye of my heart: 27 writers reveal the hidden pleasures and perils of being a grandmother* (pp. 125–133). New York, NY: HarperCollins.

Golden, Neville H.; Yang, Wei; Jacobson, Marc S.; Robinson, Thomas N. & Shaw, Gary M. (2012). Expected body weight in adolescents: Comparison between weight-for-stature and BMI methods. *Pediatrics*, *130*(6), e1607–e1613.

Golden, Rachel Lynn; Furman, Wyndol & Collibee, Charlene. (2016). The risks and rewards of sexual debut. *Developmental Psychology*, *52*(11), 1913–1925.

Goldfarb, Sally F. (2014). Who pays for the 'boomerang generation'?: A legal perspective on financial support for young adults. *Harvard Journal of Law and Gender*, *37*, 46–106.

Goldin-Meadow, Susan. (2015). From action to abstraction: Gesture as a mechanism of change. *Developmental Review*, *38*, 167–184.

Goldin-Meadow, Susan & Alibali, Martha W. (2013). Gesture's role in speaking, learning, and creating language. *Annual Review of Psychology*, *64*, 257–283.

Goldman-Mellor, Sidra; Caspi, Avshalom; Arseneault, Louise; Ajala, Nifemi; Ambler, Antony; Danese, Andrea, . . . Moffitt, Terrie E. (2016). Committed to work but vulnerable: Self-perceptions and mental health in NEET 18-year-olds from a contemporary British cohort. *Journal of Child Psychology and Psychiatry*, *57*(2), 196–203.

Goldschmidt, Andrea B.; Wall, Melanie M.; Zhang, Jun; Loth, Katie A. & Neumark-Sztainer, Dianne. (2016). Overeating and binge eating in emerging adulthood: 10-year stability and risk factors. *Developmental Psychology*, *52*(3), 475–483.

Goldstein, Thalia R. & Lerner, Matthew D. (2018). Dramatic pretend play games uniquely improve emotional control in young children. *Developmental Science, 21*(4), e12603.

Golinkoff, Roberta M. & Hirsh-Pasek, Kathy. (2016). *Becoming brilliant: What science tells us about raising successful children*. Washington, DC: American Psychological Association.

Göncü, Artin & Gaskins, Suzanne. (2011). Comparing and extending Piaget's and Vygotsky's understandings of play: Symbolic play as individual, sociocultural, and educational interpretation. In Anthony D. Pellegrini (Ed.), *The Oxford handbook of the development of play* (pp. 48–57). New York, NY: Oxford University Press.

Goniewicz, Maciej L.; Gawron, Michal; Smith, Danielle M.; Peng, Margaret; Jacob, Peyton & Benowitz, Neal L. (2017). Exposure to nicotine and selected toxicants in cigarette smokers who switched to electronic cigarettes: A longitudinal within-subjects observational study. *Nicotine & Tobacco Research, 19*(2), 160–167.

Gonyea, Judith G. (2013). Midlife, multigenerational bonds, and caregiving. In Ronda C. Talley & Rhonda J. V. Montgomery (Eds.), *Caregiving across the lifespan: Research, practice, policy* (pp. 105–130). New York, NY: Springer.

González, Hector M.; Tarraf, Wassim; Jian, Xueqiu; Vásquez, Priscilla M.; Kaplan, Robert; Thyagarajan, Bharat, . . . Fornage, Myriam. (2018). Apolipoprotein E genotypes among diverse middle-aged and older Latinos: Study of Latinos-Investigation of Neurocognitive Aging results (HCHS/SOL). *Scientific Reports, 8*(1).

Goodlad, James K.; Marcus, David K. & Fulton, Jessica J. (2013). Lead and Attention-deficit/hyperactivity disorder (ADHD) symptoms: A meta-analysis. *Clinical Psychology Review, 33*(3), 417–425.

Goodman, R.; Meltzer, H. & Bailey, V. (1998). The strengths and difficulties questionnaire: A pilot study on the validity of the self-report version. *European Child & Adolescent Psychiatry, 7*(3), 125–130.

Goodnight, Jackson A.; D'Onofrio, Brian M.; Cherlin, Andrew J.; Emery, Robert E.; Van Hulle, Carol A. & Lahey, Benjamin B. (2013). Effects of multiple maternal relationship transitions on offspring antisocial behavior in childhood and adolescence: A cousin-comparison analysis. *Journal of Abnormal Child Psychology, 41*(2), 185–198.

Gopnik, Alison. (2012). Scientific thinking in young children: Theoretical advances, empirical research, and policy implications. *Science*, 337(6102), 1623–1627.

Gopnik, Alison. (2016). *The gardener and the carpenter: What the new science of child development tells us about the relationship between parents and children*. New York, NY: Farrar, Strauss and Giroux.

Gopnik, Alison; Meltzoff, Andrew N. & Kuhl, Patricia K. (1999). *The scientist in the crib: Minds, brains, and how children learn*. New York, NY: William Morrow.

Gorbatov, Sergey & Lane, Angela. (2018). Is HR missing the point on performance feedback? *MIT Sloan Management Review, 59*(4).

Gordon, Ilanit; Zagoory-Sharon, Orna; Leckman, James F. & Feldman, Ruth. (2010). Oxytocin and the development of parenting in humans. *Biological Psychiatry, 68*(4), 377–382.

Gordon, Linda. (2017). *The second coming of the KKK: The Ku Klux Klan of the 1920s and the American political tradition*. New York, NY: Liveright.

Gordon-Hollingsworth, Arlene T.; Becker, Emily M.; Ginsburg, Golda S.; Keeton, Courtney; Compton, Scott N.; Birmaher, Boris B., . . . March, John S. (2015). Anxiety disorders in Caucasian and African American children: A comparison of clinical characteristics, treatment process variables, and treatment outcomes. *Child Psychiatry & Human Development, 46*(5), 643–655.

Gorham, Lisa S.; Jernigan, Terry; Hudziak, Jim & Barch, Deanna M. (2019). Involvement in sports, hippocampal volume, and depressive symptoms in children. *Biological Psychiatry, 4*(5), 484–492.

Gottesman, Irving I.; Laursen, Thomas Munk; Bertelsen, Aksel & Mortensen, Preben Bo. (2010). Severe mental disorders in offspring with 2 psychiatrically ill parents. *Archives of General Psychiatry, 67*(3), 252–257.

Gottman, John & Gottman, Julie. (2017). The natural principles of love. *Journal of Family Theory & Review, 9*(1), 7–26.

Gough, Ethan K.; Moodie, Erica E. M.; Prendergast, Andrew J.; Johnson, Sarasa M. A.; Humphrey, Jean H.; Stoltzfus, Rebecca J., . . . Manges, Amee R. (2014). The impact of antibiotics on growth in children in low and middle income countries: Systematic review and meta-analysis of randomised controlled trials. *BMJ, 348*, g2267.

Graber, Julia A.; Nichols, Tracy R. & Brooks-Gunn, Jeanne. (2010). Putting pubertal timing in developmental context: Implications for prevention. *Developmental Psychobiology*, 52(3), 254–262.

Grady, Denise. (2012, May 5). When illness makes a spouse a stranger. *New York Times*.

Grady, Jessica Stoltzfus & Hastings, Paul D. (2018). Becoming prosocial peers: The roles of temperamental shyness and mothers' and fathers' elaborative emotion language. *Social Development*, 27(4), 858–875.

Grady, Sarah. (2017, September 26). A fresh look at homeschooling in the U.S. [Web log post]. Institute of Education Sciences. Retrieved from https://nces.ed.gov/blogs/nces/post/a-fresh-look-at-homeschooling-in-the-u-s

Grady, Sue C.; Frake, April N.; Zhang, Qiong; Bene, Matlhogonolo; Jordan, Demetrice R.; Vertalka, Joshua, . . . Kutch, Libbey. (2017). Neonatal mortality in East Africa and West Africa: A geographic analysis of district-level demographic and health survey data. *Geospatial Health, 12*(1).

Graham, Carol; Laffan, Kate & Pinto, Sergio. (2018). Well-being in metrics and policy. *Science, 362*(6412), 287–288.

Graham, Jesse; Haidt, Jonathan; Koleva, Sena; RavilYer, MattMotyl; Wojcik, Sean P. & Ditto, Peter H. (2013). Moral foundations theory: The pragmatic validity of moral pluralism. In Patricia Devine & Ashby Plant (Eds.), *Advances in Experimental Social Psychology* (Vol. 47, pp. 55–130). San Diego, CA: Academic Press.

Grainger, Sarah A.; Henry, Julie D.; Phillips, Louise H.; Vanman, Eric J. & Allen, Roy. (2017). Age deficits in facial affect recognition: The influence of dynamic cues. *The Journals of Gerontology. Series B, Psychological Sciences and Social Sciences*, 72(4), 622–632.

Grajower, Martin M. & Horne, Benjamin D. (2019). Clinical management of intermittent fasting in patients with diabetes mellitus. *Nutrients, 11*(4), 873.

Granqvist, Pehr & Kirkpatrick, Lee A. (2013). Religion, spirituality, and attachment. In Kenneth I. Pargament (Ed.), *APA handbook of psychology, religion, and spirituality* (Vol. 1). Washington, DC: American Psychological Association.

Graybill, Emily; Self-Brown, Shannon; Lai, Betty; Vinoski, Erin; McGill, Tia & Crimmins, Daniel. (2016). Addressing disparities in parent education: Examining the effects of learn the signs/act early parent education materials on parent outcomes. *Early Childhood Education Journal, 44*(1), 31–38.

Grayson, David S. & Fair, Damien A. (2017). Development of large-scale functional networks from birth to adulthood: A guide to the neuroimaging literature. *NeuroImage, 160*, 15–31.

Grazioplene, Rachael G.; Ryman, Sephira G.; Gray, Jeremy R.; Rustichini, Aldo; Jung, Rex E. & DeYoung, Colin G. (2015). Subcortical intelligence: Caudate volume predicts IQ in healthy adults. *Human Brain Mapping*, 36(4), 1407–1416.

Greco, Daniel. (2014). Could KK be OK? *The Journal of Philosophy, 111*(4), 169–197.

Gredebäck, Gustaf; Astor, Kim & Fawcett, Christine. (2018). Gaze following is not dependent on ostensive cues: A critical test of natural pedagogy. *Child Development, 89*(6), 2091–2098.

Green, James A.; Whitney, Pamela G. & Potegal, Michael. (2011). Screaming, yelling, whining, and crying: Categorical and intensity differences in vocal expressions of anger and sadness in children's tantrums. *Emotion, 11*(5), 1124–1133.

Green, Lorraine & Grant, Victoria. (2008). "Gagged grief and beleaguered bereavements?" An analysis of multidisciplinary theory and research relating to same sex partnership bereavement. *Sexualities, 11*(3), 275–300.

Green, Lawrence W.; Fielding, Jonathan E. & Brownson, Ross C. (2018). The debate about electronic cigarettes: Harm minimization or the precautionary principle. *Annual Review of Public Health*, 39, 189–191.

Green, Ronald. (2015). Designer babies. In Henk ten Have (Ed.), *Encyclopedia of global bioethics*. Living Reference Work: Springer International Publishing.

Greene, Melissa L. & Way, Niobe. (2005). Self-esteem trajectories among ethnic minority adolescents: A growth curve analysis of the patterns and predictors of change. *Journal of Research on Adolescence, 15*(2), 151–178.

Greenfield, Emily A.; Scharlach, Andrew; Lehning, Amanda J. & Davitt, Joan K. (2012). A conceptual framework for examining the promise of the NORC program and Village models to promote aging in place. *Journal of Aging Studies*, 26(3), 273–284.

Greenfield, Patricia M. (2009). Technology and informal education: What is taught, what is learned. *Science, 323*(5910), 69–71.

Greenough, William T.; Black, James E. & Wallace, Christopher S. (1987). Experience and brain development. *Child Development,* 58(3), 539–559.

Greenough, William T. & Volkmar, Fred R. (1973). Pattern of dendritic branching in occipital cortex of rats reared in complex environments. *Experimental Neurology, 40*(2), 491–504.

Gregori, Elena Barberà; Zhang, Jingjing; Galván-Fernández, Cristina & Fernández-Navarro, Francisco de Asís. (2018). Learner support in MOOCs: Identifying variables linked to completion. *Computers & Education, 122,* 153–168.

Gregson, Joanna. (2010). *The culture of teenage mothers.* Albany, NY: SUNY.

Greyson, Bruce. (2009). Near-death experiences and deathbed visions. In Allan Kellehear (Ed.), *The study of dying: From autonomy to transformation* (pp. 253–275). New York, NY: Cambridge University Press.

Griffith, Derek M.; Bruce, Marino A. & Thorpe Jr., Roland J. (Eds.). (2019). *Men's health equity: A handbook.* New York, NY: Routledge.

Griffin, James A.; McCardle, Peggy & Freund, Lisa S. (Eds.). (2016). *Executive function in preschool-age children: Integrating measurement, neurodevelopment, and translational research.* Washington, DC: American Psychological Association.

Griffith, Patrick & Lopez, Oscar. (2009). Disparities in the diagnosis and treatment of Alzheimer's disease in African American and Hispanic patients: A call to action. *Generations,* 33(1), 37–46.

Griffiths, Thomas L. (2015). Manifesto for a new (computational) cognitive revolution. *Cognition, 135,* 21–23.

Grivell, Rosalie M.; Reilly, Aimee J.; Oakey, Helena; Chan, Annabelle & Dodd, Jodie M. (2012). Maternal and neonatal outcomes following induction of labor: A cohort study. *Acta Obstetricia et Gynecologica Scandinavica, 91*(2), 198–203.

Grobman, Kevin H. (2008). Learning & teaching developmental psychology: Attachment theory, infancy, & infant memory development. DevPsy.

Grogan-Kaylor, Andrew; Ma, Julie & Graham-Bermann, Sandra A. (2018). The case against physical punishment. *Current Opinion in Psychology, 19,* 22–27.

Groh, Ashley M.; Narayan, Angela J.; Bakermans-Kranenburg, Marian J.; Roisman, Glenn I.; Vaughn, Brian E.; Fearon, R. M. Pasco & van IJzendoorn, Marinus H. (2017). Attachment and temperament in the early life course: A meta-analytic review. *Child Development,* 88(3), 770–795.

Groh, Ashley M.; Roisman, Glenn I.; van IJzendoorn, Marinus H.; Bakermans-Kranenburg, Marian J. & Fearon, R. Pasco. (2012). The significance of insecure and disorganized attachment for children's internalizing symptoms: A meta-analytic study. *Child Development,* 83(2), 591–610.

Grønkjær, Marie; Osler, Merete; Flensborg-Madsen, Trine; Sørensen, Holger J. & Mortensen, Erik L. (2019). Associations between education and age-related cognitive changes from early adulthood to late midlife. *Psychology and Aging,* 34(2), 177–186.

Grönqvist, Hans; Nilsson, J. Peter & Robling, Per Olof. (2014). *Childhood lead exposure and criminal behavior: Lessons from the Swedish phase-out of leaded gasoline.* Stockholm: Swedish Institute for Social Research. Working Paper 9/2014.

Gröpel, Peter & Mesagno, Christopher. (2017). Choking interventions in sports: A systematic review. *International Review of Sport and Exercise Psychology, 12*(1).

Gross, James J. (Ed.). (2014). *Handbook of emotion regulation* (2nd ed.). New York, NY: Guilford Press.

Grossman, Matthew; Seashore, Carl & Holmes, Alison V. (2017). Neonatal abstinence syndrome management: A review of recent evidence. *Reviews on Recent Clinical Trials, 12*(4), 226–232.

Grossmann, Klaus E.; Bretherton, Inge; Waters, Everett & Grossmann, Karin (Eds.). (2014). *Mary Ainsworth's enduring influence on attachment theory, research, and clinical applications.* New York, NY: Routledge.

Grossmann, Tobias. (2017). The eyes as windows into other minds: An integrative perspective. *Perspectives on Psychological Science, 12*(1), 107–121.

Grotevant, Harold D. & McDermott, Jennifer M. (2014). Adoption: Biological and social processes linked to adaptation. *Annual Review of Psychology, 65,* 235–265.

Grotevant, Harold D.; Lo, Albert Y. H.; Fiorenzo, Lisa & Dunbar, Nora D. (2017). Adoptive identity and adjustment from adolescence to emerging adulthood: A person-centered approach. *Developmental Psychology,* 53(11), 2195–2204.

Grov, Christian; Gillespie, Brian Joseph; Royce, Tracy & Lever, Janet. (2011). Perceived consequences of casual online sexual activities on heterosexual relationships: A U.S. online survey. *Archives of Sexual Behavior, 40*(2), 429–439.

Gruber, Staci A.; Sagar, Kelly A.; Dahlgren, Mary K.; Gonenc, Atilla; Smith, Rosemary T.; Lambros, Ashley M., . . . Lukas, Scott E. (2018). The grass might be greener: Medical marijuana patients exhibit altered brain activity and improved executive function after 3 months of treatment. *Frontiers in Pharmacology,* 8(1), 983.

Grusec, Joan E.; Danyliuk, Tanya; Kil, Hali & O'Neill, David. (2017). Perspectives on parent discipline and child outcomes. *International Journal of Behavioral Development, 41*(4), 465–471.

Guassi Moreira, João F. & Telzer, Eva H. (2018). Family conflict is associated with longitudinal changes in insular-striatal functional connectivity during adolescent risk taking under maternal influence. *Developmental Science, 21*(5), e12632.

Guerra, Nancy G.; Williams, Kirk R. & Sadek, Shelly. (2011). Understanding bullying and victimization during childhood and adolescence: A mixed methods study. *Child Development,* 82(1), 295–310.

Guerri, Consuelo & Pascual, María. (2010). Mechanisms involved in the neurotoxic, cognitive, and neurobehavioral effects of alcohol consumption during adolescence. *Alcohol, 44*(1), 15–26.

Gulbas, L. E.; Zayas, L. H.; Yoon, H.; Szlyk, H.; Aguilar-Gaxiola, S. & Natera, G. (2016). Deportation experiences and depression among U.S. citizen-children with undocumented Mexican parents. *Child,* 42(2), 220–230.

Gulia, Kamalesh K. & Kumar, Velayudhan Mohan. (2018). Sleep disorders in the elderly: A growing challenge: Sleep in elderly. *Psychogeriatrics, 18*(3), 155–165.

Güngör, Derya; Bornstein, Marc H.; De Leersnyder, Jozefien; Cote, Linda; Ceulemans, Eva & Mesquita, Batja. (2013). Acculturation of personality: A three-culture study of Japanese, Japanese Americans, and European Americans. *Journal of Cross-Cultural Psychology, 44*(5), 701–718.

Guo, Siying. (2016). A meta-analysis of the predictors of cyberbullying perpetration and victimization. *Psychology in the Schools,* 53(4), 432–453.

Guo, Yuming; Gasparrini, Antonio; Armstrong, Ben G.; Tawatsupa, Benjawan; Tobias, Aurelio; Lavigne, Eric, . . . Tong, Shilu. (2017). Heat wave and mortality: A multicountry, multicommunity study. *Environmental Health Perspectives, 125*(8).

Gutchess, Angela. (2014). Plasticity of the aging brain: New directions in cognitive neuroscience. *Science,* 346(6209), 579–582.

Gutierrez-Galve, Leticia; Stein, Alan; Hanington, Lucy; Heron, Jon & Ramchandani, Paul. (2015). Paternal depression in the postnatal period and child development: Mediators and moderators. *Pediatrics, 135*(2), e339–e347.

Guyer, Amanda E.; Pérez-Edgar, Koraly & Crone, Eveline A. (2018). Opportunities for neurodevelopmental plasticity from infancy through early adulthood. *Child Development,* 89(3), 687–697.

Guyon-Harris, Katherine L.; Humphreys, Kathryn L.; Fox, Nathan A.; Nelson, Charles A. & Zeanah, Charles H. (2018). Course of disinhibited social engagement disorder from early childhood to early adolescence. *Journal of the American Academy of Child & Adolescent Psychiatry,* 57(5), 329–335.e322.

Guzman, Natalie S. de & Nishina, Adrienne. (2014). A longitudinal study of body dissatisfaction and pubertal timing in an ethnically diverse adolescent sample. *Body Image, 11*(1), 68–71.

Guzzo, Karen Benjamin. (2014). Trends in cohabitation outcomes: Compositional changes and engagement among never-married young adults. *Journal of Marriage and Family,* 76(4), 826–842.

Gyllenberg, Frida; Juselius, Mikael; Gissler, Mika & Heikinheimo, Oskari. (2018). Long-acting reversible contraception free of charge, method initiation, and abortion rates in Finland. *American Journal of Public Health, 108*(4), 538–543.

Gypen, Laura; Vanderfaeillie, Johan; De Maeyer, Skrallan; Belenger, Laurence & Van Holen, Frank. (2017). Outcomes of children who grew up in foster care: Systematic-review. *Children and Youth Services Review, 76,* 74–83.

Hackett, Geoffrey Ian. (2016). Testosterone replacement therapy and mortality in older men. *Drug Safety, 39*(2), 117–130.

Hackett, Ruth A.; Davies-Kershaw, Hilary; Cadar, Dorina; Orrell, Martin & Steptoe, Andrew. (2018). Walking speed, cognitive function, and dementia risk in the English Longitudinal Study of Ageing. *Journal of the American Geriatrics Society, 66*(9), 1670–1675.

Hagopian, Jesse (Ed.). (2014). *More than a score: The new uprising against high-stakes testing.* Chicago, IL: Haymarket.

Haidt, Jonathan. (2013). *The righteous mind: Why good people are divided by politics and religion.* New York, NY: Vintage Books.

Haight, Sarah C.; Ko, Jean Y.; Tong, Van T.; Bohm, Michele K. & Callaghan, William M. (2018, August 10). *Opioid use disorder documented at delivery hospitalization — United States, 1999–2014. Morbidity and Mortality Weekly Report, 67*(31), 845–849. Atlanta, GA: Centers for Disease Control and Prevention.

Halberda, Justin. (2018). Logic in babies. *Science, 359*(6381), 1214–1215.

Hales, Craig M.; Carroll, Margaret D.; Fryar, Cheryl D. & Ogden, Cynthia L. (2017, October). *Prevalence of obesity among adults and youth: United States, 2015–2016.* Atlanta, GA: Centers for Disease Control and Prevention: National Center for Health Statistics.

Halim, May Ling; Ruble, Diane N.; Tamis-LeMonda, Catherine S.; Zosuls, Kristina M.; Lurye, Leah E. & Greulich, Faith K. (2014). Pink frilly dresses and the avoidance of all things "girly": Children's appearance rigidity and cognitive theories of gender development. *Developmental Psychology, 50*(4), 1091–1101.

Hall, Jeffrey A. (2011). Sex differences in friendship expectations: A meta-analysis. *Journal of Social and Personal Relationships, 28*(6), 723–747.

Hall, Kelli Stidham; Sales, Jessica McDermott; Komro, Kelli A. & Santelli, John. (2016). The state of sex education in the United States. *Journal of Adolescent Health, 58*(6), 595–597.

Hall, Matthew L.; Eigsti, Inge-Marie; Bortfeld, Heather & Lillo-Martin, Diane. (2017). Auditory deprivation does not impair executive function, but language deprivation might: Evidence from a parent-report measure in deaf native signing children. *Journal of Deaf Studies and Deaf Education, 22*(1), 9–21.

Hall, Victoria; Banerjee, Emily; Kenyon, Cynthia; Strain, Anna; Griffith, Jayne; Como-Sabetti, Kathryn, . . . Ehresmann, Kristen. (2017, July 14). *Measles outbreak — Minnesota April–May 2017. Morbidity and Mortality Weekly Report, 66*(27), 713–717. Atlanta, GA: Centers for Disease Control and Prevention.

Hallers-Haalboom, Elizabeth T.; Mesman, Judi; Groeneveld, Marleen G.; Endendijk, Joyce J.; van Berkel, Sheila R.; van der Pol, Lotte D. & Bakermans-Kranenburg, Marian J. (2014). Mothers, fathers, sons and daughters: Parental sensitivity in families with two children. *Journal of Family Psychology, 28*(2), 138–147.

Halperin, Jeffrey M. & Healey, Dione M. (2011). The influences of environmental enrichment, cognitive enhancement, and physical exercise on brain development: Can we alter the developmental trajectory of ADHD? *Neuroscience & Biobehavioral Reviews, 35*(3), 621–634.

Halpern-Meekin, Sarah; Manning, Wendy D.; Giordano, Peggy C. & Longmore, Monica A. (2013). Relationship churning, physical violence, and verbal abuse in young adult relationships. *Journal of Marriage and Family, 75*(1), 2–12.

Hambrick, David Z.; Burgoyne, Alexander P.; Macnamara, Brooke N. & Ullén, Fredrik. (2018). Toward a multifactorial model of expertise: Beyond born versus made. *Annals of the New York Academy of Sciences, 14231*(1), 284–295.

Hambrick, David Z.; Macnamara, Brooke N.; Campitelli, Guillermo; Ullén, Fredrik & Mosing, Miriam A. (2016). Beyond born versus made: A new look at expertise. *Psychology of Learning and Motivation, 64,* 1–55.

Hamdy, Sherine. (2018). All eyes on Egypt: Islam and the medical use of dead bodies amidst Cairo's political unrest. In Antonius C. G. M. Robben (Ed.), *Death, mourning, and burial: A cross-cultural reader* (pp. 102–114). Hoboken, NJ: Wiley-Blackwell.

Hamerton, John L. & Evans, Jane A. (2005). Sex chromosome anomalies. In Merlin G. Butler & F. John Meaney (Eds.), *Genetics of developmental disabilities* (pp. 585–650). Boca Raton, FL: Taylor & Francis.

Hamill, Paul J. (1991). Triage: An essay. *The Georgia Review, 45*(3), 463–469.

Hamilton, Alice. (1914). Lead poisoning in the United States. *American Journal of Public Health, 4*(6), 477–480.

Hamilton, Brady E.; Martin, Joyce A.; Osterman, Michelle J. K.; Curtin, Sally C. & Mathews, T. J. (2015, December 23). *Births: Final data for 2014. National Vital Statistics Reports, 64*(12). Hyattsville, MD: National Center for Health Statistics.

Hamlat, Elissa J.; Shapero, Benjamin G.; Hamilton, Jessica L.; Stange, Jonathan P.; Abramson, Lyn Y. & Alloy, Lauren B. (2014a). Pubertal timing, peer victimization, and body esteem differentially predict depressive symptoms in African American and Caucasian girls. *Journal of Early Adolescence, 35*(2), 378–402.

Hamlat, Elissa J.; Stange, Jonathan P.; Abramson, Lyn Y. & Alloy, Lauren B. (2014b). Early pubertal timing as a vulnerability to depression symptoms: Differential effects of race and sex. *Journal of Abnormal Child Psychology, 42*(4), 527–538.

Hamlett, Eric D.; Ledreux, Aurélie; Potter, Huntington; Chial, Heidi J.; Patterson, David; Espinosa, Joaquin M., . . . Granholm, Ann-Charlotte. (2018). Exosomal biomarkers in Down syndrome and Alzheimer's disease. *Free Radical Biology and Medicine, 114,* 110–121.

Hamlin, J. Kiley. (2014). The origins of human morality: Complex socio-moral evaluations by preverbal infants. In Jean Decety & Yves Christen (Eds.), *New frontiers in social neuroscience* (pp. 165–188). New York, NY: Springer.

Hamlin, J. Kiley & Van de Vondervoort, Julia W. (2018). Infants' and young children's preferences for prosocial over antisocial others. *Human Development, 61*(4/5), 214–231.

Hamm, Jeremy M.; Chipperfield, Judith G.; Perry, Raymond P.; Parker, Patti C. & Heckhausen, Jutta. (2017). Tenacious self-reliance in health maintenance may jeopardize late life survival. *Psychology and Aging, 32*(7), 628–635.

Hamplová, Dana; Le Bourdais, Céline & Lapierre-Adamcyk, Évelyne. (2014). Is the cohabitation–marriage gap in money pooling universal? *Journal of Marriage and Family, 76*(5), 983–997.

Han, Hyemin; Dawson, Kelsie J.; Thoma, Stephen J. & Glenn, Andrea L. (2019). Developmental level of moral judgment influences behavioral patterns during moral decision-making. *The Journal of Experimental Education,* (In Press).

Han, Kihye; Trinkoff, Alison M.; Storr, Carla L.; Lerner, Nancy & Yang, Bo Kyum. (2017). Variation across U.S. assisted living facilities: Admissions, resident care needs, and staffing. *Journal of Nursing Scholarship, 49*(1), 24–32.

Han, S. Duke; Olsen, Bonnie J. & Mosqueda, Laura A. (2019). Elder abuse identification and intervention. In Lisa D. Ravdin & Heather L. Katzen (Eds.), *Handbook on the neuropsychology of aging and dementia* (pp. 197–203). Cham, Switzerland: Springer.

Haney, Alison M. & Rollock, David. (2018). A matter of faith: The role of religion, doubt, and personality in emerging adult mental health. *Psychology of Religion and Spirituality,* (In Press).

Hank, Karsten & Korbmacher, Julie M. (2013). Parenthood and retirement: Gender, cohort, and welfare regime differences. *European Societies, 15*(3), 446–461.

Hanna-Attisha, Mona; LaChance, Jenny; Sadler, Richard Casey & Schnepp, Allison Champney. (2016). Elevated blood lead levels in children associated with the Flint drinking water crisis: A spatial analysis of risk and public health response. *American Journal of Public Health, 106*(2), 283–290.

Hannon, Erin E.; Schachner, Adena & Nave-Blodgett, Jessica E. (2017). Babies know bad dancing when they see it: Older but not younger infants discriminate between synchronous and asynchronous audiovisual musical displays. *Journal of Experimental Child Psychology, 159,* 159–174.

Hanushek, Eric A.; Schwerdt, Guido; Woessmann, Ludger & Zhang, Lei. (2017). General education, vocational education, and labor-market outcomes over the lifecycle. *Journal of Human Resources, 52*(1), 48–87.

Hanushek, Eric A. & Woessmann, Ludger. (2007). *The role of education quality in economic growth. World Bank Policy Research Working Paper No. 4122.* Washington, DC: World Bank.

Hanushek, Eric A. & Woessmann, Ludger. (2010). *The high cost of low educational performance: The long-run economic impact of improving PISA outcomes.* Paris: OECD Publishing.

Hanushek, Eric A. & Woessmann, Ludger. (2015). *The knowledge capital of nations: Education and the economics of growth*. Cambridge, MA: MIT Press.

Harden, K. Paige & Tucker-Drob, Elliot M. (2011). Individual differences in the development of sensation seeking and impulsivity during adolescence: Further evidence for a dual systems model. *Developmental Psychology*, *47*(3), 739–746.

Hargreaves, Andy. (2012). Singapore: The Fourth Way in action? *Educational Research for Policy and Practice*, *11*(1), 7–17.

Hari, Riitta. (2017). From brain–environment connections to temporal dynamics and social interaction: Principles of human brain function. *Neuron*, *94*(5), 1033–1039.

Harkness, Sara. (2014). Is biology destiny for the whole family? Contributions of evolutionary life history and behavior genetics to family theories. *Journal of Family Theory & Review*, *6*(1), 31–34.

Harkness, Sara; Super, Charles M. & Mavridis, Caroline J. (2011). Parental ethnotheories about children's socioemotional development. In Xinyin Chen & Kenneth H. Rubin (Eds.), *Socioemotional development in cultural context* (pp. 73–98). New York, NY: Guilford Press.

Harper, Casandra E. & Yeung, Fanny. (2013). Perceptions of institutional commitment to diversity as a predictor of college students' openness to diverse perspectives. *The Review of Higher Education*, *37*(1), 25–44.

Harris Insights and Analytics. (2014, February 19). *6 in 10 Americans say they or someone they know have been bullied*. New York, NY: Harris Interactive.

Harris, Judith R. (1998). *The nurture assumption: Why children turn out the way they do*. New York, NY: Free Press.

Harris, Judith R. (2002). Beyond the nurture assumption: Testing hypotheses about the child's environment. In John G. Borkowski, et al. (Eds.), *Parenting and the child's world: Influences on academic, intellectual, and social-emotional development* (pp. 3–20). Mahwah, NJ: Erlbaum.

Harris, Michelle A.; Wetzel, Eunike; Robins, Richard W.; Donnellan, M. Brent & Trzesniewski, Kali H. (2017). The development of global and domain self-esteem from ages 10 to 16 for Mexican-origin youth. *International Journal of Behavioral Development*, (In Press).

Harris, Paul L. (2108). Children's understanding of death: From biology to religion. *Philosophical Transactions of the Royal Society B: Biological Sciences*, 373(1754).

Harrison, Kristen; Bost, Kelly K.; McBride, Brent A.; Donovan, Sharon M.; Grigsby-Toussaint, Diana S.; Kim, Juhee, . . . Jacobsohn, Gwen Costa. (2011). Toward a developmental conceptualization of contributors to overweight and obesity in childhood: The Six-Cs model. *Child Development Perspectives*, 5(1), 50–58.

Harrison, Linda J.; Elwick, Sheena; Vallotton, Claire D. & Kappler, Gregor. (2014). Spending time with others: A time-use diary for infant-toddler child care. In Linda J. Harrison & Jennifer Sumsion (Eds.), *Lived spaces of infant-toddler education and care: Exploring diverse perspectives on theory, research and practice* (pp. 59–74). Dordrecht, the Netherlands: Springer.

Harry Weger, Megan Cole & Valerie Akbulut (2019) Relationship maintenance across platonic and non-platonic cross-sex friendships in emerging adults, The Journal of Social Psychology, 159:1, 15-29.

Hart, Betty & Risley, Todd R. (1995). *Meaningful differences in the everyday experience of young American children*. Baltimore, MD: P. H. Brookes.

Hart, Chantelle N.; Cairns, Alyssa & Jelalian, Elissa. (2011). Sleep and obesity in children and adolescents. *Pediatric Clinics of North America*, 58(3), 715–733.

Hart, Daniel & Van Goethem, Anne. (2017). The role of civic and political participation in successful early adulthood. In Laura M. Padilla-Walker & Larry J. Nelson (Eds.), *Flourishing in emerging adulthood: Positive development during the third decade of life* (pp. 139–166). New York, NY: Oxford University Press.

Harter, Susan. (2012). *The construction of the self: Developmental and sociocultural foundations* (2nd ed.). New York, NY: Guilford Press.

Hartig, Hannah & Geiger, Abigail. (2018, October 8). *About six-in-ten Americans support marijuana legalization. Fact Tank*. Washington, DC: Pew Research Center.

Hartley, Catherine A. & Somerville, Leah H. (2015). The neuroscience of adolescent decision-making. *Current Opinion in Behavioral Sciences*, 5, 108–115.

Hartshorne, Joshua K. & Germine, Laura T. (2015). When does cognitive functioning peak? The asynchronous rise and fall of different cognitive abilities across the life span. *Psychological Science*, 26(4), 433–443.

Hasson, Ramzi & Fine, Jodene Goldenring. (2012). Gender differences among children with ADHD on continuous performance tests: A meta-analytic review. *Journal of Attention Disorders*, *16*(3), 190–198.

Hatch, J. Amos. (2012). From theory to curriculum: Developmental theory and its relationship to curriculum and instruction in early childhood education. In Nancy File, et al. (Eds.), *Curriculum in early childhood education: Re-examined, rediscovered, renewed*. New York, NY: Routledge.

Hatfield, Elaine; Bensman, Lisamarie & Rapson, Richard L. (2012). A brief history of social scientists' attempts to measure passionate love. *Journal of Social and Personal Relationships*, 29(2), 143–164.

Hauck, Fern & Tanabe, Kawai O. (2017). Beyond "back to sleep": Ways to further reduce the risk of sudden infant death syndrome. *Pediatric Annals*, *46*(8), e284–e290.

Haushofer, Johannes & Fehr, Ernst. (2014). On the psychology of poverty. *Science*, *344*(6186), 862–867.

Hawkes, Kristen & Coxworth, James E. (2013). Grandmothers and the evolution of human longevity: A review of findings and future directions. *Evolutionary Anthropology*, 22(6), 294–302.

Hawthorne, Joanna. (2009). Promoting development of the early parent-infant relationship using the Neonatal Behavioural Assessment Scale. In Jane Barlow & P. O. Svanberg (Eds.), *Keeping the baby in mind: Infant mental health in practice* (pp. 39–51). New York, NY: Routledge.

Hayden, Elizabeth P. & Mash, Eric J. (2014). Child psychopathology: A developmental-systems perspective. In Eric J. Mash & Russell A. Barkley (Eds.), *Child psychopathology* (3rd ed., pp. 3–72). New York, NY: Guilford Press.

Hayes, DeMarquis; Blake, Jamilia J.; Darensbourg, Alicia & Castillo, Linda G. (2015). Examining the academic achievement of Latino adolescents: The role of parent and peer beliefs and behaviors. *Journal of Early Adolescence*, 35(2), 141–161.

Hayes, Peter. (2013). International adoption, "early" puberty, and underrecorded age. *Pediatrics*, *131*(6), 1029–1031.

Hayflick, Leonard. (2004). "Anti-aging" is an oxymoron. *The Journals of Gerontology Series A: Biological Sciences and Medical Sciences*, 59(6), 573–578.

Hayman, Karen J.; Kerse, Ngaire & Consedine, Nathan S. (2017). Resilience in context: The special case of advanced age. *Aging & Mental Health*, *21*(6), 577–585.

Hayne, Harlene; Scarf, Damian & Imuta, Kana. (2015). Childhood memories. In James D. Wright (Ed.), *International encyclopedia of the social & behavioral sciences* (2nd ed., pp. 465–470). New York, NY: Elsevier.

Hayne, Harlene & Simcock, Gabrielle. (2009). Memory development in toddlers. In Mary L. Courage & Nelson Cowan (Eds.), *The development of memory in infancy and childhood* (2nd ed., pp. 43–68). New York, NY: Psychology Press.

Haynie, Dana L.; Soller, Brian & Williams, Kristi. (2014). Anticipating early fatality: Friends', schoolmates' and individual perceptions of fatality on adolescent risk behaviors. *Journal of Youth and Adolescence*, *43*(2), 175–192.

Hayslip, Bert & Smith, Gregory C. (Eds.). (2013). *Resilient grandparent caregivers: A strengths-based perspective*. New York, NY: Routledge.

He, Li; Mao, Yu; Sun, Jiangzhou; Zhuang, Kaixiang; Zhu, Xingxing; Qiu, Jiang & Chen, Xiaoyi. (2018). Examining brain structures associated with emotional intelligence and the mediated effect on trait creativity in young adults. *Frontiers in Psychology*, *9*(925).

Head, Katharine J.; Noar, Seth M.; Iannarino, Nicholas T. & Harrington, Nancy Grant. (2013). Efficacy of text messaging-based interventions for health promotion: A meta-analysis. *Social Science & Medicine*, *97*, 41–49.

Healthy Children. (Updated 2012, April 2). Breastfeeding mealtime milestones.

Healy, Jack. (2017, June 23). Out of high school, into real life. *New York Times*.

Heiman, Julia R.; Long, J. Scott; Smith, Shawna N.; Fisher, William A.; Sand,

Michael S. & Rosen, Raymond C. (2011). Sexual satisfaction and relationship happiness in midlife and older couples in five countries. *Archives of Sexual Behavior, 40*(4), 741–753.

Heimlich, Russell. (2011, June 2). *Purpose of college education. Fact Tank.* Washington, DC: Pew Research Center.

Henderson, Heather A.; Pine, Daniel S. & Fox, Nathan A. (2015). Behavioral inhibition and developmental risk: A dual-processing perspective. *Neuropsychopharmacology Reviews, 40*(1), 207–224.

Hendlin, Yogi Hale. (2018). I am a fake loop: The effects of advertising-based artificial selection. *Biosemiotics*, (In Press).

Hendry, Leo B. & Kloep, Marion. (2011). Lifestyles in emerging adulthood: Who needs stages anyway? In Jeffrey Jensen Arnett, et al. (Eds.), *Debating emerging adulthood: Stage or process?* (pp. 77–104). New York, NY: Oxford University Press.

Hendry, Mandy P. & Ledbetter, Andrew M. (2017). Narrating the past, enhancing the present: The associations among genealogical communication, family communication patterns, and family satisfaction. *Journal of Family Communication, 17*(2), 117–136.

Henrich, Joseph. (2015). Culture and social behavior. *Current Opinion in Behavioral Sciences*, 3, 84–89.

Henrich, Joseph; Heine, Steven J. & Norenzayan, Ara. (2010). The weirdest people in the world? *Behavioral and Brain Sciences*, 33(2/3), 61–83.

Henry, David B.; Deptula, Daneen P. & Schoeny, Michael E. (2012). Sexually transmitted infections and unintended pregnancy: A longitudinal analysis of risk transmission through friends and attitudes. *Social Development, 21*(1), 195–214.

Hentges, Rochelle F. & Wang, Ming-Te. (2018). Gender differences in the developmental cascade from harsh parenting to educational attainment: An evolutionary perspective. *Child Development, 89*(2), 397–413.

Herlofson, Katharina & Hagestad, Gunhild. (2012). Transformations in the role of grandparents across welfare states. In Sara Arber & Virpi Timonen (Eds.), *Contemporary grandparenting: Changing family relationships in global contexts* (pp. 27–49). Chicago, IL: Policy Press.

Hernández, Maciel M.; Robins, Richard W.; Widaman, Keith F. & Conger, Rand D. (2017). Ethnic pride, self-esteem, and school belonging: A reciprocal analysis over time. *Developmental Psychology*, 53(12), 2384–2396.

Heron, Melonie. (2018, July 26). *Deaths: Leading causes for 2016. National Vital Statistics Reports, 67*(6): National Vital Statistics System.

Herr, M.; Jeune, B.; Andersen-Ranberg, K.; Ankri, J.; Arai, Y.; Cubaynes, S., . . . Robine, J.-M. (2018). Frailty and associated factors among centenarians in the 5-COOP countries. *Gerontology, 64*, 521–531.

Herrman, Judith W.; Waterhouse, Julie K. & Chiquoine, Julie. (2011). Evaluation of an infant simulator intervention for teen pregnancy prevention. *Journal of Obstetric, Gynecologic & Neonatal Nursing, 40*(3), 322–328.

Herrmann, Julia; Schmidt, Isabelle; Kessels, Ursula & Preckel, Franzis. (2016). Big fish in big ponds: Contrast and assimilation effects on math and verbal self-concepts of students in within-school gifted tracks. *British Journal of Educational Psychology, 86*(2), 222–240.

Herschensohn, Julia R. (2007). *Language development and age.* New York, NY: Cambridge University Press.

Hertzog, Christopher. (2010). Regarding methods for studying behavioral development: The contributions and influence of K. Warner Schaie. *Research in Human Development*, 7(1), 1–8.

Herzog, Patricia Snell; Beadle, De Andre' T.; Harris, Daniel E.; Hood, Tiffany E. & Venugopal, Sanjana. (2016). Moral and cultural awareness in emerging adulthood: Preparing for multi-faith workplaces. *Religions*, 7(4).

Herzog, Serge. (2018). Financial aid and college persistence: Do student loans help or hurt? *Research in Higher Education, 59*(3), 273–301.

Hess, Thomas M.; Growney, Claire M. & Lothary, Allura F. (2019). Motivation moderates the impact of aging stereotypes on effort expenditure. *Psychology and Aging, 34*(1), 56–67.

Hewer, Mariko. (2014). Selling sweet nothings: Science shows food marketing's effects on children's minds — and appetites. *Observer*, 27(10).

Heyer, Djai B. & Meredith, Rhiannon M. (2017). Environmental toxicology: Sensitive periods of development and neurodevelopmental disorders. *NeuroToxicology*, 58, 23–41.

Heyes, Cecilia. (2016). Who knows? Metacognitive social learning strategies. *Trends in Cognitive Sciences, 20*(3), 204–213.

Heyes, Cecilia. (2018). Empathy is not in our genes. *Neuroscience and Biobehavioral Reviews, 95*, 499–507.

Heyman, Gene M. (2013). Quitting drugs: Quantitative and qualitative features. *Annual Review of Clinical Psychology, 9*, 29–59.

Hidalgo, Marco A. & Chen, Diane. (2019). Experiences of gender minority stress in cisgender parents of transgender/gender-expansive prepubertal children: A qualitative study. *Journal of Family Issues, 40*(7), 865–886.

Higgins, Matt. (2006, August 7). A series of flips creates some serious buzz. *New York Times*.

Hilgard, Joseph; Engelhardt, Christopher R. & Rouder, Jeffrey N. (2017). Overstated evidence for short-term effects of violent games on affect and behavior: A reanalysis of Anderson et al. (2010). *Psychological Bulletin, 143*(7), 757–774.

Hill, Erica & Hageman, Jon B. (Eds.). (2016). *The archaeology of ancestors: Death, memory, and veneration.* Gainesville, FL: University Press of Florida.

Hill, Patrick L.; Duggan, Peter M. & Lapsley, Daniel K. (2012). Subjective invulnerability, risk behavior, and adjustment in early adolescence. *Journal of Early Adolescence, 32*(4), 489–501.

Hill, Sarah E.; Prokosch, Marjorie L.; DelPriore, Danielle J.; Griskevicius, Vladas & Kramer, Andrew. (2016). Low childhood socioeconomic status promotes eating in the absence of energy need. *Psychological Science, 27*(3), 354–364.

Hillman, Charles H. (2014). An introduction to the relation of physical activity to cognitive and brain health, and scholastic achievement. *Monographs of the Society for Research in Child Development*, 79(4), 1–6.

Hinduja, Sameer & Patchin, Justin W. (2018). Connecting adolescent suicide to the severity of bullying and cyberbullying. *Journal of School Violence*, (In Press).

Hinnant, J. Benjamin; Nelson, Jackie A.; O'Brien, Marion; Keane, Susan P. & Calkins, Susan D. (2013). The interactive roles of parenting, emotion regulation and executive functioning in moral reasoning during middle childhood. *Cognition and Emotion, 27*(8), 1460–1468.

Hinton, Lisa; Dumelow, Carol; Rowe, Rachel & Hollowell, Jennifer. (2018). Birthplace choices: What are the information needs of women when choosing where to give birth in England? A qualitative study using online and face to face focus groups. *BMC Pregnancy and Childbirth, 18*(1).

Hirsh-Pasek, Kathy & Golinkoff, Roberta M. (2016, March 11). The preschool paradox: It's time to rethink our approach to early education [Review of the book *The importance of being little: What preschoolers really need from grownups*, by Erika Christakis]. *Science, 351*(6278), 1158.

Hitlin, Paul. (2018, September 28). *Internet, social media use and device ownership in U.S. have plateaued after years of growth.* Washington, DC: Pew Research Center.

Ho, Emily S. (2010). Measuring hand function in the young child. *Journal of Hand Therapy, 23*(3), 323–328.

Hoare, Carol Hren. (2002). *Erikson on development in adulthood: New insights from the unpublished papers.* New York, NY: Oxford University Press.

Hochman, Oshrat & Lewin-Epstein, Noah. (2013). Determinants of early retirement preferences in Europe: The role of grandparenthood. *International Journal of Comparative Sociology*, 54(1), 29–47.

Hodge, Samuel R.; Sato, Takahiro; Mukoyama, Takahito & Kozub, Francis M. (2013). Development of the physical educators' judgments about inclusion instrument for Japanese physical education majors and an analysis of their judgments. *International Journal of Disability, Development and Education, 60*(4), 332–346.

Hodson, Gordon; Crisp, Richard J.; Meleady, Rose & Earle, Megan. (2018). Intergroup contact as an agent of cognitive liberalization. *Perspectives on Psychological Science, 13*(5), 523–548.

Hofer, Claire; Eisenberg, Nancy; Spinrad, Tracy L.; Morris, Amanda S.; Gershoff, Elizabeth; Valiente, Carlos, . . . Eggum, Natalie D. (2013). Mother-adolescent conflict: Stability, change, and relations with externalizing and internalizing behavior problems. *Social Development, 22*(2), 259–279.

Hoff, Erika. (2013). Interpreting the early language trajectories of children from low-SES and language minority homes: Implications for closing achievement gaps. *Developmental Psychology, 49*(1), 4–14.

Hoff, Erika. (2018). Bilingual development in children of immigrant families. *Child Development Perspectives, 12*(2), 80–86.

Hoffman, Jessica L.; Teale, William H. & Paciga, Kathleen A. (2014). Assessing vocabulary learning in early childhood. *Journal of Early Childhood Literacy, 14*(4), 459–481.

Höjer, Ingrid & Sjöblom, Yvonne. (2014). Voices of 65 young people leaving care in Sweden: "There is so much I need to know!". *Australian Social Work, 67*(1), 71–87.

Holden, Constance. (2010). Myopia out of control. *Science, 327*(5961), 17.

Holland, James D. & Klaczynski, Paul A. (2009). Intuitive risk taking during adolescence. *Prevention Researcher, 16*(2), 8–11.

Holland, John L. (1997). *Making vocational choices: A theory of vocational personalities and work environments* (3rd ed.). Odessa, FL: Psychological Assessment Resources.

Holzer, Jessica; Canavan, Maureen & Bradley, Elizabeth. (2014). County-level correlation between adult obesity rates and prevalence of dentists. *JADA, 145*(9), 932–939.

Hong, David S. & Reiss, Allan L. (2014). Cognitive and neurological aspects of sex chromosome aneuploidies. *The Lancet Neurology, 13*(3), 306–318.

Hong, Jun Sung & Garbarino, James. (2012). Risk and protective factors for homophobic bullying in schools: An application of the social–ecological framework. *Educational Psychology Review, 24*(2), 271–285.

Hood, Michelle; Creed, Peter A. & Mills, Bianca J. (2017). Loneliness and online friendships in emerging adults. *Personality and Individual Differences,* (In Press).

Hook, Jennifer L. (2012). Working on the weekend: Fathers' time with family in the United Kingdom. *Journal of Marriage and Family, 74*(4), 631–642.

Hope, Elan C.; Hoggard, Lori S. & Thomas, Alvin. (2015). Emerging into adulthood in the face of racial discrimination: Physiological, psychological, and sociopolitical consequences for African American youth. *Translational Issues in Psychological Science, 1*(4), 342–351.

Horn, Stacey S. (2019). Sexual orientation and gender identity-based prejudice. *Child Development Perspectives, 13*(1), 21–27.

Horta, Bernardo L.; Hartwig, Fernando P. & Victora, Cesar G. (2018). Breastfeeding and intelligence in adulthood: Due to genetic confounding? *The Lancet Global Health, 6*(12), Pe1276–e1277.

Horton, Megan K.; Kahn, Linda G.; Perera, Frederica; Barr, Dana B. & Rauh, Virginia. (2012). Does the home environment and the sex of the child modify the adverse effects of prenatal exposure to chlorpyrifos on child working memory? *Neurotoxicology and Teratology, 34*(5), 534–541.

Hostinar, Camelia E.; Johnson, Anna E. & Gunnar, Megan R. (2015). Parent support is less effective in buffering cortisol stress reactivity for adolescents compared to children. *Developmental Science, 18*(2), 281–297.

Hostinar, Camelia E.; Nusslock, Robin & Miller, Gregory E. (2018). Future directions in the study of early-life stress and physical and emotional health: Implications of the neuroimmune network hypothesis. *Journal of Clinical Child & Adolescent Psychology, 47*(1), 142–156.

Howard, Kimberly S. (2010). Paternal attachment, parenting beliefs and children's attachment. *Early Child Development and Care, 180*(1/2), 157–171.

Howard, Sasha R. (2018). Genes underlying delayed puberty. *Molecular and Cellular Endocrinology, 476*, 119–128.

Howe, Tsu-Hsin; Sheu, Ching-Fan; Hsu, Yung-Wen; Wang, Tien-Ni & Wang, Lan-Wan. (2016). Predicting neurodevelopmental outcomes at preschool age for children with very low birth weight. *Research in Developmental Disabilities, 48*, 231–241.

Howell, Diane M.; Wysocki, Karen & Steiner, Michael J. (2010). Toilet training. *Pediatrics in Review, 31*(6), 262–263.

Hoyert, Donna L.; Kung, Hsiang-Ching & Smith, Betty L. (2005). *Deaths: Preliminary data for 2003. National Vital Statistics Reports, 53*(15). Hyattsville, MD: National Center for Health Statistics.

Hoyert, Donna L. & Xu, Jiaquan. (2012). *Deaths: Preliminary data for 2011. National Vital Statistics Reports, 61*(6). Hyattsville, MD: National Center for Health Statistics.

Hoyme, H. Eugene; Kalberg, Wendy O.; Elliott, Amy J.; Blankenship, Jason; Buckley, David; Marais, Anna-Susan, . . . May, Philip A. (2016). Updated clinical guidelines for diagnosing fetal alcohol spectrum disorders. *Pediatrics, 138*(2), e20154256.

Hrdy, Sarah B. (2009). *Mothers and others: The evolutionary origins of mutual understanding*. Cambridge, MA: Harvard University Press.

Hsu, William C.; Araneta, Maria Rosario G.; Kanaya, Alka M.; Chiang, Jane L. & Fujimoto, Wilfred. (2015). BMI cut points to identify at-risk Asian Americans for type 2 diabetes screening. *Diabetes Care, 38*(1), 150–158.

Hu, Youna; Shmygelska, Alena; Tran, David; Eriksson, Nicholas; Tung, Joyce Y. & Hinds, David A. (2016). GWAS of 89,283 individuals identifies genetic variants associated with self-reporting of being a morning person. *Nature Communications*, 7(10448).

Huang, Chiungjung. (2010). Mean-level change in self-esteem from childhood through adulthood: Meta-analysis of longitudinal studies. *Review of General Psychology, 14*(3), 251–260.

Huang, Jidong; Duan, Zongshuan; Kwok, Julian; Binns, Steven; Vera, Lisa E.; Kim, Yoonsang, . . . Emery, Sherry L. (2019). Vaping versus JUULing: How the extraordinary growth and marketing of JUUL transformed the US retail e-cigarette market. *Tobacco Control, 28*(2), 146.

Hughes, Claire & Devine, Rory T. (2015). Individual differences in theory of mind: A social perspective. In Richard M. Lerner (Ed.), *Handbook of child psychology and developmental science* (7th ed., Vol. 3). New York, NY: Wiley.

Hughes, Matthew L.; Geraci, Lisa & De Forrest, Ross L. (2013). Aging 5 years in 5 minutes: The effect of taking a memory test on older adults' subjective age. *Psychological Science, 24*(12), 2481–2488.

Hülür, Gizem; Wolf, Henrike; Riese, Florian & Theill, Nathan. (2019). Cognitive change at the end of life in nursing home residents: Differential trajectories of terminal decline. *Gerontology, 65*(1), 57–67.

Hunt, Earl B. (2011a). *Human intelligence*. New York, NY: Cambridge University Press.

Hunt, Earl B. (2011b). Where are we? Where are we going? Reflections on the current and future state of research on intelligence. In Robert J. Sternberg & Scott Barry Kaufman (Eds.), *The Cambridge handbook of intelligence*. New York, NY: Cambridge University Press.

Hunter, Jonathan & Maunder, Robert (Eds.). (2016). *Improving patient treatment with attachment theory: A guide for primary care practitioners and specialists*. New York, NY: Springer.

Huston, Aletha C.; Bobbitt, Kaeley C. & Bentley, Alison. (2015). Time spent in child care: How and why does it affect social development? *Developmental Psychology, 51*(5), 621–634.

Hutchinson, Esther A.; De Luca, Cinzia R.; Doyle, Lex W.; Roberts, Gehan & Anderson, Peter J. (2013). School-age outcomes of extremely preterm or extremely low birth weight children. *Pediatrics, 131*(4), e1053–e1061.

Huynh, Jimmy L. & Casaccia, Patrizia. (2013). Epigenetic mechanisms in multiple sclerosis: Implications for pathogenesis and treatment. *The Lancet Neurology, 12*(2), 195–206.

Hvistendahl, Mara. (2013). China heads off deadly blood disorder. *Science, 340*(6133), 677–678.

Hyde, Janet S. (2007). New directions in the study of gender similarities and differences. *Current Directions in Psychological Science, 16*(5), 259–263.

Hyde, Janet S. (2016). Sex and cognition: Gender and cognitive functions. *Current Opinion in Neurobiology*, 38, 53–56.

Hyslop, Anne. (2014). *The case against exit exams. New American Education Policy Brief*. Washington DC: New America Education Policy Program.

Iida, Hiroko & Rozier, R. Gary. (2013). Mother-perceived social capital and children's oral health and use of dental care in the United States. *American Journal of Public Health, 103*(3), 480–487.

Ikeda, Martin J. (2012). Policy and practice considerations for response to intervention: Reflections and commentary. *Journal of Learning Disabilities, 45*(3), 274–277.

Ilieva, Irena P. & Farah, Martha J. (2013). Enhancement stimulants: Perceived motivational and cognitive advantages. *Frontiers in Neuroscience*, 7(198).

Im, Myung Hee; Hughes, Jan N.; Cao, Qian & Kwok, Oi-Man. (2016). Effects of extracurricular participation during middle school on academic motivation and achievement at grade 9. *American Educational Research Journal*, 53(5), 1343–1375.

Inan, Hatice Z.; Trundle, Kathy C. & Kantor, Rebecca. (2010). Understanding natural sciences education in a Reggio Emilia-inspired preschool. *Journal of Research in Science Teaching*, 47(10), 1186–1208.

Inceoglu, Ilke; Segers, Jesse & Bartram, Dave. (2012). Age-related differences in work motivation. *Journal of Occupational and Organizational Psychology*, 75(2), 300–329.

Inhelder, Bärbel & Piaget, Jean. (1958). *The growth of logical thinking from childhood to adolescence: An essay on the construction of formal operational structures*. New York, NY: Basic Books.

Inhelder, Bärbel & Piaget, Jean. (1964). *The early growth of logic in the child: Classification and seriation*. New York, NY: Harper & Row.

Inhelder, Bärbel & Piaget, Jean. (2013a). *The early growth of logic in the child: Classification and seriation*. New York, NY: Routledge.

Inhelder, Bärbel & Piaget, Jean. (2013b). *The growth of logical thinking from childhood to adolescence: An essay on the construction of formal operational structures*. New York, NY: Routledge.

Insel, Thomas R. (2014). Mental disorders in childhood: Shifting the focus from behavioral symptoms to neurodevelopmental trajectories. *JAMA*, *311*(17), 1727–1728.

Insurance Institute for Highway Safety. (2018, December). Child safety: Motor vehicle crashes are a leading cause of death for children younger than 13.

Insurance Institute for Highway Safety. (2018, December). General statistics: Crashes took 37,133 lives in the U.S. in 2017.

Insurance Institute for Highway Safety, Highway Loss Data Institute. (2019, May). Older drivers.

Inzlicht, Michael & Schmader, Toni. (2012). *Stereotype threat: Theory, process, and application*. New York, NY: Oxford University Press.

Irwin, Scott; Galvez, Roberto; Weiler, Ivan Jeanne; Beckel-Mitchener, Andrea & Greenough, William. (2002). Brain structure and the functions of FMR1 protein. In Randi Jenssen Hagerman & Paul J. Hagerman (Eds.), *Fragile X syndrome: Diagnosis, treatment, and research* (3rd ed., pp. 191–205). Baltimore, MD: Johns Hopkins University Press.

Ivarsson, Andreas; Johnson, Urban; Andersen, Mark; Tranaeus, Ulrika; Stenling, Andreas & Lindwall, Magnus. (2017). Psychosocial factors and sport injuries: Meta-analyses for prediction and prevention. *Sports Medicine*, 47(2), 353–365.

Ivcevic, Zorana & Brackett, Marc. (2014). Predicting school success: Comparing conscientiousness, grit, and emotion regulation ability. *Journal of Research in Personality*, 52, 29–36.

Jack, Jordynn. (2014). *Autism and gender: From refrigerator mothers to computer geeks*. Urbana, IL: University of Illinois Press.

Jackson, Jeffrey B.; Miller, Richard B.; Oka, Megan & Henry, Ryan G. (2014). Gender differences in marital satisfaction: A meta-analysis. *Journal of Marriage and Family*, 76(1), 105–129.

Jackson, James C.; Santoro, Michael J.; Ely, Taylor M.; Boehm, Leanne; Kiehl, Amy L.; Anderson, Lindsay S. & Ely, E. Wesley. (2014). Improving patient care through the prism of psychology: Application of Maslow's hierarchy to sedation, delirium, and early mobility in the intensive care unit. *Journal of Critical Care*, 29(3), 438–444.

Jackson, James S.; Govia, Ishtar O. & Sellers, Sherrill L. (2011). Racial and ethnic influences over the life course. In Robert H. Binstock & Linda K. George (Eds.), *Handbook of aging and the social sciences* (7th ed., pp. 91–103). San Diego, CA: Academic Press.

Jaffe, Arthur C. (2011). Failure to thrive: Current clinical concepts. *Pediatrics in Review*, 32(3), 100–108.

Jamal, Ahmed; Phillips, Elyse; Gentzke, Andrea S.; Homa, David M.; Babb, Stephen D.; King, Brian A. & Neff, Linda J. (2018, January 19). *Current cigarette smoking among adults — United States, 2016. Morbidity and Mortality Weekly Report*, 67(2), 53–59. Atlanta, GA: Centers for Disease Control and Prevention.

Jambon, Marc & Smetana, Judith G. (2014). Moral complexity in middle childhood: Children's evaluations of necessary harm. *Developmental Psychology*, 50(1), 22–33.

James, Jenée; Ellis, Bruce J.; Schlomer, Gabriel L. & Garber, Judy. (2012). Sex-specific pathways to early puberty, sexual debut, and sexual risk taking: Tests of an integrated evolutionary–developmental model. *Developmental Psychology*, 48(3), 687–702.

James, Jacquelyn B.; McKechnie, Sharon & Swanberg, Jennifer. (2011). Predicting employee engagement in an age-diverse retail workforce. *Journal of Organizational Behavior*, 32(2), 173–196.

James, Karin H. (2017). The importance of handwriting experience on the development of the literate brain. *Current Directions in Psychological Science*, 26(6), 502–508.

James, Lori; Schmank, Christopher; Castro, Nichol & Buchanan, Tony. (2018). Tip of the tongue states increase under evaluative observation. *Journal of Psycholinguistic Research*, 47(1), 169–178.

James, Will. (2012, May 25). Report faults doctors: Long Island grand jury blames physicians, pharmacists for epidemic of abuse. *Wall Street Journal*.

James-Kangal, Neslihan; Weitbrecht, Eliza; Francis, Trenel & Whitton, Sarah. (2018). Hooking up and emerging adults' relationship attitudes and expectations. *Sexuality & Culture*, 22(3), 706–723.

Jankovic, Joseph. (2018). Parkinson's disease tremors and serotonin. *Brain*, *141*(3), 624–626.

Janse, Benjamin; Huijsman, Robbert; de Kuyper, Ruben Dennis Maurice & Fabbricotti, Isabelle Natalina. (2014). The effects of an integrated care intervention for the frail elderly on informal caregivers: A quasi-experimental study. *BMC Geriatrics*, *14*(1).

Jarcho, Johanna M.; Fox, Nathan A.; Pine, Daniel S.; Etkin, Amit; Leibenluft, Ellen; Shechner, Tomer & Ernst, Monique. (2013). The neural correlates of emotion-based cognitive control in adults with early childhood behavioral inhibition. *Biological Psychology*, *92*(2), 306–314.

Jaschke, Artur C.; Honing, Henkjan & Scherder, Erik J. A. (2018). Longitudinal analysis of music education on executive functions in primary school children. *Frontiers in Neuroscience*, *12*(103).

Jayson, Sharon. (2014, April 26). Shotgun weddings becoming relics of another time. *USA Today*.

Jednoróg, Katarzyna; Altarelli, Irene; Monzalvo, Karla; Fluss, Joel; Dubois, Jessica; Billard, Catherine, . . . Ramus, Franck. (2012). The influence of socioeconomic status on children's brain structure. *PLoS ONE*, 7(8), e42486.

Jenssen, Brian P. & Walley, Susan C. (2019). E-cigarettes and similar devices. *Pediatrics*, *143*(2).

Jha, Prabhat; Ramasundarahettige, Chinthanie; Landsman, Victoria; Rostron, Brian; Thun, Michael; Anderson, Robert N., . . . Peto, Richard. (2013). 21st-century hazards of smoking and benefits of cessation in the United States. *New England Journal of Medicine*, 368, 341–350.

Jia, Jianping; Wang, Fen; Wei, Cuibai; Zhou, Aihong; Jia, Xiangfei; Li, Fang, . . . Dong, Xiumin. (2014). The prevalence of dementia in urban and rural areas of China. *Alzheimer's & Dementia*, *10*(1), 1–9.

Jiang, Jingjing. (2018, May 2). *Millennials stand out for their technology use, but older generations also embrace digital life. Fact Tank*. Washington, DC: Pew Research Center.

Jimerson, Shane R.; Burns, Matthew K. & VanDerHeyden, Amanda M. (Eds.). (2016). *Handbook of response to intervention: The science and practice of multi-tiered systems of support*. New York, NY: Springer.

Johnson, Jonni L.; McWilliams, Kelly; Goodman, Gail S.; Shelley, Alexandra E. & Piper, Brianna. (2016). Basic principles of interviewing the child eyewitness. In William T. O'Donohue & Matthew Fanetti (Eds.), *Forensic interviews regarding child sexual abuse* (pp. 179–195). New York, NY: Springer.

Johnson, Matthew D. (2012). Healthy marriage initiatives: On the need for empiricism in policy implementation. *American Psychologist*, 67(4), 296–308.

Johnson, Michael P. (2008). *A typology of domestic violence: Intimate terrorism, violent resistance, and situational couple violence*. Hanover, NH: Northeastern University Press.

Johnson, Wendi; Giordano, Peggy; Manning, Wendy & Longmore, Monica. (2015). The Age–IPV curve: Changes in the perpetration of intimate partner violence during adolescence and young adulthood. *Journal of Youth and Adolescence*, 44(3), 708–726.

Johnson, Wendy; McGue, Matt & Deary, Ian J. (2014). Normative cognitive aging. In Deborah Finkel & Chandra A. Reynolds (Eds.), *Behavior genetics of cognition across the lifespan: Advances in behavior genetics* (Vol. 1, pp. 135–167). New York, NY: Springer.

Jonas, Eric & Kording, Konrad Paul. (2017). Could a neuroscientist understand a microprocessor? *PLoS Computational Biology, 13*(1), e1005268.

Jonas, Wibke; Bisceglia, Rossana; Meaney, Michael J.; Dudin, Aya; Fleming, Alison S. & Steiner, Meir. (2018). The role of breastfeeding in the association between maternal and infant cortisol attunement in the first postpartum year. *Acta Paediatrica, 107*(7), 1205–1217.

Jones, Andrea M. & Morris, Tracy L. (2012). Psychological adjustment of children in foster care: Review and implications for best practice. *Journal of Public Child Welfare, 6*(2), 129–148.

Jones, Catherine R. G.; Simonoff, Emily; Baird, Gillian; Pickles, Andrew; Marsden, Anita J. S.; Tregay, Jenifer, . . . Charman, Tony. (2018). The association between theory of mind, executive function, and the symptoms of autism spectrum disorder. *Autism Research, 11*(1), 95–109.

Jones, Jeffrey M. (2015, October 21). *In U.S., 58% back legal marijuana use*. Washington, DC: Gallup.

Jones, Mary C. (1965). Psychological correlates of somatic development. *Child Development, 36*(4), 899–911.

Jones, Owen R. & Vaupel, James W. (2017). Senescence is not inevitable. *Biogerontology, 18*(6), 965–971.

Jong, Jonathan; Ross, Robert; Philip, Tristan; Chang, Si-Hua; Simons, Naomi & Halberstadt, Jamin. (2018). The religious correlates of death anxiety: A systematic review and meta-analysis. *Religion, Brain & Behavior, 8*(1), 4–20.

Jong, Jyh-Tsorng; Kao, Tsair; Lee, Liang-Yi; Huang, Hung-Hsuan; Lo, Po-Tsung & Wang, Hui-Chung. (2010). Can temperament be understood at birth? The relationship between neonatal pain cry and their temperament: A preliminary study. *Infant Behavior and Development, 33*(3), 266–272.

Jopp, Daniela & Rott, Christoph. (2006). Adaptation in very old age: Exploring the role of resources, beliefs, and attitudes for centenarians' happiness. *Psychology and Aging, 21*(2), 266–280.

Jorgensen, Nathan & Nelson, Larry. (2018). Moving toward and away from others: Social orientations in emerging adulthood. *Journal of Applied Developmental Psychology, 58*, 66–76.

Jorgenson, Alicia Grattan; Hsiao, Ray Chih-Jui & Yen, Cheng-Fang. (2016). Internet addiction and other behavioral addictions. *Child & Adolescent Psychiatric Clinics, 25*(3), 509–520.

Jorm, Anthony F. (2000). Does old age reduce the risk of anxiety and depression? A review of epidemiological studies across the adult life span. *Psychological Medicine, 30*(1), 11–22.

Joseph, Michelle A.; O'Connor, Thomas G.; Briskman, Jacqueline A.; Maughan, Barbara & Scott, Stephen. (2014). The formation of secure new attachments by children who were maltreated: An observational study of adolescents in foster care. *Development and Psychopathology, 26*(1), 67–80.

Joshi, Kshamta & Billick, Stephen. (2017). Biopsychosocial causes of suicide and suicide prevention outcome studies in juvenile detention facilities: A review. *Psychiatric Quarterly, 88*(1), 141–153.

Julian, Megan M. (2013). Age at adoption from institutional care as a window into the lasting effects of early experiences. *Clinical Child and Family Psychology Review, 16*(2), 101–145.

Jung, Courtney. (2015). *Lactivism: How feminists and fundamentalists, hippies and yuppies, and physicians and politicians made breastfeeding big business and bad policy*. New York, NY: Basic Books.

Juster, Robert-Paul; Russell, Jennifer J.; Almeida, Daniel & Picard, Martin. (2016). Allostatic load and comorbidities: A mitochondrial, epigenetic, and evolutionary perspective. *Development and Psychopathology, 28*(4), 1117–1146.

Juvonen, Jaana & Graham, Sandra. (2014). Bullying in schools: The power of bullies and the plight of victims. *Annual Review of Psychology, 65*, 159–185.

Kaczynski, Andrew T.; Besenyi, Gina M.; Child, S.; Hughey, Morgan; Colabianchi, Natalie; McIver, Kevin L., . . . Pate, Russell R. (2018). Relationship of objective street quality attributes with youth physical activity: Findings from the Healthy Communities Study. *Pediatric Obesity, 13*(Suppl. 1), 7–13.

Kaestle, Christine E. & Evans, Larissa M. (2018). Implications of no recent sexual activity, casual sex, or exclusive sex for college women's sexual well-being depend on sexual attitudes. *Journal of American College Health, 66*(1), 32–40.

Kagan, Sarah H. (2018). When respect for our elders is ageism. *Geriatric Nursing, 39*(5), 604–606.

Kahana, Eva; Bhatta, Tirth; Lovegreen, Loren D.; Kahana, Boaz & Midlarsky, Elizabeth. (2013). Altruism, helping, and volunteering: Pathways to well-being in late life. *Journal of Aging and Health, 25*(1), 159–187.

Kahneman, Daniel. (2011). *Thinking, fast and slow*. New York, NY: Farrar, Straus and Giroux.

Kail, Robert V. (2013). Influences of credibility of testimony and strength of statistical evidence on children's and adolescents' reasoning. *Journal of Experimental Child Psychology, 116*(3), 747–754.

Kalanithi, Paul. (2016). *When breath becomes air*. New York, NY: Random House.

Kalaria, Raj N. (2018). The pathology and pathophysiology of vascular dementia. *Neuropharmacology, 134*, 226–239.

Kallio, Eeva. (2011). Integrative thinking is the key: An evaluation of current research into the development of adult thinking. *Theory Psychology, 21*(6), 785–801.

Kalshoven, Karianne & Taylor, Scott. (2018). Leadership: Philosophical perspectives and qualitative analysis of ethics—looking back, looking forward, looking around. *Journal of Business Ethics, 148*(1), 1–3.

Kalsner, Louisa & Chamberlain, Stormy J. (2015). Prader-Willi, Angelman, and 15q11-q13 Duplication syndromes. *The Pediatric Clinics of North America, 62*(3), 587–606.

Kaltiala-Heino, Riittakerttu; Fröjd, Sari & Marttunen, Mauri. (2015). Depression, conduct disorder, smoking and alcohol use as predictors of sexual activity in middle adolescence: A longitudinal study. *Health Psychology and Behavioral Medicine, 3*(1), 25–39.

Kandel, Denise B. (Ed.). (2002). *Stages and pathways of drug involvement: Examining the gateway hypothesis*. New York, NY: Cambridge University Press.

Kandel, Eric R. (2018). *The disordered mind: What unusual brains tell us about ourselves*. New York, NY: Farrar, Straus and Giroux.

Kandler, Christian. (2012). Nature and nurture in personality development: The case of neuroticism and extraversion. *Current Directions in Psychological Science, 21*(5), 290–296.

Kang, Hye-Kyung. (2014). Influence of culture and community perceptions on birth and perinatal care of immigrant women: Doulas' perspective. *The Journal of Perinatal Education, 23*(1), 25–32.

Kanner, Leo. (1943). Autistic disturbances of affective contact. *Nervous Child, 2*, 217–250.

Kapp, Steven K.; Gillespie-Lynch, Kristen; Sherman, Lauren E. & Hutman, Ted. (2013). Deficit, difference, or both? Autism and neurodiversity. *Developmental Psychology, 49*(1), 59–71.

Karbach, Julia & Unger, Kerstin. (2014). Executive control training from middle childhood to adolescence. *Frontiers in Psychology, 5*(390).

Karl, Katherine & Peluchette, Joy. (2016). Breaking boundaries and leaving bad impressions: Toward understanding workplace encounters with helicopter parents. *Journal of Organizational Psychology, 16*(1), 93–105.

Karlson, Kristian Bernt. (2019). College as equalizer? Testing the selectivity hypothesis. *Social Science Research, 80*, 216–229.

Karmiloff-Smith, Annette. (2010). A developmental perspective on modularity. In Britt Glatzeder, et al. (Eds.), *Towards a theory of thinking* (pp. 179–187). Heidelberg, Germany: Springer.

Karnatovskaia, Lioudmila V.; Gajic, Ognjen; Bienvenu, O. Joseph; Stevenson, Jennifer E. & Needham, Dale M. (2015). A holistic approach to the critically ill and Maslow's hierarchy. *Journal of Critical Care, 30*(1), 210–211.

Karraker, Amelia; DeLamater, John & Schwartz, Christine R. (2011). Sexual frequency decline from midlife to later life. *The Journals of Gerontology Series B: Psychological Sciences and Social Sciences, 66B*(4), 502–512.

Kärtner, Joscha; Borke, Jörn; Maasmeier, Kathrin; Keller, Heidi & Kleis, Astrid. (2011). Sociocultural influences on the development of self-recognition and self-regulation in Costa Rican and Mexican toddlers. *Journal of Cognitive Education and Psychology, 10*(1), 96–112.

Kärtner, Joscha; Keller, Heidi & Yovsi, Relindis D. (2010). Mother–infant interaction during the first 3 months: The emergence of culture-specific contingency patterns. *Child Development, 81*(2), 540–554.

Kastbom, Åsa A.; Sydsjö, Gunilla; Bladh, Marie; Priebe, Gisela & Svedin, Carl-Göran. (2015). Sexual debut before the age of 14 leads to poorer psychosocial health and risky behaviour in later life. *Acta Paediatrica, 104*(1), 91–100.

Kauffman, Jeffery. (2013). Culture, socialization, and traumatic death. In David K. Meagher & David E. Balk (Eds.), *Handbook of thanatology: The essential body of knowledge for the study of death, dying, and bereavement* (2nd ed.). New York, NY: Routledge.

Kauffman, James M.; Anastasiou, Dimitris & Maag, John W. (2017). Special education at the crossroad: An identity crisis and the need for a scientific reconstruction. *Exceptionality, 25*(2), 139–155.

Kaufman-Parks, Angela; DeMaris, Alfred; Giordano, Peggy; Manning, Wendy & Longmore, Monica. (2018). Intimate partner violence perpetration from adolescence to young adulthood: Trajectories and the role of familial factors. *Journal of Family Violence, 33*(1), 27–41.

Kaup, Allison R.; Xia, Feng; Launer, Lenore J.; Sidney, Stephen; Nasrallah, Ilya; Erus, Guray, . . . Yaffe, Kristine. (2018). Occupational cognitive complexity in earlier adulthood is associated with brain structure and cognitive health in midlife: The CARDIA study. *Neuropsychology, 32*(8), 895–905.

Kaur, Arshdeep. (2019). My child transformed me: Reflections of involved fathers. In Rajalakshmi Sriram (Ed.), *Fathering in India* (pp. 141–152). Singapore: Springer.

Kavanaugh, Robert D. (2011). Origins and consequences of social pretend play. In Anthony D. Pellegrini (Ed.), *The Oxford handbook of the development of play* (pp. 296–307). New York, NY: Oxford University Press.

Keating, Nancy L.; Herrinton, Lisa J.; Zaslavsky, Alan M.; Liu, Liyan & Ayanian, John Z. (2006). Variations in hospice use among cancer patients. *Journal of the National Cancer Institute, 98*(15), 1053–1059.

Keck, Carson & Taylor, Marian. (2018). Emerging research on the implications of hormone replacement therapy on coronary heart disease. *Current Atherosclerosis Reports, 20*(12).

Keers, Robert & Pluess, Michael. (2017). Childhood quality influences genetic sensitivity to environmental influences across adulthood: A life-course Gene × Environment interaction study. *Development and Psychopathology, 29*(5), 1921–1933.

Keller, Heidi. (2014). Introduction: Understanding relationships. In Hiltrud Otto & Heidi Keller (Eds.), *Different faces of attachment: Cultural variations on a universal human need* (pp. 3–25). New York, NY: Cambridge University Press.

Keller, Heidi; Borke, Jörn; Chaudhary, Nandita; Lamm, Bettina & Kleis, Astrid. (2010). Continuity in parenting strategies: A cross-cultural comparison. *Journal of Cross-Cultural Psychology, 41*(3), 391–409.

Keller, Peggy S.; El-Sheikh, Mona; Granger, Douglas A. & Buckhalt, Joseph A. (2012). Interactions between salivary cortisol and alpha-amylase as predictors of children's cognitive functioning and academic performance. *Physiology & Behavior, 105*(4), 987–995.

Kellogg, Ronald T. (2018). Professional writing expertise. In K. Anders Ericsson, et al. (Eds.), *The Cambridge handbook of expertise and expert performance* (pp. 413–430). New York, NY: Cambridge University Press.

Kelly, John R. (1993). *Activity and aging: Staying involved in later life*. Newbury Park, CA: Sage.

Kemmler, W.; Bebenek, M.; Kohl, M. & Stengel, S. (2015). Exercise and fractures in postmenopausal women. Final results of the controlled Erlangen Fitness and Osteoporosis Prevention Study (EFOPS). *Osteoporosis International*, 26(10), 2491–2499.

Kempe, Ruth S. & Kempe, C. Henry. (1978). *Child abuse*. Cambridge, MA: Harvard University Press.

Kemper, Susan. (2015). Language production in late life. In Annette Gerstenberg & Anja Voeste (Eds.), *Language development: The lifespan perspective* (pp. 59–75). Philadelphia, PA: John Benjamins.

Kempermann, Gerd. (2012). New neurons for 'survival of the fittest'. *Nature Reviews Neuroscience, 13*(10), 727–736.

Kempermann, Gerd. (2016). Adult neurogenesis: An evolutionary perspective. *Cold Spring Harbor Perspectives in Biology*, (In Press).

Kempermann, Gerd; Song, Hongjun & Gage, Fred H. (2015). Neurogenesis in the adult hippocampus. *Cold Spring Harbor Perspectives in Biology*, 7, a018812.

Kendall-Taylor, Nathaniel; Lindland, Eric; O'Neil, Moira & Stanley, Kate. (2014). Beyond prevalence: An explanatory approach to reframing child maltreatment in the United Kingdom. *Child Abuse & Neglect*, 38(5), 810–821.

Kendler, Howard H. (2002). Unified knowledge: Fantasy or reality? *Contemporary Psychology: APA Review of Books*, 47(5), 501–503.

Kennedy, Brian K. (2016). Advances in biological theories of aging. In Vern L. Bengtson & Richard Settersten (Eds.), *Handbook of theories of aging* (3rd ed., pp. 107–112). New York, NY: Springer Publishing Group.

Kenrick, Douglas T.; Griskevicius, Vladas; Neuberg, Steven L. & Schaller, Mark. (2010). Renovating the pyramid of needs: Contemporary extensions built upon ancient foundations. *Perspectives on Psychological Science*, 5(3), 292–314.

Keown, Louise J. & Palmer, Melanie. (2014). Comparisons between paternal and maternal involvement with sons: Early to middle childhood. *Early Child Development and Care, 184*(1), 99–117.

Kern, Ben D.; Graber, Kim C.; Shen, Sa; Hillman, Charles H. & McLoughlin, Gabriella. (2018). Association of school-based physical activity opportunities, socioeconomic status, and third-grade reading. *Journal of School Health*, 88(1), 34–43.

Kersken, Verena; Zuberbühler, Klaus & Gomez, Juan-Carlos. (2017). Listeners can extract meaning from non-linguistic infant vocalisations cross-culturally. *Scientific Reports*, 7.

Keselman, Alla; Smith, Catherine; Murcko, Anita & Kaufman, David R. (2019). Evaluating the quality of health information in a changing digital ecosystem. *Journal of Medical Internet Research, 21*(2), e11129.

Kesselring, Thomas & Müller, Ulrich. (2011). The concept of egocentrism in the context of Piaget's theory. *New Ideas in Psychology*, 29(3), 327–345.

Kessler, Ronald C.; Avenevoli, Shelli; Costello, E. Jane; Georgiades, Katholiki; Green, Jennifer G.; Gruber, Michael J., . . . Merikangas, Kathleen R. (2012). Prevalence, persistence, and sociodemographic correlates of *DSM-IV* disorders in the National Comorbidity Survey Replication Adolescent Supplement. *Archives of General Psychiatry*, 69(4), 372–380.

Keupp, Stefanie; Bancken, Christin; Schillmöller, Jelka; Rakoczy, Hannes & Behne, Tanya. (2016). Rational over-imitation: Preschoolers consider material costs and copy causally irrelevant actions selectively. *Cognition, 147*(3), 85–92.

Khandaker, Golam M.; Zimbron, Jorge; Dalman, Christina; Lewis, Glyn & Jones, Peter B. (2012). Childhood infection and adult schizophrenia: A meta-analysis of population-based studies. *Schizophrenia Research, 139*(1/3), 161–168.

Khurana, Atika; Romer, Daniel; Betancourt, Laura & Hurt, Hallam. (2018). Modeling trajectories of sensation seeking and impulsivity dimensions from early to late adolescence: Universal trends or distinct sub-groups? *Journal of Youth and Adolescence*, 47(9), 1992–2005.

Kidd, Celeste; Palmeri, Holly & Aslin, Richard N. (2013). Rational snacking: Young children's decision-making on the marshmallow task is moderated by beliefs about environmental reliability. *Cognition, 126*(1), 109–114.

Kiiski, Jouko; Määttä, Kaarina & Uusiautti, Satu. (2013). "For better and for worse, or until . . .": On divorce and guilt. *Journal of Divorce & Remarriage*, 54(7), 519–536.

Kiley, Dan. (1983). *The Peter Pan syndrome: Men who have never grown up*. New York, NY: Dodd Mead.

Kilgore, Paul E.; Grabenstein, John D.; Salim, Abdulbaset M. & Rybak, Michael. (2015). Treatment of Ebola virus disease. *Pharmacotherapy*, 35(1), 43–53.

Kim, Dong-Sik & Kim, Hyun-Sun. (2009). Body-image dissatisfaction as a predictor of suicidal ideation among Korean boys and girls in different stages of adolescence: A two-year longitudinal study. *The Journal of Adolescent Health*, 45(1), 47–54.

Kim, Hye-Jin; Min, Jin-Young; Min, Kyoung-Bok; Lee, Tae-Jin & Yoo, Seunghyun. (2018). Relationship among family environment, self-control, friendship quality, and adolescents' smartphone addiction in South Korea: Findings from nationwide data. *PLoS ONE, 13*(2), e0190896.

Kim, Hojin I. & Johnson, Scott P. (2013). Do young infants prefer an infant-directed face or a happy face? *International Journal of Behavioral Development*, 37(2), 125–130.

Kim, Heejung S. & Sasaki, Joni Y. (2014). Cultural neuroscience: Biology of the mind in cultural contexts. *Annual Review of Psychology, 65*, 487–514.

Kim, Joon Sik. (2011). Excessive crying: Behavioral and emotional regulation disorder in infancy. *Korean Journal of Pediatrics*, 54(6), 229–233.

Kim, Kyungmin; Cheng, Yen-Pi; Zarit, Steven H. & Fingerman, Karen L. (2015). Relationships between adults and parents in Asia. In Sheung-Tak Cheng, et al. (Eds.), *Successful aging* (pp. 101–122). Dordrecht, the Netherlands: Springer.

Kim, Pilyoung; Strathearn, Lane & Swain, James E. (2016). The maternal brain and its plasticity in humans. *Hormones and Behavior, 77*, 113–123.

Kim-Spoon, Jungmeen; Longo, Gregory S. & McCullough, Michael E. (2012). Parent-adolescent relationship quality as a moderator for the influences of parents' religiousness on adolescents' religiousness and adjustment. *Journal of Youth and Adolescence, 41*(12), 1576–1587.

King, Bruce M. (2013). The modern obesity epidemic, ancestral hunter-gatherers, and the sensory/reward control of food intake. *American Psychologist*, 68(2), 88–96.

King, Christian. (2018). Food insecurity and child behavior problems in fragile families. *Economics and Human Biology*, 28, 14–22.

Kirk, Elizabeth; Howlett, Neil; Pine, Karen J. & Fletcher, Ben. (2013). To sign or not to sign? The impact of encouraging infants to gesture on infant language and maternal mind-mindedness. *Child Development, 84*(2), 574–590.

Kirkham, Julie Ann & Kidd, Evan. (2017). The effect of Steiner, Montessori, and National Curriculum Education upon children's pretence and creativity. *Journal of Creative Behavior, 51*(1), 20–34.

Kirschner, Paul A. (2017). Stop propagating the learning styles myth. *Computers & Education, 106*, 166–171.

Kiserud, Torvid; Benachi, Alexandra; Hecher, Kurt; Perez, Rogelio González; Carvalho, José; Piaggio, Gilda & Platt, Lawrence D. (2018). The World Health Organization fetal growth charts: concept, findings, interpretation, and application. *American Journal of Obstetrics and Gynecology, 218*(2), S619–S629.

Kivipelto, Miia; Mangialasche, Francesca & Ngandu, Tiia. (2018). Lifestyle interventions to prevent cognitive impairment, dementia and Alzheimer disease. *Nature Reviews Neurology*, 14(11), 653–666.

Klaczynski, Paul A. (2001). Analytic and heuristic processing influences on adolescent reasoning and decision-making. *Child Development*, 72(3), 844–861.

Klaczynski, Paul A. (2011). Age differences in understanding precedent-setting decisions and authorities' responses to violations of deontic rules. *Journal of Experimental Child Psychology, 109*(1), 1–24.

Klaczynski, Paul A.; Daniel, David B. & Keller, Peggy S. (2009). Appearance idealization, body esteem, causal attributions, and ethnic variations in the development of obesity stereotypes. *Journal of Applied Developmental Psychology*, 30(4), 537–551.

Klaczynski, Paul A. & Felmban, Wejdan S. (2014). Heuristics and biases during adolescence: Developmental reversals and individual differences. In Henry Markovits (Ed.), *The developmental psychology of reasoning and decision-making* (pp. 84–111). New York, NY: Psychology Press.

Klass, Dennis & Steffen, Edith Maria (Eds.). (2017). *Continuing bonds in bereavement: New directions for research and practice*. New York, NY: Routledge.

Klaus, Marshall H. & Kennell, John H. (1976). *Maternal-infant bonding: The impact of early separation or loss on family development*. St. Louis, MO: Mosby.

Klaus, Susan F.; Ekerdt, David J. & Gajewski, Byron. (2012). Job satisfaction in birth cohorts of nurses. *Journal of Nursing Management*, 20(4), 461–471.

Klein, Denise; Mok, Kelvin; Chen, Jen-Kai & Watkins, Kate E. (2014). Age of language learning shapes brain structure: A cortical thickness study of bilingual and monolingual individuals. *Brain and Language, 131*, 20–24.

Klein, Stanley B. (2012). The two selves: The self of conscious experience and its brain. In Mark R. Leary & June Price Tangney (Eds.), *Handbook of self and identity* (pp. 617–637). New York, NY: Guilford Press.

Klein, Zoe A. & Romeo, Russell D. (2013). Changes in hypothalamic–pituitary–adrenal stress responsiveness before and after puberty in rats. *Hormones and Behavior, 64*(2), 357–363.

Klinger, Laura G.; Dawson, Geraldine; Burner, Karen & Crisler, Megan. (2014). Autism spectrum disorder. In Eric J. Mash & Russell A. Barkley (Eds.), *Child psychopathology* (3rd ed., pp. 531–572). New York, NY: Guilford Press.

Knapp, Emily A.; Bilal, Usama; Dean, Lorraine T.; Lazo, Mariana & Celentano, David D. (2019). Economic insecurity and deaths of despair in US counties. *American Journal of Epidemiology*, 188, kwz103.

Knopik, Valerie S.; Neiderhiser, Jenae M.; DeFries, John C. & Plomin, Robert. (2017). *Behavioral genetics* (7th ed.). New York, NY: Worth.

Knopman, Jaime M.; Krey, Lewis C.; Oh, Cheongeun; Lee, Jennifer; McCaffrey, Caroline & Noyes, Nicole. (2014). What makes them split? Identifying risk factors that lead to monozygotic twins after in vitro fertilization. *Fertility and Sterility, 102*(1), 82–89.

Knott, Craig S.; Coombs, Ngaire; Stamatakis, Emmanuel & Biddulph, Jane P. (2015). All cause mortality and the case for age specific alcohol consumption guidelines: Pooled analyses of up to 10 population based cohorts. *BMJ, 350*, h384.

Koch, Linda. (2015). Shaping the gut microbiome. *Nature Reviews Genetics, 16*, 2–3.

Kochanek, Kenneth D.; Murphy, Sherry L.; Xu, Jiaquan & Arias, Elizabeth. (2019, June 24). *Deaths: Final data for 2017. National Vital Statistics Reports*, 68(9). Hyattsville, MD: National Center for Health Statistics.

Kochanek, Kenneth D.; Xu, Jiaquan; Murphy, Sherry L.; Miniño, Arialdi M. & Kung, Hsiang-Ching. (2011). *Deaths: Preliminary data for 2009. National Vital Statistics Reports*, 59(4). Hyattsville, MD: National Center for Health Statistics.

Kochel, Karen P.; Ladd, Gary W.; Bagwell, Catherine L. & Yabko, Brandon A. (2015). Bully/victim profiles' differential risk for worsening peer acceptance: The role of friendship. *Journal of Applied Developmental Psychology, 41*, 38–45.

Kohlberg, Lawrence. (1963). The development of children's orientations toward a moral order: I. Sequence in the development of moral thought. *Vita Humana*, 6(1/2), 11–33.

Kohlberg, Lawrence; Levine, Charles & Hewer, Alexandra. (1983). *Moral stages: A current formulation and a response to critics*. New York, NY: Karger.

Kolb, Bryan & Gibb, Robbin. (2015). Childhood poverty and brain development. *Human Development*, 58(4/5), 215–217.

Kolb, Bryan; Harker, Allonna & Gibb, Robbin. (2017). Principles of plasticity in the developing brain. *Developmental Medicine & Child Neurology*, 59(12), 1218–1223.

Kolb, Bryan & Whishaw, Ian Q. (2013). *An introduction to brain and behavior* (4th ed.). New York, NY: Worth.

Koltko-Rivera, Mark E. (2006). Rediscovering the later version of Maslow's hierarchy of needs: Self-transcendence and opportunities for theory, research, and unification. *Review of General Psychology, 10*(4), 302–317.

Komisar, Erica. (2017). *Being there: Why prioritizing motherhood in the first three years matters*. New York, NY: TarcherPerigee.

Komp, Kathrin; van Tilburg, Theo & van Groenou, Marjolein Broese. (2010). Paid work between age 60 and 70 years in Europe: A matter of socio-economic status? *International Journal of Ageing and Later Life*, 5(1), 45–75.

Konner, Melvin. (2010). *The evolution of childhood: Relationships, emotion, mind*. Cambridge, MA: Harvard University Press.

Konner, Melvin. (2018). Nonmaternal care: A half-century of research. *Physiology & Behavior, 193*(Part A), 179–186.

Kono, Yumi; Yonemoto, Naohiro; Nakanishi, Hidehiko; Kusuda, Satoshi & Fujimura, Masanori. (2018). Changes in survival and neurodevelopmental outcomes of infants born at <25 weeks' gestation: A retrospective observational study in tertiary centres in Japan. *BMJ Paediatrics Open*, 2(1), e000211.

Konstam, Varda. (2015). *Emerging and young adulthood: Multiple perspectives, diverse narratives*. New York, NY: Springer.

Kooij, Dorien T. A. M.; Annet, H. D. E. Lange; Jansen, Paul G. W.; Kanfer, Ruth & Dikkers, Josje S. E. (2011). Age and work-related motives: Results of a meta-analysis. *Journal of Organizational Behavior*, 32(2), 197–225.

Koontz, Amanda; Norman, Lauren & Okorie, Sarah. (2019). Realistic love: Contemporary college women's negotiations of princess culture and the "reality" of romantic relationships. *Journal of Social and Personal Relationships*, 36(2), 535–555.

Kopp, Claire B. (2011). Development in the early years: Socialization, motor development, and consciousness. *Annual Review of Psychology*, 62, 165–187.

Korber, Maïlys & Oesch, Daniel. (2019). Vocational versus general education: Employment and earnings over the life course in Switzerland. *Advances in Life Course Research*, 40.

Kordas, Katarzyna; Burganowski, Rachael; Roy, Aditi; Peregalli, Fabiana; Baccino, Valentina; Barcia, Elizabeth, . . . Queirolo, Elena I. (2018). Nutritional status and diet as predictors of children's lead concentrations in blood and urine. *Environment International*, 111, 43–51.

Koretz, Daniel. (2017). *The testing charade: Pretending to make schools better*. Chicago, IL: University of Chicago Press.

Korte, J.; Bohlmeijer, E. T.; Cappeliez, P.; Smit, F. & Westerhof, G. J. (2012). Life review therapy for older adults with moderate depressive symptomatology: A pragmatic randomized controlled trial. *Psychological Medicine*, 42(6), 1163–1173.

Kosminsky, Phyllis. (2017). Working with continuing bonds from an attachment theoretical perspective. In Dennis Klass & Edith Maria Steffen (Eds.), *Continuing bonds in bereavement: New directions for research and practice*. New York, NY: Routledge.

Koster-Hale, Jorie & Saxe, Rebecca. (2013). Functional neuroimaging of theory of mind. In Simon Baron-Cohen, et al. (Eds.), *Understanding other minds: Perspectives from developmental social neuroscience* (3rd ed., pp. 132–163). New York, NY: Oxford University Press.

Kotsopoulos, Joanne; Gronwald, Jacek; Karlan, Beth Y.; Huzarski, Tomasz; Tung, Nadine; Moller, Pal, . . . Narod, Steven A. (2018). Hormone replacement therapy after oophorectomy and breast cancer risk among BRCA1 mutation carriers. *JAMA Oncology*, (In Press).

Kotter-Grühn, Dana; Kornadt, Anna E. & Stephan, Yannick. (2016). Looking beyond chronological age: Current knowledge and future directions in the study of subjective age. *Gerontology*, 62(1), 86–93.

Kozhimannil, Katy B. & Kim, Helen. (2014). Maternal mental illness. *Science*, 345(6198), 755.

Kozo, Justine; Sallis, James F.; Conway, Terry L.; Kerr, Jacqueline; Cain, Kelli; Saelens, Brian E., . . . Owen, Neville. (2012). Sedentary behaviors of adults in relation to neighborhood walkability and income. *Health Psychology*, 31(6), 704–713.

Kramer, Karen; Pak, Sunjin & Park, So Young. (2018). 'Can't have it all': A longitudinal analysis of the effect of parental leave on early-career wage growth. *SSRN*, (In Press).

Krampe, Ralf T. & Charness, Neil. (2018). Aging and expertise. In K. Anders Ericsson, et al. (Eds.), *The Cambridge handbook of expertise and expert performance* (pp. 835–856). New York, NY: Cambridge University Press.

Krans, Elizabeth E. & Davis, Matthew M. (2012). *Preventing Low Birthweight*: 25 years, prenatal risk, and the failure to reinvent prenatal care. *American Journal of Obstetrics and Gynecology*, 206(5), 398–403.

Krause, Elizabeth D.; Vélez, Clorinda E.; Woo, Rebecca; Hoffmann, Brittany; Freres, Derek R.; Abenavoli, Rachel M. & Gillham, Jane E. (2018). Rumination, depression, and gender in early adolescence: A longitudinal study of a bidirectional model. *Journal of Early Adolescence*, 38(7), 923–946.

Kreager, Derek A.; Molloy, Lauren E.; Moody, James & Feinberg, Mark E. (2016). Friends first? The peer network origins of adolescent dating. *Journal of Research on Adolescence*, 26(2), 257–269.

Krebs, Erin E.; Gravely, Amy; Nugent, Sean; Jensen, Agnes C.; DeRonne, Beth; Goldsmith, Elizabeth S., . . . Noorbaloochi, Siamak. (2018). Effect of opioid vs nonopioid medications on pain-related function in patients with chronic back pain or hip or knee osteoarthritis pain: The SPACE randomized clinical trial. *JAMA*, 319(9), 872–882.

Kremen, William S.; Moore, Caitlin S.; Franz, Carol E.; Panizzon, Matthew S. & Lyons, Michael J. (2014). Cognition in middle adulthood. In Deborah Finkel & Chandra A. Reynolds (Eds.), *Behavior genetics of cognition across the lifespan: Advances in behavior genetics* (Vol. 1, pp. 105–134). New York, NY: Springer.

Krisberg, Kim. (2014). Public health messaging: How it is said can influence behaviors: Beyond the facts. *The Nation's Health*, 44(6), 1, 20.

Kroger, Jane & Marcia, James E. (2011). The identity statuses: Origins, meanings, and interpretations. In Seth J. Schwartz, et al. (Eds.), *Handbook of identity theory and research* (pp. 31–53). New York, NY: Springer.

Kroncke, Anna P.; Willard, Marcy & Huckabee, Helena. (2016). Optimal outcomes and recovery. In, *Assessment of autism spectrum disorder: Critical issues in clinical, forensic and school settings* (pp. 23–33). New York, NY: Springer.

Krouse, William J. (2012, November 14). *Gun control legislation. CRS Report for Congress*. Washington, DC: Congressional Research Service. RL32842

Krueger, Robert F. & Eaton, Nicholas R. (2015). Transdiagnostic factors of mental disorders. *World Psychiatry*, 14(1), 27–29.

Kruse, Gina R.; Kalkhoran, Sara & Rigotti, Nancy A. (2017). Use of electronic cigarettes among U.S. adults with medical comorbidities. *AJPM*, 52(6), 798–804.

Krzych-Fałta, Edyta; Furmanczyk, Konrad; Piekarska, Barbara; Raciborski, Filip; Tomaszewska, Aneta; Walkiewicz, Artur, . . . Samoliński, Bolesław Krzysztof. (2018). Extent of protective or allergy-inducing effects in cats and dogs. *Annals of Agricultural and Environmental Medicine*, 25(2), 268–273.

Kubin, Laura. (2019). Is there a resurgence of vaccine preventable diseases in the U.S.? *Journal of Pediatric Nursing*, 44, 115–118.

Kübler-Ross, Elisabeth. (1975). *Death: The final stage of growth*. Englewood Cliffs, NJ: Prentice-Hall.

Kübler-Ross, Elisabeth. (1997). *On death and dying*. New York, NY: Scribner.

Kübler-Ross, Elisabeth & Kessler, David. (2005). *On grief and grieving: Finding the meaning of grief through the five stages of loss*. New York, NY: Scribner.

Kuete, Victor (Ed.). (2017). *Medicinal spices and vegetables from Africa: Therapeutic potential against metabolic, inflammatory, infectious and systemic diseases*. San Diego, CA: Academic Press.

Kuhl, Patricia K. (2004). Early language acquisition: Cracking the speech code. *Nature Reviews Neuroscience*, 5(11), 831–843.

Kuhn, Deanna. (2013). Reasoning. In Philip D. Zelazo (Ed.), *The Oxford handbook of developmental psychology* (Vol. 1, pp. 744–764). New York, NY: Oxford University Press.

Kulke, Louisa; Von Duhn, Britta; Schneider, Dana & Rakoczy, Hannes. (2018). Is implicit theory of mind a real and robust phenomenon? Results from a systematic replication study. *Psychological Science*, 29(6), 888–900.

Kumar, Gayathri S.; Pan, Liping; Park, Sohyun; Lee-Kwan, Seung Hee; Onufrak, Stephen & M., Blanck. Heidi. (2014, August 15). *Sugar-sweetened beverage consumption among adults — 18 States, 2012. Morbidity and Mortality Weekly Report*, 63(32), 686–690. Atlanta, GA: Centers for Disease Control and Prevention.

Kumar, Shaina A. & Mattanah, Jonathan F. (2018). Interparental conflict, parental intrusiveness, and interpersonal functioning in emerging adulthood. *Personal Relationships*, 25(1), 120–133.

Kundu, Tapas K. (Ed.). (2013). *Epigenetics: Development and disease*. New York, NY: Springer.

Kuperberg, Arielle. (2012). Reassessing differences in work and income in cohabitation and marriage. *Journal of Marriage and Family*, 74(4), 688–707.

Kurdek, Lawrence A. (2006). Differences between partners from heterosexual, gay, and lesbian cohabiting couples. *Journal of Marriage and Family*, 68(2), 509–528.

Kutob, Randa M.; Senf, Janet H.; Crago, Marjorie & Shisslak, Catherine M. (2010). Concurrent and longitudinal predictors of self-esteem in elementary and middle school girls. *Journal of School Health*, 80(5), 240–248.

Kuvaas, Bård; Buch, Robert; Weibel, Antoinette; Dysvik, Anders & Nerstad, Christina G. L. (2017). Do intrinsic and extrinsic motivation relate differently to employee outcomes? *Journal of Economic Psychology, 61*, 244–258.

Kuwahara, Keisuke; Kochi, Takeshi; Nanri, Akiko; Tsuruoka, Hiroko; Kurotani, Kayo; Pham, Ngoc Minh, . . . Mizoue, Tetsuya. (2014). Flushing response modifies the association of alcohol consumption with markers of glucose metabolism in Japanese men and women. *Alcoholism: Clinical and Experimental Research*, 38(4), 1042–1048.

Kvalvik, Liv G.; Haug, Kjell; Klungsøyr, Kari; Morken, Nils-Halvdan; Deroo, Lisa A. & Skjærven, Rolv. (2017). Maternal smoking status in successive pregnancies and risk of having a small for gestational age infant. *Paediatric and Perinatal Epidemiology, 31*(1), 21–28.

Kypri, Kypros; Davie, Gabrielle; McElduff, Patrick; Connor, Jennie & Langley, John. (2014). Effects of lowering the minimum alcohol purchasing age on weekend assaults resulting in hospitalization in New Zealand. *American Journal of Public Health, 104*(8), 1396–1401.

Kypri, Kypros; Voas, Robert B.; Langley, John D.; Stephenson, Shaun C. R.; Begg, Dorothy J.; Tippetts, A. Scott & Davie, Gabrielle S. (2006). Minimum purchasing age for alcohol and traffic crash injuries among 15- to 19-year-olds in New Zealand. *American Journal of Public Health, 96*(1), 126–131.

La Fauci, Luigi. (2018). The changing sexual life course of gay men and lesbians in contemporary Italy. *European Societies*, (In Press).

Labouvie-Vief, Gisela. (2015). *Integrating emotions and cognition throughout the lifespan*. New York, NY: Springer.

Lachs, Mark S. & Pillemer, Karl A. (2015, November 12). Elder abuse. *New England Journal of Medicine*, 373(20), 1947–1956.

Ladd, Helen F. & Sorensen, Lucy C. (2017). Returns to teacher experience: Student achievement and motivation in middle school. *Education Finance and Policy, 12*(2), 241–279.

Lagattuta, Kristin H. (2014). Linking past, present, and future: Children's ability to connect mental states and emotions across time. *Child Development Perspectives*, 8(2), 90–95.

Lai, Stephanie A.; Benjamin, Rebekah G.; Schwanenflugel, Paula J. & Kuhn, Melanie R. (2014). The longitudinal relationship between reading fluency and reading comprehension skills in second-grade children. *Reading & Writing Quarterly: Overcoming Learning Difficulties*, 30(2), 116–138.

Laier, Christian; Pawlikowski, Mirko & Brand, Matthias. (2014). Sexual picture processing interferes with decision-making under ambiguity. *Archives of Sexual Behavior, 43*(3), 473–482.

Lake, Stephanie & Kerr, Thomas. (2017). The challenges of projecting the public health impacts of marijuana legalization in Canada. *International Journal of Health Policy Management*, 6(5), 285–287.

Lalande, Kathleen M. & Bonanno, George A. (2006). Culture and continuing bonds: A prospective comparison of bereavement in the United States and the People's Republic of China. *Death Studies, 30*(4), 303–324.

Lam, Chun Bun; McHale, Susan M. & Crouter, Ann C. (2012). Parent–child shared time from middle childhood to late adolescence: Developmental course and adjustment correlates. *Child Development, 83*(2), 2089–2103.

Lamb, Michael E. (1982). Maternal employment and child development: A review. In Michael E. Lamb (Ed.), *Nontraditional families: Parenting and child development* (pp. 45–69). Hillsdale, NJ: Erlbaum.

Lambert, Scott & Lyons, Christopher. (2016). *Taylor and Hoyt's pediatric ophthalmology and strabismus* (5th ed.). New York, NY: Elsevier.

Lamichhane, Bidhan; McDaniel, Mark; Waldum, Emily & Braver, Todd. (2018). Age-related changes in neural mechanisms of prospective memory. *Cognitive, Affective, & Behavioral Neuroscience, 18*(5), 982–999.

Lamm, Bettina; Keller, Heidi; Teiser, Johanna; Gudi, Helene; Yovsi, Relindis D.; Freitag, Claudia, . . . Lohaus, Arnold. (2018). Waiting for the second treat: Developing culture-specific modes of self-regulation. *Child Development,* 89 (3), e261–e277.

Lander, Eric S. (2016). The heroes of CRISPR. *Cell, 164*(1/2), 18–28.

Lando, Amy M. & Lo, Serena C. (2014). Consumer understanding of the benefits and risks of fish consumption during pregnancy. *American Journal of Lifestyle Medicine*, 8(2), 88–92.

Lane, Jonathan D. & Harris, Paul L. (2014). Confronting, representing, and believing counterintuitive concepts: Navigating the natural and the supernatural. *Perspectives on Psychological Science*, 9(2), 144–160.

Langeslag, Sandra J. E.; Muris, Peter & Franken, Ingmar H. A. (2013). Measuring romantic love: Psychometric properties of the infatuation and attachment scales. *The Journal of Sex Research*, 50(8), 739–747.

Långström, Niklas; Rahman, Qazi; Carlström, Eva & Lichtenstein, Paul. (2010). Genetic and environmental effects on same-sex sexual behavior: A population study of twins in Sweden. *Archives of Sexual Behavior, 39*(1), 75–80.

Laninga-Wijnen, Lydia; Gremmen, Mariola C.; Dijkstra, Jan Kornelis; Veenstra, René; Vollebergh, Wilma A. M. & Harakeh, Zeena. (2019). The role of academic status norms in friendship selection and influence processes related to academic achievement. *Developmental Psychology*, 55(2), 337–350.

Lansford, Jennifer E.; Sharma, Chinmayi; Malone, Patrick S.; Woodlief, Darren; Dodge, Kenneth A.; Oburu, Paul, . . . Di Giunta, Laura. (2014). Corporal punishment, maternal warmth, and child adjustment: A longitudinal study in eight countries. *Journal of Clinical Child & Adolescent Psychology*, 43(4), 670–685.

Lapan, Candace & Boseovski, Janet J. (2017). When peer performance matters: Effects of expertise and traits on children's self-evaluations after social comparison. *Child Development*, 88(6), 1860–1872.

Lara-Cinisomo, Sandraluz; Fuligni, Allison Sidle & Karoly, Lynn A. (2011). Preparing preschoolers for kindergarten. In DeAnna M. Laverick & Mary Renck Jalongo (Eds.), *Transitions to early care and education* (Vol. 4, pp. 93–105). New York, NY: Springer.

Larose, Joanie; Boulay, Pierre; Sigal, Ronald J.; Wright, Heather E. & Kenny, Glen P. (2013). Age-related decrements in heat dissipation during physical activity occur as early as the age of 40. *PLoS ONE*, 8(12), e83148.

Larsen, Peter A. (2018). Transposable elements and the multidimensional genome. *Chromosome Research*, 26(1/2), 1–3.

Larzelere, Robert E. & Cox, Ronald B. (2013). Making valid causal inferences about corrective actions by parents from longitudinal data. *Journal of Family Theory & Review*, 5(4), 282–299.

Larzelere, Robert E.; Cox, Ronald B. & Swindle, Taren M. (2015). Many replications do not causal inferences make: The need for critical replications to test competing explanations of nonrandomized studies. *Perspectives on Psychological Science, 10*(3), 380–389.

Larzelere, Robert E.; Gunnoe, Marjorie Lindner; Roberts, Mark W. & Ferguson, Christopher J. (2017). Children and parents deserve better parental discipline research: Critiquing the evidence for exclusively "positive" parenting. *Marriage & Family Review*, 53(1), 24–35.

Lattanzi-Licht, Marcia. (2013). Religion, spirituality, and dying. In David K. Meagher & David E. Balk (Eds.), *Handbook of thanatology: The essential body of knowledge for the study of death, dying, and bereavement* (2nd ed., pp. 9–16). New York, NY: Routledge.

Laurent, Heidemarie K. (2014). Clarifying the contours of emotion regulation: Insights from parent–child stress research. *Child Development Perspectives*, 8(1), 30–35.

Laurino, Mercy Y.; Bennett, Robin L.; Saraiya, Devki S.; Baumeister, Lisa; Doyle, Debra L.; Leppig, Kathleen, . . . Raskind, Wendy H. (2005). Genetic evaluation and counseling of couples with recurrent miscarriage: Recommendations of the National Society of Genetic Counselors. *Journal of Genetic Counseling, 14*(3), 165–181.

Laursen, Brett; Hartl, Amy C.; Vitaro, Frank; Brendgen, Mara; Dionne, Ginette & Boivin, Michel. (2017). The spread of substance use and delinquency between adolescent twins. *Developmental Psychology*, 53(2), 329–339.

Lauster, Nathanael T. (2008). Better homes and families: Housing markets and young couple stability in Sweden. *Journal of Marriage and Family, 70*(4), 891–903.

Law, James; Rush, Robert; King, Tom; Westrupp, Elizabeth & Reilly, Sheena. (2018). Early home activities and oral language skills in middle childhood: A quantile analysis. *Child Development*, 89(1), 295–309.

Layton, Jill; Li, Xiaochen; Shen, Changyu; de Groot, Mary; Lange, Leslie; Correa, Adolfo & Wessel, Jennifer. (2018). Type 2 diabetes genetic risk scores are associated with increased type 2 diabetes risk among African Americans by cardiometabolic status. *Clinical Medicine Insights: Endocrinology and Diabetes, 11*.

Le Duc, James W. & Yuan, Zhiming. (2018). Network for safe and secure labs. *Science, 362*(6412), 267.

Leach, Penelope. (2011). The EYFS and the real foundations of children's early years. In Richard House (Ed.), *Too much, too soon?: Early learning and the erosion of childhood*. Stroud, UK: Hawthorn.

Leavitt, Judith W. (2009). *Make room for daddy: The journey from waiting room to birthing room*. Chapel Hill, NC: University of North Carolina Press.

LeBlanc, Nicole J.; Simon, Naomi M.; Reynolds, Charles F.; Shear, M. Katherine; Skritskaya, Natalia & Zisook, Sidney. (2019). Relationship between complicated grief and depression: Relevance, etiological mechanisms, and implications. In João Quevedo et al. (Eds.), *Neurobiology of depression: Road to novel therapeutics* (pp. 231–239). London: Academic Press.

LeCuyer, Elizabeth A. & Swanson, Dena Phillips. (2016). African American and European American mothers' limit setting and their 36-month-old children's responses to limits, self-concept, and social competence. *Journal of Family Issues*, 37(2), 270–296.

Lee, Barbara Coombs. (2019). *Finish strong: Putting your priorities first at life's end*. Portland, OR: Compassion & Choices.

Lee, Chun-Chia & Chiou, Wen-Bin. (2016). More eagerness, more suffering from search bias: Accuracy incentives and need for cognition exacerbate the detrimental effects of excessive searching in finding romantic partners online. *Journal of Behavioral Decision Making, 29*(1), 3–11.

Lee, Dohoon; Brooks-Gunn, Jeanne; McLanahan, Sara S.; Notterman, Daniel & Garfinkel, Irwin. (2013). The Great Recession, genetic sensitivity, and maternal harsh parenting. *Proceedings of the National Academy of Sciences, 110*(34), 13780–13784.

Lee, David M.; Nazroo, James; O'Connor, Daryl B.; Blake, Margaret & Pendleton, Neil. (2015). Sexual health and well-being among older men and women in England: Findings from the English longitudinal study of ageing. *Archives of Sexual Behavior*, (In Press).

Lee, Grace Y. & Kisilevsky, Barbara S. (2014). Fetuses respond to father's voice but prefer mother's voice after birth. *Developmental Psychobiology, 56*(1), 1–11.

Lee, Moosung; Oi-yeung Lam, Beatrice; Ju, Eunsu & Dean, Jenny. (2016). Part-time employment and problem behaviors: Evidence from adolescents in South Korea. *Journal of Research on Adolescence*, (In Press).

Lee, RaeHyuck; Zhai, Fuhua; Brooks-Gunn, Jeanne; Han, Wen-Jui & Waldfogel, Jane. (2014). Head Start participation and school readiness: Evidence from the early childhood longitudinal study–birth cohort. *Developmental Psychology, 50*(1), 202–215.

Lee, Soojeong & Shouse, Roger C. (2011). The impact of prestige orientation on shadow education in South Korea. *Sociology of Education, 84*(3), 212–224.

Lee, Shawna J. & Altschul, Inna. (2015). Spanking of young children: Do immigrant and U.S.-born Hispanic parents differ? *Journal of Interpersonal Violence, 30*(3), 475–498.

Lee, Shawna J.; Altschul, Inna & Gershoff, Elizabeth T. (2015). Wait until your father gets home? Mother's and fathers' spanking and development of child aggression. *Children and Youth Services Review*, 52, 158–166.

Lee, Yuan-Hsuan; Ko, Chih-Hung & Chou, Chien. (2015). Re-visiting Internet addiction among Taiwanese students: A cross-sectional comparison of students' expectations, online gaming, and online social interaction. *Journal of Abnormal Child Psychology, 43*(3), 589–599.

Lehner, Ben. (2013). Genotype to phenotype: Lessons from model organisms for human genetics. *Nature Reviews Genetics, 14*(3), 168–178.

Leiter, Valerie & Herman, Sarah. (2015). Guinea pig kids: Myths or modern Tuskegees? *Sociological Spectrum*, 35(1), 26–45.

Leman, Patrick J. & Björnberg, Marina. (2010). Conversation, development, and gender: A study of changes in children's concepts of punishment. *Child Development, 81*(3), 958–971.

Lemieux, André. (2012). Post-formal thought in gerontagogy or beyond Piaget. *Journal of Behavioral and Brain Science*, 2(3), 399–406.

Lemish, Daphna & Kolucki, Barbara. (2013). Media and early childhood development. In Pia Rebello Britto, et al. (Eds.), *Handbook of early childhood development research and its impact on global policy*. New York, NY: Oxford University Press.

Lengua, Liliana J.; Garstein, Maria A. & Prinzie, Peter. (2019). Temperament and personality trait development in the family: Interactions and transactions with parenting from infancy through adolescence. In Dan P. Mcadams, et al. (Eds.), *Handbook of personality development* (pp. 201–220). New York, NY: Guilford.

Lenhart, Amanda. (2015, April 9). *Teen, social media and technology overview 2015: Smartphone facilitate shifts in communication landscape for teens. Pew Research Center: Internet, Science & Tech*. Washington, DC: Pew Research Center.

Lenhart, Amanda; Anderson, Monica & Smith, Aaron. (2015, October 1). *Teens, technology and romantic relationships. Pew Research Center: Internet, Science & Tech*. Washington, DC: Pew Research Center.

Leonard, Hayley C. & Hill, Elisabeth L. (2014). Review: The impact of motor development on typical and atypical social cognition and language: A systematic review. *Child and Adolescent Mental Health, 19*(3), 163–170.

Leonard, Julia A.; Lee, Yuna & Schulz, Laura E. (2017). Infants make more attempts to achieve a goal when they see adults persist. *Science, 357*(6357), 1290–1294.

Leonoff, Arthur. (2015). *The good divorce: A psychoanalyst's exploration of separation, divorce, and childcare*. New York, NY: Routledge.

Leopold, Thomas & Skopek, Jan. (2015a). The delay of grandparenthood: A cohort comparison in East and West Germany. *Journal of Marriage and Family*, 77(2), 441–460.

Leopold, Thomas & Skopek, Jan. (2015b). The demography of grandparenthood: An international profile. *Social Forces, 94*(2), 801–832.

Lepousez, Gabriel; Nissant, Antoine & Lledo, Pierre-Marie. (2015). Adult neurogenesis and the future of the rejuvenating brain circuits. *Neuron, 86*(2), 387–401.

Lerner, Richard M.; Overton, F. Willis; Freund, Alexandra M. & Lamb, Michael E. (2010). *The handbook of life-span development*. Hoboken, NJ: Wiley.

Leshner, Alan I. & Dzau, Victor J. (2018). Good gun policy needs research. *Science*, 359(6381), 1195.

Leslie, Mitch. (2012). Gut microbes keep rare immune cells in line. *Science, 335*(6075), 1428.

Lessne, Deborah & Yanez, Christina. (2016, December 20). *Student reports of bullying: Results from the 2015 School Crime Supplement to the National Crime Victimization Survey*. Washington, DC: National Center for Education Statistics.

Lester, Barry M.; Conradt, Elisabeth; Lagasse, Linda L.; Tronick, Edward Z.; Padbury, James F. & Marsit, Carmen J. (2018). Epigenetic programming by maternal behavior in the human infant. *Pediatrics, 142*(4), e20171890.

Lester, Patricia; Leskin, Gregory; Woodward, Kirsten; Saltzman, William; Nash, William; Mogil, Catherine, . . . Beardslee, William. (2011). Wartime deployment and military children: Applying prevention science to enhance family resilience. In Shelley MacDermid Wadsworth & David Riggs (Eds.), *Risk and resilience in U.S. military families* (pp. 149–173). New York, NY: Springer.

Leung, Sumie; Mareschal, Denis; Rowsell, Renee; Simpson, David; Laria, Leon; Grbic, Amanda & Kaufman, Jordy. (2016). Oscillatory activity in the infant brain and the representation of small numbers. *Frontiers in Systems Neuroscience, 10*(4).

Leuzy, Antoine; Heurling, Kerstin; Ashton, Nicholas; Schöll, Michael & Zimmer, Eduardo R. (2018). *In vivo* detection of Alzheimer's disease. *Yale Journal of Biology and Medicine, 91*(3), 291–300.

Levey, Emma K. V.; Garandeau, Claire F.; Meeus, Wim & Branje, Susan. (2019). The longitudinal role of self-concept clarity and best friend delinquency in adolescent delinquent behavior. *Journal of Youth and Adolescence, 48*(6), 1068–1081.

Levine, Phillip B. & McKnight, Robin. (2017). Firearms and accidental deaths: Evidence from the aftermath of the Sandy Hook school shooting. *Science*, 358(6368), 1324–1328.

Levy, David T.; Borland, Ron; Lindblom, Eric N.; Goniewicz, Maciej L.; Meza, Rafael; Holford, Theodore R., . . . Abrams, David B. (2018). Potential deaths averted in USA by replacing cigarettes with e-cigarettes. *Tobacco Control*, 27(1), 18–25.

Levy, Marion; Boulle, Fabien; Steinbusch, Harry; Hove, Daniël; Kenis, Gunter & Lanfumey, Laurence. (2018). Neurotrophic factors and neuroplasticity pathways in the pathophysiology and treatment of depression. *Psychopharmacology*, 235(8), 2195–2220.

Lewandowski, Lawrence J. & Lovett, Benjamin J. (2014). Learning disabilities. In Eric J. Mash & Russell A. Barkley (Eds.), *Child psychopathology* (3rd ed., pp. 625–669). New York, NY: Guilford Press.

Lewin, Alisa. (2018). Intentions to live together among couples living apart: Differences by age and gender. *European Journal of Population, 34*(5), 721–743.

Lewin, Kurt. (1945). The Research Center for Group Dynamics at Massachusetts Institute of Technology. *Sociometry, 8*(2), 126–136.

Lewis, Ariane & Greer, David. (2017). Current controversies in brain death determination. *Nature Reviews Neurology, 13*, 505–509.

Lewis, John D.; Theilmann, Rebecca J.; Townsend, Jeanne & Evans, Alan C. (2013). Network efficiency in autism spectrum disorder and its relation to brain overgrowth. *Frontiers in Human Neuroscience, 7*, 845.

Lewis, Kristen & Burd-Sharps, Sarah. (2010). *The measure of America 2010–2011: Mapping risks and resilience*. New York, NY: New York University Press.

Lewis, Lawrence B.; Antone, Carol & Johnson, Jacqueline S. (1999). Effects of prosodic stress and serial position on syllable omission in first words. *Developmental Psychology, 35*(1), 45–59.

Lewis, Michael. (2010). The emergence of human emotions. In Michael Lewis, et al. (Eds.), *Handbook of emotions* (3rd ed.). New York, NY: Guilford Press.

Lewis, Michael & Brooks, Jeanne. (1978). Self-knowledge and emotional development. In Michael Lewis & L. A. Rosenblum (Eds.), *Genesis of behavior* (Vol. 1, pp. 205–226). New York, NY: Plenum Press.

Lewis, Michael & Kestler, Lisa (Eds.). (2012). *Gender differences in prenatal substance exposure*. Washington, DC: American Psychological Association.

Lewis, Marc D. (2013). The development of emotional regulation: Integrating normative and individual differences through developmental neuroscience. In Philip D. Zelazo (Ed.), *The Oxford handbook of developmental psychology* (Vol. 2, pp. 81–97). New York, NY: Oxford University Press.

Li, Jin; Fung, Heidi; Bakeman, Roger; Rae, Katharine & Wei, Wanchun. (2014). How European American and Taiwanese mothers talk to their children about learning. *Child Development, 85*(3), 1206–1221.

Li, Liman Man Wai; Masuda, Takahiko & Russell, Matthew J. (2014). The influence of cultural lay beliefs: Dialecticism and indecisiveness in European Canadians and Hong Kong Chinese. *Personality and Individual Differences, 68*, 6–12.

Li, Ting & Zhang, Yanlong. (2015). Social network types and the health of older adults: Exploring reciprocal associations. *Social Science & Medicine, 130*(2), 59–68.

Li, Weilin; Farkas, George; Duncan, Greg J.; Burchinal, Margaret R. & Vandell, Deborah Lowe. (2013). Timing of high-quality child care and cognitive, language, and preacademic development. *Developmental Psychology, 49*(8), 1440–1451.

Li, Yaoran; Garza, Veronica; Keicher, Anne & Popov, Vitaliy. (2018). Predicting high school teacher use of technology: Pedagogical beliefs, technological beliefs and attitudes, and teacher training. *Technology, Knowledge and Learning*, (In Press).

Li, Yibing & Lerner, Richard M. (2011). Trajectories of school engagement during adolescence: Implications for grades, depression, delinquency, and substance use. *Developmental Psychology, 47*(1), 233–247.

Liben, Lynn S. (2016). We've come a long way, baby (but we're not there yet): Gender past, present, and future. *Child Development, 87*(1), 5–28.

Libertus, Klaus & Hauf, Petra. (2017). Editorial: Motor skills and their foundational role for perceptual, social, and cognitive development. *Frontiers in Psychology, 8*(301).

Libertus, Melissa E.; Feigenson, Lisa & Halberda, Justin. (2013). Is approximate number precision a stable predictor of math ability? *Learning and Individual Differences, 25*, 126–133.

Liew, Jeffrey. (2012). Effortful control, executive functions, and education: Bringing self-regulatory and social-emotional competencies to the table. *Child Development Perspectives, 6*(2), 105–111.

Lillard, Angeline S. (2013). Playful learning and Montessori education. *American Journal of Play, 5*(2), 157–186.

Lillard, Angeline S.; Lerner, Matthew D.; Hopkins, Emily J.; Dore, Rebecca A.; Smith, Eric D. & Palmquist, Carolyn M. (2013). The impact of pretend play on children's development: A review of the evidence. *Psychological Bulletin, 139*(1), 1–34.

Lillard, Angeline S. & Taggart, Jessica. (2018). Pretend play and fantasy: What if Montessori was right? *Child Development Perspectives*, (In Press).

Lim, Cher Ping; Zhao, Yong; Tondeur, Jo; Chai, Ching Sing & Tsai, Chin-Chung. (2013). Bridging the gap: Technology trends and use of technology in schools. *Educational Technology & Society, 16*(2), 59–68.

Lin, Frank R.; Yaffe, Kristine; Xia, Jin; Xue, Qian-Li; Harris, Tamara B.; Purchase-Helzner, Elizabeth, . . . Simonsick, Eleanor M. (2013). Hearing loss and cognitive decline in older adults. *JAMA Internal Medicine, 173*(4), 293–299.

Lin, Lin; Cockerham, Deborah; Chang, Zhengsi & Natividad, Gloria. (2016). Task speed and accuracy decrease when multitasking. *Technology, Knowledge and Learning, 21*(3), 307–323.

Lin, Phoebe. (2016). Risky behaviors: Integrating adolescent egocentrism with the theory of planned behavior. *Review of General Psychology, 20*(4), 392–398.

Lindberg, Laura Duberstein; Maddow-Zimet, Isaac & Boonstra, Heather. (2016). Changes in adolescents' receipt of sex education, 2006–2013. *Journal of Adolescent Health*, 58(6), 621–627.

Lipton, Eric. (2017, March 29). E.P.A. chief, rejecting agency's science, chooses not to ban insecticide. *New York Times*.

Liu, Andrew H. (2015). Revisiting the hygiene hypothesis for allergy and asthma. *The Journal of Allergy and Clinical Immunology, 136*(4), 860–865.

Liu, Chang & Neiderhiser, Jenae M. (2017). Using genetically informed designs to understand the environment: The importance of family-based approaches. In Patrick H. Tolan & Leventhal Bennett L. (Eds.), *Gene-environment transactions in developmental psychopathology: The role in intervention research* (pp. 95–110). New York: NY: Springer.

Liu, Cindy H.; Stevens, Courtney; Wong, Sylvia H. M.; Yasui, Miwa & Chen, Justin A. (2019). The prevalence and predictors of mental health diagnoses and suicide among U.S. college students: Implications for addressing disparities in service use. *Depression and Anxiety, 36*(1), 8–17.

Liu, Dong & Xin, Ziqiang. (2014). Birth cohort and age changes in the self-esteem of Chinese adolescents: A cross-temporal meta-analysis, 1996–2009. *Journal of Research on Adolescence*.

Liu, Junsheng; Chen, Xinyin; Coplan, Robert J.; Ding, Xuechen; Zarbatany, Lynne & Ellis, Wendy. (2015). Shyness and unsociability and their relations with adjustment in Chinese and Canadian children. *Journal of Cross-Cultural Psychology, 46*(3), 371–386.

Liu, Ning; Vigod, Simone N.; Farrugia, M. Michèle; Urquia, Marcelo L. & Ray, Joel G. (2018). Intergenerational teen pregnancy: A population-based cohort study. *BJOG, 125*(13), 1766–1774.

Liu, Peiwei & Feng, Tingyong. (2017). The overlapping brain region accounting for the relationship between procrastination and impulsivity: A voxel-based morphometry study. *Neuroscience, 360*, 9–17.

Liu, Xiaojing; Gao, Xiaodong; Zhang, Li; Yuan, Zilong; Zhang, Chen; Lu, Weizhao, . . . Xie, Jindong. (2018). Age-related changes in fiber tracts in healthy adult brains: A generalized q-sampling and connectometry study. *Journal of Magnetic Resonance Imaging, 48*(2), 369–381.

Liu, Zuyun; Chen, Brian H.; Assimes, Themistocles L.; Ferrucci, Luigi; Horvath, Steve & Levine, Morgan E. (2019). The role of epigenetic aging in education and racial/ethnic mortality disparities among older U.S. women. *Psychoneuroendocrinology, 104*, 18–24.

Livas-Dlott, Alejandra; Fuller, Bruce; Stein, Gabriela L.; Bridges, Margaret; Mangual Figueroa, Ariana & Mireles, Laurie. (2010). Commands, competence, and *cariño*: Maternal socialization practices in Mexican American families. *Developmental Psychology, 46*(3), 566–578.

Livingston, Gretchen & Brown, Anna. (2017, May 18). *Intermarriage in the U.S. 50 years after Loving v. Virginia. Social & Demographic Trends*. Washington, DC: Pew Research Center.

Livingston, Lucy Anne & Happé, Francesca. (2017). Conceptualising compensation in neurodevelopmental disorders: Reflections from autism spectrum disorder. *Neuroscience and Biobehavioral Reviews, 80*, 729–742.

Lo, June C.; Lee, Su Mei; Lee, Xuan Kai; Sasmita, Karen; Chee, Nicholas I. Y. N.; Tandi, Jesisca, . . . Chee, Michael W. L. (2018). Sustained benefits of delaying school start time on adolescent sleep and well-being. *Sleep, 41*(6).

LoBue, Vanessa. (2013). What are we so afraid of? How early attention shapes our most common fears. *Child Development Perspectives*, 7(1), 38–42.

Lochman, John E.; Dishion, Thomas J.; Powell, Nicole P.; Boxmeyer, Caroline L.; Qu, Lixin & Sallee, Meghann. (2015). Evidence-based preventive intervention for preadolescent aggressive children: One-year outcomes following randomization to group versus individual delivery. *Journal of Consulting and Clinical Psychology*, 83(4), 728–735.

Löckenhoff, Corinna E.; De Fruyt, Filip; Terracciano, Antonio; McCrae, Robert R.; De Bolle, Marleen; Costa, Paul T., . . . Yik, Michelle. (2009). Perceptions of aging across 26 cultures and their culture-level associates. *Psychology and Aging*, 24(4), 941–954.

Lockhart, Kristi L.; Goddu, Mariel K. & Keil, Frank C. (2018). When saying "I'm best" is benign: Developmental shifts in perceptions of boasting. *Developmental Psychology*, 54(3), 521–535.

Lockhart, Kristi L. & Keil, Frank C. (2018). What heals and why? Children's understanding of medical treatments. *Monographs of the Society for Research in Child Development*, 83(2).

Lodge, Amy C. & Umberson, Debra. (2012). All shook up: Sexuality of mid- to later life married couples. *Journal of Marriage and Family*, 74(3), 428–443.

Loeb, Susanna & Byun, Erika. (2019). Testing, accountability, and school improvement. *The ANNALS of the American Academy of Political and Social Science*, 683(1), 94–109.

Loeber, Rolf & Burke, Jeffrey D. (2011). Developmental pathways in juvenile externalizing and internalizing problems. *Journal of Research on Adolescence*, 21(1), 34–46.

Loeber, Rolf; Capaldi, Deborah M. & Costello, Elizabeth. (2013). Gender and the development of aggression, disruptive behavior, and delinquency from childhood to early adulthood. In Patrick H. Tolan & Bennett L. Leventh (Eds.), *Disruptive behavior disorders* (pp. 137–160). New York, NY: Springer.

Lønfeldt, Nicole N.; Verhulst, Frank C.; Strandberg-Larsen, Katrine; Plessen, Kerstin J. & Lebowitz, Eli R. (2018). Assessing risk of neurodevelopmental disorders after birth with oxytocin: A systematic review and meta-analysis. *Psychological Medicine*, (In Press).

Lopez, Anna B.; Huynh, Virginia W. & Fuligni, Andrew J. (2011). A longitudinal study of religious identity and participation during adolescence. *Child Development*, 82(4), 1297–1309.

Lopez-Hartmann, Maja; Wens, Johan; Verhoeven, Veronique & Remmen, Roy. (2012). The effect of caregiver support interventions for informal caregivers of community-dwelling frail elderly: A systematic review. *International Journal of Integrated Care*, 12, 1–16.

López-Otín, Carlos; Blasco, Maria A.; Partridge, Linda; Serrano, Manuel & Kroemer, Guido. (2013). The hallmarks of aging. *Cell*, 153(6), 1194–1217.

López-Pinar, Carlos; Martínez-Sanchís, Sonia; Carbonell-Vayá, Enrique; Fenollar-Cortés, Javier & Sánchez-Meca, Julio. (2018). Long-term efficacy of psychosocial treatments for adults with attention-deficit/hyperactivity disorder: A meta-analytic review. *Frontiers in Psychology*, 9(638).

Lorthe, Elsa; Torchin, Héloïse; Delorme, Pierre; Ancel, Pierre-Yves; Marchand-Martin, Laetitia; Foix-L'Hélias, Laurence, . . . Kayem, Gilles. (2018). Preterm premature rupture of membranes at 22–25 weeks' gestation: Perinatal and 2-year outcomes within a national population-based study (EPIPAGE-2). *American Journal of Obstetrics and Gynecology*, 219(3), 298.e291–298.e214.

Lou, Wutao; Wang, Defeng; Wong, Adrian; Chu, Winnie C. W.; Mok, Vincent C. T. & Shi, Lin. (2019). Frequency-specific age-related decreased brain network diversity in cognitively healthy elderly: A whole-brain data-driven analysis. *Human Brain Mapping*, 40(1), 340–351.

Loucks, Jeff & Price, Heather L. (2019). Memory for temporal order in action is slow developing, sensitive to deviant input, and supported by foundational cognitive processes. *Developmental Psychology*, 55(2), 263–273.

Loughrey, David G.; Kelly, Michelle E.; Kelley, George A.; Brennan, Sabina & Lawlor, Brian A. (2018). Association of age-related hearing loss with cognitive function, cognitive impairment, and dementia: A systematic review and meta-analysis. *JAMA Otolaryngology*, 44(2), 115–126.

Lourenço, Orlando. (2012). Piaget and Vygotsky: Many resemblances, and a crucial difference. *New Ideas in Psychology*, 30(3), 281–295.

Love, Heather A.; Spencer, Chelsea M.; May, Scott A.; Mendez, Marcos & Stith, Sandra M. (2018). Perpetrator risk markers for intimate terrorism and situational couple violence: A meta-analysis. *Trauma, Violence & Abuse*, (In Press).

Lovell, Brian & Wetherell, Mark A. (2011). The cost of caregiving: Endocrine and immune implications in elderly and non elderly caregivers. *Neuroscience & Biobehavioral Reviews*, 35(6), 1342–1352.

Loyd, Aerika Brittian & Gaither, Sarah E. (2018). Racial/ethnic socialization for White youth: What we know and future directions. *Journal of Applied Developmental Psychology*, 59, 54–64.

Lubienski, Christopher; Puckett, Tiffany & Brewer, T. Jameson. (2013). Does homeschooling "work"? A critique of the empirical claims and agenda of advocacy organizations. *Peabody Journal of Education*, 88(3), 378–392.

Lubke, Gitta H.; Mcartor, Daniel B.; Boomsma, Dorret I. & Bartels, Meike. (2018). Genetic and environmental contributions to the development of childhood aggression. *Developmental Psychology*, 54(1), 39–50.

Lucca, Kelsey & Wilbourn, Makeba Parramore. (2018). Communicating to learn: Infants' pointing gestures result in optimal learning. *Child Development*, 89(3), 941–960.

Ludmer, Jaclyn A.; Gonzalez, Andrea; Kennedy, James; Masellis, Mario; Meinz, Paul & Atkinson, Leslie. (2018). Association between maternal childhood maltreatment and mother-infant attachment disorganization: Moderation by maternal oxytocin receptor gene and cortisol secretion. *Hormones and Behavior*, 102, 23–33.

Ludwig-Mayerhofer, Wolfgang; Solga, Heike; Leuze, Kathrin; Dombrowski, Rosine; Künster, Ralf; Ebralidze, Ellen, . . . Kühn, Susanne. (2019). Vocational education and training and transitions into the labor market. In Hans-Peter Blossfeld & Hans-Günther Roßbach (Eds.), *Education as a lifelong process* (pp. 277–295). Wiesbaden, Germany: Springer.

Luecken, Linda J.; Lin, Betty; Coburn, Shayna S.; MacKinnon, David P.; Gonzales, Nancy A. & Crnic, Keith A. (2013). Prenatal stress, partner support, and infant cortisol reactivity in low-income Mexican American families. *Psychoneuroendocrinology*, 38(12), 3092–3101.

Luengo-Prado, María J. & Sevilla, Almudena. (2012). Time to cook: Expenditure at retirement in Spain. *The Economic Journal*, 123(569), 764–789.

Luhmann, Maike & Hawkley, Louise C. (2016). Age differences in loneliness from late adolescence to oldest old age. *Developmental Psychology*, 52(6), 943–959.

Luhmann, Maike; Hofmann, Wilhelm; Eid, Michael & Lucas, Richard E. (2012). Subjective well-being and adaptation to life events: A meta-analysis. *Journal of Personality and Social Psychology*, 102(3), 592–615.

Luna, Beatriz; Paulsen, David J.; Padmanabhan, Aarthi & Geier, Charles. (2013). The teenage brain: Cognitive control and motivation. *Current Directions in Psychological Science*, 22(2), 94–100.

Lundahl, Alyssa; Kidwell, Katherine M. & Nelson, Timothy D. (2014). Parental underestimates of child weight: A meta-analysis. *Pediatrics*, 133(3), e689–e703.

Lundberg, Shelly; Pollak, Robert A. & Stearns, Jenna. (2016). Family inequality: Diverging patterns in marriage, cohabitation, and childbearing. *Journal of Economic Perspectives*, 30(2), 79–102.

Lundquist, Gunilla; Rasmussen, Birgit H. & Axelsson, Bertil. (2011). Information of imminent death or not: Does it make a difference? *Journal of Clinical Oncology*, 29(29), 3927–3931.

Luo, Rufan; Tamis-LeMonda, Catherine S.; Kuchirko, Yana; Ng, Florrie F. & Liang, Eva. (2014). Mother–child book-sharing and children's storytelling skills in ethnically diverse, low-income families. *Infant and Child Development*, 23(4), 402–425.

Lupski, James R. (2013). Genome mosaicism: One human, multiple genomes. *Science*, 341(6144), 358–359.

Lushin, Viktor; Jaccard, James & Kaploun, Victor. (2017). Parental monitoring, adolescent dishonesty and underage drinking: A nationally representative study. *Journal of Adolescence*, 57, 99–107.

Luthar, Suniya S. (2015). Resilience in development: A synthesis of research across five decades.

In Dante Cicchetti & Donald J. Cohen (Eds.), *Developmental psychopathology* (2nd ed., Vol. 3). Hoboken, NJ: Wiley.

Luthar, Suniya S.; Cicchetti, Dante & Becker, Bronwyn. (2000). The construct of resilience: A critical evaluation and guidelines for future work. *Child Development*, *71*(3), 543–562.

Luthar, Suniya S.; Small, Phillip J. & Ciciolla, Lucia. (2018). Adolescents from upper middle class communities: Substance misuse and addiction across early adulthood. *Development and Psychopathology*, *30*(1), 315–335.

Lutz, Wolfgang; Muttarak, Raya & Striessnig, Erich. (2014). Universal education is key to enhanced climate adaptation. *Science*, *346*(6213), 1061–1062.

Luyckx, Koen; Klimstra, Theo A.; Duriez, Bart; Van Petegem, Stijn & Beyers, Wim. (2013). Personal identity processes from adolescence through the late 20s: Age trends, functionality, and depressive symptoms. *Social Development*, *22*(4), 701–721.

Lyall, Donald M.; Inskip, Hazel M.; Mackay, Daniel; Deary, Ian J.; McIntosh, Andrew M.; Hotopf, Matthew, . . . Smith, Daniel J. (2016). Low birth weight and features of neuroticism and mood disorder in 83,545 participants of the UK Biobank cohort. *British Journal of Psychiatry Open*, *2*(1), 38–44.

Lynch, Scott M. & Brown, J. Scott. (2011). Stratification and inequality over the life course. In Robert H. Binstock & Linda K. George (Eds.), *Handbook of aging and the social sciences* (7th ed., pp. 105–117). San Diego, CA: Academic Press.

Lyons, Michael J.; Panizzon, Matthew S.; Liu, Weijian; Mckenzie, Ruth; Bluestone, Noah J.; Grant, Michael D., . . . Xian, Hong. (2017). A longitudinal twin study of general cognitive ability over four decades. *Developmental Psychology*, *53*(6), 1170–1177.

Lyons, Sophie; Arcara, Jennet; Deardorff, Julianna & Gomez, Anu Manchikanti. (2019). Financial strain and contraceptive use among women in the United States: Differential effects by age. *Women's Health Issues*, *29*(2), 153–160.

Lyssens-Danneboom, Vicky & Mortelmans, Dimitri. (2014). Living apart together and money: New partnerships, traditional gender roles. *Journal of Marriage and Family*, *76*(5), 949–966.

Ma, Defu; Ning, Yibing; Gao, Hongchong; Li, Wenjun; Wang, Junkuan; Zheng, Yingdong, . . . Wang, Peiyu. (2014). Nutritional status of breast-fed and non-exclusively breast-fed infants from birth to age 5 months in 8 Chinese cities. *Asia Pacific Journal of Clinical Nutrition*, *23*(2), 282–292.

Ma-Kellams, Christine; Or, Flora; Baek, Ji Hyun & Kawachi, Ichiro. (2016). Rethinking suicide surveillance Google search data and self-reported suicidality differentially estimate completed suicide risk. *Clinical Psychological Science*, *4*(3), 480–484.

Mac Dougall, Kristin; Beyene, Yewoubdar & Nachtigall, Robert D. (2013). Age shock: Misperceptions of the impact of age on fertility before and after IVF in women who conceived after age 40. *Human Reproduction*, *28*(2), 350–356.

MacDorman, Marian F. & Rosenberg, Harry M. (1993). *Trends in infant mortality by cause of death and other characteristics, 1960–88. Vital and Health Statistic*, *20*(20). Hyattsville, MD: National Center for Health Statistics.

Macgregor, Stuart; Lind, Penelope A.; Bucholz, Kathleen K.; Hansell, Narelle K.; Madden, Pamela A. F.; Richter, Melinda M., . . . Whitfield, John B. (2009). Associations of ADH and ALDH2 gene variation with self report alcohol reactions, consumption and dependence: An integrated analysis. *Human Molecular Genetics*, *18*(3), 580–593.

Machado, Liana; Thompson, Laura M. & Brett, Christopher H. R. (2019). Visual analogue mood scale scores in healthy young versus older adults. *International Psychogeriatrics*, *31*(3), 417–424.

Mackenzie, Karen J.; Anderton, Stephen M. & Schwarze, Jürgen. (2014). Viral respiratory tract infections and asthma in early life: Cause and effect? *Clinical & Experimental Allergy*, *44*(1), 9–19.

MacKenzie, Michael J.; Nicklas, Eric; Brooks-Gunn, Jeanne & Waldfogel, Jane. (2011). Who spanks infants and toddlers? Evidence from the fragile families and child well-being study. *Children and Youth Services Review*, *33*(8), 1364–1373.

Macmillan, Ross & Copher, Ronda. (2005). Families in the life course: Interdependency of roles, role configurations, and pathways. *Journal of Marriage and Family*, *67*(4), 858–879.

MacNeill, Leigha A.; Ram, Nilam; Bell, Martha Ann; Fox, Nathan A. & Pérez-Edgar, Koraly. (2018). Trajectories of infants' biobehavioral development: Timing and rate of A-not-B performance gains and EEG maturation. *Child Development*, *89*(3), 711–724.

Macosko, Evan Z. & McCarroll, Steven A. (2013). Our fallen genomes. *Science*, *342*(6158), 564–565.

MacSwan, Jeff. (2018). Academic English as standard language ideology: A renewed research agenda for asset-based language education. *Language Teaching Research*, (In Press).

MacWhinney, Brian. (2015). Language development. In Richard M. Lerner (Ed.), *Handbook of child psychology and developmental science* (7th ed., Vol. 2, pp. 296–338). New York, NY: Wiley.

Maddox, Keith B. & Perry, Jennifer M. (2018). Racial appearance bias: Improving evidence-based policies to address racial disparities. *Policy Insights from the Behavioral and Brain Sciences*, *5*(1), 57–65.

Madigan, Sheri; Browne, Dillon; Racine, Nicole; Mori, Camille & Tough, Suzanne. (2019). Association between screen time and children's performance on a developmental screening test. *JAMA Pediatrics*, *173*(3), 244–250.

Malina, Robert M.; Bouchard, Claude & Bar-Or, Oded. (2004). *Growth, maturation, and physical activity* (2nd ed.). Champaign, IL: Human Kinetics.

Mallett, Christopher A. (2016). The school-to-prison pipeline: A critical review of the punitive paradigm shift. *Child and Adolescent Social Work Journal*, *33*(1), 15–24.

Malloy, Lindsay C.; Shulman, Elizabeth P. & Cauffman, Elizabeth. (2014). Interrogations, confessions, and guilty pleas among serious adolescent offenders. *Law and Human Behavior*, *38*(2), 181–193.

Malpas, Jean. (2011). Between pink and blue: A multi-dimensional family approach to gender nonconforming children and their families. *Family Process*, *50*(4), 453–470.

Mandelbaum, David E. & de la Monte, Suzanne M. (2017). Adverse structural and functional effects of marijuana on the brain: Evidence reviewed. *Pediatric Neurology*, *66*, 12–20.

Mani, Kartik; Javaheri, Ali & Diwan, Abhinav. (2018). Lysosomes mediate benefits of intermittent fasting in cardiometabolic disease: The janitor is the undercover boss. *Comprehensive Physiology*, *8*(4), 1639–1667.

Mann, Joshua R.; McDermott, Suzanne; Bao, Haikun & Bersabe, Adrian. (2009). Maternal genitourinary infection and risk of cerebral palsy. *Developmental Medicine & Child Neurology*, *51*(4), 282–288.

Manning, Wendy D. (2015). Cohabitation and child wellbeing. *Marriage and Child Wellbeing Revisited*, *25*(2), 51–66.

Manning, Wendy D.; Longmore, Monica A. & Giordano, Peggy C. (2018). Cohabitation and intimate partner violence during emerging adulthood: High constraints and low commitment. *Journal of Family Issues*, *39*(4), 1030–1055.

Mansukhani, Meghna P.; Kolla, Bhanu Prakash & Somers, Virend K. (2019, 10 July). Hypertension and cognitive decline: Implications of obstructive sleep apnea. *Frontiers in Cardiovascular Medicine*, *6*(96).

Mantua, Janna & Spencer, Rebecca M. C. (2017). Exploring the nap paradox: Are mid-day sleep bouts a friend or foe? *Sleep Medicine*, *37*, 88–97.

Mar, Raymond A. (2011). The neural bases of social cognition and story comprehension. *Annual Review of Psychology*, *62*, 103–134.

Marazita, John M. & Merriman, William E. (2010). Verifying one's knowledge of a name without retrieving it: A U-shaped relation to vocabulary size in early childhood. *Language Learning and Development*, *7*(1), 40–54.

Marcia, James E. (1966). Development and validation of ego-identity status. *Journal of Personality and Social Psychology*, *3*(5), 551–558.

Marcovitch, Stuart; Clearfield, Melissa W.; Swingler, Margaret; Calkins, Susan D. & Bell, Martha Ann. (2016). Attentional predictors of 5-month-olds' performance on a looking A-not-B task. *Infant and Child Development*, *25*(4), 233–246.

Marcus, Gary F. & Rabagliati, Hugh. (2009). Language acquisition, domain specificity, and descent with modification. In John Colombo, et al. (Eds.), *Infant pathways to language: Methods, models, and research disorders* (pp. 267–285). New York, NY: Psychology Press.

Mareschal, Denis & Kaufman, Jordy. (2012). Object permanence in infancy: Revisiting Baillargeon's drawbridge study. In Alan M. Slater & Paul C. Quinn (Eds.), *Developmental psychology:*

Revisiting the classic studies. Thousand Oaks, CA: Sage.

Margolis, Rachel & Arpino, Bruno. (2018). The demography of grandparenthood in 16 European countries and two North American countries. In Virpi Timonen (Ed.), *Grandparenting practices around the world*. Chicago, IL: Policy Press.

Markey, Charlotte N. & Markey, Patrick M. (2012). Emerging adults' responses to a media presentation of idealized female beauty: An examination of cosmetic surgery in reality television. *Psychology of Popular Media Culture, 1*(4), 209–219.

Markova, Gabriela. (2018). The games infants play: Social games during early mother–infant interactions and their relationship with oxytocin. *Frontiers in Psychology, 9*(1041).

Markovitch, Noam; Luyckx, Koen; Klimstra, Theo; Abramson, Lior & Knafo-Noam, Ariel. (2017). Identity exploration and commitment in early adolescence: Genetic and environmental contributions. *Developmental Psychology,* 53(11), 2092–2102.

Marks, Amy K.; Ejesi, Kida & García Coll, Cynthia. (2014). Understanding the U.S. immigrant paradox in childhood and adolescence. *Child Development Perspectives,* 8(2), 59–64.

Marotta, Phillip L. & Voisin, Dexter R. (2017). Testing three pathways to substance use and delinquency among low-income African American adolescents. *Children and Youth Services Review,* 75, 7–14.

Marshall, Eliot. (2014). An experiment in zero parenting. *Science, 345*(6198), 752–754.

Martin, Carmel. (2014). *Common Core implementation best practices. New York State Office of the Governor Common Core Implementation Panel.* Washington, DC: Center for American Progress.

Martin, Carol L.; Fabes, Richard; Hanish, Laura; Leonard, Stacie & Dinella, Lisa. (2011). Experienced and expected similarity to same-gender peers: Moving toward a comprehensive model of gender segregation. *Sex Roles,* 65(5/6), 421–434.

Martin, Joyce A.; Hamilton, Brady E.; Osterman, Michelle J. K.; Driscoll, Anne K. & Drake, Patrick. (2018, January 31). *Births: Final data for 2016. National Vital Statistics Reports,* 67(1). Hyattsville, MD: National Center for Health Statistics.

Martin, Michael O.; Mullis, Ina V. S.; Foy, Pierre & Hooper, Martin. (2016). *TIMSS 2015 international results in science.* Chestnut Hill, MA: TIMSS & PIRLS International Study Center, Boston College.

Martin-Uzzi, Michele & Duval-Tsioles, Denise. (2013). The experience of remarried couples in blended families. *Journal of Divorce & Remarriage,* 54(1), 43–57.

Martincorena, Iñigo & Campbell, Peter J. (2015). Somatic mutation in cancer and normal cells. *Science, 349*(6255), 1483–1489.

Martinez, Maureen; Shukla, Hemant; Nikulin, Joanna; Wadood, Mufti Zubair; Hadler, Stephen; Mbaeyi, Chukwuma, . . . Ehrhardt, Derek. (2017, August 18). *Progress toward poliomyelitis eradication — Afghanistan, January 2016–June 2017. Morbidity and Mortality Weekly Report,* 66(32), 854–858. Atlanta, GA: Centers for Disease Control and Prevention.

Martinson, Melissa L. & Reichman, Nancy E. (2016). Socioeconomic inequalities in low birth weight in the United States, the United Kingdom, Canada, and Australia. *American Journal of Public Health, 106*(4), 748–754.

Masarik, April S. & Conger, Rand D. (2017). Stress and child development: A review of the Family Stress Model. *Current Opinion in Psychology, 13,* 85–90.

Mascarelli, Amanda. (2013). Growing up with pesticides. *Science, 341*(6147), 740–741.

Mascaro, Jennifer S.; Rentscher, Kelly E.; Hackett, Patrick D.; Mehl, Matthias R. & Rilling, James K. (2017). Child gender influences paternal behavior, language, and brain function. *Behavioral Neuroscience,* 131(3), 262–273.

Masci, David; Brown, Anna & Kiley, Jocelyn. (2017, June 26). *5 facts about same-sex marriage. Fact Tank.* Washington, DC: Pew Research Center.

Masfety, Viviane; Aarnink, Carlijn; Otten, Roy; Bitfoi, Adina; Mihova, Zlatka; Lesinskiene, Sigita, . . . Husky, Mathilde. (2019). Three-generation households and child mental health in European countries. *Social Psychiatry and Psychiatric Epidemiology,* 54(4), 427–436.

Maskileyson, Dina. (2014). Healthcare system and the wealth–health gradient: A comparative study of older populations in six countries. *Social Science & Medicine, 119,* 18–26.

Maslow, Abraham H. (1954). *Motivation and personality* (1st ed.). New York, NY: Harper & Row.

Maslow, Abraham H. (1997). *Motivation and personality* (3rd ed.). New York, NY: Pearson.

Mâsse, Louise C.; Perna, Frank; Agurs-Collins, Tanya & Chriqui, Jamie F. (2013). Change in school nutrition-related laws from 2003 to 2008: Evidence from the School Nutrition-Environment State Policy Classification System. *American Journal of Public Health, 103*(9), 1597–1603.

Masten, Ann S. (2013). Risk and resilience in development. In Philip D. Zelazo (Ed.), *The Oxford handbook of developmental psychology* (Vol. 2, pp. 579–607). New York, NY: Oxford University Press.

Masten, Ann S. (2014). *Ordinary magic: Resilience in development.* New York, NY: Guilford Press.

Mathews, T. J.; Menacker, Fay & MacDorman, Marian F. (2003). *Infant mortality statistics from the 2001 period linked birth/infant death data set. National Vital Statistics Reports,* 52(2). Hyattsville, MD: National Center for Health Statistics.

Matsumoto, David; Hwang, Hyi Sung & Yamada, Hiroshi. (2012). Cultural differences in the relative contributions of face and context to judgments of emotion. *Journal of Cross-Cultural Psychology,* 43(2), 198–218.

Matsumoto, Yasuyo; Yamabe, Shingo; Sugishima, Toru & Geronazzo, Dan. (2011). Perception of oral contraceptives among women of reproductive age in Japan: A comparison with the USA and France. *Journal of Obstetrics and Gynaecology Research,* 37(7), 887–892.

Matthews, Fiona E.; Arthur, Antony; Barnes, Linda E.; Bond, John; Jagger, Carol; Robinson, Louise & Brayne, Carol. (2013). A two-decade comparison of prevalence of dementia in individuals aged 65 years and older from three geographical areas of England: Results of the Cognitive Function and Ageing Study I and II. *The Lancet,* 382(9902), 1405–1412.

Matthews, Karen A.; Hall, Martica H.; Lee, Laisze; Kravitz, Howard M.; Chang, Yuefang; Appelhans, Bradley M., . . . Joffe, Hadine. (2019). Racial/ethnic disparities in women's sleep duration, continuity, and quality, and their statistical mediators: Study of Women's Health Across the Nation. *Sleep, 42*(5).

Matthews, Timothy C. (2018). Perspectives on financial abuse of elders in Canada. *Trusts & Trustees,* 24(1), 73–78.

Mattick, Richard P.; Clare, Philip J.; Aiken, Alexandra; Wadolowski, Monika; Hutchinson, Delyse; Najman, Jackob, . . . Degenhardt, Louisa. (2018). Association of parental supply of alcohol with adolescent drinking, alcohol-related harms, and alcohol use disorder symptoms: A prospective cohort study. *The Lancet Public Health,* 3(2), e64–e71.

Maume, David J. & Sebastian, Rachel A. (2012). Gender, nonstandard work schedules, and marital quality. *Journal of Family and Economic Issues,* 33(4), 477–490.

Maxfield, Molly; Pyszczynski, Tom; Kluck, Benjamin; Cox, Cathy R.; Greenberg, Jeff; Solomon, Sheldon & Weise, David. (2007). Age-related differences in responses to thoughts of one's own death: Mortality salience and judgments of moral transgressions. *Psychology and Aging,* 22(2), 341–353.

May, Lillian; Byers-Heinlein, Krista; Gervain, Judit & Werker, Janet F. (2011). Language and the newborn brain: Does prenatal language experience shape the neonate neural response to speech? *Frontiers in Psychology,* 2, 222.

Mayberry, Rachel I. & Kluender, Robert. (2018). Rethinking the critical period for language: New insights into an old question from American Sign Language. *Bilingualism: Language and Cognition,* 21(5), 938–944.

Mazza, Julia Rachel; Pingault, Jean-Baptiste; Booij, Linda; Boivin, Michel; Tremblay, Richard; Lambert, Jean, . . . Côté, Sylvana. (2017). Poverty and behavior problems during early childhood: The mediating role of maternal depression symptoms and parenting. *International Journal of Behavioral Development,* 41(6), 670–680.

McAdams, Tom A.; Neiderhiser, Jenae M.; Rijsdijk, Fruhling V.; Narusyte, Jurgita; Lichtenstein, Paul & Eley, Thalia C. (2014). Accounting for genetic and environmental confounds in associations between parent and child characteristics: A systematic review of children-of-twins studies. *Psychological Bulletin,* 140(4), 1138–1173.

McAlister, Anna R. & Peterson, Candida C. (2013). Siblings, theory of mind, and executive functioning in children aged 3–6 years: New longitudinal evidence. *Child Development, 84*(4), 1442–1458.

McCabe, Sean Esteban; Veliz, Philip; Wilens, Timothy E. & Schulenberg, John E. (2017). Adolescents' prescription stimulant use and adult functional outcomes: A national prospective study. *Journal of the American Academy of Child and Adolescent Psychiatry, 56*(3), 226–233.e224.

McCabe, Sean Esteban; West, Brady T.; Teter, Christian J. & Boyd, Carol J. (2014). Trends in medical use, diversion, and nonmedical use of prescription medications among college students from 2003 to 2013: Connecting the dots. *Addictive Behaviors, 39*(7), 1176–1182.

McCall, Robert B. (2013). The consequences of early institutionalization: Can institutions be improved?—Should they? *Child and Adolescent Mental Health, 18*(4), 193–201.

McCallion, Gail & Feder, Jody. (2013, October 18). *Student bullying: Overview of research, federal initiatives, and legal issues*. Washington, DC: Congressional Research Service. R43254.

McCarthy, Neil & Eberhart, Johann K. (2014). Gene–ethanol interactions underlying fetal alcohol spectrum disorders. *Cellular and Molecular Life Sciences, 71*(14), 2699–2706.

McClain, Natalie M. & Garrity, Stacy E. (2011). Sex trafficking and the exploitation of adolescents. *Journal of Obstetric, Gynecologic, & Neonatal Nursing, 40*(2), 243–252.

McClung, Nancy M.; Gargano, Julia W.; Park, Ina U.; Whitney, Erin; Abdullah, Nasreen; Ehlers, Sara, . . . HPV-IMPACT Working Group. (2019, April 19). *Estimated number of cases of high-grade cervical lesions diagnosed among women — United States, 2008 and 2016. Morbidity and Mortality Weekly Report, 68*(15), 337–343.

McCormick, Cheryl M.; Mathews, Iva Z.; Thomas, Catherine & Waters, Patti. (2010). Investigations of HPA function and the enduring consequences of stressors in adolescence in animal models. *Brain and Cognition, 72*(1), 73–85.

McCoy, Shelly; Dimler, Laura; Samuels, Danielle & Natsuaki, Misaki N. (2019). Adolescent susceptibility to deviant peer pressure: Does gender matter? *Adolescent Research Review, 4*(1), 59–71.

McCray, Jennifer S.; Chen, Jie-Qi & Sorkin, Janet Eisenband (Eds.). (2018). *Growing mathematical minds: Conversations between developmental psychologists and early childhood teachers*. New York, NY: Routledge.

McEwen, Bruce S. & Karatsoreos, Ilia N. (2015). Sleep deprivation and circadian disruption: Stress, allostasis, and allostatic load. *Sleep Medicine Clinics, 10*(1), 1–10.

McEwen, Craig A. & McEwen, Bruce S. (2017). Social structure, adversity, toxic stress, and intergenerational poverty: An early childhood model. *Annual Review of Sociology, 43*, 445–472.

McFarland, Joel; Hussar, Bill; Wang, Xiaolei; Zhang, Jijun; Wang, Ke; Rathbun, Amy, . . . Mann, Farrah Bullock. (2018, May). *The condition of education 2018*. Washington, DC: National Center for Education Statistics. NCES 2018-144.

McFarlane, Alexander C. & Van Hooff, Miranda. (2009). Impact of childhood exposure to a natural disaster on adult mental health: 20-year longitudinal follow-up study. *The British Journal of Psychiatry, 195*(2), 142–148.

McGill, Rebecca K.; Hughes, Diane; Alicea, Stacey & Way, Niobe. (2012). Academic adjustment across middle school: The role of public regard and parenting. *Developmental Psychology, 48*(4), 1003–1018.

McGillion, Michelle; Herbert, Jane S.; Pine, Julian; Vihman, Marilyn; dePaolis, Rory; Keren-Portnoy, Tamar & Matthews, Danielle. (2017). What paves the way to conventional language? The predictive value of babble, pointing, and socioeconomic status. *Child Development, 88*(1), 156–166.

McGrath, Mary H. & Mukerji, Sanjay. (2000). Plastic surgery and the teenage patient. *Journal of Pediatric & Adolescent Gynecology, 13*(3), 105–118.

McGue, Matt; Irons, Dan & Iacono, William G. (2014). The adolescent origins of substance use disorders: A behavioral genetic perspective. In Scott F. Stoltenberg (Ed.), *Genes and the motivation to use substances* (pp. 31–50). New York, NY: Springer.

McKay, Gareth J.; Silvestri, Giuliana; Chakravarthy, Usha; Dasari, Shilpa; Fritsche, Lars G.; Weber, Bernhard H., . . . Patterson, Chris C. (2011). Variations in apolipoprotein E frequency with age in a pooled analysis of a large group of older people. *American Journal of Epidemiology, 173*(12), 1357–1364.

McKee-Ryan, Frances & Maitoza, Robyn. (2018). Job loss, unemployment, and families. In Ute-Christine Klehe & Edwin van Hooft (Eds.), *The Oxford handbook of job loss and job search*. New York, NY: Oxford University Press.

McKeever, Pamela M. & Clark, Linda. (2017). Delayed high school start times later than 8:30 a.m. and impact on graduation rates and attendance rates. *Sleep Health, 3*(2), 119–125.

McKenzie, Sarah C. & Ritter, Gary W. (2017). School discipline in Arkansas. *Policy Briefs, 14*(4).

McKinney, Lyle & Burridge, Andrea Backscheider. (2015). Helping or hindering? The effects of loans on community college student persistence. *Research in Higher Education, 56*(4), 299–324.

McLean, Robert R. & Kiel, Douglas P. (2015). Developing consensus criteria for sarcopenia: An update. *Journal of Bone and Mineral Research, 30*(4), 588–592.

McLendon, Amber N. & Shelton, Penny S. (2011–2012). New symptoms in older adults: Disease or drug? *Generations, 35*(4), 25–30.

McLeod, Bryce D.; Wood, Jeffrey J. & Weisz, John R. (2007). Examining the association between parenting and childhood anxiety: A meta-analysis. *Clinical Psychology Review, 27*(2), 155–172.

McLoyd, Vonnie C. (2019). How children and adolescents think about, make sense of, and respond to economic inequality: Why does it matter? *Developmental Psychology, 55*(3), 592–600.

McManus, I. Chris; Moore, James; Freegard, Matthew & Rawles, Richard. (2010). Science in the making: Right hand, left hand. III: Estimating historical rates of left-handedness. *Laterality: Asymmetries of Body, Brain and Cognition, 15*(1/2), 186–208.

McMillin, Stephen Edward; Hall, Lacey; Bultas, Margaret W.; Grafeman, Sarah E.; Wilmott, Jennifer; Maxim, Rolanda & Zand, Debra H. (2015). Knowledge of child development as a predictor of mother-child play interactions. *Clinical Pediatrics, 54*(11), 1117–1119.

McMurtrie, Beth. (2014). Why colleges haven't stopped students from binge drinking. *Chronicle of Higher Education, 61*(14), A23–A26.

McNeil, Donald G. (2019, April 3). Scientists thought they had measles cornered: They were wrong. *New York Times*.

McNeil, Michele & Blad, Evie. (2014). U.S. comes up short on education equity, federal data indicate. *Education Week, 33*(26), 8.

McPherson, Gary E.; Osborne, Margaret S.; Evans, Paul & Miksza, Peter. (2019). Applying self-regulated learning microanalysis to study musicians' practice. *Psychology of Music, 47*(1), 18–32.

McQuillan, Geraldine; Kruszon-Moran, Deanna; Flagg, Elaine W. & Paulose-Ram, Ryne. (2018, February). *Prevalence of herpes simplex virus type 1 and type 2 in persons aged 14–49: United States, 2015–2016. NCHS Data Brief, 304*. Hyattsville, MD: National Center for Health Statistics.

Meagher, David K. (2013). Ethical and legal issues and loss, grief, and mourning. In David K. Meagher & David E. Balk (Eds.), *Handbook of thanatology: The essential body of knowledge for the study of death, dying, and bereavement* (2nd ed.). New York, NY: Routledge.

Meczekalski, Blazej; Podfigurna-Stopa, Agnieszka & Katulski, Krzysztof. (2013). Long-term consequences of anorexia nervosa. *Maturitas, 75*(3), 215–220.

Medaglia, John D.; Satterthwaite, Theodore D.; Kelkar, Apoorva; Ciric, Rastko; Moore, Tyler M.; Ruparel, Kosha, . . . Bassett, Danielle S. (2018). Brain state expression and transitions are related to complex executive cognition in normative neurodevelopment. *NeuroImage, 166*, 293–306.

Medford, Anthony & Vaupel, James W. (2019). Human lifespan records are not remarkable but their durations are. *PLoS ONE, 14*(3), e0212345.

Meece, Judith L. & Eccles, Jacquelynne S. (Eds.). (2010). *Handbook of research on schools, schooling, and human development*. New York, NY: Routledge.

Meeus, Wim. (2011). The study of adolescent identity formation 2000–2010: A review of longitudinal research. *Journal of Research on Adolescence, 21*(1), 75–94.

Meeus, Wim. (2017). Adolescent ethnic identity in social context: A commentary. *Child Development, 88*(3), 761–766.

Mehler, Philip S. (2018). Medical complications of anorexia nervosa and bulimia nervosa. In W. Stewart Agras & Athena Robinson (Eds.), *The*

Oxford handbook of eating disorders (2nd ed.). New York, NY: Oxford University Press.

Meier, Ann; Hull, Kathleen E. & Ortyl, Timothy A. (2009). Young adult relationship values at the intersection of gender and sexuality. *Journal of Marriage and Family, 71*(3), 510–525.

Meier, Emily A.; Gallegos, Jarred V.; Thomas, Lori P. Montross; Depp, Colin A.; Irwin, Scott A. & Jeste, Dilip V. (2016). Defining a good death (successful dying): Literature review and a call for research and public dialogue. *The American Journal of Geriatric Psychiatry*, 24(4), 261–271.

Meldrum, Ryan; Kavish, Nicholas & Boutwell, Brian. (2018). On the longitudinal association between peer and adolescent intelligence: Can our friends make us smarter? *PsyArXiv*, (In Press).

Mellerson, Jenelle L.; Maxwell, Choppell B.; Knighton, Cynthia L.; Kriss, Jennifer L.; Seither, Ranee & Black, Carla L. (2018, October 12). *Vaccination coverage for selected vaccines and exemption rates among children in kindergarten — United States, 2017–18 school year. Morbidity and Mortality Weekly Report*, 67(40), 1115–1122. Atlanta, GA: Centers for Disease Control and Prevention.

Meltzoff, Andrew N. & Gopnik, Alison. (2013). Learning about the mind from evidence: Children's development of intuitive theories of perception and personality. In Simon Baron-Cohen, et al. (Eds.), *Understanding other minds: Perspectives from developmental social neuroscience* (3rd ed., pp. 19–34). New York, NY: Oxford University Press.

Mendle, Jane; Harden, K. Paige; Brooks-Gunn, Jeanne & Graber, Julia A. (2010). Development's tortoise and hare: Pubertal timing, pubertal tempo, and depressive symptoms in boys and girls. *Developmental Psychology, 46*(5), 1341–1353.

Mendle, Jane; Harden, K. Paige; Brooks-Gunn, Jeanne & Graber, Julia A. (2012). Peer relationships and depressive symptomatology in boys at puberty. *Developmental Psychology, 48*(2), 429–435.

Mercer, Neil & Howe, Christine. (2012). Explaining the dialogic processes of teaching and learning: The value and potential of sociocultural theory. *Learning, Culture and Social Interaction, 1*(1), 12–21.

Merchant, Lisa V. & Whiting, Jason B. (2018). A grounded theory study of how couples desist from intimate partner violence. *Journal of Marital and Family Therapy*, 44(4), 590–605.

Merewether, Jane. (2018). Listening with young children: enchanted animism of trees, rocks, clouds (and other things). *Pedagogy, Culture & Society*, (In Press).

Merikangas, Kathleen R.; He, Jian-ping; Rapoport, Judith; Vitiello, Benedetto & Olfson, Mark. (2013). Medication use in US youth with mental disorders. *JAMA Pediatrics, 167*(2), 141–148.

Mermelshtine, Roni. (2017). Parent–child learning interactions: A review of the literature on scaffolding. *British Journal of Educational Psychology*, 87(2), 241–254.

Merriam, Sharan B. (2009). *Qualitative research: A guide to design and implementation*. San Francisco, CA: Jossey-Bass.

Mersky, Joshua P.; Topitzes, James & Reynolds, Arthur J. (2013). Impacts of adverse childhood experiences on health, mental health, and substance use in early adulthood: A cohort study of an urban, minority sample in the U.S. *Child Abuse & Neglect*, 37(11), 917–925.

Merz, Emily C. & McCall, Robert B. (2011). Parent ratings of executive functioning in children adopted from psychosocially depriving institutions. *Journal of Child Psychology and Psychiatry*, 52(5), 537–546.

Messinger, Daniel M.; Ruvolo, Paul; Ekas, Naomi V. & Fogel, Alan. (2010). Applying machine learning to infant interaction: The development is in the details. *Neural Networks*, 23(8/9), 1004–1016.

Metcalfe, Lindsay A.; Harvey, Elizabeth A. & Laws, Holly B. (2013). The longitudinal relation between academic/cognitive skills and externalizing behavior problems in preschool children. *Journal of Educational Psychology, 105*(3), 881–894.

Meyer, Madonna Harrington. (2014). *Grandmothers at work: Juggling families and jobs*. New York, NY: New York University Press.

Michaeli, Yossi; Kalfon Hakhmigari, Maor; Dickson, Daniel J.; Scharf, Miri & Shulman, Shmuel. (2018). The role of change in self-criticism across young adulthood in explaining developmental outcomes and psychological wellbeing. *Journal of Personality*, 87(4), 785–798.

Miciak, Jeremy; Cirino, Paul T.; Ahmed, Yusra; Reid, Erin & Vaughn, Sharon. (2019). Executive functions and response to intervention: Identification of students struggling with reading comprehension. *Learning Disability Quarterly*, 42(1), 17–31.

Miech, Richard A.; Johnston, Lloyd D.; O'Malley, Patrick M.; Bachman, Jerald G. & Schulenberg, John E. (2016). *Monitoring the future, national survey results on drug use, 1975–2015: Volume I, secondary school students*. Ann Arbor, MI: Institute for Social Research, The University of Michigan.

Miech, Richard A.; Johnston, Lloyd D.; O'Malley, Patrick M.; Bachman, Jerald G.; Schulenberg, John E. & Patrick, Megan E. (2017a). *Monitoring the future, national survey results on drug use, 1975–2016: Volume I, secondary school students*. Ann Arbor, MI: Institute for Social Research, The University of Michigan.

Miech, Richard A.; Johnston, Lloyd D.; O'Malley, Patrick M.; Bachman, Jerald G.; Schulenberg, John E. & Patrick, Megan E. (2018). *Monitoring the future, national survey results on drug use, 1975–2017: Volume I secondary school students*. Ann Arbor, MI: Institute for Social Research, The University of Michigan.

Miech, Richard A.; Johnston, Lloyd D.; O'Malley, Patrick M.; Bachman, Jerald G.; Schulenberg, John E. & Patrick, Megan E. (2019). *Monitoring the future, national survey results on drug use, 1975–2018: Volume I secondary school students*. Ann Arbor, MI: Institute for Social Research, The University of Michigan.

Miech, Richard A.; Patrick, Megan E.; O'Malley, Patrick M. & Johnston, Lloyd D. (2017b). E-cigarette use as a predictor of cigarette smoking: Results from a 1-year follow-up of a national sample of 12th grade students. *Tobacco Control, 26*, e106–e111.

Mihailidis, Paul & Viotty, Samantha. (2017). Spreadable spectacle in digital culture: Civic expression, fake news, and the role of media literacies in "post-fact" society. *American Behavioral Scientist, 61*(4), 441–454.

Miklowitz, David J. & Cicchetti, Dante (Eds.). (2010). *Understanding bipolar disorder: A developmental psychopathology perspective*. New York, NY: Guilford Press.

Mikolajczyk, Rafael T.; Zhang, Jun; Grewal, Jagteshwar; Chan, Linda C.; Petersen, Antje & Gross, Mechthild M. (2016). Early versus late admission to labor affects labor progression and risk of cesarean section in nulliparous women. *Frontiers in Medicine*, 3(26).

Milkman, Katherine L.; Chugh, Dolly & Bazerman, Max H. (2009). How can decision making be improved? *Perspectives on Psychological Science*, 4(4), 379–383.

Miller, Cindy F.; Martin, Carol Lynn; Fabes, Richard A. & Hanish, Laura D. (2013). Bringing the cognitive and the social together: How gender detectives and gender enforcers shape children's gender development. In Mahzarin R. Banaji & Susan A. Gelman (Eds.), *Navigating the social world: What infants, children, and other species can teach us* (pp. 306–313). New York, NY: Oxford University Press.

Miller, Evonne; Donoghue, Geraldine; Sullivan, Debra & Buys, Laurie. (2018). Later life gardening in a retirement community: Sites of identity, resilience and creativity. In David Davenport, et al. (Eds.), *Resilience and ageing: Creativity, culture and community*. Bristol, UK: Policy Press.

Miller, Melissa K.; Dowd, M. Denise; Harrison, Christopher J.; Mollen, Cynthia J.; Selvarangan, Rangaraj & Humiston, Sharon. (2015). Prevalence of 3 sexually transmitted infections in a pediatric emergency department. *Pediatric Emergency Care, 31*(2), 107–112.

Miller, Patricia H. (2011). *Theories of developmental psychology* (5th ed.). New York, NY: Worth Publishers.

Miller, Susan W. (2011–2012). Medications and elders: Quality of care or quality of life? *Generations*, 35(4), 19–24.

Miller-Cotto, Dana & Byrnes, James P. (2016). Ethnic/racial identity and academic achievement: A meta-analytic review. *Developmental Review, 41*, 51–70.

Miller-Perrin, Cindy & Wurtele, Sandy K. (2017). Sex trafficking and the commercial sexual exploitation of children. *Women & Therapy, 40*(1/2), 123–151.

Mills-Koonce, W. Roger; Garrett-Peters, Patricia; Barnett, Melissa; Granger, Douglas A.; Blair, Clancy & Cox, Martha J. (2011). Father contributions to cortisol responses in infancy and toddlerhood. *Developmental Psychology*, 47(2), 388–395.

Milton, James & Treffers-Daller, Jeanine. (2013). Vocabulary size revisited: The link between vocabulary size and academic achievement. *Applied Linguistics Review*, *4*(1), 151–172.

Milunsky, Aubrey & Milunsky, Jeff M. (2016). *Genetic disorders and the fetus: Diagnosis, prevention, and treatment* (7th ed.). Hoboken, NJ: Wiley-Blackwell.

Mindell, Jodi A.; Sadeh, Avi; Wiegand, Benjamin; How, Ti Hwei & Goh, Daniel Y. T. (2010). Cross-cultural differences in infant and toddler sleep. *Sleep Medicine*, *11*(3), 274–280.

Miniño, Arialdi M.; Heron, Melonie P.; Murphy, Sherry L. & Kochanek, Kenneth D. (2007). *Deaths: Final data for 2004. National Vital Statistics Reports*, *55*(19). Hyattsville, MD: National Center for Health Statistics.

Mischel, Walter. (2014). *The marshmallow test: Mastering self-control*. New York, NY: Little, Brown.

Mischel, Walter; Ebbesen, Ebbe B. & Raskoff Zeiss, Antonette. (1972). Cognitive and attentional mechanisms in delay of gratification. *Journal of Personality and Social Psychology*, *21*(2), 204–218.

Misra, Dawn P.; Caldwell, Cleopatra; Young, Alford A. & Abelson, Sara. (2010). Do fathers matter? Paternal contributions to birth outcomes and racial disparities. *American Journal of Obstetrics and Gynecology*, *202*(2), 99–100.

Missana, Manuela; Rajhans, Purva; Atkinson, Anthony P. & Grossmann, Tobias. (2014). Discrimination of fearful and happy body postures in 8-month-old infants: An event-related potential study. *Frontiers in Human Neuroscience*, *8*, 531.

Mitchell, Edwin A. & Krous, Henry F. (2015). Sudden unexpected death in infancy: A historical perspective. *Journal of Paediatrics and Child Health*, *51*(1), 108–112.

Mitchell, Kimberly J.; Jones, Lisa M.; Finkelhor, David & Wolak, Janis. (2013). Understanding the decline in unwanted online sexual solicitations for U.S. youth 2000–2010: Findings from three Youth Internet Safety Surveys. *Child Abuse & Neglect*, *37*(12), 1225–1236.

Miyata, Susanne; MacWhinney, Brian; Otomo, Kiyoshi; Sirai, Hidetosi; Oshima-Takane, Yuriko; Hirakawa, Makiko, . . . Itoh, Keiko. (2013). Developmental sentence scoring for Japanese. *First Language*, *33*(2), 200–216.

Mize, Krystal D.; Pineda, Melannie; Blau, Alexis K.; Marsh, Kathryn & Jones, Nancy A. (2014). Infant physiological and behavioral responses to a jealousy provoking condition. *Infancy*, *19*(3), 338–348.

MMWR. (2000, March 31). *Reducing falls and resulting hip fractures among older women. Morbidity and Mortality Weekly Report*, *49*(RR02), 1–12. Atlanta, GA: U.S. Department of Health and Human Services, Centers for Disease Control and Prevention.

MMWR. (2008, January 18). *School-associated student homicides — United States, 1992–2006. Morbidity and Mortality Weekly Report*, *57*(2), 33–36. Atlanta, GA: U.S. Department of Health and Human Services, Centers for Disease Control and Prevention.

MMWR. (2010, June 4). *Youth risk behavior surveillance — United States, 2009. Morbidity and Mortality Weekly Report Surveillance Summaries*, *59*(SS05). Atlanta, GA: U.S. Department of Health and Human Services, Centers for Disease Control and Prevention.

MMWR. (2012, June 8). *Youth risk behavior surveillance — United States, 2011. Morbidity and Mortality Weekly Report*, *61*(4). Atlanta, GA: U.S. Department of Health and Human Services, Centers for Disease Control and Prevention.

MMWR. (2013, April 5). *Blood lead levels in children aged 1–5 Years — United States, 1999–2010. Morbidity and Mortality Weekly Report*, *62*(13), 245–248. Atlanta, GA: U.S. Department of Health and Human Services, Centers for Disease Control and Prevention.

MMWR. (2013, January 11). *Vital signs: Binge drinking among women and high school girls — United States, 2011. Morbidity and Mortality Weekly Report*, *62*, 9–13. Atlanta, GA: Department of Health and Human Services, Centers for Disease Control and Prevention.

MMWR. (2014, July 25). *Human papillomavirus vaccination coverage among adolescents, 2007–2013, and postlicensure vaccine safety monitoring, 2006–2014 — United States. Morbidity and Mortality Weekly Report*, *63*(29). Atlanta, GA: U.S. Department of Health and Human Services, Centers for Disease Control and Prevention.

MMWR. (2014, June 13). *Youth risk behavior surveillance — United States, 2013. Morbidity and Mortality Weekly Report*, *63*(4). Atlanta, GA: U.S. Department of Health and Human Services, Centers for Disease Control and Prevention.

MMWR. (2014, March 28). *Prevalence of autism spectrum disorder among children aged 8 years — Autism and Developmental Disabilities Monitoring Network, 11 sites, United States, 2010. Morbidity and Mortality Weekly Report*, *63*(2). Atlanta, GA: U.S. Department of Health and Human Services, Centers for Disease Control and Prevention.

MMWR. (2014, September 5). *Prevalence of smokefree home rules — United States, 1992–1993 and 2010–2011. Morbidity and Mortality Weekly Report*, *63*(35), 765–769. Atlanta, GA: Department of Health and Human Services, Centers for Disease Control and Prevention.

MMWR. (2016, June 10). *Youth risk behavior surveillance — United States, 2015. Morbidity and Mortality Weekly Report*, *65*(6). Atlanta, GA: U.S. Department of Health and Human Services, Centers for Disease Control and Prevention.

MMWR. (2016, October 14). *QuickStats: Gestational weight gain among women with full-term, singleton births, compared with recommendations — 48 states and the District of Columbia, 2015. Morbidity and Mortality Weekly Report*, *65*(40), 1121. Atlanta, GA: Centers for Disease Control and Prevention.

MMWR. (2018, June 15). *Youth risk behavior surveillance — United States, 2017. Morbidity and Mortality Weekly Report*, *67*(8). Atlanta, GA: U.S. Department of Health and Human Services, Centers for Disease Control and Prevention.

Moffitt, Terrie E. (2003). Life-course-persistent and adolescence-limited antisocial behavior: A 10-year research review and a research agenda. In Benjamin B. Lahey, et al. (Eds.), *Causes of conduct disorder and juvenile delinquency* (pp. 49–75). New York, NY: Guilford Press.

Moffitt, Terrie E.; Caspi, Avshalom; Rutter, Michael & Silva, Phil A. (2001). *Sex differences in antisocial behaviour: Conduct disorder, delinquency, and violence in the Dunedin Longitudinal Study*. New York, NY: Cambridge University Press.

Mokrova, Irina L.; O'Brien, Marion; Calkins, Susan D.; Leerkes, Esther M. & Marcovitch, Stuart. (2013). The role of persistence at preschool age in academic skills at kindergarten. *European Journal of Psychology of Education*, 28(4), 1495–1503.

Moldavsky, Maria & Sayal, Kapil. (2013). Knowledge and attitudes about Attention-deficit/hyperactivity disorder (ADHD) and its treatment: The views of children, adolescents, parents, teachers and healthcare professionals. *Current Psychiatry Reports*, *15*, 377.

Moles, Laura; Manzano, Susana; Fernández, Leonides; Montilla, Antonia; Corzo, Nieves; Ares, Susana, . . . Espinosa-Martos, Irene. (2015). Bacteriological, biochemical, and immunological properties of colostrum and mature milk from mothers of extremely preterm infants. *Journal of Pediatric Gastroenterology & Nutrition*, *60*(1), 120–126.

Møller, Signe J. & Tenenbaum, Harriet R. (2011). Danish majority children's reasoning about exclusion based on gender and ethnicity. *Child Development*, 82(2), 520–532.

Molnar, Lisa J.; Eby, David W.; Bogard, Scott E.; LeBlanc, David J. & Zakrajsek, Jennifer S. (2018). Using naturalistic driving data to better understand the driving exposure and patterns of older drivers. *Traffic Injury Prevention*, *19*(Suppl. 1), S83–S88.

Monahan, Kathryn C.; Steinberg, Laurence; Cauffman, Elizabeth & Mulvey, Edward P. (2013). Psychosocial (im)maturity from adolescence to early adulthood: Distinguishing between adolescence-limited and persisting antisocial behavior. *Development and Psychopathology*, 25(4), 1093–1105.

Montero-Odasso, Manuel M.; Sarquis-Adamson, Yanina; Speechley, Mark; Borrie, Michael J.; Hachinski, Vladimir C.; Wells, Jennie, . . . Muir-Hunter, Susan. (2017). Association of dual-task gait with incident dementia in mild cognitive impairment: Results from the gait and brain study. *JAMA Neurology*, 74(7), 857–865.

Montgomery, Heather. (2015). Understanding child prostitution in Thailand in the 1990s. *Child Development Perspectives*, 9(3), 154–157.

Monthly Vital Statistics Report. (1980). *Final mortality statistics, 1978: Advance report. Monthly Vital Statistics Report*, 29(6, Suppl. 2). Hyattsville, MD: National Center for Health Statistics.

Monti, Jennifer D.; Rudolph, Karen D. & Miernicki, Michelle E. (2017). Rumination about social stress mediates the association between peer victimization and depressive symptoms during middle childhood. *Journal of Applied Developmental Psychology*, 48, 25–32.

Montirosso, Rosario; Casini, Erica; Provenzi, Livio; Putnam, Samuel P.; Morandi, Francesco; Fedeli, Claudia & Borgatti, Renato. (2015). A categorical approach to infants' individual differences during the Still-Face paradigm. *Infant Behavior and Development, 38*, 67–76.

Montirosso, Rosario; Tronick, Ed & Borgatti, Renato. (2017). Promoting neuroprotective care in neonatal intensive care units and preterm infant development: Insights from the neonatal adequate care for quality of life study. *Child Development Perspectives, 11*(1), 9–15.

Monto, Martin A. & Carey, Anna G. (2014). A new standard of sexual behavior? Are claims associated with the "hookup culture" supported by general social survey data? *The Journal of Sex Research, 51*(6), 605–615.

Moody, Myles. (2016). From under-diagnoses to over-representation: Black children, ADHD, and the school-to-prison pipeline. *Journal of African American Studies, 20*(2), 152–163.

Moody, Raymond A. (1975). *Life after life: The investigation of a phenomenon—Survival of bodily death*. Atlanta, GA: Mockingbird Books.

Moore, Kendra A.; Rubin, Emily B. & Halpern, Scott D. (2016). The problems with physician orders for life-sustaining treatment. *JAMA, 315*(3), 259–260.

Moore, Kelly L.; Boscardin, W. John; Steinman, Michael A. & Schwartz, Janice B. (2012). Age and sex variation in prevalence of chronic medical conditions in older residents of U.S. nursing homes. *Journal of the American Geriatrics Society, 60*(4), 756–764.

Moore, Keith L.; Persaud, T. V. N. & Torchia, Mark G. (2015). *The developing human: Clinically oriented embryology* (10th ed.). Philadelphia, PA: Saunders.

Moore, Mary Ruth & Sabo-Risley, Constance (Eds.). (2017). *Play in America: Essays in honor of Joe L. Frost*. Bloomington, IL: Archway Publishing.

Morales, Angelica; Jones, Scott; Ehlers, Alissa; Lavine, Jessye & Nagel, Bonnie. (2018). Ventral striatal response during decision making involving risk and reward is associated with future binge drinking in adolescents. *Neuropsychopharmacology, 43*(9), 1884–1890.

Moran, Lyndsey R.; Lengua, Liliana J. & Zalewski, Maureen. (2013). The interaction between negative emotionality and effortful control in early social-emotional development. *Social Development, 22*(2), 340–362.

Moran, Lauren V.; Masters, Grace A.; Pingali, Samira; Cohen, Bruce M.; Liebson, Elizabeth; Rajarethinam, R. P. & Ongur, Dost. (2015). Prescription stimulant use is associated with earlier onset of psychosis. *Journal of Psychiatric Research, 71*, 41–47.

Morawska, Alina & Sanders, Matthew. (2011). Parental use of time out revisited: A useful or harmful parenting strategy? *Journal of Child and Family Studies, 20*(1), 1–8.

Morcos, Roy N. & Kizy, Thomas. (2012). Gynecomastia: When is treatment indicated? *Journal of Family Practice, 61*(12), 719–725.

Moreira, Pollyana De Lucena; Rique Neto, Júlio; Sabucedo, José Manuel & Camino, Cleonice Pereira Dos Santos. (2018). Moral judgment, political ideology and collective action. *Scandinavian Journal of Psychology, 59*(6), 610–620.

Moreno, Sylvain; Lee, Yunjo; Janus, Monika & Bialystok, Ellen. (2015). Short-term second language and music training induces lasting functional brain changes in early childhood. *Child Development, 86*(2), 394–406.

Morgan, Ali Zaremba; Keiley, Margaret K.; Ryan, Aubrey E.; Radomski, Juliana Groves; Gropper, Sareen S.; Connell, Lenda Jo, . . . Ulrich, Pamela V. (2012). Eating regulation styles, appearance schemas, and body satisfaction predict changes in body fat for emerging adults. *Journal of Youth and Adolescence, 41*(9), 1127–1141.

Morgan, David L. (2018). Living within blurry boundaries: The value of distinguishing between qualitative and quantitative research. *Journal of Mixed Methods Research, 12*(3), 268–279.

Morgan, Ian G.; Ohno-Matsui, Kyoko & Saw, Seang-Mei. (2012). Myopia. *The Lancet, 379*(9827), 1739–1748.

Morones, Alyssa. (2013). Paddling persists in U.S. schools. *Education Week, 33*(9), 1, 10–11.

Morris, Danielle H.; Jones, Michael E.; Schoemaker, Minouk J.; Ashworth, Alan & Swerdlow, Anthony J. (2011). Familial concordance for age at natural menopause: Results from the Breakthrough Generations Study. *Menopause, 18*(9), 956–961.

Morris, Vivian G. & Morris, Curtis L. (2013). A call for African American male teachers: The supermen expected to solve the problems of low-performing schools. In Chance W. Lewis & Ivory A. Toldson (Eds.), *Black male teachers: Diversifying the United States' teacher workforce* (pp. 151–165). Bingley, UK: Emerald Group.

Morrongiello, Barbara A. (2018). Preventing unintentional injuries to young children in the home: Understanding and influencing parents' safety practices. *Child Development Perspectives, 12*(4), 217–222.

Mortimer, Jeylan T. (2010). The benefits and risks of adolescent employment. *Prevention Researcher, 17*(2), 8–11.

Mortimer, Jeylan T. (2013). Work and its positive and negative effects on youth's psychosocial development. In Carol W. Runyan, et al. (Eds.), *Health and safety of young workers: Proceedings of a U.S. and Canadian series of symposia* (pp. 66–79). Washington, DC: U.S. Department of Health and Human Services, Centers for Disease Control and Prevention, National Institute for Occupational Safety and Health.

Moshman, David. (2011). *Adolescent rationality and development: Cognition, morality, and identity* (3rd ed.). New York, NY: Psychology Press.

Moultrie, Fiona; Goksan, Sezgi; Poorun, Ravi & Slater, Rebeccah. (2016). Pain in neonates and infants. In Anna A. Battaglia (Ed.), *An introduction to pain and its relation to nervous system disorders* (pp. 283–293). New York, NY: Wiley.

Mowry, James B.; Spyker, Daniel A.; Brooks, Daniel E.; Mcmillan, Naya & Schauben, Jay L. (2015). 2014 Annual report of the American Association of Poison Control Centers' National Poison Data System (NPDS): 32nd Annual report. *Clinical Toxicology, 53*(10), 962–1146.

Mrug, Sylvie; Elliott, Marc N.; Davies, Susan; Tortolero, Susan R.; Cuccaro, Paula & Schuster, Mark A. (2014). Early puberty, negative peer influence, and problem behaviors in adolescent girls. *Pediatrics, 133*(1), 7–14.

Mueller, Noel T.; Mao, G.; Bennett, Wendy L.; Hourigan, Suchi K.; Dominguez-Bello, Maria G.; Appel, Lawrence J. & Wang, Xiaobin. (2017). Does vaginal delivery mitigate or strengthen the intergenerational association of overweight and obesity? Findings from the Boston Birth Cohort. *International Journal of Obesity, 41*, 497–501.

Muennig, Peter A.; Reynolds, Megan; Fink, David S.; Zafari, Zafar & Geronimus, Arline T. (2018). America's declining well-being, health, and life expectancy: Not just a White problem. *American Journal of Public Health, 108*(12), 1626–1631.

Mukku, Shiva Shanker Reddy; Harbishettar, Vijaykumar & Sivakumar, P. T. (2018). Psychological morbidity after job retirement: A review. *Asian Journal of Psychiatry*, 37, 58–63.

Mullis, Ina V. S.; Martin, Michael O.; Foy, Pierre & Arora, A. (2012a). *TIMSS 2011 international results in mathematics*. Chestnut Hill, MA: TIMSS & PIRLS International Study Center, Boston College.

Mullis, Ina V. S.; Martin, Michael O.; Foy, Pierre & Drucker, Kathleen T. (2012b). *PIRLS 2011 international results in reading*. Chestnut Hill, MA: TIMSS & PIRLS International Study Center, Boston College.

Mullis, Ina V. S.; Martin, Michael O.; Foy, Pierre & Hooper, Martin. (2016). *TIMSS 2015 international results in mathematics*. Chestnut Hill, MA: TIMSS & PIRLS International Study Center, Boston College.

Mullis, Ina V. S.; Martin, Michael O.; Foy, Pierre & Hooper, Martin. (2017). *International results in reading PIRLS 2016*. Chestnut Hill, MA: TIMSS & PIRLS International Study Center, Boston College.

Munson, Michelle R.; Lee, Bethany R.; Miller, David; Cole, Andrea & Nedelcu, Cristina. (2013). Emerging adulthood among former system youth: The ideal versus the real. *Children and Youth Services Review, 35*(6), 923–929.

Murawski, Wendy W. & Scott, Kathy Lynn (Eds.). (2019). *What really works with universal design for learning*. Thousand Oaks, CA: Corwin.

Muris, Peter & Meesters, Cor. (2014). Small or big in the eyes of the other: On the developmental psychopathology of self-conscious emotions as shame, guilt, and pride. *Clinical Child and Family Psychology Review, 17*(1), 19–40.

Murphy, Colleen; Gardoni, Paolo & McKim, Robert (Eds.). (2018). *Climate change and its impacts: Risks and inequalities*. Cham, Switzerland: Springer.

Murphy, Sherry L.; Kochanek, Kenneth D.; Xu, Jiaquan & Arias, Elizabeth. (2015, December). *Mortality in the United States, 2014*.

NCHS Data Brief, (229). Hyattsville, MD: National Center for Health Statistics.

Murphy, Sherry L.; Xu, Jiaquan & Kochanek, Kenneth D. (2012). *Deaths: Preliminary data for 2010. National Vital Statistics Reports, 60*(4). Hyattsville, MD: National Center for Health Statistics.

Murphy, Sherry L.; Xu, Jiaquan; Kochanek, Kenneth D. & Arias, Elizabeth. (2018). *Mortality in the United States, 2017. NCHS Data Brief*, (328). Hyattsville, MD: National Center for Health Statistics.

Murphy, Sherry L.; Xu, Jiaquan; Kochanek, Kenneth D.; Curtin, Sally C. & Arias, Elizabeth. (2017, November 27). *Deaths: Final data for 2015. National Vital Statistics Reports, 66*(6). Hyattsville, MD: National Center for Health Statistics.

Murray, Joseph L. & Arnett, Jeffrey Jensen (Eds.). (2019). *Emerging adulthood and higher education: A new student development paradigm*. New York, NY: Routledge.

Murray, Kristen; Rieger, Elizabeth & Byrne, Don. (2018). Body image predictors of depressive symptoms in adolescence. *Journal of Adolescence, 69*, 130–139.

Murray, Thomas H. (2014). Stirring the simmering "designer baby" pot. *Science, 343*(6176), 1208–1210.

Musselwhite, Charles. (2018). Transportation and promoting physical activity among older people. In Samuel R. Nyman, et al. (Eds.), *The Palgrave handbook of ageing and physical activity promotion*. Cham, Switzerland: Palgrave Macmillan.

Mustanski, Brian; Birkett, Michelle; Greene, George J.; Hatzenbuehler, Mark L. & Newcomb, Michael E. (2014). Envisioning an America without sexual orientation inequities in adolescent health. *American Journal of Public Health, 104*(2), 218–225.

Myers, David G. (2019). Getting people with hearing loss in the loop. *Perspectives on Psychological Science, 14*(1), 29–33.

Nadal, Kevin L.; Mazzula, Silvia L.; Rivera, David P. & Fujii-Doe, Whitney. (2014). Microaggressions and Latina/o Americans: An analysis of nativity, gender, and ethnicity. *Journal of Latina/o Psychology, 2*(2), 67–78.

Næss, Kari-Anne B. (2016). Development of phonological awareness in Down syndrome: A meta-analysis and empirical study. *Developmental Psychology, 52*(2), 177–190.

NAEYC. (2014). *NAEYC Early Childhood Program Standards and Accreditation Criteria & Guidance for Assessment*. Washington, DC: National Association for the Education of Young Children.

Nagl, Michaela; Jacobi, Corinna; Paul, Martin; Beesdo-Baum, Katja; Hofler, Michael; Lieb, Roselind & Wittchen, Hans-Ulrich. (2016). Prevalence, incidence, and natural course of anorexia and bulimia nervosa among adolescents and young adults. *European Child & Adolescent Psychiatry, 25*(8), 903–918.

Nahata, Leena; Morgan, Taylor L.; Ferrante, Amanda C.; Caltabellotta, Nicole M.; Yeager, Nicholas D.; Rausch, Joseph R., . . . Gerhardt, Cynthia A. (2019). Congruence of reproductive goals and fertility-related attitudes of adolescent and young adult males and their parents after cancer treatment. *Journal of Adolescent and Young Adult Oncology, 8*(3).

Nanji, Ayaz. (2005, February 8). World's smallest baby goes home. *CBS News*. AP.

Narvaez, Darcia; Gleason, Tracy; Wang, Lijuan; Brooks, Jeff; Lefever, Jennifer Burke & Cheng, Ying. (2013). The evolved development niche: Longitudinal effects of caregiving practices on early childhood psychosocial development. *Early Childhood Research Quarterly, 28*(4), 759–773.

Nash, Erin J. (2018). In defense of "targeting" some dissent about science. 26(3), 325–359.

Natarajan, Mangai (Ed.). (2017). *Drugs of abuse*. New York, NY: Routledge.

National Alliance on Mental Health. (2019). Mental health by the numbers.

National Assessment of Educational Progress. (2019, May 6). Public, private, and charter schools dashboard. The nation's report card.

National Center for Education Statistics. (2017, December). *Table 306.10. Total fall enrollment in degree-granting postsecondary institutions, by level of enrollment, sex, attendance status, and race/ethnicity of student: Selected years, 1976 through 2016*. Washington, DC: Institute of Education Sciences, U.S. Department of Education.

National Center for Education Statistics. (2018). The nation's report card.

National Center for Education Statistics. (2018, January). *Table 103.20. Percentage of the population 3 to 34 years old enrolled in school, by age group: Selected years, 1940 through 2016*. Washington, DC: Institute of Education Sciences, U.S. Department of Education.

National Center for Education Statistics. (2018, September). *Table 502.30. Median annual earnings of full-time year-round workers 25 to 34 years old and full-time year-round workers as a percentage of the labor force, by sex, race/ethnicity, and educational attainment: Selected years, 1995 through 2017*. Washington, DC: Institute of Education Sciences, U.S. Department of Education.

National Center for Education Statistics. (2019, February). *Indicator 24: Degrees awarded. Status and trends in the education of racial and ethnic groups*. Washington, DC: Institute of Education Sciences, U.S. Department of Education.

National Center for Education Statistics. (2019, May). Public high school graduation rates. The Condition of Education.

National Center for Health Statistics. (2012). *Health, United States, 2011: With special feature on socioeconomic status and health*. Hyattsville, MD: U.S. Department of Health and Human Services, Centers for Disease Control and Prevention.

National Center for Health Statistics. (2014). *Health, United States, 2013: With special feature on prescription drugs*. Hyattsville, MD: U.S. Department of Health and Human Services, Centers for Disease Control and Prevention.

National Center for Health Statistics. (2016). *National ambulatory medical care survey*. Hyattsville, MD: U.S. Department of Health and Human Services, Centers for Disease Control and Prevention.

National Center for Health Statistics. (2017). *Health, United States, 2016: With chartbook on long-term trends in health*. Hyattsville, MD: U.S. Department of Health and Human Services.

National Center for Health Statistics. (2018). *Health, United States, 2017: With a special feature on mortality*. Hyattsville, MD: U.S. Department of Health and Human Services.

National Foundation for Educational Research. (2010). *Tellus4 national report*. Berkshire, UK: National Foundation for Educational Research. DCSF Research Report 218.

National Institute of Population and Social Security Research. (2019, August). Population statistics of Japan 2017.

Naughton, Michelle J.; Yi-Frazier, Joyce P.; Morgan, Timothy M.; Seid, Michael; Lawrence, Jean M.; Klingensmith, Georgeanna J., . . . Loots, Beth. (2014). Longitudinal associations between sex, diabetes self-care, and health-related quality of life among youth with type 1 or type 2 diabetes mellitus. *The Journal of Pediatrics, 164*(6), 1376–1383.e1371.

Neale, Joanne; Bradford, Julia & Strang, John. (2017). Development of a proto-typology of opiate overdose onset. *Addiction, 112*(1), 168–175.

Neary, Karen R. & Friedman, Ori. (2014). Young children give priority to ownership when judging who should use an object. *Child Development, 85*(1), 326–337.

Neary, Marianne T. & Breckenridge, Ross A. (2013). Hypoxia at the heart of sudden infant death syndrome? *Pediatric Research, 74*(4), 375–379.

Needleman, Herbert L. & Gatsonis, Constantine A. (1990). Low-level lead exposure and the IQ of children: A meta-analysis of modern studies. *JAMA, 263*(5), 673–678.

Needleman, Herbert L.; Schell, Alan; Bellinger, David; Leviton, Alan & Allred, Elizabeth N. (1990). The long-term effects of exposure to low doses of lead in childhood. *New England Journal of Medicine, 322*(2), 83–88.

Neggers, Yasmin & Crowe, Kristi. (2013). Low birth weight outcomes: Why better in Cuba than Alabama? *Journal of the American Board of Family Medicine, 26*(2), 187–195.

Nehme, Eileen K.; Oluyomi, Abiodun O.; Calise, Tamara Vehige & Kohl, Harold W. (2016). Environmental correlates of recreational walking in the neighborhood. *American Journal of Health Promotion, 30*(3), 139–148.

Neimeyer, Robert A. (2017). Series foreword. In Dennis Klass & Edith Maria Steffen (Eds.), *Continuing bonds in bereavement: New directions for research and practice*. New York, NY: Routledge.

Neisser, Ulric. (1988). Five kinds of self knowledge. *Philosophical Psychology, 1*(1), 35–59.

Nelson, Charles A.; Fox, Nathan A. & Zeanah, Charles H. (2014). *Romania's abandoned children: Deprivation, brain development, and the struggle for recovery*. Cambridge, MA: Harvard University Press.

Nelson, Geoffrey & Caplan, Rachel. (2014). The prevention of child physical abuse and neglect: An update. *Journal of Applied Research on Children, 5*(1).

Nelson, Sarah C.; Kling, Johanna; Wängqvist, Maria; Frisén, Ann & Syed, Moin. (2018). Identity and the body: Trajectories of body esteem from adolescence to emerging adulthood. *Developmental Psychology, 54*(6), 1159–1171.

Nesdale, Drew; Zimmer-Gembeck, Melanie J. & Roxburgh, Natalie. (2014). Peer group rejection in childhood: Effects of rejection ambiguity, rejection sensitivity, and social acumen. *Journal of Social Issues, 70*(1), 12–28.

Neuman, Susan B.; Kaefer, Tanya & Pinkham, Ashley M. (2018). A double dose of disadvantage: Language experiences for low-income children in home and school. *Journal of Educational Psychology, 110*(1), 102–118.

Nevanen, Saila; Juvonen, Antti & Ruismäki, Heikki. (2014). Does arts education develop school readiness? Teachers' and artists' points of view on an art education project. *Arts Education Policy Review, 115*(3), 72–81.

Nevin, Rick. (2007). Understanding international crime trends: The legacy of preschool lead exposure. *Environmental Research, 104*(3), 315–336.

Ng, Florrie Fei-Yin; Pomerantz, Eva M. & Deng, Ciping. (2014). Why are Chinese mothers more controlling than American mothers? "My child is my report card". *Child Development*, 85(1), 355–369.

Ng, Rowena; Lai, Philip; Brown, Timothy T.; Järvinen, Anna; Halgren, Eric; Bellugi, Ursula & Trauner, Doris. (2017). Neuroanatomical correlates of emotion-processing in children with unilateral brain lesion: A preliminary study of limbic system organization. *Social Neuroscience*, (In Press).

Ngui, Emmanuel; Cortright, Alicia & Blair, Kathleen. (2009). An investigation of paternity status and other factors associated with racial and ethnic disparities in birth outcomes in Milwaukee, Wisconsin. *Maternal and Child Health Journal, 13*(4), 467–478.

Nguyen, Jacqueline; O'Brien, Casey & Schapp, Salena. (2016). Adolescent inhalant use prevention, assessment, and treatment: A literature synthesis. *Drug Policy, 31*, 15–24.

Niakan, Kathy K.; Han, Jinnuo; Pedersen, Roger A.; Simon, Carlos & Reijo Pera, Renee A. (2012). Human pre-implantation embryo development. *Development, 139*, 829–841.

Nic Gabhainn, Saoirse; Baban, Adriana; Boyce, William & Godeau, Emmanuelle. (2009). How well protected are sexually active 15-year-olds? Cross-national patterns in condom and contraceptive pill use 2002–2006. *International Journal of Public Health, 54*(Suppl. 2), 209–215.

Nichols, Emma; Szoeke, Cassandra E. I.; Vollset, Stein Emil; Abbasi, Nooshin; Abd-Allah, Foad; Abdela, Jemal, . . . Murray, Christopher J. L. (2019). Global, regional, and national burden of Alzheimer's disease and other dementias, 1990–2016: A systematic analysis for the Global Burden of Disease Study 2016. *The Lancet Neurology, 18*, 88–106.

Nichols, Shaun; Strohminger, Nina; Rai, Arun & Garfield, Jay. (2018). Death and the self. *Cognitive Science, 42*(Supp. 1), 314–332.

Niclasen, Janni; Andersen, Anne-Marie N.; Strandberg-Larsen, Katrine & Teasdale, Thomas W. (2014). Is alcohol binge drinking in early and late pregnancy associated with behavioural and emotional development at age 7 years? *European Child & Adolescent Psychiatry*, 23(12), 1175–1180.

Nicolaisen, Magnhild; Moum, Torbjørn & Thorsen, Kirsten. (2017). Mastery and depressive symptoms: How does mastery influence the impact of stressors from midlife to old age? *Journal of Aging and Health*, (In Press).

Nielsen, Mark & Tomaselli, Keyan. (2010). Overimitation in Kalahari Bushman children and the origins of human cultural cognition. *Psychological Science, 21*(5), 729–736.

Nielsen, Mark; Tomaselli, Keyan; Mushin, Ilana & Whiten, Andrew. (2014). Exploring tool innovation: A comparison of Western and Bushman children. *Journal of Experimental Child Psychology, 126*, 384–394.

Nieto, Marta; Romero, Dulce; Ros, Laura; Zabala, Carmen; Martínez, Manuela; Ricarte, Jorge J., . . . Latorre, Jose M. (2019). Differences in coping strategies between young and older adults: The role of executive functions. *The International Journal of Aging and Human Development*, (In Press).

Nieto, Sonia. (2000). *Affirming diversity: The sociopolitical context of multicultural education* (3rd ed.). New York, NY: Longman.

Nigg, Joel T. & Barkley, Russell A. (2014). Attention-deficit/hyperactivity disorder. In Eric J. Mash & Russell A. Barkley (Eds.), *Child psychopathology* (3rd ed., pp. 75–144). New York, NY: Guilford Press.

Nikitin, Dmitriy; Timberlake, David S. & Williams, Rebecca S. (2016). Is the e-liquid industry regulating itself? A look at e-liquid Internet vendors in the United States. *Nicotine & Tobacco Research, 18*(10), 1967–1972.

Nikolopoulos, Thomas P. (2015). Neonatal hearing screening: What we have achieved and what needs to be improved. *International Journal of Pediatric Otorhinolaryngology, 79*(5), 635–637.

Nilsson, Kristine Kahr & de López, Kristine Jensen. (2016). Theory of mind in children with specific language impairment: A systematic review and meta-analysis. *Child Development, 87*(1), 143–153.

Nilwik, Rachel; Snijders, Tim; Leenders, Marika; Groen, Bart B. L.; van Kranenburg, Janneau; Verdijk, Lex B. & van Loon, Luc J. C. (2013). The decline in skeletal muscle mass with aging is mainly attributed to a reduction in type II muscle fiber size. *Experimental Gerontology, 48*(5), 492–498.

Nisbett, Richard E.; Peng, Kaiping; Choi, Incheol & Norenzayan, Ara. (2001). Culture and systems of thought: Holistic versus analytic cognition. *Psychological Review, 108*(2), 291–310.

Nishina, Adrienne; Bellmore, Amy; Witkow, Melissa R.; Nylund-Gibson, Karen & Graham, Sandra. (2018). Mismatches in self-reported and meta-perceived ethnic identification across the high school years. *Journal of Youth and Adolescence, 47*(1), 51–63.

Nkomo, Palesa; Naicker, Nisha; Mathee, Angela; Galpin, Jacky; Richter, Linda M. & Norris, Shane A. (2018). The association between environmental lead exposure with aggressive behavior, and dimensionality of direct and indirect aggression during mid-adolescence: Birth to Twenty Plus cohort. *Science of the Total Environment, 612*, 472–479.

Nocentini, Annalaura; Fiorentini, Giada; Di Paola, Ludovica & Menesini, Ersilia. (2019). Parents, family characteristics and bullying behavior: A systematic review. *Aggression and Violent Behavior, 45*, 41–50.

Noël-Miller, Claire M. (2013a). Repartnering following divorce: Implications for older fathers' relations with their adult children. *Journal of Marriage and Family, 75*(3), 697–712.

Noël-Miller, Claire M. (2013b). Former stepparents' contact with their stepchildren after midlife. *The Journals of Gerontology Series B: Psychological Sciences and Social Sciences, 68*(3), 409–419.

Noll, Jennie G.; Guastaferro, Kate; Beal, Sarah J.; Schreier, Hannah M. C.; Barnes, Jaclyn; Reader, Jonathan M. & Font, Sarah A. (2018). Is sexual abuse a unique predictor of sexual risk behaviors, pregnancy, and motherhood in adolescence? *Journal of Research on Adolescence*, (In Press).

Noll, Jennie G.; Trickett, Penelope K.; Long, Jeffrey D.; Negriff, Sonya; Susman, Elizabeth J.; Shalev, Idan, . . . Putnam, Frank W. (2017). Childhood sexual abuse and early timing of puberty. *Journal of Adolescent Health, 60*(1), 65–71.

Norman, Geoffrey R.; Grierson, Lawrence E. M.; Sherbino, Jonathan; Hamstra, Stanley J.; Schmidt, Henk G. & Mamede, Silvia. (2018). Expertise in medicine and surgery. In K. Anders Ericsson, et al. (Eds.), *The Cambridge handbook of expertise and expert performance* (2nd ed., pp. 331–355). New York, NY: Cambridge University Press.

Normile, Dennis. (2018). Biologist unveils China's first private research university. *Science*, 359(6378).

Norrman, Emma; Petzold, Max; Bergh, Christina & Wennerholm, Ulla-Britt. (2018). School performance in singletons born after assisted reproductive technology. *Human Reproduction*, 33(10), 1948–1959.

North, Michael S. (2015). Ageism stakes its claim in the social sciences. *Generations*, 39(3), 29–33.

Norton, Michael I. & Ariely, Dan. (2011). Building a better America: One wealth quintile at a time. *Perspectives on Psychological Science*, 6(1), 9–12.

Nowak, Elisabeth & Schaub, Bianca. (2018). Prevention of allergies. In Ioana Agache & Peter Hellings (Eds.), *Implementing precision medicine* *in best practices of chronic airway diseases* (pp. 63–71). Cambridge, MA: Elsevier.

Nowaskie, Dustin; Austrom, Mary & Morhardt, Darby. (2019). Understanding the challenges, needs, and qualities of frontotemporal dementia family caregivers. *The American Journal of Geriatric Psychiatry*, 27(3, Suppl.), S98–S99.

Nwosisi, Christopher; Ferreira, Alexa; Rosenberg, Warren & Walsh, Kelly. (2016). A study of the flipped classroom and its effectiveness in flipping thirty percent of the course content. *International Journal of Information and Education Technology*, 6(5), 348–351.

O'Brien, Edward. (2019, March 15). Missoula high-schoolers demand action on climate change. *Montana Public Radio*.

O'Donnell, Michael; Nelson, Leif D.; Ackermann, Evi; Aczel, Balazs; Akhtar, Athfah; Aldrovandi, Silvio, . . . Briggs, Jessie C. (2018). Registered replication report: Dijksterhuis and van Knippenberg (1998). *Perspectives on Psychological Science*, 13(2), 268–294.

O'Dougherty, Maureen. (2013). Becoming a mother through postpartum depression: Narratives from Brazil. In Charlotte Faircloth, et al. (Eds.), *Parenting in global perspective: Negotiating ideologies of kinship, self and politics* (pp. 184–199). New York, NY: Routledge.

O'Meara, Madison S. & South, Susan C. (2019). Big Five personality domains and relationship satisfaction: Direct effects and correlated change over time. *Journal of Personality*, (In Press).

Oakes, J. Michael. (2009). The effect of media on children: A methodological assessment from a social epidemiologist. *American Behavioral Scientist*, 52(8), 1136–1151.

Obama, Michelle. (2018). *Becoming*. New York, NY: Crown.

Ocobock, Abigail. (2013). The power and limits of marriage: Married gay men's family relationships. *Journal of Marriage and Family*, 75(1), 191–205.

OECD. (2010). *PISA 2009 results: Learning to learn: Student engagement, strategies and practices* (Vol. 3). Paris: PISA, OECD Publishing.

OECD. (2011). *Education at a glance 2011: OECD indicators*. Paris, France: Organisation for Economic Cooperation and Development.

OECD. (2013). *Education at a glance 2013: OECD indicators*. Paris, France: Organisation for Economic Cooperation and Development.

OECD. (2014). *Education at a glance 2014: OECD Indicators*. Paris, France: Organisation for Economic Cooperation and Development.

OECD. (2015). Life expectancy at birth. In *Health at a glance 2015: OECD indicators* (pp. 46–47). Paris, France: Organisation for Economic Cooperation and Development.

OECD. (2016). *PISA 2015 results: Excellence and equity in education* (Vol. 1). Paris: PISA, OECD Publishing.

OECD. (2018). *Education at a glance 2018: OECD indicators*. Paris, France: Organisation for Economic Cooperation and Development.

OECD. (2019). Secondary graduation rate: Upper secondary, men / upper secondary, women, percentage, 2016. OECDiLibrary.

Oesterdiekhoff, Georg W. (2014). The role of developmental psychology to understanding history, culture and social change. *Journal of Social Sciences, 10*(4), 185–195.

Ogden, Cynthia L.; Fakhouri, Tala H.; Carroll, Margaret D.; Hales, Craig M.; Fryar, Cheryl D.; Li, Xianfen & Freedman, David S. (2017, December 22). *Prevalence of obesity among adults, by household income and education — United States, 2011–2014. Morbidity and Mortality Weekly Report*, 66(50), 1369–1373. Atlanta, GA: Centers for Disease Control and Prevention.

Ogolsky, Brian G. & Gray, Christine R. (2016). Conflict, negative emotion, and reports of partners' relationship maintenance in same-sex couples. *Journal of Family Psychology*, 30(2), 171–180.

Ohlsson, Stellan. (2018). The dialectic between routine and creative cognition. In Frédéric Vallée-Tourangeau (Ed.), *Insight: On the origins of new ideas*. New York, NY: Routledge.

Okazaki, Sumie. (2018). Culture, psychology, and social justice: Toward a more critical psychology of Asians and Asian Americans. In Phillip L. Hammack (Ed.), *The Oxford handbook of social psychology and social justice*. New York, NY: Oxford University Press.

Okun, Morris A.; Yeung, Ellen WanHeung & Brown, Stephanie. (2013). Volunteering by older adults and risk of mortality: A meta-analysis. *Psychology and Aging*, 28(2), 564–577.

Olfson, Mark; Crystal, Stephen; Huang, Cecilia & Gerhard, Tobias. (2010). Trends in antipsychotic drug use by very young, privately insured children. *Journal of the American Academy of Child and Adolescent Psychiatry*, 49(1), 13–23.

Oliver, David. (2019). When is it time for older drivers to stop? *BMJ*, 364(l403).

Oliver, Taylor L.; Meana, Marta & Snyder, Joel S. (2016). Sex differences in concordance rates between auditory event-related potentials and subjective sexual arousal. *Psychophysiology*, 53(8), 1272–1281.

Ollo-López, Andrea & Goñi-Legaz, Salomé. (2017). Differences in work–family conflict: Which individual and national factors explain them? *The International Journal of Human Resource Management*, 28(3), 499–525.

Olson, Kristina R. & Dweck, Carol S. (2009). Social cognitive development: A new look. *Child Development Perspectives*, 3(1), 60–65.

Olson, Sheryl L.; Lopez-Duran, Nestor; Lunkenheimer, Erika S.; Chang, Hyein & Sameroff, Arnold J. (2011). Individual differences in the development of early peer aggression: Integrating contributions of self-regulation, theory of mind, and parenting. *Development and Psychopathology*, 23(1), 253–266.

Olweus, Dan. (1999). Sweden. In Peter K. Smith, et al. (Eds.), *The nature of school bullying: A cross-national perspective* (pp. 7–27). New York, NY: Routledge.

Olweus, Dan & Limber, Susan P. (2018). Some problems with cyberbullying research. *Current Opinion in Psychology*, 19, 139–143.

Open Science Collaboration. (2015). Estimating the reproducibility of psychological science. *Science*, 349(6251), 943.

Oregon Public Health Division. (2018). *Oregon Death with Dignity Act: 2017 data summary*. Portland, OR: Oregon Health Authority, Public Health Division.

Oregon Public Health Division. (2019, February 15). *Oregon Death with Dignity Act: 2018 data summary*. Portland, OR: Oregon Health Authority, Public Health Division.

Orth, Ulrich; Erol, Ruth Yasemin & Luciano, Eva C. (2018). Development of self-esteem from age 4 to 94 years: A meta-analysis of longitudinal studies. *Psychological Bulletin, 144*(10), 1045–1080.

Orth, Ulrich & Robins, Richard W. (2014). The development of self-esteem. *Current Directions in Psychological Science*, 23(5), 381–387.

Orzabal, Marcus R.; Lunde-Young, Emilie R.; Ramirez, Josue I.; Howe, Selene Y. F.; Naik, Vishal D.; Lee, Jehoon, . . . Ramadoss, Jayanth. (2019). Chronic exposure to e-cig aerosols during early development causes vascular dysfunction and offspring growth deficits. *Translational Research*, 207, 70–82.

Osgood, D. Wayne; Ragan, Daniel T.; Wallace, Lacey; Gest, Scott D.; Feinberg, Mark E. & Moody, James. (2013). Peers and the emergence of alcohol use: Influence and selection processes in adolescent friendship networks. *Journal of Research on Adolescence*, 23(3), 500–512.

Osilla, Karen Chan; Miles, Jeremy N. V.; Hunter, Sarah B. & Amico, Elizabeth J. D. (2015). The longitudinal relationship between employment and substance use among at-risk adolescents. *Journal of Child & Adolescent Behavior Genetics*, 3(3).

Ostrov, Jamie M.; Kamper, Kimberly E.; Hart, Emily J.; Godleski, Stephanie A. & Blakely-McClure, Sarah J. (2014). A gender-balanced approach to the study of peer victimization and aggression subtypes in early childhood. *Development and Psychopathology*, 26(3), 575–587.

Ottesen, Ninja M.; Meluken, Iselin; Scheike, Thomas; Kessing, Lars V.; Miskowiak, Kamilla W. & Vinberg, Maj. (2018). Clinical characteristics, life adversities and personality traits in monozygotic twins with, at risk of and without affective disorders. *Frontiers in Psychiatry*, 9(401).

Over, Harriet & Gattis, Merideth. (2010). Verbal imitation is based on intention understanding. *Cognitive Development*, 25(1), 46–55.

Ovink, Sarah M. (2017). "In today's society, it's a necessity": Latino/a postsecondary plans in the college-for-all era. *Social Currents*, 4(2).

Owsley, Cynthia. (2011). Aging and vision. *Vision Research*, 51(13), 1610–1622.

Oza-Frank, Reena & Narayan, K. M. Venkat. (2010). Overweight and diabetes prevalence among U.S. immigrants. *American Journal of Public Health*, 100(4), 661–668.

Ozernov-Palchik, Ola; Norton, Elizabeth S.; Sideridis, Georgios; Beach, Sara D.; Wolf, Maryanne; Gabrieli, John D. E. & Gaab, Nadine. (2017). Longitudinal stability of pre-reading skill profiles of kindergarten children: Implications for early screening and theories of reading. *Developmental Science, 20*(5), e12471.

Paarlberg, Robert; Mozaffarian, Dariush; Micha, Renata & Chelius, Carolyn. (2018). Keeping soda in SNAP: Understanding the other iron triangle. *Society*, 55(4), 308–317.

Paat, Yok-Fong & Markham, Christine. (2019). The roles of family factors and relationship dynamics on dating violence victimization and perpetration among college men and women in emerging adulthood. *Journal of Interpersonal Violence, 34*(1), 81–114.

Padilla-Walker, Laura; Memmott-Elison, Madison & Nelson, Larry. (2017). Positive relationships as an indicator of flourishing during emerging adulthood. In Laura M. Padilla-Walker & Larry J. Nelson (Eds.), *Flourishing in emerging adulthood: Positive development during the third decade of life* (pp. 212–235). New York, NY: Oxford University Press.

Padilla-Walker, Laura; Nelson, Larry; Fu, Xinyuan & Barry, Carolyn. (2018). Bidirectional relations between parenting and prosocial behavior for Asian and European-American emerging adults. *Journal of Adult Development*, 25(2), 107–120.

Padilla-Walker, Laura M. & Nelson, Larry J. (Eds.). (2017). *Flourishing in emerging adulthood: Positive development during the third decade of life*. New York, NY: Oxford University Press.

Padilla-Walker, Laura M.; Nelson, Larry J. & Carroll, Jason S. (2012). Affording emerging adulthood: Parental financial assistance of their college-aged children. *Journal of Adult Development, 19*(1), 50–58.

Pahlke, Erin & Hyde, Janet Shibley. (2016). The debate over single-sex schooling. *Child Development Perspectives, 10*(2), 81–86.

Pahlke, Erin; Hyde, Janet Shibley & Allison, Carlie M. (2014). The effects of single-sex compared with coeducational schooling on students' performance and attitudes: A meta-analysis. *Psychological Bulletin, 140*(4), 1042–1072.

Pahwa, Rajesh & Lyons, Kelly E. (Eds.). (2013). *Handbook of Parkinson's disease* (5th ed.). Boca Raton, FL: CRC Press.

Paik, Anthony. (2011). Adolescent sexuality and the risk of marital dissolution. *Journal of Marriage and Family*, 73(2), 472–485.

Palatini, Paolo. (2015). Coffee consumption and risk of type 2 diabetes. *Diabetologia, 58*(1), 199–200.

Palmer, Sally B. & Abbott, Nicola. (2018). Bystander responses to bias-based bullying in schools: A developmental intergroup approach. *Child Development Perspectives*, *12*(1), 39–44.

Pankow, James F.; Kim, Kilsun; McWhirter, Kevin J.; Luo, Wentai; Escobedo, Jorge O.; Strongin, Robert M., . . . Peyton, David H. (2017). Benzene formation in electronic cigarettes. *PLoS ONE, 12*(3), e0173055.

Panksepp, Jaak & Watt, Douglas. (2011). What is basic about basic emotions? Lasting lessons from affective neuroscience. *Emotion Review*, 3(4), 387–396.

Papandreou, Maria. (2014). Communicating and thinking through drawing activity in early childhood. *Journal of Research in Childhood Education, 28*(1), 85–100.

Papapetrou, Eirini P. (2016). Induced pluripotent stem cells, past and future. *Science*, 353(6303), 991–992.

Parade, Stephanie H.; Armstrong, Laura M.; Dickstein, Susan & Seifer, Ronald. (2018). Family context moderates the association of maternal postpartum depression and stability of infant temperament. *Child Development, 89*(6), 2118–2135.

Park, Daeun; Yu, Alisa; Baelen, Rebecca N.; Tsukayama, Eli & Duckworth, Angela L. (2018). Fostering grit: Perceived school goal-structure predicts growth in grit and grades. *Contemporary Educational Psychology*, 55, 120–128.

Park, Hyun; Bothe, Denise; Holsinger, Eva; Kirchner, H. Lester; Olness, Karen & Mandalakas, Anna. (2011). The impact of nutritional status and longitudinal recovery of motor and cognitive milestones in internationally adopted children. *International Journal of Environmental Research and Public Health*, 8(1), 105–116.

Park, Jong-Tae; Jang, Yoonsun; Park, Min Sun; Pae, Calvin; Park, Jinyi; Hu, Kyung-Seok, . . . Kim, Hee-Jin. (2011). The trend of body donation for education based on Korean social and religious culture. *Anatomical Sciences Education*, 4(1), 33–38.

Parke, Ross D. (2013). Gender differences and similarities in parental behavior. In Bradford Wilcox & Kathleen K. Kline (Eds.), *Gender and parenthood: Biological and social scientific perspectives* (pp. 120–163). New York, NY: Columbia University Press.

Parker, Andrew. (2012). *Ethical problems and genetics practice*. New York, NY: Cambridge University Press.

Parker, Emily; Atchison, Bruce & Workman, Emily. (2016). *State pre-K funding for 2015–16 fiscal year: National trends in state preschool funding. 50-state review*. Denver, CO: Education Commission of the States.

Parker, Kim; Horowitz, Juliana Menasce & Stepler, Renee. (2017, December 5). *On gender differences, no consensus on nature vs. nurture: Americans say society places a higher premium on masculinity than on femininity. Social & Demographic Trends*. Washington, DC: Pew Research Center.

Parker, Samantha E.; Mai, Cara T.; Canfield, Mark A.; Rickard, Russel; Wang, Ying; Meyer, Robert E., . . . Correa, Adolfo. (2010). Updated national birth prevalence estimates for selected birth defects in the United States, 2004–2006. *Birth Defects Research Part A: Clinical and Molecular Teratology*, 88(12), 1008–1016.

Parten, Mildred B. (1932). Social participation among pre-school children. *The Journal of Abnormal and Social Psychology*, 27(3), 243–269.

Partridge, Bradley J.; Bell, Stephanie K.; Lucke, Jayne C.; Yeates, Sarah & Hall, Wayne D. (2011). Smart drugs "as common as coffee": Media hype about neuroenhancement. *PLoS ONE*, 6(11), e28416.

Pärtty, Anna & Kalliomäki, Marko. (2017). Infant colic is still a mysterious disorder of the microbiota–gut–brain axis. *Acta Paediatrica, 106*(4), 528–529.

Pascarella, Ernest T.; Martin, Georgianna L.; Hanson, Jana M.; Trolian, Teniell L.; Gillig, Benjamin & Blaich, Charles. (2014). Effects of diversity experiences on critical thinking skills over 4 years of college. *Journal of College Student Development*, 55(1), 86–92.

Pascarella, Ernest T. & Terenzini, Patrick T. (1991). *How college affects students: Findings and insights from twenty years of research*. San Francisco, CA: Jossey-Bass.

Pasco Fearon, R. M. & Roisman, Glenn I. (2017). Attachment theory: Progress and future directions. *Current Opinion in Psychology, 15*, 131–136.

Patel, Ayush; Medhekar, Rohan; Ochoa-Perez, Melissa; Aparasu, Rajender R.; Chan, Wenyaw; Sherer, Jeffrey T., . . . Chen, Hua. (2017). Care provision and prescribing practices of physicians treating children and adolescents with ADHD. *Psychiatric Services, 68*(7), 681–688.

Patel, Cyra; Brotherton, Julia Ml; Pillsbury, Alexis; Jayasinghe, Sanjay; Donovan, Basil; Macartney, Kristine & Marshall, Helen. (2018). The impact of 10 years of human papillomavirus (HPV) vaccination in Australia: What additional disease burden will a nonavalent vaccine prevent? *Eurosurveillance*, 23(41).

Patel, Dhaval; Steinberg, Joel & Patel, Pragnesh. (2018). Insomnia in the elderly: A review. *Journal of Clinical Sleep Medicine, 14*(6), 1017–1024.

Pathela, Preeti & Schillinger, Julia A. (2010). Sexual behaviors and sexual violence: Adolescents with opposite-, same-, or both-sex partners. *Pediatrics, 126*(5), 879–886.

Patil, Rakesh N.; Nagaonkar, Shashikant N.; Shah, Nilesh B. & Bhat, Tushar S. (2013). A cross-sectional study of common psychiatric morbidity in children aged 5 to 14 years in an urban slum. *Journal of Family Medicine and Primary Care*, 2(2), 164–168.

Patton, Mary H.; Blundon, Jay A. & Zakharenko, Stanislav S. (2019). Rejuvenation of plasticity in the brain: Opening the critical period. *Current Opinion in Neurobiology*, *54*, 83–89.

Paúl, Constança; Teixeira, Laetitia & Ribeiro, Oscar. (2013). What about happiness in later life? In Constantinos Phellas (Ed.), *Aging in European societies: Healthy aging in Europe* (pp. 83–96). New York, NY: Springer.

Pauwels, Lisa; Chalavi, Sima & Swinnen, Stephan P. (2018). Aging and brain plasticity. *Aging, 10*(8), 1789–1790.

Pellegrini, Anthony D. (2011). Introduction. In Anthony D. Pellegrini (Ed.), *The Oxford handbook of the development of play* (pp. 3–6). New York, NY: Oxford University Press.

Pellegrini, Anthony D. (2013). Play. In Philip D. Zelazo (Ed.), *The Oxford handbook of developmental psychology* (Vol. 2, pp. 276–299). New York, NY: Oxford University Press.

Pellegrini, Anthony D.; Roseth, Cary J.; Van Ryzin, Mark J. & Solberg, David W. (2011). Popularity as a form of social dominance: An evolutionary perspective. In Antonius H. N. Cillessen, et al. (Eds.), *Popularity in the peer system* (pp. 123–139). New York, NY: Guilford Press.

Pellis, Sergio M.; Himmler, Brett T.; Himmler, Stephanie M. & Pellis, Vivien C. (2018). Rough-and-tumble play and the development of the social brain: What do we know, how do we know it, and what do we need to know? In Robbin Gibb & Bryan Kolb (Eds.), *The neurobiology of brain and behavioral development* (pp. 315–337). San Diego, CA: Academic Press.

Peng, Peng; Yang, Xiujie & Meng, Xiangzhi. (2017). The relation between approximate number system and early arithmetic: The mediation role of numerical knowledge. *Journal of Experimental Child Psychology*, 157, 111–124.

Pennington, Charlotte R.; Heim, Derek; Levy, Andrew R. & Larkin, Derek T. (2016). Twenty years of stereotype threat research: A review of psychological mediators. *PLoS ONE, 11*(1), e0146487.

Peper, Jiska S. & Dahl, Ronald E. (2013). The teenage brain: Surging hormones — brain-behavior interactions during puberty. *Current Directions in Psychological Science*, 22(2), 134–139.

Pepper, Edward J.; Pathmanathan, Sasi; Mcilrae, Shona; Rehman, Faiz-Ur & Cardno, Alastair G. (2018). Associations between risk factors for schizophrenia and concordance in four monozygotic twin samples. *American Journal of Medical Genetics Part B: Neuropsychiatric Genetics*, 177(5), 503–510.

Perels, Franziska; Merget-Kullmann, Miriam; Wende, Milena; Schmitz, Bernhard & Buchbinder, Carla. (2009). Improving self-regulated learning of preschool children: Evaluation of training for kindergarten teachers. *British Journal of Educational Psychology*, 79(2), 311–327.

Perner, Josef. (2000). Communication and representation: Why mentalistic reasoning is a lifelong endeavour. In Peter Mitchell & Kevin John Riggs (Eds.), *Children's reasoning and the mind* (pp. 367–401). Hove, UK: Psychology Press.

Perone, Sammy; Palanisamy, Jeeva & Carlson, Stephanie M. (2018). Age-related change in brain rhythms from early to middle childhood: Links to executive function. *Developmental Science*, 21(6), e12691.

Perreira, Krista M. & Pedroza, Juan M. (2019). Policies of exclusion: Implications for the health of immigrants and their children. *Annual Review of Public Health*, 40, 7.1–7.20.

Perrin, Andrew & Anderson, Monica. (2019, April 10). *Share of U.S. adults using social media, including Facebook, is mostly unchanged since 2018. Fact Tank.* Washington, DC: Pew Research Center.

Perrin, Robin; Miller-Perrin, Cindy & Song, Jeongbin. (2017). Changing attitudes about spanking using alternative biblical interpretations. *International Journal of Behavioral Development, 41*(4), 514–522.

Perry, William G. (1970). *Forms of intellectual and ethical development in the college years: A scheme.* New York, NY: Holt, Rinehart and Winston.

Perry, William G. (1981). Cognitive and ethical growth: The making of meaning. In Arthur Chickering (Ed.), *The modern American college: Responding to the new realities of diverse students and a changing society* (pp. 76–116). San Francisco, CA: Jossey-Bass.

Perry, William G. (1998). *Forms of intellectual and ethical development in the college years: A scheme.* San Francisco, CA: Jossey-Bass.

Perry-Fraser, Charity & Fraser, Rick. (2018). A qualitative analysis of the stepparent role on transition days in blended families. *Open Journal of Social Sciences*, 6(8), 240–251.

Perszyk, Danielle R. & Waxman, Sandra R. (2018). Linking language and cognition in infancy. *Annual Review of Psychology*, 69, 231–250.

Peters, Stacey L.; Lind, Jennifer N.; Humphrey, Jasmine R.; Friedman, Jan M.; Honein, Margaret A.; Tassinari, Melissa S., . . . Broussard, Cheryl S. (2013). Safe lists for medications in pregnancy: Inadequate evidence base and inconsistent guidance from Web-based information, 2011. *Pharmacoepidemiology and Drug Safety*, 22(3), 324–328.

Petersen, Inge; Martinussen, Torben; McGue, Matthew; Bingley, Paul & Christensen, Kaare. (2011). Lower marriage and divorce rates among twins than among singletons in Danish birth cohorts 1940–1964. *Twin Research and Human Genetics, 14*(2), 150–157.

Petrenko, Christie L. M.; Friend, Angela; Garrido, Edward F.; Taussig, Heather N. & Culhane, Sara E. (2012). Does subtype matter? Assessing the effects of maltreatment on functioning in preadolescent youth in out-of-home care. *Child Abuse & Neglect*, 36(9), 633–644.

Pew Research Center. (2009, June 29). *Growing old in America: Expectations vs. reality.* Washington, DC: Pew Research Center.

Pew Research Center. (2014, April 16). *Global views on morality: Compare values across 40 countries. Global Attitudes & Trends.* Washington, DC: Pew Research Center.

Pew Research Center. (2014, February 11). *The rising cost of not going to college. Social & Demographic Trends.* Washington, DC: Pew Research Center.

Pew Research Center. (2015, December 17). *Parenting in America: Outlook, worries, aspirations are strongly linked to financial situation. Social & Demographic Trends.* Washington, DC: Pew Research Center.

Pew Research Center. (2015, May 12). *America's changing religious landscape: Christians decline sharply as share of population; unaffiliated and other faiths continue to grow. Religion & Public Life.* Washington, DC: Pew Research Center.

Pew Research Center. (2015, November 3). *U.S. public becoming less religious: Modest drop in overall rates of belief and practice, but religiously affiliated Americans are as observant as before. Religion & Public Life.* Washington, DC: Pew Research Center.

Pew Research Center. (2016, May 12). *Changing attitudes on gay marriage. Religion & Public Life.* Washington, DC: Pew Research Center.

Pew Research Center. (2018, June 13). *The age gap in religion around the world. Religion & Public Life.* Washington, DC: Pew Research Center.

Pew Research Center. (2019, June 12). *Social media fact sheet. Internet & Technology.* Washington, DC: Pew Research Center.

Pew Research Center. (2019, March 14). *Political independents: Who they are, what they think. U.S. Politics and Policy.* Washington, DC: Pew Research Center.

Pexman, Penny M. (2017). The role of embodiment in conceptual development. *Language, Cognition and Neuroscience*, (In Press).

Pfaus, James G.; Scepkowski, Lisa A.; Marson, Lesley & Georgiadis, Janniko R. (2014). Biology of the sexual response. In Deborah L. Tolman, et al. (Eds.), *APA handbook of sexuality and psychology* (Vol. 1, pp. 145–203). Washington, DC: American Psychological Association.

Phelan, Suzanne; Phipps, Maureen G.; Abrams, Barbara; Darroch, Francine; Schaffner, Andrew & Wing, Rena R. (2011). Practitioner advice and gestational weight gain. *Journal of Women's Health*, 20(4), 585–591.

Phillips, Deborah A.; Fox, Nathan A. & Gunnar, Megan R. (2011). Same place, different experiences: Bringing individual differences to research in child care. *Child Development Perspectives*, 5(1), 44–49.

Piaget, Jean. (1932). *The moral judgment of the child.* London, UK: K. Paul, Trench, Trubner & Co.

Piaget, Jean. (1950). *The psychology of intelligence.* London, UK: Routledge & Paul.

Piaget, Jean. (1952). *The origins of intelligence in children.* Oxford, UK: International Universities Press.

Piaget, Jean. (1954). *The construction of reality in the child.* New York, NY: Basic Books.

Piaget, Jean. (2001). *The psychology of intelligence.* New York, NY: Routledge.

Piaget, Jean. (2011). *The origins of intelligence in children.* New York, NY: Routledge.

Piaget, Jean. (2013a). *The construction of reality in the child.* New York, NY: Routledge.

Piaget, Jean. (2013b). *The moral judgment of the child.* New York, NY: Routledge.

Piaget, Jean. (2013c). *Play, dreams and imitation in childhood.* New York, NY: Routledge.

Piaget, Jean & Inhelder, Bärbel. (1956). *The child's conception of space.* London, UK: Routledge.

Piaget, Jean & Inhelder, Bärbel. (1972). *The psychology of the child.* New York, NY: Basic Books.

Piaget, Jean & Inhelder, Bärbel. (2013). *The child's conception of space.* New York, NY: Routledge.

Piaget, Jean; Voelin-Liambey, Daphne & Berthoud-Papandropoulou, Ioanna. (2015). Problems of class inclusion and logical implication. In Robert L. Campell (Ed.), *Studies in reflecting abstraction* (pp. 105–137). Hove, UK: Psychology Press.

Piekny, Jeanette & Maehler, Claudia. (2013). Scientific reasoning in early and middle childhood: The development of domain-general evidence evaluation, experimentation, and hypothesis generation skills. *British Journal of Developmental Psychology, 31*(2), 153–179.

Piérard, Gérald E.; Hermanns-Lê, Trinh; Piérard, Sébastien & Piérard-Franchimont, Claudine. (2015). Effects of hormone replacement therapy on skin viscoelasticity during climacteric aging. In Miranda A. Farage, et al. (Eds.), *Skin, mucosa and menopause: Management of clinical issues* (pp. 97–103). New York, NY: Springer.

Pietrantonio, Anna Marie; Wright, Elise; Gibson, Kathleen N.; Alldred, Tracy; Jacobson, Dustin & Niec, Anne. (2013). Mandatory reporting of child abuse and neglect: Crafting a positive process for health professionals and caregivers. *Child Abuse & Neglect, 37*(2/3), 102–109.

Pietromonaco, Paula R. & Powers, Sally I. (2015). Attachment and health-related physiological stress processes. *Current Opinion in Psychology, 1*, 34–39.

Pietschnig, Jakob & Voracek, Martin. (2015). One century of global IQ gains: A formal meta-analysis of the Flynn Effect (1909–2013). *Perspectives on Psychological Science, 10*(3), 282–306.

Piili, Reetta P.; Metsänoja, Riina; Hinkka, Heikki; Kellokumpu-Lehtinen, Pirkko-Liisa I. & Lehto, Juho T. (2018). Changes in attitudes towards hastened death among Finnish physicians over the past sixteen years. *BMC Medical Ethics, 19*(1).

Pilarz, Alejandra Ros & Hill, Heather D. (2014). Unstable and multiple child care arrangements and young children's behavior. *Early Childhood Research Quarterly, 29*(4), 471–483.

Pilkauskas, Natasha. (2014). Breastfeeding initiation and duration in coresident grandparent, mother and infant households. *Maternal and Child Health Journal, 18*(8), 1955–1963.

Pinderhughes, Ellen E. & Rosnati, Rosa. (2015). Introduction to special issue: Adoptees' ethnic identity within family and social contexts. *New Directions for Child and Adolescent Development, 150*, 1–3.

Pinker, Steven. (1999). *Words and rules: The ingredients of language*. New York, NY: Basic Books.

Pinker, Steven. (2003). *The blank slate: The modern denial of human nature*. New York, NY: Penguin.

Pinker, Steven. (2018). *Enlightenment now: The case for reason, science, humanism, and progress*. New York, NY: Viking.

Pinquart, Martin & Kauser, Rubina. (2018). Do the associations of parenting styles with behavior problems and academic achievement vary by culture? Results from a meta-analysis. *Cultural Diversity and Ethnic Minority Psychology, 24*(1), 75–100.

Pinquart, Martin & Silbereisen, Rainer K. (2006). Socioemotional selectivity in cancer patients. *Psychology and Aging, 21*(2), 419–423.

Piteo, A. M.; Roberts, R. M.; Nettelbeck, T.; Burns, N.; Lushington, K.; Martin, A. J. & Kennedy, J. D. (2013). Postnatal depression mediates the relationship between infant and maternal sleep disruption and family dysfunction. *Early Human Development, 89*(2), 69–74.

Pittenger, Samantha L.; Huit, Terrence Z. & Hansen, David J. (2016). Applying ecological systems theory to sexual revictimization of youth: A review with implications for research and practice. *Aggression and Violent Behavior, 26*, 35–45.

Pittenger, Samantha L.; Pogue, Jessica K. & Hansen, David J. (2018). Predicting sexual revictimization in childhood and adolescence: A longitudinal examination using ecological systems theory. *Child Maltreatment, 23*(2), 137–146.

Pizot, Cécile; Boniol, Mathieu; Mullie, Patrick; Koechlin, Alice; Boniol, Magali; Boyle, Peter & Autier, Philippe. (2016). Physical activity, hormone replacement therapy and breast cancer risk: A meta-analysis of prospective studies. *European Journal of Cancer, 52*, 138–154.

Plomin, Robert & Deary, Ian J. (2015). Genetics and intelligence differences: Five special findings. *Molecular Psychiatry, 20*, 98–108.

Plomin, Robert; DeFries, John C.; Knopik, Valerie S. & Neiderhiser, Jenae M. (2013). *Behavioral genetics*. New York, NY: Worth Publishers.

Plows, Alexandra. (2011). *Debating human genetics: Contemporary issues in public policy and ethics*. New York, NY: Routledge.

Pluess, Michael. (2015). Individual differences in environmental sensitivity. *Child Development Perspectives, 9*(3), 138–143.

Pluess, Michael & Belsky, Jay. (2010). Differential susceptibility to parenting and quality child care. *Developmental Psychology, 46*(2), 379–390.

Plutzer, Eric & Hannah, A. Lee. (2018). Teaching climate change in middle schools and high schools: Investigating STEM education's deficit model. *Climatic Change, 149*(3), 305–317.

Podsiadlowski, Astrid & Fox, Stephen. (2011). Collectivist value orientations among four ethnic groups: Collectivism in the New Zealand context. *New Zealand Journal of Psychology, 40*(1), 5–18.

Pogrebin, Abigail. (2010). *One and the same: My life as an identical twin and what I've learned about everyone's struggle to be singular*. New York, NY: Anchor.

Polanczyk, Guilherme V.; Willcutt, Erik G.; Salum, Giovanni A.; Kieling, Christian & Rohde, Luis A. (2014). ADHD prevalence estimates across three decades: An updated systematic review and meta-regression analysis. *International Journal of Epidemiology, 43*(2), 434–442.

Polderman, Tinca J. C.; Kreukels, Baudewijntje P. C.; Irwig, Michael S.; Beach, Lauren; Chan, Yee-Ming; Derks, Eske M., . . . Davis, Lea K. (2018). The biological contributions to gender identity and gender diversity: Bringing data to the table. *Behavior Genetics, 48*(2), 95–108.

Polesel, John; Dulfer, Nicky & Turnbull, Malcolm. (2012). *The experience of education: The impacts of high stakes testing on school students and their families. Literature review*. Rydalmere NSW, Australia: The Whitlam Institute within the University of Western Sydney.

Pollina, Laura Di; Guessous, Idris; Petoud, Véronique; Combescure, Christophe; Buchs, Bertrand; Schaller, Philippe, . . . Gaspoz, Jean-Michel. (2017). Integrated care at home reduces unnecessary hospitalizations of community-dwelling frail older adults: A prospective controlled trial. *BMC Geriatrics, 17*(53).

Pollock, Ross D.; O'Brien, Katie A.; Daniels, Lorna J.; Nielsen, Kathrine B.; Rowlerson, Anthea; Duggal, Niharika A., . . . Harridge, Stephen D. R. (2018). Properties of the vastus lateralis muscle in relation to age and physiological function in master cyclists aged 55–79 years. *Aging Cell, 17*(2), e12735.

Pons, Ferran & Lewkowicz, David J. (2014). Infant perception of audio-visual speech synchrony in familiar and unfamiliar fluent speech. *Acta Psychologica, 149*, 142–147.

Poole, Kristie L.; Jetha, Michelle K. & Schmidt, Louis A. (2017). Linking child temperament, physiology, and adult personality: Relations among retrospective behavioral inhibition, salivary cortisol, and shyness. *Personality and Individual Differences, 113*, 68–73.

Poon, Kean. (2018). Hot and cool executive functions in adolescence: Development and contributions to important developmental outcomes. *Frontiers in Psychology, 8*(2311).

Popham, Lauren E. & Hess, Thomas M. (2015). Age differences in the underlying mechanisms of stereotype threat effects. *Journal of Gerontology Series B, 70*(2), 223–232.

Portnoy, Jill; Gao, Yu; Glenn, Andrea L.; Niv, Sharon; Peskin, Melissa; Rudo-Hutt, Anna, . . . Raine, Adrian. (2013). The biology of childhood crime and antisocial behavior. In Chris L. Gibson & Marvin D. Krohn (Eds.), *Handbook of life-course criminology: Emerging trends and directions for future research* (pp. 21–42). New York, NY: Springer.

Posada, Germán E. & Waters, Harriet Salatas. (2018). The mother-child attachment partnership in early childhood: Secure base behavioral and representational processes. *Monographs of the Society for Research in Child Development, 83*(4).

Posner, Michael I. & Rothbart, Mary K. (2017). Integrating brain, cognition and culture. *Journal of Cultural Cognitive Science, 1*(1), 3–15.

Poushter, Jacob; Fetterolf, Janell & Tamir, Christine. (2019, April 22). *A changing world: Global views on diversity, gender equality, family life and the importance of religion*. Washington, DC: Pew Research Center.

Pouwels, J. Loes; Lansu, Tessa A. M. & Cillessen, Antonius H. N. (2016). Participant roles of bullying in adolescence: Status characteristics, social behavior, and assignment criteria. *Aggressive Behavior, 42*(3), 239–253.

Pouwels, J. Loes; Salmivalli, Christina; Saarento, Silja; Van Den Berg, Yvonne H. M.; Lansu, Tessa A. M. & Cillessen, Antonius H. N. (2017). Predicting adolescents' bullying participation from developmental trajectories of social status and behavior. *Child Development*, (In Press).

Powell, Cynthia M. (2013). Sex chromosomes, sex chromosome disorders, and disorders of sex development. In Steven L. Gersen & Martha B. Keagle (Eds.), *The principles of clinical cytogenetics* (pp. 175–211). New York, NY: Springer.

Powell, Kendall. (2006). Neurodevelopment: How does the teenage brain work? *Nature, 442*(7105), 865–867.

Powell, Katie; Wilcox, John; Clonan, Angie; Bissell, Paul; Preston, Louise; Peacock, Marian & Holdsworth, Michelle. (2015). The role of social networks in the development of overweight and obesity among adults: A scoping review. *BMC Public Health, 15*(996).

Powell, Shaun; Langlands, Stephanie & Dodd, Chris. (2011). Feeding children's desires? Child and parental perceptions of food promotion to the "under 8s". *Young Consumers: Insight and Ideas for Responsible Marketers, 12*(2), 96–109.

Powers, Alisa & Casey, B. J. (2015). The adolescent brain and the emergence and peak of psychopathology. *Journal of Infant, Child, and Adolescent Psychotherapy, 14*(1), 3–15.

Pozzoli, Tiziana & Gini, Gianluca. (2013). Why do bystanders of bullying help or not? A multidimensional model. *Journal of Early Adolescence*, 33(3), 315–340.

Prasad, Sahdeo; Gupta, Subash C. & Aggarwal, Bharat B. (2012). Micronutrients and cancer: Add spice to your life. In Sharmila Shankar & Rakesh K. Srivastava (Eds.), *Nutrition, Diet and Cancer* (pp. 23–48).

Pratt, Laura A.; Brody, Debra J. & Gu, Qiuping. (2017, August). *Antidepressant use among persons aged 12 and over: United States, 2011–2014. NCHS Data Brief*, 283. Hyattsville, MD: National Center for Health Statistics.

Preckel, Katrin; Kanske, Philipp & Singer, Tania. (2018). On the interaction of social affect and cognition: Empathy, compassion and theory of mind. *Current Opinion in Behavioral Sciences, 19*, 1–6.

Preston, Tom & Kelly, Michael. (2006). A medical ethics assessment of the case of Terri Schiavo. *Death Studies, 30*(2), 121–133.

Price, Debora; Ribe, Eloi; Di Gessa, Giorgio & Glaser, Karen. (2018). Grandparental childcare: A reconceptualisation of family policy regimes. In Virpi Timonen (Ed.), *Grandparenting practices around the world* (pp. 43–64). Chicago, IL: Policy Press.

Priess, Heather A.; Lindberg, Sara M. & Hyde, Janet Shibley. (2009). Adolescent gender-role identity and mental health: Gender intensification revisited. *Child Development*, 80(5), 1531–1544.

Proctor, Laura J. & Dubowitz, Howard. (2014). Child neglect: Challenges and controversies. In Jill E. Korbin & Richard D. Krugman (Eds.), *Handbook of child maltreatment* (pp. 27–61). New York, NY: Springer.

Propper, Cathi B. & Holochwost, Steven J. (2013). The influence of proximal risk on the early development of the autonomic nervous system. *Developmental Review*, 33(3), 151–167.

Prothero, Arianna. (2016, April 20). Charters help alums stick with college. *Education Week*, 35(28), 1, 13.

Proud2Bme. (2012, March 26). Overall, do social networking sites like Facebook and Twitter help or hurt your body confidence.

Pruden, Shannon M. & Levine, Susan C. (2017). Parents' spatial language mediates a sex difference in preschoolers' spatial-language use. *Psychological Science, 28*(11), 1583–1596.

Puertas, Alberto; Magan-Fernandez, Antonio; Blanc, Vanessa; Revelles, Laura; O'Valle, Francisco; Pozo, Elena, . . . Mesa, Francisco. (2018). Association of periodontitis with preterm birth and low birth weight: A comprehensive review. *Journal of Maternal-Fetal and Neonatal Medicine, 31*(5), 597–602.

Puetz, Vanessa B.; Parker, Drew; Kohn, Nils; Dahmen, Brigitte; Verma, Ragini & Konrad, Kerstin. (2017). Altered brain network integrity after childhood maltreatment: A structural connectomic DTI-study. *Human Brain Mapping*, 38(2), 855–868.

Puhl, Rebecca M. & Heuer, Chelsea A. (2010). Obesity stigma: Important considerations for public health. *American Journal of Public Health, 100*(6), 1019–1028.

Pulvermüller, Friedemann. (2018). Neural reuse of action perception circuits for language, concepts and communication. *Progress in Neurobiology, 160*, 1–44.

Putnam, Robert D. (2015). *Our kids: The American dream in crisis*. New York, NY: Simon & Schuster.

Qin, Desiree B. & Chang, Tzu-Fen. (2013). Asian fathers. In Natasha J. Cabrera & Catherine S. Tamis-LeMonda (Eds.), *Handbook of father involvement: Multidisciplinary perspectives* (2nd ed., pp. 261–281). New York, NY: Routledge.

Qin, Jiabi; Sheng, Xiaoqi; Wang, Hua; Liang, Desheng; Tan, Hongzhuan & Xia, Jiahui. (2015). Assisted reproductive technology and risk of congenital malformations: A meta-analysis based on cohort studies. *Archives of Gynecology and Obstetrics*, 292(4), 777–798.

Qiu, A.; Anh, T. T.; Li, Y.; Chen, H.; Rifkin-Graboi, A.; Broekman, B. F. P., . . . Meaney, M. J. (2015). Prenatal maternal depression alters amygdala functional connectivity in 6-month-old infants. *Translational Psychiatry*, 5, e508.

Qiu, Chengxuan; von Strauss, Eva; Bäckman, Lars; Winblad, Bengt & Fratiglioni, Laura. (2013). Twenty-year changes in dementia occurrence suggest decreasing incidence in central Stockholm, Sweden. *Neurology, 80*(20), 1888–1894.

Quindlen, Anna. (2012). *Lots of candles, plenty of cake*. New York, NY: Random House.

Quinn, Rand & Cheuk, Tina. (2018). *School vouchers in the Trump era: How political ideology and religion shape public opinion*. Philadelphia, PA: Consortium for Policy Research in Education. CPRE Policy Briefs. PB #2018-1.

Rabkin, Nick & Hedberg, Eric C. (2011). *Arts education in America: What the declines mean for arts participation*. Washington, DC: National Endowment for the Arts.

Raby, K. Lee; Labella, Madelyn H.; Martin, Jodi; Carlson, Elizabeth A. & Roisman, Glenn I. (2017). Childhood abuse and neglect and insecure attachment states of mind in adulthood: Prospective, longitudinal evidence from a high-risk sample. *Development and Psychopathology*, 29(2), 347–363.

Raeburn, Paul. (2014). *Do fathers matter?: What science is telling us about the parent we've overlooked*. New York, NY: Farrar, Straus and Giroux.

Rahilly, Elizabeth P. (2015). The gender binary meets the gender-variant child: Parents' negotiations with childhood gender variance. *Gender & Society*, 29(3), 338–361.

Rahman, Muhammad A.; Todd, Charlotte; John, Ann; Tan, Jacinta; Kerr, Michael; Potter, Robert, . . . Brophy, Sinead. (2018). School achievement as a predictor of depression and self-harm in adolescence: Linked education and health record study. *The British Journal of Psychiatry, 212*(4), 215–221.

Raipuria, Harinder Dosanjh; Lovett, Briana; Lucas, Laura & Hughes, Victoria. (2018). A literature review of midwifery-led care in reducing labor and birth interventions. *Nursing for Women's Health*, 22(5), 387–400.

Rajendran, Khushmand; Trampush, Joey W.; Rindskopf, David; Marks, David J.; O'Neill, Sarah & Halperin, Jeffrey M. (2013). Association between variation in neuropsychological development and trajectory of ADHD severity in early childhood. *The American Journal of Psychiatry*, 170(10), 1205–1211.

Rakic, Snezana; Jankovic Raznatovic, Svetlana; Jurisic, Aleksandar; Anicic, Radomir & Zecevic, Nebojsa. (2016). Fetal neurosonography and fetal behaviour: Genesis of fetal movements and motor reflexes. *Ultrasound in Obstetrics and Gynecology*, 48(Suppl. 1), 196.

Ramani, Geetha B.; Brownell, Celia A. & Campbell, Susan B. (2010). Positive and negative peer interaction in 3- and 4-year-olds in relation to regulation and dysregulation. *Journal of Genetic Psychology, 171*(3), 218–250.

Ramírez, Naja Ferjan; Ramírez, Rey R.; Clarke, Maggie; Taulu, Samu & Kuhl, Patricia K. (2017). Speech discrimination in 11-month-old bilingual and monolingual infants: A magnetoencephalography study. *Developmental Science, 20*(1), e12427.

Ramscar, Michael & Dye, Melody. (2011). Learning language from the input: Why innate constraints can't explain noun compounding. *Cognitive Psychology*, 62(1), 1–40.

Ranciaro, Alessia; Campbell, Michael C.; Hirbo, Jibril B.; Ko, Wen-Ya; Froment, Alain; Anagnostou, Paolo, . . . Tishkoff, Sarah A. (2014). Genetic origins of lactase persistence and the spread of pastoralism in Africa. *The American Journal of Human Genetics, 94*(4), 496–510.

Rand, David G. & Nowak, Martin A. (2016). Cooperation among humans. In Dirk Messner & Silke Weinlich (Eds.), *Global cooperation and the human factor in international relations* (pp. 113–138). New York, NY: Routledge.

Rank, Otto. (1929). *The trauma of birth*. New York, NY: Harcourt, Brace.

Rankin, Jay. (2017). Physicians disagree on legal age for cannabis. *CMAJ, 189*(4), E174–E175.

Rasberry, Catherine N.; Lee, Sarah M.; Robin, Leah; Laris, B. A.; Russell, Lisa A.; Coyle, Karin K. & Nihiser, Allison J. (2011). The association between school-based physical activity, including physical education, and academic performance: A systematic review of the literature. *Preventive Medicine, 52*, S10–S20.

Raspberry, Kelly A. & Skinner, Debra. (2011). Negotiating desires and options: How mothers who carry the fragile X gene experience reproductive decisions. *Social Science & Medicine, 72*(6), 992–998.

Rastrelli, Giulia; Guaraldi, Federica; Reismann, Yacov; Sforza, Alessandra; Isidori, Andrea M.; Maggi, Mario & Corona, Giovanni. (2019). Testosterone replacement therapy for sexual symptoms. *Sexual Medicine Reviews, 7*(3), 464–475.

Rau, Barbara L. & Adams, Gary A. (2014). Recruiting older workers: Realities and needs of the future workforce. In Daniel M. Cable, et al. (Eds.), *The Oxford handbook of recruitment* (pp. 88–109). New York, NY: Oxford University Press.

Rauers, Antje; Blanke, Elisabeth & Riediger, Michaela. (2013). Everyday empathic accuracy in younger and older couples: Do you need to see your partner to know his or her feelings? *Psychological Science, 24*(11), 2210–2217.

Rauh, Virginia A. (2018). Polluting developing brains — EPA failure on chlorpyrifos. *New England Journal of Medicine, 378*(13), 1171–1174.

Ravesteijn, Bastian; Van Kippersluis, Hans & Van Doorslaer, Eddy. (2017). The wear and tear on health: What is the role of occupation? *Health Economics, 27*(2), e69–e86.

Rawlins, William K. (2016). Foreword. In Mahzad Hojjat & Anne Moyer (Eds.), *The psychology of friendship*. New York, NY: Oxford University Press.

Ray, Brian D. (2013). Homeschooling rising into the twenty-first century: Editor's introduction. *Peabody Journal of Education, 88*(3), 261–264.

Raymond, Jaime & Brown, Mary Jean. (2017, January 20). *Childhood blood lead levels in children aged <5 Years — United States, 2009–2014. Morbidity and Mortality Weekly Report, 66*(3), 1–10. Atlanta, GA: Centers for Disease Control and Prevention.

Rea, Irene M.; Mills, Ken I. & ACUME2 Project. (2018). Living long and aging well: Are lifestyle factors the epigenetic link in the longevity phenotype. In Alexey Moskalev & Alexander M. Vaiserman (Eds.), *Epigenetics of aging and longevity* (Vol. 4). San Diego, CA: Academic Press.

Reardon, Sean F. (2013). The widening income achievement gap. *Educational Leadership, 70*(8), 10–16.

Reczek, Corinne; Liu, Hui & Spiker, Russell. (2014). A population-based study of alcohol use in same-sex and different-sex unions. *Journal of Marriage and Family, 76*(3), 557–572.

Reddy, Sunita; Patel, Tulsi; Kristensen, Malene Tanderup & Nielsen, Birgitte Bruun. (2018). Surrogacy in India: Political and commercial framings. In Sayani Mitra, et al. (Eds.), *Cross-cultural comparisons on surrogacy and egg donation: Interdisciplinary perspectives from India, Germany and Israel*. Cham, Switzerland: Palgrave Macmillan.

Reed, Andrew E.; Chan, Larry & Mikels, Joseph A. (2014). Meta-analysis of the age-related positivity effect: Age differences in preferences for positive over negative information. *Psychology and Aging, 29*(1), 1–15.

Reich, Justin. (2015). Rebooting MOOC research. *Science, 347*(6217), 34–35.

Reid, Keshia M.; Forrest, Jamie R. & Porter, Lauren. (2018, June 1). *Tobacco product use among youths with and without lifetime asthma — Florida, 2016. Morbidity and Mortality Weekly Report, 67*(21), 599–601. Atlanta, GA: Centers for Disease Control and Prevention.

Reid, Vincent M.; Kaduk, Katharina & Lunn, Judith. (2019). Links between action perception and action production in 10-week-old infants. *Neuropsychologia, 126*, 69–74.

Reilly, Steven K. & Noonan, James P. (2016). Evolution of gene regulation in humans. *Annual Review of Genomics and Human Genetics, 17*, 45–67.

Reimann, Zakary; Miller, Jacob R.; Dahle, Kaitana M.; Hooper, Audrey P.; Young, Ashley M.; Goates, Michael C., . . . Crandall, AliceAnn. (2018). Executive functions and health behaviors associated with the leading causes of death in the United States: A systematic review. *Journal of Health Psychology*, (In Press).

Reinehr, Thomas & Roth, Christian Ludwig. (2019). Is there a causal relationship between obesity and puberty? *The Lancet Child & Adolescent Health, 3*(1), 44–54.

Reiss, Ira. (1964). The scaling of premarital sexual permissiveness. *Journal of Marriage and the Family, 26*(2), 188–198.

Reitz, Anne K. & Staudinger, Ursula M. (2017). Getting older, getting better? Toward understanding positive personality development across adulthood. In Jule Specht (Ed.), *Personality Development Across the Lifespan* (pp. 219–241). Cambridge, MA: Academic Press.

Remington, Gary & Seeman, Mary V. (2015). Schizophrenia and the influence of male gender. *Clinical Pharmacology & Therapeutics, 98*(6), 578–581.

Renfrew, Mary J.; McFadden, Alison; Bastos, Maria Helena; Campbell, James; Channon, Andrew Amos; Cheung, Ngai Fen, . . . Declercq, Eugene. (2014). Midwifery and quality care: Findings from a new evidence-informed framework for maternal and newborn care. *The Lancet, 384*(9948), 1129–1145.

Rest, James. (1993). Research on moral judgment in college students. In Andrew Garrod (Ed.), *Approaches to moral development: New research and emerging themes* (pp. 201–211). New York, NY: Teachers College Press.

Retelas, George. (2017, December 12). Interview with Sheri Sheppard, Grace Young, Emily Bohl, Maria Filsinger, Marina Dimitrov, and Ariana Qayumi by undergraduate students at Stanford University. EngineerGirl @ Stanford University.

Reynolds, Arthur J. (2000). *Success in early intervention: The Chicago Child-Parent Centers*. Lincoln, NE: University of Nebraska Press.

Reynolds, Arthur J. & Ou, Suh-Ruu. (2011). Paths of effects from preschool to adult well-being: A confirmatory analysis of the Child-Parent Center Program. *Child Development, 82*(2), 555–582.

Reynolds, Jamila E. & Gonzales-Backen, Melinda A. (2017). Ethnic-racial socialization and the mental health of African Americans: A critical review. *Journal of Family Theory & Review, 9*(12), 182–200.

Rhoades, Brittany L.; Greenberg, Mark T.; Lanza, Stephanie T. & Blair, Clancy. (2011). Demographic and familial predictors of early executive function development: Contribution of a person-centered perspective. *Journal of Experimental Child Psychology, 108*(3), 638–662.

Rhodes, Marjorie. (2013). The conceptual structure of social categories: The social allegiance hypothesis. In Mahzarin R. Banaji & Susan A. Gelman (Eds.), *Navigating the social world: What infants, children, and other species can teach us* (pp. 258–262). New York, NY: Oxford University Press.

Rhodes, Marjorie & Wellman, Henry M. (2017). Moral learning as intuitive theory revision. *Cognition, 167*, 191–200.

Rice, Eric; Craddock, Jaih; Hemler, Mary; Rusow, Joshua; Plant, Aaron; Montoya, Jorge & Kordic, Timothy. (2018). Associations between sexting behaviors and sexual behaviors among mobile phone-owning teens in Los Angeles. *Child Development, 89*(1), 110–117.

Rich, Motoko. (2013, April 11). Texas considers backtracking on testing. *New York Times*.

Richards, Jennifer S.; Hartman, Catharina A.; Franke, Barbara; Hoekstra, Pieter J.; Heslenfeld, Dirk J.; Oosterlaan, Jaap, . . . Buitelaar, Jan K. (2014). Differential susceptibility to maternal expressed emotion in children with ADHD and their siblings? Investigating plasticity genes, prosocial and antisocial behaviour. *European Child & Adolescent Psychiatry, 24*(2), 209–217.

Richards, Morgan K.; Flanagan, Meghan R.; Littman, Alyson J.; Burke, Alson K. & Callegari, Lisa S. (2016). Primary cesarean section and adverse delivery outcomes among women of very advanced maternal age. *Journal of Perinatology, 36*, 272–277.

Rideout, Victoria. (2017). *The Common Sense Census: Media use by kids age zero to eight*. San Francisco, CA: Common Sense Media.

Riediger, Michaela; Voelkle, Manuel C.; Schaefer, Sabine & Lindenberger, Ulman. (2014). Charting the life course: Age differences and validity of beliefs about lifespan development. *Psychology and Aging, 29*(3), 503–520.

Riegel, Klaus F. (1975). Toward a dialectical theory of development. *Human Development, 18*(1/2), 50–64.

Riglin, Lucy; Frederickson, Norah; Shelton, Katherine H. & Rice, Frances. (2013). A longitudinal study of psychological functioning and academic attainment at the transition to secondary school. *Journal of Adolescence*, 36(3), 507–517.

Riordan, Jan & Wambach, Karen (Eds.). (2009). *Breastfeeding and human lactation* (4th ed.). Sudbury, MA: Jones and Bartlett.

Rioux, Charlie; Castellanos-Ryan, Natalie; Parent, Sophie & Séguin, Jean R. (2016). The interaction between temperament and the family environment in adolescent substance use and externalizing behaviors: Support for diathesis–stress or differential susceptibility? *Developmental Review*, *40*(10), 117–150.

Rivera, Juan Ángel; de Cossío, Teresita González; Pedraza, Lilia S.; Aburto, Tania C.; Sánchez, Tania G. & Martorell, Reynaldo. (2014). Childhood and adolescent overweight and obesity in Latin America: A systematic review. *The Lancet Diabetes & Endocrinology*, 2(4), 321–332.

Rizza, Wanda; Veronese, Nicola & Fontana, Luigi. (2014). What are the roles of calorie restriction and diet quality in promoting healthy longevity? *Ageing Research Reviews*, *13*, 38–45.

Rizzo, Michael T. & Killen, Melanie. (2016). Children's understanding of equity in the context of inequality. *British Journal of Developmental Psychology*, 34(4), 569–581.

Roane, David M.; Landers, Alyssa; Sherratt, Jackson & Wilson, Gillian S. (2017). Hoarding in the elderly: A critical review of the recent literature. *International Psychogeriatrics*, *29*(7), 1077–1084.

Robben, Antonius C. G. M. (2018). Death and anthropology: An introduction. In Antonius C. G. M. Robben (Ed.), *Death, mourning, and burial: A cross-cultural reader* (2nd ed., pp. 1–16). Hoboken, NJ: Wiley-Blackwell.

Robelen, Erik W. (2011). More students enrolling in Mandarin Chinese. *Education Week*, 30(27), 5.

Robert, L. & Labat-Robert, J. (2015). Longevity and aging: Role of genes and of the extracellular matrix. *Biogerontology*, *16*(1), 125–129.

Roberts, Andrea G. & Lopez-Duran, Nestor L. (2019). Developmental influences on stress response systems: Implications for psychopathology vulnerability in adolescence. *Comprehensive Psychiatry*, 88, 9–21.

Roberts, Andrew W.; Ogunwole, Stella U.; Blakeslee, Laura & Rabe, Megan A. (2018). *The population 65 years and older in the United States: 2016. American Community Survey Reports*. Washington, DC: U.S. Census Bureau. ACS-38.

Roberts, Brent W. & Davis, Jordan P. (2016). Young adulthood is the crucible of personality development. *Emerging Adulthood*, 4(5), 318–326.

Roberts, Leslie. (2017, April 7). Nigeria's invisible crisis. *Science*, 356(6333), 18–23.

Roberts, Soraya. (2010, January 1). Travis Pastrana breaks world record for longest rally car jump on New Year's Eve. *New York Daily News*.

Robertson, Cassandra & O'Brien, Rourke. (2018). Health endowment at birth and variation in intergenerational economic mobility: Evidence from U.S. county birth cohorts. *Demography*, 55(1), 249–269.

Robertson, Deirdre A.; King-Kallimanis, Bellinda L. & Kenny, Rose Anne. (2016). Negative perceptions of aging predict longitudinal decline in cognitive function. *Psychology and Aging*, *31*(1), 71–81.

Robinson, Eric & Sutin, Angelina R. (2017). Parents' perceptions of their children as overweight and children's weight concerns and weight gain. *Psychological Science*, 28(3), 320–329.

Robinson, Julia T. & Murphy-Nugen, Amy B. (2018). It makes you keep trying: Life review writing for older adults. *Journal of Gerontological Social Work*, *61*(2), 171–192.

Robinson, Leah E.; Wadsworth, Danielle D.; Webster, E. Kipling & Bassett, David R. (2014). School reform: The role of physical education policy in physical activity of elementary school children in Alabama's Black Belt region. *American Journal of Health Promotion*, 38(Suppl. 3), S72–S76.

Robinson, Richard M. (2019). Reasoned managerial discourse. In Richard M. Robinson (Ed.), *Imperfect duties of management* (pp. 89–128). New York, NY: Springer.

Robson, Ruthann. (2010). Notes on my dying. In Nan Bauer Maglin & Donna Marie Perry (Eds.), *Final acts: Death, dying, and the choices we make* (pp. 19–28). New Brunswick, NJ: Rutgers University Press.

Rochat, Philippe. (2013). Self-conceptualizing in development. In Philip D. Zelazo (Ed.), *The Oxford handbook of developmental psychology* (Vol. 2, pp. 378–397). New York, NY: Oxford University Press.

Rock, Jacoba; Geier, Charles F.; Noll, Jennie G. & De Bellis, Michael D. (2018). Developmental traumatology: Brain development in maltreated children with and without PTSD. In Jennie G. Noll & Idan Shalev (Eds.), *The biology of early life stress* (pp. 45–56). Cham, Switzerland: Springer.

Rodkey, Elissa N. & Riddell, Rebecca Pillai. (2013). The infancy of infant pain research: The experimental origins of infant pain denial. *Journal of Pain*, *14*(4), 338–350.

Rodrigues, Daniela; Padez, Cristina & Machado-Rodrigues, Aristides M. (2018). Active parents, active children: The importance of parental organized physical activity in children's extracurricular sport participation. *Journal of Child Health Care*, 22(1), 159–170.

Roelfs, David J.; Shor, Eran; Davidson, Karina W. & Schwartz, Joseph E. (2011). Losing life and livelihood: A systematic review and meta-analysis of unemployment and all-cause mortality. *Social Science Medicine*, 72(6), 840–854.

Roenneberg, Till; Allebrandt, Karla; Merrow, Martha & Vetter, Céline. (2012). Social jetlag and obesity. *Current Biology*, 22(10), 939–943.

Rogoff, Barbara. (2003). *The cultural nature of human development*. New York, NY: Oxford University Press.

Rohsenow, Damaris J.; Tidey, Jennifer W.; Martin, Rosemarie A.; Colby, Suzanne M. & Eissenberg, Thomas. (2018). Effects of six weeks of electronic cigarette use on smoking rate, CO, cigarette dependence, and motivation to quit smoking: A pilot study. *Addictive Behaviors*, *80*, 65–70.

Romeo, Russell D. (2013). The teenage brain: The stress response and the adolescent brain. *Current Directions in Psychological Science*, 22(2), 140–145.

Romeo, Rachel R.; Leonard, Julia A.; Robinson, Sydney T.; West, Martin R.; Mackey, Allyson P.; Rowe, Meredith L. & Gabrieli, John D. E. (2018). Beyond the 30-million-word gap: Children's conversational exposure is associated with language-related brain function. *Psychological Science*, 29(5), 700–710.

Rønneberg, Vibeke & Torrance, Mark. (2019). Cognitive predictors of shallow-orthography spelling speed and accuracy in 6th grade children. *Reading and Writing*, 32(1), 197–216.

Rook, Graham A. W.; Lowry, Christopher A. & Raison, Charles L. (2014). Hygiene and other early childhood influences on the subsequent function of the immune system. *Brain Research*, (Corrected Proof).

Roopnarine, Jaipaul L. & Hossain, Ziarat. (2013). African American and African Caribbean fathers. In Natasha J. Cabrera & Catherine S. Tamis-LeMonda (Eds.), *Handbook of father involvement: Multidisciplinary perspectives* (2nd ed., pp. 223–243). New York, NY: Routledge.

Rose, Amanda J. & Asher, Steven R. (2017). The social tasks of friendship: Do boys and girls excel in different tasks? *Child Development Perspectives*, *11*(1), 3–8.

Rose, Nikolas. (2016). Reading the human brain: How the mind became legible. *Body & Society*, 22(2), 140–177.

Rose, Steven. (2008). Drugging unruly children is a method of social control. *Nature*, *451*(7178), 521.

Roseberry, Lynn & Roos, Johan. (2016). *Bridging the gender gap: Seven principles for achieving gender balance*. New York, NY: Oxford University Press.

Rosen, Meghan. (2016). Concern grows over Zika birth defects. *Science News*, *190*(9), 14–15.

Rosenbaum, James E. (2011). The complexities of college for all. *Sociology of Education*, 84(2), 113–117.

Rosenblatt, Paul C. (2013). Culture, socialization, and loss, grief, and mourning. In David K. Meagher & David E. Balk (Eds.), *Handbook of thanatology: The essential body of knowledge for the study of death, dying, and bereavement* (2nd ed., pp. 121–126). New York, NY: Routledge.

Rosenblum, Gianine D. & Lewis, Michael. (1999). The relations among body image, physical attractiveness, and body mass in adolescence. *Child Development*, 70(1), 50–64.

Rosenfeld, Michael; Thomas, Reuben J. & Sonia, Hausen. (2019). Disintermediating your friends. *Proceedings of the National Academy of Sciences*, *116*(36), 17753–17758.

Rosenfeld, Michael J. & Roesler, Katharina. (2019). Cohabitation experience and cohabitation's association with marital dissolution: The short-term benefits of cohabitation. *Journal of Marriage and Family*, *81*(1), 42–58.

Rosenfield, Sarah. (2012). Triple jeopardy? Mental health at the intersection of gender, race, and class. *Social Science & Medicine, 74*(11), 1791–1801.

Rosow, Irving. (1985). Status and role change through the life cycle. In Robert H. Binstock & Ethel Shanas (Eds.), *Handbook of aging and the social sciences* (2nd ed., pp. 62–93). New York, NY: Van Nostrand Reinhold.

Ross, Josephine; Anderson, James R. & Campbell, Robin N. (2011). *I remember me: Mnemonic self-reference effects in preschool children*. Boston, MA: Wiley-Blackwell.

Ross, Josephine; Yilmaz, Mandy; Dale, Rachel; Cassidy, Rose; Yildirim, Iraz & Zeedyk, M. Suzanne. (2017). Cultural differences in self-recognition: The early development of autonomous and related selves? *Developmental Science, 20*(3), e12387.

Ross, Robert; Hudson, Robert; Stotz, Paula J. & Lam, Miu. (2015). Effects of exercise amount and intensity on abdominal obesity and glucose tolerance in obese adults: A randomized trial. *Annals of Internal Medicine, 162*(5), 325–334.

Rosselli, Mónica; Ardila, Alfredo; Lalwani, Laxmi N. & Vélez-Uribe, Idaly. (2016). The effect of language proficiency on executive functions in balanced and unbalanced Spanish–English bilinguals. *Bilingualism: Language and Cognition, 19*(3), 489–503.

Rossignol, Michel; Chaillet, Nils; Boughrassa, Faiza & Moutquin, Jean-Marie. (2014). Interrelations between four antepartum obstetric interventions and cesarean delivery in women at low risk: A systematic review and modeling of the cascade of interventions. *Birth, 41*(1), 70–78.

Rostila, Mikael; Saarela, Jan & Kawachi, Ichiro. (2013). Suicide following the death of a sibling: A nationwide follow-up study from Sweden. *BMJ Open, 3*(4), e002618.

Roth, B. J.; Crea, T. M.; Jani, J.; Underwood, D.; Hasson, R. G.; Evans, K. & Zuch, M. (2019). Detached and afraid: U.S. immigration policy and the practice of forcibly separating parents and young children at the border. *Children Welfare*, (In Press).

Roth, Lauren W. & Polotsky, Alex J. (2012). Can we live longer by eating less? A review of caloric restriction and longevity. *Maturitas, 71*(4), 315–319.

Rothbart, Mary Klevjord. (2011). *Becoming who we are: Temperament and personality in development*. New York, NY: Guilford.

Rothstein, Mark A. (2015). The moral challenge of Ebola. *American Journal of Public Health, 105*(1), 6–8.

Roubinov, Danielle S. & Boyce, William Thomas. (2017). Parenting and SES: Relative values or enduring principles? *Current Opinion in Psychology, 15*, 162–167.

Rovee-Collier, Carolyn. (1987). Learning and memory in infancy. In Joy Doniger Osofsky (Ed.), *Handbook of infant development* (2nd ed., pp. 98–148). New York, NY: Wiley.

Rovee-Collier, Carolyn. (1990). The "memory system" of prelinguistic infants. *Annals of the New York Academy of Sciences, 608*, 517–542.

Rowe, Meredith L.; Denmark, Nicole; Harden, Brenda Jones & Stapleton, Laura M. (2016). The role of parent education and parenting knowledge in children's language and literacy skills among White, Black, and Latino families. *Infant and Child Development, 25*(2), 198–220.

Rübeling, Hartmut; Keller, Heidi; Yovsi, Relindis D.; Lenk, Melanie & Schwarzer, Sina. (2011). Children's drawings of the self as an expression of cultural conceptions of the self. *Journal of Cross-Cultural Psychology, 42*(3), 406–424.

Rubertsson, C.; Hellström, J.; Cross, M. & Sydsjö, G. (2014). Anxiety in early pregnancy: Prevalence and contributing factors. *Archives of Women's Mental Health, 17*(3), 221–228.

Rubin, Kenneth H.; Bowker, Julie C.; McDonald, Kristina L. & Menzer, Melissa. (2013). Peer relationships in childhood. In Philip D. Zelazo (Ed.), *The Oxford handbook of developmental psychology* (Vol. 2, pp. 242–275). New York, NY: Oxford University Press.

Ruch, Donna A.; Sheftall, Arielle H.; Schlagbaum, Paige; Fontanella, Cynthia A.; Campo, John V. & Bridge, Jeffrey A. (2019). Characteristics and precipitating circumstances of suicide among incarcerated youth. *Journal of the American Academy of Child & Adolescent Psychiatry, 58*(5), 514–524.e511.

Rudaz, Myriam; Ledermann, Thomas; Margraf, Jürgen; Becker, Eni S. & Craske, Michelle G. (2017). The moderating role of avoidance behavior on anxiety over time: Is there a difference between social anxiety disorder and specific phobia? *PLoS ONE, 12*(7), e0180298.

Rudolph, Karen D. (2014). Puberty as a developmental context of risk for psychopathology. In Michael Lewis & Karen D. Rudolph (Eds.), *Handbook of developmental psychopathology* (pp. 331–354). New York, NY: Springer.

Runions, Kevin C. & Shaw, Thérèse. (2013). Teacher–child relationship, child withdrawal and aggression in the development of peer victimization. *Journal of Applied Developmental Psychology, 34*(6), 319–327.

Russell, Ashley. (2018). Human trafficking: A research synthesis on human-trafficking literature in academic journals from 2000–2014. *Journal of Human Trafficking, 4*(2), 114–136.

Russell, Allison; Nyame-Mensah, Ama; Wit, Arjen & Handy, Femida. (2019). Volunteering and wellbeing among ageing adults: A longitudinal analysis. *VOLUNTAS, 30*(1), 115–128.

Russell, Charlotte K.; Robinson, Lyn & Ball, Helen L. (2013). Infant sleep development: Location, feeding and expectations in the postnatal period. *The Open Sleep Journal, 6*(Suppl. 1: M9), 68–76.

Russell, Stephen T.; Everett, Bethany G.; Rosario, Margaret & Birkett, Michelle. (2014). Indicators of victimization and sexual orientation among adolescents: Analyses from youth risk behavior surveys. *American Journal of Public Health, 104*(2), 255–261.

Russo, Theresa J. & Fallon, Moira A. (2014). Coping with stress: Supporting the needs of military families and their children. *Early Childhood Education Journal, 43*(5), 407–416.

Ruthig, Joelle C.; Trisko, Jenna & Stewart, Tara L. (2012). The impact of spouse's health and well-being on own well-being: A dyadic study of older married couples. *Journal of Social and Clinical Psychology, 31*(5), 508–529.

Rutter, Michael. (2012). Resilience as a dynamic concept. *Development and Psychopathology, 24*(2), 335–344.

Sabol, T. J.; Soliday Hong, S. L.; Pianta, R. C. & Burchinal, M. R. (2013). Can rating pre-K programs predict children's learning? *Science, 341*(6148), 845–846.

Sackett, Paul R. & Kuncel, Nathan R. (2018). Eight myths about standardized admissions testing. In Jack Buckley, et al. (Eds.), *Measuring success: Testing, grades, and the future of college admissions* (pp. 13–39). Baltimore, MD: Johns Hopkins University Press.

Sadana, Ritu; Budhwani, Suman; Blas, Erik; Posarac, Ana; Koller, Theadora & Paraje, Guillermo. (2019). Healthy ageing and health equity: Broader determinants of health with a spotlight on climate change. In Jean-Pierre Michel (Ed.), *Prevention of chronic diseases and age-related disability* (pp. 169–183). Cham, Switzerland: Springer.

Sadeh, Avi; Mindell, Jodi A.; Luedtke, Kathryn & Wiegand, Benjamin. (2009). Sleep and sleep ecology in the first 3 years: A web-based study. *Journal of Sleep Research, 18*(1), 60–73.

Sadeh, Avi; Tikotzky, Liat & Scher, Anat. (2010). Parenting and infant sleep. *Sleep Medicine Reviews, 14*(2), 89–96.

Sader, Josette; Roy, Camille & Guay, Stephane. (2018). Intimate partner violence and psychological distress among young couples: The role of the pattern of violence. *Violence and Victims, 33*(3), 547–561.

Sadler, Troy D.; Romine, William L.; Stuart, Parker E. & Merle-Johnson, Dominike. (2013). Game-based curricula in biology classes: Differential effects among varying academic levels. *Journal of Research in Science Teaching, 50*(4), 479–499.

Sadler, Thomas W. (2015). *Langman's medical embryology* (13th ed.). Philadelphia, PA: Lippincott Williams & Wilkins.

Saegert, Susan; Fields, Desiree & Libman, Kimberly. (2011). Mortgage foreclosure and health disparities: Serial displacement as asset extraction in African American populations. *Journal of Urban Health, 88*(3), 390–402.

Saey, Tina Hesman. (2016). Neandertal DNA poses health risks. *Science News, 189*(5), 18–19.

Saffran, Jenny R. & Kirkham, Natasha Z. (2018). Infant statistical learning. *Annual Review of Psychology, 69*, 181–203.

Sahlberg, Pasi. (2011). *Finnish lessons: What can the world learn from educational change in Finland?* New York, NY: Teachers College Press.

Sahlberg, Pasi. (2015). *Finnish lessons 2.0: What can the world learn from educational change in Finland?* (2nd. ed.). New York, NY: Teachers College.

Sahoo, Krushnapriya; Sahoo, Bishnupriya; Choudhury, Ashok Kumar; Sofi, Nighat Yasin; Kumar, Raman & Bhadoria, Ajeet Singh. (2015). Childhood obesity: Causes and consequences. *Journal of Family Medicine and Primary Care, 4*(2), 187–192.

Salpeter, Shelley R.; Luo, Esther J.; Malter, Dawn S. & Stuart, Brad. (2012). Systematic review of noncancer presentations with a median survival of 6 months or less. *The American Journal of Medicine, 125*(5), 512.e511–512.e516.

Salthouse, Timothy A. (2010). *Major issues in cognitive aging*. New York, NY: Oxford University Press.

Salthouse, Timothy A. (2019). Trajectories of normal cognitive aging. *Psychology and Aging*, 34(1), 17–24.

Samaras, Nikolass; Frangos, Emilia; Forster, Alexandre; Lang, P. O. & Samaras, Dimitrios. (2012). Andropause: A review of the definition and treatment. *European Geriatric Medicine*, 3(6), 368–373.

Samek, Diana R.; Goodman, Rebecca J.; Erath, Stephen A.; McGue, Matt & Iacono, William G. (2016). Antisocial peer affiliation and externalizing disorders in the transition from adolescence to young adulthood: Selection versus socialization effects. *Developmental Psychology*, 52(5), 813–823.

SAMHSDA. (2019). Substance Abuse and Mental Health Services Administration (SAMHSA)'s public online data analysis system: Data from the national survey on drug use and health, 2017.

Sampaio-Baptista, Cassandra; Sanders, Zeena-Britt & Johansen-Berg, Heidi. (2018). Structural plasticity in adulthood with motor learning and stroke rehabilitation. *Annual Review of Neuroscience, 41*, 25–40.

Samuels, Christina A. (2013). Study reveals gaps in graduation rates: Diplomas at risk. *Education Week*, 32(32), 5.

Sánchez, Alan & Singh, Abhijeet. (2018). Accessing higher education in developing countries: Panel data analysis from India, Peru, and Vietnam. *World Development, 109*, 261–278.

Sanchez, Gabriel R. & Vargas, Edward D. (2016). Taking a closer look at group identity: The link between theory and measurement of group consciousness and linked fate. *Political Research Quarterly, 69*(1), 160–174.

Sandberg, Sheryl & UC Berkeley (Producer). (2016). Sheryl Sandberg gives UC Berkeley Commencement keynote speech.

Sándor, Judit. (2019). Editing human reproduction? Legal and ethical aspects of genome editing. In E. Scott Sills & Gianpiero D. Palermo (Eds.), *Human embryos and preimplantation genetic technologies: Ethical, social, and public policy aspects* (pp. 185–197). San Diego, CA: Academic Press.

Sangrigoli, S.; Pallier, C.; Argenti, A.-M.; Ventureyra, V. A. G. & De Schonen, S. (2005). Reversibility of the other-race effect in face recognition during childhood. *Psychological Science, 16*(6), 440–444.

Santelli, John S.; Kantor, Leslie M.; Grilo, Stephanie A.; Speizer, Ilene S.; Lindberg, Laura D.; Heitel, Jennifer, . . . Ott, Mary A. (2017). Abstinence-only-until-marriage: An updated review of U.S. Policies and programs and their impact. *Journal of Adolescent Health, 61*(3), 273–280.

Santini, Ziggi Ivan; Koyanagi, Ai; Tyrovolas, Stefanos; Mason, Catherine & Haro, Josep Maria. (2015). The association between social relationships and depression: A systematic review. *Journal of Affective Disorders, 175*, 53–65.

Santos, Carlos E.; Kornienko, Olga & Rivas-Drake, Deborah. (2017). Peer influence on ethnic-racial identity development: A multisite investigation. *Child Development*, 88(3), 725–742.

Santos-Lozano, Alejandro; Santamarina, Ana; Pareja-Galeano, Helios; Sanchis-Gomar, Fabian; Fiuza-Luces, Carmen; Cristi-Montero, Carlos, . . . Garatachea, Nuria. (2016). The genetics of exceptional longevity: Insights from centenarians. *Maturitas, 90*, 49–57.

Sanz Cruces, José Manuel; Hawrylak, María Fernández & Delegido, Ana Benito. (2015). Interpersonal variability of the experience of falling in love. *International Journal of Psychology and Psychological Therapy, 15*(1), 87–100.

Saracho, Olivia N. (2016). *Contemporary perspectives on research on bullying and victimization in early childhood education*. Charlotte, NC: Information Age.

Saraiva, Linda; Rodrigues, Luís P.; Cordovil, Rita & Barreiros, João. (2013). Influence of age, sex and somatic variables on the motor performance of pre-school children. *Annals of Human Biology, 40*(5), 444–450.

Saroglou, Vassilis. (2012). Adolescents' social development and the role of religion. In Gisela Trommsdorff & Xinyin Chen (Eds.), *Values, religion, and culture in adolescent development* (pp. 391–423). New York, NY: Cambridge University Press.

Şaşmaz, Tayyar; Öner, Seva; Kurt, A. Öner; Yapıcı, Gülçin; Yazıcı, Aylin Ertekin; Buğdaycı, Resul & şiş, Mustafa. (2014). Prevalence and risk factors of Internet addiction in high school students. *European Journal of Public Health*, 24(1), 15–20.

Sassler, Sharon & Miller, Amanda Jayne. (2017). *Cohabitation nation: Gender, class, and the remaking of relationships*. Oakland, CA: University of California Press.

Satterwhite, Catherine Lindsey; Torrone, Elizabeth; Meites, Elissa; Dunne, Eileen F.; Mahajan, Reena; Ocfemia, M. Cheryl Bañez, . . . Weinstock, Hillard. (2013). Sexually transmitted infections among US women and men: Prevalence and incidence estimates, 2008. *Sexually Transmitted Diseases*, 40(3), 187–193.

Saudi, A Nur Aulia; Hartini, Nurul & Bahar, Bahar. (2018). Teenagers' motorcycle gang community aggression from the Personal Fable and risk-taking behavior perspective. *Psychology Research and Behavior Management, 11*, 305–309.

Sauer, Mark V.; Wang, Jeff G.; Douglas, Nataki C.; Nakhuda, Gary S.; Vardhana, Pratibashri; Jovanovic, Vuk & Guarnaccia, Michael M. (2009). Providing fertility care to men seropositive for human immunodeficiency virus: Reviewing 10 years of experience and 420 consecutive cycles of in vitro fertilization and intracytoplasmic sperm injection. *Fertility and Sterility, 91*(6), 2455–2460.

Saunders, Gerda. (2019). *Memory's last breath: Field notes on my dementia*. New York, NY: Hachette.

Savage, Jeanne E.; Jansen, Philip R.; Stringer, Sven; Watanabe, Kyoko; Bryois, Julien; de Leeuw, Christiaan A., . . . Posthuma, Danielle. (2018). Genome-wide association meta-analysis in 269,867 individuals identifies new genetic and functional links to intelligence. *Nature Genetics*, 50(7), 912–919.

Savioja, Hanna; Helminen, Mika; Fröjd, Sari; Marttunen, Mauri & Kaltiala-Heino, Riittakerttu. (2015). Sexual experience and self-reported depression across the adolescent years. *Health Psychology and Behavioral Medicine*, 3(1), 337–347.

Saw, Seang-Mei; Cheng, Angela; Fong, Allan; Gazzard, Gus; Tan, Donald T. H. & Morgan, Ian. (2007). School grades and myopia. *Ophthalmic and Physiological Optics*, 27(2), 126–129.

Saxbe, Darby E. (2017). Birth of a new perspective? A call for biopsychosocial research on childbirth. *Current Directions in Psychological Science*, 26(1), 81–86.

Saxton, Matthew. (2010). *Child language: Acquisition and development*. Thousand Oaks, CA: Sage.

Scarborough, William J.; Sin, Ray & Risman, Barbara. (2019). Attitudes and the stalled gender revolution: Egalitarianism, traditionalism, and ambivalence from 1977 through 2016. *Gender & Society*, 33(2), 173–200.

Scarr, Sandra. (1985). Constructing psychology: Making facts and fables for our times. *American Psychologist*, 40(5), 499–512.

Scelzo, Anna; Di Somma, Salvatore; Antonini, Paola; Montross, Lori; Schork, Nicholas; Brenner, David & Jeste, Dilip V. (2018). Mixed-methods quantitative-qualitative study of 29 nonagenarians and centenarians in rural Southern Italy: Focus on positive psychological traits. *International Psychogeriatrics*, 30(1), 31–38.

Schacter, Hannah L. & Juvonen, Jaana. (2018). Dynamic changes in peer victimization and adjustment across middle school: Does friends' victimization alleviate distress? *Child Development*, (In Press).

Schafer, Markus H.; Morton, Patricia M. & Ferraro, Kenneth F. (2014). Child maltreatment and adult health in a national sample: Heterogeneous relational contexts, divergent effects? *Child Abuse & Neglect*, 38(3), 395–406.

Schaie, K. Warner. (1958). Rigidity-flexibility and intelligence: A cross-sectional study of the adult life span from 20 to 70 years. *Psychological Monographs*, 72(9), 1–26.

Schaie, K. Warner. (2005). *Developmental influences on adult intelligence: The Seattle*

Longitudinal Study. New York, NY: Oxford University Press.

Schaie, K. Warner. (2013). *Developmental influences on adult intelligence: The Seattle Longitudinal Study* (2nd ed.). New York, NY: Oxford University Press.

Schanler, Richard. J. (2011). Outcomes of human milk-fed premature infants. *Seminars in Perinatology*, 35(1), 29–33.

Scharf, Miri. (2014). Parenting in Israel: Together hand in hand, you are mine and I am yours. In Helaine Selin (Ed.), *Parenting across cultures: Childrearing, motherhood and fatherhood in non-Western cultures* (pp. 193–206). Dordrecht: Springer.

Scherbaum, Stefan; Frisch, Simon; Holfert, Anna-Maria; O'Hora, Denis & Dshemuchadse, Maja. (2018). No evidence for common processes of cognitive control and self-control. *Acta Psychologica, 182*, 194–199.

Schermerhorn, Alice C.; D'Onofrio, Brian M.; Turkheimer, Eric; Ganiban, Jody M.; Spotts, Erica L.; Lichtenstein, Paul, . . . Neiderhiser, Jenae M. (2011). A genetically informed study of associations between family functioning and child psychosocial adjustment. *Developmental Psychology*, 47(3), 707–725.

Schienkiewitz, Anja; Brettschneider, Anna-Kristin; Damerow, Stefan & Rosario, Angelika Schaffrath. (2018). Overweight and obesity among children and adolescents in Germany: Results of the cross-sectional KiGGS Wave 2 study and trends. *Journal of Health Monitoring*, 3(1), 15–22.

Schneider, Daniel & Harknett, Kristen. (2019). Consequences of routine work-schedule instability for worker health and well-being. *American Sociological Review*, 84(1), 82–114.

Schneider, William; Waldfogel, Jane & Brooks-Gunn, Jeanne. (2017). The Great Recession and risk for child abuse and neglect. *Children and Youth Services Review*, 72, 71–81.

Schnitzspahn, Katharina M.; Ihle, Andreas; Henry, Julie D.; Rendell, Peter G. & Kliegel, Matthias. (2011). The age-prospective memory-paradox: An exploration of possible mechanisms. *International Psychogeriatrics*, 23(4), 583–592.

Schnitzspahn, Katharina M.; Stahl, Christoph; Zeintl, Melanie; Kaller, Christoph P. & Kliegel, Matthias. (2013). The role of shifting, updating, and inhibition in prospective memory performance in young and older adults. *Developmental Psychology*, 49(8), 1544–1553.

Schoebi, Dominik; Karney, Benjamin R. & Bradbury, Thomas N. (2012). Stability and change in the first 10 years of marriage: Does commitment confer benefits beyond the effects of satisfaction? *Journal of Personality and Social Psychology*, 102(4), 729–742.

Schofield, Thomas J.; Martin, Monica J.; Conger, Katherine J.; Neppl, Tricia M.; Donnellan, M. Brent & Conger, Rand D. (2011). Intergenerational transmission of adaptive functioning: A test of the interactionist model of SES and human development. *Child Development*, 82(1), 33–47.

Schore, Allan & McIntosh, Jennifer. (2011). Family law and the neuroscience of attachment: Part I. *Family Court Review*, 49(3), 501–512.

Schroeder, Steven A. (2013). New evidence that cigarette smoking remains the most important health hazard. *New England Journal of Medicine*, 368(4), 389–390.

Schübel, Ruth; Nattenmüller, Johanna; Sookthai, Disorn; Nonnenmacher, Tobias; Graf, Mirja E.; Riedl, Lena, . . . Kühn, Tilman. (2018). Effects of intermittent and continuous calorie restriction on body weight and metabolism over 50 wk: A randomized controlled trial. *American Journal of Clinical Nutrition, 108*(5), 933–945.

Schubert, Anna-Lena; Hagemann, Dirk & Frischkorn, Gidon T. (2017). Is general intelligence little more than the speed of higher-order processing? *Journal of Experimental Psychology, 146*(10), 1498–1512.

Schulenberg, John; O'Malley, Patrick M.; Bachman, Jerald G. & Johnston, Lloyd D. (2005). Early adult transitions and their relation to well-being and substance use. In Richard A. Settersten, et al. (Eds.), *On the frontier of adulthood: Theory, research, and public policy* (pp. 417–453). Chicago, IL: University of Chicago Press.

Schulenberg, John; Patrick, Megan E.; Maslowsky, Julie & Maggs, Jennifer L. (2014). The epidemiology and etiology of adolescent substance use in developmental perspective. In Michael Lewis & Karen D. Rudolph (Eds.), *Handbook of Developmental Psychopathology* (pp. 601–620). New York, NY: Springer.

Schulzke, Eric. (2017, January 19). Why one Utah woman is planning to end her life on her own terms. *Desert News*.

Schupp, Justin & Sharp, Jeff. (2012). Exploring the social bases of home gardening. *Agriculture and Human Values*, 29(1), 93–105.

Schwartsmann, Carlos Roberto; Spinelli, Leandro de Freitas; Boschin, Leonardo Carbonera; Yépez, Anthony Kerbes; Crestani, Marcus Vinicius & Silva, Marcelo Faria. (2015). Correlation between patient age at total hip replacement surgery and life expectancy. *Acta Ortopedica Brasileira*, 23(6), 323–325.

Schwartz, Seth & Petrova, Mariya. (2019). Prevention science in emerging adulthood: A field coming of age. *Prevention Science*, 20(3), 305–309.

Schwarz, Alan. (2016). *ADHD nation: Children, doctors, big pharma, and the making of an American epidemic*. New York, NY: Scribner.

Schweinhart, Lawrence J.; Montie, Jeanne; Xiang, Zongping; Barnett, W. Steven; Belfield, Clive R. & Nores, Milagros. (2005). *Lifetime effects: The High/Scope Perry Preschool Study through age 40*. Ypsilanti, MI: High/Scope Press.

Schweinhart, Lawrence J. & Weikart, David P. (1997). *Lasting differences: The High/Scope Preschool curriculum comparison study through age 23*. Ypsilanti, MI: High/Scope Educational Research Foundation.

Scott, Diane L.; Lee, Chang-Bae; Harrell, Susan W. & Smith-West, Mary B. (2013). Permanency for children in foster care: Issues and barriers for adoption. *Child & Youth Services*, 34(3), 290–307.

Scott, Lisa S. & Monesson, Alexandra. (2010). Experience-dependent neural specialization during infancy. *Neuropsychologia*, 48(6), 1857–1861.

Sears, William & Sears, Martha. (2001). *The attachment parenting book: A commonsense guide to understanding and nurturing your baby*. Boston, MA: Little Brown.

Seaton, Eleanor K. & Iida, Masumi. (2019). Racial discrimination and racial identity: Daily moderation among Black youth. *American Psychologist*, 74(1), 117–127.

Seaton, Eleanor K.; Quintana, Stephen; Verkuyten, Maykel & Gee, Gilbert C. (2017). Peers, policies, and place: The relation between context and ethnic/racial identity. *Child Development*, 88(3), 683–692.

Sedgh, Gilda; Finer, Lawrence B.; Bankole, Akinrinola; Eilers, Michelle A. & Singh, Susheela. (2015). Adolescent pregnancy, birth, and abortion rates across countries: Levels and recent trends. *Journal of Adolescent Health*, 56(2), 223–230.

Sedlak, Andrea J. & Ellis, Raquel T. (2014). Trends in child abuse reporting. In Jill E. Korbin & Richard D. Krugman (Eds.), *Handbook of child maltreatment* (pp. 3–26). New York, NY: Springer.

Seelaar, Harro; Rohrer, Jonathan D.; Pijnenburg, Yolande A. L.; Fox, Nick C. & van Swieten, John C. (2011). Clinical, genetic and pathological heterogeneity of frontotemporal dementia: A review. *Journal of Neurology, Neurosurgery, & Psychiatry*, 82(5), 476–486.

Seemiller, Eric S.; Cumming, Bruce G. & Candy, T. Rowan. (2018). Human infants can generate vergence responses to retinal disparity by 5 to 10 weeks of age. *Journal of Vision, 18*(6).

Seider, Scott; Clark, Shelby; Graves, Daren; Kelly, Lauren Leigh; Soutter, Madora; El-Amin, Aaliyah & Jennett, Pauline. (2019). Black and Latinx adolescents' developing beliefs about poverty and associations with their awareness of racism. *Developmental Psychology*, 55(3), 509–524.

Sekeres, Mikkael A. (2013, January 31). A doctor's struggle with numbers. *New York Times*.

Selita, Fatos & Kovas, Yulia. (2019). Genes and Gini: What inequality means for heritability. *Journal of Biosocial Science*, 51(1), 18–47.

Şendil, Çağla Öneren & Erden, Feyza Tantekin. (2014). Peer preference: A way of evaluating social competence and behavioural well-being in early childhood. *Early Child Development and Care, 184*(2), 230–246.

Senese, Vincenzo Paolo; Azhari, Atiqah; Shinohara, Kazuyuki; Doi, Hirokazu; Venuti, Paola; Bornstein, Marc H. & Esposito, Gianluca. (2019). Implicit associations to infant cry: Genetics and early care experiences influence caregiving propensities. *Hormones and Behavior*, 108, 1–9.

Seppa, Nathan. (2013a). Urban eyes: Too much time spent indoors may be behind a surge in nearsightedness. *Science News*, *183*(3), 22–25.

Seppa, Nathan. (2013b). Home births more risky than hospital deliveries: Records suggest babies born at home are more prone to unresponsiveness after five minutes. *Science News*, *184*(8), 14.

Seron, Carroll; Silbey, Susan S.; Cech, Erin & Rubineau, Brian. (2016). Persistence is cultural: Professional socialization and the reproduction of sex segregation. *43*(2), 178–214.

Servick, Kelly. (2015). Mind the phone. *Science*, *350*(6266), 1306–1309.

Seth, Puja; Scholl, Lawrence; Rudd, Rose A. & Bacon, Sarah. (2018). *Overdose deaths involving opioids, cocaine, and psychostimulants — United States, 2015–2016. Morbidity and Mortality Weekly Report*, *67*(12), 349–358. Atlanta, GA: Centers for Disease Control and Prevention.

Seto, Elizabeth & Schlegel, Rebecca J. (2018). Becoming your true self: Perceptions of authenticity across the lifespan. *Self and Identity*, *17*(3), 310–326.

Settersten, Richard A. (2015). Relationships in time and the life course: The significance of linked lives. *Research in Human Development*, *12*(3/4), 217–223.

Severson, Kim & Blinder, Alan. (2014, January 7). Test scandal in Atlanta brings more guilty pleas. *New York Times*.

Shah, Nirvi. (2011). Policy fight brews over discipline. *Education Week*, *31*(7), 1, 12.

Shah, Tushaar; Ray, Chittaranjan & Lele, Uma. (2018). How to clean up the Ganges? *Science*, *362*(6414), 503.

Shanahan, Timothy & Lonigan, Christopher J. (2010). The National Early Literacy Panel: A summary of the process and the report. *Educational Researcher*, *39*(4), 279–285.

Shanholtz, Caroline E.; Brown, Sacha Devine; Davidson, Ryan D. & Beck, Connie J. (2019). Distress in emerging adults: Further evaluation of the painful feelings about divorce scale. *Journal of Divorce & Remarriage*, *60*(2), 141–151.

Shapiro, Joan Poliner & Stefkovich, Jacqueline A. (2016). *Ethical leadership and decision making in education: Applying theoretical perspectives to complex dilemmas* (4th ed.). New York, NY: Routledge.

Sharkey, Shirlee & Lefebre, Nancy. (2017). Leadership perspective: Bringing nursing back to the future through people-powered care. *Nursing Leadership*, *30*(1), 11–22.

Sharot, Tali. (2017). *The influential mind: What the brain reveals about our power to change others*. New York, NY: Henry Holt.

Shawar, Yusra Ribhi & Shiffman, Jeremy. (2017). Generation of global political priority for early childhood development: The challenges of framing and governance. *The Lancet*, 389(10064), 119–124.

Shechner, Tomer; Fox, Nathan A.; Mash, Jamie A.; Jarcho, Johanna M.; Chen, Gang; Leibenluft, Ellen, . . . Britton, Jennifer C. (2018). Differences in neural response to extinction recall in young adults with or without history of behavioral inhibition. *Development and Psychopathology*, *30*(1), 179–189.

Shek, Daniel T. L. & Yu, Lu. (2016). Adolescent Internet addiction in Hong Kong: Prevalence, change, and correlates. *Journal of Pediatric & Adolescent Gynecology*, 29(1 Suppl.), S22–S30.

Sheridan, Margaret A.; Mclaughlin, Katie A.; Winter, Warren; Fox, Nathan; Zeanah, Charles & Nelson, Charles A. (2018). Early deprivation disruption of associative learning is a developmental pathway to depression and social problems. *Nature Communications*, *9*(1), 2216.

Sherlock, James M. & Zietsch, Brendan P. (2018). Longitudinal relationships between parents' and children's behavior need not implicate the influence of parental behavior and may reflect genetics: Comment on Waldinger and Schulz (2016). *Psychological Science*, *29*(1), 154–157.

Shi, Bing & Xie, Hongling. (2012). Popular and nonpopular subtypes of physically aggressive preadolescents: Continuity of aggression and peer mechanisms during the transition to middle school. *Merrill-Palmer Quarterly*, *58*(4), 530–553.

Shi, Rushen. (2014). Functional morphemes and early language acquisition. *Child Development Perspectives*, *8*(1), 6–11.

Shields, Grant S.; Doty, Dominique; Shields, Rebecca H.; Gower, Garrett; Slavich, George M. & Yonelinas, Andrew P. (2017). Recent life stress exposure is associated with poorer long-term memory, working memory, and self-reported memory. *Stress*, *20*(6), 598–607.

Shim, Woo-Jeong & Perez, Rosemary Jane. (2018). A multi-level examination of first-year students' openness to diversity and challenge. *Journal of Higher Education*, *89*(4), 453–477.

Shimizu, Mina; Park, Heejung & Greenfield, Patricia M. (2014). Infant sleeping arrangements and cultural values among contemporary Japanese mothers. *Frontiers in Psychology*, *5*, 718.

Shin, Huiyoung & Ryan, Allison M. (2017). Friend influence on early adolescent disruptive behavior in the classroom: Teacher emotional support matters. *Developmental Psychology*, *53*(1), 114–125.

Shiovitz-Ezra, Sharon & Litwin, Howard. (2015). Social network type and health among older Americans. In Fredrica Nyqvist & Anna K. Forsman (Eds.), *Social capital as a health resource in later life: The relevance of context* (pp. 15–31). Dordrecht, the Netherlands: Springer.

Shneidman, Laura & Woodward, Amanda L. (2016). Are child-directed interactions the cradle of social learning? *Psychological Bulletin*, *142*(1), 1–17.

Shpancer, Noam & Schweitzer, Stefanie N. (2016). A history of non-parental care in childhood predicts more positive adult attitudes towards non-parental care and maternal employment. *Early Child Development and Care*, (In Press).

Shulman, Elizabeth P. & Cauffman, Elizabeth. (2014). Deciding in the dark: Age differences in intuitive risk judgment. *Developmental Psychology*, *50*(1), 167–177.

Shulman, Elizabeth P.; Monahan, Kathryn C. & Steinberg, Laurence. (2017). Severe violence during adolescence and early adulthood and its relation to anticipated rewards and costs. *Child Development*, *88*(1), 16–26.

Shulman, Shmuel & Connolly, Jennifer. (2013). The challenge of romantic relationships in emerging adulthood: Reconceptualization of the field. *Emerging Adulthood*, *1*(1), 27–39.

Shutts, Kristin; Kinzler, Katherine D. & DeJesus, Jasmine M. (2013). Understanding infants' and children's social learning about foods: Previous research and new prospects. *Developmental Psychology*, *49*(3), 419–425.

Shwalb, David W.; Shwalb, Barbara J. & Lamb, Michael E. (Eds.). (2013). *Fathers in cultural context*. New York, NY: Psychology Press.

Siddiqui, Ayesha; Cuttini, Marina; Wood, Rachel; Velebil, Petr; Delnord, Marie; Zile, Irisa, . . . Macfarlane, Alison. (2017). Can the Apgar score be used for international comparisons of newborn health? *Paediatric and Perinatal Epidemiology*, *31*(4), 338–345.

Siegal, Michael & Surian, Luca (Eds.). (2012). *Access to language and cognitive development*. New York, NY: Oxford University Press.

Siegel, Shepard. (2016). The heroin overdose mystery. *Current Directions in Psychological Science*, *25*(6), 375–379.

Siegler, Robert S. (2009). Improving the numerical understanding of children from low-income families. *Child Development Perspectives*, 3(2), 118–124.

Siegler, Robert S. (2016). Continuity and change in the field of cognitive development and in the perspectives of one cognitive developmentalist. *Child Development Perspectives*, *10*(2), 128–133.

Siegler, Robert S. & Braithwaite, David W. (2017). Numerical development. *Annual Review of Psychology*, *68*, 187–213.

Sigurdson, J. F.; Wallander, J. & Sund, A. M. (2014). Is involvement in school bullying associated with general health and psychosocial adjustment outcomes in adulthood? *Child Abuse & Neglect*, *38*(10), 1607–1617.

Silbey, Susan S. (2016, August 23). Why do so many women who study engineering leave the field? [Web log post]. Harvard Business Review.

Silk, Jessica & Romero, Diana. (2014). The role of parents and families in teen pregnancy prevention: An analysis of programs and policies. *Journal of Family Issues*, *35*(10), 1339–1362.

Silventoinen, Karri; Hammar, Niklas; Hedlund, Ebba; Koskenvuo, Markku; Ronnemaa, Tapani & Kaprio, Jaakko. (2008). Selective international migration by social position, health behaviour and personality. *European Journal of Public Health*, *18*(2), 150–155.

Sim, Zi L. & Xu, Fei. (2017). Learning higher-order generalizations through free play: Evidence from 2- and 3-year-old children. *Developmental Psychology*, *53*(4), 642–651.

Simmons, Joseph P.; Nelson, Leif D. & Simonsohn, Uri. (2011). False-positive psychology: Undisclosed flexibility in data collection and analysis allows presenting anything as significant. *Psychological Science, 22*(11), 1359–1366.

Simmons, Sandra F. & Rahman, Anna N. (2014). Next steps for achieving person-centered care in nursing homes. *JAMDA, 15*(9), 615–619.

Simon, Laura & Daneback, Kristian. (2013). Adolescents' use of the Internet for sex education: A thematic and critical review of the literature. *International Journal of Sexual Health, 25*(4), 305–319.

Simpson, Elizabeth A.; Jakobsen, Krisztina V.; Damon, Fabrice; Suomi, Stephen J.; Ferrari, Pier F. & Paukner, Annika. (2017). Face detection and the development of own-species bias in infant macaques. *Child Development, 88*(1), 103–113.

Simpson, Jeffry A. & Kenrick, Douglas. (2013). *Evolutionary social psychology*. Hoboken, NJ: Taylor & Francis.

Simpson, Jeffry A. & Rholes, W. Steven (Eds.). (2015). *Attachment theory and research: New directions and emerging themes*. New York, NY: Guilford.

Singanayagam, Aran; Ritchie, Andrew I. & Johnston, Sebastian L. (2017). Role of microbiome in the pathophysiology and disease course of asthma. *Current Opinion in Pulmonary Medicine, 23*(1), 41–47.

Singer, Judith D. & Braun, Henry I. (2018). Testing international education assessments. *Science, 360*(6384), 38–40.

Singh, Amika; Uijtdewilligen, Léonie; Twisk, Jos W. R.; van Mechelen, Willem & Chinapaw, Mai J. M. (2012). Physical activity and performance at school: A systematic review of the literature including a methodological quality assessment. *Archives of Pediatrics & Adolescent Medicine, 166*(1), 49–55.

Singh, Krishneil A.; Gignac, Gilles E.; Brydges, Christopher R. & Ecker, Ullrich K. H. (2018). Working memory capacity mediates the relationship between removal and fluid intelligence. *Journal of Memory and Language, 101*, 18–36.

Sinnott, Jan D. (2008). Cognitive and representational development in adults. In Kelly B. Cartwright (Ed.), *Literacy processes: Cognitive flexibility in learning and teaching* (pp. 42–68). New York, NY: Guilford.

Sinnott, Jan D. (2009). Cognitive development as the dance of adaptive transformation: Neo-Piagetian perspectives on adult cognitive development. In M. Cecil Smith & Nancy DeFrates-Densch (Eds.), *Handbook of research on adult learning and development* (pp. 103–134). New York, NY: Routledge.

Sinnott, Jan D. (2014). *Adult development: Cognitive aspects of thriving close relationships*. New York, NY: Oxford University Press.

Sisk, Cheryl L. (2016). Hormone-dependent adolescent organization of socio-sexual behaviors in mammals. *Current Opinion in Neurobiology, 38*, 63–68.

Sisson, Susan B.; Krampe, Megan; Anundson, Katherine & Castle, Sherri. (2016). Obesity prevention and obesogenic behavior interventions in child care: A systematic review. *Preventive Medicine, 87*, 57–69.

Skinner, B. F. (1953). *Science and human behavior*. New York, NY: Macmillan.

Skinner, B. F. (1957). *Verbal behavior*. New York, NY: Appleton-Century-Crofts.

Skoog, Therése & Stattin, Håkan. (2014). Why and under what contextual conditions do early-maturing girls develop problem behaviors? *Child Development Perspectives, 8*(3), 158–162.

Slaughter, Anne-Marie. (2012). Why women still can't have it all. *The Atlantic, 310*(1), 84–102.

Slining, Meghan; Adair, Linda S.; Goldman, Barbara D.; Borja, Judith B. & Bentley, Margaret. (2010). Infant overweight is associated with delayed motor development. *The Journal of Pediatrics, 157*(1), 20–25.e21.

Sloan, Mark. (2009). *Birth day: A pediatrician explores the science, the history, and the wonder of childbirth*. New York, NY: Ballantine Books.

Slot, Pauline Louise; Mulder, Hanna; Verhagen, Josje & Leseman, Paul. (2017). Preschoolers' cognitive and emotional self-regulation in pretend play: Relations with executive functions and quality of play. *Infant and Child Development, 26*(6), e2038.

Slotnick, Scott D. (2017). *Cognitive neuroscience of memory*. New York, NY: Cambridge University Press.

Small, Meredith F. (1998). *Our babies, ourselves: How biology and culture shape the way we parent*. New York, NY: Anchor Books.

Smart, Andrew; Bolnick, Deborah A. & Tutton, Richard. (2017). Health and genetic ancestry testing: Time to bridge the gap. *BMC Medical Genomics, 10*(1).

Smetana, Jan; Chlibek, Roman; Shaw, Jana; Splino, Miroslav & Prymula, Roman. (2018). Influenza vaccination in the elderly. *Human Vaccines & Immunotherapeutics, 14*(3), 540–549.

Smetana, Judith G. (2013). Moral development: The Social Domain Theory view. In Philip D. Zelazo (Ed.), *The Oxford handbook of developmental psychology* (Vol. 1, pp. 832–866). New York, NY: Oxford University Press.

Smetana, Judith G.; Ahmad, Ikhlas & Wray-Lake, Laura. (2016). Beliefs about parental authority legitimacy among refugee youth in Jordan: Between- and within-person variations. *Developmental Psychology, 52*(3), 484–495.

Smith, Christian & Snell, Patricia. (2009). *Souls in transition: The religious and spiritual lives of emerging adults*. New York, NY: Oxford University Press.

Smith, Douglas H.; Johnson, Victoria E.; Trojanowski, John Q. & Stewart, William. (2019). Chronic traumatic encephalopathy — confusion and controversies. *Nature Reviews Neurology, 15*(3), 179.

Smith, Hannah E.; Ryan, Kelsey N.; Stephenson, Kevin B.; Westcott, Claire; Thakwalakwa, Chrissie; Maleta, Ken, . . . Manary, Mark J. (2014). Multiple micronutrient supplementation transiently ameliorates environmental enteropathy in Malawian children aged 12–35 months in a randomized controlled clinical trial. *Journal of Nutrition, 144*(12), 2059–2065.

Smith, Jacqueline; Boone, Anniglo; Gourdine, Ruby & Brown, Annie W. (2013). Fictions and facts about parents and parenting older first-time entrants to foster care. *Journal of Human Behavior in the Social Environment, 23*(2), 211–219.

Smith, Michelle I.; Yatsunenko, Tanya; Manary, Mark J.; Trehan, Indi; Mkakosya, Rajhab; Cheng, Jiye, . . . Gordon, Jeffrey I. (2013). Gut microbiomes of Malawian twin pairs discordant for kwashiorkor. *Science, 339*(6119), 548–554.

Smith, Peter K. (2010). *Children and play: Understanding children's worlds*. Malden, MA: Wiley-Blackwell.

Smith, Sharon G.; Zhang, Xinjian; Basile, Kathleen C.; Merrick, Melissa T.; Wang, Jing; Kresnow, Marcie-jo & Chen, Jieru. (2018). *The National Intimate Partner and Sexual Violence Survey (NISVS): 2015 Data Brief – Updated Release*. Atlanta, GA: National Center for Injury Prevention and Control, Centers for Disease Control and Prevention.

Smithells, R. W.; Sheppard, S.; Schorah, C. J.; Seller, M. J.; Nevin, N. C.; Harris, R., . . . Fielding, D. W. (2011). Apparent prevention of neural tube defects by periconceptional vitamin supplementation. *International Journal of Epidemiology, 40*(5), 1146–1154.

Snellman, Kaisa; Silva, Jennifer M.; Frederick, Carl B. & Putnam, Robert D. (2015). The engagement gap: Social mobility and extracurricular participation among American youth. *The ANNALS of the American Academy of Political and Social Science, 657*(1), 194–207.

Snider, Terra Ziporyn. (2012). Later school start times are a public-health issue. *Education Week, 31*(31), 25, 27.

Snow, J. B. (2015). *Narcissist and the Peter Pan syndrome: Emotionally unavailable and emotionally immature men*. Amazon Digital Services LLC: J. B. Snow Publishing.

Snyder, Thomas D.; de Brey, Cristobal & Dillow, Sally A. (2018). *Digest of education statistics, 2017*. Washington, DC: National Center for Education Statistics, Institute of Education Sciences, U.S. Department of Education. NCES 2018-070.

Snyder, Thomas D. & Dillow, Sally A. (2013). *Digest of education statistics, 2012*. Washington, DC: National Center for Education Statistics, Institute of Education Sciences, U.S. Department of Education.

Society for Developmental and Behavioral Pediatrics. (2018, July 18). SDBP statement related to the separation of children from families at the border [Press release]. McLean, VA: Society for Developmental and Behavioral Pediatrics.

Soderstrom, Melanie; Ko, Eon-Suk & Nevzorova, Uliana. (2011). It's a question? Infants attend differently to yes/no questions and declaratives. *Infant Behavior and Development, 34*(1), 107–110.

Solheim, Elisabet; Wichstrøm, Lars; Belsky, Jay & Berg-Nielsen, Turid Suzanne. (2013). Do time in child care and peer group exposure predict poor socioemotional adjustment in Norway? *Child Development, 84*(5), 1701–1715.

Solomon, Andrew. (2012). *Far from the tree: Parents, children, and the search for identity*. New York, NY: Scribner.

Somerville, Leah H. (2013). The teenage brain: Sensitivity to social evaluation. *Current Directions in Psychological Science*, 22(2), 121–127.

Son, Daye & Padilla-Walker, Laura M. (2019). Whereabouts and secrets: A person-centered approach to emerging adults' routine and self-disclosure to parents. *Emerging Adulthood*, (In Press).

Sonesh, Shirley C.; Lacerenza, Christina; Marlow, Shannon & Salas, Eduardo. (2018). What makes an expert team? A decade of research. In K. Anders Ericsson, et al. (Eds.), *The Cambridge handbook of expertise and expert performance* (2nd ed., pp. 506–532). New York, NY: Cambridge University Press.

Sonuga-Barke, Edmund J. S.; Kennedy, Mark; Kumsta, Robert; Knights, Nicky; Golm, Dennis; Rutter, Michael, . . . Kreppner, Jana. (2017). Child-to-adult neurodevelopmental and mental health trajectories after early life deprivation: The young adult follow-up of the longitudinal English and Romanian Adoptees study. *The Lancet*, 389(10078), 1539–1548.

Sophian, Catherine. (2013). Vicissitudes of children's mathematical knowledge: Implications of developmental research for early childhood mathematics education. *Early Education and Development*, 24(4), 436–442.

Sormunen, Taina; Aanesen, Arthur; Fossum, Bjöörn; Karlgren, Klas & Westerbotn, Margareta. (2018). Infertility-related communication and coping strategies among women affected by primary or secondary infertility. *Journal of Clinical Nursing*, 27(1/2), e335–e344.

Sorrells, Shawn F.; Paredes, Mercedes F.; Cebrian-Silla, Arantxa; Sandoval, Kadellyn; Qi, Dashi; Kelley, Kevin W., . . . Alvarez-Buylla, Arturo. (2018). Human hippocampal neurogenesis drops sharply in children to undetectable levels in adults. *Nature*, 555, 377–381.

Soto-Rubio, Ana; Pérez-Marín, Marián & Barreto, Pilar. (2017). Frail elderly with and without cognitive impairment at the end of life: Their emotional state and the wellbeing of their family caregivers. *Archives of Gerontology and Geriatrics*, 73, 113–119.

Sotomayor, Sonia. (2014). *My beloved world*. New York, NY: Vintage Books.

Soulsby, Laura K. & Bennett, Kate M. (2017). When two become one: Exploring identity in marriage and cohabitation. *Journal of Family Issues*, 38(3), 358–380.

Sousa, David A. (2014). *How the brain learns to read* (2nd ed.). Thousand Oaks, CA: SAGE.

Sowell, Elizabeth R.; Thompson, Paul M. & Toga, Arthur W. (2007). Mapping adolescent brain maturation using structural magnetic resonance imaging. In Daniel Romer & Elaine F. Walker (Eds.), *Adolescent psychopathology and the developing brain: Integrating brain and prevention science* (pp. 55–84). New York, NY: Oxford University Press.

Spape, Jessica; Timmers, Amanda D.; Yoon, Samuel; Ponseti, Jorge & Chivers, Meredith L. (2014). Gender-specific genital and subjective sexual arousal to prepotent sexual features in heterosexual women and men. *Biological Psychology*, *102*, 1–9.

Sparks, Sarah D. (2016, July 20). Dose of empathy found to cut suspension rates. *Education Week*, 35(36), 1, 20.

Spearman, Charles E. (1927). *The abilities of man, their nature and measurement*. New York, NY: Macmillan.

Spelke, Elizabeth S. (1993). Object perception. In Alvin I. Goldman (Ed.), *Readings in philosophy and cognitive science* (pp. 447–460). Cambridge, MA: MIT Press.

Spencer, Justine M. Y.; Sekuler, Allison B.; Bennett, Patrick J.; Giese, Martin A. & Pilz, Karin S. (2016). Effects of aging on identifying emotions conveyed by point-light walkers. *Psychology and Aging*, *31*(1), 126–138.

Spencer, Steven J.; Logel, Christine & Davies, Paul G. (2016). Stereotype threat. *Annual Review of Psychology*, 67, 415–437.

Sperry, Debbie M. & Widom, Cathy S. (2013). Child abuse and neglect, social support, and psychopathology in adulthood: A prospective investigation. *Child Abuse & Neglect*, 37(6), 415–425.

Spijker, Jeroen & MacInnes, John. (2013). Population ageing: The timebomb that isn't? *BMJ*, *347*, f6598.

Spinrad, Tracy L. & Gal, Diana E. (2018). Fostering prosocial behavior and empathy in young children. *Current Opinion in Psychology*, *20*, 40–44.

Spira, Adam P. (2018). Sleep and health in older adulthood: Recent advances and the path forward. *Journal of Gerontology Series A*, 73(3), 357–359.

Sprecher, Susan; Econie, Alexis & Treger, Stanislav. (2018). Mate preferences in emerging adulthood and beyond: Age variations in mate preferences and beliefs about change in mate preferences. *Journal of Social and Personal Relationships*, (In Press).

Sprecher, Susan; Treger, Stanislav & Sakaluk, John. (2013). Premarital sexual standards and sociosexuality: Gender, ethnicity, and cohort differences. *Archives of Sexual Behavior*, *42*(8), 1395–1405.

Spreng, R. Nathan & Turner, Gary R. (2019). The shifting architecture of cognition and brain function in older adulthood. *Perspectives on Psychological Science*, *14*(4), 523–542.

Sprietsma, Maresa. (2010). Effect of relative age in the first grade of primary school on long-term scholastic results: International comparative evidence using PISA 2003. *Education Economics*, *18*(1), 1–32.

Springsteen, Bruce. (2017). *Born to run*. New York, NY: Simon & Schuster.

Srinivasan, Sharada & Li, Shuzhuo. (2018). Unifying perspectives on scarce women and surplus men in China and India. In Sharada Srinivasan & Shuzhuo Li (Eds.), *Scarce women and surplus men in China and India* (pp. 1–23). Cham, Switzerland: Springer.

Sriram, Rajalakshmi. (2019). A global perspective on fathering. In Rajalakshmi Sriram (Ed.), *Fathering in India* (pp. 19–34). Singapore: Springer.

Staff, Jeremy & Schulenberg, John. (2010). Millennials and the world of work: Experiences in paid work during adolescence. *Journal of Business and Psychology*, 25(2), 247–255.

Stahl, Aimee E. & Feigenson, Lisa. (2017). Expectancy violations promote learning in young children. *Cognition*, *163*, 1–14.

Standing, E. M. (1998). *Maria Montessori: Her life and work*. New York, NY: Plume.

Starr, Christine R. & Zurbriggen, Eileen L. (2016). Sandra Bem's gender schema theory after 34 years: A review of its reach and impact. *Sex Roles*, (In Press).

Stattin, Håkan; Hussein, Oula; Özdemir, Metin & Russo, Silvia. (2017). Why do some adolescents encounter everyday events that increase their civic interest whereas others do not? *Developmental Psychology*, 53(2), 306–318.

Steele, Claude M. (1997). A threat in the air: How stereotypes shape intellectual identity and performance. *American Psychologist*, 52(6), 613–629.

Stefansen, Kari; Smette, Ingrid & Strandbu, Åse. (2018). Understanding the increase in parents' involvement in organized youth sports. *Sport, Education and Society*, 23(2), 162–172.

Steffensmeier, Darrell; Painter-Davis, Noah & Ulmer, Jeffery. (2017). Intersectionality of race, ethnicity, gender, and age on criminal punishment. *Sociological Perspectives*, *60*(4), 810–833.

Steinberg, Laurence. (2004). Risk taking in adolescence: What changes, and why? *Annals of the New York Academy of Sciences*, *1021*, 51–58.

Steinberg, Laurence. (2009). Should the science of adolescent brain development inform public policy? *American Psychologist*, *64*(8), 739–750.

Steinberg, Laurence. (2014). *Age of opportunity: Lessons from the new science of adolescence*. Boston, MA: Houghton Mifflin Harcourt.

Steinberg, Laurence. (2015). The neural underpinnings of adolescent risk-taking: The roles of reward-seeking, impulse control, and peers. In Gabriele Oettingen & Peter M. Gollwitzer (Eds.), *Self-regulation in adolescence* (pp. 173–192). New York, NY: Cambridge University Press.

Steinberg, Laurence & Monahan, Kathryn C. (2011). Adolescents' exposure to sexy media does not hasten the initiation of sexual intercourse. *Developmental Psychology*, 47(2), 562–576.

Stenseng, Frode; Belsky, Jay; Skalicka, Vera & Wichstrøm, Lars. (2015). Social exclusion predicts impaired self-regulation: A 2-year longitudinal panel study including the transition from preschool to school. *Journal of Personality*, 83(2), 212–220.

Stepler, Renee. (2017, March 9). *Led by baby boomers, divorce rates climb for America's 50+ population. Fact Tank*. Washington, DC: Pew Research Center.

Sterling, Peter. (2012). Allostasis: A model of predictive regulation. *Physiology & Behavior*, *106*(1), 5–15.

Stern, Gavin. (2015). For kids with special learning needs, roadblocks remain. *Science, 349*(6255), 1465–1466.

Stern, Mark; Clonan, Sheila; Jaffee, Laura & Lee, Anna. (2015). The normative limits of choice: Charter schools, disability studies, and questions of inclusion. *Educational Policy, 29*(3), 448–477.

Stern, Peter. (2013). Connection, connection, connection . . . *Science, 342*(6158), 577.

Sternberg, Robert J. (1988). Triangulating love. In Robert J. Sternberg & Michael L. Barnes (Eds.), *The psychology of love* (pp. 119–138). New Haven, CT: Yale University Press.

Sternberg, Robert J. (2003). *Wisdom, intelligence, and creativity synthesized.* New York, NY: Cambridge University Press.

Sternberg, Robert J. (2004). A triangular theory of love. In H. T. Reis & C. E. Rusbult (Eds.), *Close relationships: Key readings*(pp. 213–227). Philadelphia, PA: Taylor & Francis.

Sternberg, Robert J. (2008). Schools should nurture wisdom. In Barbara Z. Presseisen (Ed.), *Teaching for intelligence* (2nd ed., pp. 61–88). Thousand Oaks, CA: Corwin Press.

Sternberg, Robert J. (2011). The theory of successful intelligence. In Robert J. Sternberg & Scott Barry Kaufman (Eds.), *The Cambridge handbook of intelligence* (pp. 504–526). New York, NY: Cambridge University Press.

Sternberg, Robert J. (2012). Why I became an administrator . . . and why you might become one too: Applying the science of psychology to the life of a university. *Observer, 25*(2), 21–22.

Sternberg, Robert J. (2015). Multiple intelligences in the new age of thinking. In Sam Goldstein, et al. (Eds.), *Handbook of intelligence* (pp. 229–241). New York, NY: Springer.

Sternberg, Robert J. (2018). Speculations on the role of successful intelligence in solving contemporary world problems. *Journal of Intelligence, 6*(1).

Sterzing, Paul R.; Gibbs, Jeremy J.; Gartner, Rachel E. & Goldbach, Jeremy T. (2018). Bullying victimization trajectories for sexual minority adolescents: Stable victims, desisters, and late-onset victims. *Journal of Research on Adolescence, 28*(2), 368–378.

Stevenson, Robert G. (2017). Children and death: What do they know and when do they learn it? In Robert G. Stevenson & Gerry R. Cox (Eds.), *Children, adolescents, and death: Questions and answers.* New York, NY: Routledge.

Stierand, Marc & Dörfler, Viktor. (2016). The role of intuition in the creative process of expert chefs. *Journal of Creative Behavior, 50*(3), 178–185.

Stiles, Joan & Jernigan, Terry. (2010). The basics of brain development. *Neuropsychology Review, 20*(4), 327–348.

Stiner, Mary C. (2017). Love and death in the stone age: What constitutes first evidence of mortuary treatment of the human body? *Biological Theory, 12*(4), 248–261.

Stipek, Deborah. (2013). Mathematics in early childhood education: Revolution or evolution? *Early Education & Development, 24*(4), 431–435.

Stolk, Lisette; Perry, John R. B.; Chasman, Daniel I.; He, Chunyan; Mangino, Massimo; Sulem, Patrick, . . . Lunetta, Kathryn L. (2012). Meta-analyses identify 13 loci associated with age at menopause and highlight DNA repair and immune pathways. *Nature Genetics, 44,* 260–268.

Stolt, Suvi; Matomäki, Jaakko; Lind, Annika; Lapinleimu, Helena; Haataja, Leena & Lehtonen, Liisa. (2014). The prevalence and predictive value of weak language skills in children with very low birth weight – A longitudinal study. *Acta Paediatrica, 103*(6), 651–658.

Stolzenberg, Ellen Bara; Eagan, Kevin; Aragon, Melissa C.; Cesar-Davis, Natacha M.; Jacobo, Sidronio; Couch, Victoria & Rios-Aguilar, Cecilia. (2019). *The American freshman: National norms fall 2017.* Los Angeles, CA: Higher Education Research Institute, UCLA.

Strait, Dana L.; Parbery-Clark, Alexandra; O'Connell, Samantha & Kraus, Nina. (2013). Biological impact of preschool music classes on processing speech in noise. *Developmental Cognitive Neuroscience, 6,* 51–60.

Strasburger, Victor C.; Wilson, Barbara J. & Jordan, Amy B. (2009). *Children, adolescents, and the media* (2nd ed.). Los Angeles, CA: Sage.

Stremmel, Andrew J. (2012). A situated framework: The Reggio experience. In Nancy File, et al. (Eds.), *Curriculum in early childhood education: Re-examined, rediscovered, renewed* (pp. 133–145). New York, NY: Routledge.

Stroebe, Margaret S.; Abakoumkin, Georgios; Stroebe, Wolfgang & Schut, Henk. (2012). Continuing bonds in adjustment to bereavement: Impact of abrupt versus gradual separation. *Personal Relationships, 19*(2), 255–266.

Stroebe, Wolfgang & Strack, Fritz. (2014). The alleged crisis and the illusion of exact replication. *Perspectives on Psychological Science, 9*(1), 59–71.

Strohminger, Nina & Nichols, Shaun. (2015). Neurodegeneration and identity. *Psychological Science, 26*(9), 1469–1479.

Strouse, Gabrielle A. & Ganea, Patricia A. (2017). Toddlers' word learning and transfer from electronic and print books. *Journal of Experimental Child Psychology, 156,* 129–142.

Stults, Christopher B.; Javdani, Shabnam; Kapadia, Farzana & Halkitis, Perry N. (2019). Determinants of intimate partner violence among young men who have sex with men: The P18 cohort study. *Journal of Interpersonal Violence,* (In Press).

Su, Ya-Hui. (2011). The constitution of agency in developing lifelong learning ability: The 'being' mode. *Higher Education, 62*(4), 399–412.

Suárez-Orozco, Carola. (2017). Conferring disadvantage: Behavioral and developmental implications for children growing up in the shadow of undocumented immigration status. *Journal of Developmental & Behavioral Pediatrics, 38*(6), 424–428.

Suberi, Moriya; Morag, Iris; Strauss, Tzipora & Geva, Ronny. (2018). Feeding imprinting: The extreme test case of premature infants born with very low birth weight. *Child Development, 89*(5), 1553–1566.

Suchy, Frederick J.; Brannon, Patsy M.; Carpenter, Thomas O.; Fernandez, Jose R.; Gilsanz, Vicente; Gould, Jeffrey B., . . . Wolf, Marshall A. (2010). National Institutes of Health Consensus Development Conference: Lactose intolerance and health. *Annals of Internal Medicine, 152*(12), 792–796.

Sue, Derald Wing (Ed.). (2010). *Microaggressions and marginality: Manifestation, dynamics, and impact.* Hoboken, NJ: Wiley.

Sugimoto, Taiki; Sakurai, Takashi; Ono, Rei; Kimura, Ai; Saji, Naoki; Niida, Shumpei, . . . Arai, Hidenori. (2018). Epidemiological and clinical significance of cognitive frailty: A mini review. *Ageing Research Reviews, 44.*

Sugimura, Kazumi; Crocetti, Elisabetta; Hatano, Kai; Kaniušonytė, Goda; Hihara, Shogo & Žukauskienė, Rita. (2018). A cross-cultural perspective on the relationships between emotional separation, parental trust, and identity in adolescents. *Journal of Youth and Adolescence,* 47(4), 749–759.

Sugimura, Kazumi; Matsushima, Kobo; Hihara, Shogo; Takahashi, Masami & Crocetti, Elisabetta. (2019). A culturally sensitive approach to the relationships between identity formation and religious beliefs in youth. *Journal of Youth and Adolescence, 48*(4), 668–679.

Sugiura, Motoaki. (2016). Functional neuroimaging of normal aging: Declining brain, adapting brain. *Ageing Research Reviews, 30,* 61–72.

Suleiman, Ahna B. & Brindis, Claire D. (2014). Adolescent school-based sex education: Using developmental neuroscience to guide new directions for policy and practice. *Sexuality Research and Social Policy, 11*(2), 137–152.

Sulek, Julia P. (2013, April 30). Audrie Pott suicide: Parents share grief, quest for justice in exclusive interview. *San Jose Mercury News.*

Sullivan, Jas M. & Ghara, Alexandra. (2015). Racial identity and intergroup attitudes: A multiracial youth analysis. *Social Science Quarterly, 96*(1), 261–272.

Sullivan, Kevin J.; Dodge, Hiroko H.; Hughes, Tiffany F.; Chang, Chung-Chou H.; Zhu, Xinmei; Liu, Anran & Ganguli, Mary. (2018). Declining incident dementia rates across four population-based birth cohorts. *The Journals of Gerontology: Series A,* (In Press).

Sullivan, Patrick F.; Neale, Michael C. & Kendler, Kenneth S. (2000). Genetic epidemiology of major depression: Review and meta-analysis. *American Journal of Psychiatry, 157*(10), 1552–1562.

Sullivan, Sheila. (1999). *Falling in love: A history of torment and enchantment.* London, UK: Macmillan.

Sulmasy, Daniel. (2018). The last low whispers of our dead: When is it ethically justifiable to render a patient unconscious until death? *Theoretical Medicine and Bioethics,* 39(3), 233–263.

Sun, Jianing; Liu, Qinxue & Yu, Si. (2019). Child neglect, psychological abuse and smartphone addiction among Chinese adolescents: The roles of emotional intelligence and coping style. *Computers in Human Behavior, 90*, 74–83.

Sun, Li; Guo, Xin; Zhang, Jing; Liu, Henghui; Xu, Shaojun; Xu, Yuanyuan & Tao, Fangbiao. (2016). Gender specific associations between early puberty and behavioral and emotional characteristics in children. *Zhonghua Liu Xing Bing Xue Za Zhi*, 37(1), 35–39.

Sun, Min & Rugolotto, Simone. (2004). Assisted infant toilet training in a Western family setting. *Journal of Developmental & Behavioral Pediatrics*, 25(2), 99–101.

Sun, Qian (Chayn); Xia, Jianhong (Cecilia); Li, Yongfu; Foster, Jonathan; Falkmer, Torbjörn & Lee, Hoe. (2018). Unpacking older drivers' maneuver at intersections: Their visual-motor coordination and underlying neuropsychological mechanisms. *Transportation Research Part F*, 58, 11–18.

Sunita, T. H. & Desai, Rathnamala M. (2013). Knowledge, attitude and practice of contraception among women attending a tertiary care hospital in India. *International Journal of Reproduction, Contraception, Obstetrics and Gynecology*, 2(2), 172–176.

Suomi, Steven J. (2002). Parents, peers, and the process of socialization in primates. In John G. Borkowski, et al. (Eds.), *Parenting and the child's world: Influences on academic, intellectual, and social-emotional development* (pp. 265–279). Mahwah, NJ: Erlbaum.

Super, Charles M.; Harkness, Sara; Barry, Oumar & Zeitlin, Marian. (2011). Think locally, act globally: Contributions of African research to child development. *Child Development Perspectives*, 5(2), 119–125.

Sutaria, Shailen; Devakumar, Delan; Yasuda, Sílvia Shikanai; Das, Shikta & Saxena, Sonia. (2019). Is obesity associated with depression in children? Systematic review and meta-analysis. *Archives of Disease in Childhood, 104*(1), 64–74.

Sutton-Smith, Brian. (2011). The antipathies of play. In Anthony D. Pellegrini (Ed.), *The Oxford handbook of the development of play* (pp. 110–115). New York, NY: Oxford University Press.

Suurland, Jill; van der Heijden, Kristiaan B.; Huijbregts, Stephan C. J.; Smaling, Hanneke J. A.; de Sonneville, Leo M. J.; Van Goozen, Stephanie H. M. & Swaab, Hanna. (2016). Parental perceptions of aggressive behavior in preschoolers: Inhibitory control moderates the association with negative emotionality. *Child Development*, 87(1), 256–269.

Suzumori, Nobuhiro; Kumagai, Kyoko; Goto, Shinobu; Nakamura, Akira & Sugiura-Ogasawara, Mayumi. (2015). Parental decisions following prenatal diagnosis of chromosomal abnormalities: Implications for genetic counseling practice in Japan. *Journal of Genetic Counseling*, 24(1), 117–121.

Swaab, D. F. & Hofman, M. A. (1984). Sexual differentiation of the human brain: A historical perspective. *Progress in Brain Research, 61*, 361–374.

Swanson, H. Lee. (2013). Meta-analysis of research on children with learning disabilities. In H. Lee Swanson, et al. (Eds.), *Handbook of learning disabilities* (2nd ed., pp. 627–642). New York, NY: Guilford Press.

Sweeney, Melanie D.; Kisler, Kassandra; Montagne, Axel; Toga, Arthur W. & Zlokovic, Berislav V. (2018). The role of brain vasculature in neurodegenerative disorders. *Nature Neuroscience, 21*(10), 1318–1331.

Swit, Cara & McMaugh, Anne. (2012). Relational aggression and prosocial behaviours in Australian preschool children. *Australasian Journal of Early Childhood*, 37(3), 30–34.

Swit, Cara; McMaugh, Anne & Warburton, Wayne. (2018). Teacher and parent perceptions of relational and physical aggression during early childhood. *Journal of Child and Family Studies*, 27(1), 118–130.

Szanton, Sarah L.; Wolff, Jennifer L.; Leff, Bruce; Roberts, Laken; Thorpe, Roland J.; Tanner, Elizabeth K., . . . Gitlin, Laura N. (2015). Preliminary data from Community Aging in Place, advancing better living for elders, a patient-directed, team-based intervention to improve physical function and decrease nursing home utilization: The first 100 individuals to complete a Centers for Medicare and Medicaid Services innovation project. *Journal of the American Geriatrics Society*, 63(2), 371–374.

Tabassum, Faiza; Mohan, John & Smith, Peter. (2016). Association of volunteering with mental well-being: A lifecourse analysis of a national population-based longitudinal study in the UK. *BMJ Open*, 6(8), 6:e011327.

Tacken, Mart & van Lamoen, Ellemieke. (2005). Transport behaviour and realised journeys and trips. In Heidrun Mollenkopf, et al. (Eds.), *Enhancing mobility in later life: Personal coping, environmental resources and technical support: The out-of-home mobility of older adults in urban and rural regions of five European countries* (pp. 105–139). Amsterdam, the Netherlands: IOS Press.

Tackett, Jennifer L.; Herzhoff, Kathrin; Harden, K. Paige; Page-Gould, Elizabeth & Josephs, Robert A. (2014). Personality × hormone interactions in adolescent externalizing psychopathology. *Personality Disorders: Theory, Research, and Treatment*, 5(3), 235–246.

Taga, Keiko A.; Markey, Charlotte N. & Friedman, Howard S. (2006). A longitudinal investigation of associations between boys' pubertal timing and adult behavioral health and well-being. *Journal of Youth and Adolescence*, 35(3), 380–390.

Tagar, Michal Reifen; Hetherington, Chelsea; Shulman, Deborah & Koenig, Melissa. (2017). On the path to social dominance? Individual differences in sensitivity to intergroup fairness violations in early childhood. *Personality and Individual Differences, 113*, 246–250.

Taillieu, Tamara L.; Afifi, Tracie O.; Mota, Natalie; Keyes, Katherine M. & Sareen, Jitender. (2014). Age, sex, and racial differences in harsh physical punishment: Results from a nationally representative United States sample. *Child Abuse & Neglect*, 38(12), 1885–1894.

Tajalli, Hassan & Garba, Houmma A. (2014). Discipline or prejudice? Overrepresentation of minority students in disciplinary alternative education programs. *Urban Review, 46*(4), 620–631.

Talhelm, T.; Zhang, X.; Oishi, S.; Shimin, C.; Duan, D.; Lan, X. & Kitayama, S. (2014). Large-scale psychological differences within China explained by rice versus wheat agriculture. *Science, 344*(6184), 603–608.

Talley, Ronda C. & Montgomery, Rhonda J. V. (2013). Caregiving: A developmental lifelong perspective. In Ronda C. Talley & Rhonda J. V. Montgomery (Eds.), *Caregiving across the lifespan: Research, practice, policy* (pp. 3–10). New York, NY: Springer.

Tamis-LeMonda, Catherine S.; Bornstein, Marc H. & Baumwell, Lisa. (2001). Maternal responsiveness and children's achievement of language milestones. *Child Development*, 72(3), 748–767.

Tamm, Leanne; Epstein, Jeffery N.; Denton, Carolyn A.; Vaughn, Aaron J.; Peugh, James & Willcutt, Erik G. (2014). Reaction time variability associated with reading skills in poor readers with ADHD. *Journal of the International Neuropsychological Society*, 20(3), 292–301.

Tamnes, Christian K.; Overbye, Knut; Ferschmann, Lia; Fjell, Anders M.; Walhovd, Kristine B.; Blakemore, Sarah-Jayne & Dumontheil, Iroise. (2018). Social perspective taking is associated with self-reported prosocial behavior and regional cortical thickness across adolescence. *Developmental Psychology*, 54(9), 1745–1757.

Tamura, Naomi; Hanaoka, Tomoyuki; Ito, Kumiko; Araki, Atsuko; Miyashita, Chihiro; Ito, Sachiko, . . . Kishi, Reiko. (2018). Different risk factors for very low birth weight, term-small-for-gestational-age, or preterm birth in Japan. *International Journal of Environmental Research and Public Health*, 15(2), 369.

Tan, Cheryl H.; Denny, Clark H.; Cheal, Nancy E.; Sniezek, Joseph E. & Kanny, Dafna. (2015, September 25). *Alcohol use and binge drinking among women of childbearing age — United States, 2011–2013. Morbidity and Mortality Weekly Report*, 64(37), 1042–1046. Atlanta, GA: Centers for Disease Control and Prevention.

Tan, Joseph S.; Hessel, Elenda T.; Loeb, Emily L.; Schad, Megan M.; Allen, Joseph P. & Chango, Joanna M. (2016). Long-term predictions from early adolescent attachment state of mind to romantic relationship behaviors. *Journal of Research on Adolescence*, 26(4), 1022–1035.

Tan, Patricia Z.; Armstrong, Laura M. & Cole, Pamela M. (2013). Relations between temperament and anger regulation over early childhood. *Social Development*, 22(4), 755–772.

Taneri, Petek Eylul; Jong, Jessica C. Kiefte-de; Bramer, Wichor M.; Daan, Nadine M. P.; Franco, Oscar H. & Muka, Taulant. (2016). Association of alcohol consumption with the onset of natural menopause: A systematic review and meta-analysis. *Human Reproduction Update*, 22(4), 516–528.

Tang, Jie; Yu, Yizhen; Du, Yukai; Ma, Ying; Zhang, Dongying & Wang, Jiaji. (2014). Prevalence of Internet addiction and its association with stressful life events and psychological symptoms among adolescent Internet users. *Addictive Behaviors, 39*(3), 744–747.

Tanumihardjo, Sherry A.; Gannon, Bryan & Kaliwile, Chisela. (2016). Controversy regarding widespread vitamin A fortification in Africa and Asia. *Advances in Nutrition, 7*, 5A.

Tarbetsky, Ana L.; Collie, Rebecca J. & Martin, Andrew J. (2016). The role of implicit theories of intelligence and ability in predicting achievement for Indigenous (Aboriginal) Australian students. *Contemporary Educational Psychology, 47*, 61–71.

Tarun, Kumar; Kumar, Singh Sanjeet; Manish, Kumar; Sunita & Ashok, Sharan. (2016). Study on relationship between anemia and academic performance of adolescent girls. *International Journal of Physiology, 4*(1), 81–86.

Tassell-Matamua, Natasha; Lindsay, Nicole; Bennett, Simon; Valentine, Hukarere & Pahina, John. (2017). Does learning about near-death experiences promote psycho-spiritual benefits in those who have not had a near-death experience? *Journal of Spirituality in Mental Health, 19*(2), 95–115.

Taveras, Elsie M.; Gillman, Matthew W.; Kleinman, Ken P.; Rich-Edwards, Janet W. & Rifas-Shiman, Sheryl L. (2013). Reducing racial/ethnic disparities in childhood obesity: The role of early life risk factors. *JAMA Pediatrics, 167*(8), 731–738.

Tay, Marc Tze-Hsin; Au Eong, Kah Guan; Ng, C. Y. & Lim, M. K. (1992). Myopia and educational attainment in 421,116 young Singaporean males. *Annals Academy of Medicine Singapore, 21*(6), 785–791.

Taylor, John H. (Ed.). (2010). *Journey through the afterlife: Ancient Egyptian Book of the Dead*. Cambridge, MA: Harvard University Press.

Taylor, Paul. (2014). *The next America: Boomers, millennials, and the looming generational showdown*. New York, NY: PublicAffairs.

Taylor, Roy. (2019). Calorie restriction for long-term remission of type 2 diabetes. *Clinical Medicine, 19*(1), 37–42.

Taylor, Rachael W.; Murdoch, Linda; Carter, Philippa; Gerrard, David F.; Williams, Sheila M. & Taylor, Barry J. (2009). Longitudinal study of physical activity and inactivity in preschoolers: The FLAME study. *Medicine & Science in Sports & Exercise, 41*(1), 96–102.

Taylor, Zoe E.; Eisenberg, Nancy; Spinrad, Tracy L.; Eggum, Natalie D. & Sulik, Michael J. (2013). The relations of ego-resiliency and emotion socialization to the development of empathy and prosocial behavior across early childhood. *Emotion, 13*(5), 822–831.

Tedeschi, Richard; Orejuela-Davila, Ana & Lewis, Paisley. (2017). Posttraumatic growth and continuing bonds. In Dennis Klass & Edith Maria Steffen (Eds.), *Continuing bonds in bereavement: New directions for research and practice*. New York, NY: Routledge.

Telzer, Eva H.; Ichien, Nicholas T. & Qu, Yang. (2015). Mothers know best: Redirecting adolescent reward sensitivity toward safe behavior during risk taking. *Social Cognitive and Affective Neuroscience, 10*(10), 1383–1391.

Teoh, Yee San & Lamb, Michael E. (2013). Interviewer demeanor in forensic interviews of children. *Psychology, Crime & Law, 19*(2), 145–159.

Teresi, Dick. (2012). *The undead: Organ harvesting, the ice-water test, beating-heart cadavers—How medicine is blurring the line between life and death*. New York, NY: Pantheon Books.

Terry, Nicole Patton; Connor, Carol McDonald; Johnson, Lakeisha; Stuckey, Adrienne & Tani, Novell. (2016). Dialect variation, dialect-shifting, and reading comprehension in second grade. *Reading and Writing, 29*(2), 267–295.

Terry-McElrath, Yvonne M.; Turner, Lindsey; Sandoval, Anna; Johnston, Lloyd D. & Chaloupka, Frank J. (2014). Commercialism in US elementary and secondary school nutrition environments: Trends from 2007 to 2012. *JAMA Pediatrics, 168*(3), 234–242.

Tessier, Karen. (2010). Effectiveness of hands-on education for correct child restraint use by parents. *Accident Analysis & Prevention, 42*(4), 1041–1047.

Teti, Douglas M.; Crosby, Brian; McDaniel, Brandon T.; Shimizu, Mina & Whitesell, Corey J. (2015). Marital and emotional adjustment in mothers and infant sleep arrangements during the first six months. *Monographs of the Society for Research in Child Development, 80*(1), 160–176.

Tetley, Josie; Lee, David M.; Nazroo, James & Hinchliff, Sharron. (2018). Let's talk about sex – what do older men and women say about their sexual relations and sexual activities? A qualitative analysis of ELSA Wave 6 data. *Ageing & Society, 38*(3), 497–521.

Tetzlaff, Anne & Hilbert, Anja. (2014). The role of the family in childhood and adolescent binge eating. A systematic review. *Appetite, 76*(1), 208.

Thaler, Richard H. & Sunstein, Cass R. (2008). *Nudge: Improving decisions about health, wealth, and happiness*. New Haven, CT: Yale University Press.

Tham, Diana Su Yun; Woo, Pei Jun & Bremner, J. Gavin. (2019). Development of the other-race effect in Malaysian-Chinese infants. *Developmental Psychobiology, 61*(1), 107–115.

Thiam, Melinda A.; Flake, Eric M. & Dickman, Michael M. (2017). Infant and child mental health and perinatal illness. In Melinda A. Thiam (Ed.), *Perinatal mental health and the military family: Identifying and treating mood and anxiety disorders*. New York, NY: Routledge.

Thomaes, Sander; Brummelman, Eddie & Sedikides, Constantine. (2017). Why most children think well of themselves. *Child Development, 88*(6), 1873–1884.

Thomaes, Sander; Reijntjes, Albert; Orobio de Castro, Bram; Bushman, Brad J.; Poorthuis, Astrid & Telch, Michael J. (2010). I like me if you like me: On the interpersonal modulation and regulation of preadolescents' state self-esteem. *Child Development, 81*(3), 811–825.

Thomas, Dylan. (2003). *The poems of Dylan Thomas* (Rev. ed.). New York, NY: New Directions.

Thomas, Dennis; Dickerson, Anne E.; Blomberg, Richard D.; Graham, Lindsey A.; Wright, Timothy J.; Finstad, Kraig A. & Romoser, Matthew E. (2018). *Older drivers and navigation devices*. Washington, DC: National Highway Traffic Safety Administration. DOT HS 812 587.

Thomas, Jim. (2018). Religion: Help or hindering moral judgment. *International Journal for Innovation Education and Research, 6*(8), 112–132.

Thomason, Moriah E.; Scheinost, Dustin; Manning, Janessa H.; Grove, Lauren E.; Hect, Jasmine; Marshall, Narcis, . . . Romero, Roberto. (2017). Weak functional connectivity in the human fetal brain prior to preterm birth. *Scientific Reports, 7*(39286).

Thompson, Charis. (2014). Reproductions through technology. *Science, 344*(6182), 361–362.

Thompson, Richard; Kaczor, Kim; Lorenz, Douglas J.; Bennett, Berkeley L.; Meyers, Gabriel & Pierce, Mary Clyde. (2017). Is the use of physical discipline associated with aggressive behaviors in young children? *Academic Pediatrics, 17*(1), 34–44.

Thomson, Samuel; Marriott, Michael; Telford, Katherine; Law, Hou; McLaughlin, Jo & Sayal, Kapil. (2014). Adolescents with a diagnosis of anorexia nervosa: Parents' experience of recognition and deciding to seek help. *Clinical Child Psychology Psychiatry, 19*(1), 43–57.

Thornberg, Robert & Jungert, Tomas. (2013). Bystander behavior in bullying situations: Basic moral sensitivity, moral disengagement and defender self-efficacy. *Journal of Adolescence, 36*(3), 475–483.

Thorup, Bianca; Crookes, Kate; Chang, Paul P. W.; Burton, Nichola; Pond, Stephen; Li, Tze Kwan, . . . Rhodes, Gillian. (2018). Perceptual experience shapes our ability to categorize faces by national origin: A new other-race effect. *British Journal of Psychology, 109*(3), 583–603.

Tiggemann, Marika & Slater, Amy. (2014). NetTweens: The Internet and body image concerns in preteenage girls. *Journal of Early Adolescence, 34*(5), 606–620.

Timonen, Virpi (Ed.). (2018). *Grandparenting practices around the world*. Chicago, IL: Policy Press.

Tindale, Lauren C.; Salema, Diane & Brooks-Wilson, Angela R. (2019). 10-year follow-up of the Super-Seniors Study: Compression of morbidity and genetic factors. *BMC Geriatrics, 19*(1).

Tippett, Lynette J.; Prebble, Sally C. & Addis, Donna Rose. (2018). The persistence of the self over time in mild cognitive impairment and Alzheimer's disease. *Frontiers in Psychology, 9*(94).

Tishkoff, Sarah A.; Reed, Floyd A.; Friedlaender, Françoise R.; Ehret, Christopher; Ranciaro, Alessia; Froment, Alain, . . . Williams, Scott M. (2009). The genetic structure and history of Africans and African Americans. *Science, 324*(5930), 1035–1044.

Tobey, Emily A.; Thal, Donna; Niparko, John K.; Eisenberg, Laurie S.; Quittner, Alexandra L. & Wang, Nae-Yuh. (2013). Influence of implantation age on school-age language performance in pediatric cochlear implant users. *International Journal of Audiology*, 52(4), 219–229.

Tolman, Deborah L.; Davis, Brian R. & Bowman, Christin P. (2016). "That's just how it is": A gendered analysis of masculinity and femininity ideologies in adolescent girls' and boys' heterosexual relationships. *Journal of Adolescent Research, 31*(1), 3–31.

Tolman, Deborah L. & McClelland, Sara I. (2011). Normative sexuality development in adolescence: A decade in review, 2000–2009. *Journal of Research on Adolescence, 21*(1), 242–255.

Tomasello, Michael. (2006). Acquiring linguistic constructions. In William Damon & Richard M. Lerner (Eds.), *Handbook of child psychology* (6th ed., Vol. 2, pp. 255–298). Hoboken, NJ: Wiley.

Tomasello, Michael. (2016). The ontogeny of cultural learning. *Current Opinion in Psychology*, 8, 1–4.

Tomasello, Michael & Herrmann, Esther. (2010). Ape and human cognition. *Current Directions in Psychological Science, 19*(1), 3–8.

Tong, Stephanie T.; Hancock, Jeffrey T. & Slatcher, Richard B. (2016). Online dating system design and relational decision making: Choice, algorithms, and control. *Personal Relationships*, 23(4), 645–662.

Toossi, Mitra. (2002). *A century of change: The U.S. labor force, 1950–2050. Monthly Labor Review*, 15–28. Washington, DC: U.S. Bureau of Labor Statistics, United States Department of Labor.

Topooco, Naira; Berg, Matilda; Johansson, Sofie; Liljethörn, Lina; Radvogin, Ella; Vlaescu, George, . . . Andersson, Gerhard. (2018). Chat- and Internet-based cognitive-behavioural therapy in treatment of adolescent depression: Randomised controlled trial. *BJPsych Open*, 4(4), 199–207.

Toporek, Bryan. (2012). Sports rules revised as research mounts on head injuries. *Education Week, 31*(22), 8.

Torre, Lindsey A.; Bray, Freddie; Siegel, Rebecca L.; Ferlay, Jacques; Lortet-Tieulent, Joannie & Jemal, Ahmedin. (2015). Global cancer statistics. *CA: A Cancer Journal for Clinicians*, 65(2), 87–108.

Tough, Paul. (2012). *How children succeed: Grit, curiosity, and the hidden power of character*. Boston, MA: Houghton Mifflin Harcourt.

Townsend, Apollo; March, Alice L. & Kimball, Jan. (2017). Can faith and hospice coexist: Is the African American church the key to increased hospice utilization for African Americans? *Journal of Transcultural Nursing*, 28(1), 32–39.

Trahan, Lisa H.; Stuebing, Karla K.; Fletcher, Jack M. & Hiscock, Merrill. (2014). The Flynn Effect: A meta-analysis. *Psychological Bulletin, 140*(5), 1332–1360.

Travers, Brittany G.; Tromp, Do P. M.; Adluru, Nagesh; Lange, Nicholas; Destiche, Dan; Ennis, Chad, . . . Alexander, Andrew L. (2015). Atypical development of white matter microstructure of the corpus callosum in males with autism: A longitudinal investigation. *Molecular Autism*, 6.

Trawick-Smith, Jeffrey. (2012). Teacher–child play interactions to achieve learning outcomes: Risks and opportunities. In Robert C. Pianta (Ed.), *Handbook of early childhood education* (pp. 259–277). New York, NY: Guilford Press.

Traynor, Victoria; Veerhui, Nadine & Gopalan, Shiva. (2018). Evaluating the effects of a physical activity program on agitation and wandering experienced by individuals living with a dementia in care homes. *Australian Nursing & Midwifery Journal*, 25(7), 44.

Treas, Judith & Gubernskaya, Zoya. (2012). Farewell to moms? Maternal contact for seven countries in 1986 and 2001. *Journal of Marriage and Family*, 74(2), 297–311.

Triana, María Del Carmen; Jayasinghe, Mevan; Pieper, Jenna R.; Delgado, Dora María & Li, Mingxiang. (2018). Perceived workplace gender discrimination and employee consequences: A meta-analysis and complementary studies considering country context. *Journal of Management*, (In Press).

Trivedi, Daksha. (2015). Cochrane Review Summary: Massage for promoting mental and physical health in typically developing infants under the age of six months. *Primary Health Care Research & Development, 16*(1), 3–4.

Troll, Lillian E. & Skaff, Marilyn McKean. (1997). Perceived continuity of self in very old age. *Psychology and Aging, 12*(1), 162–169.

Trommsdorff, Gisela & Cole, Pamela M. (2011). Emotion, self-regulation, and social behavior in cultural contexts. In Xinyin Chen & Kenneth H. Rubin (Eds.), *Socioemotional development in cultural context* (pp. 131–163). New York, NY: Guilford Press.

Trompeter, Susan E.; Bettencourt, Ricki & Barrett-Connor, Elizabeth. (2012). Sexual activity and satisfaction in healthy community-dwelling older women. *The American Journal of Medicine, 125*(1), 37–43.e31.

Tronick, Edward. (1989). Emotions and emotional communication in infants. *American Psychologist, 44*(2), 112–119.

Tronick, Edward & Weinberg, M. Katherine. (1997). Depressed mothers and infants: Failure to form dyadic states of consciousness. In Lynne Murray & Peter J. Cooper (Eds.), *Postpartum depression and child development* (pp. 54–81). New York, NY: Guilford Press.

Tsai, Ya-Hsun; Lin, Chien-Hung; Hong, Jon-Chao & Tai, Kai-Hsin. (2018). The effects of metacognition on online learning interest and continuance to learn with MOOCs. *Computers & Education, 121*, 18–29.

Tsang, Christine; Falk, Simone & Hessel, Alexandria. (2017). Infants prefer infant-directed song over speech. *Child Development*, 88(4), 1207–1215.

Ttofi, Maria M.; Bowes, Lucy; Farrington, David P. & Lösel, Friedrich. (2014). Protective factors interrupting the continuity from school bullying to later internalizing and externalizing problems: A systematic review of prospective longitudinal studies. *Journal of School Violence, 13*(1), 5–38.

Tu, Kristie N.; Lie, Janette D.; Wan, Chew King Victoria; Cameron, Madison; Austel, Alaina G.; Nguyen, Jenny K., . . . Hyun, Diana. (2018). Osteoporosis: A review of treatment options. *P & T, 43*(2), 92–104.

Turley, Ruth N. López & Desmond, Matthew. (2011). Contributions to college costs by married, divorced, and remarried parents. *Journal of Family Issues*, 32(6), 767–790.

Turner, Heather A.; Finkelhor, David; Ormrod, Richard; Hamby, Sherry; Leeb, Rebecca T.; Mercy, James A. & Holt, Melissa. (2012). Family context, victimization, and child trauma symptoms: Variations in safe, stable, and nurturing relationships during early and middle childhood. *American Journal of Orthopsychiatry*, 82(2), 209–219.

Tuttle, Robert & Garr, Michael. (2012). Shift work and work to family fit: Does schedule control matter? *Journal of Family and Economic Issues*, 33(3), 261–271.

Twenge, Jean M.; Joiner, Thomas E.; Rogers, Megan L. & Martin, Gabrielle N. (2018). Increases in depressive symptoms, suicide-related outcomes, and suicide rates among U.S. adolescents after 2010 and links to increased new media screen time. *Clinical Psychological Science*, 6(1), 3–17.

Twenge, Jean M. & Park, Heejung. (2019). The decline in adult activities among U.S. Adolescents, 1976–2016. *Child Development, 90*(2), 638–654.

Tynes, Brendesha M.; Lozada, Fantasy T.; Smith, Naila A. & Stewart, Ashley M. (2018). From racial microaggressions to hate crimes: A model of online racism based on the lived experiences of adolescents of color. In Gina C. Torino, et al. (Eds.), *Microaggression theory: Influence and implications*. Newark, NJ: Wiley.

U.S. Bureau of Labor Statistics. (2016, February 25). *Volunteering in the United States — 2015*. Washington, DC: U.S. Department of Labor.

U.S. Bureau of Labor Statistics. (2016a). *Local area unemployment statistics: Latest numbers, unemployment rates, seasonally adjusted*. Washington, DC: U.S. Department of Labor.

U.S. Bureau of Labor Statistics. (2016b). *Labor force statistics from the current population survey: Employed persons by detailed occupation, sex, race, and Hispanic or Latino ethnicity. Household data annual averages*. Washington, DC: U.S. Department of Labor.

U.S. Bureau of Labor Statistics. (2018, August). *Labor force characteristics by race and ethnicity, 2017. BLS Reports*. Washington, DC: U.S. Bureau of Labor Statistics.

U.S. Bureau of Labor Statistics. (2018, June 15). *Local area unemployment statistics for May*

2018. Washington, DC: U.S. Bureau of Labor Statistics.

U.S. Bureau of Labor Statistics. (2019, January 18). *Labor force statistics from the current population survey: Employed persons by detailed occupation, sex, race, and Hispanic or Latino ethnicity. Household data annual averages*. Washington, DC: U.S. Department of Labor.

U.S. Cancer Statistics Working Group. (2019, June). *U.S. cancer statistics data visualizations tool, based on November 2018 submission data (1999–2016)*. U.S. Department of Health and Human Services, Centers for Disease Control and Prevention and National Cancer Institute.

U.S. Census Bureau. (1907). *Statistical abstract of the United States 1906*. Washington, DC: U.S. Department of Commerce.

U.S. Census Bureau. (2013a). *America's families and living arrangements: 2012*. Washington, DC: U.S. Department of Commerce, Economics and Statistics Administration, U.S. Census Bureau.

U.S. Census Bureau. (2013b). *2009–2013 American Community Survey 5-year estimates: Poverty. American FactFinder*. Washington, DC: U.S. Department of Commerce, United States Census Bureau.

U.S. Census Bureau. (2015). *America's families and living arrangements: 2015: Households (H table series). Table H3: Households by race and Hispanic origin of household reference person and detailed type*. Washington, DC: U.S. Department of Commerce, Economics and Statistics Administration, U.S. Census Bureau.

U.S. Census Bureau. (2015). *American community survey*. Washington, DC: U.S. Census Bureau.

U.S. Census Bureau. (2016). *Living arrangements of adults 18 years and over by age: Population 18 years and over in households more information 2016 American Community Survey 1-Year Estimates. American FactFinder*. Washington, DC: Department of Commerce.

U.S. Census Bureau. (2016, November 17). Living arrangements of children under age 18. Cencus.gov.

U.S. Census Bureau. (2016a). *Selected population profile in the United States: 2014 American community survey 1-year estimates. American FactFinder*. Washington, DC: U.S. Department of Commerce.

U.S. Census Bureau. (2016b). *Selected population profile in the United States: 2009 American community survey 1-year estimates. American FactFinder*. Washington, DC: U.S. Department of Commerce.

U.S. Census Bureau. (2018). *American community survey*. Washington, DC: U.S. Census Bureau.

U.S. Census Bureau. (2018, February 19). CPS historical time series tables: Table A-1. Years of school completed by people 25 years and over, by age and sex: Selected years 1940 to 2018.

U.S. Census Bureau. (2018, November). Historical living arrangements of children: Living arrangements of children under 18 years old: 1960 to present.

U.S. Census Bureau. (2018, October 30). The population 65 years and older: 2016.

U.S. Census Bureau. (2018, September 18). Mid-year population by five year age groups and sex – custom region – Germany.

U.S. Census Bureau. (2019, February 21). Educational attainment in the United States: 2018.

U.S. Census Bureau, Current Population Survey. (2018). Annual Social and Economic Supplement. https://www.census.gov/data/tables/time-series/demo/income-poverty/cps-hinc/hinc-02.html

U.S. Census Bureau, Population Division. (2010, June). *Monthly resident population estimates by age, sex, race and Hispanic origin for the United States: April 1, 2000 to July 1, 2009*. Washington, DC: U.S. Census Bureau.

U.S. Department of Agriculture. (2018, September 5). *Key statistics & graphics: Food insecurity in the U.S.* Washington, DC: U.S. Department of Agriculture.

U.S. Department of Commerce. (1975). *Historical statistics of the United States, colonial times to 1970* (Bicentennial ed.). Washington, DC: U.S. Bureau of the Census.

U.S. Department of Education. (2015, April). *A matter of equity: Preschool in America*. Washington, DC: U.S. Department of Education.

U.S. Department of Health and Human Services. (1999, December 31). *Child maltreatment 1999*. Washington, DC: Administration on Children, Youth and Families, Children's Bureau.

U.S. Department of Health and Human Services. (2000, December 31). *Child maltreatment 2000*. Washington, DC: Administration on Children, Youth and Families, Children's Bureau.

U.S. Department of Health and Human Services. (2005, December 31). *Child maltreatment 2005*. Washington, DC: Administration on Children, Youth and Families, Children's Bureau.

U.S. Department of Health and Human Services. (2010). *Head Start impact study: Final report*. Washington, DC: Administration for Children and Families.

U.S. Department of Health and Human Services. (2010, January). *Child maltreatment 2009*. Washington, DC: Administration for Children and Families, Administration on Children, Youth and Families, Children's Bureau.

U.S. Department of Health and Human Services. (2011). *The Surgeon General's call to action to support breastfeeding*. Washington, DC: U.S. Department of Health and Human Services, Office of the Surgeon General.

U.S. Department of Health and Human Services. (2016, January 25). *Child maltreatment 2014*. Washington, DC: Administration for Children and Families, Administration on Children, Youth and Families, Children's Bureau.

U.S. Department of Health and Human Services. (2017, January 19). *Child maltreatment 2015*. Washington, DC: Administration for Children and Families, Administration on Children, Youth and Families, Children's Bureau.

U.S. Department of Health and Human Services. (2018, February 1). *Child maltreatment 2016*. Washington, DC: Administration for Children and Families, Administration on Children, Youth and Families, Children's Bureau.

U.S. Department of Health and Human Services. (2019, January 28). *Child maltreatment 2017*. Washington, DC: Administration for Children and Families, Administration on Children, Youth and Families, Children's Bureau.

U.S. Department of State. (2019). Adoption statistics—Adoptions by year. Travel.State.gov.

U.S. National Library of Medicine. (2019, August 6). Genetics home reference: Your guide to understanding genetic conditions.

U.S. Preventive Services Task Force. (2002). Postmenopausal hormone replacement therapy for primary prevention of chronic conditions: Recommendations and rationale. *Annals of Internal Medicine, 137*(10), 834–839.

U.S. Preventive Services Task Force. (2018). Screening for intimate partner violence, elder abuse, and abuse of vulnerable adults US Preventive Services Task Force final recommendation statement. *JAMA, 320*(16), 1678–1687.

U.S. Social Security Administration. (2018). Popular names by birth year.

Uchida, Mai; Spencer, Thomas J.; Faraone, Stephen V. & Biederman, Joseph. (2018). Adult outcome of ADHD: An overview of results from the MGH longitudinal family studies of pediatrically and psychiatrically referred youth with and without ADHD of both sexes. *Journal of Attention Disorders, 22*(6), 523–534.

Uddin, Monica; Koenen, Karestan C.; de los Santos, Regina; Bakshis, Erin; Aiello, Allison E. & Galea, Sandro. (2010). Gender differences in the genetic and environmental determinants of adolescent depression. *Depression and Anxiety, 27*(7), 658–666.

Umberson, Debra; Pudrovska, Tetyana & Reczek, Corinne. (2010). Parenthood, childlessness, and well-being: A life course perspective. *Journal of Marriage and Family, 72*(3), 612–629.

Underwood, Emily. (2013). Why do so many neurons commit suicide during brain development? *Science, 340*(6137), 1157–1158.

Underwood, Emily. (2014, February 28). Can Down syndrome be treated? *Science, 343*(6174), 964–967.

Underwood, Emily. (2014, October 31). An easy consciousness test? *Science, 346*(6209), 531–532.

Underwood, Marion K. & Ehrenreich, Samuel E. (2017). The power and the pain of adolescents' digital communication: Cyber victimization and the perils of lurking. *American Psychologist, 72*(2), 144–158.

UNESCO. (2014). *Country profiles. UNESCO Institute for Statistics Data Centre*. Montreal, Canada: UNESCO, Université de Montréal at the Montreal's École des hautes études.

UNESCO. (2018, February). *One in five children, adolescents and youth is out of school. Fact Sheet No. 48*. Montreal, Canada: UNESCO. UIS/FS/2018/ED/48.

UNICEF. (2015). *Rapid survey on children (RSOC) 2013–14: National report.* Ministry of Women and Child Development, Government of India.

UNICEF. (2017, January 13). *Global overview child malnutrition 1990–2015. UNICEF Data and Analytics: Joint Malnutrition Estimates 2016 Edition.* New York: NY: United Nations.

UNICEF. (2018, July). Infant and young child feeding. UNICEF Data: Monitoring the situation of children and women.

UNICEF. (2018, September 18). Child mortality estimates.

United Nations. (2004). *Facing the future together: Report of the Secretary-General's Task Force on Women, Girls and HIV/AIDS in southern Africa.* New York, NY: United Nations.

United Nations. (2016a). *Life expectancy at birth, females.* United Nations Statistics Division.

United Nations. (2016b). *Life expectancy at birth, males.* United Nations Statistics Division.

United Nations. (2017). *World population ageing 2017 — Highlights.* New York, NY: United Nations, Department of Economic and Social Affairs, Population Division. ST/ESA/SER.A/397.

United Nations. (2019, June 17). *UN Data: Life expectancy at birth for both sexes combined (years).*

United Nations, Department of Economic and Social Affairs, Population Division. (2017). *World population prospects: The 2017 revision.* New York, NY.

United Nations, Department of Economic and Social Affairs, Population Division. (2018). *2018 Revision of world urbanization prospects.* New York, NY.

Ursache, Alexandra; Blair, Clancy; Stifter, Cynthia & Voegtline, Kristin. (2013). Emotional reactivity and regulation in infancy interact to predict executive functioning in early childhood. *Developmental Psychology, 49*(1), 127–137.

Vadillo, Miguel A.; Kostopoulou, Olga & Shanks, David R. (2015). A critical review and meta-analysis of the unconscious thought effect in medical decision making. *Frontiers in Psychology, 6*(636).

Valentine, Christine. (2017). Identity and continuing bonds in cross-cultural perspective: Britain and Japan. In Dennis Klass & Edith Maria Steffen (Eds.), *Continuing bonds in bereavement: New directions for research and practice.* New York, NY: Routledge.

Valsiner, Jaan. (2006). Developmental epistemology and implications for methodology. In Richard M. Lerner & William Damon (Eds.), *Handbook of child psychology* (6th ed., Vol. 1, pp. 166–209). Hoboken, NJ: Wiley.

van Batenburg-Eddes, Tamara; Butte, Dick & van de Looij-Jansen, Petra. (2012). Measuring juvenile delinquency: How do self-reports compare with official police statistics? *European Journal of Criminology, 9*(1), 23–37.

van de Bongardt, Daphne; Reitz, Ellen; Sandfort, Theo & Deković, Maja. (2015). A meta-analysis of the relations between three types of peer norms and adolescent sexual behavior. *Personality and Social Psychology Review, 19*(3), 203–234.

Van De Vondervoort, Julia W. & Hamlin, J. Kiley. (2016). Evidence for intuitive morality: Preverbal infants make sociomoral evaluations. *Child Development Perspectives, 10*(3), 143–148.

van den Akker, Alithe; Deković, Maja; Prinzie, Peter & Asscher, Jessica. (2010). Toddlers' temperament profiles: Stability and relations to negative and positive parenting. *Journal of Abnormal Child Psychology, 38*(4), 485–495.

van den Pol, Anthony N.; Mao, Guochao; Yang, Yang; Ornaghi, Sara & Davis, John N. (2017). Zika virus targeting in the developing brain. *Journal of Neuroscience, 37*(8), 2161–2175.

Van Dongen, Rachel. (2019, March 15). The Energy 202: Kids are skipping school today—to protest climate change. *Washington Post.*

Van Dyke, Miriam E.; Cheung, Patricia C.; Franks, Padra & Gazmararian, Julie A. (2018). Socioeconomic and racial/ethnic disparities in physical activity environments in Georgia elementary schools. *American Journal of Health Promotion, 32*(2), 453–463.

van Eeden-Moorefield, Brad & Pasley, Kay. (2013). Remarriage and stepfamily life. In Gary W. Peterson & Kevin R. Bush (Eds.), *Handbook of marriage and the family* (pp. 517–546). New York, NY: Springer.

van Goozen, Stephanie H. M. (2015). The role of early emotion impairments in the development of persistent antisocial behavior. *Child Development Perspectives, 9*(4), 206–210.

Van Harmelen, A.-L.; Kievit, R. A.; Ioannidis, K.; Neufeld, S.; Jones, P. B.; Bullmore, E., . . . Goodyer, I. (2017). Adolescent friendships predict later resilient functioning across psychosocial domains in a healthy community cohort. *Psychological Medicine, 47*(13), 2312–2322.

Van Hecke, Wim; Emsell, Louise & Sunaert, Stefan (Eds.). (2016). *Diffusion tensor imaging: A practical handbook.* New York, NY: Springer.

Van Horn, Linda V.; Bausermann, Robert; Affenito, Sandra; Thompson, Douglas; Striegel-Moore, Ruth; Franko, Debra & Albertson, Ann. (2011). Ethnic differences in food sources of vitamin D in adolescent American girls: The National Heart, Lung, and Blood Institute Growth and Health Study. *Nutrition Research, 31*(8), 579–585.

Van Houtte, Mieke. (2016). Lower-track students' sense of academic futility: Selection or effect? *Journal of Sociology, 52*(4), 874–889.

van IJzendoorn, Marinus H.; Bakermans-Kranenburg, Marian J.; Pannebakker, Fieke & Out, Dorothée. (2010). In defence of situational morality: Genetic, dispositional and situational determinants of children's donating to charity. *Journal of Moral Education, 39*(1), 1–20.

van Nunen, Karolien; Kaerts, Nore; Wyndaele, Jean-Jacques; Vermandel, Alexandra & Van Hal, Guido. (2015). Parents' views on toilet training (TT): A quantitative study to identify the beliefs and attitudes of parents concerning TT. *Journal of Child Health Care, 19*(2), 265–274.

Van Rheenen, Derek. (2012). A century of historical change in the game preferences of American children. *Journal of American Folklore, 125*(498), 411–443.

Van Ryzin, Mark J. & Dishion, Thomas J. (2013). From antisocial behavior to violence: A model for the amplifying role of coercive joining in adolescent friendships. *Journal of Child Psychology and Psychiatry, 54*(6), 661–669.

van Tilburg, Theo G.; Aartsen, Marja J. & van der Pas, Suzan. (2015). Loneliness after divorce: A cohort comparison among Dutch young-old adults. *European Sociological Review, 31*(3), 243–252.

Van Vonderen, Kristen E. & Kinnally, William. (2012). Media effects on body image: Examining media exposure in the broader context of internal and other social factors. *American Communication Journal, 14*(2), 41–57.

Vandenbosch, Laura & Eggermont, Steven. (2015). The role of mass media in adolescents' sexual behaviors: Exploring the explanatory value of the three-step self-objectification process. *Archives of Sexual Behavior, 44*(3), 729–742.

Vanderberg, Rachel H.; Farkas, Amy H.; Miller, Elizabeth; Sucato, Gina S.; Akers, Aletha Y. & Borrero, Sonya B. (2016). Racial and/or ethnic differences in formal sex education and sex education by parents among young women in the United States. *Journal of Pediatric and Adolescent Gynecology, 29*(1), 69–73.

VanderEnde, Kristin; Gacic-Dobo, Marta; Diallo, Mamadou S.; Conklin, Laura M. & Wallace, Aaron S. (2018, November 16). *Global routine vaccination coverage — 2017. Morbidity and Mortality Weekly Report, 67*(45), 1261–1264: Centers for Disease Control and Prevention.

Vanhalst, Janne; Luyckx, Koen; Scholte, Ron H. J.; Engels, Rutger C. M. E. & Goossens, Luc. (2013). Low self-esteem as a risk factor for loneliness in adolescence: Perceived – but not actual – social acceptance as an underlying mechanism. *Journal of Abnormal Child Psychology, 41*(7), 1067–1081.

Vardaki, Sophia; Dickerson, Anne E.; Beratis, Ion; Yannis, George & Papageorgiou, Sokratis G. (2016). Simulator measures and identification of older drivers with mild cognitive impairment. *American Journal of Occupational Therapy, 70*(2).

Varga, Mary Alice & Paletti, Robin. (2013). Life span issues and dying. In David K. Meagher & David E. Balk (Eds.), *Handbook of thanatology: The essential body of knowledge for the study of death, dying, and bereavement* (2nd ed., pp. 25–31). New York, NY: Routledge.

Vargas Lascano, Dayuma I.; Galambos, Nancy L.; Krahn, Harvey J. & Lachman, Margie E. (2015). Growth in perceived control across 25 years from the late teens to midlife: The role of personal and parents' education. *Developmental Psychology, 51*(1), 124–135.

Vaughn, Byron P.; Rank, Kevin M. & Khoruts, Alexander. (2019). Fecal microbiota transplantation: Current status in treatment of GI and liver disease. *Clinical Gastroenterology and Hepatology, 17*(2), 353–361.

Vedantam, Shankar. (2011, December 5). *What's behind a temper tantrum? Scientists deconstruct the screams. Hidden Brain*. Washington DC: National Public Radio.

Veenstra, René; Lindenberg, Siegwart; Munniksma, Anke & Dijkstra, Jan Kornelis. (2010). The complex relation between bullying, victimization, acceptance, and rejection: Giving special attention to status, affection, and sex differences. *Child Development, 81*(2), 480–486.

Veldheer, Susan; Yingst, Jessica; Midya, Vishal; Hummer, Breianna; Lester, Courtney; Krebs, Nicolle, . . . Foulds, Jonathan. (2019). Pulmonary and other health effects of electronic cigarette use among adult smokers participating in a randomized controlled smoking reduction trial. *Addictive Behaviors, 91*, 95–101.

Verdine, Brian N.; Golinkoff, Roberta Michnick; Hirsh-Pasek, Kathy & Newcombe, Nora S. (2017). Spatial skills, their development, and their links to mathematics. *Monographs of the Society for Research in Child Development, 82*(1).

Verona, Sergiu. (2003). Romanian policy regarding adoptions. In Victor Littel (Ed.), *Adoption update* (pp. 5–10). New York, NY: Nova Science.

Verschoor, Chris P. & Tamim, Hala. (2019). Frailty is inversely related to age at menopause and elevated in women who have had a hysterectomy: An analysis of the Canadian longitudinal study on aging. *The Journals of Gerontology Series A: Biological Sciences & Medical Sciences, 74*(5), 675–682.

Victora, Cesar G.; Bahl, Rajiv; Barros, Aluísio J. D.; França, Giovanny V. A.; Horton, Susan; Krasevec, Julia, . . . Rollins, Nigel C. (2016). Breastfeeding in the 21st century: Epidemiology, mechanisms, and lifelong effect. *The Lancet, 387*(10017), 475–490.

Vijayakumar, Nandita; Op de Macks, Zdena; Shirtcliff, Elizabeth A. & Pfeifer, Jennifer H. (2018). Puberty and the human brain: Insights into adolescent development. *Neuroscience and Biobehavioral Reviews, 92*, 417–436.

Viljaranta, Jaana; Aunola, Kaisa; Mullola, Sari; Virkkala, Johanna; Hirvonen, Riikka; Pakarinen, Eija & Nurmi, Jari-Erik. (2015). Children's temperament and academic skill development during first grade: Teachers' interaction styles as mediators. *Child Development, 86*(4), 1191–1209.

Villa, Virginia. (2019, March 19). *5 facts about vaccines in the U.S. Fact Tank*. Washington, DC: Pew Research Center.

Vilppu, Henna; Mikkilä-Erdmann, Mirjamaija; Södervik, Ilona & Österholm-Matikainen, Erika. (2016). Exploring eye movements of experienced and novice readers of medical texts concerning the cardiovascular system in making a diagnosis. *Anatomical Sciences Education*, (In Press).

Vinters, H. V.; Zarow, C.; Borys, E.; Whitman, J. D.; Tung, S.; Ellis, W. G., . . . Chui, H. C. (2018). Vascular dementia: Clinicopathologic and genetic considerations. *Neuropathology and Applied Neurobiology, 44*(3), 247–266.

Visscher, Peter M.; Wray, Naomi R.; Zhang, Qian; Sklar, Pamela; McCarthy, Mark I.; Brown, Matthew A. & Yang, Jian. (2017). 10 years of GWAs discovery: Biology, function, and translation. *AJHG, 101*(1), 5–22.

Vitale, Susan; Sperduto, Robert D. & Ferris, Frederick L. (2009). Increased prevalence of myopia in the United States between 1971–1972 and 1999–2004. *Archives of Ophthalmology, 127*(12), 1632–1639.

Vittner, Dorothy; Mcgrath, Jacqueline; Robinson, Joann; Lawhon, Gretchen; Cusson, Regina; Eisenfeld, Leonard, . . . Cong, Xiaomei. (2018). Increase in oxytocin from skin-to-skin contact enhances development of parent–infant relationship. *Biological Research for Nursing, 20*(1), 54–62.

Vlachos, George S. & Scarmeas, Nikolaos. (2019). Dietary interventions in mild cognitive impairment and dementia. *Dialogues in Clinical Neuroscience, 21*(1), 69–82.

Vladeck, Fredda & Altman, Anita. (2015). The future of the NORC-supportive service program model. *Public Policy Aging Report, 25*(1), 20–22.

Voegtline, Kristin M.; Costigan, Kathleen A.; Pater, Heather A. & DiPietro, Janet A. (2013). Near-term fetal response to maternal spoken voice. *Infant Behavior and Development, 36*(4), 526–533.

Voelcker-Rehage, Claudia; Niemann, Claudia & Hübner, Lena. (2018). Structural and functional brain changes related to acute and chronic exercise effects in children, adolescents and young adults. In Romain Meeusen, et al. (Eds.), *Physical activity and educational achievement: Insights from exercise neuroscience* (pp. 143–163). New York: Routledge.

Vöhringer, Isabel A.; Kolling, Thorsten; Graf, Frauke; Poloczek, Sonja; Fassbender, Iina; Freitag, Claudia, . . . Knopf, Monika. (2018). The development of implicit memory from infancy to childhood: On average performance levels and interindividual differences. *Child Development, 89*(2), 370–382.

Volkovich, Ella; Ben-Zion, Hamutal; Karny, Daphna; Meiri, Gal & Tikotzky, Liat. (2015). Sleep patterns of co-sleeping and solitary sleeping infants and mothers: A longitudinal study. *Sleep Medicine, 16*(11), 1305–1312.

von Hippel, Courtney; Kalokerinos, Elise K.; Haanterä, Katri & Zacher, Hannes. (2019). Age-based stereotype threat and work outcomes: Stress appraisals and rumination as mediators. *Psychology and Aging, 34*(1), 68–84.

von Salisch, Maria. (2018). Emotional competence and friendship involvement: Spiral effects in adolescence. *European Journal of Developmental Psychology, 15*(6), 678–693.

Vos, Bodil C.; Nieuwenhuijsen, Karen K. & Sluiter, Judith K. (2018). Consequences of traumatic brain injury in professional American football players: A systematic review of the literature. *Clinical Journal of Sport Medicine, 28*(2), 91–99.

Vos, Miriam B.; Kaar, Jill L.; Welsh, Jean A.; Van Horn, Linda V.; Feig, Daniel I.; Anderson, Cheryl A. M., . . . Johnson, Rachel K. (2017). Added sugars and cardiovascular disease risk in children: A scientific statement from the American Heart Association. *Circulation, 135*(9), 135:e1017–e1034.

Votruba-Drzal, Elizabeth & Dearing, Eric (Eds.). (2017). *Handbook of early childhood development programs, practices, and policies*. New York, NY: Wiley.

Vygotsky, Lev S. (1980). *Mind in society: The development of higher psychological processes*. Cambridge, MA: Harvard University Press.

Vygotsky, Lev S. (1987). Thinking and speech. In Robert W. Rieber & Aaron S. Carton (Eds.), *The collected works of L. S. Vygotsky* (Vol. 1, pp. 39–285). New York, NY: Springer.

Vygotsky, Lev S. (1994a). The development of academic concepts in school aged children. In René van der Veer & Jaan Valsiner (Eds.), *The Vygotsky reader* (pp. 355–370). Cambridge, MA: Blackwell.

Vygotsky, Lev S. (1994b). Principles of social education for deaf and dumb children in Russia. In Rene van der Veer & Jaan Valsiner (Eds.), *The Vygotsky reader* (pp. 19–26). Cambridge, MA: Blackwell.

Vygotsky, Lev S. (2012). *Thought and language*. Cambridge, MA: MIT Press.

Waber, Deborah P.; Bryce, Cyralene P.; Fitzmaurice, Garrett M.; Zichlin, Miriam L.; McGaughy, Jill; Girard, Jonathan M. & Galler, Janina R. (2014). Neuropsychological outcomes at midlife following moderate to severe malnutrition in infancy. *Neuropsychology, 28*(4), 530–540.

Waber, Deborah P.; Bryce, Cyralene P.; Girard, Jonathan M.; Fischer, Laura K.; Fitzmaurice, Garrett M. & Galler, Janina R. (2018). Parental history of moderate to severe infantile malnutrition is associated with cognitive deficits in their adult offspring. *Nutritional Neuroscience, 21*(3), 195–201.

Wade, Lisa. (2017). *American hookup: The new culture of sex on campus*. New York, NY: Norton.

Wade, Mark; Prime, Heather; Jenkins, Jennifer; Yeates, Keith; Williams, Tricia & Lee, Kang. (2018). On the relation between theory of mind and executive functioning: A developmental cognitive neuroscience perspective. *Psychonomic Bulletin & Review, 25*(6), 2119–2140.

Wade, Tracey D.; O'Shea, Anne & Shafran, Roz. (2016). Perfectionism and eating disorders. In Fuschia M. Sirois & Danielle S. Molnar (Eds.), *Perfectionism, health, and well-being* (pp. 205–222). New York, NY: Springer.

Wagmiller, Robert L. (2015). The temporal dynamics of childhood economic deprivation and children's achievement. *Child Development Perspectives, 9*(3), 158–163.

Wagner, Erica. (2017). *Chief engineer: Washington Roebling, the man who built the Brooklyn Bridge*. New York, NY: Bloomsbury.

Wagner, Jenny; Lüdtke, Oliver & Robitzsch, Alexander. (2019). Does personality become more stable with age? Disentangling state and trait effects for the Big Five across the life span using local structural equation modeling. *Journal of Personality and Social Psychology, 116*(4), 666–680.

Wagner, Katie; Dobkins, Karen & Barner, David. (2013). Slow mapping: Color word learning as a gradual inductive process. *Cognition, 127*(3), 307–317.

Wagner, Paul A. (2011). Socio-sexual education: A practical study in formal thinking and teachable moments. *Sex Education: Sexuality, Society and Learning, 11*(2), 193–211.

Waldinger, Robert & Schulz, Marc. (2018). The blind psychological scientists and the elephant: Reply to Sherlock and Zietsch. *Psychological Science, 29*(1), 158–160.

Waldorf, Kristina M. Adams; Nelson, Branden R.; Stencel-Baerenwald, Jennifer E.; Studholme, Colin; Kapur, Raj P.; Armistead, Blair, . . . Rajagopal, Lakshmi. (2018). Congenital Zika virus infection as a silent pathology with loss of neurogenic output in the fetal brain. *Nature Medicine, 24*, 368–374.

Walk, Laura M.; Vaidya, Chandan; Evers, Wiebke F.; Quante, Sonja & Hille, Katrin. (2018). Evaluation of a teacher training program to enhance executive functions in preschool children. *PLoS ONE, 13*(5), e0197454.

Walker, Christa L. Fischer; Rudan, Igor; Liu, Li; Nair, Harish; Theodoratou, Evropi; Bhutta, Zulfiqar A., . . . Black, Robert E. (2013). Global burden of childhood pneumonia and diarrhoea. *The Lancet, 381*(9875), 1405–1416.

Walker, Lauren; Stefanis, Leonidas & Attems, Johannes. (2019). Clinical and neuropathological differences between Parkinson's disease, Parkinson's disease dementia and dementia with Lewy bodies – current issues and future directions. *Journal of Neurochemistry, 150*(5), 467–474.

Walker, Renee; Block, Jason & Kawachi, Ichiro. (2014). The spatial accessibility of fast food restaurants and convenience stores in relation to neighborhood schools. *Applied Spatial Analysis and Policy*, 7(2), 169–182.

Wallace, Helen & Jones, Tracey. (2017). Managing procedural pain on the neonatal unit: Do inconsistencies still exist in practice? *Journal of Neonatal Nursing*, 23(3), 119–126.

Walle, Eric A. & Campos, Joseph J. (2014). Infant language development is related to the acquisition of walking. *Developmental Psychology, 50*(2), 336–348.

Wallis, Claudia. (2014). Gut reactions: Intestinal bacteria may help determine whether we are lean or obese. *Scientific American, 310*(6), 30–33.

Wallis, Christopher J. D.; Lo, Kirk; Lee, Yuna; Krakowsky, Yonah; Garbens, Alaina; Satkunasivam, Raj, . . . Nam, Robert K. (2016). Survival and cardiovascular events in men treated with testosterone replacement therapy: An intention-to-treat observational cohort study. *The Lancet Diabetes & Endocrinology*, 4(6), 498–506.

Walter, Melissa Clucas & Lippard, Christine N. (2017). Head Start teachers across a decade: Beliefs, characteristics, and time spent on academics. *Early Childhood Education Journal*, 45(5), 693–702.

Wambach, Karen & Riordan, Jan. (2014). *Breastfeeding and human lactation* (5th ed.). Burlington, MA: Jones & Bartlett.

Wanberg, Connie R. (2012). The individual experience of unemployment. *Annual Review of Psychology, 63*, 369–396.

Wang, Chao; Xue, Haifeng; Wang, Qianqian; Hao, Yongchen; Li, Dianjiang; Gu, Dongfeng & Huang, Jianfeng. (2014). Effect of drinking on all-cause mortality in women compared with men: A meta-analysis. *Journal of Women's Health*, 23(5), 373–381.

Wang, Limin; Gao, Pei; Zhang, Mei; Huang, Zhengjing; Zhang, Dudan; Deng, Qian, . . . Wang, Linhong. (2017). Prevalence and ethnic pattern of diabetes and prediabetes in China in 2013. *JAMA, 317*(24), 2515–2523.

Wang, Meifang & Liu, Li. (2018). Reciprocal relations between harsh discipline and children's externalizing behavior in China: A 5-year longitudinal study. *Child Development*, 89(1), 174–187.

Wang, Teresa W.; Gentzke, Andrea; Sharapova, Saida; Cullen, Karen A.; Ambrose, Bridget K. & Jamal, Ahmed. (2018, June 8). *Tobacco product use among middle and high school students — United States, 2011–2017. Morbidity and Mortality Weekly Report*, 67(22), 629–633. Atlanta, GA: Centers for Disease Control and Prevention.

Ward, Emma V.; Berry, Christopher J. & Shanks, David R. (2013). Age effects on explicit and implicit memory. *Frontiers in Psychology, 4*, 639.

Warneken, Felix. (2015). Precocious prosociality: Why do young children help? *Child Development Perspectives*, 9(1), 1–6.

Warner, Lisa M.; Wolff, Julia K.; Ziegelmann, Jochen P. & Wurm, Susanne. (2014). A randomized controlled trial to promote volunteering in older adults. *Psychology and Aging*, 29(4), 757–763.

Wastesson, Jonas W.; Parker, Marti G.; Fastbom, Johan; Thorslund, Mats & Johnell, Kristina. (2012). Drug use in centenarians compared with nonagenarians and octogenarians in Sweden: A nationwide register-based study. *Age and Ageing, 41*(2), 218–224.

Watson, John B. (1924). *Behaviorism*. New York, NY: The People's Institute Pub. Co.

Watson, John B. (1928). *Psychological care of infant and child*. New York, NY: Norton.

Watson, John B. (1972). *Psychological care of infant and child*. New York, NY: Arno Press.

Watson, John B. (1998). *Behaviorism*. New Brunswick, NJ: Transaction.

Watts, Nicolas; Amann, Markus; Ayeb-Karlsson, Sonja; Belesova, Kristine; Bouley, Timothy; Boykoff, Maxwell, . . . Costello, Anthony. (2018). The *Lancet* Countdown on health and climate change: From 25 years of inaction to a global transformation for public health. *The Lancet, 391*(10120), 581–630.

Webb, Alexandra R.; Heller, Howard T.; Benson, Carol B. & Lahav, Amir. (2015). Mother's voice and heartbeat sounds elicit auditory plasticity in the human brain before full gestation. *Proceedings of the National Academy of Sciences, 112*(10), 3152–3157.

Weber, Ann; Fernald, Anne & Diop, Yatma. (2017). When cultural norms discourage talking to babies: Effectiveness of a parenting program in rural Senegal. *Child Development*, 88(5), 1513–1526.

Weber, Daniela; Dekhtyar, Serhiy & Herlitz, Agneta. (2017). The Flynn effect in Europe—Effects of sex and region. *Intelligence, 60*, 39–45.

Webster, Collin A. & Suzuki, Naoki. (2014). Land of the rising pulse: A social ecological perspective of physical activity opportunities for schoolchildren in Japan. *Journal of Teaching in Physical Education*, 33(3), 304–325.

Wechsler, Konstantin; Drescher, Uwe; Janouch, Christin; Haeger, Mathias; Voelcker-Rehage, Claudia & Bock, Otmar. Multitasking during simulated car driving: A comparison of young and older persons. *Frontiers in Psychology*, 9(910).

Weger, Harry; Cole, Megan & Akbulut, Valerie. (2019). Relationship maintenance across platonic and non-platonic cross-sex friendships in emerging adults. *The Journal of Social Psychology*, 159(1), 15–29.

Wegrzyn, Lani R.; Tamimi, Rulla M.; Rosner, Bernard A.; Brown, Susan B.; Stevens, Richard G.; Eliassen, A. Heather, . . . Schernhammer, Eva S. (2017). Rotating night-shift work and the risk of breast cancer in the nurses' health studies. *American Journal of Epidemiology, 186*(5), 532–540.

Wei, Si. (2013). A multitude of people singing together. *International Journal of Community Music*, 6(2), 183–188.

Weiland, Christina & Yoshikawa, Hirokazu. (2013). Impacts of a prekindergarten program on children's mathematics, language, literacy, executive function, and emotional skills. *Child Development, 84*(6), 2112–2130.

Weinshenker, Naomi J. (2014). Teenagers and body image. Education.

Weinstein, Netta & DeHaan, Cody. (2014). On the mutuality of human motivation and relationships. In Netta Weinstein (Ed.), *Human motivation and interpersonal relationships: Theory, research, and applications* (pp. 3–25). New York, NY: Springer.

Weiss, David & Lang, Frieder R. (2012). "They" are old but "I" feel younger: Age-group dissociation as a self-protective strategy in old age. *Psychology and Aging*, 27(1), 153–163.

Weiss, Noel S. & Koepsell, Thomas D. (2014). *Epidemiologic methods: Studying the occurrence of illness* (2nd ed.). New York, NY: Oxford University Press.

Weissberg, Roger P.; Durlak, Joseph A.; Domitrovich, Celene E. & Gullotta, Thomas P. (2016). Social and emotional learning: Past, present, and future. In Joseph A. Durlak, et al. (Eds.), *Handbook of social and emotional learning: Research and practice* (pp. 3–19). New York: Guilford Press.

Weisskirch, Robert S. (2017a). A developmental perspective on language brokering. In Robert S. Weisskirch (Ed.), *Language brokering in immigrant families: Theories and contexts*. New York, NY: Routledge.

Weisskirch, Robert S. (2017b). *Language brokering in immigrant families: Theories and contexts*. New York, NY: Routledge.

Weisz, John R.; Kuppens, Sofie; Ng, Mei Yi; Eckshtain, Dikla; Ugueto, Ana M.;

Vaughn-Coaxum, Rachel, . . . Fordwood, Samantha R. (2017). What five decades of research tells us about the effects of youth psychological therapy: A multilevel meta-analysis and implications for science and practice. *American Psychologist*, 72(2), 79–117.

Wellman, Henry M. (2014). *Making minds: How theory of mind develops*. New York, NY: Oxford University Press.

Wellman, Henry M. (2018). Theory of mind: The state of the art. *European Journal of Developmental Psychology*, *15*(6), 728–755.

Wellman, Henry M.; Fang, Fuxi & Peterson, Candida C. (2011). Sequential progressions in a theory-of-mind scale: Longitudinal perspectives. *Child Development*, *82*(3), 780–792.

Wen, Ming; Ren, Qiang; Korinek, Kim & Trinh, Ha N. (2019). Living in skipped generation households and happiness among middle-aged and older grandparents in China. *Social Science Research*, *80*, 145–155.

Wendelken, Carter; Baym, Carol L.; Gazzaley, Adam & Bunge, Silvia A. (2011). Neural indices of improved attentional modulation over middle childhood. *Developmental Cognitive Neuroscience*, *1*(2), 175–186.

Wendland, Claire. (2018). Who counts? What counts? Place and the limits of perinatal mortality measures. *AMA Journal of Ethics*, *20*(1), 278–287.

Werker, Janet F. & Hensch, Takao K. (2015). Critical periods in speech perception: New directions. *Annual Review of Psychology*, *66*, 173–196.

Wesche, Rose; Walsh, Jennifer L.; Shepardson, Robyn L.; Carey, Kate B. & Carey, Michael P. (2018). The association between sexual behavior and affect: Moderating factors in young women. *The Journal of Sex Research*, (In Press).

Westerhof, Gerben J.; Miche, Martina; Brothers, Allyson F.; Barrett, Anne E.; Diehl, Manfred; Montepare, Joann M., . . . Wurm, Susanne. (2014). The influence of subjective aging on health and longevity: A meta-analysis of longitudinal data. *Psychology and Aging*, 29(4), 793–802.

Weymouth, Bridget B.; Buehler, Cheryl; Zhou, Nan & Henson, Robert A. (2016). A meta-analysis of parent–adolescent conflict: Disagreement, hostility, and youth maladjustment. *Journal of Family Theory & Review*, 8(1), 95–112.

Whalley, Lawrence J.; Duthie, Susan J.; Collins, Andrew R.; Starr, John M.; Deary, Ian J.; Lemmon, Helen, . . . Staff, Roger T. (2014). Homocysteine, antioxidant micronutrients and late onset dementia. *European Journal of Nutrition*, 53(1), 277–285.

Wheeler, Lorey A.; Zeiders, Katharine H.; Updegraff, Kimberly A.; Umaña-Taylor, Adriana J.; Rodríguez de Jesús, Sue A. & Perez-Brena, Norma J. (2017). Mexican-origin youth's risk behavior from adolescence to young adulthood: The role of familism values. *Developmental Psychology*, 53(1), 126–137.

Whisman, Mark A.; Gilmour, Anna L. & Salinger, Julia M. (2018). Marital satisfaction and mortality in the United States adult population. *Health Psychology*, 37(11), 1041–1044.

Whitbourne, Susan K. & Whitbourne, Stacey B. (2014). *Adult development and aging: Biopsychosocial perspectives* (5th ed.). Hoboken, NJ: Wiley.

White, Rebecca M. B.; Deardorff, Julianna; Liu, Yu & Gonzales, Nancy A. (2013). Contextual amplification or attenuation of the impact of pubertal timing on Mexican-origin boys' mental health symptoms. *Journal of Adolescent Health*, 53(6), 692–698.

White-Traut, Rosemary C.; Rankin, Kristin M.; Yoder, Joe; Zawacki, Laura; Campbell, Suzann; Kavanaugh, Karen, . . . Norr, Kathleen F. (2018). Relationship between mother-infant mutual dyadic responsiveness and premature infant development as measured by the Bayley III at 6 weeks corrected age. *Early Human Development*, *121*, 21–26.

Wicks, Elizabeth. (2012). The meaning of 'life': Dignity and the right to life in international human rights treaties. *Human Rights Law Review*, *12*(2), 199–219.

Widman, Laura; Choukas-Bradley, Sophia; Helms, Sarah W.; Golin, Carol E. & Prinstein, Mitchell J. (2014). Sexual communication between early adolescents and their dating partners, parents, and best friends. *The Journal of Sex Research*, *51*(7), 731–741.

Widom, Cathy Spatz; Czaja, Sally J. & DuMont, Kimberly A. (2015a). Intergenerational transmission of child abuse and neglect: Real or detection bias? *Science*, 347(6229), 1480–1485.

Widom, Cathy Spatz; Horan, Jacqueline & Brzustowicz, Linda. (2015b). Childhood maltreatment predicts allostatic load in adulthood. *Child Abuse & Neglect*, 47, 59–69.

Wierenga, Lara M.; van den Heuvel, Martijn P.; Oranje, Bob; Giedd, Jay N.; Durston, Sarah; Peper, Jiska S., . . . Crone, Eveline A. (2018). A multisample study of longitudinal changes in brain network architecture in 4–13-year-old children. *Human Brain Mapping*, *39*(1), 157–170.

Wieten, Sarah. (2018). Expertise in evidence-based medicine: A tale of three models. *Philosophy, Ethics, and Humanities in Medicine*, *13*(1).

Wigger, J. Bradley. (2018). Invisible friends across four countries: Kenya, Malawi, Nepal and the Dominican Republic. *International Journal of Psychology*, 53(Suppl. 1), 46–52.

Wigginton, Nicholas S.; Fahrenkamp-Uppenbrink, Julia; Wible, Brad & Malakoff, David. (2016). Cities are the future. *Science*, 352(6288), 904–905.

Wiik, Kenneth Aarskaug; Keizer, Renske & Lappegård, Trude. (2012). Relationship quality in marital and cohabiting unions across Europe. *Journal of Marriage and Family*, 74(3), 389–398.

Wijdicks, Eelco F. M.; Varelas, Panayiotis N.; Gronseth, Gary S. & Greer, David M. (2010). Evidence-based guideline update: Determining brain death in adults; Report of the quality standards subcommittee of the American Academy of Neurology. *Neurology*, 74(23), 1911–1918.

Wilcox, W. Bradford (Ed.). (2011). *The sustainable demographic dividend: What do marriage and fertility have to do with the economy?* New York, NY: Social Trends Institute.

Wilcox, William B. & Kline, Kathleen K. (2013). *Gender and parenthood: Biological and social scientific perspectives*. New York, NY: Columbia University Press.

Wilkinson, Stephen. (2015). Prenatal screening, reproductive choice, and public health. *Bioethics*, 29(1), 26–35.

Williams, Anne M.; Chantry, Caroline; Geubbels, Eveline L.; Ramaiya, Astha K.; Shemdoe, Aloisia I.; Tancredi, Daniel J. & Young, Sera L. (2016). Breastfeeding and complementary feeding practices among HIV-exposed infants in coastal Tanzania. *Journal of Human Lactation*, *32*(1), 112–122.

Williams, Joshua L.; Corbetta, Daniela & Guan, Yu. (2015). Learning to reach with "sticky" or "non-sticky" mittens: A tale of developmental trajectories. *Infant Behavior and Development*, 38, 82–96.

Williams, Katie M. & Hammond, Christopher J. (2016). GWAS in myopia: Insights into disease and implications for the clinic. *Expert Review of Ophthalmology*, *11*(2), 101–110.

Williams, Lela Rankin; Fox, Nathan A.; Lejuez, C. W.; Reynolds, Elizabeth K.; Henderson, Heather A.; Perez-Edgar, Koraly E., . . . Pine, Daniel S. (2010). Early temperament, propensity for risk-taking and adolescent substance-related problems: A prospective multimethod investigation. *Addictive Behaviors*, 35(2), 1148–1151.

Williams, Shanna; Moore, Kelsey; Crossman, Angela M. & Talwar, Victoria. (2016). The role of executive functions and theory of mind in children's prosocial lie-telling. *Journal of Experimental Child Psychology*, *141*, 256–266.

Williamson, Victoria; Stevelink, Sharon A. M.; Da Silva, Eve & Fear, Nicola T. (2018). A systematic review of wellbeing in children: A comparison of military and civilian families. *Child and Adolescent Psychiatry and Mental Health*, *12*(46).

Willoughby, Michael T.; Mills-Koonce, W. Roger; Gottfredson, Nisha C. & Wagner, Nicholas J. (2014). Measuring callous unemotional behaviors in early childhood: Factor structure and the prediction of stable aggression in middle childhood. *Journal of Psychopathology and Behavioral Assessment*, 36(1), 30–42.

Wilmshurst, Linda. (2011). *Child and adolescent psychopathology: A casebook* (2nd ed.). Thousand Oaks, CA: Sage.

Wilson, Jennifer; Andrews, Glenda; Hogan, Christy; Wang, Si & Shum, David H. K. (2018). Executive function in middle childhood and the relationship with theory of mind. *Developmental Neuropsychology*, 43(3), 163–182.

Winegard, Bo; Winegard, Benjamin & Geary, David C. (2018). The evolution of expertise. In K. Anders Ericsson, et al. (Eds.), *The Cambridge handbook of expertise and expert performance* (pp. 40–48). New York, NY: Cambridge University Press.

Winn, Phoebe; Acharya, Krishna; Peterson, Erika & Leuthner, Steven R. (2018). Prenatal counseling and parental decision-making following a fetal diagnosis of trisomy 13 or 18. *Journal of Perinatology*, 38(7), 788–796.

Winner, Brooke; Peipert, Jeffrey F.; Zhao, Qiuhong; Buckel, Christina; Madden,

Tessa; Allsworth, Jenifer E. & Secura, Gina M. (2012). Effectiveness of long-acting reversible contraception. *New England Journal of Medicine, 366*, 1998–2007.

Wolchik, Sharlene A.; Ma, Yue; Tein, Jenn-Yun; Sandler, Irwin N. & Ayers, Tim S. (2008). Parentally bereaved children's grief: Self-system beliefs as mediators of the relations between grief and stressors and caregiver-child relationship quality. *Death Studies, 32*(7), 597–620.

Wolf, Norman S. (Ed.). (2010). *Comparative biology of aging*. New York, NY: Springer.

Wolff, Jason J.; Gerig, Guido; Lewis, John D.; Soda, Takahiro; Styner, Martin A.; Vachet, Clement, . . . Piven, Joseph. (2015). Altered corpus callosum morphology associated with autism over the first 2 years of life. *Brain, 138*(7), 2046–2058.

Wolff, Mary S.; Teitelbaum, Susan L.; McGovern, Kathleen; Pinney, Susan M.; Windham, Gayle C.; Galvez, Maida, . . . Biro, Frank M. (2015). Environmental phenols and pubertal development in girls. *Environment International, 84*, 174–180.

Womack, Sean R.; Taraban, Lindsay; Shaw, Daniel S.; Wilson, Melvin N. & Dishion, Thomas J. (2018). Family turbulence and child internalizing and externalizing behaviors: Moderation of effects by race. *Child Development*, (In Press).

Wong, Jaclyn S. (2018). Toward a theory of gendered projectivity and linked lives in the transition to adulthood. *Journal of Family Theory & Review, 10*(1), 126–140.

Wong, Jaclyn S. & Waite, Linda J. (2015). Marriage, social networks, and health at older ages. *Journal of Population Ageing, 8*(1/2), 7–25.

Woodward, Amanda L. & Markman, Ellen M. (1998). Early word learning. In Deanna Kuhn & Robert S. Siegler (Eds.), *Handbook of child psychology* (5th ed., Vol. 2, pp. 371–420). Hoboken, NJ: Wiley.

Woollett, Katherine; Spiers, Hugo J. & Maguire, Eleanor A. (2009). Talent in the taxi: A model system for exploring expertise. *Philosophical Transactions of the Royal Society of London, 364*(1522), 1407–1416.

Woolley, Jacqueline D. & Ghossainy, Maliki E. (2013). Revisiting the fantasy–reality distinction: Children as naïve skeptics. *Child Development, 84*(5), 1496–1510.

World Bank. (2014). *Table 2.11: World Development indicators, participation in education*. Washington, DC: World Bank.

World Bank. (2017). World development indicators: Mortality rate, infant (per 1,000 live births).

World Bank. (2019). World Bank open data. World Bank.

World Bank. (2019, August). GDP per capita (current US$).

World Bank. (2019, August 26). Population ages 65 and above (% of total population)—World Bank staff estimates based on age/sex distributions of United Nations Population Division's World Population Prospects: 2017 Revision.

World Bank. (2019, August 27). Population ages 0-14 (% of total population)—World Bank staff estimates based on age/sex distributions of United Nations Population Division's World Population Prospects: 2017 Revision.

World Bank. (2019, July). GINI index (World Bank estimate).

World Health Organization. (2019, February 15). Immunization, vaccines and biologicals: Data, statistics and graphics.

World Health Organization. (2018, July 15). WHO-UNICEF estimates of BCG coverage.

World Health Organization. (2006). WHO Motor Development Study: Windows of achievement for six gross motor development milestones. *Acta Paediatrica, 95*(Suppl. 450), 86–95.

World Health Organization. (2014). Infant and young child feeding data by country.

World Health Organization. (2015). *Global status report on road safety 2015*. Geneva, Switzerland: World Health Organization.

World Health Organization. (2017, April 28). Measles vaccines: WHO position paper – April 2017. *Weekly Epidemiological Record, 17*(92), 205–228.

World Health Organization. (2017, September 29). Global Health Observatory data repository: Prevalence of obesity among children and adolescents, BMI>+2 standard deviation above the median, crude estimates by country, among children aged 5–19 years.

World Health Organization. (2019). Global Health Observatory (GHO) data: Overweight and obesity.

World Health Organization. (2019, May 14). Dementia: Key facts [Press release]. Geneva, Switzerland: World Health Organization.

World Health Organization. (2019, May 29). WHO vaccine-preventable diseases: Monitoring system—2019 global summary: Global and regional immunization profile.

Wörmann, Viktoriya; Holodynski, Manfred; Kärtner, Joscha & Keller, Heidi. (2012). A cross-cultural comparison of the development of the social smile: A longitudinal study of maternal and infant imitation in 6- and 12-week-old infants. *Infant Behavior and Development, 35*(2), 335–347.

Wosje, Karen S.; Khoury, Philip R.; Claytor, Randal P.; Copeland, Kristen A.; Hornung, Richard W.; Daniels, Stephen R. & Kalkwarf, Heidi J. (2010). Dietary patterns associated with fat and bone mass in young children. *American Journal of Clinical Nutrition*, 92(2), 294–303.

Wright, Emily M. & Cain, Calli M. (2018). Women in prison. In John Wooldredge & Paula Smith (Eds.), *The Oxford handbook of prisons and imprisonment*. New York, NY: Oxford University Press.

Wright, Vince. (2018). Vygotsky and a global perspective on scaffolding in learning mathematics. In Joseph Zajda (Ed.), *Globalisation and education reforms: Globalisation, comparative education and policy research* (pp. 123–135). Dordrecht: Springer.

Wrzus, Cornelia & Neyer, Franz J. (2016). Co-development of personality and friendships across the lifespan: An empirical review on selection and socialization. *European Psychologist, 21*(4), 254–273.

Wu, Ming-Yih & Ho, Hong-Nerng. (2015). Cost and safety of assisted reproductive technologies for human immunodeficiency virus-1 discordant couples. *World Journal of Virology, 4*(2), 142–146.

Wynberg, Rachel & Laird, Sarah A. (2018). Fast science and sluggish policy: The Herculean task of regulating biodiscovery. *Trends in Biotechnology, 36*(1), 1–3.

Xu, Fei. (2013). The object concept in human infants: Commentary on Fields. *Human Development, 56*(3), 167–170.

Xu, Fei & Kushnir, Tamar. (2013). Infants are rational constructivist learners. *Current Directions in Psychological Science, 22*(1), 28–32.

Xu, Guifeng; Strathearn, Lane; Liu, Buyun; O'Brien, Matthew; Kopelman, Todd G.; Zhu, Jing, . . . Bao, Wei. (2019). Prevalence and treatment patterns of autism spectrum disorder in the United States, 2016. *JAMA Pediatrics, 173*(2), 153–159.

Xu, Guifeng; Strathearn, Lane; Liu, Buyun; Yang, Binrang & Bao, Wei. (2018). Twenty-year trends in diagnosed attention-deficit/hyperactivity disorder among US children and adolescents, 1997–2016. *JAMA Network Open, 1*(4), e181471.

Xu, Jiaquan; Murphy, Sherry L.; Kochanek, Kenneth D. & Arias, Elizabeth. (2016, December). *Mortality in the United States, 2015. NCHS Data Brief*, (267). Hyattsville, MD: National Center for Health Statistics.

Xu, Richard; Poole, Kristie L.; Van Lieshout, Ryan J.; Saigal, Saroj & Schmidt, Louis A. (2018). Shyness and sociability among extremely low birth weight survivors in the third and fourth decades of life: Associations with relationship status. *Journal of Personality*, (In Press).

Xu, Yaoying. (2010). Children's social play sequence: Parten's classic theory revisited. *Early Child Development and Care, 180*(4), 489–498.

Yackobovitch-Gavan, Michal; Wolf Linhard, D.; Nagelberg, Nessia; Poraz, Irit; Shalitin, Shlomit; Phillip, Moshe & Meyerovitch, Joseph. (2018). Intervention for childhood obesity based on parents only or parents and child compared with follow-up alone. *Pediatric Obesity, 13*(11), 647–655.

Yadav, Priyanka; Banwari, Girish; Parmar, Chirag & Maniar, Rajesh. (2013). Internet addiction and its correlates among high school students: A preliminary study from Ahmedabad, India. *Asian Journal of Psychiatry, 6*(6), 500–505.

Yan, J.; Han, Z. R.; Tang, Y. & Zhang, X. (2017). Parental support for autonomy and child depressive symptoms in middle childhood: The mediating role of parent–child attachment. *Journal of Child and Family Studies, 26*(7), 1970–1978.

Yang, Rongwang; Zhang, Suhan; Li, Rong & Zhao, Zhengyan. (2013). Parents' attitudes toward stimulants use in China. *Journal of Developmental & Behavioral Pediatrics*, *34*(3), 225.

Yeager, David S.; Dahl, Ronald E. & Dweck, Carol S. (2018). Why interventions to influence adolescent behavior often fail but could succeed. *Perspectives on Psychological Science*, *13*(1), 101–122.

Yerkes, Robert Mearns. (1923). Testing the human mind. *Atlantic Monthly*, *131*, 358–370.

Yip, Tiffany. (2018). Ethnic/racial identity—a double-edged sword? Associations with discrimination and psychological outcomes. *Current Directions in Psychological Science*, 27(3), 170–175.

Yon, Yongjie; Mikton, Christopher R.; Gassoumis, Zachary D. & Wilber, Kathleen H. (2017). Elder abuse prevalence in community settings: A systematic review and meta-analysis. *The Lancet Global Health*, 5(2), e147–e156.

Yoon, Cynthia; Jacobs, David R.; Duprez, Daniel A.; Dutton, Gareth; Lewis, Cora E.; Neumark-Sztainer, Dianne, . . . Mason, Susan M. (2018). Questionnaire-based problematic relationship to eating and food is associated with 25 year body mass index trajectories during midlife: The Coronary Artery Risk Development In Young Adults (CARDIA) Study. *International Journal of Eating Disorders*, *51*(1), 10–17.

Yorgason, Jeremy B.; Draper, Thomas W.; Bronson, Haley; Nielson, Makayla; Babcock, Kate; Jones, Karolina, . . . Howard, Myranda. (2018). Biological, psychological, and social predictors of longevity among Utah centenarians. *International Journal of Aging and Human Development*, 87(3), 225–243.

Young, Marisa & Schieman, Scott. (2018). Scaling back and finding flexibility: Gender differences in parents' strategies to manage work–family conflict. *Journal of Marriage and Family*, *80*(1), 99–118.

Yu, Edward & Lippert, Adam M. (2016). Neighborhood crime rate, weight-related behaviors, and obesity: A systematic review of the literature. *Sociology Compass*, *10*(3), 187–207.

Yu, Jing; Cheah, Charissa S. L.; Hart, Craig H. & Yang, Chongming. (2018). Child inhibitory control and maternal acculturation moderate effects of maternal parenting on Chinese American children's adjustment. *Developmental Psychology*, *54*(6), 1111–1123.

Yudell, Michael; Roberts, Dorothy; DeSalle, Rob & Tishkoff, Sarah. (2016). Taking race out of human genetics. *Science*, *351*(6273), 564–565.

Zagheni, Emilio; Zannella, Marina; Movsesyan, Gabriel & Wagner, Brittney. (2015). Time is economically valuable: Production, consumption and transfers of time by age and sex. In Emilio Zagheni, et al. (Eds.), *A comparative analysis of European time transfers between generations and genders* (pp. 19–33). New York, NY: Springer.

Zahran, Hatice S.; Bailey, Cathy M.; Damon, Scott A.; Garbe, Paul L. & Breysse, Patrick N. (2018). *Vital signs: Asthma in children — United States, 2001–2016. Morbidity and Mortality Weekly Report*, 67(5), 149–155. Atlanta, GA: Centers for Disease Control and Prevention.

Zak, Nikolay. (2019). Evidence that Jeanne Calment died in 1934—not 1997. *Rejuvenation Research*, *22*(1), 3–12.

Zak, Paul J. (2012). *The moral molecule: The source of love and prosperity*. New York, NY: Dutton.

Zalenski, Robert J. & Raspa, Richard. (2006). Maslow's hierarchy of needs: A framework for achieving human potential in hospice. *Journal of Palliative Medicine*, *9*(5), 1120–1127.

Zametkin, Alan J. & Solanto, Mary V. (2017). A Review of *ADHD nation* [Review of the book *ADHD nation: Children, doctors, big pharma, and the making of an American epidemic*, by Alan Schwarz]. *The ADHD Report*, 25(2), 6–10.

Zatorre, Robert J. (2013). Predispositions and plasticity in music and speech learning: Neural correlates and implications. *Science*, *342*(6158), 585–589.

Zeiders, Katharine H.; Umaña-Taylor, Adriana J. & Derlan, Chelsea L. (2013a). Trajectories of depressive symptoms and self-esteem in Latino youths: Examining the role of gender and perceived discrimination. *Developmental Psychology*, *49*(5), 951–963.

Zeiders, Katharine H.; Updegraff, Kimberly A.; Umaña-Taylor, Adriana J.; Wheeler, Lorey A.; Perez-Brena, Norma J. & Rodríguez, Sue A. (2013b). Mexican-origin youths trajectories of depressive symptoms: The role of familism values. *Journal of Adolescent Health*, 53(5), 648–654.

Zeifman, Debra M. (2013). Built to bond: Coevolution, coregulation, and plasticity in parent-infant bonds. In Cindy Hazan & Mary I. Campa (Eds.), *Human bonding: The science of affectional ties* (pp. 41–73). New York, NY: Guilford Press.

Zeitlin, Marian. (2011). *New information on West African traditional education and approaches to its modernization.* Dakar, Senegal: Tostan.

Zelazo, Philip D. (2018). Abstracting and aligning essential features of cognitive development. *Human Development*, *61*(1), 43–48.

Zhan, Min; Xiang, Xiaoling & Elliott, William. (2018). How much is too much: Educational loans and college graduation. *Educational Policy*, 32(7), 993–1017.

Zhang, Limei. (2018). *Metacognitive and cognitive strategy use in reading comprehension: A structural equation modelling approach*. Singapore: Springer.

Zhang, Linlin & Eggum-Wilkens, Natalie D. (2018). Correlates of shyness and unsociability during early adolescence in urban and rural China. *Journal of Early Adolescence*, 38(3), 408–421.

Zhao, Fei; Franco, Heather L.; Rodriguez, Karina F.; Brown, Paula R.; Tsai, Ming-Jer; Tsai, Sophia Y. & Yao, Humphrey H.-C. (2017). Elimination of the male reproductive tract in the female embryo is promoted by COUP-TFII in mice. *Science*, 357(6352), 717–720.

Zhao, Jinxia & Wang, Meifang. (2014). Mothers' academic involvement and children's achievement: Children's theory of intelligence as a mediator. *Learning and Individual Differences*, 35, 130–136.

Zhou, Cindy Ke; Levine, Paul H.; Cleary, Sean D.; Hoffman, Heather J.; Graubard, Barry I. & Cook, Michael B. (2016). Male pattern baldness in relation to prostate cancer–specific mortality: A prospective analysis in the NHANES I Epidemiologic Follow-Up Study. *American Journal of Epidemiology*, *183*(3), 210–217.

Zhu, Qi; Song, Yiying; Hu, Siyuan; Li, Xiaobai; Tian, Moqian; Zhen, Zonglei, . . . Liu, Jia. (2010). Heritability of the specific cognitive ability of face perception. *Current Biology*, *20*(2), 137–142.

Zimmer-Gembeck, Melanie J. (2016). Peer rejection, victimization, and relational self-system processes in adolescence: Toward a transactional model of stress, coping, and developing sensitivities. *Child Development Perspectives*, *10*(2), 122–127.

Zimmerman, Marc A.; Stoddard, Sarah A.; Eisman, Andria B.; Caldwell, Cleopatra H.; Aiyer, Sophie M. & Miller, Alison. (2013). Adolescent resilience: Promotive factors that inform prevention. *Child Development Perspectives*, 7(4), 215–220.

Zimmermann, Camilla. (2012). Acceptance of dying: A discourse analysis of palliative care literature. *Social Science & Medicine*, 75(1), 217–224.

Zinzow, Heidi M. & Thompson, Martie. (2015). Factors associated with use of verbally coercive, incapacitated, and forcible sexual assault tactics in a longitudinal study of college men. *Aggressive Behavior*, *41*(1), 34–43.

Zosel, Amy; Bartelson, Becki Bucher; Bailey, Elise; Lowenstein, Steven & Dart, Rick. (2013). Characterization of adolescent prescription drug abuse and misuse using the Researched Abuse Diversion and Addiction-Related Surveillance (RADARS[R]) System. *Journal of the American Academy of Child & Adolescent Psychiatry*, 52(2), 196-204.e192.

Zubrzycki, Jackie. (2017). 1 in 5 public school students in the class of 2016 passed an AP exam [Web log post]. Education Week: Curriculum Matters.

Zuk, Jennifer; Benjamin, Christopher; Kenyon, Arnold & Gaab, Nadine. (2014). Behavioral and neural correlates of executive functioning in musicians and non-musicians. *PLoS ONE*, *9*(6), e99868.

Zurcher, Jessica D.; Holmgren, Hailey G.; Coyne, Sarah M.; Barlett, Christopher P. & Yang, Chongming. (2018). Parenting and cyberbullying across adolescence. *Cyberpsychology, Behavior, and Social Networking*, *21*(5), 294–303.

Zych, Izabela; Farrington, David P.; Llorent, Vicente J. & Ttofi, Maria M. (Eds.). (2017). *Protecting children against bullying and its consequences*. Cham, Switzerland: Springer.

NAME INDEX

Note: "f" indicates the reference is to a figure; "t" indicates the reference is to a table; "p" indicates the reference is to a photo.

Aarnoudse-Moens, Cornelieke S. H., 105
Abar, Caitlin C., 409
Abbott, Nicola, 342
Abraham, Eyal, 181, 185
Abramovitch, Amitai, 283
Accardo, Pasquale, 54
Acharya, Arnab, 128
Acharya, Kartikey, 79
Ada (child), 197
Adams, Gary A., 573
Adams, Melissa, 562p
Adamson, Lauren B., 157, 227
Addati, Laura, 189f
Adler, Alfred, 36
Adler, Caleb, 211p, 446
Adler, Lynn Peters, 656
Adolph, Karen E., 91, 130, 131, 132
Aesop, 224
Aggarwal, Bharat B., 128
Ahler, Douglas J., 20
Ahles, Tim A., 434
Ahmadabadi, Zohre, 498
Ailshire, Jennifer A., 593
Ainsworth, Mary D., 59f, 175, 177
Aizpitarte, Alazne, 407
Akhtar, Nameera, 11
Al Otaiba, Stephanie, 292
Albert, Dustin, 359, 384, 420, 420f
Aldwin, Carolyn M., 512, 519
Alegre, Alberto, 259
Alesi, Marianha, 282
Alex (adolescent), 412p
Alexander, Karl L., 23
Alexandre-Heymann, Laure, 361
Al-Hashim, Aqeela H., 202
Alibali, Martha W., 226
Alice (adopted child), 179, 179p
Allen, Sian, 432
Allen, Tony, 419p
Allendorf, Keera, 495
Al-Namlah, Abdulrahman S., 228
Alper, Meryl, 229
Altaye, Mekibib, 211p
Altman, Anita, 644
Altmann, Andre, 622
Altschul, Inna, 257
Alvarado, Louis, 277
Alvira-Hammond, Marta, 498
Amato, Michael S., 211
Amato, Paul R., 563
Ameade, Evans Paul Kwame, 359
American Academy of Pediatrics, 165t, 229, 253, 271f, 356
American Heart Association, 200
American Medical Association, 669
American Pediatric Association, 423
American Psychiatric Association, 169, 287, 366, 639
American Psychological Association, A–1
Amin, Avnika, 136
Anandakumar, Jeya, 385
Anderin, Claes, 524
Anderson, Craig A., 22
Anderson, Daniel R., 160
Anderson, Hans Christian, 290
Anderson, Michael, 677
Anderson, Monica, 388, 427f
Andreas, Nicholas J., 136
Andrews, Timothy, 281
Ang, Shannon, 641
Angelou, Maya, 216p
Anita (emerging adult), 436, 437
Ann (twin), 330
Ansado, Jennyfer, 202
Ansmann, Lena, 601
Antonucci, Toni C., 564
Apgar, Virginia, 95, 549
Ardelt, Monika, 630
Arden, Rosalind, 532
Argyrides, Marios, 365
Arias, Elizabeth, 659f
Ariely, Dan, 573
Aristotle, 58f
Armstrong, Kim, 433
Armstrong, Zan, 97
Arnett, Jeffrey, 59f, 432, 433
Arnett, Jeffrey Jensen, 432, 433
Aron, Arthur, 489
Arpino, Bruno, 570
Arshad, S. Hasan, 96
Arterburn, David E., 524
Arthur (adolescent), 412p
Arum, Richard, 470
Asa (author's grandson), 89, 197, 221, 247, 585
Asad, Ghaden, 384p
Ashley (cardiologist), 519
Ashraf, Quamrul, 64
Ashwin, Sarah, 334
Aslin, Richard N., 155
Association for Psychological Science, A–2
Association of American Medical Colleges, 549f
Atamna, Hani, 434
Attaran, Amir, 674
Atzaba-Poria, Naama, 250
Atzil, Shir, 174
Aud, Susan, 307f
Augustine, Vineet, 437
Aunola, Kaisa, 259
Ava (child), 205p
Avery, Rosemary J., 487
Aviv, Abraham, 606
Ayotte, Brian J., 626
Ayoub, Mona, 254
Ayyanathan, Kasirajan, 63
Azrin, Nathan H., 54

Babadjouni, Robin M., 210
Babchishin, Lyzon K., 187
Babcock, Renée L., 586
Bachman, Heather J., 301
Baert, Stijn, 440
Bagchi, Debasis, 280
Bagot, Kara, 424
Bailey, J. Michael, 413
Baillargeon, Renée, 154
Baio, Jon, 14
Bakeman, Roger, 157
Baker, Darren J., 624
Baker, Jeffrey P., 133
Baker, Lindsey A., 571
Baker, Olesya, 396
Baker, Simon T. E., 383
Bakken, Jeremy P., 409
Balk, David, 663
Ball, Helen L., 120
Baltes, Margret M., 53, 541, 542
Baltes, Paul B., 7, 53, 457, 541, 542, 630
Baly, Michael W., 393
Bandura, Albert, 39, 59f, 612p
Banks, James R., 281
Bannon, Michael J., 73
Baranowski, Tom, 280
Barbey, Aron K., 533, 538
Barkley, Russell A., 288, 289
Barnes, J. C., 39
Barnett, W. Steven, 240, 241, 242
Baron-Cohen, Simon, 229, 231
Barone, Joseph, 55
Barr, Rachel, 160
Barrett, Anne E., 587
Barrios, Yasmin V., 361
Barry, Carolyn McNamara, 463
Bartels, Meike, 329
Basseches, Michael, 457
Bassok, Daphna, 239, 239f
Bateson, Mary Catherine, 630
Bateson, Patrick, 251
Bathory, Eleanor, 120
Baude, Amandine, 334
Bauer, Clemens C. C., 122
Baumrind, Diana, 59f, 254, 255t
Bax, Trent, 389
Bayley, Nancy, 534
BBC News, 377
Bea, Megan Doherty, 484, 485, 487
Beal, Susan, 133
Bearak, Jonathan, 441, 442
Beatles, The, 15

Beauchaine, Theodore P., 329
Beck, Melinda, 95
Bedford, Elliott Louis, 670
Bee, Margaret, 89
Beebe, Beatrice, 174
Bell, Beth T., 365
Bell, Georgie, 168
Bell, Linda G., 561
Bell, Martha Ann, 249
Belsky, Daniel W., 433, 518
Belsky, Jay, 329, 361
Beltran, Alicia, 105p
Bem, Sandra L., 263
Benatar, David, 673
Bender, Heather L., 258
Benigno, Joann P., 228
Benn, Peter, 79
Bennett, Kate M., 562
Bennett, Tamara, 500
Benoit, Amelie, 362
Bentley, Gillian R., 91t
Bercovitz, Katherine, 614
Berg, Jeremy, 34
Bergelson, Elika, 145, 145t
Berger, Kathleen S. (author, citations), 210, 646, 647
Berger, Kathleen S. (author, personal anecdotes), 3, 16–17, 33, 61, 73–74, 89, 117, 157, 167, 186, 197, 207, 221, 226, 262, 275, 293, 312, 411, 431, 453, 479, 495, 507, 531, 550, 555, 580, 585, 611, 635
Bergmann, Olaf, 510
Berken, Jonathan A., 8
Berko, Jean, 234
Berkowitz, C., 620
Berlin, Lisa J., 187
Bernard, Jessie S., 560
Bernard, Kristin, 173
Bernat, James L., 671
Bernaud, Jean-Luc, 484
Betancourt, Theresa S., 327
Bethany (author's daughter), 117, 167, 208, 262
Bettelheim, Bruno, 14
Bhatia, Tej K., 235
Bialik, Kristen, 553f
Bialystok, Ellen, 235, 308
Bieber, Justin, 201
Biemiller, Andrew, 233
Biffen, Stevie C., 202
Bill (author's nephew), 17p
Bill (older adult), 645
Bill-Axelson, Anna, 601
Billick, Stephen, 420
Billy (adult), 507, 526
Binet, Alfred, 58f, 284
Biro, Frank M., 354, 359
Bishop, Jacob, 474
Bjorklund, David F., 50, 52, 148, 248
Björnberg, Marina, 346, 346f
Black, Dennis M., 600
Black, Maureen M., 570
Blad, Evie, 316
Blair, Clancy, 231, 304
Blakemore, Sarah-Jayne, 42, 384, 385
Blalock, Garrick, 664
Blanchard-Fields, Fredda, 461
Blanchflower, David G., 637
Blank, Grant, 489
Blas, Erik, 522
Bleidorn, Wiebke, 433, 484, 642
Blieszner, Rosemary, 648
Blinder, Alan, 396
Block, Robert, 125
Blomqvist, Ylva Thernström, 119
Blum-Kulka, Shoshana, 264
Blurton-Jones, Nicholas G., 252
Bodner-Adler, Barbara, 95
Bøe, Tormod, 337
Boerma, Ties, 96
Bögels, Susan M., 169
Bogle, Kathleen A., 493
Bohannon, John, 5
Bohn, Manuel, 157
Boisvert, Stéphanie, 433
Boldrini, Maura, 511, 612
Bolk, Jenny, 282
Bollyky, Thomas J., 522
Bonanno, George A., 680
Bonanno, Rina A., 390
Bone, Anna E., 667
Bonora, Massimo, 69
Booker, Erik, 524p
Booth, Alan, 334
Bordini, Gabriela Sagebin, 442
Borke, Jörn, 183
Bornstein, Marc H., 11, 258, 264, 265, 550
Boseovski, Janet J., 325
Bosworth, Hayden B., 626
Bourdain, Anthony, 82
Bourguignon, Jean-Pierre, 360
Bouter, Lex M., 5
Bowlby, John, 59f, 175
Bowman, Nicholas A., 472
Boyce, W. Thomas, 7, 337
boyd, danah, 380, 387, 391
Boyd, Wendy, 187
Boyle, J., 639
Boyle, Patricia A., 626
Braams, Barbara R., 359
Brackett, Marc, 315
Bradley, Rachel, 109
Bradshaw, Matt, 644
Braithwaite, David W., 305
Brame, Robert, 418
Brandone, Amanda C., 153
Brandt, Hella E., 668t
Brandt, Martina, 487
Branje, Susan, 408
Braun, Henry I., 314, 316, 397
Braun, Katharina, 123
Braver, Sanford L., 334, 564
Brazelton, T. Berry, 54
Breckenridge, Ross A., 134
Bremner, J. Gavin, 154, 158
Brennan, Arthur, 109
Breslow, Lori, 473
Bridge, Jeffrey A., 417
Bridgers, Sophie, 229
Bridges, Moziah, 32p
Bridgett, David J., 249
Briley, Daniel A., 636
Brindis, Claire D., 415
Brint, Steven, 466
Brix, Nis, 354, 359, 364
Broberg, Thomas, 597
Brodsky, Michael C., 127
Brody, Gene H., 407, 408, 408f
Brody, Jane E., 102
Broekhuizen, Martine L., 187
Bronfenbrenner, Urie, 9, 10f, 59f, 89
Broockman, David, 454
Brooks, Jeanne, 170
Brooten, Dorothy, 677
Broström, Stig, 227
Brotto, Lori A., 514
Brouwer, Rachel M., 286
Brown, Anna, 457
Brown, B. Bradford, 409
Brown, Christia Spears, 325
Brown, J. Scott, 638
Brown, James, 15
Brown, Kay, 323, 344
Brown, Louise, 70, 70p
Brown, Mary Jean, 211
Brown, Steven D., 66
Brownell, Celia A., 266
Brubaker, Christopher J., 211p
Brubaker, Matthew S., 616
Bruder, Gerard E., 202
Brummelman, Eddie, 251
Brunborg, Geir Scott, 435
Brunham, Robert C., 515
Bucx, Freek, 487, 565
Buddha, 464
Budiman, Abby, 180
Bueno, Clarissa, 119
Buiting, Hilde, 672
Bulmer, Maria, 672
Burchinal, Margaret R., 189
Burd-Sharps, Sarah, 525
Burén, Jonas, 413
Burgoyne, Alexander P., 537
Burke, Brian L., 664
Burlina, Alessandro P., 510
Burnette, Jeni L., 394
Burri, Andrea, 514
Burridge, Andrea Backscheider, 467
Bursztyn, Leonardo, 410, 411
Burt, S. Alexandra, 329
Bush, George H. W., 201
Buss, David M., 49
Buss, Kristin A., 43
Butler, Ashley M., 256
Butler, Robert N., 628, 629
Butterworth, Brian, 290
Butterworth, Peter, 574
Butts, Donna, 572
Byard, Roger W., 126
Byers-Heinlein, Krista, 145
Byrnes, James P., 406
Byun, Erika, 396, 397

Cabrera, Natasha, 15
Caccamo, Alexandra, 443
Cacioppo, Stephanie, 63
Calarco, Jessica McCrory, 312

Caleb (author's grandson), 226
Calkins, Susan D., 249
Callaghan, Tara, 223
Calment, Jeanne, 604
Calment, Yvonne, 604
Calvo, Rocío, 641, 642
Camhi, Sarah M., 482
Campbell, Frances A., 241, 241p
Campbell, Peter J., 605
Canadian Medical Association, 674
Candelario, Abraham, 102p
Candelario, Carlos, 102p
Candelario, Francisca, 102p
Cao, Zhipeng, 420
Caplan, Rachel, 215
Cappelletti, Marinella, 614
Cardozo, Eden R., 516
Carey, Anna G., 493
Carey, Nessa, 14
Carlsen, Karin C. Lødrup, 423
Carlson, Robert G., 24
Carlson, Scott, 395
Carlyann (child), 205p
Carmichael, Cheryl L., 489
Carocho, Márcio, 606
Carr, Deborah, 646
Carra, Cecilia, 183
Carrese, Joseph A., 462
Carroll, Linda J., 435
Carson, Valerie, 253
Carson (child), 334p
Carstensen, Laura L., 53, 564, 638, 665
Carter (child), 334p
Caruso, Federica, 238
Carwile, Jenny L., 359
Casaccia, Patrizia, 65
Casey, B. J., 358
Caspi, Avshalom, 330
Cassandra (mythlogy), 82
Castellacci, Fulvio, 489
Castro-Martin, Teresa, 498
Cattell, Raymond, 537
Caudle, Kristina, 358
Cauffman, Elizabeth, 444, 447
Cavalari, Rachel N. S., 202
Ceauşescu, Nicolae, 176, 177
Ceballo, Rosario, 308
Cecil, Kim M., 211p
Cenegy, Laura Freeman, 334, 563
Center for Education Policy, 395
Centers for Disease Control and Prevention, 68, 133, 141, 211f, 369, 434, 443, 600, 658, 669f
Cesana-Arlotti, Nicoló, 146
Cespedes, Elizabeth M., 198
Chamberlain, Stormy J., 65
Champagne, Frances A., 110
Chan, Kit Yee, 621
Chancer, Lynn S., 567
Chandler, Kevan, 564p
Chang, Alicia, 263
Chang, Tzu-Fen, 181
Chang, Yevvon Yi-Chi, 454
Charise, Andrea, 629
Charness, Neil, 545, 548
Charnigo, Richard, 386
Chartier, Karen G., 76
Chaudhury, S. Raj, 474
Chelsea (emerging adult), 495
Chen, Diane, 325
Chen, Edith, 407, 408, 526
Chen, Feinian, 571
Chen, Hong, 365
Chen, Irit, 538
Chen, M. Keith, 18, 19
Chen, Mu-Hong, 289, 289f, 524
Chen, Ruijia, 653
Chen, Xinyin, 304, 340
Cheng, Diana, 102
Cher, 602p
Cherlin, Andrew, 560
Chernev, Alexander, 494
Cherng, Hua-Yu Sebastian, 316
Cheslack-Postava, Keely, 101
Chestnut, Joey, 524p
Cheuk, Tina, 319
Chikritzhs, Tanya, 522
Child Development Institute, A–3
Child Trends Data Bank, 211f, 401f
Child Welfare Information Gateway, 569
Chiou, Wen-Bin, 454, 494
Chlebowski, Rowan T., 517
Cho, Youngmin, 576, 577
Choe, Daniel E., 259, 266
Choi, Hyunkyung, 112
Choi, Rhea, 612
Choi, Yool, 472
Chomsky, Noam, 161
Chong, Jessica X., 78
Chopin, Frederick, 6p
Choshen-Hillel, Shoham, 573
Choudhury, Ananyo, 74
Choukas-Bradley, Sophia, 414
Christakis, Dimitri A., 125, 239
Christian, Cindy W., 125
Christian, Kimberly M., 99
Christoforides, Michael, 302
Chu, Shuyuan, 96
Churchill, Winston, 290
Cianciolo, Anna T., 539
Cicchetti, Dante, 173, 176, 287, 289
Cicconi, Megan, 229
Cierpka, Astrid, 169
Cierpka, Manfred, 169
Cillessen, Antonius H. N., 340
Claessen, Jacques, 345
Clark, Caron A. C., 105
Clark, Kenneth, 58f
Clark, Lee Anna, 287
Clark, Linda, 356
Clark, Mamie, 58f
Clarke, Philippa, 640
Clinton, Bill, 201
Clinton, Hillary, 19
Coe, Jesse L., 328
Coffelt, Tina A., 414
Coggin, Alexander, 469
Cohen, Joel E., 311
Cohen, Jon, 27, 70, 599
Cohn, D'Vera, 560f, 565, 581f
Colby, Reggie, 448p
Cole, Pamela M., 172, 266
Coleman, Barbara, 679p
Coleman, Patrick A., 488
Coleman-Jensen, Alisha, 106
Coles, Robert, 343
Coley, Nicola, 625
Coley, Rebekah Levine, 188
Collett, DeShana, 500
Collin-Vézina, Delphine, 371
Colson, Eve R., 120
Colver, Allan, 455
Committee on Health Care for Underserved Women, 104
Common Sense Media, 253f
Compian, Laura J., 362
Compton, Wilson M., 574
Confer, Jaime C., 50
Conger, Rand D., 336
Connolly, Jennifer, 493
Conti, Aldo Alberto, 625
Cook, Peta S., 636
Coon, Carleton S., 12
Copeland, William E., 342
Copher, Ronda, 486
Coplan, Robert J., 307
Corballis, Michael C., 202
Cordina-Duverger, Emilie, 577
Corenblum, Barry, 325
Cornelis, Marilyn C., 521
Cornwall, Claudia, 540
Corps, Kara N., 510
Corr, Charles A., 676
Corr, Donna M., 676
Cosgrave, James F., 447
Costa, Albert, 235, 308
Côté, James E., 404
Couch, Mahalia, 97p
Council on Communications and Media, 297f
Couzin-Frankel, Jennifer, 65, 81, 84, 200
Covington-Ward, Yolanda, 654
Cowen, Joshua M., 317
Cox, Ronald B., 258, 259
Coxworth, James E., 51
Coyne, Sarah M., 542
Craig (father), 299
Crain, William C., 224
Cree, Robyn A., 309
Crenshaw, David A., 681
Crenshaw, Kimberlé, 13
Cripe, Larry D., 668
Crone, Eveline A., 420
Crosnoe, Robert, 240
Crossley, Nicolas A., 304
Crowe, Kristi, 105
Crowe, Laura, 574
Cruikshank, Margaret, 596
Csibra, Gergely, 146
Csikszentmihalyi, Mihaly, 547, 629
Culpin, Iryna, 361
Cumming, Elaine, 640
Cunningham, F. Gary, 91t
Curley, James P., 110
Curry, Andrew, 52
Curtin, Nancy, 676
Cutler, David M., 602
Cuzzolaro, Massimo, 365
Cyrus, Miley, 414p

Dabbagh, Alya, 134, 135
Dahl, Ronald E., 354, 356
Dahmen, Brigitte, 123
Daley, Tamara C., 285
Dall'Alba, Gloria, 544
Damasio, Antonio R., 43, 202
Daneback, Kristian, 414
D'Angelo, Jonathan D., 494
Daniel (child), 79p
Danielsbacka, Mirkka, 563
Dantchev, Slava, 342
Darweesh, Sirwan K. L., 623
Darwin, Charles, 49, 58f, 293
Darwin, Zoe, 109
Dasgupta, Rajib, 138
Daugherty, Ana M., 613
Dave (adult), 562
David (author's nephew), 16–17, 17p, 17t, 30, 285
Davidai, Shai, 573
Davis, Corey S., 21
Davis, Jordan P., 484
Davison, Glen, 519
Dawson, Chris, 577
Day, Felix R., 361
Day, Melissa D., 652p
Dayanim, Shoshana, 160
De Boeck, Paul, 5
de Boer, Anouk, 421
de Jong Gierveld, Jenny, 561
de Jonge, Ank, 97
de Jonge, Guustaaf Adolf, 133
de Jonge, Huub, 678
de la Monte, Suzanne M., 15
de la Torre, Pedro, 482
De Lima, Liliana, 674
de López, Kristine Jensen, 231
De Neys, Wim, 382
de Oliveira Cardoso, Caroline, 306
De Raedt, Rudi, 665
De Vos, Ans, 548
de Vos, Paul, 437
de Vries, Dian A., 365
de Vrieze, Jop, 22
De Wilde, Arno, 626
Dean, Angela J., 276
Dean, Ethan, 81p
Dean, James, 663, 664
Dearing, Eric, 188, 237, 277
Deary, Ian J., 532
Deater-Deckard, Kirby, 257, 258
Dees, Marianne K., 672
Dehaene-Lambertz, Ghislaine, 162
Deindl, Christian, 487
Del Giudice, Marco, 361
DeLamater, John, 514
Delasobera, B. Elizabeth, 446
Delaunay-El Allam, Maryse, 128
DeLiema, Marguerite, 638
Delon-Martin, Chantal, 548
Demartini, Julie K., 434
Deming, Michelle E., 493
Demir, Melikşah, 564
Demosthene, Anne, 387p
Denq, William, 446
Dent, Lauren, 415
Deresiewicz, William, 470
Desai, Rathnamala M., 514
Desai, Rishi J., 102
Desmond, Matthew, 335
Devine, Rory T., 231, 615
Devitt, Aleea L., 617
DeVos, Betsy, 645
DeVos, Julie, 154
DeYoung, Colin G., 558p
Diamond, Adele, 222, 223
Diamond, Marian C., 125
Diana (adult), 561p
Diana (author's friend), 611–612
Didion, Joan, 675
Dietrich, Kim N., 211p
Digest of Education Statistics, 317f
Dijksterhuis, Ap, 6, 545, 545f
Dillman Carpentier, Francesca, 414
Dillow, Sally A., 317
Dim, Anna, 384p
Dimler, Laura M., 360
Dingemans, Ellen, 642
Dinh, Michael M., 210
Diseth, Åge, 394
Dishion, Thomas J., 407, 412
Ditch the Label, 427f
Dittmar, Helga, 365
Dix, Theodore, 172
Doka, Kenneth J., 668, 677
Domina, Thurston, 395
Dominguez, Cynthia O., 544
Dominguez-Folgueras, Marta, 498
Don (father), 330
Dong, XinQi, 653, 654
Donovick, Peter J., 202
Doom, Jenalee R., 410
Dora (mother), 299
Dorais, Michel, 371
Dörfler, Viktor, 544
Doris (author's friend), 635–636, 636p, 639
Dot (author's sister-in-law), 16–17, 17p
Dotterer, Aryn M., 393
Doucet, Andrea, 567
Dougherty, Rachel, 66
Dovey-Pearce, Gail, 455
Dow-Edwards, Diana, 15
Down, Langdon, 79
Downing, Katherine L., 253
Drake, Patrick, 106
Drewelies, Johanna, 636
Driemeyer, Wiebke, 367
Drover, James, 136
Drury, Stacy S., 606
Dubowitz, Howard, 212
Duckett, Stephen, 670
Duckworth, Angela L., 315, 398
Duckworth, Tammy, 515p
Duffey, Kiyah J., 438
Dugas, Lara R., 64
Duggan, Maeve, 427f
Dumas, A., 101
Dunbar, R. I. M., 564
Duncan, Dustin T., 439
Duncan, Greg J., 241
Dunn, Erin C., 215
Dunn, Judy, 334
Dunn, Kristy, 154
Dunning, David, 265
DuPont, Robert L., 15
Durso, Francis T., 546
Dutton, Donald G., 499
Duval-Tsioles, Denise, 335
Dvornyk, Volodymyr, 359
Dweck, Carol S., 184, 325, 326, 394
Dyer, Nazly, 256, 649
Dylan, Bob, 15
Dzau, Victor J., 28

Eagly, Alice H., 260, 263
Early Child Care Network, 188
Eaton, Nicholas R., 287
Eberhart, Johann K., 101
Eccles, Jacquelynne S., 392, 393, 416
Edmonds, Tyler, 419
Edmonson, Lwrence, 387p
Education Resources Information Center (ERIC), A-3
Egelhoff, John C., 211p
Egger, Sam J., 601
Eggermont, Steven, 414
Eggum-Wilkens, Natalie D., 265, 340
Eginton, Margaret L., 629
Ehrenberg, Rachel, 77
Ehrenreich, Samuel E., 390
Ehrlich, Sara Z., 264
Einav, Liran, 668t
Einstein, Albert, 293
Eisenberg, Nancy, 222, 248
Elangovan, Ilayaraja, 211p
Elder, Glen H., 486
Elissa (author's daughter), 4, 89, 117, 167, 262, 262f
Eliza (adolescent), 366p
Elizabeth II (British queen), 596p
Elkind, David, 251, 378
Ellefson, Michelle R., 357
Ellie (child), 74p
Elliot, Ari J., 652p
Elliott, Sinikka, 414
Ellis, Bruce J., 7, 248, 360, 361
Ellis, Raquel T., 213
Ellison, Christopher G., 258
El-Sheikh, Mona, 119, 120
Emanuel, Ezekiel J., 674
Emery, Carolyn A., 209
Emma (child), 261p
Emmen, Rosanneke A. G., 336
Endendijk, Joyce J., 566
Engelberts, Adèle C., 133
England, Paula, 441, 442
Englander, Elizabeth, 413
English, Tammy, 564
Ennis, Linda Rose, 176
Enough Is Enough, 427f
Enserink, Martin, 73
Epps, Chad, 76
Epstein, Robert, 492
Erden, Feyza Tantekin, 251
ERIC (Education Resources Information Center), A-3
Erickson, Anders C., 104
Ericsson, K. Anders, 548

Erikson, Erik H., 34, 35t, 36p, 53t, 54, 56, 59f, 182, 248–250, 324, 403, 404, 480t, 483, 485, 489, 490, 502, 556, 556t, 557, 559, 566, 628, 637
Erikson, Joan, 36p
Ernst, Monique, 385
Erola, Jani, 565
Erreygers, Sara, 390
Errichiello, Luca, 366
Esposito, Gianluca, 119, 120
Espy, Kimberly Andrews, 222
Eun, John, 409
European Society of Human Reproduction and Embryology, 70
Evans, Angela D., 230, 230f, 231
Evans, Jane A., 80t
Evans, Larissa M., 442
Evans, M. D. R., 309
Eyer, Diane E., 109

Fackler, Clayton, 642p
Fagot, Delphine, 536
Fair, Damien A., 455
Fairbank, John, 331
Fairhurst, Merle T., 128
Fallahi (child), 378
Fan, Hung, 443
Farah, Martha J., 471
Farber, Annalu, 675
Farber, Stu, 675
Fareed, Mohd, 75
Fassino, Secondo, 365
Fast, Anne A., 261
Fawkes, Guy, 357p
FBI (Federal Bureau of Investigation), 589f
Fearon, R. M. Pasco, 177
Feder, Jody, 427f
Federal Bureau of Investigation (FBI), 589f
Fedewa, Michael V., 437
Feeley, Nancy, 110
Fehr, Ernst, 471, 640
Feld, Barry C., 419
Feldman, Ruth, 181, 185
Feliciano, Cynthia, 481
Felicilda-Reynaldo, Rhea, 557
Felmban, Wejdan S., 384
Feng, Tingyong, 203
Ferguson, Christopher J., 22, 258
Fernando, Dulini, 66
Ferrari, Laura, 482
Ferrari, Marco, 43f
Fikkan, Janna L., 440
Filippa, Manuela, 129
Fine, Jodene Goldenring, 290
Finer, Lawrence B., 70, 104, 106
Fingerman, Karen L., 7, 486, 488, 572
Finlay, Ilora G., 673
Finn, Amy S., 318, 319
Fins, Joseph J., 671
Fischer, Nantje, 594
Fischetti, Mark, 97
Fiset, Sylvain, 154
Fisher, Helen E., 492, 493
Fiske, Amy, 644
Flannery, Jessica E., 330
Flegal, Katherine M., 524
Fleming, Peter, 120
Fletcher, Erica N., 253
Fletcher, Richard, 181
Flood, Tryphona, 638p
Flores, Andrew R., 454
Flynn, Heather Kohler, 410
Flynn, James, 534, 536
Fontana, Luigi, 602
Forbes, Deborah, 238
Forbes, Thomas A., 202
Ford, Carole L., 547
Ford, Gerald, 201
Forestell, Catherine A., 181
Forrest, Ray, 640
Forrest, Walter, 497
Foster, Eugene A., 69
Foulkes, Lucy, 42
Fowler, James W., 463, 464
Fox, Molly, 105
Fox, Nathan A., 171, 171f
Fox, Stephen, 575
Foxx, Richard M., 54
Fraley, R. Chris, 177, 558
Franchak, John M., 91, 130, 132
Francis Ferdinand (archduke), 679
Franco, Marcia R., 588, 603
Frankel, Richard M., 668
Frankenburg, William K., 130t
Franklin, Aretha, 665p
Fraser, Rick, 569
Fraundorf, Scott H., 616
Frayer, David W., 62
Frazier, A. Lindsay, 200
Frederick, David A., 513, 514
Fredricks, Jennifer A., 416
Freeman, Joan, 293
Frejka, Tomas, 567
French, Ruth, 623
Freud, Anna, 418
Freud, Sigmund, 34–36, 34p, 35t, 46, 53t, 54, 56, 58f, 149, 182, 261, 262, 293, 418, 556t, 559

Freund, Alexandra M., 461
Freundlich, Madelyn, 487
Fried, Terri R., 625
Friedman, Naomi P., 223
Friedman, Ori, 266
Friedman, Zack, 467
Friedmann, Naama, 127
Friend, Stephen H., 63
Fries, James F., 599
Frisén, Ann, 489
Frost, Randy O., 639
Fry, Douglas P., 252
Fryar, Cheryl D., 199
Fujiwara, Takeo, 123
Fuligni, Allison Sidle, 239
Fuller, Bruce, 308
Fulmer, C. Ashley, 558
Furstenberg, Frank F., 486
Fury, Gail, 48
Fusaro, Maria, 180

Gabrieli, John D. E., 290
Gaither, Sarah E., 405
Galak, Jeff, 250
Galasso, Vincenzo, 186
Gallagher, Annabella, 407
Gallagher, Shaun, 636
Gallo, Vittorio, 202
Gallup, 271f
Galor, Oded, 64
Galván, Adriana, 359
Galvao, Tais F., 362
Gambaro, Ludovica, 236, 237
Ganapathy, Thilagavathy, 109
Ganchimeg, Togoobaatar, 370
Gandhi, Mohandas, 464
Ganea, Patricia A., 160
Gao, Wei, 123, 124, 150, 172
Gao, Yuan, 624
Garba, Houmma A., 39
Garbarino, James, 341
Garcia, Daniel, 454p
Garcia, Lizalia, 240p
García Coll, Cynthia T., 308, 576
Gardner, Howard, 59f, 286, 286p, 537, 540
Gardner, Paula, 134f
Gariépy, Geneviève, 355
Garr, Michael, 577
Garrett, Mallory, 414
Garrison, Mary, 676
Garrity, Stacy E., 370
Garthus-Niegel, Susan, 171
Garti, Helene Akpene, 359
Gaskins, Audrey Jane, 515
Gaskins, Suzanne, 251
Gassin, Elizabeth A., 680
Gates, Bill, 201
Gatsonis, Constantine A., 210
Gattario, Kristina Holmqvist, 489
Gattis, Merideth, 230
Gawande, Atul, 668
Gaydosh, Lauren, 605
Ge, Xinting, 93
Geary, David C., 532
Geiger, Abigail, 16f
Geiger, Jennifer Mullins, 569
Gelbgiser, Dafna, 471
Gelder, Elke Van, 382
Gellert, Anna S., 239
Gendron, Brian P., 390
Gentile, Douglas A., 389
Geoff (adult), 567
Geoffroy, Marie-Claude, 390
George, R., 673
Georgeson, Jan, 236
Gergely, György, 146
Gerholz, Karl-Heinz, 474
Germano, Roy, 482
Germine, Laura T., 617
Gernhardt, Ariane, 48
Gershoff, Elizabeth T., 257
Gervais, Will M., 383
Ghara, Alexandra, 12
Ghossainy, Maliki E., 305
Gibb, Robbin, 309
Gibbons, Ann, 200
Giblin, Chris, 446
Gidley, Jennifer M., 454

Giedd, Jay N., 286
Gignac, Gilles E., 533
Gilbert, Daniel T., 5
Gilchrist, Julie, 208
Gillen, Meghan M., 439
Gillespie, Brian Joseph, 490, 491f
Gilligan, Carol, 345
Gillon, Raanan, 27
Gilmer, Diane Fox, 512, 519
Gilmore, John H., 93
Gilovich, Thomas, 573
Gina (adult), 562
Giovanna (adult), 648
Giumetti, Gary W., 390
Glauber, Rebecca, 652p
Gleb (father), 73p
Glen (author's brother-in-law), 17p
Glenberg, Arthur M., 43
Glenn, Dana E., 285
Global Burden of Disease Neurological Disorders Collaborator Group, 620
Glover, Crystal Polite, 566
Gobert, Fernald, 545
Goddings, Anne-Lise, 286, 354, 355, 359
Godinet, Meripa T., 215
Godon-Decoteau, Danielle, 482
Goel, Sunny, 522
Golant, Stephen M., 654
Golden, Marita, 571
Golden, Neville H., 363, 368
Goldfarb, Sally F., 334
Goldin-Meadow, Susan, 156, 226
Goldman-Mellor, Sidra, 574
Goldschmidt, Andrea B., 438
Goldstein, Bradley J., 612
Goldstein, Thalia R., 253
Golinkoff, Roberta M., 239
Göncü, Artin, 251
Goniewicz, Maciej L., 423
Goñi-Legaz, Salomé, 577
Gonyea, Judith G., 572
Gonzales-Backen, Melinda A., 325
González, Hector M., 604
Goodlad, James K., 211
Goodman, R., 44
Goodnight, Jackson A., 569
Gopnik, Alison, 144, 229, 234, 261
Gorbatov, Sergey, 614
Gordon, Ilanit, 121
Gordon, Linda, 12
Gordon-Hollingsworth, Arlene T., 288
Gorham, Lisa S., 282
Gottesman, Irving I., 82
Gottman, John, 59f, 457
Gottman, Julie, 457
Gough, Ethan K., 138
Graber, Julia A., 370
Grady, Sarah, 317
Grady, Denise, 623
Grady, Jessica Stoltzfus, 183
Graham, Jesse, 465
Graham, Sandra, 342
Grainger, Sarah, 615
Grajower, Martin M., 603
Grande, Ariana, 665p
Granqvist, Pehr, 644
Grant, Victoria, 676
Gray, Christine R., 562
Graybill, Emily, 550
Grayson, David S., 455
Grazioplene, Rachael G., 533
Greco, Daniel, 544
Gredebäck, Gustaf, 146
Green, James A., 169
Green, Lorraine, 676
Greene, Melissa L., 416
Greenfield, Emily A., 644
Greenfield, Patricia M., 388
Greenough, William T., 124, 125
Greer, David, 670
Gregori, Elena Barberà, 473
Greyson, Bruce, 666
Griffin, James A., 223
Griffith, Derek, 576
Griffith, Patrick, 651
Grivell, Rosalie M., 97
Groh, Ashley M., 176
Grønkjær, Marie, 536
Grönqvist, Hans, 211
Gröpel, Peter, 546
Gross, James J., 247
Grossman, Matthew, 129
Grossmann, Tobias, 127, 175
Grotevant, Harold D., 178, 179
Gruber, Staci A., 15
Grusec, Joan E., 260
Guassi Moreira, João F., 420
Gubernskaya, Zoya, 565
Guerra, Nancy G., 340, 341
Guerri, Consuelo, 422
Gulbas, L. E., 416
Gulia, Kamalesh K., 586, 588
Güngör, Derya, 558
Guo, Siying, 390
Guo, Yuming, 434
Guthrie, Woody, 80
Gutierrez-Galve, Leticia, 109
Guyon-Harris, Katherine L., 178
Guzman, Natalie S. de, 379
Guzzo, Karen Benjamin, 497
Gyllenberg, Frida, 444
Gypen, Laura, 569

Hackett, Geoffrey Ian, 518
Hackett, Ruth A., 614
Hageman, Jon B., 662
Hagestad, Gunhild, 646
Hagopian, Jesse, 397
Haidt, Jonathan, 40, 345, 464, 465
Haight, Sarah C., 129
Hailey (child), 256
Halberda, Justin, 146
Hales, Craig M., 280, 280fp, 297
Halim, May Ling, 260, 263
Hall, Jeffrey A., 490
Hall, Kelli Stidham, 415
Hall, Matthew L., 135, 156
Hallers-Haalboom, Elizabeth T., 263
Halperin, Jeffrey M., 270
Halpern-Meekin, Sarah, 497
Halsey (singer), 482p
Hambrick, David Z., 6
Hamerton, John L., 80t
Hamill, Paul J., 543
Hamilton, Alice, 210
Hamilton, Brady E., 516
Hamlat, Elissa J., 362
Hamlett, Eric D., 79
Hamlin, J. Kiley, 265, 343
Hamm, Jeremy M., 639, 652
Hammond, Christopher J., 76
Hamplová, Dana, 497, 561
Han, Kihye, 655
Han, S. Duke, 462, 654
Haney, Alison M., 486
Hank, Karsten, 642
Hanna-Attisha, Mona, 210, 211
Hannah, A. Lee, 388
Hannon, Erin E., 168
Hanson, Katherine G., 160
Hanushek, Eric A., 312, 392, 397
Happé, Francesca, 287, 291
Harden, K. Paige, 386, 386f
Hargreaves, Andy, 396
Hari, Riitta, 174
Harkness, Sara, 258, 361
Harknett, Kristen, 576
Harlow, Harry, 59f
Harper, Casandra E., 473
Harris, Paul L., 663
Harris, Michelle A., 362
Harris, Paul L., 180, 226
Harris Insights and Analytics, 427f
Harrison, Kristen, 280
Harrison, Linda J., 187
Harrison (child), 73p
Harsin, Amanda, 561
Hart, Betty, 308
Hart, Chantelle N., 280
Hart, Daniel, 405
Harter, Susan, 183
Hartig, Hannah, 16f
Hartley, Catherine A., 358, 383, 385, 420, 421
Hartshorne, Joshua K., 617
Hasson, Ramzi, 290
Hastings, Paul D., 183
Hatch, J. Amos, 236
Hatfield, Elaine, 491
Hauck, Fern, 134
Hauf, Petra, 131
Haushofer, Johannes, 471, 640
Hawkes, Kristen, 51
Hawking, Stephen, 532p
Hawkins, Larycia, 473p
Hawkley, Louise C., 489
Hawthorne, Joanna, 107
Hayden, Elizabeth P., 287
Hayes, DeMarquis, 393
Hayflick, Leonard, 605
Hayman, Karen J., 636
Hayne, Harlene, 149
Haynie, Dana L., 380
Hayslip, Bert, 571
He, Li, 455
Healey, Dione M., 270
Healy, Jack, 471
Heath, Tobin, 432p
Hedberg, Eric C., 317

Hegel, Georg Wilhelm Friedrich, 457
Heiman, Julia R., 594
Heimlich, Russell, 475
Helen (older adult), 595
Henderson, Kevin E., 502
Henderson, Heather A., 383
Hendlin, Yogi Hale, 389
Hendrix, Jimi, 201
Hendry, Leo B., 488
Hendry, Mandy P., 572
Henrich, Joseph, 433
Henry, David B., 414
Henry, William Earl, 640
Henry (child), 210p
Hensch, Takao K., 8
Hentges, Rochelle F., 410
Herlofson, Katharina, 646
Herman, Sarah, 27
Hernández, Maciel M., 325
Heron, Melonie, 447
Herrmann, Esther, 160
Herschensohn, Julia R., 232
Hertzog, Christopher, 536
Herzog, Patricia Snell, 462
Herzog, Serge, 467
Hess, Thomas M., 456, 616
Heuer, Chelsea A., 524
Heyer, Djai B., 103
Heyes, Cecilia, 228
Heyman, Gene M., 448
Hidalgo, Marco A., 325
Higgins, Matt, 446
Hilbert, Anja, 366
Hilgard, Joseph, 22
Hill, Erica, 662
Hill, Heather D., 186
Hill, Patrick L., 379, 380
Hill, Sarah E., 198
Hillman, Charles H., 270
Hinduja, Sameer, 390
Hinnant, J. Benjamin, 345
Hinton, Lisa, 97
Hirsh-Pasek, Kathy, 239
Hitlin, Paul, 494
Ho, Emily S., 131
Ho, Hong-Nerng, 516
Hoare, Carol Hren, 556t
Hochman, Oshrat, 642
Hodson, Gordon, 19
Hofer, Claire, 408
Hoff, Erika, 308
Hoffman, Jessica L., 233
Hofman, M. A., 41
Höjer, Ingrid, 487
Holden, Constance, 77
Holland, John L., 483
Hollenstein, Tom, 172
Holochwost, Steven J., 125
Holt, Lynn, 76
Holzer, Jessica, 25
Homer, 532
Hong, David S., 79
Hong, Jun Sung, 341
Hood, Michelle, 489
Hook, Jennifer L., 577
Hopkins, Will, 432
Horn, John, 537
Horn, Stacey S., 406
Horne, Benjamin D., 603
Horney, Karen, 36
Hornung, Richard, 211p
Horton, Megan K., 103
Hossain, Ziarat, 181
Hostinar, Camelia E., 173, 410
Houston, Whitney, 664
Howard, Kimberly S., 550
Howard, Sasha R., 359
Howard, Vivian, 547p
Howe, Christine, 302
Howe, Tsu-Hsin, 105, 309
Howell, Diane M., 55
Hoyert, Donna L., 134f
Hoyme, H. Eugene, 99, 101
Hrdy, Sarah B., 51, 184
Hsu, William C., 604
Hu, Youna, 355
Huang, Jidong, 423
Hudson, Bettie L., 134f
Hughes, Claire, 231, 615
Hughes, Matthew L., 616, 618
Huisman, Henk, 652p
Huisman, Ria, 652p
Hülür, Gizem, 627
Hunt, Earl B., 532
Hunter, Jonathan, 175
Hutchinson, Esther A., 105
Huynh, Jimmy L., 65
Hvistendahl, Mara, 83
Hyde, Janet S., 490
Hymel, Shelley, 390
Hyslop, Anne, 396

Ifrah, Chaim, 343p
Iida, Hiroko, 276
Iida, Masumi, 390
Ilies, Remus, 502
Ilieva, Irena P., 471
Im, Myung Hee, 393
Inan, Hatice Z., 238
Inceoglu, Ilke, 573
Inhelder, Bärbel, 40, 223, 381
Insel, Thomas R., 123
Insurance Institute for Highway Safety, 209, 209f, 356, 609f
International Association of Hospice and Palliative Care, 674
Inzlicht, Michael, 456
Irene (older adult), 595
Irma (older adult), 645
Irwin, Scott, 124
Isaac (author's grandson), 89, 157, 167, 247
Isupova, Olga, 334
Ivarsson, Andreas, 364
Ivcevic, Zorana, 315

Jack, Jordynn, 14
Jackson, James C., 557
Jackson, James S., 641
Jackson, Jeffrey B., 560
Jackson, Michael, 679
Jackson, Todd, 365
Jacqueline (child), 128p
Jaffe, Arthur C., 118
Jamal, Ahmed, 525
Jambon, Marc, 343
James, Jacquelyn B., 642
James, Jenée, 360
James, Karin H., 282
James, Lori, 616
James, Will, 522
James-Kangal, Neslihan, 493
Jankovic, Joseph, 623
Janse, Benjamin, 652
Jarcho, Johanna M., 171
Jarvis, Kelly, 211p
Jaschke, Artur C., 279, 282
Jaswal, Vikram K., 11
Jayson, Sharon, 441
Jeannette (informant), 83
Jednoróg, Katarzyna, 309
Jeff (twin), 330
Jefferson, Thomas, 69
Jenner, Edward, 58f
Jenny (adult), 507, 525–526
Jensen, Robert, 410, 411
Jenssen, Brian P., 423
Jernigan, Terry, 93, 124, 125
Jesus (Christ), 51
Jha, Prabhat, 508
Jia, Jianping, 621
Jim (older adult), 595
Jimmy (prisoner), 445
Jobs, Steve, 293
John Hancock Life & Health Insurance Company, 655
Johnson, Jonni L., 204
Johnson, Matthew D., 561
Johnson, Scott P., 168
Johnson, Wendi, 499
Johnson, Wendy, 536
Jonas, Wibke, 121
Jonathan (adult), 561p
Jones, Andrea M., 216
Jones, Catherine R. G., 290
Jones, Jeffrey M., 16f
Jones, Mary C., 362
Jones, Owen R., 602
Jones, Tracey, 129
Jong, Jonathan, 664
Jong, Jyh-Tsorng, 170
Jopp, Daniela, 593
Jorgensen, Nathan, 485
Jorgenson, Alicia Grattan, 389
Jorm, Anthony F., 612
Joseph, Michelle A., 570
Joshi, Kshamta, 420
Jung, Carl Gustav, 36
Jung, Courtney, 137
Jungert, Tomas, 342
Juster, Robert-Paul, 276
Juvonen, Jaana, 341, 342

Kaczynski, Andrew T., 205
Kaestle, Christine E., 442
Kagan, Sarah H., 586, 589
Kahana, Eva, 643
Kahneman, Daniel, 573

Kalanithi, Paul, 668
Kalaria, Raj N., 622
Kalfur, Monica, 165f
Kalinsky, Amanda, 80p
Kalinsky, Bradley, 80p
Kalla, Joshua, 454
Kallio, Eeva, 454
Kalliomäki, Marko, 129
Kalshoven, Karianne, 462
Kalsner, Louisa, 65
Kaltiala-Heino, Riittakerttu, 368
Kamaludeen, Ahmed, 384p
Kandel, Denise B., 15
Kandel, Eric R., 14
Kandler, Christian, 558
Kang, Hye-Kyung, 94
Kanner, Leo, 290
Kapp, Steven K., 286
Karatsoreos, Ilia N., 435
Karbach, Julia, 306
Karen (woman), 83p
Karl, Katherine, 488
Karmiloff-Smith, Annette, 542
Karnatovskaia, Lioudmila V., 557
Karraker, Amelia, 594
Kärtner, Joscha, 183
Kastbom, Åsa A., 369
Katrina (child), 169
Kauffman, James M., 293
Kauffman, Jeffery, 676
Kaufman-Parks, Angela, 500
Kaur, Arshdeep, 181
Kauser, Rubina, 255, 260
Kavanaugh, Robert D., 253
Keating, Nancy L., 668t
Keck, Carson, 517
Keers, Robert, 9
Keil, Frank C., 302
Kelemen, Deb, 21p
Keller, Heidi, 433
Keller, Heidi, 177
Keller, Peggy S., 204
Kellogg, Ronald T., 546
Kelly, John R., 640
Kelly, Ryan J., 119, 120
Kemmler, W., 600
Kempe, C. Henry, 212
Kempe, Ruth S., 212
Kemper, Susan, 589
Kempermann, Gerd, 510, 613
Kendall-Taylor, Nathaniel, 212
Kendler, Howard H., 465
Kennedy, Brian K., 602
Kennell, John H., 109
Kenrick, Douglas T., 49, 557
Kent, Blake Victor, 644
Kent (emerging adult), 495
Kern, Ben D., 278
Kern, Margaret L., 315
Kerr, Thomas, 422
Kersken, Verena, 158
Keselman, Alla, 388
Kessler, David, 668
Kessler, Ronald C., 82, 416
Kestler, Lisa, 101
Keupp, Stefanie, 228
Keysar, Boaz, 44
Khandaker, Golam M., 135
Khurana, Atika, 386
Kidd, Celeste, 249
Kidd, Evan, 238
Kiel, Douglas P., 650
Kiiski, Jouko, 458
Kilburn, John, 22
Kiley, Dan, 351
Kilgore, Paul E., 53
Killen, Melanie, 343
Kim, Dong-Sik, 365
Kim, Helen, 108
Kim, Hojin I., 168
Kim, Hye-Jin, 389
Kim, Hyun-Sun, 365
Kim, Joon Sik, 168
Kim, Kyungmin, 646
Kim, Pilyoung, 42
Kim-Spoon, Jungmeen, 404
King, Bruce M., 50
King, Martin Luther, Jr., 464, 637p
Kirk, Elizabeth, 156
Kirkham, Julie Ann, 238
Kirkham, Natasha Z., 159
Kirkpatrick, Lee A., 644
Kirschner, Paul A., 48
Kiserud, Torvid, 94
Kivipelto, Miia, 624
Kizy, Thomas, 367
Kjerulff, Kristen, 97
Kkeli, Natalie, 365
Klaczynski, Paul A., 383, 384
Klass, Dennis, 662, 680
Klaus, Marshall H., 109
Klaus, Susan F., 577
Klein, Denise, 235
Klein, Stanley B., 637
Klein, Zoe A., 355
Kline, Kathleen K., 260
Klinger, Laura G., 291, 307
Kloep, Marion, 488
Kluender, Robert, 232
Knapp, Emily A., 576
Knieval, Evel, 446, 447
Knopik, Valerie S., 82
Knopman, Jaime M., 72
Knott, Craig S., 522
Koch, Linda, 64
Kochanek, Kenneth D., 134f
Kochel, Karen P., 341
Koedinger, Kenneth, 473
Koepke, Rachel, 238p
Koepsell, Thomas D., 81
Kohlberg, Lawrence, 263, 344, 345, 463, 464
Kolb, Bryan, 122, 173, 309
Koltko-Rivera, Mark E., 668
Kolucki, Barbara, 160
Komisar, Erica, 176
Komp, Kathrin, 642
Konner, Melvin, 51, 126, 184
Kono, Yumi, 92
Konstam, Varda, 480, 483
Konstantinsler, Wechlser, 542
Kooij, Dorien T. A. M., 573
Koontz, Amanda, 495
Korbmacher, Julie M., 642
Kordas, Katarzyna, 211
Koretz, Daniel, 396
Korte, J., 629
Koster-Hale, Jorie, 231
Kotsopoulos, Joanne, 518
Kotter-Grühn, Dana, 587
Kovas, Yulia, 292, 508
Kowalski, Robin M., 390
Köymen, Bahar, 157
Kozhimannil, Katy B., 108
Kozo, Justine, 519
Kramer, Karen, 578
Krause, Elizabeth D., 379
Krebs, Erin E., 523
Kremen, William S., 536
Krisberg, Kim, 424
Kroger, Jane, 404
Krous, Henry F., 133
Krouse, William J., 210
Krueger, Robert F., 287
Krzych-Fałta, Edyta, 7
Kubin, Laura, 291
Kübler-Ross, Elisabeth, 667, 668
Kuete, Victor, 128
Kuhl, Patricia K., 144
Kumar, Gayathri S., 438
Kumar, Shaina A., 488
Kumar, Velayudhan Mohan, 586, 588
Kuncel, Nathan R., 397
Kundu, Tapas K., 73
Kunzmann, Ute, 616
Kuperberg, Arielle, 560
Kurdek, Lawrence A., 500
Kurup, Anand Sivasankara, 522
Kushnir, Tamar, 155
Kutob, Randa M., 416
Kuvaas, Bård, 573
Kuwahara, Keisuke, 76
Kvalvik, Liv G., 101
Kyle (child), 157
Kypri, Kypros, 422

La Fauci, Luigi, 368
Labat-Robert, J., 508
Labouvie-Vief, Gisela, 454, 455
Lachs, Mark S., 653
Ladd, Helen F., 392, 393
Lady Gaga, 201, 371p
Lagattuta, Kristin H., 328
Lai, Stephanie A., 304
Laier, Christian, 514
Laird, Sarah A., 63
Lake, Stephanie, 422
Lalande, Kathleen M., 680
Lam, Chun Bun, 325
Lamb, Michael E., 109, 204
Lambert, Scott, 127
Lamichhane, Bidhan, 617
Lamm, Bettina, 249
Lamolie, Paulette, 604p
Lamolie, Simone, 604p
Lander, Eric S., 70
Lane, Angela, 614
Lane, Jonathan D., 226

Lang, Frieder R., 587
Lang, Kevin, 396
Langeslag, Sandra J. E., 492
Långström, Niklas, 329
Laninga-Wijnen, Lydia, 339
Lanphear, Bruce P., 211p
Lansford, Jennifer E., 257, 258
Lapan, Candace, 325
Lara-Cinisomo, Sandraluz, 237
Larose, Joanie, 434
Larzelere, Robert E., 5, 256, 258, 259
Lattanzi-Licht, Marcia, 665, 678
Laura (emerging adult), 459
Laurent, Heidemarie K., 7
Laursen, Brett, 411
Lauster, Nathanael T., 492
Law, James, 309
Layton, Jill, 605
Le Duc, James W., 27
Leach, Penelope, 239
Leacock, Stephen, 474
Leavitt, Judith W., 109
LeBlanc, Nicole J., 676
LeCuyer, Elizabeth A., 248
Ledbetter, Andrew M., 572
Lee, Barbara Combs, 667
Lee, Chun-Chia, 494
Lee, David M., 513
Lee, Kathleen, 223
Lee, Shawna J., 257
Lee, Soojeong, 396
Lee, Yuan-Hsuan, 389
Lefebre, Nancy, 656
Lefkowitz, Eva S., 439
Leiter, Valerie, 27
Leman, Patrick J., 346, 346f
Lemieux, André, 455, 457
Lemish, Daphna, 160
Lengua, Liliana J., 171
Lenhart, Amanda, 387–388
Lent, Robert W., 66
Leonard, Julia A., 148
Leonoff, Arthur, 458
Leopold, Thomas, 643
Lepousez, Gabriel, 510
Lerner, Matthew D., 253
Lerner, Richard M., 7, 398, A–2
Leshner, Alan I., 28
Leslie, Mitch, 281
Lessne, Deborah, 427f
Lester, Barry M., 121
Leung, Sumie, 150
Leuzy, Antoine, 626
Levine, Charles, 404
Levine, Phillip B., 210
Levine, Susan C., 263
Levinson, Sam, 648p
Levy, Marion J. F., 612
Lewandowski, Lawrence J., 290, 304
Lewin, Alisa, 560
Lewin, Kurt, 34
Lewin-Epstein, Noah, 642
Lewis, Ariane, 670
Lewis, John, 637p
Lewis, John D., 124
Lewis, Kristen, 525
Lewis, Lawrence B., 157
Lewis, Marc D., 247, 249
Lewis, Michael, 101, 170
Lewkowicz, David J., 156
Li, Jin, 315
Li, Liman Man Wai, 460
Li, Shuzhuo, 68
Li, Ting, 560
Li, Weilin, 189
Li, Yaoran, 387
Li, Yibing, 398
Liben, Lynn S., 263
Libertus, Klaus, 131
Libertus, Melissa E., 306
Lieberman, Jeffrey A., 15
Lillard, Angeline S., 237, 252
Lim, Cher Ping, 318
Limber, Susan P., 390
Lin, Frank R., 615
Lin, Lin, 542
Lin, Phoebe, 380
Lincoln, Abraham, 328, 360, 360p
Lindberg, Laura Duberstein, 415
Lippard, Christine N., 239
Lippert, Adam M., 437
Lipton, Eric, 103
Litwin, Howard, 648
Liu, Andrew H., 281
Liu, Chang, 330
Liu, Jia-Lin, 316
Liu, Li, 256, 257
Liu, Ning, 370, 455, 470
Liu, Peiwei, 203
Livas-Dlott, Alejandra, 256
Livingston, Gretchen, 457
Livingston, Lucy Anne, 287, 291
Lo, June C., 356
LoBue, Vanessa, 146
Lochman, John E., 412
Locke, John, 58f
Löckenhoff, Corinna E., 630
Lockhart, Kristi L., 248, 302
Lodge, Amy C., 595
Loeb, Susanna, 396, 397
Lohan, Baba Ram Devi, 516p
Lohan, Rajo, 516p
Lopez, Anna B., 405
Lopez, Mark Hugo, 180
Lopez, Oscar, 651
Lopez-Hartmann, Maja, 652
López-Otín, Carlos, 605
López-Pinar, Carlos, 289
Lord, Aysna, 566p
Lorenz, Kaylee, 370p
Lorthe, Elsa, 92
Lou, Wutao, 614
Loucks, Jeff, 301
Loughrey, David G., 616
Lourenço, Orlando, 301, 302
Lovato, Demi, 365p
Love, Heather A., 499
Lovett, Benjamin J., 290, 304
Loyd, Aerika Brittian, 405
Lubienski, Christopher, 319
Lucca, Kelsey, 144
Lucy (child), 74p
Ludmer, Jaclyn A., 121
Ludwig-Mayerhofer, Wolfgang, 397
Luecken, Linda J., 105
Luengo-Prado, María J., 643
Luhmann, Maike, 489, 574
Luna, Beatriz, 358
Lundahl, Alyssa, 199
Lundberg, Shelly, 498
Lunde, Carolina, 413
Lundquist, Gunilla, 668
Luo, Rufan, 227
Lushin, Viktor, 409
Luthar, Suniya S., 326, 337
Lutz, Christoph, 489
Lutz, Wolfgang, 549
Luyckx, Koen, 480
Lyall, Donald M., 105
Lynch, Scott M., 638
Lyons, Christopher, 127
Lyons, Kelly E., 623
Lyons, Michael J., 536
Lyons, Sophie, 444
Lyssens-Danneboom, Vicky, 561

Ma, Defu, 137
Mac Dougall, Kristin, 516
MacDorman, Marian F., 134f
Macgregor, Stuart, 76
Machado, Liana, 612
MacInnes, John, 592
Mackenzie, Karen J., 281
MacKenzie, Michael J., 257
Macky (adoptive parent), 179, 179p
Macmillan, Ross, 486
MacNeill, Leigha A., 154
MacSwan, Jeff, 308
MacWhinney, Brian, 156
Maddox, Keith B., 439
Madigan, Sheri, 253
Madison, James, 360, 360p
Maehler, Claudia, 306
Magnuson, Katherine, 241
Magnuson (doctor), 586p
Maitoza, Robyn, 574
Maldonado, Giovanni, 471
Malik, Zayn, 365p
Malin, Martin B., 311
Malina, Robert M., 363f
Mallett, Christopher A., 39
Malloy, Lindsay C., 419
Maloney, Patricia, 415
Malpas, Jean, 261
Mandelbaum, David E., 15
Mani, Kartik, 603
Mann, Joshua R., 98
Manning, Wendy D., 498
Mansukhani, Meghna P., 626
Mantua, Janna, 509
Mar, Raymond A., 231
Marcia, James E., 404
Marcus, Gary F., 161
Margolis, Rachel, 570
Maricruz (mother), 256
Mariela (emerging adult), 495p
Markey, Charlotte N., 439
Markey, Patrick M., 439

Markham, Christine, 500
Markman, Ellen M., 233
Markova, Gabriela, 173
Markovitch, Noam, 404
Marks, Amy K., 105, 576
Marks, Peter E. L., 340
Marley, Bob, 15
Marotta, Phillip L., 418
Marshall, Eliot, 172, 176, 179
Martin, Carmel, 316
Martin, Carol L., 263
Martin, Joyce A., 106, 369
Martin, Meagan, 562p
Martin, Michael O., 337
Martin, Paul, 251
Martincorena, Iñigo, 605
Martinez, Maureen, 134, 451f
Martinson, Melissa L., 104
Martin-Uzzi, Michele, 335
Masarik, April S., 336
Mascarelli, Amanda, 103
Mascaro, Jennifer S., 263
Masci, David, 441
Mascie-Taylor, C. G. Nicholas, 91t
Masfety, Viviane, 570
Mash, Eric J., 287
Maskileyson, Dina, 466
Maslow, Abraham H., 53, 59f, 557, 557f, 559, 570p, 628, 667, 668
Masten, Ann S., 315, 326–328, 331, 336
Mathews, T. J., 134f
Matsa, Katerina Eva, 553f
Matsumoto, David, 460
Matsumoto, Yasuyo, 514
Mattanah, Jonathan F., 488
Matthews, Fiona E., 621
Matthews, Karen A., 509
Matthews, Timothy C., 654, 655
Mattick, Richard P., 422
Maume, David J., 577
Maunder, Robert, 175
Maxfield, Molly, 664
May, Lillian, 42
Mayberry, Rachel I., 232
Maynard, Brittany, 672, 672p
McAdams, Tom A., 330
McAlister, Anna R., 231
McCabe, Sean Esteban, 289, 424
McCain, John, 665p
McCall, Robert B., 178, 180
McCallion, Gail, 427f
McCallum, Jared, 508p
McCarthy, Neil, 101
McClain, Natalie M., 370
McClung, Nancy M., 371
McCormick, Cheryl M., 392
McCoy, Shelly, 410
McCray, Jennifer S., 225
McDermott, Jennifer M., 178, 179
McEwen, Bruce S., 276, 435
McEwen, Craig A., 276
McFarland, Joel, 292, 308, 318
McFarlane, Alexander C., 327
McGill, Rebecca K., 392, 393
McGillion, Michelle, 156
McGrath, Mary H., 365
McGue, Matt, 24
McIntosh, Jennifer, 121
McKay, Gareth J., 604
McKee-Ryan, Frances, 574
McKeever, Pamela M., 356
McKenzie, Sarah C., 259
McKinney, Lyle, 467
McKnight, Robin, 210
McLean, Robert R., 650
McLendon, Amber N., 626
McLoyd, Vonnie C., 309
McManus, I. Chris, 201
McMillin, Stephen Edward, 550
McMurtrie, Beth, 448
McNeil, Michele, 316
McNulty, Chris, 516p
McNulty, Cole, 516p
McNulty, Kyle, 516p
McPherson, Gary E., 547
Mead, Margaret, 517
Meagher, David K., 677
Mecca, Marcia C., 625
Meczekalski, Blazej, 366
Medaglia, John D., 386
Medford, Anthony, 604
Meece, Judith L., 393
Meesters, Cor, 326
Meeus, Wim, 404, 406
Mehler, Philip S., 366
Meier, Ann, 496
Meier, Emily A., 666
Meldrum, Ryan, 339
Mellerson, Jenelle L., 141f
Meltzoff, Andrew N., 229, 234
Mendle, Jane, K., 362
Menna-Barreto, Luiz, 119
Mennella, Julie A., 181
Mercer, Neil, 302
Merchant, Lisa V., 500
Meredith, Rhiannon M., 103
Merewether, Jane, 224
Merikangas, Kathleen R., 288
Mermelshtine, Roni, 227
Merriam, Sharan B., 26
Mersky, Joshua P., 215
Merz, Emily C., 178
Merz, Eva-Maria, 561
Mesagno, Christopher, 546
Messinger, Daniel M., 174
Metcalfe, Lindsay A., 203
Meyer, Madonna Harrington, 571
Mia (child), 265
Michael (author's nephew), 17p
Michaeli, Yossi, 484
Michelangelo, 629
Miciak, Jeremy, 292
Miech, Richard A., 15, 422, 422f, 423
Mihailidis, Paul, 388
Mike (twin), 330
Miklowitz, David J., 289
Mikolajczyk, Rafael T., 97
Milburn, Peter, 566p
Miller, Amanda Jayne, 498
Miller, Cindy F., 265
Miller, Evonne, 643
Miller, Gregory E., 526
Miller, Melissa K., 371
Miller, Patricia H., 43, 381
Miller, Susan W., 626
Miller-Cotto, Dana, 406
Miller-Perrin, Cindy, 370
Mills-Koonce, W. Roger, 168
Milton, James, 233
Milunsky, Aubrey, 78, 80
Milunsky, Jeff M., 78, 80
Mindell, Jodi A., 120, 120f
Miniño, Arialdi M., 134f
Miranda, Lin-Manuel, 539p
Mischel, Walter, 249
Misra, Dawn P., 104
Missana, Manuela, 172
Mitchell, Allen, 102
Mitchell, Edwin A., 133
Mitchell, Kimberly J., 388
Miyake, Akira, 223
Miyata, Susanne, 159
Miyazaki, Hedikichi, 603p
Mize, Krystal D., 170
MMWR (*Morbidity and Mortality Weekly Report*), 21, 22f, 210, 291, 294, 356f, 357, 364, 365, 368f, 369, 371, 375f, 413, 417, 417f, 423f, 448, 498, 600
Moffitt, Terrie E., 418, 419
Mokrova, Irina L., 250
Moldavsky, Maria, 288
Moles, Laura, 136
Møller, Signe J., 261
Molnar, Lisa J., 596
Monahan, Kathryn C., 414, 419
Monesson, Alexandra, 147
Montero-Odasso, Manuel M., 614
Montessori, Maria, 58f, 237, 237p
Montgomery, Heather, 370
Montgomery, Rhonda J. V., 571
Monthly Vital Statistics Report, 134f
Monti, Jennifer D., 394
Montirosso, Rosario, 129, 174, 175
Monto, Martin A., 493
Moody, Myles, 289
Moody, Raymond A., 665
Moore, Keith L., 8
Moore, Kelly L., 653
Moore, Kendra A., 671
Moore, Mary Ruth, 205
Morales, Angelica, 421
Moran, Seana, 286
Morawska, Alina, 259
Morbidity and Mortality Weekly Report. See MMWR
Morcos, Roy N., 367
Moreira, Pollyana De Lucena, 462
Moreno, Sylvain, 285
Morgan, Daniel M., 517
Morgan, Ali Zaremba, 440
Morgan, David L., 26
Morgan, Ian G., 77
Morones, Alyssa, 257
Morris, Curtis L., 393
Morris, Danielle H., 516
Morris, Pamela A., 9
Morris, Tracy L., 216
Morris, Vivian G., 393

Morrongiello, Barbara A., 207
Mortelmans, Dimitri, 561
Moses (prophet), 51
Moshman, David, 382, 460, 461
Mother Teresa, 464
Motz, Ryan, 39
Moultrie, Fiona, 129
Mowry, James B., 208
Mozart, Wolfgang Amadeus, 293
Mrug, Sylvie, 362
Mueller, Noel T., 96
Muennig, Peter A., 534
Muhammad (prophet), 464
Mujanovic, Denis, 384p
Mukerji, Sanjay, 365
Mukku, Shiva Shanker Reddy, 642
Mullis, Ina V. S., 313f, 314, 337f
Munson, Michelle R., 433
Murawski, Wendy W., 598
Muris, Peter, 326
Murphy, Colleen, 23, 534
Murphy, Sherry L., 134f, 276
Murphy-Nugen, Amy B., 629
Murray, Conrad, 679
Murray, Joseph L., 433
Murray, Kristen, 365
Murray, Thomas H., 68
Musselwhite, Charles, 597
Mustanski, Brian, 413
Mwamba, Guyauma Ngoyi, 27p
Myers, David G., 598

Nadal, Kevin L., 575
NAEP (National Assessment of Educational Progress), 321f
NAEYC (National Association for the Education of Young Children), 189, 270
Nahata, Leena, 441
Namy, Laura L., 160
Nanji, Ayaz, 92p
Narayan, K. M. Venkat, 438
Narvaez, Darcia, 184
Nash, Erin J., 5
Nassar, Larry, 370p
National Administration for Children and Families, 214
National Assessment of Educational Progress (NAEP), 321f
National Association for the Education of Young Children (NAEYC), 189, 270
National Center for Education Statistics, 292, 396f, 401f, 468, 472f, 477f
National Center for Health Statistics, 206, 210, 212f, 276, 433, 433t, 434, 447f, 508, 520, 521, 521f, 588f, 589, 592, 593, 601f, 605, 625, 637, 639, 664f, A–3
National Foundation for Educational Research, 427f
National Institute of Child Health and Human Development, 188
National Institute of Mental Health, 82, 83, 612
National Institute of Population and Social Security Research, 591f
National Rifle Association, 679
National Safety Council, 664
Natsuaki, Misaki N., 360
Naughton, Michelle J., 276
Naveh-Benjamin, Moshe, 616
Neary, Karen R., 266
Neary, Marianne T., 134
Needleman, Herbert L., 210
Neesha (child), 335, 336
Neggers, Yasmin, 105
Nehme, Eileen K., 437
Neiderhiser, Jenae M., 330
Neimeyer, Robert A., 680
Neisser, Ulric, 636
Nelson, Charles A., 178, 204
Nelson, Geoffrey, 215
Nelson, Larry J., 479, 485
Nelson, Sarah C., 439
Neuman, Susan B., 309
Nevanen, Saila, 317
Nevin, Rick, 211
Newton, Isaac, 293
Neyer, Franz J., 339
Ng, Florrie Fei-Yin, 315
Ng, Rowena, 123
Nguyen, Jacqueline, 422
Niakan, Kathy K., 90
Nichols, Shaun, 663
Nichols, Emma, 633f
Nichols, Shaun, 637
Nick (adoptive parent), 179, 179p
Niclasen, Janni, 101
Nicola (mother), 73p
Nicolaisen, Magnhild, 637
Nielsen, Mark, 227, 228
Nieto, Marta, 222
Nieto, Sonia, 339
Nigg, Joel T., 288, 289
Nikitin, Dmitriy, 422
Nikolopoulos, Thomas P., 127
Nilsson, Kristine Kahr, 231
Nilwik, Rachel, 519
Nisbett, Richard E., 460
Nishina, Adrienne, 379, 405
Nixon, Richard M., 15
Nkomo, Palesa, 211
Noah, Trevor, 13p
Nocentini, Annalaura, 342
Noël-Miller, Claire M., 563
Noll, Jennie G., 360, 371
Norenzayan, Ara, 383
Norman, Geoffrey R., 70, 545
Normile, Dennis, 466
North, Michael S., 586
Norton, Michael I., 573
Nowak, Elisabeth, 200
Nowak, Martin A., 52
Nowaskie, Dustin, 622
Nwosisi, Christopher, 474

Oakes, J. Michael, 391
Obama, Barack, 59f, 70, 103, 201, 360p, 679
Obama, Michelle, 199
O'Brien, Edward, 378
O'Brien, Rourke, 104
Occupational Outlook Handbook, 192
Ocobock, Abigail, 563
O'Connell, Becky, 569p
Oden, Melita H., 534
O'Donnell, Michael, 6
O'Dougherty, Maureen, 108
OECD (Organisation for Economic Co-operation and Development), 50, 349f, 397, 398, 401f, 466, 467f, 470f, 525f
Oedipus (mythology), 261
Oesterdiekhoff, Georg W., 224
Ogden, Cynthia L., 529f
Ogolsky, Brian G., 562
Ohlsson, Stellan, 457
Okazaki, Sumie, 460
Okun, Morris A., 643
Olascoaga, Jesse, 398p
Oliver, David, 596
Oliver, Taylor L., 514
Olivia (child), 73p, 168p
Ollo-López, Andrea, 577
Olson, Kristina R., 184, 261
Olweus, Dan, 341, 390
O'Meara, Madison S., 559
Open Science Collaboration, 5
Oregon Public Health Division, 672t, 673f
Organisation for Economic Co-operation and Development. *See* OECD
Orth, Ulrich, 325
Orzabal, Marcus R., 423
Osborne, Gabby, 240p
Oswald, Andrew, 637
Ottesen, Ninja M., 82
Ou, Suh-Ruu, 241
Ovellos, Sandra, 99p
Over, Harriet, 230
Ovink, Sarah M., 471
Owsley, Cynthia, 512
Oza-Frank, Reena, 438
Ozernov-Palchik, Ola, 239

Paarlberg, Robert, 280
Paat, Yok-Fong, 500
Padilla-Walker, Laura M., 479, 485, 486, 487, 488
Pagnini, Francesco, 614
Pahwa, Rajesh, 623
Paik, Anthony, 370
Palatini, Paolo, 521
Paletti, Robin, 663
Palmer, Sally B., 342
Pandian, Roshan K., 495
Panksepp, Jaak, 169
Papapetrou, Eirini P., 69
Parade, Stephanie H., 109
Park, Daeun, 398
Park, Hyun, 178
Parke, Ross D., 181
Parker, Andrew, 84
Parker, Emily, 242
Parker, Erin M., 208
Parker, Kim, 260, 260f
Parker, Samantha E., 79
Parten, Mildred B., 252
Partridge, Bradley J., 470
Pärtty, Anna, 129
Pascarella, Ernest T., 469, 472, 473
Pascual, María, 422
Pasley, Kay, 335
Passel, Jeffrey S., 565, 581f

Pastrana, Travis, 446, 447
Patchin, Justin W., 390
Patel, Ayush, 289
Patel, Cyra, 443
Patel, Dhaval, 586
Pathela, Preeti, 414
Patil, Rakesh N., 335
Patton, Mary H., 285
Paúl, Constança, 593
Paul (child), 339
Paula (mother), 187
Pauwels, Lisa, 613
Pavlak, Piotr, 6p
Pavlov, Ivan, 34, 36, 37, 37p, 38, 46, 58f, 547
Pawar, Sunny, 294p
Payler, Jane, 236
Pedroza, Juan M., 328
Pelé, 201
Pellegrini, Anthony D., 252, 341
Pellis, Sergio M., 252
Peluchette, Joy, 488
Penelope (adopted child), 179, 179p
Peng, Peng, 306
Pennington, Charlotte R., 456
Peper, Jiska S., 354, 356
Pepper, Edward J., 82
Perels, Franziska, 228
Perez, José, 398p
Perez, Rosemary Jane, 473
Perner, Josef, 231
Perone, Sammy, 309
Perreira, Krista M., 328
Perrin, Robin, 258
Perry, Jennifer M., 439
Perry, William G., 469
Perry-Fraser, Charity, 569
Perszyk, Danielle R., 162
Peters, Stacey L., 102
Petersen, Inge, 565
Petersen, Ronald C., 624
Peterson, Candida C., 231
Petrenko, Christie L. M., 215
Petrova, Mariya, 485
Pew Research Center, 405, 413f, 442f, 451f, 463, 471, 503f, 553f, 587, 644, 645
Pexman, Penny M., 282
Pfaus, James G., 514
Phelan, Suzanne, 102
Philip, Duke of Edinburgh (British prince), 596
Philip (child), 299, 302
Phillips, Deborah A., 189
Piaget, Jean, 34, 40–41, 40p, 40t, 44–46, 58f, 149, 150p, 151–155, 162, 168, 221, 223–226, 225f, 237, 299–303, 315, 344–346, 380–382, 381f, 454, 455, 463, 474
Picasso, Pablo, 293
Piekny, Jeanette, 306
Piérard, Gérald E., 511
Pietromonaco, Paula R., 177
Pietschnig, Jakob, 285
Piili, Reetta, 671
Pilarz, Alejandra Ros, 186
Pilkauskas, Natasha, 370
Pillemer, Karl A., 653
Pinderhughes, Ellen E., 482
Pinker, Steven, 25, 50, 59f, 161
Pinquart, Martin, 255, 260, 665f
Piteo, A. M., 119
Pittenger, Samantha L., 9, 371
Pizot, Cécile, 519
Plato, 58f
Plomin, Robert, 81, 532
Plourde, Vickie, 154
Pluess, Michael, 8, 9, 329
Plutzer, Eric, 388
Pocheptsov, George, 286p
Podsiadlowski, Astrid, 575
Pogrebin, Abigail, 71
Pohl, Brenda, 424p
Pohl, Erika, 424p
Polanczyk, Guilherme V., 288
Polderman, Tinca J. C., 67
Pollina, Laura Di, 652
Pollock, Ross D., 603
Polotsky, Alex J., 602
Pons, Ferran, 156
Poole, Kristie L., 171
Poon, Kean, 222
Popham, Lauren E., 456
Porchon-Lynch, Tao, 599p
Posada, Germán E., 183
Posner, Michael I., 203
Pott, Audrie, 390
Poulin, François, 433
Poushter, Jacob, 483
Pouwels, J. Loes, 341
Powell, Katie, 564
Powell, Kendall, 358f
Powell, Shaun, 280
Powers, Sally I., 177
Prasad, Sahdeo, 128
Pratt, Laura A., 520
Preckel, Katrin, 231
Price, Debora, 570, 646
Price, Heather L., 301
Priess, Heather A., 406
Prince (singer), 523p, 664, 679
Proctor, Laura J., 212
Propper, Cathi B., 125
Prothero, Arianna, 317
Proud2Bme, 375f
Pruden, Shannon M., 263
Puertas, Alberto, 200
Puetz, Vanessa B., 204
Puhl, Rebecca M., 524
Pulvermüller, Friedemann, 162
Putnam, Robert D., 277
Putnick, Diane L., 264, 265

Qin, Desiree B., 181
Qiu, A., 123
Qiu, Chengxuan, 621
Quaresima, Valentina, 43f
Quindlen, Anna, 636
Quinn, Rand, 319

Rabagliati, Hugh, 161
Rabkin, Nick, 317
Raby, K. Lee, 177
Rachel (adult), 293
Rachel (author's daughter), 73, 117, 262, 353
Raeburn, Paul, 109, 252
Rahilly, Elizabeth P., 260, 261
Rahman, Anna N., 655
Rahman, Hiba, 92p
Rahman, Muhammad A., 393
Rahman, Rumaisa, 92p
Raipuria, Harinder Dosanjh, 95
Rakic, Snezana, 91
Ramani, Geetha B., 266
Ramírez, Naja Ferjan, 145
Ranciaro, Alessia, 52
Rand, David G., 52
Rank, Otto, 129
Rankin, Jay, 422
Rasberry, Catherine N., 393
Raspa, Richard, 667
Raspberry, Kelly A., 112
Rau, Barbara L., 573
Rauers, Antje, 618, 619f
Rauh, Virginia A., 103
Raver, C. Cybele, 231
Ravesteijn, Bastian, 602
Rawlins, William K., 564
Ray, Brian D., 317, 319
Raymond, Jaime, 211
Rea, Irene M., 508
Reagan, Nancy, 15
Reagan, Ronald, 201
Reardon, Sean F., 318
Reczek, Corinne, 562
Reddy, Sunita, 70
Reed, Andrew E., 638
Reef, Shai, 343p
Reich, Justin, 473
Reichman, Nancy E., 104
Reid, Keshia M., 664
Reid, Vincent M., 131
Reimann, Zakary, 222
Reinehr, Thomas, 359
Reiss, Allan L., 79
Reiss, Ira, 441
Reitz, Anne K., 630
Renfrew, Mary J., 95
Rest, James, 461, 462
Retelas, George, 66
Reynolds, Arthur J., 241
Reynolds, Jamila E., 325
Rhoades, Brittany L., 223
Rhodes, Marjorie, 249
Rholes, W. Steven, 175
Rice, Eric, 391
Rich, Motoko, 396
Richards, Morgan K., 96
Riddell, Rebecca Pillai, 129
Rideout, Victoria, 297f
Riediger, Michaela, 587, 587t
Riegel, Klaus F., 457
Riglin, Lucy, 393
Riordan, Jan, 136, 137t
Rioux, Charlie, 410
Risley, Todd R., 308
Ritchie, William C., 235
Ritter, Gary W., 259
Rizza, Wanda, 602
Rizzo, Michael T., 343
Rizzolatti, Giacomo, 59f

Roane, David M., 639
Rob (young adult), 656
Robben, Antonius C. G. M., 661
Robelen, Erik W., 317
Robert, L., 508
Roberts, Brent W., 484
Roberts, Leslie, 138
Roberts, Soraya, 446
Robertson, Cassandra, 104, 659f
Robertson, Deirdre A., 587
Robins, Richard W., 325
Robinson, Richard M., 575
Robinson, Eric, 199
Robinson, Julia T., 629
Robinson, Scott, 132
Rock, Jacoba, 204
Rodkey, Elissa N., 129
Rodrigues, Daniela, 277
Roe, Jennifer, 511p
Roebling, Emily, 66
Roelfs, David J., 574
Roenneberg, Till, 355
Roeser, Robert W., 392
Roesler, Katharina, 496, 497
Rogoff, Barbara, 59f
Rohla, Ryne, 18, 19
Roisman, Glenn I., 177
Roksa, Josipa, 470
Rollock, David, 486
Romeo, Rachel R., 309
Romeo, Russell D., 355, 357
Romero, Diana, 414
Rønneberg, Vibeke, 304
Rook, Graham A. W., 198
Roopnarine, Jaipaul L., 181
Rose, Katherine K., 186
Rose, Steven, 288
Rosen, Meghan, 99
Rosenbaum, James E., 395
Rosenberg, Harry M., 134f
Rosenfeld, Michael J., 496, 497
Rosenfield, Sarah, 641
Rosnati, Rosa, 482
Rosow, Irving, 640
Ross, Josephine, 170, 183
Ross, Robert, 519
Rosselli, Mónica, 235
Rossignol, Michel, 98
Rostila, Mikael, 677
Roth, B. J., 180
Roth, Christian Ludwig, 359
Roth, Lauren W., 602
Rothausen, Teresa J., 502
Rothbart, Mary K., 171, 203
Rothblum, Esther D., 440
Rothstein, Mark A., 27
Rott, Christoph, 593
Roubinov, Danielle S., 337
Rousseau, Jean Jacques, 58f
Rovee-Collier, Carolyn, 59f, 150, 150p
Rozier, R. Gary, 276
Rübeling, Hartmut, 48
Rubertsson, C., 103
Rubin, Kenneth H., 338, 342, 343
Ruch, Donna A., 417
Rudaz, Myriam, 169
Rugolotto, Simone, 54
Rumbaut, Rubén G., 481
Rusou, Dana, 127
Russell, Allison, 643
Russell, Ashley, 442
Russell, Charlotte K., 119
Russell, Stephen T., 414
Ruth, Babe, 201
Ruthig, Joelle C., 645
Ryan, Allison M., 412

Sabol, T. J., 237
Sabo-Risley, Constance, 205
Sackett, Paul R., 397
Sacks, Oliver, 293
Sadana, Ritu, 378
Sadeh, Avi, 119
Sader, Josette, 499
Sadler, Thomas W., 90, 91
Saffran, Jenny R., 159
Sahlberg, Pasi, 312, 313, 397, 426
Sahoo, Krushnapriya, 199
Salpeter, Shelley R., 668t
Salthouse, Timothy A., 536, 612, 617, 619
Samaras, Nikolass, 518
Samek, Diana R., 412
SAMHSA (Substance Abuse and Mental Health Services Administration), 83f, 448f
Sampaio-Baptista, Cassandra, 510
Samuels, Christina A., 396
Sánchez, Alan, 468
Sanchez, Gabriel R., 12
Sandberg, Sheryl, 675
Sanders, Matthew, 259
Sangrigoli, S., 147
Santelli, John S., 415
Santini, Ziggi Ivan, 564
Santos, Carlos E., 405
Santos-Lozano, Alejandro, 604
Sanz Cruces, José Manuel, 491
Saporita, Vincent, 287p
Saracho, Olivia N., 266
Sarah (author's daughter), 4, 117, 130, 262
Sarah-Maria (woman), 23p
Saraiva, Linda, 279
Saroglou, Vassilis, 405
Şaşmaz, Tayyar, 389
Sassler, Sharon, 498
Satterwhite, Catherine Lindsey, 371
Saudi, A Nur Aulia, 380
Saul/Paul of Tarsus, 464
Saunders, Cecily, 668
Saunders, Gerda, 627
Savage, Jeanne E., 532
Savioja, Hanna, 368
Saw, Seang-Mei, 77
Saxbe, Darby E., 94
Saxe, Rebecca, 231
Saxton, Matthew, 157
Sayal, Kapil, 288
Scarborough, William J., 567
Scarmeas, Nikolaos, 625
Scarr, Sandra, 210
Scelzo, Anna, 26
Schacter, Daniel L., 617
Schacter, Hannah L., 341
Schadt, Eric E., 63
Schaie, K. Warner, 24, 59f, 509, 535, 535f, 536, 539
Scharf, Miri, 183
Schaub, Bianca, 200
Scherbaum, Stefan, 248
Schermerhorn, Alice C., 337
Schieman, Scott, 567, 568
Schienkiewitz, Anja, 199
Schillinger, Julia A., 414
Schlegel, Rebecca J., 636
Schmader, Toni, 456
Schneider, Daniel, 576
Schneider, William, 574
Schnitzspahn, Katharina M., 617, 618
Schoebi, Dominik, 492
Schore, Allan, 121
Schroeder, Steven A., 521
Schübel, Ruth, 603
Schubert, Anna-Lena, 614
Schulenberg, John, 484, 485f
Schulz, Marc, 330
Schulzke, Eric, 627
Schupp, Justin, 643
Schwaba, Ted, 642
Schwartsmann, Carlos Roberto, 600
Schwartz, Seth, 485
Schwarz, Alan, 288
Schweinhart, Lawrence J., 241
Schweitzer, Stefanie N., 186
Scott, Diane L., 216
Scott, Kathy Lynn, 598
Scott, Lisa S., 147
Sears, Martha, 120, 176
Sears, William, 120, 176
Seaton, Eleanor K., 390, 407, 481
Sebastian, Rachel A., 577
Sebastián-Gallés, Núria, 235
Sedlak, Andrea J., 213
Seelaar, Harro, 622
Seemiller, Eric S., 127
Sekeres, Mikkael A., 661
Seles, Monica, 201
Selita, Fatos, 508
Şendil, Çağla Öneren, 251
Senese, Vincenzo Paolo, 181
Seppa, Nathan, 77
September, Shirley Jade, 550
Seron, Carroll, 66
Servick, Kelly, 519
Seth, Puja, 522, 523f
Seto, Elizabeth, 636
Settersten, Richard A., 486
Severson, Kim, 396
Sevilla, Almudena, 643
Shah, Tushaar, 50
Shakespeare, William, 532
Shanholtz, Caroline E., 458
Shapiro, Joan Poliner, 462
Sharkey, Shirlee, 656
Sharot, Tali, 143
Sharp, Jeff, 643
Shayer, Michael, 534, 536
Shaywitz, Sally E., 294
Shechner, Tomer, 171

Shek, Daniel T. L., 389
Shelton, Penny S., 626
Sheppard, Sheri, 66
Sheridan, Margaret A., 172
Shi, Bing, 340
Shi, Rushen, 160
Shields, Grant S., 616
Shim, Woo-Jeong, 473
Shimizu, Mina, 120
Shin, Huiyoung, 412
Shiovitz-Ezra, Sharon, 648
Shneidman, Laura, 183
Shouse, Roger C., 396
Shpancer, Noam, 186
Shulman, Elizabeth P., 38, 444, 447
Shulman, Shmuel, 493
Shutts, Kristin, 180
Shwalb, David W., 181
Sidden (reverend), 562p
Siddiqui, Ayesha, 95
Siegal, Michael, 235
Siegler, Robert S., 302, 305
Sigurdson, J. F., 388
Silbereisen, Rainer K., 665f
Silbey, Susan S., 66
Silk, Jessica, 414
Silva, Lindsay, 15
Silverstein, Merril, 571
Sim, Zi L., 239
Simmons, Joseph P., 27
Simmons, Sandra F., 655
Simon, Laura, 414
Simon, Melissa A., 654
Simpson, Elizabeth A., 147
Simpson, Jeffry A., 49, 175
Simpson, Nancy, 586p
Singanayagam, Aran, 281
Singer, Judith D., 314, 316, 397
Singh, Abhijeet, 468
Singh, Amika, 282
Singh, Krishneil A., 537
Sinnott, Jan D., 454, 457, 459, 460
Sisk, Cheryl L., 355
Sisson, Susan B., 199
Sjöblom, Yvonne, 487
Skaff, Marilyn McKean, 638
Skinner, B. F., 34, 38, 38p, 59f, 159, 474
Skinner, Debra, 112
Skoog, Therése, 362
Skopek, Jan, 643
Slade, Pauline, 109
Slater, Amy, 375f
Slaughter, Anne-Marie, 578
Sloan, Mark, 109
Slot, Pauline Louise, 248
Slotnick, Scott D., 616
Small, Meredith F., 550
Smart, Andrew, 112
Smetana, Jan, 599
Smetana, Judith G., 267, 343, 409
Smith, Sharon G., 499
Smith, Christian, 463
Smith, Douglas H., 623
Smith, Gregory C., 571
Smith, Jacqueline, 569
Smith, Jacqui, 630
Smith, Lucretia, 557
Smith, Maggie, 593p
Smith, Michelle I., 138
Smith, Peter K., 251
Smithells, R. W., 101
Snell, Patricia, 463
Snider, Terra Ziporyn, 356
Snyder, Thomas D., 317, 472
Society for Developmental and Behavioral Pediatrics, 328
Society for Research in Child Development, A–1, A–2
Soderstrom, Melanie, 161
Solanto, Mary V., 288
Solheim, Elisabet, 187
Solomon, Andrew, 82, 291
Somerville, Leah H., 358, 380, 383, 385, 420, 421
Son, Daye, 488
Sonesh, Shirley C., 546
Sonuga-Barke, Edmund J. S., 178
Sophia (emerging adult), 488p
Sophian, Catherine, 226
Sophocles, 262
Sorensen, Lucy C., 392, 393
Sormunen, Taina, 515
Sorrells, Shawn F., 511
Sotomayor, Sonia, 520, 520p, 578
Soulsby, Laura K., 562
South, Susan C., 559
Spape, Jessica, 514
Sparks, Sarah D., 312
Sparrow, Joshua D., 54
Spearman, Charles E., 283, 532
Spector, Timothy, 514
Spencer, Justine M. Y., 615
Spencer, Rebecca M. C., 509
Spencer, Steven J., 456
Sperb, Tania Mara, 442
Sperry, Debbie M., 215
Spijker, Jeroen, 592
Spira, Adam P., 509
Spota (local attorney general), 522
Sprecher, Susan, 440, 441, 442
Spreng, R. Nathan, 612, 615
Sprietsma, Maresa, 302
Springsteen, Bruce, 82
Srinivasan, Sharada, 68
Sriram, Rajalakshmi, 181
Stahl, Aimee E., 146
Starr, Christine R., 264
Stattin, Håkan, 362, 405
Staudinger, Ursula M., 630
Steele, Claude M., 456
Stefansen, Kari, 277
Steffen, Edith Maria, 662, 680
Steffensmeier, Darrell, 13
Stefkovich, Jacqueline A., 462
Steinberg, Laurence, 358, 384, 414
Steiner, Rudolf, 238
Stenseng, Frode, 340
Stepler, Renee, 563
Sterling, Peter, 438
Stern, Gavin, 294
Stern, Mark, 317
Stern, Peter, 304
Sternberg, Robert J., 286, 491, 491t, 538–541, 539t, 561
Sterzing, Paul R., 413
Stevens, Elise, 414
Stevens, Laura, 318p
Stevenson, Robert G., 663
Stierand, Marc, 544
Stiles, Joan, 93, 124, 125
Stipek, Deborah, 237
Stolk, Lisette, 516
Stolt, Suvi, 105
Stolzenberg, Ellen Bara, 472
Strack, Fritz, 5
Strait, Dana L., 279
Strasburger, Victor C., 424
Stravinsky, Igor, 540
Stroebe, Margaret S., 680
Stroebe, Wolfgang, 5
Strohminger, Nina, 637
Strouse, Gabrielle A., 160
Stults, Christopher B., 500
Suárez-Orozco, Carola, 416
Suberi, Moriya, 149, 152
Substance Abuse and Mental Health Services Administration (SAMHSA), 83f, 448f
Suchy, Frederick J., 52
Sudo, Miki, 524p
Sue, Derald Wing, 575
Sugimoto, Taiki, 614
Sugimura, Kazumi, 404, 405
Suleiman, Ahna B., 415
Sulek, Julia P., 390
Sullivan, Jas M., 12
Sullivan, Kevin J., 621
Sullivan, Patrick F., 82
Sullivan, Sheila, 492
Sulmasy, Daniel, 670
Sun, Jianing, 389
Sun, Li, 362
Sun, Min, 54
Sun, Qian (Chayn), 596
Sunita, T. H., 514
Suomi, Steven J., 110
Surian, Luca, 235
Susan (twin), 330
Suskind, Owen, 291p
Sutaria, Shailen, 199
Sutin, Angelina R., 199
Sutton, Ward, 323, 344
Suzuki, Naoki, 278
Swaab, D. F., 41
Swanson, Dena Phillips, 248
Swanson, H. Lee, 290
Sweeney, Melanie D., 509
Swingley, Daniel, 145, 145t
Swit, Cara, 267
Syers, Ricky, 636p
Szanton, Sarah L., 644

Tabassum, Faiza, 643
Tacken, Mart, 590
Taga, Keiko A., 362
Taillieu, Tamara L., 258
Tajalli, Hassan, 39
Talley, Ronda C., 571
Tamim, Hala, 517

Tamis-LeMonda, Catherine S., 131, 159
Tamm, Leanne, 304
Tamnes, Christian K., 44
Tamura, Naomi, 106
Tan, Cheryl H., 102
Tan, Joseph S., 175
Tanabe, Kawai O., 134
Taneri, Petek Eylul, 516
Tang, Jie, 389
Tanumihardjo, Sherry A., 77
Tassell-Matamua, Natasha, 666
Taveras, Elsie M., 280
Tay, Marc Tze-Hsin, 77
Taylor, John H., 662
Taylor, Marian, 517
Taylor, Paul, 405
Taylor, Rachael W., 205
Taylor, Roy, 603
Taylor, Scott, 462
Tedeschi, Richard, 661, 678
Telzer, Eva H., 359, 420
Tenenbaum, Harriet R., 261
Teoh, Yee San, 204
Terenzini, Patrick T., 469
Teresi, Dick, 671
Terry, Nicole Patton, 307
Tessier, Karen, 208
Teti, Douglas M., 120
Tetley, Josie, 594
Tetzlaff, Anne, 366
Tham, Diana Su Yun, 147
Thiam, Melinda A., 168
Thomaes, Sander, 325
Thomas, Dennis, 597
Thomas, Dylan, 664
Thomas, Jim, 464
Thomas, Sonya, 524p
Thomason, Moriah E., 93
Thompson, Charis, 70
Thompson, Martie, 448
Thompson, Richard, 256, 257, 259
Thomson, Samuel, 366
Thornberg, Robert, 342
Thorup, Bianca, 147
Tiago (emerging adult), 495p
Tiggemann, Marika, 375f
Timonen, Virpi, 570, 646
Tindale, Lauren C., 604
Tippett, Lynette J., 637
Titus, Courtney, 256
Tobey, Emily A., 127
Todd, Gillian, 117
Todd (Mrs.), 117, 130, 148
Tolen, Megan, 638p
Tolman, Deborah L., 368
Tom (adult), 564p
Toma, Catalina L., 494
Tomaselli, Keyan, 227
Tomasello, Michael, 160, 228
Tomopoulos, Suzy, 120
Tong, Stephanie T., 494
Topooco, Naira, 387
Toporek, Bryan, 277
Torrance, Mark, 304
Tough, Paul, 315, 398
Townsend, Apollo, 669
Trahan, Lisa H., 285
Travers, Brittany G., 202
Traynor, Victoria, 651
Treas, Judith, 565
Treffers-Daller, Jeanine, 233
Triana, María Del Carmen, 440
Trivedi, Daksha, 128
Troll, Lillian E., 638
Trommsdorff, Gisela, 266
Tronick, Edward, 174
Trump, Donald, 19, 22, 103, 360, 360p, 679
Tsai, Ya-Hsun, 473
Tsang, Christine, 156
Ttofi, Maria M., 342
Tu, Kristie N., 600
Tucker-Drob, Elliot M., 386, 386f, 636
Turley, Ruth N. López, 335
Turner, Gary R., 612, 615
Turner, Heather A., 331, 337, 342
Tuttle, Robert, 577
Tveito, Vegard, 489
Twenge, Jean M., 417
Tynes, Brendesha M., 390
Tyrone (child), 336

UC Berkeley, 675
Uchida, Mai, 289
Uddin, Monica, 416
Umberson, Debra, 561, 595
Underwood, Emily, 79, 92, 671
Underwood, Marion K., 390
UNESCO, 310, 401f
Unger, Kerstin, 306
UNICEF, 105, 138, 138f
United Nations, 68, 132, 133, 441, 443, 524, 525f, 590, 592, 633f. *See also* UNESCO; UNICEF; World Health Organization
United States. *See entries beginning "U.S." and other specific U.S. agencies and organizations—e.g.,* Centers for Disease Control and Prevention
Ursache, Alexandra, 172
U.S. Bureau of Labor Statistics, 187, 270, 426, 451f, 468f, 484, 502, 574, 574f, 580, 641f, 643, 643f, 658
U.S. Census Bureau, 31f, 307f, 332f, 333t, 349f, 451f, 456, 477f, 487, 494, 496f, 503f, 560f, 581f, 659f, 664f
U.S. Department of Agriculture, 106, 106f
U.S. Department of Commerce, 429
U.S. Department of Education, 241, 468
U.S. Department of Health and Human Services, 104f, 212–214, 213f, 240, 259, 436, 466, 598
U.S. Department of Justice, 68
U.S. Department of Labor, 112
U.S. Department of State, 180f
U.S. Office of Disease Prevention and Health Promotion, 436
U.S. Preventive Services Task Force, 517, 654
U.S. Social Security Administration, 10, 11t
U.S. Youth Risk Behavior Survey, 369

Vadillo, Miguel A., 545
Valentine, Christine, 678
van Batenburg-Eddes, Tamara, 419
van de Bongardt, Daphne, 369, 412
Van De Vondervoort, Julia W., 265, 343
van den Akker, Alithe, 170
van den Pol, Anthony N., 99
Van Dongen, Rachel, 378
Van Dyke, Miriam E., 278
van Eeden-Moorefield, Brad, 335
Van Goethem, Anne, 405
Van Gogh, Vincent, 82, 540
van Goozen, Stephanie H. M., 172
Van Harmelen, A.-L., 413
Van Hecke, Wim, 43f
Van Hooff, Miranda, 327
Van Horn, Linda V., 365
van IJzendoorn, Marinus H., 343
van Knippenberg, Ad, 6
van Lamoen, Ellemieke, 590
van Nunen, Karolien, 55
Van Ryzin, Mark J., 412
van Tilburg, Theo G., 563
Vandenbosch, Laura, 414
Vanderberg, Rachel H., 414
VanderEnde, Kristin, 135
Vanessa (emerging adult), 469
Vanhalst, Janne, 379
Vardaki, Sophia, 597
Varga, Mary Alice, 663
Vargas, Edward D., 12
Vargas Lascano, Dayuma I., 484
Vaughn, Byron P., 64
Vaupel, James W., 602, 604
Vedantam, Shankar, 169
Veenstra, René, 341
Veldheer, Susan, 423
Verdine, Brian N., 228, 229
Verleger, Matthew A., 474
Verona, Sergiu, 176
Verschoor, Chris P., 517
Victora, Cesar G., 137t
Vijayakumar, Nandita, 354
Viljaranta, Jaana, 313
Vilppu, Henna, 546
Vinters, H. V., 622
Viotty, Samantha, 388
Visscher, Peter M., 604
Vitale, Susan, 77
Vittner, Dorothy, 121
Vlachos, George S., 625
Vladeck, Fredda, 644
Voegtline, Kristin M., 127
Voelcker-Rehage, Claudia, 282
Vöhringer, Isabel A., 149
Voisin, Dexter R., 418
Volkmar, Fred R., 125
Volkovich, Ella, 120
Volpe, Lane E., 120
von Hippel, Courtney, 619
von Salisch, Maria, 410
Voracek, Martin, 285
Vos, Bodil C., 446
Vos, Miriam B., 200
Votruba, Ashley M., 334, 564
Votruba-Drzal, Elizabeth, 237
Vygotsky, Lev S., 46–47, 46p, 58f, 221, 222, 226–229, 237, 299–303, 315

Waber, Deborah P., 138
Wachs, Theodore D., 158
Wade, Tracey D., 416
Wade, Mark, 231
Wagner, Erica, 66
Wagner, Jenny, 558
Wagner, Katie, 233
Wagner, Paul A., 414
Waite, Linda J., 645
Waldinger, Robert, 330
Waldorf, Kristina M. Adams, 99
Walk, Laura M., 222
Walker, Lauren, 623
Walker, Lenore, 654p
Walker, Renee, 138
Wallace, Helen, 129
Walley, Susan C., 423
Wallis, Christopher J. D., 518
Wallis, Claudia, 96
Walter, Melissa Clucas, 239
Wambach, Karen, 136, 137t
Wanberg, Connie R., 573, 574
Wang, Teresa W., 423f
Wang, Chao, 76
Wang, Limin, 604
Wang, Meifang, 256, 257, 394
Wang, Ming-Te, 410
Waqar-ul-Haq, 359
Ward, Emma V., 616
Warneken, Felix, 170
Warner, Lisa M., 643
Wastesson, Jonas W., 593
Watkins, Alice, 680p
Watson, John B., 37, 37p, 58f, 182
Watt, Douglas, 169
Watts, Nicolas, 378
Waxman, Sandra R., 162
Way, Niobe, 416
Webb, Alexandra R., 92
Weber, Ann, 158
Weber, Daniela, 285
Weber, Max, 58f
Webster, Collin A., 278
Wechsler, David, 283
Weeks, Murray, 307
Weger, Harry, 490
Wegrzyn, Lani R., 577
Wei, Si, 629
Weikart, David P., 241
Weiland, Christina, 242
Weinberg, M. Katherine, 174
Weiss, David, 587
Weiss, Noel S., 81
Weissberg, Roger P., 343
Weisskirch, Robert S., 328
Wellman, Henry M., 180, 306
Wen, Ming, 571
Wendelken, Carter, 282
Wendland, Claire, 97
Werker, Janet F., 8
Werner, Emmy, 59f
Wessel, Stephanie, 211p
Westerhof, Gerben J., 589
Weymouth, Bridget B., 408
Whalley, Lawrence J., 625
Wheeler, Lorey A., 410
Whishaw, Ian Q., 122
Whisman, Mark A., 561
Whitbourne, Stacey B., 432, 439, 511, 512
Whitbourne, Susan K., 432, 439, 511, 512
White, Rebecca M. B., 362
White-Traut, Rosemary C., 168, 172
Whiting, Jason B., 500
WHO. *See* World Health Organization
Wicks, Elizabeth, 673
Widman, Laura, 415
Widom, Cathy Spatz, 215, 439
Wieck, Cornelia, 616
Wierenga, Lara M., 304
Wieten, Sarah, 544
Wigger, J. Bradley, 251
Wiik, Kenneth Aarskaug, 563
Wijdicks, Eelco F. M., 670
Wilbourn, Makeba Parramore, 144
Wilcox, W. Bradford, 349f
Wilcox, William B., 260
Wilkinson, Stephen, 68
Williams, Anne M., 137
Williams, Joshua L., 132
Williams, Katie M., 76
Williams, Lela Rankin, 171
Williams, Robin, 623p
Williams, Shanna, 230
Williamson, Victoria, 331
Willoughby, Michael T., 342
Willstrand, Tania Dukic, 597
Wilmshurst, Linda, 336
Wilson, Jennifer, 306
Winegard, Bo, 547
Winfrey, Oprah, 201, 328
Winn, Phoebe, 112
Winner, Brooke, 444
Woessmann, Ludger, 312, 392
Wolchik, Sharlene A., 663
Wolf, Norman S., 604
Wolff, Jason J., 202
Womack, Sean R., 331
Wonder, Stevie, 512p
Wong, Jaclyn S., 645
Wood, Wendy, 260, 263
Woodward, Amanda L., 183, 233
Woolf, Virginia, 82
Woollett, Katherine, 548, 549
Woolley, Jacqueline D., 305
World Bank, 103
World Health Organization (WHO), 92, 103, 130t, 135f, 136, 137, 141, 207, 287, 297f, 529f, 600, 620, 633f
Wörmann, Viktoriya, 168
Wosje, Karen S., 199
Wright, Frank Lloyd, 629
Wright, Vince, 302
Wrzus, Cornelia, 339
Wu, Ming-Yih, 516
Wurtele, Sandy K., 370
Wynberg, Rachel, 63
Xie, Hongling, 340
Xu, Fei, 153, 155, 239
Xu, Guifeng, 105, 276f, 288, 290
Xu, Jiaquan, 134f
Xu, Yaoying, 252

Yackobovitch-Gavan, Michal, 280
Yadav, Priyanka, 389
Yan, J., 325
Yan, Ni, 172
Yanez, Christina, 427f
Yang, Rongwang, 288, 521
Yaniv, Ilan, 573
Yeager, David S., 408
Yerkes, Robert Mearns, 533
Yeung, Fanny, 473
Yi, Youngmin, 484, 485, 487
Yip, Tiffany, 482
Yolanda (child), 339
Yon, Yongjie, 653
Yoon, Cynthia, 439
Yore, Larry D., 547
Yorgason, Jeremy B., 638
Yoshikawa, Hirokazu, 242
Yost, Debora, 128
Young, Marisa, 567, 568
Young, Ralph, 646p
Young, Ruth, 646p
Yu, Edward, 437
Yu, Lu, 389
Yuan, Zhiming, 27
Yudell, Michael, 12
Yule, Morag A., 514
Yusof, Sufiah, 293

Zachrisson, Henrik D., 188
Zagheni, Emilio, 508
Zahran, Hatice S., 281
Zak, Nikolay, 604
Zak, Paul J., 265
Zalenski, Robert J., 667
Zametkin, Alan J., 288
Zatorre, Robert J., 285
Zeiders, Katharine H., 416
Zeifman, Debra M., 107, 108, 126, 146
Zeitlin, Marian, 158
Zelazo, Philip D., 533
Zhan, Min, 467
Zhang, Linlin, 340
Zhang, Yanlong, 560
Zhao, Fei, 91
Zhao, Jinxia, 394
Zhou, Cindy Ke, 511
Zhou, Qing, 222
Zhu, Qi, 285
Zimmer-Gembeck, Melanie J., 394
Zimmerman, Marc A., 12
Zimmermann, Camilla, 637
Zinzow, Heidi M., 448
Zolna, Mia R., 70, 104, 106
Zuk, Jennifer, 279
Zurbriggen, Eileen L., 264
Zurcher, Jessica D., 390
Zych, Izabela, 342

SUBJECT INDEX

Note: Boldface indicates pages where key terms are called out; "f" indicates the reference is to a figure; "t" indicates the reference is to a table; "p" indicates the reference is to a photo.

Abacus, 227p
Abecedarian Project, 241, 241p
Abortion
 rates of, 369
 in sex selection, 68, 68p
 spontaneous abortion, 91t
 trisomies and, 112
Absent grief, **676**
Abstinence, 415
Abuse. *See* Child abuse; Child maltreatment; Domestic abuse; Drug use and abuse; Elder abuse; Sexual abuse
Abusive head trauma, 125–126
Academic achievement
 analytic intelligence and, 538, 539t
 automatization and, 304–305
 emotional regulation and, 249
 family function and, 338, 338f
 gender differences in, 314–316
 in high school, 395–398
 intrinsic motivation and, 250
 in middle childhood, 314–316
 in middle school, 392–394
 parent–child relationships and, 410
Accident bump, 445
Accident prevention. *See* Harm reduction
Accidents, 207–209, 209f, 609f, 664, 664f. *See also* Harm reduction; Injuries
Accommodation, **41,** 41f, 151t, 152
Ache people, 550
Achievement, 283. *See also* Academic achievement
Active euthanasia, **671**
Activities of daily life (ADLs), **649**–651, 659f
Activity theory, **640**
AD. *See* Alzheimer's disease
Adaptation, 41, 41f, 149, 149p, 151t, 152, 153
 selective adaptations, 51–52, 51f
Adderall, 422f
Addiction. *See also* Drug use and abuse
 brain function and, 510
 computer addiction, 389
 in emerging adulthood, 448, 448p
 in newborns, 129
 to opioids, 522–523, 523p
 substance use disorder, 24, 37
Additive heredity, 73–74
ADHD. *See* Attention-deficit/hyperactivity disorder
ADLs (activities of daily life), **649**–651, 659f
Adolescence, 8t, 350–427
 adoption and, 568
 anger in, 408, 416, 417–418
 biosocial development in, 353–375. *See also* Puberty
 body image in, 355p, 365–366, 375f, 378–379, 391
 boys and, 353–354, 357–359, 358f, 362–369, 362p
 brain development in, 356–357, 358–359, 358f, 383, 385–386, 420–421, 420f, 455
 cognitive development in, 377–401
 death and dying and, 663, 664f
 delinquency and defiance in, 362, 411–412, 417–421, 418p, 419p
 depression in, 406, 409, 416–417
 diseases and disorders in, 364–366, 370–372, 406, 409, 416–421
 driving in, 356, 357, 420–421, 420f, 546
 drug use and abuse in, 15, 421–424, 421p, 422f, 424p
 education in, 356, 380–381, 387–388, 387p, 391–399, 394p, 395p, 398p, 401f
 egocentrism in, 378–380, 379p, 380p, 391, 393
 emotions and emotional development in, 355, 357, 358, 368, 375f, 379, 384, 385–386, 386f, 416–421
 families in, 370, 407–410, 409p, 416
 friendships in, 385, 394, 410–413, 412p, 413p, 427f
 genetics and, 63p
 girls and, 353–355, 355p, 357–368, 368f, 370–371
 growth during, 363–364
 identity in, 403–406, 404p, 405p, 406p
 impulsivity and impulse control in, 379, 385–386, 386f, 390–391, 420–421
 LGBTQ individuals in, 406, 413–414, 413f
 logic in, 380–386
 nonmaternal infant care and, 189
 nutrition during, 359–360, 364–366, 364p
 parents and parenting in, 388, 390, 393, 404–405, 406–410, 409p, 414–415, 422, 426
 peers in, 375f, 385, 387, 391, 393, 407, 410–415, 410p, 413p, 420–421, 420f, 427f
 in psychodynamic perspectives, 35t
 psychopathology in, 370, 416–421
 psychosocial development in, 403–427
 race in, 12
 risk in, 359, 379, 380, 385, 412p, 420–421, 420f
 sexual abuse in, 360, 361, 370–371, 370p, 371p, 388–389
 sexuality during, 21–22, 22f, 354–355, 367–372, 388–389, 412–415, 414p, 415p
 sleep in, 355–356, 356f
 technology in, 386–391, 387p, 388p, 390p
Adolescence-limited offenders, **419**
Adolescent egocentrism, **378**–380, 379p, 380p, 391, 393
Adoption and adopted children
 difficulties in, 216
 family structure and, 333t
 identity development and, 482
 international adoptions, 180, 180f, 482
 parenthood and, 568, 568p
 from Romanian orphanages, 176, 178–179, 178p, 204
Adrenal glands, **354**
Adult children, 565, 570–572, 572p
Adulthood, 8t, 504–581
 aging in, 508–518
 attachment in, 177
 balancing needs in, 577–578
 biosocial development in, 507–529
 brain development in, 509–511, 510p, 533, 536, 538, 542, 547–549, 548p, 558p
 caregiving in, 571–572
 cognitive development in, 531–553
 death and dying and, 664
 drug use and abuse in, 521–523, 523f
 employment in, 572–577
 exercise in, 519–520
 expert cognition in, 543–550, 543p, 547p, 548p
 families in, 564–566, 565p, 581f
 friendships in, 564, 564p
 habits and routines in, 518–526
 health in, 509, 517–525
 intelligence in, 532–541
 intimacy in, 560–566
 marriage in, 505, 560–563, 560f, 561t, 562p
 nutrition in, 523–524
 parenthood in, 566–571, 567p, 568p, 570p, 572p
 personality development in, 555, 556–559
 pharmaceutical use in, 520
 plasticity in, 510–511, 548, 548p
 in psychodynamic perspectives, 35t
 psychosocial development in, 555–581
 risk taking in, 420–421, 420f
 romance and romantic relationships in, 560–563, 561p
 selective optimization with compensation in, 541–543
 sexual-reproductive system in, 513–518
 sexual urges, thoughts, and activity in, 513–514, 518
Advance directives, **672**–675
Advertising, and smoking, 424, 521p
Aerobic exercise, 436, 436t
Afghanistan
 maternity leave in, 189f
 polio in, 134
Africa. *See also specific nations*
 cesarean sections in, 96
 Ebola in, 27, 27p
 infant care in, 186
 premarital sex in, 442f
 walking development in, 132
African Americans
 ADHD and, 289
 adolescent sexuality in, 369
 in college, 466p, 472f, 477f

African Americans (*Continued*)
corporal punishment among, 257
distribution of, by age and region, 31f
e-cigarettes and, 423f
ethnic identity among, 481
family structure and, 332f
genetic variation in, 74
graduation rates of, 451f
in high-stakes testing, 396f
home ownership of, 640
hospice and, 669
income and obesity in, 529f
in labor force, 574, 574f
in NAEP, 316
obesity among, 280f
parent–child relationships of, 407–408, 408f
puberty onset in, 359, 362
racial/ethnic pride among, 12
sickle-cell disease and, 81
Afterlife, 662–663, 662p, 662t
Age. *See also* Adolescence; Adulthood; Ageism; Aging; Cohorts; Early childhood; Emerging adulthood; Infancy; Late adulthood; Middle childhood; Norms
addiction and, 76
Big Five and, 558
centenarians, 593, 603p, 604, 604p, 628, 638, 662t
cesarean sections and, 96
cognition and, 587, 587t
death and dying and, 663–665
demographic shift and, 590–593, 591f
divorce and, 563
dizygotic twins and, 72
driving and, 609f
drug use and, 421–422
empathy and, 618–619, 619f
employment and, 573
ethnicity and, in United States, 31
exercise and, 568f
expertise and, 548–549
fertility and, 515
friendships and, 491f
gestational age, 90t
of grandparenthood, 570
intelligence and, 533, 533p, 534, 536, 540
intimate partner violence and, 499f
IVF and, 70
living arrangements and, 581f
mental age, 284
physician-assisted suicide and, 673, 673f
psychopathology and, 82, 83f
at puberty, 351, 353–354, 357–362
self-comparisons and, 587, 587t
social media use and, 553f
stratification and, 640
Age in place, **643**–644, 644p, 648
Age of viability, **91**–92, 92p, 93
Ageism, 583, **586**–593, 619, 620, 628, 638, 639p, 640, 641, 655
Age–prospective memory paradox, 618
Aggression. *See also* Bullying
corporal punishment and, 257
in early childhood, 266–267, 267t
Aging
in adulthood, 508–518
aging in place, 643–644, 644p, 648
depression and, 612
in emerging adulthood, 433–434
employment and, 602
in late adulthood, 599–606, 643–644, 644p, 648
nutrition and, 602–603
physical therapy and, 580
theories of, 602–606
Agreeableness, 555, 558, 558p, 559, 578
Airline pilots, 546
Airplane accidents, 664
Alabama, high-stakes testing in, 396
Alcohol use. *See also* Alcohol use disorder; Fetal alcohol syndrome
in adolescence, 422, 422f
in adulthood, 522
cerebellum affected by, 122
in emerging adulthood, 448, 448f, 451f
for insomnia, 586
postformal thought about, 459
in pregnancy, 101, 102
in same-sex relationships, 562
women and, 76p
Alcohol use disorder, 76, 522
attachment and, 178t
Algeria, maternity leave in, 189f
Alleles, **62**, 101. *See also* Genes
longevity and, 604
Allergies, in early childhood, 200, 200p
Allocare, **185**, 187–189, 188f, 189f. *See also* Day care
Alloparents, 185
Allostasis, **435**
Allostatic load, **435**–436, 435f, 438
Alzheimer's disease (AD), 510, **621**–622, 621p, 621t, 622f, 622p, 624
bilingualism and, 235
Down syndrome and, 79
"Ambiguous genitals," 64p
Amnesia, 616–617
Amphetamines, 422f
Amygdala, 122f, 123, 172, 203, 357
Anal personality, 182
Anal stage, 35, 35t, 182
Analytic intelligence, **538,** 539p, 539t, 540
Analytic thought, **383**–384, 386
Ancestry, and genetic counseling, 112
Ancient Egypt, 662, 662p
Ancient Greece, 662
Androgens, 354
Andropause, **518**
Anemia, 364–365
Anencephaly, 101
Angelman syndrome, 65, 65p
Anger. *See also* Aggression
in adolescence, 408, 416, 417–418
in infancy, 168, 168t, 169
Angola, life expectancy in, 525f
Animism, **224**
Anorexia nervosa, **366,** 366p
Anoxia, **98**
Antipathy, **266**
Antisocial behavior, **265,** 266–267, 266p. *See also* Aggression
Antithesis, **457**
Anxiety. *See also* Insecure-resistant/ambivalent attachment
stranger anxiety, 169
AP (Advanced Placement), 395
Apgar scale, **95,** 98, 113f
APOE gene, 604, 622
Apoptosis, 92
Appalachia, 17, 17t, 97p
Appearance. *See also* Body image
in adulthood, 511–512, 511p
in emerging adulthood, 439–440, 439p
in middle childhood, 338
Apprenticeship in thinking, **46**–47
Apprenticeship in Thinking (Rogoff), 59f
Aptitude, 283, 285
Arkansas
corporal punishment in, 257–259
moral development in, 462–463
Arranged marriages, 487, 492, 495
Art
drawings by children, 48, 49f
by gifted child, 286p
in late adulthood, 629, 629p
in middle childhood, 279, 317, 323
psychopathology and, 82
ART. *See* Assisted reproductive technology
ASD. *See* Autism spectrum disorder
Asexual individuals, 514
Asia and Asians. *See also specific nations*
co-sleeping in, 120, 120f
nearsightedness in, 77
premarital sex and, 442f
Asian Americans
in college, 472f, 477f
distribution of, by age and region, 31f
family structure and, 332f
graduation rates of, 451f
in high-stakes testing, 396f
income and obesity in, 529f
in labor force, 574, 574f
in NAEP, 316
obesity among, 280f, 529f
Asperger's syndrome, 290
Assimilation, **41,** 41f
Assisted living, 655–656, 659f
Assisted reproductive technology (ART), 515–516, 515p, 516p. *See also* In vitro fertilization
Associative play, 252
Asthma, 7, **280**–281, 281p, 364
At About This Time. *See* Norms
Athletics. *See* Sports
Attachment, 59f, **175**–180, 193f
adoption and, 568
foster care and, 569–570
harm reduction and, 215
nonmaternal care and, 188–189
religion and, 644
Strange Situation and, 59f, 177, 193f
Attachment parenting, 120, 176
Attempted suicide, 417
Attention, 282
Attention-deficit/hyperactivity disorder (ADHD), 279, **288**–290, 289f
gross motor skills and, 270
overstimulation in infancy and, 125
Audition. *See* Hearing
Auditory cortex, 122f, 123
Australia
co-sleeping in, 120f
college education in, 467f
infant care in, 187
life expectancy in, 525f
overimitation study in, 227–228

parental leave in, 189f
problem-solving skills in, 470f
SIDS in, 133
TIMSS and PIRLS scores in, 313t
weight in early childhood in, 199
Austria
parental leave in, 189f
problem-solving skills in, 470f
voting age in, 451f
Authoritarian parenting, **254**–255, 255t, 256
Authoritative parenting, **255,** 255t
Autism spectrum disorder (ASD), **290**–292, 291f, 292f
multidisciplinary approach to, 14
pragmatics and, 307
in second-born children, 101
synaptic pruning in, 124
Automatization, **304**–305, 305p
in expertise, 544–545
Autonomy versus shame and doubt, 35t, **182,** 480t
Autosomes, 64–65
Average life expectancy, **590**–591. *See also* Life expectancy
Avoidance. *See* Insecure-avoidant attachment
Axons, **121**

Babbling, **156,** 156p, 156t, 159
Babinski reflex, 108
Baby blues, 108–109
"Baby signs," 160
"Baby" teeth, 200
"Back to Sleep," 133–134
Balancing a scale, 381, 381f
Balding, 511
Bali, Indonesia
Hindu cremation procession in, 678p
wedding in, 440p
Baltimore, Maryland
curfew in, 356
longitudinal study in, 23
Bangladesh, boat classroom in, 307p
Bariatric surgery, 524
Base for exploration, 175
Base pairs, 62
Baseball, 282
Beanpole families, 646, 647f
Bed-sharing, **119,** 120
Behavior. *See* Antisocial behavior; Child abuse; Child maltreatment; Delinquency and defiance; Domestic abuse; Drug use and abuse; Elder abuse; Exercise; Prosocial behavior; Risk and risk taking; Sexual abuse; Sexual urges, thoughts, and activity
Behavioral teratogens, 99, **100**
Behaviorism, **36**–40, 53t
on gender differences, 263
on infant psychosocial development, 173–174
language development and, 159
teacher-directed programs and, 239
toilet training in, 54
Beijing, China
prayer meeting in, 640p
taxi driving in, 541p
Belgium
parental leave in, 189f
problem-solving skills in, 470f
TIMSS scores in, 313t
toilet training in, 55
Benzene, 423
Bereavement, 680–681. *See also* Grief; Mourning
Beta-amyloid, 621, 624
Bicycle riding, 47–48, 590, 603
Big Five (personality theory), 555, 558–559, 558p, 559p
Bilingual education, **308**
Bilingualism, 145, 233–234, 235–236, 235p, 307–308, 307f. *See also* Second language learning
Binge eating disorder, **366**
Binocular vision, 127
Biology. *See also* Biosocial development; Genetics
race and, 12
Biomarkers, 43, 620
Biorhythms, 355. *See also* Circadian rhythm
Biosocial development. *See also* Body changes
in adolescence, 353–375
in adulthood, 507–529
in emerging adulthood, 431–451
in infancy, 115–141
in late adulthood, 585–609
in middle childhood, 275–297
of prenatal brain, 93
Birth, 94–96. *See also* Labor and delivery; Newborns
due date for, 90t
as trauma, 129
Birth control. *See* Abortion; Abstinence; Contraception
Birth control pills, 514
Birth defects, 59f, 100–102, 102p. *See also* Teratogens
genetic counseling and, 83
types and timing of, 100f
Birth rate, in emerging adulthood, 440
Birthweight
low birthweight, 103–107
small for gestational age, 104
Bisexuality. *See* LGBTQ individuals
Bisphenol A (BPA), 23
Black Death, 338
Black Panther (movie), 326p
Blastocysts, 70
Blended family, 333t
Blind (in research studies), 658, **A-4**
Blindness, 77
Blood–brain barrier, 509
BMI (body mass index), 198, 280, 363–364, **437**–438, 438t
Body changes. *See also* Age; Brain and brain development; Death and dying; Diseases and disorders; Growth; Health; Hearing; Height; Motor skills; Puberty; Vision; Weight
in adulthood, 511–512
in early childhood, 198–200, 198p
in emerging adulthood, 432–433
in infancy, 118–126
Body fat, and puberty, 359–360
Body image
in adolescence, 355p, 365–366, 375f, 378–379, 391
in emerging adulthood, 489
Body mass index (BMI), 198, 280, 363–364, **437**–438, 438t
Body temperature
heat waves and, 434
reflexes of, 107
Bonding. *See* Attachment; Social referencing; Synchrony
Bone density testing, 600
Bones, and osteoporosis, 600
Boomers, 16f
Boston, Massachusetts, 387p
Botox, 511p
Bottle feeding. *See* Formula feeding
Bottom-up reasoning, 82
Bovine spongiform encephalopathy (BSE), 509, 623
Boys. *See also* Gender differences; Gender identity; Males
ADHD in, 289–290, 289f
breast growth in, 367
as bullies, 341
depression in, 416
early maturation in, 362
first names of, 11t
gender identity and, 406
height of, in early childhood, 219f
inhibited temperament in, 171
nonmaternal care and, 188
obesity in, 280f
play by, 251p, 252
puberty and adolescence in, 353–354, 357–359, 358f, 362–369, 362p
running speed of, 363, 363f
sexual abuse of, 371
sexuality of, in adolescence, 368–369, 368f
BPA (bisphenol A), 23
BRAC1 gene, 517–518
Brain and brain development. *See also* Cerebral cortex; Inside the Brain; Neuroimaging; Neuroscience; *other specific brain areas and structures*
activation in brain regions, 126p
in adolescence, 356–357, 358–359, 358f, 383, 385–386, 420–421, 420f, 455
in adulthood, 509–511, 510p, 533, 536, 538, 542, 547–549, 548p, 558p
anoxia and, 98
bilingualism and, 235
in early childhood, 201–206, 231, 249–250, 252, 270
in emerging adulthood, 455, 455f
emotions and, 171, 172–173, 172f
epigenetics and, 63
executive function and, 223
experience in, 124–125, 231
in expertise, 547–549, 548p
head measurement and, 41
in infancy, 121–125, 121p
intelligence and, 533, 536, 538
language development and, 235, 309
in late adulthood, 612–615, 613p
lead poisoning and, 210–211, 211p
in middle childhood, 282–286, 303–306, 309
personality and, 558p
postformal thought and, 455, 455f
poverty and, 309
in prenatal development, 92, 93, 93f
rough-and-tumble play and, 252
in selective optimization, 542
shrinkage of brain, 613–615, 613p
stress and, 203–204
structures and functions of, 122, 122f
BRAIN (Brain Research Through Advancing Innovative Technologies), 59f

Brain death, 670, 670t
Brain diseases and disorders. *See also* Neurocognitive disorders
in adulthood, 509–510
cerebral palsy, 98
fetal alcohol syndrome, 99, 101
in infancy, 125–126
teratogens and, 59f, 98–100
Brain Research Through Advancing Innovative Technologies (BRAIN), 59f
Brain scans. *See* Neuroimaging
Brain stem, 93f
Brassieres, 367
Brazelton Neonatal Behavioral Assessment Scale (NBAS), **107**–108
Brazil
life expectancy in, 525f
maternity leave in, 189f
overweight prevalence and GDP of, 529f
voting age in, 451f
Zika virus in, 99
Breast cancer
exercise and, 519
hormone replacement therapy and, 517
Breast feeding, 136–137, 136p, 137t
oxytocin and, 121
of preterm babies, 149
sleep and, 119
Breasts, 367
Breathing disorders, 508–509
Bridge jobs, 642
Britain. *See* United Kingdom
Brooklyn, New York, 329p
Brooklyn Bridge, 66
BSE (bovine spongiform encephalopathy), 509, 623
Bulgaria, parental leave in, 189f
Bulimia nervosa, **366**
Bully-victims, **341**
Bullying, **340**
in adolescence, 413, 427f
cyberbullying, 340, 341, 390, 390p, 427f
in middle childhood, 340–343, 340p, 342p
Bullying aggression, **267,** 267t. *See also* Bullying
Buttoning, 226p

C-sections. *See* Cesarean sections
Calcium, 199, 364–365
California
IVF and, 70
public colleges in, 466
teachers in, 393p
California Medical Board, 70
Calorie restriction, **602**–603
Camel herding, 541p
Cameroon
children's drawings in, 48, 49f
maternity leave in, 189f
Canada
aging in place in, 644p
co-sleeping in, 120f
college education in, 467f
elderly population in, 590
extroversion in, 558
graduation rates in, 401f
infant care in, 187, 188f
life expectancy in, 525f
marijuana legalization in, 422
parental leave in, 189f
problem-solving skills in, 470f
refugees in, 343p
smoking in, 424
TIMSS and PIRLS scores in, 313t, 337f
Cancer
breast cancer, 517, 519
death and dying and, 605, 664, 665f, 670, 671, 672p
HPV and, 371
IVF and, 516
lung cancer, 23, 521, 521f
male pattern baldness and, 511
prostate cancer, 511, 601
in United States, 212f, 433t
Car accidents. *See* Motor vehicle accidents
Car seats, 208
CARDIA (Coronary Artery Risk Development in Adulthood), 426, 438, 439
Care homes, 667
Career Alert
The Career Counselor, 502
The Developmental Scientist, 658
The Genetic Counselor, 122
The Pediatrician and the Pediatric Nurse, 192
The Physical Therapist, 580
The Preschool Teacher, 270
The Teacher, 426
Career counselors, 502
Caregiving and caregivers. *See also* Adoption and adopted children; Attachment; Discipline; Foster care; Parents and parenting
in adulthood, 571–572
in day care, 189–190, 190t
in early childhood, 216, 254–268, 271f
evolutionary perspective on, 184–185
for frail elderly, 651–656
gaze-following and, 146–147
grandparents in, 647–648, 648p
harm reduction and, 216
in infancy, 146–147, 169, 169p, 172–174, 174p, 180–181, 184–190, 190t
in late adulthood, 622, 633f, 638, 642, 646, 647, 650, 651–656, 669, 670, 674
long-term care, 653–656
NCDs and, 622, 633f
in nursing homes, 653–655
palliative care, 669, 670, 674
styles of caregiving, 254–256, 255t
Caribbean region
cesarean sections in, 96
Carrier, **74**–75, 75f, 75t
recessive disorders and, 80–81
Case to Study
Behavioral Teratogens, 99
The Benefits of Marriage, 562
The Berger Daughters, 260
Biting the Policeman, 384
Can We Bear This Commitment?, 179
David, 16–17
Early Speech, 157
Generation to Generation, 471
The Gifted and Talented, 293
Happiness or High Grades?, 315
A Hero for Millions, 446
How Hard Is It to Be a Kid?, 336
The More You Know . . . , 627
"My Baby Swallowed Poison," 208
My Students, My Daughters, and Me, 495–496
The Naiveté of Your Author, 411
Parenting Expertise, 550
Saving Old Newspapers, 639
Scientist at Work, 133–134
Sex Among Older Adults, 595
Stones in the Belly, 226
A Trusted Sister, 654
What Is Your Intention?, 670
Women Engineers, 66
Cataracts, 597t
Cattle raising, 52
Caudate nucleus, 455f
Causes of death. *See* Mortality rates
Cell phones
adults' use of, 553f
multitasking and, 542
Cells, 69, 69p. *See also* Neurons
aging of, 605–606
Cellular aging, **605**–606, 605p
Census (U.S.), 456–457
Centenarians, 593, 603p, 604, 604p, 628, 638, 639p, 662t
Centers for Disease Control and Prevention (U.S.), 28
Central African Republic, 524
Central nervous system, 90, 91, 93. *See also* Brain and brain development
Centration, **224,** 225
Cephalocaudal development, **91**
Cerebellum, 122, 122f
Cerebral cortex, 44, 93, 122–123, 122f, 358f. *See also* Hemispheres of brain
Cerebral palsy, **98**
Cerebrum, 122
Cesarean sections, **96,** 97
Charter schools, 317, 317p, 318
Chef and the Farmer, 547p
Chess expertise, 545, 548
Child abuse, **212**. *See also* Child sexual abuse
The Speech Therapist, 348
in United States, 212, 213f, 216p
Child-centered programs, 237–238, 239, 239f, 241, 242, 245f
Child culture, **338**–339, 339p
moral rules of, 343
Child maltreatment. *See also* Child abuse; Child neglect
brain effects of, 204
consequences of, 215
in early childhood, 204, 212–215, 213f, 214t, 215p
medical professionals and, 192
reported maltreatment, 212–213
substantiated maltreatment, 212, 213, 213f
Child mortality. *See* Infant mortality
Child neglect, **212**
in United States, 212, 213f, 216p
Child sexual abuse, **370**–371, 370p, 371p. *See also under* Sexual abuse
puberty onset and, 360, 361
in United States, 212, 213f
Childhood obesity, **280,** 280f. *See also under* Obesity
Childhood overweight, **280**. *See also under* Overweight
Child–Parent Centers, 241

Children. *See also* Adolescence; Adoption and adopted children; Early childhood; Families; Infancy; Middle childhood; Parents and parenting; Stepparents and stepfamilies
adult children, 565, 570–572, 572p
custody of, 334, 563–564
drawings by, 48, 49f
Chile
infant mortality in, 132–133
parental leave in, 189f
special education in, 79p
China
ADHD in, 288
alcohol use in, 451f
breast feeding in, 137
cesarean sections in, 98p
co-sleeping in, 120f
cognitive testing in, 58f
college education in, 77p, 466, 473p
early childhood motor skills in, 205p
international testing in, 313, 313t, 314
life expectancy in, 525f
middle childhood in, 324p
obesity in, 437p
overweight prevalence and GDP of, 529f
prayer meeting in, 640p
rock climbing in, 445p
sex selection in, 68
technology addiction in, 389
teen pregnancies in, 369
TIMSS and PIRLS scores in, 313, 313t
Chinese Americans, 227
puberty onset in, 359
Chinese people
dialectical thought among, 460
SIDS among, 133
Chinese Taipei. *See* Taiwan
Chlamydia, 371
Chlorpyrifos, 103
Choice overload, **494**
Chromosomal anomalies, 78–79, 80t
Chromosomes, **61**–62, 64p. *See also* DNA; Genes; Sex chromosomes
autosomes, 64–65
chromosomal anomalies, 78–79, 80t
duplication of, 69
in siblings, 64
Chronic traumatic encephalopathy (CTE), 510, 623
Chronosystem, **9,** 10f
Churning, 497, 497f
Cigarettes. *See* E-cigarettes; Tobacco use
Cingulate cortex, 455f
Circadian rhythm, **355**–356, 355p, 364, 586, 618
Circular reactions, 151t, 152–155, 152f
Cisgender identification, 406
Class size, 318
Classical conditioning, 36–**37,** 37p, 39t
Classification, **300**
Climate change, 377–378, 378p
Clinical practice guidelines, 625
Clothes, in middle childhood, 338
Cluster feeding, 119
Cluster suicides, **417**
Co-sleeping, **119,** 120, 120f
Cocaine, 422f
Cochlear implants, 127
Code of ethics, 26–27
Code-switching, 233–234
Coffee, 521
Cognition. *See* Cognitive development; Cognitive theory; Information processing and information-processing theory; Intelligence
Cognitive development. *See also* Education; Egocentrism; Intelligence; Language and language development; Logic; Mathematics; Morality and moral development; Piagetian perspective; Reading; Vygotskian perspective
in adolescence, 377–401
in adulthood, 531–553
breast feeding and, 149
children's theories in, 229–231
college and, 469–472, 470f
core knowledge in, 146–148
dual processing in, 383–384, 383f
in early childhood, 221–245
in emerging adulthood, 453–477
equilibrium and disequilibrium in, 40–41, 41f
evolutionary theory and, 148–149
in executive function, 222–223
face recognition in, 146–147
hearing in, 144–145
in infancy, 143–165
information processing and, 148
in late adulthood, 611–633
learning to learn in, 148
memory in, 149–150, 150p
in middle childhood, 299–321, 344–346, 346f
preoperational intelligence in, 223–226
resilience and, 328
sensorimotor intelligence in, 151–155, 151t, 152f, 153p, 155p
social learning in, 226–229, 226p, 227p, 228p
sucking reflex in, 149, 149p
technology and, 386–391, 387p, 388p, 390p
vision in, 145–146
Cognitive disequilibrium, 41, 41f
Cognitive equilibrium, **40**–41, 41f
Cognitive theory, **40**–45, 53t. *See also* Information processing and information-processing theory; Piagetian perspective
on gender differences, 263–264
on infant psychosocial development, 183–184
toilet training in, 54
Cohabitation, 451f, **496**–498, 496f, 560–562
Cohort-sequential research. *See* Cross-sequential research
Cohorts, **10**
drug use by, 448f
exercise and, 520
family structure and, 332
generational forgetting and, **424**
IQ and, 534
marijuana and, 15, 16f
marriage and, 560f
media use by, 553f
nonmaternal infant care and, 189–190
political identity in, 483
premarital sex and, 441
religious affiliation in, 464f
in Seattle Longitudinal Study, 536
sexual orientation and, 413, 413f
Colic, 129, 168
Collagen, 511
College, 466–475
alcohol use at, 448
beginnings of, 58f
cognition and, 469–472, 470f
diversity and, 472–473, 472f
health and wealth and, 23, 466–469, 477f
high school as preparation for, 395–398
intimate partner violence in, 500
technology in, 473–475, 473p, 474p
in United States, 451f, 466–475, 466p, 467f, 468f, 470f, 472f, 473p, 474p, 477f
Colombia
college education in, 467f
day-care program in, 182p
Zika virus in, 99p
Color blindness, 75, 75t
Colorado, special education in, 292p
Colostrum, 136
Coma, 670, 670t
Comedians, 13p
Commitment in intimate relationships, 485, 491t, 492–493, 494, 496–498, 503f, 513, 513p, 561. *See also* Moratorium
Communities
driving by elderly and, 596–597
exercise and, 437
Comorbidity, **287**
Comparing oneself to others. *See* Social comparison
Comparison group, 20, 20f
Complicated grief, **676**
Compression of morbidity, **599**–601, 599p
Compulsive hoarding, **636,** 638p, 639
Computer addiction, 389
Computers. *See also* Technology
adults' use of, 553f
information-processing theory and, 41, 302
in middle childhood education, 318
Conception, 369, 515. *See also* Assisted reproductive technology
Concrete operational intelligence, 40t, **300**–301, 300p, 663
Conditioning
classical conditioning, 36–37, 37p, 39t
operant conditioning, 38–39, 39t, 59f
Condoms, 443p
Confirmation bias, 465
Conflict in families, 18–19, 337, 408
Congenital syphilis, 371–372, 443
Congo, Democratic Republic of, 27p
Conjunctive faith, 464
Conscientiousness, 558, 558p, 559
Conservation, **225**–226, 225f
Consummate love, 491t, 492–493, 561
Contact-maintaining, 175, 179
Contexts of development, 8–10, 17t. *See also* Culture; Ecological-systems approach; Families; Socioeconomic status
Continuing bonds, **680**
Continuity in development, 8
Contraception, 415, 441, 442p, 443p, 444, 468, 514
Control group, 20, 20f
Control processes, **306**
in late adulthood, 617–618, 618p
Conventional moral reasoning, **344**–345
Convergent thinkers, 285
Conviviencia, 342
Convoy. *See* Social convoy
Cooperative play, 252
Copy number variations, 80, 81
Core knowledge, 146–148
Corporal punishment, **257**–259, 257p

Corpus callosum, 122f, **201**, 202, 304
Correlation, **25**–26, 25t, 26p, 278
Cortex. *See* Cerebral cortex
Cortisol, **121**, 123, 125, 168, 204, 328, 355, 358
Cosmetic surgery, 439, 511p
Cost-benefit analysis, 19t
Cot death. *See* Sudden infant death syndrome
Counseling
career counseling, 502
genetic counseling and testing, 81–84, 83p, 112, 122, 128p
Couvade, **109**
Crawling, 130p, 130t
Creative intelligence, **539**, 539p, 539t, 540
Creativity, in late adulthood, 629, 629p
Creeping. *See* Crawling
Crib death. *See* Sudden infant death syndrome
Crime and criminal justice system
in adolescence, 418–421, 419p
intersectionality and, 13
lead poisoning and, 211
sexual behavior and, 211
Criminology, and psychology, 14p
CRISPR, 69–70, 99
Critical period, **8**, 100–101, 232
Cross-fostering, 109–110
Cross-sectional research, **22**–23, 24t, 535
Cross-sequential research, **23**–24, 24t, 535
Crying, 107, 129, 168
Crystallized intelligence, **538**, 538p
CTE. *See* Chronic traumatic encephalopathy
Cuba
calorie restriction in, 603
late adulthood in, 655
Cultural variations. *See also* Ethnicity and ethnic groups; International comparisons
in Apgar scoring, 95
in belief in afterlife, 662–663
in breast feeding, 136
in child maltreatment, 214
in co-sleeping, 120, 120f
in cognition, 460
in delayed gratification, 249
in eating skills, 205, 206p
in emerging adulthood, 487, 488, 492
in emotional regulation, 248
in gender differences, 264–265, 264p
in imaginary friends, 251
in language development, 158
in LGBTQ attitudes, 413
in motor skills development, 131–132
in mourning, 678
in parenting style, 256, 550
in scaffolding, 227
in self-esteem, 326
in sexual orientation, 413
in SIDS rates, 133–134
in sociodramatic play, 253
Culture. *See also* Child culture; Cultural variations; Ethnicity and ethnic groups; Nature–nurture interaction; Social learning and social learning theory; Sociocultural theory
Big Five and, 558, 559p
bilingualism and, 235–236
brain development and, 231
developmental scientists and, 658
intelligence and, 540–541, 541p
in late adulthood, 637
in life-span perspective on development, 10–13
parent–child relationships and, 409–410, 410p
replication and, 6
self-esteem and, 236
Curfews, 356
Curiosity, 168, 168t
Curriculum, 310–312, 311p
Custody of children, 334, 563–564
Cyprus, thalassemia in, 83
Cystic fibrosis, 81, 81p
Czech Republic
college education in, 467f
problem-solving skills in, 470f

Dandelions (in differential susceptibility), 7
Dating sites, 494, 495p
Day care, 186–190, 186p, 188f, 190t. *See also* Early-childhood schooling
weight in early childhood and, 199
Deafness
in infancy, 127, 161
sign language and, 156, 161
Death and dying, 661–682, 662t. *See also* Homicide; Infant mortality; Mortality rates; Suicide
accidental deaths, 209–210, 209f, 210p
advance directives and, 672–675
blame and meaning and, 679–680
choices in, 666–675
deciding when death occurs, 669–671, 670t
diverse reactions to, 680–681
in early childhood, 209–210, 209f, 210p, 212f
ethical issues in, 669–672
good death, 666–668
grief and, 675–677
hope and, 661–666
hospitals and, 662t, 667, 667p, 668–669, 669f
life-span perspective on, 663–665
mourning and, 677–679
near-death experiences, 665–666
pain and pain management in, 666–667, 669, 672, 672t
palliative care and, 669, 670, 674
process and stages of, 662t, 668–672, 670t
religion and, 662–663, 662p, 663p, 664, 666, 669–670, 672, 677–678, 678p
terror management theory and, 664
DEATH (dressing, eating, ambulating, toileting, hygiene), 649
Death rates. *See* Mortality rates
Debt for college, 467, 469
Deductive reasoning, **382**
Deferred imitation, 155, 155p
Deficiencies, nutritional. *See* Malnutrition
Defining Issues Test (DIT), **462**
Delay discounting, 385–386
Delayed gratification, 249
Delinquency and defiance in adolescence, 362, 411–412, 417–421, 418p, 419p
Dementia, 620. *See also* Alzheimer's disease; Major neurocognitive disorder
Demographic pyramid, 590
Demographic shift, 311, **590**–593, 591f
Dendrites, **121**, 121p, 123–124, 612, 612p, 614, 622
Denmark
middle childhood in, 277p
PIRLS scores in, 313t
problem-solving skills in, 470f
psychopathology in, 82
twins in, 565
Dental health. *See* Oral health
Dentate gyrus, 510
Dentists, 25
Deoxyribonucleic acid. *See* DNA
Dependent variable, **20**, 20f
Depression
in adolescence, 406, 409, 416–417
aging and, 612
cyberbullying and, 390
in late adulthood, 624–625
postpartum depression, 108–109
"Designer babies," 70
Development. *See also* Biosocial development; Brain and brain development; Cognitive development; Developmental theories; Emotions and emotional development; Eriksonian perspective; Freudian perspective; Life-span perspective; Morality and moral development; Piagetian perspective; Prenatal development; Psychosocial development; Science of human development; Stages of development; Visualizing Development; Vygotskian perspective
patterns of growth in, 8, 8f
WEIRD group and, 433
Developmental crises, 35t, 36
Developmental psychopathology, **287**–291
Developmental theories, **34**–59. *See also* Behaviorism; Cognitive theory; Eclectic perspective; Evolutionary theory and evolutionary perspective; Psychodynamic theory
Deviancy training, **412**
Diabetes
baby weight and, 106
bariatric surgery and, 524
exercise and, 436, 519
genetics and, 73
in immigrants' offspring, 438
in late adulthood, 602, 603, 604–605, 626
medication for, 520, 520p, 521
obesity and, 524
text messaging in prevention of, 47
Diagnostic and Statistical Manual of Mental Disorders (DSM), 59f
on ADHD, 287, 288
on ASD, 290, 291
on binge eating disorder, 366
on compulsive hoarding, 639
gender identity in, 406
on infant emotional disorders, 169
on insomnia, 586
on NCDs, 620
on reactive attachment disorder, 568
on specific learning disorders, 290
Dialectic, 457
Dialectical thought, **457**–461, 465
Dictator task, 44, 45f
Diet. *See* Nutrition
Difference-equals-deficit error, **11**–12, 12p, 286
Differences. *See* Cultural variations; Ethnicity and ethnic groups; Gender differences; International comparisons; Sex differences
Differential susceptibility, **7**, 101, 172, 361, 410
Differentiation of cells, 69, 90

Diffusion tensor imaging. *See* DTI
Digital and online technology. *See* Internet; Screen time; Social media; Television watching
Digital divide, 387
Digital natives, 387
Directories, A-2–A-3
Disabilities. *See* Deafness; Frail elderly; Neurocognitive disorders; Special needs and special education
Discipline, 38–39, 259, 259p
corporal punishment, 257–259, 257p
in early childhood, 254–260
in middle childhood, 338–339
parenting styles and, 254–256, 255t
Discontinuity in development, 8
Discrimination. *See* Prejudice and discrimination
Diseases and disorders. *See also* Brain diseases and disorders; Frail elderly; Genetic disorders; Health; Neurocognitive disorders; Psychopathology; *other specific diseases and disorders—e.g., Cancer, Depression*
in adolescence, 364–366, 371–372
allostatic load and, 438
breathing disorders, 508–509
chromosomal anomalies, 78–79, 80t
death caused by, 664f
eating disorders, 365p, 366, 366p
genotype and phenotype and, 73
hormone replacement therapy and, 517
in infancy, 133–136, 138
malnutrition and, 138
during menopause, 516–517
in middle childhood, 280–281
NCDs caused by, 623
Disenfranchised grief, **676**
Disengagement theory, **640**
Disinhibited social engagement disorder, 178
Disorganized attachment, **176,** 178t, 193f
Disruptive mood dysregulation disorder, 289
Distal parenting, **183**
DIT (Defining Issues Test), **462**
Divergent thinkers, 285
Diversity. *See* Cultural variations; Ethnicity and ethnic groups; Gender differences; International comparisons; Sex differences
Division of cells, 69
Divorce
in adulthood, 505, 563–564
cohabitation and, 497
custody of children and, 334, 563–564
dialectical thought about, 458
in United States, 503f
Dizygotic twins (DZ twins), **72,** 73p, 87f, 330
DNA (deoxyribonucleic acid), **61**. *See also* Chromosomes; Genetic code; Genome
testing of, 69
DNR (do not resuscitate) order, **671**
Doctors. *See* Medical doctors and medical professionals
Doctors without Borders, 559p
Dogs, 146p
Domestic abuse, 497, 497f, 498–500, 499f
Dominant genes, **74**–75, 74p
Dominant–recessive heredity, 74–75
in genetic disorders, 80–81
Dominican Republic
cesarean sections in, 96
imaginary friends in, 251
Double effect, **669, 670**
Double standard, 368
Doula, **94**
Down syndrome, **79,** 79p, 112
Drawings by children, 48, 49f
Dreamers, 482
Dreaming, 119
DRI allele, 604
Drinking. *See* Alcohol use
Driving
in adolescence, 356, 357, 420–421, 420f, 546
age and, 609f
cell phones and, 542
expertise in, 545–546
in late adulthood, 596–597, 596p, 597p, 609f
Dropout rates, 396f. *See also* Graduation rates
Drowning deaths, 207–208
Drug use and abuse. *See also* Alcohol use; Marijuana; Opioids; Pharmaceuticals; Tobacco use; *other specific drugs*
ADHD and, 289
in adolescence, 15, 421–424, 421p, 422f, 424p
in adulthood, 521–523, 523f
blame for, 679
brain damage from, 509
in college, 470–471
in emerging adulthood, 447–448, 448f, 448p
infant temperament and, 171
intimate partner violence and, 498
low birthweight and, 104, 106
polypharmacy and, 625–626
prevention of, 424, 424p
substance use disorder, 24, 37
surveys on, 21
Drugs (medications). *See* Pharmaceuticals
DSM. *See Diagnostic and Statistical Manual of Mental Disorders*
DTI (diffusion tensor imaging), 43t
Dual processing, **383**–384, 383f
Due date for birth, 90t
Duplication of chromosomes, 69
Dying. *See* Death and dying
Dynamic-systems approach, **14**–17, 457–458. *See also* Plasticity
Dyscalculia, **290**
Dysgraphia, 290
Dyslexia, **290,** 290p
DZ twins. *See* Dizygotic twins

E-cigarettes, 422, 423, 423f
e-waste, 23
Early Child Care Network, 188
Early childhood (ages 2 to 6), 8t, 195–271
accidents and injuries in, 206–211
biosocial development in, 197–219
body changes in, 198–200, 198p
brain development in, 201–206, 231, 249–250, 252, 270
caregivers and caregiving in, 254–268
child maltreatment in, 212–215, 214t
cognitive development in, 221–245
death and dying in, 209–210, 209f, 210p, 212f, 661, 663, 663p
discipline in, 254–260
education in, 225–226, 236–242, 245f
emotional development in, 247–251, 663
gender in, 260–265, 261p
harm and harm prevention in, 206–216
impulsivity and impulse control in, 203, 207, 214t
language development in, 229–230, 232–236, 232t, 233p, 234p, 235p
logic in, 224–226, 233
maltreatment in, 204, 212–215, 213f, 214t, 215p
moral development in, 265–267, 266p
motivation in, 250–251
motor skills in, 130–131, 130p, 130t, 131p, 205–206, 206p, 219f
nutrition in, 198–200, 199p
parenting styles in, 254–256, 255t
play in, 251–254, 271f
prosocial behavior in, 230, 265–266, 266p
in psychodynamic perspectives, 35t
psychosocial development in, 247–271
screen time in, 229, 270, 271f
social learning in, 226–229, 226p, 227p, 228p
Early-childhood schooling, 236–242, 245f
child-centered programs, 237–238, 239, 239f, 241, 242, 245f
intervention programs, 240
long-term gains from, 240–242, 241p
preschool teachers in, 270
teacher-directed programs, 238–239, 239f, 245f
Eating. *See also* Nutrition
competitive eating, 524p
fine motor skills in, 205, 206p
Eating disorders, 365p, 366, 366p
Ebola, 27, 27p, 52–53, 679p
Eclectic perspective, **55**
Ecological-systems approach, **9**–10, 10f, 59f, 413
Ecological validity, **618**–619
Ecuador, language development in, 161p
Education. *See also* Academic achievement; College; International testing; Schools; Secondary education; Social learning and social learning theory; Special needs and special education; STEM learning; Teaching and teachers
about sex, 414–415, 414p
in adolescence, 356, 380–381, 387–388, 387p, 391–399, 394p, 395p, 398p, 401f
bilingual education, 308
on bullying, 427f
compulsory schooling, 58f
corporal punishment and, 257–259
curriculum in, 310–312, 311p
cyberbullying and, 390
of developmental scientists, 658
in early childhood, 225–226, 236–242, 245f
employment and, 502
high-stakes tests and, 395, 396–397
infant mortality and, 133
intermarriage and, 457
marriage and, 498
marriage and divorce and, 562
in middle childhood, 300–306, 309–319, 321f
moral reasoning and, 462
morning school start times and, 356
multiple intelligences and, 286
physician-assisted suicide and, 673f
preoperational intelligence and, 225–226
technology in, 387–388
in United States, 451f, 466–475, 466p, 467f, 468f, 470f, 472f, 473p, 474p, 477f
Edwards syndrome, 79
EEG (electroencephalography), 42t, 124p

Effect size, 19t, **A-5**
Effortful control, 171, **248,** 315. *See also* Emotional regulation
Egocentrism, **224,** 226, 232, 233p. *See also* Adolescent egocentrism
ELBW (extremely low birthweight), **103,** 105
Elder abuse, 653, 654
Elderly. *See* Frail elderly; Late adulthood
Elderspeak, **589**
Electroencephalography (EEG), 42t, 124p
Electronic devices. *See* Computers; Internet; Screen time; Social media; Television watching
ELLs (English language learners), **308**
Emanuel African Methodist Episcopal Church shooting, 680
Embodied cognition, 282
Embryo, **90,** 90p
Embryonic period, **90**–91, 90p, 91t
Emerging adulthood, 8t, 428–503, **432**
aging in, 433–434
alcohol use in, 448, 448f, 451f
appearance in, 439–440, 439p
biological universals of, 432–440
biosocial development in, 431–451
body systems in, 432–433
cognitive development in, 453–477
cultural variations in, 487, 488, 492
death and dying and, 663, 664f
dialectical thought in, 457–461
drug use and abuse in, 447–448, 448f, 448p, 451f
emotions and emotional development in, 454–460, 455f
Eriksonian stages of development in, 480t
ethics and religion in, 461–466
ethnic identity in, 480–483, 482p
exercise in, 435–437, 436p
friendships in, 488–491, 489p, 491f
gender in, 439–440, 447, 447f, 451f
health, sickness, load, and balancing in, 433–439
higher education in, 466–475, 477f
identity in, 479–485, 480t
independence in, 451f, 483–485
intimacy in, 485, 486p, 490, 491–493, 491t
marriage in, 494–500, 503f
morality and moral development in, 461–465
moratoria in, 480
nutrition and weight in, 437–439, 438t
parents and parenting in, 485, 486–488, 488p, 495, 572
personality in, 484–485, 485f
postformal thought in, 454–457
psychosocial development in, 479–503
religion in, 462–465, 462p
risk taking in, 431, 444–448, 444p, 445p, 446p
romantic relationships in, 491–500, 491t, 494p, 495p
sexual activity in, 440–444
sleep in, 435, 435f
sports in, 432, 432p, 438–439, 445–447, 445p
violent and abusive relationships in, 498–500, 499f
vocational identity in, 483–484
weight in, 437–439, 438t
well-being in, 484–485, 485f
Emotional disorders. *See* Psychopathology
Emotional regulation, **247**–248, 248p. *See also* Effortful control; Impulsivity and impulse control
in adolescence, 357, 358, 384–386, 386f
in early childhood, 203, 203p
Emotions and emotional development. *See also* Anger; Anxiety; Autism spectrum disorder; Depression; Emotional regulation; Fear; Happiness; Impulsivity and impulse control; Love; Motivation; Romance and romantic relationships; Sadness; Sexual urges, thoughts, and activity; Stress
brain and, 122, 122f, 123, 455, 455f
in death and dying, 661–666, 667–668, 675–681
in early childhood, 247–251, 663
in emerging adulthood, 454–460, 455f
in infancy, 167–173, 184–185, 188–189
lateralization and, 202
in middle childhood, 326
norms in, 168t
in puberty and adolescence, 355, 357, 358, 368, 375f, 379, 384, 385–386, 386f, 416–421
Empathy, 169p, 183, **265**–266, 343, 618–619, 619f
Empirical evidence, **5**
Employment. *See also* Career Alert; Unemployment
in adulthood, 572–577
age at, 451f
aging and, 602
career counseling and, 502
diversity and, 574–575, 574f
expertise and, 548–549
extrinsic and intrinsic rewards of, 573
in late adulthood, 641–643
location changes in, 575–576
parenthood and, 567
schedule changes in, 576–577, 577p
vocational identity and, 483–484, 483f
Empty nest, 487, **562**
Engineers, women as, 66
England. *See also* United Kingdom
climate change protest in, 377–378
hospice in, 668, 668t
NCDs in, 655
puberty onset in, 361
resilience in, 327
TIMSS and PIRLS scores in, 313t, 337f
English as a second language (ESL), **308**
English language learners (ELLs), **308**
Entity theory of intelligence, **394**
Environment. *See also* Cultural variations; Epigenetics; Nature–nurture interaction
climate change and, 377–378, 378p
longitudinal research and, 23
in puberty onset, 360
Epidurals, 97
Epigenetics, **63**
aging and, 605
MZ twins and, 71
phenotype and, 73
Equifinality, **287**
Erectile dysfunction, 595
Eriksonian perspective, 35t, 36, 480t
on adolescent psychosocial development, 403–404
on adult psychosocial development, 556–557, 556t
dialectical thought in, 457
on early childhood psychosocial development, 248
on infant psychosocial development, 173
on late adulthood psychosocial development, 628, 637
on middle childhood psychosocial development, 324
ERPs (event-related potentials), 42t
ESL (English as a second language), **308**
Estradiol, **354**
Estrogens, 354, 517
Ethics. *See also* Morality and moral development
CRISPR and IVF and, 70–71
death and dying and, 669–672
in emerging adulthood, 461–463
of genetic counseling, 84
in scientific research, 26–28, 27p, 658
Ethiopia, mosquito netting used in, 133p
Ethnic group, **12**. *See also* Ethnicity and ethnic groups
Ethnic identity, 405–406. *See also* Ethnicity and ethnic groups
in emerging adulthood, 480–483, 482p
Ethnicity and ethnic groups. *See also* African Americans; Asian Americans; Cultural variations; European Americans; Hispanic Americans; *other specific groups*
ADHD and, 288
alcohol use and, 522
college and, 472–473, 472f
corporal punishment and, 257
digital technology and, 387
dizygotic twins and, 72
employment and, 574–575, 574f
ethnic identity and, 405–406
family structure and, 332f
genetic risks and, 604–605
graduation rates and, 451f
high school dropout rates and, 396f
hospice and, 669
income and obesity and, 529f
in intermarriage, 456–457
intersectionality and, 13f
in life-span perspective on development, 12
marriage and divorce and, 456–457, 561
in middle school, 393
obesity and, 280f, 529f
own-race effect and, 147
parent–child relationships and, 410
physician-assisted suicide and, 673f
puberty onset and, 359, 362
sleep among, 509
social comparison and, 325
stratification and, 639–640
teachers and, 311–312, 393p
tobacco use and, 423f
in United States, diversity of, 31, 31f
Europe. *See also specific nations*
Flynn effect in, 285
premarital sex and, 442f
European Americans
adolescent sexuality in, 369
in college, 477f
corporal punishment among, 257
distribution of, by age and region, 31f
family structure and, 332f
graduation rates of, 451f
in high-stakes testing, 396f

hospice and, 669
income and obesity in, 529f
in labor force, 574, 574f
in NAEP, 316
obesity among, 280f, 529f
racial/ethnic pride among, 12
Euthanasia, 671–672, 672p, 672t, 673–674, 673f
Eveningness, 355
Event-related potentials (ERPs), 42t
Every Student Succeeds Act (ESSA), 396
Evidence, empirical, **5**
Evolutionary psychology. *See* Evolutionary theory and evolutionary perspective
Evolutionary theory and evolutionary perspective, **49**–53, 53t
children's understanding of, 21p
on cognitive development in infancy, 148–149, 160–161
on gender differences, 265
on infant psychosocial development, 184–185
on language development, 160–161
puberty onset in, 361
toilet training in, 54
Executive function, **222**–223, 230–231, 279, 282, 306, 308, 357. *See also* Emotional regulation
Executive processes. *See* Control processes
Exercise. *See also* Physical activity
in adulthood, 519–520
age and, 568f
body dissatisfaction and, 375f
in emerging adulthood, 435–437, 436p
health and, 519
in late adulthood, 588–589, 588f, 603, 603p, 624, 624p, 650–651, 650p
U.S. standards for, 436, 436t
Exosystem, **9,** 10f, 597–598
Expansion microscopy, 43p
Experience. *See also* Culture; Environment; Nature–nurture interaction
in brain development, 124–125, 172–173, 231
expertise and, 544, 548–549
in Piagetian perspective, 41, 41f
Experience-dependent growth, **124**–125, 128, 147, 161
Experience-expectant growth, **124,** 128, 147, 161, 174
Experiment, **20,** 20f, 21p
Experimental group, 20, 20f
Experimental variable, 20, 20f
Experts and expertise, 543–550, 543p, **544,** 547p, 548p
Explicit memory, 149–150, 616
Extended family, **332,** 333t, 335
Extramarital sex, 493
Extremely low birthweight (ELBW), **103,** 105
Extrinsic motivation, **250**–251
Extrinsic rewards of work, **573**
Extroversion, 558, 558p, 559, 578
Exuberance, 171
Eye color, 74, 75f

Fables, in adolescent cognition, 380
Facebook, 387
Faces
aging of, 511
face recognition in infancy, 146–147
perception of, 127, 127p
Facilitation of behavior, 412
Factor analysis, 19t
FAE (fetal alcohol effects), 101
Failed suicide. *See* Parasuicide
Failure to thrive, 118–119
Falls in late adulthood, 600, 650
False confessions, 418–419
False positives, **102**
Families. *See also* Children; Family function; Family structure; Grandparents; Marriage; Nuclear families; Parents and parenting; Siblings
in adolescence, 407–410, 409p, 416
in adulthood, 564–566, 565p
beanpole families, 646, 647f
death and dying and, 665, 665f
in emerging adulthood, 486–488
employment changes and, 576–577, 577p
executive function and, 223
experimental design for research on, 20–21
fictive kin in, 565–566, 566p
filial responsibility and, 646, 651–652, 652p
food insecurity of, 106f
kinkeepers in, 572
during labor and delivery, 94
in middle childhood, 327–328, 329–337, 333t, 349f
newborns in, 107–110
resilience and, 327–328
same-sex relationships in, 563
weddings and, 440p
Familism, **409**
Family function, **329**
adolescent sexual activity and, 370
conflict and, 18–19, 337
eating disorders and, 366
in middle childhood, 329–331, 332–337
puberty onset and, 360, 361
Family leave. *See* Maternity leave; Parental leave; Paternity leave
Family-stress model, 336
Family structure, **329**
in adulthood, 581f
in middle childhood, 331–336, 332f, 332p, 333t, 335p, 349f
FAS (fetal alcohol syndrome), 99, **101**
Fast food, 297
Fast-mapping, **233,** 233p, 240
Fat. *See* Body fat; Body mass index; Obesity; Overweight
Fathers
adult children and, 572p
child care by, 263p, 265p
low birthweight and, 104–105
of newborns, 108p, 109
physical activity in middle childhood and, 277
roles of, 566–568, 567p
single fathers, 332f, 333t, 334, 335p
in social referencing, 181
Fear
in early childhood, 203
of flying, 664
in infancy, 125, 168t, 169, 171
Feces, medical use of, 64
Feeding reflexes, 107
Feelings. *See* Emotions and emotional development
Female–male differences. *See* Gender differences; Sex differences
Females. *See also* Gender differences; Gender identity; Girls; Mothers; Sex differences; Women
chromosomal anomalies in, 80t
in demographic pyramid, 591f
infant weight of, 118f
karyotype of, 64p
ratio of, at birth, 67
sex selection and, 68
teratogens and, 101
Fentanyl, 522, 523p
Fertility and infertility. *See also* Assisted reproductive technology
in adolescence, 354, 369
in adulthood, 514–516, 515p
IVF and, 70
Fetal alcohol effects (FAE), 101
Fetal alcohol syndrome, 99, **101**
Fetal period, **90**–94, 91t
Fetus, **91**. *See also* Fetal period
hearing in, 127
Fictive kin, **565**–566, 566p
"File-drawer problem," 22
Filial responsibility, **646,** 651–652, 652p
Films. *See* Motion pictures
Financial issues. *See* Income; Poverty; Socioeconomic status
Fine motor skills, **131**
in early childhood, 205–206, 206p, 219f
in infancy, 131, 131t, 132p
in middle childhood, 278–279
Finland
active euthanasia study in, 671
college education in, 467f
contraception in, 444
graduation rates in, 401f
high-stakes testing in, 396–397
independent living in, 451f
international testing in, 312–313
problem-solving skills in, 470f
psychological control in, 259
TIMSS and PIRLS scores in, 313t, 337f
Firearms. *See* Guns and gun control
First acquired adaptations, 151t, 152
First names, 10, 11t
First two years. *See* Infancy
First words, 156t, 157, 165f
5-HTTLPR gene, 408, 408f, 416
Flexibility, 203–204, 222, 223
expertise and, 547
Flint, Michigan, lead poisoning crisis, 211
Flipped classroom, 474
Florida
aging in place in, 643
child maltreatment in, 215p
elementary school classroom in, 311p
transgender stereotyping in, 454–456
Flu and flu shots, 434, 599
Fluid intelligence, **537,** 538, 538p
"Flying storks," 97
Flynn effect, **285,** 534
fMRI (functional magnetic resonance imaging), 42, 42t
fNIRS (functional near-infrared spectroscopy), 42, 43t
Focus on appearance, **224,** 225
Folic aid, 101–102
Folk psychology, 230

Fontanels, 92
Food. *See* Nutrition
Food insecurity, 106, 106f
Football, 277, 446
Forebrain, 93f, 122
Foreclosure, **404**
Formal code, 307
Formal operational intelligence, 40t, **380**–382, 381f
Formula feeding, 121, 136–137, 137t, 138, 149
Foster care, **216**, 487, 569–570, 569p
Fragile X syndrome, **81**, 112, 124
Frail elderly, **649**–656
  ADLs and IADLs and, 649–651, 650t, 659f
  caregiving for, 651–656
  prevention of frailty, 649–651, 649p, 650p
France
  child safety in, 207p
  college education in, 467f
  independent living in, 451f
  infant care in, 186
  life expectancy in, 525f
  overweight prevalence and GDP of, 529f
  parental leave in, 189f
  PIRLS scores in, 313t
  preterm babies in, 92
  TIMSS scores in, 337f
  voting age in, 451f
Franciscan University, 470
Fraternal twins. *See* Dizygotic twins
Free radicals, 606
Freudian perspective, 34–36, 34p, 35t
  on infant psychosocial development, 173
Friendships. *See also* Peers, peer groups, and peer relationships
  in adolescence, 385, 394, 410–413, 412p, 413p, 427f
  in adulthood, 564, 564p
  for bullying victims, 341
  in emerging adulthood, 488–491, 489p, 491f
  exercise and, 437
  in late adulthood, 648
  in middle childhood, 339, 341, 343
  peer pressure and, 411–412
  selection and facilitation in, 412
  self-comparisons about, 587t
Frontotemporal lobar degeneration, 622
Frontotemporal NCDs, **622**–623
Full-term babies, 90t, 94
Functional magnetic resonance imaging (fMRI), 42, 42t
Functional near-infrared spectroscopy (fNIRS), 42, 43t
Fusiform face area, 146

g (general intelligence), **283**–285, **532**–533. *See also* Intelligence quotient
Gamete, **62**. *See also* Ovum; Sperm
Ganges, 50, 50p
Gardenia, California, 393p
Gardening, 643
Gays and lesbians. *See* LGBTQ individuals
Gaze-following, 146–147
GDP (gross domestic product), overweight prevalence and, 529f
Gen X, 16f
Gender, 67
Gender differences, 67, **260**–265, 260f. *See also* Gender identity
  in academic achievement, 314–316
  in ADHD, 289–290
  in adolescent sexuality, 367–369, 368f
  in body dissatisfaction, 375f
  in bullying, 341
  in education and income, 468, 468f
  in emerging adulthood, 447, 447f, 451f, 468, 468f, 490, 491f, 493
  friendships and, 490, 491f
  in frontotemporal disorders, 623
  in graduation rates, 401f
  in hearing, 512
  in hookups, 493
  in income and obesity, 529f
  in major depression, 416
  in marriage, 560
  in middle childhood, 277, 279, 280f, 289–290, 314–316, 314p, 341
  in motor skills, 206, 279
  in obesity, 280f
  in parenthood, 566–568, 567p
  in peer pressure effects, 421
  physical activity in middle childhood and, 277
  in puberty onset, 357–359
  in retirement age, 642
  in risky behavior, 410
  in rumination, 379
  in sex in late adulthood, 595
  in sexual responses, 514
  social referencing and, 181
  stratification and, 638–639
  in tobacco use, 521
Gender dysphoria, 406
Gender identity, 67, **406**. *See also* LGBTQ individuals; Sexual orientation; Transgender identification
  in adolescence, 406
  in early childhood, 260–265, 261p
  in emerging adulthood, 439–440, 490, 491f
  friendships and, 490, 491f
  intersectionality and, 13f
  in middle childhood, 325
  social comparison and, 325
Gender schema, **263**–264
Gene–gene interactions, 73–75
General intelligence. *See g*
Generational forgetting, **424**
Generativity versus stagnation, 35t, 480t, 556t, **557**, 566–578, 638
Genes, **61**–62, 62p. *See also* Alleles; Chromosomes; DNA; Epigenetics; Genetic counseling and testing; Genetic disorders; Genetics; Genome; Genotype; Nature–nurture interaction; Twins and twin studies
  brain effects of, 510
  in gene–gene interactions, 73–75
Genetic code, 61–62
Genetic counseling and testing, 81–84, 83p, 112, 122, 128p
Genetic disorders, 65, 80–84, 80p, 81p. *See also* Genetic counseling and testing
  MZ twins and, 71
Genetic diversity, 64
Genetics, 51–53, 61–87. *See also* Chromosomes; Epigenetics; Genes; Genotype; Innateness; Nature–nurture interaction
  adolescent biology and, 407–408, 408f
  aging and, 508, 604–605
  of Alzheimer's disease, 621–622, 622p
  asthma and, 281
  eveningness and, 355
  family conflict and, 337
  family structure and, 329
  intelligence and, 532, 536
  in life-span perspective on development, 13–14
  professions and, 66
  psychopathology and, 82–83
  of puberty onset, 359
  race and, 12
  in teratogen susceptibility, 101–102
Genital stage, 35, 35t
Genome, **62**. *See also* Genetic counseling and testing
Genome-wide association study (GWAS), 112, 604
Genotype, **64**, 73–76, 74p, 75t
Georgia, parent–child relationships in, 407–408, 408f
German measles, 16–17
Germany
  alcohol use in, 451f
  drawings by children in, 48, 49f
  early childhood motor skills in, 206p
  graduation rates in, 401f
  infant care in, 187
  kindergartens in, 58f
  life expectancy in, 525f
  overweight prevalence and GDP of, 529f
  parental leave in, 189f
  problem-solving skills in, 470f
  TIMSS and PIRLS scores in, 313t, 337f
  weight in early childhood in, 199
Germinal period, 69, 69p, **90**, 91t
Gerontology, 58f
Gerstmann-Straussler-Schenker disease, 80p
Gestational age, 90t
Gesturing, in infancy, 156, 160
Ghana, menarche in, 359
Gifted and talented children, 286p, 293, 294, 294p
Gig economy, 484
Girls. *See also* Females; Gender differences; Gender identity
  anemia in, 364–365
  body image of, 355p
  as bullies, 341
  depression in, 416
  early maturation in, 361–362
  first names of, 11t
  height of, in early childhood, 219f
  inhibited temperament in, 171
  obesity among, 280f
  puberty and adolescence in, 353–355, 355p, 357–368, 368f, 370–371
  rumination by, 379
  running speed of, 363, 363f
  sexual abuse of, 370–371, 370p, 371p
  sexuality of, in adolescence, 368–369, 368f
  in sports, 359p
Glaucoma, 597t
Global warming. *See* Climate change
GnRH (gonadotropin-releasing hormone), 354
Goals, in infancy, 153
Gonadotropin-releasing hormone. *See* GnRH
Gonads, **354**
Google, 573p
Government
  frail elderly care and, 652–653

infant care and, 186–187, 187p, 188f
pesticides regulated by, 103
sex selection and, 68
Graduation rates, 396, 396f, 401f
Grammar, **158**–159
in early childhood, 229–230, 232t, 234–235, 234p
Grand theories, 34. *See also* Behaviorism; Cognitive theory; Psychodynamic theory
Grandmother hypothesis, 51
Grandmothers
childcare by, 184p
in grandchildren's households, 570
Grandparents, 184p, 570–571, 570p
family structure and, 333t
in intergenerational relationships, 646–648, 647f, 648p
shared custody and, 564
in skipped-generation families, 571
"Granny midwife," 94
Grasping reflex, 108, 113p
Gray matter (brain), 358f, 613
Great Britain. *See* United Kingdom
Great-grandparents, 647, 647f
Greece
Art of Motion festival in, 445p
graduation rates in, 401f
late adulthood in, 651p
Greece, ancient, 58f
Grief, **675**–677. *See also* Mourning
Grit, 315
Gross domestic product (GDP), overweight prevalence and, 529f
Gross motor skills, **130**–131, 130p, 130t, 131p, 278
Grounded theory, 595
Group loyalty, 249
Growth. *See also* Height; Weight
during puberty, 363–364
secular trend and, 360
Growth spurt, **363**
Guatemala, maternity leave in, 189f
Guided participation, **47,** 227, 302. *See also* Mentors and mentoring
Guns and gun control, 28, 210, 357, 679–680, 679p
Gustation. *See* Taste
GWAS (genome-wide association study), 112, 604
Gyri, 93

Habits and routines
in adulthood, 518–526
in early childhood, 250
in infancy, 152–153
Hair (head and body), 353–354, 364, 367, 511–512
Haiti, overweight prevalence and GDP of, 529f
Handwriting
dysgraphia and, 290
obsolescence and, 544
reading and, 282
Happiness
of grandparents, 571
in infancy, 168
marital happiness, 514, 560, 561, 561t, 566
in middle childhood, 315
Happiness paradox, 641
Harm reduction
in early childhood, 215–216
levels of prevention and, 208, 209–210
Harm to children. *See also* Child maltreatment; Child sexual abuse; Harm reduction
from drugs, 422, 423
families and, 331, 331p, 337
Hatching, 72
Hayflick limit, **605**
Head-sparing, **121**
Head Start, 59f, 239, 240p, 241, 242, **242**
Health. *See also* Diseases and disorders; Health care; Nutrition; Oral health
in adulthood, 509, 517–525
calorie restriction and, 602–603
cesarean sections and, 96
e-cigarettes and, 423
education and, 466
in emerging adulthood, 433–439
employment schedules and, 576–577
exercise and, 519
friendship and, 564
genetics of, 68
intermittent fasting and, 603
Internet and, 387, 388
in late adulthood, 26, 586–590, 592–593, 592p, 593p, 599–601
low birthweight and, 105
in middle childhood, 276–281
puberty onset and, 360–361
religion and, 644
SES and, 524–526
Health care. *See also* Genetic counseling and testing; Hospitals and hospitalization; Medical doctors and medical professionals; Pharmaceuticals; Prenatal testing, diagnosis, and care
at birth, 95–96, 97
feces used in, 64
hormone replacement therapy, 517–518
hospice and, 668–669, 668t
in late adulthood, 600–601, 603
low birthweight and, 106
NCDs and, 633f
zone of proximal development in, 47
Health care proxy, **674**
Hearing. *See also* Deafness
in adulthood, 512
in David (author's nephew), 16
in infancy, 127, 144–145
in late adulthood, 589, 598
in prenatal development, 92
Hearing loop, 598, 598p
Heart, 364
Heart disease
exercise and, 519
sex ratios in, 68
in United States, 433t
Heat stroke, 434
Height
in adolescence, 363
in adulthood, 512
in early childhood, 198, 219f
in emerging adulthood, 432
heritability of, 77
in infancy, 118, 138, 138f
Helicopter parents, **487**–488
Hemispheres of brain, 122f, 201, 201p, 202
Herd immunity, 135
Heredity, 73–75
Heritability, **77**
Heroin, 24, 522
Heterozygous genes, **65**
HGA (hypothalamus-pituitary-gonad) axis, **354**
Hiccups reflex, 107
Hidden curriculum, **311,** 311p
Hierarchy of needs, 59f, 557, 557f
High school, 356, 393p, 394–398, 394p, 396f, 398p, 401f, 477f
High-stakes tests, **395,** 396–397
Higher education. *See* College
Hindbrain, 93f, 122
Hip fractures and hip replacements, 600
Hippocampus, 93, 122f, 123, 282, 309, 510, 613, 621
Hispanic Americans. *See also* Latinos/Latinas; Mexican Americans
ADHD among, 288
in college, 472f, 477f
corporal punishment among, 257
distribution of, by age and region, 31f
e-cigarettes and, 423f
ethnic identity of, 405
family structure and, 332f
graduation rates of, 451f
in high-stakes testing, 396f
income and obesity in, 529f
in labor force, 574, 574f
in NAEP, 316
obesity among, 280f, 529f
racial/ethnic pride among, 12
Hispanic paradox. *See* Immigrant paradox
Historical context, 10
HIV/AIDS, 442–443, 509
assisted reproductive technology and, 52
breast feeding and, 136–137
genetics and, 52
Hoarding, compulsive, **636,** 638p, 639
Holophrase, **157**
Home births, 97
Home deaths, 662t, 667, 669f, 673f
Home ownership, 640
Home schooling, 317, 317f, 318, 319
Homeostasis, **434**–439, 508
Homicide, 664f
among children in United States, 212f
among intimate partners, 499
victims of, by age, 589f
Homosexuality. *See* LGBTQ individuals; Same-sex relationships
Homozygous genes, **65**
Hong Kong
co-sleeping in, 120f
computer addiction in, 389
emotional regulation in, 248p
life expectancy in, 524
TIMSS and PIRLS scores in, 313t
Hookup culture, 493
Hookups, **493**
Hope, and death, 661–666
Hormone replacement therapy, **517**
Hormones. *See also specific hormones*
in infancy, 121–123
in puberty, 353, 354–355, 357, 359, 360, 367–369
Hospice, 667p, **668**–669, 668t

Hospitals and hospitalization
  birth in, 95–96
  death and dying in, 662t, 667, 667p, 668–669, 669f
  elderly and, 593
"Hot yoga," 436p
Housework, 643
Housing crisis, 640
Howard University, 466p
HPA (hypothalamus-pituitary-adrenal) axis, **354**
HPV. *See* Human papillomavirus
Hubs (brain), 304
Human Genome Project, **73**
Human papillomavirus (HPV), 371, 443
Humanism, **557**
Hungary, Chinese-Hungarian school in, 235p
Hunger. *See* Food insecurity; Malnutrition
Huntington's disease, 80, 623
Hurricane Maria, 677p
Hutchinson-Gilford syndrome, 604
Hydrofracking, 23
Hygiene hypothesis, 281
Hypervigilance, 214t
Hypothalamus, 122f, 123, 173
Hypothesis, **5**
Hypothetical thought, 381–**382**
Hysterectomies, 517

IADLs (instrumental activities of daily life), **649**–651, 650t, 659f
Ice hockey, 277
Iceland
  alcohol use in, 451f
  parental leave in, 189f
Identical twins. *See* Monozygotic twins
Identity. *See also* Ethnic identity; Gender identity; Self-concept; Sexual identity
  in adolescence, 403–406, 404p, 405p, 406p
  in emerging adulthood, 479–485, 480t
  intersectionality and, 12–13, 13f, 13p
  political identity, 405, 483
  religious identity, 404–405, 405p
  vocational identity, 483–484
Identity achievement, **403**–404, 479–485
Identity versus role confusion, 35t, **403**–404, 480t, 556t
IEP (individual education plan), **292**
If-then propositions, 382
Imaginary audience, **379**–380
Imaginary friends, 251
Imagination in early childhood. *See* Pretend play
Imitation, deferred, 155, 155p
Immersion, **308**
Immigrant paradox, **104**–105
Immigrants and immigration. *See also* Refugees
  attachment and, 180
  birthweight and, 104–105
  caregiving and, 654
  child maltreatment and, 215p
  difference-equals-deficit error and, 11–12
  Dreamers and, 482
  employment and, 576
  happiness and, 641
  health among, 438
  religion and, 644
  in United States, 328, 438
Immunity and immune system. *See also* Immunization
  in abused children, 173
  asthma and, 281
  HPV and, 371
Immunization. *See also* Vaccines and vaccination
  in infancy, 133–136, 135f
Implantation, 70, 90
Implicit memory, 149–150, 616
Imprinting, 65
Impulsivity and impulse control, **203**
  in adolescence, 379, 385–386, 386f, 390–391, 420–421
  in early childhood, 203, 207, 214t
In vitro fertilization (IVF), 515–516, 515p, 516p
  genetic testing and, 80p
  MZ twins and, 71
Income. *See also* Poverty; Socioeconomic status
  attitudes about, 573
  college and, 468, 468f, 477f
  in emerging adulthood, 487
  family function and, 336–337
  obesity and, 529f
  of preschool teachers, 270
  in socioeconomic status, 10
  stratification and, 639–640
Incomplete grief, **676**–677
Incremental theory of intelligence, **394**
Independence
  of adult children, 565
  in emerging adulthood, 451f, 483–485
  in late adulthood, 636, 641–656
  in middle childhood, 338
Independent variable, **20**, 20f
India
  college education in, 468
  computer addiction in, 389
  contraception in, 514
  couvade in, 109
  Ganges in, 50, 50p
  hospice in, 667p
  life expectancy in, 525f
  malnutrition in, 138
  marriage in, 495
  overweight prevalence and GDP of, 529f
  psychopathology in, 335
  sex selection in, 68p
  Tibetans in, 237p
  toothbrushing in, 276p
Individual education plan (IEP), **292**
Individual-reflective faith, 463
Indonesia
  co-sleeping in, 120f
  cremation procession in, 678p
  maternity leave in, 189f
  mourning in, 678
  overweight prevalence and GDP of, 529f
Induced labor, 97, 98
Induction, **259**
Inductive reasoning, **382**
Indulgent parenting. *See* Permissive parenting
Industry versus inferiority, 35t, **324**, 480t
Infancy (first two years), 8t, 115–193. *See also* Newborns
  adaptation in, 149, 149p, 151t, 152, 153
  anger in, 168, 168t, 169
  biosocial development in, 115–141
  body changes in, 118–126
  brain development in, 121–125, 121p
  caregiving and caregivers in, 169, 169p, 172–174, 174p, 180–181, 184–190
  cognitive development in, 143–165
  core knowledge in, 146–148
  deafness in, 127, 161
  diseases and disorders in, 133–136
  emotions and emotional development in, 167–173, 184–185, 188–189
  evolutionary theory and, 148–149
  face recognition in, 146–147
  fear in, 125, 168t, 169, 171
  health and survival in, 132–139. *See also* Sudden infant death syndrome
  hearing in, 127, 144–145
  height in, 118, 138
  immunization in, 133–136
  information processing and, 148
  language development in, 127, 144–145, 155–162, 156p, 156t, 159f, 165f
  learning in, 144–148
  malnutrition in, 137–139, 138f
  memory in, 149–150, 150p
  motor skills in, 130–132, 131p, 131t, 132p, 132t
  nutrition in, 136–137
  pain and pain management in, 128–129, 128p
  play in, 251
  protection of babies during, 51
  in psychodynamic perspectives, 35t
  psychosocial development in, 167–193
  sadness in, 168, 169, 172
  sensation and perception in, 126–129, 126p, 127p, 128p
  sensorimotor intelligence in, 151–155, 151t, 152f, 153p, 155p
  sleep in, 119, 120
  smiling in, 127, 127p, 168t, 174, 174p
  social bonds in, 173–181
  sucking reflex in, 149, 149p
  synchrony in, 173–175, 174p
  temperament in, 170–172, 171f, 171p
  toilet training in, 54–55
  vaccination in, 133–136, 135f, 141f
  vision in, 127, 127p, 145–146
  weight in, 118–119, 118f, 138
Infant amnesia, 149, 150p
Infant mortality, 132–133
Infanticide, 51
Infants. *See* Infancy; Newborns
Infertility, **514**. *See also* Fertility and infertility
Influenza. *See* Flu and flu shots
Informal code, 307
Information processing and information-processing theory, **41**–45
  on infant cognitive development, 148
  in late adulthood, 615–619
  on middle childhood cognitive development, 302–306, 305p, 306p
Inhalants, 421–422
Inhibited temperament, 171
Inhibition, 203–204, 222
Initiative versus guilt, 35t, **248**, 480t
Injuries
  in early childhood, 207–211, 214t
  in emerging adulthood, 447, 447f
  sports injuries, 364
Injury control, **208**
Innateness. *See also* Nature–nurture interaction
  of differential susceptibility, 7, 101, 172, 361

in language development, 160–161
of temperament, 170
of traits, 6
Insecure-avoidant attachment, **175**–176, 178t, 193f
Insecure-resistant/ambivalent attachment, **176,** 178t, 193f
Inside Out (movie), 224p
Inside the Brain
Brains from Back to Front, 122
Connected Hemispheres, 202
Coordination and Capacity, 304
Essential Connections, 93
The Growth of Emotions, 172–173
Impulses, Rewards, and Reflection, 420–421
Lopsided Growth, 358–359
Measuring Mental Activity, 41–43
Neurons Forming in Adulthood, 510–511
A New Stage?, 455
The Role of Experience, 231
Stop and Think? No!, 385–386
Thinking About Marijuana, 15–16
Insomnia, 586–588
Instant vs. delayed gratification, 249
Instincts, 50, 51
Institutional Review Board (IRB), 27
Instrumental activities of daily life (ADLs), **649**–651, 650t, 659f
Instrumental aggression, **266,** 267t
Instrumental conditioning. *See* Operant conditioning
Insula, 455f
Integrated care, **652**–653
Integrity versus despair, 35t, 480t, 556t, 626, **637,** 637p
Intelligence. *See also g;* Intelligence quotient
in adulthood, 532–541
age and, 533, 533p, 534, 536, 540
in Alzheimer's disease and vascular disease, 622f
components of, 537–541
of David (author's nephew), 17, 17t
entity theory and incremental theory of, 394
middle childhood friendships and, 339
selective optimization with compensation and, 542
Intelligence quotient (IQ), 283–285, 284f
age and, 533, 533p, 534, 536
inborn IQ, 532
physical activity and, 282
plasticity of, 17t
Intergenerational relationships, 646, 647f
Intermarriage, 456–457
Intermittent fasting, **603**
International adoptions, 180, 180f
International comparisons. *See also* Cultural variations
of ADHD treatments, 288
of alcohol use, 451f
of belief in afterlife, 662–663
of breast feeding, 137
of co-sleeping, 120, 120f
of cohabitation, 496–498
of college education, 466, 467f
of computer addiction, 389
of corporal punishment, 257
of delayed gratification, 249
of demographic shift, 590
of educational testing, 312–316, 313p, 313t, 321f, 337f, 396–397
of elementary school enrollments, 310
of emerging adulthood, 451f
of family financial help, 487
of family function, 338, 338f, 487
of family structure, 349f
of Flynn effect, 285
of graduation rates, 401f
of infant care, 186–188, 188f
of infant disease rates, 134–136
of IQ, 534
of lead poisoning, 211
of life expectancy, 524–525, 525f
of low birthweight, 105–107
of NCDs, 633f
of obesity in childhood, 297f
of obesity-reduction policies, 280
of overweight prevalence and GDP, 529f
of parental leave, 189f
of PISA scores, 398
of premarital sex, 442f
of problem-solving skills, 470f
of science education, 337f
of secondary school enrollment, 401f
of sex education, 415
of sexual activity in late adulthood, 594
of stunting, 138f
of voting age, 451f
International testing, 312–316, 313p, 313t, 337f, 397–398
Internet, 387–391, 473, 473p, 474p, 489, 494, A-2–A-3. *See also* Social media
Intersectionality, **12**–13, 13f, 13p, 486, 641
Intervention programs, 240
Intimacy. *See also* Families; Friendships; Marriage; Romance and romantic relationships
in adulthood, 560–566
in emerging adulthood, 485, 486p, 490, 491–493, 491t
Intimacy versus isolation, 35t, 36, 480t, **485, 556,** 556t
Intimate terrorism, **499**–500, 499f
Intrinsic motivation, **250**–251, 394
Intrinsic rewards of work, **573,** 573p
Intuitive-projective faith, 463
Intuitive thought, **383**–384, 386
in expertise, 544
Invincibility fable, **380**
Invisible friends. *See* Imaginary friends
Iowa, land-grant college in, 466
Ipecac, 208
IQ. *See* Intelligence quotient
Iran
emerging adulthood in, 494p
TIMSS and PIRLS scores in, 313t
IRB (Institutional Review Board), 27
Ireland. *See also* Northern Ireland
college education in, 467f
PIRLS scores in, 313t
problem-solving skills in, 470f
Iron (dietary), 364–365
Irreversibility, **224,** 225
Israel
graduation rates in, 401f
parental leave in, 189f
PIRLS scores in, 313t
Italy
college education in, 467f
double standard in, 368
elderly population in, 590
independent living in, 451f
overweight prevalence and GDP of, 529f
TIMSS and PIRLS scores in, 313t, 337f
IVF. *See* In vitro fertilization

Jacob's syndrome, 80t
Jakarta, Indonesia, 543p
Japan
co-sleeping in, 120, 120f
college education in, 467f
demographic shift in, 591f
early childhood motor skills in, 206p
elderly population in, 590, 591f
extroversion in, 558
graduation rates in, 401f
life expectancy in, 525f
overweight prevalence and GDP of, 529f
parental leave in, 189f
physical activity in middle childhood in, 278, 278p
preterm babies in, 92
problem-solving skills in, 470f
TIMSS scores in, 313t, 337f
voting age in, 451f
Jobs. *See* Employment; Unemployment
Jordan, refugees in, 409
Jumping, 130t
Junior ROTC, 404p
Junk DNA, 63
JUUL, 423
Juvenile delinquency. *See* Delinquency and defiance in adolescence

Kangaroo care, **109,** 109p
Karyotype, 64p
Kentucky, Western Kentucky Physics Olympics in, 384p
Kenya, maternity leave in, 189f
KIDI test, 550
Kindergartens, 239, 239f, 242. *See also* Early-childhood schooling
beginnings of, 58f
Kinkeepers, **572**
Kinship care, **216**
Klinefelter syndrome, 80t
Knowledge. *See also* Education
replication and, 6
Knowledge base, **305,** 306p
Korea. *See* South Korea
Kosovo, 405p
Kuwait, TIMSS scores in, 313t

Labor and delivery, 94, 95p. *See also* Birth
interventions in, 97
risks in, 98
Lactivism, 137
Lactose intolerance, 52, 365
LAD (language acquisition device), **161**
Land-grant colleges, 466
Language acquisition device (LAD), **161**
Language and language development. *See also* Bilingualism; Grammar; Reading; Vocabulary
developmental research and, 658
dyslexia and, 290
in early childhood, 222–223, 228, 231, 232–236, 232t, 233p, 235p
elderspeak, 589

Language and language development (*Continued*)
genetic basis of, 62
in infancy, 127, 144–145, 145t, 155–162, 156p, 156t, 159f, 165f
in late adulthood, 589, 617–618
in middle childhood, 290, 306–309, 317, 348
norms in, 156t, 165f
second language learning, 8, 317
sensitive and critical periods in, 8, 222–223, 232
speech therapy and, 348
theories of, 159–162
Vygotskian perspective on, 228
Language Instinct, The (Pinker), 59f
Language shift, 235
LAT (live apart together), 560–561, 561p
Late adulthood, 8t, 583–659
activities in, 641–648
aesthetic sense and creativity in, 628–629
ageism in, 583, 586–593
aging in, 599–606, 643–644, 644p, 648
biosocial development in, 585–609
brain development in, 612–615, 613p
caregiving and caregivers in, 638, 642, 646, 647, 650, 651–656
cognitive development in, 611–633
cognitive failure in, 651
death and dying and, 665
demography of, 590–593
destructive protection in, 589–590
diabetes in, 602, 603, 604–605, 626
driving in, 596–597, 596p, 597p, 609f
elderspeak and, 589
employment in, 641–643, 641f, 642p, 643f
Eriksonian perspective on, 628, 637
exercise in, 588–589, 588f, 603, 603p, 624, 624p, 650–651, 650p
for frail elderly, 649–656
health and health care in, 26, 586–590, 592–593, 592p, 593p, 599–601, 603
hearing in, 589, 598
independence in, 636, 641–656
information processing in, 615–619, 615p
marriage in, 645–646, 646p, 652, 652p
memory in, 612, 616–619, 621, 624–625, 627
primary and secondary aging in, 599–601
psychosocial development in, 635–659
religion in, 644–645
self-actualization in, 628
self-concept in, 587, 587t
self theories of, 636–638
senses in, 597–598, 615–616
sexual activity in, 594–596, 594p
sleep in, 586–587
slower thinking in, 614
stratification theories of, 638–641
theories of, 636–641
wisdom in, 630
Latency, 35, 35t
Lateralization, **201,** 202, 204
Latin America. *See also specific nations*
cesarean sections in, 96
infant care in, 186
Latinos/Latinas. *See also* Hispanic Americans
adolescent sexuality in, 369
Laughter
in Angelman syndrome, 65p
in infancy, 168, 168t
Laws and legal issues. *See also* Crime and criminal justice system
adolescence and, 421
euthanasia and, 671–672, 672p, 673–674
family structure and, 329
gun regulation, 28
on high-stakes testing, 396
IVF and, 70
LBW (low birthweight), **103**–107
Lead poisoning, 210–211, 211p
Learning. *See also* Cognitive development; Conditioning; Education; Information processing and information-processing theory; Language and language development; Social learning and social learning theory
in infancy, 144–148
Learning theory. *See* Behaviorism; Social learning and social learning theory
Least restrictive environment (LRE), **292**
Lebanon, maternity leave in, 189f
Left-handedness, 201
Left hemisphere of brain, 122f
Legal system. *See* Crime and criminal justice system; Laws and legal issues
Legos, 228p
Lesbians and gays. *See* LGBTQ individuals
Levels of prevention, 208, 209–210
Lewy body disease, **623,** 623p
LGBTQ individuals (lesbian, gay, bisexual, transgender, queer). *See also* Same-sex relationships; Transgender identification
in adolescence, 406, 413–414, 413f
Lies. *See* Lying
Life after death (afterlife), 662–663, 662p, 662t
Life Animated (movie), 291p
Life-course-persistent offenders, **419**
Life expectancy, 525f, 590–591, 662, 662t
in United States, 525, 525f, 534, 605
Life review, 629
Life-span perspective, **7**–18. *See also* Contexts of development; Culture; Ecological-systems approach; Genetics; Plasticity; Socioeconomic status
critical period in, 8, 100–101, 232
on death and dying, 663–665
multicontextual development in, 8–10, 17t
multicultural development in, 10–13, 17t
multidirectional development in, 7–8, 8f, 8t, 17t
multidisciplinary approach in, 13–14, 17t
sensitive period in, 8, 222–223, 232
Limbic system, 122f, 123, 172–173, 357, 420. *See also* Amygdala; Hippocampus; Hypothalamus
Linguistic codes, 307
Linked lives, **486**–487, 561
Lion (movie), 294p
Literacy. *See* Reading
Lithuania, college education in, 467f
"Little scientist," 151t, **154**–155
Live apart together (LAT), 560–561, 561p
Living will, **674**
Loans for college, 467, 469
Locked-in syndrome, 670–671, 670t
Logic. *See also* Mathematics
in adolescence, 380–386
in early childhood, 224–226, 233
in infancy, 146
in middle childhood, 300–301, 302, 303
Logical extension, 233–234
London, England
"hot yoga" in, 436p
taxi driving in, 548–549, 548p
Loneliness
divorce and, 563
in emerging adulthood, 489
Long-term care, 653–656
Longevity, 604, 604p. *See also* Centenarians; Life expectancy
Longitudinal research, **23,** 23p, 24t, 177
on intelligence, 535–536
Love, 491–493, 491t, 561. *See also* Romance and romantic relationships; Sexual urges, thoughts, and activity
marriage and, 495, 495p
Love marriages, 495
Low birthweight (LBW), **103**–107
Low income. *See* Poverty; Socioeconomic status
Loyalty, 249
LRE (least restrictive environment), **292**
Lung cancer, 23, 521, 521f
Lungs, 364
Luxembourg, college education in, 467f
Lying, 230–231, 230f, 231p
Lymphoid system, 364

Macrosystem, **9,** 10f, 596–597
Macular degeneration, 597t
Mad cow disease, 509, 623
Madrid, Spain, 171p
Magnetic resonance imaging. *See* MRI
Maine
elementary school in, 279p
teaching award in, 318p
Major depression, **416**–417
Major neurocognitive disorder, 435
Making interesting sights last, 151t, 153, 168
Malaria, netting as protection against, 133p
Malawi, Doctors without Borders in, 559p
Malaysia
co-sleeping in, 120f
face recognition study in, 147
intimacy in, 485p
wedding in, 440p
Male menopause, 518
Male pattern baldness, 511
Male–female differences. *See* Gender differences; Sex differences
Males. *See also* Boys; Fathers; Gender differences; Gender identity; Men
chromosomal anomalies in, 80t
in demographic pyramid, 591f
dizygotic twins and, 72
infant weight of, 118f
karyotype of, 64p
ratio of, at birth, 67
sex selection and, 68
teratogens and, 101
Mali, elderly men in, 630p
Malnutrition. *See also* Food insecurity
in early childhood, 199–200
head-sparing and, 121
in infancy, 137–139, 138f
in late adulthood, 625
low birthweight and, 104
puberty onset and, 359–360
Malta, elderly men in, 615p

Maltreatment of children. *See also* Child abuse
Romanian orphans/adoptees, 176, 178–179, 178p, 204
shared parenting and, 334
Management paradox, 548
Mandated reporters, 212–213
Maori, 575
Marathon running, 508–509, 509p
Marijuana
in adolescence, 422, 422f
attitudes toward, 15, 16f
brain effects of, 15
laws on, 15, 16f
Marriage. *See also* Arranged marriages; Cohabitation; Divorce
in adulthood, 505, 560–563, 560f, 561t, 5562p
age at, 451f
benefits of, 562
dialectical thought about, 458
in emerging adulthood, 494–500, 503f
family function and, 334
family structure and, 332f, 332p
frail elderly care and, 652, 652p
intermarriage rates, 456–457
in late adulthood, 645–646, 646p, 652, 652p
in United States, 451f, 494, 497, 498, 503f
Marshmallow test, 249
Massachusetts, in international testing, 316
Massification, **466,** 467f, 470f, 471
Massive open online courses (MOOCs), **473**
Mastery motivation, 394
Masturbation, 367
Maternity leave, 189f, 515p
Mathematics
in adolescence, 381
in early childhood, 228–229
in middle childhood, 301, 305, 310t, 312–314, 313t, 314p, 316, 321f, 324
norms in, 310t
in PISA test, 397–398
in Seattle Longitudinal Study, 536
self-comparisons about, 587t
Matthew effect, 467
Maximum life span, **604**
McDonald's, 437p
Mean length of utterance (MLU), 156t, **158,** 165f
Means to the end, 153
Measles, 134p, 135, 135f, 141f
Media. *See also* Motion pictures; Social media; Television watching
in adolescence, 414, 417
in United States, 553f
Medicaid, 669
Medical doctors and medical professionals. *See also* Health care; Hospitals and hospitalization
birth process and, 97
death and dying and, 666–672, 667p, 668
in emerging adulthood, 433–434
expertise in, 546
humanism and, 557
in integrated care, 652–653, 653p
interventions in birth process by, 97
in late adulthood, 586p, 625–627, 633f
NCDs and, 626–627, 633f
opioids and, 522–523
pediatricians and pediatric nurses, 192
polypharmacy and, 625–626
postformal thought by, 454p
prenatal diagnosis and treatment by, 102
women as, 549, 549f
Medicare, 669
Medications. *See* Pharmaceuticals
Memory. *See also* Hippocampus; Working memory
in infancy, 149–150, 150p
in late adulthood, 612, 616–619, 621, 624–625, 627
self-comparisons about, 587t
stress and, 204
visual-spatial memory, 279
working memory, 222
Men. *See also* Fathers; Gender differences; Gender identity; Males
andropause and, 518
appearance and, 439p
college and, 468, 468f
in emerging adulthood, 485f
fertility in, 515
friendships of, 490, 491f
on gender differences, 260, 260f
in hookups, 493
income and obesity in, 529f
in intimate partner violence, 498–500, 499f
in labor force, 574
life expectancy of, 525f
marriage and, 503f
as medical doctors, 549, 549f
in Seattle Longitudinal Study, 535–536, 535f
sex in late adulthood and, 595
tobacco use by, 521
Menarche, **353**–354, 357, 359, 361
Menopause, **516**–517
Mental age, 284
Mental combinations, 151t, 155
Mental illness. *See* Psychopathology
Mentors and mentoring, 46–47, 226p, 227, 233, 238, 247. *See also* Guided participation
Mercy killing. *See* Euthanasia
Mesosystem, **9,** 10f
Meta-analysis, **22, A-4,** A-5
Metabolic syndrome, 435–436
Methylation, 62
Mexican Americans, 227
ethnic identity among, 481
mothers among, 256
parent–child relationships among, 410
puberty onset among, 362
Mexico
alcohol use in, 451f
college education in, 467f
life expectancy in, 525f
maternity leave in, 189f
overweight prevalence and GDP of, 529f
voting age in, 451f
Mice. *See* Mouse research
Michigan, Christian rally in, 405p
Michigan State University, 370p
Micro-aggressions, 575
Microbiome, **63**–64, 96, 281
Microcephaly, 99, 99p
Microsystem, **9,** 10f, 594–596
Midbrain, 93f, 122
Middle childhood (ages 6 to 11), 8t, 273–349
art in, 279, 317, 323
biosocial development in, 275–297
brain development in, 282–286, 303–306, 309
bullying in, 340–343, 340p, 342p
child culture in, 338–339, 339p
cognitive development in, 299–321, 344–346, 346f
death and dying and, 663
education in, 287–295, 292f, 292p, 300–306, 309–319, 321f
families during, 327–337, 332f, 332p, 333t, 335p, 349f
friendships in, 339, 341, 343
gender differences in, 277, 279, 280f, 289–290, 314–316, 314p, 341
health in, 276–281
international testing in, 312–316, 313p, 313t
language development in, 306–309
logic in, 300–301, 302, 303
mathematics in, 301, 305, 310t, 312–314, 313t, 314p, 316, 321f
moral development in, 343–346, 343p, 346f
motor skills in, 278–279
natural selection understood in, 21p
nature of the child during, 323–324
needs during, 331
parents and parenting in, 277, 291, 309, 314–316, 318–319, 324–325, 342, 344
peer groups during, 338–346
popularity and unpopularity in, 340
in psychodynamic perspectives, 35t
psychosocial development in, 323–349, 324t
reading in, 278, 282, 304, 309, 310t, 321f
resilience and stress in, 326–329
self-concept in, 325–326, 326p
special needs and special education in, 287–295, 292f, 292p
Middle East, premarital sex in, 442f
Middle school, **392**–394, 394p
Midwives, 94, 95, 97, 97p
Mild cognitive impairment, 619–**620,** 624
Military service, in adolescence, 404p
Milk, 365. *See also* Lactose intolerance
Millennials, 16f
Mind. *See* Brain and brain development; Cognitive development; Theory of mind
Ministrokes, 622
Minnesota, immunization in, 135
Mirror neurons, 59f
Mirror self-recognition, 170, 170p
Miscarriage, 91t
Misdiagnosis of NCDs, 626–627
Mitochondria, 69
MMR vaccine, 135, 141f
Mobiles, 150, 150p
Modeling, **39**–40
Mongolia, walking development in, 132
Monitoring the Future, 422f
Monkeys
face recognition and, 147
rough-and-tumble play by, 252
Monozygotic twins (MZ twins), **71**–72, 71p, 87f
differences between, 13
nonshared environments of, 330
psychopathology in, 82
self-awareness in, 170, 170p
Montessori schools, **237,** 237p
MOOCs (massive open online courses), **473**
Mood disorders, 82

Morality and moral development
in early childhood, 265–267, 266p
in emerging adulthood, 461–465
foundational beliefs in, 464–465
in middle childhood, 343–346, 343p, 346f
Moratorium, **404,** 480
Morbidity, 620. *See also* Compression of morbidity; Death and dying
Moro reflex, 108
Morphine, 129
Mortality. *See* Death and dying; Infant mortality; Mortality rates
Mortality rates
by age group, 276, 276f, 433t, 664f
breathing disorders in, 508
from lung cancer, 521, 521f
from opioids, 522, 523f
by sex, 67, 68
volunteer work and, 643
Mo's Bows, 302p
Mosaicism, 79
Mosquitoes
netting as protection against, 133p
Zika virus and, 99, 99p
Mothers. *See also* Birth; Breast feeding; Labor and delivery; Pregnancy; Prenatal development
ASD and, 291
in attachment parenting, 176
autism spectrum disorder and, 14
co-sleeping and, 120
emotional regulation and, 250
exclusive infant care by, 186–188, 188f
language development and, 158, 158f
in Mexican American families, 256
in middle childhood, 315
of monozygotic twins, 330
of newborns, 108–109, 108p, 121
roles of, 566–568, 567p
single mothers, 332f, 333t
in still-face technique, 174–175
of teenagers, 409p, 420
Motion pictures
Black Panther, 326p
Inside Out, 224p
Life Animated, 291p
Lion, 294p
Reefer Madness, 15
Motivation
in early childhood, 250–251
in international testing, 314
mastery motivation, 394
Motocross, 446, 446p
Motor cortex, 123
Motor skills. *See also* Fine motor skills; Gross motor skills
in early childhood, 202, 204–206, 205p, 206p, 219f
in infancy, 130–132, 131p, 131t, 132p, 132t
in middle childhood, 278–279
Motor vehicle accidents, death from, 208, 209, 209f, 664
Mourning, **677**–679
Mouse research, 173
Movies. *See* Motion pictures
MRI (magnetic resonance imaging), 42t
Müllerian ducts, 91
Multi-infarct dementia, 622
Multiethnic Americans, 31f
Multifactorial traits, 73
Multifinality, **287**
Multiple intelligences, 285–**286**
Multiple Intelligences (Gardner), 59f
Multiple sclerosis, 65, 623
Multiples (twins, triplets, etc.), 70, 71. *See also* Dizygotic twins; Monozygotic twins; Twins and twin studies
low birthweight and, 104
Multitasking, 542
Mumps, 135
Muscle development, 363–364, 432, 436, 436t, 512, 519, 650–651
Music
expertise in, 547
in middle childhood, 279
Mutations, 69
Myelin, **121**
Myelination, **201,** 201p, 202, 283, 421
Myopia (nearsightedness), 76–77
Mythic-literal faith, 463
MZ twins. *See* Monozygotic twins

NAEP. *See* National Assessment of Educational Progress
Naloxone, 523
Names. *See* First names
Naming explosion, 156t, **157**–158
National Assessment of Educational Progress (NAEP), **316,** 321f
National Rifle Association (NRA), 679, 679p
National Study of Youth and Religion (NYSR), 462
Native Americans
in college, 472f
distribution of, by age and region, 31f
Natural pedagogy, 146
Natural selection. *See* Evolutionary theory and evolutionary perspective
Naturally occurring retirement communities (NORCs), **644**
Nature, **5**–6. *See also* Nature–nurture interaction
Nature–nurture interaction, 76–78. *See also* Culture; Differential susceptibility; Environment; Epigenetics; Genes; Phenotype; Twins and twin studies
in alcohol use disorder, 76
debate about, 5–7
in health, 68
in nearsightedness, 76–77
in prodigies, 6p
in professions, choice of, 66
on risky behavior in adolescence, 407–408, 408f
in temperament and personality, 171
thalidomide in, 8
NBAS (Brazelton Neonatal Behavioral Assessment Scale), **107**–108
NCDs. *See* Neurocognitive disorders
Neanderthals, 62, 662
Near-death experiences, 665–666
Nearsightedness, 76–77
NEET (not in education, employment, or training), 498
Negative identity, 404
Negative mood, 171
Neglect. *See* Child neglect
Neglectful/uninvolved parenting, **255**
Neighborhoods. *See* Communities
Neonatal intensive care units (NICUs), 119, 129
Neonates. *See* Newborns
Nepal
imaginary friends in, 251
measles in, 134p
Netflix, 417
Netherlands
euthanasia in, 672, 674
face covering in, 465
frail elderly care in, 652p
home births in, 97
infant care in, 187, 188f
life reviews in, 629
priming study in, 6
problem-solving skills in, 470f
retirement in, 642
SIDS in, 133
Neural progenitor cells, 93
Neural tube, 90, 93, 93f
Neural-tube defects, 101
Neurocognitive disorders (NCDs), **619**–627. *See also* Alzheimer's disease; *other specific disorders*
ageism and, 620
frontotemporal disorders, 622–623
malnutrition and, 625
mild cognitive impairment, 619–620
misdiagnosis of, 626–627
polypharmacy and, 625–626
prevalence of, 620–621, 633f
prevention of impairment from, 624, 651
types of, 619–623
vascular disease, 622, 622f, 627
Neurodiversity, **286,** 291
Neurogenesis, 93, 509, 510–511
Neuroimaging, 42–43, 286. *See also* EEG; fMRI; PET
Neurons, 43p, 121, 203
in adulthood, 509–511, 510p
in Alzheimer's disease, 621
apoptosis of, 92
infant development of, 121, 121p
in late adulthood, 612, 613
in Parkinson's disease and Lewy body disease, 623
prenatal development of, 93
Neuroscience. *See also* Brain and brain development; Neuroimaging
brain activity measurement in, 41–43, 42t
language development and, 161–162
Neuroticism, 558, 558p, 559, 578
Neurotransmitters, 614
New adaptation and anticipation, 151t, 153
New Orleans, Louisiana, ReNEW Cultural Arts Academy in, 317p
New York City, measles in, 135
New York City Marathon, 509p
New York State, NAEP in, 316
New Zealand
alcohol use in, 422
co-sleeping in, 120, 120f
parental leave in, 189f
TIMSS and PIRLS scores in, 313t, 337f
workforce diversity in, 575
Newborns. *See also* Birth; Labor and delivery; Prenatal development; Preterm babies
addiction in, 129
on Apgar scale, 95, 98, 113f
at birth, 95, 95p

body size of, 118–119
emotions in, 168
families of, 107–110
full-term newborns, 90t
reflexes in, 107–108
sensation and perception in, 126–129, 126p, 127p, 128p
sleep in, 119, 120
weight of, 92–94. *See also* Low birthweight
News sources, 553f
Nicotine, 423. *See also* Tobacco use
NICUs (neonatal intensive care units), 119, 129, 149
Niger, overweight prevalence and GDP of, 529f
Nigeria
malnutrition in, 138
polio in, 134
Nonshared environment, 329, 329p, 336
NORCs (naturally occurring retirement communities), **644**
Norms
of emotional development, 168t
of infant weight, 118f
of language development, 156t, 165f, 232t
of marital happiness, 561t
of mathematics, 310t
of motor skills, 131t, 132t, 219f
of psychosocial development in middle childhood, 324t
of reading, 310t
of sleep in newborns, 119
North America. *See specific nations*
North Carolina, aquarium in, 306p
Northern Ireland, TIMSS and PIRLS scores in, 313t
Norway
college education in, 467f
family function in, 337
infant care in, 186–187, 188f
middle childhood sports in, 277
problem-solving skills in, 470f
NRA (National Rifle Association), 679, 679p
Nso (people), 49f, 249
NSYR (National Study of Youth and Religion), 462
Nuclear families, **331,** 331t, 332, 332f, 335, 335p, 349f. *See also* Stepparents and stepfamilies
Nucleus accumbens, 359
Numbers. *See* Mathematics
Nurse practitioners, 192
Nursery schools. *See* Early-childhood schooling
Nurses, 192
Nursing homes, 653–655, 654p, 667, 669f
Nurture, **5**–6. *See also* Culture; Environment; Nature–nurture interaction
Nutrition. *See also* Breast feeding; Eating; Eating disorders; Malnutrition
in adolescence, 359–360, 364–366, 364p
in adulthood, 523–524
aging and, 602–603
body dissatisfaction and, 375f
in early childhood, 198–200, 199p
in emerging adulthood, 437–439
food insecurity and, 106, 106f
in infancy, 136–137
lactose intolerance and, 52, 365
in pregnancy, 102
puberty onset and, 359–360

Obesity
in adulthood, 524, 529f
childhood obesity worldwide, 297f
dentists and, 25
in early childhood, 198–199
in middle childhood, 280, 280f
Object permanence, **153,** 153p, 154
Odds ratio, 19t
Oedipus complex, **261**–262
Oedipus Rex (Sophocles), 262
Ohio, family structure in, 334p
Old-old, **592**
Oldest-old, **592**
Olfaction. *See* Smell
Online technology. *See* Internet; Screen time; Social media
Onlooker play, 252
Ontario (Canada), TIMSS scores in, 313t
Openness, 555, 558, 558p, 578
Operant conditioning, **38**–39, 39t, 59f
Operational definition, 177, **A-4**
Opioids, 102, 424p
in adulthood, 522–523, 523f, 523p
in newborns, 129
Opposing Perspectives
Accommodating Diversity, 575
Comparing Child-Centered and Teacher-Directed Preschools, 239
Drug Treatment for ADHD and Other Disorders, 288–289
E-Cigarettes: Path to Addiction or Health?, 423
High-Stakes Testing, 396–397
Interventions in the Birth Process, 97
Making Divorce More Likely?, 497
Object Permanence, 154
Parents Versus Peers, 344
Premarital Sex, 441
The "Right to Die"?, 673–674
Slower Thinking, 614
Spare the Rod?, 258
Toilet Training—How and When?, 54–55
Too Many Boys?, 68
Two or Twenty Pills a Day, 303
Where Should Babies Sleep?, 120
Who Is Smarter, the College Student or the Retiree?, 535
Why Doesn't Everyone Agree?, 186–187
Optimism, 248, 578
Oral fixation, 182
Oral health
in early childhood, 200
in middle childhood, 276, 276p
Oral stage, 35, 35t, 182
Orchids (in differential susceptibility), 7
Oregon, and physician-assisted suicide, 672, 672p, 672t, 673–674
Organ donation, 671
Organ growth, 364
Organ reserve, **434,** 508
Orphanages, Romanian, 176, 178–179, 178p
Osteoporosis, 365, **600**
Outward appearance. *See* Appearance
Overimitation, **227**–228
Overregulation, **234**
Overweight. *See also* Obesity
in adulthood, 524, 529f
friendship and, 564
in middle childhood, 280

Ovum
with dizygotic twins, 72
in IVF, 70
in multiple births, 87f
Own-race effect, 147
Ownership. *See* Possessions and ownership
Oxidative stress, 606
OxyContin, 422f
Oxygen for breathing, 508
Oxygen supply reflexes, 107
Oxytocin, 94, 97, **121**–123

Pacific Islander Americans, 31f
Paddling in school, 257–259
Pain and pain management
in death and dying, 666–667, 669, 672, 672t
in infancy, 128–129, 128p
medications for, 102, 522–523
Paint, lead in, 210
Pakistan, polio in, 134
Palliative care, **669,** 670, 674
Palmar grasping reflex, 108, 113p
Parallel play, 252
Parasuicide, **417**
Parental imprinting, 65
Parental leave, 187p. *See also* Maternity leave; Paternity leave
international comparisons of, 189f, 577
Parental monitoring, **409**
Parent–infant bond, **109**–110
Parents and parenting. *See also* Attachment; Caregiving and caregivers; Discipline; Families; Genetics; Single-parent family
in adolescence, 361, 388, 390, 393, 404–405, 406–410, 409p, 414–415, 422, 426
adult children and, 565, 570–572, 572p
in adulthood, 566–571, 567p, 568p, 570p, 572p
ASD and, 291
attachment parenting, 176
beginning age of, 451f
bilingualism and, 145
body dissatisfaction and, 375f
bullying and, 342, 390
cohabitation and, 498
cyberbullying and, 390
divorce and, 561
in emerging adulthood, 485, 486–488, 488p, 495
empty nest and, 562
evolutionary perspective on, 184–185
expertise in, 550
failure to thrive and, 118–119
first words for, 165f
food insecurity and, 106f
helicopter parents, 487–488
infant sleep and, 119, 120
Internet dangers and, 388
language development and, 145, 157, 160, 309
medical professionals and, 192
in middle childhood, 277, 291, 309, 314–316, 318–319, 324–325, 342, 344
in middle school, 393
multiple intelligences and, 286
nonshared environments and, 330
in parent–infant bond, 109–110
physical activity in middle childhood and, 277
proximal parenting and distal parenting, 183
puberty onset and, 361
in same-sex relationships, 562

Parents and parenting (*Continued*)
sex education and, 414
sex selection by, 68, 68p
snowplow parents, 488
styles of parenting, 254–255, 255t
weight in early childhood and, 198–199
Paris Opera House, 564p
Parkinson's disease, **623,** 623p
Parkland, Florida, mass shooting, 679–680, 679p
PARO (robot), 626p
Part-time employment, 577
Participants, **A-3**
Passionate love, 491–492, 491t
Passive euthanasia, **671**
Patau syndrome, 79
Paternity leave, 187, 189f
Patience and impatience, 249
Peanut allergies, 200
Pediatric nurses, 192
Pediatricians, 192
Peer pressure, **410**–411
Peer review, 658
Peers, peer groups, and peer relationships. *See also* Bullying; Friendships; Playmates
in adolescence, 375f, 385, 387, 391, 393, 407, 410–415, 410p, 413p, 420–421, 420f, 427f
body dissatisfaction and, 375f
in middle childhood, 338–346
moral development and, 345–346
play with, 251–253
sex education and, 414–415
social comparison and, 235
Pelvic inflammatory disease (PID), 515
Pennsylvania, high-stakes testing in, 396
Percentile, **118**
Perception, **126**
in infancy, 126–129
in late adulthood, 615–616
Perfumers, 548
Periods of development. *See* Stages of development
Permanency planning, **216**
Permissive parenting, **255,** 255t
Perry program, 241
Perseveration, **203**
Persistence, 148, 315
Personal fable, **380**
Personality
addiction and, 76
in adulthood, 555, 556–559, 578
anal personality, 182
in behaviorism, 182–183
Big Five of, 555, 558–559, 558p, 559p
brain activity and, 558p
in emerging adulthood, 484–485, 485f
Maslow's theory of, 557, 557f
vs. temperament, 171
Perspective taking, 44–45, 45f
Peru
adolescent sexual abuse in, 361
birth in, 95p
Pessimism, 578
Pester power, 280
Pesticides, 102p, 103
PET (positron emission tomography), 43t
Peter Pan syndrome, 351
Phallic stage, 35, 35t, **261**–262
Pharmaceuticals, 422f
in adulthood, 520
birth control pills, 514
death and dying and, 669–674
for insomnia, 588
middle childhood cognition on, 303, 303f
in physician-assisted suicide, 672, 673–674
polypharmacy and, 625–626
pregnancy and, 102
psychoactive drugs, 288–289, 421–424, 520
Phenotype, **72**–78, 75t
Philippines
Carabao Kneeling Festival in, 254p
co-sleeping in, 120f
elementary school classroom in, 311p
kangaroo care in, 109p
maternity leave in, 189f
Phobias, 50
Phrenology, 41
Phthalates, 23
Physical activity. *See also* Exercise
brain development and, 282
in middle childhood, 276–278, 276p, 278p
Physical appearance. *See* Appearance
Physical bullying, 340
Physical development. *See* Body changes
Physical punishment. *See* Corporal punishment
Physical therapy, 580
Physician-assisted suicide, 671–**672,** 672p, 672t, 673–674, 673f
Physicians. *See* Medical doctors and medical professionals
Piagetian perspective, 40–41, 40t, 41f
concrete operational intelligence in, 40t, 300–301, 300p, 663
dialectical thought in, 457
on early childhood cognition, 223–226
formal operational intelligence in, 40t, 380–382, 381f
on infant cognition, 151–155, 151t
on middle childhood cognition, 300–301
preoperational intelligence in, 40t, 223–226
sensorimotor intelligence in, 40t, 151–155, 151t, 152f, 153p, 155p
Pick disease, 622
Picture books, 233
PID (pelvic inflammatory disease), 515
Pilots, 546
PIRLS (Progress in International Reading Literacy Study), 312–316, 313t, 397
PISA (Programme for International Student Assessment), 312–313, 397–398
Pituitary gland, 122f, **354**
Placenta, 90
Plaques (in brain), **621**
Plastic surgery. *See* Cosmetic surgery
Plasticity, **14**–17, 17t
in adulthood, 510–511, 548, 548p
experience and, 124, 128
expertise and, 548, 548p
intelligence and, 284–285
middle childhood cognition and, 304
in synapse formation, 121
in taste and smell, 128
Play, 251–254, 271f. *See also* Physical activity; Screen time
Play face, 252
Playmates, 251–253, 251p
Plumbism. *See* Lead poisoning
Pointing, 156–157, 157p
Poisoning, 208, 210–211, 211f
Poland
college education in, 467f
families in, 565p
graduation rates in, 401f
parental leave in, 189f
PIRLS scores in, 313t
Polio, 134, 135f
Political identity, 405, 483
Politics and political views
in adolescence, 405
climate change and, 377–378, 378p
of college students, 472–473
international adoptions and, 18–19
in late adulthood, 645, 645p
political identity and, 405
during Thanksgiving holiday after 2016 election, 18–19
Pollution, of Ganges, 50, 50p
POLST (physician-ordered life-sustaining treatment), **671**
Polyandry, 333t
Polygamous family, **332,** 333t
Polygenic traits, 73
Polypharmacy, **625**–626
Popularity and unpopularity, in middle childhood, 340
Population, **A-3**. *See also* Cohorts; Demographic shift
elderly in, 590–593
Pornography, 514
revenge porn, 391
Positivity effect, **638**
Positron emission tomography (PET), 43t
Possessions and ownership, 266, 326. *See also* Sharing
Post-traumatic growth, 678–679
Postconventional moral reasoning, **344**–345
Postformal thought, **454**–457, 454p
Postpartum depression, 108–109
Postpartum psychosis, 108
Posttraumatic stress disorder (PTSD), **215**
Poverty. *See also* Socioeconomic status
asthma and, 281
college and, 471
health and, 525–526
language development and, 308–309
stratification and, 640
Practical intelligence, **539**–540, 539p, 539t
Practice, 304–305
Prader-Willi syndrome, 65, 65p
Pragmatics, **235,** 307
Prayer, 328p
Pre-K classes. *See* Early-childhood schooling
Pre-primary programs. *See* Early-childhood schooling
Preconventional moral reasoning, **344**–345
Predictions, and expertise, 545, 545f
Prefrontal cortex, 122f, 172
maturation of, 202–203, 203p, 231, 304, 357, 358, 389, 455f
Pregnancy. *See also* Abortion; Assisted reproductive technology; Birth; Conception; Fertility and infertility; Labor and delivery; Prenatal development
in emerging adulthood, 444
planning for, 100, 100f
prenatal care in, 102
stages of, 90t
in teenagers, 369, 370

Prejudice and discrimination. *See also* Ageism; Stereotype threat
in adolescence, 384
intersectionality and, 13
in middle childhood, 325
race and, 12
Premarital sex, 441–444, 441p
Prenatal development, 89–94
of brain, 92, 93, 93f
low birthweight and, 103–107
prenatal diagnosis and care and, 102
teratogens and, 98–102
Prenatal testing, diagnosis, and care, 102
in sex selection, 68
Preoperational intelligence, 40t, **223**–226
Presbycusis, 512
Preschool years. *See* Early childhood
Preschools. *See* Early-childhood schooling
Prescribing cascade, 625
Prescription drugs. *See* Pharmaceuticals
Presidential Award for Excellence in Math and Science Teaching, 318p
Pretend play, 252, 253p
Preterm babies, 91–93, 92p, **103,** 105
breast feeding of, 149
sleep of, 119
smiling in, 168
Pride, 12, 248, 249p, 324. *See also* Self-esteem
Primary aging, **599**–601
Primary circular reactions, 151t, **152**–153, 152f
Primary prevention, **209,** 215
Primary sex characteristics, **367**
Priming, 6
Primitive streak, 90, 93
Prions, 509
Private schools, 316, 317f, 318
Private speech, **228**
Proactive cognitive control, 617
Problem solving, 460–461, 470f
Procrastination, 203
Professional journals and books, A-1–A-2
Progeria, 604
Progesterone, 517
Programme for International Student Assessment (PISA), 312–313, 397–398
Progress in International Reading Literacy Study (PIRLS), 312–316, 313t, 397
Property. *See* Possessions and ownership
Prosocial behavior, 230, **265**–266, 266p
Prosopagnosia, 146
Prospective memory, 617, 618
Prospective research, A-3–A-4
Prostate cancer, 511, 601
Protective optimism, 248
Protein-calorie malnutrition, **137**–138
Protest movements, 377–378, 378p, 418p
Provocative victims. *See* Bully-victims
Proximal parenting, **183**
Proximity-seeking, 175, 179
Proximodistal development, **91,** 93
Pruning, 123–124
Psychoactive drugs, 288–289, 421–424, 520
Psychodynamic theory, 34–36, 53t. *See also* Eriksonian perspective; Freudian perspective
beginnings of, 58f
on gender differences, 261–262
on infant psychosocial development, 173
toilet training in, 54
Psychological control, **259**
Psychological disorders. *See* Psychopathology
Psychopathology. *See also* Attention-deficit/hyperactivity disorder; Autism spectrum disorder; Depression; *Diagnostic and Statistical Manual of Mental Disorders;* Neurocognitive disorders
in adolescence, 370, 416–421
bullying and, 342
in college, 470–471
corporal punishment and, 258
corpus callosum and, 202
developmental psychopathology, 287–291
disorganized attachment and, 176
in Eriksonian stages of development, 480t
family structure and, 335, 336
genetics and, 82–83
IQ and, 284
in LGBTQ individuals, 413
menopause and, 517
physician-assisted suicide and, 673–674
in Romanian orphans, 178–179, 178p
sex differences and, 354
Zika virus and, 99
Psychosexual development. *See* Freudian perspective
Psychosocial development. *See also* Attachment; Caregiving and caregivers; Egocentrism; Emotions and emotional development; Families; Friendships; Intimacy; Marriage; Morality and moral development; Parents and parenting; Peers, peer groups, and peer relationships; Personality; Romance and romantic relationships; Social learning and social learning theory
in adolescence, 403–427
in adulthood, 555–581
in early childhood, 247–271
in emerging adulthood, 479–503
in infancy, 167–193
in late adulthood, 635–659
in middle childhood, 323–349, 324t
Psychosocial theory. *See* Eriksonian perspective
PTSD (posttraumatic stress disorder), **215**
Puberty, **353**–362
age at, 351, 353–354, 357–362
behavioral problems during, 392–393
body rhythms in, 355–356, 356f
boys and, 353–354, 357–359, 358f, 362–369, 362p
brain development during, 356–357, 358–359, 358f
girls and, 353–355, 355p, 357–368, 368f, 370–371
growth during, 363–364
hormones in, 353, 354–355, 357, 359, 360, 367–369
overview of, 353–354
sex characteristics in, 367
Pubic hair. *See* Hair (head and body)
Public schools, 316, 317f, 318
Publication bias, 22
Puerto Rico, 677p
Pushing away reflex, 107

Qualitative research, **26**
Quantitative research, **26**
Quebec (Canada)
aging in place in, 644p
infant care in, 188f
TIMSS scores in, 313t

Race, **12**. *See also* Ethnicity and ethnic groups
Racial/ethnic prejudice. *See under* Prejudice and discrimination; *specific groups—e.g.,* African Americans
Racial pride. *See under* Pride
Random sample, A-3
Rape, 493
Rationality and irrationality. *See* Logic
Rats, research with, 125, 252
Reaction time, **283**
Reactive aggression, **266,** 267t
Reactive attachment disorder, 568
Reading
automatization and, 304
brain development and, 304
dyslexia and, 290, 290p
handwriting and, 282
language development and, 309
in middle childhood, 278, 282, 304, 309, 310t, 321f, 324
norms in, 310t
of picture books, 233
SES and, 278
Reasoning. *See* Logic
Recessive genes, **74**–75. *See also* Dominant–recessive heredity
Reefer Madness (movie), 15
Reflexes, 94, **107**–108, 113f
gross motor skills and, 130
in primary circular reactions, 151t, 152
Reflux, 168
"Refrigerator mothers," 291
Refugees, 12p, 343p
familism in, 409
Reggio Emilia, **238,** 238p
Reinforcement, **38**–39, 38p
Relational aggression, **267,** 267t
Relational bullying, 340
Relationships. *See* Caregiving and caregivers; Children; Families; Friendships; Intimacy; Marriage; Parents and parenting; Peers, peer groups, and peer relationships; Romance and romantic relationships
Religion
in ancient times, 662
corporal punishment and, 258
death and dying and, 662–663, 662p, 663p, 664, 666, 669–670, 672, 677–678, 678p
in emerging adulthood, 462–465, 462p
in late adulthood, 644–645
in middle childhood education, 311, 317
religious identity and, 404–405, 405p
stages of religious development, 463–464
at Wheaton College, 473p
Religious identity, 404–405, 405p
REM (rapid eye movement sleep), **119**
Remarriage, 563
ReNEW Cultural Arts Academy, 317p
Replication, **5**
of priming studies, 6
of quantitative and qualitative research, 26
Replication crisis, 5
Reported maltreatment, **212**–213
Representative sample, **A-3**
Research and research methods, A-1–A-5. *See also* Longitudinal research; Replication; Scientific method
correlation and causation in, 25–26, 25t, 26p
cross-sectional research, 22–23, 23p, 24f

Research and research methods (*Continued*)
cross-sequential research, 23–24, 24f
by developmental scientists, 658
ecological validity in, 618
ethics in, 26–28, 27p
experiments in, 20–21, 20f, 21p
Internet in, A-2–A-3
meta-analyses in, 22
observation in, 18–19
participation in, A-3–A-4
professional journals and books in, A-1–A-2
quantitative research and qualitative research, 26
reporting results in, A-4–A-5
research design and, A-4
statistical measures used in, 19t
surveys in, 21–22, 22f
Resilience, **326**–328, 327t, 328p, 336
Resilient Coders, 387p
Respiration. *See* Breathing disorders
Respondent conditioning. *See* Classical conditioning
Response to intervention (RTI), **292**
Restitution versus retribution. *See* Retribution versus restitution
Retirement, 642
Retribution versus restitution, 345–346, 346f
Retrospective research, A-4
Revenge porn, 391
Ribonucleic acid (RNA), 62–63
Right hemisphere of brain, 122f
"Right to die." *See* Euthanasia
"Ring around the rosy" (rhyme), 338
Risk and risk taking. *See also* Sensation seeking
in adolescence, 359, 379, 380, 385, 412p, 420–421, 420f
of birth defects, 98, 100–102, 100f
in emerging adulthood, 431, 444–448, 444p, 445p, 446p
in labor and delivery, 98
resilience and, 327t
Ritalin, 288, 422f
RNA (ribonucleic acid), 62–63
Robot helpers, 626p
Rock climbing, 445p
Role confusion, **404**
Romance and romantic relationships, 367p. *See also* Commitment; Love; Marriage; Same-sex relationships; Sexual urges, thoughts, and activity
in adolescence, 388–389, 412–414
in adulthood, 560–563, 561p
in emerging adulthood, 491–500, 491t, 494p, 495p
Internet and, 388–389, 494
postformal thought and, 456–457, 458
Romanian orphans/adoptees, 176, 178–179, 178p, 204
Rooting reflex, 107
Rough-and-tumble play, **252,** 264–265
Routines. *See* Habits and routines
RTI (response to intervention), **292**
Rubella, 16–17
Rumination, **379**
Running, 130t, 363f
Russia
college education in, 467f
international adoptions from, 180
life expectancy in, 525f
overweight prevalence and GDP of, 529f
physical activity in middle childhood in, 278p
single men in, 334
TIMSS and PIRLS scores in, 313t

Sadness. *See also* Depression
in infancy, 168, 169, 172
Safety. *See also* Harm reduction
of co-sleeping, 120
in early childhood, 207p
of pesticides, 103
of pharmaceuticals, 102
Saint Joseph's College, 488p
Salaries. *See* Income
Same-sex relationships, 562–563, 562p
in adolescence, 413
cohabitation in, 497, 497f
family structure and, 333t
U.S. attitudes on, 413f, 441
Sample, **A-3**
San Francisco, California, maternity leave in, 187p
San (people), 227–228
Sandwich generation, **572**
Santa Claus, 168p
Sarcopenia, 650
Saudi Arabia
camel herding in, 541p
maternity leave in, 189f
overweight prevalence and GDP of, 529f
Scaffolding, **227**–228, 232, 233
Schizophrenia, 82
Schools. *See also* College; Early-childhood schooling; Education; High school; Middle school
bullying in, 427f
special education in, 79p
suspension as punishment in, 38–39
Science education. *See also* STEM learning
in adolescence, 381
international comparisons in, 337f
Science of human development, 3, **4**–31. *See also* Development; Nature–nurture interaction; View from Science
developmental scientists in, 658
life-span perspective in, 7–18
nature–nurture controversy in, 5–7, 6p
scientific method in, 4–5, 6, 18–24
Scientific method, **4**–5, 4f. *See also* Research and research methods
Scientific observation, **18**–19
Screen time, 160, 160p
in early childhood, 229, 253–254, 253f, 270, 271f
obesity and, 297f
Search engines, A-2–A-3
Seattle Longitudinal Study, 24, 59f, **535**–536, 535f
Second language learning, 8, 317
Secondary aging, **599**–601
Secondary circular reactions, 151t, 152f, **153**
Secondary education, 391–399, **392,** 401f. *See also* High school; Middle school
Secondary prevention, **209,** 215
Secondary sex characteristics, **367,** 368p
Secular trend, **360**
Secure attachment, **175**–176, 178t, 193f
Seeing. *See* Vision
Selection bias, A-3
Selection of relationships, 412
Selective adaptation, **51**–52, 51f
Selective attention, 282
Selective optimization with compensation, **541**–543, 548, 594–597, 601, 603, 638, 644, 646, 656
Self-actualization, **628**
Self-awareness, **170,** 170p
Self-concept, **248**. *See also* Identity
in late adulthood, 587, 587t
in middle childhood, 325–326, 326p
Self-consciousness. *See* Egocentrism
Self-control. *See* Emotional regulation
Self-employment, 577
Self-esteem. *See also* Pride
culture and, 236
Self-expansion, 488–489
Self-fulfilling prophecy, 586
Self-respect. *See* Self-esteem
Self theories, **636**–638
Self-transcendence, 668
Selfies, 379p
Senegal, language development in, 158
Senescence, **508**–512. *See also* Aging
Senility, 620
Sensation, **126**–129
Sensation seeking, 386, 386f
Senses. *See also* Hearing; Sensation; Smell; Taste; Touch; Vision
in adulthood, 512, 512p
in late adulthood, 597–598, 615–616
Sensitive period, **8,** 222–223, 232
Sensorimotor intelligence, 40t, **151**–155, 151t, 152f, 153p, 155p
Sensory threshold, 615
Separation anxiety, **169**
Seriation, **300**–301, 301p
SES. *See* Socioeconomic status
Set point, **437**
Sex. *See also* Same-sex relationships
determination of, 65, 67, 67f
prenatal development of, 91
selection of, 68
Sex chromosomes, **65**–67. *See also* X chromosome; Y chromosome
in color blindness, 75t
syndromes and, 79, 80t
Sex differences, 67, **260**. *See also* Gender differences
in adolescence, 367–369
psychopathology and, 354
Sex education, 414–415, 415p
Sex hormones, in puberty, 354–355
Sex ratios, 67, 68
Sex trafficking, 360
Sexting, **390**–391
Sexual abuse. *See also* Child sexual abuse
in adolescence, 388–389
ecological-systems approach on, 9–10
in same-sex relationships, 414
Sexual double standard, 441–442
Sexual identity, 406. *See also* Gender identity
Sexual intercourse. *See also* Premarital sex
in adolescence, 370, 413
in late adulthood, 594–596
Sexual orientation, **413**–414, 482p. *See also* Gender identity; LGBTQ individuals
friendships and, 490, 491f
intersectionality and, 13f
Sexual-reproductive system. *See* Birth; Labor and delivery; Pregnancy; Sexual urges, thoughts, and activity; Sexually transmitted infections

Sexual urges, thoughts, and activity. *See also* LGBTQ individuals; Romance and romantic relationships; Same-sex relationships; Sexual intercourse
in adolescence, 21–22, 22f, 354–355, 361, 367–372, 388–389, 412–415
in adulthood, 513–514, 518
in emerging adulthood, 440–444
in hookups, 493
in late adulthood, 594–596, 594p
sexting and, 390–391
Sexually transmitted infections (STIs), 369, **371**–372, 414, 442–444. *See also* HIV/AIDS; *other specific STIs*
SGA (small for gestational age), **104**
Shaken baby syndrome, 125–126
Shanghai Jiao Tong University, 77p
Shared environment, 329, 329p
Sharing, 266. *See also* Possessions and ownership
Shifting. *See* Flexibility
Shivering reflex, 107
Short-term memory, 222
Shotgun wedding, 441
Shyness, 171
Siblings, 74p. *See also* Twins and twin studies
brain development and, 231
bullying and, 342
in early childhood, 222p
genetics in, 64
shared and nonshared environments of, 329, 329p
Sickle-cell disease, 81, 507
SIDS. *See* Sudden infant death syndrome
Sierra Leone
life expectancy in, 525f
resilience in, 327
Sign language, 156, 161
Significance (statistics), 19t
Silent generation, 16f
"Silos" of research, 14
Simon Says, 202–203
Sing Sing Correctional Facility, 445, 456
Singapore
high-stakes testing in, 396
TIMSS and PIRLS scores in, 313, 313t
Single-nucleotide polymorphisms (SNPs), 62
Single-parent family, 106f, **331,** 331t, 332, 332f, 334–335, 349f
Sitting, 130, 130t
Situational couple violence, **498**–499, 499f
Skin and skin color, 12, 81, 364
in adulthood, 511
in emerging adulthood, 439, 439p
Skipped-generation family, 333t
Sleep
in adolescence, 355–356, 356f
in adulthood, 509
allostatic load and, 435, 435f
in emerging adulthood, 435, 435f
in infancy, 119, 120
in late adulthood, 586–587
SIDS and, 133–134
Sleep hygiene, 120, 588
Slovak Republic
problem-solving skills in, 470f
puberty onset in, 362
Slow-wave sleep, 119
Small for gestational age (SGA), **104**
Smallpox, 134
Smartphones. *See* Cell phones
Smell
in infancy, 127–128
in perfumers, 548
Smiling in infancy, 127, 127p, 168t, 174, 174p
Smoking. *See* E-cigarettes; Tobacco use
Snakes, fear of, 50
Sneezing reflex, 107
Snowplow parents, **488**
SNPs (single-nucleotide polymorphisms), 62
Soccer predictions, 545, 545f
Social awareness, 169–170
Social bonds, in infancy, 173–181
Social class. *See* Socioeconomic status
Social comparison, **325,** 325p, 326
Social construction, **11**
Social context, 9
Social convoy, **564,** 645
Social development. *See* Psychosocial development
Social games, 173
Social interactions. *See* Friendships; Marriage; Peers, peer groups, and peer relationships; Play; Psychosocial development; Romance and romantic relationships
Social learning and social learning theory, **39**–40, 39t, 59f. *See also* Perspective taking
in early childhood, 226–229, 226p, 227p, 228p
on gender differences, 263, 263p
in infancy, 183
Social media
in adolescence, 388, 389–391, 427f
adults' use of, 553f
body dissatisfaction and, 375f
cyberbullying and, 427f
in emerging adulthood, 489, 494
Social mediation, **228,** 229
Social networks. *See* Social media
Social perspective taking. *See* Perspective taking
Social play, 252–253
Social referencing, **180**–181
Social smile, **168,** 168t, 172
Social stratification. *See* Stratification theories
Social studies, 381
Society for Research on Child Development, 58, 58f
Sociocultural context. *See* Cultural variations; Culture; International comparisons
Sociocultural theory, **46**–49, 53t. *See also* Vygotskian perspective
on gender differences, 264–265, 264p
on infant psychosocial development, 185
language development in, 160
toilet training in, 54
Sociodramatic play, **253**
Socioeconomic status (SES). *See also* Income; Poverty
asthma and, 281
cohabitation and, 498
contraception and, 444
corporal punishment and, 257, 258
depression and, 416–417
as developmental context, 10
education and, 23, 312, 393, 466–469, 468f, 471
family function and, 336–337
health and, 524–525
hidden curriculum and, 312
hormone replacement therapy and, 517
intersectionality and, 13f
language development and, 308–309
low birthweight and, 104–105
middle school and, 393
NORCs and, 644
obesity and, 198
physical activity in middle childhood and, 277
reading skills and, 278
resilience and, 328
in same-sex relationships, 563
SIDS and, 134
tobacco use and, 521–522
Socioemotional selectivity theory, **638**
Soda consumption, 438
Soft skills, 318
Software, for early childhood, 229
Solitary play, 252
SORL gene, 622
Source amnesia, 616–617
South Africa
burial in, 678p
early childhood in, 222p
HIV/AIDS in, 443
South America. *See specific nations*
South Asia, infant care in, 186
South Korea
college education in, 467f
coming of age ceremony in, 480p
graduation rates in, 401f
high-stakes testing in, 396
infant fortune telling in, 143
problem-solving skills in, 470f
TIMMS scores in, 313t
South Sudan, cesarean sections in, 96
Spain
cohabitation in, 498
college education in, 467f
Cortylandia Christmas show in, 171p
intimacy in, 485p
parental leave in, 189f
PIRLS scores in, 313t
Spanking, 257–259
Special needs and special education, 79p. *See also* Attention-deficit/hyperactivity disorder; Autism spectrum disorder
David (author's nephew) and, 16–17, 17t
in middle childhood, 287–295, 292f, 292p
speech therapy and, 348
Species, 62
Specific learning disorders, **290,** 292f
Speech. *See* Language and language development
Speech sounds, learning of, 144–145, 145t
Speech therapists, 348
Sperm
in IVF, 70
in multiple births, 87f
Sperm count, 515
Spermarche, **354,** 357
Spices, 128
Spina bifida, 101
Spinal cord, 122f
Spitting up reflex, 107
Sports
in adolescence, 359p, 364
attention in, 282
brain development and, 282
in emerging adulthood, 432, 432p, 438–439, 445–447, 445p
extreme sports, 445–447, 445p
injuries in, 364
in middle childhood, 277, 282
in middle school, 393

SRY gene, 65
Stage of first habits, 152
Stage of reflexes, 151t, 152
Stages of development, 7–8. *See also* Adolescence; Adulthood; Early childhood; Eriksonian perspective; Infancy; Late adulthood; Middle childhood; Piagetian perspective
age ranges for, 8t
in psychodynamic theories, 35–36, 35t
Stalking, 499f
Standing, 130t
Stanford-Binet intelligence scale, 284
Starbucks, 437p
Static reasoning, **224,** 225, 226
Statistical significance, A-4
Statistics, 19t, 658, A-4–A-5
misleading use of, 591–592
STDs. *See* Sexually transmitted infections
Stem cells, **69, 69**–70
STEM learning. *See also* Mathematics; Science education; Trends in Math and Science Study
in early childhood, 228–229
income and, 468
in middle childhood, 314–316, 314p, 337f
Step reflex, 108, 113p
Stepparents and stepfamilies, 333t, 335, 568–569
Stereotype threat, **456,** 456p, 482, 616
Stereotypes and stereotyping. *See also* Ageism
in adolescence, 384
of late adulthood, 587, 587t, 640
postformal thought and, 454–456
Sterilization (contraception), 514
Still-face technique, **174**–175
Stillbirths, 91t
Stimulation, and brain development, 125
Stimulus and response, 36–37, 38
STIs. *See* Sexually transmitted infections
Strange Situation, 59f, **177,** 193f
Stranger wariness, **169**
Strategic thinking, 546–547
Stratification theories, **638**–641
Stress. *See also* Posttraumatic stress disorder; Resilience
aging and, 606
attachment and, 178t
brain development and, 125–126
cortisol and, 121
cumulative nature of, 327
in early childhood, 203–204
executive function and, 223
puberty onset and, 360, 361
sleep and, 509
social referencing and, 181
sports injuries and, 364
Stroke, 510, 622
Studies on Hysteria (Freud), 58f
Stunting, **138,** 138f
Subiculum, 613
Subjects. *See* Participants
Substance abuse. *See* Alcohol use; Drug use and abuse; Opioids; Substance use disorder
Substance use disorder (SUD), 24, 37
Substantiated maltreatment, **212,** 213, 213f
Sucking reflex, 107, 113p, 149, 149p, 152
SUD. *See* Substance use disorder
Sudden infant death syndrome (SIDS), **133,** 133–134, 134f
co-sleeping and, 120
Sugar and sweetened foods, 199–200
Suicidal ideation, **417**
Suicide, 336, 417, 417f, 637, 664f, 672, 677
physician-assisted suicide, 671–672, 672p, 672t, 673–674, 673f
Sulci, 93
Superego, **262**
Supreme Court (U.S.), 468, 562
Surgery
at birth, 96
for obesity, 524
Surveys, **21**–22, 22f
Suspension from school, 38–39
Swallowing reflex, 107
Sweden
bed-sharing in, 119
centenarians in, 593
couples' stability in, 492
foster care in, 487
lead poisoning in, 211
parental leave in, 189f
problem-solving skills in, 470f
puberty onset in, 362
suicide in, 677
TIMSS scores in, 313t, 337f
Swimming pools, 207–208
Swimming reflex, 108
Switzerland, college education in, 467f
Symbolic thought, **223**–224, 224p
Synapses, **121,** 123–124
Synchrony, **173**–175, 174p
Syndrome, 79, 80t
Synthesis, **457**
Synthetic-conventional faith, 463
Syphilis, 371–372, 443
Syrian refugees, 12p

Table manners, 48
Tacit intelligence. *See* Practical intelligence
Taiwan
ADHD in, 289–290, 289f
co-sleeping in, 120f
parenting in, in middle childhood, 315
Talking. *See* Language and language development
Tangles (in brain), **621**
Taste, in infancy, 127–128, 128p
Tattoos, 495p
Tau, 621
Taxi driving, 541p, 548–549, 548p
TBI (traumatic brain injury), 510
Teacher-directed programs, 238–239, 239f, 245f
Teaching and teachers
careers in, 426
in college, 473–474
in Finland, 313
flexibility in, 547
kindergarten teachers, 239f
in middle childhood, 311–312, 318
in middle school, 393, 431
postformal thought about, 459–460
preschool teachers, 270
sex education and, 415
speech therapists, 348
in teacher-directed programs, 238–239, 239f, 245f
technology and, 387–388
Team sports. *See* Sports
Technology. *See also* Computers
in adolescence, 386–391, 387p, 388p, 390p
in adulthood, 470f
in college, 473–474, 473p, 474p
Teeth. *See* Oral health
Television watching. *See also* Screen time
obesity and, 297f
sexual learning by, 414
Telomerase, 606
Telomeres, 605p, **606**
Temper tantrums, 169
Temperament, **170**–173
attachment and, 178t
dimensions of, 171
emotional regulation and, 247
in infancy, 170–172, 171f, 171p
Temperature. *See* Body temperature
Temporary employment, 577
Teratogens, 59f, **98**
behavioral teratogens, 99, 100
Terminal decline, 626–627
Terror management theory, **664**
TERSIS, 102
Tertiary circular reactions, 151t, 152f, **154**–155, 155p
Tertiary prevention, **209**–210, 215–216
Testosterone, **354,** 518
Tests and testing. *See* High-stakes tests; International testing; National Assessment of Educational Progress
Texas, high-stakes testing in, 396
Text messaging, 318p
while driving, 357
expertise in, 544
in health care, 47
Thailand, co-sleeping in, 120f
Thalamus, 122f
Thalidomide, 59f
Thanksgiving holiday, after 2016 election, 18–19
Theories, in early childhood, 229–231
Theories of development. *See* Developmental theories
Theory of mind, **230**–231, 234, 290, 306
Theory-theory, **229**–230
Thesis, **457**
Thinking. *See* Cognitive development
Threshold effect, **101**
TIAs (transient ischemic attacks), 622
Tibet and Tibetans, 237p
Time-out, **259,** 259p
Time-sequential research. *See* Cross-sequential research
TIMSS (Trends in Math and Science Study), 312–316, 313t, 337f, 397
"Tip-of-the-tongue" experience, 616
Tobacco use
in adolescence, 423, 423f
in adulthood, 521, 521f, 521p
e-cigarettes, 422, 423, 423f
in emerging adulthood, 448f
lung cancer and, 23
pregnancy risks of, 101, 102p
Toddlers. *See* Infancy
Toilet training, 182p
theoretical perspectives on, 54–55
Top-down reasoning, 382
Toronto, Ontario, 543p
Touch, in infancy, 128–129
Tracking, 294
Traits and genetic expression. *See* Genotype; Phenotype

Transgender identification. *See also* LGBTQ individuals
in early childhood, 260–261, 261p
in middle childhood, 325
stereotypes about, 454–456
Transient exuberance, **123**
Transient ischemic attacks (TIAs), 622
Transitional sleep, 119
Transphobia, 454
Traumatic brain injury (TBI), 510
Trebuchets, 384p
Trends in Math and Science Study (TIMSS), 312–316, 313t, 337f, 397
Trilingualism, 236
Trimesters, 90t
Triple X syndrome, 80t
Trisomies, 79, 112
Trisomy-21. *See* Down syndrome
Trust versus mistrust, 35t, **182**, 480t
Tucking legs reflex, 107
Turkey
college education in, 467f
computer addiction in, 389
graduation rates in, 401f
life expectancy in, 525f
TIMSS scores in, 337f
Turner syndrome, 79, 80t
23rd pair of chromosomes, **65**. *See also* Sex chromosomes
Twins and twin studies, 71–72, 330. *See also* Multiples
delinquency and, 411
family conflict and, 337
family experiences and, 565
longevity and, 604p, 639p
Two-parent families, 332–334, 333t, 349f. *See also* Nuclear families
Type A attachment. *See* Insecure-avoidant attachment
Type B attachment. *See* Secure attachment
Type C attachment. *See* Insecure-resistant/ambivalent attachment
Type D attachment. *See* Disorganized attachment

Uganda
attachment in, 175
maternity leave in, 189f
Unemployment, 573–574
United Arab Emirates, 469p
United Kingdom. *See also* England; Northern Ireland
birth in, 95p
co-sleeping in, 120f
college education in, 467f
graduation rates in, 401f
home births in, 97
infant care in, 188f
life expectancy in, 525f
parental leave in, 189f
problem-solving skills in, 470f
United Nations International School, 312
United States. *See also specific groups—e.g.,* African Americans, *European Americans,* Hispanic Americans; *specific states, cities, etc.*
2016 election in, 18–19, 483
ADHD in, 288
adolescent criminality in, 418–419
adolescent sexuality in, 21–22, 22f, 369
adoptees in, 482
aging in place in, 643
alcohol use in, 522
AP (Advanced Placement) in, 395
ASD in, 290
asthma in, 281
autism in, 14
behaviorism in, 37–38
bicycle riding in, 590
bilingualism in, 307–308, 307f
birth in, 94
birth rate in, 440
BMI in, 438
"boomerang children" in, 565
breathing disorders in, 508
cancer in, 212f, 521, 521f, 605
causes of death in, 433t, 447, 605
centenarians in, 593
cesarean sections in, 96
child maltreatment in, 212–214, 212f, 213f, 215p
child safety in, 207p
climate change protest in, 378
co-sleeping in, 120, 120f
cohabitation in, 496f, 497, 503f
college in, 451f, 466–475, 466p, 467f, 468f, 470f, 472f, 473p, 474p, 477f
computer addiction in, 389
congenital syphilis in, 443
contraception in, 444, 514
corporal punishment in, 257–259
couvade in, 109
demographic shift in, 311, 590–593
divorce in, 563
domestic abuse in, 498, 499f
Dreamers in, 482
driving in, by age, 609f
drug use in, 21, 422, 422f, 423, 423f, 448, 448f, 448p, 522–523, 523f
early-childhood motor skills in, 205p
early-childhood schooling in, 239, 239f, 240–242
education in, 239, 239f, 240–242, 292–293, 292f, 311–312, 316–319, 317f, 317p, 318p, 321f, 395–398, 395p, 401f, 451f, 466–475, 466p, 467f, 468f, 470f, 472f, 473p, 474p, 477f
ELLs in, 308
employment in, 574, 576, 641–643, 641f, 642p, 643f
ethnic diversity in, 31, 31f
ethnic identity in, 405, 481–482
exercise in, 520, 588f
family structures in, 331, 332f, 333t, 334p, 335p, 349f, 581f
fertility and infertility in, 514, 514p
food insecurity in, 106, 106f
foster care in, 569
funding for schools in, 316–317
gifted and talented children in, 294
graduation rates in, 401f, 451f
grandparents in, 647–648
gun research in, 28
harm and harm reduction in, 206, 207–208, 209f, 210–211, 211f, 212–214, 212f, 213f
health and SES in, 525, 525f
health ratings in, 601f
hearing loss in, 598, 598p
high school in, 395–398, 395p, 401f
high-stakes testing in, 396
hookups in, 493
hospice in, 668t
hospitalization in, 593
hysterectomies in, 517
IADLs in, 650t
immigrants and immigration in, 328, 438, 481–482
income and obesity in, 529f
independent living by elderly in, 659f
infant care in, 187, 188f
intermarriages in, 456–457
international adoptions in, 180, 180f
IQ in, 533
IVF in, 70
labor and delivery in, 97
lead poisoning in, 210–211, 211f
life expectancy in, 525, 525f, 534, 605
low birthweight in, 103, 104t, 106
lung cancer in, 521, 521f
marijuana in, 15, 16f
marriage in, 451f, 494, 497, 498, 503f, 560, 560f, 563
maternal age in, 515
measles in, 135
media use by adults in, 553f
medical school graduates in, 549, 549f
middle childhood schooling in, 316–319, 317f, 317p, 318p, 321f
mortality rates in, 276, 276f, 433t
motor skills development in, 132
motor vehicle accident deaths in, 208, 209, 209f
murder victims in, by age, 589f
nearsightedness in, 77
nursing homes in, 654–655, 654p
obesity in, 280f, 297f, 524, 529f
opioid use in, 522–523, 523f, 523p
overweight prevalence and GDP of, 529f
parental leave in, 187, 187p, 189f
parenting and parenthood in, 315, 487, 567
PISA scores in, 398
political identity and activity in, 483, 645, 645p
premarital sex in, 441, 442f
prescription drug use in, 520
presidents' height in, 360, 360p
primary and secondary aging in, 599
problem-solving skills in, 470f
psychopathology in, 82, 83f, 416, 417, 417f
religion in, 464f, 645
retirement in, 642
second language learning in, 317
sex education in, 415
sexual attitudes and behavior in, 441, 493, 513, 594
SIDS in, 134, 134f
skipped-generation families in, 571
special education in, 292–293, 292f
STIs in, 371–372, 443
suicide, suicidal ideation, and parasuicide in, 417, 417f, 637
teacher ethnicity and expectations in, 311–312
teen pregnancies in, 369, 370
TIMSS and PIRLS scores in, 313, 313t, 337f
tobacco use in, 521, 521p, 525
unemployment in, 451f
volunteer work in, 643, 643f
weight in early childhood in, 199
workplace diversity in, 574, 576
workweek in, 576
Universal design, **598,** 644
Universalizing faith, 464
Universities. *See* College

Vaccines and vaccination
ASD and, 291
in emerging adulthood, 434
ethics and, 27, 27p
flu shots, 434, 599
HPV and, 443
in infancy, 133–136, 135f, 141f
medical professionals and, 192
risks of, 83
for smallpox, 58f
Values. *See* Ethics; Morality and moral development
Vaping. *See* E-cigarettes
Variables, 20, 20f
correlations between, 25–26, 25t, 26p
Vascular disease, **622**, 622f, 627
Vectors, 443
Vegetative state, 670, 670t
Venezuela, maternity leave in, 189f
Ventral striatum, 385, 420
Verbal bullying, 340
Verrazano Narrows Bridge, 509p
Very low birthweight (VLBW), **103**
Vibrato, 17
Vicodin, 422f
Victims
of bullying, 341
of intimate terrorism, 499–500, 499f
Video games
addiction to, 389
in early childhood, 229
violent behavior and, 22
Videos, for language development, 160
Vietnam
co-sleeping in, 120, 120f
college education in, 468
View from Science
Addiction in Newborns, 129
Face Recognition, 147
The Flynn Effect, 285
The Genes of Psychological Disorders, 82–83
"I Always Dressed One in Blue Stuff . . . ," 330
I'm Not Like Those Other Old People, 587
Lead in the Environment, 210–211
Measuring Attachment, 177
Priming, 7
The Skipped-Generation Family, 571
Stress and Puberty, 361
Teens and Genes, 407–408
Universal or WEIRD?, 433
Waiting for the Marshmallow, 249
Walk a Mile, 44–45
What Is Safe?, 103
Who Wins in Soccer?, 545
Women and College, 468
Violence. *See also* Domestic abuse; Sexual abuse
intimate partner violence, 498–500
video games and, 22
Virginia, middle childhood in, 324p
Virginia Military Institute, 468
Viruses. *See also* Flu and flu shots
brain damage from, 509
Vision
in adulthood, 512
in infancy, 127, 127p, 145–146
in late adulthood, 597–598, 597t
nearsightedness, 76–77
Visual cortex, 122f, 123
Visual-spatial memory, 279
Visualizing Development
Adolescent Bullying, 427
Adult Overweight Around the World, 529
The Apgar, 113
Childhood Obesity Around the World, 297
Developing Attachment, 193
Developing Motor Skills, 219
Diverse Complexities, 31
Early-Childhood Schooling, 245
Early Communication and Language, 165
Education in Middle Childhood, 321
Elders Behind the Wheel, 609
Family Connections, 581
Family Structures Around the World, 349
Global Prevalence of Major NCD, 633
Highlights in the Journey to Adulthood, 451
Historical Highlights of Developmental Science, 58–59
How Many Adolescents Are in School?, 401
Immunization, 141
Living Independently After Age 65, 659
Marital Status in the United States, 503
Media Use Among U.S. Adults, 553
More Play Time, Less Screen Time, 271
One Baby or More?, 87
Satisfied with Your Body?, 375
Why Study?, 477
Vital Involvement in Old Age (Erikson), 628
Vitamin A, 77
Vitamin C, 200
Vitamin D, 365
VLBW (very low birthweight), **103**
Vocabulary
in early childhood, 232–233, 232t, 240
in infancy, 157–158, 159f
in middle childhood, 307
in naming explosion, 157–158
Vocational education, 395–397, 398p
Vocational identity, 483–484
Voices, in prenatal development, 92
Volunteer work, 642–643, 643f
Voting age, 451f
Vouchers, 317
Vygotskian perspective, 46–47
on early childhood cognition, 226–229
on middle childhood cognition, 301–302

WAIS (Wechsler Adult Intelligence Scale), 284
Waldorf schools, **238**
Walking, 130–131, 130t, 131p, 132
War
calorie restriction and, 602–603
resilience and, 327–328
Wariness, 169
Wasting, **138**
Wear-and-tear theory, **602**–603
Wechsler scales. *See* WIPPSI; WISC
Weddings, 440p. *See also* Marriage
shotgun weddings, 441
Weight. *See also* Body mass index; Obesity; Overweight
in adolescence, 363–364
bariatric surgery and, 524
body dissatisfaction and, 375f
in early childhood, 198
in emerging adulthood, 437–439, 438t
in infancy, 118–119, 118f, 138
intermittent fasting and, 603
low birthweight, 103–107
of newborns, 92–94
in pregnancy, 102
wasting and, 138
WEIRD (Western, Educated, Industrialized, Rich Democracies), **432,** 433
Wernicke-Korsakoff syndrome, 509
Western Kentucky Physics Olympics, 384p
Wheaton College, 473p
White matter (brain), 358f, 613
Whites. *See* European Americans
WIPPSI (Wechsler Preschool and Primary Scale of Intelligence), 284
WISC (Wechsler Intelligence Scale for Children), 284
Wisdom, 630
Wolffian ducts, 91
Women. *See also* Females; Gender differences; Gender identity; Mothers
alcohol use by, 76, 76p, 448
college and, 468, 468f
in emerging adulthood, 485f
as engineers, 66
as experts, 549–550, 549f
fertility in, 515
friendships of, 490, 491f
on gender differences, 260f
in hookups, 493
income and obesity in, 529f
in intimate partner violence, 498–500, 499f
IVF and, 70
in labor force, 574
in late adulthood, 595, 637
life expectancy of, 525f
marriage and, 495–496, 503f
as medical doctors, 549, 549f
menopause in, 516–517
premarital sex and, 441–442
in Seattle Longitudinal Study, 535–536, 535f
sex in late adulthood and, 595
tobacco use by, 521
"Women's work," 550
Work. *See* Employment; Unemployment
Working memory, 222
Working model, **183**–184
World Cup (soccer), 432p
World War I, 679
Writing. *See* Handwriting

X chromosome, 64p, 65–67, 67f, 75, 81
X-linked genes, 67f, **75,** 75t
XX chromosomes, **65**
XY chromosomes, **65**

Y chromosome, 64p, 65–67, 67f, 69, 75
Yoga, 436p
Young-old, **592**
Youth Risk Behavior Survey, 21–22, 368f, 371

Zika virus (ZIKV), 99
Zone of proximal development (ZPD), **47**–48, 47f, **227,** 228, 233, 247
Zygote, **62,** 65, 67, 67f, 69, 69p, 70, 78, 80p, 87f, 90, 91t. *See also* Dizygotic twins; Monozygotic twins